www.wadsworth.com

wadsworth.com is the World Wide Web site for Wadsworth Publishing Company and is your direct source to dozens of online resources.

At *wadsworth.com* you can find out about supplements, demonstration software, and student resources. You can also send e-mail to many of our authors and preview new publications and exciting new technologies.

wadsworth.com
Changing the way the world learns®

Seventh Edition

CRIMINAL LAW

JOEL SAMAHA

University of Minnesota

WADSWORTH

THOMSON LEARNING

Australia • Canada • Mexico • Singapore • Spain • United Kingdom • United States

WADSWORTH

★

THOMSON LEARNING

™

Executive Editor, Criminal Justice: Sabra Horne
Development Editor: Terri Edwards
Assistant Editor: Dawn Mesa
Editorial Assistant: Lee McCracken
Marketing Manager: Jennifer Somerville
Marketing Assistant: Karyl Davis
Project Manager, Editorial Production: Jennie Redwitz
Print/Media Buyer: Karen Hunt
Technology Project Manager: Susan DeVanna
Permissions Editor: Joohee Lee

Production Service: Ruth Cottrell
Text Designer: Adriane Bosworth
Photo Researcher: Laura Murray
Copy Editor: Kevin Gleason
Illustrator: Abby Balz, Judith Ogus
Cover Designer: Yvo Riezebos
Cover Image: PhotoDisc
Cover Printer: Phoenix Color Corp.
Compositor: R&S Book Composition
Printer: R. R. Donnelley/Willard

Printed in the United States of America
3 4 5 6 7 05 04 03

Library of Congress Cataloging-in-Publication Data
Samaha, Joel.
      Criminal law/Joel Samaha.—7th ed.
         p. cm.
      Includes index.
   ISBN 0-534-56358-9
   1. Criminal law—United States—Cases. I. Title.
   KF9218.S26 2001
   345.73—dc21   2001026299

Instructor's Edition ISBN: 0-534-56361-9

Wadsworth/Thomson Learning
10 Davis Drive
Belmont, CA 94002-3098
USA

For more information about our products, contact us:
Thomson Learning Academic Resource Center
1-800-423-0563
http://www.wadsworth.com

International Headquarters
Thomson Learning
International Division
290 Harbor Drive, 2nd Floor
Stamford, CT 06902-7477
USA

UK/Europe/Middle East/South Africa
Thomson Learning
Berkshire House
168-173 High Holborn
London WC1V 7AA
United Kingdom

Asia
Thomson Learning
60 Albert Street, #15-01
Albert Complex
Singapore 189969

Canada
Nelson Thomson Learning
1120 Birchmount Road
Toronto, Ontario M1K 5G4
Canada

For Doug and my students

About the Author

Professor Joel Samaha teaches Criminal Law, Criminal Procedure, Introduction to Criminal Justice, and The Supreme Court and the Bill of Rights at the University of Minnesota. He is both a lawyer and an historian whose primary research interest is the history of criminal justice. He received his B.A., J.D., and Ph.D. from Northwestern University. Professor Samaha also studied under the late Sir Geoffrey Elton at Cambridge University, England.

Professor Samaha was admitted to the Illinois Bar in 1962. He taught at UCLA before coming to the University of Minnesota in 1971. At the University of Minnesota, he served as Chair of the Department of Criminal Justice Studies from 1974 to 1978. He now teaches and writes full time. He has taught both television and radio courses in criminal justice and has co-taught a National Endowment for the Humanities seminar in legal and constitutional history. He was named Distinguished Teacher at the University of Minnesota in 1974.

Professor Samaha is an active scholar. In addition to his monograph, *Law and Order in Historical Perspective,* an analysis of law enforcement in pre-industrial English society, he has transcribed and written a scholarly introduction to a set of criminal justice records in the reign of Elizabeth I. He has also written several articles on the history of criminal justice, published in *Historical Journal, The American Journal of Legal History, Minnesota Law Review, William Mitchell Law Review,* and *Journal of Social History.* In addition to *Criminal Law,* he has written two other textbooks, *Criminal Procedure* and *Criminal Justice,* both in their fifth editions.

Contents

Preface   xi

CHAPTER 1

The Nature and Purposes of Criminal Law   1

Introduction   2

The Nature of Criminal Law   4

Classifying and Grading Crimes   4
   Crime, Tort, and Nonlegal Responses
      to Social Harms   5
   The General and Special Parts
      of Criminal Law   6
   Grading Schemes   6

Punishment   8
   Retribution   10
   Prevention   12
   Trends in Punishment   15

Criminal Law in a Federal System   16

Sources of Criminal Law   17
   The Common-Law Origins
      of Criminal Law   18
   Criminal Codes   19
   Common-Law Crimes and Modern
      Criminal Law   20
   "Rational Criminal Law"   22

Nonlegal Influences on Criminal Law   23
   The Influence of Ideology   23
   The Influence of Irrationality   25
   The Influence of History   26
   The Influence of an "Ethical Core"   27

Summary   28

CHAPTER 2

Constitutional Limits on Criminal Law   35

Introduction   36

The Rule of Law   37

Ex Post Facto Laws   37

Void-for-Vagueness Doctrine   38

HOW TO READ, BRIEF,
AND FIND CASES   39

Equal Protection of the Laws   47

Free Speech   50

Right to Privacy   57

Cruel and Unusual Punishments   70

Summary   74

CHAPTER 3

The General Principles of Criminal Liability: The Requirement of Action   78

Introduction   79

Actus Reus   82

Status as *Actus Reus*   85

Failure to Act   91

Possession   105

Summary   113

CHAPTER 4

The General Principles of Criminal Liability: *Mens Rea,* Concurrence, Causation 116

Introduction 117

Determining *Mens Rea* 118

Four Levels of *Mens Rea* 118
Purpose 119
Knowledge 125
Standards for Determining Purpose and Knowledge 128
Recklessness and Negligence 129
Strict Liability 133

Concurrence 137

Causation 137

Grading Offenses 142

Summary 142

CHAPTER 5

Parties to Crime and Vicarious Liability 145

Introduction 146

Parties to Crime 147
Actus Reus of Accomplice Liability 148
Mens Rea of Accomplice Liability 152
Complicity Following Crime 155

Vicarious Liability 158
Corporate Vicarious Liability 159
Individual Vicarious Liability 163
Vicarious Liability of Parents 167

Summary 170

CHAPTER 6

Uncompleted Crimes: Attempt, Conspiracy, and Solicitation 172

Introduction 173

Attempt 173
History of the Law of Attempt 174
Theories of Criminal Attempt 175
The Elements of Criminal Attempt 175
Legal and Factual Impossibility 185
Abandonment 191
Summary of Attempt Law 194

Conspiracy 194
Conspiracy *Actus Reus* 194
Conspiracy *Mens Rea* 195
The Objective of the Conspiracy 196
Parties to the Conspiracy 197
Summary of Conspiracy Law 202

Solicitation 203

Summary 208

CHAPTER 7

Defenses to Criminal Liability: Justifications 211

Introduction 212

Self-Defense 214
Elements of Self-Defense 215
The Retreat Doctrine 241
Defense of Others 244
Defense of Home and Property 244

Execution of Public Duties 251

Resisting Unlawful Arrest 255

Choice-of-Evils Defense 259
The Elements of the Choice-of-Evils Defense 261

Consent 265

Summary 270

CHAPTER 8

Defenses to Criminal Liability: Excuses 274

Introduction 275

Insanity 275
Right-Wrong Test 276
Irresistible Impulse Test 282
Substantial Capacity Test 283
Burden of Proof 289

Diminished Capacity 290

Intoxication 291

Age 297

Duress 303

Mistake 308

Entrapment 308

Syndromes 316

Summary 319

CHAPTER 9

Crimes Against Persons I: Criminal Homicide 323

Introduction 324

History of Criminal Homicide 325

Elements of Criminal Homicide 325
  Taking a Life 326
  Causing Another's Death 334

Murder 336
  First-Degree Murder 337
  Second-Degree Murder 349
  Felony Murder 352
  Corporate Murder 359

Manslaughter 363
  Voluntary Manslaughter 363
  Involuntary Manslaughter 372

Summary 379

CHAPTER 10

Crimes Against Persons II: Criminal Sexual Conduct and Others 383

Introduction 384

Criminal Sexual Conduct 385
  History of Rape 385

The Elements of Modern Rape 389
  The *Actus Reus* of Rape 389
  The *Mens Reus* of Rape 396

Assault and Battery 409
  The Elements of Battery 410
  Grading Battery 412
  The Elements of Assault 413
  A Comprehensive Model Assault
    and Battery Statute 416

False Imprisonment 417

Kidnapping 417

Summary 424

CHAPTER 11

Crimes Against Habitation: Burglary and Arson 427

Introduction 428

Burglary 428
  Burglary *Actus Reus* 430

Circumstance Elements 431
  Burglary *Mens Rea* 435
  Grading Burglary 435

Arson 436
  History and Rationale of Arson 436
  Burning: The Arson *Actus Reus* 437
  Arson *Mens Rea* 440
  Property in Arson 441
  Grading Arson 441

Summary 441

CHAPTER 12

Crimes Against Property 444

Introduction 445

History of Theft 445

Larceny 446
  Larceny *Actus Reus* 447
  The Property and Its Value 450
  Larceny *Mens Rea* 451

Embezzlement 451

False Pretenses—Stealing by Deceit 452

General Theft Statutes 454

Computer Crime 455

Receiving Stolen Property 463

Forgery and Uttering 467
  Forgery 467
  Uttering 469

Robbery and Extortion 469
  Robbery 470
  Extortion 474

Summary 477

CHAPTER 13

Crimes Against Public Order and Morals 481

Introduction 482

Street People 484
  Loitering 485
  Panhandling 493

Street Gangs 501

Summary 513

APPENDIX

Constitution of the
United States   517

Glossary   533

Table of Cases   539

Index   545

Preface

I've loved the exciting subject of criminal law since I studied it at Northwestern University Law School in 1958. I've also loved writing *Criminal Law*. What a privilege it is to write seven editions of a book about a subject I care so much about. To have my modest innovation to the study of criminal law—the text/casebook—meet with such success is (to borrow a word from my students' lexicon) "awesome."

Criminal Law, Seventh Edition, like its predecessors, stresses both the general principles that apply to all of criminal law and the specific elements of particular crimes that prosecutors have to prove beyond a reasonable doubt. Learning the principles of criminal law isn't just good mental exercise, although it has stimulated countless students to use their minds through six previous editions of *Criminal Law*. Understanding the general principles is a tool for understanding the elements of specific crimes. The general principles have lasted for centuries. The elements of specific crimes, on the other hand, differ from state to state and from time to time because they have to meet varied and changing needs of new times and different places. That the principles have stood the test of time testifies to their strength as a framework for explaining the elements of crimes as they are defined in 50 states and the U.S. criminal codes. But there is more to their importance than durability. Knowledge of the principles is also practical. The general principles are the bases both of the elements that prosecutors have to prove beyond a reasonable doubt to convict defendants and of the defenses that justify or excuse the guilt of defendants.

Criminal Law, Seventh Edition, therefore, rests on a solid foundation. But it can't stand still, any more than the subject of criminal law can remain frozen in time. There's so much I still haven't learned; so much of what I know that I have to think about again; so many existing cases I haven't found yet; and so many new cases that weren't decided by the time the last edition was printed.

I feel deeply obligated to incorporate as much as I can of this rethinking and these recent discoveries. I hope it will benefit both the teachers who use and the students who buy *Criminal Law*, Seventh Edition. Obligated yes, but there's so much more. Obligation doesn't describe the thrill, the fascination—the sheer pleasure—that preparing new editions of *Criminal Law* brings me. Finding cases that not only elaborate on a principle in clear terms but also stimulate students to think about subjects worth thinking about is the most exciting part of teaching and writing. Looking for, and better yet finding, cases with facts that will get students to pay attention to fundamental issues of good and evil, right and wrong, justifications and excuse and at the same time give them pleasure are my favorite pastimes.

Criminal Law, Seventh Edition, continues the interactive approach to learning that lies at the heart of the text/casebook method. The use of text to explain general principles and their application to specific crimes, followed by specific cases that apply the general principles to facts, was successful in previous editions. The text/case approach invites students to participate actively in learning. They can agree or disagree with the application made by the court in its opinion, but they have to *understand* the principles and definitions in order to apply them. The text/case approach demonstrates that students not only *understand* what they've learned, that they not only actually *enjoy* what they've learned, but also that they *remember* what they've learned. Perhaps the most gratifying part of teaching criminal law by the text/case method is having students tell me many years after they've taken the course that they remember the cases and the principles the cases stood for.

The case excerpts portray the criminal law in action because they apply the general principles to real-life events. Students have to think about, to formulate their own interpretations of, and to apply the principles of criminal law to these real-life events. Students in my classes have to act as legislators, prosecutors, defense attorneys, judges, and juries so they can see the principles and rules of criminal law from all perspectives. They have to show that they understand the principles and rules first by stating them as the text presents them and then by applying them to the facts and reasoning of the case excerpts. This close relationship between the principles and rules appearing in the text and the case excerpts remains central to *Criminal Law,* seventh edition.

Case excerpts in *Criminal Law,* Seventh Edition, remain tailored to teach students the principles, doctrines, and rules of criminal law, but with an eye toward policy rather than toward the technical knowledge needed by lawyers. The case excerpts remain distinct from the text, as they have in previous editions. The text covers all of the main points so it can stand alone as an analysis of the criminal law. So, instructors can choose to omit the cases altogether from assignments; they can use them as illustrations and elaborations of the points made in the text; they can use them to test students' grasp of the text; or they can integrate them fully into the course.

A **case question** introduces each case, focusing students' attention on the point that the case excerpt elaborates. Introductions to the case excerpts state the case history, including the outcome of the case, and the sentence imposed if it is known. The excerpts present the facts and the opinion of the case in the actual words of the court. **Case discussions** follow the excerpts. The case discussions test the students' understanding of the principle, doctrine, and rule of the case excerpt. They also test the students' mastery of the facts. Finally, the case discussion questions provoke students to evaluate, criticize, and propose alternatives to the arguments and the decisions of the court as presented in the case excerpt.

Note cases elaborate further and often present a different application of the principle, doctrine, or rule covered in the main case excerpt. Instructors and students have convinced me that the note cases are a valuable tool both in understanding and applying the topics covered in the text.

A special section, **"How to Read, Brief, and Find Cases,"** appears in Chapter 2. This section explains in detail the major parts of an appellate court opinion and tells students how they can look for an opinion in the printed reports.

ORGANIZATION OF CHAPTERS

The chapters in the text follow a traditional arrangement. The first eight chapters cover the general part of the criminal law, which includes the following topics: the nature, origins, structure, and purposes of criminal law; the constitutional limits on the criminal law; the general principles of criminal liability; the doctrines of complicity and inchoate crimes; and the defenses of justification and excuse to criminal liability. The next five chapters cover the special part of the criminal law: the part that deals with the major crimes against persons, habitation, property, public order, and public morals. The logic of the arrangement is to first treat the principles and doctrines common to all crimes and then to apply the general principles and doctrines to the crimes against persons, habitation, property, public order, and public morals. For example, Chapters 3 and 4 examine the general principles of criminal liability—*actus reus, mens rea,* concurrence, causation, and resulting harm. Chapter 9 applies these general principles to the rules governing criminal homicide. In other words, Chapter 9 examines the *actus reus, mens rea,* concurrent, causation, and resulting harm required to satisfy the requirements of the law of homicide. Similarly, Chapter 10 applies the general principles to the law of criminal sexual conduct, assault, and kidnapping. Chapter 11 applies the principles to the law of burglary and arson. Chapter 12 applies them to the major property crimes. Chapter 13 addresses some of the traditional public order and morals crimes in the context of "quality of life" crimes. It invites debate about the use of criminal law to regulate not only conduct that physically injures people, their homes, and their property, but also behavior that creates community disorder by "offending respectable people."

NEW TO THIS EDITION

New Cases *Criminal Law,* Seventh Edition, contains thirty-nine new cases and many reedited cases from the previous edition. Why so many new and reedited cases? First is the need to keep the cases current. Second is the discovery of cases that explain the general principles better and apply the facts in clearer and more interesting ways than cases in previous editions. Third, some cases from previous editions require reediting after continued use in the classroom.

"The Rest of the Story" Too often we forget that the cases involve real people; they don't just apply an impersonal legal principle. Students frequently want to get beyond the confines of the case excerpt; they wonder what happened to criminals and their victims before, during, and after the crime; they even want to know what they looked like—like Paul Harvey's "the rest of the story." This "rest of the story" is difficult and even impossible to know in most cases. But I've been able to supply it for four cases' excerpts: *Bowers v. Hardwicke,* in Chapter 2; *The Kitty Genovese Case,* in Chapter 3; *People v. Goetz,* in Chapter 7; and *Snowden v. State,* in Chapter 9. My students really liked them when I tried them out in my classes.

Interactive CD-ROM Linked to the Internet The words I used to introduce the CD-ROM included with *Criminal Law,* Seventh Edition, capture the essence of my purpose in supplying the Internet links: "Criminal law is a fascinating subject, as I hope you're already finding out from the book. But the book is only a glimpse at the riches you can find on the Internet. I designed this CD-ROM to introduce you to those riches. I want research to be as exciting for you as it has been for me for forty years."

Approximately forty text references to the CD-ROM are highlighted with an icon. Some of the links on the CD-ROM enrich students' knowledge of a case and its principles by taking students to oral arguments, briefs, and other case documents.

Others provide students research opportunities to compare the principles, statutes, and opinions in the book with those in their own states. Still others take students to cases and other materials that come to contrasting conclusions to those in the book. Students can access these cases and other materials by a few mouse clicks on the hot links on the CD-ROM. I tried them out in my classes and students really liked them.

Four goals have guided the creation of the links:

1. *Make them as specific as possible.* I've tried to make it possible for students to use a single mouse click to get to specific cases, briefs, oral arguments, transcripts, statutes, and constitutional provisions. Of course, I couldn't do this for students who are looking for these and other materials from their own states, but I've tried to get these students as close as possible to them, and I've included hints for searching within their own state codes, constitutions, and cases.

2. *Make them stable.* We all know the frustration of clicking on a potentially valuable link and finding the dreaded "This page can't be found..." message. I've tried to reduce the chance of this by using stable sites. Fortunately, most of the sites are state and U.S. government sites. We are blessed with this great fact about the contents of these sites: Cases, statutes, constitutional provisions, and other such materials don't disappear or get replaced, they just keep accumulating and getting deeper and richer. This is one government program that I think we all agree we want to keep growing!

3. *Make them meaningful.* All of these links take students to information and analyses that enrich and deepen their understanding of the important concepts in criminal law. Although my students were sometimes frustrated because they couldn't find what they were looking for, or because it took them so long to find it or because the information was so hard to find, *every single one* thought what they found was worth finding when they found it. That was worth all of the work I put into creating the links.

4. *Make them interesting.* "Unfortunately, not everything that's worth knowing is interesting," I have to remind my students. But, fortunately in criminal law a lot that's worth knowing is interesting too. I believe, and my students agree, that the links go to interesting as well as meaningful places. I hope other students and their instructors will also agree.

SUPPLEMENTS

Instructor's Manual with Testbank This valuable resource has been fully updated and includes such key features as learning objectives, a detailed chapter outline, class discussion topics and student activities, as well as recommended readings and a test bank—all designed to help you smoothly correlate and plan your classes.

Criminal Law: A Microsoft® PowerPoint® Tool I created these PowerPoint presentations for use in my own Criminal Law class Fall Semester 2000. They were so successful that I've provided them for use with this edition of *Criminal Law* as well. The slides cover the key topics, concepts, terms, and laws on a chapter-by-chapter basis.

Guides to Criminal Law These state-specific guides to criminal law for California, Florida, Maryland, New York, Tennessee, and Texas offer a convenient way to explore state-specific laws and cases, with chapter introductions and overviews of codes and implications, as well as exercises for state-specific penal codes.

Student Study Guide Students can supplement their classroom experience with this integral tool that provides a detailed outline, key words and concepts with definitions, and a practice test bank for each chapter.

Web Site for *Criminal Law*, Seventh Edition Designed exclusively for this edition, this text-specific Web site, located at *http://cj.wadsworth.com,* offers a variety of online resources for students and instructors. Students can enhance their learning experience with book-specific and chapter-based resources. Web links, periodicals, and InfoTrac College Edition offer valuable and reliable sources for researching specific topics. Projects and quizzing activities provide immediate feedback and can be emailed to instructors. Online homework assignments integrate Web site research with textbook activities. Student study tips provide a well-developed guide to encourage student success. Instructor downloads and Web links for professionals offer an array of resources for curriculum development.

The Wadsworth Criminal Justice Video Library You can select from an exciting collection of videos to enrich your lectures, including the *Court TV Library Series* video, *A&E American Justice Series* videos, *National Institute of Crime File* videos, *ABC News* videos, and *MPI Home* videos. Available to qualified adopters.

Thomson Learning *WebTutor*™ on WebCT and Blackboard Professors can use *WebTutor* to provide virtual office hours, post their syllabi, set up threaded discussions, and track student progress with quizzing material. For students, *WebTutor* offers real-time access to a full array of study tools, including flash cards (with audio), practice quizzes and tests, online tutorials, and much more!

***ExamView*®** *ExamView* helps you create and customize tests in minutes. You can easily edit and import your own questions and graphics, change test layout, and move questions. The test appears on screen just as it will print. *ExamView* also offers flexible delivery and the ability to test and grade online.

Key Cases, Comments, and Questions on Substantive Criminal Law Providing students with examinations of key cases (with comments) and analyses, this text will help them grasp challenging material and test their knowledge through discussion questions and fully integrated pedagogy.

Black's Handbook of Basic Law Terms Coming from the premier publisher of legal textbooks, West Group, this paperback dictionary includes key terms used in the criminal justice field. It fully defines more than 7,500 terms, is readable and easy to use, is authoritative and up to date, and is built on the tradition of the world's most widely used law dictionary.

The Field Guide to Law Enforcement Provides clear, concise, and current statements of the rule of law commonly encountered by police officers in the field.

Careers in Criminal Justice Interactive CD-ROM (Dual platform Windows®/ Macintosh®) This engaging self-exploration provides students with a personalized profile and an interactive discovery of the wide range of careers in criminal justice.

Seeking Employment in Criminal Justice and Related Fields, Third Edition
Assists students in developing a job search strategy through resumes, cover letters, and interview techniques.

Guide to Careers in Criminal Justice This concise booklet provides a brief introduction on opportunities in law enforcement, courts, and corrections—and how to land these jobs.

InfoTrac® College Edition Opening the door to the full text of countless articles from hundreds of publications, this online library is expertly indexed and easy to use. Updated daily with articles going back as far as four years, it enables students, through a simple keyword search, to quickly generate a comprehensive list of related articles from thousands of possibilities. (Available to North American college students only.)
　　Also available: *InfoTrac®* College Edition Activities for Criminal Justice

Internet Investigator III An all-new updated version of our popular tri-fold brochure—this revised version includes up-to-date URLs that direct students to relevant Web sites for information on research, statistics, careers, the courts, and more as well as fun sites to blow off a little criminal justice steam!

Internet Activities for Criminal Justice This 60-page booklet illustrates how to best utilize the Internet for research through various searches and Internet activities.

Internet Guide for Criminal Justice Developed with the novice user in mind, the first half of this 80-page booklet provides the vocabulary and background information necessary for successfully navigating the Internet, while the second half concentrates on criminal justice–related Web sites as well as project ideas.

ACKNOWLEDGMENTS

Criminal Law, Seventh Edition, didn't get here just by my efforts. Others have also contributed. I gratefully acknowledge the contributions of the following reviewers: Phyllis Gerstenfeld, California State University, Stanislaus; Craig Hemmens, Boise State University; William Hyatt, Western Carolina University; William E. Kelly, Auburn University; Susette M. Talarico, University of Georgia; and Lee S. Weinberg, University of Pittsburgh.

　　Criminal Justice Editor Sabra Horne has enthusiastically supported me at every stage of the book. Susan DeVanna helped to develop the CD-ROM. Dawn Mesa edited the PowerPoint presentations. Jennie Redwitz and Terri Edwards kept me on track—and that's not easy with me—in getting the parts of the book ready for publication. Ruth Cottrell's calm efficiency, warm kindness, careful editing, and extraordinary patience were as welcome (and necessary) in this edition as they have been in so many others. Once again, Kevin Gleason's superb copyediting definitely improved the text; his keen wit and sense of humor were big bonuses.

　　Julia Shaw, my former student and now my teaching assistant, compiled a superb index. I'm always turning to the indexes of books I read. Because I believe they're so important, I always used to make my own indexes. In recent years, when I've turned to others to compile the indexes, I've usually been disappointed. But not this time! I knew I could count on Julia because everything she does is outstanding. I should have known that she would outdo herself in compiling the index. She did.

Abbey Baltz has definitely enriched the "Rest of the Stories" with her superb drawings of Michael Hardwick, Katherine Genovese, and Cora Dean. How she could turn the awful original newspaper photos into these excellent drawings is a mystery to me. But then she's an artist and I'm a teacher.

What would I do without Sally, who keeps on praising my work and me, even when I don't deserve it? It's a marvel (and a boon) to me how she keeps on doing detective work, leg work, eye work, and just plain grunt work year after year and edition after edition. Then there's Doug, who's always there to take me there and get me here and everywhere, filling out forms and completing paperwork, day in and day out, days that now have stretched into years. And, like Sally, he does all of this while putting up with my mercurial temperament. Only those who really know me can understand how trying for even the most patient that can be! Friends and associates like these have made *Criminal Law,* Seventh Edition, a better book. All its failings are, naturally, mine.

Joel Samaha

CHAPTER 1

The Nature and Purposes of Criminal Law

Chapter Outline

I. Introduction

II. The Nature of Criminal Law

III. Classifying and Grading Crimes

IV. Punishment

V. Criminal Law in a Federal System

VI. Sources of Criminal Law

VII. Nonlegal Influences on Criminal Law

VIII. Summary

CHAPTER MAIN POINTS

1. Criminal law consists of the power and limits of government authority to define, prohibit, grade, and punish socially harmful behavior.

2. Criminal law is distinguished from all other law because it carries with it the moral condemnation of the whole community.

3. Rational criminal law is criminal law that is based on a principle of limits.

4. There is a criminal law for every local government, every state, and the federal government.

5. The general part of the criminal law consists of general principles of criminal liability, parties to crime, uncompleted crimes, and the defenses.

6. The special part of criminal law consists of the definitions of the elements of crimes against the state, persons, habitation, property, and public order and morals.

7. Criminal law distinguishes among criminal conduct, illegal but not criminal conduct, and reprehensible but not illegal conduct.

8. Criminal law grades criminal behavior according to several schemes.

9. Criminal punishment requires the infliction of pain, prescribed by law, administered intentionally by the state.

10. The general purposes of criminal punishment are retribution and prevention.

11. The ideological, irrational, historical, and ethical core perspectives enrich our understanding of how and why the principles, doctrines, and rules of criminal law originated.

Police Officer: "There ought to be a big billboard at our city limits that reads: 'Welcome to Bloomington, you're under arrest.'"
Professor: "Why?"
Police Officer: "Because everything in Bloomington is a crime."
Professor: "But Bloomington is a city in the freest country in the history of the world."

INTRODUCTION

Throughout our history we have relied heavily on criminal law to prohibit and punish everything from murder to playing loud music. In Palo Alto, California, "harboring overdue library books" is punishable by thirty days in jail. In Minnesota, it's a crime to fornicate with a bird. In some communities, it's a crime to park your car on your lawn, hang laundry out in your back yard, eat on a bus, or hang out in shopping malls.

Why do we have criminal law? What is it good for? Two reasons are obvious:

1. Prevent wrongdoing.
2. Punish wrongdoers.

Three others are just as important, even if they're not so obvious:

1. Define exactly what behavior is criminal.
2. Grade crimes according to their seriousness.
3. Fix the punishment for each crime.

Think about the following scenarios. Which of the behaviors in them would you define as crimes? Rank these crimes from what you think is the most to least serious. Fix a punishment for each instance of what you consider a crime. Give a reason for the punishment you prescribed. If you think an episode doesn't describe a crime, does it still deserve some kind of legal response? For example, should the law regulate the behavior by taxing it, or by requiring a license to engage in it? Should the law allow the "victims" to sue the person who injured them? Why should the victims win or lose? If you think the scenario doesn't deserve legal action, does it call for some informal response? Do any of the people in the scenarios deserve condemnation by families and friends but not the label of "criminal" and its accompanying criminal punishment? Do some deserve no sanction at all? Do any deserve praise or other reward?

1. Sheila hates Rosemary because Rosemary is richer and smarter than Sheila. Sheila reaches the breaking point when a prestigious medical school accepts Rosemary, while the law school at the same university rejects Sheila. Enraged, Sheila decides to murder Rosemary. Sheila waits patiently for the right time to commit the murder. She gets her chance when Rosemary invites Sheila to a celebration party. Sheila poisons Rosemary's drink and watches with immense pleasure as Rosemary writhes in pain and dies a slow, agonizing death.

2. Tom's wife suffers excruciating pain from what the doctors say is terminal bone cancer. The family has exhausted its insurance coverage and savings in order to keep her alive. For the past few weeks now, every time Tom sees his

wife, she pleads, "Tom, please put me out of my misery. I can't take this anymore." Tom loves his wife dearly and cannot bear her pain. An avid hunter, he takes one of his guns and shoots her in the head, killing her instantly.

3. Driving down an icy city street, Nathan steps on the gas when he approaches a particularly slick spot, hoping for the thrill of feeling the car spin out. As it does, Nathan sees a frail old man crossing the street in front of him. He tries to swerve away but cannot. He hits the old man. "Oh, my God!" cries Nathan. "This is the last thing I wanted to happen." Two days later, while still in the hospital for treatment of his injuries, the man dies of a heart attack.

4. Scott is drowning in a lake. Foy, his lifelong enemy, sees Scott struggling but walks on, laughing at the thought of getting Scott out of the way. Scott drowns.

5. Every night when he gets home from work, Doug watches child pornography videos. He finds them highly erotic, especially when they involve sex between teenage girls. After getting his "release," Doug falls asleep until it's time to get up for work the next morning.

6. Michael is a demonstrative person who really likes women. He goes into a singles bar, where he is immediately drawn to Marietta. Michael puts his arm around her waist and introduces himself. Marietta, offended by a stranger touching her, says firmly, "Stop that!" Michael doesn't remove his arm, saying, "Don't be such a prude, I'm just trying to be friendly."

7. Adam sees a radio in a department store that he wants. When the clerk walks away, Adam takes the radio.

8. Bill is addicted to crystal meth.

9. Jessica, a highly successful attorney in a major law firm, smokes marijuana on weekends.

10. Michelle cheats on her boyfriend, Cameron, with Cameron's best friend, D. J. Cameron is so distraught when he catches them that he loses his business and becomes an alcoholic.

11. Monty tells his boyfriend Brad that he's HIV negative. It's a lie. Monty is HIV positive.

12. A major pharmaceutical corporation introduced a drug used to treat high blood pressure. Although knowing that the drug had been reported to cause death and liver damage, the corporation labeled the product saying that no cause-and-effect relationship existed between the drug and liver damage. After the drug was linked to thirty-six deaths and more than five hundred cases of liver and kidney damage, the corporation withdrew the drug from the U.S. market.

13. Hilary, a gynecologist, recommends a hysterectomy for Jane, who suffers from back pain. After the surgery, the pain continues. Another doctor discovers that the source of Jane's pain is the difference in length between her left and right leg. He recommends platform shoes, and Jane's pain disappears.

14. Duran burns the American flag while chanting, "I hate America."

15. Matt dances nude in a local tavern. A sign outside the bar reads: "All male strippers. Adults welcome."

Can you state specifically why you defined, classified, and graded the examples the way you did? Can you explain why you believe some examples deserve criminal prohibition and punishment? Write down your answers. Reconsider these hypotheticals and your preliminary answers to them as you study this and the remaining chapters.

THE NATURE OF CRIMINAL LAW

Criminal law is the power of government to ban and punish behavior. In a constitutional democracy, like that of the United States, this power is limited. So, students of criminal law in a constitutional democracy have to learn not only what behavior government *can* but also what it *can't* ban and punish. Criminal law has six fundamental characteristics:

1. *It is a list of commands, of dos and don'ts telling people what they must do or refrain from doing.* Common don'ts include "Don't murder, rape, rob, steal, panhandle, fornicate outside marriage, or urinate in public." Common dos include "Pay your taxes, support your children, report child abuse."

2. *These commands are enacted into law.* Only commands that legislatures pass into law or that were established by courts hundreds of years ago in the common law (discussed later in this chapter) qualify as crimes.

3. *The law prescribes a punishment to accompany the crime.* Criminal laws are not bare commands; they also order painful consequences for those who don't obey the commands.

4. *The dos and don'ts apply to everyone under the authority that created the criminal law.* The commands "speak to all members of the community . . . in the community's behalf, with all the power and prestige of the community behind them."

5. *Crimes injure both individual victims and society.* A mugging not only injures the victim of that particular mugging, it also puts the whole community in fear; forgery not only cheats the particular victim, it undermines public confidence in all kinds of dealings that allow everyday life to go on.[1]

6. *Conviction and punishment is a formal public condemnation backed up by the weight of the whole community's moral judgment.*

The first five characteristics aren't unique to criminal law. They also describe civil law, or the law that controls private rights like contracts, property, and personal injuries (torts). Moral condemnation is what sets criminal law apart from the rest of law. In his classic "The Aims of the Criminal Law," the legal philosopher Henry M. Hart, Jr. writes of this unique characteristic of criminal law:

> The essence . . . lies in the criminal conviction itself. One may lose more money on the stock market than in a court-room; a prisoner of war camp may well provide a harsher environment than a state prison; death on the field of battle has the same characteristics as death by sentence of law. It is the expression of the community's hatred, fear, or contempt for the convict which alone characterizes physical hardship as punishment.[2]

CLASSIFYING AND GRADING CRIMES

Throughout U.S. history, legislators, courts, and scholars have created various schemes to describe the different features of criminal law just discussed. Although not the most exciting part of your study of criminal law, the basics of these schemes are important to learn right at the beginning. Why? For at least three reasons.

1. All of the schemes focus on the nature of criminal law.
2. Professionals use the schemes to think about the subject.
3. The schemes are an excellent way to help you think critically and effectively about the many fascinating aspects of criminal law.

CRIME, TORT, AND NONLEGAL RESPONSES TO SOCIAL HARMS

Before we examine the schemes, we need to spend a little time putting criminal law into a bigger picture that incorporates three kinds of social control—two legal and one nonlegal. Most social control has nothing to do with law. It's the condemnation of your friends, neighbors and others whose approval matters to you. Or, it might take the form of getting thrown out of an organization you really want to be a member of. The two legal forms are civil law and criminal law. **Civil law** is most familiar to you in the form of a suit brought by one private party (called a **plaintiff**) against a **defendant** (either a person, business, or government) to collect money (called damages). The formal title to a civil action reflects these individual and private qualities—for example, Marconi (plaintiff, the injured person who brings the suit) v. (versus or against) Yu (defendant, the person sued). These lawsuits are called torts, personal injury, or product liability cases. **Damages** are not fines. Damages are compensation paid to individuals for their injuries; fines are penalties paid to the state as criminal punishment. Although tort actions can include **punitive damages** (damages intended to punish the wrongdoer), their primary purpose is to restore injured persons to the position they enjoyed before defendants injured them. Damages usually cover medical expenses, lost wages, disability, and sometimes pain and suffering.

Unlike civil law, criminal law considers society to be the injured party. Why? Because crimes not only hurt individuals and their property but they also undermine social security, harmony, and well-being. The government prosecutes criminal defendants to protect the social interest in harmony, order, peace, and security. The titles of criminal cases—*State v. Wenz, People v. Twohy, Commonwealth v. McDonald,* or *United States v. Storlie*—denote the societal nature of criminal prosecution. The stigma attached to criminal conviction and incarceration is far greater than that associated with losses in private lawsuits, even though the financial cost may be lower.

Civil actions and criminal prosecution are not mutually exclusive responses to social harms. States can prosecute, injured parties can sue, friends might censure, and conscience may pang the same person, all for a single event. In our law, most crimes are also torts: Burglary is the tort of trespass, theft is the tort of conversion, and there is both civil and criminal assault. Burglary victims can sue burglars for trespass, and states can prosecute the same burglars for burglary. The double jeopardy clause in the United States Constitution—"no person shall . . . be subject for the same offence to be twice put in jeopardy of life or limb"—does not prohibit tort and criminal actions for the same conduct. Defendants in tort actions do not lose "life or limb"; they can only lose money.

As you study criminal law, keep this range of alternative responses—personal and private sanctions, tort, and criminal prosecution—in mind. Rational criminal law systems designate only the worst injuries crimes. Murder, rape, robbery, and burglary are the obvious examples; they call for society's strongest response—imprisonment and sometimes even death. Criminal law is society's last resort. To summarize, where something less will do, then something more should not be done. So, if friends' disapproval makes avaricious people less greedy, then making avarice a crime doesn't make sense.[3]

THE GENERAL AND SPECIAL PARTS OF CRIMINAL LAW

With the broad picture just sketched in mind, let's turn to the centuries-old scheme by which criminal law is divided into two classes. The **general part of criminal law** covers principles that apply to all crimes: constitutional principles found in the U.S. and state constitutions (Chapter 2); principles of criminal liability included in state statutes and court opinions (Chapters 3 and 4); principles that define the liability for accomplices and accessories to crime (Chapter 5); liability for the uncompleted crimes of attempt, conspiracy, and solicitation (Chapter 6); and finally the general principles of justification and excuse known as the defenses to crimes, such as self-defense and insanity (Chapters 7 and 8).[4]

The **special part of criminal law** defines the specific crimes, such as murder, rape, robbery, theft, and disturbing the peace (Chapters 9 through 13). The definitions in the special part must agree with the principles set out in the general part. For example, the general principle *actus reus* says that liability depends on what people do, not what they think or who they are. So, all specific crimes include an action—killing in murder, breaking and entering in burglary, taking someone else's stuff in theft.

GRADING SCHEMES

Not all bad conduct is criminal, nor should it be. A "creep" is not necessarily a criminal! Fairness calls for a measured response, one proportional to the wrong. As the ancient saying goes, "Let the punishment fit the crime." So, the conscience of the wrongdoer is enough punishment for some conduct. Some conduct, while reprehensible, still doesn't need a criminal law response; private sanctions are enough. These might include suspending students who cheat on exams; docking the pay of lazy workers; and scorning liars and unfaithful spouses.

Felony, Misdemeanor, and Violation

One scheme for grading criminal offenses focuses on punishments. From most severe to least severe, the penalty categories are capital felonies, felonies, gross misdemeanors, petty misdemeanors, and violations. In states with capital punishment, **capital felony** means the death penalty; in states without the death penalty, it means life in prison without hope of release before death. In the United States, aggravated murder is currently the only capital felony punishable by death. However, some states have recently enacted life-without-parole statutes for some drug law violations. Michigan, for example, punishes the possession of more than 650 grams of cocaine with life imprisonment without parole. And, as we will see in Chapter 2, at least one state now permits the death penalty for the rape of a child under 12 years old.[5]

The differences between **felonies** and **misdemeanors** are the *length* and *place* of imprisonment. Felonies are crimes punishable by incarceration of at least one year in state prisons; misdemeanors are punishable by incarceration in local jails for less than one year. Misdemeanors are also punishable by fines. Although there are many differences among the states, **gross misdemeanors** usually carry maximum penalties of close to one year in jail, misdemeanors are usually punishable in the ninety-day range, and **petty misdemeanors** result in a jail sentence of up to thirty days. **Violations**, consisting mainly of traffic offenses punishable by fines, aren't designated criminal convictions in most jurisdictions and they don't become part of your criminal record.[6]

One problem with grading is the large number of offenses and penalties in most criminal codes. At one time, Oregon had 1,413 separate offenses and 466 different sentencing levels! Someone called this "anarchy in sentencing." The highly respected criminal law professor, Herbert Wechsler, called it "nonsense." According to Wechsler,

> The human mind cannot draw an infinite number of distinctions about crime. You can see the most serious crimes and the less serious ones, and you can see some gradations in between. And there may be some difference of opinion whether you can see three or four or six or seven categories. But there is a finite number that it is prudent to attempt to perceive.[7]

Wrongs *Mala in Se* and *Mala Prohibita*

Another grading scheme divides crimes between inherently evil conduct, ***malum in se***, and merely prohibited conduct, ***malum prohibitum***. Murder, rape, robbery, burglary, arson, larceny are *malum in se* because they would be evil even if the law didn't make them crimes. On the other hand, if you make an illegal left turn or commit most of the long list of offenses that regulate life in the twenty-first century, no one will treat you as a bad person even though you broke the law. The law prohibits them but they're not naturally bad like murder and rape.

Classifications According to Subject

At least as early as the sixteenth century, crimes were classified according to their subject matter. Most states still classify crimes similarly. Typically, state criminal codes divide the special part of criminal law into the following subject classifications:

- *Crimes against the state,* including treason and sedition.
- *Crimes against persons,* including murder, manslaughter, rape, kidnapping, assault, and battery.
- *Crimes against habitation,* including burglary and arson.
- *Crimes against property,* including larceny, embezzlement, false pretenses, malicious mischief, and robbery (really a combination of a crime against a person and property).
- *Crimes against public order,* including disorderly conduct and public drunkenness.
- *Crimes against the administration of justice,* including obstruction of justice and bribery.
- *Crimes against public morals,* including prostitution, fornication, and profanity.

❊ 1-1 State Criminal Codes

Professors Andrew von Hirsch and Nils Jareborg have worked out a subject matter grading system called a **living standard analysis** of criminal harm. Living standard means the quality of life, including both economic well-being and noneconomic wherewithal that affect the quality of a person's life. According to von Hirsch and Jareborg, crimes invade four general interests that affect the quality of life:

1. Physical integrity.
2. Material support and amenity.
3. Freedom from humiliation.
4. Privacy and autonomy.

How much a crime invades these interests tells us how serious an offense it is.[8]

PUNISHMENT

Banning and grading are necessary aims of criminal law, but they are not enough. Criminal law also has to punish wrongdoers. Punishment takes many forms. A teenager grounded for staying out too late; a worker fired for too many absences; a student suspended for truancy—all are punished because they have felt the unpleasant consequences of breaking rules. But these punishments aren't *criminal* punishment. Why? Because, to qualify as criminal punishment, penalties have to meet four conditions:

1. impose pain or other unpleasant consequences
2. be prescribed by the law
3. be administered intentionally
4. be administered by the state

The last three are clear enough. But "pain or other unpleasant consequences" doesn't spell out the purpose of the pain or other unpleasant consequence. A violent mental patient confined indefinitely to a padded cell in a state security hospital clearly suffers more pain than a person incarcerated for three days in the county jail for disorderly conduct. However, only the jail sentence is criminal punishment. Why? The *reason* for the pain. The mental patient is confined in the hospital for treatment and in the padded cell for safety. The pain is an unfortunate side effect, not the reason for the patient's confinement. On the other hand, confinement in jail is the intentional infliction of pain for the purpose of punishment. (See Table 1.1.)

Pain and pleasure don't always distinguish punishment from treatment. Shock treatment inflicts more pain on mental patients than confinement in "Club Fed" minimum-security prisons inflicts on federal offenders. So, if pain is the measure, punishment trumps treatment. Indeed, some critics maintain that "helping" a patient justifies extreme measures: massive surgery, castration, and lobotomy. One of my professors once said, "Whenever someone says, 'I'm going to help you,' turn around and run as fast as you can because it's going to hurt like hell." Professor Herbert Packer resolved the dilemma of treatment and punishment by adding a fifth element of criminal punishment—the purpose of punishment.[9]

Two purposes underlie all criminal punishment: retribution and prevention. **Retribution** looks back to the crime committed, punishing it because it is right to do so. **Prevention** looks forward, punishing offenders in order to prevent crimes in the future. Prevention takes four forms: general deterrence, special deterrence, incapacitation, and rehabilitation.

TABLE 1.1 "What Types of Sentences Usually Are Given to Offenders?"

DEATH PENALTY	For the most serious crimes such as murder, the courts in most states may sentence an offender to death by lethal injection, electrocution, exposure to lethal gas, hanging, or other method specified by state law. • As of 2000, 37 states had laws providing for the death penalty. • All death penalty sentences are for murder. • 500 persons had been executed from 1976 to 1991. • 3,452 persons were under sentence of death on January 1, 1999.
INCARCERATION	Incarceration is the confinement of a convicted criminal in a federal or state prison or a local jail to serve a court-imposed sentence. Confinement is usually in a jail, administered locally; or in a prison, operated by the state or federal government. In many states offenders sentenced to 1 year or less are held in a jail; those sentenced to longer terms are committed to a state prison. More than 4,200 correctional facilities are maintained by federal, state, and local governments. They include 47 federal facilities, 922 state-operated adult confinement and community-based correctional facilities, and 3,300 local jails, which usually are county operated. • 1,302,019 Americans were locked up in federal and state prisons and jails on January 1, 1999.
PROBATION	Probation is the sentencing of an offender to community supervision by a probation agency, often as a result of suspending a sentence to confinement. Such supervision normally entails specific rules of conduct while in the community. If the rules are violated, a sentence to confinement may be imposed. Probation is the most widely used correctional disposition in the United States. State or local governments operate more than 2,000 probation agencies. • 3,417,613 Americans were on probation on January 1, 1999.
SPLIT SENTENCES, SHOCK PROBATION, AND INTERMITTENT CONFINEMENT	These are penalties that explicitly require the convicted person to serve a brief period of confinement in a local, state, or federal facility (the "shock") followed by a period of probation. This penalty attempts to combine the use of community supervision with a short incarceration experience. Some sentences are periodic rather than continuous; for example, an offender may be required to spend a certain number of weekends in jail.
RESTITUTION AND VICTIM COMPENSATION	In these dispositions, the offender is required to provide financial repayment—or, in some jurisdictions, services in lieu of monetary restitution—for the losses incurred by the victim. Nearly all states have statutory provisions for the collection and disbursement of restitution funds. A restitution law was enacted at the federal level in 1982.
COMMUNITY SERVICE	The offender is required to perform a specified amount of public service work, such as collecting trash in parks or other public facilities. Many states authorize community service work orders. Community service often is imposed as a specific condition of probation.

(continued)

TABLE 1.1   Continued

FINES	A fine is an economic penalty that requires the offender to pay a specified sum of money within limits set by law. Fines often are imposed in addition to probation or as alternatives to incarceration. The Victims of Crime Act of 1984 authorizes the distribution of fines and forfeited criminal profits to support state victim-assistance programs, with priority given to programs that aid victims of sexual assault, spouse abuse, and child abuse. These programs, in turn, provide assistance and compensation to crime victims. Many laws that govern the imposition of fines are being revised. The revisions often provide for more flexible means of ensuring equity in the imposition of fines, flexible fine schedules, "day fines" geared to the offender's daily wage, installment payment of fines, and the imposition of confinement only when there is an intentional refusal to pay. One study reports that ". . . more than three-fourths of criminal courts use fines extensively, and that fines levied each year exceed $1 billion."

Source: Bureau of Justice Statistics, *Capital Punishment 1998* (December 1999); *Prisoners in the U.S. 1998* (April 1999); *Probation and Parole in the U.S. 1998* (August 1999)

RETRIBUTION

Striking out to hurt what hurts us is a natural impulse. It's what makes us kick the table leg we stub our toe on. It's the heart of the idea of retribution, summed up in the words of the Old Testament: "When one man strikes another and kills him, he shall be put to death. When one man injures and disfigures his fellow-countryman, it shall be done to him as he had done; fracture for fracture, eye for eye, tooth for tooth." The nineteenth-century English judge and historian of the criminal law, Sir James F. Stephen, wrote:[10]

> The infliction of punishment by law gives definite expression and a solemn ratification and justification to the hatred which is excited by the commission of the offense. The criminal law thus proceeds upon the principle that it is morally right to hate criminals, and it confirms and justifies that sentiment by inflicting on criminals punishments which express it. I think it highly desirable that criminals should be hated, that the punishments inflicted upon them should be so contrived as to give expression to that hatred, and to justify it so far as the public provision of means for expressing and gratifying a healthy natural sentiment can justify and encourage it. The forms in which deliberate anger and righteous disapprobation are expressed, and the execution of criminal justice is the most emphatic of such forms, stand to the one set of passions in the same relation in which marriage stands to sexual passion.[11]

Retribution is two-edged: It benefits society by retaliation and it benefits criminals by "paying their debt to society." Retribution assumes that offenders are free to choose between committing and not committing crimes. Because offenders have this choice, society can blame them for making the wrong choice. We call this blameworthiness culpability. **Culpability** means that offenders are responsible for their actions and must suffer the consequences if they act irresponsibly.

Retribution has several appealing qualities. First, it assumes that we have free will and individual autonomy. We're not mere pawns at the mercy of forces we can't control. Instead, we are the masters of and are responsible for our own destinies. Second, retribution seems in accord with human nature. Hating what and who hurts us—especially murderers, rapists, robbers, and other violent criminals—is a natural impulse.[12]

From the Old Testament's philosophy of taking an eye for an eye, to the nineteenth-century Englishman's claim that it is right to hate and hurt criminals, to the modern idea of "three strikes and you're out" and "lock 'em up and throw away the key," the desire for retribution has run strong and deep in religion, in criminal justice, and in society as a whole. Retributionists see this long tradition as proof of its worth, as if its sheer tenacity validates its use. The long and strong life of retribution lies mainly in its dependence on the idea of culpability. Simply put, we can't punish those we can't blame; and, we can't blame those who aren't responsible. But justice demands that we *do* punish the blameworthy.

It's difficult to translate *abstract* justice into specific penalties. What are a rapist's just deserts? Is castration justice? How many years in prison is robbery worth? How much offender suffering will repay the pain of a disfigured assault victim? Critics of retribution say that we can't and—what's more we shouldn't even try—to perform such calculations because, as Henry Wiehofen maintained, retribution is the last hold-out of barbarism:

> All of this abstract philosophizing about punishment as requital for crime has a musty smell about it, a smell of the professor's study. The people who have the responsibility for fighting crime and dealing with criminals have learned that it is pointless to talk about "how much punishment" is deserved. In the nineteenth century it had its appeal. But the modern behavioral sciences have shown that armchair abstractions about the "justice" of retribution by philosophers who reject human experience are sadly defective in human understanding, not to say human sympathy. The retributive approach is too subjective and too emotional to solve problems that have their roots in social conditions and the consequent impact on individual personality.[13]

Wiehofen flatly rejects the assumption that the urge to retaliate is part of human nature. According to Wiehofen, retributionsts have no proof that a bloodthirsty human nature craves vengeance. Therefore, the law should get rid of vengeance.

Many criminologists reject the most basic assumption of retribution—free will. They suggest that forces beyond human will control, or determine, individual behavior. Their research has demonstrated a relationship between social conditions and crime. (Of course, relationship doesn't prove cause and effect.) Psychiatrists point to subconscious forces, beyond the conscious will's control, that determine criminal conduct. Some biologists have linked violent crime to an extra Y chromosome. Medical doctors have tried to show a link between brain chemistry and violence. There is no satisfying empirical proof of any of these claims for determinism. But neither are the claims of free will documented in the empirical research. In any event, determinism undermines the legitimacy of retribution to the extent that we act according to "forces" either inside or outside our conscious minds instead of choosing our behavior.[14]

Probably the strongest argument against retribution is that most criminal laws aren't based on moral blameworthiness. A vast number of crimes do not require intentional wrongdoing to qualify for criminal punishment. To cite but two of many examples: Statutory rape is not excused by either the consent of the victim or an honest and reasonable mistake about the victim's age. Pulling the trigger of a gun believed to be unloaded does not justify or excuse a death resulting from the shots. Throughout the book, you'll find examples of crimes in which the actors didn't intend to do wrong.[15]

PREVENTION

Retribution justifies punishment on the ground that it's right to hurt criminals. Prevention inflicts pain not for its own sake but to prevent future crimes. **General prevention**, also called **general deterrence**, aims by threat of punishment to prevent the general population who have not committed crimes from doing so. **Special deterrence** by inflicting pain on individual offenders aims to deter them from committing future crimes. **Incapacitation** also aims to prevent specific convicted criminals from committing future crimes by confining them or, more rarely, by altering them surgically, or at the extreme by executing them. **Rehabilitation** aims to prevent crime by changing individuals so that they will obey the law. These purposes all have in common the premise that pain is necessary only to prevent future crime. They differ from retribution in this essential respect: Retribution purposely inflicts pain to give criminals their "just deserts" for past criminal conduct.

Deterrence

Jeremy Bentham, the great eighteenth-century English philosopher and law reformer, promoted deterrence as the only purpose of punishment in a "civilized" society. Bentham was heavily influenced by the intellectual movement of his time called the Enlightenment. At the core of the movement was the notion that natural laws govern both the physical universe and society. One of these natural laws of society, **hedonism**, states that human beings seek pleasure and avoid pain. A related law, **rationalism**, states that the desire to maximize pleasure and minimize pain lies behind all human action. Reason, a distinct human quality, permits human beings to apply natural laws mechanistically (according to rules), rather than by discretion (individual judgment of the decision makers).

These ideas (oversimplified here) led Bentham to formulate his **deterrence theory**. It states that rational human beings won't commit crimes if they know that the pain of punishment outweighs the pleasure of committing crimes. According to the natural law of hedonism, if would-be criminals fear future punishment more than they want the pleasure of present crime, they won't commit crimes.

Deterrence is considerably more complex than Bentham's crime prevention model suggests. Threatened punishment doesn't always deter—it goads some people to do the very thing the threat is supposed to prevent. During the Vietnam War, for example, Congress made burning draft cards a crime. Instead of avoiding draft card burning, protesters turned out in scores to burn their cards.[16]

Preventionists rely on the **principle of utility**—the state can inflict only enough pain to prevent crime. English playwright George Bernard Shaw, a strong deterrence supporter, put it this way: "Vengeance is *mine* sayeth the Lord; which means it is *not* the Lord Chief Justice's." According to this argument, only God, the angels, or some other divine being can measure just deserts, but social scientists can determine how much pain can prevent crime.

Preventionists concede that there are impediments to translating theory into practice. The emotionalism that surrounds punishment cuts into objectivity, and penalties often rest more on faith than evidence. For example, one economist in the 1970s found that every execution saves about eight lives by deterring potential murderers from killing. This finding sparked a controversy having little to do with the study's empirical validity. Instead, the arguments turned to ethics—whether killing anyone is right, no matter what social benefits it produces. This shift from science to ethics is graphically illustrated in a conversation about the study that I had with one state legislator, a strong preventionist. When I told him about the study, he said, "That study can't be right." "What if it is right?" I persisted. His reply, "Well, then we'll have to 'deep-six' that study."[17]

Critics attack deterrence from several angles. First, they claim that the rational, free-will individual of deterrence theory is as far from reality as the eighteenth-century world that gave birth to the idea. Complex forces within the human organism and in the external environment, both of which are beyond individual control, strongly influence behavior. Individual behavior is too unpredictable to reduce to a mechanistic formula. The mere existence of criminal law deters some people from committing crimes; others require more. We don't have enough information about who these others are and of what the "more" consists to base policy on it.

Second, severity isn't the only ingredient in effective punishment. Certainty and celerity (speed) probably have a greater deterrent effect than severity, according to empirical findings.[18]

Third, threats don't affect all crimes or would-be criminals equally. Crimes of passion, such as murder and rape, are probably little affected by threats; whereas speeding, drunken driving, and corporate crime are probably greatly affected by threats. The leading deterrence theorist, Johannes Andenaes, sums up the state of our knowledge about deterrence:

> There is a long way to go before research can give quantitative forecasts. The long-term moral effects of the criminal law and law enforcement are especially hard to isolate and quantify. Some categories of crime are so intimately related to specific social situations that generalizations of a quantitative kind are impossible. An inescapable fact is that research will always lag behind actual developments. When new forms of crime come into existence, such as hijacking of aircraft or terrorist acts against officers of the law, there cannot possibly be a body of research ready as a basis for the decisions that have to be taken. Common sense and trial by error have to give the answers.[19]

Finally, critics maintain that even if we could get convincing empirical support for criminal punishment, deterrence is unjust because it punishes for example's sake. Supreme Court Justice Oliver Wendell Holmes described the example dimension to deterrence:

> If I were having a philosophical talk with a man I was going to have hanged (or electrocuted) I should say, "I don't doubt that your act was inevitable for you but to make it more avoidable by others we propose to sacrifice you to the common good. You may regard yourself as a soldier dying for your country if you like. But the law must keep its promises."[20]

Punishment shouldn't be a sacrifice to the common good. According to retributionists, it is just only if it aims at redeeming the person being punished. Punishment is personal and individual, not general and societal. Preventionists answer that so long as offenders are in fact guilty, punishing them is personal; hence, it is just to use individual punishment for society's benefit.

Incapacitation

Incapacitation restrains offenders from committing further crimes. At the extreme, incapacitation includes mutilation—castration, amputation, and lobotomy—or even death in capital punishment. Incapacitation in most cases means imprisonment. Incapacitation works: Dead people can't commit crimes, and prisoners don't commit them, at least not outside prison walls. Incapacitation, then, offers a lot to a society determined to repress crime. According to criminologist James Q. Wilson:

> The chances of a persistent robber or burglar living out his life, or even going a year with no arrest are quite small. Yet a large proportion of repeat offenders suffer little or no loss of freedom. Whether or not one believes that such penalties, if inflicted, would act as a deterrent, it is obvious that they could serve to incapacitate these offenders and, thus, for the period of the incapacitation, prevent them from committing additional crimes.[21]

Like deterrence and retribution, incapacitation has its share of critics. The basic problem with incapacitation is prediction, particularly the prediction of violent behavior. Kleptomaniacs will almost surely steal again, exhibitionists will expose themselves, and addicts will continue to use chemicals. But when will murderers, rapists, or bank robbers strike again? Nobody really knows. So, punishment is based on a poor guess about future danger.[22]

Furthermore, critics argue, incapacitation merely shifts criminality from outside prisons to inside prisons. Sex offenders and other violent criminals find victims among other inmates; property offenders get and sell contraband and other smuggled items. Moreover, incarceration is expensive. According to current estimates, it costs over $100,000 to construct a prison cell and as much as $35,000 a year to feed, house, and clothe a prisoner. Finally, critics maintain that several incapacitative measures—death, psychosurgery, and mutilation—violate the Eighth Amendment "cruel and unusual punishment" clause of the U.S. Constitution.[23] (See Chapter 2.)

Rehabilitation

In his now classic *The Limits of the Criminal Sanction,* Herbert Packer succinctly summarized the aims of rehabilitation: "The most immediately appealing justification for punishment is the claim that it may be used to prevent crimes by so changing the personality of the offender that he will conform to the dictates of law; in a word, by reforming him."[24]

Rehabilitation borrows a lot from medicine, leading to the descriptions of it as the **medical model of punishment.** According to the medical model, crime is a "disease" that criminals have caught. The major purpose of punishment is to "cure" criminal patients through "treatment." The length of imprisonment depends upon when the cure takes effect. On its face, rehabilitation is the most humane form of criminal punishment. Its proponents contend that treating offenders is more civilized than other forms of punishment.

Two assumptions underlie rehabilitation theory. First, forces beyond the control of individual offenders control their criminality. So, when it comes to the *causes* of crime, rehabilitationists are determinists. The second assumption is that experts can modify the behavior of offenders so they won't commit any more crimes. Treatment restores free will so that former criminals can control their own destinies. So, when it comes to the *cure* for crime, rehabilitationists subscribe to free will. Criminals can choose to change their life habits, and after they do, society can hold them responsible for their actions.

The view that criminals are sick has profoundly affected criminal law and has generated acrimonious debate. The reason is not that reform and rehabilitation are new ideas; quite the contrary. The nineteenth-century scholar Sir Francis Palgrave summed up a 700-year-old attitude when he stated the medieval church's position on punishment: It was not to be "thundered in vengeance for the satisfaction of the state, but imposed for the good of the offender; in order to afford the means of amendment and to lead the transgressor to repentance, and to mercy." Sixteenth-century Elizabethan pardon statutes were laced with the language of repentance and reform. By granting pardons to criminals, the queen hoped to reform criminals by mercy, not vengeance. Even Jeremy Bentham, most closely associated with deterrence, claimed that punishment would "contribute to the reformation of the offender, not only through fear of being punished again, but by a change in his character and habits."[25]

Throughout its long history, rehabilitation has suffered serious attacks. The most fundamental criticism is that rehabilitation is based on false, or at least unproven, assumptions. The causes of crime are so complex, and the wellsprings of human behavior as yet so undetermined, that sound policy cannot rest on treatment. A second criticism is that it makes no sense to brand everyone who violates the criminal law as sick and needing treatment.[26]

Some critics call rehabilitation inhumane because the desire to cure tears away the limits to administering large doses of pain. British literary critic C. S. Lewis put it this way:

> My contention is that good men (not bad men) consistently acting upon that position would act as cruelly and unjustly as the greatest tyrants. They might in some respects act even worse. Of all tyrannies a tyranny sincerely exercised for the good of its victims may be the most oppressive. It may be better to live under robber barons than under omnipotent moral busybodies. The robber baron's cruelty may sometimes sleep, his cupidity may at some point be satiated; but those who torment us for our own good will torment us without end for they do so with the approval of their own conscience. They may be more likely to go to Heaven yet at the same time likelier to make a Hell of earth. Their very kindness stings with intolerable insult. To be "cured" against one's will and cured of states which we may not regard as disease is to be put on a level with those who have not yet reached the age of reason or those who never will; to be classed with infants, imbeciles, and domestic animals. But to be punished, however severely, because we have deserved it, because we "ought to have known better," is to be treated as a human person made in God's image.[27]

The answers to the problem of punishment call for a division of labor. Scientific researchers should answer the empirical question, "What kind of punishment and how much works, and why?" Policymakers should focus on the answer to the questions, "Is this particular punishment and the amount of it wise, and is it consistent with our humane values? Lawyers should answer the questions, "Is it legal? Does the Constitution allow it?" And philosophers and moralists should guide us to decide, "Is it right?" For instance, empirical research might demonstrate that the death penalty for rape prevents rape, and state legislatures may decide that it is sound public policy, but the United States Supreme Court has declared that capital punishment for rape violates the Eighth Amendment of the Constitution. And religion and other moral compasses should guide our final decision as to the rightness or wrongness of punishment in general and particular punishments.[28] (See Chapter 2.)

TRENDS IN PUNISHMENT

In all times, societies have justified punishment on the grounds of retribution, deterrence, incapacitation, and rehabilitation. But the weight given to each shifts over the centuries. Retribution and rehabilitation, for example, run deep in English criminal law from at least the year 1200. The church's emphasis on atoning for sins and rehabilitating sinners affected criminal law variously. Sometimes the aims of punishment and reformation conflict in practice.

In Elizabethan England, for example, the letter of the law was retributionist: hanging was the penalty for all felonies, including stealing 12 cents. In practice, however, most convicted felons were never executed. For example, legal technicalities freed all first-time thieves from the noose because the penalty was considered disproportionate to the crime. Many felons were freed because of their chances for rehabilitation. The queen's general pardon, issued almost every year around Christmas, gave blanket clemency to all condemned criminals in the hope that criminals, by this act of mercy, would change their erring ways.[29]

Gradually, retribution came to dominate penal policy. Then, in the eighteenth century, deterrence and incapacitation were introduced to replace what contemporary humanitarian reformers considered ineffective, brutal, and barbaric punishments inflicted in the name of retribution. By 1900, humanitarian reformers concluded that deterrence was neither effective nor humane. So, once again, rehabilitation replaced deterrence as the aim of criminal sanctions and remained the dominant form of criminal punishment. By 1960, most states had enacted indeterminate sentencing laws that made prison release dependent on rehabilitation. Most prisons created treatment programs intended to reform criminals.[30]

Rehabilitation never won the hearts of most criminal justice professionals despite their strong public talk to the contrary. And, by 1970, there was little empirical evidence to prove that rehabilitation programs reformed offenders. A "nothing works" theme dominated reform discussions, prompted by a highly touted, widely publicized, and largely negative study evaluating the effectiveness of rehabilitation programs. At the same time that academics and policymakers were becoming disillusioned with rehabilitation, public opinion was demanding harsh punishment to curb steeply rising crime rates. The time was clearly ripe for a comeback of retribution. And it did.[31]

California, a pioneer in the rehabilitation movement, shifted to retribution in 1976. In its Uniform Determinate Sentencing Law, the California legislature abolished the indeterminate sentence, baldly claiming that "the purpose of imprisonment is punishment," not treatment or rehabilitation. Called just deserts or even simply deserts, retribution was touted as "right" and "just" by conservatives who believed in punishment's morality and as "humane" by liberals convinced that rehabilitation was cruel and discriminatory. Public opinion supported it, largely on the ground that criminals deserve to be punished.[32]

Since the middle of the 1980s, reformers have heralded retribution and incapacitation as the primary criminal punishments. There are, to be sure, some powerful holdouts. One is the *Model Penal Code,* first published in 1961, when rehabilitation dominated penal policy. In the 1980s, after thoroughly reviewing current research and debate, its reporters decided to retain rehabilitation as the primary form of punishment.[33]

CRIMINAL LAW IN A FEDERAL SYSTEM

Throughout this book, you will see the term criminal law used in the singular. This use is not accurate. In our federal system of government, there are many criminal codes—a federal criminal code, fifty state criminal codes, and countless city ordinances containing myriad violations. The result of this system is that the United States has federal crimes, state crimes, and local crimes. In practice, the use of the term criminal law in the singular refers to the similarities in most state codes. And there are many similarities. For example, all state codes include the most serious crimes—murder, rape, robbery, burglary, arson, theft, and assault; all allow the most common defenses—self-defense and insanity; and all punish serious crimes by imprisonment. However, they don't all define a particular crime the same way. For example, in some states, burglary requires unlawful breaking and entering; in others, it requires only entering without breaking; and in still others, it requires merely unlawfully remaining in a building entered lawfully, such as hiding until after closing time in a department store rest room lawfully entered during business hours (Chapter 11).

The defenses to crime also vary from state to state. In some states, insanity requires proof both that defendants didn't know what they were doing and that they didn't know that it was wrong to do it. In other states, it's enough to prove either that defendants didn't know what they were doing or that they didn't know that it was wrong (Chapter 8). Some states permit individuals to use deadly force to protect homes from intruders; others require proof that the occupants in the home were in danger of serious bodily harm or death before they can shoot intruders (Chapter 7).

Criminal penalties also differ widely among jurisdictions. Several states prescribe death for some convicted murderers; others, life imprisonment. Hence, where murderers kill can determine whether those murderers will live or die. It also determines how they will die: by electrocution, lethal injection, the gas chamber, hanging, or even the firing squad.

The death penalty is only the most dramatic example of different penalties, and it affects only a few individuals. Other, less dramatic examples affect far more people. Some states subject those who engage in "open and notorious" sexual intercourse to fines; others make the mere fact of living together outside marriage punishable by up to five years of prison. Some states imprison individuals who possess small quantities of marijuana; others have protected private marijuana use as a constitutional right.[34]

These differences in crime and punishment among jurisdictions stem from several sources related to the type of community, the period in time, and the social problems of particular localities. In Texas, for example, stealing property valued between $750 and $20,000 is a third-degree felony, but it's also a third-degree felony to steal crude oil "regardless of the value" (Chapter 12).[35]

SOURCES OF CRIMINAL LAW

The main sources of criminal law include:

- U.S. Constitution
- State constitutions
- U.S. Criminal Code
- State criminal codes
- Municipal ordinances
- Common law of England and the United States
- Judicial decisions interpreting codes and the common law

Most criminal law is *state* criminal law, consisting of definitions of crimes and punishments in state criminal codes, and state court decisions interpreting state criminal statutes. There is also a rapidly growing federal criminal law found in the U.S.

Criminal Code and interpreted by the federal courts. The U.S. Code has grown rapidly since the 1970s because of the increase in the number of federal drug and weapons crimes. Municipal codes in towns and cities throughout the country include long lists of minor offenses, such as traffic violations and disorderly conduct on streets and sidewalks and buses and in parks, stadiums, and other public buildings. State criminal law and sometimes municipal ordinances are the focus of this book because that is where most criminal law is made and enforced.

✸ 1-2 Municipal Ordinances

THE COMMON-LAW ORIGINS OF CRIMINAL LAW

State criminal codes didn't spring full-grown from state legislatures. They evolved from a long history of offenses called the **common-law crimes**. These crimes didn't come into being in the way that we are used to, that is, by legislation. Before legislatures existed, social order depended on obedience to unwritten rules—the *lex non scripta*—based on local community customs and mores. Common-law crimes originated in the ancient customs of the English people. These traditions were passed on from generation to generation and changed from time to time to meet changed conditions. These unwritten rules were eventually incorporated into court decisions. These incorporated traditions became the **common law.**

The eighteenth-century English jurist Sir William Blackstone, whose *Commentaries on the Laws and Customs of England* was the only law book most American lawyers read until well into nineteenth century, described the common law as follows:

> As to general customs, or the common law, properly so called, this is that law, by which proceedings and determinations in the king's ordinary courts of justice are guided and directed. This, for the most part, settles . . . the several species of temporal offenses, with the manner and degree of punishment . . . ; all these are doctrines that are not set down in any written statute or ordinance, but depend merely upon immemorial usage, that is, upon the common law, for their support.[36]

By the seventeenth century, the English courts had created a substantial list of common-law felonies and misdemeanors. Most have familiar names today, and many have kept the core of their original meaning. The common-law felonies included murder, suicide, manslaughter, burglary, arson, robbery, larceny, rape, sodomy, and mayhem. The common-law misdemeanors included assault, battery, false imprisonment, libel, perjury, corrupting morals, and disturbing the peace.[37]

Exactly how the common law began is a mystery, but like the traditions it incorporated, the common law grew and changed to meet new conditions. At first, its growth depended mainly on judicial decisions. The courts formulated basic principles, rules, and standards based on the common law. They considered these the law of the land. Judges felt bound to follow these common-law principles, standards, and rules, and interpreted new cases according to them. As judges decided more cases according to them, common law became more detailed. The prior decisions that judges relied on to interpret new situations came to be called **precedent**. Common-law judges devised the principle of *stare decisis* that bound them to follow these precedents. U.S. Supreme Court Justice Benjamin Cardozo, in an enormously influential lecture about precedent and *stare decisis,* explained why he relied on prior scholars' work in preparing his lecture. In doing so, he also explained precedent itself:

It is easier to follow the beaten track than it is to clear another. In doing this, I shall be treading in the footsteps of my predecessors, and illustrating the process that I am seeking to describe, since the power of precedent, when analyzed, is the power of the beaten path.[38]

You'll realize how important precedent and *stare decisis* are when you read the cases excerpted in this book, beginning in Chapter 2. Court opinions contain many references to prior cases, relying on them to decide the case under review. Sometimes, an opinion expresses regret about having to make an undesirable decision but explains that precedent and *stare decisis* bind the court to follow the prior cases even if they don't produce the best result. *Stare decisis* doesn't absolutely prohibit courts from ever changing precedent. Precedent binds courts only in cases with similar facts. So, one way to get around precedent is to **distinguish cases**; that is, to decide that the facts of the prior case aren't similar enough to the one being decided to bind the court. For example, in Chapter 7, you'll read about a court that applied the battered woman defense to a woman who killed her batterer while he was awake. But when another battered woman killed her battering husband while he was asleep, the court didn't feel bound to follow the prior case.

Courts can also throw out a precedent directly, although they do it rarely and reluctantly. Directly throwing out a precedent is called **overruling a case**. In one case, a court had earlier ruled that a defendant who obtained money by false pretenses had a defense if the victim participated in the crime. Later, it reconsidered its decision. The court overruled its precedent and abolished the defense because it is a bad rule to allow one criminal to escape punishment simply because the victim was also a criminal ("two wrongs don't make a right").[39]

As legislatures became more established, they added crimes to the common law. They did so for a number of reasons: to clarify existing common law; to fill in blanks left by the common law; and to adjust the common law to new conditions. Judicial decisions interpreting the statutes became part of the growing body of precedent making up the common law.

The English colonists brought this common law with them to the New World and incorporated the common-law crimes into their legal systems. Following the American Revolution, the thirteen original states adopted the common law. Almost every state created after that enacted "reception statutes" that adopted the English common law. For example, the Florida reception statute reads: "The Common Law of England in relation to crimes . . . shall be of full force in this state where there is no existing provision by statute on the subject."[40]

CRIMINAL CODES

Periodically, reformers have called for the abolition of the common law. The first appeared in 1648, the work of the New England Puritans. The *Laws and Liberties of Massachusetts* **codified** (put into writing) the criminal law, defining crimes and prescribing punishments. The authors stated their case for a code this way: "So soon as God had set up political government among his people Israel he gave them a body of laws for judgment in civil and criminal causes. . . . For a commonwealth without laws is like a ship without rigging and steerage."[41]

Although some of the offenses sound odd today (witchcraft, cursing parents, blasphemy, idolatry, and adultery), others, such as rape—

> If any man shall ravish any maid or single woman, committing carnal copulation with her by force, against her own will, that is above ten years of age he shall be punished either with death or some other grievous punishment—

and murder—

> If any man shall commit any wilful murder, which is manslaughter, committed upon premeditate malice, hatred, or cruelty not in a man's necessary and just defense, nor by mere casualty against his will, he shall be put to death—

sound familiar.[42]

Hostility to English institutions after the American Revolution led reformers to call again for written legislative codes to replace the English common law. The eighteenth-century Enlightenment, with its emphasis on reason and natural law, inspired reformers to put aside the piecemeal "irrational" common law scattered throughout judicial decisions and to replace it with criminal codes based on a natural law of crimes. Despite anti-British feeling, Blackstone's *Commentaries* remained popular with reformers who hoped to transform Blackstone's complete and orderly outline of criminal law into criminal codes.

Reformers contended that judge-made law was not only disorderly and incomplete but also antidemocratic. They believed that legislatures that reflected the popular will should make laws, not aloof judges out of touch with public opinion. Thomas Jefferson proposed such a penal code for Virginia. The proposed Virginia code never passed the Virginia legislature, not because it codified the law but because it recommended too many drastic reductions in criminal punishments.[43]

Fears of anti-democratic tyranny by courts seemed to be realized when a federal court in Connecticut attempted to create a new common law of libel early in the nineteenth century. The defendants were indicted for "a libel against the President and Congress of the United States, contained in the *Connecticut Courant* of 7th May, 1806, charging them with having in secret voted $2,000,000 as a present to [Napoléon] Bonaparte, for leave to make a treaty with Spain." There was no such criminal statute.

On appeal, in *Hudson v. Goodwin,* the United States Supreme Court only partly eased the reformers' fear of judge-made law. The Court said that *federal* courts had no power to create common-law crimes. According to the Court, "the legislative authority of the Union must first make an act a crime, affix a punishment to it, and declare the court that shall have jurisdiction over the offense." However, *Hudson v. Goodwin* said nothing about prohibiting *state* courts from creating common-law crimes.[44]

The codification movement had an uneven history, but it gathered strength during the twentieth century. The American Law Institute supported codification, and the earliest drafts of the *Model Penal Code* abolished common-law crimes in § 1.05: "All Offenses Defined by Statute. (1) No conduct constitutes an offense unless it is a crime or violation under this Code or another statute of this State."

COMMON-LAW CRIMES AND MODERN CRIMINAL LAW

Since the American Law Institute adopted § 1.05, twenty-five states have abolished the common-law crimes and ten others have proposed to do so. Several states, however, still recognize the common law of crimes, at least in part. Abolishing the common-law crimes doesn't render the common law useless. Most states that have abolished common-law offenses (these states are called code jurisdictions) retain the common-law defenses, such as self-defense and insanity. Furthermore, statutes frequently contain the terms murder, manslaughter, robbery, burglary, rape, and assault without defining them, and courts have to rely on the common-law meanings of those terms. For example, the 1975 Alabama Criminal Code provides as follows: "Any person who commits . . . voluntary manslaughter, shall be guilty of a felony. Voluntary manslaughter is punishable as a Class 5 felony."[45]

California, a code jurisdiction, went even further by including all of the common-law felonies in its criminal code. The California Supreme Court reviewed the common law to determine the meaning of its murder statute in *Keeler v. Superior Court*. Keeler's wife was pregnant with another man's child. Keeler kicked his pregnant wife in the stomach, causing her to abort the fetus. The California court had to decide whether fetuses were included in the murder statute. The court, in the following passage, reveals the importance of the common law in interpreting present statutes:

> Penal code § 187 provides: "Murder is the unlawful killing of a human being, with malice aforethought." The dispositive question is whether the fetus which petitioner is accused of killing was, on February 23, 1969, a "human being" within the meaning of this statute. . . . We therefore undertake a brief review of the origins and development of the common law of abortional homicide. . . . From that inquiry it appears that by the year 1850—the date with which we are concerned—an infant could not be the subject of homicide at common law unless it had been born alive. . . . Perhaps the most influential statement of the "born alive" rule is that of Coke, in mid-seventeenth century: "If a woman be quick with childe and by a potion or otherwise killeth it in her wombe, or if a man beat her, whereby the childe dyeth in her body, and she is delivered of a dead childe, this is a great misprision (i.e., misdemeanor), and no murder; but if the childe be born alive and dyeth of the potion, battery, or other cause, this is murder; for in law it is accounted a reasonable creature . . . when it is born alive." (3 Coke, *Institutes* 58 (1648)) . . .
>
> We hold that in adopting the definition of murder in Penal Code § 187 the Legislature intended to exclude from its reach the act of killing an unborn fetus.[46]

As a result of the court's decision, the California legislature changed the criminal homicide statute to include fetuses.[47]

Jurisdictions that still recognize the common-law crimes (these are called **common-law jurisdictions**) have created many offenses, particularly misdemeanors, that extend far beyond the common-law felonies. All of the following are crimes without statutes in some states: conspiring, attempting, and soliciting to commit crimes; uttering grossly obscene language in public; burning a body in a furnace; keeping a house of prostitution; maliciously killing a horse; being a common scold; negligently permitting a prisoner to escape; discharging a gun near a sick person; being drunk in public; using libel; committing an indecent assault; and eavesdropping.[48]

What if both statutes and common law cover the same conduct? Some states say that the words of the statute have to in exact words either repeal the common law or take over the whole field of law covered by the common law. For example, where a state conspiracy statute listed five criminal conspiracies while the common law listed many more, a court held that the statute was not meant to take over the whole field of conspiracy. So, the conspiracies not listed in the statute remained common-law crimes.[49]

What conduct is included in a common-law crime? Courts approach this subject from two perspectives. Some courts eagerly define new crimes without precedent;

others do so only reluctantly. The perspective that courts adopt depends on their view of the common law. If they consider that decided cases merely illustrate broad principles of the unwritten common law, then defining new offenses requires no precedent. According to this view, the common law can expand to meet new conditions. In other words, courts aren't inventing new crimes; they are only applying existing common-law principles to new problems. Courts following this view of the common law are likely to define new crimes without looking for precedent. Other courts view the decisions themselves as embodying the whole of common law. These courts maintain that U.S. courts cannot define new crimes. Therefore, they depend on specific precedent to justify expanding the scope of common-law crimes.

"RATIONAL CRIMINAL LAW"

During the nineteenth century, discontent with the disorganized and illogical state of criminal law and the complex scheme of punishments led to calls for a more rational organization of criminal law and punishments. The phrase **"rational criminal law"** applies four criteria to criminal law:

1. It is based on general principles, not on the discretion and personal philosophies of legislators and judges.
2. The general principles of criminal law apply to all crimes.
3. Criminal law grades punishment according to both the seriousness of the harm and the blameworthiness of the conduct.
4. Criminal law prescribes no greater penalty than punishment and prevention require.

A rational criminal law follows a **principle of limited methods**; that is, the principle that criminal law is the last resort of social control. According to this principle, if informal private sanctions work, criminal law has no role to play. If informal sanctions fail and civil actions work, then criminal law still has no role to play. If civil actions don't secure obedience, and criminal law becomes necessary, if a lesser penalty is as effective as a greater penalty, the lesser penalty is the rational one. Rational criminal law rests on the core values of individual autonomy and social economy. In a rational criminal law, government should intervene in human actions only when absolutely necessary and should spend no more money and use no more power than are required to prevent and punish antisocial conduct.[50]

The American Law Institute's *Model Penal Code* has substantially advanced the pursuit of a rational criminal code. The American Law Institute (ALI) is a private association whose membership includes eminent lawyers, judges, and professors. Founded in 1923, it works to clarify and improve the law. In 1950, with Rockefeller Foundation aid, it undertook a major effort to establish a rational criminal law. The ALI created a large advisory committee drawn from all disciplines concerned with criminal justice and charged it with drafting a model penal code. For ten years, these specialists met and drafted, redrafted, and finally in 1961 completed the *Model Penal Code and Commentaries,* a learned and influential document.[51]

As its title indicates, the code is a model to guide actual legislation. Jurisdictions vary in which specific provisions meet their needs. By 1985, when the ALI published an updated code and commentary, thirty-four states had enacted widespread criminal law revision and codification based on its provisions; fifteen hundred courts had cited its provisions and referred to its commentary. The *Model Penal Code* fulfills the criteria outlined at the beginning of this section for a rational criminal code, but it's not the final word on the subject. Much of the criminal law is not "rational" as the term is defined here. Moreover, rational doesn't necessarily mean "best." Finally, some jurisdictions, such as the state of California, haven't followed much of what the model code proposes.

NONLEGAL INFLUENCES ON CRIMINAL LAW

Prosecutors, defense attorneys, and judges look at criminal law through practitioners' eyes. They accept the definitions of crime in the criminal law and proceed from there to argue and decide cases. But practicing lawyers aren't the only people who study and think about criminal law. Historians, philosophers, doctors, and social scientists, to name but a few, have studied criminal law too. However, instead of focusing on what criminal law is and how to apply it to specific cases, they have tried to find out how and why criminal law came to be what it is. They have shown us the importance of morality, history, social forces and processes, and ideology in the creation, development, and operation of our criminal law. You should keep these influences in mind as you study the topics in the remainder of this book. These influences don't necessarily contradict the legal definition of crime. Rather, they enrich our understanding of when, how, and why the principles, doctrines, and definitions of specific crimes developed.

THE INFLUENCE OF IDEOLOGY

Political scientists and sociologists study the political and social influences on criminal law. All crimes are political in the sense that the legislatures that enact criminal codes are political bodies. Also, community standards informally influence judges when they interpret the law. Statutes outline broad categories of conduct, leaving judges room in which to fit particular cases. In applying broad categories to individual cases, judges' own ideas and community standards influence their decisions. So, applying criminal law to individual cases is never a value-neutral exercise.[52]

Two opposing theories inform the ideological perspective. The **democratic-consensus theory**, originating in the insights of the great French sociologist Emile Durkheim, holds that elected representatives define crime. The criminal law expresses the will of the people through their elected representatives. Criminal law represents society's stand against conduct that violates its values and describes what punishments society inflicts on those who flout its values. This reading of the legislative process rests on two assumptions: First, politics and laws reflect consensus; people work together and compromise their individual interests so the state can work efficiently and effectively to satisfy the majority's collective needs. Second, criminal statutes embody the people's will. In fact, research suggests that criminal codes express neither the will of the people nor the will of their legislators; instead, criminal justice professionals write most criminal laws that legislatures passively enact and the public passively accepts.[53]

The **conflict-elitist theory** assumes that society operates according to conflict, not consensus. Interest groups, each ensconced in a bailiwick, come out fighting for their selfish interests—interests promoted only at the expense of other groups' interests. The most powerful interest group wins every major contest and then imposes its values on the rest of society. The rich and powerful use the legal system to protect their wealth and secure their dominant position of power. The ruling elite brandish the criminal laws as weapons to coerce weaker elements of society into submission.[54]

The conflict-elitist theory is considerably more complicated than this brief summary suggests. First, the criminal process is rarely so personal and purposely exploitative. Second, the ruling elite often disagree over which criminal laws best serve their interests. Third, not all laws promote the dominant class's interests, at least not in the short term.[55]

Both the democratic-consensus and the conflict-elitist theories reflect part of the social reality of criminal law. Without question, much criminal law exhibits consensus. Most people, for example, agree that murder, rape, and robbery should be crimes; in fact, widespread agreement exists about the seriousness of more than one hundred crimes. Legislatures represent most people when they enact these statutes, as do judges when they apply them. Much criminal law, however, does not represent consensus. Historically, the powerful have used vagrancy laws to keep in their place certain elements of society—the poor, the unattached, and others on the fringes of "respectable" society. Vagrancy legislation therefore supports the claim of the conflict-elitist theory that criminal law results from the ruling class's effort to keep the "lower orders" in line. Similarly, recent ordinances against "aggressive panhandling," sleeping on park benches, and camping within city limits represent efforts of the middle class to control the public behavior of "street people."[56]

Both theories also display considerable naiveté. The democratic-consensus theory fails to account for the powerful effects that money, class, race, and other social factors have on both the political and the legal processes. Decisions throughout every stage of the criminal process—reporting crimes; arresting suspects; prosecuting, trying, and convicting defendants; and sentencing or releasing offenders—require judgments, or discretion, the amount of freedom that victims, police officers, prosecutors, judges, or juries have in making these decisions.[57]

There is a debate as old as law itself over how much leeway law officers and the public should have in enforcing criminal law. Good reasons support tempering the letter of the law with flexibility to do justice in individual cases. In his advice to new judges, Sir Nicholas Bacon, a sixteenth-century English lord chancellor, stressed that legislators could not possibly write statutes clear enough or complete enough to cover all cases. Because of this, "the judge is not always so narrowly to weigh the words of the law, but sometimes in respect of the person, place, time and occasion or other circumstance to qualify and moderate such extremities as the particular words of the law written may offer."

Sir Nicholas was no fool. Realizing that discretion was equally a means to evil as well as good, he warned his new judges accordingly:

> For albeit his knowledge be never so great and his discretion equal to it, if he will suffer them to be subject and governed by fear, by love, by malice or gain, then shall all his judgments be such as his affections be and not such as knowledge and discretion doth require.[58]

Class, wealth, power, and prejudice influence the operation of the law, perhaps even more than they influence its creation. Selective enforcement has characterized the administration of criminal law from as early as the sixteenth century. For example, in one English town in the 1570s, poor, wandering people without family or other community ties were arrested more often, prosecuted more vigorously, and punished more harshly than were "respectable," established residents.[59]

Discretion creates a gap between what law books say and what law officers do because class, race, economics, and politics influence discretionary action. Victims who never report crimes, suspects whom police could arrest but don't, arrested suspects whom prosecutors could charge but don't, and offenders who could be punished but aren't—they, as much as any statute or universal moral code, shape the criminal law. Commenting on social forces and their current impact on the administration of justice, the late criminologist Donald R. Cressey concluded that there is a great deal of evidence that current statutes calling for punishment of lawbreakers are not administered uniformly, or with celerity or certainty. This suggests that the actual reactions to crime are not really reflected in the laws governing the administration of justice. Statutes are so severe they have to be mitigated in the interests of justice, and in order to maintain the consent of the governed. The following conclusions have been drawn by so many investigators that they may be accepted as factual:

1. Blacks are more likely to be arrested than whites.
2. Blacks are more likely to be indicted than whites.
3. Blacks have a higher conviction rate than whites.
4. Blacks are usually punished more severely than whites, but this is not true for all crimes, especially those in which a black person victimizes a black person.
5. Blacks are less likely to receive probation and suspended sentences.
6. Blacks receive pardons less often than do whites.
7. Blacks have less chance of having a death sentence commuted than do whites.[60]

The conflict-elitist theory, no more than the democratic-consensus theory, fully explains the origins and nature of criminal laws. Just as the democratic-consensus theory minimizes the pluralistic conflict of interests in society, the conflict-elitist theory ignores the very real core of values about which wide agreement exists. The same sixteenth-century English town that favored established members of the community over poor, wandering strangers also exhibited wide consensus on some values. Town officials stuck to the principle of legality in the administration of justice, enforcing procedural safeguards such as rules of proof requiring reliable witnesses to bring charges and testify in court against the accused. They also firmly recognized that despite the letter of the law prescribing death as a punishment for all felonies—from murder to the theft of a chicken—only murderers and some other violent criminals should hang for their crimes. This consensus persists today.

THE INFLUENCE OF IRRATIONALITY

Both the conflict-elitist and the democratic-consensus theories share a common flaw: neither takes into account the influence of chance and the irrational on criminal law. Human institutions, including criminal law and its administration, rarely develop and operate purely according to democratic-consensus and conflict-elitist theories. Police officers on patrol, for example, may arrest citizens as much because they are tired, irritable, or bored as because they revere law and order. A question endlessly repeated to my generation of law students in explaining why a court made a particular decision was, "What did the judge have for dinner the night before she decided the case?"

Irrational forces give rise to more than erratic individual decisions. They affect criminal codes as well, as sex psychopath laws illustrate. Shortly after World War II, a small spate of brutal sex crimes generated public fear. One ghoulish man dismembered and killed several young girls after sexually assaulting them. In response, most states hastily passed sex psychopath statutes, enabling states to confine potential sex offenders indefinitely without a trial. Some experts questioned the effectiveness, propriety, and constitutionality of these statutes. Critics argued that the statutes were unconstitutional because they denied procedural safeguards to those affected by them. Furthermore, they rested on the erroneous assumption that society could predict who would commit sex offenses.[61]

Considerable empirical evidence since the passage of sex psychopath legislation has demonstrated the shortcomings of the laws. Yet, despite this knowledge, the laws remain largely in force today. Fear and panic explain their enactment. Any complete explanation of the nature and origins of criminal law must account for the unpredictable, irrational, and chance elements in human behavior.[62]

THE INFLUENCE OF HISTORY

The great jurist and United States Supreme Court justice, Oliver Wendell Holmes, maintained that in understanding the law, "a page of history is worth a volume of logic." He meant that real-life experience, not abstract reasoning, creates law. Most crimes originate in the circumstances of time and place. In addition to law's response to time and place, lawyers' reverence for precedent enhances the power of history to shape the law. Imbued with the importance of precedent, lawyers approach change in the law cautiously. As a result, the current body of criminal law retains laws that were once believed necessary but are no longer relevant. The great English legal historian, William Maitland, noted that the past rules us from the grave. The ghosts of the past stalk silently through our courts and legislatures, ruling our modern law by means of outdated and irrelevant but venerated ancient principles and doctrines. Thus, history plays a powerful part in maintaining, in today's criminal law, that which yesterday's social, economic, political, and philosophical considerations created.[63]

The development of the modern law of theft illustrates the historical perspective on criminal law. In early times, larceny—forcibly taking and carrying away another's cattle—was the only theft. The original crime resembles the modern law of robbery—taking another's property by force or by threat of force (see Chapter 11). Later, larceny came to include taking another's property by stealth (from which our word stealing descends). Getting another's property by trickery was not a crime; it was shrewd or clever. Neither was taking property left for safekeeping (examples would be taking a car left in an attended parking lot or clothes left at a dry cleaner's); it was the owner's folly. Hence, only stealing or forcibly taking another's property constituted larceny; cheating was not a crime.[64]

Such was the law of theft in medieval England before commerce and industry had advanced beyond the most rudimentary stages. Most people lived in small communities, rarely dealt with strangers, and had few personal property items available to misappropriate. Furthermore, larceny was a felony, punishable by death. Judges were reluctant to expand the definition of larceny if doing so meant hanging more property offenders.

The complexities of modern life changed all this. More people, personal property, and strangers; a greater need to leave property and money with strangers; and less bloody punishments for larceny all led to alterations in theft law. Larceny came to include the theft of most movable personal property, such as jewelry, furniture, clothing, and utensils. Then it was expanded to include the stealing of paper instruments representing ownership, such as checks, bank notes, and deeds. Finally, new crimes were created to embrace more misappropriations than the taking of property by force or stealth. Misappropriating money entrusted to another became embezzlement, tricking another out of money became false pretenses; both became felonies.

Theft law developed to meet the needs of a complex society and to ameliorate a harsh criminal law; these historical facts explain theft law. In the past twenty years, thirty states have overcome this history by consolidating larceny, embezzlement, false pretenses, and other theft offenses into one crime. The remaining twenty states cling to a host of theft offenses, of which the arcane larceny, embezzlement, fraud, and false pretenses are only the most common.

To cite one more example, the criminal law enacted in seventeenth-century New England to secure Puritan religious values, despite its clear irrelevance to modern behavior, remains surprisingly intact. For example, until their recent demise in the face of a constitutional assault on their validity, vagrancy statutes were based on the needs of sixteenth-century England. Yet, until the 1970s, American vagrancy statutes copied their sixteenth-century English legal forebears verbatim. Fornication, profanity, and curfews still remain on the books, although they are rarely enforced. The retention of these "morals" offenses demonstrates that the past rules the present in criminal law.[65]

THE INFLUENCE OF AN "ETHICAL CORE"

Political, legal, historical, and irrational theories assume that environment determines criminal law: Crime doesn't reflect permanent values; it is relative to time and place. In other words, irrational outbursts, ideology, social conditions, and other circumstances shape what society condemns in its criminal law. What one age considers evil, another may tolerate, even promote as good.

The **ethical core theory** is a fundamentally different approach. It assumes that crime is the embodiment of universal, permanent, inherent evil. According to this theory, lawmaking, politics, history, and emotional outbursts can't affect this ethical core of criminal law. The ethical core theory stems in part from religion. For example, some proponents maintain that criminal law reflects universally accepted commands found in the Ten Commandments: "Thou shalt not kill" and "Thou shalt not steal" illustrate this view. However, other commandments are not part of modern criminal law. For example, "Thou shalt not covet thy neighbor's wife" violates the basic principle that the state cannot punish evil thoughts (see Chapter 3).

The ethical core theory isn't strictly religious; sometimes it's cast in more general moral terms. For instance, criminal law manifests the universally high value placed on the rights to life, liberty, and property. The English common law first enshrined these rights; then Americans entrenched them in constitutions, statutes, and court decisions. The ethical core theory strikes a responsive chord in those who accept that life, liberty, and property are widely valued, uniformly defined, and universally protected by law. But the theory does not fully match reality. Take, for example, the enormous body of regulatory traffic offenses. Although driving seventy-five miles per hour in a sixty-five-mile-an-hour zone may violate the law, few would call it an inherently evil act, violating some ethical core of values. On the other hand, even though many might believe that breaking someone's heart on purpose violates an ethical core of values, the law doesn't and shouldn't make breaking hearts a crime.

Some critics argue that equating values or notions of good and bad with crime, as the ethical core theory does, is both dangerous and improper. Professor Louis B.

Schwartz criticized the statement of purpose in the Federal Criminal Justice Reform Act of 1973 on the ground that

> the bill injects a new, false, and dangerous notion that the criminal code "aims at the articulation of the nation's public values" and its vindication through punishment. A criminal code necessarily falls far short of expressing the nation's morality. Many things are evil or undesirable without being at all appropriate for imprisonment: lying, overcharging for goods and services, marital infidelity, lack of charity or patriotism. Nothing has been more widely recognized in modern criminal law scholarship than the danger of creating more evil by ill-considered use of the criminal law than is caused by the target misconduct. Accordingly, the failure to put something under the ban of the penal code is not an expression of a favorable "value" of the non-penalized behavior. It is a fatal confusion of values to see the Criminal Code as anything but a list of those most egregious misbehaviors, which according to a broad community consensus, can be usefully dealt with by social force.[66]

Several of the *hypothetical cases* presented earlier in this chapter illustrate other weaknesses in the ethical core theory. They demonstrate that the meaning of life, liberty, and property is by no means settled. Controversy surrounds such issues as whether looking at pornography, smoking marijuana, or even using methamphetamines should be crimes. Also, just what do life and property, not to mention liberty, really mean? The answers vary from place to place and over time.

One major theme in criminal law is the need to reconcile stability with change. Changed conditions, new knowledge, and shifts in ideals all require that the law advance beyond what it was in the eighteenth, nineteenth, and even the twentieth centuries. Stealing a chicken was once a capital offense. Wives who scolded their husbands were considered criminals in the not-too-distant past. Most of the adult population in India can remember a time when a widow's burning herself to death after her husband died was considered the highest form of love. Recent cases involving people whose hearts are beating and who are still breathing but whose brains have stopped functioning have raised new questions about the meanings of life and death. A term has even been created to describe this new dilemma: brain death. Equally controversial is the heated debate over whether a fetus is property subject to contract law and whether it is a life for purposes of criminal law (see Chapter 9).

SUMMARY

Criminal law is a method, or way of doing things, that aims to reduce crime and punish criminals. It's a list of commands, or dos and don'ts, written into law, with penalties attached that apply to everyone in the jurisdiction or under the authority of the government making the law. Criminal law shares these qualities with other forms of law, but it has another distinctive feature: Criminal conviction carries with it the formal moral condemnation of the community.

Criminal law has two parts. The general part establishes the general principles of criminal law that apply to all crimes. These include the principles of criminal liability; accomplice liability; uncompleted crimes of attempt, conspiracy, and solicitations; and the principles of justification and excuse. The special part consists of the definitions of specific crimes.

Crimes are classified according to several schemes. One scheme, the felony, misdemeanor, violation scheme, organizes crimes according to the penalty. Capital felonies are punishable by death or life imprisonment without parole. Felonies are punishable by incarceration in prisons for one year or more. Misdemeanors are punishable by fine or incarceration in local jails for up to one year. Violations, often not designated crimes at all, are punishable by fine only. Another classification scheme ranks crimes according to their degree of "badness" or "evil." Crimes *mala in se*, like rape and murder, are inherently evil. Crimes *mala prohibita*, such as parking violations, are illegal but not evil. Another scheme classifies crimes according to their subject matter, including crimes against the state, crimes against the person, crimes against habitation, crimes against property, crimes against the administration of justice, crimes against public order, and crimes against public morals.

Criminal punishment rests on two basic purposes: retribution and prevention. Retribution is meant to inflict pain on the person who harmed another in order to give offenders their just deserts. The major types of prevention are (1) deterrence, or using the threat of punishment to deter people generally from future crime; (2) incapacitation, or preventing specific offenders from committing future crimes; and (3) rehabilitation, or changing individual offenders' behavior so that they will not commit crimes in the future.

Throughout history, criminal law has reflected these purposes, but the emphasis has shifted among them over time. During most of early history, retribution predominated; during the first sixty years of the twentieth century, rehabilitation held sway; during the last two decades, retribution and incapacitation have returned to prominence.

The United States does not have a unified criminal law. Each of the fifty states has its own criminal law; the federal government has a separate criminal code, and cities and towns have municipal codes. The states and federal criminal codes share similarities in general terms, but the specific definitions of crimes—and the penalties attached—differ widely across jurisdictions.

There are federal, state, and municipal criminal codes, but most criminal law is state criminal law. Definitions of crimes in statutes, and defenses to crimes, require reference to the common law, another major source of criminal law. Some states have retained the common-law crimes; others have abolished the common-law crimes but retained the common-law defenses. All, however, require reference to the common law for definition of terms. A final source of criminal law is judicial opinions interpreting constitutions, statutes, and the common law.

The common-law origins of criminal law eventually produced a disorganized, illogical arrangement of crimes and punishments. By contrast, a rational criminal law rests on fundamental principles, universally applied, that grade and punish crimes according to their seriousness and blameworthiness. Criminal law acts economically to use only that punishment needed to reduce crime and punish criminals. Criminal law, therefore, is a limited instrument of social control. It consists of both government power and limits on that power.

Studying the principles, doctrines, and rules of criminal law reveals the body of criminal law. However, it doesn't tell us how or why the criminal law established the principles, doctrines, and rules. Sociology, political science, psychology, history, and philosophy shed light on the rationale, policies, and values of the criminal law and how they developed in the context of specific times and places; we find that criminal law did not spring full-grown from rational minds. Social forces, political power, emotions, past traditions and practices, and philosophy have shaped the criminal law as we know it today.

 Go to the Criminal Law 7e CD-ROM for Internet exercises.

REVIEW QUESTIONS

1. Why do we say criminal law is a method, or way, of doing things?

2. Describe the major characteristics of criminal law. How do they compare and contrast with other branches of law? What one characteristic most distinguishes criminal law from other branches of law?

3. Why is it incorrect to use the term criminal law in the singular?

4. Explain the major characteristics of a "rational criminal law."

5. Describe the general and special parts of the criminal law.

6. Identify and describe the four main characteristics of criminal punishment.

7. What is the difference between retribution and prevention?

8. Explain general deterrence, special deterrence, incapacitation, and rehabilitation. What do they all have in common?

9. Identify and describe the major classification schemes for organizing and grading crimes.

KEY TERMS

capital felonies—felonies punishable by death or life imprisonment without parole.

civil law—the law that deals with private rights and remedies.

codified—put into writing.

common law—the body of law consisting of all the statutes and case law background of England and the colonies before the American Revolution, based on principles and rules that derive from usages and customs of antiquity.

common-law crimes—crimes originating in the English common law.

common-law jurisdictions—jurisdictions that still recognize the common-law crimes.

conflict-elitist theory—assumes that society operates according to conflict among interest groups.

culpability—deserving of punishment because of individual responsibility for actions.

damages—money awarded in civil lawsuits for injuries.

defendant—the person against whom a civil or criminal action is brought.

democratic-consensus theory—originating in the insights of the great French sociologist Emile Durkheim, holds that elected representatives define crime.

deterrence theory—states that rational human beings will not commit crimes if they know that the pain of punishment outweighs the pleasure gained from committing crimes.

distinguish cases—to find that facts differ enough from those in a prior case to release judges from the precedent of the decision in that case.

ethical core theory—assumes that crime is the embodiment of universal, permanent, inherent evil.

felonies—serious crimes generally punishable by one year or more in prison.

general deterrence or prevention—preventing crime by threatening potential lawbreakers.

general part of criminal law—principles that apply to all crimes.

gross misdemeanor—offense with a maximum penalty of close to one year in jail.

hedonism—human beings seek pleasure and avoid pain.

incapacitation—punishment by imprisonment, mutilation, and even death.

lex non scripta—based on local community customs and mores.

living standard analysis—classification based on injury to quality of life.

malum in se—a crime inherently bad, or evil.

malum prohibitum—a crime not inherently bad, or evil, but merely prohibited.

medical model of punishment—crime as a disease.

misdemeanor—a minor crime for which the penalty is usually less than one year in jail or a fine.

Model Penal Code—the code developed by the American Law Institute to guide reform in criminal law.

overruling a case—throwing out a precedent.

petty misdemeanor—offense punishable by a jail sentence of up to thirty days.

plaintiff—the person who sues another party in a civil action.

precedent—prior court decision that guides judges in deciding future cases.

prevention—the punishing of offenders in order to prevent crimes in the future.

principle of limited methods—criminal law is the last resort of social control.

principle of utility—allows only the minimum amount of pain necessary to prevent crime.

punitive damages—payments to injured parties intended to punish the wrongdoer.

rational criminal law—if informal private sanctions can secure compliance, criminal law has no role to play.

rationalism—desire to maximize pleasure and minimize pain.

rehabilitation—prevention of crime by treatment.

retribution—punishment based on just deserts.

special deterrence—the threat of punishment aimed at individual offenders in the hope of deterring future criminal conduct.

special part of criminal law—defines the elements of specific crimes.

stare decisis—the principle that binds courts to stand by prior decisions and to leave undisturbed settled points of law.

tort—a legal wrong for which the injured party may sue the injuring party.

violation—a minor legal infraction subject to a small fine.

SUGGESTED READINGS

1. Wayne R. LaFave and Austin W. Scott, Jr., *Criminal Law,* 2d ed. (St. Paul, Minn.: West Publishing Company, 1986). This updated version of a classic law school textbook is a good place for the undergraduate to research further the problems of criminal law.

2. Rollin M. Perkins and Ronald N. Boyce, *Criminal Law,* 3d ed. (Mineola, N.Y.: Foundation Press, 1982). This is a law school hornbook (textbook) covering the general and special parts of criminal law. It is an excellent reference book for anyone who wishes to pursue in further detail topics suggested here.

3. George P. Fletcher, *Rethinking Criminal Law* (Boston: Little, Brown, 1978). Fletcher's provocative effort to write a comprehensive theory of criminal law is challenging and difficult but well worth the serious student's efforts.

4. Lawrence M. Friedman, *A History of American Law* (New York: Simon and Schuster, 1973). Friedman has written an interesting history of American law for the general public. Although it covers all law, sections on criminal law are clearly set apart and can be read separately without difficulty.

5. American Law Institute, *Model Penal Code* (Philadelphia: American Law Institute, 1954–1961); and *American Law Institute, Model Penal Code and Commentaries* (Philadelphia: American Law Institute, 1980, 1985). These are excellent works full of the latest scholarship, thoughtful analyses, and commentary by some of the leading judges, lawyers, and academics in American law. The works present, in imposing fashion, the democratic-consensus approach to criminal law; but their value stretches well beyond. They contain the most comprehensive coverage of American criminal law in existence.

6. Lawrence M. Friedman, *American Law* (New York: Norton, 1984). This is a general introduction to American law, filled with anecdotes and discussion intended to explain the nature and processes of American law to the general reader. It is a vivid picture of American law and its role in American life. Well worth the time spent reading it.

7. Jerome Hall, *General Principles of Criminal Law,* 2d ed. (Indianapolis, Ind.: Bobbs-Merrill, 1960). Hall covers the general principles and doctrines of criminal law, arranging them into a theory of criminal law. This text is a classic in the literature of criminal law.

8. Leo Katz, *Bad Acts and Guilty Minds* (Chicago: University of Chicago, 1987). The author presents an interesting, thought-provoking look at the philosophy of criminal law. He focuses on the basic problems of criminal law, using real cases from several countries, many challenging hypothetical cases, and critical suggestions. Difficult to read, but well worth the effort.

9. Henry M. Hart, Jr., "The Aims of the Criminal Law," *Law and Contemporary Problems* 23 (1958): 104–141. This essay is the best brief statement about the nature of criminal law and its characteristics.

10. Jeffrey H. Reiman, *The Rich Get Richer and the Poor Get Prison,* 2d ed. (New York: Wiley, 1984). In this book, Reiman forcefully presents the conflict-elitist theory.

NOTES

1. These characteristics modify and expand on those listed in Henry M. Hart, Jr.'s classic, "The Aims of the Criminal Law," *Law and Contemporary Problems* 23 (1958):403–405.

2. Ibid., p. 405.

3. American Law Institute, *Model Penal Code and Commentaries,* vol. 1 (Philadelphia: American Law Institute, 1985), pp. 1–30; Norval Morris and Gordon Hawkins, *The Honest Politician's Guide to Crime Control* (Chicago: University of Chicago Press, 1969), chapter 1.

4. See Jerome Hall, *The General Principles of Criminal Law,* 2d ed. (Indianapolis: Bobbs-Merrill, 1960), pp. 16–26, for a detailed discussion of the differences among principles, doctrines, and rules.

5. See *Harmelin v. Michigan,* 501 U.S. 957 (1991) for a discussion of the Michigan statute. For an excellent discussion of capital crimes and punishment, see Hugo Adam Bedau, ed., *The Death Penalty in America,* 3d ed. (New York: Oxford University Press, 1982).

6. For a thorough summary of the wide disparity in existing misdemeanor classification, see American Law Institute, *Model Penal Code and Commentaries,* vol. 1, pp. 1–30.

7. Ibid., p. 34.

8. Andrew von Hirsch and Nils Jareborg, "Gauging Criminal Harm: A Living-Standard Analysis," *Oxford Journal of Legal Studies,* 11 (1991):1–38.

9. Thomas Szasz, M.D., *Law, Liberty, and Psychiatry* (New York: Collier Books, 1963); Herbert Packer, *The Limits of the Criminal Sanction* (Palo Alto, Calif.: Stanford University Press, 1968), pp. 33–34.

10. *Leviticus,* 24:20.

11. *A History of the Criminal Law of England,* vol. 3 (London: Macmillan, 1883), pp. 81–82.

12. There is a full discussion of free will in James Q. Wilson and Richard Herrnstein, *Crime and Human Nature,* chap. 19 (New York: Simon and Schuster, 1985); see also psychiatrist Willard Gaylin's fascinating *The Killing of Bonnie Garland* (New York: Simon and Schuster, 1982).

13. Henry E. Wiehofen, "Retribution Is Obsolete," in *Responsibility,* ed. C. Friedrich, Nomos series, no. 3 (New York: Lieber-Atherton, 1960), pp. 116, 119–120.

14. These theories are discussed at length in James Q. Wilson and Richard Herrnstein, *Crime and Human Nature.* An intriguing case study applying the theories to one criminal homicide is Andre Mayer and Michael Wheeler, *The Crocodile Man: A Case of Brain Chemistry and Criminal Violence* (Boston: Houghton Mifflin, 1982).

15. John L. Diamond, "The Myth of Morality and Fault in Criminal Law," *American Criminal Law,* 34 (1996):111–131 discusses this problem with a criminal law system based on morality and fault.

16. Joseph Goldstein, "Psychoanalysis and Jurisprudence," *Yale Law Journal* 77 (1968):1071–1072.

17. This topic is explored fully in Bedau, ed., *The Death Penalty in America,* chap. 4.

18. See *Wilson and Herrnstein, Crime and Human Nature,* for a full discussion; Johannes Andenaes, "Deterrence," *Encyclopedia of Crime and Justice,* Sanford H. Kadish, ed. (New York: Free Press, 1983), pp. 2, 593.

19. Ibid., p. 596.

20. Mark DeWolfe Howe, ed., *Holmes-Laski Letters* (Cambridge, Mass.: Harvard University Press, 1953), p. 806.

21. James Q. Wilson, *Thinking About Crime* (New York: Basic Books, 1975).

22. See Mark H. Moore et al., *Dangerous Offenders: The Elusive Target of Justice* (Cambridge, Mass.: Harvard University Press, 1984).

23. Sandra Gleason, "Hustling: The 'Single' Economy of a Prison," *Federal Probation* (June 1978), pp. 32–39; Samuel Walker, *Sense and Nonsense about Crime: A Policy Guide* (Monterey, Calif.: Brooks/Cole, 1985), pp. 59–61; Steven R. Donziger, ed., *The Real War on Crime* (New York: Harper Perennial, 1996).

24. Packer, *The Limits of the Criminal Sanction,* p. 50.

25. For these early reformation ideas, see Joel Samaha, "Hanging for Felony," *Historical Journal* 21 (1979); and "Some Reflections on the Anglo-Saxon Heritage of Discretionary Justice," in Lawrence E. Abt and Irving R. Stuart, eds., *Social Psychology and Discretionary Law* (New York: Van Nostrand, 1979), pp. 4–16.

26. See Richard D. Schwartz, "Rehabilitation," in *Encyclopedia of Crime and Justice,* pp. 1364–1373.

27. "The Humanitarian Theory of Punishment," *Res Judicatae* 6 (1953):224.

28. *Coker v. Georgia,* 433 U.S. 584 (1977).

29. Joel Samaha, *Law and Order in Historical Perspective* (New York: Academic Press, 1974); Samaha, "Hanging for Felony."

30. See David J. Rothman, *Conscience and Convenience* (Boston: Little, Brown, 1980), for the history of rehabilitation during the early twentieth century.

31. Robert Martinson, "What Works? Questions and Answers about Prison Reform," *The Public Interest* 35 (Spring 1974):22–54.

32. Quoted in Malcom M. Feeley, *Court Reform on Trial* (New York: Basic Books, 1983), 139; Walker, *Sense and Nonsense about Crime,* chapters 1, 5, 6, and 11.

33. See the excellent review of these issues in American Law Institute, *Model Penal Code and Commentaries,* 3, 11–30.

34. *Ravin v. State,* 537 P.2d 494 (Alaska 1975).

35. *Texas Penal Code,* § 31.03(5)(a)(1) (St. Paul, Minn.: West Publishing Co., 1988).

36. Sir William Blackstone, *Commentaries,* book IV.

37. LaFave and Scott, *Criminal Law,* p. 59.

38. *The Growth of the Law* (New Haven, Conn.: Yale University Press, 1924), p. 62.

39. *State v. Mellenberger,* 163 Or. 233, 95 P.2d 70 (1939) overruling *State v. Alexander,* 76 Or. 329, 148 P. 1136 (1915).

40. West's Florida Statutes Annotated (1991), Title XLVI, § 775.01.

41. Max Farrand, ed., *The Laws and Liberties of Massachusetts* (Cambridge, Mass.: Harvard University Press, 1929), A2.

42. Ibid., pp. 5, 6.

43. Julian P. Bond, ed., *The Papers of Thomas Jefferson,* vol. 2 (Princeton, N.J.: Princeton University Press, 1950) reprints this proposed code and Jefferson's fascinating notes about it. Also, Kathryn Preyer's "Crime, the Criminal Law and Reform in Post-Revolutionary Virginia," *Law and History Review* 1 (1983):53–85, contains an informative discussion about Jefferson's code.

44. *United States v. Hudson and Goodwin,* 11 U.S. (7 Cranch) 32, 3 L.Ed. 259 (1812).

45. American Law Institute, *Model Penal Code and Commentaries,* part I, § 1.01 to 2.13 (Philadelphia: American Law Institute, 1985), 75–80; § 13A-1-4, Code of Alabama 1975.

46. 2 Cal. 3d 619, 87 Cal.Rptr. 481, 470 P.2d 617 (Cal. 1970).

47. West's California Penal Code (St. Paul, Minn.: West Publishing Company, 1988) § 187(a).

48. LaFave and Scott, *Criminal Law,* pp. 68–69.

49. *State v. McFeely,* 25 N.J. Misc. 303, 52 A.2d 823 (Quar.Sess. 1947).

50. Herbert Packer, "The Aims of the Criminal Law Revisited: A Plea for a New Look at 'Substantive Due Process,'" *Southern California Law Review* 44 (1970–71):490–498.

51. A useful survey of the *Model Penal Code* written by its leading light can be found in Herbert Wechsler, "The Model Penal Code and the Codification of American Criminal Law," Roger Hood, ed., *Crime, Criminology, and Public Policy* (London: Heineman, 1974), pp. 419–468; *American Law Institute, tentatwe drafts* 1–13 (Philadelphia: American Law Institute, 1954–61).

52. An excellent discussion of some of these matters appears in David W. Neubauer, *Criminal Justice in Middle America* (Morristown, N.J.: General Learning Press, 1974), pp. 86–105. For an earlier but provocative analysis, see Jerome Frank, *Courts on Trial: Myth and Reality in American Justice* (Princeton, N.J.: Princeton University Press, 1949), chap. 14.

53. Emile Durkheim, *The Division of Labor in Society* (New York: Free Press, 1933), pp. 73–80; the insight concerning policy formulation stems from the research of Timothy Lenz, Department of Political Science, University of Minnesota.

54. George B. Vold and Thomas J. Bernard, *Theoretical Criminology,* 3d ed. (New York: Oxford University Press, 1986); Chapters 14 through 16 develop these points fully.

55. For good introductions to this theory, see Richard Quinney, *Criminology,* 2d ed. (Boston: Little, Brown, 1979), pp. 120–125; and William Chambliss and Robert Seidman, *Law, Order, and Power,* 2d ed. (Reading, Mass.: Addison-Wesley, 1982), pp. 171–207.

56. Peter Rossi et al., "The Seriousness of Crimes: Normative Structure and Individual Differences," *American Sociological Review* 39 (1974): 224–237; William J. Chambliss, "The Law of Vagrancy," in *Criminal Law in Action,* 2d ed., edited by William J. Chambliss (New York: Macmillan, 1984), pp. 33–42.

57. An excellent introduction to discretion is Kenneth Culp Davis, *Discretionary Justice* (Baton Rouge, La.: Louisiana State University Press, 1969).

58. Sir Nicholas Bacon, quoted in Joel Samaha, "Hanging for Felony," *Historical Journal* (1979):75.

59. Ibid., pp. 769–771.

60. Edwin H. Sutherland and Donald R. Cressey, *Criminology,* 10th ed., rev. (Philadelphia: Lippincott, 1978), pp. 333–334.

61. Edwin Sutherland, "The Sexual Psychopath Laws," *Journal of Criminal Law, Criminology, and Police Science* 40 (1950):543–554.

62. Francis A. Allen, *The Borderland of Criminal Justice* (Chicago: University of Chicago Press, 1964), p. 15.

63. Holmes's famous aphorism appears in *New York Trust Company v. Eisner,* 256 U.S. 345, 41 S.Ct. 506, 65 L.Ed. 963 (1921), 349.

64. See Rollin M. Perkins and Ronald N. Boyce, *Criminal Law,* 3d ed. (Mineola, N.Y.: Foundation Press, 1982), pp. 289–292; and American Law Institute, *Model Penal Code and Commentaries,* vol. 2, pp. 128–130. For a full and interesting treatment of the relationship of history and society to theft, see Jerome Hall, *Theft, Law, and Society* (Indianapolis, Ind.: Bobbs-Merrill, 1952).

65. Joel Samaha, "John Winthrop and the Criminal Law," *William Mitchell Law Review* (1989):217.

66. Quoted in Sanford Kadish and Manfred Paulson, *Criminal Law and Its Processes,* 3d ed., rev. (Boston and Toronto: Little, Brown, 1975), p. 40.

2 Constitutional Limits on Criminal Law

Chapter Outline

I. Introduction

II. The Rule of Law

III. *Ex Post Facto* Laws

IV. Void-for-Vagueness Doctrine

V. How to Read, Brief, and Find Cases

VI. Equal Protection of the Laws

VII. Free Speech

VIII. Right to Privacy

IX. Cruel and Unusual Punishments

X. Summary

CHAPTER MAIN POINTS

1. The United States Constitution creates a balance between the power of the government to control crime and the rights of individuals against excesses of government power.

2. The Constitution requires that the law define crimes and prescribe penalties *before* individuals are prosecuted and punished.

3. The Constitution requires that criminal statutes define crimes clearly enough both to notify individuals as to what the law prohibits and to control the discretion of officials when they enforce the law.

4. Equal protection doesn't mean that the law has to treat everyone exactly alike, but classifications cannot be arbitrary.

5. The Constitution doesn't mention privacy, but the right of privacy nevertheless limits the power of legislatures to create crimes.

6. The First Amendment prohibits making it a crime to express some ideas and feelings.

7. The "cruel and unusual punishment" clause of the U.S. Constitution prohibits both "barbaric" punishments and punishments out of proportion to the seriousness of the crime.

Was Metzger's Behavior Indecent, Immodest, or Filthy?

Metzger lived in Lincoln, Nebraska, in a garden-level apartment with a large window facing a parking lot. At about 7:45 A.M., on April 30, 1981, another resident of the building was parking his automobile in a space directly in front of Metzger's apartment window. While doing so, he observed, for a period of 5 seconds, Metzger standing naked in the window with his arms at his sides. The resident testified that he saw Metzger's body from the thighs up.

The resident called the police, and two officers arrived at the apartment at about 8 A.M. The officers testified that they observed Metzger standing in front of the window, within a foot of it, eating a bowl of cereal, and that his naked body was visible from the mid-thigh up.

INTRODUCTION

The authors of the United States Constitution were suspicious of power, especially power in the hands of government officers. They were also passionately devoted to the right of individuals to control their own destinies free of government interference. But they were realists too. They knew that freedom depends on order, and order depends on control. So, they created a Constitution that balanced the power of government and the liberty of individuals. No one has put the purpose of the Constitution better than James Madison, fourth president of the United States:

> If men were angels, no government would be necessary. If angels were to govern men, neither external nor internal controls on government would be necessary. In framing a government which is to be administered by men over men, the great difficulty is this: You must first enable the government to control the governed; and in the next place, oblige it to control itself.[1]

We live in a constitutional democracy, not a pure democracy. In a pure democracy the majority can have whatever it wants. In a *constitutional* democracy, the majority can't make a crime out of what the Constitution protects as a fundamental right. No matter if all the people want to make it a crime to say, "God damn the President of the United States," they can't. Why? Because, as we'll see later in this chapter, the First Amendment says that legislatures can't pass laws against free speech. A central feature of criminal law in a constitutional democracy is the limits that are placed on the power of government to create crimes. Chapter 1 described the limits imposed by the common-law tradition and by our federal system of government. Chapters 3 through 7 examine the boundaries drawn by the general principles of criminal liability, justification, and excuse; and by the doctrines of attempt, conspiracy, solicitation, complicity, and vicarious liability. Chapters 8 through 12 analyze how the definitions of specific crimes further restrict the reach of the criminal law. This chapter focuses on the limits imposed by the U.S. and state constitutions. These limits include:

1. The rule of law.
2. The prohibition against *ex post facto* laws.

3. The right to "due process of law."
4. The right to "equal protection of the law."
5. The right to free speech, association, press, and religion.
6. The right to privacy.
7. The right against "cruel and unusual punishment."

THE RULE OF LAW

Deeply embedded in our constitutional system is the principle that the government can punish people only if there is an exact law that both defines and prescribes the punishment for criminal behavior. This principle is called the **rule of law**, also known as the **principle of legality**. The U.S. and state constitutions, federal and state laws, and court decisions are all based on the rule of law.

This is a grand principle, but in fact challenging the constitutionality of laws isn't easy. One reason is another principle—that the will of the people should prevail in a democracy. So, courts are extremely reluctant to overturn popular will enacted into law. Second, the government doesn't have to prove that its laws *are* constitutional; challengers have to prove that they *aren't*. Put in technical terms, there is a strong presumption in favor of the constitutionality of laws, and challengers carry the **burden of proof** that the laws are unconstitutional. This is a heavy burden, sometimes requiring that challengers prove unconstitutionality beyond a reasonable doubt, the heaviest burden known to the law. In fact, it's the same burden that the government has to carry to convict defendants of crimes (see Chapter 3). That's why the great Supreme Court Justice Oliver Wendell Holmes called constitutional arguments the "last resort" of lawyers. So, it's no surprise that most defendants rarely challenge the constitutionality of laws, and when they do they usually lose.

EX POST FACTO LAWS

"No crime without law; no punishment without law." So goes the ancient maxim of Western law. The Roman Civil Law read: "A penalty is not inflicted unless it is expressly imposed by law, or by some other authority." In the fierce struggle between king and Parliament in seventeenth-century England, the great jurist Lord Edward Coke said: "It is against the law, that men should be committed [to prison] and no cause showed..." Article I, Section 9 of the U.S. Constitution adopts this ancient principle by providing: "No state shall... pass any *ex post facto* law...." (a law that punishes crimes defined after the conduct occurs). Most state constitutions contain similar provisions.[2]

The *ex post facto* prohibition has two major goals:

1. To give fair warning to private individuals.

2. To prevent arbitrary action by government officials.

The U.S. Supreme Court has interpreted the *ex post facto* clause liberally. In 1798, the Court ruled that the clause prohibits laws that

1. Punish actions committed before the laws were enacted.

2. Aggravate the degree of the crime after it was committed.

3. Increase the punishment for a specific crime after the crime was committed.
4. Reduce the amount or alter the kind of evidence required for conviction when the offense was committed.[3]

Ex post facto laws that *benefit* defendants don't come within its prohibition. For example, the *ex post facto* clause doesn't stand in the way of a statute that retroactively reduces the punishment for murder. In one case, a defendant was convicted of first degree murder when the penalty was death. Then the state retroactively reduced the penalty for first degree murder from death to life imprisonment. The *ex post facto* prohibition didn't apply because the defendant benefited by having his death sentence reduced to life imprisonment.[4]

VOID-FOR-VAGUENESS DOCTRINE

Like *ex post facto* laws, vaguely defined laws fail to warn private individuals and permit **arbitrary action** by government officials. (Arbitrary means without reason or standards.) According to the U.S. Supreme Court, vague laws violate the **due process clauses** of the U.S. Constitution. In the words of the Court,

> It is a basic principle of due process that an enactment is void for vagueness if its prohibitions are not clearly defined. Vague laws offend... important values. First, because we assume that man is free to steer between lawful and unlawful conduct, we insist that laws give the person of ordinary intelligence a reasonable opportunity to know what is prohibited, so that he may act accordingly. Vague laws may trap the innocent by not providing fair warning. Second, if arbitrary and discriminatory enforcement is to be prevented, laws must provide explicit standards for those who apply them. A vague law impermissibly delegates basic policy matters to policemen, judges, and juries for resolution on an ad hoc and subjective basis, with the attendant dangers of arbitrary and discriminatory application.... Uncertain meanings inevitably lead citizens to steer far wider of the unlawful zone... than if the boundaries of the forbidden areas were clearly marked.[5]

The rule that vague laws violate due process is called the **void-for-vagueness doctrine**. The reasoning behind the doctrine goes like this:

1. Criminal punishment involves the deprivation of life (capital punishment), liberty (imprisonment), or property (fines).
2. The Fifth and Fourteenth Amendments to the U.S. Constitution prohibit both federal and state governments from taking any person's "life, liberty, or property without due process of law."
3. Failure to adequately warn private persons what the law prohibits and/or allowing officials the chance to arbitrarily define what the law prohibits denies people life, liberty, and/or property without due process of law.[6]

The Court has adopted a two-pronged test to determine whether laws are void-for-vagueness. Do they:

1. Provide fair warning to individuals as to what the law prohibits?
2. Prevent arbitrary and discriminatory criminal justice administration?

Notice that the first prong is aimed at private individuals, the second at criminal justice officials. In early cases, the Supreme Court focused on the fair warning to private individuals prong. For example, in 1939, in *Lanzetta v. New Jersey,* the Court struck down a New Jersey statute that made it a crime to be a member of a "gang." After holding that the word *gang* was too vague to give fair warning, the Court commented:

> No one may be required at peril of life, liberty, or property to speculate as to the meaning of penal statutes. All are entitled to be informed as to what the State commands or forbids.... [A] statute which either forbids or requires the doing of an act in terms so vague that men of common intelligence must necessarily guess at its meaning and differ as to its application, violates the first essential of due process of law.[7]

Despite the importance of giving fair warning to individuals, by 1983, in the case of *Kolender v. Lawson,* the Supreme Court decided that the "more important aspect of the vagueness doctrine is not actual notice [to private individuals], but the other principal element of the vagueness doctrine—the requirement that a legislature establish minimal guidelines to govern law enforcement."[8]

✳ 2-1 *Kolender v. Lawson* Oral Argument, Transcript, and Briefs

Whether the emphasis is on notice to individuals or control of officials, the void-for-vagueness doctrine can never cure the uncertainty in all laws. After all, laws are made up of words. And concerning the use of words, U.S. Supreme Court Justice Thurgood Marshall wrote that, "Condemned to the use of words, we can never expect mathematical certainty from our language." It's not just the natural uncertainty of words that creates problems. It's also that the variety of human behavior and the limits of human imagination make it impossible for lawmakers to predict all the variations that might arise under the provisions of statutes. As a result, courts allow considerable leeway in the degree of certainty required to pass the two prongs of fair warning and avoidance of arbitrary law enforcement.

The strong presumption of constitutionality referred to earlier requires that challengers prove that the law is vague, "not in the sense that it requires a person to conform his conduct to an imprecise but comprehensible normative standard, but rather in the sense that no standard of conduct is specified at all."[9] The Ohio supreme court summarized the heavy burden of proof placed on those who challenge statutes on the grounds that they are void for vagueness:

> The challenger must show that upon examining the statute, an individual of ordinary intelligence would not understand what he is required to do under the law. Thus, to escape responsibility... [the challenger] must prove that he could not reasonably understand that .. [the statute] prohibited the acts in which he engaged.... The party alleging that a statute is unconstitutional must prove this assertion beyond a reasonable doubt.[10]

The first case excerpt, *Sterling v. State,* is a good example of how one court applied the void-for-vagueness doctrine to uncertain words in an Alabama disorderly conduct law.

HOW TO READ, BRIEF, AND FIND CASES

For most students, reading and discussing the cases are their favorite part of the book. That's good, not only because the cases make criminal law more interesting for you but also because they help you to grasp the important issues and learn the

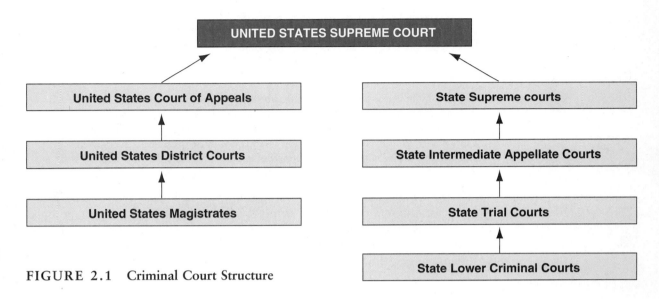

FIGURE 2.1   Criminal Court Structure

important concepts in criminal law. Cases bring criminal law to life by applying the abstract general principles, doctrines, and rules described in the text to real events in the lives of real people. But, judges write the reports of the cases and they don't all write with college students in mind; reading them takes some getting used to and guidance. This section is designed to help you get the most out of the cases.

The cases in this book are all excerpts; that is, they are edited versions of the complete reports of the cases. When you see the three (...) or four (....) dots called ellipses, you'll know I've cut something out that I don't think you need to know at this point in the text. When you see text inside brackets ([ ]), that text is something I've added, usually to define a technical term or explain a concept that you need to know in order to understand the case.

In almost all of the case excerpts, you'll be reading reports of appeals of convictions. In other words, the defendant has been convicted and has asked a higher court to review the conviction. You'll never read a review of a case in which a defendant was acquitted. In the criminal law of the United States, a "not guilty" verdict is final and not subject to review.

Most states and the federal government have two levels of appeals courts (see Figure 2.1), an intermediate court of appeals and a supreme court. The usual procedure is to appeal first to the intermediate court of appeals and then to the state supreme court. In a few cases involving issues about the U.S. Constitution, the case may go to the U.S. Supreme Court. The first case following this section, *Sterling v. State,* is a typical appeal from an Alabama trial court to the Alabama intermediate appeals court.

Cases like *Sterling v. State* are called appellate cases. The parties who appeal them are called **appellants,** and the parties appealed against are called **appellees.** The case title reveals who is the appellant and who is the appellee. The party who brings the appeal is the first name in the title. The party appealed against is the appellee. So, in *Sterling v. State,* Sterling is the appellant (the convicted defendant in the trial court), the "v." is the abbreviation for the Latin *versus,* which means "against," and State (in this case, the state of Alabama) is the appellee. You'll see two other names for states, "People" and "Commonwealth." Most case excerpts in this book are like *Sterling v. State*—convicted defendants appealing against the state to get their convictions overturned, or **reversed**.

In cases involving constitutional questions, defendants may seek a different kind of review called **collateral attack**. Collateral attacks are separate legal actions from the criminal proceeding. They are lawsuits that challenge either the authority of a court to hear a case or the legality of a detention in a prison or jail. The most frequent collateral attack is habeas corpus. Habeas corpus begins with the habeas corpus petition. In this petition, a prisoner asks for a court order demanding that the person in charge of the prison or jail detaining the prisoner demonstrate that the agency has the legal authority to incarcerate the prisoner. In the few case excerpts in the book involving habeas corpus proceedings, the person challenging imprisonment is called the petitioner; these petitioners are the defendants in the criminal case. You can tell whether the case is a collateral attack by its title. The title contains two individuals' names—the name of the petitioner who would be the defendant in the criminal case and the name of the respondent who is the warden of the prison or whoever is in charge of the facility holding the petitioner.

PARTS OF THE CASE EXCERPTS

Title

The case title consists of the names of the parties, either appellants and appellees or petitioners and respondents.

Citation

The **citation** is like the footnote or endnote in any text; it tells you where to find the case. (See below on "Finding cases.")

Case History

The case history is a brief description of the case from its beginning to the decision in the appeals court reporting the case.

Judge

The name of the judge who wrote the opinion in the case.

Facts

The facts of the case are the critical starting point in reading and analyzing cases. If you don't know the facts, you can't understand the principle the case is teaching. One of my favorite law professors used to tell us again and again: "Remember cases are stories with a point. You can't get the point if you don't know the story." He also told us something else that I think will help you. "Forget you're lawyers. Tell me the story as if you were telling it to your grandmother who doesn't know anything about the law." Take Professor Hill's advice, even though he's been dead and gone for a long time. I do, because it's still good advice.

Opinion

The court's opinion is "the point of the story." In the opinion the court applies the law to the facts of the case. The law in the case excerpts includes the constitutional principles in this chapter; the principles of criminal liability in Chapters 3 and 4; the law of parties to crime and incomplete offenses in Chapters 5 and 6; the defenses in Chapters 7 and 8; and the law of crimes against persons, burglary and arson, property, and public order in Chapters 9 through 13. The opinion contains two essential ingredients:

1. The court's **holding**—the legal rule that the court has decided applies to the facts of the cases.

2. The court's **reasoning**—the reasons the court gives to support its holding.

In some cases, there are majority and dissenting opinions. A **majority opinion**, as its name indicates, is the opinion of the majority of the justices on the court who participated in the case. The majority opinion is the law of the case. Although the majority opinion represents the established law of the case, **dissenting opinions** present a plausible alternative to the majority opinion. Dissents of former times frequently become the law of later times. For example, many dissents in U.S. Supreme Court opinions of the 1930s became the law in the 1960s; and many of the dissents of the 1960s became the law by the 1990s. Occasionally, you'll see a **concurring opinion**. In concurring opinions, justices agree with the conclusions of either the majority or dissenting opinion, but they have separate reasons for reaching the conclusion. Sometimes, enough justices agree with the result in the case so that there is a majority decision, but not enough justices agree on the reasoning to make up a majority opinion. In these cases, there is a **plurality opinion**, an opinion that represents the reasoning of the greatest number of justices but that falls short of a majority. So, there is no majority opinion. All of the differing perspectives in the opinions get you to think about the principles of criminal law. They also clearly demonstrate that there is almost always more than one reasonable way to look at important questions.

Briefing the Cases

To get the most from the cases, you should write out the answers to the following questions about each case excerpt. This is what we call briefing a case.

1. *What are the facts?* State the facts in simple narrative form in chronological order. As Professor Hill said, "Tell me the story as if you were telling it to your grandmother." Then, select, sort, and arrange the facts into the following categories:
   a. Actions of the defendant. (Notice that the actions of defendants are always relevant because there is no criminal case without the acts of the defendant.)
   b. Intent of the defendant; if not relevant, say none.
   c. Harm; if not relevant, say none.
   d. Cause of the harm; if not relevant, say none.
   e. Justification or excuse (defense); if not relevant, say none.

2. *What is the legal issue in the case?* State the principle and/or the rule of criminal law raised by the facts of the case.

3. *What is the court's holding?* State the answer that the court gives to the issue in the case.

4. *What is the court's opinion?* State the reasons that the court gives for its decision and holdings. How did it arrive at the conclusions it reached? The court's reasoning, or opinion, applies the general principle, doctrine, and rule to the facts of the case.

5. *What is the court's decision?* State how the court disposed of the case. The most common decisions include:
   a. **Affirmed** (agree with and uphold the lower court's decision).
   b. **Reversed** (overturned the lower court decision).
   c. Reversed in part (overturned part of lower court's decision and affirmed the rest).
   d. Reversed and **remanded** (overturned lower court's decision and sent the case back to the lower court for further proceedings in accord with the appellate court's decision).

You can't answer all these questions in every case. The answers depend on the knowledge that you will accumulate as the text and your instructor introduce more principles, doctrines, and rules. Furthermore, courts don't necessarily follow the same procedure in reviewing an appeal as that outlined above. Finally, not all of the questions come up in every case. Only one question comes up in every case— What did the defendant do? That is because there is no criminal case without some action.

Developing the skills needed to sort out the elements of the case excerpts requires practice but is worth the effort. Answering the questions given here can challenge you to think not only about the basic principles, doctrines, and rules of criminal law but also about your own fundamental values regarding life, property, privacy, and morals.

Finding Cases

Knowing how to read and brief cases is important. So is knowing how to find cases. It will help you to complete the Internet exercises on the CD that accompanies the text. Also, you might want to look up cases on your own, either on-line or in the library. These cases might include those that your instructor talks about in class, and those that are discussed in the text but not excerpted. You may also want to read the whole case that is excerpted in the book. Or, you may even want to look up a case that you read or hear about outside of class. If you want to go further and read the full cases excerpted here, or read cases referred to in either the text or the cases, I've included the case citation. The citation consists of the numbers, letters, and punctuation that follow the title of a case in the excerpts, or in the endnote referencing cases in the text. These letters and numbers tell you where to locate the full case report. For example, in the first excerpt that follows this section, just after the title of the case, *Sterling v. State,* you read "701 So.2nd 71 (1997 Ala. App.)." This citation indicates that you can find this case reported in Volume 701 of the *Southern Reports, second series,* (abbreviated "So.2nd") beginning on page 71. *Southern Reports* is a multivolume set in two series that reports published appellate cases in Alabama and several other states in the southern region of the United States. There are comparable *Reports* for other regions, including the *Northeast, Northwest, Southeast,* and *Pacific.* There is also one each for New York and for California. Case citations always follow the same order. The volume number always comes before the title of a report and the page always come immediately after the title. The abbreviation for the name of the court and the year the case was decided follows the page number in parentheses. You can tell if the court was the highest or an intermediate appellate court by the abbreviation. For example, in *Sterling* the court is the intermediate appellate court in Alabama, designated as "Ala. App." If the Alabama supreme court had decided the case, you would see only "Ala."

C A S E **Did He Make "Unreasonable Noise"?**

Sterling v. State
701 So.2d 71 (1997 Ala. App.)

Henry Sterling was convicted in the Randolph District Court, of disorderly conduct. He appealed. Following trial de novo [a new trial, as if Sterling has never been tried], he was convicted in the Randolph Circuit Court and sentenced to perform community service or, in the alternative, to serve 60 days in the Randolph County jail. He appealed. The Court of Criminal Appeals affirmed.

FACTS

Sterling applied for a pistol permit with the Randolph County Sheriff's Department. After routine processing, the application was denied. Sterling came to the sheriff's office, which is located in the county courthouse, and inquired about the status of his application. Sterling was told that his application had been denied. When he asked why, the sheriff told him that permits could be issued only to county residents (Sterling was not a resident of Randolph County). Sterling continued to ask the sheriff why his application had been denied and raised his voice with each successive question. The sheriff repeatedly gave him the same reason—that he was not a resident of the county. Sterling, trailing closely behind the sheriff, followed him out of the office and into the courthouse hallway and again demanded to know why his application had been denied. His voice was now loud enough that workers in other offices along the hallway heard him and stopped their work to see what was happening. The sheriff then warned Sterling that he would be arrested if he did not cease; Sterling responded that he "was not scared of your jail." When Sterling continued to ask, in the same tone of voice, why his permit application had been denied, the sheriff arrested him.

OPINION

Sterling claims that § 13A-11-7(a)(2) is unconstitutionally vague because it does not provide a reasonable person with notice as to the type of conduct it proscribes. He also claims that this statute is overbroad because it also prohibits constitutionally protected speech. Although he raises these issues separately in his brief on appeal, we will address them together here. Section 13A-11-7(a), Code of Alabama 1975 reads, in pertinent part:

> "(a) A person commits the crime of disorderly conduct if, with intent to cause public inconvenience, annoyance or alarm, or recklessly creating a risk thereof, he:
> "...
> "(2) Makes unreasonable noise...."

... To withstand a challenge of vagueness, a statute must: 1) give a person of ordinary intelligence a reasonable opportunity to know what is prohibited, and, 2) provide explicit standards to those who apply the laws.

"This prohibition against excessive vagueness does not invalidate every statute which a reviewing court believes could have been drafted with greater precision. Many statutes will have some inherent vagueness, for 'in most English words and phrases there lurk uncertainties.' *Robinson v. United States*, 324 U.S. 282, 286, 65 S.Ct. 666, 668, 89 L.Ed. 944 (1945). Even trained lawyers may find it necessary to consult legal dictionaries, treatises, and judicial opinions before they may say with any certainty what some statutes may compel or forbid. A defendant who challenges a statute on the ground of vagueness must demonstrate that the statute under attack is vague as applied to his own conduct, regardless of the potentially vague applications to others...."

We have found no instance in which the appellate courts of Alabama have addressed the issue whether § 13A-11-7(a)(2) is unconstitutionally vague.... Section 13A-11-7 is virtually identical to New York Revised Penal Law § 240.20; in fact, the Alabama statute was adapted from the New York law. The Court of Appeals of New York addressed the constitutionality of § 240.20 in *People v. Bakolas,* 59 N.Y.2d 51, 462 N.Y.S.2d 844, 449 N.E.2d 738 (N.Y.1983). In *Bakolas,* two defendants were charged with violating, among other laws, subdivision 2 of § 240.20, which states that "[a] person is guilty of disorderly conduct when, with intent to cause public inconvenience, annoyance or alarm, or recklessly creating a risk thereof ... [h]e makes unreasonable noise." The Rochester, New York, City Court held that subdivision 2 was unconstitutionally vague "because the meaning of the term 'unreasonable noise' depends on the ear and mind of the listener." On appeal, the County Court of Monroe County, New York, reversed that ruling, holding that "the culpability requirement ('with intent to cause public inconvenience, annoyance or alarm, or recklessly creating a risk thereof') saved the statute." The Court of Appeals affirmed the order of the county court, stating that "[t]he term 'unreasonable noise' is not incapable of definition. Rather, it describes a noise of a type or volume that a reasonable person, under the circumstances, would not tolerate." The court further stated that the standard for "unreasonable noise" is that it be "'an assault on public sensibilities'" such that "the noise be intended to cause, or recklessly create a risk of, public inconvenience, annoyance or alarm" and that this standard "narrows the definition [of unreasonable noise], so that no inadvertently disturbing act may be punished." The Court of Appeals also stated that this statute was based on the objective standard of public disturbance rather than the subjective standard of the annoyance of a particular person which could result in "enforcement according to the 'malice or animosity of a cantankerous neighbor'" or the "'boiling point of a particular person.'" ... Sterling has not "demonstrated that § 13A-11-7(a)(2), Code of Alabama 1975 is vague as applied to his own conduct." ...

The judgment of the trial court is affirmed.

QUESTIONS FOR DISCUSSION

1. Was Sterling making "unreasonable noise"?
2. To whom should the noise be unreasonable? To the people who actually heard it?
3. Or, to a reasonable person? Explain and defend your answer.
4. Do you believe that the words "unreasonable noise" fairly warn individuals and adequately guard against arbitrary and discriminatory criminal justice administration? Defend your answer.

NOTE CASES

1. Section 147-1 of the Washington, New Jersey, Township Code states:

It shall be unlawful for any person to make, continue or cause to be made or continued any loud, unnecessary or unusual noise or any noise which either annoys, disturbs, injures or endangers the comfort repose, health, peace or safety of others within the limits of the Township of Washington.

Section 147-2, in relevant part, provides:

The following acts, among others, are declared to be loud, disturbing and unnecessary noises in violation of this chapter, but said enumeration shall not be deemed to be exclusive: ... Animals, birds, etc. The keeping of any animal or bird which by causing frequent or long-continued noise shall disturb the comfort or repose of any person in the vicinity.

Washington Township issued eight separate summonses to the Friedmans for violation of Washington Township Ordinance 147-2(E) based upon complaints by their neighbor Naomi Theisz, that the defendants' dog, a Collie named Whitney, repeatedly woke her up in the early morning hours. After hearing the testimony of the complainant, Theisz, and the defendants, the Municipal Court Judge found defendants guilty on all eight summonses. Defendants appealed to the Law Division and moved to dismiss the Washington Township summonses on the ground that the Township's anti-noise ordinance was unconstitutional. The Law Division determined that the ordinance was constitutional and that although the barking complained of was very brief in duration, it occurred with sufficient frequency to sustain a conviction under the ordinance.

The Friedmans argue, as they did in the Law Division, that Washington Township's anti-noise ordinance is vague and provides a completely subjective standard for determining what constitutes a disturbing noise. Essentially, they contend that *State v. Holland*, 132 N.J.Super. 17, 25-27, 331 A.2d 626 (App.Div.1975), requires courts to utilize a standard of objective reasonableness when determining what type of conduct violates the anti-noise ordinance and that the Law Division, as did the Municipal Court Judge, applied a subjective "any person" standard. They thus contend that the ordinance is vague on its face and may only be constitutionally applied when interpreted to require that a defendant act unreasonably for there to be a violation of the ordinance.

Was the ordinance void for vagueness? Yes, according to the New Jersey Superior Court:

Neither the Law Division Judge nor the Municipal Court Judge considered the reasonableness of the Friedmans' conduct in determining whether their dog's barking violated the anti-noise ordinance. A purely subjective standard of behavior was utilized to determine whether the dog's barking constituted a disturbance of the peace; such a standard is unconstitutionally vague. Hence, section 147-2(E) of the Washington Township Code is defective because it proscribes noise which disturbs "the comfort or repose of any person in the vicinity." Such a standard does not provide any guidance as to what constitutes a violation of the statute, leaving the determination as to whether a violation has occurred "to any person who feels a dog's frequent or habitual barking is annoying or disturbing." Although the ordinance does provide a relatively detailed list of conduct which violates its proscription, its articulation of the standard of conduct as it applies to animals is extremely vague.

Despite the ordinance's vagueness, under our law the ordinance is not facially unconstitutional. As numerous decisions regarding such ordinances make clear, such general language is permissible so long as courts utilize a reasonableness standard when applying it. Hence, the Law Division's failure to consider the reasonableness of the Friedmans' conduct in determining whether the ordinance was violated makes the application of the ordinance in this case unconstitutional as to them.

"A dog is not a nuisance per se.... But it has also been of the essence of civilized society, where many individuals live as neighbors, for each to exercise his rights with due regard to the rights of

all. Barking is "a natural canine act" and the ordinance, as applied in this case, does not provide a sufficient basis for concluding that the kind of barking that occurred here is prohibited. Certainly the township has authority to prohibit barking that constitutes a public nuisance. To the extent Section 147-2(E) does so, it is constitutional and may be applied, as written, to prohibit such conduct. This ordinance, however, cannot proscribe reasonable noises associated with common, acceptable behavior. Such an application would deprive defendants of due process. Reversed.

State v. Friedman, 697 A.2d 947 (N.J. Sup. Ct. 1997)

2. Metzger lived in a garden-level apartment located in Lincoln, Nebraska. A large window in the apartment faces a parking lot which is situated on the north side of the apartment building. At about 7:45 A.M., on April 30, 1981, another resident of the apartment, while parking his automobile in a space directly in front of Metzger's apartment window, observed Metzger standing naked with his arms at his sides in his apartment window for a period of 5 seconds. The resident testified that he saw Metzger's body from the thighs on up. The resident called the police department and two officers arrived at the apartment at about 8 A.M. The officers testified that they observed Metzger standing in front of the window eating a bowl of cereal. They testified that Metzger was standing within a foot of the window and his nude body, from the mid-thigh on up, was visible.

... The pertinent portion of § 9.52.100... under which Metzger was charged, provides as follows:

"It shall be unlawful for any person within the City of Lincoln ... to commit any indecent, immodest or filthy act in the presence of any person, or in such a situation that persons passing might ordinarily see the same."...

Was the ordinance void for vagueness? Yes, said the Nebraska supreme court. According to the court:

The ordinance in question makes it unlawful for anyone to commit any "indecent, immodest or filthy act." We know of no way in which the standards required of a criminal act can be met in those broad, general terms. There may be those few who believe persons of opposite sex holding hands in public are immodest, and certainly who might believe that kissing in public is immodest. Such acts cannot constitute a crime. Certainly one could find many who would conclude that today's swimming attire found on many beaches or beside many pools is immodest. Yet, the fact that it is immodest does not thereby make it illegal, absent some requirement related to the health, safety, or welfare of the community.

The dividing line between what is lawful and what is unlawful in terms of "indecent," "immodest," or "filthy" is simply too broad to satisfy the constitutional requirements of due process. Both lawful and unlawful acts can be embraced within such broad definitions. That cannot be permitted. One is not able to determine in advance what is lawful and what is unlawful. We do not attempt, in this opinion, to determine whether Metzger's actions in a particular case might not be made unlawful, nor do we intend to encourage such behavior. Indeed, it may be possible that a governmental subdivision using sufficiently definite language could make such an act as committed by Metzger unlawful. We simply do not decide that question at this time because of our determination that the ordinance is so vague as to be unconstitutional. We therefore believe that § 9.52.100 of the Lincoln Municipal Code must be declared invalid. Because the ordinance is therefore declared invalid, the conviction cannot stand. Reversed and Dismissed.

State v. Metzger, 211 Neb. 593, 319 N.W.2d 459 (1982)

EQUAL PROTECTION OF THE LAWS

In addition to the due process guarantee, the Fourteenth Amendment to the United States Constitution provides that "no state shall deny to any person within its jurisdiction the equal protection of the laws." Equal protection doesn't require the government to treat everybody exactly alike. Statutes frequently classify particular groups of people and types of conduct for special treatment. For example, statutes classify embezzlement by public officials as a more serious crime than embezzlement by private individuals. Almost every state ranks premeditated killings as more serious than negligent homicides. Several states punish habitual criminals more severely than first-time offenders. None of these classifications based on occupation, state of mind, and type of person violates the equal protection clause. The courts almost always uphold these kinds of statutory classification schemes. Why? Because they make sense. Or, as the courts say, they have a "rational basis."[11]

Arbitrary classifications, especially those based on race, are another matter. The U.S. Supreme Court subjects all racial classifications to **strict scrutiny**; that is, they have to further a "compelling state interest." Practically speaking, strict scrutiny means that race-based classifications are never justified. According to the U.S. Supreme Court, any statute that "invidiously classifies similarly situated people on the basis of the immutable characteristics with which they were born ... *always* [emphasis added] violates the Constitution, for the simple reason that, so far as the Constitution is concerned, people of different races are always similarly situated." Gender classifications are scrutinized more carefully than the general classifications that require only a "rational basis" but less so than race classifications that demand the impossible-to-satisfy "strict scrutiny." The Supreme Court has had difficulty deciding exactly how carefully to scrutinize gender classifications in criminal statutes. The plurality, but not a majority, of the justices in *Michael M. v. Superior Court of Sonoma County* agreed that gender classifications must have a "fair and substantial relationship" to legitimate state ends. The Alaska Court of Appeals applied the equal protection clauses of both the United States and the Alaska constitution to an age-based possession of marijuana criminal statute in *Allam v. State*.[12]

C A S E   Did the Age Distinction Violate the Equal Protection Clause?

Allam v. State
830 P.2d 435 (Alaska App. 1992)

Peter Allam pleaded no contest to a charge of possession of marijuana by a person under the age of 19. When he entered his plea, Allam preserved the right to challenge the constitutionality of this statute on appeal. The court imposed a suspended imposition of sentence conditioned on his good behavior for a period of 90 days, his performance of 24 hours of community work, and his being screened by the Alcohol Safety Action Program. The Alaska Court of Appeals affirmed. Judge Mannheimer wrote the opinion for the court.

FACTS

On May 15, 1990, Allam was 18 years old and a senior at Dimond High School in Anchorage. He and the rest of his high school class were at Kincaid Park, participating in "Senior Fun Day," a school-sponsored event. Allam and three other boys, one of whom was also 18 years old and two of whom were under 18 years of age, left the main group of students and went off by themselves to an area several hundred yards away. A school official found the four of them rolling marijuana cigarettes. The boys were taken back to the high school, where school officials called the police. Allam and the other 18-year-old were arrested.

OPINION

Allam asserts that, under former AS 11.71.060(a), he and all other 18-year-olds were denied the equal protection of the law. He contends that the legislature unreasonably put 18-year-olds in a class by themselves: a person older than 18 who possessed up to four ounces of marijuana committed no crime, an 18-year-old like Allam who possessed the same amount of marijuana would be criminally prosecuted, while persons 17 years old or younger who possessed marijuana would be dealt with under the juvenile justice system. AS 47.10.010(a)(1). We reject Allam's attack on the statute and affirm his conviction.

The Alaska Supreme Court has recognized that the legislature may restrict minors' freedom in ways that would be unconstitutional if applied to adults. In *Hanby v. State,* 479 P.2d 486, 498 (Alaska 1970), the court upheld a criminal statute that prohibited the distribution or showing of certain sexually oriented material to minors, even though the material did not qualify as "obscene" and thus could not be banned for the general population. Similarly, in *Anderson v. State,* 562 P.2d 351, 358–59 (Alaska 1977), the court upheld criminal prohibitions on consensual sexual activity with minors. Lastly, in *Ravin v. State,* 537 P.2d 494, 511 & n. 69 (Alaska 1977), when the court declared that the Alaska Constitution protected marijuana possession and use in the privacy of one's home, the court emphasized that this rule did not apply to minors....

Allam concedes that he has no fundamental or protected right to smoke or possess marijuana. He argues, however, that if the legislature allows people 19 years of age or older to engage in these activities then the equal protection clauses of the federal and state constitutions (United States Constitution, Fourteenth Amendment, Section 1; Alaska Constitution, Article I, Section 1) require the legislature to extend the same freedom of action to 18-year-olds.... Under federal equal protection law, when neither a fundamental right nor a suspect or quasi-suspect classification is involved, a statute will satisfy the requirement of equal protection if it is rationally related to furthering a legitimate state interest. Under this test, a statute will not be invalidated unless its "varying treatment of different groups or persons is so unrelated to the achievement of any combination of legitimate purposes that...the legislature's actions were irrational."...

Former AS 11.71.060(a)(3) established 19 years as the age of majority for the purpose of regulating the possession of marijuana. This statute was passed in 1982, when the general age of majority was 18 years. Nevertheless... for purposes of possessing and using marijuana, the legislature intended to set the age of majority at 19 years.... While the Alaska legislature has, since 1977, been willing to recognize 18-year-olds as legal adults in most respects, the legislature has consistently affirmed its view that, for purposes of alcohol and drug use, the age of majority should be set higher.

To satisfy the requirement of . . . [equal protection] legislation must be rationally related to a valid legislative purpose. The Alaska Supreme Court has repeatedly recognized the protection of minors as a valid legislative purpose. Within our system of government, subject to constitutional limitations, it is the legislature's prerogative to restrict or forbid the use of dangerous intoxicants and, if a restriction is based on age, to establish the age at which persons can presumably be trusted to handle those intoxicants in a mature and socially acceptable manner. Former AS 11.71.060(a)(3) set the age for marijuana use at 19 years. We conclude that this choice was rational.

Allam concedes that the legislature's current decision to establish the drinking age at 21 years is supported by "years of scientific study and years of conscious legislative debate." If a drinking age of either 19 years (Alaska law until 1983) or 21 years (current Alaska law) is constitutional, then we have no difficulty concluding that reasonable people could also conclude that 19 years should be the minimum age for using marijuana, another intoxicant.

The facts of Allam's particular case demonstrate another rationale for establishing the age of marijuana use at 19 years. Allam and another 18-year-old were found sharing marijuana with two other high school students who were under the age of 18 years. Like Allam, many 18-year-olds attend high school and regularly associate with students under the age of 18 years. Establishment of a minimum age of 19 years for marijuana use is justified by the danger that, if 18-year-olds were allowed to possess and use marijuana, they would share the drug with other younger students or would at least frequently expose those younger students to drug use. . . .

The final question is whether former AS 11.71.060(a)(3) violated the Alaska Constitution's equal protection guarantee. . . . This court must first identify the individual interest impaired by the statute and evaluate its importance; we then identify the social purposes underlying the statute and evaluate their importance. The level of justification required for the statute rises in proportion to the importance of the individual interest it affects. Depending upon the importance of that individual interest, the government's interest in enacting the statute must fall somewhere on a continuum between "mere legitimacy" to a "compelling interest."

Second, if the government's interest in enacting the statute is sufficiently strong, this court must examine the connection between the social policies underlying the statute and the means adopted in the statute to further those policies. Again, depending upon the importance of the individual interest affected, this nexus between ends and means must fall somewhere on a continuum between "substantial relationship" and "least restrictive alternative."

Here, Allam concedes that he has no protected interest in possessing or using marijuana. Even if Allam had not conceded this point, we would recognize the legislature's legitimate interest in regulating marijuana. Indeed, the Alaska Supreme Court has already held that, except for personal use of marijuana by adults in their own home, the legislature is justified in regulating the possession and use of this drug.

The second prong of the equal protection test is also satisfied. Because Allam has no interest in possessing or using marijuana, the classification drawn by former AS 11.71.060(a)(3) between people at least 19 years old and people younger than 19 years must bear a "substantial relationship" to the policy interests underlying the regulation of marijuana. We conclude that, given the relationship between age and discretion, the establishment of a minimum age of 19 years for marijuana use bears a substantial relationship to the social interests advanced by marijuana regulation. . . .

For these reasons, we conclude that the Alaska legislature acted constitutionally when they enacted former AS 11.71.060(a)(3), establishing 19 years as the minimum age for possession and use of marijuana guarantee, and when they left the maximum age for juvenile jurisdiction at 18 years, so that 18-year-olds who violated former AS 11.71.060(a)(3) would be prosecuted as adults. . . .

The judgement of the district court is AFFIRMED.

QUESTIONS FOR DISCUSSION

1. What exactly are Allam's arguments as to why the Alaska statute denies him equal protection of the laws?

2. How does the Alaska court answer Allam's arguments?

3. What are the two prongs of the equal protection clause to which the court refers?

4. Do you agree with Allam or the court? Defend your answer.

5. What arguments can you give for making special rules for marijuana use that are different from those governing the drinking age?

NOTE CASE

1. Colorado prohibits the possession, use, and sale of "narcotic drugs." It defines narcotic drug as "coca leaves, opium, cannabis [i.e., marijuana], isonipecaine, amidone, isoamidone, ketobemidone, and every other substance neither chemically nor physically distinguishable from them, and any other drug to which the federal narcotic laws may apply." Stark was convicted of possessing marijuana and argued that the classification of cannabis in the same category as addicting narcotic drugs denied him the equal protection of the law.

Was he right? The Colorado Supreme Court said no:

We recognize that differences of opinion exist as to whether cannabis causes physical or psychological addiction. This fact is not material in determining what drugs may be included within the classification of "narcotic drugs" in an exercise of police powers by a state. The important and pivotal consideration is whether the classification bears a reasonable relation "to the public purpose sought to be achieved by the legislation involved." Clearly, the use of marijuana and other drugs identified in the Colorado statute presents a danger to the public safety and welfare of the community since they are clearly related to each other and to the commission of crime. *People v. Stark,* 400 P.2d 923 (1965)

Of course, this decision is 35 years old. However, according to the most recent survey of the law, the case was still good law on December 31, 1999.[13]

FREE SPEECH

The First Amendment commands: "Congress shall make no law...abridging the freedom of speech." The U.S. Supreme Court has expanded the prohibition beyond this already sweeping scope. First, although the Amendment refers only to "speech," the Court has ruled that the protection of the amendment "does not end with the spoken or written word." It also includes **expressive conduct**, meaning actions that communicate ideas and feelings. So, free speech includes wearing black arm bands to protest war, "sitting in" to protest racial segregation, picketing to support all kinds of causes from abortion to animal rights. It even includes giving money to political candidates. Second, although the Amendment directs its prohibition only at the U.S. Congress, the Court has applied the prohibition to the States since 1925. In *Gitlow v. New York,* the Court ruled that a *state* law restricting free speech was a denial of liberty without due process of law under the Fourteenth Amendment.[14]

A further protection against government limits on free speech and expression is the Court's decision that free speech is a *fundamental* right, one that enjoys preferred status. This means that the government has to provide more than a rational basis for restricting speech and other forms of expression. It has the much higher burden of proving that a compelling interest justifies the restrictions.

Despite these broad prohibitions and the heavy burden the government faces in justifying them, the First Amendment doesn't mean that you can express yourself any where, any time, any place, on any subject. According to the Supreme Court, there are five categories of expression that the Amendment does not protect:

1. **Obscenity,** material whose predominant appeal is to nudity, sex, or excretion.
2. **Profanity,** irreverence toward sacred things, particularly an irreverent use of the name God.

3. **Libel** and **slander,** the former defamation expressed by print, writing, pictures, or signs and the latter defamation by the spoken word.

4. **Fighting words,** words that are likely to provoke the average person to retaliation, and thereby to cause a "breach of the peace."

5. Expression that creates a clear and present danger of an evil that legislatures have a right to prohibit.[15]

Why doesn't the First Amendment protect these forms of expression? Because they are not an "essential element of any exposition of ideas, and are of such slight value as a step to truth that any benefit that may be derived from them is clearly outweighed by the social interest in order and morality."[16]

These exceptions create the opportunity for the government to make expression a crime, depending on the manner, time, and place of expression. For example, under the **clear and present danger doctrine** the government can punish words "that produce clear and present danger of a serious substantive evil that rises far above public inconvenience, annoyance, or unrest." So, the First Amendment didn't save Walter Chaplinsky from conviction under a New Hampshire statute that made it a crime to call anyone "any offensive or derisive name" in public. Chaplinsky had called the marshal of the City of Rochester, New Hampshire "a God damned racketeer." In perhaps the most famous reference to the doctrine, U.S. Supreme Court Justice Oliver Wendell Holmes wrote: "The most stringent protection of free speech would not protect a man in falsely shouting fire in a theatre and causing a panic."[17]

The most difficult problem in making speech and expressive conduct criminal is laws that reach so far that they ban not only expression that the Constitution prohibits but also expression that it protects. According to the **void-for-overbreadth doctrine,** laws that include not only prohibited but also protected expression are void because they deny people freedom of expression without due process of law. Why? Because people will hesitate to express themselves if they fear criminal prosecution. This "chilling effect" on the exercise of the fundamental right to freedom of expression violates the right to liberty guaranteed by the Fifth and Fourteenth Amendments to the U.S. Constitution. The Illinois Appellate Court dealt with the problem of free speech and hate crimes in *People v. Rokicki.*

| C A S E | Does the Hate Crime Statute Violate Free Speech? |

People v. Rokicki
307 Ill.App.3d 645, 718 N.E.2d 333, 240
Ill.Dec. 852 (Ill.App. 1999)

Kenneth Rokicki was charged in a single-count indictment with a hate crime based on the predicate [underlying] offense of disorderly conduct. Before trial, Rokicki moved to dismiss the charges alleging, among other things, that the hate crime statute was unconstitutional. The trial court denied his motion. Rokicki waived his right to a jury, and the matter proceeded to a bench trial (trial without a jury). Rokicki was convicted, sentenced to two years' probation, and ordered to perform 100 hours of community service and to attend anger management counseling. He appealed, contending that the hate crime statute is unconstitutionally overly broad and chills expression protected by the first amendment to the United States Constitution. The Illinois Appellate court affirmed the conviction and sentence.

HUTCHINSON, J. delivered the opinion of the court.

FACTS

Donald Delaney testified that he is the store manager of a Pizza Hut in South Elgin. On October 20,

1995, at approximately 1:30 p.m., defendant entered the restaurant. The victim was a server there and took defendant's order. The victim requested payment, and defendant refused to tender payment to him. Delaney, who was nearby, stepped in and completed the sale. Defendant told Delaney not to let "that faggot" touch his food. When defendant's pizza came out of the oven, Delaney was on the telephone, and the victim began to slice the pizza. Delaney saw defendant approaching the counter with an irritated expression and hung up the telephone. Before Delaney could intervene, defendant leaned over the counter and began yelling at the victim and pounding his fist on the counter. Defendant directed a series of epithets at the victim including "Mary," "faggot," and "Molly Homemaker." Defendant continued yelling for 10 minutes and, when not pounding his fist, shook his finger at the victim. Delaney asked defendant to leave several times and threatened to call the police. However, Delaney did not call the police because he was standing between the victim and defendant and feared that defendant would physically attack the victim if Delaney moved. Eventually Delaney returned defendant's money and defendant left the establishment.

The victim testified that he was working at the South Elgin Pizza Hut on October 20, 1995. Defendant entered the restaurant and ordered a pizza. When defendant's pizza came out of the oven, the victim began to slice it. Defendant then began yelling at the victim and pounding his fist on the counter. Defendant appeared very angry and seemed very serious. The victim, who is much smaller than defendant, testified that he was terrified by defendant's outburst and remained frightened for several days thereafter. Eventually, the manager gave defendant a refund and defendant left the restaurant. The victim followed defendant into the parking lot, recorded the license number of his car, and called the police.

Christopher Merritt, a sergeant with the South Elgin police department, testified that, at 2:20 p.m. on October 20, 1995, defendant entered the police station and said he wished to report an incident at the Pizza Hut. Defendant told Merritt that he was upset because a homosexual was working at the restaurant and he wanted someone "normal" to touch his food. Defendant stated that he became angry when the victim touched his food. He called the victim a "Mary," pounded on the counter, and was subsequently kicked out of the restaurant.

Merritt asked defendant what he meant by a "Mary," and defendant responded that a "Mary" was a homosexual. Merritt conducted only a brief interview of defendant because shortly after defendant arrived at the police station Merritt was dispatched to the Pizza Hut.

Deborah Hagedorn, an employee at the Pizza Hut in St. Charles, testified that in 1995 defendant came into the restaurant and asked for the address of the district manager for Pizza Hut. When asked why he wanted the address, defendant complained that he had been arrested at the South Elgin restaurant because he did not want a "f——— faggot" touching his food.

Defendant testified that he was upset because the victim had placed his fingers in his mouth and had not washed his hands before cutting the pizza. Defendant admitted calling the victim "Mary" but denied that he intended to suggest the victim was a homosexual. Defendant stated that he used the term "Mary" because the victim would not stop talking and "it was like arguing with a woman." Defendant denied yelling and denied directing other derogatory terms towards the victim. Defendant admitted giving a statement to Merritt but denied telling him that he pounded his fist on the counter or used homosexual slurs. Defendant testified that he went to the St. Charles Pizza Hut but that Hagedorn was not present during his conversation with the manager. Defendant testified that he complained about the victim's hygiene but did not use any homosexual slurs.

The trial court found defendant guilty of hate crime. In a posttrial motion, defendant again argued that the hate crime statute was unconstitutional. The trial court denied defendant's motion and sentenced him to two years' probation. As part of the probation, the trial court ordered defendant not to enter Pizza Hut restaurants, not to contact the victim, to perform 100 hours' community service, and attend anger management counseling. Defendant timely appeals.

OPINION

On appeal, defendant does not challenge the sufficiency of the evidence against him. Defendant contends only that the hate crime statute is unconstitutional when the predicate offense is disturbing the peace. Defendant argues that the statute is overly broad and impermissibly chills free speech.

...The Illinois hate crime... reads in part as follows:

> A person commits hate crime when, by reason of the actual or perceived race, color, creed, religion, ancestry, gender, sexual orientation, physical or mental disability, or national origin of another individual or group of individuals, [she or] he commits assault, battery, aggravated assault, misdemeanor theft, criminal trespass to residence, misdemeanor criminal damage to property, criminal trespass to vehicle, criminal trespass to real property, mob action or disorderly conduct.... 720 ILCS 5/12-7.1(a) (West 1994).

...Defendant's conviction was based on the predicate offense of disorderly conduct. A person commits disorderly conduct when she or he knowingly "[d]oes any act in such unreasonable manner as to alarm or disturb another and to provoke a breach of the peace." Disorderly conduct is punishable as a Class C misdemeanor. However, hate crime is punishable as a Class 4 felony for a first offense and a Class 2 felony for a second or subsequent offense.

Defendant notes that the Appellate Court, Third District, was faced with a similar challenge to the hate crime statute in *People v. Nitz*, 285 Ill.App.3d 364, 221 Ill.Dec. 9, 674 N.E.2d 802 (1996). The *Nitz* court held that the hate crime statute, when predicated on disorderly conduct, was constitutional and neither infringed upon a defendant's free speech rights directly nor was overly broad because of its "chilling effect" on free speech. However, defendant urges us to reconsider the Nitz analysis and hold the hate crime statute overly broad.

Infringement upon Free Speech Rights

The issue presented in this case highlights the limits imposed by the first amendment on a state's power to regulate its citizens' speech and thought. In a pair of cases decided in 1992 and 1993, the Supreme Court staked out the boundary between a state's unconstitutional regulation of unpopular beliefs in the marketplace of ideas and the permissible regulation of conduct motivated by those beliefs. See *R.A.V. v. City of St. Paul*, 505 U.S. 377, 112 S.Ct. 2538, 120 L.Ed.2d 305 (1992); *Wisconsin v. Mitchell*, 508 U.S. 476, 113 S.Ct. 2194, 124 L.Ed.2d 436 (1993). Our analysis of defendant's claims is controlled by these two cases, and we will begin by examining them.

In *R.A.V.*, the petitioner was alleged to have burned a crudely constructed wooden cross on the lawn of the residence of an African-American family and was charged with violating St. Paul's Bias-Motivated Crime Ordinance. The ordinance declared that anyone who places a burning cross, Nazi swastika, or other symbol on private or public property knowing that the symbol would arouse "'anger, alarm or resentment in others on the basis of race, color, creed, religion, or gender commits disorderly conduct and shall be guilty of a misdemeanor.'" The Minnesota Supreme Court found that the ordinance was constitutional because it could be construed to reach only "fighting words," which are outside the protection of the first amendment. The United States Supreme Court held that, even when a statute addresses speech that is otherwise proscribable, the state may not discriminate on the basis of the content. The *R.A.V.* Court then found that the St. Paul ordinance violated the first amendment because it would allow the proponents of racial tolerance and equality to use fighting words to argue in favor of tolerance and equality but would prohibit similar use by those opposed to racial tolerance and equality.

One year later, the United States Supreme Court revisited the issue in *Mitchell*. The defendant in *Mitchell* was convicted of aggravated battery, which carried a maximum term of two years' incarceration. However, the defendant was sentenced to a term of four years' incarceration under a Wisconsin statute that enhanced the penalty for an offense when the defendant intentionally selected a victim because of his or her "'race, religion, color, disability, sexual orientation, national origin or ancestry.'" The Wisconsin Supreme Court reversed the conviction and held that the statute was unconstitutional under *R.A.V.*, holding that the legislature cannot "criminalize bigoted thought with which it disagrees."

The *Mitchell* Court held that, unlike the ordinance in *R.A.V.*, the Wisconsin statute was aimed solely at conduct unprotected by the first amendment. The Court noted that, although a defendant may not be punished for his or her abstract beliefs, motive has traditionally been used as a factor in sentencing. The Court also observed that, although the statute punished the defendant for his discriminatory motive, motive played the same role in federal and state antidiscrimination statutes that had withstood first amendment challenges. The Court further held that a state legislature could reasonably conclude that bias-motivated crimes cause greater societal harm warranting stiffer penalties because such offenses are more likely to provoke retaliatory crimes, inflict distinct emotional harms on their victims, and incite community unrest. Consequently, the Court found that the Wisconsin statute did not infringe upon free speech rights....

In *Nitz,* 285 Ill.App.3d 364, 221 Ill.Dec. 9, 674 N.E.2d 802, the Appellate Court, Third District, followed *Mitchell*... and rejected the defendant's argument that predicating a hate crime on disorderly conduct can result in punishment based solely on speech.... Defendant acknowledges that these precedents seem to have settled the issue of whether the hate crime statute infringes upon free speech. However, he... urges us not to follow... *Nitz.* Defendant argues that the *Nitz* court failed to recognize some of the practical consequences of predicating hate crime on disorderly conduct. Defendant argues... that the conduct necessary to support a charge of disorderly conduct is judged on a sliding scale and is inversely proportional to the offensiveness of the speech. After positing this sliding scale, defendant concludes that conduct that would otherwise go unpunished will be treated as disorderly conduct and enhanced to hate crime if the accused expresses certain unpopular beliefs. We decline to follow defendant down this slippery slope.

The overbreadth doctrine protects the freedom of speech guaranteed by the first amendment by invalidating laws so broadly written that the fear of prosecution would discourage people from exercising that freedom. A law regulating conduct is facially overly broad if it (1) criminalizes a substantial amount of protected behavior, relative to the law's plainly legitimate sweep, and (2) is not susceptible to a limiting construction that avoids constitutional problems. A statute should not be invalidated for being overly broad unless its overbreadth is both real and substantial

Defendant's argument ignores the longstanding principle that speech alone cannot form the basis for a disorderly conduct charge. See *People v. Bradshaw,* 116 Ill.App.3d 421, 422, 72 Ill.Dec. 209, 452 N.E.2d 141 (1983). As the Bradshaw court observed: "Vulgar language, however distasteful or offensive to one's sensibilities, does not evolve into a crime because people standing nearby stop, look, and listen. The State's concern becomes dominant only when a breach of the peace is provoked by the language." Consequently, the hate crime statute does not reach those who, in defendant's words, simply "express themselves loudly and in a highly-animated, passionate manner" but applies only when their conduct is unreasonable and provokes a breach of the peace.

In this case, defendant is not being punished merely because he holds an unpopular view on homosexuality or because he expressed those views loudly or in a passionate manner. Defendant was charged with hate crime because he allowed those beliefs to motivate unreasonable conduct. Defendant remains free to believe what he will regarding people who are homosexual, but he may not force his opinions on others by shouting, pounding on a counter, and disrupting a lawful business. Defendant's conduct exceeded the bounds of spirited debate, and the first amendment does not give him the right to harass or terrorize anyone. Therefore, because the hate crime statute requires conduct beyond mere expression, we follow *Nitz* and conclude that... the Illinois hate crime statute constitutionally regulates conduct without infringing upon free speech.

Content Discrimination

Defendant cites *R.A.V.* and argues that the hate crime statute is constitutionally impermissible because it discriminates based on the content of an offender's beliefs. Defendant argues that the statute enhances disorderly conduct to hate crime when the conduct is motivated by, e.g., an offender's views on race or sexual orientation but that it treats identical conduct differently if motivated, e.g., by an offender's beliefs regarding abortion or animal rights. The *R.A.V.* Court invalidated the St. Paul ordinance because it favored some political views over others....However,...the Court recognized several limitations to its content discrimination analysis, including statutes directed at conduct rather than speech, which sweep up a particular subset of proscribable speech....We too decide that the legislature was free to determine as a matter of sound public policy that bias-motivated crimes create greater harm than identical conduct not motivated by bias and should be punished more harshly. Consequently, we reject defendant's content discrimination argument.

Chilling Effect

Defendant also argues that the hate crime statute chills free expression because individuals will be deterred from expressing unpopular views out of fear that such expression will later be used to justify a hate crime charge. We disagree. The overbreadth doctrine should be used sparingly and only when the constitutional infirmity is both real and substantial.... [W]e find defendant's argument speculative, and we cannot conclude that individuals will refrain from expressing controversial beliefs simply because they fear that their statements might be used as evidence of motive if they later commit an offense identified in the hate crime statute.

Conlusion

We hold that the hate crime statute is not facially unconstitutional when the predicate offense is disorderly conduct because (1) the statute reaches only conduct and does not punish speech itself; (2) the statute does not impermissibly discriminate based on content; and (3) the statute does not chill the exercise of first amendment rights. Defendant contends only that the statute is unconstitutional and does not challenge the sufficiency of the evidence against him or assert any other basis for reversal. Accordingly, we affirm defendant's conviction.

Affirmed.

QUESTIONS FOR DISCUSSION

1. According to the court, why doesn't the Illinois "hate crime" statute violate Rokicki's right to free speech?
2. In your opinion, does the statute punish speech or nonexpressive conduct?
3. Do you think the purpose of this statute is to prevent disorderly conduct or expression?
4. Does the defendant have a point when he argues that the statute prohibits only some kinds of hatred—race, ethnic, and sexual orientation—but not other kinds, like hate for animal rights and abortion? Defend your answer.

✳ 2-2 In re *Rosencrantz*

NOTE CASES

1. The New York Transit Authority, which has the authority to make rules equivalent to laws, made it unlawful to panhandle or beg in the New York subways. Several homeless people argued that the rule violated their right to free speech. The United States Second Circuit Court of Appeals ruled: "Common sense tells us that begging is much more 'conduct' than it is 'speech.'" The court acknowledged that the conduct had an element of expression in it, but said: "The only message that we are able to espy as common to all acts of begging is that beggars want to exact money from those whom they accost. Such conduct, therefore, is subject to regulation." Research and other experts indicated that panhandlers and beggars frighten passengers; this provides adequate grounds to regulate them. *Young v. New York City Transit Authority*, 903 F.2d 146 (2d Cir.1990) See Chapter 12 for a full discussion of panhandling and the criminal law.

2. An Indiana statute prohibits nude dancing in public. Glen Theatre, a bar that featured nude dancing, sought an injunction against enforcing the law, arguing that it violated the First Amendment. The law permitted erotic dancing, so long as the dancers wore "G-strings" and "pasties." It prohibited only totally nude dancing. Dancers can express themselves erotically without total nudity. The United States Supreme Court ruled that it did not unduly restrict expressive conduct. *Barnes v. Glen Theatre*, Inc., et al., 501 U.S. 560, 111 S.Ct. 2456, 115 L.Ed.2d 504 (1991)

3. While the Republican National Convention was taking place in Dallas in 1984, Johnson participated in a political demonstration dubbed the "Republican War Chest Tour." As explained in literature distributed by the demonstrators and in speeches made by them, the purpose of this event was to protest the policies of the Reagan administration and of certain Dallas-based corporations. The demonstrators marched through the Dallas streets, chanting political slogans and stopping at several corporate locations to stage "die-ins" intended to dramatize the consequences of nuclear war. On several occasions they spray-painted the walls of buildings and overturned potted plants, but Johnson himself took no part in such activities. He did, however, accept an American flag handed to him by a fellow protestor who had taken it

from a flag pole outside one of the targeted buildings.

The demonstration ended in front of Dallas City Hall, where Johnson unfurled the American flag, doused it with kerosene, and set it on fire. While the flag burned, the protestors chanted, "America, the red, white, and blue, we spit on you." After the demonstrators dispersed, a witness to the flag-burning collected the flag's remains and buried them in his backyard. No one was physically injured or threatened with injury, though several witnesses testified that they had been seriously offended by the flag-burning.

Johnson was charged and convicted under Texas's "desecration of a venerated object" statute, sentenced to one year in prison, and fined $2,000. Did the flag burning statute violate Johnson's right to free speech? Yes, said a divided U.S Supreme Court. According to the majority:

... The First Amendment literally forbids the abridgment only of "speech," but we have long recognized that its protection does not end at the spoken or written word. While we have rejected "the view that an apparently limitless variety of conduct can be labeled 'speech' whenever the person engaging in the conduct intends thereby to express an idea, we have acknowledged that conduct may be sufficiently imbued with elements of communication to fall within the scope of the First and Fourteenth Amendments."...

Texas claims that its interest in preventing breaches of the peace justifies Johnson's conviction for flag desecration. However, no disturbance of the peace actually occurred or threatened to occur because of Johnson's burning of the flag. Although the State stresses the disruptive behavior of the protestors during their march toward City Hall, it admits that "no actual breach of the peace occurred at the time of the flag burning or in response to the flag burning."...

Nor does Johnson's expressive conduct fall within that small class of "fighting words" that are "likely to provoke the average person to retaliation, and thereby cause a breach of the peace." No reasonable onlooker would have regarded Johnson's generalized expression of dissatisfaction with the policies of the Federal Government as a direct personal insult or an invitation to exchange fisticuffs.

We thus conclude that the State's interest in maintaining order is not implicated on these facts. The State need not worry that our holding will

disable it from preserving the peace. We do not suggest that the First Amendment forbids a State to prevent "imminent lawless action."...

If there is a bedrock principle underlying the First Amendment, it is that the Government may not prohibit the expression of an idea simply because society finds the idea itself offensive or disagreeable. We have not recognized an exception to this principle even where our flag has been involved. Justice Jackson described one of our society's defining principles in words deserving of their frequent repetition: "If there is any fixed star in our constitutional constellation, it is that no official, high or petty, can prescribe what shall be orthodox in politics, nationalism, religion, or other matters of opinion or force citizens to confess by word or act their faith therein."...

Although Justice Kennedy concurred, the flag burning obviously disturbed him.

... The hard fact is that sometimes we must make decisions we do not like. We make them because they are right, right in the sense that the law and the Constitution, as we see them, compel the result. And so great is our commitment to the process that, except in the rare case, we do not pause to express distaste for the result, perhaps for fear of undermining a valued principle that dictates the decision. This is one of those rare cases. Our colleagues in dissent advance powerful arguments why respondent may be convicted for his expression, reminding us that among those who will be dismayed by our holding will be some who have had the singular honor of carrying the flag in battle. And I agree that the flag holds a lonely place of honor in an age when absolutes are distrusted and simple truths are burdened by unneeded apologetics.... The case here today forces recognition of the costs to which [our]... beliefs commit us. It is poignant but fundamental that the flag protects those who hold it in contempt.... So I agree with the court that he must go free.

Four justices dissented. Perhaps none of the justices felt more strongly than the World War II naval officer Justice Stevens, who wrote:

... The ideas of liberty and equality have been an irresistible force in motivating leaders like Patrick Henry, Susan B. Anthony, and Abraham Lincoln, schoolteachers like Nathan Hale and Booker T. Washington, the Philippine Scouts who fought at Bataan, and the soldiers who scaled the bluff at

Omaha Beach. If those ideas are worth fighting for—and our history demonstrates that they are—it cannot be true that the flag that uniquely symbolizes their power is not itself worthy of protec-tion from unnecessary desecration. I respectfully dissent.

Texas v. Johnson, 491 U.S. 397, 109 S.Ct. 2533, 105 L.Ed.2d 342 (1989)

RIGHT TO PRIVACY

Unlike the right to freedom of speech, which is clearly spelled out in the First Amendment, you will search in vain for the word "privacy" in the U.S. Constitution. Nevertheless, the U.S. Supreme Court has held that there is a constitutional right to privacy, a right that prohibits "all governmental invasions of the sanctity of a man's home and the privacies of life." And, like free speech, the right to privacy is a fundamental right that requires that the government prove that a compelling interest justifies invading it. According to the Court, the fundamental right to privacy originates in six amendments to the U.S. Constitution:

1. The First Amendment prohibition against laws that infringe on the right to free expression, association, and belief.
2. The Third Amendment prohibition against the quartering of soldiers in private homes.
3. The Fourth Amendment right to be secure in one's "person, house, papers, and effects" from "unreasonable searches."
4. The Ninth Amendment provision that "The enumeration in the Constitution, of certain rights, shall not be construed to deny or disparage others retained by the people."
5. The Fifth and Fourteenth Amendment prohibition against government denial of "liberty without due process of law."[18]

This cluster of amendments sends the strong if only implied message that the people have the right to be let alone by government. In the First Amendment it is our beliefs and expression of them and our associations with other people that are protected from the government. In the Third and Fourth Amendments, our homes are the object of protection. And, in the Fourth Amendment, it's not only our homes but our bodies, our private papers, and even our property that fall under its protection. The Ninth, or catch-all, Amendment acknowledges that we have rights not listed in the Constitution. According to the Court, one of these unlisted rights is privacy. Finally, according to the Court, liberty would mean little without a zone of autonomy that promotes individual personality and relationships central to the meaning of life in a free society. (See the Appendix for the full text of these amendments.)

The Court has strictly limited the right of privacy to the intimate relationships within the traditional family and home. In the leading case on the point, *Griswold v. Connecticut,* the Court struck down a criminal statute that made it a crime for married couples to use contraceptives. Justice Douglas, writing for the majority, said that the law

operates directly on an intimate relation of husband and wife.... The present case ... concerns a relationship lying within the zone of privacy created by several different fundamental constitutional guarantees. And it concerns a law which, in forbidding the use of contraceptives rather than regulating their manufacture or sale, seeks to achieve its goals by means having a maximum destructive impact upon that relationship. Such a law cannot stand.[19]

Four years later, in *Stanley v. Georgia,* it looked like the Court might take a more expanded view of the right to privacy. In *Stanley,* the Court struck down a statute that made it a crime to possess pornography within the privacy of a home. Some supporters of the right to privacy hoped that the Court had permanently locked the criminal law out of private homes, believing that the Court's holding meant that except for committing serious felonies, what people do at home is none of the law's business.[20] The Court took up the issue of the right to privacy in the highly controversial case of *Bowers v. Hardwick,* decided in 1986.

 2-3 State Constitution Right to Privacy

C A S E   **Did He Have a Right to Practice Consensual Sodomy?**

Bowers v. Hardwick
478 U.S. 186 (1986)

Michael Hardwick, a practicing homosexual, challenged the constitutionality of the Georgia sodomy statute. The United States District Court for the Northern District of Georgia granted defendant's (attorney general of Georgia Michael Bowers) motion to dismiss, and Hardwick appealed. The Court of Appeals reversed and remanded. After rehearing was denied defendants petitioned for *certiorari* [an order to a lower court from the U.S. Supreme Court to send the record of the lower court to the Supreme Court for review]. The Supreme Court reversed.

WHITE, J.

FACTS

[A police officer went to Hardwick's (the respondent's) house on August 3, 1982, to serve a warrant because Hardwick had failed to pay a fine for public drunkenness. The officer asked the man who answered the door if Hardwick was at home. The man said he wasn't sure but he told the officer that he could check if he wanted to. The officer walked down a hall to a bedroom where the door was ajar. He saw Hardwick, 29, and another man performing oral sex. He arrested the two men and charged them with sodomy, a felony in Georgia punishable by up to 20 years in prison.][21]

Georgia Code Ann. § 16-6-2 (1984) provides, in pertinent part, as follows:

"(a) A person commits the offense of sodomy when he performs or submits to any sexual act in-

volving the sex organs of one person and the mouth or anus of another....

"(b) A person convicted of the offense of sodomy shall be punished by imprisonment for not less than one nor more than 20 years...."

After a preliminary hearing, the District Attorney decided not to present the matter to the grand jury unless further evidence developed. Respondent then brought suit in the Federal District Court, challenging the constitutionality of the statute insofar as it criminalized consensual sodomy. He asserted that he was a practicing homosexual, that the Georgia sodomy statute, as administered by the defendants, placed him in imminent danger of arrest, and that the statute... violates the Federal Constitution. The District Court granted the defendant's motion to dismiss for failure to state a claim. A divided panel of the Court of Appeals for the Eleventh Circuit reversed.... Because other Courts of Appeals have arrived at judgments contrary to that of the Eleventh Circuit in this case, we granted the Attorney General's petition for certiorari questioning the holding that the sodomy statute violates the fundamental rights of homosexuals. We agree with petitioner that the Court of Appeals erred, and hence reverse its judgment.

OPINION

... The issue presented is whether the Federal Constitution confers a fundamental right upon homosexuals to engage in sodomy and hence invalidates the laws of the many States that still make such conduct illegal and have done so for a very long time....

We first register our disagreement with the Court of Appeals and with respondent that the Court's prior cases have construed the Constitution to confer a right of privacy that extends to homosexual sodomy and for all intents and purposes have decided this case. The reach of this line of cases... [was] described as dealing with child rearing and education; with family relationships; with procreation; with marriage; with contraception; and with abortion.... Accepting the decisions in these cases..., we think it evident that none of the rights announced in those cases bears any resemblance to the claimed constitutional right of homosexuals to engage in acts of sodomy that is asserted in this case. No connection between family, marriage, or procreation on the one hand and homosexual activity on the other has been demonstrated.... Moreover, any claim that these cases nevertheless stand for the proposition that any kind of private sexual conduct between consenting adults is constitutionally insulated from state proscription is unsupportable....

... [Despite these prior cases,] respondent would have us announce... a fundamental right to engage in homosexual sodomy. This we are quite unwilling to do. It is true that despite the language of the Due Process Clauses of the Fifth and Fourteenth Amendments, which appears to focus only on the processes by which life, liberty, or property is taken, the cases are legion in which those Clauses have been interpreted to have substantive content, subsuming rights that to a great extent are immune from federal or state regulation or proscription. Among such cases are those recognizing rights that have little or no textual support in the constitutional language....

Striving to assure itself and the public that announcing rights not readily identifiable in the Constitution's text involves much more than the imposition of the Justices' own choice of values on the States and the Federal Government, the Court has sought to identify the nature of the rights qualifying for heightened judicial protection. In *Palko v. Connecticut,* 302 U.S. 319, 325, 326, 58 S.Ct. 149, 151, 152, 82 L.Ed. 288 (1937), it was said that this category includes those fundamental liberties that are "implicit in the concept of ordered liberty," such that "neither liberty nor justice would exist if [they] were sacrificed." A different description of fundamental liberties appeared in *Moore v. East Cleveland,* 431 U.S. 494, 503, 97 S.Ct. 1932,

1937, 52 L.Ed.2d 531 (1977) where they are characterized as those liberties that are "deeply rooted in this Nation's history and tradition." See also *Griswold v. Connecticut,* 381 U.S., at 506, 85 S.Ct., at 1693.

It is obvious to us that neither of these formulations would extend a fundamental right to homosexuals to engage in acts of consensual sodomy. Proscriptions against that conduct have ancient roots. Sodomy was a criminal offense at common law and was forbidden by the laws of the original thirteen States when they ratified the Bill of Rights. In 1868, when the Fourteenth Amendment was ratified, all but 5 of the 37 States in the Union had criminal sodomy laws. In fact, until 1961, all 50 States outlawed sodomy, and today, 24 States and the District of Columbia continue to provide criminal penalties for sodomy performed in private and between consenting adults. Against this background, to claim that a right to engage in such conduct is "deeply rooted in this Nation's history and tradition" or "implicit in the concept of ordered liberty" is, at best, facetious.

Nor are we inclined to take a more expansive view of our authority to discover new fundamental rights imbedded in the Due Process Clause. The Court is most vulnerable and comes nearest to illegitimacy when it deals with judge-made constitutional law having little or no cognizable roots in the language or design of the Constitution.... There should be, therefore, great resistance to expand the substantive reach of those Clauses, particularly if it requires redefining the category of rights deemed to be fundamental. Otherwise, the Judiciary necessarily takes to itself further authority to govern the country without express constitutional authority. The claimed right pressed on us today falls far short of overcoming this resistance.

Respondent, however, asserts that the result should be different where the homosexual conduct occurs in the privacy of the home. He relies on *Stanley v. Georgia,* 394 U.S. 557, 89 S.Ct. 1243, 22 L.Ed.2d 542 (1969), where the Court held that the First Amendment prevents conviction for possessing and reading obscene material in the privacy of one's home: "If the First Amendment means anything, it means that a State has no business telling a man, sitting alone in his house, what books he may read or what films he may watch."

Stanley did protect conduct that would not have been protected outside the home, and it partially prevented the enforcement of state obscenity laws; but the decision was firmly grounded in the First Amendment. The right pressed upon us here has no similar support in the text of the Constitution, and it does not qualify for recognition under the prevailing principles for construing the Fourteenth Amendment. Its limits are also difficult to discern. Plainly enough, otherwise illegal conduct is not always immunized whenever it occurs in the home. Victimless crimes, such as the possession and use of illegal drugs, do not escape the law where they are committed at home. *Stanley* itself recognized that its holding offered no protection for the possession in the home of drugs, firearms, or stolen goods. And if respondent's submission is limited to the voluntary sexual conduct between consenting adults, it would be difficult, except by fiat, to limit the claimed right to homosexual conduct while leaving exposed to prosecution adultery, incest, and other sexual crimes even though they are committed in the home. We are unwilling to start down that road.

Even if the conduct at issue here is not a fundamental right, respondent asserts that there must be a rational basis for the law and that there is none in this case other than the presumed belief of a majority of the electorate in Georgia that homosexual sodomy is immoral and unacceptable. This is said to be an inadequate rationale to support the law. The law, however, is constantly based on notions of morality, and if all laws representing essentially moral choices are to be invalidated under the Due Process Clause, the courts will be very busy indeed. Even respondent makes no such claim, but insists that majority sentiments about the morality of homosexuality should be declared inadequate. We do not agree, and are unpersuaded that the sodomy laws of some 25 States should be invalidated on this basis.

Accordingly, the judgment of the Court of Appeals is Reversed.

CONCURRING OPINIONS

BURGER, CJ. concurring.

... Decisions of individuals relating to homosexual conduct have been subject to state intervention throughout the history of Western civilization. Condemnation of those practices is firmly rooted in Judeo-Christian moral and ethical standards. Homosexual sodomy was a capital crime under Roman law. During the English Reformation when

powers of the ecclesiastical courts were transferred to the King's Courts, the first English statute criminalizing sodomy was passed. 25 Hen. VIII, ch. 6. Blackstone described "the infamous crime against nature" as an offense of "deeper malignity" than rape, a heinous act "the very mention of which is a disgrace to human nature," and "a crime not fit to be named." The common law of England, including its prohibition of sodomy, became the received law of Georgia and the other Colonies. In 1816 the Georgia Legislature passed the statute at issue here, and that statute has been continuously in force in one form or another since that time. To hold that the act of homosexual sodomy is somehow protected as a fundamental right would be to cast aside millennia of moral teaching....

POWELL, J. concurring.

I join the opinion of the Court. I agree with the Court that there is no fundamental right—i.e., no substantive right under the Due Process Clause—such as that claimed by respondent Hardwick, and found to exist by the Court of Appeals. This is not to suggest, however, that respondent may not be protected by the Eighth Amendment of the Constitution. The Georgia statute at issue in this case, Ga.Code Ann. § 16-6-2 (1984), authorizes a court to imprison a person for up to 20 years for a single private, consensual act of sodomy. In my view, a prison sentence for such conduct—certainly a sentence of long duration—would create a serious Eighth Amendment issue. Under the Georgia statute a single act of sodomy, even in the private setting of a home, is a felony comparable in terms of the possible sentence imposed to serious felonies such as aggravated battery, first-degree arson, and robbery. Among those States that continue to make sodomy a crime, Georgia authorizes one of the longest possible sentences. In this case, however, respondent has not been tried, much less convicted and sentenced. Moreover, respondent has not raised the Eighth Amendment issue below. For these reasons this constitutional argument is not before us.

DISSENT

BLACKMUN, J., joined by BRENNAN, MARSHALL, and STEVENS, JJ.

This case is no more about "a fundamental right to engage in homosexual sodomy," as the

Court purports to declare, than *Stanley v. Georgia,* 394 U.S. 557, 89 S.Ct. 1243, 22 L.Ed.2d 542 (1969), was about a fundamental right to watch obscene movies, or *Katz v. United States,* 389 U.S. 347, 88 S.Ct. 507, 19 L.Ed.2d 576 (1967), was about a fundamental right to place interstate bets from a telephone booth. Rather, this case is about "the most comprehensive of rights and the right most valued by civilized men," namely, "the right to be let alone." *Olmstead v. United States,* 277 U.S. 438, 478, 48 S.Ct. 564, 572, 72 L.Ed. 944 (1928) (Brandeis, J., dissenting).

... Ga.Code Ann. § 16-6-2 (1984), denies individuals the right to decide for themselves whether to engage in particular forms of private, consensual sexual activity. The Court concludes that § 16-6-2 is valid essentially because "the laws of... many States... still make such conduct illegal and have done so for a very long time."... I believe that "it is revolting to have no better reason for a rule of law than that so it was laid down in the time of Henry IV. It is still more revolting if the grounds upon which it was laid down have vanished long since, and the rule simply persists from blind imitation of the past." Holmes, The Path of the Law, 10 Harv.L.Rev. 457, 469 (1897).

... "Our cases long have recognized that the Constitution embodies a promise that a certain private sphere of individual liberty will be kept largely beyond the reach of government." In construing the right to privacy, the Court has proceeded along two somewhat distinct, albeit complementary, lines. First, it has recognized a privacy interest with reference to certain decisions that are properly for the individual to make. Second, it has recognized a privacy interest with reference to certain places without regard for the particular activities in which the individuals who occupy them are engaged. The case before us implicates both the decisional and the spatial aspects of the right to privacy.

The Court concludes today that none of our prior cases dealing with various decisions that individuals are entitled to make free of governmental interference "bears any resemblance to the claimed constitutional right of homosexuals to engage in acts of sodomy that is asserted in this case." While it is true that these cases may be characterized by their connection to protection of the family, the Court's conclusion that they extend no further than this boundary ignores the warning in *Moore v. East Cleveland,* 431 U.S. 494, 501, 97 S.Ct.

1932, 1936, 52 L.Ed.2d 531 (1977) (plurality opinion), against "clos[ing] our eyes to the basic reasons why certain rights associated with the family have been accorded shelter under the Fourteenth Amendment's Due Process Clause." We protect those rights not because they contribute, in some direct and material way, to the general public welfare, but because they form so central a part of an individual's life. "The concept of privacy embodies the 'moral fact that a person belongs to himself and not others nor to society as a whole.'" And so we protect the decision whether to marry precisely because marriage "is an association that promotes a way of life, not causes; a harmony in living, not political faiths; a bilateral loyalty, not commercial or social projects." *Griswold v. Connecticut,* 381 U.S., at 486, 85 S.Ct., at 1682. We protect the decision whether to have a child because parenthood alters so dramatically an individual's self-definition, not because of demographic considerations or the Bible's command to be fruitful and multiply. And we protect the family because it contributes so powerfully to the happiness of individuals, not because of a preference for stereotypical households. The Court recognized in *Roberts,* 468 U.S., at 619, 104 S.Ct., at 3250, that the "ability independently to define one's identity that is central to any concept of liberty" cannot truly be exercised in a vacuum; we all depend on the "emotional enrichment from close ties with others."

Only the most willful blindness could obscure the fact that sexual intimacy is "a sensitive, key relationship of human existence, central to family life, community welfare, and the development of human personality," The fact that individuals define themselves in a significant way through their intimate sexual relationships with others suggests, in a Nation as diverse as ours, that there may be many "right" ways of conducting those relationships, and that much of the richness of a relationship will come from the freedom an individual has to choose the form and nature of these intensely personal bonds.

... The Court claims that its decision today merely refuses to recognize a fundamental right to engage in homosexual sodomy; what the Court really has refused to recognize is the fundamental interest all individuals have in controlling the nature of their intimate associations with others. The behavior for which Hardwick faces prosecution occurred in his own home, a place to which the

Fourth Amendment attaches special significance. The Court's treatment of this aspect of the case is symptomatic of its overall refusal to consider the broad principles that have informed our treatment of privacy in specific cases. Just as the right to privacy is more than the mere aggregation of a number of entitlements to engage in specific behavior, so too, protecting the physical integrity of the home is more than merely a means of protecting specific activities that often take place there. Even when our understanding of the contours of the right to privacy depends on "reference to a 'place,'" *Katz v. United States*, 389 U.S., at 361, 88 S.Ct., at 516 (Harlan, J., concurring), "the essence of a Fourth Amendment violation is 'not the breaking of [a person's] doors, and the rummaging of his drawers,' but rather is 'the invasion of his indefeasible right of personal security, personal liberty and private property.'"

> "'The makers of our Constitution undertook to secure conditions favorable to the pursuit of happiness. They recognized the significance of man's spiritual nature, of his feelings and of his intellect. They knew that only a part of the pain, pleasure and satisfactions of life are to be found in material things. They sought to protect Americans in their beliefs, their thoughts, their emotions and their sensations.'" *Olmstead v. United States*, 277 U.S., at 478, 48 S.Ct., at 572 (Brandeis, J., dissenting).

. . .

The right of an individual to conduct intimate relationships in the intimacy of his or her own home seems to me to be the heart of the Constitution's protection of privacy.

. . . The core of petitioner's defense of § 16-6-2 . . . is that respondent and others who engage in the conduct prohibited by § 16-6-2 interfere with Georgia's exercise of the "'right of the Nation and of the States to maintain a decent society,'" Essentially, petitioner argues, and the Court agrees, that the fact that the acts described in § 16-6-2 "for hundreds of years, if not thousands, have been uniformly condemned as immoral" is a sufficient reason to permit a State to ban them today. I cannot agree that either the length of time a majority has held its convictions or the passions with which it defends them can withdraw legislation from this Court's scrutiny. As Justice Jackson wrote so eloquently for the Court in *West Virginia Board of Education v. Barnette*, 319 U.S. 624, 641-642, 63 S.Ct. 1178, 1187, 87 L.Ed. 1628 (1943), "we apply the limitations of the Constitution with no fear that freedom to be intellectually and spiritually diverse or even contrary will disintegrate the social organization.... [F]reedom to differ is not limited to things that do not matter much. That would be a mere shadow of freedom. The test of its substance is the right to differ as to things that touch the heart of the existing order." It is precisely because the issue raised by this case touches the heart of what makes individuals what they are that we should be especially sensitive to the rights of those whose choices upset the majority....

The assertion that "traditional Judeo-Christian values proscribe" the conduct involved cannot provide an adequate justification for § 16-6-2. That certain, but by no means all, religious groups condemn the behavior at issue gives the State no license to impose their judgments on the entire citizenry. The legitimacy of secular legislation depends instead on whether the State can advance some justification for its law beyond its conformity to religious doctrine.... A State can no more punish private behavior because of religious intolerance than it can punish such behavior because of racial animus. "The Constitution cannot control such prejudices, but neither can it tolerate them. Private biases may be outside the reach of the law, but the law cannot, directly or indirectly, give them effect." No matter how uncomfortable a certain group may make the majority of this Court, we have held that "[m]ere public intolerance or animosity cannot constitutionally justify the deprivation of a person's physical liberty."

Nor can § 16-6-2 be justified as a "morally neutral" exercise of Georgia's power to "protect the public environment," Certainly, some private behavior can affect the fabric of society as a whole. Reasonable people may differ about whether particular sexual acts are moral or immoral, but "we have ample evidence for believing that people will not abandon morality, will not think any better of murder, cruelty and dishonesty, merely because some private sexual practice which they abominate is not punished by the law." H.L.A. Hart, Immorality and Treason, reprinted in The Law as Literature 220, 225 (L. Blom-Cooper ed. 1961). Petitioner and the Court fail to see the difference between laws that protect public sensibilities and those that enforce private morality. Statutes banning public sexual activity are entirely consistent with protecting the individual's liberty interest in decisions concerning sexual relations: the same recognition that those decisions are intensely private which justifies protecting them from governmental interference can justify protecting individuals from unwilling exposure to the sexual activities of others. But the mere fact that intimate behavior may be punished when it takes place in public cannot dictate how States can regulate intimate behavior that occurs in intimate places. . . .

This case involves no real interference with the rights of others, for the mere knowledge that other individuals do not adhere to one's value system cannot be a legally cognizable interest, let alone an interest that can justify invading the houses, hearts, and minds of citizens who choose to live their lives differently. . . .

I dissent.

STEVENS, J., joined by BRENNAN and MARSHALL, JJ.

Like the statute that is challenged in this case, the rationale of the Court's opinion applies equally to the prohibited conduct regardless of whether the parties who engage in it are married or unmarried, or are of the same or different sexes. Sodomy was condemned as an odious and sinful type of behavior during the formative period of the common law. That condemnation was equally damning for heterosexual and homosexual sodomy. Moreover, it provided no special exemption for married couples. The license to cohabit and to produce legitimate offspring simply did not include any permission to engage in sexual conduct that was considered a "crime against nature."

. . . Our prior cases make two propositions abundantly clear. First, the fact that the governing majority in a State has traditionally viewed a particular practice as immoral is not a sufficient reason for upholding a law prohibiting the practice; neither history nor tradition could save a law prohibiting miscegenation from constitutional attack. Second, individual decisions by married persons, concerning the intimacies of their physical relationship, even when not intended to produce offspring, are a form of "liberty" protected by the Due Process Clause of the Fourteenth Amendment. Moreover, this protection extends to intimate choices by unmarried as well as married persons.

In consideration of claims of this kind, the Court has emphasized the individual interest in privacy, but its decisions have actually been animated by an even more fundamental concern. As I wrote some years ago:

> "These cases do not deal with the individual's interest in protection from unwarranted public attention, comment, or exploitation. They deal, rather, with the individual's right to make certain unusually important decisions that will affect his own, or his family's, destiny. The Court has referred to such decisions as implicating 'basic values,' as being 'fundamental,' and as being dignified by history and tradition. The character of the Court's language in these cases brings to mind the origins of the American heritage of freedom—the abiding interest in individual liberty that makes certain state intrusions on the citizen's right to decide how he will live his own life intolerable. Guided by history, our tradition of respect for the dignity of individual choice in matters of conscience and the restraints implicit in the federal system, federal judges have accepted the responsibility for recognition and protection of these rights in appropriate cases."

Society has every right to encourage its individual members to follow particular traditions in expressing affection for one another and in gratifying their personal desires. It, of course, may prohibit an individual from imposing his will on another to satisfy his own selfish interests. It also may prevent an individual from interfering with, or violating, a legally sanctioned and protected relationship, such as marriage. And it may explain the relative advantages and disadvantages of different forms of intimate expression. But when individual married couples are isolated from observation by others, the way in which they voluntarily choose to conduct their intimate relations is a matter for them—not the State—to decide. The essential "liberty" that animated the development of the law . . . surely embraces the right to engage in nonreproductive, sexual conduct that others may consider offensive or immoral.

Paradoxical as it may seem, our prior cases thus establish that a State may not prohibit sodomy within "the sacred precincts of marital bedrooms," or, indeed, between unmarried heterosexual adults. In all events, it is perfectly clear that the State of Georgia may not totally prohibit the conduct proscribed by § 16-6-2 of the Georgia Criminal Code.

. . . The Court has posited as a justification for the Georgia statute "the presumed belief of a majority of the electorate in Georgia that homosexual sodomy is immoral and unacceptable." But the

Georgia electorate has expressed no such belief—instead, its representatives enacted a law that presumably reflects the belief that all sodomy is immoral and unacceptable. Unless the Court is prepared to conclude that such a law is constitutional, it may not rely on the work product of the Georgia Legislature to support its holding. For the Georgia statute does not single out homosexuals as a separate class meriting special disfavored treatment.

Nor, indeed, does the Georgia prosecutor even believe that all homosexuals who violate this statute should be punished. This conclusion is evident from the fact that the respondent in this very case has formally acknowledged in his complaint and in court that he has engaged, and intends to continue to engage, in the prohibited conduct, yet the State has elected not to process criminal charges against him. As Justice POWELL points out, moreover, Georgia's prohibition on private, consensual sodomy has not been enforced for decades. The record of nonenforcement, in this case and in the last several decades, belies the Attorney General's representations about the importance of the State's selective application of its generally applicable law.

...Both the Georgia statute and the Georgia prosecutor thus completely fail to provide the Court with any support for the conclusion that homosexual sodomy is considered unacceptable conduct in that State, and that the burden of justifying a selective application of the generally applicable law has been met....

I respectfully dissent.

QUESTIONS FOR DISCUSSION

1. Summarize the arguments of the majority opinion denying that consensual sodomy is included in the right to privacy. Do you agree with the arguments? Defend your answer.
2. How does the argument of the concurring opinion differ from the majority?
3. Do you agree or disagree with the concurring opinion? Defend your answer. Summarize the arguments of the dissent in favor of a privacy right to practice adult consensual sodomy.
4. In your opinion, is there a federal constitutional right to privacy at all? Explain your answer.

THE REST OF THE STORY *What Happened to Michael Hardwick?*

HOW THE CASE STARTED

A. Balz

MICHAEL HARDWICK: This girlfriend that had pulled me out four years earlier [after a bad relationship] was living in Atlanta, so I went down there to visit her, which is how this whole case started. I had been working for about a year, in a gay bar that was getting ready to open up a discotheque. I was there one night until seven o'clock in the morning, helping them put in insulation. When I left, I went up to the bar and they gave me a beer. I was kind of debating whether I wanted to leave, because I was pretty exhausted, or stay and finish the beer. I decided to leave, and I opened the door and threw the beer bottle into this trash can by the front door of the bar. I wasn't really in the mood for the beer.

Just as I did that I saw a cop drive by. I walked about a block, and he turned around and came back and asked me where the beer was. I told him I had thrown it in the trash can in front of the bar. He insisted I had thrown the beer bottle right as he pulled up. He made me get in the car and asked me what

I was doing. I told him that I worked there, which immediately identified me as a homosexual, because he knew it was a homosexual bar. He was enjoying his position as opposed to my position.

After about twenty minutes of bickering he drove me back so I could show him where the beer bottle was. There was no way of getting out of the back of a cop car. I told him it was in the trash can and he said he couldn't see it from the car. I said fine, just give me a ticket for drinking in public. He was just busting my chops because he knew I was gay.

Anyway, the ticket had a court date on the top and a date in the center and they didn't coincide; they were one day apart. Tuesday was the court date, and the officer had written Wednesday on top of the ticket. So Tuesday, two hours after my court date, he was at my house with a warrant for my arrest. This was Officer Torick. This was unheard of, because it takes forty-eight hours to process a warrant. What I didn't realize, and didn't find out until later, was that he had personally processed a warrant for the first time in ten years. So I think there is reason to believe that he had it out for me.

I wasn't there when he came with the warrant. I got home that afternoon and my roommate said there was a cop here with a warrant. I said, That's impossible; my court date isn't until tomorrow. I went and got my ticket and realized the court date was Tuesday, not Wednesday. I asked my roommate if he'd seen the warrant and he said he hadn't. So I went down to the county clerk and showed him the discrepancy on the ticket. He brought it before the judge, and he fined me $50. I told the county clerk the cop had already been at my house with a warrant and he said that was impossible. He said it takes forty-eight hours to process a warrant. He wrote me a receipt just in case I had any problems with it further down the road. That was that, and I thought I had taken care of it and everything was finished, and I didn't give it much thought.

Three weeks went by, and my mom had come up to visit me. I came home one morning after work at 6:30 and there were three guys standing in front of my house. I cannot say for sure that they had anything to do with this, but they were very straight, middle thirties, civilian clothes. I got out of the car, turned around, and they said "Michael" and I said yes, and they proceeded to beat the hell out of me. Tore all the cartilage out of my nose, kicked me in the face, cracked about six of my ribs. I passed out. I don't know how long I was unconscious. When I came to, all I could think of was, God, I don't want my mom to see me like this!

I managed to crawl up the stairs into the house, into the back bedroom. What I didn't realize was that I'd left a trail of blood all the way back. My mom woke up, found this trail of blood, found me passed out, and just freaked out. I assured her that everything was okay, that it was like a fluke accident, these guys were drunk or whatever. They weren't drunk, they weren't ruffians, and they knew who I was. I convinced her everything was okay and she left to go visit a friend in Pennsylvania.

THE ARREST

OFFICER K.R. TORICK'S STORY: At 8:30 in the morning on August 3, 1982, Officer K.R. Torick arrived at Michael Hardwick's house armed with a warrant for Hardwick's arrest for failing to appear in court on a public drinking ticket. One of Hardwick's housemates answered the door and let the officer in. "The room-mate told me he didn't know if Hardwick was home but said I could come in to look for him. While walking down the hallway inside the house, I saw a bedroom door partially open." He saw Hardwick and another man engaged in oral sodomy. He entered the room and arrested both men for violating the Georgia sodomy statute. While Hardwick and the other man dressed, Officer Torick searched the bedroom and found a small amount of marijuana, which he confiscated.

MICHAEL HARDWICK'S STORY: I had a friend come in ... from out of town ... to apply for a government job. He waited for me to get off work [as a bartender in the gay bar], we went home, and then my roommate left for work. That night at work another friend of mine had gotten really drunk, and I took his car keys, put him in a cab, and sent him to my house, so he passed out on the couch in the living room. He did not hear me and my friend come in. I retired with my friend. He had left the front door open, and Officer Torick came into my house about 8:30 in the morning. He had a warrant that had not been valid for three weeks and that he didn't bother to call in and check on. [Hardwick had paid the ticket for public drinking.] Officer Torick came in and woke up the guy who was passed out on my couch, who didn't now I was there and had a friend with me.

Officer Torick then came to my bedroom. The door was cracked, and the door opened up and I looked up and there was nobody there. I just blew it off as the wind and went back to what I was involved in, which was mutual oral sex. About thirty-five seconds went by and I heard another noise and I looked up, and this officer is standing in my bedroom. He identified himself when he realized that I had seen him. He said, my name is Officer Torick. Michael Hardwick, you are under arrest. I said, For what? What are you doing in my bedroom? He said, I have a warrant for your arrest. I told him the warrant isn't any good. He said, It doesn't matter because I was acting under good faith.

I asked Torick if he would leave the room so we could get dressed and he said, There's no reason for that because I have already seen you in your most intimate aspect. He stood there and watched us get dressed, and then he brought us over to a substation. We waited in the car for about twenty-five minutes, handcuffed to the back floor. Then he brought us downtown; brought us in and made sure everyone in the holding cells and the guards and people who were processing us knew I was in there for "c————-g" and that I should be able to get what I was looking for. The guards were having a *real* good time with that.

There was somebody there to get me out of jail within an hour, but it took them twelve hours to get me out. In the meantime, after they processed me and kept me in a holding cell for about four hours, they brought me up to the third floor, where there was convicted criminals. I had no business being up there. They again told all the people in the cells what I was in there for. It was not a pleasant experience....

THE COURTS

I didn't realize when I went into all of this that I was going to be suing the police commissioner, nor did I realize that while in the federal courts I had to continue to live in a city where the KKK was rather strong. The case lasted about five years, and in that time I moved and got an apartment in someone else's name; my phone bills, electric bills, everything was in someone else's name. I was still working as a bartender, plus I had opened up a floral shop with a friend of mine, but all in his name again, because I didn't want them to have any way of tracing me, especially after the beating. I lived very incognito for the rest of the five years.

After the appeals court decided in my favor, the state brought it into the Supreme Court. At that time I wanted to get out of the city. I'd been living there in fear for three years and I just wanted to leave the city, but my lawyers said it might hurt the case in the Supreme Court, and there was only six months to go. I stuck it out for about five more months and moved down to Miami about a month before the case was argued before the Supreme Court.

Then I went to the Supreme Court and was there for the hearing. No one knew who I was. At that point, I had not done any interviews or speaking in public. The issue was privacy, and I wanted to keep it a private issue. My lawyers had informed me from the very beginning that it would be better to keep a low profile because we did not want the personal aspects of the case to come into it, which I agreed with. They thought that if there was a lot of personal publicity it would affect the decision of the Supreme Court.

It was an education to be there. I had forty-two lawyers working on my case, plus Laurence Tribe of Harvard Law School arguing the case for me. I had met with all of them early that morning for breakfast, and we were kind of psyching each other up. I was going to be sitting with one of the people who wrote the *amicus* brief for Lamda, which does gay legal defense in New York, and they once again assured me that no one knew who I was. So I sat in the Supreme Court as a completely anonymous person. The whole omnipresence of the room, the procedure of the judges coming in, is sort of overpowering. I expected the room to be huge, but it wasn't; it was a very small room. You could see the judges' faces and their expressions no matter where you sat.

The guy from the state came up first and argued for about five minutes and he was an idiot. He kept going on about how the state *did* have a justified government interest in continuing to enforce the law because it prevented adultery and retarded children and bestiality, and that if they changed the law all of those things would be legal. He made absolutely no sense. I think it was Justice Burger who asked why, if they had my head on a silver platter, if they had such a justified government interest in enforcing this law, did they refuse to prosecute me. At which point, his answer was that he wasn't at liberty to discuss that. The nine justices and the whole place cracked up and he pretty much ended his argument.

Then Laurence Tribe got up and articulately argued for about forty-five minutes. He was incredible. I've never seen any person more in control of his senses than he was. When he got done, everyone was very much pre-victory. They were *sure* I would win. About forty of us went to lunch around the corner, and everything seemed very positive and optimistic, and I flew back to Miami to work.

Then came the waiting period. That was the worst phase for me, because we never knew when the decision was coming. I would be on pins and needles, and every time the phone rang I'd be jumping. They made it the last decision of the year, of course. They waited until just after all of the Gay Pride parades around the country.

I was at work when I heard about the decision. I cater a complimentary buffet for about a hundred people a day, so I go into work about four or five hours before anyone else gets there to do all my prep work. On this particular morning I could not sleep, and I got to work about nine o'clock. A friend of mine had been watching cable news and had seen it and knew where to find me and came over. When I opened the door he was crying and saying that he was sorry, and I didn't know what the hell he was talking about. Finally I calmed him down and he told me what had happened: that I had lost by a five-to-four vote.

AFTERWORD

I was totally stunned. My friend took off and I was there for about four hours by myself and that's when it really sunk in. I just cried—not so much because I had failed but because to me it was frightening to think that in the year of 1986 our Supreme Court, next to God, could make a decision that was more suitable to the mentality of the Spanish Inquisition. It was frightening and it stunned me. I was scared. I had been fighting this case for five years and everyone had seemed so confident that I was really not expecting this decision the way that they handed it down.

So I called Kathy Wilde and I called Laurence Tribe. I think he was more devastated than I was. Nobody expected it. I was calling for some kind of reaffirming that everything was going to be okay and that something could be done. But they said, That's it! There's nothing we can do. I learned later that I originally *had* five votes in my favor on the Supreme Court. Justice Powell came out a week later and said to the press that he had originally decided in my favor. I still don't understand why Powell changed his mind in my case. What a half-assed decision!

At that time, everyone thought I was still in Atlanta. And I thought this was okay, I'll just get through this personally. People who knew what I was doing kept coming into the bar and saying, I'm sorry. And I'd say that I'd rather not talk about it. I figured the best place for me would be behind the bar, because it would make me pull myself out of it.

About eight o'clock that night, in comes this woman from Channel 11 news, with a man behind her with a camera on his shoulder. This is in a gay club. I was stunned. All of a sudden it sunk in that they could find me. I asked her how she knew where I was, and she said she was very resourceful. She wanted to do an interview, and I immediately left the bar and went upstairs. I was shaking. She got pissed off because she couldn't do an interview with me, and on the eleven o'clock news she's talking about Michael Hardwick, and the whole time she has the camera focused on the bar I worked at.

About two days went by where I was just kind of stunned. There wasn't anything I could do to change the way I feel, and I'm normally a very positive person. It wasn't that I was negative, I was just nonresponsive to anything. Then all of a sudden I started getting pissed off, angry. Kathy called me two days later and she said that *Newsweek* magazine just came out with a national poll that said 57 percent of the people were opposed to the decision. And she said, By the way, Phil Donahue called and wants to know if you'll do his show. She was very clever, letting me know the nation was behind me, and then hitting me with the Donahue show. Up until then, they had all advised me to keep it private. But she said, This is one approach you can take: You can come out and let people know this was not a homosexual decision, as they tried to put it out, but that it affects everyone as individuals, as consenting adults. And the only way you're going to get that across to them is to use this opportunity.

That was the first time I'd ever spoken publicly. Donahue called and said he was putting me on with Jerry Falwell, and I said I wouldn't do the show—it wasn't a religious issue. So he called back and said, We got rid of Falwell, but you'll have to do the whole show by yourself. Okay. So I flew up there and did that, and that was probably the hardest thing I've ever done in my life. But it went very well, and everyone who saw the program said I was a good spokesman. That started something I had never anticipated. I did a lot of talk shows after that, a lot of newspaper interviews.

. . .

Because of my personal perspective in life, I have a tendency to dwell on the positive instead of the negative. I feel very fortunate I was given the opportunity to do it. Speaking and coming out nationally was a very healthy experience for me, because it made me develop a confidence I never would have had if I had gone along with my individual life. It also gave me a sense of importance, because right now there is a very strong need for the gay community to pull together, and also for the heterosexual community to pull together, against something that's affecting both of us. I feel that no matter what happens, I gave it my best shot. I will continue to give it my best shot.

Source: Reprinted with permission of The Free Press, a Division of Simon & Schuster, Inc., from *The Courage of Their Convictions* by Peter Irons. Copyright © by Peter Irons.

✳ *2-4 State v. Powell*

NOTE CASES

1. Florida prosecuted Borras for possession of marijuana in his home. Borras argued that "the primary purpose of smoking marijuana is the 'psychological reaction' it produces in the user and that by smoking marijuana he was 'merely asserting the right to satisfy his intellectual and emotional needs' in the privacy of his own home."

Did the law violate Borras's right to privacy? No, according to the Florida Supreme Court. The court ruled:

This Court is aware that commission of other types of crime, particularly violent crimes, has an emotional effect on the perpetrator. This, however, does not give a constitutional right to commit the crime.... Marijuana is a harmful, mind-altering drug. An individual might restrict his possession of marijuana to the privacy of his home, but the effects of the drug are not so restricted. The interest of the state in preventing harm to the individual and to the public at large amply justifies the outlawing of marijuana, in private and elsewhere.

Borras v. State, 229 So.2d 244 (Fla. 1969)

Unlike the U.S. Constitution, several state constitutions contain specific provisions guaranteeing the right to privacy. For example, the Florida Declaration of Rights provides: "Every natural person has the right to be let alone and free from governmental intrusion into his private life." Other states have followed the example of the U.S. Supreme Court and implied a state constitutional right to privacy. Ironically, in 1998, Georgia's supreme court not only implied a constitutional right to privacy but struck down, under Georgia's implied right to privacy, the very statute that the U.S. Supreme Court upheld under the U.S. Constitution's implied right to privacy.

This difference in result demonstrates an important principle of our constitutional system: States are free to *expand* a federal right under their own state constitutions, but they are not free to *reduce* a constitutional right beneath the federal standard.[22]

CRUEL AND UNUSUAL PUNISHMENTS

The Eighth Amendment says that "excessive fines" shall not be "imposed" and that "cruel and unusual punishments" shall not be "inflicted." In this section we discuss only the prohibition against cruel and unusual punishments. The U.S. Supreme Court has ruled that two kinds of punishments are cruel and unusual:

1. "Barbaric" punishments.
2. Punishments that are disproportionate to the crime committed.[23]

Barbaric punishments are punishments that are no longer acceptable to civilized society. At the time of the Amendment, these included drawing and quartering, boiling in oil, beheading, and other medieval forms of torture and mutilation.

For more than a hundred years after the adoption of the Bill of Rights, no "cruel and unusual" punishment cases reached the U.S. Supreme Court because these medieval forms of execution weren't used in the United States. But in 1885, the governor of the state of New York in his annual message to the legislature wrote, "The present mode of executing criminals by hanging has come down to us from the dark ages, and it may well be questioned whether the science of the present day cannot provide a means for taking... life... in a less barbarous manner." The legislature appointed a commission to study the matter. The commission reported that electrocution was "the most humane and practical method [of execution] known to modern science." In 1888, the legislature replaced the hangman's noose with the electric chair.[24]

William Kemmler, convicted for murdering his wife, and sentenced to die in the electric chair, argued that electrocution was "cruel and unusual punishment." The U.S. Supreme Court disagreed. The Court said that electrocution was certainly unusual but it isn't cruel. For the first time, the Court defined what "cruel" means in the Eighth Amendment. According to the Court, punishment by death isn't cruel so long as it isn't "something more than the mere extinguishment of life." The Court spelled out what it meant by this phrase. First, the Court said, death has to be both instantaneous and painless. Second, it can't involve unnecessary mutilation of the body. So, according to the Court, beheading is cruel because it mutilates the body. Crucifixion is doubly cruel because it inflicts a "lingering" death *and* mutilates the body.[25]

The principle of proportionality, namely that punishment should fit the crime, has an ancient history. The Magna Carta, adopted in 1215 before imprisonment was a form of punishment, prohibited "excessive" fines. The English Bill of Rights in 1689 repeated the principle of proportionality in language that later appeared in the Eighth Amendment.[26]

The U.S. Supreme Court first applied proportionality as a principle required by the Eighth Amendment in 1910. In *Weems v. United States,* Weems was convicted of falsifying a public document. The trial court first sentenced him to fifteen years in prison at hard labor in chains and then took away all of his civil rights for life. The Court ruled that the punishment was "cruel and unusual" because it was disproportionate to his crime. In imposing the cruel and unusual punishment ban to state criminal justice in the 1960s, the Court in *Robinson v. California* reaffirmed its commitment to the proportionality principle. The Court majority ruled that a ninety-day sentence for drug addiction was disproportionate because addiction is an illness, and it is cruel and unusual to punish persons for being sick. "Even one day in prison would be a cruel and unusual punishment for the 'crime' of having a common cold," wrote Justice Marshall for the Court majority. However, cases decided during the 1980s reflected disagreement as to whether the principle of proportionality should apply to sentences of imprisonment. A majority of the Court has consistently agreed that the proportionality principle applies to death penalty cases. For example, it held that the death penalty for raping an adult woman violated the principle of proportionality. In fact, it looked as if a majority of the Court was committed to the idea that the death penalty is always disproportionate except in some aggravated murders. The state of Louisiana has challenged this notion by making child rape a capital offense. The Louisiana supreme court dealt with the proportionality of capital punishment for child rape in *State v. Wilson*.[27]

C A S E Is The Death Penalty for Child Rape Cruel and Unusual?

State v. Wilson
685 So.2d 1063 (La. 1996)

Anthony Wilson was charged by a grand jury indictment with aggravated rape of a five-year-old girl. He moved to quash [dismiss] the indictment. The Criminal District Court, Parish of New Orleans, quashed defendant's indictment for aggravated rape of a five-year-old. The Fourth Judicial District Court, Parish of Ouachita, quashed the indictment of another defendant, Patrick Dewayne Bethley charged with raping three girls under the age of 12. The cases were consolidated. The Supreme Court of Louisiana reversed and vacated; remanded.

BLEICH, J.

FACTS

On December 21, 1995, Anthony Wilson was charged by grand jury indictment with the aggravated rape of a five-year-old girl. He moved to quash the indictment, alleging that the crime of rape could never be punished with the death penalty. The trial court granted Wilson's motion to quash, resulting in this appeal by the state. Patrick Dewayne Bethley was charged with raping three girls, one of whom was his daughter, between December 1, 1995, and January 10, 1996. The ages of the little girls at the time of the rape were five, seven, and nine. Furthermore, the State alleges that at the time of the alleged crimes, Bethley knew that he was HIV positive. Bethley filed a motion to quash urging the unconstitutionality of La. R.S. 14:42(C). The trial court granted Bethley's motion to quash. Although finding La. R.S. 14:42(C) would pass constitutional muster under the Eighth Amendment and the Equal Protection clause of the United States Constitution and Article I, § 20 of the Louisiana Constitution, the trial court held La. R.S. 14:42(C) unconstitutional because the class of death eligible defendants was not sufficiently limited. That ruling resulted in an appeal.

OPINION

The thrust of both defendants' arguments is that the imposition of the death penalty for a crime not resulting in a death is "cruel and unusual punishment" and therefore unconstitutional under the Eighth Amendment to the United States Constitution and Article I, § 20 of the Louisiana Constitution of 1974. The phrase "cruel and unusual punishment" found in the Eighth Amendment and in Article I, § 20 takes its roots from the English Bill of Rights of 1689. The English version of the phrase appears to prohibit punishments unauthorized by statute and beyond the jurisdiction of the court, as well as those disproportionate to the offense committed. However, the American drafters of the Eighth Amendment were primarily concerned with proscribing "tortures" and other "barbarous" methods of punishment such as pillorying, decapitation, and drawing and quartering. Therefore, the American courts virtually ignored the Eighth Amendment since the barbaric practices proscribed had become obsolete.

Not until the nineteenth century did the Supreme Court recognize that the scope of the Eighth Amendment might be broader than originally thought and include the prohibition of disproportionately excessive sentences. See *Weems v. United* States, 217 U.S. 349, 30 S.Ct. 544, 54 L.Ed.

793 (1910). The years since *Weems* have seen a development of the Eighth Amendment's "cruel and unusual punishment" clause. As Chief Justice Warren said, "(t)he Amendment must draw its meaning from the evolving standards of decency that mark the maturing society." *Trop v. Dulles,* 356 U.S. 86, 101, 78 S.Ct. 590, 598, 2 L.Ed.2d 630 (1958). Therefore, the Eighth Amendment bars not only those punishments that are barbaric but also those that are excessive.

A punishment is excessive and unconstitutional if it (1) makes no measurable contribution to acceptable goals of punishment and hence is nothing more that the purposeful and needless imposition of pain and suffering; or (2) is grossly out of proportion to the severity of the crime. *Gregg v. Georgia,* 428 U.S. 153, 96 S.Ct. 2909, 49 L.Ed.2d 859 (1976).

Excessive Punishment Argument

The defendants' primary argument is that death is a disproportionate penalty for the crime of rape. The defendants' contention is based on *Coker v. Georgia,* 433 U.S. 584, 97 S.Ct. 2861, 53 L.Ed.2d 982 (1977) decided by the Supreme Court in a plurality opinion.

2-5 *Coker v. Georgia*

The *Coker* court rejected capital punishment as a penalty for the rape of an adult woman saying: "Although rape deserves serious punishment, the death penalty, which is unique in its severity and irrevocability, is an excessive penalty for the rapist who, as such and as opposed to the murderer, does not take human life." *Coker,* supra at 585, 97 S.Ct. at 2862. The plurality took great pains in referring only to the rape of adult women throughout their opinion, leaving open the question of the rape of a child. The defendants argue that the *Coker* findings cannot be limited to the rape of an adult. They contend the following words used by the Court would apply with equal force to the crime of statutory rape when no life is taken:

> "Rape is without doubt deserving of serious punishment; but in terms of moral depravity and of the injury to the person and to the public, it does not compare with murder, which does involve the unjustified taking of human life. Although it may be accompanied by another crime, rape by definition does not include the death or even the serious

injury to another person. The murderer kills; the rapist, if no more than that, does not. Life is over for the victim of the murderer; for the rape victim, life may not be nearly so happy as it was, but it is not over and normally is not beyond repair. We have the abiding conviction that the death penalty, which is unique in its severity and irrevocability, ... is an excessive penalty for the rapist who, as such, does not take human life." *Coker,* supra at 598, 97 S.Ct. at 2869.

The contention that the harm caused by a rapist is less serious than that caused by a murderer is apparently not subscribed to by all rape victims. In some cases women have preferred death to being raped or have preferred not to continue living after being raped.

. . .

La. R.S. 14:42(C) was amended by Acts 1995, No. 397, § 1 to allow for the death penalty when the victim of rape is under the age of twelve. Rape of a child less than twelve years of age is like no other crime. Since children cannot protect themselves, the State is given the responsibility to protect them. Children are a class of people that need special protection; they are particularly vulnerable since they are not mature enough nor capable of defending themselves. A "maturing society," through its legislature has recognized the degradation and devastation of child rape, and the permeation of harm resulting to victims of rape in this age category. The damage a child suffers as a result of rape is devastating to the child as well as to the community. As noted previously, in determining whether a penalty is excessive, the Supreme Court has declared that we should take into account the "evolving standards of decency," and in making this determination, the courts should not look to their own subjective conceptions, but should look instead to the conceptions of modern American society as reflected by objective evidence. As evidence of society's attitudes, we look to the judgment of the state legislators who are representatives of society.

Louisiana's legislature determined a "standard of decency" by amending La. R.S. 14:42(C) to permit the death penalty in cases of aggravated rape when the victim is less than twelve, and deference must be given to that decision. The legislature alone determines what are punishable as crimes and the proscribed penalties. The legislature is not required to select the least severe penalty for the crime as long as the selected penalty is not cruelly inhumane or disproportionate to the offense. Furthermore, legislative enactments are presumed constitutional under both the Federal and the State Constitutions. The party challenging the constitutionality of a statute bears a heavy burden in proving the statute to be unconstitutional. This is true in part because the constitutional test is intertwined with an assessment of contemporary standards, and the decisions of the legislature are indicative of such standards. "In a democratic society legislatures, not courts, are constituted to respond to the will and consequently the moral values of the people." The courts must exercise caution in asserting their views over those of the people as announced through their elected representatives.

. . .

Crime without Death

It has been argued that the death penalty should not be an option when the crime committed produces no death. The Supreme Court has held that the death penalty is an excessive penalty for a robber who does not take a human life. *Enmund v. Florida*, 458 U.S. 782, 102 S.Ct. 3368, 73 L.Ed.2d 1140 (1982). In *Enmund*, the defendant was the driver of the getaway car. His accomplices had robbed and shot two people. The shooter and Enmund were convicted of first degree murder and sentenced to death. The Supreme Court overturned Enmund's sentence of death holding that the Eight Amendment does not permit the imposition of the death penalty of a defendant who aids and abets a felony in course of which murder is committed by others but who does not himself kill, attempt to kill, or intend that killing take place or that lethal force will be employed. The Court goes on to say that "we have no doubt that robbery is a serious crime deserving serious punishment. It is not, however, a crime 'so grievous an affront to humanity that the only adequate response may be the penalty of death.' The Court focused on Enmund's conduct in determining the appropriateness of the death penalty. In Enmund, the defendant simply aided and abetted a robbery which, as the Court holds, is not deserving of the death penalty. However, La. R.S. 14:42(C) contemplates a defendant who rapes a child. The legislature has determined that this crime is deserving of the death penalty because of its deplorable nature, being a "grievous affront to humanity."

. . .

While the Eighth Amendment bars the death penalty for minor crimes under the concept of disproportionality, the crime of rape when the victim is under the age of twelve is certainly not a minor crime. The *Coker* Court recognized the possibility that the degree of harm caused by an offense could be measured not only by the injury to a particular victim but also by the resulting public injury. This implies that some offenses, in particular the rape of a child, might be so injurious to the public that death would not be disproportionate in relation to the crime for which it is imposed. "In part, capital punishment is an expression of society's moral outrage at particularly offensive conduct. This function may be unappealing to many, but it is essential in an ordered society that asks its citizens to rely on legal processes rather than self-help to vindicate their wrongs."

Thus, we conclude that given the appalling nature of the crime, the severity of the harm inflicted upon the victim, and the harm imposed on society, the death penalty is not an excessive penalty for the crime of rape when the victim is a child under the age of twelve years old.

Arbitrary and Capricious

. . .

Much has been made of why eleven year old children are protected by such severe penalties but not twelve year olds. This is not a decision for this Court to make. The legislature is given the power to make the laws and they determined where the line should be drawn, and they drew it between the ages of eleven and twelve. La. R.S. 14:30, first degree murder, as well as La.C.Cr.P. art. 905.4(10) use the same line. Distinctions must be drawn and the legislature is in the best position to make these distinctions.

. . .

Goals of Punishment

Two legitimate goals of punishment are retribution and deterrence. The defendants argue that the death sentence in the case of child rape fails to meet either of these goals. They say the imposition of the death penalty will have a chilling effect on the already inadequate reporting of this crime. Since arguably, most child abusers are family members, the victims and other family members are concerned about the legal, financial and emotional consequences of coming forward. According to defendants, permitting the death penalty for the crime will further decrease the reporting since no child wants to be responsible for the death of a family member. But what defendants fail to understand is that the child is not the one responsible. The child is the innocent victim. The offender is responsible for his own actions. The subject punishment is for the legislature to determine, not this Court.

Self-help is not permitted in our society, so there is a need for retribution in our criminal sanctions. The death penalty for rape of a child less than twelve years old would be deterrence to the commission of that crime. There are a range of possible penalties for such a crime, but as Justice Burger notes in his dissent in *Coker*: "We cannot know which among this range of possibilities is correct, but today's holding (finding the death penalty for rape of an adult woman to be unconstitutional) forecloses the very exploration we have said federalism was intended to offer."

While Louisiana is the only state that permits the death penalty for the rape of a child less than twelve, it is difficult to believe that it will remain alone in punishing rape by death if the years ahead demonstrate a drastic reduction in the incidence of child rape, an increase in cooperation by rape victims in the apprehension and prosecution of rapists, and a greater confidence in the role of law on the part of the people. This experience will be a consideration for this and other states' legislatures.

Our holding today permits the death penalty without a death actually occurring. In reaching this conclusion, we give great deference to our legislature's determination of the appropriateness of the penalty. This is not to say, however, that the legislature has free reign in proscribing penalties. They must still conform to the mandates of the Eighth Amendment and Article I, § 20 of the Louisiana Constitution, and they are still subject to judicial review by the courts. We hold only that in the case of the rape of a child under the age of

twelve, the death penalty is not an excessive punishment nor is it susceptible of being applied arbitrarily and capriciously.

For the reasons stated above, we find La. R.S. 14:42(C) to be constitutional. The motion to quash in each case is reversed and vacated. These cases are remanded to the respective trial courts.

. . .

DISSENT

CALOGERO, CJ.

No other State in the union imposes the death penalty for the aggravated rape of a child under twelve years of age. The reason for this, in my view, is that the statute fails constitutional scrutiny under the decisions of the United States Supreme Court in *Coker v. Georgia*, 433 U.S. 584, 97 S.Ct. 2861, 53 L.Ed.2d 982 (1977), *Furman v. Georgia*, 408 U.S. 238, 92 S.Ct. 2726, 33 L.Ed.2d 346 (1972), and *Gregg v. Georgia*, 428 U.S. 153, 96 S.Ct. 2909, 49 L.Ed.2d 859 (1976). I therefore dissent and would hold R.S. 14:42(C) facially unconstitutional under the Eighth Amendment to the United States Constitution.

QUESTIONS FOR DISCUSSION

1. According to the court, why is death a proportionate penalty for child rape? Do you agree? Explain your reasons

2. Who should make the decision as to what is the appropriate penalty for crimes? Courts? Legislatures? Juries? Defend your answer.

3. In deciding whether the death penalty for child rape is cruel and unusual, is it relevant that Louisiana is the only state that punishes child rape with death?

4. According to the court, some crimes are worse than death. Do you agree? Is child rape one of them? Why? Why not?

SUMMARY

The U.S. Constitution limits the entire criminal law. Constitutional limits differ from other limits because they overarch all parts of the criminal law. The other limits apply only to some of the criminal law. The principles of criminal liability control only the elements of crimes that the prosecution has to prove beyond a reasonable doubt

(Chapters 3 and 4). The doctrines of complicity and incomplete crimes (Chapters 5 and 6) and the principles of justification and excuses (Chapters 7 and 8) may or may not apply to a particular case or crime. The definitions of specific crimes, obviously, each apply only to one crime (Chapters 9–13). The constitutional limits, on the other hand, affect all the elements, doctrines, excuses, justifications, definitions, and penalties.

The Constitution imposes at least three general limits on the creation of crimes: (1) the *ex post facto* clause forbids making conduct criminal after it occurs; (2) the void-for-vagueness doctrine requires the law to state with precision what conduct it prohibits; and (3) the guarantee of equal protection of the laws prohibits unreasonable classifications.

The Constitution protects a number of specific individual rights from criminal prohibition. The right to free speech protects the freedom to express ideas and feelings consistent with a free society. The right to privacy—the right to be let alone by the government—protects conduct that occurs within the intimate sphere of the traditional family and home life. It does not protect nontraditional intimate conduct whether inside or outside the home.

The Constitution also bans "cruel and unusual punishments." According to the U.S. Supreme Court, cruel and unusual punishments include two kinds of punishments: barbaric punishments like boiling in oil that inflict more pain than is required to kill a person; and punishments disproportionate to the seriousness of the crime. A majority of the Court has agreed that the principle of proportionality applies to all criminal punishments. Some members of the Court, however, have argued that the principle of proportionality applies only to capital punishment.

Go to the Criminal Law 7e CD-ROM for Internet exercises.

REVIEW QUESTIONS

1. Describe the "great difficulty" James Madison identified in the quote on government that appears at the beginning of this chapter.

2. Define the rule of law.

3. Define *ex post facto* law. Identify the two goals of *the ex post facto* clause in the U.S. Constitution.

4. List the four types of laws that the *ex post facto* clause prohibits.

5. Explain the void-for-vagueness doctrine. Identify the two "prongs" of the void-for-vagueness test.

6. What kinds of classifications does the equal protection clause prohibit?

7. According to the U.S. Supreme Court, what kinds of privacy does the Constitution protect?

8. According to the Supreme Court, what does the First Amendment protect from criminal law?

9. Define cruel and unusual punishment, as the Supreme Court has interpreted it.

10. Explain the principle of proportionality as it relates to the cruel and unusual punishments clause.

KEY TERMS

affirm—to uphold a trial court's decision.
appellant—a party who appeals a lower court decision.
appellee—the party against whom an appeal is filed.
arbitrary action—unreasonable action
burden of proof—the affirmative duty to prove a point in dispute

certiorari—an order to a lower court from the U.S. Supreme Court to send the record of the lower court to the Supreme Court for review.

citation—a reference to the published report of a case.

clear and present danger doctrine—criminal statutes can prohibit words that threaten a serious public danger that rises above public inconvenience, annoyance, and unrest.

collateral attack—a proceeding asking an appellate court to rule against the trial court's jurisdiction to decide a question or case.

concurring opinion—an opinion that supports the court's result but not its reasoning.

dissenting opinion—the opinion of the minority of justices.

due process clauses—clauses within the U.S. Constitution stating that government cannot deny citizens life, liberty, or property without notice, hearing, and other established procedures.

***ex post facto* laws**—laws passed after the occurrence of the conduct constituting the crime.

expressive conduct—conduct that communicates an idea or emotion without using words.

fighting words—words likely to provoke the average person to breaching the peace by retaliation.

habeas corpus—a request for a court action to review an individual's detention by the government.

holding—the legal principle or rule that a case enunciates.

libel—defamation expressed in print.

majority opinion—the opinion of the majority of justices.

obscenity—material whose predominant appeal is to nudity, sex, or excretion.

plurality opinion—an opinion that announces the result of the case but whose reasoning does not command a majority of the court.

principle of legality—a principle stating that there can be no crime or punishment if there are no specific laws forewarning citizens that certain specific conduct will result in a particular punishment.

principle of proportionality—a principle of law stating that the punishment must be proportionate to the crime committed.

profanity—irreverence toward sacred things.

reasoning—the reasons a court gives to support its holding.

remand—to send a case back to a trial court for further proceedings consistent with the reviewing court's decision.

reverse—to set aside the decision of the trial court and substitute a different decision.

rule of law—the principles that require that established written rules and procedures define, prohibit, and prescribe punishments for crimes.

slander—defamation by spoken word.

strict scrutiny—statutory classifications that require proof that they further a compelling state interest.

void-for-overbreadth doctrine—the principle that a statute is unconstitutional if it includes in its definition of undesirable behavior conduct protected under the U.S. Constitution.

void-for-vagueness doctrine—the principle that statutes violate due process if they do not clearly define crime and punishment in advance.

SUGGESTED READINGS

1. Herbert L. Packer, *The Limits of the Criminal Sanction* (Palo Alto, Calif.: Stanford University Press, 1968). Packer's book is a necessary starting point for anyone seriously interested in the aims and purposes of criminal law in general and in criminal punishment in particular. Packer takes the approach that he is writing for the generalists, not the criminal justice specialist. He especially addresses what he calls the rational lawmaker, one who "stops, looks, and listens" before passing laws. The book is written in a thoughtful, clear, easy-to-read style.

2. Lois G. Forer, *Criminals and Victims* (New York: Norton, 1980). Written by a judge with many years of experience in sentencing criminal defendants, this book explores the difficulties in applying general purposes to concrete cases. Forer analyzes the few alternatives judges have in sentencing, particularly the heavy emphasis on imprisonment, which she believes satisfies neither victims nor society. Well documented with interesting, challenging cases from her courtroom, the book is lively, easy to read, and provocative.

3. Andrew von Hirsch, *Doing Justice* (New York: Hill and Wang, 1976). This book is a brief, clear, and concise argument for just deserts. Based on deliberations by the Committee for the Study of Incarceration, it resulted from serious consideration of returning to retribution as the proper aim of punishment.

4. Norval Morris, *The Future of Imprisonment* (Chicago: University of Chicago Press, 1974).

Morris, a criminal justice expert, has written an influential book in which he recommends a set of principles upon which punishment should rest. His principles are aimed at preserving what is the best of the rehabilitative ideal in the realities of twentieth-century prisons. These ideas are argued convincingly and written clearly, so that general readers can profit from reading the book.

5. David J. Rothman, *Conscience and Convenience* (Boston: Little, Brown, 1980). Rothman, a professor of history, surveys the origins and historical development of rehabilitation in the early years of the twentieth century. This book is excellent for anyone interested in the history of the rehabilitative ideal.

6. Johannes Andenaes, "Deterrence," in *Encyclopedia of Crime and Justice,* vol. 2, ed. Sanford H. Kadish (New York: Free Press, 1983). This is a brief, excellent summary of deterrence theory and research and of the problems of applying deterrence theory in practice, written by the world's leading deterrence theorist. The article includes a valuable bibliography on deterrence, which can lead to fruitful examination of this basic justification for criminal punishment.

7. Jerome Hall, *General Principles of Criminal Law,* 2d ed. (Indianapolis, Ind.: Bobbs-Merrill, 1960). This book gives the most comprehensive treatment of the general principles of legality and proportionality. Hall, a law professor, writes for the specialist, but his challenging arguments and his knowledge of history, law, and philosophy make the book well worth the effort for the layperson.

NOTES

1. James Madison, "The Federalist No. 51," Jacob E Cooke, ed., *The Federalist* (Middletown, Conn.: Wesleyan University Press, 1961), p. 349.

2. Quotes from Roman Civil Law and Lord Coke appear in Jerome Hall, *General Principles of Criminal Law,* 2d ed. (Indianapolis, Ind.: Bobbs-Merrill, 1960), pp. 31–32.

3. United States Constitution, Art. 1, § 9, cl. 3 prohibits the federal government from passing *ex post facto laws*; Art. 10 § 10, cl. 1 prohibits the states from doing so; *Calder v. Bull,* 3 U.S. (3 Dall.) 386, 390, 1 L.Ed. 648 (1798) defined *ex post facto.*

4. *People ex rel. Lonschein v. Warden,* 43 Misc. 2d 109, 250 N.Y.S.2d 15 (1964) (change from death penalty to life imprisonment effective retroactively).

5. *Grayned v. City of Rockford,* 408 U.S. 104, 108–109 (1972).

6. Rollin M. Perkins and Ronald N. Boyce, *Criminal Law,* 3d ed. (Mineola, N.Y.: Foundation Press, 1982), 6–7.

7. *Lanzetta v. New Jersey,* 306 U.S. 451, 453, 59 S.Ct. 618, 619, 83 L.Ed. 888 (1939).

8. *Kolender v. Lawson,* 461 U.S. 352, 357, 358, 103 S.Ct. 1855, 1858, 1859, 75 L.Ed.2d 903 (1983).

9. *Coates v. Cincinnati,* 402 U.S. 611, 614 (1971).

10. *State v. Anderson,* 566 N.E. 2d 1224, 1226–1227, 1226 (Oh. 1991).

11. *Buck v. Bell,* 274 U.S. 200, 208, 47 S.Ct. 584, 585, 71 L.Ed. 1000 (1927) (equal protection argument the last resort).

12. *Michael M. v. Superior Court of Sonoma County,* 450 U.S. 464, 477, 101 S.Ct. 1200, 1208, 67 L.Ed.2d 437 (1981).

13. *American Jurisprudence.* 2d, volume 25, Drugs and Controlled Substances § 36 (1996), 1999 supplement.

14. *Johnson v. Texas,* 491 U.S. 397 (1989), 404.

15. *Chaplinsky v. State of New Hampshire,* 315 U.S. 568 (1942), 574.

16. Ibid., 572.

17. *Gitlow v. New York,* 268 U.S. 652, 45 S.Ct. 625, 69 L.Ed 1138 (1925); *Chaplinsky v. New Hampshire,* 315 U.S. 568, 62 S.Ct. 766, 86 L.Ed. 1031 (1942); *Terminiello v. Chicago,* 337 U.S. 1 (1949), 4; *Schenck v. United States,* 249 U.S. 47, (1919), 52 (shouting fire in theater).

18. *Roe v. Wade,* 410 U.S. 113, 93 S.Ct. 705, 35 L.Ed.2d 147 (1973) (abortion); *Bowers v. Hardwick,* 478 U.S. 186, 106 S.Ct. 2841, 92 L.Ed.2d 140 (1986) (sexual orientation).

19. *Griswold v. Connecticut,* 381 U.S. 479, 85 S.Ct. 1678, 14 L.Ed.2d 510 (1965).

20. Jed Rubenfeld, "The Right to Privacy," *Harvard Law Review* 102 (1989):737–807. This article includes a detailed, extended discussion of the concept and development in constitutional law of privacy.

21. The facts are taken from Editorial, "Striking Down Sodomy Laws," *New York Times,* November 25, 1986.

22. Florida Constitution, Article I, § 23.

23. *Solem v. Helm,* 463 U.S. 277, 284, 103 S.Ct. 3001, 3006, 77 L.Ed.2d 637 (1983).

24. *In re Kemmler,* 136 U.S. 436 (1890), 444.

25. Ibid., 446–447.

26. *Solem v. Helm,* 103 S.Ct. at 3007.

27. *Weems v. United States,* 217 U.S. 349, 30 S.Ct. 544, 54 L.Ed. 793 (1910); *Robinson v. California,* 370 U.S. 660, 82 S.Ct. 1417, 8 L.Ed.2d 758 (1962).

CHAPTER

3

The General Principles of Criminal Liability: The Requirement of Action

Chapter Outline

I. Introduction

II. *Actus Reus*

III. Status as *Actus Reus*

IV. Failure to Act

V. Possession

CHAPTER MAIN POINTS

1. Every crime consists of separate elements, each of which the prosecution has to prove beyond a reasonable doubt.

2. There are two categories of crimes, crimes of criminal conduct and crimes requiring the causation of a particular result.

3. Crimes of criminal conduct consist of three elements: *actus reus,* concurrence, and *mens rea.*

4. Crimes requiring the causation of a particular result consist of five elements: *actus reus, mens rea,* concurrence, causation, and resulting harm.

5. Each element of a specific crime forms the basis of a general principle of criminal liability.

6. The first principle of criminal liability is *actus reus.*

7. *Actus reus* includes not only voluntary bodily movements but also omissions, possession, and some involuntary actions and conditions.

Did Mrs. Cogdon Murder Pat?

Mrs. Cogdon went to sleep. She dreamt that "the war was all around the house," that soldiers were in her daughter Pat's room, and that one soldier was on the bed attacking Pat. Mrs. Cogdon, still asleep, got up, left her bed, got an axe from a woodpile outside the house, entered Pat's room, and struck her two accurate forceful blows on the head with the blade of the axe, thus killing her.

INTRODUCTION

Crooking your finger ordinarily doesn't attract anyone's attention. But if you crook it around the trigger of a gun, squeeze the trigger, and kill someone, crooking your finger suddenly takes on great significance—it can help to prove that you committed murder. Stripping naked before you take a shower is hardly worth mentioning; but if you did it in your criminal law class, that's a different story. So, what you'll learn in this chapter is that under extraordinary circumstances, the stuff of daily life becomes the **elements of crimes.**

In practical terms the elements of crime are what the prosecution has to prove beyond a reasonable doubt to convict defendants. Based on these elements, there are two types of crimes:[1]

1. **Crimes of criminal conduct.** Legally speaking, conduct means an act triggered by intent; criminal conduct means an act triggered by criminal intent. Put more technically, criminal conduct is the concurrence of criminal intent and action.

2. **Crimes of cause and result.** These are crimes in which criminal conduct (the joining of a criminal act with a criminal intent) causes a harm that the law specifically prohibits.

In crimes of criminal conduct a criminal act has to join with a criminal intent. Therefore, crimes of criminal conduct consist of three elements:

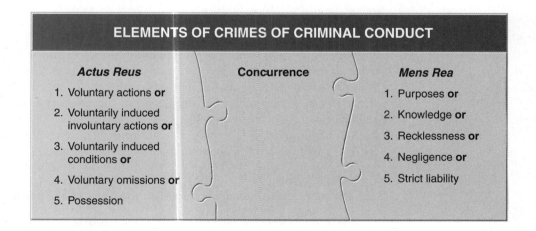

ELEMENTS OF CRIMES OF CRIMINAL CONDUCT

Actus Reus	Concurrence	*Mens Rea*
1. Voluntary actions **or**		1. Purposes **or**
2. Voluntarily induced involuntary actions **or**		2. Knowledge **or**
3. Voluntarily induced conditions **or**		3. Recklessness **or**
4. Voluntary omissions **or**		4. Negligence **or**
5. Possession		5. Strict liability

ELEMENTS OF CRIMES REQUIRING THE CAUSING OF A PARTICULAR RESULT

Actus Reus	Concurrence	*Mens Rea*	Causation	Resulting Harm
1. Voluntary actions **or**		1. Purposes **or**	1. Factual (but for) **and**	
2. Voluntarily induced involuntary actions **or**		2. Knowledge **or**	2. Legal (proximate)	
3. Voluntarily induced conditions **or**		3. Recklessness **or**		
4. Voluntary omissions **or**		4. Negligence **or**		
5. Possession		5. Strict liability		

1. *Actus reus*, a criminal act: the physical element, sometimes called the objective element because it can be determined without reference to the intent of the actor;

2. *Mens rea*, a criminal intent: the mental element, sometimes called the subjective element because intent resides inside the person who has it; and

3. **Concurrence**, act and intent are joined in the exact sense that the criminal intent sets the criminal act in motion.

Let's look at burglary as an example of a crime of criminal conduct. It consists of the *actus reus* (criminal act) of breaking and entering joined with the *mens rea,* the intent to commit a crime (such as stealing a MP3 player) once inside the house. The crime of burglary is complete whether or not the intended crime to be committed inside the house (in our example, stealing a DVD player) is completed. The crime of burglary, therefore, is criminal conduct whether or not it causes any harm beyond the conduct itself.

Crimes of cause and result consist of five elements:

1. *Actus reus*
2. *Mens rea*
3. Concurrence
4. Causation
5. Resulting harm

In all crimes consisting of conduct that causes a particular result, the requirement of concurrence applies not only to the union of action and intention but also to the union of criminal conduct and the cause of the particular result, such as the conduct of one who intentionally shoots another, causing the other's death (Chapter 9). Other crimes of cause and result are battery, conduct that causes bodily injury (Chapter 10); conduct that causes injury to property in arson (Chapter 11); and conduct that causes the loss of property in false pretenses (Chapter 12). Remember that in all cause and result crimes, there are *two* concurrences:

1. The joining of act and intent.
2. The joining of criminal conduct with the cause of the particular result.[2]

Each of the five elements of specific crimes relates to a **general principle of criminal liability**. Table 3.1 uses the example of criminal homicide to show the link be-

TABLE 3.1   Elements of Crime and General Principles of Liability

ELEMENTS OF HOMICIDE	GENERAL PRINCIPLE OF LIABILITY
Criminal act: shooting a gun	*Actus Reus*: the requirement of a voluntary act, omission, or possession
Criminal intent: shooting the gun on purpose	*Mens Rea*: acting intentionally, knowingly, recklessly, or negligently
Joining act and intent: the intent to shoot produced the act of shooting the gun	Concurrence: the requirement of a causal relation between act and intent
Causation: shooting caused the victim's death	Causation: that criminal conduct caused the harm specifically prohibited by the law
Harm: the death of the victim	Harmful result: criminal conduct has to produce a harm specifically defined in the law

tween the practical elements of crimes and the general principles of liability, which will be discussed in this chapter and applied to specific offenses in Chapters 9 through 13.

Action is the essence of the principle of *actus reus,* literally the "evil act." Intention is the heart of the principle of *mens rea,* the "evil mind" (Chapter 4). The union of act and intent in the sense that the criminal intent set the criminal act in motion is the principle of concurrence (Chapter 4). That the criminal conduct causes a harm prohibited by the law is the principle of **causation** (Chapter 4). Causation is another concurrence, this time between criminal conduct and criminal result. That criminal conduct has to cause a criminal result is the principle of **harmful result.** These general principles allow us to organize the content of the special part of the criminal law (the part that defines the elements of the specific crimes included in Chapters 9 through 12) into a logical, orderly theoretical framework. For example, in murder, the intent to kill unites with the act of killing; in illegal left turn violations, the intent to turn unites with the act of turning. So, the elements of every specific crime have to fit within the parameters of the general principles of *actus reus, mens rea* and concurrence; and, where relevant, causation and result.

 3-1 General Principles of Liability in State Codes

The prestigious American Law Institute, in its widely cited Model Penal Code, succinctly summarizes the main aspects of the general principle of actus reus in the following provision:

> Section 2.01 Requirement of Voluntary Act; Omission as Basis of Liability; Possession as an Act.
> (1) A person is not guilty of an offense unless his liability is based on conduct that includes a voluntary act or the omission to perform an act of which he is physically capable.
> (2) The following are not voluntary acts within the meaning of this section:
>   (a) a reflex of convulsion;
>   (b) a bodily movement during unconsciousness or sleep;
>   (c) conduct during hypnosis or resulting from hypnotic suggestion;

(d) a bodily movement that otherwise is not a product of the effort or determination of the actor, either conscious or habitual.

(3) Liability for the commission of an offense may not be based on an omission unaccompanied by action unless
  (a) the omission is expressly made sufficient by the law defining the offense; or
  (b) a duty to perform the omitted act is otherwise imposed by law. . . .

(4) Possession is an act, within the meaning of this Section, if the possessor knowingly procured or received the thing possessed or was aware of his control thereof for a sufficient period to have been able to terminate his possession.

ACTUS REUS

Consider a statute that makes it a crime merely to *intend* to kill another person. Why does such a statute strike us as absurd? One reason is that intent alone is impossible to prove. In the words of a medieval judge, "The thought of man is not triable, for the devil himself knoweth not the thought of man." Furthermore, intentions by themselves do no harm. Although the moral law may condemn those who have immoral thoughts, the criminal law demands conduct—intention turned into action. So, punishing the intent to kill, even if we could prove it, misses the harm of the statute's aim—another's death.[3]

Another problem with punishing intent is that it's terribly hard to separate daydreaming and fantasy from intent. The angry thought, "I'll kill you for that!" rarely turns into actual killing (or for that matter even an attempt to kill) because it's almost always just a blunt way of saying, "I'm really angry." Punishment has to wait for proof in the form of enough action that angry thoughts demonstrate that the speaker really means to commit a crime (Chapter 6). Punishing thoughts stretches the reach of the criminal law too far when it puts within its grasp a "mental state that the accused might be too irresolute even to begin to translate into action." So, thoughts are barred from *actus reus* because punishing them is impractical, inequitable, and unjust.[4]

Now you know why the first principle of criminal liability is the requirement of a voluntary act. This requirement is as old as our law. Long before there was a principle of criminal intent, there was the requirement of a criminal act. The requirement that intentions have to turn into deeds is called **manifest criminality**. Manifest criminality leaves no doubt about the criminal nature of the action. The modern phrase "caught red-handed" comes from the ancient idea of manifest criminality. Then it meant catching murderers with the blood still on their hands; now, it means catching someone in the act of wrongdoing. For example, if bank customers see several people enter the bank, draw guns, threaten to shoot if the tellers don't hand over money, take the money the tellers give them, and leave the bank with the money, their criminality—the *actus reus* and *mens rea* of robbery—is manifest.[5]

The *actus reus* requirement serves several purposes. For one, it helps to prove the *mens rea*. We can't observe intentions; we can only infer them from actions. Furthermore, the *actus reus* reserves the harsh sanction of the criminal law for cases of actual danger, and protects the privacy of individuals. The law need not pry into the thoughts of individuals unless the thinker crosses "the threshold of manifest criminality." Many axioms illustrate the *actus reus* principle: "Thoughts are free"; "We're punished for what we do, not for who we are"; "Criminal punishment depends on conduct, not status"; "We're punished for what we have done, not for what we might do." Although simple to state as a general rule, much in the principle of *actus reus* complicates its apparent simplicity.[6]

One complication is that the act has to be voluntary. In the words of the great justice and legal philosopher Oliver Wendell Holmes, "An act . . . is a muscular contraction, and something more. . . . The contraction of muscles must be willed." So, *actus reus* consists of two ideas: bodily movements and free will. Reflexes and spasms are not voluntary; a spasm that lurches an arm forcefully into someone's face in its path does not satisfy the *actus reus* of assault and battery. The bizarre case of *The King v. Cogdon* deals with the intriguing question whether sleepwalking can be a voluntary criminal act.[7]

CASE | Is Killing While Asleep a Voluntary Act?

The King v. Cogdon[8]

Mrs. Cogdon was charged with the murder of her only child, a daughter called Pat, aged nineteen. Pat had for some time been receiving psychiatric treatment for a relatively minor neurotic condition of which, in her psychiatrist's opinion, she was now cured. Despite this, Mrs. Cogdon continued to worry unduly about her. Describing the relationship between Pat and her mother, Mr. Cogdon testified: "I don't think a mother could have thought any more of her daughter. I think she absolutely adored her." On the conscious level, at least, there was no reason to doubt Mrs. Cogdon's deep attachment to her daughter. To the charge of murdering Pat, Mrs. Cogdon pleaded not guilty. Her story, though somewhat bizarre, was not seriously challenged by the Crown, and led to her acquittal.

FACTS

She told how, on the night before her daughter's death, she had dreamt that their house was full of spiders and that these spiders were crawling all over Pat. In her sleep, Mrs. Cogdon left the bed she shared with her husband, went into Pat's room, and awakened to find herself violently brushing at Pat's face, presumably to remove the spiders. This woke Pat. Mrs. Cogdon told her she was just tucking her in. At the trial, she testified that she still believed, as she had been told, that the occupants of a nearby house bred spiders as a hobby, preparing nests for them behind the pictures on their walls. It was these spiders which in her dreams had invaded their home and attacked Pat. There had also been a previous dream in which ghosts had sat at the end of Mrs. Cogdon's bed and she had said to them, "Well, you have come to take Pattie." It does

not seem fanciful to accept the psychological explanation of these spiders and ghosts as the projections of Mrs. Cogdon's subconscious hostility towards her daughter; a hostility which was itself rooted in Mrs. Cogdon's own early life and marital relationship.

The morning after the spider dream she told her doctor of it. He gave her a sedative and, because of the dream and certain previous difficulties she had reported, discussed the possibility of psychiatric treatment. That evening Mrs. Cogdon suggested to her husband that he attend his lodge meeting, and asked Pat to come with her to the cinema. After he had gone Pat looked through the paper, not unusually found no tolerable programme, and said that as she was going out the next evening she thought she would rather go to bed early. Later, while Pat was having a bath preparatory to retiring, Mrs. Cogdon went into her room, put a hot water bottle in the bed, turned back the bedclothes, and placed a glass of hot milk beside the bed ready for Pat. She then went to bed herself. There was some desultory conversation between them about the war in Korea, and just before she put out her light Pat called out to her mother, "Mum, don't be so silly worrying there about the war, it's not on our front door step yet."

Mrs. Cogdon went to sleep. She dreamt that "the war was all around the house," that soldiers were in Pat's room, and that one soldier was on the bed attacking Pat. This was all of the dream she could later recapture. Her first "waking" memory was of running from Pat's room, out of the house to the home of her sister who lived next door. When her sister opened the front door Mrs. Cogdon fell into her arms, crying "I think I've hurt Pattie."

In fact Mrs. Cogdon had, in her somnambulistic state, left her bed, fetched an axe from the woodheap, entered Pat's room, and struck her two accurate forceful blows on the head with the blade of the axe, thus killing her.

OPINION

Mrs. Cogdon's story was supported by the evidence of her physician, a psychiatrist, and a psychologist. The jury believed Mrs. Cogdon. The jury concluded that Mrs. Cogdon's account of her mental state at the time of the killing, and by the unanimous support given to it by the medical and psychological evidence completely rebutted the presumption that Mrs. Cogdon intended the natural consequences of her acts. It must be stressed that insanity was not pleaded as a defence because the experts agreed that Mrs. Cogdon was not psychotic. [See chapter 8.] The jury acquitted her because the act of killing itself was not, in law, regarded as her act at all.

QUESTIONS FOR DISCUSSION

1. Was Mrs. Cogdon's act of killing Pat involuntary?
2. Could she have done anything to prevent it?
3. It is widely held that it is wrong to punish those who cannot be blamed. Would it be "right" to punish Mrs. Cogdon? Why or why not?

NOTE CASES

1. Emil Decina suffered an epileptic seizure while driving his car. During the seizure, he struck and killed four children. Was the killing an "involuntary act" because it occurred during the seizure? The court said no:

   This defendant knew he was subject to epileptic attacks at any time. He also knew that a moving vehicle uncontrolled on a public highway is a highly dangerous instrumentality capable of unrestrained destruction. With this knowledge, and without anyone accompanying him, he deliberately took a chance by making a conscious choice of a course of action, in disregard of the consequences which he knew might follow from his conscious act, which in this case did ensue.

   People v. Decina, 138 N.E.2d 799 (N.Y.1956)

2. Bobby George was convicted of aggravated assault. George put a gun to a friend's head and demanded a dollar. After he cocked the hammer, it "slipped off [his] thumb" and the "gun went off." George did not mean for the gun to go off. He did not intend to hurt his friend; it was an accident. In its opinion, the Texas Court of Criminal Appeals said:

   "[T]here is no law and defense of accident in the present penal code," but . . . the Legislature had not jettisoned the notion. "The function of the former defense of accident is performed now by the requirement of . . . § 6.01(a), that, A person commits an offense if he voluntarily engages in conduct . . ." If the issue is raised by the evidence, a jury may be charged that a defendant should be acquitted if there is a reasonable doubt as to whether he voluntarily engaged in the conduct of which he is accused.". . .

   If the hammer "slipped off [his] thumb," it had to be that the thumb holding the hammer partially back released just enough pressure for the hammer to "slip" forward. However slight, that is "bodily movement" within the meaning of § 1.07(a)(1), and there is no evidence that it was involuntary.

   George v. State, 681 S.W.2d 43 (Tex.Crim.App.1984)

3. In a Danish case, Bjorn Nielson masterminded a robbery by hypnotizing his friend Palle Hardrup. While in the hypnotic trance, Hardrup held up a Copenhagen bank, shooting and killing a teller and director. Nielson was sentenced to life imprisonment because he masterminded the holdup, even though he was nowhere near the bank when the robbery took place. Hardrup was sent to a mental hospital. He was not tried for robbery because his acts during the holdup were not considered voluntary.[9]

4. Robert Brian Fulcher got into a fight in a bar, passed out, and was picked up by the police. He was taken to jail, where he brutally stomped on another jail inmate and shouted ethnic slurs at him. Fulcher testified that he remembers nothing after passing out in the bar. At the trial, Doctor LeBegue testified that Fulcher suffered from a concussion incurred during the bar fight, and that it caused a brain injury that put Fulcher "in a state of traumatic automatism at the time of his attack on Hernandez . . . the state of mind

in which a person does not have conscious and willful control over his actions. . . ." Was Fulcher liable? No, said the court. Unconscious automatism is an affirmative defense because "[T]he rehabilitative value of imprisonment for the automatistic offender who has committed the offense unconsciously is nonexistent. The cause of the act was an uncontrollable physical disorder that may never recur and is not a moral deficiency." *Fulcher v. State,* 633 P.2d 142 (Wyo.1981)

5. Bruce Jerrett terrorized Dallas and Edith Parsons—he robbed them, killed Dallas, and kidnapped Edith. At trial, Jerrett testified that he could remember nothing of what happened until he was arrested, and that he had suffered previous blackouts following exposure to Agent Orange during military service in Vietnam. The trial judge refused to instruct the jury on the defense of automatism. The North Carolina Supreme Court reversed, and ordered a new trial. *State v. Jerrett,* 309 N.C. 239, 307 S.E.2d 339 (1983)

Hypnosis and sleepwalking aren't really voluntary acts. Speaking precisely, they are voluntarily induced involuntary acts. Less bizarre acts than hypnosis and sleepwalking fall in this category. Many involve drivers of vehicles: Drowsy drivers fall asleep while they're driving; drunk drivers aren't in control; drivers with dangerously high blood pressure suffer strokes while they're driving; epileptics have seizures when they're driving. Why stretch the meaning of voluntary to include them within the grasp of the voluntary act requirement? Because it might deter people whose voluntary acts create risks of involuntarily hurting innocent people.

STATUS AS *ACTUS REUS*

Most conditions, like involuntary acts, don't qualify as *actus reus.* As opposed to action that refers to *what* we *do,* condition (status) refers to *who* we *are.* Status arises in two ways. Sometimes it results from prior voluntary acts—methamphetamine addicts voluntarily used methamphetamine the first time and alcoholics voluntarily took their first drink. Other conditions result from no act at all. The most obvious examples are sex, age, race, and ethnicity.

In his novel about the imaginary land called Erewhon, Samuel Butler deals with the criminal code of the Erewhonians, which makes it a crime to have tuberculosis. Following conviction for tuberculosis, the judge pronounced sentence on one defendant in these words:

> It only remains for me to pass such a sentence on you, as shall satisfy the ends of the law. That sentence must be a very severe one. It pains me much to see one who is yet so young, and whose prospects in life were otherwise so excellent, brought to this distressing condition by a constitution which I can only regard as radically vicious; but yours is no case for compassion: this is not your first offense: you have led a career of crime, and have only profited by the leniency shown you upon past occasions, to offend yet more seriously against the laws and institutions of your country. You were convicted of aggravated bronchitis last year: and I find that though you are but twenty-three years old, you have been imprisoned on no less than fourteen occasions for illnesses of a more or less hateful character; in fact, it is not too much to say that you have spent the greater part of your life in jail.
>
> It is all very well for you to say that you came of unhealthy parents, and had a severe accident in your childhood which permanently undermined your constitution; excuses such as these are the ordinary refuge of the criminal; but they cannot

for one moment be listened to by the ear of justice. I am not here to enter upon curious metaphysical questions as to the origins of this or that—questions to which there would be no end were their introduction once tolerated, and which would result in throwing the only guilt on the tissues of the primordial cell, or on the elementary gasses. There is no question of how you came to be wicked, but only this—namely, are you wicked or not? This has been decided in the affirmative, neither can I hesitate for a single moment to say that it has been decided justly. You are a bad and dangerous person. . . .

I do not hesitate to sentence you to imprisonment, with hard labor, for the rest of your miserable existence.[10]

Why does it strike as wrong to sentence someone to life imprisonment for having tuberculosis? Because the voluntary acts of the defendant didn't cause the disease. In *Robinson v. California,* the U.S. Supreme Court took up this problem of punishment for the status of drug addiction. It was a crime in California not only to manufacture, sell, buy, and use narcotics but also to "be addicted" to them. Robinson was convicted and sentenced for being a heroin addict. The Court ruled that punishing Robinson for his addiction to heroin was cruel and unusual punishment prohibited by the Eighth Amendment to the U.S. Constitution (discussed in Chapter 2). According to the Court, it's cruel and unusual punishment to sentence someone to "even one day" for an illness. Why? Because a disease is not an act. If addiction results from no act at all, as in the addiction of a baby born to an addicted mother, the baby isn't responsible for the addiction. We can't blame people who aren't responsible for their conditions. And, if we can't blame them then it's not fair to punish them. Of course, Robinson differs from the fictional defendant with tuberculosis in that Robinson's addiction resulted from a prior voluntary act.

 3-2 *Robinson v. California,* Oral Argument

What about acts that result from conditions? In *Powell v. Texas,* the U.S. Supreme Court had to decide whether to extend the prohibition against punishing the status of drug addiction resulting from the prior voluntary act of drug use to an alcoholic's act of public drunkenness resulting from his alcoholism.

| C A S E | Drunkenness an Act? |

Powell V. Texas,
392 U.S. 514, 88 S.Ct. 2145, 20 L.Ed.2d
1254 (1968)

Leroy Powell was found guilty of public drunkenness. He appealed on the ground that punishing his drunkenness was cruel and unusual punishment because it punished a status. The Supreme Court affirmed the conviction.

MARSHALL, J. announced the judgment of the Court and delivered an opinion joined by WARREN, CJ., BLACK, and HARLAN, JJ.

FACTS

In late December 1966, appellant was arrested and charged with being found in a state of intoxication in a public place, in violation of Vernon's Ann. Texas Penal Code, Art. 477 (1952), which reads as follows: "Whoever shall get drunk or be found in a state of intoxication in any public place, or at any private house except his own, shall be fined not exceeding one hundred dollars." Appellant was tried in the Corporation Court of Austin, Texas., found guilty, and fined $20. He appealed to the County

Court at Law No. 1 of Travis County, Texas, where a trial *de novo* was held. His counsel urged that appellant was "afflicted with the disease of chronic alcoholism," that "his appearance in public (while drunk was)... not of his own volition," and therefore that to punish him criminally for that conduct would be cruel and unusual, in violation of the Eighth and Fourteenth Amendments to the United States Constitution. The trial judge in the county court, sitting without a jury ... ruled ... that chronic alcoholism was not a defense to the charge. He found appellant guilty, and fined him $50. There being no further right to appeal within the Texas judicial system, appellant appealed to this Court. ...

Appellant testified [at his trial] concerning the history of his drinking problem. He reviewed his many arrests for drunkenness; testified that he was unable to stop drinking; stated that when he was intoxicated he had no control over his actions and could not remember them later, but that he did not become violent; and admitted that he did not remember his arrest on the occasion for which he was being tried. On cross-examination, appellant admitted that he had had one drink on the morning of the trial and had been able to discontinue drinking. In relevant part, the cross-examination went as follows:

Q. You took that one at eight o'clock because you wanted to drink?

A. Yes, sir.

Q. And you knew that if you drank it, you could keep on drinking and get drunk?

A. Well, I was supposed to be here on trial, and I didn't take but that one drink.

Q. You knew you had to be here this afternoon, but this morning you took one drink and then you knew that you couldn't afford to drink any more and come to court; is that right?

A. Yes, sir, that's right.

Q. So you exercised your will power and kept from drinking anything today except that one drink?

A. Yes, sir, that's right.

Q. Because you knew what you would do if you kept drinking that you would finally pass out or be picked up?

A. Yes, sir.

Q. And you didn't want that to happen to you today?

A. No, sir.

Q. Not today?

A. No, sir.

Q. So you only had one drink today?

A. Yes, sir.

On redirect examination, appellant's lawyer elicited the following:

Q. Leroy, isn't the real reason why you just had one drink today because you just had enough money to buy one drink?

A. Well, that was just give to me.

Q. In other words, you didn't have any money with which you could buy any drinks yourself?

A. No, sir, that was give to me.

Q. And that's really what controlled the amount you drank this morning, isn't it?

A. Yes, sir.

Q. Leroy, when you start drinking, do you have any control over how many drinks you can take?

A. No, sir.

... Dr. David Wade, a Fellow of the American Medical Association, duly certificated in psychiatry [testified at length]. ... Dr. Wade sketched the outlines of the "disease" concept of alcoholism; noted that there is no generally accepted definition of "alcoholism"; alluded to the ongoing debate within the medical profession over whether alcohol is actually physically "addicting" or merely psychologically "habituating"; and concluded that in either case a "chronic alcoholic" is an "involuntary drinker," who is "powerless not to drink," and who "loses his self-control over his drinking." He testified that he had examined appellant, and that appellant is a "chronic alcoholic," who "by the time he has reached (the state of intoxication) ... is not able to control his behavior, and (who) ... has reached this point because he has an uncontrollable compulsion to drink." Dr. Wade also responded in the negative to the question whether appellant has "the willpower to resist the constant excessive consumption of alcohol." He added that in his opinion jailing appellant without medical attention would operate neither to rehabilitate him nor to lessen his desire for alcohol.

On cross-examination, Dr. Wade admitted that when appellant was sober he knew the difference between right and wrong, and he responded affirmatively to the question whether appellant's act in taking the first drink in any given instance when he was sober was a "voluntary exercise of his will." Qualifying his answer, Dr. Wade stated that "these individuals have a compulsion, and this compulsion, while not completely overpowering, is a very strong influence, an exceedingly strong influence, and this compulsion coupled with the firm belief in their mind that they are going to be able to handle it from now on causes their judgment to be somewhat clouded."

Evidence in the case then closed. The State made no effort to obtain expert psychiatric testimony of its own, or even to explore with appellant's witness the question of appellant's power to control the frequency, timing, and location of his drinking bouts, or the substantial disagreement within the medical profession concerning the nature of the disease, the efficacy of treatment and the prerequisites for effective treatment. It did nothing to examine or illuminate what Dr. Wade might have meant by his reference to a "compulsion" which was "not completely overpowering," but which was "an exceedingly strong influence," or to inquire into the question of the proper role of such a "compulsion" in constitutional adjudication. Instead, the State contented itself with a brief argument that appellant had no defense to the charge because he "is legally sane and knows the difference between right and wrong."

[Powell was found guilty] and fined $20. He appealed to the County Court at Law No. 1 of Travis County, Texas, where a trial *de novo* [a new trial as if the first had not occurred and no decision rendered] was held. His counsel urged that appellant was "afflicted with the disease of chronic alcoholism," that "his appearance in public [while drunk was] . . . not of his own volition," and therefore that to punish him criminally for that conduct would be cruel and unusual, in violation of the Eighth and Fourteenth Amendments to the United States Constitution.

Following this abbreviated exposition of the problem before it, the trial court indicated its intention to disallow appellant's claimed defense of

chronic alcoholism. Thereupon defense counsel submitted, and the trial court entered, the following findings of fact:

(1) That chronic alcoholism is a disease which destroys the afflicted person's will power to resist the constant, excessive consumption of alcohol.

(2) That a chronic alcoholic does not appear in public by his own volition but under a compulsion symptomatic of the disease of chronic alcoholism.

(3) That Leroy Powell, defendant herein, is a chronic alcoholic who is afflicted with the disease of chronic alcoholism.

[Note: According to Justice Marshall, "Whatever else may be said of them, those are not 'findings of fact' in any recognizable, traditional sense in which that term has been used in a court of law; they are the premises of a syllogism transparently designed to bring this case within the scope of this Court's opinion in Robinson v. State of California, 370 U.S. 660, 82 S.Ct. 1417, 8 L.Ed.2d 758 (1962). Nonetheless, the dissent [see dissent] would have us adopt these 'findings' without critical examination; it would use them as the basis for a constitutional holding that 'a person may not be punished if the condition essential to constitute the defined crime is part of the pattern of his disease and is occasioned by a compulsion symptomatic of the disease.'"]

OPINION

. . . Appellant seeks to come within the application of the Cruel and Unusual Punishment Clause announced in *Robinson v. California*, 370 U.S. 660, 82 S.Ct. 1417, 8 L.Ed.2d 758 (1962), which involved a state statute making it a crime to "be addicted to the use of narcotics." This Court held there that "a state law which imprisons a person thus afflicted (with narcotic addiction) as a criminal, even though he has never touched any narcotic drug within the State or been guilty of any irregular behavior there, inflicts a cruel and unusual punishment. . . ."

On its face the present case does not fall within that holding, since appellant was convicted, not for being a chronic alcoholic, but for being in public while drunk on a particular occasion. The State of Texas thus has not sought to punish a mere status, as California did in *Robinson*; nor has it attempted to regulate appellant's behavior in the privacy of his own home. Rather, it has imposed upon appellant a criminal sanction for public behavior which may create substantial health and safety hazards, both for appellant and for members of the general public, and which offends the moral and esthetic sensibilities of a large segment of the community. This seems a far cry from convicting one for being an addict, being a chronic alcoholic, being "mentally ill, or a leper. . . ."

Robinson so viewed brings this Court but a very small way into the substantive criminal law. . . . The entire thrust of *Robinson's* interpretation of the Cruel and Unusual Punishment Clause is that criminal penalties may be inflicted only if the accused has committed some act, has engaged in some behavior, which society has an interest in preventing, or perhaps in historical common-law terms, has committed some *actus reus.* . . .

Traditional common-law concepts of personal accountability and essential considerations of federalism lead us to disagree with appellant. We are unable to conclude, on the state of this record or on the current state of medical knowledge, that chronic alcoholics in general, and Leroy Powell in particular, suffer from such an irresistible compulsion to drink and to get drunk in public that they are utterly unable to control their performance of either or both of these acts and thus cannot be deterred at all from public intoxication. And in any event this Court has never articulated a general constitutional doctrine of *mens rea.*

We cannot cast aside the centuries-long evolution of the collection of interlocking and overlapping concepts which the common law has utilized to assess the moral accountability of an individual for his antisocial deeds. The doctrines of *actus reus, mens rea,* insanity, mistake, justification, and duress have historically provided the tools for a constantly shifting adjustment of the tension between the evolving aims of the criminal law and changing religious, moral, philosophical, and medical views of the nature of man. This process of adjustment has always been thought to be the province of the States. . . .

But formulating a constitutional rule would reduce, if not eliminate . . . fruitful experimentation, and freeze the developing productive dialogue between law and psychiatry into a rigid constitutional mold. It is simply not yet the time to write the Constitutional formulas cast in terms whose meaning, let alone relevance, is not yet clear either to doctors or to lawyers.

Affirmed.

CONCURRING OPINION

BLACK, J., joined by HARLAN, J.

. . . Punishment for a status is particularly obnoxious, and in many instances can reasonably be called cruel and unusual, because it involves punishment for a mere propensity, a desire to commit an offense; the mental element is not simply one part of the crime but may constitute all of it. This is a situation universally sought to be avoided in our criminal law; the fundamental requirement that some action be proved is solidly established even for offenses most heavily based on propensity, such as attempt, conspiracy, and recidivist crimes. In fact, one eminent authority has found only one isolated instance, in all of Anglo-American jurisprudence, in which criminal responsibility was imposed in the absence of any act at all.

The reasons for this refusal to permit conviction without proof of an act are difficult to spell out, but they are nonetheless perceived and universally expressed in our criminal law. Evidence of propensity can be considered relatively unreliable and more difficult for a defendant to rebut; the requirement of a specific act thus provides some protection against false charges. Perhaps more fundamental is the difficulty of distinguishing, in the absence of any conduct, between desires of the daydream variety and fixed intentions that may pose a real threat to society; extending the criminal law to cover both types of desire would be unthinkable, since "(t)here can hardly be anyone who has never thought evil. When a desire is inhibited it may find expression in fantasy; but it would be absurd to condemn this natural psychological mechanism as illegal."

In contrast, crimes that require the State to prove that the defendant actually committed some proscribed act involve none of these special problems. In addition, the question whether an act is "involuntary" is . . . an inherently elusive question, and one which the State may, for good reasons, wish to regard as irrelevant. In light of all these considerations, our limitation of our Robinson holding to pure status crimes seems to me entirely proper. . . .

. . . I would hold that *Robinson v. California* establishes a firm and impenetrable barrier to the punishment of persons who, whatever their bare desires and propensities, have committed no proscribed wrongful act. But I would refuse to plunge from the concrete and almost universally recognized premises of *Robinson* into the murky problems raised by the insistence that chronic alcoholics cannot be punished for public drunkenness, problems that no person, whether layman or expert, can claim to understand, and with consequences that no one can safely predict. I join in affirmance of this conviction.

WHITE, J.

If it cannot be a crime to have an irresistible compulsion to use narcotics, *Robinson v. California,* 370 U.S. 660, 82 S.Ct. 1417, 8 L.Ed.2d 758, I do not see how it can constitutionally be a crime to yield to such a compulsion. Punishing an addict for using drugs convicts for addiction under a different name. Distinguishing between the two crimes is like forbidding criminal conviction for being sick with flu or epilepsy but permitting punishment for running a fever or having a convulsion. Unless *Robinson* is to be abandoned, the use of narcotics by an addict must be beyond the reach of the criminal law. Similarly, the chronic alcoholic with an irresistible urge to consume alcohol should not be punishable for drinking or for being drunk.

Powell's conviction was for the different crime of being drunk in a public place. Thus even if Powell was compelled to drink, and so could not constitutionally be convicted for drinking, his conviction in this case can be invalidated only if there is a constitutional basis for saying that he may not be punished for being in public while drunk. The statute involved here, which aims at keeping drunks off the street for their own welfare and that of others, is not challenged on the ground that it interferes unconstitutionally with the right to frequent public places. No question is raised about applying this statute to the nonchronic drunk, who has no compulsion to drink, who need not drink to excess, and who could have arranged to do his drinking in private or, if he began drinking in public, could have removed himself at an appropriate point on the path toward complete inebriation.

DISSENT

FORTAS, J., joined by DOUGLAS, BRENNAN, and STEWART, JJ.

. . . It is settled that the Federal Constitution places some substantive limitation upon the power of state legislatures to define crimes for which the imposition of punishment is ordered. . . . *Robinson v. California* . . . stands upon a principle which, despite its subtlety, must be simply stated and respectfully applied because it is the foundation of individual liberty and the cornerstone of the relations between a civilized state and its citizens: Criminal penalties may not be inflicted upon a person for being in a condition he is powerless to change.

In all probability, Robinson at some time before his conviction elected to take narcotics. But the crime as defined did not punish this conduct. The statute imposed a penalty for the offense of "addiction"—a condition which Robinson could not control. Once Robinson had become an addict, he was utterly powerless to avoid criminal guilt. He was powerless to choose not to violate the law.

In the present case, appellant is charged with a crime composed of two elements—being intoxicated and being found in a public place while in that condition. The crime, so defined, differs from that in *Robinson.* The statute covers more than a mere status. But the essential constitutional defect here is the same as in *Robinson,* for in both cases the particular defendant was accused of being in a condition which he had no capacity to change or avoid.

The trial judge sitting as trier of fact found upon the medical and other relevant testimony, that Powell is a "chronic alcoholic." He defined appellant's "chronic alcoholism" as "a disease which destroys the afflicted person's willpower to resist the constant, excessive consumption of alcohol.". . . I would reverse the judgment below.

QUESTIONS FOR DISCUSSION

1. According to *Powell v. Texas,* is *actus reus* not only a general principle of criminal liability but also a constitutional requirement? Explain.

2. Does it make sense to punish Powell if he was drunk in public because of his alcoholism? Why or why not?

3. Was his alcoholism a condition?

4. If so, did it result from a voluntary act?

5. Was his alcoholism a "disease"?

6. Does the public drunkenness statute punish Powell for being "sick"?

7. Which opinion do you agree with, the plurality or the dissent? Why?

FAILURE TO ACT

Those who rape, murder, and rob deserve punishment because their actions caused harm. What about people who stand by and do nothing while bad things are happening around them? As Professor George Fletcher describes these people, "They get caught in a situation in which they falter. Someone needs help and they cannot bring themselves to render it." Can these failures to act satisfy the *actus reus* requirement? Yes, when it is outrageous for someone to fail to do something to help someone in danger.[11]

Failure to act, called **criminal omission**, takes two forms. One is the simple failure to act, usually the failure to file some kind of report required by law, such as reporting an accident or child abuse, filing an income tax return, registering a firearm, or notifying sexual partners of positive HIV status. The other type of omission is the failure to intervene to prevent injuries and death to persons or the damage and destruction of property. Only the failure to act or intervene when there is a legal duty to act can qualify as a criminal omission. Legal duties can arise in three ways:

1. Statutes
2. Contracts
3. Special relationships.

Statutes create legal duties to file income tax returns, to report accidents and child abuse, and to register firearms. Individuals can also contract to perform duties. For example, police officers agree to "protect and serve" the people; failure to perform those duties can create criminal liability. The main special relationships that create legal duties include the parent-child relationship, the doctor-patient relationship, the employer-employee relationship, the carrier-passenger relationship, and, in some states, the husband-wife relationship.

Failure to perform *moral* duties does not qualify as a criminal omission. According to Professors Wayne LaFave and Austin Scott:

> Generally one has no legal duty to aid another person in peril, even when that aid can be rendered without danger or inconvenience to himself. He need not shout a warning to a blind man headed for a precipice or to an absent-minded one walking into a gunpowder room with a lighted candle in hand. He need not pull a neighbor's baby out of a pool of water or rescue an unconscious person stretched across the railroad tracks, though the baby is drowning or the whistle of the approaching train is heard in the distance. A doctor is not legally bound to answer a desperate call from the frantic parents of a sick child, at least if it is not one of his regular patients. A moral duty to take affirmative action is not enough to impose a legal duty to do so. But there are situations which do give rise to legal duties.[12]

There are two approaches to defining what is a legal duty giving rise to criminal liability. One approach is the **Good Samaritan doctrine**, which "imposes a legal duty to render or summon aid for imperiled strangers." Only a few jurisdictions follow the Good Samaritan doctrine. Nearly all jurisdictions follow the second approach called the **American bystander rule.** According to the bystander rule, there is no legal duty to rescue or call for help to aid someone who is in danger even if helping poses no risk whatsoever to the potential rescuer. So, shameful as it might be morally, an Olympic swimmer has no duty to rescue or even call 911 for a child drowning in front of her eyes.[13]

Limiting criminal omissions to the failure to perform legal duties is based on three assumptions:

 3-3 Omission Statute

1. Individual conscience, peer pressure, and other informal mechanisms condemn and prevent behavior more effectively than criminal prosecution.

2. Prosecuting omissions unduly burdens an already overburdened criminal justice system.

3. Criminal law cannot compel "Good Samaritans" to help those in need.[14]

In *State v. Miranda,* the court dealt with legal duties and failure to act.

C A S E	Did He Have a Legal Duty to the Children?

State v. Miranda
245 Conn. 209, 715 A.2d 680 (1998)

Santos Miranda, the defendant, was convicted in the Superior Court, Judicial District of New Haven, of assault in the first degree, and he appealed. The Appellate Court reversed the conviction. The Connecticut Supreme Court reversed and remanded.

KATZ, J.

FACTS

Santos Miranda, the defendant, commenced living with his girlfriend and her two children in an apartment in September, 1992. On January 27, 1993, the defendant was twenty-one years old, his girlfriend was sixteen, her son was two, and her daughter, the victim in this case, born on September 21, 1992, was four months old. Although he was not the biological father of either child, the defendant took care of them and considered himself to be their stepfather. He represented himself as such to the people at Meriden Veteran's Memorial Hospital where, on January 27, 1993, the victim was taken for treatment of her injuries following a 911 call by the defendant that the child was choking on milk. Upon examination at the hospital, it was determined that the victim had multiple rib fractures that were approximately two to three weeks old, two skull fractures that were approximately seven to ten days old, a brachial plexus injury to her left arm, a rectal tear that was actively "oozing blood" and bilateral subconjunctival nasal hemorrhages. On the basis of extensive medical evidence, the trial court determined that the injuries had been sustained on three or more occasions and that none of the injuries had been the result of an accident, a fall, events that took place at the time

of the child's birth, cardiopulmonary resuscitation, a blocked air passageway or the child choking on milk. Rather, the trial court found that the injuries, many of which created a risk of death, had been caused by great and deliberate force.

The trial court further found in accordance with the medical evidence that, as a result of the nature of these injuries, at the time they were sustained the victim would have screamed inconsolably, and that her injuries would have caused noticeable physical deformities, such as swelling, bruising and poor mobility, and finally, that her intake of food would have been reduced. The court also determined that anyone who saw the child would have had to notice these injuries, the consequent deformities and her reactions. Indeed, the trial court found that the defendant had been aware of the various bruises on her right cheek and the subconjunctival nasal hemorrhages, as well as the swelling of the child's head, that he knew she had suffered a rectal tear, as well as rib fractures posteriorly on the left and right sides, and that he was aware that there existed a substantial and unjustifiable risk that the child was exposed to conduct that created a risk of death. The trial court concluded that despite this knowledge, the defendant "failed to act to help or aid [the child] by promptly notifying authorities of her injuries, taking her for medical care, removing her from her circumstances and guarding her from future abuses. As a result of his failure to help her, the child was exposed to conduct which created a risk of death to her and the child suffered subsequent serious physical injuries. . . ."

The trial court concluded that the defendant had a legal duty to protect the health and well-being of the child based on the undisputed facts that he had established a familial relationship with the child's mother and her two children, that he had voluntarily assumed responsibility for the care and welfare of both children, and that he considered himself the victim's stepfather. On the basis of these circumstances, the trial court found the defendant guilty of one count of § 53-21 and six counts of § 53a-59 (a)(3).

OPINION

The issue . . . is whether a person who is not the biological or legal parent of a child but who establishes a familial relationship with a woman and her infant child, voluntarily assumes responsibility for the care and welfare of the child, and considers himself the child's stepfather, has a legal duty to protect the child from abuse, such that the breach of that duty exposes the person to criminal liability pursuant to General Statutes § 53a- 59 (a)(3). General Statutes § 53a-59 provides in relevant part: "Assault in the first degree: Class B felony: Nonsuspendable sentences. (a) A person is guilty of assault in the first degree when . . . (3) under circumstances evincing an extreme indifference to human life he recklessly engages in conduct which creates a risk of death to another person, and thereby causes serious physical injury to another person. . . ."

After a court trial, the defendant, Santos Miranda, was convicted of six counts of assault in the first degree in violation of § 53a-59 (a)(3). . . . The court concluded that the defendant had established a familial relationship with the victim and her mother, that his failure to help and protect the child from abuse constituted a gross deviation from the standard of conduct that a reasonable person would observe in the situation, and that such reckless conduct resulted in serious physical injuries to the child. Although the trial court never stated who actually had caused the injuries, we take judicial notice that the child's mother entered a plea of nolo contendere to the crimes of intentional assault in the first degree and risk of injury to a minor. She received a sentence of twelve years incarceration suspended after seven years. The trial court found the defendant not guilty of nineteen counts of assault in the first degree. Those counts had charged him with either personally inflicting the injuries or not preventing the child's mother from inflicting the injuries. The court imposed a total effective sentence of forty years imprisonment.

The defendant appealed to the Appellate Court . . . which reversed the assault convictions concluding that the defendant had no legal duty to act under the circumstances of this case. This court granted the state's petition for certification limited to the following issue: "Under the circumstances of this case, did the Appellate Court properly conclude that the defendant could not be convicted of violating General Statutes § 53a-59 (a)(3) because he had no legal duty to protect the victim from parental abuse." We conclude that, based upon the trial court's findings that the defendant had established a familial relationship with the victim's mother and her two children, had assumed responsibility for the welfare of the children, and had taken care of them as though he were their father, the defendant had a legal duty to protect the victim from abuse. Accordingly, we reverse the judgment of the Appellate Court.

Before addressing the certified issue of whether the facts and circumstances of this case were sufficient to create a legal duty to protect the victim from parental abuse pursuant to § 53a-59 (a)(3), we turn our attention to the question of whether, even if we assume such a duty exists, the failure to act can create liability under that statute. In other words, by failing to act in accordance with a duty, does a defendant commit a crime, such as assault in the first degree in violation of § 53a-59 (a)(3), that is not specifically defined by statute in terms of an omission to act but only in terms of cause and result? Whether a failure to discharge a legal duty to protect a child constitutes an omission punishable as an assault is a question of law subject to *de novo* review by this court.

The trend of Anglo-American law has been toward enlarging the scope of criminal liability for failure to act in those situations in which the common law or statutes have imposed an affirmative responsibility for the safety and well-being of others. Criminal liability of parents based on a failure to act in accordance with common-law affirmative duties to protect and care for their children is well recognized in many jurisdictions. See, e.g., *People v. Stanciel*, 153 Ill.2d 218, 180 Ill.Dec. 124, 606 N.E.2d 1201 (1992) (mother guilty of homicide by allowing known abuser to assume role of disciplinarian over child); *Smith v. State*, 408 N.E.2d 614 (Ind.App.1980) (mother held criminally responsible for failing to prevent fatal beating of child by her lover); *State v. Walden*, 306 N.C. 466, 293 S.E.2d 780 (1982) (mother guilty of assault for failure to prevent beating); *State v. Williquette*, 129

Wis.2d 239, 385 N.W.2d 145 (1986) (mother guilty of child abuse for allowing child to be with person known previously to have been abusive and who subsequently abused child again). In light of this duty to protect and care for children, courts in these jurisdictions have concluded that, where this duty exists and injury results, the failure to protect the child from harm will be "deemed to be the cause of those injuries" and the person bearing the duty may face criminal sanctions. *State v. Peters,* 116 Idaho 851, 855, 780 P.2d 602 (1989).

Although our research has revealed no case by this court in which we expressly have held a parent criminally liable for failure to act to save his or her child from harm, the Appellate Court has recognized that criminal liability may attach not only to overt acts but also to an omission to act when there is a legal duty to do so. *State v. Jones,* 34 Conn.App. 807, 812-13, 644 A.2d 355, cert. denied, 231 Conn. 909, 648 A.2d 158 (1994) (defendant's failure to call ambulance or seek help for his obviously injured child indicated "conscious disregard of a substantial risk of death" within meaning of § 53a-59 [a][3]). We agree that criminal conduct can arise not only through overt acts, but also by an omission to act when there is a legal duty to do so. "Omissions are as capable of producing consequences as overt acts. Thus, the common law rule that there is no general duty to protect limits criminal liability where it would otherwise exist. The special relationship exception to the 'no duty to act' rule represents a choice to retain liability for some omissions, which are considered morally unacceptable." Therefore, had the defendant been the victim's parent—[someone with an undisputed affirmative legal obligation to protect and provide for his minor child]— we would conclude that his failure to protect the child from abuse could constitute a violation of § 53a-59 (a)(3).

We next turn to the issue of whether the duty to protect can be imposed on the defendant, an adult member of the household unrelated to the child. Both the state and the defendant recognize that the determination of the existence of a legal duty is a question of law subject to *de novo* review by this court.

The defendant argues that there is no statutory or common-law precept "authorizing the expansion of assault under § 53a-59 (a)(3)." The state argues that there is both. We conclude that, based on the trial court's findings that the defendant had

established a family-like relationship with the mother and her two children, that he had voluntarily assumed responsibility for the care and welfare of both children, and that he had considered himself the victim's stepfather, there existed a common-law duty to protect the victim from her mother's abuse, the breach of which can be the basis of a conviction under § 53a-59 (a)(3).

. . .

"'Duty is a legal conclusion about relationships between individuals, made after the fact. . . . The nature of the duty, and the specific persons to whom it is owed, are determined by the circumstances surrounding the conduct of the individual.'" Although one generally has no legal duty to aid another in peril, even when the aid can be provided without danger or inconvenience to the provider, there are four widely recognized situations in which the failure to act may constitute breach of a legal duty: (1) where one stands in a certain relationship to another; (2) where a statute imposes a duty to help another; (3) where one has assumed a contractual duty; and (4) where one voluntarily has assumed the care of another. The state argues that this case falls within both the first and fourth situations, or some combination thereof.

We begin with the duty based upon the relationship between the parties. One standing in a certain personal relationship to another person has some affirmative duties of care with regard to that person. "Legal rights and duties . . . may arise out of those complex relations of human society which create correlative rights and duties the performance of which is so necessary to the good order and well-being of society that the state makes their observance obligatory."

It is undisputed that parents have a duty to provide food, shelter and medical aid for their children and to protect them from harm. "The inherent dependency of a child upon his parent to obtain medical aid, i.e., the incapacity of a child to evaluate his condition and summon aid by himself, supports imposition of such a duty upon the parent." Additionally, "'[t]he commonly understood general obligations of parenthood entail these minimum attributes: (1) express love and affection for the child; (2) express personal concern over the health, education and general well-being of the child; (3) the duty to supply the necessary food, clothing, and medical care; (4) the duty to provide an adequate domicile; and (5) the duty to furnish social and religious guidance.'" Indeed, the status relationship giving rise to a duty to provide and protect that has been before the courts more often than any other relationship and, at the same time, the one relationship that courts most frequently assume to exist without expressly so stating, is the relationship existing between a parent and a minor child.

In addition to biological and adoptive parents and legal guardians, there may be other adults who establish familial relationships with and assume responsibility for the care of a child, thereby creating a legal duty to protect that child from harm. See, e.g., *Cornell v. State,* 159 Fla. 687, 32 So.2d 610 (1947) (grandmother guilty of manslaughter in death of grandchild where she had assumed care of child but became so intoxicated that she allowed child to smother to death). "Recognizing the primary responsibility of a natural parent does not mean that an unrelated person may not also have some responsibilities incident to the care and custody of a child. Such duties may be regarded as derived from the primary custodian, i.e., the natural parent, or arise from the nature of the circumstances." *People v. Berg,* 171 Ill.App.3d 316, 320, 121 Ill.Dec. 515, 525 N.E.2d 573 (1988); see 1 W. LaFave & A. Scott, supra, § 3.3(a), p. 286 ("if two people, though not closely related, live together under one roof, one may have a duty to act to aid the other who becomes helpless").

. . .

. . . The traditional approach in this country is to restrict the duty to save others from harm to certain very narrow categories of cases. We are not prepared now to adopt a broad general rule covering other circumstances. We conclude only that, in accordance with the trial court findings, when the defendant, who considered himself the victim's parent, established a familial relationship with the victim's mother and her children and assumed the role of a father, he assumed, under the common law, the same legal duty to protect the victim from the abuse as if he were, in fact, the victim's guardian. Under these circumstances, to require the defendant as a matter of law to take affirmative action to prevent harm to the victim or be criminally responsible imposes a reasonable duty. That duty does not depend on an ability to regulate the mother's discipline of the victim or on the defendant having exclusive control of the victim when the injuries occurred. Nor is the duty contingent

upon an ability by the state or the mother to look to the defendant for child support. Certainly, if the defendant had been the biological father of only one of the two children, it would be absurd to suggest that he would have had an obligation to stop the mother from abusing one of the children but not the other. Moreover, whether the defendant had created a total in loco parentis relationship with the victim by January, 1993, is not dispositive of whether the defendant had assumed a responsibility for the victim. "If immediate or emergency medical attention is required from a child's custodian it should not matter that such custodian is not the primary care provider or for that matter a legally designated surrogate."

. . . We recognize the continuing demographic trend reflecting a significant increase in nontraditional alternative family arrangements. Consequently, more and more children will be living with or may depend upon adults who do not qualify as a natural or adoptive parent. The attachment by children to the adults who care for them does not, however, depend exclusively upon whether the caregiver is the natural or adoptive parent or another person who has assumed the caretaker role. Children become attached to people who care for them, and this attachment is "rooted inevitably in the infant's inability to ensure his own survival. . . ." To distinguish among children in deciding which ones are entitled to protection based upon whether their adult caregivers have chosen to have their relationships officially recognized hardly advances the public policy of protecting children from abuse.

The defendant acknowledges that he could not simply close his eyes to evidence of the brutality the child suffered and that his failure to protect her was punishable. . . . Nevertheless, the defendant argues that . . . he did not have a duty under § 53a-59 (a)(3) [the first degree assault provision]. . . . We conclude that the defendant had a duty, under the facts and circumstances of this case, to protect the victim and prevent further harm to her, and that for violating that duty to her, he can be found guilty of having violated § 53a-59 (a)(3).

The defendant has argued that he did not actually know that the child had been abused by her mother and that knowledge of her injuries should not be equated with knowledge of their cause. He also argues that there was no evidence that he had the ability to prevent any harm from occurring to the child. Those claims of insufficiency of evidence are to be considered on the merits by the Appellate Court on remand.

The judgment of the Appellate Court is reversed and the case is remanded to that court for consideration of the defendant's remaining claims . . .

DISSENT

BERDON, J.

Cases, such as the one before us, that present revolting facts concerning the physical abuse of a four-month-old child, test the foundation of our democracy. The rule of law must be upheld even when confronted with alarming allegations of improper acts, indeed allegations of loathsome conduct on the part of the defendant. The question for this court, in cases such as this, is whether the legislature intended to make the conduct with which the defendant was charged criminal under General Statutes § 53a-59 (a)(3), assault in the first degree. It is not whether this court, were it sitting as a legislature, would have proscribed the conduct at issue. "Such action by a legislature may well be commendable, but by a court condemnable." Simply put, we cannot craft a substantive offense *ex post facto* [after the fact] in order to include conduct that we find abhorrent to our sensitivities and that of the general public. It is this judicial restraint that sharply puts into focus one of the essential differences between democratic and totalitarian forms of government. . . .

The majority addresses an issue that is necessarily implied in the certified question—that is, whether the "conduct" referred to in § 53a-59 (a)(3) includes the failure to act. I disagree with the majority's very tenuous argument that it does. Section 53a-59 (a) provides in part that "[a] person is guilty of assault in the first degree when . . . (3) under circumstances evincing an extreme indifference to human life he recklessly engages in conduct which creates a risk of death to another person, and thereby causes serious physical injury to another person. . . ." Although "conduct" can include the failure to act under circumstances when there is a duty to act, the majority points to nothing in the text of § 53a-59 (a)(3), or its legislative history, to support its conclusion that conduct under § 53a-59 (a)(3) includes the failure to

act. In fact, both the common definition of assault—"a violent attack with physical means"—"any willful attempt or threat to inflict injury upon the person of another" belie the majority's claim.

Moreover, by construing § 53a-59 (a)(3) to include the duty to act, the majority stands a long-standing and fundamental principle of statutory construction on its head: Penal statutes "are to be expounded strictly against an offender, and liberally in his favor. This can only be accomplished, by giving to them a literal construction, so far as they operate penally. . . ." While a criminal statute is not to be defeated by an unreasonably strict construction of its language, it must be rather strictly construed so that the conduct made criminal will be ascertainable with reasonable certainty from a careful reading of the statute. . . . A careful reading of § 53a-59 (a)(3) would never lead a rational reader to believe that a person was subject to criminal liability under the statute for the failure to act—whether the person is a stranger, a live-in boyfriend, or a parent. . . .

The legislature will be very much surprised to discover that we have in place, under § 53a-59 (a)(3), a law that provides that the failure to act is punishable criminal conduct. Although the legislature recently has grappled with the issue of imposing an affirmative obligation on the part of a parent and an unrelated adult to protect children from abuse; see Substitute House Bill No. 5283 (1988) (H.B. No. 5283), entitled "An Act Concerning Facilitation of Abuse of a Child"; it did not enact the proposed legislation. Nevertheless, the majority of this court, without any understanding of the implications of its decision today and without the aid of expert advice that is available to the legislature through the public hearing process, impetuously and presumptuously crafts a crime of assault that was never intended by the legislature. Clearly, if the legislature agreed with the majority that, pursuant to § 53a-59 (a)(3), parents as well as unrelated adults had an affirmative legal obligation to protect children from abuse, it never would have had a need to consider H.B. No. 5283, a bill that explicitly criminalizes the conduct with which the defendant was charged in the present case.

. . . I would affirm the judgment of the Appellate Court. Accordingly, I dissent.

NOTE CASES

1. Bonnie Kuntz and Warren Becker, who had never married but had lived together for approximately six years, were in the process of ending a stormy relationship. Kuntz and Becker had argued the morning of April 18, 1998. At some point during the day, both parties left the trailer home. When Kuntz arrived at the mobile home that night, she discovered that many of her personal belongings had been destroyed, the interior of the home "trashed," and the phone ripped from the wall. At or before midnight, a physical altercation ensued.

Kuntz told sheriff's deputies who had been sent to the trailer that she went into the kitchen where Becker physically attacked her, and at one point grabbed her by the hair, shook her, and slammed her into the stove. Kuntz told the deputies that she could not clearly remember what happened, only that she had pushed Becker away and had then gone outside by the kitchen door to "cool off." When she thought that the fight was over, and that it was safe to go back inside, she returned to the kitchen. She discovered a trail of blood leading from the kitchen through the living room and out onto the front porch where she found Becker collapsed face-down on the porch. She alleges that she rolled him over. Becker was unresponsive.

Then, according to Kuntz, she found Becker's car keys in one of his pockets, got in his vehicle, drove to a friend's house several miles away, and called her mother. Kuntz's sister-in-law, who lived next door to Kuntz's mother, called for medical assistance sometime within an hour after the stabbing. Kuntz returned to the trailer home where she waited for the deputies and medics to arrive.

The state charged Kuntz with negligent homicide, alleging that Kuntz caused the death of Becker by stabbing him once in the chest with a knife and by failing to call for medical assistance. Kuntz pleaded not guilty. Kuntz filed a motion to dismiss the amended information or in the alternative to strike the allegation that the failure to seek medical assistance constituted negligent homicide.

Was Kuntz's failure to call for medical assistance a criminal omission? It depends, said the court.

For criminal liability to be based upon a failure to act, there must be a duty imposed by the law to act, and the person must be physically capable of performing the act. . . . [T]he parties here have identified . . . "the American bystander rule." This rule imposes no legal duty on a person to rescue or summon aid for another person who is at risk or in danger, even though society recognizes that a moral obligation might exist. This is true even "when that aid can be rendered without danger or inconvenience to" the potential rescuer. . . . Thus, an Olympic swimmer may be deemed by the community as a shameful coward, or worse, for not rescuing a drowning child in the neighbor's pool, but she is not a criminal.

But this rule if far from absolute. [There are a number of] . . . exceptions to the American bystander rule: 1) a duty based on a personal relationship, and 2) a duty based on creation of the peril. . . . A breach of one of these legal duties by failing to take action, therefore, may give rise to criminal liability. . . . [T]his Court held that under certain circumstances a husband has a duty to summon medical aid for his wife and breach of that duty could render him criminally liable. . . .

Applying the . . . [rule] to the facts here, we conclude that Kuntz and Becker, having lived together for approximately six years, owed each other [a] . . . "personal relationship" duty. . . . This duty . . . mutual reliance . . . would include circumstances involving two people, though not closely related, [who] live together under one roof. To hold otherwise would result in an untenable rule that would not . . . impose a legal duty to summon medical aid on persons in a relationship involving cohabitation. Nevertheless, this holding is far from dispositive in establishing a legal duty under the facts presented.

. . . The duty based on "creation of the peril" is far more closely aligned with the factual circumstances here. Undoubtedly, when a person places another in a position of danger, and then fails to safeguard or rescue that person, and the person subsequently dies as a result of this omission, such an omission may be sufficient to support criminal liability. *State v. Morgan* (1997), (imposing criminal liability for supplying cocaine leading to victim's overdose); *United States v. Hatatley* (10th Cir 1997), 130 F.3d 1399, 1406 (imposing criminal liability for leaving victim badly beaten and shirtless in a freezing, remote desert).

This duty may include peril resulting from a defendant's criminal negligence, as alleged here. . . . The legal duty based on creation of the peril has been . . . cases of self-defense . . . The legal duty imposed on personal relationships and those who create peril are not absolute; i.e., there are exceptions to these exceptions. The personal relationship legal duty, for example, does not require a person to jeopardize his own life. Furthermore, the duty does not arise unless the spouse "unintentionally entered a helpless state," or was otherwise incompetent to summon medical aid on his or her own behalf.

Similarly, the law does not require that a person, who places another person in a position of peril, risk bodily injury or death in the performance of the legally imposed duty to render assistance. . . . Therefore, where self-preservation is at stake, the law does not require a person to "save the other's life by sacrificing his own," and therefore no crime can be committed by the person who "in saving his own life in the struggle for the only means of safety," causes the death of another. Even states such as Vermont that have adopted a "Good Samaritan Doctrine" which—contrary to the American bystander rule— imposes a legal duty to render or summon aid for imperiled strangers, do not require that the would-be rescuer risk bodily injury or death. Thus, although a person may still be held accountable for the results of the peril into which he or she placed another, the law does not require that he or she risk serious bodily injury or death in order to perform a legal duty.

. . . We hold that when a person justifiably uses force to fend off an aggressor, that person has no duty to assist her aggressor in any manner that may conceivably create the risk of bodily injury or death to herself, or other persons. This absence of a duty necessarily includes any conduct that would require the person to remain in, or return to, the zone of risk created by the original aggressor. We find no authority that suggests that the law should require a person, who is justified in her use of force, to subsequently check the pulse of her attacker, or immediately dial 911, before retreating to safety.

Under the [facts of this case] . . . we conclude that the victim has but one duty after fending off an attack, and that is the duty owed to one's self—as a matter of self-preservation—to seek and secure safety away from the place the attack occurred. Thus, the person who justifiably acts in self-defense is temporarily afforded the same status as the innocent bystander under the American rule.

Finally, we conclude that the duty to summon aid may in fact be "revived". . . but only after the victim of the aggressor has fully exercised her right to seek and secure safety from personal harm. Then, and only then, may a legal duty be imposed to summon aid for the person placed in peril by an act of self-defense. We further hold that preliminary to imposing this duty, it must be shown that 1) the person had knowledge of the facts indicating a duty to act; and 2) the person was physically capable of performing the act. . . . This . . . raises the possibility that after a person is found to have justifiably used force, and reasonably exercised her right to secure her own safety, she may still be found criminally liable for the ultimate death the force caused. In other words, if the duty to summon aid may be revived, as we have just held, may the failure to perform this legal duty give rise to criminal liability, even though the underlying use of force was justified?

Not all of the justices agreed with the majority. The dissenting judge wrote:

. . . I disagree with . . . the majority's conclusion that at some point, a victim of aggression who has justifiably defended herself has a "revived" obligation to come to the assistance of the person against whom it was necessary for her to defend herself. The majority has concluded that although circumstances occur which are so extreme that a woman is justified in the use of deadly force to defend herself, a jury can, after the fact, in the safe confines of the jury room, conclude that at some subsequent point she was sufficiently free from danger that she should have made an effort to save her assailant and that because she didn't she is still criminally liable for his death even though at some previous point in time she was justified in taking his life. This result is simply unworkable as a practical matter and makes poor public policy.

. . . I conclude that when a person is attacked by another and reasonably believes that deadly force is necessary to prevent imminent death or serious bodily injury to herself and therefore uses deadly force to defend herself, she has no duty, "revived" or otherwise, to summon aid for her assailant. The fact that the use of force by her was justifiable as defined by statute is a complete defense to any charge based on her assailant's death. . . . A person driven to the point of having to violently defend herself from a violent attack should not, at the risk of criminal punishment, be required to know that at some undefined point in time she has a duty to save that same person. A normal person under those circumstances is incapable of undertaking such an intellectual process. To require her to do so is inconsistent with the traditional notion that when criminal liability is based on the failure to perform a duty, it must be a plain duty which leaves no doubt as to its obligatory force.

State v. Kuntz 995 P.2d 951 (2000)

2. Carol Ann Oliver met Carlos Cornejo in the afternoon when she was with her boyfriend at a bar. She and her boyfriend purchased jewelry from Cornejo. In the late afternoon, when Oliver was leaving the bar to return home, Cornejo got into the car with her, and she drove home with him. At the time, he appeared to be extremely drunk. At her house, he asked her for a spoon and went into the bathroom. She went to the kitchen, got a spoon and brought it to him. She knew he wanted the spoon to take drugs. She remained in the living room while Cornejo "shot up" in the bathroom. He then came out and collapsed onto the floor in the living room. She tried but was unable to rouse him. Oliver then called the bartender at the bar where she had met Cornejo. The bartender advised her to leave him and come back to the bar, which appellant did.

Oliver's daughter returned home at about 5 P.M. that day with two girlfriends. They found Cornejo unconscious on the living room floor. When the girls were unable to wake him, they searched his pockets and found eight dollars. They did not find any wallet or identification. The daughter then called Oliver on the telephone. Oliver told her to drag Cornejo outside in case he woke up and became violent. The girls dragged Cornejo outside and put him behind a shed so that he would not be in the view of the neighbors. He was snoring when the girls left him there. About a half hour later, appellant returned home with her boyfriend. She, the boyfriend, and the girls went outside to look at Cornejo. Oliver told the girls that she had watched him "shoot up" with drugs and then pass out.

The girls went out to eat and then returned to check on Cornejo later that evening. He had a pulse and was snoring. In the morning, one of the girls heard appellant tell her daughter that Cornejo might be dead. Cornejo was purple and had flies around him. Oliver called the bartender at about 6 A.M. and told her she thought Cornejo had died in her backyard. Oliver then told the girls to call the police and she left for work. The police were called.

Oliver was convicted of involuntary manslaughter and appealed. Did Oliver have a "special relationship" with Cornejo that created a legal duty? Yes, said the appeals court:

We conclude that the evidence of the combination of events which occurred between the time appellant left the bar with Cornejo through the time he fell to the floor unconscious, established as a matter of law a relationship which imposed upon appellant a duty to seek medical aid. At the time appellant left the bar with Cornejo, she observed that he was extremely drunk, and drove him to her home. In so doing, she took him from a public place where others might have taken care to prevent him from injuring himself, to a private place—her home—where she alone could provide care. To a certain, if limited, extent, therefore, she took charge of a person unable to prevent harm to himself. She then allowed Cornejo to use her bathroom, without any objection on her part, to inject himself with narcotics, an act involving the definite potential for fatal consequences.

When Cornejo collapsed to the floor, appellant should have known that her conduct had contributed to creating an unreasonable risk of harm for Cornejo—death. At that point, she owed Cornejo a duty to prevent that risk from occurring by summoning aid, even if she had not previously realized that her actions would lead to such risk. Her failure to summon any medical assistance whatsoever and to leave him abandoned outside her house warranted the jury finding a breach of that duty. . . . The judgment is affirmed.

People v. Oliver, 258 Cal.Rptr. 138 (1989)

Only *unreasonable* failures to perform legal duties are criminal omissions. For example, in one case, a sea captain allowed a crew member who had fallen overboard to drown in order to save other crew members and passengers from a dangerous storm. The court held that failure to try and save the one crew member was not a criminal omission because it was reasonable to allow one crew member to die in order to save many others. Neither is it a criminal omission for a baby-sitter who could not swim to fail to dive into deep water to save the child he was watching.

A famous incident occurring in New York City, the failure of residents to take action to save Kitty Genovese from a brutal murder, raises both the questions of when a legal duty arises and what acts amount to a reasonable fulfillment of a legal duty, once the duty arises.

CASE ▌ Did the Bystanders Have a Legal Duty?

FACTS

In 1964, Winston Moseley was going on 30; he made a good living as a business machine technician; he supported his wife and children; he was quiet and very neat. But what Moseley liked to do most was go out into the streets in the early morning hours looking for men to rob and women to kill. He didn't need money, but he got a thrill out of overpowering men and taking their money. Much more thrilling to him was to find a woman alone walking or driving. If she was driving, he'd follow her until she stopped and parked her car. Then he tracked her on foot for the kill. According to Moseley, he did it at least five times before he saw Catherine Genovese driving alone in a red car.[15]

During his trial, the following testimony was recorded:

Q: Now, on this night did you intend killing?

A: Yes.

Q: What if anything did you do to prepare for that?

A: Well, I had a hunting knife that I had taken from a previous burglary, and I took that with me.

Q: Had you any specific type of individual in mind?

A: Well, I knew it would be a woman.

Q: Is there any reason why now you intended to kill a white woman as distinguished from the two prior times that you thought you killed colored?

A: No, unless perhaps I might have been thinking there might have been some difference between them.

Q: Now tell us what you did, please.

A: Well, I left the house about one-thirty or two o'clock, and it took me until about three o'clock to find one that was driving where I could actually catch up with her . . . I followed [her red car] for about ten blocks, and then it pulled into what I thought was a parking lot.

Q: Did you make your mind up to kill her?

A: Yes.

Q: Can you tell us any reasons why?

A: No, I can't give you any reasons why.

Q. [The court:] Was [money] one of the factors?

A: It possibly was, but it was not a primary factor.

Q: You tell us exactly what happened, Winston.

A: As soon as she got out of the car she saw me and ran. I ran after her and I had a knife in my hand, then I caught up with her and I stabbed her twice in the back.

According to the police: Twenty-eight-year-old Catherine Genovese, who was called Kitty by almost everyone in the neighborhood, was returning home from her job as manager of a bar in Hollis. She parked her red Fiat in a lot adjacent to the Kew Gardens Long Island Rail Road Station, facing Mowbray Place. Like many residents of the neighborhood, she had parked there day after day since her arrival from Connecticut a year ago, although the railroad frowns on the practice. She turned off the lights of her car, locked the door and started to walk the 100 feet to the entrance of her apartment at 82-70 Austin Street, which is in a Tudor building, with stores on the first floor and apartments on the second.

The entrance to the apartment is in the rear of the building because the front is rented to retail stores. At night the quiet neighborhood is shrouded in the slumbering darkness that marks most residential areas. Miss Genovese noticed a man at the far end of the lot, near a seven-story apartment house at 82-40 Austin Street. She halted. Then, nervously, she headed up Austin Street toward Lefferts Boulevard, where there is a call box to the 102d Police Precinct in nearby Richmond Hill.

He testified that he stabbed her in the chest and stomach as well as the back, that somebody called out the window, but that he "did not think that person would come down to help her." Moseley also testified that later he had heard somebody open an apartment door and shout down, but he "didn't feel these people" were coming down the stairs. So he lifted her skirt, cut off her underclothes, including her brassiere. After he had stabbed her repeatedly he began to worry that somebody might have seen his car and noted the color, make, or license. So he walked back to the outdoor parking lot where he had left it to stalk her on foot. He moved the car around the corner. Then he took off his hat, a stocking cap, and put on a fedora he had in the car.

Q: [from *the prosecutor*] *Why?*

A: Well, I felt that perhaps if I had not killed the girl and had to leave what I started unfinished, she would have only seen the bottom half of my face.

Q: In other words, you thought you could disguise your face better by putting on a different hat.

A: That's right.

Q: Now, when you came back, you were thinking, weren't you, about what you were going to do?

A: That's right.

Q: What?

A: That's right.

Moseley said he heard some yelling from windows, but it had stopped by the time he got back to Catherine Genovese, whom he had left lying in the street. He did not think that anybody would come down "regardless to the fact that she had screamed." "So I came back but I didn't see her . . . I tried the first door in the row of those back houses, which was locked. The second door was open and she was in there. As soon as she saw me she started screaming so I stabbed her a few other times, once in the neck. She only moaned after that."

Q: You also knew that people at three o'clock in the morning on a cold morning would not take the trouble to even come down and investigate if someone had been killed?

A: I thought that way, yes.

Q: And as she started to scream, you stabbed her, didn't you?

A: Yes, I did.

Q: You stabbed her in the throat?

A: Right.

Q: That is where the voice was coming from, isn't that right?

A: That's right.

Moseley testified that he saw that she was exposed, decided to rape her, stabbed her again, that she kept moaning, that he took off one of his gloves to pull down his zipper, took out his penis, laid on top of her but could not attain—"What was the word?" he asked the judge. "Erection," said the court.

Did he have an orgasm, the court asked. Moseley said yes. He also said she was menstruating at the time. He took the money from the wallet.

Q: Forty-nine dollars you put in your pocket, hah?

A: That's being practical.

Q: Being practical?

A: Yes. Why would I throw money away?

He left. Somebody then did call the police. A half hour had gone by in the two attacks on Catherine Genovese, what with seventeen stabbings, Moseley's back and forth from the parking lot, cutting her clothes off, raping her, and so on. She died soon after arrival in the hospital. If the call had come more quickly, the police said later, her life could have been saved. Moseley said he did not know for sure that she was dead until he read it in the newspapers the next day. He committed at least three robberies between the time of the murder and the day the police arrested him. The trial took three days. He was convicted and sentenced to death.

According to *The New York Times*

For more than half an hour 37 respectable, law-abiding citizens in Queens watched a killer stalk and stab a woman in three separate attacks in Kew Gardens. Twice the sound of their voices and the sudden glow of their bedroom lights interrupted him and frightened him off. Each time he returned, sought her out and stabbed her again. Not one person telephoned the police during the assault; one witness called after the woman was dead. But Assistant Chief Inspector Frederick M. Lussen, in charge of the borough's detectives and a veteran of 25 years of homicide investigations, is still shocked. He can give a matter of fact recitation of many murders. But the Kew Gardens slaying baffles him—not because it is a murder, but because the "good people" failed to call the police. "As we have reconstructed the crime," he said, "the assailant had three chances to kill this woman during a 35-minute period. He returned twice to complete the job. If we had been called when he first attacked, the woman might not be dead now."

She got as far as a street light in front of a bookstore before the man grabbed her. She screamed. Lights went on in the 10-story apartment house at 82-67 Austin Street, which faces the bookstore. Windows slid open and voices punctured the early morning stillness. Miss Genovese screamed: "Oh, my God, he stabbed me! Please help me! Please help me!" From one of the upper windows in the apartment house, a man called down: "Let that girl alone!"

The assailant looked up at him, shrugged and walked down Austin Street toward a white sedan parked a short distance away. Miss Genovese struggled to her feet. Lights went out. The killer returned to Miss Genovese, now trying to make her way around the side of the building by the parking lot to get to her apartment. The assailant stabbed her again. "I'm dying!" she shrieked. "I'm dying!"

Windows were opened again, and lights went on in many apartments. The assailant got into his car and drove away. Miss Genovese staggered to her feet. A city bus, Q i 10, the Lefferts Boulevard line to Kennedy International Airport, passed. It was 3:35 A.M.

The assailant returned. By then, Miss Genovese had crawled to the back of the building, where the freshly painted brown doors to the apartment house held out hope of safety. The killer tried the first door; she wasn't there. At the second door, 82-62 Austin Street, he saw her slumped on the floor at the foot of the stairs. He stabbed her a third time—fatally.

It was 3:50 by the time the police received their first call, from a man who was a neighbor of Miss Genovese. In two minutes they were at the scene. The neighbor, a 70-year-old woman, and another woman were the only persons on the street. Nobody else came forward.

The man explained that he had called the police after much deliberation. He had phoned a friend in Nassau County for advice and then he had crossed the roof of the building to the apartment of the elderly woman to get her to make the call. "I didn't want to get involved," he sheepishly told the police.

The police stressed how simple it would have been to have gotten in touch with them. "A phone call," said one of the detectives, "would have done it." The police may be reached by dialing "0" for operator or SPring 7-3100. Today, witnesses from the neighborhood, which is made up of one-family homes in the $35,000 to $60,000 range with the exception of the two apartment houses near the railroad station, find it difficult to explain why they didn't call the police.

Lieut. Bernard Jacobs, who handled the investigation by the detectives, said: "It is one of the better neighborhoods. There are few reports of crimes.". . .

The police said most persons had told them they had been afraid to call, but had given meaningless answers when asked what they had feared. "We can understand the reticence of people to become involved in an area of violence," Lieutenant Jacobs said, "but where they are in their homes, near phones, why should they be afraid to call the police?"

Witnesses—some of them unable to believe what they had allowed to happen—told a reporter why. A housewife, knowingly if quite casual, said, "We thought it was a lover's quarrel." A husband and wife both said, "Frankly, we were afraid." They seemed aware of the fact that events might have been different. A distraught woman, wiping her hands in her apron, said, "I didn't want my husband to get involved.". . . A man peeked out from a slight opening in the doorway to his apartment and rattled off an account of the killer's second attack. Why hadn't he called the police at the time? "I was tired," he said without emotion." I went back to bed." It was 4:25 A.M. when the ambulance arrived for the body of Miss Genovese. It drove off. "Then," a solemn police detective said, "the people came out." (Copyright © 1964 by the New York Times Company. Reprinted by permission.)

QUESTIONS FOR DISCUSSION

1. Did the residents have a legal duty to intervene? A moral duty? What is the basis of the duty?

2. Should the "neighborly" relationship give rise to a duty? Why?

3. Should a statute impose a duty of individuals to intervene? Why or why not?

4. Assuming there is a duty, what does it consist of?

5. What, if any, penalty would you impose for failing to intervene?

6. Consider two other incidents. In the first, an assailant raped and beat an eighteen-year-old switchboard operator. The victim ran naked and bleeding from the building onto the street, screaming for help. A crowd of forty people gathered and watched, in broad daylight, while the rapist tried to drag her back into the building. No onlooker intervened; two police officers happened on the scene and arrested the assailant. In the second incident, eleven people watched while an assailant stabbed seventeen-year-old Andrew Melmille in the stomach on a subway. The assailant left the subway at the next stop. Not one of the eleven people on the train helped Melmille. He bled to death. Is there a legal duty to act in either of these incidents?[16]

7. What is the duty?

8. How, if at all, do these incidents differ from the Genovese incident?

THE REST OF THE STORY *What Ever Happened to Winston Moseley?*

AP/Wide World Photos

A. Balz

Winston Moseley appealed his murder conviction because the trial judge refused to permit evidence that mental illness reduced Moseley's ability to control his actions.

1967: The Court of Appeals, New York's highest court, commuted Moseley's death sentence to life imprisonment. Why? Because the trial judge didn't allow into evidence enough information about the mitigating circumstances surrounding the crime, such as Moseley's mental illness.

Moseley cut himself with a bottle in Attica state prison. He was sent to a prison hospital in Buffalo, where he overpowered a guard and escaped. Before he was caught four days later, he tied up a man and his wife and raped the woman while the husband was forced to watch. **1971:** Moseley earned a college degree.

1977: April 16, 1977: Letter from Winston Moseley to the *New York Times* from Attica prison.

More than a decade ago, I committed a crime I genuinely regret. No one should murder or can justify it. Society was rightly outraged. One of its members had been murdered. The murderer should have been speedily apprehended and punished. I've been imprisoned many years now, and I've wished so many times that I could bring Kitty Genovese back to life, back to her family and friends.

My perpetual torment and agony will not resurrect her but if my arrest, conviction, and even execution would have served to deter others, if my death would have somehow balanced the scales of justice, then in accordance with the laws in force in 1964, my life should have been taken. The crime was tragic, but it did serve society, urging it, as it did to come to the aid of its members in distress or danger.

Newspapers, and The New York Times specifically, acted conscientiously and responsibly. You informed the public and suggested that it can't in good conscience afford the luxury of being indifferent to the fate of other human beings.

Pre-eminent journalism focused attention on a senseless murder and heightened the public's awareness as to apathy. A salient reminder that all people should care and be concerned about others was long overdue. To help others is both good and right. It is necessary to sometimes get involved.

Those sent to prison are ultimately society's responsibility too. Prison and prisoners involve everyone in one way or another. Prison as it presently stands is an inherently evil place that insidiously and systematically works to destroy imprisoned persons. It should rather be a place that builds better human beings. Men can and do change for the better despite the miasma of imprisonment, however.

I went through a trial of fire and death. The '71 Attica rebellion profoundly affected me. Misunderstanding, suspicion, animosity, hostility, and virulent hate lashed out and killed viciously and indiscriminately. I saw all that and more and was sickened. I vowed then and there that I was going to get on the right track and make amends for my own past wrongdoing. I learned that human life has great value. In the future I would act responsibly.

My life in 1973, however, was still a bit harsh and chaotic, and it was pretty much an empty shell. In that year college courses were offered here, and I availed myself of that positive opportunity. Now, I have earned a B.A. degree in sociology.

One professor, Sister Mary Frances Welch, has been particularly instrumental in helping me remold my character and my way of thinking. Another woman, Dorothy Tishler, came into my life and filled it with goodness and sunshine. She provided me with specific direction and exact guidance. The bright miracle of her faith, deep devotion, and the inspirational, affectionate love she gives that covers all, accounts for the final stages, of my transformation.

Transformation, a new outlook, caused me to get involved. I began applying myself to problems that periodically plague Attica. I've been both president and vice president of the inmate liaison committee here. I've made reasonable suggestions to state officials about prison reform, and I exercised my influence and used my expertise to the utmost in the formulation of the peaceful demonstration that began here Aug. 23. Many prisoners, then as now, felt that they had many legitimate grievances and complaints badly in need of an airing and redress.

I tried and succeeded in doing something good, and it was something that came out right. In striking contrast to the '71 rebellion, intelligent dialogue triumphed over emotional rancor, and a peaceful settlement ensued this time.

The man who killed Kitty Genovese in Queens in 1964 is no more. He was also destroyed in that calamity and its aftermath. Another vastly different individual has emerged, a Winston Moseley intent and determined to do constructive, not destructive things.

Today I'm a man who wants to be an asset to society, not a liability to it.

1984 parole hearing: A parole commissioner told Moseley that he sounded like he was suggesting that "it was difficult . . . for a person like yourself, as it is for your victim." Moseley responded, "In a sense, yes. For a victim outside, it's a one-time or one-hour or one-minute affair, but for the person who's caught, it's forever." The shocked commissioner responded, "Well, that's one way to look at it.... Miss Genovese [is] no longer with us.... But, you're here ... at least it's debatable that you're as bad off as Miss Genovese."

1990 parole hearing: The following exchange took place about the rape of a woman during Moseley's prison escape:

> Moseley: "I wrote to the victims to apologize for the inconvenience I have caused."
> Commissioner: "That's a good way to say it. They were inconvenienced."
> Moseley: "No one was hurt."
> Commissioner: "Someone was hurt. You don't rape someone without them being hurt."
> Moseley: "Physically injured," he corrected the commissioner.

1995 request for a new trial: Now 61 years old, Moseley asked for a new trial on the ground that his lawyer didn't effectively represent him. The judge denied the motion for a new trial. The sister and brothers of Catherine Genovese were present. So was Moseley's original lawyer and the prosecutor. They had not attended the original trial. The family was satisfied with the decision. So was the prosecutor who said that the only reason Moseley is alive is because of the effective representation of his lawyer who saved Moseley from the electric chair.[17]

POSSESSION

In addition to voluntary acts and the failure to reasonably perform legal duties, the possession of some things—usually weapons, illegal drugs, stolen property, and pornography—can qualify as a criminal act. Possession itself is not action, but obviously you have to act to get possession. For example, if I put marijuana in my pocket, my voluntary act was responsible for my possessing marijuana. If, on the other hand, my enemy plants marijuana on me without my knowledge, I've taken no action to gain possession of it.

Possession can be either actual or constructive. **Actual possession** means physical possession; that is, the substance or item is on the person of the possessor. I actually possess a gun, for example, if it's in my pocket. **Constructive possession** means that the substance or item is under the control of the possessor. Constructive possession requires that possessors *know* what they possess and that they are in a "position to exercise dominion or control" over it, "either personally or through others." For example, owners are in a "position to exercise dominion or control" over their homes, even though they don't physically possess cocaine that a weekend guest keeps in the guest room.[18]

Possession also can be either knowing possession or mere possession. **Knowing possession** means that possessors are aware of what they possess. Hence, those who buy crystal meth, conscious that it is crystal meth, knowingly possess it. They don't need to know that the possession of crystal meth is illegal; it's enough that they know that it is crystal meth. **Mere possession** means that possessors don't know what they possess. One who does a friend a favor by carrying a brown paper bag without knowing that the bag contains stolen money has mere possession of the money.

All states except Washington and North Dakota require knowing possession in order to satisfy the *actus reus* in the form of possession. In Washington, however, the court has created a defense of unwitting possession in order to protect against punishing people who don't know that they possess illegal substances or objects. In *State v. Staley,* unbeknownst to Staley, someone had rolled up cocaine in a dollar bill and put it in Staley's tip jar at a night club where Staley played guitar. The Washington Supreme Court ruled that Staley was entitled to the defense of unwitting possession.[19]

The U.S. Court of Appeals for the District of Columbia fully examined the problem of constructive possession in *United States v. Lucas.*

C A S E　Did He Possess the Drugs?

U.S. v. Lucas
67 F.3d 956, 314 U.S.App.D.C. 262 (D.C. 1995)

After a trial by jury, Charles Lucas, the defendant, was convicted, in the United States District Court for the District of Columbia, of possession with intent to distribute at least 100 grams of heroin, possession of marijuana, and knowingly and intentionally making his apartment available for the purpose of unlawfully manufacturing, storing, distributing, and using heroin. Lucas appealed. The Court of Appeals reversed.

EDWARDS, CJ.

FACTS

In late 1991, a team of police officers searched an apartment in southeast Washington, D.C., and found drugs, drug paraphernalia, cash, and a gun concealed in a number of places, whereupon they arrested Alphonso Lucas ("Al") who was in the apartment at the time. Al's cousin, Charles Lucas, the appellant in this case, had rented the apartment in 1977. But appellant had moved out of the apartment in 1984, at which time he sublet the residence to Al. From 1984 until 1992 appellant lived with his wife in their home in Temple Hills, Maryland, and he worked as a correctional counselor in the D.C. Department of Corrections. There is no evidence that he had any regular connection with the apartment, other than occasionally collecting rent from Al. Indeed, he did not even retain a key to the apartment.

Even though appellant had vacated the apartment in 1984, had no ongoing contact there, and had no apparent connection to the drugs, paraphernalia, and cash found there, he was arrested and indicted for possession of marijuana, possession of heroin with intent to distribute, and knowingly and intentionally making the apartment available for drug trafficking. It is undisputed that appellant remained the nominal "tenant" of the apartment, but the Government offered no other meaningful evidence to connect him to the apartment or the activities therein. Rather, the Government attempted to prove appellant's knowledge of drugs and drug-dealing in the apartment through a single, ambiguously dated laundry receipt and some undated, randomly discovered fingerprints. Despite the prosecution's lack of any meaningful evidence, the jury convicted appellant on all three counts.

The indictment, returned against Charles Lucas on December 19, 1991, charged appellant and his cousins, Al and Gregory Lucas ("Greg"), each with one count of possession with intent to distribute at least 100 grams of heroin, and one count of possession of marijuana. . . . Just before opening statements on March 9, 1992, Al Lucas pleaded guilty to the two drug possession counts. Appellant and Greg Lucas then proceeded to trial before a jury. The Government presented little evidence linking appellant to the apartment in the months or even years before the raid. The Government did not dispute that appellant had moved out of the apartment in 1984, and had lived with his wife in Temple Hills, Maryland, ever since. Appellant and his wife testified that he sublet the apartment informally to Al, because Al was "family" and could not rent an apartment himself due to his bad credit history. Al either paid directly or reimbursed appellant for paying the post-1984 rent and utility bills, which the Government introduced. The Government stipulated that Al forged appellant's signature on the money orders used to pay bills. The apartment manager explained the need for this arrangement by testifying that the landlord does not permit subletting and insists that checks or money orders used to pay rent bear the lessee's name.

In an attempt to show that appellant occasionally had entered the apartment after moving out, the Government introduced a laundry receipt found in a bedroom closet that bore the handwritten name "C. Lucas" and argued that it was dated "7/25/91." On cross-examination, the officer who presented the receipt conceded that he had no personal knowledge of its age, and that the year could have been "81," but opined that it looked more like "91." Neither this nor any other evidence contradicted appellant's testimony that he rarely visited the apartment and did not have a key. If he needed to pick up money for rent or bills from Al, appellant testified that he would usually call ahead and meet Al at the door or in the parking lot. Appellant said he would occasionally briefly enter the apartment to use the bathroom, but he never saw drugs or drug paraphernalia. Almost all the drugs and drug paraphernalia found by the police were hidden in a locked cabinet, in a safe in a closet, in a shoe box under a bed, and in the pocket of a jacket in a closet. Only one small wax-paper packet of heroin was found unconcealed. So, even if appellant had occasionally entered the apartment between 1984 and 1991, there was nothing to suggest that he would have seen any drugs.

The Government introduced evidence to prove the presence of drugs and drug paraphernalia at the apartment. But the prosecutor could not connect them to appellant. Appellant's fingerprints were found on the shoe box, but the Government could not date the prints, and Al's and Greg's fingerprints were also on the box. Appellant explained that during a brief visit "quite a while" ago, he had seen the shoe box, opened it, and set it down after seeing only women's shoes in it. While no other drug-related evidence bore appellant's fingerprints, the locked cabinet bore the fingerprints of Al and Greg. The police also found a key in the apartment that later turned out to open a bank safe deposit box containing a large amount of cash. However, the evidence showed that appellant had never entered the safe deposit box, and was not among those authorized to open it.

The court denied appellant's motion for judgment of acquittal, but did acquit Greg. On March 12, 1992, the jury convicted appellant of all three counts. On May 12, 1992, the court sentenced appellant to two terms of 63 months and one term of 12 months of incarceration to run concurrently, to be followed by three consecutive terms of supervised release.

On January 7, 1993, appellant moved for a new trial. The District Court denied the motion on October 18, 1993. This appeal was deferred until resolution of post-conviction proceedings in the District Court. Unfortunately, this caused part of the three-and-a-half-year delay between appellant's conviction and argument on his appeal. Appellant has now served approximately 42 months of his 63-month sentence. . . . At the time of trial appellant was 48 years old, and had been employed as a correctional counselor for the D.C. Department of Corrections for the last eight years. Before that he had been a police officer, a railroad brakeman, and had been in the army. During trial, appellant attempted to present two character witnesses, but the court struck the testimony. . . .

OPINION

In assessing the sufficiency of the evidence, we do not lightly overturn a jury's determination of guilt. We review the evidence *de novo* [starting over as if the evidence had not been reviewed], in a light most favorable to the Government and we determine whether "any rational trier of fact could have found the essential elements of the crime beyond a reasonable doubt." After careful consideration of the record in this case, we conclude that, even under this highly deferential standard, no rational jury could have found that the Government proved appellant's knowledge of the drugs or drug paraphernalia beyond a reasonable doubt.

The Government does not contend that appellant had actual possession of the marijuana or heroin. Therefore, we look for evidence of constructive possession, which "requires that the defendant knew of, and was in a position to exercise dominion and control over, the contraband." *United States v. Byfield*, 928 F.2d 1163, 1166 (D.C.Cir.1991). "The essential question is whether there is 'some action, some word, or some conduct that links the individual to the narcotics and indicates that he had some stake in them, some power over them.'" The heroin possession count also charged appellant with aiding and abetting in violation of 18 U.S.C. § 2 (1988). To prove aiding and abetting the Government must demonstrate "sufficient knowledge and participation to indicate that [the defendant] knowingly and wilfully participated in the offense in a manner that indicated he intended to make it succeed." Therefore, if appellant did not know of the presence of drugs in the apartment, he cannot be guilty of possessing marijuana, or of possessing heroin with intent to distribute, either as a principal or as an accessory. . . .

At oral argument the Government conceded that the fingerprints on the shoe box were the only evidence tending to link appellant to the drugs and the drug paraphernalia. Indeed, of the various drug stashes, only the shoe box contained appellant's fingerprints. However, the box also contained fingerprints of Greg and Al. The Government could not date any of the prints and conceded that fingerprints remain on items for extended periods of time. The Government presented nothing to link appellant to the locked cabinet, the safe, or the bank safe deposit box, which together held most of the incriminating evidence. Neither could the Government link appellant to the six wax-paper packets of heroin found in a jacket in a closet or to the one packet of heroin found on the floor.

The evidence tended to show that Al had actual possession of the drugs in the apartment. Al was appellant's subtenant and cousin. The Government could show nothing more about their relationship. The jury had no evidence that appellant was particularly close to Al, saw him regularly, or was in a position to know that Al concealed drugs or drug paraphernalia at the apartment. The mere act of subletting the apartment to his cousin does not prove knowledge. If it did, anyone who rents an apartment to a relative could be liable for the tenant's misconduct.

In certain circumstances, juries may infer that a person exercises constructive possession over items found in his home. However, it is undisputed that appellant moved out of the apartment about seven years before the police raid. Though appellant remained the tenant of record, his subtenant paid the rent and the utility bills. The fact that appellant left behind some personal papers and mementos dating from 1982 and earlier showed only that he lived in the apartment before 1984.

The Government's sole evidence that appellant may have entered the apartment anytime close to the November 20, 1991 raid was an ambiguously dated laundry receipt. Even assuming that the date was "7/25/91," the receipt would only permit the jury to conclude that appellant may have entered the apartment at some time in the four months before the raid. That does not prove that he knew about the concealed drugs and drug paraphernalia. The Government presented no evidence of how long the drugs and drug paraphernalia had been present in the apartment.

Overall, the evidence indicated that appellant had very little connection to the apartment: he moved out seven years ago, he did not have a key, he only occasionally met his cousin, he rarely entered the apartment, and, when he did so, he stayed only briefly. No witness testified to having seen appellant in or near the apartment. While generally "[m]ere proximity to the drugs or association with others possessing drugs will not suffice" to prove constructive possession, *Byfield*, 928 F.2d at 1166, here the Government could not even prove appellant's proximity to the drugs and had no evidence that his association with Al was related to drugs. Therefore, we hold that evidence adduced at trial was insufficient to support the verdict as a matter of law. No rational jury could find beyond a reasonable doubt that appellant knew that drugs and drug paraphernalia were hidden in the apartment. The verdict was based on pure speculation, and it cannot stand. ("A jury is entitled to draw a vast range of reasonable inferences from evidence, but may not base a verdict on mere speculation.")

The courts of appeals have not been hesitant to reverse convictions where the evidence does not suffice to prove one or more of the elements of the alleged crime. In this case, knowledge is fundamental, because without knowledge there could be no criminal purpose or intent. Obviously, absence of proof of knowledge is fatal to the Government's case. For example, despite evidence stronger than present here, the court in *United States v. Onick*, 889 F.2d 1425, 1431 (5th Cir.1989) (as amended Feb. 6, 1990), reversed, *inter alia* [among other reasons], for insufficient evidence of knowledge of drugs, a conviction of a defendant who was arrested at, but did not live in, an apartment containing drugs. See also *United States v. Zeigler*, 994 F.2d 845, 848 (D.C.Cir.1993) (The court reversed a conviction based on constructive possession of drugs for insufficient evidence of knowledge or control of drugs that were found in a locked briefcase in a locked laundry room of an apartment where defendant was frequently present.); *United States v. Clavis*, 956 F.2d 1079, 1093-94, (11th Cir.) (The court held that evidence that defendant had lived on the premises where drugs were found five days after his arrest, and that he had distributed cocaine elsewhere, was insufficient to support a § 856(a)(1) conviction that requires proof that defendant knowingly maintained the premises for proscribed purposes.), cert. denied, 504 U.S. 990, 112 S.Ct. 2979, 119 L.Ed.2d 597 (1992); *United States v. Johnson*, 952 F.2d 1407, 1411-12 (D.C.Cir.1992) (The court found insufficient evidence of constructive possession of drugs and reversed a conviction where the defendant was arrested in codefendant's apartment in which drugs and paraphernalia were in plain view, and defendant was found with $127 cash but no drugs on his person; the court held that the evidence failed to demonstrate a special relationship between defendant and codefendant, and that there was no basis for imputing to defendant any control over the drugs found in codefendant's apartment.).

Here, there can be no doubt that the evidence was insufficient to prove knowledge. Indeed, at oral argument, Government counsel could offer no plausible argument to connect appellant to drugs found at the apartment. Appellant, no less than Greg, should have received the benefit of a judgment of acquittal. Instead, he has spent almost four years in jail for crimes that the Government did not come close to proving.

Appellant's convictions are hereby reversed because the evidence adduced at trial was insufficient to support the verdict as a matter of law. No rational jury could find beyond a reasonable doubt that appellant knew of the concealed drugs or drug paraphernalia. The District Court shall enter a judgment of acquittal forthwith, and appellant shall be promptly released without conditions. The mandate in this case shall be issued with the issuance of this opinion.

So ordered.

QUESTIONS FOR DISCUSSIONS

1. List all of the facts relevant to deciding whether Lucas possessed heroin and marijuana.

2. How does the court define constructive possession?

3. Summarize the court's arguments for holding that Lucas didn't possess heroin and marijuana. Do you agree? Defend your answer.

4. Assume you are the prosecutor. Relying on the facts, argue that Lucas did possess the heroin and marijuana.

NOTE CASES

1. On August 18, 1989, Wayne Byfield and a young girl took Amtrak's "Night Owl" train from New York to Washington, D.C. Thomas Maher, an Amtrak detective, testified that Byfield and the young girl sat together and talked quietly during the trip. Maher followed them off the train and into Union Station. He testified that they looked "very nervous." Byfield had no luggage, but the young girl carried a tote bag. They stood next to each other and talked as they rode an escalator from the train platform. Byfield then moved ahead of the girl in the station, but she approached him again and had a brief conversation while they walked "very swiftly." Byfield went ahead, looking back at the girl and pushing downward with both hands, evidently motioning her to stay back away from him.

Maher observed Byfield repeat these furtive hand gestures at least two more times. Detective Maher alerted two Metropolitan Police Department ("MPD") detectives on duty at Union Station. Maher and Detective Zattau approached the girl, who was approximately 20–30 feet behind Byfield at this time. Zattau described her as "very hesitant and very nervous" when they talked with her, and testified that "[s]he would look in front of her and . . . up ahead of her towards Mr. Byfield." When asked if she had a ticket, the girl apparently pointed to Byfield. During a consensual search of her tote bag, the detectives found a shoe box for Etonics Transam trainers (size $8\frac{1}{2}$ men's, white and light grey) containing an old pair of New Balance shoes and six plastic bags holding over 600 grams of crack cocaine. The tote bag also contained men's clothing (all size extra-large), but no women's clothing.

William Buss, the other MPD detective, approached Byfield outside the station near the taxicab waiting area. When questioned, Byfield said that he lived in New York and was planning to stay in Washington, D.C. for a couple of days. Byfield added that he had traveled alone and carried no luggage because he had clothing at the place he was going to visit. Byfield consented to a pat-down search and left after Buss found nothing on him. About 15 minutes later, Detective Maher saw Byfield sitting on a wall across the street and proceeded to arrest him. Byfield was wearing a "muscle shirt" (like those found in the tote bag), shorts, and new Etonic running shoes matching the model, size, and color of those identified on the shoe box found in the tote bag. (Byfield insists that the government never tried to definitively link the shoes he was wearing with the shoe box in the tote bag.)

Wayne Byfield was charged . . . with one count of possession with intent to distribute more than 50 grams of cocaine base, in violation of 21 U.S.C. § 841(a)(1) & (b)(1)(A)(iii). At a jury trial commencing on December 6, 1989, the government presented testimony from the detectives involved in the case, along with expert testimony to the effect that it is "a very common practice" for adults to use young people as drug couriers because of the lesser penalties faced by juveniles. . . . Was Byfield guilty of possessing cocaine? Yes, according to the U.S. Court of Appeals:

. . . [O]ur review of the evidence presented by both sides convinces us that a reasonable jury could find Mr. Byfield guilty of constructive possession. Constructive possession requires that the defendant knew of, and was in a position to exercise dominion and control over, the contraband, "either personally or through others." The essential question is whether there is "some action, some word, or some conduct that links the individual to the narcotics and indicates that he had some stake in them, some power over them." Mere proximity to the drugs or association with others possessing drugs will not suffice. . . . There is ample evidence from which a jury could infer that they were in fact traveling together. In defense counsel's opening statement, Byfield's attorney argued that Byfield was planning to travel with [a man named] Larry and the girl, but that Larry backed out at the last moment. This is consistent with the behavior observed by the detectives on the train and in

the station. There is also evidence that Byfield exercised some control over the girl as they walked through the station, especially by signaling her to stay behind him. Although such conduct may not be as strong as prior cases where the defendant had exercised control over the drugs themselves, it suffices to prove control over the person carrying the drugs. Here, we do not have a case where the defendant merely sat beside or was acquainted with a person carrying contraband.

The government also points to the shoes, which it contends strongly tied Byfield to the tote bag and the cocaine. They add that other circumstantial evidence also linked Byfield to the contents of the tote bag (e.g., the men's clothing generally consistent with his size). Finally, the government points to expert testimony describing the modus operandi of using juveniles as couriers. All of this circumstantial evidence removes any potential doubts raised by the direct evidence concerning a controlling connection between Byfield and the girl. As defense counsel points out, however, Byfield's general cooperativeness distinguishes this from previous constructive possession cases where there was clearer evasion of the police, but that alone would not make constructive possession unavailable on these facts. Although hardly conclusive, the evidence introduced by both the government and the defense in this case would allow a reasonable jury to convict the defendant on a theory of constructive possession.

United States v. Byfield, 928 F.2d 1163 (D.C. Cir. 1991)

2. The Omaha Police Department was engaged in a reverse sting operation. Kevan Barbour, a narcotics officer, sold crack cocaine to parties who approached him. After the purchase, Barbour signaled fellow officers, who arrested the purchasers. Earl Clark approached Officer Barbour, asking for a "twenty" ($20 worth of crack cocaine). Barbour handed Clark a sack. After examining it, Clark handed it back, saying it was "too small." Barbour then handed Clark a larger sack. According to Barbour, Clark then handed him $20. Barbour signaled for the arrest. While being arrested, Clark dropped the crack. In a trial without a jury for possessing crack cocaine, the court believed Barbour's testimony and convicted Clark.

According to Clark's testimony, he handed back the first package because it was too small. But, when given the larger package, he held it for about a minute and a half while trying to decide whether to buy it. Officer Barbour snatched the $20 from him and signaled for the arrest. Did Clark criminally possess the smaller package? If his story is true, did Clark possess the larger package of crack? *State v. Clark,* 236 Neb. 475, 461 N.W.2d 576 (1990)

3. Leonard Dawkins was convicted of possession of heroin and "controlled paraphernalia." The police testified that when they entered a Baltimore, Maryland, hotel room, Dawkins held a tote bag in his hand. The police searched the bag, finding in it narcotics paraphernalia and a bottle cap containing heroin residue. Dawkins testified that the tote bag belonged to his girlfriend, who had asked him to carry the bag to her hotel room. He testified further that he had arrived only a few minutes before the police and that he did not know what was in the bag. Dawkins's girlfriend produced a receipt for the purchase of the bag and testified that she owned the bag. The trial court refused Dawkins's request for an instruction to the effect that knowledge was a requirement of criminal possession. The Maryland statute prohibits "possession of controlled substances." It is silent on intent, but it defines possession as "the exercise of actual or constructive dominion or control over a thing by one or more persons."

   Did Dawkins criminally possess heroin and controlled substance paraphernalia, even if he did not know the bag contained them? The Maryland Supreme Court decided that he did not. It said in part: "[A]n individual ordinarily would not be deemed to exercise 'dominion or control' over an object about which he is unaware. Knowledge of the presence of an object is normally a prerequisite to exercising dominion or control." *Dawkins v. State,* 313 Md. 638, 547 A.2d 1041 (1988)

4. Seattle police armed with a search warrant entered Velma Sykes's boyfriend's apartment and found her sleeping in a bedroom with her two children. Sykes's boyfriend was not present. In a second bedroom police found marijuana in matchboxes stacked on a nightstand. In the closet were both men's and women's clothes and more matchboxes with marijuana. Did Sykes possess the marijuana? The trial court found her guilty of possession of marijuana. On appeal, Sykes argued that she did not know the marijuana was in the apartment. The Supreme Court of Washington held that mere constructive possession is sufficient to impose liability for possession of controlled substances. Washington and North Dakota are the only two states that do not require knowledge as an element of possession. *State v. Cleppe,* 96 Wash. 2d 373, 635 P.2d 435 (1981)

5. In the summer of 1997, INN News (Fox Television) advertised for intelligent, fast-thinking women who appeared young, but who were over 18 years of age. Jennifer Hersey, a 20-year-old woman who appeared quite youthful, was hired. Her duties were to pose as a 13-year-old girl and to talk on the Internet with persons seeking sexual encounters with underage women. Hersey referred to such persons as "stalkers." Hersey posed as two different girls, "Stacie" and "Lisa," and posted on the Internet biographical information, stating that each of them was 13 years old. Hersey then waited to be contacted by men. David Hatch, a kindergarten teacher in Oceanside, California, was one of the men who contacted her. After much communication on line, they finally met. During the meeting, Hatch masturbated; Hersey photographed him; the police arrested him.

   Hatch was charged with violating section 311.11, subdivision (a) of the California Penal Code, which proscribes knowingly possessing any matter depicting a person under 18 years of age engaging in or simulating sexual conduct knowing that the matter depicts a person under 18 years of age. This count was based on computer and floppy discs containing digitized photographs seized by police during the search of Hatch's home. An expert who viewed the pictures embedded on the floppy discs opined the pictures qualified as child pornography. As long as Hatch knew the digitized photographs depicted persons under age 18 engaging in sexual conduct, the precise dates on which he may have last viewed the photographs is irrelevant.

Was there enough evidence to prosecute Hatch for possession of child pornography? Yes, according to the California Court of Appeals:

There was ample evidence to support the inference Hatch knew the digitized photographs depicted persons under age 18 engaging in sexual conduct. First, there was evidence Hatch was able, at some point in time, to view the photographs. The expert testified that although Hatch's computer did not have the software needed to view the photographs on the discs, the photographs could be viewed either elsewhere or by reinstalling the necessary software, and the photographs had at one time been viewable on Hatch's computer. Other evidence also supports the inference Hatch had the capability of viewing images that, like the images on the floppy disks, were digitized photographs. For example, Lisa electronically transmitted a digitized picture of herself to Hatch during their initial September 15, 1997, conversation and Hatch responded "wow lisa!!! you are beautiful!!!!". He also told Lisa three days later that he masturbated while "looking at [her] pretty picture." Hatch also sent Lisa a "JPG" formatted digitized picture of a nude girl, apparently under 18, and asked Lisa whether she had "pointy and pink nipples like [the girl depicted in the photograph]," which was a detail Hatch could not have known unless he had viewed the transmitted photograph at some point in time. Finally, a trier of fact could infer that Hatch, having manifested a clear interest in younger girls, would not have possessed these images and a computer capable of viewing them without having viewed them.

Because the evidence permits the inference Hatch had the ability to and did view the proscribed photographs, we consider whether a person viewing these photographs would have known they depicted persons under the age of 18 years engaged in the sexual conduct. The evidence showed that at least one photograph on the floppy discs depicted a child engaged in sexual conduct with an adult male. This child was so young, the court, in striking the expert's statement the child appeared to be five or six years old, stated "for someone obviously small, then I don't need an expert opinion; if someone is five or six years old, I don't think that's beyond the expertise of the average person." Other photographs depicting young participants were also found on the discs. The evidence permits the inference that a viewer of these photographs would have known the depicted participants were under the age of 18 years.

Hatch v. Superior Court, 94 Cal.Rptr.2d 453 (Cal.App. 2000)

Punishing criminal possession strikes at future harm. It aims to prevent possessors from putting prohibited items and substances to use, like taking drugs, shooting guns, and using burglary tools. The law of criminal possession is based on the belief that preventive justice is the best justice. It parallels the medical belief that prevention is better than cure. Nevertheless, the crime of possession runs against the grain of a basic premise—our criminal law punishes people only for what they *have done*, not for what they *might do*. The mere possession of drugs, weapons, and other prohibited substances and objects is not action, it is a passive state; and by itself it can do no harm. All the harm comes from doing something with whatever is possessed. The punishment of possession also increases the risk that criminal law will punish status and condition—the status or condition of dangerous persons. People who possess drugs, burglary tools, and the like are considered dangerous. The law of criminal possession punishes them for *being* burglars or drug addicts, not for *committing* burglary or *using* illegal drugs. Throughout history when fears of violence, illegal drug use, and disorder increase, preventive justice plays a larger part in the making of criminal law. One way to measure public fear is to examine the breadth of the law of criminal possession.[20]

The objections that criminal possession punishes future actions and status have led to the recommendation that possession should qualify as *actus reus* only when possessors know that they are in possession of substances and objects that unambiguously threaten serious bodily harm. According to this view, the criminal law appropriately includes the prohibition against the possession of guns, explosives, and, increasingly, a number of illegal drugs. The possession of obscene materials, on the other hand, does not threaten serious bodily harm; therefore, the criminal law should not include it. In addition, proponents of a limited definition of criminal possession as *actus reus* maintain that the criminal law ought to exclude substances or items that possessors may use for either harmless or harmful purposes. These include burglary tools, such as lock picks, and drug paraphernalia, such as hypodermic needles and pipes.

SUMMARY

Crimes are of two general types: crimes of conduct and crimes that require that criminal conduct cause a particular harmful result. Crimes of conduct comprise three elements: *actus reus, mens rea,* and concurrence. Crimes requiring the causing of a particular result have two elements in addition to the three just named: causation and resulting harm. As a practical matter, the prosecution must prove each element beyond a reasonable doubt in order to convict defendants. Each element is also the basis for a general principle of criminal liability. So, the element of *actus reus* of a particular crime, such as shooting or stabbing in murder, also reflects the general principle of *actus reus*. The *mens rea* of the intent to kill also reflects the general principle of *mens rea,* and so on for each of the elements in particular crimes.

The *actus reus* includes voluntary bodily movements; omissions, or failures to perform legal duties; and possession. The meanings of these types of *actus reus* vary from jurisdiction to jurisdiction. Whether sleepwalking and hypnosis are voluntary movements, whether harms resulting from failures to act are based on legal duties, and whether criminal possession requires knowledge of the thing possessed and whether it requires actual possession or the much broader constructive possession—the answers to these questions alter the reach of criminal law. In times of public fear of crime, these definitions work to expand the criminal law. In times of public calm, definitions confine the criminal law in narrower bounds. Therefore, the definitions of *actus reus,* like the definitions of all of the principles of criminal law, bear heavily on criminal policy, reflecting the basic values that a community hopes its criminal law will uphold and protect.

 Go to the Criminal Law 7e CD-ROM for Internet exercises.

REVIEW QUESTIONS

1. Identify the two types of crime and the elements of each that give rise to the general principles of criminal liability.

2. Identify, and fully explain, all of the general principles of criminal liability.

3. What are the purposes of the requirement of *actus reus* as an element in criminal liability?

4. Under what circumstances might a status satisfy the *actus reus* requirement?

5. What are the reasons for excluding thoughts from *actus reus*?

6. Under what circumstances might an involuntary act satisfy the *actus reus* requirement?

7. When can words amount to *actus reus*?

8. Explain when and why omissions can qualify as *actus reus*. What are the two forms criminal omissions can take?

9. When can possession qualify as *actus reus*?

KEY TERMS

actual possession—physical possession; on the possessor's person.

actus reus—the criminal act or the physical element in criminal liability.

American bystander rule—there is no legal duty to rescue or call for help to aid someone who is in danger even if helping poses no risk whatsoever to the potential rescuer.

causation—concurrence between criminal conduct and criminal result.

concurrence—the requirement that *actus reus* must join with *mens rea* to produce criminal conduct or that conduct cause a harmful result.

constructive possession—legal possession or custody of an item or substance.

crimes of cause and result—crimes in which criminal conduct (the joining of a criminal act with a criminal intent) causes a harm that the law specifically prohibits.

crime of criminal conduct—an act triggered by criminal intent.

criminal omission—two forms: (1) mere failure to act or (2) failure to intervene in order to prevent a serious harm.

elements of crime—the parts of a crime that the prosecution must prove beyond a reasonable doubt, such as *actus reus, mens rea,* concurrence, causation, and harmful result.

general principles of criminal liability The theoretical foundation for the elements of *actus reus, mens rea,* concurrence, causation, and harm.

Good Samaritan doctrine—doctrine that imposes a legal duty to render or summon aid for imperiled strangers.

harmful result—a harm defined by criminal law.

knowing possession—awareness of physical possession.

manifest criminality—the requirement in law that intentions have to turn into criminal deeds to be punishable.

mens rea—the mental element in crime, including purpose, knowledge, recklessness, and negligence.

mere possession—physical possession.

SUGGESTED READINGS

1. George Fletcher, *Rethinking Criminal Law* (Boston: Little, Brown, 1978), pt. II. A thorough and thought-provoking discussion of the principles of criminal liability. Difficult in places but worth the effort.

2. Jerome Hall, *General Principles of Criminal Law,* 2d ed. (Indianapolis, Ind.: Bobbs-Merrill, 1960). Difficult but rewarding reading.

3. Hyman Gross, *A Theory of Criminal Justice* (New York: Oxford University Press, 1979), chap. 4. Untangles knotty questions surrounding *actus reus.*

4. American Law Institute, *Model Penal Code and Commentaries* (Philadelphia: American Law Institute, 1985), pt. I. The fullest treatment of the general principles of criminal liability.

5. Rollin M. Perkins and Ronald N. Boyce, *Criminal Law,* 3d ed. (Mineola, N.Y.: Foundation Press, 1982), chaps. 6 and 7. A straightforward analysis of *actus reus, mens rea,* and causation.

NOTES

1. Oliver Wendell Holmes, *The Common Law* (Boston: Little, Brown and Company, 1963), pp. 45–47.

2. Paul H. Robinson and Jane A. Grall, "Element Analysis in Defining Criminal Liability: The Model Criminal Code and Beyond," *Stanford Law Review* 35 (1983):681–762, esp. 691–705.

3. See Herbert Morris, *On Guilt and Innocence* (Los Angeles: University of California Press, 1976), chap. 1, "Punishing Thoughts."

4. Glanville Williams, *Criminal Law,* 2d ed. rev. (London: Stevens and Sons, 1961), pp. 1–2.

5. *Hales v. Petit,* 1 Plowd. 253, 259; 75 Eng. Rep. 387, 397 (cannot punish thoughts); George Fletcher, *Rethinking Criminal Law* (Boston: Little, Brown and Company, 1978), pp. 115–116 (manifest criminality).

6. Fletcher, *Rethinking Criminal Law,* p. 117.

7. Holmes, *The Common Law,* pp. 46–47.

8. Narrated in Norval Morris, "Somnambulistic Homicide: Ghosts, Spiders, and North Koreans," *Res Judicata* 5 (1951):29.

9. Joseph Goldstein et. al., *Criminal Law: Theory and Process* (New York: Free Press, 1974), p. 766.

10. Samuel Butler, *Erewhon* (New York: Modern Library, 1927), pp. 104–111.

11. George Fletcher, *Rethinking Criminal Law*, p. 635.

12. Wayne R. LaFave, *Criminal Law*, 2d ed. (St. Paul, Minn.: West Publishing Co., 1986), p. 203.

13. *State v. Kuntz* 995 P.2d 951 (2000).

14. Ibid., pp. 581–633.

15. This excerpt is based largely on A.M. Rosenthal, *Thirty Eight Witnesses*, (Berkeley: University of California Press, 1999).

16. Bib Latane and John Darley, *The Unresponsive Bystander: Why Doesn't He Help?* (New York: Appleton-Crofts, 1970), pp. 1–2.

17. *New York Times,* April 16, 1977, p. 25; July 25, 1995, p. B-1; August 5, 1995, p. 4; A.M. Rosenthal, *Thirty-Eight Witnesses,* (Berkeley: University of California Press, 1999), Introduction.

18. American Law Institute, *Model Penal Code and Commentaries,* vol. 1 (Philadelphia: American Law Institute, 1985), p. 24; See also *Jenkins v. State,* 215 Md. 70, 137 A.2d 115 (1957) for a case that adopts the mere possession rule.

19. *State v. Staley,* 123 Wash.2d 794, 872 P.2d 502 (1994).

20. *Robinson v. California,* 370 U.S. 660 82 S.Ct. 1417, 8 L.Ed.2d 758 (1962); Fletcher, *Rethinking Criminal Law,* pp. 202–205.

The General Principles of Criminal Liability: *Mens Rea,* Concurrence, Causation

Chapter Outline

I. Introduction

II. Determining *Mens Rea*

III. Four Levels of *Mens Rea*

IV. Concurrence

V. Causation

VI. Grading Offenses

VII. Summary

CHAPTER MAIN POINTS

1. The requirement of a criminal intent ensures that only the blameworthy receive criminal punishment.

2. The principle of *mens rea* includes four levels of culpability—purpose, knowledge, recklessness, and negligence.

3. Strict liability crimes don't require proof of *mens rea* because they impose lesser penalties than other crimes and because they endanger large numbers of persons.

4. The principle of concurrence requires that *mens rea* prompt action in crimes of criminal conduct and that criminal conduct cause a particular result in crimes of cause and result—crimes requiring the causation of a particular result.

5. The principle of causation requires proof of both factual and legal causation.

6. *Mens rea* is the principal means of grading the seriousness of an offense.

Was He Guilty if He Didn't Know about an Open Bottle in Someone Else's Car?

Police officers stopped Steven Loge for speeding. During a routine search of the automobile, the officers found a nearly empty bottle of beer in a brown paper bag underneath the front passenger seat. Based on this finding, they charged Loge with keeping an open bottle containing intoxicating liquor in an automobile. At trial, Loge testified that the car he was driving belonged to his father and that he, as well as others, had driven it for the past two weeks. He also testified that the open bottle did not belong to him and that he did not know it was in the car.

INTRODUCTION

The idea that a criminal intent (**mens rea**) has to accompany *actus reus* is fundamental to criminal liability. The child's "I didn't mean to" captures this basic idea that to be punishable actions have to be blameworthy or culpable. So does Justice Holmes's remark that "Even a dog distinguishes between being stumbled over and being kicked." *Mens rea* is the most complex concept in criminal law. In 1931, Professor Francis Sayre summed up the history of *mens rea,* in words that are just as true today: "No problem of criminal law is of more fundamental importance or has proved more baffling through the centuries than the determination of the precise mental element or *mens rea.*"[1]

Several things account for the complexity of *mens rea.* First, courts and legislatures define *mens rea* in varying and confusing terminology. According to the Commentary on *mens rea* accompanying the Alabama Criminal Code:

> It would be impossible to review, much less reconcile and make clear and uniform, the myriad of Alabama statutes and cases that have employed or discussed some term of mental culpability. Such mental terms and concepts, while necessarily difficult to articulate, sometimes have been vaguely or only partly defined, or otherwise seem imprecise or inconclusive, unclear or ambiguous, even confusing or contradictory, or over refined with technical, obscure and often subtle, if not dubious, distinctions. These adverbial terms include, e.g.: "intentionally," "willfully," "purposely," "designedly," "knowingly," "deliberately," "maliciously," "with premeditation," "recklessly," "negligently," "with culpable negligence," "with gross negligence," "with criminal negligence," "without due caution," "wickedly," "unlawfully," "wrongfully" and scores of others.[2]

Second, there are four levels of *mens rea.* Third, *mens rea* can relate to one or more elements of particular crimes. So, it is possible that one state of mind is required for *actus reus,* another for causation, and still another for circumstance elements. Fourth, proving *mens rea* can create difficult practical problems for prosecutors in criminal cases.[3]

DETERMINING *MENS REA*

Intent is invisible. The finest instruments of modern technology can't detect it. Electroencephalograms can record brain waves, and X-rays can photograph brain tissue, but the medieval judge's words still ring true: "The thought of man is not triable, for the devil himself knoweth not the thought of man." St. Thomas Aquinas put it even more pointedly: "Man, the framer of human law, is competent to judge only of outward acts, because man seeth those things that appear . . . while God alone, the framer of the Divine law, is competent to judge of the inward movement of wills."[4]

Confessions are the only direct evidence of *mens rea*. Since defendants rarely confess their true intentions, proof of *mens rea* has to rely on indirect evidence, that is, **circumstantial evidence**. Action is the most common circumstantial evidence. In everyday experience, we rely on people's actions to tell us their intentions. For example, most people don't break into strangers' houses at night unless they intend to commit crimes. Thus, the acts of breaking into and entering someone else's house allows us to draw the reasonable inference that the intruder intends to commit a crime while inside. Hence, we can know indirectly what people intend by observing directly what they do.

FOUR LEVELS OF *MENS REA*

Courts and legislatures don't define *mens rea* precisely or consistently. Instead, they use a host of vague terms to identify the mental element. For example, one survey found that the United States Criminal Code used 79 separate words and phrases to define *mens rea*. All of these definitions boil down to four mental states of intent that qualify as *mens rea*: general, specific, transferred, and constructive intent.[5]

General intent refers to crimes of criminal conduct. Specifically, general intent refers to the intent to commit the criminal act. For example, the *actus reus* in burglary is breaking and entering, in larceny the taking and carrying away of another's property, and in rape sexual penetration. **Specific intent** applies to crimes of cause and result. So, in addition to the intent to commit the criminal act, specific intent includes the intent to cause a particular result, such as homicide, which requires the intent to cause death. **Transferred intent** applies to cases in which actors intend to harm one victim but instead harm another. For example, if Nathan shoots at his enemy Doug but hits Michelle when she steps in front of Doug to block the shot, the law transfers Nathan's intent to kill Doug to the intent to kill Michelle. Transferred intent is sometimes called "bad aim intent" because the cases frequently involve misfired guns; however, the law also transfers intent in other situations. If Matt intends to burn down Michael's restaurant but mistakenly burns down Paul's house instead, Matt has committed arson. Only the intent to cause similar harms transfers. The intent to assault a man by throwing a rock at him doesn't transfer to the intent to break a window when the rock intended to hit the man hits the window instead. **Constructive intent** refers to cases in which actors cause harms greater than they intend or expect. For example, if Laila drives above the speed limit on an icy street and her car veers out of control, killing Irmgard, Laila has the constructive intent to kill.[6]

The *Model Penal Code* has refined these four types of intent in its *mens rea* provision. After enormous effort and sometimes heated debate, the drafters sorted out, identified, and defined four criminal mental states. From most to least blameworthy, they are:

1. Purpose
2. Knowledge
3. Recklessness
4. Negligence

The Model Code levels of **culpability** are roughly equivalent to but more elaborate and precise than general, specific, transferred, and constructive intent. The *Code* specifies that all crimes requiring a mental element (some do not) must include one of these mental states. They are defined in Section 2.02, reproduced here.

§ 2.02.
General Requirements of Culpability.
1. Minimum Requirements of Culpability. . . . [A] person is not guilty of an offense unless he acted purposely, knowingly, recklessly or negligently . . . with respect to each material element of the offense.
2. Kinds of Culpability Defined
   a. *Purposely.* A person acts purposely with respect to a material element of an offense when:
      i. if the element involves the nature of his conduct or a result thereof, it is his conscious object to engage in conduct of that nature or to cause such a result; and
   b. *Knowingly.* A person acts knowingly . . . when:
      i. if the element involves the nature of his conduct . . . he is aware that his conduct is of that nature . . . and
      ii. if the element involves a result of his conduct, he is aware that it is practically certain that his conduct will cause such a result.
   c. *Recklessly.* A person acts recklessly with respect to a material element of an offense when he consciously disregards a substantial and unjustifiable risk that the material element exists or will result from his conduct. The risk must be of such a nature and degree that, considering the nature and purpose of the actor's conduct and the circumstances known to him, its disregard involves a gross deviation from the standard of conduct that a law-abiding person would observe in the actor's situation.
   d. *Negligently.* A person acts negligently with respect to a material element of an offense when he should be aware of a substantial and unjustifiable risk that the material element exists or will result from his conduct. The risk must be of such a nature and degree that the actor's failure to perceive it, considering the nature and purpose of his conduct and the circumstances known to him, involves a gross deviation from the standard of care that a reasonable person would observe in the actor's situation. . . .[7]

PURPOSE

Purpose in *mens rea* is roughly the same as the everyday "you did that on purpose." Translated into criminal law, it means the specific intent either to engage in crimes of criminal conduct or to act with the conscious object of causing a particular result in crimes of cause and result. For example, common-law burglary requires that the burglar break into and enter a house on purpose, and larceny requires that the thief take and carry away another's property on purpose. In murder, the murderer's "conscious object" is the victim's death. The court in *State v. Stark* examined the mental state of purpose required in the Washington assault statute.

C A S E   Did He Expose His Victims to HIV on Purpose?

State v. Stark,
66 Wash.App. 423, 832 P.2d 109 (1992)

Calvin Stark was convicted in the Superior Court of two counts of second-degree assault for intentionally exposing his sexual partners to the human immunodeficiency virus (HIV), and he appealed. The Court of Appeals affirmed and remanded the case for resentencing.
PETRICH, CJ.

FACTS

On March 25, 1988, Calvin Stark tested positive for HIV, which was confirmed by further tests on June 25 and on June 30, 1988. From June 30, 1988, to October 3, 1989, the staff of the Clallam County Health Department had five meetings with Stark during which Stark went through extensive counseling about his infection. He was taught about "safe sex," the risk of spreading the infection, and the necessity of informing his partners before engaging in sexual activity with them. On October 3, 1989, Dr. Locke, the Clallam County Health Officer, after learning that Stark had disregarded this advice and was engaging in unprotected sexual activity, issued a cease and desist order as authorized by RCW 70.24.024(3)(b).

Stark did not cease and desist, and, consequently, on March 1, 1990, Dr. Locke went to the County prosecutor's office. . . . The prosecutor . . . had Dr. Locke complete a police report. The State then charged Stark with three counts of assault in the second degree under RCW 9A.36.021(1)(e). [RCW 9A.36.021(1)(e) provides:

"(1) A person is guilty of assault in the second degree if he or she, under circumstances not amounting to assault in the first degree: . . .
(e) With intent to inflict bodily harm, exposes or transmits human immunodeficiency virus as defined in chapter 70.24 RCW; . . ."]

Each count involved a different victim:
Count One: The victim and Stark engaged in sexual intercourse on October 27 and October 29, 1989. On both occasions, Stark withdrew his penis from the victim prior to ejaculation. The victim, who could not become pregnant because she had

previously had her fallopian tubes tied, asked Stark on the second occasion why he withdrew. He then told her that he was HIV positive.

Count Two: The victim and Stark had sexual relations on at least six occasions between October, 1989, and February, 1990. Stark wore a condom on two or three occasions, but on the others, he ejaculated outside of her body. On each occasion, they had vaginal intercourse. On one occasion Stark tried to force her to have anal intercourse. They also engaged in oral sex. When she told Stark that she had heard rumors that he was HIV positive, he admitted that he was and then gave the victim an AZT pill "to slow down the process of the AIDS."

Count Three: The victim and Stark had sexual relations throughout their brief relationship. It was "almost nonstop with him," "almost every night" during August 1989. Stark never wore a condom and never informed the victim he was HIV positive. When pressed, Stark denied rumors about his HIV status. The victim broke off the relationship because of Stark's drinking, after which Stark told her that he carried HIV and explained that if he had told her, she would not have had anything to do with him.

. . . At the jury trial, the victim in count one testified to her contacts with Stark and the jury received Dr. Locke's deposition testimony regarding the Health Department's contacts with Stark. Stark did not testify. In the bench trial [trial without a jury], Dr. Locke testified. There the State also presented the testimony of one of Stark's neighborhood friends. She testified that one night Stark came to her apartment after drinking and told her and her daughter that he was HIV positive. When she asked him if he knew that he had to protect himself and everybody else, he replied, "I don't care. If I'm going to die, everybody's going to die."

The jury found Stark guilty on count one. A second trial judge found Stark guilty of the second and third counts at a bench trial. On count one, Stark was given an exceptional sentence of 120 months based on his future danger to the community. The standard range for that offense was 13 to 17 months. On counts two and three, Stark was given the low end of the standard range, 43 months each, to be served concurrently, but consecutively to count one.

OPINION

. . .

Stark contends that there is insufficient evidence to prove that he "exposed" anyone to HIV or that he acted with intent to inflict bodily harm. Since Stark is undisputedly HIV positive, he necessarily exposed his sexual partners to the virus by engaging in unprotected sexual intercourse. The testimony of the three victims supports this conclusion.

The testimony supporting the element of intent to inflict bodily harm includes Dr. Locke's statements detailing his counseling sessions with Stark. With regard to the first victim, we know that Stark knew he was HIV positive, that he had been counseled to use "safe sex" methods, and that it had been explained to Stark that coitus interruptus will not prevent the spread of the virus. While there is evidence to support Stark's position, all the evidence viewed in a light most favorable to the State supports a finding of intent beyond a reasonable doubt. The existence of noncriminal explanations does not preclude a finding that a defendant intended to harm his sexual partners.

With regard to the later victims, we have, in addition to this same evidence, Stark's neighbor's testimony that Stark, when confronted about his sexual practices, said, "I don't care. If I'm going to die, everybody's going to die." We also have the testimony of the victim in count two that Stark attempted to have anal intercourse with her and did have oral sex, both methods the counselors told Stark he needed to avoid. See also *Commonwealth v. Brown,* — Pa.Super. —, 605 A.2d 429 (1992) (Defendant threw his feces into face of prison guard. Court found that there was sufficient evidence to support finding of intent to inflict bodily harm when defendant had been counseled by both a physician and a nurse about being tested HIV positive and that he could transmit the virus through his bodily fluids.); *State v. Haines,* 545 N.E.2d 834 (Ind.App.1989) (sufficient evidence to convict of attempted murder when defendant, knowing he was HIV positive, spit, bit, scratched, and threw blood at officer); *Scroggins v. State,* 198 Ga.App. 29, 401 S.E.2d 13 (1990) (sufficient evidence to convict of aggravated assault with intent to murder when defendant, knowing he was HIV positive, sucked up excess sputum, bit an officer, and laughed about it later); *Zule v. State,* 802 S.W.2d 28 (Tex.App.1990) (sufficient evidence that defendant transmitted virus to victim).

. . .

Stark also contends that the trial court erred in imposing an exceptional sentence based solely on future dangerousness. [Washington has a guidelines scheme of sentencing. Judges can sentence outside the guidelines if they provide written reasons for doing so. According to Washington law, "[t]he reasons must be substantial and compelling. . . . Once substantial and compelling factors exist to support an exceptional sentence, the length of the sentence is left to the discretion of the sentencing court."]

The trial court reasoned:

2. By his behavior the defendant has not demonstrated that he will do anything to protect others. He has and he will continue to be a danger to those persons with whom he comes into contact. His past behavior as outlined in testimony and exhibits indicates that he presents a grave risk to the community.

3. The purpose[s] of the Sentencing Reform Act include imposing sufficient punishment upon the offender and protecting the public. Given the history of this defendant and corroborating evidence, the Court concludes that the defendant presents extreme danger to the community. It is the Court's conclusion that the threat posed to the community by this defendant is greater than that which could be ameliorated by incarceration for a period of time limited to the standard range (13 to 17 months).

While future dangerousness is an appropriate factor when there is a demonstrated history of similar criminal acts coupled with a finding of nonamenability to treatment, the Washington Supreme Court has recently held that future dangerousness is an inappropriate factor for justifying an exceptional sentence in nonsexual offense cases. As the State did not convict Stark of a sexual offense, it cannot use a finding of future dangerousness to justify an exceptional sentence.

Furthermore, the trial court abused its discretion in imposing a 10-year sentence. In order to commit this crime, a person has to know he or she is HIV positive, know how the virus is transmitted, and engage in activity with intent to cause harm.

Although such conduct is by nature very serious and reprehensible, the Legislature fixed the same relatively light standard range term that applies in all other second degree assault cases. Significantly, since "transmitting" the virus is an alternative means of committing the offense, the standard range remains the same even if the victim acquires the virus.

Here, there was no evidence that as of the date of the trial that any of the victims had contracted the virus, and Stark's conduct does not seem to be the "worst possible" example of this offense. The trial court, therefore, abused its discretion in imposing a 10-year term. Cf. *State v. Farmer,* 116 Wash.2d 414, 431-32, 805 P.2d 200, 812 P.2d 858 (1991) (upholding exceptional 7½-year sentence based on finding of deliberate cruelty where defendant knowingly exposed his two minor victims to HIV).

"The standard to be used when determining whether a case should be remanded for resentencing is if the appellate court deems the invalidated facts to be facts upon which the trial court placed considerable weight in determining the sentence, then remand is necessary. As future dangerousness was the only basis for the exceptional sentence imposed, this court must remand for resentencing on count one within the standard range.

. . .

We affirm the convictions, but remand for resentencing on count one.

QUESTIONS FOR DISCUSSION

1. Identify all of the facts relevant to determining Stark's *mens rea.*
2. Using the common-law definition of specific intent and the *Model Penal Code* definitions of purposely, knowingly, recklessly, and negligently, and relying on the relevant facts, identify Stark's intention with respect to his acts.
3. Is motive important in this case?
4. Do you agree that the sentence should fall within the standard range, or was it proper to make it more severe, as the trial court did? Defend your answer.

Disturbed by what appears to be a trend in church burning, race and ethnic violence, and gay bashing, many state legislatures have passed church burning, hate crime, ethnic intimidation, gay bashing, and similar criminal laws. For example, a commission in California concluded that "minorities had been harassed, intimidated, assaulted, and even murdered in virtually every part of the state, and further found that the rate of such hate crimes was increasing, and that existing laws were inadequate to protect Californians from hate-motivated violence." A statute followed that created heavy criminal penalties aimed at both preventing and punishing "acts of hate violence." The court in *Commonwealth v. Barnette* applied the Massachusetts hate crime statute to a race and ethnic altercation.

C A S E | **Did He Assault for the Purpose of Ethnic Intimidation?**

Commonwealth v. Barnette
45 Mass.App.Ct. 486, 699 N.E.2d 1230 (1998)

Aubrey Barnette was convicted by a jury in the District Court Department, Concord Division, Middlesex County, of two counts of assault and battery for purpose of intimidation and two counts of threatening to commit a crime. Defendant appealed the convictions and the denial of a motion for new trial. The Appeals Court affirmed.

LENK, J.

FACTS

In the early evening of September 21, 1995, Maria Acuna (Acuna) was working at her computer on the second floor of her home in Lexington, where she had been living with her son, Israel Rodriguez (Rodriguez), since May, 1995. The defendant, Aubrey Barnette, was next door at his sister's house babysitting his niece. Acuna heard a loud noise, like someone banging or shaking a wooden fence, looked out her window, and saw the defendant trying to enter her back yard to retrieve his niece's ball. Concerned that the defendant was going to break her fence, Acuna called through the window to the defendant to please not trespass, and that she would come downstairs to help him out.

The defendant shouted, "You bitch, I just came to pick up my ball." Acuna went downstairs and walked into her backyard, and observed that the defendant had entered her yard, and was turning to leave. As the defendant left her yard, he repeatedly called her a "bitch" and told her that she could keep the ball the next time. Acuna walked towards the fence to latch the gate and the defendant said: "You bitch. You don't fit here. What are you doing here, you damn Mexican. Why don't you go back to your country? All of you come and get our jobs and our houses. Get out of here. You don't fit here. I'll kill you and your son." The defendant's tirade continued in the same vein: "I am a black man. I have been living here for seven years. I can go inside your house or anyplace I want to. Because nobody will stop me, you bitch, and I will kill you if you say something. Why don't you just go back to your country? Why don't you just go back to Mexico? You don't fit here. . . . By the way, do you speak English? Greasy bitch."

While standing next to the fence shouting at Acuna, the defendant thrust his fist towards her face so that she "could almost feel the hit of his fist" in her nose and face. The defendant then threw his fingers in a forking motion towards her, coming to within an inch of her eyes. The defendant was yelling at Acuna so loudly that Rodriguez awoke from his nap and came outside to the backyard. Rodriguez testified that he could hear the defendant shouting "fuck," "shit," and "Mexican," "Get the hell out of the country," "You don't belong here," and "Mexicans don't belong here" at his mother. He pulled his mother away from the fence and demanded to know from the defendant what was going on. The defendant now attempted to hit Rodriguez with his fists, from the other side of the fence, rattling the gate, trying to enter the backyard, and saying: "You little shit. Come up here. I'm going to take the fucking shit out of you and your mother together. I will beat you both to death." The defendant continued saying, "Damn Mexicans. What are you doing here?" Acuna and Rodriguez both testified that they felt afraid and threatened by the defendant's rage and determination to hit them.

At the time of the incident, the defendant's neighbor, Michael Townes, was barbecuing in his backyard, approximately twenty feet away. Townes heard the defendant yell at Acuna and Rodriguez "You should go back to where you're from," and refer to "whupping" Rodriguez's ass. Townes came over and, smelling alcohol on the defendant's breath, told the defendant to "Let it go" and to go home and "sleep it off." Townes put his hands on the defendant and led him away. Rodriguez went inside and, after calling Townes to express his gratitude, called the police.

Officer Paul Callahan responded to the call and arrived at Acuna's residence to find her and her son visibly upset. Callahan filed an incident report and tried, unsuccessfully, to locate the defendant. The next day, Detective Charles Mercer returned to the neighborhood and interviewed the defendant. In response to the detective's questions, the defendant asserted that he entered the yard to retrieve the ball only after knocking on the fence and not receiving a response, that Acuna had appeared and yelled at him for not going around to ring the bell, and that he did not swear at or threaten Acuna. Nonetheless, the defendant did admit that he had said that Acuna should "go back to where she came from," but claims to have said it to his neighbor Townes, not directly to Acuna.

OPINION

. . .

General Laws c. 265, § 39, as inserted by St.1983, c. 165, § 1, is a so-called "hate crime" statute. It provides that "[w]hoever commits an assault or a battery upon a person . . . for the purpose of intimidation because of said person's race, color, religion, or national origin, shall be punished. . . ." As instructed by the trial judge, the essential elements of the crime are: (1) the commission of an assault or battery (2) with the intent to intimidate (3) because of a person's race, color, religion, or national origin. In general, a hate crime is "a crime in which the defendant's conduct was motivated by hatred, bias, or prejudice, based on the actual or perceived race, color, religion, national origin, ethnicity, gender, or sexual orientation of another individual or group of individuals." Thus, hate crime laws such as G.L. c. 265, § 39, operate to "enhance the penalty of criminal conduct when it is motivated by racial hatred or bigotry." It is not the conduct but the underlying motivation that distinguishes the crime.

Here, the defendant was convicted of assaulting the victims for the purpose of intimidation. The intent required by G.L. c. 265, § 39, was not only that required to establish the underlying assault, i.e., the intent either to cause a battery or to cause apprehension of immediate bodily harm, but also the intent to intimidate because of the victim's membership in a protected class. The defendant argues that, in order to satisfy the intimidation element, the Commonwealth was required to but did not prove that he had the specific intent to put Acuna and Rodriguez in fear for the purpose of compelling or deterring their conduct.

The defendant urges us, in construing G.L. c. 265, § 39, to employ a definition of "intimidation" that has been used in the context of the Massachusetts Civil Rights Act, G.L. c. 12, § 11H. There, the concept of intimidation has been defined as "putting in fear for the purpose of compelling or deterring conduct." We decline the invitation. General Laws c. 12, § 11H, is not a criminal statute. It provides a civil cause of action against those who interfere or attempt to interfere with a person's constitutional rights by threats, intimidation, or coercion. In the context of c. 12, § 11H, intimidation describes the prohibited conduct itself and not any underlying intent. We discern neither reason nor necessity to transplant this definition of intimidation to the hate crime at issue. *Webster's Third New International Dictionary* 1184 (1993), to which this court often resorts in construing criminal statutes, defines the verb intimidate as: "to make timid or fearful: inspire or affect with fear."

The defendant next argues that, if intimidation does not mean to compel or deter the victim's conduct but simply means to put the victims in fear, the intimidation element of the hate crime becomes redundant of the intent requirement of the underlying assault. The intent requirement of the underlying assault, namely, the intent to cause a battery or to cause apprehension of an imminent battery, would not, however, standing alone, be sufficient to satisfy the intimidation element of G.L. c. 265, § 39. The latter is satisfied only by establishing that the defendant had the specific intent to put his victims in fear because of their membership in a protected class, not simply the intent to put them in fear of an imminent battery. There is no redundancy here.

At trial, Acuna and Rodriguez both testified that, throughout the altercation that gave rise to this case, the defendant repeatedly called them "damn Mexicans," and demanded that they "[g]et out of here." Acuna testified that the defendant verbally attacked her, saying that she should go back to her country and that he would kill her and her son. Rodriguez testified that the defendant told him that he was going to beat up Rodriguez and his "bitchy" mother. Both Acuna and Rodriguez also testified that they felt threatened by the defendant's behavior. The Commonwealth presented ample evidence that the defendant assaulted Acuna and Rodriguez with the intent to intimidate them because of their national origin in violation of c. 265, § 39. A rational trier of fact could find that the defendant's repetition of the phrase "damn Mexican," accompanied by his repeated demand that Acuna and Rodriguez "Get out of here," demonstrated a purpose of intimidation because of the victims' national origin. The trial judge did not err in denying the defendant's motion for a required finding of not guilty.

The defendant also contends that the trial judge erred in not reading the Model Jury Instruction on specific intent, as a supplement to the judge's instructions on the crime of assault or battery for the purpose of intimidation. Although the defendant failed to object to this omission at trial, he now claims that it created a substantial risk of a miscarriage of justice. The judge's instructions to the jury here were brief. The instructions on all six charges against the defendant take up only three pages of trial transcript. Although the judge did not dwell on the subtleties of each element of the crimes charged, he did correctly explain all the necessary elements. The judge explained to the jury, for example, that one of the three elements of assault or battery for the purpose of intimidation is that the defendant acted "for the purpose of intimidation." He explained that one of the three elements of threatening another person with a crime is that the defendant communicated "an intent to injure . . . now or in the future," and, with respect to the assault charges, the judge explained to the jury that they must find "that the defendant intended to commit a battery" or that the defendant "intended to put Maria Acuna or Israel Rodriguez in fear of an imminent battery." It is not necessary for a judge "to refer to the defendant's specific intent to do something as an element of a crime. A reference to intent is sufficient." Although an instruction on specific intent very well might have given the jury better guidance in their deliberations, its omission did not create a substantial risk of a miscarriage of justice.

. . .

The defendant contends that his outburst at Acuna and Rodriguez was motivated by his anger at being called a trespasser and was not motivated by any anti-Mexican sentiment. The defendant believes that the fact that his niece is of Puerto Rican descent demonstrates that he lacks any anti-Hispanic bias or prejudice. The uncontroverted evidence at trial, however, was that the defendant was shouting specifically anti-Mexican slurs at Acuna and Rodriguez, not that he expressed any more generalized anti-Hispanic animus. Moreover, the evidence submitted in conjunction with the defendant's motion for new trial established merely that the defendant's niece was of Puerto Rican descent not that the defendant thought favorably of Puerto Ricans or Hispanics in general. The trial judge found that the fact that the defendant has an Hispanic niece was not necessarily relevant to whether the victims in the instant case were subjected to racial invective and actions on the part of the defendant. . . . The trial judge did not err in denying the defendant's motion for new trial.

Judgments affirmed. Order denying motion for new trial affirmed.

QUESTIONS FOR DISCUSSION

1. List all of the facts relevant to determining whether the crime was motivated by ethnic hatred.
2. Does the defendant have a point when he argues that the crime was motivated by the trespass and not ethnic hatred? Explain.
3. It was objected in this case, as it is frequently in hate crime cases, that the statutes violate guarantees of free speech. Do you agree? Defend your answer.
4. Which of the following do you think is the best response to acts motivated by group hatred: Punishing them as hate crimes? Increasing the penalty for existing crimes if hate motivated the crime? Keeping the criminal law out of the business of punishing hate, relying instead on informal sanctions against prejudice? Defend your choice.

KNOWLEDGE

You can't intend to cause harm without knowing it, but you can knowingly cause harm without intending it. So, a surgeon who removes a cancerous uterus to save a pregnant woman's life knowingly kills the fetus in her womb. But killing the fetus is not the purpose (conscious object) of the removal. Rather, the death of the fetus is an unwelcome side effect to removing the cancerous uterus. Similarly, treason, the only crime defined in the U.S. Constitution, requires that traitors provide aid and comfort to enemies *for the purpose of overthrowing the government.* Defendants may provide aid and comfort to enemies of the United States knowing that doing so is practically certain to contribute to overthrowing the government. But that isn't enough; they have to provide them for the purpose of overthrowing the U.S. government. If their conscious object was to get rich, then they haven't committed treason. The purpose requirement in treason led to the enactment of other statutes to fill the void, like making it a crime to provide secrets to the enemy, an offense that requires only that defendants purposely provide such secrets. The need to distinguish between knowledge and purpose arises most frequently in attempt, conspiracy, and solicitation (Chapter 6).

In *State v. Barnes* and the note case following it, the Oregon Court of Appeals grappled with the "knowing" requirement in the state's assault statute. These cases clearly show just how complicated the application of "knowingly" to the facts of specific cases can get.[8]

C A S E   Did He Knowingly Cause Injury?

State v. Barnes
150 Or.App. 128, 945 P.2d 627 (1997)

Edward Forrest Barnes, the defendant, was convicted following jury trial in the Circuit Court, Lincoln County, of resisting arrest and assault in the second degree. Defendant appealed. The Court of Appeals affirmed the conviction for resisting arrest and remanded for resentencing and reversed the conviction for assault in the second degree and remanded for a new trial.

De MUNIZ, J.

FACTS

The charges arose following an incident at the Newport Seafood and Wine Festival in February 1994. Defendant and his wife Debra were at the marina building with another couple, Dean and Dana Chase. Defendant had had four or five glasses of wine at the festival when, around 6:00 p.m., the incident started. Newport Chief of Police Rivers testified that breaking wine glasses had become "kind of a tradition" and that the crowd at the marina numbered about 3,500, the limit the security personnel tried to maintain. Rivers heard glass being broken in the area where defendant, his wife and the Chases were. Rivers sent officers Miller and Simpson to the area. Simpson testified that he asked Dana Chase to leave, and she refused. Simpson then physically removed her and outside, after she tried to slap and kick him, Simpson told her that she was under arrest. She tried to run, and when he caught her she continued to fight. Debra Barnes then jumped on his back, as did defendant. Simpson said that Miller took defendant off his back and, as Simpson rolled over, he saw defendant throwing punches at Miller.

Paul Rose was working as a security guard. He testified that he saw a police officer coming out with a female who was yelling and screaming and that he saw her try to slap and kick the officer and try to run. Rose testified that he saw Miller go down and that Rose stepped forward with his hands out, intending to keep the crowd back. Defendant struck Rose in the right eye. Rose suffered a "blow-out fracture" of the eye socket—a fracture of a thin layer of bone at the floor of the

socket. The injury resulted in double vision and required surgery. Rose still has some double vision and a "sunken" eye.

Defendant was indicted for "unlawfully and knowingly caus[ing] serious physical injury to Paul Rose" under ORS 163.175(1)(a), which provides: "(1) A person commits the crime of assault in the second degree if the person: (a) Intentionally or knowingly causes serious physical injury to another[.]" In turn, ORS 161.085(8) provides: "'Knowingly' or 'with knowledge,' when used with respect to conduct or to a circumstance described by a statute defining an offense, means that a person acts with an awareness that the conduct of the person is of a nature so described or that a circumstance so described exists."

OPINION

Defendant first assigns error to the denial of his requested jury instruction on assault in the second degree and to the instruction given. Defendant's requested instruction stated, in part, that, to find the crime of assault in the second degree, the state had to prove:

> "3. [Defendant] caused serious physical injury to Paul Rose. Serious physical injury means a physical injury that either (1) creates a substantial risk of death, or (2) causes serious and protracted disfigurement, or (3) causes protracted impairment of health, or (4) causes protracted loss or impairment of the function of any bodily organ; and
> "4. That the defendant caused said physical injury knowingly. To act knowingly in this case the defendant had to have acted with an awareness that his conduct would cause a serious physical injury. A person achieves a particular result knowingly when he is practically certain that his conduct will cause that result. A person who is aware of and consciously disregards a substantial and unjustifiable risk that a serious physical injury will occur acts recklessly, but not knowingly[.]"

The trial court rejected defendant's instruction, instead instructing the jury that

> "a person acts 'knowingly' if that person acts with an awareness that his or her conduct is of a particular nature. Oregon law provides that a person

commits the crime of Assault in the Second Degree if that person knowingly—I've defined the term 'knowingly'— causes serious physical injury—and I've defined 'serious physical injury'—to another. "In this case to establish Assault in the Second Degree, the State must prove beyond a reasonable doubt the following three elements:

"* * * * *

"Number three, that [defendant] knowingly caused serious physical injury to Paul Rose."

The court also gave the state's special instruction:

"You are instructed when knowingly suffices to establish a culpable mental state, it is also established if a person acts intentionally."

Neither party makes an argument specifically directed to that instruction. However, we note that "intent" and "knowledge" are distinct concepts under the criminal code.

Defendant argues that the statutory definitions of "intentionally," "recklessly" and "criminal negligence", ORS 161.085(7); ORS 161.085(9); ORS 161.085(10), all refer to "a result * * * described by a statute defining an offense," but that "result" is absent from the definition of "knowingly." Defendant contends, however, that assault in the second degree is a "result offense" and requires proof that the person knowingly caused serious physical injury. Defendant argues that the instructions given did not distinguish between conduct and result. He argues that the instructions must inform the jury that there must be proof beyond a reasonable doubt that he intended a serious physical injury to occur or that he was conscious of the result of the blow and was almost certain that a serious physical injury would occur. He further argues that here the instruction permitted the jury to find him guilty of assault in the second degree if they found that he knowingly struck Rose, even though he did not intend or was not almost certain that Rose would suffer serious physical injury from the blow.

The state responds that the court's elements instruction specifically stated that, to establish second-degree assault, the state had to prove that defendant "knowingly caused serious physical injury to Paul Rose." It argues that the court's instructions "tracked" the uniform jury instructions and relevant statutes and accurately stated the law. It contends that, given the juxtaposition of "knowingly" and "caused" in the instruction, as well as

the court's instruction that "a person acts 'knowingly' if that person acts with an awareness that his or her conduct is of a particular nature," the jury could not reasonably have understood the instructions to mean anything but that defendant had to be aware that his act of punching Rose in the face would cause serious physical injury. It argues that, taken as a whole, the instructions could not have been understood to mean that the state only had to prove that defendant knew he struck Rose in the face.

The drafters of the Oregon Criminal Code sought to restrict the concept of "knowingly" to awareness of the nature of one's conduct or to the existence of specified circumstances. Thus, ORS 161.085(8) specifically provides that the definition of "knowledge" applies "when [knowingly] is used with respect to conduct or to a circumstance described by a statute defining an offense[.]" However, despite that general definition, "knowingly" in ORS 163.175(1)(a) is not used with respect to conduct or a circumstance. It is used instead, as defendant contends, with a result.

. . .

Unlike sexual abuse, assault in the second degree under ORS 163.175(1)(a) proscribes a result—causing serious physical injury. The trial court concluded that one who intends the act must live with the consequences, i.e. that "you take the victim as you find them." However, the clear language of ORS 163.175(1)(a) does not proscribe conduct resulting in serious physical injury; it requires intentionally or knowingly causing that injury. Here, the trial court instructed the jury according to the statutory definition of "knowingly" and incorporated that definition in its instructions on the elements of assault in the second degree. However, the statutory definition of "knowingly" is restricted to awareness of conduct; it does not define awareness as to result. It is the result that must be proved for the offense of assault in the second degree, and an instruction using only the statutory definition of "knowingly" does not sufficiently inform the jury of the nexus between conduct and knowledge of the result of the conduct to satisfy the elements of ORS 163.175(1)(a).

. . .

Conviction for resisting arrest affirmed and remanded for resentencing; conviction for assault in the second degree reversed and remanded for a new trial.

QUESTIONS FOR DISCUSSION

1. List all of the facts relevant to determining Barnes's state of mind.
2. According to the court, what *mens rea* does the assault statute require?
3. Explain why it makes a difference whether assault is a crime of criminal conduct or a crime of causing a result.
4. Explain the difference between the defendant's requested instruction and the one the trial court gave. According to the court, what is wrong with the instruction that the trial court gave? Should it make a difference? Defend your answer.

NOTE CASE

Pete Jantzi, the defendant, accompanied Diane Anderson, who shared a house with defendant and several other people, to the home of her estranged husband, Rex. While Diane was in the house talking with Rex, Jantzi was using the blade of his knife to let the air out of the tires on Rex's van. Another person put sugar in the gas tank of the van. While the Andersons were arguing, Diane apparently threatened damage to Rex's van and indicated that someone might be tampering with the van at that moment. Rex's roommate ran out of the house and saw two men beside the van. He shouted and began to run toward the men. Rex ran from the house and began to chase Jantzi, who ran down a bicycle path. Jantzi, still holding his open knife, jumped into the bushes beside the path and landed in the weeds. He crouched there, hoping that Rex would not see him and would pass by. Rex, however, jumped on top of defendant and grabbed his shirt. They rolled over and Rex was stabbed in the abdomen by defendant's knife. Jantzi could not remember making a thrusting or swinging motion with the knife; he did not intend to stab Rex.

An indictment charged that Jantzi "did unlawfully and knowingly cause physical injury to Rex Anderson by means of a deadly weapon, to-wit: knife, by stabbing the said Rex Anderson with said knife." According to the same Oregon assault statute as that in *State. v. Barnes,* "A person commits the crime of assault in the second degree if he intentionally or knowingly causes physical injury to another . . ."

Did Jantzi knowingly assault Rex Anderson? The trial court said yes. But, according to the appellate court:

> Although the trial judge found defendant guilty of "knowingly" causing physical injury to Anderson, what he described in his findings is recklessness. The court found that defendant knew he had a dangerous weapon and that a confrontation was going to occur. The court believed that defendant did not intend to stab Anderson. The court's conclusion seems to be based on the reasoning that because defendant knew it was possible that an injury would occur, he acted "knowingly." However, a person who "is aware of and consciously disregards a substantial and unjustifiable risk" that an injury will occur acts "recklessly," not "knowingly. Recklessly causing physical injury to another is assault in the third degree.

State v. Jantzi, 56 Or.App. 57, 641 P.2d 62 (1982)

STANDARDS FOR DETERMINING PURPOSE AND KNOWLEDGE

Most jurisdictions apply a subjective standard to determine whether defendants intentionally or knowingly engaged in conduct or caused harmful results. The rationale for the subjective standard is that culpability for serious criminal conduct ought to depend on what defendants *actually* intended or knew, not on what reasonable people *would have* intended or should have known. Some jurisdictions adopt an objective standard for determining purpose and knowledge. For example, the Washington state criminal code provides:

> A person acts knowingly or with knowledge when:
> (i) he is aware of a fact, facts, circumstances or result . . . ; or
> (ii) he has information which would lead a reasonable man in the same situation to believe that facts exist.[9]

The Michigan code permits objective criteria in determining *mens rea* but only for the purpose of inferring the actual intent of defendants. According to the statute, a person acts

> intentionally with respect to a result or conduct . . . when his conscious objective is to cause that result or engage in that conduct. In finding that a person acted intentionally with respect to a result the finding of fact may rely upon proof that such result was the natural and probable consequence of the person's act.[10]

RECKLESSNESS AND NEGLIGENCE

Reckless people consciously (knowingly) create *risks* of harm; they don't intend to cause harm itself. **Recklessness** resembles purpose and knowledge because it requires conscious action. But consciously creating the risk of harm isn't as blameworthy as acting either with the purpose to cause harm itself or with the knowledge that a harmful result is practically certain to follow. Recklessness deals in probabilities; purpose and knowledge, in certainties.

Recklessness requires more than awareness of ordinary risks; it requires awareness of *substantial* and *unjustifiable* risks. The American Law Institute's *Model Penal Code* proposes that fact finders determine recklessness according to a two-pronged test:

1. Were defendants aware how substantial and unjustifiable the risks that they disregarded were? Under this prong, notice that even a substantial risk isn't by itself reckless. For example, a doctor who performs life-saving surgery has created a substantial risk. But the risk is justifiable because the doctor took it to save the life of the patient. This prong doesn't answer the important questions of *how* substantial and *how* unjustifiable the risk amounts to recklessness. So, the second prong gives guidance to juries.

2. Does defendants' disregard of risk amount to so "gross [a] deviation from the standard" that a law-abiding person would observe in that situation? This prong requires juries to make the judgment whether the risk is substantial and unjustifiable enough to deserve condemnation in the form of criminal liability.

This test has both a subjective and an objective component. The first prong of the test is subjective; it focuses on a defendant's actual awareness. The second prong is objective; it measures conduct according to how it deviates from what reasonable people do.

Actual harm isn't the conscious object of reckless wrongdoers. In fact, most reckless actors probably hope that they don't hurt anyone. Or, at most, they don't care if they hurt anyone. But the heart of their culpability is that in the full knowledge of the risks, they act anyway. For example, in one case, a large drug company knew that a medication it sold to control high blood pressure had caused severe liver damage and even death in some patients; it sold the drug anyway. The company's officers, who made the decision to sell the drug, didn't want to hurt anyone (indeed, they hoped no one would die or suffer liver damage). They sought only profit for the company. But they were prepared to risk the deaths of their customers in order to make a profit.[11]

Like reckless wrongdoers, negligent wrongdoers create risks of harm. But there is a critical difference between them. Negligent wrongdoers *should* know that they are creating risks, but they don't *actually* know it. So, recklessness is conscious risk creation; **negligence** is unconscious risk creation. The standard for negligence is wholly objective—actors should have known, even though in fact they did not know, that they were creating risks. For example, a reasonable person should know that driving fifty miles an hour down a crowded street creates a risk of harm, even though in fact the driver doesn't know it. The driver who should know this but doesn't is negligent. The driver who knows it but drives too fast anyway is reckless. Negligence, like **recklessness**, requires that defendants create substantial and unjustifiable risks, risks that grossly deviate from the ordinary standards of behavior.

C A S E | **Did He Kill His Wife Recklessly or Negligently?**

Koppersmith v. State
1999 Wl 463469 (Ala.Crim.App. 1999)

Gregory Thaddeus Koppersmith, the appellant, was charged with the murder of his wife, Cynthia ("Cindy") Michel Koppersmith. He was convicted of reckless manslaughter, a violation of § 13A-6-3(a)(1), Ala.Code 1975, and the trial court sentenced him to 20 years in prison. The Alabama Court of Appeals reversed and remanded.

BASCHAB, J.

FACTS

Koppersmith (appellant) and his wife were arguing in the yard outside of their residence. Cindy tried to enter the house to end the argument, but the appellant prevented her from going inside. A physical confrontation ensued, and Cindy fell off of a porch into the yard. She died as a result of a skull fracture to the back of her head.

In a statement he made to law enforcement officials after the incident, the appellant gave the following summary of the events leading up to Cindy's death. He and Cindy had been arguing and were on a porch outside of their residence. Cindy had wanted to go inside the house, but he had wanted to resolve the argument first. As she tried to go inside, he stepped in front of her and pushed her back. Cindy punched at him, and he grabbed her. When Cindy tried to go inside again, he wrapped his arms around her from behind to stop her. Cindy bit him on the arm, and he "slung" her to the ground. He then jumped down and straddled her, stating that he "had her by the head" and indicating that he moved her head up and down, as if slamming it into the ground. When Cindy stopped struggling, he rolled her over and found a

brick covered with blood under her head. The appellant stated that, although Cindy fell near a flowerbed, he did not know there were bricks in the grass.

At trial, the appellant testified that Cindy had tried to go into the house two or three times, but he had stopped her from doing so. During that time, she punched at him and he pushed her away from him. At one point, he put his arms around her from behind to restrain her, and she turned her head and bit him. When she bit him, he pulled her by her sweater and she tripped. He then "slung" her off of him, and she tripped and fell three to four feet to the ground. He jumped off of the porch and straddled her, grabbing her by the shoulders and telling her to calm down. When he realized she was not moving, he lifted her head and noticed blood all over his hands.

The appellant testified that, when he grabbed Cindy from behind, he did not intend to harm her. He also testified that, when he "slung" her away from him off of the porch, he was not trying to hurt her and did not intend to throw her onto a brick. Rather, he stated that he simply reacted after she bit his arm. He also testified that he did not know there were bricks in the yard, that he had not attempted to throw her in a particular direction, and that he was not aware of any risk or harm his actions might cause. He further testified that, when he grabbed and shook her after she fell, he did not intend to harm her, he did not know there was a brick under her head, and he did not intend to hit her head on a brick or anything else. Instead, he testified that he was trying to get her to calm down.

The medical examiner, Dr. Gregory Wanger, testified that the pattern on the injury to the victim's skull matched the pattern on one of the bricks found at the scene. He stated that, based on the position of the skull fracture and the bruising to the victim's brain, the victim's head was moving when it sustained the injury. He testified that her injuries could have been caused by her falling off of the porch and hitting her head on a brick or from her head being slammed into a brick.

The indictment in this case alleged that the appellant "did, with the intent to cause the death of Cynthia Michel Koppersmith, cause the death of Cynthia Michel Koppersmith, by striking her head against a brick, in violation of § 13A-6-2 of the Code of Alabama. (C.R.11.)" The appellant requested that the trial court instruct the jury on criminally negligent homicide as a lesser included offense of murder. However, the trial court denied that request, and it instructed the jury only on the offense of reckless manslaughter.

OPINION

The appellant argues that the trial court erred in denying his request that it instruct the jury on criminally negligent homicide. An individual accused of the greater offense has a right to have the court charge on the lesser offenses included in the indictment, when there is a reasonable theory from the evidence supporting his position. . . . [E]very accused is entitled to have charges given, which would not be misleading, which correctly state the law of his case, and which are supported by any evidence, however, weak, insufficient, or doubtful in credibility.

Section 13A-6-3(a), Ala.Code 1975, provides that a person commits the crime of manslaughter if he recklessly causes the death of another person.

> A person acts recklessly with respect to a result or to a circumstance described by a statute defining an offense when he is aware of and consciously disregards a substantial and unjustifiable risk that the result will occur or that the circumstance exists. The risk must be of such nature and degree that disregard thereof constitutes a gross deviation from the standard of conduct that a reasonable person would observe in the situation. A person who creates a risk but is unaware thereof solely by reason of voluntary intoxication, as defined in subdivision (e)(2) of Section 13A-3-2 acts recklessly with respect thereto.

§ 13A-2-2(3), Ala.Code 1975. "A person commits the crime of criminally negligent homicide if he causes the death of another person by criminal negligence." § 13A-6-4(a), Ala.Code 1975.

> A person acts with criminal negligence with respect to a result or to a circumstance which is defined by statute as an offense when he fails to perceive a substantial and unjustifiable risk that the result will occur or that the circumstance exists. The risk must be of such nature and degree that the failure to perceive it constitutes a gross deviation from the standard of care that a reasonable person would observe in the situation. A court or jury may consider statutes or ordinances regulating the defendant's conduct as bearing upon the question of criminal negligence.

. . . The only difference between manslaughter under Section 13A-6-3(a)(1) and criminally negligent homicide is the difference between recklessness and criminal negligence. The reckless offender is aware of the risk and "consciously disregards" it. On the other hand, the criminally negligent offender is not aware of the risk created ("fails to perceive") and, therefore, cannot be guilty of consciously disregarding it. The difference between the terms "recklessly" and "negligently" . . . is one of kind, rather than degree. Each actor creates a risk or harm. The reckless actor is aware of the risk and disregards it; the negligent actor is not aware of the risk but should have been aware of it.

. . .

Thus, we must determine whether there was any evidence before the jury from which it could have concluded that the appellant did not perceive that his wife might die as a result of his actions. We conclude that there was evidence from which the jury could have reasonably believed that his conduct that caused her to fall was unintentional and that he was not aware he was creating a risk to his wife. He testified that, after she bit him, his reaction—which caused her to fall to the ground—was simply reflexive. He also testified that he did not know there were bricks in the yard. Even in his statement to the police in which he said he was slamming her head against the ground, the appellant said he did not know at that time that there was a brick under her head. Finally, he stated that he did not intend to throw her onto a brick or harm her in any way when he "slung" her, and that he did not intend to hit her head on a brick or otherwise harm her when he grabbed and shook her after she had fallen. Because there was a reasonable

theory from the evidence that would have supported giving a jury instruction on criminally negligent homicide, the trial court erred in refusing to
instruct the jury on criminally negligent homicide.
Thus, we must reverse the trial court's judgment
and remand this case for a new trial.
     REVERSED AND REMANDED.

QUESTIONS FOR DISCUSSION

1. List all of the facts relevant to determining
   Koppersmith's mental state with respect both
   to his acts and the results of his actions.
2. In your opinion, was Koppersmith reckless or
   negligent? Support your answer with relevant
   facts.
3. Is it possible to argue that Koppersmith
   knowingly or even purposely killed his wife?
   What facts, if any, support these two states of
   mind?

NOTE CASES

1. Robert Strong, 57 years old at the time of
   trial, had left his native Arabia at the age of
   19, emigrating first to China and then coming
   to the United States three years later. He had
   lived in Rochester only a short time before
   committing the acts which formed the basis
   for this homicide charge. He testified that he
   had been of the Sudan Muslim religious faith
   since birth, and had become one of the sect's
   leaders, claiming a sizable following. Defendant articulated the three central beliefs of
   this religion as "cosmic consciousness, mind
   over matter and physiomatic psychomatic
   consciousness." He stated that the second of
   these beliefs, "mind over matter," empowered
   a "master," or leader, to lie on a bed of nails
   without bleeding, to walk through fire or on
   hot coals, to perform surgical operations
   without anesthesia, to raise people up off the
   ground, and to suspend a person's heartbeat,
   pulse, and breathing while that person remained conscious. In one particular type of
   ceremony, defendant, purportedly exercising
   his powers of "mind over matter," claimed he
   could stop a follower's heartbeat and breathing and plunge knives into his chest without
   any injury to the person. There was testimony from at least one of defendant's follow-

ers that he had successfully performed this
ceremony on previous occasions. Defendant
himself claimed to have performed this ceremony countless times over the previous 40
years without once causing an injury. Unfortunately, on January 28, 1972, when defendant performed this ceremony on Kenneth
Goings, a recent recruit, the wounds from the
hatchet and three knives which defendant had
inserted into him proved fatal.

   Did Strong knowingly, recklessly, or negligently kill Goings? According to the majority
of the court:

The essential distinction between the crimes of
manslaughter, second degree, and criminally negligent homicide is the mental state of the defendant
at the time the crime was committed. In one, the
actor perceives the risk, but consciously disregards
it. In the other, he negligently fails to perceive the
risk. We view the record as warranting the submission of the lesser charge of criminally negligent
homicide since there is a reasonable basis upon
which the jury could have found that the defendant failed to perceive the risk inherent in his
actions.

   The defendant's conduct and claimed lack of
perception, together with the belief of the victim
and defendant's followers, if accepted by the jury,
would justify a verdict of guilty of criminally negligent homicide. There was testimony, both from defendant and from one of his followers, that the
victim himself perceived no danger, but in fact vol-
unteered to participate. Additionally, at least one
of the defendant's followers testified that the defendant had previously performed this ritual without causing injury. Assuming that a jury would
not believe that the defendant was capable of performing the acts in question without harm to the
victim, it still could determine that this belief held
by the defendant and his followers was indeed sin-
cere and that defendant did not in fact perceive
any risk of harm to the victim.

   According to the dissent:

Testimony was adduced that just prior to being
stabbed, Goings, a voluntary participant up to that
point, objected to continuance of the ceremony
saying "No, father" and that defendant, obviously
evincing an awareness of the possible result of his
actions, answered, "It will be all right, son." Defendant testified that after the ceremony, he noticed
blood seeping from the victim's wounds and that
he attempted to stop the flow by bandaging the

mortally wounded Goings. Defendant further stated that when he later learned that Goings had been removed to another location and had been given something to ease the pain, he became "up-tight," indicating, of course, that defendant appreciated the risks involved and the possible consequences of his acts.

Can it be reasonably claimed or argued that, when the defendant inflicted the several stab wounds, one of which penetrated the victim's heart and was four and three-quarter inches deep, the defendant failed to perceive the risk? The only and obvious answer is simply "no." Moreover, the record is devoid of evidence pointing toward a negligent lack of perception on defendant's part. *People v. Strong*, 37 N.Y.2d 568 (1975)

2. On September 11, 1996, Dean Michaud caused the death of Thomas Maki ("Maki") by drowning him in the St. John River in Frenchville, Maine. Prior to the incident, Maki had recently begun courting Michaud's former girlfriend, Barbie Ouellette ("Ouellette"). After an "on again, off again" romantic relationship that lasted approximately fourteen months, Michaud broke up with Ouellette for the third and final time on September 3, 1996. Maki met Ouellette during the same week and began spending time with her, much to Michaud's chagrin. Michaud became jealous because Ouellette showed a growing interest in Maki. After many unsuccessful attempts to salvage his relationship with Ouellette, Michaud asked Maki to accompany him to the St. John River to talk on September 11, 1996. An altercation broke out between Michaud and Maki in the shallow water near the rocky shore of the river. During the struggle, Michaud pushed or struck Maki and caused him to fall on his back and hit his head on the rocks. While grappling in the shallow water with Michaud on top of him, Maki inhaled water while his head was below the surface. At the time of the drown-

ing, Michaud was an eighteen-year-old student at the University of Maine at Fort Kent ("UMFK") and a citizen of New Brunswick, Canada. Maki was a twenty-year-old UMFK student. Michaud was approximately 6'4" tall and weighed around 180 to 200 pounds. Maki was 5'10" tall and weighed 150 pounds. An autopsy examination revealed numerous injuries to Maki's head, throat, neck, and back. Michaud had no injuries except for one or two small red spots on his face.

Was Michaud guilty of reckless homicide? Yes, according to the Maine Supreme Court:

Reckless manslaughter consists of "[r]ecklessly . . . caus[ing] the death of another human being." 17-A M.R.S.A. § 203(1). Recklessness involves a conscious disregard of risk that grossly deviates from "the standard of conduct that a reasonable and prudent person would observe in the same situation." 17-A M.R.S.A. § 35(3) (1983 & Supp.1998). . . . [I]t is reasonable to infer from the record that Michaud forcefully caused Maki to fall on his back and strike his head on rocks and that Maki inhaled water while Michaud straddled him and held his head under water. Such behavior certainly involves a conscious disregard of risk that grossly deviates from a reasonable and prudent standard of care, particularly in light of Michaud's size advantage over Maki.

The [trial] court found that "Michaud acted in conscious disregard that his actions created the risk of death to Maki, and his actions were a gross deviation from how a reasonable and prudent person would act under the circumstances." Upon "[v]iewing the evidence in the light most favorable to the State and drawing all reasonable inferences therefrom," the evidence was clearly sufficient to support a finding of recklessness beyond a reasonable doubt. Therefore, the [trial] court did not err in finding Michaud guilty of reckless manslaughter. Judgment of guilt and sentence of 19 to 20 years were affirmed. *State v. Michaud*, 724 A.2d 1222 (1998)

STRICT LIABILITY

Traditionally, criminal liability has required some degree of blameworthiness. But in large numbers of minor offenses, culpability is not required. In these **strict liability** (liability without *mens rea*) offenses, the prosecution has to prove only that defendants committed the criminal act and, in cause and result crimes, that the criminal act caused the harm set out in the statute. Proponents of traditional criminal law only reluctantly accept strict liability as legitimate. However, no court, including the U.S. Supreme Court, has questioned the authority of legislatures to create strict liability offenses in order to protect the "public health and safety." Legislatures may do so as long as they make clear that their intent is to impose liability without the *mens rea* requirement.

Two main arguments support strict liability. First, a strong public interest justifies eliminating *mens rea*. Strict liability arose during the industrial revolution when manufacturing, mining, and commerce exposed large numbers of the public to death, disability, and disease in the form of noxious gases, unsafe railroads and other workplaces, and adulterated foods and other products. Second, strict liability offenses carry minimum penalties, usually fines. The combined strong public interest and moderate penalty justify extending criminal liability to cases where there is no *mens rea,* according to supporters.[12]

Despite these arguments, opponents of strict liability criticize it on the grounds that it is too easy to expand it beyond public welfare offenses that seriously endanger the public. They also contend that strict liability weakens the force of criminal law because too many people acting innocently are caught within its net. In turn, this weakened force reduces respect for criminal law, which properly should punish only the blameworthy. The critics say that it does no good, and probably considerable harm, to punish those who have not purposely, knowingly, recklessly, or negligently harmed others. In the end, critics maintain, strict liability is inconsistent with the basic nature of criminal law: to serve as a stern moral code based on culpability. To punish those who accidentally injure others violates that moral code. The court decided whether Minnesota's open bottle law is a strict liability offense in *State v. Loge.*

C A S E | **Did He Have to "Know" There Was an Open Bottle in the Car?**

State v. Loge
589 N.W.2d 491, (Minn. App. 1999)

Steven Mark Loge (defendant) was convicted in the District Court, Freeborn County, of keeping an opened bottle of intoxicating liquor in an automobile while on a public highway, and he appealed. The Court of Appeals held that Loge could be convicted despite his lack of knowledge that an opened beer bottle was under the front seat of the borrowed pickup truck. Affirmed.

HOLTAN, J.

FACTS

In September 1997, Albert Lea police officers stopped Steven Mark Loge for speeding. During a routine search of the automobile, the officers found a nearly empty bottle of beer in a brown paper bag underneath the front passenger seat. Based on this finding, they charged Loge with keeping an open bottle containing intoxicating liquor in an automobile, in violation of Minn.Stat. § 169.122, subd. 3.

At trial, Loge testified that the car he was driving belonged to his father and that he, as well as others, had driven it for the past two weeks. He also testified that the open bottle did not belong to him and that he did not know it was in the car. Notwithstanding Loge's testimony, the trial court convicted him, reasoning that Minn.Stat. § 169.122, subd. 3, "creates an absolute liability for Mr. Loge to inspect and determine[,] when he is going to operate the pickup truck [,] whether there are any containers that would violate the open receptacle law in Minnesota."

On appeal, Loge claims the trial court erred in concluding that Minn.Stat. § 169.122, subd. 3, creates a strict liability offense. The state agrees with Loge and asks that the case be remanded for a determination of whether Loge knew the open bottle was in the car.

OPINION

This appeal raises an issue of statutory interpretation. The interpretation of statutes is a question of law, which this court reviews *de novo* [as if it had not been heard before]. Minn.Stat. § 169.122, subd. 2 (1996), imposes a general rule applicable to all occupants of a motor vehicle. It provides that "[n]o person shall have in possession while in a private motor vehicle upon a public highway, any bottle or receptacle containing intoxicating liquor . . . which has been opened." Possession means "either that the person had actual possession of the bottle or receptacle or that the person consciously exercised dominion and control over the bottle or receptacle." We agree with Loge that the legislature defined "possession" in a way that makes it clear that subdivision 2 of the statute requires proof that the occupants acted knowingly.

In contrast, subdivision 3, under which Loge was charged, imposes a limited rule applicable only to the owner of a private motor vehicle and to the driver if the owner is not present. It makes it unlawful for either one of them to "keep or allow to be kept in a motor vehicle when such vehicle is upon the public highway any bottle or receptacle containing intoxicating liquors . . . which has been opened." Minn.Stat. § 169.122, subd. 3 (1996). We conclude that unlike subdivision 2, subdivision 3 does not require proof of *mens rea*. Instead, it imposes an affirmative duty on the owner and the driver of a private motor vehicle, without regard to fault, to ensure compliance with the open bottle law. Had the legislature intended to subject the owner and the driver to the same liability as the occupants, it would have done so in subdivision 2.

Although strict liability offenses are disfavored, *Staples v. United States,* 511 U.S. 600, 606, 114 S.Ct. 1793, 1797, 128 L.Ed.2d 608 (1994), states may create strict liability by defining criminal offenses without an element of *scienter* [knowledge], see, e.g., *State v. Morse,* 281 Minn. 378, 380-82, 161 N.W.2d 699, 700-02 (1968) (excluding mistake of age as a defense to sexual conduct between an adult and a child under the age of consent). To impose criminal liability for conduct unaccompanied by fault, however, "the legislative intent to do so should be clear."

The legislature's intent to impose strict liability in this case is clear. A reading of Minn.Stat. § 169.122 (1996) as a whole suggests that by carving a special rule for the owner and the driver of a private motor vehicle, rather than including them within the general prohibition in subdivision 2, the legislature intended, in the exercise of its police power for the protection of the public at large, to distinguish between the liability of occupants, who do not have charge of the automobile, and the liability of the owner and the driver, who do. Specifically, the legislature intended to hold the owner and the driver strictly liable for failing to ascertain that the car contained no open bottles before it entered a public highway, while holding other occupants liable only if they acted knowingly.

. . .

[Furthermore,] Minn.Stat. § 169.122, subd. 3, like other provisions within the same chapter, is a regulatory statute designed to promote highway safety. The express language of subdivision 3 does not require proof of mens rea on the driver's part any more than other traffic regulations within the same chapter do. See, e.g., Minn.Stat. § 169.14 (1996) (forbidding drivers from exceeding speed restrictions); Minn.Stat. § 169.34 (1996) (prohibiting drivers from parking a vehicle in certain specified locations including a public or private driveway and an intersection); Minn.Stat. § 169.48 (1996) (requiring vehicles to display specific lighted lamps and illuminating devices). The full protection regulatory statutes are designed to afford could not be secured if knowledge was a necessary element of the offense. Evasion would be so easy that the statutes would practically fail. It is reasonable to assume, therefore, that had the legislature intended to depart from its standard practice with respect to regulatory statutes and make knowledge of the open bottle an element of the offense, it would have done so expressly by forbidding the owner and the driver from knowingly or intentionally keeping or allowing to be kept in a motor vehicle an open bottle containing intoxicating liquor.

The burden subdivision 3 imposes on the owner and the driver of an automobile is minimal compared to the mischief the legislature intended to prevent, namely, drinking intoxicating beverages while driving. The magnitude of the problems associated with drinking while driving fully justifies the minimal burden the legislature placed on the owner and the driver. Admittedly, subdivision 3 exposes unsuspecting owners and drivers to criminal liability. On occasion, this exposure may result in the conviction of what may be viewed as an innocent person. The greater public good, however, justifies an occasional, but only apparent, injustice. Moreover, any injustice resulting from the imposition of strict liability could be effectively remedied at the time of sentencing. Strict liability, therefore, is not too high a price to pay for public safety and a legitimate legislative purpose. Thus, despite the severity of excluding lack of knowledge as a defense, we conclude that Minn.Stat. § 169.122, subd. 3, creates a strict liability offense.

The evidence, which establishes that officers saw an open bottle containing intoxicating liquor underneath the passenger seat of the automobile Loge was driving on a public highway, is sufficient to support Loge's conviction under Minn.Stat. § 169.122, subd. 3. Proof that Loge knew the bottle was in the automobile is not required to sustain the conviction.

Affirmed.

DISSENT

RANDALL, J.

I respectfully dissent. I conclude that Minn.Stat. § 169.122, subd. 3 (1998), has to include a scienter [knowledge] element. The only way this subdivision can read to include basic fairness and due process is that the driver/owner must knowingly allow an open bottle to be kept in the car. . . . The plain meaning of Minn.Stat.§ 169.122, subd. 3, indicates that the legislature intended to criminalize only the knowing possession of an open bottle in a motor vehicle. . . . It is unlawful under subdivision 3 "to keep or allow to be kept" an open bottle containing intoxicating liquor in a motor vehicle. The phrase "to keep or allow to be kept" requires knowledge by the actor. Logic and fairness mandate only that conclusion. To "keep" is to "maintain, or cause to stay or continue in a specified condition, position, etc." *Webster's New Universal Unabridged Dictionary* 997 (Jean L. McKechnie ed., 2d ed.1983). To "allow" is "to permit." One cannot "cause" or "permit" something to stay in a specified condition if one has absolutely no knowledge that it exists. The statute's plain language incorporates a mens rea requirement.

. . . A determination that Minn.Stat. § 169.122, subd. 3, imposes strict criminal liability on innocent drivers and owners would lead to a variety of unreasonable results the legislature could not have intended. For example, it would expose all unsuspecting drivers, young and old, to criminal liability if they offer a ride to a friend or colleague who happens to have a concealed open bottle on his or her person. . . . It would also expose innocent parents or other adults to criminal liability if they loan their car to their children, or anyone else, who, unknown to the parents, buy a container of liquor, open it, and leave it under the seat of the car or some other place not readily apparent when returning the vehicle. . . . A strict-liability open bottle law would drag in both the "hot rodder" whose buddies had open beers in the car and the unsuspecting, kind old gentleman who drove home from church with the little old lady with the open flask of communion wine in her handbag. *People v. Hutchison*, 46 Ill.App.3d 725, 5 Ill.Dec. 189, 361 N.E.2d 328, 330 (Ill.App.Ct.1977) (Mill, J., dissenting), overruled by *People v. Graven*, 124 Ill.App.3d 990, 80 Ill.Dec. 149, 464 N.E.2d 1132 (Ill.App.Ct.1984)).

Finally, to determine legislative intent, this court may also consider "[t]he occasion and necessity for the law" and "[t]he mischief to be remedied" by the law. As the majority points out, the purpose of this statute is to prevent drinking while driving. A scienter or knowledge requirement does not hinder that purpose. If the driver has no knowledge that there is an open bottle in the vehicle, there is no danger that the driver will drink alcohol while driving. If the driver does know there is an open bottle in the vehicle, then, in that case, the driver clearly comes under the purview of subdivision 3. But that is not this case. The same clear logic is true with owners who are not present in the car but have loaned the car to someone else. If, upon turning over the car, the owner is aware that the recipient has containers, then you can legitimately impose criminal liability on the owner under subdivision 3. That makes sense. The owner has every right, and in fact a legal obligation, to have open containers of alcohol known to him removed from the car before turning it over. Once that lack of knowledge becomes actual knowledge, and that is an element of proof for the state, the driver or owner loses the protection of "no knowledge" and is now properly subject to criminal liability under subdivision 3. This principle of law is in no way hampered by not imposing strict liability on innocent drivers and owners. . . .

QUESTIONS FOR DISCUSSION

1. What words, if any, in the statute indicate a *mens rea* requirement?
2. What *mens rea*, if any, do the words in the statute require?
3. Summarize the arguments that the majority of the court gives to support strict liability offenses.
4. What arguments did the dissent give in response to the majority's arguments?
5. Do you agree with the majority or the dissent? Defend your answer.

✺ 4-1 Open Bottle Laws

CONCURRENCE

Suppose that you and your friend agree to meet at her house on a cold winter night. She is late because her car won't start. She calls you on her cell phone and tells you to break the lock on her front door so you can wait inside safe from the cold. Once inside, you decide to steal her new Tivo. Have you committed burglary? No, because the principle of **concurrence** requires that a criminal intent (*mens rea*) trigger a criminal act (*actus reus*). You decided to steal her Tivo *after* you broke into and entered her house. Burglary requires that the intent to steal set in motion the acts of breaking and entering. So, in crimes of criminal conduct, *mens rea* has to come before *actus reus* (see Chapter 11).[13]

CAUSATION

The principle of **causation** applies only to crimes of cause and result. The main examples include the various kinds and degrees of criminal homicide. Determining whether criminal conduct causes a particular result requires that the facts support the answer yes to two questions:

1. Was the conduct the **cause in fact** of the harmful result? If so:
2. Was the conduct the **legal cause** of the harmful result?

What is the cause in fact of a result? This is an empirical question. Often called **"but for"** or *sine qua non* **causation** or **factual causation**, cause in fact means that the defendant's conduct sets in motion a chain of events that, sooner or later, leads to the harmful result; hence the expression "but for" causation. You might think of cause in fact this way: "If it hadn't been for the defendant's conduct, the harm would not have happened when it did."

Cause in fact is necessary but not sufficient to impose criminal liability. The prosecution has to also prove legal cause, frequently called **proximate cause**. What is the proximate cause of a result is a policy question. It asks, "Is it just to hold the defendant accountable for this harm, even if her conduct in fact caused the result?" Proximate cause is decided case by case. To satisfy the requirement of proximate cause, the prosecution has to prove in each case that justice demands that the criminal law hold particular defendants accountable for a chain of events that their criminal actions set in motion. Most cases satisfy both the factual and proximate cause requirements.

Proximate cause problems arise when something in addition to the conduct of the actor contributes to the result, something that the actor can't control, didn't foresee, or couldn't reasonably have foreseen. Put another way, proximate causation almost always involves harms caused by recklessness and negligence. Suppose that Jennifer, preoccupied with a conversation on her cell phone, doesn't notice a red light. She drives through it and hits Marcy. Marcy dies in the hospital following negligent surgery. But for Jennifer's conduct, Marcy wouldn't be in the hospital. But, if it weren't for the negligent surgery, Marcy would be alive. Is Jennifer criminally liable for Marcy's death? The question boils down to who is it "just" to blame? Chief Justice Schwab of the Oregon Supreme Court expressed the idea of proximate cause in this excellent statement in *State v. Peterson:*

> The problem . . . is not "causation in fact," it is "legal causation." . . . [W]hether certain conduct is deemed to be the legal cause of a certain result is ultimately a policy question. The question of legal causation thus blends into the question of whether we are willing to hold a defendant responsible for a prohibited result. Or, stated differently, the issue is not causation, it is responsibility.[14]

What is just? Some have answered the question this way: Proximate cause doesn't extend to consequences set in motion by an act beyond the point where the consequences have "come to rest in a position of apparent safety." Suppose, for example, someone rolled a boulder down a hill where a crowd of people gathered below. Halfway down the hill, the boulder caught on a tree trunk that stopped its rolling toward the crowd. Several months later, a vibration dislodged the boulder and it rolled the rest of the way down the hill, striking and killing an unlucky person standing in its path. The person who initially set the boulder in motion is not the legal cause of the death; the boulder had literally come safely to rest on the tree, where an outside force later set in motion the chain of events that killed the ultimate victim.[15]

Another way to determine the justice of holding defendants accountable for the results of their reckless and negligent conduct is the idea of intervening cause (sometimes called a **supervening cause**). **Intervening causes** either significantly interrupt the chain of events set in motion by the actions of a defendant or at least substantially contribute to results. Suppose a driver injures a pedestrian while negligently driving her car. While the pedestrian is in the hospital seeking treatment, an inexperienced intern injects her with a fatal dose of a painkiller, given to the intern by a drunken nurse. The intern's inexperience and the drunken nurse's action contributed to the death at least as much as the negligent driving; arguably, they intervened and became themselves the main, dominant, or proximate cause. It is unjust to impose criminal liability in cases where the harmful results of actions are far remote from the initial actions that set a chain of events in motion. Therefore, we are led to conclude that the drunken nurse is an intervening, or supervening, cause of the death of the pedestrian in the hypothetical example.

Intervening causes may be either external forces or responses to the actions of defendants. Courts rarely impose liability when the proximate cause is an outside force. Suppose a robber leaves the victim of the robbery on a country road and the victim climbs over a fence into a field and falls asleep. A horse kicks the victim in the head and the victim dies. The kick is an outside force too remote from the robbery to impose liability for criminal homicide. Where, instead, the defendants' actions generate a direct human response from victims, courts are more likely to impose liability. In one case, Wilson threatened to castrate Armstrong if he didn't hand over two $100 bills. In escaping, Armstrong ran into the Missouri River, where he drowned. The Nebraska Supreme Court affirmed Wilson's conviction for murder because Armstrong's attempt to escape was a direct response to Wilson's threat to castrate him. One type of legal causation case involves medical personnel who treat wounded crime victims. The court dealt with actual, proximate, and intervening cause in a nonmedical setting in *People v. Armitage.*

C A S E   Did He Cause the Drowning?

People v. Armitage
239 Cal.Rptr. 515, (1987)

On a drunken escapade on the Sacramento River in the middle of a spring night, David James Armitage flipped his boat over and caused his companion to drown. As a result of this accident, defendant was convicted of the felony of drunk boating causing death in violation of former Harbors and Navigation Code. The Court of Appeal affirmed the judgment.

SPARKS, J.

FACTS

On the evening of May 18, 1985, defendant and his friend, Peter Maskovich, were drinking in a bar in the riverside community of Freeport. They were observed leaving the bar around midnight. In the early morning hours defendant and Maskovich wound up racing defendant's boat on the Sacramento River while both of them were intoxicated. The boat did not contain any personal flotation devices. At about 3 A.M. Gary Bingham, who lived in a house boat in a speed zone (five miles per hour, no wake), was disturbed by a large wake. He went out to yell at the boaters and observed a small aluminum boat with two persons in it at the bend in the river. The boaters had the motor wide open, were zigzagging, and had no running lights on at the time. About the same time, Rodney and Susan Logan were fishing on the river near the Freeport Bridge when they observed an aluminum boat with two men in it coming up the river without running lights. The occupants were using loud and vulgar language, and were operating the boat very fast and erratically.

James Snook lives near the Sacramento River in Clarksburg. Some time around 3 A.M. defendant came to his door. Defendant was soaking wet and appeared quite intoxicated. He reported that he had flipped his boat over in the river and had lost his buddy. He said that at first he and his buddy

had been hanging on to the overturned boat, but that his buddy swam for shore and he did not know whether he had made it. As it turned out, Maskovich did not make it; he drowned in the river.

Mr. Snook notified the authorities of the accident. Deputy Beddingfield arrived and spent some time with defendant in attempting to locate the scene of the accident or the victim. Eventually Deputy Beddingfield took defendant to the sheriff's boat shed to meet with officers who normally work on the river. At the shed they were met by Deputy Snyder. Deputy Snyder attempted to question defendant about the accident and defendant stated that he had been operating the boat at a high rate of speed and zigzagging until it capsized. Defendant also stated that he told the victim to hang on to the boat but his friend ignored his warning and started swimming for the shore. As he talked to defendant, the officer formed the opinion that he was intoxicated. Deputy Snyder then arrested defendant and informed him of his rights. Defendant waived his right to remain silent and repeated his statement.

OPINION

. . .

Defendant . . . contends his actions were not the proximate cause of the death of the victim. In order to be guilty of felony drunk boating the defendant's act or omission must be the proximate cause of the ensuing injury or death. (Harb. & Nav.Code, § 655, subd. (a).) Defendant asserts that after his boat flipped over he and the victim were holding on to it and the victim, against his advice, decided to abandon the boat and try to swim to shore. According to defendant the victim's fatally reckless decision should exonerate him from criminal responsibility for his death.

We reject defendant's contention. The question whether defendant's acts or omissions criminally caused the victim's death is to be determined according to the ordinary principles governing proximate causation. (1 Witkin, Cal.Crimes (1963) § 78, p. 79.) Proximate cause of a death has traditionally been defined in criminal cases as "a cause which, in natural and continuous sequence, produces the death, and without which the death would not have occurred." (CALJIC Nos. 8.55 (1987 Revision)), 8.93 (1987 Revision); Thus, as Witkin notes, "[p]roximate cause is clearly established where the act is directly connected with the resulting injury, with no intervening force operating." (1 Witkin, Cal. Crimes, supra, § 79, p. 79.)

Defendant claims that the victim's attempt to swim ashore, whether characterized as an intervening or a superseding cause, constituted a break in the natural and continuous sequence arising from the unlawful operation of the boat. The claim cannot hold water. It has long been the rule in criminal prosecutions that the contributory negligence of the victim is not a defense. In order to exonerate a defendant the victim's conduct must not only be a cause of his injury, it must be a superseding cause. "A defendant may be criminally liable for a result directly caused by his act even if there is another contributing cause. If an intervening cause is a normal and reasonably foreseeable result of defendant's original act the intervening act is 'dependent' and not a superseding cause, and will not relieve defendant of liability." As Witkin further notes, "[a]n obvious illustration of a dependent cause is the victim's attempt to escape from a deadly attack or other danger in which he is placed by the defendant's wrongful act." (1 Witkin, Cal. Crimes, supra, § 82, p. 81.) Thus, it is only an unforeseeable intervening cause, an extraordinary and abnormal occurrence, which rises to the level of an exonerating, superseding cause. Consequently, in criminal law a victim's predictable effort to escape a peril created by the defendant is not considered a superseding cause of the ensuing injury or death. As leading commentators have explained it, an unreflective act in response to a peril created by defendant will not break a causal connection. In such a case, the actor has a choice, but his act is nonetheless unconsidered. "When defendant's conduct causes panic an act done under the influence of panic or extreme fear will not negate causal connection unless the reaction is wholly abnormal." (Hart & Honore, *Causation in the Law* (2d ed. 1985) p. 149.)

Here defendant, through his misconduct, placed the intoxicated victim in the middle of a dangerous river in the early morning hours clinging to an overturned boat. The fact that the panic stricken victim recklessly abandoned the boat and tried to swim ashore was not a wholly abnormal reaction to the perceived peril of drowning. Just as "[d]etached reflection cannot be demanded in the presence of an uplifted knife" (*Brown v. United States* (1921) 256 U.S. 335, 343, 41 S.Ct. 501, 502, 65 L.Ed. 961, 963, Holmes, J.), neither can caution be required of a drowning man. Having placed the inebriated victim in peril, defendant cannot obtain exoneration by claiming the victim should have reacted differently or more prudently. In sum, the evidence establishes that defendant's acts and omissions were the proximate cause of the victim's death.

The judgment is affirmed.

QUESTIONS FOR DISCUSSION

1. State all of the facts relevant to determining whether Armitage caused his friend's death.
2. According to these facts, do you agree that Armitage is both the actual and the proximate cause of his friend's death?
3. Do you agree with the court that his friend's actions were not an intervening cause of his death? Defend your answer.

NOTE CASES

1. At about 2:30 A.M., Isaac Alejandro Velazquez met the deceased Adalberto Alvarez at a Hardee's restaurant in Hialeah, Florida. The two had never previously met, but in the course of their conversation agreed to race each other in a "drag race" with their automobiles. They accordingly left the restaurant and proceeded to set up a quarter-mile drag race course on a nearby public road that ran perpendicular to a canal alongside the Palmetto Expressway in Hialeah; a guardrail and a visible stop sign stood between the end of this road and the canal. The two men began their drag race at the end of this road and proceeded away from the canal in a westerly direction for one quarter mile. Upon completing the course without incident, the deceased

Alvarez suddenly turned his automobile 180 degrees around and proceeded east toward the starting line and the canal; Velazquez did the same and followed behind Alvarez. Alvarez proceeded in the lead and attained an estimated speed of 123 m.p.h.; he was not wearing a seat belt and subsequent investigation revealed that he had a blood alcohol level between .11 and .12. Velasquez, who had not been drinking, trailed Alvarez the entire distance back to the starting line and attained an estimated speed of 98 m.p.h. As both drivers approached the end of the road, they applied their brakes, but neither could stop. Alvarez, who was about a car length ahead of Velazquez, crashed through the guardrail first and was propelled over the entire canal, landing on its far bank; he was thrown from his car upon impact, was pinned under his vehicle when it landed on him, and died instantly from the resulting injuries. Velazquez also crashed through the guardrail, but landed in the canal where he was able to escape from his vehicle and swim to safety uninjured.

Velazquez was charged with vehicular homicide. Were his actions in participating in the drag race the legal or proximate cause of Alvarez's death? No, according to the appeals court:

The "proximate cause" element of vehicular homicide in Florida embraces more . . . than . . . "but for" causation-in-fact. . . . Even where a defendant's conduct is a cause-in-fact of a prohibited result, as where a defendant's reckless operation of a motor vehicle is a cause-in-fact of the death of a human being, Florida and other courts throughout the country have for good reason declined to impose criminal liability (1) where the prohibited result of the defendant's conduct is beyond the scope of any fair assessment of the danger created by the defendant's conduct, or (b) where it would otherwise be unjust, based on fairness and policy considerations, to hold the defendant criminally responsible for the prohibited result.

. . . [A] driver-participant in an illegal "drag race" on a public road cannot be held criminally responsible for the death of another driver participant when (a) the deceased, in effect, kills himself by his own reckless driving during the race, and (b) the sole basis for attaching criminal liability

for his death is the defendant's participation in the "drag race." The policy reasons for reaching this result are best expressed in *State v. Petersen*, 270 Or. 166, 526 P.2d 1008 (1974):

"[T]he question is whether defendant's reckless conduct 'caused' the death of the victim. The problem here is not 'causation in fact,' it is 'legal causation.' In unusual cases like this one, whether certain conduct is deemed to be the legal cause of a certain result is ultimately a policy question. The question of legal causation thus blends into the question of whether we are willing to hold a defendant responsible for a prohibited result. Or, stated differently, the issue is not causation, it is responsibility. In my opinion, policy considerations are against imposing responsibility for the death of a participant in a race on the surviving racer when his sole contribution to the death is the participation in the activity mutually agreed upon. . .

. . . [I]t is clear that the defendant's reckless operation of a motor vehicle in participating in the "drag race" with the deceased was, technically speaking, a cause-in-fact of the deceased's death under the "but for" test. But for the defendant's participation in the subject race, the deceased would not have recklessly raced his vehicle at all and thus would not have been killed. However, . . . the defendant's participation in the subject "drag race" was not a proximate cause of the deceased's death because, simply put, the deceased, in effect, killed himself by his own volitional reckless driving—and, consequently, it would be unjust to hold the defendant criminally responsible for this death. Reversed and remanded. *Velazquez v. State*, 561 So.2d 347 (Fla.App. 1990)

2. Barry Kibbe and a companion, Roy Krall, met George Stafford in a bar on a cold winter night. They noticed Stafford had a lot of money and was drunk. When Stafford asked them for a ride, they agreed, having already decided to rob him. "The three men entered Kibbe's automobile and began the trip toward Canandaigua. Krall drove the car while Kibbe demanded that Stafford turn over any money he had. In the course of an exchange, Kibbe slapped Stafford several times, took his money, then compelled him to lower his trousers and to take off his shoes to be certain that Stafford had given up all his money; and when they were satisfied that Stafford

had no more money on his person, the defendants forced Stafford to exit the Kibbe vehicle.

As he was thrust from the car, Stafford fell onto the shoulder of the rural two-lane highway on which they had been traveling. His trousers were still down around his ankles, his shirt was rolled up towards his chest, he was shoeless and he had also been stripped of any outer clothing. Before the defendants pulled away, Kibbe placed Stafford's shoes and jacket on the shoulder of the highway. Although Stafford's eyeglasses were in Kibbe's vehicle, the defendants, either through inadvertence or perhaps by specific design, did not give them to Stafford before they drove away.

Michael W. Blake, a college student, was driving at a reasonable speed when he saw Stafford in the middle of the road with his hands in the air. Blake could not stop in time to avoid striking Stafford and killing him.

Who legally caused Stafford's death? The court said Kibbe and his companion.

The defendants do not dispute the fact that their conduct evinced a depraved indifference to human life which created a grave risk of death, but rather they argue that it was just as likely that Stafford would be miraculously rescued by a good samaritan. We cannot accept such an argument. There can be little doubt but that Stafford would have frozen to death in his state of undress had he remained on the shoulder of the road. The only alternative left to him was the highway, which in his condition, for one reason or another, clearly foreboded the probability of resulting death.

People v. Kibbe, 35 N.Y.2d 407, 362 N.Y.S.2d 848, 321 N.E.2d 773 (1974)

GRADING OFFENSES

The seriousness of an offense depends on several considerations. First, and perhaps most important, is the harm done. Harms to persons are generally considered most serious, followed by harms to habitation, property, public order, and public morals. Chapters 9 through 13 follow this order. Uncompleted harms are less serious than completed ones (see Chapter 6). Sometimes seriousness depends on *actus reus,* such as in especially brutal murders. Sometimes, it depends on *mens rea.* As we noted at the beginning of the chapter, purpose or specific intent is the most blameworthy, followed by knowledge, recklessness, negligence, and strict liability. Penalties reflect these degrees of blameworthiness.

SUMMARY

Criminal conduct requires that the *mens rea* triggered the *actus reus* and, in crimes requiring a particular result, that the *actus reus* caused the result. The principle of causation requires a causal relationship between criminal conduct and a harmful result. This causal relation is expressed both as factual causation, that is, "but for" or *sine qua non* cause, and as legal or proximate cause, the cause the law looks to in justifying criminal liability. Problems arise when the resulting harm exceeds what actors intended, expected, or should have expected. Reckless and negligent wrongdoers are held accountable only for substantial and unjustifiable risks that deviate grossly from the reasonable behavior of ordinary people under similar circumstances. This is another way of saying that we punish only those who it is just to hold accountable.

 Go to the Criminal Law 7e CD-ROM for Internet exercises.

REVIEW QUESTIONS

1. How can we determine *mens rea*?

2. Identify and define the four types of common-law *mens rea*.

3. Identify and define the four levels of culpability under the *Model Penal Code*.

4. Distinguish accurately and completely among the four levels of culpability.

5. According to the *Model Penal Code,* to what three elements can *mens rea* refer?

6. Define strict liability and explain how it originated and under what circumstances it usually applies.

7. Explain the principle of concurrence.

8. Define factual causation and legal causation. Specifically identify the differences between them.

9. What are the main grounds for grading offenses in terms of the general principles of criminal liability?

KEY TERMS

"but for" or *sine qua non* **causation**—the actor's conduct sets in motion a chain of events that, sooner or later, leads to a result.

causation—the requirement that criminal conduct cause a particular result.

cause in fact—actual cause of the harmful result.

circumstantial evidence—indirect evidence.

concurrence—the requirement that *actus reus* must join with *mens rea* to produce criminal conduct or that conduct cause a harmful result.

constructive intent—intent in which the actors do not intend any harm but should have known that their behavior created a high risk of injury.

culpability—blameworthiness based on *mens rea.*

factual causation—conduct that in fact leads to a harmful result.

general intent—intent to commit the *actus reus*—the act required in the definition of the crime.

intervening or supervening cause—the cause that either interrupts a chain of events or substantially contributes to a result.

legal causation—cause recognized by law to impose criminal liability.

mens rea—the mental element in crime, including purpose, knowledge, recklessness, and negligence.

negligence—the unconscious creation of substantial and unjustifiable risks.

proximate cause—the main cause of the result of criminal conduct.

recklessness—the conscious creation of substantial and unjustifiable risk.

specific intent—the intent to do something beyond the *actus reus.*

strict liability—liability without fault, or in the absence of *mens rea.*

transferred intent—actor intends to harm one victim but instead harms another.

SUGGESTED READINGS

1. George Fletcher, *Rethinking Criminal Law* (Boston: Little, Brown, 1978), pt. II. A thorough and thought-provoking discussion of the principles of criminal liability. Difficult in places but worth the effort.

2. Jerome Hall, *General Principles of Criminal Law,* 2d ed. (Indianapolis, Ind.: Bobbs-Merrill, 1960). Difficult but rewarding reading.

3. Hyman Gross, *A Theory of Criminal Justice* (New York: Oxford University Press, 1979), chap. 2. Untangles knotty questions surrounding *actus reus.*

4. American Law Institute, *Model Penal Code and Commentaries* (Philadelphia: American Law Institute, 1985), pt. I. The fullest treatment of the general principles of criminal liability.

5. Rollin M. Perkins and Ronald N. Boyce, *Criminal Law,* 3d ed. (Mineola, N.Y.: Foundation Press, 1982), chaps. 6 and 7. A straightforward analysis of *actus reus, mens rea,* and causation.

NOTES

1. Francis Bowes Sayre, "*Mens rea,*" *Harvard Law Review* 45 (1931–32):974.

2. *Burnette v. State,* 1999 WL 722698 (Ala. App. 1999).

3. Holmes, *The Common Law,* p. 7; American Law Institute, *Model Penal Code,* tentative draft no. 11 (1955).

4. Glanville Williams, *Criminal Law,* 1; quoted in Jerome Hall, *General Principles of Criminal Law,* 2d ed. (Indianapolis, Ind.: Bobbs-Merrill, 1960), p. 153.

5. Quoted in Joseph Goldstein et al., *Criminal Law: Theory and Process.*

6. Wayne R. LaFave and Austin W. Scott, Jr., *Handbook on Criminal Law,* 2d ed. (St. Paul, Minn.: West Publishing Co., 1972), pp. 201–202; Jerome Hall, *General Principles of Criminal Law,* pp. 142–144.

7. American Law Institute, *Model Penal Code and Commentaries,* pt. I, p. 229.

8. *Haupt v. United States,* 330 U.S. 631, 67 S.Ct. 874, 91 L.Ed. 1145 (1947) (treason).

9. West's Revised Code Wash. Ann. 9A.08010(1)(b).

10. Michigan Statutes 82; § 305(a) and (b).

11. *New York Times* (September 14, 1985).

12. Rollin M. Perkins and Ronald N. Boyce, *Criminal Law,* 3d ed. (Mineola, N.Y.: Foundation Press, 1982), pp. 896–907.

13. *The Penal Code of California,* § 20, West's California Penal Codes, 1988 compact ed. (St. Paul, Minn.: West Publishing Company, 1988), p. 7; Hall, *General Principles of Criminal Law,* pp. 185–190.

14. Katz, *Bad Acts and Guilty Minds,* chap. 4; *State v. Peterson,* 522 P.2d 912, 920 (1974).

15. Perkins and Boyce, *Criminal Law,* pp. 776–777.

5

Parties to Crime and Vicarious Liability

Chapter Outline

I. Introduction

II. Parties to Crime

III. Vicarious Liability

IV. Summary

CHAPTER MAIN POINTS

1. Parties to crime deal with group participation in crime.

2. Accomplice liability attributes the *actus reus* and *mens rea* of one person to other participants before and during the commission of a crime.

3. Accessory liability depends on participation after the commission of a felony.

4. Vicarious liability imposes liability for a relationship with someone who commits a crime.

5. Parties before and during crime are liable for the principal crime; parties following crime are liable for separate, lesser offenses.

6. Vicarious liability may be imposed either with or without culpability.

Was David's Mother a Party to the Crime?

When David Hoffman's wife, Carol, refused to make love with him, he lost his temper and choked her to death. He called down to the basement to wake his mother, asking her to come upstairs to sit on the living room couch. From there she would be able to see the kitchen, bathroom, and bedroom doors and could stop his daughter if she awoke and tried to use the bathroom. His mother came upstairs to lie on the couch. In the meantime David had moved the body to the bathtub. His mother was aware that while she was in the living room her son was dismembering the body, but she turned her head away so that she could not see. After dismembering the body and putting it in bags, Hoffman cleaned the bathroom, took the body to a lake and disposed of it. On returning home he told his mother to wash the cloth covers from the bathroom toilet and tank, which she did. David fabricated a story about Carol leaving the house the previous night after an argument, and his mother agreed to corroborate it. David phoned the police with a missing person report and during the ensuing searches and interviews with the police, he and his mother continued to tell the fabricated story.

INTRODUCTION

"Two heads are better than one." "The whole is greater than the sum of its parts." We've all heard these expressions of the positive side of working together. When working together turns malicious, it becomes complicity in criminal law. A group of young men playing football generates no criminal liability; a gang rape—teamwork turned malicious—is worse than each individual rape. The **doctrine of complicity**— also called the doctrine of parties to crime—establishes the conditions under which two or more persons incur liability for the conduct of another before, during, and after the commission of crimes. Complicity assigns the *actus reus* and the *mens rea* of one person to the actions and intentions of someone else. It doesn't matter whether the defendant, someone else, or both together contribute to the elements of the crime. Everybody who joins with others to commit crimes is accountable as if they had committed the crime alone.

Vicarious liability bases criminal liability on the *relationship* between someone who commits a crime and someone else. The vicariously liable person doesn't need to act or intend to commit a crime; some kind of relationship substitutes for both. The most common of these relationships are employer-employee, manager-corporation, buyer-seller, producer-consumer, service provider-recipient. But vicarious liability can also arise in other situations, such as making the owner of a car liable for the driver's traffic violations and holding parents liable for their minor children's crimes.

PARTIES TO CRIME

The common law recognized four parties to crime:

1. Principals in the first degree—those who actually commit the crime.
2. Principals in the second degree—aiders and abettors present when crimes are committed, such as lookouts, getaway drivers, and co-conspirators.
3. Accessories before the fact—aiders and abettors not present when crimes are committed, such as those who provide the weapons that others use in murders.
4. Accessories after the fact—individuals who give aid and comfort to persons known to have committed crimes, such as those who harbor fugitives.

The significance of these distinctions lay largely in the rule that only after principals were convicted could the government try accomplices. If principals were not convicted before the government brought accomplices to trial, common-law complicity shielded accomplices even in the face of certain proof of their guilt. The doctrine was one way to avoid the death penalty during a period in history when all felonies were capital offenses. As the number of capital crimes diminished, so did the need to distinguish between principals and accessories. Modern statutes have abolished the common-law distinction by declaring accessories both before and during crime to be principals. These principals are called **accomplices**. In most states, complicity after crimes—the common-law **accessory** after the fact—is a separate, lesser offense.

The distinguished federal judge Learned Hand nicely summed up the doctrine of complicity as requiring that defendants "in some sort associate [themselves] with the venture, that they participate in it as in something that they wish . . . to bring about, that they seek by . . . their action to make it succeed."[1]

Accomplice liability is often confused with conspiracy. They are related only in the sense that they both involve more than one party. Otherwise, they are two completely different crimes. Conspiracy is an agreement to commit some other crime. A conspiracy to commit murder is not murder; it is the lesser offense of agreeing to commit murder (see Chapter 6). Participating in a murder is the crime of murder itself. For example, two people agree to commit a murder. They go and buy a gun and drive together to the victim's house. One acts as a lookout while the other kills the victim. They drive away together. They have committed both conspiracy to commit murder and murder itself. The rule that conspiracy and the underlying crime are separate offenses is called the *Pinkerton* rule. The name derives from the leading U.S.

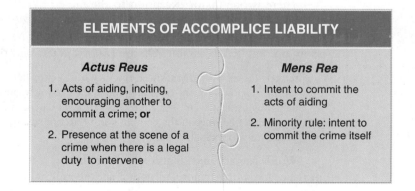

ELEMENTS OF ACCOMPLICE LIABILITY

Actus Reus

1. Acts of aiding, inciting, encouraging another to commit a crime; **or**
2. Presence at the scene of a crime when there is a legal duty to intervene

Mens Rea

1. Intent to commit the acts of aiding
2. Minority rule: intent to commit the crime itself

Supreme Court case involving both offenses, *Pinkerton v. United States*. In the case, two brothers conspired to evade taxes. Both were found guilty of both conspiracy to evade taxes and tax evasion itself. According to Justice Douglas, who wrote the opinion for the Court, "It has been long and consistently recognized by the Court that the commission of the substantive offense and a conspiracy to commit it are separate and distinct offenses."[2]

ACTUS REUS OF ACCOMPLICE LIABILITY

Modern statutes have redefined the common-law parties to crime. But the *actus reus* of accomplice liability remains similar to the old law. Statutes use words like "aid," "abet," "assist," "counsel," "procure," "hire," or "induce" to define accomplice *actus reus*. What the words are trying to convey is "some positive act in aid of the commission of the offense." How much aid is enough can be difficult to decide, but all of the following qualify:

- Providing guns, supplies, or other instruments of crime
- Serving as a lookout
- Driving a getaway car
- Sending the victim to the principal
- Preventing warnings from reaching the victim.[3]

Mere presence at the scene of a crime is not enough. According to the **mere presence rule**, even presence at the scene of a crime followed by flight is not enough action to satisfy the *actus reus* requirement of accomplice liability. In *Bailey v. United States,* Bailey spent most of the afternoon shooting craps with another man. Then, when a man carrying cash walked by, Bailey's craps partner pulled a gun and robbed the man with the cash. Both Bailey and the other man fled the scene. Bailey was caught; the other man never was. The court held that although flight from the scene of a crime can be taken into account, it's not enough to prove accomplice *actus reus*. According to the court,

> We no longer hold tenable the notion that "the wicked flee when no man pursueth, but the righteous are as bold as a lion." The proposition that "one flees shortly after a criminal act is committed or when he is accused of something does so because he feels some guilt concerning the act" is not absolute as a legal doctrine "since it is a matter of common knowledge that men who are entirely innocent do sometimes fly from the scene of a crime through fear of being apprehended as guilty parties or from an unwillingness to appear as witnesses."[4]

There is one major exception to the mere presence rule. When defendants have a legal duty to act, presence alone is enough. In *State v. Walden*, Walden stood by and did nothing while her boyfriend beat her young son. A jury found Walden guilty as an accomplice to assault. On appeal, the court said that

> the trial court properly allowed the jury . . . to consider a verdict of guilty of assault . . . upon a theory of aiding and abetting, solely on the ground that the defendant was present when her child was brutally beaten. . . . A person who so aids or abets under another in the commission of a crime is equally guilty with that other person as a principal.[5]

Words can amount to accomplice *actus reus* if they encourage and show approval of the crime. Furthermore, although actions following the crime aren't themselves accomplice *actus reus,* they are circumstances from which juries can infer participation. In *State v. Ulvinen,* the court dealt with the problem of words as accomplice *actus reus,* and also grappled with two additional problems in accomplice liability:

1. Imposing liability if defendants aren't present when crimes are committed.
2. Inferring participation in crimes from actions taken after the commission of crimes.

| **C A S E** | **Was She an Accomplice to Murder?** |

State v. Ulvinen
313 N.W.2d 425 (Minn. 1981)

Helen Ulvinen was convicted of first degree murder pursuant to Minn.Stat. § 609.05, subd. 1 (1980), which imposes criminal liability on one who "intentionally aids, advises, hires, counsels, or conspires with or otherwise procures" another to commit a crime. The Minnesota supreme court reversed.

OTIS, J.

FACTS

Carol Hoffman, Helen Ulvinen's (appellant's) daughter-in-law, was murdered late on the evening of August 10th or the very early morning of August 11th by her husband, David Hoffman. She and David had spent an amicable evening together playing with their children, and when they went to bed David wanted to make love to his wife. However, when she refused him he lost his temper and began choking her. While he was choking her he began to believe he was "doing the right thing" and that to get "the evil out of her" he had to dismember her body.

After his wife was dead, David called down to the basement to wake his mother, asking her to come upstairs to sit on the living room couch. From there she would be able to see the kitchen, bathroom, and bedroom doors and could stop the older child if she awoke and tried to use the bathroom. Appellant didn't respond at first but after being called once, possibly twice more, she came upstairs to lie on the couch. In the meantime David had moved the body to the bathtub. Appellant was aware that while she was in the living room her son was dismembering the body but she turned her head away so that she could not see.

After dismembering the body and putting it in bags, Hoffman cleaned the bathroom, took the body to Weaver Lake and disposed of it. On returning home he told his mother to wash the cloth covers from the bathroom toilet and tank, which she did. David fabricated a story about Carol leaving the house the previous night after an argument, and Helen agreed to corroborate it. David phoned the police with a missing person report and during the ensuing searches and interviews with the police, he and his mother continued to tell the fabricated story.

On August 19, 1980, David confessed to the police that he had murdered his wife. In his statement he indicated that not only had his mother helped him cover up the crime but she had known of his intent to kill his wife that night. After hearing Hoffman's statement the police arrested appellant and questioned her with respect to her part in the cover up. Police typed up a two-page statement which she read and signed. The following day a detective questioned her further regarding events surrounding the crime, including her knowledge that it was planned.

Appellant's relationship with her daughter-in-law had been a strained one. She moved in with the Hoffmans on July 26, two weeks earlier to act as a live-in babysitter for their two children. Carol was unhappy about having her move in and told friends that she hated Helen, but she told both David and his mother that they could try the arrangement to see how it worked. On the morning of the murder Helen told her son that she was going to move out of the Hoffman residence because "Carol had been so nasty to me." In his statement to the police David reported the conversation that morning as follows:

> . . . Sunday morning I went downstairs and my mom was in the bedroom reading the newspaper and she had tears in her eyes, and she said in a very frustrated voice, "I've got to find another

house." She said, "Carol don't want me here," and she said, "I probably shouldn't have moved in here." And I said then, "Don't let what Carol said hurt you. It's going to take a little more period of readjustment for her." Then I told mom that I've got to do it tonight so that there can be peace in this house.

Q. What did you tell your mom that you were going to have to do that night?

A. I told my mom I was going to have to put her to sleep.

Q. Dave, will you tell us exactly what you told your mother that morning, to the best of your recollection?

A. I said I'm going to have to choke her tonight and I'll have to dispose of her body so that it will never be found. That's the best of my knowledge.

Q. What did your mother say when you told her that?

A. She just—she looked at me with very sad eyes and just started to weep. I think she said something like "it will be for the best."

David spent the day fishing with a friend of his. When he got home that afternoon he had another conversation with his mother. She told him at that time about a phone conversation Carol had had in which she discussed taking the children and leaving home. David told the police that during the conversation with his mother that afternoon he told her "Mom, tonight's got to be the night."

Q. When you told your mother, "Tonight's got to be the night," did your mother understand that you were going to kill Carol later that evening?

A. She thought I was just kidding her about doing it. She didn't think I could. . . .

Q. Why didn't your mother think that you could do it?

A. . . . Because for some time I had been telling her I was going to take Carol scuba diving and make it look like an accident.

Q. And she said?

A. And she always said, "Oh, you're just kidding me.". . .

Q. But your mother knew you were going to do it that night?

A. I think my mother sensed that I was really going to do it that night.

Q. Why do you think your mother sensed you were really going to do it that night?

A. Because when I came home and she told me what had happened at the house, and I told her, "Tonight's got to be the night," I think she said, again I'm not certain, that ["]it would be the best for the kids."

OPINION

. . . It is well-settled in this state that presence, companionship, and conduct before and after the offense are circumstances from which a person's participation in the criminal intent may be inferred. The evidence is undisputed that appellant was asleep when her son choked his wife. She took no active part in the dismembering of the body but came upstairs to intercept the children, should they awake, and prevent them from going into the bathroom.

She cooperated with her son by cleaning some items from the bathroom and corroborating David's story to prevent anyone from finding out about the murder. She is insulated by statute from guilt as an accomplice after-the-fact for such conduct because of her relation as a parent of the offender. See Minn. Stat. § 609.495, subd. 2 (1980). The jury might well have considered appellant's conduct in sitting by while her son dismembered his wife so shocking that it deserved punishment. Nonetheless, these subsequent actions do not succeed in transforming her behavior prior to the crime to active instigation and encouragement. Minn.Stat. § 609.05, subd. 1 (1980) implies a high level of activity on the part of an aider and abettor in the form of conduct that encourages another to act. Use of terms such as "aids," "advises," and "conspires" requires something more of a person than mere inaction to impose liability as a principal.

The evidence presented to the jury at best supports a finding that appellant passively acquiesced in her son's plan to kill his wife. The jury might have believed that David told his mother of his intent to kill his wife that night and that she neither actively discouraged him nor told anyone in time to prevent the murder. Her response that "it would be the best for the kids" or "it will be the best" was not, however, active encouragement or instigation. There is no evidence that her remark had any influence on her son's decision to kill his wife. Minn.Stat. § 609.05, subd. 1 (1980), imposes liability for actions which affect the principal, encouraging him to take a course of action which he might not otherwise have taken.

The state has not proved beyond a reasonable doubt that appellant was guilty of anything but passive approval. However morally reprehensible it may be to fail to warn someone of their impending death, our statutes do not make such an omission a criminal offense. We note that mere knowledge of a contemplated crime or failure to disclose such information without evidence of any further involvement in the crime does not make that person liable as a party to the crime under any state's statutes. . . .

David told many people besides appellant of his intent to kill his wife but no one took him seriously. He told a co-worker, approximately three times a week that he was going to murder his wife, and confided two different plans for doing so. Another co-worker heard him tell his plan to cut Carol's air hose while she was scuba diving, making her death look accidental, but did not believe him. Two or three weeks before the murder, David told a friend of his that he and Carol were having problems and he expected Carol "to have an accident sometime." None of these people has a duty imposed by law, to warn the victim of impending danger, whatever their moral obligation may be. . . .

Her conviction must be reversed.

QUESTIONS FOR DISCUSSION

1. What were Mrs. Ulvinen's specific actions relevant to her liability?

2. Did she participate in the murder?

3. Are Mrs. Ulvinen's actions after the killing relevant to determining her complicity, if any, before and during the crime? Why or why not?

4. If she is not an accomplice, should she nevertheless be guilty of some crime?

5. Do you agree with the court that however morally reprehensible her behavior, she nonetheless did not commit a crime?

6. Why should she not be guilty of accessory after the fact?

7. Why isn't her remark that "it would be for the best" sufficient to amount to the *actus reus*? Should it be? Explain.

NOTE CASES

1. Carl Pace, his wife, and one child were in the front seat of their car driving from South Bend to LaPorte, Indiana. Rootes and another of the Pace children sat in the back seat. Pace, after receiving his wife's permis-

sion, picked up Reppert, a hitchhiker. Later, Rootes pulled a knife on Reppert and took his wallet. Just before Reppert got out of the car, Rootes took Reppert's watch. Pace said nothing during the entire episode. Was he an accomplice to robbery? He was convicted, but on appeal, the supreme court said:

We have found no evidence . . . which might demonstrate that the appellant aided and abetted in the alleged crime. While he was driving his car, nothing was said nor did he act in any manner to indicate his approval or countenance of the robbery. While there is evidence from which a jury might reasonably infer that he knew the crime was being committed, his situation was not one which would demonstrate a duty to oppose it.

State v. Pace, 224 N.E.2d 312 (Ind.1967)

2. Ella Mobley's boyfriend John Fagan beat Mobley's young child, threw her in the air and let her drop on the concrete floor, burned her with cigarettes, and told her to run and pushed her over. These, and a series of other violent actions over a period of weeks, eventually led to the child's death. Mobley did not intervene in any of the actions Fagan took because, according to her, she was afraid Fagan would leave her. Was Mobley an accomplice to murder? The court said yes:

It is true that mere presence of a person at the scene of a crime is insufficient to constitute him a principal therein. In the absence of anything in his conduct showing a design to encourage, incite, aid, abet or assist in the crime, the trier of the facts may consider failure of such person to oppose the commission of the crime in connection with other circumstances and conclude therefrom that he assented to the commission of the crime, lent his countenance and approval thereto and thereby aided and abetted it. This, it seems to us, is particularly true when the person who fails to interfere owes a duty to protect as a parent owes to a child.

Mobley v. State, 85 N.E.2d 489 (Ind.1949)

3. Frank Roberts's wife suffered from multiple sclerosis, which according to her doctor was incurable. She asked Roberts to get her some poison so she could kill herself. She could not do it herself because the disease had disabled her so she could no longer walk. Roberts complied with the request, placing the poison

in a glass by her bed. She took the poison and died. Was Roberts an accomplice to murder? The court said yes:

Where one person advises, aids, or abets another to commit suicide, and the other by reason thereof kills himself, and the adviser is present when he does so, he is guilty of murder as a principal. . . . It is said by counsel that suicide is no crime . . . and that therefore there can be no accessories or principals . . . in suicide. This is true. But the real criminal act charged here is not suicide, but the administering of poison. . . . We are of the opinion

that, when defendant mixed the paris green with water and placed it within reach of his wife to enable her to put an end to her suffering by putting an end to her life, he was guilty of murder by means of poison within the meaning of the statute, even though she requested him to do so. By this act he deliberately placed within her reach the means of taking her own life, which she could have obtained in no other way by reason of her helpless condition.

People v. Roberts, 178 N.W. 690 (Mich.1920)

MENS REA OF ACCOMPLICE LIABILITY

Confusion surrounds the *mens rea* of accomplices because criminal intent can refer both to the acts of aiding and abetting and to the crime that defendants aid and abet. Most courts hold that accomplice liability requires both of the following:

1. The specific intent or purpose to commit the acts that amount to aiding another to commit a crime;
2. The specific intent or purpose to commit the crime itself.

A minority of courts, however, hold that the *mens rea* of accomplice liability requires

1. Purpose to commit the acts of aiding and abetting; and
2. Knowledge of the perpetrator's criminal purpose.

Further confusion arises because both recklessness and negligence can satisfy the *mens rea* requirement. For example, if participants can predict that aiding and abetting one crime might reasonably lead to another crime, they are guilty of both. The court dealt with this problem in *People v. Poplar.*

C A S E | **Did He Have Accomplice *Mens Rea?***

People v. Poplar
20 Mich.App. 132, 173 N.W.2d 732 (1970)

Marathon Poplar, the defendant, was charged as an aider and abettor of breaking and entering and of assault with intent to commit murder. He moved for a directed verdict on both charges, claiming that there wasn't enough evidence to submit the case to the jury. The motions were denied. Poplar was found guilty on both counts by a jury in the Circuit Court, Genesee. The Court of Appeals affirmed.
      GILLIS, J.

FACTS

Alfred Williams and Clifford Lorrick broke into and entered the Oak Park recreation building in Flint in the early morning of December 3, 1964. When the manager of the building discovered the two men, Williams shot him in the face with a shotgun. Poplar, the defendant, allegedly acted as a lookout. Williams was tried as a codefendant and was convicted, along with this defendant, of breaking and entering and of assault with intent to commit murder. Williams' application for a delayed appeal was denied by this Court on April 18, 1967.

Lorrick pled guilty to breaking and entering on January 25, 1965, and testified for the prosecution at defendant's trial. He stated that he met defendant and Williams in a bar the night before the breaking and entering and left with them and two others. The five men allegedly drove around for a while before stopping to pick up some tools. They then took the tools and placed them in back of the bowling alley. An unsuccessful attempt to enter was made at that time. The group continued to drive around and during that time a shotgun that was in the car accidentally discharged, blowing a hole in the windshield. Just before the actual breaking and entering, the defendant, after getting out of the car with Lorrick and Williams, proceeded to a house directly across from the bowling alley. Lorrick testified that defendant went to see if anybody was watching.

Defendant took the stand and testified that he was in no way involved in the plans of Lorrick and Williams. He stated that the purpose of his going to the house across the street was to seek a friend who he thought would help him find employment.

OPINION

. . . It [was not] error for the trial court to deny defendant's motion for directed verdict on the issue of whether defendant aided and abetted in the breaking and entering by acting as a lookout. The circumstances leading up to the offense, coupled with Lorrick's testimony, present sufficient evidence which, if believed by the jury, would support a conviction under the statute.

. . . A more difficult question is whether defendant may be found guilty, as an aider and abettor, of assault with intent to commit murder. Where a crime requires the existence of a specific intent, an alleged aider and abettor cannot be held as a principal unless he himself possessed the required intent or unless he aided and abetted in the perpetration of the crime knowing that the actual perpetrator had the required intent. . . . It is the knowledge of the wrongful purpose of the actor plus the encouragement provided by the aider and abettor that makes the latter equally guilty. Although the guilt of the aider and abettor is dependent upon the actor's crime, the criminal intent of the aider and abettor is presumed from his actions with knowledge of the actor's wrongful purpose.

There was no evidence that defendant harbored any intent to commit murder. Therefore, knowledge of the intent of Williams to kill the deceased is a necessary element to constitute Poplar a principal. This, however, may be established either by direct or circumstantial evidence from which knowledge of the intent may be inferred.

A typical case of this kind is one where, as here, a crime not specifically within the common intent and purpose is committed during an escape. Convictions for aiding and abetting such crimes have been carefully scrutinized. In *People v. Knapp*, the defendant had gathered with several other men in an upper story of his building for the purpose of having forcible sexual intercourse with the deceased against her will. In order to avoid arrest, all the parties jumped out of a window. After the defendant had jumped, the deceased was either pushed or thrown out of the window by one of the other men present. As a result, she suffered injuries from which she died. Knapp was tried separately on an information charging him and the others with murder and was convicted of manslaughter. In reversing the conviction, the Court stated,

> The conviction of manslaughter could only have been under certain portions of the charge, permitting the jury to find it in case the injury was caused in an attempt of the various persons assembled in the paint shop to avoid an arrest. The language of the court, repeated nearly in the same terms twice, was as follows:
>
> "In this case, if the jury should be satisfied (beyond the doubt that I have spoken of) that these defendants combined for the purpose of inducing this girl to go to that shop for the purpose of prostitution, and that they did induce her to go, and while at the shop all had connection with her, and, in order to avoid arrest or exposure, threw her out of the window, without the intention of killing her, but by it she received injuries which caused her death, it would be manslaughter, because they were engaged in an act against public morals, and unlawful. "
>
> And the court refused to charge that, if the act was done under these circumstances without the concurrence of Knapp, he should not be convicted. Also refused to charge, that if the parties attempted to escape, and one of them, without the knowledge or consent of the other, helped or threw the deceased out of the window, then, none but those actually engaged in the act are liable for the consequences.

The effect of these rulings was practically to hold that parties who have combined in a wrong purpose must be presumed, not only to combine in some way in escaping arrest, but also to be so far bound to each other as to be responsible severally for every act done by any of them during the escape.

It is impossible to maintain such a doctrine. It is undoubtedly possible for parties to combine in order to make an escape effectual, but no such agreement can lawfully be inferred from a combination to do the original wrong. There can be no criminal responsibility for any thing not fairly within the common enterprise, and which might be expected to happen if occasion should arise for any one to do it. In other words, the principle is quite analogous to that of agency, where the liability is measured by the express or implied authority. And the authorities are quite clear, and reasonable, which deny any liability for acts done in escaping, which were not within any joint purpose or combination.

This ruling must have been of controlling weight with the jury. There is evidence tending to show that some person other than Knapp pushed, or threw, the deceased out of the window; but, if the testimony is all before us, it has very little, if any, bearing upon Knapp's complicity in the act which caused her death. He jumped out first, according to the clear current of evidence, and it is not easy to discover in the record, proof of his part in any conspiracy or agreement, in pursuance or execution of which it can be inferred she was put out of the window

Whether the crime committed was fairly within the scope of the common unlawful enterprise is a question of fact for the jury. In the present case, the evidence tends to show that the gun with which the victim was shot was removed from the trunk of the car to the front seat. It is not clear whether the defendant was present when the gun was moved but he was aware of its presence inside the car. Since the record also fails to reveal whether or not defendant knew that the gun was taken into the bowling alley, the question is whether it was proper for the jury to infer from the circumstantial evidence that the defendant entertained the requisite intent to render him liable as a principal for assault with intent to commit murder.

In our opinion the jury could reasonably infer from the defendant's knowledge of the fact that a shotgun was in the car that he was aware of the fact that his companions might use the gun if they were discovered committing the burglary or in making their escape. If the jury drew that inference, then it could properly conclude that the use of the gun was fairly within the scope of the common unlawful enterprise and that the defendant was criminally responsible for the use by his confederates of the gun in effectuating their escape.

Affirmed.

QUESTIONS FOR DISCUSSION

1. List all of the relevant facts to determine the mental state of Poplar.

2. On the basis of these facts, did Poplar intend to kill? Did he do so knowingly? Recklessly? Negligently?

3. According to the Court, what is the *mens rea* required for accomplice liability?

4. Is it just and does it make sense to hold Poplar criminally liable for manslaughter? Defend your answer.

NOTE CASES

1. Harry Wren was driving his friend Steve Lewis's car. On the way from Atkins to Morrilton, they purchased twelve cans of beer and drank a considerable amount of beer and gin from 7 P.M. until immediately before colliding head on with another car. Occupants of both automobiles were seriously injured, and Mrs. Pounds, driver of the other car, died from her injuries three days later. Was Lewis guilty of criminal homicide? The court said yes:

   If the owner of a dangerous instrumentality like an automobile knowingly puts that instrumentality in the immediate control of a careless and reckless driver, sits by his side, and permits him without protest so recklessly and negligently to operate the car as to cause the death of another, he is as much responsible as the man at the wheel.

   Lewis et al. v. State, 220 Ark. 914, 251 S.W.2d 490 (1952)

2. Michael Foster believed Bill had raped Foster's girlfriend. Foster beat Bill up. He handed his friend Otha a knife, telling him to

keep Bill from leaving until Foster returned from getting his girlfriend to verify the rape. After Foster left, Otha got nervous and stabbed Bill, who died from the stab wounds. Was Foster an accomplice to negligent homicide? The courts said yes, because even though Foster did not intend to kill Bill, he was negligent with respect to the death: He should have foreseen the consequences of leaving Otha, armed with the knife, to guard Bill. *State v. Foster,* 202 Conn. 520, 522 A.2d 277 (1987)

COMPLICITY FOLLOWING CRIME

The common law included accessories after the fact—complicity following the commission of crimes—within the scope of liability for the main offense. For example, one who gave a burglar a place to hide was an accessory after the fact and as such was also guilty of burglary. Modern statutes impose liability for complicity following commission of the main crime, but the liability is for separate, less serious offenses, such as obstructing justice, interfering with prosecution, and aiding in escape.

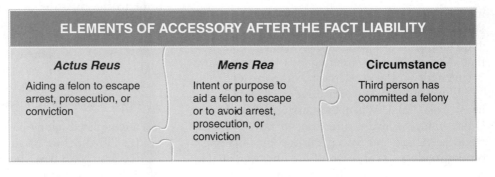

ELEMENTS OF ACCESSORY AFTER THE FACT LIABILITY

Actus Reus	*Mens Rea*	*Circumstance*
Aiding a felon to escape arrest, prosecution, or conviction	Intent or purpose to aid a felon to escape or to avoid arrest, prosecution, or conviction	Third person has committed a felony

Most statutes retain the following common-law requirements for accessories after the fact:

1. A third person has actually committed a felony.
2. The accessory knew of the commission of the felony.
3. The accessory personally aided the third person with the intent to hinder the prosecution of the third person.

The Supreme Court of Louisiana dealt with that state's accessory-after-the-fact statute in *State v. Chism.*

C A S E	Was He an Accessory after the Fact?

State v. Chism,
436 So.2d 464 (La.1983)

Brian Chism was convicted by a judge of being an accessory after the fact, and sentenced to three years in prison, with two and one-half years suspended. He was placed on supervised probation for two years. The supreme court affirmed.

DENNIS, J.

FACTS

On the evening of August 26, 1981 in Shreveport, Tony Duke gave the defendant Brian Chism a ride in his automobile. Brian Chism was impersonating a female, and Duke was apparently unaware of Chism's disguise. After a brief visit at a friend's house the two stopped to pick up some beer at the residence of Chism's grandmother. Chism's one-legged uncle, Ira Lloyd, joined them, and the three continued on their way, drinking as Duke drove the automobile. When Duke expressed a desire to have sexual relations with Chism, Lloyd announced that he wanted to find his ex-wife Gloria for the same purpose. Shortly after midnight, the trio arrived at the St. Vincent Avenue Church of Christ and persuaded Gloria Lloyd to come outside. As Ira Lloyd stood outside the car attempting to persuade Gloria to come with them, Chism and Duke hugged and kissed on the front seat as Duke sat behind the steering wheel.

Gloria and Ira Lloyd got into an argument, and Ira stabbed Gloria with a knife several times in the stomach and once in the neck. Gloria's shouts attracted the attention of two neighbors, who unsuccessfully tried to prevent Ira from pushing Gloria into the front seat of the car alongside Chism and Duke. Ira Lloyd climbed into the front seat also, and Duke drove off. One of the bystanders testified that she could not be sure but she thought she saw Brian's foot on the accelerator as the car left.

Lloyd ordered Duke to drive to Willow Point, near Cross Lake. When they arrived, Chism and Duke, under Lloyd's direction, removed Gloria from the vehicle and placed her in some high grass on the roadway, near a wood line. Ira was unable to help the two because his wooden leg had come off. Afterwards, as Lloyd requested, the two drove off, leaving Gloria with him. There was no evidence that Chism or Duke protested, resisted or attempted to avoid the actions which Lloyd ordered them to take. Although Lloyd was armed with a knife, there was no evidence that he threatened either of his companions with harm.

Duke proceeded to drop Chism off at a friend's house, where he changed to male clothing. He placed the blood-stained women's clothes in a trash bin. Afterward, Chism went with his mother to the police station at 1:15 A.M. He gave the police a complete statement, and took the officers to the place where Gloria had been left with Ira Lloyd. The police found Gloria's body in some tall grass several feet from the spot. An autopsy indicated that stab wounds had caused her death. Chism's discarded clothing disappeared before the police arrived at the trash bin.

OPINION

An accessory after the fact is any person, who, after the commission of a felony, shall harbor, con-

ceal, or aid the offender, knowing or having reasonable ground to believe that he has committed the felony, and with the intent that he may avoid or escape from arrest, trial, conviction, or punishment. La. R.S. 14:25

> [A] person may be punished as an accessory after the fact if he aids an offender personally, knowing or having reasonable ground to believe that he has committed the felony, and has a specific or general intent that the offender will avoid or escape from arrest, trial, conviction, or punishment. . . .

An accessory after the fact may be tried and convicted, notwithstanding the fact that the principal felon may not have been arrested, tried, convicted, or amenable to justice. . . . [I]t is essential to prove that a felony was committed and completed prior to the time the assistance was rendered the felon, although it is not also necessary that the felon already have been charged with the crime. . . .

We must determine whether, after viewing the evidence in the light most favorable to the prosecution, any rational trier of fact could have found beyond a reasonable doubt that

(a) a completed felony had been committed by Ira Lloyd before Brian Chism rendered him the assistance described below;

(b) Chism knew or had reasonable grounds to know of the commission of the felony by Lloyd; and

(c) Chism gave aid to Lloyd personally under circumstances that indicate either that he actively desired that the felon avoid or escape arrest, trial, conviction, or punishment or that he believed that one of these consequences was substantially certain to result from his assistance.

There was clearly enough evidence to justify the finding that a felony had been completed before any assistance was rendered to Lloyd by the defendant. The record vividly demonstrates that Lloyd fatally stabbed his ex-wife before she was transported to Willow Point and left in the high grass near the wood line. Thus, Lloyd committed the felonies of attempted murder, aggravated battery, and simple kidnapping, before Chism aided him in any way. . . .

The evidence overwhelmingly indicates that Chism had reasonable grounds to believe that Lloyd had committed a felony before any assistance was rendered. In his confessions and his testimony Chism indicates that the victim was bleeding profusely when Lloyd pushed her into the vehicle, that she was limp and moaned as they drove to Willow Point, and that he knew Lloyd had inflicted her wounds with a knife. . . .

The closest question presented is whether any reasonable trier of fact could have found beyond a reasonable doubt that Chism assisted Lloyd under circumstances that indicate that either Chism actively desired that Lloyd would avoid or escape arrest, trial, conviction, or punishment, or that Chism believed that one of these consequences was substantially certain to result from his assistance. After carefully reviewing the record, we conclude that the prosecution satisfied its burden of producing the required quantity of evidence. . . .

(1) Chism did not protest or attempt to leave the car when his uncle, Lloyd, shoved the mortally wounded victim inside;

(2) he did not attempt to persuade Duke, his would-be lover, exit [sic] out the driver's side of the car and flee from his uncle, whom he knew to be one-legged and armed only with a knife;

(3) he did not take any of these actions at any point during the considerable ride to Willow Point;

(4) at their destination, he docilely complied with Lloyd's direction to remove the victim from the car and leave Lloyd with her, despite the fact that Lloyd made no threats and that his wooden leg had become detached;

(5) after leaving Lloyd with the dying victim, he made no immediate effort to report the victim's whereabouts or to obtain emergency medical treatment for her;

(6) before going home or reporting the victim's dire condition he went to a friend's house, changed clothing and discarded his own in a trash bin from which the police were unable to recover them as evidence;

(7) he went home without reporting the victim's condition or location;

(8) and he went to the police station to report the crime only after arriving home and discussing the matter with his mother. . . .

Therefore, we affirm the defendant's conviction. We note, however, that the sentence imposed by the trial judge was illegal. The judge imposed a sentence of three years. He suspended two and one half of years [sic] of the term. The trial judge has no authority to suspend part of a sentence in a felony case. The correct sentence would have been a suspension of all three years of the term, with a six-month term as a condition of two years of probation. . . .

DISSENT

DIXON, CJ.

I respectfully dissent from what appears to be a finding of guilt by association. The majority lists five instances of inaction, or failure to act, by defendant:

(1) did not protest or leave the car;

(2) did not attempt to persuade Duke to leave the car;

(3) did neither (1) nor (2) on ride to Willow Point;

(5) made no immediate effort to report crime or get aid for the victim;

(7) failed to report victim's condition or location after changing clothes.

The three instances of defendant's actions relied on by the majority for conviction were stated to be:

(4) complying with Lloyd's direction to remove the victim from the car and leave the victim and Lloyd at Willow Point;

(6) changing clothes and discarding bloody garments; and

(8) discussing the matter with the defendant's mother before going to the police station to report the crime.

None of these actions or failures to act tended to prove defendant's intent, specifically or generally, to aid defendant avoid arrest, trial, conviction or punishment.

QUESTIONS FOR DISCUSSION

1. Was the crime completed at the time Chism aided Lloyd? What facts show this?

2. Do you agree that Chism intended to help Lloyd avoid arrest, trial, conviction, or punishment?

3. What does the dissent mean in saying that the ruling makes a person guilty of crime by association? Do you agree?

4. In Louisiana, according to this ruling, is the *mens rea* for accessory after the fact purpose, knowledge, recklessness, or negligence? Explain.

NOTE CASE

On two separate occasions, Charles Lee Dunn was a passenger in a car when two grand larcenies occurred. He said that he didn't know that the others planned to break into cars, and didn't participate in the thefts of stereo equipment and CDs. He admitted that, after the first theft on September 4th, he voluntarily went with the others when they sold the equipment and he received a small piece of crack cocaine from the proceeds. Regarding one of the offenses, he testified that he took no active part in the theft and was taken home immediately thereafter.

The Commonwealth's evidence included testimony from the investigating officer, Detective Ramsey, that appellant told him that he knew the purpose of going to the location of the first offense was "to take equipment belonging to Mr. Roberts. It was known there was equipment in his car." As to the September 7, 1995 offense, Ramsey testified that Dunn said:

> The three of them went to a location near Mr. Jackson's house. Mr. Dunn waited in the car, and Mr. Walker and Mr. Kraegers approached Mr. Jackson's vehicle. They entered the vehicle through an unlocked door and took stereo equipment from the vehicle, brought it back to the car. [Appellant] states that they put the speaker box in the trunk,

put the amp and a CD player in the car, and he says, I think they got some CD's. That equipment was also taken to the city and traded for crack cocaine which they all used, and that property has not been recovered.

Ramsey stated that Dunn admitted to participating and taking the property to the city in exchange for crack cocaine.

Was Dunn an accessory after the fact? Yes, said the Virginia Court of Appeals:

> In order to convict as an accessory after the fact, the felony must be completed, appellant must know that the felon is guilty and he must receive, relieve, comfort, or assist him. Mere presence and consent will not suffice to make one an accomplice. It must be shown that the alleged accomplice intended to encourage or help the person committing the crime to commit it. Whether a person aids or abets another in the commission of a crime is a question which may be determined by circumstantial as well as direct evidence.
>
> While appellant contends that the evidence failed to establish that he did anything other than ride in a car with friends, the trial court was not required to accept his explanation. Appellant admitted to Ramsey that he knew that the others intended to steal on both occasions; he smoked crack cocaine purchased with the money received from disposing of the goods; and he went out with the codefendants three days after the first larceny occurred. Under the facts of this case, the Commonwealth's evidence was sufficient to prove beyond a reasonable doubt that appellant was an accessory after the fact to the two grand larcenies. Affirmed. *Dunn v. Commonwealth,* 1997 WL 147448 (1997)

✷ 5-1 Accomplice Liability

VICARIOUS LIABILITY

The doctrine of complicity applies to accomplices and accessories because they *participate* in crime. The doctrine of vicarious liability bases criminal liability on the *relationship* between the person who commits the crime and someone else. Vicarious liability applies mainly to business relationships: employer-employee, manager-corporation, buyer-seller, producer-consumer, service provider-recipient. But it can also apply to other situations, such as making the owner of a car liable for the driver's traffic violations and holding parents liable for their children's crimes.

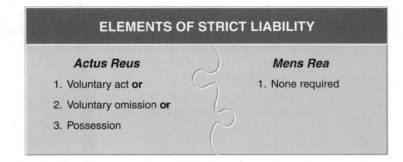

ELEMENTS OF STRICT LIABILITY

Actus Reus	*Mens Rea*
1. Voluntary act **or**	1. None required
2. Voluntary omission **or**	
3. Possession	

CORPORATE VICARIOUS LIABILITY

Conviction and punishment for business crimes on the basis of vicarious liability are difficult to obtain. Pinpointing responsibility for corporate crime is especially difficult because frequently many people are involved in a decision that breaks the law. This problem increases as corporate structures become more complex. The larger and more spread out the business, the harder it is to attribute responsibility to particular individuals. Furthermore, it's difficult to prove *mens rea* in corporate crimes. A corporation can't have a *mens rea* because it can't think. So, prosecutors have to rely on two doctrines to prove corporate criminal liability:

1. Strict liability eliminates the element of *mens rea*.
2. Vicarious liability attaches the intent of managers and agents to the corporation.

Although vicarious and strict liability work together to impose criminal liability, they are distinct doctrines: strict liability *eliminates* the *mens rea*; vicarious liability *transfers* the *actus reus* and *mens rea*.[6]

Criminal punishment based on someone else's actions, especially when there is no criminal intent, raises constitutional questions. Some courts have ruled that it violates the fundamental fairness required by due process to put someone in jail based on vicarious liability. Some courts have gone so far as to declare that even fining someone based on vicarious liability violates due process if noncriminal measures are enough to control harmful business practices. Fundamental fairness is also involved because stockholders, "most of whom ordinarily had nothing to do with the offense and were powerless to prevent it," wind up actually paying the fines.

Vicarious liability not only raises questions about fundamental fairness required by due process. There is also a question of its effectiveness. Fines probably don't deter

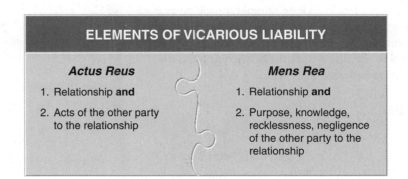

ELEMENTS OF VICARIOUS LIABILITY

Actus Reus	*Mens Rea*
1. Relationship **and**	1. Relationship **and**
2. Acts of the other party to the relationship	2. Purpose, knowledge, recklessness, negligence of the other party to the relationship

officers or other agents who don't have to pay them. Also, the deterrent effect is weakened because businesses treat fines simply as a business expense. Finally, officers suffer no stigma if they are seen as merely violating "regulations," not committing "real crimes." Quite the contrary: officers can boost their reputation for "shrewd business" practices by breaking the rules to turn a profit.[7]

The Iowa Supreme Court dealt with vicarious corporate liability in *State v. Casey's General Stores Inc. and Hy-Vee, Inc.*

C A S E	Did They Sell Liquor to Minors?

State v. Casey's General Stores, Inc. and Hy-Vee, Inc.
587 N.W.2d 559 (1998)

Casey's General Stores, Inc., and Hy-Vee, Inc, corporate defendants, were convicted in District Court, Mahaska County of the simple misdemeanors of selling alcoholic beverages to minors, and they appealed. The Court of Appeals affirmed, and defendants were granted discretionary review. The Supreme Court reversed and remanded for dismissal.

TERNUS, J.

FACTS

Casey's General Stores, Inc., and Hy-Vee, Inc., operate stores in Oskaloosa, Iowa. On October 26, 1996, cashiers in both stores sold alcoholic beverages to underage customers without requiring identification or attempting to ascertain the customer's age. The underage customers were part of a reverse sting operation by the local police. These sales violated policies and procedures established by the corporations to prevent the sale of alcoholic beverages to minors.

Both corporations were charged with the crime of selling alcoholic beverages to an underage person in violation of Iowa Code sections 123.47 and 123.49(2)(h) (1995). These simple misdemeanor charges were tried to the court and both defendants were found guilty. Their convictions were affirmed on appeal to the district court. We then granted discretionary review. See Iowa Code § 814.6(2)(d).

OPINION

. . .

Casey's and Hy-Vee argue that there is no evidence that they, as corporate entities, engaged in cul-pable conduct so as to directly violate sections 123.47 and 123.49(2)(h). The State does not contest this assertion, but rather relies on the corporations' alleged vicarious responsibility for their employees' actions. The State first contends that corporate liability for illegal sales made by an employee is implicit in sections 123.47 and 123.49(2)(h). Alternatively, the State claims Iowa Code section 703.5(1) imposes vicarious liability upon corporate employers under the facts presented here.

The precise claim in this appeal is based on the alleged insufficiency of the evidence to support the verdict. . . . The determinative question . . . is whether the statutes in question render corporate defendants criminally responsible for the actions of their employees in selling alcoholic beverages to a minor in contravention of company policies and procedures. . . .

The primary rule of statutory interpretation is to give effect to the intention of the legislature. To ascertain that intent, we look to the language of the statute. We consider not only the commonly understood meaning of the words used in the statute, but also the context within which they appear. . . .

Do Sections 123.47 and 123.49(2)(h) Impose Vicarious Liability on a Licensee or Permittee for the Sale of Alcohol to a Minor?

Section 123.47 prohibits the sale of alcohol to a minor:

A person shall not sell . . . alcoholic liquor, wine, or beer to any person knowing or having reasonable cause to believe that person to be under the age of eighteen. . . .

Section 123.49(2)(h) contains a similar prohibition:

A person or club holding a liquor control license or retail wine or beer permit under this chapter, and the person's or club's agents or employees, shall not. . . .

. . . .

    h. Sell, give, or otherwise supply any alcoholic beverage, wine, or beer to any person, knowing or failing to exercise reasonable care to ascertain whether the person is under legal age. . . .

The State argues that the evidence supports the defendants' convictions for violating these statutes under the following rationale.

The State first points out that the statutory prohibitions apply to a "person," and that word is defined to include a corporation. See Iowa Code § 123.3(25). Because a corporation can act only through an employee, the State reasons that the legislature must have contemplated criminal liability for corporations based on the acts of their employees. We find this analysis unpersuasive because these statutes do not impose vicarious liability.

Vicarious liability occurs when "one [person] is made liable, though without personal fault, for the bad conduct of someone else.". . . This doctrine is contrary to the "basic premise of criminal justice that crime requires personal fault." La Fave, Criminal Law § 3.9, at 250; accord John J. Yeager, Ten Years with the Iowa Criminal Code, 38 *Drake L. Rev.* 831, 847 (1988-89). As La Fave explains in his treatise on criminal law,

> It is a general principle of criminal law that one is not criminally liable for how someone else acts, unless of course he directs or encourages or aids the other so to act. Thus, unlike the case with torts, an employer is not generally liable for the criminal acts of his employee even though the latter does them in furtherance of his employer's business. In other words, with crimes defined in terms of harmful acts and bad thoughts, the defendant himself must personally engage in the acts and personally think the bad thoughts, unless, in the case of a statutory crime, the legislature has otherwise provided.

Thus, if a statutory crime requires mental fault, "it is the rule that the employer must personally know or be wilful or have the requisite intention [before he will] be liable for the criminal conduct of his employee. . . ."

We begin, therefore, with an examination of the statutes to determine whether they require mental fault or whether they impose strict liability. When a statute imposes strict liability, it is only necessary to prove that the defendant committed the culpable act; it is not necessary to establish any *mens rea* or mental fault. Such an examination re-

veals that a *mens rea* element is included in both crimes.

We had the opportunity to consider whether section 123.47 required mental fault in *Bauer v. Cole,* 467 N.W.2d 221 (Iowa 1991), a negligence case premised on a violation of section 123.47. In that case, the plaintiffs, an injured minor and his parents, sued the hosts of a New Year's Eve party for injuries sustained by the minor in an automobile accident. The plaintiffs alleged the defendants had provided liquor to the minor driver causing his intoxication, which in turn caused the accident. The plaintiffs appealed from an adverse jury verdict, claiming error in the instruction submitting the plaintiffs' negligence claim based on section 123.47.

In the challenged instruction, the trial court had required the plaintiffs to prove the defendants had knowingly supplied alcohol to the minor driver. The plaintiffs argued that knowledge was not an element of the offense. In ruling that the instruction was correct, this court held that section 123.47 requires proof of the defendants' criminal intent: "[W]e conclude that defendants' knowledge of the transaction must be shown to prove a criminal violation under section 123.47." Accord, La Fave (stating if the statutory crime is worded in language such as "knowingly," "wilfully," or "with intent to," the statute requires mental fault).

We think the same conclusion is appropriate with respect to section 123.49(2)(h). Section 123.49(2)(h) requires that the defendant sell the alcoholic beverage "knowing or failing to exercise reasonable care to ascertain whether the person is under legal age." Iowa Code § 123.49(2)(h). Similarly, section 123.47 requires that the defendant "know[ ] or hav[e] reasonable cause to believe" that the person buying the alcoholic beverage is under the age of eighteen. Id. § 123.47. The similar language of section 123.49(2)(h) calls for the same interpretation given to section 123.47 in *Bauer,* namely, that proof of the defendant's criminal intent is required for a criminal violation. Thus, a licensee or permittee cannot be held strictly criminally liable for the illegal sale of alcohol to a minor; there must be proof that the sale to a minor was made "with the knowledge, or by the direction, sanction, or approval of the defendant." *Fullmer v. Tague,* 500 N.W.2d 432, 434 (Iowa 1993) (holding that a plaintiff, to prevail on a negligence claim predicated on section 123.47, "must prove the defendants' knowing and affirmative delivery of the beer to the underage person").

Because sections 123.47 and 123.49(2)(h) specifically require fault, we will not read vicarious liability into these criminal statutes, but must first find a legislative expression of an intent to impose vicarious liability. See La Fave, Criminal Law § 3.9(a), at 252 ("[I]f the statute requires mental fault, it will not be presumed that the legislature intended that the fault of the employee should suffice for conviction of the employer."). Clearly, there is no expression of such an intent in the statutory language. In contrast, we note that the legislature has imposed vicarious liability on licensees and permittees for civil fines and penalties assessed for a violation of section 123.49(2)(h). If the legislature had intended the same result with respect to criminal liability, it could easily have said so. Therefore, we reject any suggestion that chapter 123 itself imposes vicarious criminal liability on licensees and permittees for the illegal sale of alcoholic beverages to minors.

Are the Defendants Vicariously Liable Under Section 703.5?

We now consider the State's contention that the defendants can be held vicariously liable for the conduct of their employees under section 703.5(1). Section 703.5 provides for the vicarious liability of a corporation in two different situations:

> A . . . private corporation . . . shall have the same level of culpability as an individual committing the crime when any of the following are true:
> 1. The conduct constituting the offense consists of an omission to discharge a specific duty or an affirmative performance imposed on the accused by the law.
> 2. The conduct or act constituting the offense is committed by an agent, officer, director, or employee of the accused while acting within the scope of the authority of the agent, officer, director or employee and in behalf of the accused and when said act or conduct is authorized, requested, or tolerated by the board of directors or by a high managerial agent. . . .

We think the first subsection of this statute addresses crimes of omission, ones in which the criminal statute imposes an obligation on the corporation to do something, as opposed to criminal statutes prohibiting certain conduct. Iowa Code section 703.5(1) is taken almost verbatim from Model Penal Code section 2.07(1)(b). The drafters of the Model Code intended this species of vicarious liability to be very limited in scope: Subsection (1)(b) deals with a situation where the criminal law speaks explicitly to corporations. . . . The reference to a "specific" duty imposed on corporations by law is designed to make it clear that the provision does not govern in such a case as negligent homicide, where the duty violated is one that the law imposes generally. Rather, the section will apply when there is a failure, for example, to file a report of a kind that the corporation is specifically required to file, or to maintain records that the corporation is required by law to keep. *Model Penal Code* § 2.07 cmt. 1(b), at 335 (1985). See La Fave, Criminal Law § 3.3, at 202 (noting that some crimes are defined as an omission to act in the face of a legal duty to act, as opposed to more typical crimes that are committed by affirmative action, i.e., the performance of a prohibited act); *Black's Law Dictionary* 1086 (6th ed.1990) (defining "omission" as "[t]he neglect to perform what the law requires"). The second subsection of the statute addresses criminal conduct that consists of the commission of a prohibited act. See *Black's Law Dictionary* 276 (defining "commission" as "the doing or perpetration of a criminal act"). With this distinction in mind, we now consider the application of this statute to the case before us.

The State does not rely on section 703.5(2) to support the defendants' convictions. Indeed, there is no evidence in the record that these sales of alcohol to minors were "authorized, requested, or tolerated" by the companies' boards of directors or any high managerial agents of the defendants. Therefore, we must focus on the requirements of section703.5(1) and decide whether there is sufficient evidence of those requirements to support the application of this statute in this case. To determine whether section 703.5(1) applies, we must identify the "conduct constituting the offense" and then consider whether that conduct constitutes "an omission to discharge a specific duty or an affirmative performance imposed on the accused by the law." Iowa Code § 703.5(1).

The State argues that the conduct constituting the offense is the failure to use reasonable care to ascertain the purchaser's age. Prior to 1986, chapter 123 placed an affirmative obligation on employees of state liquor stores to demand evidence of legal age from a prospective purchaser of alcohol who appeared to be under the legal age. See Iowa Code

§ 123.48 (1985) (repealed 1986). No similar statute exists today. But a defendant can be convicted of a violation of sections 123.47 and 123.49(2)(h) in the absence of such evidence, for example, where the defendant knew the purchaser was a minor. Thus, the requirement of reasonable care is merely a substitute for the mens rea or knowledge element of the crime. We think "the conduct constituting the offense," as contemplated by section 703.5(1), is not the mens rea element of the crime, but rather is the core conduct of selling alcohol to a minor.

We next consider whether this conduct is "an omission to discharge a specific duty or an affirmative performance imposed on the accused by law" within the meaning of section 703.5(1). The sale of alcohol to a minor is the commission of a prohibited act; it is not the omission of a specific duty or affirmative obligation. Therefore, section 703.5(1) does not apply.

Summary.
Sections 123.47 and 123.49(2)(h) do not impose vicarious liability on licensees and permittees for illegal sales made by their employees. Therefore, the criminal culpability of Casey's and Hy-Vee's employees does not provide a basis for the convictions of these corporations. In addition, the factual prerequisites of the statute providing for a corporation's vicarious liability, section 703.5, are not satisfied under the facts before us.

We conclude, therefore, that there is insufficient evidence to support a finding that the corporate defendants violated sections 123.47 and 123.49(2)(h). Accordingly, we reverse the defendants' convictions and remand for dismissal of the charges.

REVERSED AND REMANDED.

QUESTIONS FOR DISCUSSION

1. Consider the wording of the statutes §§123.47 and 123.49(2)? Do they require mental fault, or are they strict liability statutes?

2. Why is it important to determine whether these provisions impose liability?

3. Why did the court not read vicarious liability into the these two sections? Should the court have done so? Explain your answer.

4. According to the court, are the defendants vicariously liable for their employees' selling liquor to minors under the corporate liability provisions in §703.5?

5. Do you think Hy-Vee *should* be criminally liable in this case? Explain your answer, referring to the facts, the purposes of vicarious liability, and the purposes of criminal law discussed in Chapter 1 and the principles of criminal liability discussed in Chapters 3 and 4.

INDIVIDUAL VICARIOUS LIABILITY

Vicarious liability for business crimes gets most of the attention. However, the doctrine of vicarious liability also applies to nonbusiness offenses. In *Nolan v. Iowa City,* the Iowa Supreme Court dealt with the vicarious liability of the owner of a car for the driver's offenses.

C A S E   Is Nolan Guilty of Illegal Parking?

Nolan v. Iowa City
239 N.W.2d 102 (Iowa 1976)

John Nolan, the defendant, was convicted in the Johnson District Court of three vehicle-parking violations and he appealed. The Supreme Court affirmed.

MOORE, CJ.

FACTS

John Nolan was charged in the Magistrate Division of the District Court with over a dozen vehicle parking violations under three separate Iowa City ordinances. Upon conviction, he appealed three of the charges (one under each ordinance) to the Johnson District Court, where he was found guilty under all three ordinances. He was fined a total of $20. Nolan's defense consisted of a challenge to the constitutionality of these ordinances. . . .

The case was presented to the trial court upon stipulation that the vehicle was illegally parked under the various ordinances and that defendant was the vehicle's registered owner. No evidence was offered regarding the identity of the operator of the illegally parked vehicle. The relevant Iowa City ordinances are set out as follows (in pertinent portions):

§ 6.16.2 "No operator of a vehicle shall stop, stand or park any vehicle in any of the following places * * *."

§ 6.16.9 "No person shall leave any vehicle upon any street, alley or public ground at any time for a period longer than twelve (12) hours * * *."

§ 6.30.7 "It shall be unlawful and a violation of the provisions of this chapter for any person to cause, allow, permit or suffer any vehicle registered in the name of or operated by such person to be parked overtime * * *.

"It shall be unlawful and a violation of the provisions of this chapter for any person to permit any vehicle to remain in any parking space beyond (the legal parking time)."

§ 6.54.1 "If any vehicle is found stopped, standing or parking in any manner violative of the provisions of Title 6 and the identity of the Operator cannot be determined, the Owner or person or corporation in whose name said vehicle is registered shall be held Prima facie [DF][in the absence of facts showing otherwise] responsible for said violation."

Read together, these ordinances provide for enforcement of the statutory prohibitions against both active and passive traffic violators. Sections 6.16.2, 6.16.9 and 6.30.7 define the actual violations and are made operable through section 6.54.9 which provides for punishment of the operator if he or she can be found or of the vehicle's registered owner if the operator is not available. These provisions impose a form of strict or vicarious liability upon the registered owner of an illegally parked vehicle. It is upon the constitutional validity of this vicarious liability that our decision in this appeal must rest. . . .

There is wide latitude in lawmakers to declare an offense and to exclude elements of knowledge and diligence from its definition. No general constitutional doctrine of mens rea has ever been articulated. *Powell v. Texas,* [DF][see Chapter 3],

392 U.S. 514, 535, 88 S.Ct. 2145, 2156, 20 L.Ed.2d 1254, 1269. Thus legislation delineating elements of a public welfare offense frequently dispenses with any awareness of wrongdoing. In the interest of the larger good it puts the burden of acting at hazard upon a person otherwise innocent but standing in responsible relation to a public danger.

Not only may public welfare legislation dispense with a mens rea or scienter requirement, it may, and frequently does, impose a vicarious "criminal" liability for the acts of another. We recognized such liability in *State v. Barry,* 255 Iowa 1329, 125 N.W.2d 833, affirming the conviction of a partner in a car sales agency whose employee, without defendant's knowledge, permitted a customer to use pasteboard plates without application for registration and certificate of title. We there said: "* * *. It (section 321.26, The Code, 1958 as amended) imposes a duty upon the dealer to see that this requirement is not neglected. It falls within the class of police offenses where the act is prohibited for the welfare of the state. It is in the nature of a prohibition such as is usually found in statutes that forbid a person to permit ice to accumulate before his front door on a city street. . . . [I]n such instances it is of no consequence whether the offender was cognizant of the violation of the law. The legislature may adopt such a method as the best way of preventing deleterious results to the public. . . ."

In this appeal the ordinances before us are clearly within a permissible area of regulation in the interest of people's lives and property. The tragic statistics have been so well promulgated as to be within the ordinary person's general knowledge. About 50,000 lives are lost annually through traffic accidents. A vastly greater number of persons are injured and crippled. Certainly an illegally parked vehicle on a downtown street during rush hour can seriously endanger pedestrian and vehicular travel. Under the rationale of the above authorities, a registered owner may be vicariously liable for his illegally parked vehicle and subject to punishment pursuant to a public welfare regulation. Whether he may be subjected to imprisonment is not before us now.

Under this public welfare doctrine, it is clear section 6.54.1 may impose prima facie strict criminal responsibility upon the registered owner of an illegally parked vehicle. By proving (1) the existence of an illegally parked vehicle, (2) registered in the name of the defendant, and (3) inability to determine the actual operator, the city can make out a prima facie case for imposing responsibility for the violation upon the vehicle's owner. Under prior authority of this court and others, this "prima facie" responsibility means "at first view" or "on its face" or "without more," the proof of ownership is sufficient to create a jury question on defendant's responsibility for the violation. This proof would also be sufficient to convict defendant unless the evidence indicated defendant was not in fact responsible for the violation. This permits defendant to come forward with evidence that someone was operating the vehicle without his consent or with other facts which would rebut the prima facie inference that the registered owner of a vehicle is responsible for its operation. In the area of public welfare offenses, such burden shifting is not constitutionally infirm. . . .

We hold the Iowa City ordinances considered here fall well within the permissible bounds of public welfare legislation. The inference created by section 6.54.1 does not deny due process to defendant by placing the burden of proof upon him, but rather merely shifts to him the burden of going forward with evidence that the vehicle was not operated by one who the City has a right to presume was operating the automobile with its owner's consent. The convictions must therefore be affirmed.

DISSENT

McCORMICK, J.

This is a small case which involves large principles. I am unable to agree with the majority's view of those principles. Dictum [DF][opinion of the court that goes beyond the law of the case] in *Morissette v. United States*, 342 U.S. 246, 72 S.Ct. 240, 96 L.Ed. 288 (1952), relied on in the majority opinion, does not purport to authorize state and local government to create "strict liability" crimes without limitation. Immediately after the language quoted with approval by the majority, the Supreme Court added:

> Also, penalties commonly are relatively small, and conviction does no grave damage to an offender's reputation. Under such considerations, courts have turned to construing statutes and regulations which make no mention of intent as dispensing

with it and holding that the guilty act alone makes out the crime. This has not, however, been without expressions of misgiving.

Although the *Morissette* decision does not delineate exactly how far government may go in this area, it does indicate three factors must be present: (1) the conduct must at the very least be akin to common-law negligence, (2) the penalty must be slight, and (3) the conviction must not carry a damaging stigma. Government may not make conduct criminal which is wholly passive. The Supreme Court quoted with approval the following statement from Holmes, *The Common Law*, p. 50, "A law which punished conduct which would not be blameworthy in the average member of the community would be too severe for that community to bear." I believe the construction given ordinance 6.54.1 by the majority in this case puts it in this category.

Under the majority construction of the ordinance an automobile owner is guilty of a crime when his car is illegally parked in Iowa City unless he proves the car was being operated without his consent on the occasion involved. Although the record does not show what maximum penalty is possible for such crimes in Iowa City, the conduct is a misdemeanor and may include misdemeanor penalties, a maximum fine of $100 or jail sentence of 30 days. §§ 321.236(1), 321.482, The Code. In addition, an alleged violator is subject to misdemeanor prosecution and maximum penalties for failure to appear. § 321.487, The Code. . . .

Many states do not treat ordinance violations as misdemeanors. In Iowa, without regard to the passivity of the owner's conduct, he is subject to criminal conviction and criminal penalty which may be as great at 60 days in jail, 30 days upon conviction of the parking offense, if authorized by the ordinance, and 30 days if he fails to appear as required. If an illegal parking violation is not a "true crime," as maintained in the majority opinion, it should not be called a crime nor should it carry criminal penalties. If it is a "true crime," vicarious strict liability is unreasonable and denies substantive due process of law. "Where the offense is in the nature of a true crime, that is, where it involves moral delinquency or is punishable by imprisonment or a serious penalty, it seems clear that the doctrine of **Respondeat superior** [liability of an employer for the employee's faults] must be repudiated as a foundation for criminal liability. For it is of the very essence of our deep-rooted notions of criminal liability that guilt be personal and individual. . . . "

Municipal parking regulations like those involved here utilize the machinery of criminal administration as an enforcement tool for social regulations purely civil in nature. Due process does not permit the City to have it both ways. The right not to be labeled a criminal for conduct acknowledged not to amount to a true crime is cherished and constitutionally protected. Ordinance 6.54.1 of Iowa City, as construed by the majority, deprives those convicted under it of that basic right. It thereby violates the due process clause of the Fourteenth Amendment of the United States Constitution. . . .

If illegal parking is as serious as the majority opinion contends, it should be a crime, but the government must then accept the burden of proving personal and individual guilt. However, one of the violations alleged here was under an Iowa City meter ordinance. It is difficult to equate the parking meter system with the lofty goal of preventing traffic fatalities. We are not told by the majority how failure to pay the City's rental charge for temporary storage of a vehicle in a public parking place endangers the public safety.

Moreover, the majority opinion fails to recognize the difference between strict liability and vicarious liability. The traffic ordinances under which defendant was charged purport to impose strict liability. They make illegal parking an offense without regard to the state of mind of the vehicle operator. That is strict liability as discussed in *Morissette*. Here, however, under the majority's construction of § 6.54.1, the issue is not only strict liability but vicarious liability. The majority sustains an ordinance which makes the vehicle owner culpable for conduct for which the vehicle operator is strictly liable. The owner's vicarious liability is predicated wholly on vehicle ownership and presumed authorization of its use by the operator. No relationship akin to common-law negligence is involved. No notice that the vehicle may be or was illegally parked is required. . . . [V]icarious liability is properly imposed when the person charged fails to exercise authority and supervisory responsibility in relation to the violation by another. No such authority and supervisory responsibility exists in the ordinary relationship between a motor vehicle owner and bailee [someone in charge of but not the owner of the car].

In any event, because § 6.54.1, as construed by the majority makes conduct criminal which the majority opinion says is not truly criminal, I would hold it is invalid on due process grounds.

Nor do I accept the assertion in the majority opinion that it is somehow acceptable to shift the burden of proof to a defendant in a mere "public welfare offense." The due process clause protects any accused against conviction of any crime "except upon proof beyond a reasonable doubt of every fact necessary to constitute the crime with which he is charged." Mere law enforcement or prosecutorial inconvenience does not justify trampling on rights which are constitutionally assured. This includes shifting the risk of non-persuasion on elements essential to prove guilt of crime. . . .

QUESTIONS FOR DISCUSSION

1. Under what specific circumstances do the Iowa City ordinances impose vicarious liability for traffic tickets?

2. What constitutional objections were raised to the ordinances?

3. Is this a case of strict liability, vicarious liability, or both? Is the dissent correct in saying the majority is confused about the meaning of these concepts?

4. Assume the role of the attorney for the city in the case. Argue the constitutionality of the ordinances, relying on the opinion of the majority.

5. Assume the role of Nolan's lawyer. Relying on the dissenting opinion, argue that the ordinances are unconstitutional. Identify all of the arguments made by the majority and the dissenting opinions regarding the constitutionality of the ordinances.

6. With which opinion do you agree? Defend your answer.

NOTE CASE

Peter Tomaino owns VIP Video, a video sales and rental store in Millville, Ohio. VIP Video's inventory includes only sexually oriented videotapes and materials. On October 13, 1997, Carl Frybarger, age thirty-seven, and his son Mark, age seventeen, decided that Mark should attempt to rent a video from VIP. Mark entered the store, selected a video, and presented it to the clerk along with his father's driver's license and credit card. The purchase was completed and the Frybargers contacted the Butler County Sheriff's Department. After interviewing Mark and his father, Sergeant Greg Blankenship, supervisor of the Drug and Vice Unit, determined that Mark should again attempt to purchase videos at VIP Video with marked money while wearing a radio transmitter wire. On October 14, 1997, Mark again entered the store. A different clerk was on duty. Following Sergeant Blankenship's instructions, Mark selected four videos and approached the clerk. He told her that he had been in the store the previous day and that he was thirty-seven. Mark told the clerk that he had used a credit card on that occasion and that he was using cash this time and thus did not have his identification with him. The clerk accepted the cash ($100) and did not require any identification or proof of Mark's age. It is this video transaction that constitutes the basis of the indictment.

The clerk, Billie Doan, was then informed by Sergeant Blankenship that she had sold the videos to a juvenile and that she would be arrested. Doan said that she needed to call appellant and made several unsuccessful attempts to contact appellant at different locations. The grand jury indicted Tomaine, Doan, and VIP Video on two counts. Count One charged the defendants with recklessly disseminating obscene material to juveniles and Count Two charged the defendants with disseminating matter that was harmful to juveniles.

Was Tomaino vicariously liabile for the clerk's illegal sale? No, according to the Ohio Court of Appeals:

> The state argued that appellant was reckless by not having a sign saying "no sales to juveniles."

Tomaino argued that criminal liability could not be imputed to him based on the actions of the clerk. Vicarious liability for another's criminal conduct or failure to prevent another's criminal conduct can be delineated by statute; it cannot be created by the courts. Statutes defining offenses are to be strictly construed against the state and liberally construed in favor of the accused. The elements of a crime must be gathered wholly from the statute. Where a duty of supervision is specifically enjoined by a statute, a failure to meet such a duty can be the basis for criminal liability. For instance, criminal liability for endangering children can be based on the combination of one's status as a parent, guardian, or person having custody and control of a child with either positive acts such as abuse or allowing the child to act in nudity oriented matter, or by "violating a duty of care, protection or support."

The state posited, and the trial court apparently accepted, that appellant could be criminally liable because he failed to supervise his employees and take affirmative steps to keep juveniles from entering his store and purchasing videos. However, as we have determined, no statute specifically criminalizes this failure. Although such failure may provide circumstantial evidence of appellant's complicity in the clerk's criminal actions, appellant was not indicted or prosecuted and the jury was not instructed under a complicity theory. It is undisputed that the clerk furnished the video to the minor and that appellant was not present. Because we find that a plain reading of the disseminating matter harmful to juveniles statute requires personal action by a defendant unless the issue of aiding and abetting is submitted, and does not by its terms impose vicarious or premises oriented liability, the jury was not correctly instructed in this case.

State v. Tomaino, 1999 WL 627370 (Ohio App. 12 Dist. 1999)

VICARIOUS LIABILITY OF PARENTS

In 1995, Salt Lake City enacted an ordinance that made it a crime for parents to fail to "supervise and control their children." As of 1997, seventeen states and cities had followed Salt Lake City's example. This wave of parental responsibility laws reflect fear and frustration with "juvenile crime and violence." Parental responsibility laws are nothing new. Contributing to the delinquency of a minor is an old offense. These statutes require that the acts of minor children were done at the direction or with the consent of their parents. So, in one case a father was guilty for "allowing his child to violate a curfew ordinance," and in another, a mother was convicted for "knowingly" permitting her children "to go at large in violation of a valid quarantine order." A gruesome case involved the Detroit suburb of St. Clair Shores, which has an ordinance making it a crime to fail to "exercise reasonable control" to prevent children from committing delinquent acts. Alex Provenzino, sixteen, committed a string of seven burglaries. The local police ordered his parents to "take control" of Alex. When his father tried to discipline him, Alex "punched his father." When he tried to restrain him, Alex escaped by pressing his fingers into his father's eyes. When Alex tried to attack him with a golf club, his father called the police. The parents were acquitted of both vicariously committing the seven burglaries and for failing to supervise their son.[8]

Parental responsibility statutes aren't the same as vicarious liability. They are separate offenses based on either the separate acts or more frequently failures of parents to act. There are only a few cases based on our topic, vicarious liability, that make the crimes of the child those of the parent solely on the basis of the parent-child relationship. One of the few cases is *State v. Akers,* where the New Hampshire Supreme Court dealt with a state statute making parents liable for their children's illegal snowmobile driving.[9]

C A S E | **Are the Parents Guilty of Illegal Snowmobiling?**

State v. Akers
119 N.H. 161, 400 A.2d 38 (1979)

Following a verdict of guilty for violating a statute, which seeks to impose vicarious criminal liability on parents for the acts of their children, the parents objected. The Supreme Court sustained the objections.
GRIMES, J.

FACTS

The defendants are fathers [Two other defendants, Melvin Akers and Marshall Fox, are not named in the case.] whose minor sons were found guilty of driving snowmobiles in violation of RSA 269-C:6-a II (operating on public way) and III (reasonable speed) (Supp.1977). RSA 269-C:24 IV, which pertains to the operation and licensing of off Highway Recreational Vehicles (OHRV), provides that "(t)he parents or guardians or persons assuming responsibility will be responsible for any damage incurred or for any violations of this chapter by any person under the age of 18." Following a verdict of guilty for violating RSA 269-C:24 IV the two defendants waived all right to an appeal de novo to the superior court and all questions of law were reserved and transferred by the District Court (Schroeder, J.). The defendants argue that (1) RSA 269-C:24 IV, the statute under which they were convicted, was not intended by the legislature to impose criminal

responsibility, and (2) if in fact the legislative intention was to impose criminal responsibility, then the statute would violate N.H.Const. pt. 1, art. 15 and U.S.Const. amend. XIV, § 1.

OPINION

... The language of RSA 269-C:24 IV, "parents ... will be responsible ... for any violations of this chapter by any person under the age of 18," clearly indicates the legislature's intention to hold the parents criminally responsible for the OHRV violations of their minor children. It is a general principle of this State's Criminal Code that "(a) person is not guilty of an offense unless his criminal liability is based on conduct that includes a voluntary Act or the voluntary omission to perform an act of which he is physically capable." RSA 269-C:24 IV seeks to impose criminal liability on parents for the acts of their children without basing liability on any voluntary act or omission on the part of the parent. Because the statute makes no reference at all to parental conduct or acts it seeks to impose criminal responsibility solely because of their parental status contrary to the provisions of RSA 626:1 I.

The legislature has not specified any voluntary acts or omissions for which parents are sought to be made criminally responsible and it is not a judicial function to supply them. It is fundamental to the rule of law and due process that acts or omissions which are to be the basis of criminal liability must be specified in advance and not Ex post facto. N.H.Const. pt. 1, art. 23.

It is argued that liability may be imposed on parents under the provisions of RSA 626:8 II(b), which authorizes imposing criminal liability for conduct of another when "he is made accountable for the conduct of such other person by the law defining the offense." This provision comes from the *Model Penal Code* s 2.04(2)(b). The illustrations of this type of liability in the comments to the Code all relate to situations involving employees and agents, and no suggestion is made that it was intended to authorize imposing vicarious criminal liability on one merely because of his status as a parent.

Without passing upon the validity of statutes that might seek to impose vicarious criminal liability on the part of an employer for acts of his employees, we have no hesitancy in holding that any attempt to impose such liability on parents simply because they occupy the status of parents, without more, offends the due process clause of our State constitution. N.H.Const. pt. 1, art. 15.

Parenthood lies at the very foundation of our civilization. The continuance of the human race is entirely dependent upon it. It was firmly entrenched in the Judeo-Christian ethic when "in the beginning" man was commanded to "be fruitful and multiply." Genesis I. Considering the nature of parenthood, we are convinced that the status of parenthood cannot be made a crime. This, however, is the effect of RSA 269-C:24 IV. Even if the parent has been as careful as anyone could be, even if the parent has forbidden the conduct, and even if the parent is justifiably unaware of the activities of the child, criminal liability is still imposed under the wording of the present statute. There is no other basis for criminal responsibility other than the fact that a person is the parent of one who violates the law.

One hundred and twenty seven years ago the justices of this court in giving their opinions regarding a proposed law that would have imposed vicarious criminal liability on an employer for acts of his employee stated, "(b)ut this does not seem to be in accordance with the spirit of our Constitution . . ." Opinion of the Justices, 25 N.H. 537, 542 (1852). Because the net effect of the statute is to punish parenthood, the result is forbidden by

substantive due process requirements of N.H. Const. pt. 1, art. 15.

Exceptions sustained.

DISSENT

BOIS, J.

The majority read RSA 269-C:24 IV in isolation. They conveniently ignore RSA 626:8 (Criminal Liability for Conduct of Another), which provides in subsection II that "(a) person is legally accountable for the conduct of another person when: (b) he is made accountable for the conduct of such other person by the law defining the offense. . . ." RSA 269-C:24 IV is such a law. Imposing criminal liability based on status for certain violations of a mala prohibitum nature does not offend constitutional requirements.

Even if I were to accept the majority's conclusion that the vicarious imposition of criminal liability on parents of children who have committed an OHRV violation under RSA ch. 269-C is constitutionally impermissible, I would still uphold the validity of RSA 269-C:24 IV. A closer reading of this State's Criminal Code belies the majority's reasoning that RSA 269-C:24 IV holds parents of minor offenders criminally responsible for their children's offenses solely on the basis of their parental status. RSA 626:1 I, enunciating the fundamental principle of the Criminal Code, states that all criminal liability must be based on a "voluntary act" or "voluntary omission." When RSA 269-C:24 IV is read in conjunction with RSA 626:1 I, a parental conviction can result only when the State shows beyond a reasonable doubt that a minor child has committed a violation under a provision of chapter 269-C, and that his parent voluntarily performed or omitted to perform an act such as participating in the minor's conduct, or entrusting, or negligently allowing his minor child to operate an OHRV.

When RSA 269-C:24 IV is construed to require a voluntary act or voluntary omission in accordance with RSA 626:1 I, there are no due process infirmities, either under N.H.Const. pt. 1, art. 15 or U.S. Const. amend. XIV, § 1. Culpable intent is not required to impose criminal penalties for minor infractions. "It is well settled in this jurisdiction that the Legislature may declare criminal a certain act or omission to act without requiring it to be done with intent."

When the legislature imposes criminal responsibility without requiring intent, we will override it only when such imposition violates concepts of fundamental fairness. In the present case, there is a demonstrable public interest to assure the safe operation of OHRVs, and the minor penalties imposed upon violators of RSA 269-C:24 IV are insubstantial. In such circumstances, we will not second guess the wisdom of the legislature.

Public welfare offenses requiring no criminal intent have also been held consistent with the due process requirements of U.S.Const. amend. XIV, § 1. "There is wide latitude in the lawmakers to declare an offense and to exclude elements of knowledge and diligence from its definition." "In vindicating its public policy . . . a State in punishing particular acts may provide that 'he who shall do them shall do them at his peril. . . .'"

QUESTIONS FOR DISCUSSION

1. Exactly what does the New Hampshire statute prohibit?

2. Summarize all of the arguments of the majority and dissenting opinions. Which one do you agree with? Defend your answer.

3. Apart from the legal and constitutional arguments, do you think it is good public policy to make parents criminally liable for their children's crimes? Defend your answer.

 5-2 Vicarious Liability of Parents for Their Children's Crimes

SUMMARY

The doctrine of complicity defines criminal liability when more than one person participates in crime. The common law of complicity recognized four categories of participants: (1) principals in the first degree, (2) principals in the second degree, (3) accessories before the fact, and (4) accessories after the fact. Modern statutes have combined participation before and during crime into one category—accomplices—while retaining the category of accessory after the fact. Accomplices are equally liable for the principal crime; accessories after the fact are liable for separate, lesser offenses.

Accomplice and accessory liability depend upon participation. Relationships substitute for participation in vicarious liability. Business relationships—employer-employee, principal-agent, and corporation-management—most commonly give rise to vicarious criminal liability. However, states have occasionally imposed vicarious liability on parents for minor children and on owners of cars for those who drive them. Vicarious liability may be strict, in which case the vicariously liable party lacks both *actus reus* and *mens rea*. Penalties for vicarious strict liability are limited to fines.

 Go to the Criminal Law 7e CD-ROM for Internet exercises.

REVIEW QUESTIONS

1. Distinguish between accomplice and vicarious liability.

2. Distinguish accomplices from accessories under modern law.

3. Identify the two conditions for liability before and during the commission of crimes.

4. State the *actus reus* and the *mens rea* of accomplice liability.

5. Identify and explain the main conditions of accessory liability, that is, liability following the commission of crimes.

6. State the *actus reus* and the *mens rea* of accessory liability.

7. Define and explain the differences between vicarious and strict liability. Give the arguments

in favor of and against each of the two types of liability.

8. What does it mean to say that corporate officers are a corporation's brain?

9. Who in the corporate structure should be punished for corporate crimes?

10. Summarize the arguments for and against extending vicarious liability to the parent-child relationship.

KEY TERMS

accessory—the party liable for separate, lesser offenses following a crime.
accomplices—the parties liable as principals before and during a crime.
doctrine of complicity—the principle regarding parties to crime that establishes the conditions under which more than one person incurs liability before, during, and after committing crimes.
mere presence rule—that a person's presence at the scene of a crime doesn't by itself satisfy the *actus reus* requirement of accomplice liability.
***Pinkerton* rule**—the rule that conspiracy and the underlying crime are separate offenses.
respondeat superior—the doctrine that employers are responsible for their employees' actions.
vicarious liability—the principle regarding liability for another based on relationship.

SUGGESTED READINGS

1. George P. Fletcher, *Rethinking Criminal Law* (Boston: Little, Brown, 1978), pp. 131–205, 218–232. This work contains provocative discussions about complicity, which Fletcher clearly defines in considerable detail. He also assesses participation in crime in ways that provoke considerable thought about the role of those terms in criminal law.

2. American Law Institute, *Model Penal Code and Commentaries*, vol. 1 (Philadelphia: American Law Institute, 1985), pt. 1, pp. 295–348. A detailed analysis of all elements in complicity and vicarious liability, especially of corporations, as well as arguments why these should be included in criminal law and to what extent participants should be criminally liable. This is an advanced discussion written

for experts in the field, but it is well worth the effort to read it and consider its points.

3. Rollin M. Perkins and Ronald N. Boyce, *Criminal Law*, 3d ed. (Mineola, N.Y.: Foundation Press, 1982), pp. 718–720, 911–922. The authors discuss vicarious liability and corporate crime in some detail. They also provide a brief history of how these arose.

4. John Monahan, Raymond W. Novaco, and Gilbert Geis, "Corporate Violence: Research Strategies for Community Psychology," in *Challenges to the Criminal Justice System*, ed. Theodore R. Sarbin and Daniel Adelson (New York: Human Sciences Press, 1979), pp. 117–141. An excellent, clearly written, and easy-to-understand discussion of corporate violence. It defines and describes corporate violence, and includes a thorough bibliography for those who wish to read further.

NOTES

1. *United States v. Peoni*, 100 F.2d 401 (2d. Cir. 1938)

2. *Pinkerton v. U.S.*, 328 U.S. 640 (1946), 643.

3. *Model Penal Code*, tentative draft no. 1, p. 43 (1953); *State v. Spillman*, 105 Ariz. 523, 468 P.2d 376 (1970); Wayne LaFave and Arthur Scott, *Criminal Law* (St. Paul, Minn.: West Publishing Co., 1972), 504.

4. 416 F.2d 1110 (D.C.Cir. 1969).

5. 306 N.C. 466, 293 S.E.2d 780 (1982).

6. Brian Fisse, "Sanctions against Corporations: Economic Efficiency or Legal Efficacy?" in W. Byron Groves and Graeme Newman, eds., *Punishment and Privilege* (Albany: Harrow and Heston, 1986), pp. 23–54.

7. *Commonwealth v. Koczwara*, 397 Pa. 575, 155 A.2d 825 (1959); *Davis v. Peachtree*, 251 Ga. 219, 304 S.E.2d 701 (1983).

8. *American Jurisprudence 2nd*, (1999), Vol. 59, § 124, Parent and Child; Barry Siegel, "Held Accountable for Son's Burglaries," *Los Angeles Times*, May 10, 1996, p. A1.

9. Christine Greenwood, "Holding Parents Criminally Responsible for the Delinquent Acts of their Children: Reasoned Response or 'Knee-Jerk Reaction'?" *Journal of Contemporary Law*, 23 (1997):401.

Uncompleted Crimes: Attempt, Conspiracy, and Solicitation

Chapter Outline

I. Introduction

II. Attempt

III. Conspiracy

IV. Solicitation

V. Summary

C H A P T E R   M A I N   P O I N T S

1. The doctrine of incomplete offenses imposes criminal liability on those who intend to commit crimes and take some steps toward completing them.

2. Attempts to commit crimes stand closest to completion, conspiracies are further removed, and solicitations are furthest removed.

3. The elements of attempt include the intent to commit a specific crime (*mens rea*), steps to carry out the criminal purpose (*actus reus*), and failure to complete the crime.

4. According to attempt law, those bent on committing crimes should not benefit from a stroke of luck that interrupts the fulfillment of their purpose.

5. A voluntary abandonment of a crime heading toward completion can remove liability or mitigate punishment.

6. Legal impossibility is a defense to criminal attempt; factual impossibility is not.

7. The elements of conspiracy include an agreement or combination (*actus reus*) entered into for the specific purpose of committing an unlawful act or committing a lawful act by unlawful means (*mens rea*).

8. The elements of solicitation include the specific intent to induce another to commit a crime (*mens rea*) accompanied by action—usually words—urging the other person to commit the crime (*actus reus*).

Did He Attempt to Rob the Convenience Store?

James Kimball went into a convenience store and began talking to and whistling at the Doberman Pinscher guard dog on duty at the time. Susan Stanchfield, the clerk, gave Kimball a "dirty look," because she didn't want him playing with the dog. Kimball then approached the cash register, where Stanchfield was stationed, and demanded money. Stanchfield then began fumbling with the one dollar bills until Kimball directed her to the "big bills." According to Kimball, he then said, "Hey, I'm just kidding," and something to the effect that "you're too good looking to take your money." As Kimball was leaving, Stanchfield called after him, saying that she would not call the police if "you swear never to show your face around here again." Kimball replied, "You could only get me on attempted anyway."

INTRODUCTION

So far, we have dealt with completed crimes. But it's also a crime to start to commit but not finish committing a crime These incomplete crimes are called **inchoate offenses**. There are three inchoate offenses: Attempting to commit a crime (**attempt**), agreeing with someone to commit a crime (**conspiracy**), and trying to get someone to commit a crime (**solicitation**). Each inchoate offense has its own elements, but they all share the *mens rea* of purpose, that is, the specific intent to commit the crime and the *actus reus* of taking some steps toward fulfilling the criminal purpose but not enough steps to complete the crime.

Incomplete criminal conduct poses the dilemma whether to punish someone who has harmed no one or to set free someone who is determined to commit a crime. The doctrine of inchoate crimes asks the question: How far should criminal law go to prevent crime by punishing people who have not accomplished their criminal purpose? Criminal liability for uncompleted crimes flies in the face of the notion that free societies punish people for what they have done, not for what they might do. On the other hand, the doctrine of inchoate crimes reflects the widely held belief that "an ounce of prevention is worth a pound of cure." The law of inchoate crimes tries to resolve the dilemma between limiting criminal liability to what people have done and setting free people who are determined to commit crimes in the following ways:

1. Requiring a specific intent to commit the crime.
2. Requiring some acts toward completing the crime.
3. Punishing inchoate crimes less severely than completed crimes.[1]

ATTEMPT

Failure is an unwelcome part of everyday life. In criminal law, we hope for failure. Criminal attempt is probably the best known failure in criminal law. So, we're happy when a murderer wannabe shoots at someone and misses the target and when a store detective interrupts an aspiring thief reaching to steal a CD from a bin in Best Buy.

HISTORY OF THE LAW OF ATTEMPT

How to deal with attempt in criminal law has plagued lawmakers, judges, and philosophers for centuries. In his *Laws*, the Greek philosopher Plato wrote that one who "has a purpose and intention to slay another and he [only] wounds him should be regarded as a murderer." But, he added, the law should punish such wounding less than it would murder. In the thirteenth century, the great English jurist Bracton disagreed: "For what harm did the attempt cause, since the injury took no effect?" By the fifteenth century, English judges were applying what became a famous common-law maxim: "The will shall be taken for the deed." Justice Shardlowe held that "one who is taken in the act of robbery or burglary, even though he does not carry it out, will be hanged."[2]

According to the common law, the crime of attempt required more than the bare intent to harm: "The thoughts of man shall not be tried, for the devil himself knoweth not the thought of man," as a medieval judge cogently put it. The early cases required that both substantial acts and some kind of harm flow from the intent. Two leading cases took this position. In the first, a servant, after cutting his master's throat, fled with the master's goods. In the second, a wife's lover attacked and seriously injured her husband, leaving him for dead. Both the servant and the lover were punished for attempted murder because they had not only taken substantial steps toward completing the crime, but they had also seriously injured their victims.[3]

During the 1500s, English criminal attempt law began to resemble today's attempt law. Criminal attempt law was a response to the threats to peace and safety brought on by a society known for hot, short tempers and violent, quarrelsome tendencies. The famous royal court (meaning that it was not a court that followed the common law) that met in the Star Chamber started punishing a wide range of potential harms, hoping to nip violence in the bud. Typical cases included lying in wait, threats, challenges, and even words that "tended to challenge." Surviving records are replete with efforts to punish budding violence that too often erupted into serious injury and death.[4]

In the early seventeenth century, the English common law courts began to develop a doctrine of attempt law. Stressing the need to prevent the serious harms spawned by dueling, Francis Bacon maintained that "all the acts of preparation should be punished." He argued for this criminal attempt principle:

> I take it to be a ground infallible: that wheresoever an offense is capital, or matter
> of felony, though it be not acted, there the combination or acting tending to the of-
> fense is punishable. . . . Nay, inceptions and preparations in inferior crimes, that are
> not capital have likewise been condemned.[5]

By the late eighteenth century, the English common law courts adopted a full-fledged doctrine that applied to all of the inchoate offenses. In 1784, in the great case of *Rex v. Scofield*, a servant put a lighted candle in his master's house, intending to burn the house down. The house didn't burn, but the servant was punished anyway. According to the court, "the intent may make an act, innocent in itself, criminal; nor is the completion of an act, criminal in itself, necessary to constitute criminality."[6]

By the nineteenth century, common-law attempt was well defined as follows:

> All attempts whatever to commit indictable offenses, whether felonies or misde-
> meanors . . . are misdemeanors, unless by some special statutory enactment they are
> subjected to special punishment.[7]

Some jurisdictions have kept the common law of attempt. In 1979, a Maryland appeals court judge confidently wrote that "the common law is still alive and well in
Maryland," and that the common law of attempt "still prospers on these shores." As
of August, 2000 no cases in Maryland since 1979 have disputed this claim.[8]

THEORIES OF CRIMINAL ATTEMPT

Two theories underlie criminal attempt doctrine. One focuses on *actus reus*, aiming
at dangerous *conduct*. The other focuses on *mens rea*, aiming at dangerous *persons*.
The states that follow the dangerous conduct rationale look at how close the defendant came to completing the crime. The dangerous person rationale concentrates not
on how close defendants came to completing their plans but on how fully they have
developed their criminal designs. Both rationales measure dangerousness according
to actions: The dangerous conduct rationale does so to establish closeness to completion; the dangerous person rationale to gauge development of design.[9]

THE ELEMENTS OF CRIMINAL ATTEMPT

Attempt liability boils down to three elements:

1. Intent to commit a specific crime;
2. Act or acts to carry out the intent; and
3. Failure to complete the crime.

Most states don't define attempted murder, attempted robbery, attempted rape,
and so on in separate statutes. They usually define attempt in a general attempt
statute. A typical general attempt statute might read something like "Any person who
shall attempt to commit any offense prohibited by law shall be punished."[10]

 6-1 Attempt Statutes

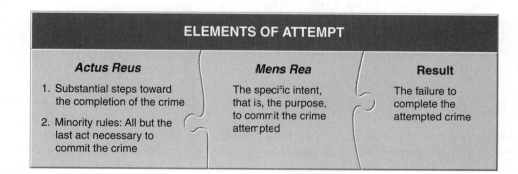

ELEMENTS OF ATTEMPT		
Actus Reus	***Mens Rea***	**Result**
1. Substantial steps toward the completion of the crime 2. Minority rules: All but the last act necessary to commit the crime	The specific intent, that is, the purpose, to commit the crime attempted	The failure to complete the attempted crime

Attempt *Mens Rea*

Attempt is a crime of purpose; it requires specific intent. There are no reckless, negligent, or strict liability attempts. According to one authority,

> "To attempt something . . . necessarily means to seek to do it, to make a deliberate effort in that direction. Intent is inherent in the notion of attempt; it is the essence of the crime. An attempt without intent is unthinkable; it cannot be."[11]

U.S. Supreme Court Justice and legal philosopher Oliver Wendell Holmes, in his classic essay, *The Common Law,* criticized the view that there can be no attempt without specific intent:

> Acts should be judged by their tendency, under the known circumstances, not by the actual intent which accompanies them. It may be true that in the region of attempts, as elsewhere, the law began with cases of actual intent, as these cases were the most obvious ones. But it cannot stop with them, unless it attaches more importance to the etymological meaning of the word attempt than to the general principles of punishment.[12]

Despite the weight of Justice Holmes' views, purpose to act or to bring about a specific result remains the linchpin of criminal attempt *mens rea.*

C A S E — **Did He Intend to Rob the Convenience Store?**

People v. Kimball,
109 Mich.App. 273, 311 N.W.2d 343 (1981)

James Kimball was charged with and convicted of attempted unarmed robbery at a bench trial. He was sentenced to a prison term of from 3 to 5 years. He appealed and the Michigan appeals court reversed the conviction. Although the appeals court found that the evidence proved that Kimball had the requisite intent, it reversed the conviction and ordered a new trial because the trial court rejected defendant's claim that voluntary abandonment was a defense to a prosecution for criminal attempt; in so doing, it never determined whether defendant's abandonment was voluntary or involuntary. Defendant was entitled to a new trial at which defendant could present such defense. (Voluntary abandonment is discussed later in this chapter.)

MAHER, J.

FACTS

It appears that on the day in question the defendant went to the home of a friend, Sandra Storey, where he proceeded to consume a large amount of vodka mixed with orange juice. Defendant was still suffering from insect stings acquired the previous day so he also took a pill called "Eskaleth 300," containing 300 milligrams of Lithium, which Storey had given him. After about an hour, the pair each mixed a half-gallon container of their favorite drinks (vodka and orange juice, in the defendant's case), and set off down the road in Storey's '74 MGB roadster.

At approximately 8:15 or 8:30 in the evening, defendant (who was driving) pulled into the parking lot of the Alpine Party Store. Although he apparently did not tell Storey why he pulled in, defendant testified that the reason for the stop was to buy a pack of cigarettes. Concerning events inside the store, testimony was presented by Susan Stanchfield, the clerk and sole employee present at the time. She testified that defendant came in and began talking to and whistling at the Doberman Pinscher guard dog on duty at the time. She gave him a "dirty look," because she didn't want him playing with the dog. Defendant then approached the cash register, where Stanchfield was stationed, and demanded money.

Stanchfield testified that she thought the defendant was joking, and told him so, until he demanded money again in a "firmer tone."

STANCHFIELD: "By his tone I knew he meant business; that he wanted the money."

PROSECUTION: "You felt he was serious?"

STANCHFIELD: "I knew he was serious."

Stanchfield then began fumbling with the one dollar bills until defendant directed her to the "big bills." Stanchfield testified that as she was separating the checks from the twenty dollar bills defendant said "I won't do it to you; you're good looking and I won't do it to you this time, but if you're here next time, it won't matter."

A woman then came in (Storey) who put a hand on defendant's shoulder and another on his stomach and directed him out of the store. Stanchfield testified that she called after the defendant, saying that she would not call the police if "you swear never to show your face around here again." To this defendant is alleged to have responded: "You could only get me on attempted anyway." Stanchfield then directed a customer to get the license plate number on defendant's car while she phoned the owner of the store.

Defendant also testified concerning events inside the store. He stated that the first thing he noticed when he walked in the door was the Doberman Pinscher. When he whistled the dog came to him and started licking his hand. Defendant testified that while he was petting the dog Stanchfield said "[w]atch out for the dog; he's trained to protect the premises."

> DEFENDANT: Well, as soon as she told me that the dog was a watchdog and a guarddog [sic], I just walked up in front of the cash register and said to Sue (Stanchfield) I said, "I want your money."
>
> I was really loaded and it just seemed to me like it was kind of a cliché because of the fact that they've got this big bad watchdog there that's supposed to watch the place and there I was just petting it, and it was kind of an open door to carry it a little further and say hey, I want all your money because this dog isn't going to protect you. It just kind of happened all at once.
>
> She said I can't quote it, but something to the effect that if this is just a joke, it's a bad joke, and I said, "Just give me your big bills."
>
> Then she started fumbling in the drawer, and before she pulled any money out of the drawer I don't know whether she went to the ones or the twenties I said as soon as she went toward the drawer to actually give me the money, I said,

"Hey, I'm just kidding," and something to the effect that you're too good-looking to take your money.

And she said, "Well, if you leave right now and don't ever come back, I won't call the police," and I said, "Okay, okay," and I started to back up.

And Sandy (Storey) I mean I don't know if I was stumbling back or stepping back, but I know she grabbed me, my arm, and said, "Let's go," and we turned around and left, and that was it.

Both Stanchfield and the defendant testified that there were other people in the store during the time that defendant was in the store, but the testimony of these people revealed that they did not hear what was said between Stanchfield and the defendant.

Storey testified that she remained in the car while defendant went into the store but that after waiting a reasonable time she went inside to see what was happening. As she approached the defendant she heard Stanchfield say "just promise you will never do that again and I won't take your license number." She then took defendant's arm, turned around, gave Stanchfield an "apologetic smile," and took defendant back to the car. Once in the car, defendant told Storey what had happened in the store, saying "but I told her (Stanchfield) I was only kidding." Defendant and Storey then drove to a shopping center where defendant was subsequently arrested.

OPINION

The general attempt statute, under which defendant was prosecuted, provides in part as follows: "Any person who shall attempt to commit an offense prohibited by law, and in such attempt shall do any act towards the commission of such offense, but shall fail in the perpetration, or shall be intercepted or prevented in the execution of the same, when no express provision is made by law for the punishment of such attempt, shall be punished. . . ."

The elements of an attempt are (1) the specific intent to commit the crime attempted and (2) an overt act going beyond mere preparation towards the commission of the crime. Considering the second element first, it is clear that in the instant case defendant committed sufficient overt acts. As the trial court noted, there was evidence on every element of an unarmed robbery except for the actual taking of money. From the evidence presented, including the evidence of defendant's intoxication, the question of whether defendant undertook these acts with the specific intent to commit an unarmed robbery is a much closer question. After hearing all the evidence, however, the trial court found that defendant possessed the requisite intent and we do not believe that finding was clearly erroneous. Reversed on other grounds.

QUESTIONS FOR DISCUSSION

1. If you were a juror and heard the testimony of Kimball and Stanchfield, who would you believe?

2. Has the prosecution proved the *mens rea* beyond a reasonable doubt?

3. What in the testimony of each specifically bears on Kimball's *mens rea*?

4. Did he have the specific intent to rob the store?

5. Is the answer as clear as the court believes? Why or why not?

NOTE CASES

1. John Thacker shot a gun through a tent, intending to "shoot the light out." The shot passed through the tent. People were inside the tent at the time Thacker fired the shot. A bullet hit the bed, barely missing the heads of a woman and her baby who were lying on the bed. Did Thacker attempt to murder them? The Virginia Supreme Court said no, because Thacker lacked the specific intent to kill. He intended to put the light out, not to kill the woman and her baby. *Thacker v. Commonwealth*, 134 Va. 767, 114 S.E. 504 (1922)

2. Robert and his mother were visiting Johnnie Shields's apartment. Robert got drunk and fell, breaking a table. Some time after Robert and his mother returned to their apartment (which was next door to Johnnie Shields's), Johnnie appeared at Robert's door with a gun, threatening to kill him. Robert and his mother fled the apartment; Johnnie chased them. Outside, Robert's mother stood in front of Robert to shield him. Johnnie told

her to step aside or he "would blow her brains out." After a scuffle over possession of the gun, Johnnie fired, wounding her. Did he attempt to murder her? The trial court instructed the jury that they could find Johnnie guilty of attempted murder if they believed that he intended to kill or cause great bodily harm. The jury found him guilty. The Illinois Supreme Court reversed, holding that attempted murder required the specific intent to kill and did not include the alternative intent to cause great bodily harm. *People v. Shields*, 72 Ill.2d 16, 17 Ill.Dec. 838, 377 N.E.2d 28 (1978)

3. On January 15, 1994, a Platte County sheriff's deputy attempted to stop Terry Hemmer for a speeding violation. When Hemmer would not stop, a high-speed chase ensued. The chase continued from Platte County through Madison County and into Pierce County, at which time there were 8 to 10 law enforcement officers from four different law enforcement agencies involved in the chase. During the chase, Hemmer ran two roadblocks set up by police. One roadblock had been set up by the Pierce County sheriff in the town of Osmond. As Hemmer's vehicle was being chased through Osmond by a State Patrol trooper, the sheriff parked his vehicle in the middle of a street in the path of the pursuit and exited the vehicle. The sheriff then attempted to "flag the Hemmer vehicle down" as it approached, but when Hemmer's vehicle did not stop, the sheriff was forced to "dive into a snowbank" to avoid being struck. Hemmer was later apprehended in a rural area after his vehicle ran out of gas.

Hemmer was charged with several crimes relating to the incident, including attempted assault on an officer in the second degree. The charge in the form of an information alleged that Hemmer attempted to "intentionally or recklessly cause bodily injury with a dangerous instrument to a peace officer." Hemmer filed a motion to quash the attempted assault charge, alleging that it is "legally impossible to commit the crime of attempting to recklessly cause bodily injury with a dangerous instrument to a peace officer."

Hemmer claims that it is legally impossible to commit a crime of attempt to recklessly cause bodily injury because the attempt statute requires that the actor intentionally attempt to commit the underlying crime. Before addressing this argument, we find it necessary to clarify the levels of culpability that are involved in the two statutes at issue in this case. Was Hemmer guilty of attempting to recklessly assault a police officer? No, said the Nebraska Supreme Court:

The attempt statute mentions two levels of culpability, "intentional" and "knowing." See § 28201(1) and (2). The crime of assault on a peace officer in the second degree has three potential levels of culpability: intentional, § 28930(1)(a); knowing, § 28930(1)(a); and reckless, § 28930(1)(b). However, the information only charged Hemmer with attempted "reckless" assault on an officer in the second degree.

In *State v. Sodders*, 208 Neb. 504, 304 N.W.2d 62 (1981), the Nebraska Supreme Court discussed the attempt statute and the requisite mental states that accompany § 28201(1)(a), (1)(b), and (2). In its discussion, the court indicated that where a particular result is an element of the underlying crime, subsections (1)(a) and (b) of the attempt statute require that the actor intended the result, i.e., an intentional *mens rea*. . . .

The underlying crime, as charged in this case, does not contain an intentional or a knowing state of mind as an element, as is required by § 28201. As charged in the amended information, the crime is not an intentional or knowing one, but, rather, a reckless one. As the Supreme Court stated in *Sodders*, the attempt statute only applies to crimes committed knowingly or intentionally. The attempt statute thus does not apply to a crime such as an attempt to recklessly cause bodily injury to a peace officer because the *mens rea* of "reckless" does not rise to the level of "knowing" or "intentional" as required by the attempt statute. See § 28201. . . .

. . . We conclude that there is no crime in the State of Nebraska for attempted reckless assault on a peace officer in the second degree. We note, however, that our decision in no way affects the validity of the crimes of attempted intentional or knowing assault on a peace officer in the second degree. The crime of attempted reckless assault on a peace officer in the second degree is not a crime under the statutes and case law of Nebraska. Hemmer, therefore, correctly asserts that the amended information was insufficient to charge a crime, and accordingly, we reverse his conviction. Reversed. *State v. Hemmer*, 531 N.W.2d 559 (Neb. 1995)

4. Thames and his friends, David Bost and Sean Rhodes, met at Rhodes's home to smoke marijuana and drink gin. Thereafter, Thames and Bost began "playing" with guns and Thames accidently shot Bost. Instead of taking Bost to a hospital, out of fear that they would be caught by the police, Thames and Rhodes put Bost in the trunk of Rhodes's car and drove around, looking for an open garage to dump the body. After Thames and Rhodes left Bost in a vacant garage, they left in the car. They returned to the garage when their car ran out of gas. When Thames and Rhodes returned, Rhodes instructed Thames to "put him [Bost] to rest." Thames shot Bost again. Thames then burned the body.

Thames was charged with attempted intentional homicide while armed with a dangerous weapon for the second shot. Thames filed a motion to dismiss, arguing that there was no probable cause to charge him with attempted intentional homicide. The trial court denied the motion. Did Thames attempt to kill Bost? Yes, according to the appeals court:

The first issue involves application of the attempt and intentional homicide statutes. See §§ 939.32(3) and 940.01(1), Stats. Section 940.01(1) states, in relevant part, that "whoever causes the death of another human being with intent to kill that person . . . is guilty of a Class A felony." Section 939.32(3) defines attempt. It provides:

> An attempt to commit a crime requires that the actor have an intent to perform acts and attain a result which, if accomplished, would constitute such crime and that the actor does acts toward the commission of the crime which demonstrate unequivocally, under all the circumstances, that the actor formed that intent and would commit the crime except for the intervention of another person or some other extraneous factor.

Thames accidently shot Bost while the two were intoxicated and had been "playing" with loaded guns. After shooting Bost, Thames saw Bost on the floor moving, with blood seeping out of his head. Afraid that Bost would inform the police about what had happened, Thames and Rhodes decided not to take Bost to a hospital. Instead, Thames and Rhodes put Bost in the trunk of a car and drove around, looking for an open garage to dump the body. After Thames and Rhodes dumped Bost in a garage, Rhodes told Thames to "put him to rest," and Thames then shot Bost again. Thames then set fire to Bost, after dousing him with gasoline. The complaint further alleges that an autopsy concluded that Bost died as a result of the bullet that entered behind his ear and lodged in his brain, the first shot, and that the second shot, the one which entered the left side of his jaw and lodged in the right side, was "nonfatal."

Thames argues that the complaint does not show that he intended to kill Bost when he shot him the second time because Bost died as a result of the first shot. We disagree. Although the complaint alleges that the first shot was the fatal shot and that the second shot was nonfatal, the complaint does not allege that Bost was already dead when Thames shot him the second time. The com-

plaint merely alleges that Bost died from the wound he received as a result of the first shot. Further, the allegations in the complaint give every indication that Thames believed that Bost was still alive immediately before he shot Bost the second time and that he fired the second shot with every intention of making sure Bost was dead. As noted, Rhodes instructed Thames to "put him to rest." Thames then shot Bost at close range. Notwithstanding Thames's argument, we find that the circumstances of the crime allow the clear inference of an intent to kill. Further, the attempt element is satisfied because the complaint establishes probable cause that Thames would have killed Bost except for the extraneous factor that the second shot was nonfatal. The allegations of Count 2 of the complaint establish probable cause to believe that Thames committed the crime of attempted first-degree intentional homicide. . . . Judgment affirmed.

State v. Thames, Unpublished Opinion, Court of Appeals, Wisconsin, No. 95-3313-CR, 1996

Attempt *Actus Reus*

Criminal attempt doesn't require a completed crime, but mere preparation to commit a crime isn't a criminal attempt. If you sit in your room plotting to kill someone, then get up and walk out to your car in order to buy a gun and then say to yourself, "What am I thinking? I can't kill him," and do no more, you haven't committed a crime. Attempt law determines at which point on the spectrum between mere intention and completed crime an attempt to commit a crime has taken place.[13]

Criminal attempt requires action or steps that go beyond plotting and preparation. However, jurisdictions vary in distinguishing between preparation and attempt. Some states require "some steps." At the other extreme, a few states demand "all but the last act." Most states require "substantial steps" toward completing the crime, the test recommended in the *Model Penal Code.* Under all three tests, if you stand over your enemy on the verge of pulling the trigger, you've committed attempted murder. Most jurisdictions require considerably less. But how much less? If you leave your house only to buy a handgun to do the job, you're merely preparing to murder. Courts distinguish mere preparation from criminal attempt according to four tests:

1. Physical proximity doctrine

2. Probable desistance approach

3. Equivocality approach

4. Substantial steps, or the *Model Penal Code* standard.

The **physical proximity doctrine** focuses on time, space, and the number of necessary acts remaining to complete the crime. The easiest point at which to justify criminal liability is when the attempter has taken all but the last act necessary to commit the crime. This was the test applied in the old and famous case, *Commonwealth v. Peaslee*. (See Note Case 3 following *Young v. State*.) The court reversed Peaslee's conviction for attempted arson because Peaslee, "the would-be criminal," had not "done his last act." According to the New York Supreme Court, the conduct has to come "dangerously near completion of the criminal endeavor before the boundary is reached where preparation ripens into punishable conduct." This rule insulates some dangerous conduct from criminal liability. Physical proximity looks to dangerous conduct, not dangerous actors. According to the physical proximity doctrine, the criminal law punishes conduct when it reaches a "dangerous proximity to success." Great importance, therefore, attaches to how close the actor's conduct has come to completing the intended crime. The physical proximity doctrine does not answer the question "how close is close enough to attempt liability?"[14]

The **probable desistance approach** considers whether an act in the ordinary course of events would lead to the commission of the crime but for some timely interference. Acts must pass the point where ordinary law-abiding citizens would think better of what they are about to do and desist from going further. The **equivocality approach** distinguishes preparation from attempt *actus reus* when the act can have no other purpose than committing the crime intended.

The *Model Penal Code* **standard** requires "substantial steps" to corroborate intent. In contrast to the proximity doctrines, the *Model Penal Code* focuses on neutralizing dangerous persons. To satisfy the *actus reus* of attempt, the code requires "substantial steps in a course of conduct planned to culminate in his [the actor's] commission of the crime" and that are "strongly corroborative of the actor's criminal purpose." These substantial steps corroborate the *mens rea*. In other words, the code requires enough action toward completing the crime, not so much to show that crimes are about to occur but to prove that attempters are determined to commit crimes.

According to the authors of the code, lying in wait for and searching for and following potential victims also satisfy the *actus reus* of criminal attempt. Many jurisdictions, however, consider these actions mere preparation. For example, in the often cited old case of *People v. Rizzo*, the court ruled that searching for a victim to rob was only preparing, it wasn't attempting, to commit robbery. Some states, like Louisiana, say that lying in wait and searching for and following are attempts but only if the defendants were armed.

Borrowing from indecent liberties statutes (which make it a crime to lure minors into cars or houses for sex) the *Model Penal Code* provides that enticement satisfies the *actus reus* of criminal attempt. The drafters of the code say that enticement clearly demonstrates the intent to commit a crime—so, enticers are dangerous enough to punish.[15]

The Model Code provides that reconnoitering—popularly called "casing a joint"—satisfies attempt *actus reus* because "scouting the scene of a contemplated crime" clearly bespeaks the intent to commit the crime. By their unlawful entries, intruders also demonstrate their criminal purpose under the Code. The unlawful entry provision particularly helps in two types of cases: entries to commit sexual abuse and entries to steal. In one case, for example, two defendants entered a car intending to steal it, but they got out when the owner unexpectedly came back to the car. According to the court, the defendants hadn't attempted to steal the car. However, under the *Model Penal Code* provision, they would have committed unlawful entry for a criminal purpose.[16]

In most states, collecting, possessing, or preparing materials used to commit crimes is preparation, not attempt. So, courts have found that buying a gun to murder someone, making a bomb to blow up a house, and collecting tools for a burglary are preparations, not attempts. Although these activities aren't criminal attempts, many criminal codes make it a crime to possess items and substances like burglary tools, illegal drugs, drug paraphernalia, and concealed weapons. Under the *Model Penal Code,* these possessions are criminal only if they "strongly corroborate" a purpose to commit a crime. The authors of the code concluded that people who carry weapons and burglary tools with the clear intent to commit crimes are dangerous enough to punish.[17]

The *Model Penal Code* also provides that bringing weapons, equipment, and other materials to the scene of a crime satisfies the *actus reus* of criminal attempts. Examples include bringing guns to a robbery, explosives to an arson, a ladder to a burglary. Only the bringing of materials that are plainly the instrumentalities of crime qualify as taking a substantial step toward completing the crime. A potential robber who takes a gun to a bank clearly falls within the scope of this provision; a would-be forger who takes a fountain pen into a bank does not.[18]

Preparation isn't criminal attempt. However, some states have created a few separate, less serious offenses involving the act of preparation. In Nevada, for example, preparing to commit arson is a crime. Preparing to manufacture illegal substances is an offense in other states. These statutes are aimed at balancing the degree of threatening behavior and the dangerousness of persons against the remoteness in time and place of the intended harm. *Young v. State* deals with the problem of distinguishing preparation from attempt.[19]

C A S E   **Did He Take Substantial Steps Toward Robbing the Bank?**

Young v. State
303 Md. 298, 493 A.2d 352 (1985)

Raymond Alexander Young was tried and convicted of attempted armed robbery and transporting a handgun. He appealed. Both the intermediate court of appeal and Maryland's highest court, the Court of Appeals, affirmed the conviction.

ORTH, J.

FACTS

Several banks in the Oxon Hill-Fort Washington section of Prince George's County had been held up. The Special Operations Division of the Prince George's Police Department set up a surveillance of banks in the area. In the early afternoon of 26 November 1982 the police . . . observed Young driving an automobile in such a manner as to give rise to a reasonable belief that he was casing several banks. They followed him in his reconnoitering. At one point when he left his car to enter a store, he was seen to clip a scanner onto his belt. The scanner later proved to contain an operable crystal number frequency that would receive Prince George's County uniform patrol transmissions. At that time Young was dressed in a brown waist-length jacket and wore sunglasses.

Around 2:00 P.M. Young came to rest at the rear of the Fort Washington branch of the First National Bank of Southern Maryland. Shortly before, he had driven past the front of the Bank and had parked in the rear of it for a brief time. He got out of his car and walked hurriedly beside the Bank toward the front door. He was still wearing the brown waist-length jacket and sunglasses, but he had added a blue knit stocking cap pulled down to the top of the sunglasses, white gloves and a black eye-patch. His jacket collar was turned up. His right hand was in his jacket pocket and his left hand was in front of his face. As one of the police officers observing him put it, he was sort of "duck[ing] his head."

It was shortly after 2:00 P.M. and the Bank had just closed. Through the windows of his office the Bank Manager saw Young walking on the "landscape" by the side of the Bank toward the front door. Young had his right hand in his jacket pocket and tried to open the front door with his left hand. When he realized that the door was locked and the Bank was closed, he retraced his steps, running past the windows with his left hand covering his face. The Bank Manager had an employee call the police.

Young ran back to his car, yanked open the door, got in, and put the car in drive "all in one movement almost," and drove away. The police stopped the car and ordered Young to get out. Young was in the process of removing his jacket. . . . The butt of what proved to be a loaded .22 caliber revolver was sticking out of the right pocket of his jacket. On the front seat of the car were a pair of white surgical gloves, a black eyepatch, a blue knit stocking cap, and a pair of sunglasses. Young told the police that his name was Morris P. Cunningham. As Young was being taken from the scene, he asked "how much time you could get for attempted robbery."

OPINION

. . . The determination of the overt act which is beyond mere preparation in furtherance of the commission of the intended crime is a most significant aspect of criminal attempts. If an attempt is to be a culpable offense serving as the basis for the furtherance of the important societal interests of crime prevention and the correction of those persons who have sufficiently manifested their dangerousness, the police must be able to ascertain with reasonable assurance when it is proper for them to intervene. It is not enough to say merely that there must be "some overt act beyond mere preparation in furtherance of the crime" as the general definition puts it.

It is true that this definition is in line with the observation of Justice Holmes that

> intent to commit a crime is not itself criminal. There is no law against a man's intending to commit a murder the day after tomorrow. The law deals only with conduct. An attempt is an overt act. O. Holmes, *The Common Law* 65 (1923). . . .

What act will suffice to show that an attempt itself has reached the stage of a completed crime has persistently troubled the courts. They have applied a number of approaches in order to determine when preparation for the commission of a crime has ceased and the actual attempt to commit it has begun. It is at the point when preparation has been completed and perpetration of the intended crime has started that a criminal attempt has been committed and culpability for that misdemeanor attaches. . . .

[Here the court defines the proximity, probable desistance, the equivocality, and *Model Penal Code* approaches.]

We believe that the preferable approach is one bottomed on the "substantial step" test as is that of *Model Penal Code* [sic]. We think that using a "substantial step" as the criterion in determining whether an overt act is more than mere preparation to commit a crime is clearer, sounder, more practical and easier to apply to the multitude of differing fact situations which may occur. . . .

We are by no means alone in the belief that an approach based on the substantial step is superior. This belief was shared by the Commission which drafted a proposed criminal code for this State following the *Model Penal Code* approach with respect to criminal attempts. Courts in eight of the federal circuits and courts or legislatures in 23 states also share this belief. . . .

When the facts and circumstances of [this] . . . case are considered in the light of the overt act standard which we have adopted, it is perfectly clear that the evidence was sufficient to prove that Young attempted the crime of armed robbery as charged. As we have seen, the police did not arrive on the scene after the fact. They had the advantage of having Young under observation for some time before his apprehension. They watched his preparations. They were with him when he reconnoitered or cased the banks. His observations of the banks were in a manner not usual for law-abiding individuals and were under circumstances that warranted alarm for the safety of persons or property.

Young manifestly endeavored to conceal his presence by parking behind the Bank which he had apparently selected to rob. He disguised himself with an eyepatch and made an identification of him difficult by turning up his jacket collar and by donning sunglasses and a knit cap which he pulled down over his forehead. He put on rubber surgical gloves. Clipped on his belt was a scanner with a police band frequency. Except for the scanner, which he had placed on his belt while casing the Bank, all this was done immediately before he left his car and approached the door of the Bank.

As he walked towards the Bank he partially hid his face behind his left hand and ducked his head. He kept his right hand in the pocket of his jacket in which, as subsequent events established, he was carrying, concealed, a loaded handgun, for which he had no lawful use or right to transport. He walked to the front door of the Bank and tried to enter the premises.

When he discovered that the door was locked, he ran back to his car, again partially concealing his face with his left hand. He got in his car and immediately drove away. He removed the knit hat, sunglasses, eyepatch and gloves, and placed the scanner over the sun visor of the car. When apprehended, he was trying to take off his jacket. His question as to how much time he could get for attempted bank robbery was not without significance.

It is clear that the evidence which showed Young's conduct leading to his apprehension established that he performed the necessary overt act towards the commission of armed robbery, which was more than mere preparation. Even if we assume that all of Young's conduct before he approached the door of the Bank was mere preparation, on the evidence, the jury could properly find as a fact that when Young tried to open the bank door to enter the premises, that act constituted a "substantial step" toward the commission of the intended crime. It was strongly corroborative of his criminal intention.

One of the reasons why the substantial step approach has received such widespread favor is because it usually enables the police to intervene at an earlier stage than do the other approaches. In this case, however, the requisite overt act came near the end of the line. Indeed, it would qualify as the necessary act under any of the approaches—the proximity approach, the probable desistance approach or the equivocality approach. It clearly met the requirements of the substantial step approach.

Since Young, as a matter of fact, could be found by the jury to have performed an overt act which was more than mere preparation, and was a substantial step towards the commission of the intended crime of armed robbery, it follows as a matter of law that he committed the offense of criminal attempt.

We think that the evidence adduced showed directly, or circumstantially, or supported a rational inference of, the facts to be proved from which the jury could fairly be convinced, beyond a reasonable doubt, of Young's guilt of attempted armed robbery as charged. Therefore, the evidence was sufficient in law to sustain the conviction. We so hold. Judgments of the Court of Special Appeals affirmed; costs to be paid by appellant.

QUESTIONS FOR DISCUSSION

1. Identify the relevant facts in the case to determine *actus reus*.
2. What four tests does the court outline to determine whether the actions of the defendant amount to the *actus reus* of attempted armed robbery?
3. What reasons does the court give for adopting the *Model Penal Code* standard?
4. Do you agree that it is the best test of attempt *actus reus*?
5. If you were deciding this case, what test would you adopt?
6. According to your test, did Young attempt an armed robbery?
7. At what point, if any, in the chronology of events did preparation become attempt? Defend your position.

NOTE CASES

1. On September 21, 1976, at Dallas State Correctional Institution, a guard discovered that the bars of the window in Richard Gilliam's cell had been cut and were being held in place by sticks and paper. The condition of the bars was such that they could be removed manually at will. The same guard observed that a shelf hook was missing from its place in the cell. A subsequent search revealed visegrips concealed inside appellant's mattress, and two knotted extention cords attached to a hook were found in a box of clothing. At trial, evidence showed that the hook had been fashioned from the missing shelf hook. The visegrips were capable of cut-

ting barbed wire of the type located along the top of the fence that was the sole barrier between appellant's cell window and the perimeter of the prison compound. Inspection of the cell immediately before it was assigned to Gilliam as its sole occupant had disclosed bars intact and the shelf hooks in place.

Did Gilliam commit the crime of attempted escape? The court said yes, because Gilliam had taken substantial steps by not only gathering the tools for his escape but also sawing through the bars. According to the court, the substantial step test "broadens the scope of attempt liability by concentrating on the acts the defendant has done and does not . . . focus on the acts remaining to be done before actual commission of the crime." *Commonwealth v. Gilliam,* 273 Pa.Super. 586, 417 A.2d 1203 (1980)

2. In *People v. Rizzo,* Charles Rizzo, Anthony J. Dorio, Thomas Milo, and John Thomasello were driving through New York City looking for a payroll clerk they intended to rob. While they were still looking for their victim, the police apprehended and arrested them. They were tried for attempted robbery but were acquitted because "they had not found or reached the presence of the person they intended to rob." The New York Court of Appeals held:

Many acts in the way of preparation are too remote to constitute the crime of attempt. The line has been drawn between those acts which are remote and those which are proximate and near to the consummation. The law must be practical, and therefore considers those acts only as tending to the commission of the crime which are so near to its accomplishment that in all reasonable probability the crime itself would have been committed but for timely interference. The cases which have been before the courts express this idea in different language, but the idea remains the same. The act or acts must come or advance very near to the accomplishment of the intended crime.

People v. Rizzo, 158 N.E. 888 (N.Y.App.1927)

3. Lincoln Peaslee had made and arranged combustibles in a building he owned so they were ready to be lighted and, if lighted, would have set fire to the building and its contents. He got within a quarter of a mile of the building, but his would-be accomplice refused to light the fire. Did Peaslee attempt to commit arson? According to the court, he did not:

A mere collection and preparation of materials in a room, for the purpose of setting fire to them, unaccompanied by any present intent to set the fire, would be too remote and not all but "the last act" necessary to complete the crime.

Commonwealth v. Peaslee, 59 N.E. 55 (Mass.1901)

LEGAL AND FACTUAL IMPOSSIBILITY

To avoid paying the tax, a man sneaks an antique book past customs. In fact, however, the law exempts antique books from custom duty. Has he committed a crime by attempting to evade customs? A woman stabs her sleeping victim. In fact, her victim died of a heart attack two hours before she stabbed him. Has she committed attempted murder? The man in the first hypothetical case represents an example of legal impossibility. **Legal impossibility** means that actors intended to commit crimes and they have done everything that they could do in order to commit them. However, the law doesn't prohibit what they did. The man intended to evade customs, and he did everything he could do to commit what he believed was a crime. But it was legally impossible to commit the crime because antique books aren't subject to the customs laws.

Stabbing an already dead victim is an example of factual impossibility. **Factual impossibility** exists when the actor intends to commit a crime but some fact or circumstance—**extraneous factor**—prevents its completion. The woman intended to commit murder. She did all that she could in order to commit it; if the facts were different, that is, if her victim had been alive, she would have committed murder.

Legal impossibility requires a different law in order to make the conduct criminal; factual impossibility requires different facts or circumstances in order to complete the crime. In most jurisdictions, legal impossibility is a defense to criminal attempt; factual impossibility is not. The principal reason for the difference is that to convict someone for conduct that the law doesn't prohibit, no matter what the actor's intentions, violates the principle of legality—no crime without a law, no punishment without a crime (see Chapter 2). Factual impossibility, on the other hand, would allow chance to determine criminal liability. A person who is determined to commit a crime, and who acts sufficiently to succeed in that determination, should not escape liability and punishment because of a stroke of good luck.[20]

C A S E   Was the Unloaded Gun a "Stroke of Luck"?

State v. Damms,
9 Wis.2d 183, 100 N.W.2d 592 (1960)

A jury convicted Ralph Damms of attempt to commit murder in the first degree. Damms was sentenced to imprisonment for not more than ten years. Damms appealed. The supreme court of Wisconsin affirmed the conviction.

CURRIE, J.

FACTS

. . . Marjory Damms, wife of the defendant, had instituted an action for divorce against him and the parties lived apart. She was thirty-nine years and he thirty-three years of age. Marjory Damms was also estranged from her mother, Mrs. Laura Grant. That morning, a little before eight o'clock, Damms drove his automobile to the vicinity in Milwaukee where he knew Mrs. Damms would take the bus to go to work. He saw her walking along the sidewalk, stopped, and induced her to enter the car by falsely stating that Mrs. Grant was ill and dying. They drove to Mrs. Grant's home. Mrs. Damms then discovered that her mother was up and about and not seriously ill. Nevertheless, the two Damms remained there nearly two hours conversing and drinking coffee. Apparently it was the intention of Damms to induce a reconciliation between mother and daughter, hoping it would result in one between himself and his wife, but not much progress was achieved in such direction.

At the conclusion of the conversation Mrs. Damms expressed the wish to phone for a taxi-cab to take her to work. Damms insisted on her getting into his car, and said he would drive her to work.

They again entered his car but instead of driving south towards her place of employment, he drove in the opposite direction. Some conversation was had in which he stated that it was possible for a person to die quickly and not be able to make amends for anything done in the past, and referred to the possibility of "judgment day" occurring suddenly. Mrs. Damms's testimony as to what then took place is as follows:

> When he was telling me about this being judgment day, he pulled a cardboard box from under the seat of the car and brought it up to the seat and opened it up and took a gun out of a paper bag. [He] aimed it at my side and he said, 'This is to show you I'm not kidding.' I tried to quiet him down. He said he wasn't fooling. I said if it was just a matter of my saying to my mother that everything was all right, we could go back and I would tell her that.

They did return to Mrs. Grant's home and Mrs. Damms went inside and Damms stayed outside. In a few minutes he went inside and asked Mrs. Damms to leave with him. Mrs. Grant requested that they leave quietly so as not to attract the attention of the neighbors. They again got into the car and this time drove out on Highway 41 towards Menomonee Falls. Damms stated to Mrs. Damms that he was taking her "up North" for a few days, the apparent purpose of which was to effect a reconciliation between them. As they approached a roadside restaurant, he asked her if she would like something to eat. She replied that she wasn't hungry but would drink some coffee. Damms then drove the car off the highway beside the restaurant and parked it with the front facing, and in close proximity to, the restaurant wall.

Damms then asked Mrs. Damms how much money she had with her and she said "a couple of dollars." He then requested to see her checkbook and she refused to give it to him. A quarrel ensued between them. Mrs. Damms opened the car door and started to run around the restaurant building screaming, "Help!"

Damms pursued her with the pistol in his hand. Mrs. Damms' cries for help attracted the attention of the persons inside the restaurant, including two officers of the State Traffic Patrol who were eating their lunch. One officer rushed out of the front door and the other the rear door. In the meantime, Mrs. Damms had run nearly around three sides of the building.

In seeking to avoid colliding with a child, who was in her path, she turned, slipped and fell. Damms crouched down, held the pistol at her head, and pulled the trigger, but nothing happened. He then exclaimed, "It won't fire. It won't fire." Damms testified that at the time he pulled the trigger the gun was pointing down at the ground and not at Mrs. Damms' head. However, the two traffic patrol officers both testified that Damms had the gun pointed directly at her head when he pulled the trigger.

The officers placed Damms under arrest. They found that the pistol was unloaded. The clip holding the cartridges, which clip is inserted in the butt of the gun to load it, they found in the cardboard box in Damms' car together with a box of cartridges.

That afternoon, Damms was questioned by a deputy sheriff at the Waukesha county jail, and a clerk in the sheriff's office typed out the questions and Damms' answers as they were given. Damms later read over such typed statement of questions and answers, but refused to sign it. In such statement Damms stated that he thought the gun was loaded at the time of the alleged attempt to murder. Both the deputy sheriff and the undersheriff testified that Damms had stated to them that he thought the gun was loaded. On the other hand, Damms testified at the trial that he knew at the time of the alleged attempt that the pistol was not loaded.

OPINION

The two questions raised on this appeal are:

1. Did the fact, that it was impossible for the accused to have committed the act of murder because the gun was unloaded, preclude his conviction of the offense of attempt to commit murder?

2. Assuming that the foregoing question is answered in the negative, does the evidence establish the guilt of the accused beyond a reasonable doubt?

§ 939.32(2), Stats., provides as follows:

> An attempt to commit a crime requires that the actor have an intent to perform acts and attain a result which, if accomplished, would constitute such crime and that he does acts toward the commission of the crime which demonstrate unequivocally, under all the circumstances, that he formed that intent and would commit the crime except for the intervention of another person or some other extraneous factor.

The issue with respect to the first . . . question boils down to whether the impossibility of accomplishment due to the gun being unloaded falls within the statutory words, "except for the intervention of . . . some other extraneous factor." We conclude that it does.

Prior to the adoption of the new criminal code by the 1955 legislature the criminal statutes of this state had separate sections making it an offense to assault with the intent to do great bodily harm, to murder, to rob, and to rape, etc. The new code did away with these separate sections by creating § 939.32, Stats., covering all attempts to commit a battery or felony, and making the maximum penalty not to exceed one-half the penalty imposed for the completed crime, except that, if the penalty for a completed crime is life imprisonment, the maximum penalty for the attempt is thirty years imprisonment.

In an article in 1956 *Wisconsin Law Review,* 350, 364, by assistant attorney general Platz, who was one of the authors of the new criminal code, explaining such code, he points out that "attempt" is defined therein in a more intelligible fashion than by using such tests as "beyond mere preparation," "locus poenitentiae" (the place at which the actor may repent and withdraw), or "dangerous proximity to success." Quoting the author

> Emphasis upon the dangerous propensities of the actor as shown by his conduct, rather than upon how close he came to succeeding, is more appropriate to the purposes of the criminal law to protect society and reform offenders or render them temporarily harmless.

Robert H. Skilton, in an article entitled, "The Requisite Act in a Criminal Attempt (1937)," advances the view, that impossibility to cause death because of the attempt to fire a defective weapon at a person, does not prevent the conviction of the actor of the crime of attempted murder:

> If the defendant does not know that the gun he fires at B is defective, he is guilty of an attempt to kill B, even though his actions under the circumstances given never come near to killing B. . . . The possibility of the success of the defendant's enterprise need only be an apparent possibility to the defendant, and not an actual possibility.

. . . Sound public policy would seem to support the majority view that impossibility not apparent to the actor should not absolve him from the offense of attempt to commit the crime he intended. An unequivocal act accompanied by intent should be sufficient to constitute a criminal attempt. Insofar as the actor knows, he has done everything necessary to insure the commission of the crime intended, and he should not escape punishment because of the fortuitous circumstance that by reason of some fact unknown to him it was impossible to effectuate the intended result. . . .

It is not a defense . . . that, because of a mistake of fact or law . . . which does not negative the actor's intent to commit the crime, it would have been impossible for him to commit the crime attempted. . . . It is our considered judgment that the fact that the gun was unloaded when Damms pointed it at his wife's head and pulled the trigger, did not absolve him of the offense charged, if he actually thought at the time that it was loaded.

We do not believe that the further contention raised in behalf of the accused, that the evidence does not establish his guilt of the crime charged beyond a reasonable doubt, requires extensive consideration on our part. The jury undoubtedly believed the testimony of the deputy sheriff and undersheriff that Damms told them on the day of the act that he thought the gun was loaded. This is also substantiated by the written statement constituting a transcript of his answers given in his interrogation at the county jail on the same day. The gun itself, which is an exhibit in the record, is the strongest piece of evidence in favor of Damms' present contention that he at all times knew the gun was unloaded. Practically the entire bottom end of the butt of the pistol is open. Such opening is caused by the absence of the clip into which the cartridges must be inserted in order to load the pistol. This readily demonstrates to anyone looking at the gun that it could not be loaded.

Because the unloaded gun with this large opening in the butt was an exhibit which went to the jury room, we must assume that the jury examined the gun and duly considered it in arriving at their verdict. We are not prepared to hold that the jury could not come to the reasonable conclusion that, because of Damms' condition of excitement when he grabbed the gun and pursued his wife, he so grasped it as not to see the opening in the end of the butt which would have unmistakably informed him that the gun was unloaded. Having so concluded, they could rightfully disregard Damms' testimony given at the trial that he knew the pistol was unloaded. Judgment affirmed. Martin, C. J., not participating.

DISSENT

Dietrich, J.

I disagree with the majority opinion in respect to their interpretations and conclusions of § 939.32(2), Stats. The issue raised on this appeal: Could the defendant be convicted of murder, under § 939.32(2), Stats., when it was impossible for the defendant to have caused the death of anyone because the gun or pistol involved was unloaded?

§ 939.32(2), Stats., provides:

> An attempt to commit a crime requires that the actor have an intent to perform acts and attain a result which, if accomplished, would constitute such crime and that he does acts toward the commission of the crime which demonstrate unequivocally, under all the circumstances, that he formed that intent and would commit the crime except for the intervention of another person or some other extraneous factor.

In view of the statute, the question arising under § 939.32(2), is whether the impossibility of accomplishment due to the pistol being unloaded falls with the statutory words "except for the intervention of . . . some other extraneous factor." In interpreting the statute we must look to the ordinary meaning of words. *Webster's New International Dictionary* defines "extraneous" as not belonging to or dependent upon a thing . . . originated or coming from without.

The plain distinct meaning of the statute is: A person must form an intent to commit a particular crime and this intent must be coupled with sufficient preparation on his part and with overt acts from which it can be determined clearly, surely and absolutely the crime would be committed except for the intervention of some independent thing or something originating or coming from someone or something over which the actor has no control.

As an example—if the defendant actor had formed an intent to kill someone, had in his possession a loaded pistol, pulled the trigger while his intended victim was within range and the pistol did not fire because the bullet or cartridge in the chamber was defective or because someone unknown to the actor had removed the cartridges or bullets or because of any other thing happening which happening or thing was beyond the control of the actor, the actor could be guilty under § 339.32(2), Stats.

But when as in the present case (as disclosed by the testimony) the defendant had never loaded the pistol, although having ample opportunity to do so, then he had never completed performance of the act essential to kill someone, through the means of pulling the trigger of the pistol. This act, of loading the pistol, or using a loaded pistol, was dependent on the defendant himself. It was in no way an extraneous factor since by definition an extraneous factor is one which originates or comes from without.

Under the majority opinion the interpretations of the statute are if a person points an unloaded gun (pistol) at someone, knowing it to be unloaded and pulls the trigger, he can be found guilty of an attempt to commit murder. This type of reasoning I cannot agree with.

He could be guilty of some offense, but not attempt to commit murder. If a person uses a pistol as a bludgeon and had struck someone, but was prevented from killing his victim because he (the actor) suffered a heart attack at that moment, the illness would be an extraneous factor within the statute and the actor could be found guilty of attempt to commit murder, provided the necessary intent was proved.

In this case, there is no doubt that the pistol was not loaded. The defendant testified that it had never been loaded or fired. The following steps must be taken before the weapon would be capable of killing. . . .

Type of Pistol: 32 semiautomatic

Assembly of Pistol
A. Pistol grip or butt hand grasp
B. Barrel
C. Slide
D. Trigger housing

Mechanism
A. To load pistol requires pulling of slide operating around barrel toward holder or operator of pistol.
B. After pulling slide to rear, safety latch is pushed into place by operator of pistol to hold pistol in position for loading.
C. A spring lock is located at one side of opening of magazine located at the bottom grip or butt of gun.
D. This spring is pulled back and the clip is inserted into magazine or bottom of pistol and closes the bottom of the grip or butt of the pistol.
E. The recoil or release of the safety latch on the slide loads the chamber of the pistol and it is now ready to fire or be used as a pistol.

The law judges intent objectively. It is impossible to peer into a man's mind particularly long after the act has been committed. Viewing objectively the physical salient facts, it was the defendant who put the gun, clip and cartridges under the car seat. It was he, same defendant, who took the pistol out of the box without taking clip or cartridges. It is plain he told the truth, he knew the gun would not fire, nobody else knew that so well. In fact his exclamation was "It won't fire. It won't fire."

The real intent showed up objectively in those calm moments while driving around the county with his wife for two hours, making two visits with her at her mother's home, and drinking coffee at the home. He could have loaded the pistol while staying on the outside at his mother-in-law's home on his second trip, if he intended to use the pistol to kill, but he did not do this required act.

The majority states: "The gun itself, which is an exhibit in the record, is the strongest piece of evidence in favor of Damms' present contention that he at all times knew the gun was unloaded. Practically the entire bottom end of the butt of the pistol is open. . . . This readily demonstrates to anyone looking at the gun that it could not be loaded." They are so correct.

The defendant had the pistol in his hand several times before chasing his wife at the restaurant and it was his pistol. He, no doubt, had examined the pistol at various times during his period of ownership—unless he was devoid of all sense of touch and feeling in his hands and fingers it would be impossible for him not to be aware or know that the pistol was unloaded.

He could feel the hole in the bottom of the butt, and this on at least two separate occasions for he handled the pistol by taking it out of the box and showing it to his wife before he took her back to her mother's home the second time, and prior to chasing her at the restaurant.

Objective evidence here raises reasonable doubt of intent to attempt murder. It negatives intent to kill. The defendant would have loaded the pistol had he intended to kill or murder or used it as a bludgeon. . . .

The Assistant Attorney General contends and states in his brief: "In the instant case, the failure of the attempt was due to lack of bullets in the gun but a loaded magazine was in the car. If defendant had not been prevented by the intervention of the two police officers, or possibly someone else, or conceivably by the flight of his wife from the scene, he could have returned to the car, loaded the gun, and killed her. Under all the circumstances the jury were justified in concluding that that is what he would have done, but for the intervention."

If that conclusion is correct, and juries are allowed to convict persons based on speculation of what might have been done, we will have seriously and maybe permanently, curtailed the basic rights of our citizenry to be tried only on the basis of proven facts. I cannot agree with his contention or conclusion. The total inadequacy of the means (in this case the unloaded gun or pistol) in the manner intended to commit the overt act of murder, precludes a finding of guilty of the crime charged under § 939.32(2), Stats.

QUESTIONS FOR DISCUSSION

1. Does it matter whether or not the gun was loaded?

2. Hasn't Damms done everything possible to commit the crime of murdering his wife?

3. What if Damms subconsciously "forgot" to load the gun because he meant only to frighten his wife?

4. Such speculation depends on a belief in Freudian psychology, but assuming that Damms forgot, was the unloaded gun then an extraneous factor, or within Damms's control?

5. Is the Wisconsin rule punishing attempts at about half the amount for completed crimes a good idea?

6. Some states punish attempts at the same level on the ground that when a person intends to commit a crime and only a fortuity prevents its commission, that person deserves punishment equal to that of the person for whom a fortuity did not prevent commission of the crime. Should criminal law consider only intent in determining the seriousness of an offense?

7. What else should it take into account?

NOTE CASE

Wagner accosted Candace I. on October 24, 1990, in a laundromat at 3910 North 76th Street in Milwaukee. He approached her from behind, put a gun to her right side, and tried to force her into the bathroom a few feet away. She struggled and escaped. On June 11, 1991, Wagner accosted Megan M. in a laundromat at 10440 West Silver Spring Drive in Milwaukee. As with Candace I. eight months earlier, he approached her from behind and put a gun to her right side. This time, however, he was able to force his victim into the laundromat's bathroom. While in the bathroom, Megan M. refused his demand that she remove her clothes. After a struggle, she escaped. Wagner was convicted of attempted kidnapping and sentenced to 72 years in prison. Was the victim's escape an extraneous factor, a stroke of luck that prevented Wagner from completing the crime? Yes, according to the Wisconsin appeals court.

State v. Wagner, Nos. 94-0978-CR and 94-1980-CR, Court of Appeals, Wisconsin, 1995

ABANDONMENT

We know from the last section that those bent on committing crimes who have taken steps to carry out their criminal plans can't escape criminal liability just because an outside force or person interrupted them. But what about those who have the intent required, take enough steps to satisfy the *actus reus* of attempt, aren't prevented from completing the crime by some outside force, and change their mind and voluntarily abandon the scheme? Should the law benefit those who themselves are the force that interrupts their crime? The traditional view is that voluntary abandonment is no defense once the *actus reus* and *mens rea* of attempt are established.[21]

Nevertheless, several respected commentators have recommended, and a significant number of states have adopted, a defense of voluntary abandonment. For example, the Michigan criminal code provides

> It is an affirmative defense . . . that, under circumstances manifesting a voluntary and complete renunciation of his criminal purpose, the actor avoided the commission of the offense attempted by abandoning his criminal effort. . . .
>
> A renunciation is not "voluntary and complete" within the meaning of this chapter if it is motivated in whole or in part by either of the following:
> (a) A circumstance which increases the probability of detection or apprehension of the defendant or another participant in the criminal operation or which makes more difficult the consummation of the crime.
> (b) A decision to postpone the criminal conduct until another time or to substitute another victim or another but similar objective.[22]

According to the *Model Penal Code,* voluntary abandonment means

> a change in the actor's purpose not influenced by outside circumstances, what may be termed repentance or change of heart. Lack of resolution or timidity may suffice. A reappraisal by the actor of the criminal sanctions hanging over his conduct would presumably be a motivation of the voluntary type as long as the actor's fear of the law is not related to a particular threat of apprehension or detection.[23]

Opponents of the defense say that it will encourage would-be criminals to take initial steps to commit crimes because they know that they can escape punishment. Supporters offer two reasons to support the defense. First, those who voluntarily renounce their criminal conduct are not the dangerous people the law of attempt is designed to punish, and probably were not bent on committing the crime in the first place. Second, the defense encourages would-be criminals to give up their criminal designs by the promise of escaping punishment. The court in *Le Barron v. State* dealt with the defense of abandonment.[24]

| **C A S E** | **Did He Voluntarily Renounce His Intent to Rape?** |

Le Barron v. State,
32 Wis.2d 294, 145 N.W.2d 79 (1966)

David Le Barron was convicted of attempted rape and sentenced to not more than fifteen years in prison. He appealed. The Wisconsin Supreme Court affirmed.
    CURRIE, J.

FACTS

On March 3, 1965 at 6:55 P.M., the complaining witness, Jodean Randen, a housewife, was walking home across a fairly well-traveled railroad bridge in Eau Claire. She is a slight woman whose normal weight is 95 to 100 pounds. As she approached the opposite side of the bridge she passed a man who was walking in the opposite direction. The man turned and followed her, grabbed her arm and demanded her purse. She surrendered her purse and at the command of the man began walking away as fast as she could. Upon discovering that the purse was empty, he caught up with her again, grabbed her arm and told her that if she did not scream he would not hurt her. He then led her—willingly, she testified, so as to avoid being hurt by him—to the end of the bridge. While walking he shoved her head down and warned her not to look up or do anything and he would not hurt her.

On the other side of the bridge along the railroad tracks there is a coal shack. As they approached the coal shack he grabbed her, put one hand over her mouth, and an arm around her shoulder and told her not to scream or he would kill her. At this time Mrs. Randen thought he had a knife in his hand. He then forced her into the shack and up against the wall. As she struggled for her breath he said, "You know what else I want," unzipped his pants and started pulling up her skirt. She finally succeeded in removing his hand from her mouth, and after reassuring him that she would not scream, told him she was pregnant and pleaded with him to desist or he would hurt her baby. He then felt her stomach and took her over to the door of the shack, where in the better light he was able to ascertain that, under her coat, she was wearing maternity clothes. He thereafter let her alone and left after warning her not to scream or call the police, or he would kill her.

OPINION

The material portions of the controlling statutes provide:

> § 944.01(1), Stats. "Any male who has sexual intercourse with a female he knows is not his wife, by force and against her will, may be imprisoned not more than 30 years."
>
> § 939.32(2), Stats.
> An attempt to commit a crime requires that the actor have an intent to perform acts and attain a result which, if accomplished, would constitute such crime and that he does acts toward the commission of the crime which demonstrate unequivocally, under all the circumstances, that he formed that intent and would commit the crime except for the intervention of another person or some other extraneous factor.

The two statutory requirements of intent and overt acts which must concur in order to have attempt to rape are as follows: (1) The male must have the intent to act so as to have intercourse with the female by overcoming or preventing her utmost resistance by physical violence, or overcoming her will to resist by the use of threats of imminent physical violence likely to cause great bodily harm; (2) the male must act toward the commission of the rape by overt acts which demonstrate unequivocally, under all the circumstances, that he formed the intent to rape and would have committed the rape except for the intervention of another person or some other extraneous factor.

The thrust of defendant's argument, that the evidence was not sufficient to convict him of the crime of attempted rape is . . . [that] the factor which caused him to desist, viz., the pregnancy of complainant, was intrinsic and not an "extraneous factor" within the meaning of § 939.32(2), Stats. . . . The argument, that the pregnancy of the instant complainant which caused defendant's desistance does not qualify as an "extraneous factor" within the meaning of § 939.32, Stats., is in conflict with our holding in *State v. Damms* [excerpted earlier in this chapter]. There we upheld a conviction of attempt to commit murder where the accused pulled the trigger of an unloaded pistol intending to kill his estranged wife thinking the pistol was loaded. It was held that the impossibility of accomplishment due to the gun being unloaded fell within the statutory words, "except for the intervention of some other extraneous factor." Particularly significant is this statement in the opinion:

> An unequivocal act accompanied by intent should be sufficient to constitute a criminal attempt. Insofar as the actor knows, he has done everything necessary to insure the commission of the crime intended, and he should not escape punishment because of the fortuitous circumstance that by reason of some fact unknown to him it was impossible to effectuate the intended result.

Affirmed.

QUESTIONS FOR DISCUSSION

1. Le Barron demonstrates how difficult it can be to apply the renunciation doctrine. Did Le Barron stop the attempted rape because he believed it was morally wrong to rape a preg-

nant woman, or did the pregnancy simply repel him sexually?

2. Should his reason make a difference?

3. Is Le Barron equally dangerous, whichever reason led to interrupting the rape?

4. Do you agree that Le Barron's victim's pregnancy was an extraneous factor?

5. The court said a jury could conclude either that it was or that Le Barron voluntarily renounced his intention to rape because the victim was pregnant. If you were a juror, how would you have voted on the pregnancy question?

NOTE CASE

On January 18, 1992, at 2:19 A.M., Rodney Herron was stopped in his automobile by the Mechanicsburg, Ohio, Police Department for driving under the influence of alcohol. After processing a DUI charge, the police officer dropped Herron off at his residence at 4:06 A.M. According to Herron, he entered his house, walked into the living room, which was dimly lit by a fluorescent light in the adjacent kitchen, and noticed a person lying on the couch on the opposite wall. Herron testified that he believed the person on the couch to be his wife, since she had been sleeping there on a frequent basis. Additionally, he testified that the person was facing the back of the couch, and had a sheet partially covering her head.

Herron further testified that he unzipped his pants, but left them on, and lay down on the couch behind the person. He testified that he unbuttoned the other person's pants, and pulled them down a little. Herron testified that he then placed the other person's hand upon his penis. Herron also testified that he might have touched the person's butt, and he might have kissed her. According to his testimony, Herron then lay his head down, heard the person "whimpering," and realized that it was not his wife, but his stepdaughter, Trisha. He testified that he immediately jumped up and ended the contact. Herron testified that the lighting in the room was adequate for him to identify the color of the person's shorts, and that had she been facing him, he would have recognized that she was not his wife.

Was Herron entitled to have the jury decide whether he was entitled to the defense of voluntary renunciation (abandonment)? Yes, according to the court:

Herron claims that he was entitled to an instruction on abandonment as a defense to the charge of Attempted Sexual Battery. He contends that there was evidence presented that he "abandoned his efforts long before the point of sexual conduct and without the application of any force, * * *." He further claims that his abandonment constituted a "complete and voluntary renunciation of his criminal purpose," since it did not arise out of any fear of discovery. The State argues that the defense of abandonment is only available "where the defendant renounces his activity before completing a significant portion of the offense."

An attempt is a failed offense. Any attempt will inevitably reach a point when it either succeeds or fails. If it is successful, it is no longer an attempt, but a completed offense; e.g. a successful rapist is not guilty of the attempt, but of the actual offense of Rape. If the attempt fails, a defendant may or may not be guilty of the attempt, depending upon the reason for the failure. For example, if the attempt is thwarted by someone or something outside of the defendant's control, or if the defendant stops the attempt due to a fear of detection, the defendant will be guilty of an attempt.

However, if the attempt fails because the defendant voluntarily abandons the attempt, the defendant will not be guilty of the attempted offense, although he may be guilty of some lesser offense. Herron is correct in his argument that abandonment is an affirmative defense to an attempt charge. It is an affirmative defense to a charge under this section [DF][the attempt provision] that the actor abandoned his effort to commit the offense or otherwise prevented its commission, under circumstances manifesting a complete and voluntary renunciation of his criminal purpose.

The burden of going forward with the evidence of an affirmative defense, and the burden of proof, by a preponderance of the evidence, for an affirmative defense, is upon the accused." Our review of the record reveals that Herron presented evidence, by way of his own testimony, that he abandoned any alleged attempt to have sexual intercourse with his stepdaughter upon realizing that he had mistaken her identity. If believed, his testimony could lead a jury to find, by a preponderance of the evidence, that Herron did voluntarily and completely renounce his purpose of committing a Sexual Battery.

State v. Herron, 1996 WL 715445 (Ohio App. 2 Dist.)

✳ 6-2 Abandonment

SUMMARY OF ATTEMPT LAW

Attempt liability requires the *mens rea* of a purpose, that is, the specific intent, to commit a crime combined with the *actus reus* of some steps that go toward committing the crime but that fall short of completing it. Several difficult issues surround attempt law. First, conflicting rationales support criminal attempt. One rationale, for example, justifies attempt as a means to control dangerous persons. Another rationale is that the law of criminal attempt prevents criminal harm. A second difficulty is the dispute over how many acts toward completion amount to attempt. Jurisdictions disagree as to whether any act toward completion, substantial steps toward completion, or all but the last act necessary to complete the crime suffices. Third, difficulties surround legal and factual impossibility. Is it attempt if it was impossible to complete the crime? Most jurisdictions say no to legal impossibility but yes to factual impossibility. Factual impossibilities are generally referred to as extraneous factors. Finally, renunciation creates problems: Should it matter if a person bent on criminal conduct has a change of heart and desists from committing the crime? If the answer is yes, does it matter whether moral or nonmoral considerations prompted the change?

CONSPIRACY

The more remote from completion, the less justifiable is punishment for uncompleted crimes. In this respect preparation, attempt, conspiracy, and solicitation stand on a continuum, with attempt closest to and solicitation furthest from the completed crime. Conspiracy "strikes against the special danger incident to group activity, facilitating prosecution of the group, and yielding a basis for imposing added penalties when combination is involved."[25]

At common law, conspiracy is a combination between two or more persons formed for the purpose of doing either an unlawful act or a lawful act by an unlawful means. In words famous in conspiracy law, Justice Oliver Wendell Holmes defined conspiracy as "a partnership in criminal purpose." Holmes's broad definition needs some refinement, but it captures the basic idea of conspiracy. Criminal conspiracy consists of two elements:

1. *Actus reus*—an agreement or combination (Holmes's "partnership")
2. *Mens rea*—the purpose of attaining either
   a. an unlawful (Holmes's "criminal") objective, or
   b. a lawful objective by an unlawful means.

CONSPIRACY *ACTUS REUS*

Conspiracy *actus reus* is an agreement. The agreement needn't be a formal signed contract; unwritten understandings suffice. This provision makes sense because conspirators rarely put their agreements in writing. Some courts hold that agreement includes "aid," even when given without another party's consent. In one case, a judge learned that someone planned to kill one of the judge's enemies. The judge wanted the plan to succeed, so he intercepted a letter warning the intended victim of the plan.

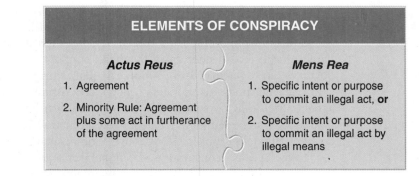

The court held that the judge committed conspiracy to commit murder because he aided the other conspirators, even though he had nothing to do with them.

Vague definitions of agreement can lead to injustice. In one famous trial during the unhappy period of the Vietnam War, the government tried the famous baby doctor turned war protestor, Dr. Benjamin Spock, for conspiracy to avoid the draft law. Videotapes showed several hundred spectators clapping while Dr. Spock urged young men to resist the draft. Spurred on by antagonism to anti-war protestors, the prosecutor in the case made the wild assertion that any person seen clapping on the videotape was a coconspirator. By virtue of their encouragement, according to the prosecutor, these people were aiding Spock, and that made the parties to a conspiracy to violate the draft law.[26]

In most jurisdictions, the agreement alone satisfies the conspiracy *actus reus* requirement. Some jurisdictions, however, require some act beyond agreeing itself. These jurisdictions differ over how much additional action the criminal design requires. Some say "some act"; in others, "any act" will do. One jurisdiction demands that conspirators "go forth for the purpose of committing" the prohibited act. The federal statute requires an "act to effect the object of the conspiracy."[27]

CONSPIRACY *MENS REA*

Conspiracy *mens rea* wasn't clearly defined at common law and most modern legislatures haven't made it any clearer. This leaves the courts to define it. The courts in turn have taken imprecise, widely divergent, and inconsistent approaches to the *mens rea* problem. According to former Supreme Court Justice Robert Jackson, "The modern crime of conspiracy is so vague that it almost defies definition."[28]

Authorities frequently call conspiracy a specific intent crime. But what does that mean? Does it mean that conspiracy involves intent to enter a criminal agreement or combination? Or must conspiracy also include an intent to attain a particular criminal objective, or at least to use a specific criminal means to attain the objective? For example, if two men agree to burn down a building, they have conspired to commit arson. However, if they don't intend to hurt anyone, do they also conspire to commit murder? Surely not, if the conspiracy *mens rea* requires an intent to attain a particular criminal objective. The example demonstrates the importance of distinguishing between the intent to make agreements or combinations and the intent to attain a particular criminal objective. If the objective is to commit a specific crime, it must satisfy that crime's *mens rea*. Hence, conspiring to take another's property is not conspiring to commit larceny unless the conspirators intended to permanently deprive the owner of possession (see the discussion of larceny in Chapter 12).

Courts further complicate conspiracy *mens rea* by not clarifying whether it requires purpose. Consider cases involving suppliers of goods and services, such as doctors who order from drug supply companies drugs that they then use or sell illegally. At what point do suppliers become coconspirators, even though they have not agreed specifically to supply drugs for illegal distribution? Must prosecutors prove that suppliers entered an agreement or combination intending specifically to further buyers' criminal purposes? Most courts require such proof, even though it is difficult to obtain, because conspirators rarely subject their purposes to written contracts. Purpose must therefore be inferred from circumstances surrounding the combination, such as sales quantities, the continuity of the supplier-recipient relationship, the seller's initiative, a failure to keep records, and the relationship's clandestine nature. Some argue that knowing, or conscious, wrongdoing ought to satisfy the conspiracy *mens rea*.[29]

THE OBJECTIVE OF THE CONSPIRACY

What objectives does the law require conspiratorial agreements to have? In some states only combinations or agreements to commit felonies qualify as conspiracies. Other states include both felonies and misdemeanors. Still others include agreements to "accomplish any unlawful object by lawful means," or "any lawful object by unlawful means," or "any unlawful object by unlawful means." Some courts have extended "unlawful" to embrace even civil wrongs. For example, an agreement to interfere unfairly with trade is not a crime in most states, but it may be still against the law. An agreement to engage in unfair trade practices has an unlawful, if not criminal, objective and is considered a conspiracy.

Some conspiracy statutes reach still further. In Alabama, for instance, conspiracy not only applies to agreements and combinations to accomplish criminal and other unlawful objectives, it also encompasses "any act injurious to public health, morals, trade, and commerce." Agreements and combinations falling within this sweeping phrase are almost limitless in number. Examples include combinations to commit fornication, to interfere with social intercourse at a picnic, and to use another person's car without permission.[30]

Reformers have urged courts to declare the most sweeping statutes void for vagueness. In *State v. Musser*, the state of Utah prosecuted Mormons for practicing polygamy. The Utah Supreme Court ruled that the "public morals" provision in Utah's conspiracy statute was unconstitutionally vague. Most efforts to limit the reach of conspiracy law have failed, however. Courts have actually expanded the federal conspiracy to defraud provision in the United States Code to encompass "virtually any impairment of the Government's operating efficiency." The United States Supreme Court remarked that these broad statutes "would seem to be warrant for conviction for agreement to do almost any act which a judge and jury might find at the moment contrary to his or its notions of what was good for health, morals, trade, commerce, justice or order."[31]

Another path toward reform is to draft narrower conspiracy statutes. The *Model Penal Code,* for example, includes only agreements or combinations with "criminal objectives." Several states have followed suit. Connecticut, Georgia, Illinois, and others now include only agreements or combinations made to pursue criminal objectives.

PARTIES TO THE CONSPIRACY

At common law and in most jurisdictions today, a conspiracy requires two or more parties to the agreement. The criminal law punishes conspiracies in part because group offenses threaten more danger than offenses committed by individuals. Thus, some have argued that when unlawful combinations do not have an element of added danger, they are not conspiracies unless they involve more than the number of parties required to commit the completed crime. According to **Wharton's rule** (named after a nineteenth-century criminal law commentator), in a crime that requires two or more persons (such as bigamy, bribery, incest, and gambling), the state must prove that three or more persons agreed to commit the offense. For example, a police officer who agreed not to arrest a person in exchange for money did not conspire to obstruct justice because bribery itself requires at least two persons—the offerer and receiver. Had two police officers agreed to take the money, then conspiracy would have occurred because three parties (the two officers and the briber) agreed to commit the crime.[32]

Some jurisdictions have abolished the Wharton rule on the ground that whether or not the completed offense required more than one party, the danger the actor poses to society justifies making the effort criminal. The *Model Penal Code* adopts this unilateral approach to liability for conspiracy.[33]

The relationship of parties to conspiracies can get intricate, particularly when they involve large operations. Most of these large-scale conspiracies fall into two major patterns: "wheel" and "chain" conspiracies. In wheel conspiracies, one or more defendants participate in every transaction. These participants make up the hub of the wheel conspiracy. Others participate in only one transaction; they are the spokes in the wheel. Chain conspiracies usually involve the distribution of some commodity, such as illegal drugs. In chain conspiracies, participants at one end of the chain may know nothing of each other, but every participant handles the same commodity at different points, such as manufacture, distribution, and sale. In *United States v. Bruno,* for example, smugglers brought narcotics into New York, middlemen purchased the narcotics, and two groups of retailers (one operating in New York and the other in Louisiana) bought narcotics from middlemen.[34]

Failure to convict one party does not prevent conviction of other parties to conspiracies. Typically, statutes similar to the Illinois Criminal Code provide:

> It shall not be a defense to conspiracy that the person or persons with whom the accused is alleged to have conspired
> 1. Has not been prosecuted or convicted, or
> 2. Has been convicted of a different offense, or
> 3. Is not amenable to justice, or
> 4. Has been acquitted, or
> 5. Lacked the capacity to commit an offense.[35]

Conspiracy is an important part of the "arsenal" of the "war on drugs" that most states and the federal government have periodically waged since the early 1900s. The court in *State v. McCart* dealt with most of the complicated issues surrounding the elements of criminal conspiracy in the "drug war" context.

C A S E   Did They Conspire to Sell Marijuana?

McCart v. State
1999 WL 784125 (Ala.Crim.App.)

William Gary McCart, Peggy Wilson McCart, and Gary Keith McCart, defendants, were convicted in the Baldwin Circuit Court of conspiracy to traffic in marijuana. Defendants appealed. The Court of Criminal Appeals affirmed the convictions and remanded for imposition of further fines.

BASCHAB, J.

FACTS

The appellants, William Gary McCart (Gary), Peggy Wilson McCart, and Gary Keith McCart (Keith), were convicted of conspiracy to traffic in marijuana, in violation of §§ 13A-12-204 and 13A-12-231(1)a., Ala.Code 1975, and unlawful possession of drug paraphernalia, in violation of § 13A-12-260(c), Ala.Code 1975. The trial court sentenced each appellant to serve 25 years in prison and ordered each to pay a $25,000 fine on the conspiracy convictions. The court also sentenced each appellant to serve one year in the Baldwin County jail and to pay a $2,000 fine on the unlawful possession of drug paraphernalia convictions. This appeal followed.

The State's evidence showed that Peggy McCart, Gary McCart, and Keith McCart lived in the same house. After investigating the McCarts for a period of time, law enforcement officers obtained a warrant to search the McCart residence. When the officers arrived at the residence to execute the search warrant, Gary McCart pointed to a Tupperware container on a table beside a chair in the living room. There was a marijuana cigarette on top of the container, and more marijuana, scissors, rolling papers, and hemostats were inside the container. Gary McCart told the officers that was all of the marijuana that was in the residence. However, after the officers mentioned that they would be using a dog to search for more marijuana, Gary McCart took the officers to the master bedroom, where they found two sets of scales, some plastic sandwich bags, and a quantity of marijuana. During their search, the officers found more marijuana in a purse in the master bedroom, in a cat food bag in a drawer under Gary and Peggy McCart's waterbed, and in a tin on top of the refrigerator in the kitchen. In Keith McCart's bedroom, the officers found more marijuana and drug paraphernalia, including pipes, bongs, scissors, plastic bags, and rolling papers. During the search, they also found a handheld scanner that would pick up the frequency used by the Sheriff's Department. Finally, in an outbuilding, officers found a setup designed for the indoor cultivation of marijuana.

After the search, the officers questioned the appellants. Gary McCart admitted that he had been selling marijuana for approximately one year. He explained that he obtained one pound of marijuana at a time from a man in Mobile, that the man would "front" him the marijuana, or give it to him on credit, and that he would pay for it after he sold it. Gary McCart admitted to the officers that he had bought and sold at least three pounds of marijuana over a short period of time. He also admitted that he had tried unsuccessfully to grow marijuana in the outbuilding. Finally, he stated that he did not document any cash sales, but that he used a calendar to keep a record of sales he made on credit. Peggy McCart admitted that she knew the marijuana was coming from a man in Mobile and was being fronted, but she denied selling marijuana. Keith McCart admitted that he had been selling marijuana for approximately one year, and he gave the officers the names of two people from whom he had bought marijuana and the names of several people to whom he had sold marijuana.

Officers found the calendar on which Gary McCart kept his record of credit sales on a counter in the kitchen. They also found similar notes with names and numbers on them in Keith McCart's bedroom. A handwriting-identification and document-examination expert testified that Peggy McCart did not make any of the drug-related entries on the calendar, but that she had entered other information on that calendar. Finally, there was testimony that there was more traffic coming and going from the house than was usual for a residence. People would come, stay a short while, and leave.

OPINION

With respect to conspiracies to commit controlled substance crimes, § 13A-12-204(a), Ala.Code 1975, provides:

"A person is guilty of criminal conspiracy to commit a controlled substance crime if he engages in the conduct defined in Section 13A-4-3(a), and the object of the conspiracy is a controlled substance crime."

Section 13A-4-3(a), Ala.Code 1975, provides:

"A person is guilty of criminal conspiracy if, with the intent that conduct constituting an offense be performed, he agrees with one or more persons to engage in or cause the performance of such conduct, and any one or more of such persons does an overt act to effect an objective of the agreement."

Finally, § 13A-12-231(1), Ala.Code 1975, defines trafficking in marijuana as follows:

"Any person who knowingly sells, manufactures, delivers, or brings into this state, or who is knowingly in actual or constructive possession of, in excess of one kilo or 2.2 pounds of any part of the plant of the genus Cannabis, whether growing or not, the seeds thereof, the resin extracted from any part of the plant, and every compound, manufacture, salt, derivative, mixture, or preparation of the plant, its seeds, or resin including the completely defoliated mature stalks of the plant, fiber produced from the stalks, oil, or cake, or the completely sterilized samples of seeds of the plant which are incapable of germination is guilty of a felony, which felony shall be known as 'trafficking in cannabis.'"

In a conspiracy prosecution, the State may rely on circumstantial evidence to show the element of agreement. The existence of a "confederation or conspiracy need not be proved by positive testimony. It seldom can be. The trier of fact is to determine its existence and extent from all the evidence in the case and the conduct of the parties. . . . Furthermore, "[a] conspiracy agreement need not be formal or express. It is sufficient if there is a meeting of the minds or a tacit agreement, its existence being generally a matter of inference from the acts of the participants." In addition, it need not be shown that the defendant knew all of the details of the alleged conspiracy as knowledge of the essential objective is sufficient to impose liability. Although association alone will not support an inference of conspiracy, association with co-conspirators may be considered as a factor. Moreover, because the appellants were charged with conspiracy to traffic in marijuana, the State was not required to show that they possessed or sold more than 2.2 pounds of marijuana at any one time. Conspiracy is a distinct and separate substantive offense from the crime intended, and does not require that the criminal offense agreed to be actually completed. The state was not required to prove the elements of trafficking in cannabis under § 13A-12-231. They only had to prove conspiracy to commit that offense pursuant to § 13A-12-204. Finally, [i]n determining whether there is sufficient evidence to support the verdict of the jury and the judgment of the trial court, we must accept as true the evidence introduced by the state, accord the state all legitimate inferences therefrom, and view the evidence in the light most favorable to the prosecution.

In this case, the State presented sufficient evidence to show that the appellants conspired to traffic in excess of 2.2 pounds of marijuana. The appellants' conduct and statements to law enforcement officers, the evidence presented at trial, and the circumstances surrounding the offense showed a conspiracy that was ongoing for approximately one year. Gary and Keith McCart had been selling marijuana from their residence for approximately one year, and Peggy McCart, at the very least, knew about and consented to the fronting and selling of marijuana from the residence. Thus, the appellants all knew that large amounts of marijuana were being sold from the residence and at least implicitly consented to the sales. Further, Gary McCart admitted that, over a short period of time, he had bought and sold in excess of 2.2 pounds of marijuana. Therefore, the State presented sufficient circumstantial evidence from which the jury could have concluded beyond a reasonable doubt that the appellants had engaged in an ongoing conspiracy to traffic in excess of 2.2 pounds of marijuana. Accordingly, the trial court properly denied the appellants' motions for a judgment of acquittal.

. . .

For the above-stated reasons, we affirm the appellants' convictions. Also, the trial court properly fined the appellants $25,000 for their conspiracy to traffic convictions, as required by § 13A-12-231(1)a., Ala.Code 1975. However, the trial court should also have imposed a fine in accordance with § 13A-12-281, Ala.Code 1975, for each of the conspiracy to traffic convictions. Section 13A-12-281, provides:

"(a) In addition to any disposition and fine authorized by Sections 13A- 12-202, 13A-12-203, 13A-12-
204, 13A-12-211, 13A-12-212, 13A-12- 213,
13A-12-215, or 13A-12-231, . . . every person convicted of, or adjudicated delinquent for, a violation
of any offense defined in the sections set forth
above, shall be assessed for each such offense an additional penalty fixed at $1,000 for first offenders,
and $2,000 for second and subsequent offenders.
"(b) All penalties provided for in this division
shall be in addition to and not in lieu of any fine
authorized by law or required to be imposed pursuant to the provision of the controlled substance
statutes set forth in subsection (a) of this section."

Therefore, we remand this case to the trial court so
that it can impose the fines required by § 13A-12-
281, Ala.Code 1975.

DISSENT

FRY, J.

I respectfully disagree with the majority's . . .
that the state presented sufficient evidence to sustain Gary, Peggy, and Keith McCart's convictions
for conspiracy to traffic in marijuana. "A person is
guilty of criminal conspiracy if, with the intent that
conduct constituting an offense be performed, he
agrees with one or more persons to engage in or
cause the performance of such conduct, and any
one or more of such persons does an overt act to
effect an objective of the agreement." Section 13A-
4-3(a), Ala.Code 1975.

To establish a prima facie case [a case that is
proven if contrary evidence is not offered] of conspiracy,
the state must prove: 1) the specific intent that a
crime be performed; 2) an agreement with at least
one other person to engage in or cause the crime
to be performed; and 3) the commission of an
overt act in furtherance of the conspiracy. The
existence of a conspiracy can rarely be shown
by direct evidence; it must be determined by the
triers of fact from the conduct of the parties, the
trial testimony, the circumstances surrounding the
criminal act, and the conduct of the defendant subsequent to the act. "[The] mere association with
persons involved in a criminal enterprise is insufficient to prove participation in a conspiracy."
Moreover, "[c]onspiracy is a distinct and separate
substantive offense from the crime intended, and
does not require that the criminal offense agreed to
be actually completed."

The essence of a conspiracy is the agreement to
engage in the prohibited conduct. A conspiracy
agreement need not be formal or express. Agreements to enter into conspiracies can be shown by
inferences from the conduct of the participants. In
addition, it need not be shown that the defendant[s] knew all the details of the alleged conspiracy as knowledge of the essential objective is
sufficient to impose liability.

Gary, Peggy, and Keith McCart were charged
with conspiring to "knowingly sell, deliver, or actually or constructively possess in excess of 2.2
pounds of marijuana." Essentially, the state had to
prove an agreement to commit the offense of trafficking in marijuana. When the facts are viewed in
the light most favorable to the state, the record
shows that Gary, Peggy, and Keith McCart lived together in the same house. Gary McCart admitted
during a period of "a month or so" that he made
at least three purchases of marijuana in approximately one-pound increments from a supplier in
Mobile and that he then sold the marijuana from
the McCarts' residence. Evidence showing the purchase of the marijuana from the supplier and its
subsequent sale to customers was found in a date
book that contained notations from December 30,
1996, to February 5, 1997, indicating the amount
of money he owed his supplier and the amount of
money his customers owed him. One notation in
the date book indicated that Keith McCart had
purchased one ounce of marijuana from Gary Mc-
Cart. Additionally, the notations indicated the
largest amount of marijuana Gary McCart sold to
any customer at one time was two ounces. In their
statements to law enforcement officers, Gary Mc-
Cart and Keith McCart admitted selling marijuana. Their statements did not indicate that they
were partners in purchasing and selling marijuana.
Keith McCart denied purchasing marijuana from
Gary McCart's supplier and provided law enforcement officers with the names of two of his suppliers. Peggy McCart denied selling marijuana. When
law enforcement officers searched the McCarts'
residence, they found approximately five ounces of
marijuana.

Although circumstantial evidence may be used
to prove the existence of an agreement, the state's
evidence is insufficient to establish that Gary,
Peggy, and Keith McCart agreed to or had the specific intent to "knowingly sell, deliver, or actually
or constructively possess in excess of 2.2 pounds of

marijuana." No evidence, either direct or circumstantial, was presented indicating that there was an agreement among Gary, Peggy, and Keith McCart to "knowingly sell, deliver, or actually or constructively possess in excess of 2.2 pounds of marijuana." The state's evidence of an agreement essentially rests, as one of the narcotics officers admitted during his testimony, on the inference that because Gary, Peggy, and Keith McCart lived in the same house and were related, family members, they were in business together. However, these two facts are insufficient to prove that Gary, Peggy, and Keith McCart had agreed to traffic in marijuana.

Moreover, the sharing of a date book by Gary and Peggy McCart does not exhibit an agreement. While the date book, which was found on the kitchen counter, does allow the inference that Gary McCart was engaged in the illegal activity of buying and selling marijuana, that Peggy McCart may have known of Gary McCart's actions, and that Keith McCart had bought marijuana from Gary McCart, this evidence does not establish an agreement to knowingly buy and sell more than 2.2 pounds of marijuana. Indeed, the evidence presented indicated that Gary, Peggy, and Keith McCart were aiding and abetting one another in the distribution of marijuana. However, evidence that a person aided or abetted another in the distribution of marijuana, although sufficient to convict the person as a principal for the offense of distributing marijuana is insufficient to convict that person of a conspiracy to commit the offense. Participation without any evidence of an agreement does not reach the level of the separate crime of conspiracy to traffic in marijuana. Furthermore, the date book and Gary McCart's statement indicate that he alone made purchases from a Mobile supplier in approximately one-pound quantities and that he alone sold the marijuana.

Based on the foregoing, no reasonable inference that Gary, Peggy, and Keith McCart agreed to obtain the common goal of "knowingly sell[ing], deliver[ing], or actually or constructively possess[ing] in excess of 2.2 pounds of marijuana" can be drawn from the evidence. While the combined circumstances of the McCarts' association with one another over a period of a month and their alleged distribution of marijuana certainly arouses suspicion that they were engaged in a joint criminal enterprise or venture, these circumstances do not prove beyond a reasonable doubt that Gary,

Peggy, and Keith McCart agreed to, and had the specific intent to, buy and sell more than 2.2 pounds of marijuana. Therefore, in my opinion, the state failed to show that there was an agreement, either by "a meeting of the minds or a tacit agreement," to "knowingly sell, deliver, or actually or constructively possess in excess of 2.2 pounds of marijuana."

I recognize that the state, to establish a prima facie case of conspiracy to traffic in marijuana, was not required to prove the elements of trafficking in marijuana under § 13A-12-231, Ala.Code 1975. My conclusion, however, does not rest upon the state's failure to recover more than 2.2 pounds of marijuana or upon the fact that the state's evidence failed to show that at any given time Gary, Peggy, and Keith McCart possessed in excess of 2.2 pounds of marijuana. These factors have no bearing on the state's ability to show an agreement among Gary, Peggy, and Keith McCart and their "specific intent" to sell or possess in excess of 2.2 pounds of marijuana.

The majority's conclusion that the state presented sufficient evidence of an agreement seems to rely on the fact that Gary, Peggy, and Keith McCart resided in the same house and on Gary McCart's admission to law enforcement officers that he had purchased three one-pound increments of marijuana over a period of time. However, to meet the threshold amount of 2.2 pounds, the majority must rely on the weight of the marijuana over a period of weeks or months—the adding of ounces and pounds from at least three separate purchases. There is no Alabama case supporting the proposition that the weight of marijuana from several distinct transactions may be combined to attain the threshold amount of 2.2 pounds in a trafficking case. . . . [T]here is no Alabama case supporting the proposition that a conviction can stand for conspiracy to traffic in marijuana in the absence of evidence of an agreement to traffic in any amount less than 2.2 pounds. While I do believe that separate transactions could be used to arrive at the threshold amount of 2.2 pounds of marijuana, the state must establish beyond a reasonable doubt that an agreement among the conspirators existed that their end goal, purpose, or objective was to "knowingly sell, deliver, or actually or constructively possess more than 2.2 pounds of marijuana."

In this case, the state's evidence at best, establishes that Gary McCart purchased and probably sold three pounds of marijuana between December 30, 1996, and February 5, 1997. Gary McCart, however, could not have conspired with himself. Keith McCart apparently purchased approximately one ounce of marijuana from his father during that period for his own resale purposes. None of the state's evidence established how much marijuana Keith McCart may have purchased from his suppliers or sold to customers. Peggy McCart, at best, was a secretary for Gary McCart—answering the telephone and informing callers when she expected Gary McCart to return home. There is no evidence that she knew how much marijuana was being purchased or sold and certainly no evidence that she and Gary McCart had an agreement or the specific intent to sell or possess 2.2 pounds or more of marijuana.

"[N]o rule is more fundamental or better settled than that convictions cannot be predicated upon surmise, speculation, and suspicion to establish the accused's criminal agency in the offense charged." "[T]he possibility that a thing may occur is not alone evidence, even circumstantially, that the thing did occur." "A conviction for crime, slight or serious, cannot be rested upon the imagination, conjecture, or guesswork" of any witness. . . .

Conspiracy has been called the "darling" of prosecutors. Having served the State of Alabama as a prosecutor for over 17 years, I am inclined to agree with this characterization. However, because of the implications of the majority's holding to sustain Gary, Peggy, and Keith McCart's convictions for conspiracy based upon "inference upon inference," I believe that this particular "darling" has opened a Pandora's box.

QUESTIONS FOR DISCUSSION

1. List all of the facts relevant to determining whether the defendants agreed to traffic in marijuana.

2. Whom do you agree with, the majority or the dissent, on the point of whether the defendants satisfied the agreement requirement of conspiracy? Cite the specific facts and arguments to support your answer.

3. Although neither the majority nor the dissent dealt with the important *mens rea* requirement of conspiracy, do you think the facts prove that they had the specific intent to traffic in marijuana, as the statute requires? What facts support your answer?

SUMMARY OF CONSPIRACY LAW

Conspiracy is further removed from completed crimes than are both attempt and preparation. Conspiracy law is based on the rationale that it not only prevents dangerous persons from completing their evil plans but also strikes at a second evil, combinations for wrongful purposes, a serious social problem in itself. Conspiracy's elements are simply stated—conspiracy is an agreement or combination intended to achieve an illegal objective—but are applied according to widely varied interpretation and meaning.

The often vague definitions of the elements in conspiracy offer considerable opportunity for prosecutorial and judicial discretion. At times, this discretion borders on abuse, leading to charges that conspiracy law is unjust. First, a general criticism is that conspiracy law punishes conduct far remote from actual crime. Second, labor organizations, civil liberties groups, and large corporations charge that conspiracy is a weapon against their legitimate interests of, respectively, collective bargaining and strikes, dissent from accepted points of view and public policies, and profit making. Critics say that when prosecutors do not have enough evidence to convict for the crime itself, they turn as a last hope to conspiracy. Conspiracy's vague definitions greatly enhance the chance for a guilty verdict.

Not often mentioned, but extremely important, is that intense media attention to conspiracy trials can lead to abuse. This happened in the conspiracy trials of Dr. Benjamin Spock and the Chicago Eight, and in other conspiracy trials involving radical politics during the 1960s. It also occurred in the Watergate conspiracy trials involving President Nixon's associates during the 1970s, and in the alleged conspiracies surrounding the sale of arms to Iran for hostages and the subsequent alleged diversion of funds during the 1980s.

Several states have made efforts to overcome these criticisms by defining conspiracy elements more narrowly. The definitions of agreement or combination are no longer as vague as they once were. The *Model Penal Code* requires acts in furtherance of agreement, and several states are following that lead. Those states have refined *mens rea* to include only purposeful conduct, that is, a specific intent to carry out the objective of the agreement or combination. Knowledge, recklessness, and negligence are increasingly attacked as insufficient culpability for an offense as remote from completion as conspiracy. Furthermore, most recent legislation restricts conspiratorial objectives to criminal ends. Phrases like "unlawful objects," "lawful objects by unlawful means," and "objectives harmful to public health, morals, trade, and commerce" are increasingly regarded as too broad and, therefore, unacceptable.

On the other hand, the Racketeer Influenced and Corrupt Organizations Act (RICO) demonstrates the continued vitality of conspiracy law. RICO reflects the need for effective means to meet the threat posed by organized crime. It imposes enhanced penalties for "all types of organized criminal behavior, that is, enterprise criminality—from simple political to sophisticated white collar schemes to traditional Mafia-type endeavors."[36]

Racketeering activity includes any act chargeable under state and federal law, including murder, kidnaping, bribery, drug dealing, gambling, theft, extortion, and securities fraud. Among other things, the statute prohibits using income from a "pattern of racketeering activity" to acquire an interest in or establish an enterprise affecting interstate commerce; conducting an enterprise through a pattern of racketeering; or conspiring to violate these provisions.[37]

RICO's drafters intended the statute to "break the back of organized crime." According to conservative columnist William Safire, the racketeers they had in mind were "loansharks, drug kingpins, prostitution overlords, and casino operators who hired murderers and arsonists to enforce and extort—you know, the designated bad guys who presumably did not deserve the rights of due process that should protect all of us." Now, however, aggressive prosecutors use RICO against white-collar crime. Rudolf Giuliani, as a U.S. Attorney, for example, caused Drexel Burnham Lambert to plead guilty to several counts of securities violations in order to avoid RICO prosecution, which would not only result in harsher legal penalties but also attach the label of "racketeer" to white-collar criminals.[38]

SOLICITATION

Most remote from its underlying substantive crime is solicitation. At common law—and under most modern statutes—solicitation is a command, urging, or request to a third person to commit a crime. Suppose I want to murder my wife but I'm afraid to do it. If I ask a friend to do it and he kills her, then we're both murderers. If he tries to kill her and fails because his gun is defective, then we have committed attempted murder. If he agrees to kill her and buys the gun but gets no further, then we have conspired to commit murder. Even urging my friend to commit murder is a crime. So, if I ask my friend to commit murder and offer her money to do it, even if she turns down the offer, I have committed the crime called solicitation to commit murder.

Opinion differs as to whether solicitation to commit a crime presents a sufficient social danger to be a crime. On one side, it is argued that solicitation is not dangerous because an independent moral agent (the person solicited) stands between solicitors and their criminal objectives. Furthermore, by soliciting others to commit crimes, solicitors demonstrate their reluctance to commit crimes themselves. On the other side, advocates argue that solicitation creates the special danger inherent in group participation in crime; in this sense, solicitation is an attempt to conspire. In addition, solicitors show masterful and intelligent manipulation of their underlings. According to the commentary of the *Model Penal Code,* "[t]here should be no doubt on this issue. Purposeful solicitation presents dangers calling for preventive intervention and is sufficiently indicative of a disposition towards criminal activity to call for liability."[39]

Solicitation consists of words, but the law imprecisely prescribes what words qualify as the *actus reus* of solicitation. Courts generally agree that statements simply favoring or approving crime do not constitute solicitation. Hence, someone who merely says, "I think it would be great if someone killed that terrorist," hasn't solicited murder. Courts demand some sort of inducement. Statutes and judicial decisions have deemed sufficient a statement that does any of the following: advises, commands, counsels, encourages, entices, entreats, importunes, incites, induces, instigates, procures, requests, solicits, or urges. Uttering the proper inducement accompanied by the required *mens rea* constitutes solicitation. In other words, criminal solicitation consists of the effort to engage another in crime, whether or not the inducement ever ripens into a completed crime. The law considers that those who urge others to commit crimes are sufficiently dangerous to punish.[40]

Does the solicitor have to address the words to particular individuals? Some say yes, but courts have ruled that public exhortations to audiences suffice. One speaker who was convicted urged his audience from a public platform to commit murder and robbery. Soliciting is a crime even if the solicitor does not personally communicate the inducement, and despite the inducement's failure to reach its object. Hence, if I send a letter to my hoped-for collaborator, offering her $30,000 to kill my enemy, I have solicited murder even if the letter gets lost in the mail. The danger of a criminal solicitation does not depend on the inducement's reaching its object. Rather, the danger lies in a solicitor bent on engaging another in crime who continues to seek for someone more willing to accept the solicitation.[41]

Some statutes restrict the objective in solicitation to felonies; in some cases to violent felonies. In other jurisdictions, it's a crime to solicit another to commit any crime, whether felony, misdemeanor, or violation. Furthermore, solicitation need not include an inducement to commit a crime. For example, suppose a robber urges a friend to borrow money and lend it to the robber for a plane ticket to escape from the jurisdiction. The robber has solicited escape, or aiding and abetting a robbery. Al-

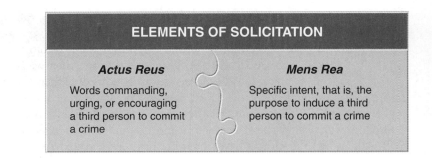

ELEMENTS OF SOLICITATION

Actus Reus	*Mens Rea*
Words commanding, urging, or encouraging a third person to commit a crime	Specific intent, that is, the purpose to induce a third person to commit a crime

though borrowing money isn't a crime, and lending money to a robber is not by itself a crime, both escape and aiding and abetting robbers are crimes. One who urges another to commit those crimes has committed the crime of solicitation.

Solicitation *mens rea* requires purpose or specific intent. The words in a solicitation must convey the author's intention to induce another to commit the substantive offense. If I urge my friend who works in an expensive jewelry shop to take a gold chain for me, I have solicited larceny. If, on the other hand, I ask another friend who works in a clothing shop to get a coat for me to use for the evening, and I plan to return the coat the next morning before anyone knows it is missing, I haven't solicited larceny because I do not intend to steal the coat, only to use it for the night (see the discussion of larceny in Chapter 12).

A problem arises when law enforcement officers solicit in order to determine whether someone is disposed to commit a crime. For example, police decoys who try to get suspected prostitutes to offer sex for money haven't solicited criminally under current law because the decoys' motive is not dangerous. Proponents of current law maintain (not without objection) that the decoys' motives are nobly addressed to upholding the law, hardly a dangerous propensity. Similarly, narcotics police or street decoys hoping to catch muggers are working to prevent and control crime, not to foster crime, according to supporters. Others argue that decoys encourage innocent people to commit crimes. Although law enforcement officers acting properly in the course of their duties may not be guilty of solicitation, their too-energetic encouragement may constitute entrapment (see Chapter 8). Solicitation, like conspiracy, is a weapon in the drug wars. But, it is also an instrument in improving the "quality of life" in neighborhoods plagued by what a majority of the people call "incivility" (Chapter 13). The objectives of reducing illegal drug use and trafficking and of improving the "quality of life" in city neighborhoods are evident in the case of *People v. Agnello*.

C A S E   Were They Guilty of Solicitation?

People v. Agnello
165 Misc.2d 855, 630 N.Y.S.2d 614 (1995)

David Agnello and at least 26 others, defendants, were charged with fifth-degree criminal solicitation, and they moved to dismiss. The City Court, Monroe County, held that defendants could not be convicted of fifth-degree criminal solicitation as charges of soliciting sale of marijuana were precluded from prosecution by exemption statute. The charges were dismissed.

JOHNSON, J.

FACTS

All of the defendants were arrested on various streets in the Northeastern section of the City of Rochester allegedly attempting to buy small amounts of marijuana. Those streets, among them

Hudson and Conkey Avenues and Berlin Street, have become known as open-air drug markets where marijuana, and in some areas cocaine and heroin, can be purchased on the streets. Those who live and work in those areas have become frustrated at the misuse of their neighborhoods for drug activity, that activity bringing with it increased public safety concerns for themselves and their families. The potential for violence in connection with the open-air drug trafficking was illustrated and underscored on January 2, 1995 with the murder of Matthew Maier. Mr. Maier, a resident of the surrounding suburb of Penfield, New York, was shot to death while reportedly attempting to purchase marijuana in one of these open-air drug markets on Berlin Street.

In response to the public safety concerns of the neighborhoods, and in direct response to the murder of Matthew Maier, the City of Rochester Police

Department in January of 1995 began to station undercover police officers on the various streets with reputations for being open-air drug markets. Those officers then arrested individuals who approached them attempting to buy marijuana and other drugs. In these cases before the Court, all of the defendants were charged with criminal solicitation in the fifth degree, a violation punishable by a maximum of 15 days in jail. The informations allege either that the defendants were soliciting the officers to sell them marijuana, or were attempting to buy a "marijuana-type substance" or "fake" marijuana.

The activities of the Rochester Police in these "sting" operations were highly publicized in the media and well received by the citizens of this city, particularly those in the neighborhoods most directly affected who had felt frustrated at the seemingly endless supply of individuals from throughout the rest of the city and suburbs who were venturing into their neighborhoods to buy drugs with no apparent consequences. The operation seemed to relieve the shared frustration of neighbors with very real concerns and fears about the atmosphere and actuality of danger that these drug markets bring and that of the police in their efforts to respond to the very real public safety concerns of citizens in the neighborhoods adversely affected. The police were responding as well to public safety concerns for those traveling to the neighborhoods to feed their habits, the very individuals who cause these open-air markets to exist and thrive.

OPINION

The Court applauds the interest of the neighbors and the police and their determination to eliminate those open-air drug markets. Unfortunately, the laws of the State of New York do not include any statute or combination of statutes that would allow for the prosecution of these defendants for the conduct alleged. On the contrary, the exemption statute in the section of the Penal Law that governs prosecutions for criminal solicitation states specifically that under certain situations "A person *is not guilty* of criminal solicitation" (emphasis added) (see, Penal Law § 100.20 Criminal solicitation; exemption). For this reason, as is more fully set forth below, the defendants' motions to dismiss the charges of criminal solicitation in the fifth degree must be granted. . . .

These defendants were charged with criminal solicitation in the fifth degree. Section 100.00 of the Penal Law, criminal solicitation in the fifth degree, reads as follows:

> A person is guilty of criminal solicitation in the fifth degree when, with intent that another person engage in conduct constituting a crime, he solicits, requests, commands, importunes or otherwise attempts to cause such other person to engage in such conduct. . . .

A charge of criminal solicitation in the fifth degree must allege, therefore, the following two elements:

1. That the defendant had the intent that another person engage in conduct constituting a crime, and,
2. That the defendant solicits, requests, commands, importunes or otherwise attempts to cause that other person to engage in such conduct.

In order for a person to be found guilty of any degree of criminal solicitation, it is not necessary that the person solicited engage in any criminal activity or even any preparation for any criminal activity. The gravamen [heart] of criminal solicitation is the request or other attempt by the defendant to the person solicited to engage in criminal conduct. In the instant cases in which the allegations are that the defendants solicited the undercover officers to sell them marijuana the people have alleged the necessary elements, that:

1. the defendants intended that the undercover officers sell them marijuana, and
2. that the defendants solicited the undercover officers to sell them marijuana.

As is more fully set forth below, the Court believes that a violation of criminal solicitation in the fifth degree is sufficiently pleaded in those cases.

Unfortunately, the inquiry does not end there. The criminal solicitation section of the Penal Law contains an exemption provision that must be considered in determining whether or not a defendant may be found guilty of any degree of criminal solicitation, in this case the fifth degree. That exemption is the result of a determination by the State Legislature that not all requests of another to engage in conduct constituting a crime would be punished as criminal solicitation. That exemption section states:

Section 100.20 Criminal solicitation, exemption:

> A person is not guilty of criminal solicitation when his solicitation constitutes conduct of a kind that is necessarily incidental to the commission of the

crime solicited. When under such circumstances the solicitation constitutes an offense other than criminal solicitation which is related to but separate from the crime solicited, the actor is guilty of such related and separate offense only and not of criminal solicitation.

. . . Penal Law § 220.00(1), defines "sale" as follows: "1. 'Sale' means to sell, exchange, give or dispose of to another, or to offer or agree to do the same." By definition, therefore, a sale involves two parties, the one actually doing the selling or exchanging and "another" who receives or is intended to receive the marijuana. In these cases a sale of marijuana, by virtue of Penal Law § 220.00, requires the existence of another person—the person to whom the transfer is made. In these cases the required "anothers" are the defendants and their conduct in soliciting the sale is, this Court finds, "necessarily incidental" to the sales of marijuana they were alleged to intend the police officers to commit. For the reasons set forth above the charges of criminal solicitation in the fifth degree as against the above defendants are dismissed.

QUESTIONS FOR DISCUSSION

1. State the elements of solicitation as defined by the New York statute.
2. Do the facts fit the definition? Refer specifically to the facts that fit the elements in the statute.
3. What is the exemption provision in the solicitation statute and what is the purpose of the provision?
4. Is the exemption provision a good idea? Why? Why not?

NOTE CASE

Harold Furr and his wife had been married about 21 years and had four children when they separated in 1973. After the separation, Furr moved his real estate office from their home to a nearby location near the square in Locust, North Carolina. His wife, Earlene, continued to live at the house on Willow Drive and Furr moved into Western Hills Mobile Home Park. The couple's relationship was apparently quite volatile and Furr exhibited increasing hostility towards Earlene after the separation. In April, 1973, Earlene filed a civil action against defendant resulting in a judgment against him in October, 1973. A year later, on his wife's motion, defendant was adjudged to be in contempt and was committed to jail. While in Stanly County jail, Furr met Raymond Clontz and Donald Owens, and related his marital problems to them, especially his concern over the property dispute. He was released from jail on December 6, 1974, upon payment of $13,623.00. After his release, Furr approached Clontz and Owens, drove them by Earlene's home and explained how to get into the house. He offered Owens $3,000.00 to kill Earlene and offered to give Clontz a lot which the latter wanted to store cars on if Clontz would do the job. Neither man accepted the offer.

Did Furr commit solicitation to murder? Yes. According to the North Carolina supreme court:

> Solicitation of another to commit a felony is a crime in North Carolina, even though the solicitation is of no effect and the crime solicited is never committed. The gravamen of the offense of soliciting lies in counseling, enticing or inducing another to commit a crime.
>
> Defendant . . . contends that there was no evidence to support three indictments alleging solicitation of Raymond Clontz to murder Earlene Furr. There is no merit to these contentions in two of the counts. [The] indictment . . . alleges that Clontz was solicited in January to murder Furr's wife. The evidence is that during that month, shortly after both men were released from jail where defendant had been quite talkative about his marital problems, Clontz and Furr met to discuss a lot which Clontz wished to purchase. Furr said he wanted $3,000.00 for the lot and Clontz agreed to take it. Then, as Clontz related at trial Furr told him not to be so hasty, that "he would make some arrangements about the payment for the lot in another way; that he wanted me to do a job for him." Clontz told Furr that he "knew what he was talking about, but that [he] wasn't interested in it." Defendant then told him he had to go to court with his wife in a few weeks and "that he had to have something done before court time or he was going to be in serious trouble. He said his wife was already getting $250.00 a week from him, and she had possession of the house, and had his property tied up and that he had to have something done." In the context, we find no other reasonable interpretation of defendant's words on this occasion than that he was requesting Clontz to kill his wife.

State v. Furr, 292 N.C. 711, 235 S.E.2d 193 (1977)

SUMMARY

Criminal laws against attempt, conspiracy, and solicitation aim primarily to prevent crime and control dangerous persons. Two theories support the punishment of conduct short of completing the crime. One is to prevent dangerous conduct; the other is to control dangerous persons. Both theories require a specific intent that triggers some act toward completing the crime. In attempt, the acts consist of steps toward completing the crime. If extraneous factors interrupt or frustrate completion—such as when police officers or others arrive at the scene—that stroke of luck shouldn't allow would-be criminals to escape punishment for attempt. However, if perpetrators voluntarily renounce their attempts, a number of states grant them the defense of abandonment both because they are no longer dangerous and because the law should encourage people to not finish their criminal plans.

In conspiracy, further removed from actual harm than attempt, the *mens rea* is the intent to commit a particular crime or to accomplish a legal goal by an unlawful means. Conspiracy *actus reus* is the agreement. Some states say that conspiracy is completed with the agreement; others require some step to carry out the agreement. In solicitation, the furthest removed from actual harm, the criminal intent is to get another person to commit a crime; the act is encouraging someone to commit a crime. The crime of solicitation is committed even if the person solicited turns down the offer; solicitation is complete upon the encouragement.

✺ Go to the Criminal Law 7e CD-ROM for Internet exercises.

REVIEW QUESTIONS

1. Identify and define the three inchoate offenses.

2. What two elements do all of the inchoate offenses share?

3. What is the dilemma posed by the inchoate offenses? How does the criminal law resolve this dilemma?

4. Identify the major steps in the history of the law of attempt.

5. Identify and explain the two theories of the law of criminal attempt.

6. State the *mens rea* of the crime of attempt. What criticisms of this requirement did Justice Holmes make?

7. Identify and explain the four main tests courts have adopted to determine the *actus reus* of criminal attempts.

8. Explain the difference between legal and factual impossibility in the law of criminal attempt.

9. Explain the defense of renunciation in the law of criminal attempt. What are the arguments in favor of allowing the defense?

10. Identify and describe the elements of the crime of conspiracy.

11. Identify the objectives that satisfy the requirements of the crime of conspiracy.

12. Explain the justification for Wharton's rule. Why have some jurisdictions abolished the rule?

13. Identify and describe the elements of the crime of solicitation.

14. Summarize the arguments for and against having a crime of solicitation.

15. Define the *actus reus* and the *mens rea* of solicitation.

KEY TERMS

attempt—taking steps toward but not completing a crime.

equivocality approach—the theory that attempt *actus reus* requires an act that can have no other purpose than the commission of a crime.

conspiracy—agreeing to commit a crime.

extraneous factor—a condition beyond the attempter's control.

factual impossibility—the defense that some extraneous factor makes it impossible to complete a crime.

inchoate offenses—offenses based on crimes not yet completed.

legal impossibility—the defense that what the actor attempted was not a crime.

***Model Penal Code* standard**—the precept that attempt *actus reus* requires substantial steps that strongly corroborate the actor's purpose.

physical proximity doctrine—the principle that the number of remaining acts in attempt determines attempt *actus reus*.

probable desistance approach—an approach that considers whether the act in attempt would naturally lead to the commission of the crime.

solicitation—trying to get someone to commit a crime.

Wharton's rule—the principle that more than two parties must conspire to commit crimes that naturally involve at least two parties.

SUGGESTED READINGS

1. Jerome Hall, *General Principles of Criminal Law,* 2d ed. (Indianapolis, Ind.: Bobbs-Merrill, 1960), chap. 15. An excellent survey of attempt law. Hall includes a good history of attempt and the theoretical justifications for it, and discusses some proper limits to be placed on it.

2. George P. Fletcher, *Rethinking Criminal Law* (Boston: Little, Brown, 1978), pp. 131–205, 218–232. Contains provocative discussions about the inchoate offenses. Fletcher clearly defines the terms in considerable detail. He also assesses the inchoate crimes and participation in crime in ways that provoke considerable thought about the roles of those terms in criminal law.

3. Jessica Mitford, *The Trial of Dr. Spock* (New York: Knopf, 1969). An excellent narrative, written for the general public. It reveals much about conspiracy within the context of a real case that attracted enormous publicity.

4. American Law Institute, *Model Penal Code and Commentaries,* vol. 1 (Philadelphia: American Law Institute, 1985), pt. 1, pp. 295–328. A detailed analysis of all elements in complicity, as well as arguments for why complicity should be included in criminal law and to what extent participants should be criminally liable. This is an advanced discussion written for experts in the field but is well worth the effort to read and consider its points. In vol. 2, pt. 1, the inchoate offenses are treated similarly.

NOTES

1. Rollin M. Perkins and Ronald N. Boyce, *Criminal Law,* 3d ed. (Mineola, N.Y.: Foundation Press, 1982), pp. 611–658, 700–714; American Law Institute, *Model Penal Code and Commentaries,* vol. 2 (Philadelphia: American Law Institute, 1985), pp. 293–298.

2. George P. Fletcher, *Rethinking Criminal Law* (Boston: Little, Brown, 1978), p. 131; Plato, *Laws,* trans. Trevor J. Saunders (Middlesex, England: Penguin Books, 1975), pp. 397–398; Jerome Hall, *General Principles of Criminal Law,* 2d ed. (Indianapolis, Ind.: Bobbs-Merrill, 1960), pp. 560–564.

3. Ibid., Hall.

4. Geoffrey R. Elton, *The Tudor Constitution* (Cambridge: Cambridge University Press, 1972), pp. 170–171.

5. Joel Samaha, *Law and Order in Historical Perspective* (New York: Academic Press, 1974); Joel Samaha, "The Recognizance in Elizabethan Law Enforcement," *American Journal of Legal History* 25 (1981): 189–204.

6. Cald. 397 (1784).

7. Sir James F. Stephen, *A History of the Criminal Law of England,* reprint (New York: Burt Franklin, 1973), p. 224.

8. Justice Moylan in *Gray v. State,* 43 Md.App. 238, 403 A.2d 853 (1979).

9. Arnold N. Enker, "*Mens Rea* and Criminal Attempt," *American Bar Foundation Research Journal* (1977):845.

10. *United States. v. Mandujano,* 499 F.2d 370, 374 (5th Cir. 1974); *Young v. State,* 303 Md. 298, 493 A.2d 352 (1985) (failure not an element); see also Perkins and Boyce, *Criminal Law,* pp. 612–617.

11. Enker, "*Mens Rea* and Criminal Attempt," p. 847.

12. Oliver Wendell Holmes, *The Common Law* (Boston: Little, Brown, 1963), pp. 54–55.

13. *United States v. Mandujano*, 499 F.2d 370, 375–376 (5th Cir. 1974) (more than intention required).

14. *Commonwealth v. Peaslee*, 177 Mass. 267, 59 N.E. 55 (1901); Fletcher, *Rethinking Criminal Law*, pp. 139–140; American Law Institute, *Model Penal Code and Commentaries*, vol. 2, pp. 321–322; *People v. Acosta*, 172 A.D.2d 103, 578 N.Y.S.2d 525 (1991).

15. *Commonwealth v. Peaslee*.

16. *Bradley v. Ward*, N.Z.L.R. 471 (1955).

17. American Law Institute, *Model Penal Code and Commentaries*, vol. 2, pp. 337–346.

18. Ibid.

19. Nev.Rev.Stat. 205.055; American Law Institute, *Model Penal Code and Commentaries*, vol. 2, pp. 354–355.

20. Fernand N. Dutile and Harold F. Moore, "Mistake and Impossibility: Arranging a Marriage between Two Difficult Partners," *Northwestern University Law Review* 74 (1979): 166, 181ff.

21. *People v. Kimball*, 311 N.W.2f 343 (Mich. 1981), p. 347.

22. Ibid., pp. 346–348.

23. American Law Institute, *Model Penal Code and Commentaries*, vol. 2, pp. 356–362.

24. Ibid.; Daniel G. Moriarty, "Extending the Defense of Renunciation," *Temple Law Review* 62 (1989):1.

25. *Model Penal Code and Commentaries*, vol. 2, p. 387.

26. Jessica Mitford, *The Trial of Dr. Spock* (New York: Knopf, 1969), pp. 70–71.

27. Fletcher, *Rethinking Criminal Law*, pp. 218, 223, 225; Kentucky Rev. Stat. 427.110 (1958).

28. Concurring in *Krulewitch v. United States*, 336 U.S. 440, 445–446, 69 S.Ct. 716, 719–720, 93 L.Ed. 790 (1949).

29. *Direct Sales Co. v. United States*, 319 U.S. 703, 63 S.Ct. 1265, 87 L.Ed. 1674 (1943).

30. Ala.Gen.tat. 54–197 (1958); *Baker v. Commonwealth*, 204 Ky. 420, 264 S.W. 1069 (1924); *State v. Ameker*, 73 S.C. 330, 53 S.E. 484 (1906); *State v. Davis*, 229 S.E. 811 (1911).

31. 118 Utah 537, 223 P.2d 193 (1950); 18 U.S.C.A.; st 371 (1976); *Musser v. Utah*, 333 U.S. 95, 97, 68 S.Ct. 397, 92 L.Ed. 562 (1948).

32. *People v. Davis*, 408 Mich. 255, 290 N.W.2d 366 (1980).

33. *Model Penal Code*, § 5.03.

34. *United States v. Bruno*, 105 F.2d 921 (2d Cir. 1939).

35. *Illinois Criminal Law and Procedure* (St. Paul, Minn.: West Publishing Co., 1988), chap. 38, § 8-4.

36. Blakely and Gettings, "Racketeer Influenced and Corrupt Organizations (RICO): Basic Concepts—Criminal and Civil Remedies," *Temple Law Quarterly* 53 (1980):1013–1014.

37. 18 U.S.C.A. § 1961 et seq.

38. William Safire, "The End of RICO," *The New York Times* (January 30, 1989), p. 19.

39. American Law Institute, *Model Penal Code and Commentaries*, vol. 2, pp. 365–366.

40. LaFave and Scott, *Criminal Law*, p. 419.

41. *State v. Schleifer*, 99 Conn. 432 121 A. 805 (1923).

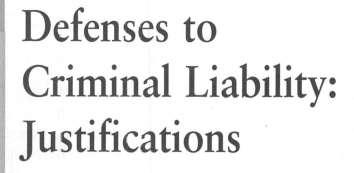

CHAPTER 7

Defenses to Criminal Liability: Justifications

Chapter Outline

I. Introduction

II. Self-Defense

III. Execution of Public Duties

IV. Resisting Unlawful Arrest

V. Choice-of-Evils Defense

VI. Consent

VII. Summary

CHAPTER MAIN POINTS

1. In the defense of justification, defendants admit responsibility but maintain that under the circumstances what they did was right.

2. In the defenses of excuse, defendants admit what they did was wrong but maintain that under the circumstances they were not responsible.

3. Self-defense justifies the use of force or threats of force to prevent attacks from individuals who the victim honestly and reasonably believes threaten imminent death or serious bodily harm and when it is reasonable for the victim to believe that force is necessary to prevent the attack.

4. Self-defense does not justify either retaliation for past attacks or preemptive strikes to prevent future, nonimminent attacks.

5. Owners may use reasonable force, sometimes including deadly force, to defend their homes and property.

6. Law enforcement officers may use force, including deadly force, when it is reasonable to use such force in order to enforce the criminal law.

7. In a few jurisdictions, citizens may use force (but not deadly force) to prevent an unlawful arrest.

8. The defense of necessity justifies otherwise criminal conduct (a lesser evil) when the commission of the lesser offense avoids a greater imminent evil.

9. Voluntary, knowing consent of the victim is a defense to minor assaults in some jurisdictions.

Was He Justified in Shooting?

Canty approached Goetz, possibly with Allen beside him, and said to Goetz, "Give me five dollars." Goetz stated that he knew from the smile on Canty's face that they wanted to "play with me." Although he was certain that none of the youths had a gun, he had a fear, based on prior experiences, of being "maimed." Goetz then established "a pattern of fire," deciding specifically to fire from left to right. His stated intention at that point was to "murder [the four youths], to hurt them, to make them suffer as much as possible." When Canty again requested money, Goetz stood up, drew his weapon, and began firing, aiming for the center of the body of each of the four. Goetz recalled that the first two he shot "tried to run through the crowd [but] they had nowhere to run." Goetz then turned to his right to "go after the other two." Cabey "tried pretending that he wasn't with [the others]" by standing still, holding on to one of the subway hand straps, and not looking at Goetz. Goetz nonetheless fired his fourth shot at him. He then ran back to the first two youths to make sure they had been "taken care of." Seeing that they had both been shot, he spun back to check on the other two. Goetz noticed that the youth who had been standing still was now sitting on a bench and seemed unhurt. As Goetz told the police, "I said '[y]ou seem to be all right, here's another,'" and he fired the shot which severed Cabey's spinal cord. Goetz added that "if I was a little more under self-control . . . I would have put the barrel against his forehead and fired." He also admitted that "if I had had more [bullets], I would have shot them again, and again, and again."

INTRODUCTION

In all criminal cases, the government has the **burden of proof**. This means that the prosecution has to prove all of the elements of criminal liability that we discussed in Chapters 3 and 4. The **defenses** allow defendants to escape criminal liability even when the government has proved the elements beyond a reasonable doubt. There are three types of defense:

1. **Alibi.** Defendants prove that they were in a different place than the scene of the crime when the crime was committed, so they couldn't have committed it.
2. **Justifications** (the subject of this chapter). Defendants accept responsibility for their actions but claim that what they did was right under the circumstances.
3. **Excuses** (Chapter 8). Defendants admit that what they did was wrong but argue that under the circumstances they were not responsible for what they did.[1]

According to the principle of justification, some circumstances justify what would otherwise be crimes. Justified conduct doesn't deserve punishment because it's not blameworthy. For example, it's wrong to blame—hence, to punish—one who has killed in self-defense. The argument of self-defense runs something like this: I killed my attacker; I intended to kill him; so, I'm responsible for killing him. But under the circumstances (being forced to choose between his life and mine) it was right to kill him. Similarly, to use a common law school example, it's not right to punish a man who was so mentally diseased that he thought he was squeezing a lemon when, in fact, he was choking his girlfriend to death. The argument of the defense of insanity runs something like this: I admit that killing my husband was wrong. However, because I was insane when I killed him, I'm not responsible for killing him (Chapter 8). The distinguished professor of criminal law, George Fletcher, sums up the difference between justification and excuse this way: "A justification speaks to the rightfulness of the act; an excuse, to whether the actor is accountable for a concededly wrongful act."[2]

Most of the justifications and excuses are what we call **affirmative defenses**. Affirmative defenses require that defendants carry some burden in presenting evidence to support it. In effect, an affirmative defense admits the crime charged but, according to the authors of a leading treatise on the criminal law, Professors LaFave and Scott, "seeks to justify, excuse, or mitigate the defendant's conduct." In all jurisdictions, defendants bear the **burden of production**. This means that defendants have to "start matters off by putting in some evidence in support" of the defense. According to LaFave and Scott, "We can assume that those who commit crimes are sane, sober, conscious, and acting freely. It makes sense, therefore, to make defendants responsible for injecting these extraordinary circumstances into the proceedings." The amount of evidence required "is not great; some credible evidence" suffices. Once defendants meet the burden of production by introducing some evidence of justification or excuse, they may or may not have the further **burden of persuasion**. This means that they have to do more than get things started; they have to prove they were justified or excused. Typically, jurisdictions require defendants to prove their defenses by a **preponderance of the evidence**. This means that more than 50% of the evidence proves justification or excuse. Occasionally, jurisdictions require that once defendants have met the burden of persuasion, the burden shifts to the prosecution to prove beyond a reasonable doubt that the defendant was *not* justified or excused.[3]

Perfect defenses, like a successful self-defense plea, lead to outright acquittal—the defendant "walks." Sometimes, evidence that doesn't amount to a perfect defense is enough to convict on a lesser charge, like when provocation reduces murder to manslaughter (Chapter 9). An **imperfect defense** can mean the difference between death or life imprisonment for murder and ten to twenty years for manslaughter (see Chapter 9). The defense of insanity is different from other defenses. Defendants who successfully plead insanity don't walk, at least not right away. Special insanity hearings follow insanity verdicts. The outcome of most of these hearings sends most insane defendants to maximum-security hospitals until they regain their sanity. Often, defendants never regain their sanity; they remain committed for life (see Chapter 8).

Evidence that doesn't amount to either a perfect or imperfect defense might still show **mitigating circumstances** that convince judges or juries that defendants don't deserve the maximum penalty. For example, words, however insulting, can't reduce murder to manslaughter in most states (Chapter 9). But they might be a mitigating circumstance that results in life without parole instead of the death penalty. So, if an African-American person killed someone in an outburst of rage brought on by the victim's relentless taunting, "nigger, nigger," the killing is still murder but the taunting might mitigate the death penalty to life without parole (Chapter 9).

Motive can also influence punishment, or sometimes even conviction itself. **Motive** refers to the reason why individuals commit crimes. Criminal law distinguishes motive from *mens rea*. *Mens rea* tells us *what* a person intended; motive tells us the reason *why*. Suppose a burglar purposely breaks into and enters a house with the intent to steal food because he is hungry. In this example, the intent is to steal; hunger is the motive. Mercy killing is another good example. The intent of the mercy killer is to kill; the motive is to stop the victim's suffering. The law doesn't recognize motive in most instances; it looks only at *mens rea*. However, motive might help to prove *mens rea*: Proving that Matt wanted to end Michael's suffering is some evidence that Matt intended to kill Michael.

The motive of mercy might also affect conviction and punishment. A jury might refuse to convict a mercy killer of first-degree murder even though the *mens rea* for murder is clearly there—the premeditated, purposeful causing of another's death (see Chapter 9). The murder conviction of Robert Latimer is a good example of this. Robert Latimer could no longer stand the constant pain from which his twelve-year-old daughter, Tracy, was suffering because of her severe and incurable cerebral palsy. She wore diapers, weighed only 38 pounds, and couldn't walk, talk, or feed herself. So, Robert put Tracy into the cab of his pickup truck on the family farm and pumped exhaust into the cab of the truck. He told the police that he stood by, ready to stop if Tracy started to cry, but that Tracy simply went quietly "to sleep. My priority was to put her out of her pain." He pleaded not guilty to first-degree murder, but the jury found him guilty of second-degree murder. Despite the verdict of guilty on the lesser charge, many people in the town agreed with an eighteen-year-old high school student who said Latimer "did what he had to do for his daughter's sake. And that's the way a lot of people in town are feeling."[4]

If a sentence is harsher than the community thinks a mercy killer deserves, officials might release the killer at the earliest possible date. This happened to seventy-eight-year-old Oscar Carlson. When Carlson could no longer bear his wife's suffering from advanced Alzheimer's disease, he shot her to death. He was convicted of murder and the judge sentenced him to prison. On his first day in prison, Carlson said, "I know it's better for me to sit here in prison than for Agnes to sit up there in the home like she was." A barrage of negative publicity surrounded his sentence to prison, generating considerable sympathy for the elderly murderer. He was released after a short time in prison.[5]

SELF-DEFENSE

Self-defense is the use of force to prevent attacks against individuals, their homes, and their property. Self-defense is the classic example of "taking the law into your own hands." Allowing private individuals to take the law into their own hands conflicts with a fundamental element of criminal law in a constitutional democracy—the rule of law (Chapter 1). Under the rule of law, the government has a monopoly on the use of force. But that monopoly carries with it the duty to protect people from illegal attacks. Sometimes, agents of the government aren't there when they're needed. Self-defense allows individuals to use force to help themselves when the government can't do it for them.

Self-defense, as the term suggests, is a *defensive* action. Those who rely on it have to act right *now* because if they don't they'll be attacked. Self-defense doesn't include warding off some *future* attack by volleying a preemptive strike. Nor does self-defense justify retaliation in the form of "pay back" for a *past* attack. In short, self-defense is about protective action required and taken right now. Preemptive strikes come too soon and retaliation too late. Individuals have to rely on conventional means to prevent future attacks, and only the state can legally punish past attacks.[6]

ELEMENTS OF SELF-DEFENSE

The law of self-defense tells us under what conditions individuals can ignore the government's monopoly of force and rely on self-help. These conditions strictly limit the use of violent self-help. According to the common law:

> A man may repel force by force in the defense of his person, habitation, or property, against one or many who manifestly intend and endeavor, by violence or surprise, to commit a known felony on either. In such a case he is not obliged to retreat, but may pursue his adversary until he finds himself out of danger; and if, in a conflict between them, he happens to kill, such killing is justifiable. The right of self-defense in cases of this kind is founded on the law of nature; and is not, nor can be, superseded by any law of society. . . . To make homicide excusable on the ground of self-defense, the danger must be actual and urgent.[7]

The modern law of self-defense has boiled down common law self-defense to four elements:

1. Reasonable belief in the danger of an attack that will cause death or serious bodily injury.
2. The danger has to be to a nonaggressor, that is, to someone who has not provoked the attack in the first place.
3. The danger has to be imminent, meaning immediate or on the verge of happening right now.
4. The force used to repel the attack can only be the amount necessary to repel the attack; that is, the force can't be excessive.

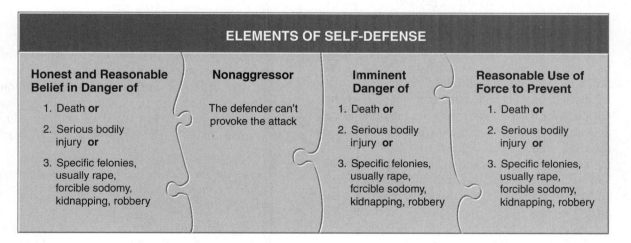

ELEMENTS OF SELF-DEFENSE

Honest and Reasonable Belief in Danger of	Nonaggressor	Imminent Danger of	Reasonable Use of Force to Prevent
1. Death **or** 2. Serious bodily injury **or** 3. Specific felonies, usually rape, forcible sodomy, kidnapping, robbery	The defender can't provoke the attack	1. Death **or** 2. Serious bodily injury **or** 3. Specific felonies, usually rape, forcible sodomy, kidnapping, robbery	1. Death **or** 2. Serious bodily injury **or** 3. Specific felonies, usually rape, forcible sodomy, kidnapping, robbery

Initial Aggressors and Defender-Provoked Attacks

Ordinarily, self-defense isn't available to someone who starts a fight or otherwise provokes an attack. However, if attackers completely withdraw from fights they start or attacks they otherwise provoke, they can defend themselves against an attack by their initial victims. In one case a little man attacked a much bigger man with a knife. Realizing that he'd taken on too much, the little man tried to get away. But the larger man was by now so angry that he ran after him. Unable to escape, the little man stood his ground and stabbed his attacker to death. He was acquitted on self-defense because the jury was satisfied that he "withdrew in good faith" and had not retreated just to regain enough strength to start the attack again. The Colorado Court of Appeals dealt with the issue of self-defense where defenders injured victims in a fight outside a bar in *People v. Silva*.[8]

C A S E | Did He Start the Fight?

People v. Silva
987 P.2d 909 (Col. App. 1999)

Steven Silva, the defendant, was convicted in the District Court, La Plata County, of attempted reckless manslaughter, first degree assault, and second degree assault. He appealed. The Court of Appeals reversed and remanded the case for a new trial.

DAVIDSON, J.

FACTS

. . . The two victims and their three friends went to a bar. However, two of the friends were denied admittance because of their age and decided to wait in the truck in which they were riding while the others went inside briefly. Also in the bar were defendant and his two friends. They left at about the same time as the victims.

Prior to the affray giving rise to the charges against defendant, there was no meeting or altercation between the two groups. However, as one of the victims' friends was about to get into the truck, he instead approached defendant and one of his friends. Words were exchanged and the other of defendant's friends came around from the far side of the truck and hit the victims' friend. The victims then came over and began hitting the person who had struck the first blow. Defendant and his friends and the victims and their friends entered into the affray.

As one of defendant's friends was fighting with the first victim, defendant jumped on his back, took out his knife, and began stabbing the first victim in the arm. The second victim, not knowing that defendant had a knife, knocked defendant off of the first victim. Defendant then turned around and swung at the second victim, stabbing him in the chest and arm. The victims and their friends fled. Defendant and his friends remained at the bar where defendant subsequently was arrested.

At trial, defendant asserted the affirmative defense of self-defense and defense of others. In support of his claim, he presented evidence that he had used justifiable force when the victims and their friend returned the first blow, made by defendant's friend, with excessive force. Therefore, he asserted, he had acted reasonably in coming to his friends' defense with his knife. Defendant was convicted of the charges from which he now appeals.

OPINION

. . . Defendant argues that the trial court violated his right to present a defense by instructing the jury on the issue of provoking the victim as an exception to self-defense. We agree. . . . The trial court, over defendant's objection, instructed the jurors, using the language of § 18-1-704(3)(a), C.R.S.1998, that:

3. A person is not justified in using physical force if:
a. with intent to cause bodily injury or death to another person, he provokes the use of unlawful physical force by that person.

Under the common law, a defendant could not avail himself of the defense of self-defense if the necessity for such defense was brought on by a deliberate act of the defendant, such as being the initial aggressor or acting with the purpose of provoking the victim into attacking. The provocation limitation on self-defense is codified under § 18-1- 704(3)(a).

According to the plain language of the statute, a defendant's assertion of self-defense is lost if he or she acted with intent to provoke the victim into attacking first in order to provide the defendant with the excuse to injure or kill the victim.

In order to warrant the giving of this instruction, the prosecution has the burden of establishing that the defendant intended to harm the victim and that he or she intended the provocation to goad the victim into attacking him or her as a pretext for injuring or killing the victim. In contrast to the initial aggressor limitation, the provocation limitation applies in situations where the defendant was not the initial aggressor.

An instruction on provoking the victim, therefore, should be given if: 1) self-defense is an issue in the case; 2) the victim makes an initial attack on the defendant; and 3) the defendant's conduct or words were intended to cause the victim to make such attack and provide a pretext for injuring the victim.

Here, although there was no dispute that there had been no confrontation between defendant and his friends and the victim and his friends either in the bar or in the parking lot as the two groups walked to their vehicles, there was conflicting evidence as to the cause of the fight. Evidence was presented that an argument started between defendant and one of his friends and one member of the other group after both groups had begun to get into their trucks; however, no witness could recall the content of the discussion or who had spoken first.

Further, the victims who were stabbed were not present when words first were exchanged. Indeed, the victims did not enter the fight until after defendant's friend had thrown the first punch.

. . . We conclude there simply was no evidence presented that defendant intended to provoke a fight with the victims or their friend so that he could inflict injury upon them under the guise of such provocation. In the absence of such evidence, it was error for the trial court to give the jury an instruction on provoking the victim. . . .

Defendant argues that the trial court erred in instructing the jurors concerning the initial aggressor exception to self-defense and defense of others. Specifically, defendant argues that, because he was not the initial aggressor, the evidence was insufficient to support the giving of this instruction. The People contend that the instruction was proper because defendant's friend, as the initial aggressor, could not assert self-defense and, therefore, likewise, defendant could not assert defense of others. Assuming that the same or similar evidence is introduced on retrial, we conclude that the evidence creates questions of fact for the jury to determine whether the friend was the initial aggressor and, if so, whether defendant was justified in using physical force to come to his friend's aid. We further conclude that the instructions given by the trial court, with some modification, will properly inform the jury of these fact questions and the law necessary to make its determination.

A reasonable belief that one is defending against the use of unlawful force is the touchstone of self-defense and, thus, of defense of others. In determining whether an initial aggressor instruction is appropriate under the circumstances of a case in which hostilities begin and escalate among a group of people, the conduct of the defendant in the context of the situation must be the focus of any analysis of the defendant's right to self-defense.

It is undisputed that defendant did not strike the first blow and, therefore, was not himself the initial aggressor. That he may have uttered some insult or engaged in an argument also would not justify identifying defendant as the initial aggressor. However, there was conflicting testimony as to how the fight actually began. Defendant's friend testified that he threw the first punch when he saw one of the other persons take an aggressive stance and draw his arm back as if to hit defendant's other friend. The victims testified, to the contrary, that defendant's friend threw the first punch without any provocation. This evidence created questions of fact for the jury as to who, other than defendant, was the initial aggressor, and whether defendant responded reasonably under the circumstances once the fight began. See *State v. Amado,* 50 Conn.App. 607, 719 A.2d 45 (1998) (person may respond with physical force to reasonably perceived threat of physical force without being the initial aggressor)

Nevertheless, the People contend that a defendant, when asserting defense of others, "stands in the shoes" of the person being defended. If, they argue, that other person is not entitled to assert self-defense, then the defendant is precluded on that basis from asserting defense of others. We disagree.

As a general rule, a person coming to the aid of a third party with a reasonable belief that his or her intervention is necessary to prevent injury to the third party is entitled to assert defense of others to absolve or mitigate a charge of assault or homicide. The affirmative defense of defense of others is not absolutely barred by the wrongful actions of the third party.

The majority of jurisdictions today, for public policy reasons, allow a defendant to assert some form of defense of others based on a reasonable belief by a defendant that intervention was necessary to protect the person he or she perceived as being under attack. See *State v. Holmes,* 208 N.J.Super. 480, 506 A.2d 366 (1986) (whether a defendant may intervene to defend a third party is determined by the subjective intent of the defendant subject to an objective finding by the jury that the defendant reasonably concluded that the third party was in danger); *State v. Chiarello,* 69 N.J.Super. 479, 174 A.2d 506 (1961) (people should not be discouraged by thought of criminal prosecution if they come to another's aid in good faith); Model Penal Code § 3.09, comment 2 (person should not be convicted of crime requiring intent if person was acting under a mistake that, had the facts been as he or she supposed, would have left that person free from guilt).

Similarly, under the Colorado statute defining self-defense, § 18-1-704(1), C.R.S.1998, a person coming to the aid of a third party must have a reasonable belief that the third party is in imminent danger of becoming the victim of unlawful force. The statute does not require that such person have actual knowledge of the circumstances surrounding the use of force by another, but requires only a reasonable belief of the necessity to intervene. See *Sanchez v. People,* 820 P.2d 1103 (Colo.1991) (person asserting self-defense may act on appearances rather than reality; question is whether the defendant's conduct was reasonable under the circumstances as he or she perceived them to be).

Thus, on retrial, regardless whether defendant's friend, and not defendant, was the initial aggressor, if the same or similar evidence is presented, questions of fact concerning defendant's action

under the circumstances of the fight are raised for the jury's determination and the jury must be instructed accordingly.

At trial, the court, over defendant's objection, instructed the jury that:

> 3. A person is not justified in using physical force if:
> . . .
> b. he is the initial aggressor, except that his use of physical force upon another person under the circumstances is justifiable if he withdraws from the encounter and effectively communicates to the other person his intent to do so, but the latter nevertheless continues or threatens the use of unlawful physical force.

The court separately instructed the jurors that:

> A man has a right to defend himself and others against what he reasonably believes to be the unlawful assaults and attacks of others. He may repel force by force.
> A man has the right to make decisions and to act upon the circumstances as they reasonably appeared to him at the time, and as they may have appeared to a reasonable person. A man may act out of apparent necessity, if his perceptions are reasonable, even though the perceived danger does not exist.
> In deciding whether or not the defendant had reasonable grounds for believing that there was imminent danger, you should determine this question from the standpoint of the defendant at the time he acted, in the circumstances in which he found himself. You must determine whether he acted as a reasonable person in those circumstances.

The trial court has a duty to instruct the jury properly concerning all the issues supported by the evidence. Generally, instructions phrased in the language of the statute are proper. However, if a statutory instruction does not fit a particular case, or if supplementary instructions are needed to state a defendant's position, then such instructions should be submitted to the jury.

Here, although no evidence was presented that defendant, himself, was the initial aggressor, as discussed, the evidence was sufficient to raise a question of fact concerning defendant's right to come to the defense of another person who might have been the initial aggressor. Thus, on remand, if the same or similar evidence is presented, it would be proper for the trial court to instruct the jury concerning the limitation on an initial aggressor's right to assert self-defense, and the right of the defendant to act upon his reasonable belief under the circumstances. However, to clarify the applicable law under the circumstances of this case, the court should also instruct the jury that defendant, in coming to the aid of another who is the initial aggressor, may defend the other only from that which he reasonably believes to be the use of excessive force. . . .

The judgment is reversed and the cause is remanded for further proceedings consistent with the views expressed in this opinion.

QUESTIONS FOR DISCUSSION

1. Summarize the provocation and aggressor exceptions to the self-defense rule. Is there a difference between them? Can you say what it is?
2. List the facts relevant to deciding whether Steven Silva is entitled to self-defense.
3. Relying on the facts, do you think that Steven Silva is entitled to self-defense or do his actions bring him within either of the exceptions that the court discusses?

Belief in Danger

The most common cases of self-defense involve someone who kills to save his or her own life. But self-defense is broader than that. It also includes killing someone who is about to kill a member of your family, or any innocent person for that matter. And you're not limited to killing someone who is going to kill you or someone else. You may kill anyone who you believe is about to hurt you or someone else badly enough to send you or them to the hospital. This is what "serious bodily injury" found in most self-defense statutes means. Some self-defense statutes go even further. They allow you to kill someone you believe is about to commit a serious felony against you that doesn't threaten either your life or serious bodily injury. These felonies usually include rape, sodomy, kidnapping, and armed robbery. The list can also include killing someone who commits crimes against your home, as we'll see in the section on defense of homes and property.

What kind of belief does self-defense require? Is it enough that you *honestly* believe that someone is going to kill you, seriously injure you, or commit some other serious felony against you or your property? No. Most statutes require not only that *you* believe that you need to use force but that a *reasonable person* in the same situation also would have believed that force was necessary. Specifically, you're justified in killing someone if you honestly *and* reasonably believe it's necessary. In the 1980s' sensational "New York Subway Vigilante case," the New York Court of Appeals examined the belief in danger of armed robbery provision in New York's self-defense statute.[9]

CASE   Did He Shoot in Self-Defense?

People v. Goetz
68 N.Y.2d 96, 506 N.Y.S.2d 18, 497 N.E.2d 41
(1986)

Bernhard Goetz, the defendant, was indicted for criminal possession of a weapon, attempted murder, assault and reckless endangerment. The Supreme Court, Trial Term, New York County, dismissed the indictment and the People appealed. The Supreme Court, Appellate Division affirmed and the People appealed. The Court of Appeals reversed, and reinstated all of the dismissed counts of the indictment.

WACHTLER, C.J.

FACTS

The precise circumstances of the incident giving rise to the charges against defendant are disputed, and ultimately it will be for a trial jury to determine what occurred. We feel it necessary, however, to provide some factual background to properly frame legal issues before us. . . .

On Saturday afternoon, December 22, 1984, Troy Canty, Darrell Cabey, James Ramseur, and Barry Allen boarded an IRT express subway train in The Bronx and headed south toward lower Manhattan. The four youths rode together in the rear portion of the seventh car of the train. Two of the four, Ramseur and Cabey, had screwdrivers inside their coats, which they said were to be used to break into the coin boxes of video machines.

Defendant Bernhard Goetz boarded this subway train at 14th Street in Manhattan and sat down on a bench towards the rear section of the same car occupied by the four youths. Goetz was carrying an unlicensed .38 caliber pistol loaded with five rounds of ammunition in a waistband holster. The train left the 14th Street station and headed towards Chambers Street.

It appears from the evidence before the Grand Jury that Canty approached Goetz, possibly with Allen beside him, and stated "give me five dollars." Neither Canty nor any of the other youths displayed a weapon. Goetz responded by standing up, pulling out his handgun and firing four shots in rapid succession. The first shot hit Canty in the chest; the second struck Allen in the back; the third went through Ramseur's arm and into his left side; the fourth was fired at Cabey, who apparently was then standing in the corner of the car, but missed, deflecting instead off of a wall of the conductor's cab. After Goetz briefly surveyed the scene around him, he fired another shot at Cabey, who was then sitting on the end bench of the car. The bullet entered the rear of Cabey's side and severed his spinal cord.

All but two of the passengers fled the car when, or immediately after, the shots were fired. The conductor, who had been in the next car, heard the shots and instructed the motorman to radio for emergency assistance. The conductor then went into the car where the shooting occurred and saw Goetz sitting on a bench, the injured youths lying on the floor or slumped against a seat, and two women who had apparently taken cover, also lying on the floor. Goetz told the conductor that the four youths had tried to rob him.

While the conductor was aiding the youths, Goetz headed towards the front of the car. The train had stopped just before the Chambers Street station and Goetz went between two of the cars, jumped onto the tracks, and fled. Police and ambulance crews arrived at the scene shortly thereafter. Ramseur and Canty, initially listed in critical condition, have fully recovered. Cabey remains paralyzed, and has suffered some degree of brain damage.

On December 31, 1984, Goetz surrendered to police in Concord, New Hampshire. . . . Later that day, after receiving Miranda warnings, he made two lengthy statements, both of which were tape recorded with his permission. In his statements, which are substantially similar, Goetz admitted that he had been illegally carrying a handgun in New York City for three years. He stated that he had first purchased a gun in 1981 after he had been injured in a mugging. Goetz also revealed that twice between 1981 and 1984 he had successfully warded off assailants simply by displaying the pistol.

According to Goetz's statement, the first contact he had with the four youths came when Canty, sitting or lying on the bench across from him, asked "how are you," to which he replied "fine." Shortly thereafter, Canty, followed by one of the other youths, walked over to the defendant and stood to his left, while the other two youths remained to his right, in the corner of the subway car. Canty then said "give me five dollars." Goetz stated that he knew from the smile on Canty's face that they wanted to "play with me." Although he was certain that none of the youths had a gun, he had a fear, based on prior experiences, of being "maimed."

Goetz then established "a pattern of fire," deciding specifically to fire from left to right. His stated intention at that point was to "murder [the four youths], to hurt them, to make them suffer as much as possible." When Canty again requested money, Goetz stood up, drew his weapon, and began firing, aiming for the center of the body of each of the four. Goetz recalled that the first two he shot "tried to run through the crowd [but] they had nowhere to run." Goetz then turned to his right to "go after the other two." One of these two "tried to run through the wall of the train, but . . . he had nowhere to go." The other youth (Cabey) "tried pretending that he wasn't with [the others]" by standing still, holding on to one of the subway hand straps, and not looking at Goetz. Goetz nonetheless fired his fourth shot at him. He then ran back to the first two youths to make sure they had been "taken care of." Seeing that they had both been shot, he spun back to check on the other two. Goetz noticed that the youth who had been standing still was now sitting on a bench and seemed unhurt. As Goetz told the police, "I said 'you seem to be all right, here's another,'" and he fired the shot which severed Cabey's spinal cord. Goetz added that "if I was a little more under self-control . . . I would have put the barrel against his forehead and fired." He also admitted that "if I had had more [bullets], I would have shot them again, and again, and again."

After waiving extradition, Goetz was brought back to New York and arraigned on a felony complaint charging him with attempted murder and criminal possession of a weapon. The matter was presented to a Grand Jury in January 1985, with the prosecutor seeking an indictment for attempted murder, assault, reckless endangerment, and criminal possession of a weapon. . . . The Grand Jury indicted defendant on one count of criminal possession of a weapon in the third degree for possessing the gun used in the subway shootings, and two counts of criminal possession of a weapon in the fourth degree. . . . It dismissed, however, the attempted murder and other charges stemming from the shootings themselves.

Several weeks after the Grand Jury's action, the People, asserting that they had newly available evidence, moved for an order authorizing them to resubmit the dismissed charges to a second Grand Jury. . . . The second Grand Jury filed a 10-count indictment, containing four charges of attempted murder, four charges of assault in the first degree, one charge of reckless endangerment in the first degree, and one charge of criminal possession of a weapon in the second degree. . . .

On October 14, 1985, Goetz moved to dismiss the charges contained in the second indictment alleging, among other things, that the evidence before the second Grand Jury was not legally sufficient to establish the offenses charged and that the prosecutor's instructions to that Grand Jury on the defense of justification were erroneous and prejudicial to the defendant so as to render its proceedings defective.

On November 25, 1985, while the motion to dismiss was pending before Criminal Term, a column appeared in the *New York Daily News* containing an interview which the columnist had conducted with Darrell Cabey the previous day in Cabey's hospital room. The columnist claimed that Cabey had told him in this interview that the other three youths had all approached Goetz with the intention of robbing him. . . .

. . . The court, after inspection of the Grand Jury minutes, . . . held . . . that the prosecutor, in a supplemental charge elaborating upon the justification defense, had erroneously introduced an objective element into this defense by instructing the grand jurors to consider whether Goetz's conduct was that of a "reasonable man in [Goetz's] situation." The court . . . concluded that the statutory test for whether the use of deadly force is justified to protect a person should be wholly subjective, focusing entirely on the defendant's state of mind when he used such force. It concluded that dismissal was required for this error because the justification issue was at the heart of the case. . . .

On appeal by the People, a divided Appellate Division affirmed Criminal Term's dismissal of the charges. . . . Justice ASCH, in a dissenting opinion in which Justice WALLACH concurred, disagreed with both bases for dismissal relied upon by Criminal Term. On the justification question, he opined that the statute requires consideration of both the defendant's subjective beliefs and whether a reasonable person in defendant's situation would have had such beliefs. . . . Justice WALLACH stressed that the plurality's adoption of a purely subjective test effectively eliminated any reasonableness requirement contained in the statute. Justice ASCH granted the People leave to appeal to this court.

OPINION

Penal Law article 35 recognizes the defense of justification, which "permits the use of force under certain circumstances." . . . Penal Law § 35.15 (1) sets forth the general principles governing all such uses of force:

> a person may . . . use physical force upon another person when and to the extent he *reasonably believes* such to be necessary to defend himself or a third person from what he *reasonably* believes to be the use or imminent use of unlawful physical force by such other person. [emphasis added] § 35.15 (2) . . . A person may not use deadly physical force upon another person under circumstances specified in subdivision one unless (a) He *reasonably*

believes that such other person is using or about to use deadly physical force . . . or (b) He *reasonably* believes that such other person is committing or attempting to commit a kidnapping, forcible rape, forcible sodomy or robbery. [emphasis added]

✳ 7-1 New York's Complete "Defense of Justification" Provision

Thus, consistent with most justification provisions, Penal Law § 35.15 permits the use of deadly physical force only where requirements as to triggering conditions and the necessity of a particular response are met. As to the triggering of conditions, the statute requires that the actor "reasonably believes" that another person either is using or about to use deadly physical force or is committing or attempting to commit one of certain enumerated felonies, including robbery. As to the need for the use of deadly physical force as a response, the statute requires that the actor "reasonably believes" that such force is necessary to avert the perceived threat.

Because the evidence before the second Grand Jury included statements by Goetz that he acted to protect himself from being maimed or to avert robbery, the prosecutor correctly chose to charge the justification defense. . . . The prosecutor properly instructed the grand jurors to consider whether the use of deadly physical force was justified to prevent, either serious physical injury or a robbery, and, in doing so, to separately analyze the defense with respect to each of the charges. . . .

When the prosecutor had completed his charge, one of the grand jurors asked for clarification of the term "reasonably believes." The prosecutor responded by instructing the grand jurors that they were to consider the circumstances of the incident and determine "whether the defendant's conduct was that of a reasonable man in the defendant's situation." It is this response by the prosecutor—and specifically his use of "a reasonable man"—which is the basis for the dismissal of the charges by the lower courts. As expressed repeatedly in the Appellate Division's plurality opinion, because § 35.15 uses the term "he reasonably believes," the appropriate test, according to that court, is whether a defendant's beliefs and reactions were "reasonable to him." Under that reading of the statute, a jury which believed a defendant's testimony that he felt that his own actions

were warranted and were reasonable would have to acquit him, regardless of what anyone else in defendant's situation might have concluded. Such an interpretation defies the ordinary meaning and significance of the term "reasonably" in a statute, and misconstrues the clear intent of the Legislature, in enacting § 35.15, to retain an objective element as part of any provision authorizing the use of deadly physical force. . . .

We cannot lightly impute to the Legislature an intent to fundamentally alter the principles of justification to allow the perpetrator of a serious crime to go free simply because the person believed his actions were reasonable and necessary to prevent some perceived harm. To completely exonerate such an individual, no matter how aberrational or bizarre his thought patterns, would allow citizens to set their own standards for the permissible use of force. It would also allow a legally competent defendant suffering from delusions to kill or perform acts of violence with impunity, contrary to fundamental principles of justice and criminal law.

We can only conclude that the Legislature retained a reasonableness requirement to avoid giving a license for such actions. The plurality's interpretation, as the dissenters . . . recognized, excises the impact of the word "reasonably." . . .

Accordingly, the order of the Appellate Division should be reversed, and the dismissed counts of the indictment reinstated.

QUESTIONS FOR DISCUSSION

Consider the following:

- New York tried Goetz for attempted murder and assault. The jury acquitted him of both charges. The jury said Goetz "was justified in shooting the four men with a silver-plated .38-caliber revolver he purchased in Florida." They did convict him of illegal possession of a firearm, for which the court sentenced Goetz to one year in jail.

- Following the sentencing, Goetz told the court: "This case is really more about the deterioration of society than it is about me. . . . I believe society needs to be protected from criminals.[10]

- Criminal law professor George Fletcher followed the trial closely. After the acquittal, he commented:

The facts of the Goetz case were relatively clear, but the primary fight was over the moral interpretation of the facts. . . . I am not in the slightest bit convinced that the four young men were about to mug Goetz. If he had said, "Listen buddy, I wish I had $5, but I don't," and walked to the other side of the car the chances are 60-40 nothing would have happened. Street-wise kids like that are more attuned to the costs of their behavior than Goetz was.[11]

1. If Professor Fletcher is right, was Goetz justified in shooting?

2. Under what circumstances can people use deadly force, according to the New York statutes cited in the opinion?

3. Do you agree with those circumstances?

4. Would you add more? Remove some? Which ones? Why?

5. Were Goetz's shots a preemptive strike? Retaliation? Necessary for self-protection? Explain.

THE REST OF THE STORY

What Happened to Bernhard Goetz?

BERNHARD GOETZ'S STORY
(excerpted with permission from the Associated Press)

AP/Wide World Photos

1981 Mugging

Goetz called himself a "cold-blooded murderer" and a "monster" during his confession. But, he said, "I wasn't a monster until several years ago in New York."

Several years ago I got jumped . . . on Canal Street. Two-thirty in the afternoon. I was jumped by three guys. Now, they deliberately went after my knee and they got it. Like I got kicked in the knee and then what hurts you—They didn't have weapons, and people—you don't have to be maimed with a weapon. What—What really hurts you is the sidewalk. They tried to push me through a plate-glass door also, you know? I pushed as hard as I could when I—when I hit that door, with my hands. I still hit that door so hard, the glass hard. The glass didn't break, thank God, you know because I—that would've been it. . . . But the handle—yeah, yeah—the handle hit my chest and it—afterwards, now, I was a wreck.[12]

Incident in Central Park North After the 1981 Mugging but Before the Subway Shootings

By accident I was up there. I got on the wrong train. I was up there and I—I quickly wanted to get back to, uh, a more civilized section, it that's what you want to call it. People use the word "civilized" section. Two fellows, uh . . . one ran up from behind me and one ran up in front of me. And . . . the guy in front of me whipped out a cane and shouted, "Okay, motherfucker, give it up." What I did is, I pulled out my gun and I was scared. He was scared. I was so scared I was shaking. I thought I was going to shoot him. He thought I was going to shoot him. I—I just didn't know, but he—his knees buckled. He—He could hardly walk. . . . And people have said, "Well, showing the gun is enough." But this was an—this was a . . .[13]

Second Incident After Mugging and Before Subway Shooting

A fellow on the street, this was just a crazy kid on drugs. He . . . asked me for some money or something, and I just kept walking. He was walking behind me and this was on Sixth Avenue at about 8:00 p.m. . . . He threatened me okay? He said, "I hope I catch up with you 'cause I'm gonna—you know—. . . because when I do" and whatever and stuff like that. And I got pissed off and pulled out the gun. And that was stupid because I didn't have to pull the gun, and showing it was enough to make him run away.

"Why did you pull the gun?" one of the interrogating officers asked.

I just—Okay, okay, it's true; I was pissed. But I didn't shoot him. He deserved to die. I—I—I—I—I told him something like, "I'm gonna blow you away" or something like that. He got scared shitless and that was that.[14]

The "Subway Shooting"

In a videotape made on New Year's Eve, 1984, in the police department in Concord, New Hampshire, where Goetz turned himself in, Goetz explained when and why he decided to shoot. Goetz insisted that "the key was the look Troy Canty gave him when he asked for or demanded five dollars."

> GOETZ: The threat, when I was surrounded—At that point pulling the gun would've been enough. But when I saw this one fellow, when I saw the gleam in his eye and the smile on his face . . . What happened is I snapped. [When Canty first asked] "How're you doing" It wasn't even a warning signal. . . . These were just kids kidding around. . . . But then two of them stood up, okay? And they walked over to my left, okay? . . . The situation, when the two move on my left and the two are on my right—Now that is a real fucking threat. I knew at that point I would have to pull the gun. I'll—I'm gonna say this: At that—At that time I was gonna pull the gun, but I wasn't gonna kill them. . . . What my intention was at this time was to follow the situation as closely as I could.
>
> [Although one youth showed a] bulge in his pocket, [Goetz didn't fear that they were armed.] Robbery had nothing to do with it. Canty's exact words were, "Give me five dollars." He said it with a smile and his eyes were bright. The words meant bullshit. Five dollars to me is bullshit. . . . I knew I had to pull the gun, but it was the look and—now, you cannot understand this—it was his eyes were shiny. He had a smile on his face. He'll claim it was all a joke. If you believe that, I accept that. When I saw the the smile on his face and the shine—and the shine in his eyes, that he was enjoying this, I knew what they were going to do. You understand? . . . And it was at that point I decided I was going to kill 'em all, murder 'em all, do anything.
>
> [ASSISTANT MANHATTAN D.A.] BRAVER: What did you think they were going to do?
>
> GOETZ: How can you ask a question like that? They were going to—They were going to have fun with me, Miss.
>
> BRAVER: What do you mean by that? What is your interpretation of that? I can't get inside your head.
>
> GOETZ: Beat the shit out of you.
>
> BRAVER: You thought they were going to beat you up? Is that what you're saying?
>
> GOETZ: You just use such a casual phrase. What are you saying, Miss? Miss, your attitude—your attitude. You are so far removed from reality, and yet they send you here as a professional, as a professional, to investigate this. It's beyond belief. Look, they—what they were going to do is enjoy me for awhile. They were going to beat the fucking shit out of me, okay?

BRAVER: Did you feel trapped?

GOETZ: Did I feel—What do you think? Oh, no, no, no. I felt free. I felt—I felt great. I was enjoying Fun City. You know, I was gonna . . .

BRAVER: I'm trying to see what you felt at the time.

GOETZ: I was just whistling Dixie, okay?

TROY CANTY'S STORY

Troy Canty, a 5 foot, 7 inches tall, 140 pound African American, grew up in a housing project with his mother and brother. He dropped out of school after ninth grade. From then until he was shot he supported himself by stealing cashboxes in video games. "On a good day," he made between $150 and $200. Also, "I used to buy items wholesale and sell them for retail, and occasionally I shoplifted in large department stores." The money he stole went for clothes and drugs.

At the time of Goetz's trial, Canty lived in "Phoenix Academy," a drug rehabilitation center. Since entering the center, he hadn't used drugs, had gone back to school and completed his high school equivalency diploma, and was set to enter a 21-month program at the Culinary Institute of America. He's worked in the kitchen at the rehab center and wanted to become a cook.

On December 22, 1984, the day Goetz shot him, Troy Canty was 5 feet, 7 inches tall and weighed 140 pounds. He and his friends were on their way to steal from the video games at Pace University. None of them had cash, which they needed to ward off suspicion while they broke open the video cash boxes with screwdrivers. When they saw Goetz, he looked like a good target to get money from. Canty testified that he was three to four feet from Goetz with his hands empty at his sides when he asked Goetz, "Mister, can I have five dollars." Goetz answered, "Yes, you can all have it."

After he was shot, *The National Enquirer* paid Canty $300 (which he split with Barry Allen) for an interview. In the interview, Canty was quoted as saying that in addition to stealing from video cash boxes, they also "learned about taking people's wallets, grabbing gold chains off people's necks and strong-arming people for money." He also was quoted as saying, "The justice system is a joke. If we get caught, we plea-bargain a felony down to a misdemeanor, then walk away."

According to the prosecutor in the Goetz case,

In the first place, you have to bear in mind this group is going downtown for a very specific purpose: to rob video machines. Troy Canty had done this for years. He knew he had a gold mine in this kind of action. . . . Canty knew that breaking into video machines was neat, clean work [that] paid rich dividends with very little risk.

How many times had he done it? Hundreds of times. How many times had he been caught? A handful. Even on those rare occasions when the authorities succeeded in nabbing him, what happened to him? He was charged with a misdemeanor. That's all. He knew that. He got what, the most, thirty days in jail? That was a small price for Troy Canty to pay for the hundreds of dollars that was available to him. But breaking into video machines is one thing. Robbing people is quite another.

Canty may not be the most highly educated person in the world, but he is not dumb. He is shrewd and he is streetwise and Troy Canty knew in December of 1984, as he knows now, that there is a big difference between robbing people and breaking into video machines. . . . Canty knew that there was a difference between a felony and a misdemeanor, big difference between going upstate to prison with murderers and rapists and spending a few weeks on Rikers Island with the boys.

Canty, I submit, is simply too shrewd to try to rob the defendant in front of a carload of passengers, [that a group] taking care to wear reversible jackets' so they could avoid apprehension [would not have tried to rob someone] in front of a trainload of passengers that they have been riding with for thirty minutes . . . , conspicuously calling attention to themselves: playing on the bars, pounding on the seats, talking to people, approaching people for matches.

The last published news of Troy Canty is that on August 8, 1996. He was *arrested* for assaulting Kim Williams, his common law wife. Canty allegedly punched and choked her when she refused to give him money. Williams suffered a cut lip during the incident. There is no published evidence whether he was *convicted.*[15]

BARRY ALLEN'S STORY

"We piled aboard a subway for a day of hassling passengers for money and this nervous-looking guy got aboard at Fourteenth Street and sat right across from us. One look at him and we could tell he was scared. We thought we had an easy victim. Nudging each other and nodding towards him, we decided to strike. All four of us gathered around him, standing over him threateningly, as he looked up at us from his seat. Troy asked him, 'Mister, can we have five dollars?'"

A JUROR'S STORY

According to Mark Lesly, an actor and member of the jury, the jury's toughest problem was to decide whether Goetz was justified in shooting Darrell Cabey, especially after Goetz said, "You don't look so bad, here's another." The specific problem was to apply Justice Crane's instruction to that shooting. Justice Crane's instruction was:

> If you conclude, beyond a reasonable doubt, that any particular shot was an unnecessary or excessive response to whatever the defendant perceived, then you must conclude that he was not legally justified in firing the shot.

Notice that the prosecution had the burden of proving beyond a reasonable doubt that Goetz was not justified, that is, that a reasonable person would not have fired that second shot. Here's how Lesly described and interpreted what Goetz said and did and the jury's deliberations:

> For a period of time, I was a cold-blooded murderer; I wanted to kill those guys; I wanted to maim those guys; I wanted to make them suffer in every way I could; if I had more bullets, I would have shot 'em all again and again; were these the comments of a man with a score to settle, a man who held the entire city of New York in contempt, and a man who had decided to take the law into his own hands and deliver his own brutal brand of justice? Or were these the words of a frightened, confused, bitter man who was just coming to terms with the fact that, as a result of what he'd done, his life had been irrevocably

changed; and the manifestations of internal turmoil, guilt, self-deprecation, self-directed rage? On the one hand, there really was no way for us to know for certain. And on the other hand it really did not matter, because although it might have made a difference concerning intent, we primarily had to judge Goetz on his actions; not on his words but on his deeds.

. . . Even as I argued to acquit Goetz for the assault of Canty, Allen, and Ramseur, then, I felt that the Cabey assault was different and made it clear to everyone where I stood. If Cabey had been shot as part of a single burst of gunfire, I believed Goetz had to be found not guilty given the verified threat he faced. If, however, the evidence proved Goetz had shot Cabey in the way he'd described—after a pause that provided him the opportunity to reflect on and to reassess his situation—I was convinced that Goetz should be found guilty of that crime.

This was the big question of the whole trial. Did Cabey get hit by a bullet that paralyzed him while standing in front of his subway seat, then fall backward into the seat as a second bullet fired at him missed, striking the wall of the conductor's cab? Or was he missed by the first volley and then coldbloodedly and unjustifiably shot while cowering in his seat?

. . . Our ultimate decision rested on the concept of reasonable doubt. Cathy Brody [an uncertain juror] was the final convert, as she had been throughout; but she acquiesced because we agreed we just couldn't be certain of what had happened. Maybe Goetz did shoot at Cabey when he was seated. I still think it is possible that that in fact is what occurred. But neither Goetz's own incriminating statements, the corroborative testimony of Christopher Boucher, nor the two bullet holes in Cabey's jacket was enough to *convince* me that it had happened. And all the other jurors, ultimately, were unconvinced as well.

After [a lot more] . . . discussion, we still had to have one final round of discussion to convince Cathy Brody that Goetz faced the threat of deadly force. She was holding out on acquitting Goetz of the assault of Cabey on this issue because Cabey was the last youth shot. We more or less repeated all our previous arguments; and I contended that at the moment when Goetz started firing it was from Cabey that he had the most to fear. I reiterated that when Goetz pulled his gun and turned to face Troy Canty, Cabey had the opportunity to grab Goetz from behind. All Cabey had to do was to have reacted quickly enough, and I argued that the fact that this hadn't happened did not eliminate it as a danger and something that Goetz could have reasonably feared. I urged Brody to accept the threat that the youths represented as one that could have resulted in Goetz's death.

Finally, Brody reluctantly agreed that there was too much reasonable doubt to support a conviction either on the basis of how Goetz shot Darrell Cabey or because of a nagging belief that the shooting of four unarmed youths on a subway train is not a reasonable act, and that somehow Goetz must have overstepped that which the law allows.

Lesly had this to say about critics of the jury's verdict and New York's self-defense law:

To you who . . . believe in Goetz's guilt on the assault and attempted murder charges, I suggest that the fault in failing to convict him lies not with the jury nor the judge nor the prosecutor, but with a deficiency in the justification laws. The law, I think, is not specific enough about the alternatives Goetz should have been required to seek before being allowed to fire his gun as a legitimate act of self-defense.

According to the law, as explained by Justice Crane, once the implied threat of deadly force is present a person can shoot to defend himself if he cannot retreat "with complete safety to himself." When a person is confronted by two or more persons within the close confines of a moving subway car, a strong argument can always be made that the person's safety is not ensured. I believe that a truly reasonable person with a proper respect for the sanctity of human life should do more than Goetz did to try to avoid shooting preemptively. Nothing more, however, is required by the law. . . . Bernhard Goetz did what the law allows . . . and I think that the law is flawed.[16]

CABEY V. GOETZ, THE CIVIL SUIT, APRIL 1996

On April 23, 1996, an 11-year civil suit in which Darrell Cabey sued Bernhard Goetz came to a close. The jury in the case awarded Darrell Cabey $43,000,000. During the civil trial, Goetz testified that Shirley Cabey, Darrell's mother "should have had an abortion instead of giving birth to Darrell," and that shooting her son was "a public service." Mrs. Cabey, a widow who had to quit her job to take care of Darrell, said that "the Cabey name had been cleared" by the jury's verdict.[17]

Juror Comments

What clinched their verdict was Goetz' testimony that after the 1984 shooting, he admitted he told Cabey: "You don't look so bad, here's another," then fired a final shot that left the youth paralyzed.

Ronald Corley, a chef's assistant from University Heights, said he sympathized with Goetz at first but later changed his mind. "[Darrell Cabey] was scared already. Now you're going to go over there and shoot him?" Corley said.

Juror Sylvester Lewis 3d, 27, a sound engineer who works at the United Nations and Apollo Theatre, agreed. "If Mr. Goetz was to end his shooting on the fourth shot, it might have been a different situation," he said.

"[Cabey] was on the floor, so why did Goetz have anything to be afraid of?" asked Elba Torres, 45, a city worker. Torres said the 4½ hours of deliberations were generally cordial, although sometimes voices including her own were raised as the six jurors grappled with the case.

According to the *New York Daily News* (reprinted with permission),

> From their first vote, the four Hispanics and two blacks on the panel knew they would reach a unanimous decision in Cabey's favor. But there was wrangling over the amount of damages. In the end, the amount totaled just $7 million less than the $50 million Cabey sought.
>
> Much of lawyer Ronald Kuby's case against Goetz centered on race and the gunman's decision to fire on four black teenagers. But, said Torres, "I don't think it was race. . . . When kids approach you, they approach you with an attitude." Mildred Richardson, an alternate juror, agreed with the verdict but disagreed that race was not a factor. "If you want to be prejudiced, that's your decision but you don't express it the way he did," she said. "That man didn't learn anything. Maybe if he had gone to jail, maybe he would have learned a thing or two," Richardson said, apparently unaware that Goetz had served time for a weapons possession violation. "Maybe he would have learned to say I'm sorry."[18]

Professor George Fletcher's Comments

The distinguished professor of criminal law, George Fletcher, had this to say after the civil case trial:

> It took two trials to do justice in the serial story of Bernhard Goetz. The first trial, the six-week criminal hearing in 1987, focused on whether Mr. Goetz overreacted after four black teen-agers surrounded him on a downtown No. 2 train and asked him for money. It was Mr. Goetz against the group his lawyers called "the predators" and "the gang of four."
>
> This month's short civil trial brought one of the youths, the paralyzed Darrell Cabey, center stage. In the lens of our time, it pitted a brain-damaged victim in a wheelchair against an eccentric gunman with hate in his heart.
>
> In the first trial, it made sense, given the political atmosphere of the day, that a racially mixed Manhattan jury acquitted Mr. Goetz of attempted murder. It also made sense that a Bronx jury yesterday found him liable to Mr. Cabey to the tune of $43 million. This tendency to split the outcomes is the way justice is now done in the United States.
>
> Our effort to give both sides their due weighs more heavily in these results than does racial politics. Black jurors played an important role in Mr. Goetz's 1987 acquittal. And if this month's civil trial had taken place in Manhattan, instead of the Bronx, my sense is that the judgment would have gone against Mr. Goetz.[19]

WHATEVER HAPPENED TO THE YOUTHS GOETZ SHOT?

Soon after the Goetz case, Barry Allen went to prison for "chain snatching." In 1991, he was released from prison after serving three years for robbery. In 1996, James Ramseur was still serving time for raping, robbing, and sodomizing an 18-year-old woman on a Bronx rooftop. Troy Canty went to Phoenix House to participate in a drug treatment program not related to the Goetz case. He was released in 1989. As of 1996, he had no further criminal record. Darrell Cabey is in a wheelchair, paralyzed for life.[20]

Imminent Attacks

Only the danger of imminent attacks, that is, attacks that are either happening or are going to happen *right now,* justifies the use of force. So, in one case, after a street gang member threw a brick at a cabdriver from the far side of an intersection, the driver justifiably shot into the gang because, despite their distance, they could have killed the driver at any moment. It is sometimes argued that *present* danger (that is, danger that *could* happen at any time but isn't going to happen right now) is good enough. For example, suppose an assailant stops attacking to get reinforcements and the victim shoots her as she's leaving. The victim may be in present danger but she isn't in immediate danger because the attack is not on the verge of happening.

The *Model Penal Code* allows self-defense to fend off present danger. A few states, such as Delaware, Hawaii, New Jersey, Nebraska, and Pennsylvania, have followed the *Model Penal Code.* Most states, however, require immediate or imminent danger. Many cases of present danger involve battered women. The Kansas Supreme Court dealt with the problem of present danger in the battered wife case of *State v. Stewart.*[21]

C A S E | Was She in "Imminent" Danger?

State v. Stewart
243 Kan. 639, 763 P.2d 572 (1988)

Peggy Stewart was charged with the first-degree murder of her husband. A jury found her not guilty. The prosecution appealed the self-defense ruling. (Of course, the state can't appeal a jury's acquittal, but it can appeal questions of law.) The Kansas supreme court sustained the appeal.

LOCKETT, J.

FACTS

. . . Following an annulment from her first husband and two subsequent divorces in which she was the petitioner, Peggy Stewart married Mike Stewart in 1974. Evidence at trial disclosed a long history of abuse by Mike against Peggy and her two daughters from one of her prior marriages. Laura, one of Peggy's daughters, testified that early in the marriage Mike hit and kicked Peggy, and that after the first year of marriage Peggy exhibited signs of severe psychological problems. Subsequently, Peggy was hospitalized and diagnosed as having symptoms of paranoid schizophrenia; she responded to treatment and was soon released. It appeared to Laura, however, that Mike was encouraging Peggy to take more than her prescribed dosage of medication.

In 1977, two social workers informed Peggy that they had received reports that Mike was taking indecent liberties with her daughters. Because the social workers did not want Mike to be left alone with the girls, Peggy quit her job. In 1978, Mike began to taunt Peggy by stating that Carla, her 12-year-old daughter, was "more of a wife" to him than Peggy.

Later, Carla was placed in a detention center, and Mike forbade Peggy and Laura to visit her. When Mike finally allowed Carla to return home in the middle of summer, he forced her to sleep in an un-air-conditioned room with the windows nailed shut, to wear a heavy flannel nightgown, and to cover herself with heavy blankets. Mike would then wake Carla at 5:30 A.M. and force her to do all the housework. Peggy and Laura were not allowed to help Carla or speak to her.

When Peggy confronted Mike and demanded that the situation cease, Mike responded by holding a shotgun to Peggy's head and threatening to kill her. Mike once kicked Peggy so violently in the chest and ribs that she required hospitalization. Finally, when Mike ordered Peggy to kill and bury Carla, she filed for divorce. Peggy's attorney in the divorce action testified in the murder trial that Peggy was afraid for both her and her children's lives.

One night, in a fit of anger, Mike threw Carla out of the house. Carla, who was not yet in her teens, was forced out of the home with no money, no coat, and no place to go. When the family heard that Carla was in Colorado, Mike refused to allow Peggy to contact or even talk about Carla. Mike's intimidation of Peggy continued to escalate. One morning, Laura found her mother hiding on the school bus, terrified and begging the driver to take her to a neighbor's home. That Christmas, Mike threw the turkey dinner to the floor, chased Peggy outside, grabbed her by the hair, rubbed her face in the dirt, and then kicked and beat her.

After Laura moved away, Peggy's life became even more isolated. Once, when Peggy was working at a cafe, Mike came in and ran all the customers off with a gun because he wanted Peggy to go home and have sex with him right that minute. He abused both drugs and alcohol, and amused himself by terrifying Peggy, once waking her from a sound sleep by beating her with a baseball bat. He shot one of Peggy's pet cats, and then held the gun against her head and threatened to pull the trigger. Peggy told friends that Mike would hold a shotgun to her head and threaten to blow it off, and indicated that one day he would probably do it.

In May 1986, Peggy left Mike and ran away to Laura's home in Oklahoma. It was the first time Peggy had left Mike without telling him. Because Peggy was suicidal, Laura had her admitted to a hospital. There, she was diagnosed as having toxic psychosis as a result of an overdose of her medication. On May 30, 1986, Mike called to say he was coming to get her. Peggy agreed to return to Kansas. Peggy told a nurse she felt like she wanted to shoot her husband. At trial, she testified that she decided to return with Mike because she was not able to get the medical help she needed in Oklahoma.

When Mike arrived at the hospital, he told the staff that he "needed his housekeeper." The hospital released Peggy to Mike's care, and he immediately drove her back to Kansas. Mike told Peggy that all her problems were in her head and he would be the one to tell her what was good for her, not the doctors. Peggy testified that Mike threatened to kill her if she ever ran away again. As soon as they arrived at the house, Mike forced Peggy into the house and forced her to have oral sex several times.

The next morning, Peggy discovered a loaded .357 magnum. She testified she was afraid of the gun. She hid the gun under the mattress of the bed in a spare room. Later that morning, as she cleaned house, Mike kept making remarks that she should not bother because she would not be there long, or that she should not bother with her things because she could not take them with her. She testified she was afraid Mike was going to kill her.

Mike's parents visited Mike and Peggy that afternoon. Mike's father testified that Peggy and Mike were affectionate with each other during the visit. Later, after Mike's parents had left, Mike forced Peggy to perform oral sex. After watching television, Mike and Peggy went to bed at 8:00 P.M.

As Mike slept, Peggy thought about suicide and heard voices in her head repeating over and over, "kill or be killed." At this time, there were two vehicles in the driveway and Peggy had access to the car keys. About 10:00 P.M. Peggy went to the spare bedroom and removed the gun from under the mattress, walked back to her bedroom, and killed her husband while he slept. She then ran to the home of a neighbor, who called the police.

When the police questioned Peggy regarding the events leading up to the shooting, Peggy stated that things had not gone quite right that day, and that when she got the chance she hid the gun under the mattress. She stated that she shot Mike to "get this over with, this misery and this torment." When asked why she got the gun out, Peggy stated to the police:

> I'm not sure exactly what . . . led up to it . . . and my head started playing games with me and I got to thinking about things and I said I didn't want to be by myself again. . . . I got the gun out because there had been remarks made about me being out there alone. It was as if Mike was going to do something again like had been done before. He had gotten me down here from McPherson one time and he went and told them that I had done something and he had me put out of the house and was taking everything I had. And it was like he was going to pull the same thing over again.

Two expert witnesses testified during the trial. The expert for the defense, psychologist Marilyn Hutchinson, diagnosed Peggy as suffering from "battered woman syndrome," or post-traumatic stress syndrome. Dr. Hutchinson testified that Mike was preparing to escalate the violence in retaliation for Peggy's running away. She testified that loaded guns, veiled threats, and increased sexual demands are indicators of the escalation of the cycle. Dr. Hutchinson believed Peggy had a repressed knowledge that she was in a "really grave lethal situation."

The State's expert, psychiatrist Herbert Modlin, neither subscribed to a belief in the battered woman syndrome nor to a theory of learned helplessness as an explanation for why women do not leave an abusive relationship. Dr. Modlin testified that abuse such as repeated forced oral sex would not be trauma sufficient to trigger a post-traumatic stress disorder. He also believed Peggy was erroneously diagnosed as suffering from toxic psychosis. He stated that Peggy was unable to escape the abuse because she suffered from schizophrenia, rather than the battered woman syndrome.

At defense counsel's request, the trial judge gave an instruction on self-defense to the jury. The jury found Peggy not guilty [of first-degree murder. Upon a special appeals procedure, the state appealed, arguing that the trial judge erred in his self-defense instruction.]:

OPINION

. . . K.S.A. 21-3211 provides:

> A person is justified in the use of force against an aggressor when and to the extent it appears to him and he reasonably believes that such conduct is necessary to defend himself or another against such aggressor's imminent use of unlawful force.

The traditional concept of self-defense has posited one-time conflicts between persons of somewhat equal size and strength. When the defendant claiming self-defense is a victim of long-term domestic violence, such as a battered spouse, such traditional concepts may not apply. Because of the prior history of abuse, and the difference in strength and size between the abused and the abuser, the accused in such cases may choose to defend during a momentary lull in the abuse, rather than during a conflict. However, in order to warrant the giving of a self-defense instruction, the facts of the case must still show that the spouse was in imminent danger close to the time of killing.

A person is justified in using force against an aggressor when it appears to that person and he or she reasonably believes such force to be necessary. A reasonable belief implies both an honest belief and the existence of facts which would persuade a reasonable person to that belief. A self-defense instruction must be given if there is any evidence to support a claim of self-defense, even if that evidence consists solely of the defendant's testimony.

Where self-defense is asserted, evidence of the deceased's long-term cruelty and violence towards the defendant is admissible. In cases involving battered spouses, expert evidence of the battered woman syndrome is relevant to a determination of the reasonableness of the defendant's perception of danger. . . .

In order to instruct a jury on self-defense, there must be some showing of an imminent threat or a confrontational circumstance involving an overt act by an aggressor. There is no exception to this requirement where the defendant has suffered long-term domestic abuse and the victim is the abuser. In such cases, the issue is not whether the defendant believes homicide is the solution to past or future problems with the batterer, but rather whether circumstances surrounding the killing were sufficient to create a reasonable belief in the defendant that the use of deadly force was necessary. . . . Here . . . there is an absence of imminent danger to defendant.

Peggy told a nurse at the Oklahoma hospital of her desire to kill Mike. She later voluntarily agreed to return home with Mike when he telephoned her. She stated that after leaving the hospital Mike threatened to kill her if she left him again. Peggy showed no inclination to leave. In fact, immediately after the shooting, Peggy told the police that she was upset because she thought Mike would leave her. Prior to the shooting, Peggy hid the loaded gun. The cars were in the driveway and Peggy had access to the car keys. After being abused, Peggy went to bed with Mike at 8 P.M. Peggy lay there for two hours, then retrieved the gun from where she had hidden it and shot Mike while he slept.

Under these facts, the giving of the self-defense instruction was erroneous. Under such circumstances, a battered woman cannot reasonably fear imminent life-threatening danger from her sleeping spouse. We note that other courts have held that the sole fact that the victim was asleep does not preclude a self-defense instruction. In *State v. Norman,* 89 N.C.App. 384, 366 S.E.2d 586 (1988) . . . the defendant's evidence disclosed a long history of abuse. Each time defendant attempted to escape, her husband found and beat her. On the day of the shooting, the husband beat defendant continually throughout the day, and threatened either to cut her throat, kill her, or cut off her breast. In the afternoon, defendant shot her husband while he napped.

The North Carolina Court of Appeals held it was reversible error to fail to instruct on self-defense. The court found that, although decedent was napping at the time defendant shot him, defendant's unlawful act was closely related in time to an assault and threat of death by decedent against defendant and that the decedent's nap was "but a momentary hiatus in a continuous reign of terror."

There is no doubt that the North Carolina court determined that the sleeping husband was an evil man who deserved the justice he received from his battered wife. Here, similar comparable and compelling facts exist. But, as one court has stated: "To permit capital punishment to be imposed upon the subjective conclusion of the [abused] individual that prior acts and conduct of the deceased justified the killing would amount to a leap into the abyss of anarchy." *Jahnke v. State,* 682 P.2d 991, 997 (Wyo.1984).

Finally, our legislature has not provided for capital punishment for even the most heinous crimes. We must, therefore, hold that when a battered woman kills her sleeping spouse when there is no imminent danger, the killing is not reasonably necessary and a self-defense instruction may not be given. To hold otherwise in this case would in effect allow the execution of the abuser for past or future acts and conduct.

One additional issue must be addressed. In its *amicus curiae* brief, the Kansas County and District Attorney Association contends the instruction given by the trial court improperly modified the law of self-defense to be more generous to one suffering from the battered woman syndrome than to any other defendant relying on self-defense. We agree. . . .

The appeal is sustained.

DISSENT

HERD, J., joined by PRAGER, C.J.

. . . It is evident . . . appellee met her burden of showing some competent evidence that she acted in self-defense, thus making her defense a jury question. She testified she acted in fear for her life, and Dr. Hutchinson corroborated this testimony. The evidence of Mike's past abuse, the escalation of violence, his threat of killing her should she attempt to leave him, and Dr. Hutchinson's testimony that appellee was indeed in a "lethal situation" more than met the minimal standard of "any evidence" to allow an instruction to be given to the jury.

The evidence showed Mike had a "Dr. Jekyll and Mr. Hyde" personality. He was usually very friendly and ingratiating when non-family persons were around, but was belligerent and domineering to family members. He had a violent temper and would blow up without reason. Mike was cruel to his two stepdaughters, Carla and Laura, as well as to the appellee. He took pride in hurting them or anything they held dear, such as their pets. Mike's violence toward appellee and her daughters caused appellee to have emotional problems with symptoms of paranoid schizophrenia. He would overdose appellee on her medication and then cut her off it altogether. Mike's cruelty would culminate in an outburst of violence, and then he would suddenly become very loving and considerate. This was very confusing to appellee. She lived in constant dread of the next outburst. . . .

It is a jury question to determine if the battered woman who kills her husband as he sleeps fears he will find and kill her if she leaves, as is usually claimed. Under such circumstances the battered woman is not under actual physical attack when she kills but such attack is imminent, and as a result she believes her life is in imminent danger. She may kill during the tension-building stage when the abuse is apparently not as severe as it sometimes has been, but nevertheless has escalated so that she is afraid the acute stage to come will be fatal to her. She only acts on such fear if she has some survival instinct remaining after the husband-induced "learned helplessness.". . .

The majority claims permitting a jury to consider self-defense under these facts would permit anarchy. This underestimates the jury's ability to recognize an invalid claim of self-defense. Although this is a case of first impression where an appeal by the State has been allowed, there have been several similar cases in which the defendant appealed on other grounds. In each of these cases where a battered woman killed the sleeping batterer, a self-defense instruction has been given when requested by the defendant. . . .

The majority bases its opinion on its conclusion appellee was not in imminent danger, usurping the right of the jury to make that determination of fact. The majority believes a person could not be in imminent danger from an aggressor merely because the aggressor dropped off to sleep. This is a fallacious conclusion. For instance, picture a hostage situation where the armed guard inadvertently drops off to sleep and the hostage grabs his gun and shoots him. The majority opinion would preclude the use of self-defense in such a case. . . . I would deny this appeal.

QUESTIONS FOR DISCUSSION

1. How does the court define imminent?

2. Can battered women ever be in imminent danger when their husbands are sleeping?

3. Should we have a special battered woman's defense of justification?

4. Or should we expand the definition of imminent or change the requirement from imminent to present, or continuing, danger?

5. Why does the court talk about putting the power of capital punishment into the hands of battered wives?

6. Consider the following comment:

   Retaliation, as opposed to defense, is a common problem in cases arising from wife battering and domestic violence. The injured wife waits for the first possibility of striking against a distracted or unarmed husband. The man may even be asleep when the wife finally reacts. Retaliation is the standard case of "taking the law into your own hands." There is no way, under the law, to justify killing a wife batterer or a rapist in retaliation or revenge, however much sympathy there may be for the wife wreaking retaliation. Private citizens cannot act as judge and jury toward each other. They have no authority to pass judgment and to punish each other for past wrongs.

   Do you agree?

7. In your opinion, was Peggy Stewart's act one of self-defense, a preemptive strike, or retaliation? Back up your answer with facts in the case.

In 1993, seven years after the Kansas Supreme Court decided the state's appeal in Peggy Stewart's case, the same court had to decide two other difficult questions regarding battered women who kill: Can evidence of the battered woman's violence toward other people rebut the claim that she suffers from battered woman's syndrome? And, what is a fair penalty for battered women who don't suffer from the syndrome who kill their husbands after years of abuse? The court answered the questions in *State v. Cramer.*

C A S E	**Can a Woman with a History of Violence Use the Battered Woman Syndrome Defense?**

State v. Cramer
17 Kan.App.2d 623, 841 P.2d 1111
(Kan. App. 1993)

Janette Cramer, the defendant, was convicted in the Finney District Court of involuntary manslaughter and sentenced to from three to five years in prison. She appealed. The Court of Appeals affirmed.

LEWIS, J.

FACTS

This is a case of an abused wife who terminated her marriage and any future abuse by fatally shooting her husband. Prior to the night of the shooting, defendant's life with the victim appears to have been one of abuse and pain.

Defendant and William Cramer were married in July 1987. The record indicates that William first began to beat defendant nine days prior to their wedding and that he continued to beat her on a regular basis up to the time of his death. It would serve little good to recite the details of all of the beatings inflicted by William on defendant. The record shows that there were many, that they were regular, and that they were accompanied by verbal abuse as well. Some of these beatings were so violent that defendant was hospitalized as a result. On one occasion, William picked defendant up and attempted to "hang" her on a nail protruding from a wall. The nail punctured her back and left a scar running up to her shoulder. Frequently, both parties were drinking when these violent episodes took place.

Finally, defendant sued William for divorce. She obtained a restraining order, which did not restrain William, who continued to beat and threaten her. After one of these beatings put defendant in

the hospital, a friend gave her a handgun for protection. It is noted that, on the night of William's death, defendant placed the handgun in a strategic position in her house.

On the evening of William's death, he came to defendant's home with her permission. He came to discuss their divorce and brought along a supply of beer and liquor. The two parties apparently sat down at the table and began to drink and discuss the terms of their divorce. As the evening wore on, William became more angry and, finally, began to pound on the table. He started to verbally abuse defendant and stood up and stepped towards her. According to defendant, she got up and retrieved the handgun from where she had placed it. She pointed the gun at William and said, "[You're not] going to beat on me again." William apparently laughed, took one step forward, and defendant shot him in the chest. William was either dead on arrival at the hospital or died shortly thereafter. According to the postmortem reports, the bullet wound was not necessarily fatal but, as a result of that gunshot, William bled to death.

Defendant was charged with second-degree murder. Her defense was self-defense, based on the battered woman's syndrome. After a three-day trial, the jury returned a verdict, finding her guilty of involuntary manslaughter. At her sentencing, defendant argued that to deny her probation amounted to "manifest injustice" under K.S.A.1991 Supp. 21-4618(3). After listening to defendant's arguments, the trial court denied her probation because of her use of a firearm and the provisions of K.S.A. 21-4618(1) and (2). She appeals her conviction and sentence. After careful consideration, we affirm on both counts.

OPINION

Defendant argues that the trial court erred in admitting evidence of specific instances of past conduct between defendant and third parties. This evidence was not complimentary to defendant and may have been prejudicial. The trial court determined that, despite its potential prejudice, the evidence was admissible. We agree with that conclusion.

In order to prove her battered woman's syndrome defense, defendant introduced the expert testimony of Dr. Stephen E. Peterson, a psychiatrist at the Menninger Clinic. He testified that, in his opinion, defendant was suffering from the battered woman's syndrome. He reached this diagnosis after a two-day examination of defendant. As a result of that examination, Dr. Peterson prepared an extensive report that gave specific details about defendant's past life and experiences. A portion of this report described several instances of violent conduct between defendant and other parties.

The State of Kansas countered Dr. Peterson's testimony by introducing testimony of Dr. Alice Brill. Dr. Brill is also a psychiatrist, and she testified that, in her opinion, defendant did not suffer from the battered woman's syndrome. Dr. Brill's opinion was based in large part on the evidence of specific instances of past conduct, to which defendant objects.

Defendant's argument is that the evidence was so prejudicial that it should not have been admitted. The State argues that the evidence was probative and admissible. It points out that much of the evidence came in as a result of the cross-examination of Dr. Peterson. Basically, the State argues that this testimony was admissible to rebut the diagnosis of the battered woman's syndrome testified to by Dr. Peterson.

Defendant is particularly aggrieved by the testimony of Melvin Fox. A recounting of his testimony will serve to illustrate the type of evidence to which defendant objects. Fox was called as a rebuttal witness by the State of Kansas. He testified that he had had a relationship of sorts with defendant. He described in graphic detail one occasion when he was in the bathroom, throwing up after a drinking spree. He testified that, while he was in this rather vulnerable state, defendant entered the bathroom wearing only steel-toed biker boots and proceeded to kick him several times.

Dr. Brill referred to the incident described by Fox in support of her opinion that defendant was not suffering from the battered woman's syndrome. Dr. Brill used other instances involving defendant and third parties in stating that defendant did not suffer from the battered woman's syndrome. Defendant insists that the testimony of Fox and the use of other instances of her past conduct were intended to prejudice the jury against her.

. . . In this instance, we find no abuse of discretion in admitting the evidence under discussion. Testimony concerning the specific instances complained of by defendant was elicited by the State in an effort to cast doubt upon Dr. Peterson's diagnosis of the battered woman's syndrome. On cross-examination, Dr. Peterson was cross-examined about an incident at a wedding party where defendant physically fought with another woman. Another incident concerned an altercation between defendant and a male bouncer at a tavern. Dr. Brill, the State's expert witness, referred to these incidents as inconsistent with those characteristics associated with the battered woman's syndrome. . . .

In the final analysis, the trial court determined that the probative value of the evidence outweighed the prejudicial effect of that evidence. This was a proper decision for the trial court, and we will not substitute our judgment for that of the trial court on this issue. . . .

The defense in this lawsuit was self-defense. This was based on the contention that defendant suffered from the battered woman's syndrome and perceived that she was protecting herself from imminent danger in shooting William. The trial court gave a self-defense instruction. . . . After the jury had retired and begun its deliberation, it submitted a question. This question bracketed the following language from the self-defense instruction: "Such justification requires both a belief on the part of the defendant and the existence of facts that would persuade a reasonable person to that belief." The jury then asked the following question:

> "Does this mean:
> (1) That a reasonable person, in the same situation, would choose the same.
> or
> (2) That a reasonable person, would believe that she believed that was her only option.
> "Need last part clarified please.
> "/s/ Gilbert Widows"

After receiving the question, the trial court adjourned the trial and retired to chambers with all parties and counsel present to formulate an answer to the question. . . . Defendant argues that the trial court should have advised the jury that the objective test is whether a "reasonably prudent battered woman would have perceived self-defense as necessary." We disagree. . . .

The defense in this case was self-defense, based on the battered woman's syndrome. The record is replete with evidence of repeated beatings inflicted upon defendant by William. Both expert witnesses agreed that defendant was a battered woman. To advise the jury that the objective test was "whether a reasonable person in defendant's circumstances would have perceived self-defense as necessary" was to advise the jury to judge defendant's conduct as that of a battered spouse. We see no other way the jury could have perceived the court's instructions and the use of the term "in defendant's circumstances." Defendant's circumstances in this case were those of a battered woman being advanced upon by her battering spouse. The instruction sufficiently advised the jury that it should consider whether a person in defendant's circumstances would perceive self-defense as necessary. We consider that to have been a proper answer to the question and one which could not possibly have confused the jury.

We have reviewed the most recent Supreme Court holdings concerning instructions where a battered spouse is defending against a charge of homicide. . . . Our reading of the Supreme Court decisions concerning battered women reveals no requirement that a jury be advised that it must employ an objective test based on how a "reasonably prudent battered woman" would react to a threat. Indeed, to employ such language would modify the law of self-defense to be more generous to one suffering from the battered woman's syndrome than to any other defendant relying on self-defense. The Supreme Court in *State v. Stewart* expressly disavowed any such interpretation of the law. Under the facts shown, the trial court's answer to the jury's question correctly stated the law and was not confusing or misleading. . . .

The defendant in this case was convicted of the crime of involuntary manslaughter, as defined by K.S.A. 21-3404. This crime was committed with the use of a firearm. Under these circumstances, the mandatory sentencing provisions of K.S.A.1991 Supp. 21-4618 are applicable. This statute requires mandatory imprisonment under the circumstances shown. The trial court sentenced defendant under K.S.A.1991 Supp. 21-4618(1) and (2) and denied her application for probation or assignment to a community corrections program. Defendant argued that the trial court erred in sentencing her in this manner.

Defendant argues that K.S.A.1991 Supp. 21-4618(3) applied and that her sentencing amounts to manifest injustice. K.S.A.1991 Supp. 21-4618(3) reads as follows: "The provisions of this section shall not apply to any crime committed by a person where such application would result in a manifest injustice." It is defendant's position that, in her case, imposition of mandatory imprisonment constitutes manifest injustice.

In a very recent decision, we dealt with a similar question. Although we concluded that the term "manifest injustice" as used in the statute was not possible of exact definition, we said: "A sentence which is 'obviously unfair' or 'shocking to the conscience' accurately and permissibly characterizes one which would result in manifest injustice." *State v. Turley,* 17 Kan.App.2d 484, Syl. ¶ 2, 840 P.2d 529 (1992). In *Turley,* we concluded that a sentence which "shocks the conscience of the court" is manifestly unjust. This is similar to saying that, while it is difficult to define "pornography," one will most certainly know it when he or she sees it. While this may not be an entirely satisfactory definition, we believe it to be the only definition possible.

In the first instance, the sentencing court in this state is the trial court. "A sentence imposed will not be disturbed on appeal if it is within the limits prescribed by law and the realm of trial court discretion and not a result of partiality, prejudice, oppression, or corrupt motive." Our standard of review in the ordinary sentencing case is abuse of discretion. We conclude that this is the standard of review to be applied in a case of this nature together with the use of the "shocking to the conscience" philosophy. . . .

We have reviewed the record carefully in the instant matter. We conclude that the trial court considered all of the necessary sentencing factors required by statute in making its decision. . . . It is not our position to second-guess the trial court in matters of sentencing. The trial judge heard all of the testimony, observed the witnesses, and had the opportunity to evaluate their credibility based on personal observance. We do not have that same opportunity. The trial court is in the best position to evaluate the sentencing factors involved, and we respect the trial court's superior knowledge and its primary responsibility in pronouncing sentence. . . .

Affirmed.

QUESTIONS FOR DISCUSSION

1. State exactly why the court approved evidence of Janette Cramer's history of violence.

2. Do you think the exact evidence of her violence against other people proves that she didn't suffer from battered woman syndrome? Defend your answer.

3. Do you think that the evidence of her violent history should play a part in sentencing her? Defend your answer.

4. Did the sentence "shock your conscience"? Would you sentence her to probation? Defend your answer.

NOTE CASES

1. Ms. Gallegos suffered a long history of physical and sexual abuse, dating back to oppressive childhood encounters with her father, her brother, and one of her mother's boyfriends. Her father beat her; her brother physically and sexually abused her; and one of her mother's lovers tied defendant to her mother's bed and fondled her while making love to her mother. Out of her turbulent relationship with the victim, George Gallegos, four children were born, but the relationship was marred with violence.

George was a heavy drinker, and she displayed to the jury scars near her eye, on her forehead, and on her nose, resulting from beatings she claimed George administered to her. Ms. Gallegos testified that George threatened to cut off her breasts with the knife if her breasts grew any larger. When she was pregnant with their second child, defendant testified that George picked her up and threw her against a wall, causing the premature birth of the child. George's gun also was put into evidence. Ms. Gallegos claimed that George would place the loaded gun at her

head and threaten to shoot her if she ever left him. On numerous occasions, Gallegos testified, George would tie her hands behind her back and sodomize her to the point of inducing rectal bleeding. He would also force her to engage in fellatio. On one occasion, according to defendant's testimony, the Gallegos' neighbors, aware that George was abusing defendant, summoned the police. The police, however, apparently failed to take action because they had not witnessed the brutality.

On the day Ms. Gallegos killed George, she had taken her older children to school. She testified that when she returned home, George sodomized her against her will, making her cry and bleed. During the course of the day, George apparently drank beer. At one point in the day, defendant said that she told George that she was tired of being hurt and that she threatened to leave him. George pulled out his gun and threatened to kill her if she left. Also, on that day, George had struck one of their sons in the face with a belt buckle.

That evening, after the children went to bed, George asked the victim why she was not a virgin when they married. She answered that she was not a virgin because of her brother. Gallegos testified that George became angry, called her a profane name, and said "you probably liked it." At that moment, when she looked at George, she saw her father, her brother, and George, all coming toward her.

George then called her into the bedroom. He added something to the effect that if she did not come, he would find someone else. Defendant testified that she feared for her life. She did not know whether George intended to kill her, to rape her, or to beat her. Gallegos picked up a loaded rifle which George kept in the living room. While George was lying on the bed, she cocked the rifle and shot him. After shooting him, she stabbed George numerous times.

Was Ms. Gallegos in imminent danger of death or serious bodily harm? Yes, according to the New Mexico Supreme Court:

In order to assert a valid self-defense claim . . . there must have been the appearance to the defendant of immediate danger of death or great bodily harm. . . . We believe that defendant presented evidence sufficient to allow reasonable minds to differ as to whether defendant believed that she was in imminent danger of death or great bodily harm. Defendant was a victim of recurrent violence. On the day of George's death, he had been drinking. Already that day he had sexually abused defendant; he had struck a child in the face with a belt buckle; he had threatened to kill defendant; and, finally, he was angry and calling her into the bedroom. Based upon that evidence, reasonable minds could believe that defendant was afraid. While one inference from George's statement, that if defendant did not come into the bedroom he would find someone else, might be that George only desired sex, another equally permissible inference could be that he was using that as a ploy to catch defendant off guard so he could harm her.

She stated she was put in fear. Dr. Cave, a clinical psychologist who regularly treats battered wife cases, testified at the trial. According to Dr. Cave's opinion, the above facts, coupled with a history of prior physical, sexual and verbal abuse and her testing of defendant, the appearance of immediate danger of "great bodily harm, even death" was present. Dr. Cave testified that the history of abuse in this case, as extensive as any she had ever seen, combined with the events of the day, created "great fear" which was real to defendant.

The fear present in this case also was prompted by more than a history of abuse. Based on the brutality which defendant testified she had experienced that day, George's anger, and her knowledge of what had happened to her in similar circumstances, George's calling her into the bedroom could provide the requisite immediacy of danger.

. . . To deny the defense of self-defense under the facts of this case would ignore reality. We, therefore, hold that the trial court erred in rejecting defendant's tendered self-defense instruction. . . . We reverse and remand this case for a new trial, consistent with this opinion.

State v. Gallegos, 719 P.2d 1268 (N.M. 1986)

2. On the night of his death, Richard Jahnke's father took Richard's mother out to dinner, apparently to celebrate the anniversary of their meeting. Earlier, 16-year-old Richard had a violent altercation with his father. His father warned Richard not to be there when he got home. While his parents were gone, Jahnke made elaborate preparation for a final confrontation with his father. He changed into dark clothing and prepared a number of weapons which he positioned at various places throughout the family home that he selected to serve as "backup" positions in case he failed in his first attempt to kill his father. These weapons included two shotguns, three rifles, a .38 caliber pistol and a Marine knife. Richard also armed his sister, Deborah, with a .30 caliber M1 carbine which he taught her how to operate so that she could protect herself in case he failed to kill his father. Richard removed the family pets from the garage to the basement to protect them from injury in a potential exchange of gunfire between him and his father, and he closed the garage door.

Then he waited inside the dark garage in a position where he couldn't be seen but where he could see the lighted driveway on the other side of the garage door. Shortly before 6:30 P.M. his parents returned, and Jahnke's father got out of the car and came to the garage door. Jahnke was armed with a 12-gauge shotgun loaded with slugs, and when he could see the head and shoulders of his father through the spacing of the slats of the shade covering the windows of the garage door, he blew his R.O.T.C. command-sergeant-major's whistle for courage, and he opened fire. All six cartridges in the shotgun were expended, and four of them in one way or another struck the father. The most serious wound was caused by a slug which entered the father on the right chest just above and to the inside of the right nipple, followed a trajectory which took it through the right rib cage and the right lobe of the liver, bruising the right lung and tearing the diaphragm along the way, into the middle of the chest cavity where it passed behind the heart nearly severing the aorta, inferior vena cava and the esophagus, then through the lower lobe of the left lung, finally lodging just under the skin in the mid-part of the victim's back. About one hour after the shooting incident the father was pronounced dead from the wounds inflicted by Jahnke.

After the shooting, and while his mother still was screaming in the driveway, Jahnke and his sister left through a window in their mother's bedroom. He and his sister then went separate ways, and Richard was arrested at his girlfriend's house. Prior to the arrival of authorities Richard told his girlfriend's father that he had shot his dad for revenge. Subsequently, after being advised of his constitutional rights, he made a statement in which he explained he had shot his father "for past things."

Richard Jahnke was tried as an adult, convicted of voluntary manslaughter, and sentenced to 5 to 15 years in prison. Did Richard Jahnke kill his father in self-defense? Although he was entitled to an instruction on self-defense, according to the Wyoming Supreme Court, there is no special defense for battered "persons." According to the court:

. . . Although many people, and the public media, seem to be prepared to espouse the notion that a victim of abuse is entitled to kill the abuser that special justification defense is antithetical to the mores of modern civilized society. It is difficult enough to justify capital punishment as an appropriate response of society to criminal acts even after the circumstances have been carefully evaluated by a number of people. To permit capital punishment to be imposed upon the subjective conclusion of the individual that prior acts and conduct of the deceased justified the killing would amount to a leap into the abyss of anarchy.

In *People v. White*, and *State v. Thomas*, the courts suggest that the true role of any evidence with respect to family abuse is to assist the jury to determine whether the defendant's belief that he was in danger of his life or serious bodily injury was reasonable under the circumstances. In those cases the courts indicate that expert testimony with respect to such an issue is neither necessary nor relevant and for that reason is best eschewed. It is clear that if such evidence has any role at all it is in assisting the jury to evaluate the reasonableness of the defendant's fear in a case involving the recognized circumstances of self-defense which include a confrontation or conflict with the deceased not of the defendant's instigation.

In a concurring opinion, one of the justices noted:

At the outset I confess to a philosophical bias against people who take the law into their own hands and execute their supposed tormentors. I am particularly opposed to patricide. After considering the news, particularly letters to the editor, I conclude that I must represent a view contrary to that of the public.

Appellant is handsome, personable, intelligent and ready of tongue. He is an all-American boy, except that he has a predilection toward patricide. Appellant and his incredible story caught the imagination of the media and public.

Richard thought about killing his father many times before November 16. On the 16th he made elaborate plans for the execution. He lay in wait for an hour and one half, then blew his ROTC whistle to freeze his victim. He fired repeatedly, propelling lead into his father's body. His first comment after the slaying was that he did it for revenge. This is a textbook case of first-degree murder.

The jury convicted appellant of killing his father voluntarily upon a sudden heat of passion. If lying in wait for one and one-half hours is a "sudden heat of passion," then appellant must have been frozen in time. This must have been the longest "sudden" in history.

In his defense appellant employed the oldest, most common and most successful tactic in homicide cases. He put the deceased on trial. His strategy was largely successful as he was convicted of a lesser offense when the uncontradicted evidence and appellant's admission pointed only to murder.

Evidence produced by appellant characterized the deceased father as a cruel, sadistic and abusive man. Experience, common sense and the conduct of Mrs. Jahnke indicated to me that the testimony in support of this characterization was greatly exaggerated. There was no one at trial to speak for the deceased. All defense witnesses were at liberty to say anything they wanted about the deceased, knowing that they could not be contradicted. Defense witnesses had a motive to make the deceased look like a bad man; they wanted to make the jury believe that appellant's father deserved to be executed. By no stretch of the imagination was this a case of self-defense. Arming and barricading himself and lying in wait for one and one-half hours for his father's return is not self-defense under the law.

The trial judge was eminently fair with appellant and resolved any doubt in his favor. Appellant was not entitled to an instruction on self-defense, nor was he entitled to an instruction on the lesser included offense of manslaughter because there was no evidence justifying either instruction. However, the judge being abundantly cautious gave these instructions.

Richard's avowed motives for gunning down his father have changed during this ordeal depending upon his forum. While he was in an excited state he told his girlfriend's father that he did it for revenge. While still exhilarated he told Officer Hildago that he killed for past things. Then his expressed reason briefly changed and he claimed self-defense at the trial. Richard now says he did it for his mother and sister. He said at a later trial he killed his father to "stop him from further abuse of his family."

Many in our society are fascinated by violence. We make folk heroes out of our criminals. Ballads and odes are written about murders. The more bizarre or unusual the murder, the greater the proliferation of songs, poems and books. The public's thirst for this sort of literature will not be stilled. If a person wants to become famous and even wealthy, he just needs to commit a grotesque crime.

John Herbert Dillinger and Alphonse Capone will live in our history for more than one hundred years. Good men, contemporaries of Dillinger and Capone, are already forgotten. "The evil that men do lives after them; the good is oft interred with their bones." Wm. Shakespeare, *Julius Caesar (The Tragedy of)*, Act 3, Scene 2.

Perhaps Richard Jahnke was entitled to compassion because of his age. The jury meted out that compassion when they found him guilty of manslaughter, despite the fact that the evidence pointed to murder. The judge's sentence evidences further compassion. He could have sentenced Richard to not less than nineteen years, eleven months and twenty-nine days. The judge and jury deserve to be commended, rather than harangued by the public. They demonstrated intelligence, good judgment and compassion.

One of the dissenting justices noted:

This case concerns itself with what happens—or can happen—and did happen when a cruel, ill-tempered, insensitive man roams, gun in hand, through his years of family life as a battering bully—a bully who, since his two children were babies, beat both of them and his wife regularly and unmercifully. Particularly, this appeal has to do with a 16-year-old boy who could stand his father's abuse no longer—who could not find solace or friendship in the public services which had been established for the purpose of providing aid, comfort and advice to abused family members—and who had no place to go or friends to help either him or his sister for whose protection he felt responsible and so in fear and fright, and with fragmented emotion, Richard Jahnke shot and killed his father one night in November of 1982. In these courts, Richard

pleads self-defense and, since the jury was given a self-defense instruction, it must be conceded that the trial judge recognized this as a viable defense theory under the evidence adduced at trial.

It is my conception that Richard Jahnke properly came to the courts of Wyoming asking—not that he be judged as one who, at the time and place in question, was insanely unreasonable—but that his 14 years of beatings and uncivilized emotional abuse be explained by a qualified expert in order that judgment be passed on the question which asks whether or not his behavior was sanely reasonable. One might wonder why—since our courts admit expert testimony with commendable regularity upon the issue of sanity when that is the ultimate fact—and the plea is insanity—it is not acceptable that a psychiatrist testify about whether behavior such as that with which this case is concerned and which is unlike that which lay jurors would understand to be the expected, is, nevertheless, sanely typical of the behavior of a reasonable person acting in the same or similar circumstances. Richard was not, however, permitted to have the impact of 14 years of abuse upon his alleged self-defensive behavior explained to the jury through the testimony of a psychiatrist even though this is the only way the fallout from brutality can be communicated.

Denied this opportunity, the appellant was forced to submit his case to the jury with what consequently presents itself as a ridiculous, unbelievable, outrageous defense. Without medical input, what possible sense could it make to a lay juror or any other nonprofessional person for the citizen accused to urge self-defense where the evidence is that, even though the recipient of untold battering and brutalizing by the victim, the defendant nevertheless contemplated the possibility of the use of deadly force as he lay in wait, gun in hand, for his father's return? How could any jury be receptive to such a defense on an informed basis if its members are not to be permitted to hear from those who understand how brutalized people—otherwise "reasonable" in all respects—entertain what, for them, is a belief that they are in imminent danger from which there is no escape and how they, with their embattled psyche, responsively behave?

Jahnke v. State, 682 P.2d 991 (Wyo. 1984)

Excessive Force

Defenders can use only the amount of force that they reasonably believe they have to use to repel an attack. This means they can't use deadly force when something less will do because that would be unreasonable. So, if an angry student is about to slap my face, I can't shoot her because that would be excessive force. On the other hand, it's always reasonable to use nondeadly force to repel deadly force. But no matter how menacing, threats by themselves don't justify the use of force. In one case, a prisoner threatened another prisoner with sodomy if the prisoner didn't immediately pay back a loan. The prisoner stabbed the would-be sodomizer. The court held that mere threats don't justify preventive assaults.[22]

THE RETREAT DOCTRINE

What if you can avoid an attack by escaping? Do you have to retreat? Or can you stand your ground and fight back? The **retreat rule** says you have to retreat. But only if you reasonably believe that backing off won't unreasonably put you in danger of death or serious bodily harm. The **stand-your-ground rule** says that if you didn't start the fight, you can stand your ground and kill. Of course you have to reasonably believe that you're in danger of death or serious bodily harm. Different values underlie these rules. The retreat rule puts a premium on human life and discourages injuring or killing another person (even an assailant). The stand-your-ground rule (sometimes called the "real man doctrine") is based on the belief that retreat forces innocent people to take a cowardly or humiliating position. Most states follow the stand-your-ground rule.[23]

States that require retreat have carved out an exception to the retreat doctrine known as the **castle exception**. According to the castle exception, when you're attacked in your home, you can stand your ground and use deadly force to fend off an unprovoked attack. But again, only if you reasonably believe that the attack threatens death or serious bodily injury. A problem arises over just what "home" means. Does it include the entryway? The sidewalk in front of the house? The property line? What if a person lives in a car, a hotel room, or under a bridge? Does it include your business? The Second Circuit U.S. District Court of Appeals dealt with retreat and the castle exception in *U.S. v. Peterson.*

| **C A S E** | **Did He Have to Retreat?** |

U.S. v. Peterson
483 F.2d 1222, 157 U.S.App.D.C. 219
(2nd Cir. 1973)

Bennie Peterson, the defendant, was convicted before the United States District Court for the District of Columbia of manslaughter, and he appealed. The District of Columbia Court of Appeals affirmed.
SPOTTSWOOD W. ROBINSON, III, J.

FACTS

Charles Keitt, the deceased, and two friends drove in Keitt's car to the alley in the rear of Peterson's house to remove the windshield wipers from Peterson's wrecked car. (The car was characterized by some witnesses as "wrecked" and by others as "abandoned." The testimony left it clear that its condition was such that it could not be operated.) While Keitt was doing so, Peterson came out of the house into the back yard to protest. After a verbal exchange, Peterson went back into the house, obtained a pistol, and returned to the yard. (Although the time lapse between Peterson's reentrance into the house and his subsequent reappearance in the yard is not precisely fixed, the testimony indicates that it was very short.) In the meantime, Keitt had reseated himself in his car, and he and his companions were about to leave.

Upon his reappearance in the yard, Peterson paused briefly to load the pistol. "If you move," he shouted to Keitt, "I will shoot." He walked to a point in the yard slightly inside a gate in the rear fence and, pistol in hand, said, "If you come in here I will kill you." Keitt alighted from his car, took a few steps toward Peterson and exclaimed, "What the hell do you think you are going to do with that?" (There was abundant evidence that Keitt was intoxicated or nearly so. His companions readily admitted to a considerable amount of drinking earlier that day, and an autopsy disclosed that he had a .29% blood-alcohol content.) Keitt then made an about-face, walked back to his car and got a lug wrench. With the wrench in a raised position, Keitt advanced toward Peterson, who stood with the pistol pointed toward him. Peterson warned Keitt not to "take another step" and, when Keitt continued onward shot him in the face from a distance of about ten feet. Death was apparently instantaneous. Shortly thereafter, Peterson left home and was apprehended 20-odd blocks away.

This description of the fatal episode was furnished at Peterson's trial by four witnesses for the Government. Peterson did not testify or offer any evidence, but the Government introduced a statement which he had given the police after his arrest, in which he related a somewhat different version. Keitt had removed objects from his car before, and on the day of the shooting he had told Keitt not to do so. After the initial verbal altercation, Keitt went to his car for the lug wrench, so he, Peterson, went into his house for his pistol. When Keitt was about ten feet away, he pointed the pistol "away of his right shoulder"; adding that Keitt was running toward him, Peterson said he "got scared and fired the gun. He ran right into the bullet." "I did not mean to shoot him," Peterson insisted, "I just wanted to scare him."

At trial, Peterson moved for a judgment of acquittal on the ground that . . . the evidence was insufficient to support a conviction. The trial judge denied the motion. After receiving instructions . . . the jury returned a verdict finding Peterson guilty of manslaughter. Judgment was entered conformably with the verdict, and this appeal followed.

OPINION

. . . Peterson's . . . position is that . . . his act was one of self-preservation. . . . The Government, on the other hand, has contended from the beginning that Keitt's slaying fell outside the bounds of lawful self-defense. The questions remaining for our decision inevitably track back to this basic dispute. . . . Self-defense . . . is as viable now as it was in Blackstone's time, and in the case before us the doctrine is invoked in its purest form. . . . Necessity is the pervasive theme of the . . . conditions which the law imposes on the right to kill or maim in self-defense. There must have been a threat, actual or apparent, of the use of deadly force against the defender. The threat must have been unlawful and immediate. The defender must have believed that he was in imminent peril of death or serious bodily harm, and that his response was necessary to save himself therefrom. These beliefs must not only have been honestly entertained, but also objectively reasonable in light of the surrounding circumstances. It is clear that no less than a concurrence of these elements will suffice.

Here the parties' opposing contentions focus on . . . the defendant's failure to utilize a safe route for retreat from the confrontation. . . . At no time did Peterson endeavor to retreat from Keitt's approach with the lug wrench. The judge instructed the jury that if Peterson had reasonable grounds to believe and did believe that he was in imminent danger of death or serious injury, and that deadly force was necessary to repel the danger, he was required neither to retreat nor to consider whether he could safely retreat. Rather, said the judge, Peterson was entitled to stand his ground and use such force as was reasonably necessary under the circumstances to save his life and his person from pernicious bodily harm. But, the judge continued, if Peterson could have safely retreated but did not do so, that failure was a circumstance which the jury might consider, together with all others, in determining whether he went further in repelling the danger, real or apparent, than he was justified in going.

Peterson contends that this imputation of an obligation to retreat was error, even if he could safely have done so. He points out that at the time of the shooting he was standing in his own yard, and argues he was under no duty to move. We are persuaded to the conclusion that in the circumstances presented here, the trial judge did not err in giving the instruction challenged.

Within the common law of self-defense there developed the rule of "retreat to the wall," which ordinarily forbade the use of deadly force by one to whom an avenue for safe retreat was open. This doctrine was but an application of the requirement of strict necessity to excuse the taking of human life, and was designed to insure the existence of that necessity. Even the innocent victim of a vicious assault had to elect a safe retreat if available, rather than resort to defensive force which might kill or seriously injure.

In a majority of American jurisdictions, contrarily to the common law rule, one may stand his ground and use deadly force whenever it seems reasonably necessary to save himself. While the law of the District of Columbia on this point is not entirely clear, it seems allied with the strong minority adhering to the common law. In 1856, the District of Columbia Criminal Court ruled that a participant in an affray "must endeavor to retreat, . . . that is, he is obliged to retreat, if he can safely." The court added that "a man may, to be sure, decline a combat when there is no existing or apparent danger, but the retreat to which the law binds him is that which is the consequence." In a much later era this court, adverting to necessity as the soul of homicidal self-defense, declared that "no necessity for killing an assailant can exist, so long as there is a safe way open to escape the conflict." Moreover, the common law rule of strict necessity pervades the District concept of pernicious self-defense, and we cannot ignore the inherent inconsistency of an absolute no-retreat rule. Until such time as the District law on the subject may become more definitive, we accept these precedents as ample indication that the doctrine of retreat persists.

That is not to say that the retreat rule is without exceptions. Even at common law it was recognized that it was not completely suited to all situations. Today it is the more so that its precept must be adjusted to modern conditions nonexistent during the early development of the common law of self-defense. One restriction on its operation comes to the fore when the circumstances apparently foreclose a withdrawal with safety. The doctrine of retreat was never intended to enhance the risk to the innocent; its proper application has never required a faultless victim to increase his assailant's safety at the expense of his own. On the contrary, he could stand his ground and use deadly force otherwise appropriate if the alternative were perilous, or if to him it reasonably appeared to be.

A slight variant of the same consideration is the principle that there is no duty to retreat from an assault producing an imminent danger of death or grievous bodily harm. "Detached reflection cannot be demanded in the presence of an uplifted knife," nor is it "a condition of immunity that one in that situation should pause to consider whether a reasonable man might not think it possible to fly with safety or to disable his assailant rather than to kill him."

The trial judge's charge to the jury incorporated each of these limitations on the retreat rule. Peterson, however, invokes another, the so-called "castle" doctrine. It is well settled that one who through no fault of his own is attacked in his home is under no duty to retreat therefrom. The oft-repeated expression that "a man's home is his castle" reflected the belief in olden days that there were few if any safer sanctuaries than the home. The "castle" exception, moreover, has been extended by some courts to encompass the occupant's presence within the curtilage outside his dwelling. Peterson reminds us that when he shot to halt Keitt's advance, he was standing in his yard and so, he argues, he had no duty to endeavor to retreat.

Despite the practically universal acceptance of the "castle" doctrine in American jurisdictions wherein the point has been raised, its status in the District of Columbia has never been squarely decided. But whatever the fate of the doctrine in the District law of the future, it is clear that in absolute form it was inapplicable here. The right of self-defense . . . cannot be claimed by the aggressor in an affray so long as he retains that unmitigated role. It logically follows that any rule of no-retreat which may protect an innocent victim of the affray would, like other incidents of a forfeited right of self-defense, be unavailable to the party who provokes or stimulates the conflict. Accordingly, the law is well settled that the "castle" doctrine can be invoked only by one who is without fault in bringing the conflict on. That, we think, is the critical consideration here.

. . . By no interpretation of the evidence could it be said that Peterson was blameless in the affair. And while, of course, it was for the jury to assess the degree of fault, the evidence well nigh dictated the conclusion that it was substantial.

The only reference in the trial judge's charge intimating an affirmative duty to retreat was the instruction that a failure to do so, when it could have been done safely, was a factor in the totality of the circumstances which the jury might consider in determining whether the force which he employed was excessive. We cannot believe that any jury was at all likely to view Peterson's conduct as irreproachable. We conclude that for one who, like Peterson, was hardly entitled to fall back on the "castle" doctrine of no retreat, that instruction cannot be just cause for complaint. . . .

The judgment of conviction appealed from is accordingly Affirmed.

QUESTIONS FOR DISCUSSION

1. List all of the facts relevant to deciding whether Bennie Peterson shot and killed Charles Keitt in self-defense.

2. Apply both the retreat and stand-your-ground rules to the facts of the case. Is Peterson guilty under both, one, or neither? Defend your answer.

3. Does the castle exception apply to the facts of the case? Rely on the specific facts in the case to back up your answer.

4. Do you favor the retreat or the stand-your-ground rule of self-defense? Why?

5. Exactly where would you draw the line in the castle exception? Or would you abolish the exception? Explain your answer.

✳ 7-2 Self-Defense

DEFENSE OF OTHERS

Historically, self-defense meant protecting both yourself and the members of your immediate families. Although several states still require a special relationship, the trend is in the opposite direction. Many states have abandoned the special relationship requirement altogether. Several states that still have the requirement have expanded it to include lovers and friends. [24]

The "others" have to have the right to defend themselves before someone else can claim the defense. This is important in cases involving abortion rights protesters. In one case, protesters argued that they had the right to prevent abortions by violating the law because they were defending the right of unborn children to live. In rejecting the defense of others, the court said:

> The "defense of others" specifically limits the use of force or violence in protection of others to situations where the person attacked would have been justified in using such force or violence to protect himself. In view of *Roe v. Wade* . . . and the provisions of the Louisiana abortion statute, defense of others as justification for the defendants' otherwise criminal conduct is not available in these cases. Since abortion is legal in Louisiana, the defendants had no legal right to protect the unborn by means not even available to the unborn themselves.[25]

DEFENSE OF HOME AND PROPERTY

The law regarding the defense of homes is deeply rooted in the common-law idea that "a man's home is his castle." As early as 1604, Sir Edward Coke, the great common-law judge, in his report of *Semayne's Case,* wrote:

> The house of everyone is to him his castle and fortress, as well for his defense against injury and violence, as for his repose; and although the life of a man is a thing precious and favored in law . . . if thieves come to a man's house to rob him, or murder, and the owner or his servants kill any of the thieves in defense of himself and his house, it is not felony and he shall lose nothing.[26]

The most impassioned statement of the supreme value placed on the sanctity of homes came from the Earl of Chatham during a debate in the British Parliament in 1764:

The poorest man may in his cottage bid defiance to all the forces of the Crown. It may be frail; its roof may shake; the wind may blow through it; the storm may enter; the rain may enter; but the King of England may not enter; all his force dares not cross the threshold of the ruined tenement.

Sir William Blackstone, in his eighteenth-century *Commentaries* (the best-known—and often the only law book known—to American lawyers at that time), writes:

If any person attempts . . . to break open a house in the nighttime (which extends also to an attempt to burn it) and shall be killed in such attempt, the slayer shall be acquitted and discharged. This reaches not to . . . the breaking open of any house in the daytime, unless it carries with it an attempt of robbery.[27]

Nearly all states allow the use of force to protect homes; some states go further and adopt provisions authorizing the use of force to protect personal property as well.

 7-3 Texas Provisions Regarding the Use of Nondeadly and Deadly Force to Protect Property

The Maryland Court of Appeals dealt with a tragic case of using deadly force to protect a home in *Law v. State*.

C A S E   Was He Justified in Killing to Protect His Home?

Law v. State
21 Md.App. 13, 318 A.2d 859 (Md. App. 1974)

James Law, the defendant, was convicted in the Circuit Court, Charles County, of murder and assault with intent to murder and he appealed. He was sentenced to 10 years in prison. The Court of Special Appeals reversed and remanded.

LOWE, J.

FACTS

When James Cecil Law, Jr., purchased a thirty-nine dollar shotgun for "house protection," he could not possibly have conceived of the ordeal it would cause him to undergo. Mr. Law, a 32-year-old black man, had recently married and moved to a predominantly white middle-class neighborhood. Within two weeks his home was broken into and a substantial amount of clothing and personal property was taken. The investigating officer testified that Mr. Law was highly agitated following the burglary and indicated that he would take the matter in his own hands. The officer quoted Mr. Law as saying: "I will take care of the job. I know who it is." The officer went on to say that Law told him

". . . he knew somebody he could get a gun from in D.C. and he was going to kill the man and he was going to take care of it." Two days later he purchased a 12-gauge shotgun and several "double ought" shells.

The intruder entered the Laws' home between 6:30 and 9:00 in the evening by breaking a windowpane in the kitchen door which opened onto a screened back porch. The intruder then apparently reached in and unlocked the door. Law later installed "double locks" which required the use of a key both inside and outside. He replaced the glass in the door window in a temporary manner by holding it in place with a few pieces of molding, without using the customary glazing compound to seal it in.

One week after the break-in a well-meaning neighbor saw a flickering light in the Laws' otherwise darkened house and became suspicious. Aware of the previous burglary, he reported to the police that someone was breaking into the Laws' home. Although the hour was 8:00 p.m., Mr. Law and his bride had retired for the evening. When the police arrived, a fuse of circumstances ignited by fear exploded into a tragedy of errors.

The police did not report to or question the calling neighbor. Instead they went about routinely checking the house seeking the possible illegal point of entry. They raised storm windows where they could reach them and shook the inside windows to see if they were locked. They shined flashlights upon the windows out of reach, still seeking evidence of unlawful entry. Finding none, two officers entered the back screened porch to check the back door, whereupon they saw the windowpane which appeared to have been temporarily put in place with a few pieces of molding. These officers apparently had not known of the repair or the cause of damage.

Upstairs Mr. and Mrs. Law heard what sounded like attempts to enter their home. Keenly aware of the recent occurrence, Mr. Law went downstairs, obtained and loaded his newly acquired shotgun and, apparently facing the rear door of the house, listened for more sounds.

In the meantime, the uniformed officers found what they thought to be the point of entry of a burglar, and were examining the recently replaced glass. While Officer Adams held the flashlight on the recently replaced pane of glass, Officer Garrison removed the molding and the glass, laid them down and stated that he was going to reach in and unlock the door from the inside to see if entry could be gained. Officer Adams testified that they "were talking in a tone a little lower than normal at this point." Officer Adams stated that Officer Garrison then tested the inside lock, discovered it was a deadlock and decided no one could have gotten in the door without a key. A law enforcement student, riding with Officer Garrison that evening, testified that he then heard a rattling noise and someone saying "if there was somebody here, he's still in there." As Officer Garrison removed his hand from the window he was hit by a shotgun blast which Law fired through the door. Officer Garrison was dead on arrival at the hospital.

Officer Potts, the officer next to arrive at the scene, saw Officer Adams running to his car to call for reinforcements. He heard another shot and Officer Adams yell "they just shot at me."

The tragedy of errors had only begun. The officers, having obtained reinforcements and apparently believing they had cornered a burglar, subjected the house to a fusillade of gun fire evidenced by over forty bullet holes in the bottom of the kitchen door and the police department transcription of a telephone conversation during the ensuing period of incomprehensible terror.

Mr. Law testified that while he stood listening to the sounds and voices at the door, fearful that someone was about to come in ". . . the gun went off, like that, and when it went off like that it scared me and I was so scared because I had never shot a shotgun before and then I heard a voice on the outside say that someone had been shot." Mr. Law was not able to hear who had been shot but he then ". . . hollered up to my wife, call a police officer, I think I shot a burglar." His wife called the police and most of her conversation was recorded. It is the most accurate portrayal of that which transpired and is repeated in full: The portion of the transcription that follows involves the conversation between a female physically located within the crime scene, 6519 Medwick Road, and Lt. Sellner who was located in the Communications Division.

S LT SELLNER   V MRS. LAW
MALE VOICE MR. LAW
LDO LONG DISTANCE OPERATOR

S Is he still downstairs?

V I beg your pardon.

S Hello, is he still downstairs?

V Who is this speaking?

S Are they still shooting?

V Hello, hello. They're shooting in my house at my husband.

S It's your husband?

V They're shooting at him. Tell them to stop.

S Alright where is he? Downstairs?

V Tell them to stop shooting.

S Alright, just hang on a minute. Hang on a minute. (Sounds of sporadic gunfire)

MALE VOICE Hey police, hey police. Hey stop shootin', please. Stop shootin'.

S Hello lady, MRS. LAW, MRS. LAW.

V Please tell them to stop shooting.

S Alright, tell him to put his hands up over his head and come out the front door.

V They keep shooting.

S Tell him to put his hands up over his head and stop his shooting.

V He's not shooting. They are shooting at him.

S Alright, he's not shooting anymore?

MALE VOICE Hey police, police, are you the police or not.

S Alright, just hang loose a minute. Hang on there now.

MALE VOICE Hey police, I'm coming out now. You hear me. Hey police you hear me. I'm coming out now.

V OK.

S Hang on a minute.

MALE VOICE I'm coming out now. Can't you hear me? Hey police, don't you hear me? (Gunfire)

S Hey lady, MRS. LAW. Alright, MRS. LAW, we're going to stop the shooting over there. Tell the man, your husband, to put his hands up over his head and go out the front door.

V Put your hands up over your head and go out the front door (Screaming) He's got to unlock the door, he's coming out. Please don't shoot him.

S Alright, tell him to put his hands up over his head.

V Hey, James, put your hands up over your head. OK, he's going to unlock the door, the front door was locked.

S OK, Steve, tell them he's going to come out the front door. Alright, he opened the front door, lady?

V Just a minute, we're trying to find the keys. (Screaming—James look in my pocketbook. James look in my pocketbook for the keys and open the front door)

V Please don't let them shoot him.

S Alright, tell him to just unlock the front door and they've stopped the shooting now, haven't they?

V Yes-unk-hah

V (Screaming) James look in my pocketbook and get the keys to the front door.

S Alright, you got the front door open?

V He hasn't got it open yet. He's trying to find the key.

S Is anybody in the house other than your husband?

V I don't know, sir. I'm still upstairs. Hey James, look in my pocketbook. Officer, please.

S Alright just tell him to do what I tell him to do. Put his hands up over his head and go out that front door. Is your husband the one who called the police or was the one who broke in or what?

V James, put your hands up over your head and go out the front door.

S Has he gone outside, ma'am?

V No, he's still trying to get the keys. Please don't let them shoot him. He didn't bother nobody.

S Alright just take and hold on there a minute. Then the cars outside have stopped shooting, right?

MALE VOICE They're not police.

V He says you're not the police. Are you a police?

S Yes.

V He said they're not.

S Who's not the police? Have you got the front door open?

V Are you sure you're the police?

S Has he got the front door open yet?

V They're breaking in.

S They're breaking in? Has he gone over to the front door yet? Hey, they're breaking in the door over there.

MALE VOICE Hey police, police please don't kill me.

MALE VOICE I don't know if you're the police.

S Hello.

S MRS. LAW, MRS. LAW, MRS. LAW, Hello.

MALE VOICE (in the background—yelling at the police)

V Hello, he's not armed.

S Hello, MRS. LAW, has he got out the front door yet?

V Just a minute. James go out the front door so nobody will hurt you.

MALE VOICE How can I go out the front door when I can't find the keys?

V The front door is locked and he can't find the keys.

S Alright, wait a minute. Can he go out the back door?

V Just a minute. Can you go out the back door, James?

MALE VOICE I support the police.

S MRS. LAW, can he get out the back door? Alright, tell him to go out the back door.

V James, he says go to the back door.

S Alright he's going to go out the back door. He can't go out the front door because the front door is locked.

V Don't fire.

S He's coming out the back door. Alright, tell him to put his hands over his head and come to the back door. Come out the back door. Alright, he's going to put his hands over his head and come out the back door.

V James, go out the back door.

S Alright, are you coming out now? Alright, tell him to open the door and put his hands over his head. If he can't get out the front door, tell him to go out the back door.

V The back door is locked also. Sir, we're not trying to harm anybody.

S You don't have a key to either door?

V Hold on James, they're the police so open the door.

MALE VOICE I'm coming out, I'm coming out. You police hold your fire.

S Did he get the door open?

V James go on out.

MALE VOICE You're not the police.

V They are the police, honey, they are (Heavy gunfire).

V Officer, officer, they're shooting at him again.

S Hey, they're shooting out there again.

S Alright just hold on there.

MALE VOICE (Screaming very loudly) They're not the police, they're not the police. They shot me in my own house. They're not the police.

V Officer, officer, please, officer, officer, officer!

S Hello MRS. LAW. Has he gone out the back door yet?

V Yes, officer, please come here in person.

S Alright hang on a minute.

(The man, apparently upstairs now, screaming unintelligibly: The woman, "James go downstairs, honey, they are the police" The man yelling)

S Alright, will you wait a minute?

MALE VOICE Hey officer, they come in my house and shoot at her and shot me. They're shooting at me. I threw my gun out the window and they shot. They shot me for no reason.

S Alright, will you go out the door with your hands over you head?

MALE VOICE (Yelling)

S Will you go out the front door with your hands over your head?

S Hello, MRS. LAW, MRS. LAW, that man is still shooting out the window.

V No my husband is not shooting, honestly.

S Alright, tell him to go out front with his hands over his head. Tell him to throw his gun out the house.

V James throw the gun out.

S Hello, yes MRS. LAW, MRS. LAW tell him to throw his gun out of the house.

V I told him to throw it out.

S Tell him to go to the front door and put his hands over his head and walk outside that house.

V He's downstairs officer.

A Alright, holler down to him and tell him to put his hands over his head and walk outside that house.

V He's downstairs officer.

S Alright, holler down to him and tell him to put his hands over his head and go out the front door. He can open it. He can open it. A while ago he opened it up and went outside and fired some shots. MRS. LAW, tell him to open the front door and go outside. MRS. LAW, is he going outside?

S Hello, MRS. LAW, MRS. LAW. Hello.

V Officer.

S Yes, MRS. LAW.

V I hear a lot of walking all over the house.

S I can't hear you.

V Are they in my house?

S I don't know ma'am, I'm not there. Did he out the front door, Hello. MRS. LAW.

V Officer, I believe they're in the house.

S What ma'am?

V I think they're in the house.

S You think the police are in the house.

V Would you tell somebody that I'm upstairs?

S Alright, Steve, tell the cars that there is a lady upstairs. MRS. LAW is upstairs. Okay, look why don't you holler down to them and tell them you are up there.

V Would you please tell them?

S Yes, we are telling them on the radio. But they don't have too many radios with them.

V I don't think anybody that has ever heard about or knows my husband been hit oh, officer, please.

V Officer . . .

S Alright, alright. You've been doing real good thru this, lady, just hang on a while longer.

V A littler while longer.

S Alright tell them someone is upstairs. His wife is upstairs. She's on the phone to me. Alright MRS. LAW you still there.

V Yes.

S Okay just stay right there. They'll be coming up in a minute. Why don't you open the door and holler down to them.

V Officer, officer, he told me to come down.

S Alright put your hands over top of your head now Ma'am and go down the steps. Alright!

V Okay.

S Bye now.

V I'm upstairs officer. Officer alright I'm coming. Officer, Officer, Officer.

S They're inside. Troops inside.

S Hello, hello, hello (background noise)

LDO Hello

S Hello.

LDO This is the long distance operator.

S Yes.

LDO Is this call finished?

S No, it is still in use.

LDO Okay Sir.

S Okay (more background noise).

MALE VOICE-not legible.

S Hello, hello, hello, hello, hello (Male voices) Hello, hello, hello.

The appellant, James Cecil Law, Jr. was found guilty of murder in the second degree and of assault with intent to murder. He was convicted by a jury in the Circuit Court for Charles County following removal from Prince George's County. Judge JAMES C. MITCHELL sentenced him to concurrent ten year terms.

OPINION

. . . There is a dearth of Maryland authority upon the question of what constitutes justifiable homicide in the defense of one's home. We hasten to note, however, that the single case directly meeting the question does so concisely and clearly. In 1962, the Court of Appeals in *Crawford v. State*, 231 Md. 354, 190 A.2d 538, reversed a conviction of manslaughter against a 42-year-old man, suffering from a nervous condition and ulcers, whose home was being broken into by a 23-year-old man and a partner. The decedent had knocked out a piece of masonite replacing one of four glass panes in the door. Crawford fired a shotgun through the door killing the attacker before he was able to enter. Certain of the circumstances of that case coincide remarkably with the case at bar. It is as remarkably distinguished, however, by the character and purpose of the decedent, who had previously beaten Crawford and was returning to rob and beat him again after threatening to do so. . . .

The defense of habitation is explained by text writers and treated in *Crawford* as an extension of the right of self-defense. The distinction between the defense of home and the defense of person is primarily that in the former there is no duty to retreat. "A man in his own house was treated as 'at the wall' and could not, by another's assault, be put under any duty to flee therefrom."

The regal aphorism that a man's home is his castle has obscured the limitations on the right to preserve one's home as a sanctuary from fear of force or violence. *Crawford* articulates the rule well, distilling it from a review of cases in many jurisdictions:

> Most American jurisdictions in which the question has been decided have taken the view that if an assault on a dwelling and an attempted forcible entry are made under circumstances which would create a reasonable apprehension that it is the design of the assailant to commit a felony or to inflict on the inhabitants injury which may result in loss of life or great bodily harm, and that the danger that the design will be carried into effect is imminent, a lawful occupant of the dwelling may prevent the entry even by the taking of the intruder's life.

The felonies the prevention of which justifies the taking of a life "are such and only such as are committed by forcible means, violence, and surprise such as murder, robbery, burglary, rape or arson."... It is "essential that killing is necessary to prevent the commission of the felony in question. If other methods would prevent its commission, a homicide is not justified; all other means of preventing the crime must first be exhausted."

The right thus rests upon real or apparent necessity. It is this need for caution in exercising the right that has been relegated to obscurity. The position espoused by appellant typifies the misunderstanding of the extent of the right to defend one's home against intrusion. He says:

> The defendant is not required to act as a reasonable, prudent and cautious individual, nor was he required to limit his force to only that that was required under the circumstances—not when the defendant was in his own home, and believed he was being set upon, or about to be set upon by would be robbers or burglars who were in the act of breaking into his home at the time.

The judgment which must usually be made precipitously under frightening conditions nevertheless demands a certain presence of mind and reasonableness of judgment. Although one is "not obliged to retreat ... but ... may even pursue the assailant until he finds himself or his property out of danger ... , this will not justify a person's firing upon everyone who forceably enters his house, even at night."... The taking of life is not justified "unless unavoidable ... Beyond this the law does not authorize the sacrifice of human life or the infliction of serious bodily injury."

In 1894 Mr. Justice HARLAN redefined the scope of the rule within its permissible limits:

> In East's Pleas of the Crown, the author, considering what sort of an attack it was lawful and justifiable to resist, even by the death of the assailant, says: "A man may repel force by force in defense of his person, habitation, or property against one who manifestly intends and endeavors, by violence or surprise, to commit a known felony, such as murder, rape, robbery, arson, burglary, and the like, upon either. In these cases he is not obliged to retreat, but may pursue his adversary until he has secured himself from all danger; and if he kill him in so doing it is called justifiable self-defense; as, on the other hand, the killing by such felon of any person so lawfully defending himself will be murder. *But a bare fear of any of these offenses, however well grounded, as that another lies in wait to take away the party's life, unaccompanied with any overt act indicative of such an intention, will not warrant in killing that other by way of prevention ....*" (My italics.) *Beard v. United States,* 158 U.S. 550, 563, 15 S.Ct. 962, 966, 39 L.Ed. 1086.

Judgments reversed; case remanded for a new trial. [The court reversed and remanded the case because the conviction was based on a coerced confession that violated *Miranda v. Arizona.*]

QUESTIONS FOR DISCUSSION

1. Exactly how does the court define the defense of habitation?

2. List all of the facts relevant to deciding whether James Cecil Law is entitled to the defense.

3. Assume that you're the prosecutor. Argue that Law was *not* justified in killing the officer. Rely on the court's definition and the facts of the case to back up your arguments.

4. Now, assume that you're the defense lawyer. Argue that Law *was* justified in killing the officer. Rely on the court's definition and the facts of the case to back up your arguments.

5. When the case was remanded and the court on remand rejected Law's defense of home defense, the court commented on the mitigating circumstances that might reduce Law's punishment:

We think the evidence ... fairly generated an issue of mitigation. At the time of the homicide, appellant and his bride of a few weeks were alone in the bedroom in their darkened house. Two weeks before the homicide their house had been burglarized. They heard noises outside. Appellant got out of bed, nude, and went downstairs to investigate the matter. He continued to hear noises like someone was "trying to get in." He obtained from the living room his shotgun, purchased for "home protection" after his house had been burglarized two weeks before. He heard a noise on his back porch, "a fiddling around with the door." There were curtains on the back door and he could see no figures on the darkened back porch. He felt that there were burglars on his porch, and "then I heard the scraping of a window pane." He next heard a voice say, "lets go in." At that time he was in the living room, "standing there with my shotgun shaking ..." because he was scared. In appellant's words, "at that time the gun went off." He said he didn't know how the gun went off; he could have pulled the trigger intentionally or accidentally; he didn't know. When the gun went off, it was held about waist high pointed toward the back door. The single shotgun blast went through the door killing police officer Garrison, who at that time was attempting to gain entrance to the house. The blast narrowly missed police officer Adams who was standing beside officer Garrison. The two officers had gone to the house in response to a call from appellant's next door neighbor who, unknown to appellant or his wife, had earlier called the police to report a suspected burglary attempt at appellant's house. The State conceded in closing argument that appellant did not knowingly shoot a police officer and that "he probably thought he shot a burglar or whatever that was outside."

Although by far the most common form of mitigation is that of a hot-blooded response to legally adequate provocation, this is not the only form of mitigation that will negate malice and will reduce what might otherwise be murder to manslaughter. . . . For example, if one man kills another intentionally, under circumstances beyond the scope of innocent homicide, the facts may come so close to justification or excuse that the killing will be classed as voluntary manslaughter rather than murder.

Law v. State, 29 Md.App. 457, 349 A.2d 295 (Md. App. 1975)

Do you think that this is evidence of mitigation or evidence of justifiable homicide in the defense of home? Explain your answer.

EXECUTION OF PUBLIC DUTIES

Public executioners throw switches to electrocute condemned murderers; soldiers shoot and kill enemy soldiers; police officers use force to make arrests or to take property pursuant to search warrants. In all these examples, individuals' lives, liberty, and property are intentionally taken away. Yet, none is a crime. Why? Because all the actors were doing their jobs, and the deprivations they caused were justified because they were carried out as public duties. These examples illustrate the justification called execution of public duty. This defense is at least as old as the sixteenth century, as its common-law definition illustrates: "A public officer is justified in using reasonable force against the person of another, or in taking his property, when he acts pursuant to a valid law, court order, or process, requiring or authorizing him so to act."[28]

The values underlying the execution-of-public-duty defense are clear: Once the state legitimately formulates laws, citizens must obey them; the law takes precedence over citizens' property, their liberty, and even their lives. Therefore, the value in enforcing the law ranks higher than individual property, liberty, and life.

The public duty defense arouses most controversy over the power of the police to kill suspects. A furious debate has raged over whether, and under what circumstances, the police may lawfully kill fleeing suspects. Some say the defense should cover officers who "need" to kill in order to make arrests. Others insist that only protecting officers' or other innocent people's lives justifies killing—that police have only the defense of self-defense belonging to private citizens. Still others believe that officers can't shoot at fleeing suspects if doing so endangers innocent lives.

At one time, state laws authorized police officers to kill when necessary to effect felony arrests, including those for property crimes. In 1985, however, the U.S. Supreme Court restricted the constitutionality of police use of deadly force under the Fourth Amendment search and seizure clause (see *Tennessee v. Garner,* excerpted later in this section). Furthermore, police departments have established rules that prescribe in detail when officers can use force, including deadly force, in arresting suspects.[29]

The argument favoring the police power to kill in order to arrest fleeing suspects is based not only on protecting lives but also on maintaining respect for law enforcement authority. One commentator said:

> I am convinced that only through truly effective power of arrest can law be satisfactorily enforced. Obviously until violators are brought before the courts the law's sanctions cannot be applied to them. But effectiveness in making arrests requires more than merely pitting the footwork of policemen against that of suspected criminals. An English director of public prosecutions once explained to me that the English police had no need to carry pistols because (1) no English criminal would think of killing a police officer, and (2) even if a suspected offender should outrun an officer in the labyrinth of London he could be found eventually in Liverpool or Birmingham. As the director put it, if a man offends in his own district everyone knows him, if he goes somewhere else everyone notices him.
>
> [Without such power, he continued] we say to the criminal, "You are foolish. No matter what you have done you are foolish if you submit to arrest. The officer dare not take the risk of shooting at you. If you can outrun him, if you are faster than he is, you are free, and God bless you." I feel entirely unwilling to give that benediction to the modern criminal.[30]

The value of general obedience to the law rests on the reasonable assumption that life, liberty, and property mean little without order. The power to kill in order to make an arrest is therefore grounded not only on the value of life but also on the need for law observance in general. On the other hand, critics contend that the police power to kill creates social problems. Commenting on the troubled time of the late 1960s, United States Attorney General Ramsey Clarke wrote:

> In these dog days of 1968, we have heard much loose talk of shooting looters. This talk must stop. The need is to train adequate numbers of police to prevent riots and looting altogether. Where prevention fails, looters must be arrested not shot. The first need in a civil disorder is to restore order. To say that when the looting starts, the shooting starts means either that shooting is preferable to arrest, or that there is not enough police protection, or the unpredictable nature of a disorder makes arrest impossible. Other techniques—including the use of tear gas—may be necessary. The use of deadly force is neither necessary, effective nor tolerable.
>
> Far from being effective, shooting looters divides, angers, embitters, drives to violence. It creates the very problems its advocates claim is their purpose to avoid. Persons under the influence of alcohol killed 25,000 Americans in automobile accidents in 1967. Fewer than 250 people have died in all riots since 1964. Looters, as such, killed no one. Why not shoot drunken drivers? What is it that causes some to call for shooting looters when no one is heard to suggest the same treatment for a far deadlier and less controllable crime?
>
> Is the purpose to protect property? Bank embezzlers steal ten times more money each year than bank robbers. Should we shoot embezzlers? What do the police themselves believe? It is the police to whom some would say, pull the trigger when looters are fleeing—perhaps dozens of looters fleeing toward a crowd; women, children; some making trouble, some committing crime, some trying to talk sense to a mob, to cool it.[31]

The U.S. Supreme Court dealt with the constitutionality of the use of deadly force by police officers in the important case of *Tennessee v. Garner.*

C A S E	Did He Use Reasonable Force to Execute the Arrest?

Tennessee v. Garner
471 U.S. 1, 105 S.Ct. 1694, 85 L.Ed.2d 1 (1985)

Cleamtee Garner, Edward Garner's father, brought an action for wrongful death when a police officer shot and killed his young son who was fleeing the scene of a suspected burglary. The trial court awarded damages. The defendant city and police department appealed.

WHITE, J., joined by BRENNAN, MARSHALL, BLACKMUN, POWELL, and STEVENS, JJ.

FACTS

At about 10:45 P.M. on October 3, 1974, Memphis Police Officers Elton Hymon and Leslie Wright were dispatched to answer a "prowler inside call." Upon arriving at the scene they saw a woman standing on her porch gesturing toward the adjacent house. She told them she had heard glass breaking and that "they" or "someone" was breaking in next door. While Wright radioed the dispatcher to say that they were on the scene, Hymon went behind the house. He heard a door slam and saw someone run across the back yard. The fleeing suspect, who was appellee-respondent's descendent, Edward Garner, stopped at a 6-foot-high chain link fence at the edge of the yard. With the aid of a flashlight, Hymon was able to see Garner's face and hands. He saw no sign of a weapon, and, though not certain, was "reasonably sure" and "figured" that Garner was unarmed. He thought Garner was 17 or 18 years old and about 5'5" or 5'7" tall. While Garner was crouched at the base of the fence, Hymon called out "police, halt" and took a few steps toward him. Garner began to climb over the fence. Convinced that if Garner made it over the fence he would elude capture, Hymon shot him. The bullet hit Garner in the back of the head. Garner was taken by ambulance to a hospital, where he died on the operating table. Ten dollars and a purse taken from the house were found on his body.

In using deadly force to prevent escape, Hymon was acting under the authority of a Tennessee statute and pursuant to Police Department policy. The statute provides that "if, after notice of the intention to arrest the defendant, he either flee or forcibly resist, the officer may use all the necessary means to effect the arrest." Tenn. Code Ann. § 40-7-108 (1982). The Department policy was slightly more restrictive than the statute, but still allowed the use of deadly force in cases of burglary. The incident was reviewed by the Memphis Police Firearms Review Board and presented to a grand jury. Neither took any action.

Garner's father then brought this action in the Federal District Court for the Western District of Tennessee, seeking damages under 42 U.S.C. § 1983 for asserted violations of Garner's constitutional rights. The complaint alleged that the shooting violated the Fourth, Fifth, Sixth, Eighth, and Fourteenth Amendments of the United States Constitution. It named as defendants Officer Hymon, the Police Department, its Director, and the Mayor and city of Memphis. After a 3-day bench trial, the District Court entered judgment for all defendants. It dismissed the claims against the Mayor and the Director for lack of evidence. It then concluded that Hymon's actions were authorized by the Tennessee statute, which in turn was constitutional. Hymon had employed the only reasonable and practicable means of preventing Garner's escape. Garner had "recklessly and heedlessly attempted to vault over the fence to escape, thereby assuming the risk of being fired upon."

The District Court . . . found that the statute, and Hymon's actions, were constitutional. The Court of Appeals reversed and remanded. . . .

OPINION

. . .

Whenever an officer restrains the freedom of a person to walk away, he has seized that person. . . . There can be no question that apprehension by the use of deadly force is a seizure subject to the reasonableness requirement of the Fourth Amendment.

A police officer may arrest a person if he has probable cause to believe that person committed a crime. Petitioners and appellant argue that if this requirement is satisfied the Fourth Amendment has nothing to say about how that seizure is made. This submission ignores the many cases in which this Court, by balancing the extent of the intrusion against the need for it, has examined the reasonableness of the manner in which a search or seizure is conducted. . . .

The use of deadly force to prevent the escape of all felony suspects, whatever the circumstances, is constitutionally unreasonable. It is not better that all felony suspects die than that they escape. Where the suspect poses no immediate threat to the officer and no threat to others, the harm resulting from failing to apprehend him does not justify the use of deadly force to do so. It is no doubt unfortunate when a suspect who is in sight escapes, but the fact the police arrive a little late or are a little slower afoot does not always justify killing the suspect. A police officer may not seize an unarmed, nondangerous suspect by shooting him dead. The Tennessee statute is unconstitutional insofar as it authorizes the use of deadly force against such fleeing suspects. . . .

Officer Hymon could not reasonably have believed that Garner—young, slight, and unarmed—posed any threat. Indeed, Hymon never attempted to justify his actions on any basis other than the need to prevent escape. . . . The fact that Garner was a suspected burglar could not, without regard to the other circumstances, automatically justify the use of deadly force. Hymon did not have probable cause to believe that Garner, whom he correctly believed to be unarmed, posed any physical danger to himself or to others.

DISSENT

O'CONNOR, J., joined by BURGER, CJ., and REHNQUIST, J.

For purposes of Fourth Amendment analysis, I agree with the Court that Officer Hymon "seized" Garner by shooting him. Whether that seizure was reasonable and therefore permitted by the Fourth Amendment requires a careful balancing of the important public interest in crime prevention and detection and the nature and quality of the intrusion upon legitimate interests of the individual. In striking this balance here, it is crucial to acknowledge that police use of deadly force to apprehend a fleeing criminal suspect falls within the "rubric of police conduct . . . necessarily [involving] swift action predicated upon the on-the-spot observations of the officer on the beat." . . .

The public interest involved in the use of deadly force as a last resort to apprehend a fleeing burglary suspect relates primarily to the serious nature of the crime. Household burglaries represent not only the illegal entry into a person's home, but also "pose a real risk of serious harm to others." According to recent Department of Justice statistics, "three-fifths of all rapes in the home, three-fifths of all home robberies, and about a third of home aggravated and simple assaults are committed by burglars." . . .

Against the strong public interests justifying the conduct at issue here must be weighed the individual interests implicated in the use of deadly force by police officers. The majority declares that "the suspect's fundamental interest in his own life need not be elaborated upon." This blithe assertion hardly provides an adequate substitute for the majority's failure to acknowledge the distinctive manner in which the suspect's interest in his life is even exposed to risk. For purposes of this case, we must recall that the police officer, in the course of investigating a nighttime burglary, had reasonable cause to arrest the suspect and ordered him to halt. The officer's use of force resulted because the suspected burglar refused to heed this command and the officer reasonably believed that there was no means short of firing his weapon to apprehend the suspect. . . . "The policeman's hands should not be tied merely because of the possibility that the suspect will fail to cooperate with legitimate actions by law enforcement personnel." . . .

QUESTIONS FOR DISCUSSION

1. State all of the facts relevant to determining whether public duty justified the use of deadly force in this case.

2. Should the Fourth Amendment prohibit the use of deadly force to arrest property felons?

3. Is residential burglary simply a property crime?

4. Do you agree with the majority or dissent? Explain.

5. Will this rule embolden criminals? Defend your answer.

RESISTING UNLAWFUL ARREST

Can individuals resist an illegal arrest by force? The answers have fluctuated over time. Historically, the common law of both England and the United States favored the right to resist arrest. Then, beginning in the 1960s, states started to curb the right to resist arrest. By 2000, the majority of states had limited the right to resist arrest. The issue is still alive, however, because of an historical suspicion, if not an outright hostility, to government power in the United States. Two policies support restrictions on the use of force against police officers:

1. Encourage obedience to police.
2. Encourage nonviolent remedies, such as suing in private lawsuits.

The majority and dissenting opinions in *State v. Valentine* dramatically demonstrate the heated debate over the individual right to resist arrest.

C A S E   Did He Lawfully Resist Arrest?

State v. Valentine,
935 P.2d 1294 (Wash. 1997)

Ronald Valentine was convicted of assaulting police officers. He appealed. The Court of Appeals affirmed. The Washington supreme court granted review and affirmed.

ALEXANDER, J.

FACTS

In the early afternoon of May 16, 1990, in downtown Spokane, Spokane Police Officer Rick Robinson observed what he believed was a "suspicious subject on the corner at First and Jefferson." Upon making this observation, Robinson radioed another Spokane police officer, John Moore, and asked him if he knew the person standing at First and Jefferson "wearing a black coat." Moore proceeded to that location and observed a person wearing a black jacket enter a car. Although Moore was unable to immediately identify that person, he followed the car as the person drove it away.

According to Moore, the car soon made a turn without signaling. Moore, who was driving an unmarked car, advised Robinson over his radio that he was going to stop the car. He then attempted to do so by placing a rotating blue light on his dashboard, flashing his headlights, and honking his horn. While attempting to stop the automobile, Moore recognized that the driver of the car he was following was Ronald Valentine. [Moore testified at trial that he was acquainted with Valentine because he had cited him on two prior occasions for front license plate violations.] Moore broadcast over his police radio that he was following Valentine and that Valentine was not heeding Moore's efforts to stop him. Shortly thereafter, Valentine stopped his automobile and Moore pulled his car in behind him. Officer Robinson also pulled in behind Moore as did several other officers who had overheard the radio broadcasts.

All of the police officers who arrived at the scene testified at trial. Their version of the events that transpired after the traffic stop varied dramatically from Valentine's version of events. Moore said that upon confronting Valentine he asked to see his license and registration. This, he indicated, prompted Valentine to ask, "Why?" Moore said that he then told Valentine that he was being cited for failing to signal for a turn. According to Moore, Valentine said that since Moore had given him a ticket a few days earlier, he had all the information that he needed. Moore said that he again asked for the driver's license and registration and Valentine responded by saying that "you . . . cops are just harassing me. I'm Black, and I'm tired of the harassment." After what Moore said was his third request of Valentine to produce his driver's license and registration, Valentine produced it.

Moore testified that he asked Valentine for his current address and that Valentine told Moore to "look it up." Moore then asked Valentine if he was going to cooperate and sign a citation and, according to Moore, Valentine said that he would not do so. Moore then informed Valentine that he was being placed under "arrest for failure to cooperate . . . and refusing to sign an infraction."

Moore also testified that after Valentine walked to the front of the car to show Moore that the car Valentine had been driving had a front license plate, Valentine returned to his car door, opened it, and started to reach inside the car. Moore said that he told Valentine to stay out of the car and grabbed Valentine's left arm to prevent him from reaching into the car. Robinson also claimed that he grabbed Valentine's right arm in a similar effort to keep Valentine from entering his car. Valentine, according to Moore, responded to their actions by spinning toward Moore and punching him in the side of the head. Robinson also claimed that he was hit in the ensuing skirmish.

Spokane Police Officers Jones, Webb, and Yates all testified that they joined the scuffle when Valentine began to struggle with Moore and Robinson. They said that they eventually subdued Valentine and forced him to the ground. Yates, who indicated that he had decided to assist Moore in effecting the traffic stop when he heard over the radio that it was Valentine who was being pursued, testified that when he became involved in the fracas, he felt Valentine's hand on his gun butt. [Yates had been involved in a verbal confrontation with Valentine in a tavern the day before the incident leading to this appeal. Yates testified that the tavern incident "probably could have been" discussed with other officers at roll call, about two hours before the incident.] He said that in order to subdue Valentine, he had to apply a "carotid hold" to Valentine's neck. [The carotid hold is a hold applied to the neck area. It is designed to inhibit the supply of blood to the brain, and when it is applied correctly, the victim of the hold will lose consciousness.]:

Valentine was eventually placed in handcuffs and was transported to jail. A nurse supervisor at the jail refused to admit Valentine because of his apparent injuries. Valentine was then taken to a hospital where Moore presented him with a citation for failing to signal for a turn. Valentine signed the citation. Valentine was later booked into the Spokane County Jail where he was charged by information with two counts of third degree assault, it being alleged that he assaulted Moore and Robinson while they were performing "official duties."

Valentine testified at trial on his own behalf. He claimed that because his turn signals were not functioning, he used hand signals to indicate his intention to turn. He also said that he stopped his car as soon as it was possible for him to do so. Valentine indicated that before reaching inside his car, he told Moore he was going to lock his car in order to protect some personal items. He denied that he told Moore to look up his address for himself. He also said that he did not throw the first punch, asserting that any blows he delivered were in self-defense and amounted to reasonable force to protect himself from an illegal arrest. Valentine contended that he would have signed a citation on the scene if he had been presented with one. Valentine was found guilty of assaulting Moore and not guilty of assaulting Robinson.

OPINION

Valentine asks us to decide whether the trial court erred in instructing the jury regarding the employment of force to resist an unlawful arrest. Instruction 17 reads as follows:

> A person unlawfully arrested by an officer may resist the arrest; the means used to resist an unlawful arrest must be reasonable and proportioned to the injury attempted upon the party sought to be arrested. The use of force to prevent an unlawful arrest which threatens only a loss of freedom, if you so find, is not reasonable.

. . . In *State v. Rousseau*, 40 Wash.2d 92, 241 P.2d 447 (1952) . . . we recited the common law rule prevalent in most jurisdictions at the time: "It is the law that a person illegally arrested by an officer may resist that arrest, even to the extent of the taking of life if his own life or any great bodily harm is threatened.". . .

In 1966, the right to resist an unlawful arrest was recognized in 45 out of 50 states. At that time the five states that had abrogated the right were Rhode Island, New Hampshire, Delaware, California, and New Jersey. Max Hochanadel & Harry W. Stege, Note, Criminal Law: The Right to Resist an Unlawful Arrest: An Out-Dated Concept?, 3 TULSA L.J. 40, 46 (1966). By 1983, however, 25 of those 45 states had revoked the common law rule either by statute or decision, and today, only 20 states have it in place, while resisting even an unlawful arrest is prohibited by law in 30 states. "This common law principle has suffered a devastating deluge of criticism." *State v. Thomas,* 262 N.W.2d 607, 610 (Iowa 1978) (rule is "an anachronistic and dangerous concept"). Thus, the hold of the common law rule has weakened substantially in the last 30 years as jurisdiction after jurisdiction has modernized its jurisprudence to reflect the differences in criminal procedure in late twentieth century America as compared to early eighteenth century England. "The trend in this country has been away from the old rule and toward the resolution of disputes in court."

Courts addressing the question have set out many cogent and compelling reasons for consigning the common law rule to the dustbin of history. For example: While society has an interest in securing for its members the right to be free of unreasonable searches and seizures, society also has an interest in the orderly resolution of disputes between its citizens and the government. Given such competing interests, we opt for the orderly resolution through the courts over what is essentially "street justice."...

We are of the opinion that the common law rule is outmoded in our modern society. A citizen, today, can seek his remedy for a policeman's unwarranted and illegal intrusion into the citizen's private affairs by bringing a civil action in the courts against the police officer and the governmental unit which the officer represents. The common law right of forceful resistance to an unlawful arrest tends to promote violence and increases the chances of someone getting injured or killed.

More important [than the existence of civil remedies], however, are the unwarranted dangers to civil order caused by this lingering artifact. Peace officers are today lethally armed and usually well trained to efficiently effect arrests. Resultantly, the resister's chances of success are seriously diminished unless he counters with equal or greater levels of force. The inevitable escalation of violence has serious consequences for both participants and innocent bystanders.

Briefly stated, a far more reasonable course is to resolve an often difficult arrest legality issue in the courts rather than on often hectic and emotion laden streets. Modern urbanized society has a strong interest in encouraging orderly dispute resolution. Confronting this is the outmoded common law rule which fosters unnecessary violence in the name of an obsolete self-help concept which should be promptly discarded.

We agree with all of these sentiments. Finally, we also associate ourselves with Judge LEARNED HAND, who said,

> The idea that you may resist peaceful arrest—and mind you, that is all it is—because you are in debate about whether it is lawful or not, instead of going to the authorities which can determine, seems to me not a blow for liberty but, on the contrary, a blow for attempted anarchy. 35 A.L.I.PROC. 254 (1958).

In the final analysis, the policy supporting abrogation of the common law rule is sound. That policy was well enunciated by Division Two of the Court of Appeals in *State v. Westlund,* 13 Wash.App. 460, 467, 536 P.2d 20, 77 A.L.R.3d 270, review denied, 85 Wash.2d 1014 (1975), where the court said:

> The arrestee's right to freedom from arrest without excessive force that falls short of causing serious injury or death can be protected and vindicated through legal processes, whereas loss of life or serious physical injury cannot be repaired in the courtroom. However, in the vast majority of cases, as illustrated by the one at bar, resistance and intervention make matters worse, not better. They create violence where none would have otherwise existed or encourage further violence, resulting in a situation of arrest by combat. Police today are sometimes required to use lethal weapons for self-protection. If there is resistance on behalf of the person lawfully arrested and others go to his aid, the situation can degenerate to the point that what should have been a simple lawful arrest leads to serious injury or death to the arrestee, the police or innocent bystanders. Orderly and safe law enforcement demands that an arrestee not resist a lawful arrest and a bystander not intervene on his behalf unless the arrestee is actually about to be seriously injured or killed.

...In sum, we hold that, although a person who is being unlawfully arrested has a right, as the trial court indicated in instruction 17, to use reasonable and proportional force to resist an attempt to inflict injury on him or her during the course of an arrest, that person may not use force against the arresting officers if he or she is faced only with a loss of freedom. We explicitly overrule *Rousseau* and other cases that are inconsistent with our holding in this case.

. . . If the rule were, as the dissent suggests it should be, that a person being unlawfully arrested may always resist such an arrest with force, we would be inviting anarchy. While we do not, as the dissent appears to suggest, condone the unlawful use of state force, we can take note of the fact that in the often heated confrontation between a police officer and an arrestee, the lawfulness of the arrest may be debatable. To endorse resistance by persons who are being arrested by an officer of the law, based simply on the arrested person's belief that the arrest is unlawful, is to encourage violence that could, and most likely would, result in harm to the arresting officer, the defendant, or both. In our opinion, the better place to address the question of the lawfulness of an arrest that does not pose harm to the arrested person is in court and not on the street. . . .

Affirmed.

DISSENT

SANDERS, J.

Ronald Valentine was brutally beaten during the course of an unlawful arrest for a minor traffic infraction. Now this court affirms the criminal conviction of the victim despite the common law rule which clearly provides Valentine a viable legal defense. Mr. Valentine would not give up his liberty without a fight. Neither should we. . . .

The facts as recounted by the majority are bad enough, yet understated. Even so they depict a bone-chilling, brutal, and nearly lethal beating of a fellow citizen for a minor traffic violation. But I would rejoin, to sustain a criminal conviction of the victim who was denied an instruction which simply would have allowed the jury to consider his defense is yet a greater outrage. Such refusal of the proposed jury instruction not only excuses the true offense perpetrated upon the victim but generalizes the wrong to all of us through its ill-conceived precedent. . . .

Claiming a new-found enlightenment not apparent to legal generations which preceded it, the majority then opines that the established common law rule has outlived its usefulness in our brave new world where resistance to unlawful infliction of state coercive power is not only futile, but also invites "anarchy." Apparently the majority believes the unlawful use of state force is not anarchy but order. Yet I suggest such circumstances are not new, nor is the seeming futility of individual resistance to the overwhelming, yet still unlawful, police power of the state. It is an age-old tale. Mr. Valentine does not need courts to tell him who is going to win a physical confrontation with the police. But he does need this court to recognize and protect his legal rights.

Ultimately the majority's rule forbidding lawful resistance to unlawful state conduct specially privileges government agents in the wrong to the prejudice of citizens in the right. This special privilege is established notwithstanding the unquestioned and continuing right of a citizen to forcibly resist an assault against his person or a trespass on his property if committed by a private citizen. Thus, in a society of equals, those who violate their public trust by stepping beyond the boundaries of their lawful authority are privileged to become the usurping masters of the public they were originally entrusted to serve. Compare, e.g., *State v. Williams*, 81 Wash.App. 738, 74344, 916 P.2d 445 (1996) (one who is assaulted in a place he has a right to be has no duty to retreat and has a right to respond with force no matter how reasonable flight may be).

Finally, I offer my condolences to a majority which makes a criminal out of a victim under a circumstance which "causes it concern." The concurrence appears to appreciate exactly what is afoot but still will deny Mr. Valentine the benefit of his legal defense. . . .

In America the tradition of resisting unlawful authority has been embraced from the early days of resisting imperial British power during the Revolution through the civil rights movement. . . . Traditionally, illegal, arbitrary abuse of state power has been regarded as even more threatening and deserving of resistance than the occasional street crime. . . .

Thomas Paine considered it common sense that

> Society in every state is a blessing, but government even in its best state is but a necessary evil; in its worst state an intolerable one; for when we suffer, or are exposed to the same miseries by a government, which we might expect in a country without government, our calamities is [sic] heightened by

reflecting that we furnish the means by which we suffer. Thomas Paine, *Common Sense* at 65 (Penguin Books 1976) (1776).

. . . The Government of the State of Washington, as well, was "established to protect and maintain individual rights." Const. art. I, § 1. It was not established to do precisely the opposite.

The age-old rule which recognizes the right to resist unlawful assertions of state power is an important deterrent to tyranny. With the rule limited to cases where the police are exceeding and abusing their authority, the police officers involved in the excess should be deterred, knowing that their abuse may spark resistance.

This rule has equal application in the twentieth and twenty-first centuries to the extent it is rooted in political theory and human nature. In a well-known passage in *The Gulag Archipelago*, Aleksandr Solzhenitsyn wonders what would have happened had the countless victims of Stalin's arbitrary state power resisted and whether the officers serving under Stalin might have acted with less zeal had they known they could face legitimate resistance and even harm in effectuating their unlawful arrests. Solzhenitsyn suggests that resistance would have been an effective deterrent; had the victims resisted, "notwithstanding all of Stalin's thirst, the cursed machine would have ground to a halt!" He then concludes that "resistance should have begun right there, at the moment of the arrest itself." What, then, would Solzhenitsyn make of the majority's claim that this rule has outlived its usefulness because resistance to unlawful arrest when perpetrated by American authority is an act of futility, as the power of our state is so omnipotent that resistance is not only futile but should be condemned?

It may be true, as the majority posits, those who resist an unlawful arrest, like Valentine, will often be the worse for it physically; however, that is not to say that their resistance is unlawful. The police power of the state is not measured by how hard the officer can wield his baton but rather by the rule of law. Yet by fashioning the rule as it has, the majority legally privileges the aggressor while insulting the victim with a criminal conviction for justifiable resistance. . . .

"In the famous language of the Massachusetts Bill of Rights, the government of the commonwealth is 'a government of laws and not of men.' For, the very idea that one man may be compelled to hold his life, or the means of living, or any material right essential to the enjoyment of life, at the mere will of another, seems to be intolerable in any country where freedom prevails, as being the essence of slavery itself."

QUESTIONS FOR DISCUSSION

1. Self-defense does not mean defense only against death or bodily injury. It also includes defending personal liberty. Resisting unlawful arrests is a good, but controversial, example.

2. Can citizens ever use force against the police, and if so, how much force can they use?

3. *State v. Valentine* represents the law in the majority of states that have rejected the common law right to resist unlawful arrest. Is it the correct policy choice? Defend your answer.

4. Identify the competing interests involved in the right to resist arrest. Rank them in order of importance. Defend your ranking.

5. Summarize the arguments in favor of and against the right to resist arrest.

6. Do you agree that times have changed, or do we still need a rule that supports the right to resist arrest? Defend your answer.

7-4 *State v. Valentine*, Oral Arguments; *State v. Tunney*, Opinion and Oral Argument

CHOICE-OF-EVILS DEFENSE

The **choice-of-evils defense**, also known as the **principle of necessity**, has a long history in the law of Europe and the Americas. Throughout that history, the defense has generated heated controversy. The great thirteenth-century jurist of English and Roman law, Bracton, declared that what "is not otherwise lawful, necessity makes lawful." Other famous English commentators, such as Sir Francis Bacon, Sir Edward

Coke, and Sir Matthew Hale in the sixteenth and seventeenth centuries, agreed with Bracton. The influential seventeenth-century English judge Hobart expressed the argument this way: "All laws admit certain cases of just excuse, when they are offended in letter, and where the offender is under necessity, either of compulsion or inconvenience."

On the other side of the debate, the distinguished nineteenth-century English historian of criminal law and judge Sir James F. Stephen believed that the defense of necessity was so vague that judges could interpret it to mean anything they wanted. In the same vein, Glanville Williams, a modern criminal law professor, writes: "It is just possible to imagine cases in which the expediency of breaking the law is so overwhelmingly great that people may be justified in breaking it, but these cases cannot be defined beforehand."[32]

Early cases record occasional instances of defendants who successfully pleaded the necessity defense. In 1500, a prisoner successfully pleaded necessity to a charge of prison break; he was trying to escape a fire that burned down the jail. The most common example in the older cases is destroying houses in order to stop fires from spreading. In 1912, a man was acquitted on the defense of necessity when he burned a strip of the owner's heather in order to prevent a fire from spreading to his house.[33]

Perhaps the most famous case involving the defense of necessity is *The Queen v. Dudley and Stephens*. Dudley and Stephens, two adults with families, and Brooks, an eighteen-year-old man without any family responsibilities, were lost in a lifeboat on the high seas. They had no food or water, except for two cans of turnips and a turtle they caught in the sea on the fourth day. After twenty days (the last eight without food), perhaps a thousand miles from land and with virtually no hope of rescue, Dudley and Stephens—after failing to get Brooks to cast lots—told Brooks that if no rescue vessel appeared by the next day, they were going to kill him for food. They explained to Brooks that his life was the most expendable because Dudley and Stephens had family responsibilities and Brooks didn't. The following day, no vessel appeared. After saying a prayer for him, Dudley and Stephens killed Brooks, who was too weak to resist. They survived on his flesh and blood for four days, when they were finally rescued. Dudley and Stephens were prosecuted, convicted, and sentenced to death for murder. They appealed, pleading the defense of necessity.

The judge, Lord Coleridge, in this famous passage, rejected the defense of necessity:

> The temptation to act . . . here was not what the law ever called necessity. Nor is this to be regretted. Though law and morality are not the same, and many things may be immoral which are not necessarily illegal, yet the absolute divorce of law from morality would be of fatal consequence; and such divorce would follow if the temptation to murder in this case were to be held by law an absolute defense of it. It is not so. . . .
>
> To preserve one's life is generally speaking a duty, but it may be the plainest and the highest duty to sacrifice it. War is full of instances in which it is a man's duty not to live, but to die. The duty, in case of shipwreck, of a captain to his crew, of the crew to the passengers, of soldiers to women and children . . . ; these duties impose on men the moral necessity, not of the preservation, but of the sacrifice of their lives for others. . . . It is not correct, therefore, to say that there is any absolute or unqualified necessity to preserve one's own life. . . .
>
> It is not needful to point out the awful danger of admitting the principle contended for. Who is to be the judge of this sort of necessity? By what measure of the comparative value of lives to be measured? Is it to be strength, or intellect, or what? It is plain that the principle leaves to him who is to profit by it to determine the necessity which will justify him in deliberately taking another's life to save his

own. In this case, the weakest, the youngest, the most unresisting, was chosen. Was it more necessary to kill him than one of the grown men? The answer must be "No"—

> "So spake the Fiend, and with necessity,
> The tyrant's plea, executed his devilish deeds."

It is not suggested that in this particular case, the deeds were "devilish," but it is quite plain that such a principle once admitted might be made the legal cloak for unbridled passion and atrocious crime.

Lord Coleridge sentenced them to death but expressed his hope that Queen Victoria would pardon them. The queen didn't pardon them but she almost did—she commuted their death penalty to six months in prison.[34]

THE ELEMENTS OF THE CHOICE-OF-EVILS DEFENSE

The linchpin of the choice-of-evils defense is making the right choice, namely choosing the lesser of two evils. The *Model Penal Code* choice-of-evils provision reads as follows:

§ 3.02. Justification Generally: Choice of Evils.
1. Conduct that the actor believes to be necessary to avoid a harm or evil to himself or to another is justifiable, provided that:
   a. the harm or evil sought to be avoided by such conduct is greater than that sought to be prevented by the law defining the offense charged; and
   b. neither the Code nor other law defining the offense provides exceptions or defenses dealing with the specific situation involved; and
   c. a legislative purpose to exclude the justification claimed does not otherwise plainly appear.
2. When the actor was reckless or negligent in bringing about the situation requiring a choice of harms or evils or in appraising the necessity for his conduct, the justification afforded by this Section is unavailable in a prosecution for any offense for which recklessness or negligence, as the case may be, suffices to establish culpability.

Twenty-one states have enacted necessity defense statutes that roughly follow the *Model Penal Code* provision.[35]

The choice-of-evils defense provision in the *Model Penal Code* requires three steps:

1. Identify the evils.
2. Rank the evils.
3. Choose the lesser evil to avoid the greater evil.

ELEMENTS OF CHOICE-OF-EVILS DEFENSE		
Identify the Evils	**Rank the Evils**	**Choose Correctly**
1. Evil committed **and**	1. Greater evil **and**	1. Avoid greater evil **and**
2. Evil avoided	2. Lesser evil	2. Commit lesser evil in order to avoid greater

Simply put, the choice-of-evils defense justifies choosing to do a lesser evil in order to avoid a greater evil. The choice of the lesser evil has to be both imminent and necessary. Those who choose to do the lesser evil have to reasonably believe that their only choice is to cause the lesser evil *right now*.

The *Model Penal Code* lists all of the following choices of evils:

1. destroying property to prevent spreading fire;
2. violating a speed limit to get a dying person to a hospital;
3. throwing cargo overboard to save a sinking vessel and its crew;
4. dispensing drugs without a prescription in an emergency; and
5. breaking and entering a mountain cabin to avoid freezing to death.

The right choice is life, safety, and health over property. Why? Because life, safety, and health trump property interests.[36]

The *Model Penal Code* doesn't leave the ranking of evils to individuals; it charges legislatures or judges and juries at trial with the task. Once an individual has made the "right" choice, either she is free or the right choice is a mitigating circumstance that can lighten the punishment. The Oregon Court of Appeals applied the Oregon choice-of-evils defense to the medical use of marijuana in *State v. Ownbey*.

C A S E   Was Using Marijuana a Lesser Evil?

State v. Ownbey
165 Or.App. 132, 996 P.2d 510 (Oregon App. 2000)

Jack Ownbey, the defendant, was convicted, in the Circuit Court, Multnomah County, of manufacture of a controlled substance, marijuana, and possession of a controlled substance, marijuana. He appealed. The Court of Appeals affirmed.

   DEITS, C.J.

FACTS

Jack Ownbey is a veteran of the Vietnam war. He has been diagnosed with Post-Traumatic Stress Disorder (PTSD). At the hearing on the state's motion *in limine* [during the proceedings], defendant argued that he should be allowed to present evidence to show that he has suffered from this disorder for some time and that, although he has sought traditional medical treatment, the only substance that alleviates his symptoms is marijuana. In his defense to the charges against him, defendant intended to show that "his actions in growing marijuana and possessing marijuana were as a result of medical necessity or choice of evils."

Before trial, defendant requested jury instructions on the choice-of-evils defense. In response to that request, the state made a motion, asking the trial court to exclude any evidence pertaining to the choice-of-evils defense. ORS 161.200, codifies that defense in Oregon. It provides:

(1) Unless inconsistent with . . . some other provision of law, conduct which would otherwise constitute an offense is justifiable and not criminal when:
   (a) That conduct is necessary as an emergency measure to avoid an imminent public or private injury; and
   (b) The threatened injury is of such gravity that, according to ordinary standards of intelligence and morality, the desirability and urgency of avoiding the injury clearly outweigh the desirability of avoiding the injury sought to be prevented by the statute defining the offense in issue.
(2) The necessity and justifiability of conduct under subsection (1) of this section shall not rest upon considerations pertaining only to the morality and advisability of the statute, either in its general application or with respect to its application to a particular class of cases arising thereunder.

The trial court granted the state's motion on the ground that, under ORS 161.200, the choice-of-evils defense was not available to defendant because it was inconsistent with other provisions of law. The court explained:

> In our case the Legislature has anticipated the choice of evils and determined the balance to be struck between competing values. And the defendants and the Court are precluded from reassessing those values to determine whether certain conduct is justified when we have a statutory construct such as we do.

OPINION

We agree with the trial court's conclusion. In *State v. Clowes*, 310 Or. 686, 801 P.2d 789 (1990), the Supreme Court articulated the analysis necessary to determine whether a choice-of-evils defense is available to a defendant. Under that analysis, we must first determine if allowing the defense would be "inconsistent with some other provision of law." If so, "it may not be asserted." Although the phrase "inconsistent with some other provision of law" is not defined in ORS 161.200, the court in *Clowes* explained that that language means "that the legislature's decision prevails if and when it makes specific value choices, and that competing values which have been foreclosed by deliberate legislative choice are excluded from the general defense of justification."

Therefore, the critical question here is whether the legislature has made deliberate choices that would exclude the choice-of-evils defense that defendant wishes to assert in this case. Defendant argues that he should be allowed the choice-of-evils defense here because his use of marijuana was medically necessary to treat a diagnosed illness and, consequently, his choice to use marijuana to treat his PTSD was a lesser evil than letting his condition remain untreated. This is an issue that the legislature has confronted several times and has made a deliberate choice. The legislature and the voters of this state have considered the use of marijuana for medical purposes and, at the time of defendant's offense, the legislature had concluded that the use of marijuana for medical treatment under these circumstances should not be allowed.

[Footnote: In 1979, the Oregon legislature enacted ORS 475.505 et seq. allowing physicians to prescribe marijuana to patients undergoing chemotherapy and for the treatment of glaucoma. The legislature repealed ORS 475.505 et seq. in 1987. The Oregon legislature again considered legalizing marijuana for medical use in 1993 and 1997, but did not do so.

The voters of the State of Oregon have also addressed this issue. In fact, since this case was briefed and argued, the 1999 legislature again addressed this issue in response to a measure passed by voters in 1998. The measure itself, the Oregon Medical Marijuana Act, allows the use of marijuana for medical purposes within specified limits. The 1999 legislature subsequently amended portions of that act to "clarify" it. Because the act establishes a defense that expressly applies only to acts or offenses committed on or after December 3, 1998, it does not affect the outcome of this case.]

Defendant argues that if "inconsistent . . . with some other provision of law" means that the legislature has considered a matter and made it illegal, that effectively does away with a choice-of-evils defense because the defense necessarily involves committing an illegal act. However, what defendant fails to recognize is that "the defense of necessity is available only in situations wherein the legislature has not itself, in its criminal statute, made a determination of values." If the legislature has not made such a value judgment, the defense would be available. However, when, as here, the legislature has already balanced the competing values that would be presented in a choice-of-evils defense and made a choice, the court is precluded from reassessing that judgment.

Finally, defendant relies on two cases from the State of Washington in which the defendants were allowed to use the medical necessity defense in response to charges of marijuana possession. *State v. Cole*, 74 Wash.App. 571, 874 P.2d 878 (1994); *State v. Diana*, 24 Wash.App. 908, 604 P.2d 1312 (1979). Of course, we are not bound by Washington case law, although we occasionally seek guidance from the reasoning of courts of other states. In any event, a more recent case from Washington reached the opposite result from that desired by defendant. The Washington court articulated its reasoning as follows:

> The decision of whether there is an accepted medical use for particular drugs has been vested in the Legislature by the Washington Constitution. The Legislature has determined that marijuana has no accepted medical use. Williams has no fundamental right to have marijuana as his preferred treatment over the State's objections. Further, if the

debate over medical treatment belongs in the political arena, it makes no sense for the courts to fashion a defense whereby jurors weigh experts' testimony on the medical uses of a Schedule I drug. Otherwise, each trial would become a battlefield of experts. But the Legislature has designated the battlefield as the Board of Pharmacy. The Washington Constitution has not enabled each individual to be the final arbiter of the medicine he is entitled to take—it is the Legislature that has been authorized to make laws to regulate the sale of medicines and drugs. *Seeley v. State,* 132 Wash.2d 776, 940 P.2d 604 (1997) by implication, overrules both *Cole* and *Diana.* Thus, our holding is that with respect to Schedule I drugs, there is not a defense of medical necessity." *State v. Williams,* 93 Wash.App. 340, 968 P.2d 26, 30 (1998), rev. den. 138 Wash.2d 1002, 984 P.2d 1034 (1999).

We conclude that the trial court here properly excluded evidence of a choice-of-evils defense.
Affirmed.

QUESTIONS

1. State the choice-of-evils defense as Oregon defines it.
2. Exactly what is the court's reason for denying Jack Ownbey the necessity defense?
3. Do you agree with the court that medical use of marijuana is not available in Oregon? Should it be? Defend your answer.

NOTE CASES

1. The prosecution proved beyond a reasonable doubt by the use of radar readings that James Dover was driving eighty miles per hour in a fifty-five mile-per-hour zone. However, the court also found that the defendant, who is a lawyer, was not guilty on the grounds that his speeding violation was justified because he was late for a court hearing in Denver as a result of a late hearing in Summit County, Colorado.

   A Colorado statute, § 42-4-1001(8)(a) provides:

   The conduct of a driver of a vehicle which would otherwise constitute a violation of this section is justifiable and not unlawful when:
   > a. It is necessary as an emergency measure to avoid an imminent public or private injury which is about to occur by reason of a situation occasioned or developed through no conduct of said driver and which is of sufficient gravity that, according to ordinary standards of intelligence and morality, the desirability and urgency of avoiding the injury clearly outweigh the desirability of avoiding the consequences sought to be prevented by this section.

   Was Dover justified in speeding because of necessity? No, said the Colorado Supreme Court:

   In this case, the defendant did not meet the foundational requirements of § 42-4-1001(8)(a). He merely testified that he was driving to Denver for a "court matter" and that he was late because of the length of a hearing in Summit County. No other evidence as to the existence of emergency as a justification for speeding was presented. The defendant did not present evidence as to the type or extent of the injury that he would suffer if he did not violate § 42-4-1001(1). He also failed to establish that he did not cause the situation or that his injuries would outweigh the consequences of his conduct. The record does not include evidence to establish a sufficient foundation to invoke the emergency justification defense provided by § 42-4-1001(8)(a). Since the defendant did not lay a proper foundation as to the existence of the defense, the prosecution was not required to prove beyond a reasonable doubt that the defendant was not justified in violating § 42-4-1001(1). § 18-1-407(2). The county court erred by finding the defendant not guilty because the defendant's speeding was justified because of an emergency. § 42-4-1001(8)(a). Accordingly, we reverse the district court and disapprove the ruling of the county court.

   People v. Dover, 790 P.2d 834 (Colo.1990)

2. On a cold winter day, William Celli and his friend, Glynis Brooks, left Deadwood, South Dakota, hoping to hitchhike to Newcastle, Wyoming, to look for work. The weather turned colder, they were afraid of frostbite, and there was no place of business open for them to get warm. Their feet were so stiff from the cold that it was difficult for them to walk. They entered the only structure around, a cabin, breaking the lock on the front door. Celli immediately crawled into a bed to warm up, and defendant Brooks attempted to light a fire in the fireplace. They rummaged through drawers to look for matches, which

they finally located and started a fire. Finally defendant Celli emerged from the bedroom, took off his wet moccasins, socks and coat, placed them near the fire, and sat down to warm himself. After warming up somewhat they checked the kitchen for edible food. That morning they had shared a can of beans, but had not eaten since. All they found was dry macaroni, which they could not cook because there was no water.

A neighbor noticed the smoke from the fireplace and notified the police. When the police entered the cabin, both defendants were warming themselves in front of the fireplace. The defendants were searched, but nothing belonging to the cabin owners was found. The trial court convicted them of fourth-degree burglary. The appellate court reversed on other grounds so it didn't get to the issue of the defense of necessity.

How would you identify and rank the evils? Did Celli and his friend choose the lesser of two evils? Defend your answer.

State v. Celli, 263 N.W.2d 145 (S.D.1978)

 7-5 Choice-of-Evils or Necessity Provisions

CONSENT

The defense of consent is based on the value of individual autonomy in a free society. If a mentally competent adult wants to be a crime victim, so the argument for the defense of consent goes, no paternalistic government should interfere with his or her choice. Consent may make sense in the large context of individual freedom and responsibility, but the criminal law is hostile to consent as a justification for committing crimes. Individuals can take their own lives and inflict injuries on themselves, but they can't authorize others to kill them or beat them. The law recognizes only three exceptions to this rule:

- No serious injury results from the consensual crime.
- Injury happens during a sporting event.
- Conduct benefits the consenting person, such as when a doctor performs surgery.[37]

Not only is consent limited to these three circumstances, but it also has to be both voluntary and knowing. That is, the consent must stem from the consenting party's own free will without either compulsion or duress. And the person consenting has to be competent to consent; youth, intoxication, or mental abnormality disables the consent. Consent obtained by fraud or deceit also renders the consent ineffective. Finally, forgiveness *after* the commission of a crime is not consent.

 7-6 Connecticut Defense of Consent Statute

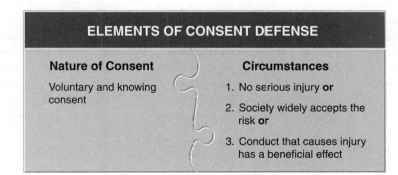

ELEMENTS OF CONSENT DEFENSE	
Nature of Consent	**Circumstances**
Voluntary and knowing consent	1. No serious injury **or**
	2. Society widely accepts the risk **or**
	3. Conduct that causes injury has a beneficial effect

The court dealt with the defense during an intramural college basketball game in *State v. Shelley.*

State v. Shelley
929 P.2d 489 (Wash. 1997)

Jason Shelley was convicted in the Superior Court, King County, of second-degree assault, arising out of an incident in which Shelley intentionally punched another basketball player during a game. Shelley appealed. The Court of Appeals affirmed the conviction.

GROSSE, J.

FACTS

On March 31, 1993, Jason Shelley and Mario Gonzalez played "pickup" basketball on opposing teams at the University of Washington Intramural Activities Building (the IMA). Pickup games are not refereed by an official; rather, the players take responsibility for calling their own fouls. During the course of three games, Gonzalez fouled Shelley several times. Gonzalez had a reputation for playing overly aggressive defense at the IMA. Toward the end of the evening, after trying to hit the ball away from Shelley, he scratched Shelley's face, and drew blood. After getting scratched, Shelley briefly left the game and then returned.

Shelley and Gonzalez have differing versions of what occurred after Shelley returned to the game. According to Gonzalez, while he was waiting for play in the game to return to Gonzalez's side of the court, Shelley suddenly hit him. Gonzalez did not see Shelley punch him. According to Shelley's version of events, when Shelley rejoined the game, he was running down the court and he saw Gonzalez make "a move towards me as if he was maybe going to prevent me from getting the ball." The move was with his hand up "across my vision." Angry, he "just reacted" and swung. He said he hit him because he was afraid of being hurt, like the previous scratch. He testified that Gonzalez continually beat him up during the game by fouling him hard.

A week after the incident, a school police detective interviewed Shelley and prepared a state-

ment for Shelley to sign based on the interview. Shelley reported to the police that Gonzalez had been "continually slapping and scratching him" during the game. Shelley "had been getting mad" at Gonzalez and the scratch on Shelley's face was the "final straw." As the two were running down the court side by side, "I swung my right hand around and hit him with my fist on the right side of his face." Shelley asserted that he also told the detective that Gonzalez waved a hand at him just before Shelley threw the punch and that he told the detective that he was afraid of being injured. Gonzalez required emergency surgery to repair his jaw. Broken in three places, it was wired shut for six weeks. His treating physician believed that a "significant" blow caused the damage.

During the course of the trial, defense counsel told the court he intended to propose a jury instruction that: "A person legally consents to conduct that causes or threatens bodily harm if the conduct and the harm are reasonably foreseeable hazards of joint participation in a lawful, athletic contest or competitive sport." Although the trial court agreed that there were risks involved in sports, it stated that "the risk of being intentionally punched by another player is one that I don't think we ever do assume." The court noted, "In basketball . . . you consent to a certain amount of rough contact. If they were both going for a rebound and Mr. Shelley's elbow or even his fist hit Mr. Gonzalez as they were both jumping for the rebound and Mr. Gonzalez's jaw was fractured in exactly the same way . . . then you would have an issue." Reasoning that "our laws are intended to uphold the public peace and regulate behavior of individuals," the court ruled "that as a matter of law, consent cannot be a defense to an assault." The court indicated that Shelley could not claim consent because his conduct "exceeded what is considered within the rules of that particular sport:"

Consent is a contact that is contemplated within the rules of the game and that is incidental to the furtherance of the goals of that particular game.

If you can show me any rule book for basketball at any level that says an intentional punch to the face in some way is a part of the game, then I would take another . . . look at your argument. I don't believe any such rule book exists.

Later Shelley proposed jury instructions on the subject of consent:

> An act is not an assault, if it is done with the consent of the person alleged to be assaulted. It is a defense to a charge of second degree assault occurring in the course of an athletic contest if the conduct and the harm are reasonably foreseeable hazards of joint participation in a lawful athletic contest or competitive sport.

The trial court rejected these and Shelley excepted. The trial court did instruct the jury about self-defense.

OPINION

First, we hold that consent is a defense to an assault occurring during an athletic contest. This is consistent with the law of assault as it has developed in Washington. A person is guilty of second degree assault if he or she "intentionally assaults another and thereby recklessly inflicts substantial bodily harm." One common law definition of assault recognized in Washington is "an unlawful touching with criminal intent." At the common law, a touching is unlawful when the person touched did not give consent to it, and [it] was either harmful or offensive. As our Supreme Court stated in *State v. Simmons,* "where there is consent, there is no assault." The State argues that because *Simmons* was a sexual assault case, the defense of consent should be limited to that realm. We decline to apply the defense so narrowly. Logically, consent must be an issue in sporting events because a person participates in a game knowing that it will involve potentially offensive contact and with this consent the "touchings" involved are not "unlawful."

The rationale that courts offer in limiting [consent as a defense] is that society has an interest in punishing assaults as breaches of the public peace and order, so that an individual cannot consent to a wrong that is committed against the public peace. Urging us to reject the defense of consent because an assault violates the public peace, the State argues that this principle precludes Shelley from being entitled to argue the consent defense on the facts of his case. In making this argument, the State ignores the factual contexts that dictated the results in the cases it cites in support.

When faced with the question of whether to accept a school child's consent to hazing or consent to a fight, *People v. Lenti,* 44 Misc.2d 118, 253 N.Y.S.2d 9 (1964), or a gang member's consent to a beating, *Helton v. State,* 624 N.E.2d 499, 514 (Ind.Ct.App.1993), courts have declined to apply the defense. Obviously, these cases present "touchings" factually distinct from "touchings" occurring in athletic competitions.

If consent cannot be a defense to assault, then most athletic contests would need to be banned because many involve "invasions of one's physical integrity." Because society has chosen to foster sports competitions, players necessarily must be able to consent to physical contact and other players must be able to rely on that consent when playing the game. This is the view adopted by the drafters of the *Model Penal Code:* "There are, however, situations in which consent to bodily injury should be recognized as a defense to crime. . . . There is . . . the obvious case of participation in an athletic contest or competitive sport, where the nature of the enterprise often involves risk of serious injury. Here, the social judgment that permits the contest to flourish necessarily involves the companion judgment that reasonably foreseeable hazards can be consented to by virtue of participation."

The more difficult question is the proper standard by which to judge whether a person consented to the particular conduct at issue. The State argues that "when the conduct in question is not within the rules of a given sport, a victim cannot be deemed to have consented to this act." The trial court apparently agreed with this approach. Although we recognize that there is authority supporting this approach, we reject a reliance on the rules of the games as too limiting. Rollin M. Perkins in *Criminal Law* explains:

> The test is not necessarily whether the blow exceeds the conduct allowed by the rules of the game. Certain excesses and inconveniences are to be expected beyond the formal rules of the game. It may be ordinary and expected conduct for minor assaults to occur. However, intentional excesses beyond those reasonably contemplated in the sport are not justified.

Instead, we adopt the approach of the *Model Penal Code* which provides:

> (2) Consent to Bodily Injury. When conduct is charged to constitute an offense because it causes or threatens bodily injury, consent to such conduct or to the infliction of such injury is a defense if: . . .
>
> > (b) the conduct and the injury are reasonably foreseeable hazards of joint participation in a lawful athletic contest or competitive sport or other concerted activity not forbidden by law.

The State argues the law does not allow "the victim to 'consent' to a broken jaw simply by participating in an unrefereed, informal basketball game." This argument presupposes that the harm suffered dictates whether the defense is available or not. This is not the correct inquiry. The correct inquiry is whether the conduct of defendant constituted foreseeable behavior in the play of the game. Additionally, the injury must have occurred as a byproduct of the game itself. In construing a similar statutory defense, the Iowa court required a "nexus between defendant's acts and playing the game of basketball." In *State v. Floyd,* a fight broke out during a basketball game and the defendant, who was on the sidelines, punched and severely injured several opposing team members. Because neither defendant nor his victims were voluntarily participating in the game, the defense did not apply because the statute "contemplated a person who commits acts during the course of play, and the exception seeks to protect those whose acts otherwise subject to prosecution are committed in furtherance of the object of the sport." As the court noted in *Floyd,* there is a "continuum, or sliding scale, grounded in the circumstances under which voluntary participants engage in sport . . . which governs the type of incidents in which an individual volunteers (i.e., consents) to participate." *State v. Floyd,* 466 N.W.2d 919, 922 (Iowa.Ct.App.1990)

The New York courts provide another example. In a football game, while tackling the defendant, the victim hit the defendant. After the play was over and all of the players got off the defendant, the defendant punched the victim in the eye. The court in *People v. Freer* held that this act was not consented to:

> Initially it may be assumed that the very first punch thrown by the complainant in the course of the tackle was consented to by defendant. The act

of tackling an opponent in the course of a football game may often involve "contact" that could easily be interpreted to be a "punch." Defendant's response after the pileup to complainant's initial act of "aggression" cannot be mistaken. Clearly, defendant intended to punch complainant. This was not a consented to act. *People v. Freer,* 86 Misc.2d 280, 381 N.Y.S.2d 976, 978 (1976).

As a corollary to the consent defense, the State may argue that the defendant's conduct exceeded behavior foreseeable in the game. Although in "all sports players consent to many risks, hazards and blows," there is "a limit to the magnitude and dangerousness of a blow to which another is deemed to consent." This limit, like the foreseeability of the risks, is determined by presenting evidence to the jury about the nature of the game, the participants' expectations, the location where the game has been played, as well as the rules of the game. Here, taking Shelley's version of the events as true, the magnitude and dangerousness of Shelley's actions were beyond the limit. There is no question that Shelley lashed out at Gonzalez with sufficient force to land a substantial blow to the jaw, and there is no question but that Shelley intended to hit Gonzalez. There is nothing in the game of basketball, or even rugby or hockey, that would permit consent as a defense to such conduct. Shelley admitted to an assault and was not precluded from arguing that the assault justified self-defense; but justification and consent are not the same inquiry. . . .

We affirm.

QUESTIONS FOR DISCUSSION

1. According to the court, why can participants in a sport consent to conduct that would otherwise be a crime?

2. Why should they be allowed to consent to such conduct when in other situations, such as those enumerated in the note cases that follow, they cannot consent?

3. Should individuals be allowed to knowingly and voluntarily consent to the commission of crimes against them? Why or why not?

4. Why was Shelley not allowed the defense of consent in this case?

5. Do you agree with the court's decision? Relying on the relevant facts in the case, defend your answer.

NOTE CASES

1. Richard Hiott and his friend Jose were playing a game of shooting at each other with BB guns. During the game Jose was hit in the eye and lost his eye as a result. Richard was charged with third-degree assault. His defense was consent. Was he entitled to the defense? No, said the Washington Court of Appeals:

Consent can be a defense to a criminal assault. . . . *State v. Shelley* [excerpted before this note] held that consent can be a defense to an assault occurring during an athletic contest. . . . Under *Shelley* . . . consent is a defense only if the game is a lawful athletic contest, competitive sport, or other concerted activity not forbidden by law. . . .

Hiott argues that . . . the game they were playing "is within the limits of games for which society permits consent." Hiott compares the boys' shooting of BB guns at each other to dodgeball, football, rugby, hockey, boxing, wrestling, "ultimate fighting," fencing, and "paint-ball." We disagree.

The games Hiott uses for comparison, although capable of producing injuries, have been generally accepted by society as lawful athletic contests, competitive sports, or concerted activities not forbidden by law. And these games carry with them generally accepted rules, at least some of which are intended to prevent or minimize injuries. In addition, such games commonly prescribe the use of protective devices or clothing to prevent injuries. Shooting BB guns at each other is not a generally accepted game or athletic contest; the activity has no generally accepted rules; and the activity is not characterized by the common use of protective devices or clothing.

Moreover, consent is not a valid defense if the activity consented to is against public policy. Thus, a child cannot consent to hazing, a gang member cannot consent to an initiation beating, and an individual cannot consent to being shot with a pistol. In *Fransua*, the New Mexico court held that consent was not a defense to aggravated battery, recognizing that criminal statutes are enacted to protect citizens and to prevent breaches of the public peace. Assaults in general are breaches of the public peace. And we consider shooting at another person with a BB gun a breach of the public peace and therefore, against public policy. We conclude that the trial court did not err in refusing to consider Jose's consent as a defense.

State v. Hiott, 97 Wash.App. 825, 987 P.2d 135 (Wash. App. 1999)

2. Mrs. Brown was an alcoholic. On the day of the alleged crime she indulged in some spirits, apparently to Reginald Brown, her husband's, dissatisfaction. As per their agreement, defendant sought to punish Mrs. Brown by severely beating her with his hands and other objects. Brown was charged with atrocious assault and battery. He contended that he was not guilty of atrocious assault and battery because he and Mrs. Brown, the victim, had an understanding to the effect that if she consumed any alcoholic beverages (and/or became intoxicated), he would punish her by physically assaulting her. The trial court refused the defense of consent.

Was Mr. Brown justified because of Mrs. Brown's consent? No, said the New Jersey appellate court:

. . . The laws . . . are simply and unequivocally clear that the defense of consent cannot be available to a defendant charged with any type of physical assault that causes appreciable injury. If the law were otherwise, it would not be conducive to a peaceful, orderly and healthy society. . . .

This court concludes that, as a matter of law, no one has the right to beat another even though that person may ask for it. Assault and battery cannot be consented to by a victim, for the State makes it unlawful and is not a party to any such agreement between the victim and perpetrator. To allow an otherwise criminal act to go unpunished because of the victim's consent would not only threaten the security of our society but also might tend to detract from the force of the moral principles underlying the criminal law. . . .

Thus, for the reasons given, the State has an interest in protecting those persons who invite, consent to and permit others to assault and batter them. Not to enforce these laws which are geared to protect such people would seriously threaten the dignity, peace, health and security of our society.

State v. Brown, 143 N.J. Super. 571, 364 A.2d 27 (1976),

3. Daniel Fransua and the victim were in a bar in Albuquerque. Fransua had apparently been drinking heavily that day and the previous day. Sometime around 3:00 P.M., after an argument, Fransua told the victim that if Fransua had a gun, he would shoot the victim. The victim then left the bar, went to his own automobile, removed a loaded pistol from the

automobile, and returned to the bar. He came up to Fransua, laid the pistol on the bar, and made the following remark: "There is the gun. If you want to shoot me, go ahead." Fransua picked up the pistol, put the barrel next to the victim's head, and pulled the trigger, wounding him seriously.

Was Fransua guilty of aggravated battery or was the victim's consent a justification? No, said the New Mexico Court of Appeals:

It is generally conceded that a state enacts criminal statutes making certain violent acts crimes for at least two reasons: One reason is to protect the persons of its citizens; the second, however, is to prevent a breach of the public peace. While we entertain little sympathy for either the victim's absurd actions or the defendant's equally unjustified act of pulling the trigger, we will not permit the defense of consent to be raised in such cases. Whether or not the victims of crimes have so little regard for their own safety as to request injury, the public has a stronger and overriding interest in preventing and prohibiting acts such as these. We hold that consent is not a defense to the crime of aggravated battery, irrespective of whether the victim invites the act and consents to the battery.

State v. Fransua, 85 N.M. 173, 510 P.2d 106, 58 A.L.R.3d 656 (App.Ct.1973)

SUMMARY

In the defenses of justification, defendants admit their responsibility for their actions but maintain that special circumstances justify their conduct or its result. The defenses of justification examined in this chapter involve cases in which defendants are confronted with a dilemma—choosing between two evils. They kill or injure persons, or violate the property of another, in order to avoid an imminent greater evil, or do so because they are performing a public duty, defending their rights against government invasion, or carrying out an agreement with the consent of the "victim."

Theoretically, these evils—and the greater ones defended against—apply the general principle of necessity to specific crimes. Practically, however, neither legislators, judges, prosecutors, nor defense attorneys think in such broad, theoretical terms. Rather, they think of specific defenses applicable to particular crimes. Hence, for example, they think in terms of self-defense as a defense to the specific crimes of criminal homicide, rape, and assault. They refer to the special defense of choice-of-evils defense, not to the general principle of necessity, when they deal with such cases as freezing people breaking into deserted cabins to keep warm.[38]

 Go to the Criminal Law 7e CD-ROM for Internet exercises.

REVIEW QUESTIONS

1. Identify and briefly describe the three situations in which defenses to crimes arise.

2. Explain the theoretical and practical differences between the defenses of justification and the defenses of excuse.

3. Explain how an affirmative defense works.

4. Explain the relationship between motive and *mens rea.* How and why does motive affect punishment?

5. What is the common-law definition of self-defense?

6. What two purposes do not justify the use of force in self-defense?

7. When can one who has provoked an attack plead self-defense?

8. What two elements must defendants demonstrate in order to plead self-defense?

9. Distinguish between imminent and present danger.

10. Explain the retreat doctrine and the castle exception to the retreat doctrine.

11. Identify the conditions under which a person can use force to protect a third person.

12. When can a person use less than deadly force to protect homes and property and when can deadly force be used?

13. Under what conditions can a public official use force, including deadly force, against citizens?

14. How much force can a citizen use against a police officer and under what circumstances? What is the rationale for prohibiting the use of force against police officers?

15. Explain the principle of necessity. What are the elements in the *Model Penal Code's* choice-of-evils defense?

16. Identify and describe the three steps in applying the choice-of-evils defense.

17. What five conditions in addition to self-defense does the *Model Penal Code* provide for the application of the choice-of-evils defense?

18. What two critical issues surround the defense of consent? Explain the situations in which consent is accepted as a defense to crime.

KEY TERMS

affirmative defense—a defense in which the defendant bears the burden of production.
alibi—a defense that places defendants in a different place from the scene at the time of the crime.
burden of persuasion—the responsibility to convince the fact finder of the truth of the defense.
burden of production—the responsibility to introduce initial evidence to support a defense.
burden of proof—the responsibility to produce the evidence to persuade the fact finder.
castle exception—the principle stating that defenders have no need to retreat when attacked in their homes.
choice-of-evils defense or the principle of necessity—defense of making the right choice, namely choosing the lesser of two evils.
defenses—justifications and excuses to criminal liability.

excuse—a defense admitting wrongdoing without criminal responsibility.
imperfect defense—defense reducing but not eliminating criminal liability.
justification—a defense deeming acceptable under the circumstances what is otherwise criminal conduct.
mitigating circumstances—facts that reduce but do not eliminate culpability.
motive—the reason why a defendant commits a crime.
perfect defense—a defense that leads to outright acquittal.
preponderance of the evidence—this means that more than 50 percent of the evidence proves justification or excuse.
retreat rule—you have to retreat, but only if you reasonably believe that backing off won't unreasonably put you in danger of death or serious bodily harm.
self-defense—the use of force to prevent attacks against individuals, their homes, and their property.
stand-your-ground rule—says that if you didn't start the fight, you can stand your ground and kill.

SUGGESTED READINGS

1. George Fletcher, "Justification," in *Encyclopedia of Crime and Justice*, vol. 3, ed. Sanford H. Kadish (New York: Free Press, 1983), pp. 941–946. An excellent introduction to the theory of justification in criminal law. Fletcher describes and assesses the scope and criteria for justification, balancing evils, and the imminent risk requirement.

2. American Law Institute, *Model Penal Code and Commentaries*, vol. 2 (Philadelphia: American Law Institute, 1985), pp. 8–22. The most complete discussion of the principle of necessity by the foremost authorities on the subject. Although written primarily for lawyers, it is worth the serious student's effort.

3. George F. Dix, "Self-Defense," in *Encyclopedia of Crime and Justice*, vol. 3, pp. 946–953. A good general discussion of self-defense. Dix covers the main elements of self-defense, the defense by battered wives who attack their husbands, the retreat doctrine, the defense of others, and the use of force to resist arrest.

4. Rollin M. Perkins and Ronald N. Boyce, *Criminal Law,* 3d ed. (Mineola, N.Y.: Foundation Press, 1982), pp. 1074–1092. The authors thoroughly discuss the consent defense in criminal law. They describe both the legal effect of consent and the crimes to which consent is a defense. They also appraise arguments both for and against consent, as well as the law as it stands in several jurisdictions.

NOTES

1. George Fletcher, *Rethinking Criminal Law* (Boston: Little, Brown, 1981), chap. 10; Rollin M. Perkins and Ronald N. Boyce, *Criminal Law,* ed. (Mineola, NY: Foundation Press, 1982), chs. 8–10; Thomas Morawetz, "Reconstructing the Criminal Defenses: The Significance of Justification," *Journal of Criminal Law and Criminology* 77 (1986):277.

2. Fletcher, *Rethinking Criminal Law,* p. 759; American Law Institute, *Model Penal Code and Commentaries,* vol. 2 (Philadelphia: American Law Institute, 1985), pt. I, p. 3.

3. See Arnold H. Loewy, *Criminal Law* (St. Paul, Minn.: West Publishing Co., 1987), pp. 192–204, for a brief introduction to the topics of burdens and amount of proof. Also, more thorough discussion appears in Wayne R. LaFave and Austin W. Scott, Jr., *Criminal Law,* 2d ed. (St. Paul, Minn.: West Publishing Company, 1986), pp. 51–56; *People v. Dover,* 790 P.2d 834 (Colo.1990).

4. *New York Times,* November 11, 1994.

5. Perkins and Boyce, *Criminal Law,* pp. 926–932; Jerome Hall, *General Principles of Criminal Law,* 2d ed. (Indianapolis, Ind.: Bobbs-Merrill, 1960), pp. 86–88, 97–102; Carol Byrne, "Was Mercy in This Killing?" *Minneapolis Star and Tribune* (May 1, 1988), 1A; Carol Byrne, "An Old Man Starts a New Life—In Prison," *Minneapolis Star and Tribune* (June 5, 1988), p. 1A.

6. George P. Fletcher, *A Crime of Self-Defense: Bernhard Goetz and the Law on Trial* (New York: Free Press, 1988), Chapter 2, especially pp. 18–19.

7. Francis Wharton, *A Treatise on the Criminal Law of the United States* (Philadelphia: Kay and Brother, 1861), § 1020.

8. *State v. Goode,* 271 Mo. 43, 195 S.W. 1006 (1917); Perkins and Boyce, *Criminal Law,* pp. 1128–1129.

9. American Law Institute, *Model Penal Code and Commentaries,* vol. 2, pt. I, pp. 30–61; George P. Fletcher, *A Crime of Self-Defense,* pp. 18–27.

10. *New York Times* (January 14, 1989), p. 9.

11. Quoted in *New York Times* (January 23, 1989); also see Fletcher, *A Crime of Self-Defense.*

12. Associated Press, "Gunman tells story of shooting on subway," *The Toronto Star,* September 27, 1990, p. H14

13. Ibid.

14. Ibid.

15. Mark Lesly, *Subway Gunman* (Latham, N.Y.: British American Publishing, 1988), pp. 75–81; *New York Daily News,* August 10, 1996, p. 8.

16. Mark Lesly, *Subway Gunman,* 310-312, 315-316.

17. *New York Times,* April 25, 1996, sec. B, p. 2.

18. Rafael Olmeda, Virginia Breen, Virginia Breen, and Jane Purse, "From First Vote Jurors Knew," *New York Daily News,* April 24, 1996, p. 3.

19. *New York Times,* April 24, 1996, sec. A, p. 21.

20. *New York Daily News,* April 24, 1996, p. 23.

21. *People v. Williams,* 56 Ill.App.2d 159, 205 N.E.2d 749 (1965); American Law Institute, *Model Penal Code and Commentaries,* art. 3.04.

22. *State v. Schroeder,* 199 Neb. 822, 261 N.W.2d 759 (1978).

23. *State v. Kennamore,* 604 S.W.2d 856 (Tenn.1980).

24. Ibid.

25. *State v. Aguillard,* 567 So.2d 674 (La.1990).

26. Quoted in *State v. Mitcheson,* 560 P.2d 1120 (Utah 1977), 1122.

27. Sir William Blackstone, *Commentaries on the Laws of England* (New York: Garland, 1978), pt. IV, p. 180.

28. LaFave and Scott, *Criminal Law,* p. 389.

29. *Mattis v. Schnarr,* 547 F.2d 1007 (8th Cir. 1976) judgment vacated 431 U.S. 171, 97 S.Ct. 1739, 52 L.Ed.2d 219 (1977). Catherine H. Milton et al., *Police Use of Deadly Force* (Washington, D.C.: The Police Foundation, 1977), contains a detailed discussion. See also Lawrence O'Donnell, Jr., *Deadly Force* (New York: Morrow, 1983), for a spirited attack on deadly force.

30. Quoted in American Law Institute, *Model Penal Code,* tentative draft no. 8, pp. 60–62.

31. Address delivered to National College of State Trial Judges, Chapel Hill, North Carolina, August

15, 1968. Quoted in Sanford Kadish and Manfred Paulson, *Criminal Law and Its Processes,* 3d ed. rev. (Boston: Little, Brown, 1975), pp. 541–542.

32. American Law Institute, *Model Penal Code and Commentaries,* vol. 3, pt. 1, p. 18; Quoted in Glanville Williams, *Criminal Law,* 2d ed. (London: Stevens & Sons, 1961), pp. 724–725.

33. Jerome Hall, *General Principles of Criminal Law,* pp. 425ff.

34. *The Queen v. Dudley and Stephens,* L.R. 14 Q.B.D. 273 (1883).

35. For a general introduction to this topic, see Edward Arnolds and Norman Garland, "The Defense of Necessity in Criminal Law: The Right to Choose the Lesser Evil," *The Journal of Criminal Law and Criminology* 65 (1974):291–293; see also American Law Institute, *Model Penal Code and Commentaries,* vol. 2, pt. 1, pp. 8–22.

36. American Law Institute, *Model Penal Code and Commentaries,* vol. 1, pt. 1, p. 18.

37. George P. Fletcher, *Rethinking Criminal Law,* p. 770; Perkins and Boyce, *Criminal Law,* pp. 1154–1160; Richard L. Binder, "The Consent Defense: Sports, Violence, and the Criminal Law," *The American Criminal Law Review* 13 (1975): 235–248.

38. American Law Institute, *Model Penal Code and Commentaries,* vol. 2, pt. I, pp. 1–5.

Defenses to Criminal Liability: Excuses

Chapter Outline

I. Introduction

II. Insanity

III. Diminished Capacity

IV. Intoxication

V. Age

VI. Duress

VII. Mistake

VIII. Entrapment

IX. Syndromes

X. Summary

CHAPTER MAIN POINTS

1. In the defenses of excuse, defendants admit the wrongfulness of their actions but argue that under the circumstances they were not responsible.

2. The main defenses of excuse are insanity, diminished capacity, intoxication, age, duress, mistake, entrapment, and syndromes.

3. Insanity is a legal concept; mental illness is a medical condition.

4. A mental disease or defect excuses criminal liability when it impairs *mens rea* and/or *actus reus*.

5. The right-wrong test of insanity focuses on reason; the irresistible impulse test focuses on will; and the *Model Penal Code* test focuses on both reason and will.

6. Insanity is an affirmative defense.

7. Diminished capacity reduces but doesn't remove responsibility when mental disease or defect less than insanity impairs *mens rea*.

8. Voluntary intoxication never excuses criminal liability; involuntary intoxication is an excuse in crimes of specific intent if the involuntary intoxication impairs specific intent.

9. Age, either old or young, may excuse criminal liability if it impairs *mens rea*.

10. Duress excuses some crimes when defendants are in immediate danger of death or serious harm.

11. Mistakes of law never excuse criminal liability; honest and reasonable mistakes of fact sometimes excuse criminal liability; legal and factual mistakes are sometimes difficult to distinguish.

12. Entrapment is a defense to criminal liability if the government induces an otherwise law-abiding citizen to commit a crime he or she would not have committed.

Were Laotian Cultural Norms an Excuse?

May Aphaylath, a Laotian refugee living in this country for approximately two years, intentionally killed his Laotian wife of one month because of his jealousy over his wife's ex-boyfriend. Under Laotian culture the conduct of the victim wife in displaying affection for another man and receiving phone calls from an unattached man brought shame on defendant and his family sufficient to trigger Aphaylath's actions.

INTRODUCTION

The defenses of excuse are based on the idea that the law should make allowances for the imperfections and frailties of human nature. Practically speaking, excuses are no more popular in criminal law than they are in daily life. I hear them from students all the time. And when I do I think (and sometimes say out loud) in exasperation: "Excuses, excuses, excuses, I'm sick of excuses!!" The criminal law's reaction is similar. The long list of available excuses hides the law's hostility to them. But you can see the hostility in the failure of almost every defendant who tried to escape criminal liability by pleading the excuses reviewed in this chapter.

Legally speaking, the defenses of excuse (with the major exception of insanity) provide defendants the same opportunity as justification (Chapter 7) to escape criminal liability. Defendants who successfully plead these defenses "walk." But they walk under a different theory. Defendants who plead justification accept responsibility for their actions but claim that what they did was right. Those who plead excuse admit what they did was wrong but deny that they were responsible. The best-known excuse is insanity, but there is a long list of others, including diminished capacity, intoxication, age, mistake, entrapment, and syndromes. Keep in mind that in criminal law as in ordinary life, excuses aren't popular. So, although the list of excuses is long, in practice most defendants fail when they try to escape criminal liability by pleading an excuse that absolves them of responsibility for their wrongdoing.

INSANITY

Thanks to CNN, the whole world knew that Lorena Bobbitt was free on an insanity plea a mere five weeks after a jury convicted her of cutting off her husband's penis. No one knew that John Smith who drove a Greyhound bus out of the New York City Port Authority bus terminal in 1980, crashed, and was acquitted of grand larceny charges "by reason of insanity," is still locked up in the Manhattan Psychiatric Center on Ward's Island in New York City. CNN may have made Lorena Bobbitt a household word throughout the world and no one but the lawyers, doctors, and hospital staff may know of John Smith, but Smith's case is typical of insanity defense cases and Bobbitt's is rare.[1]

The insanity defense attracts a lot of public and scholarly attention. But the public grossly misunderstands the way the defense works. Contrary to widespread belief, few defendants plead the insanity defense. (Only a few thousand a year, according to the largest empirical study ever conducted of the insanity defense.) The few who do plead insanity—nearly all murderers sentenced either to death or life without parole—hardly ever succeed. During 1991, for example, 60,432 individuals were indicted in Baltimore, Maryland. Of these, only 190 entered a plea of insanity, and all but eight dropped the plea before trial. The few who succeed don't go free. Courts have to decide if defendants who were insane when they committed their crimes are still insane. If they are—and this is almost always—they are locked up in maximum-security prisons called hospitals. And like John Smith and unlike Lorena Bobbitt, they stay there for a long time, often for the rest of their lives.

Despite its rarity, the insanity defense stands for the important proposition that we have often referred to—that we can only blame people who are responsible. Insanity excuses criminal liability only when it impairs *mens rea* and/or *actus reus*. If defendants were so mentally diseased that they couldn't form a criminal intent and/or control their actions, then we can't blame them for what they did, and retribution is out of order. Neither would it deter either the defendant or other mentally ill people who can't form criminal intent. As we have already noted, this doesn't mean that insane people go free. The government can invoke its power to lock up dangerous people by means of the noncriminal proceeding called **civil commitment**.

Keep in mind that insanity is a *legal* concept, not a *medical* term. What psychiatry calls mental illness may or may not be legal insanity. Mental disease is insanity only when the disease affects reason and will. Psychiatrists testify in courts to help juries decide whether defendants are legally insane, not to prove defendants are mentally ill. The verdict "guilty but mentally ill" makes this point clear. In that verdict, used in some states, juries can find that defendants weren't insane but were mentally ill when they committed crimes. These defendants receive criminal sentences and go to prison, but they may require, and are supposed to receive, treatment for their mental illness while in prison.[2]

There are two major insanity tests:

1. The right-wrong test.
2. The substantial capacity test.

Both tests look at defendants' mental capacity, but they differ in what they are looking for. The right-wrong test focuses on reason, namely on the capacity to tell right from wrong. The substantial capacity test focuses not only on reason but also on will, namely on defendants' power to control their actions. The psychologists call it volition, popularly we call it "will power."

RIGHT-WRONG TEST

The **M'Naghten rule**, or **right-wrong test**, focuses on reason, namely the capacity to distinguish right from wrong. The psychologists call it cognition. The test is based on a famous English case. In 1843, Daniel M'Naghten suffered the paranoid delusion that the prime minister, Sir Robert Peel, had masterminded a conspiracy to kill him. M'Naghten shot at Peel in delusional self-defense but killed Peel's secretary, Edward Drummond, by mistake. Following his trial for murder, the jury returned a verdict of not guilty by reason of insanity. On appeal, England's highest court, the House of Lords, created the two-pronged right-wrong test, or M'Naghten rule of insanity. The test requires proof of two elements:

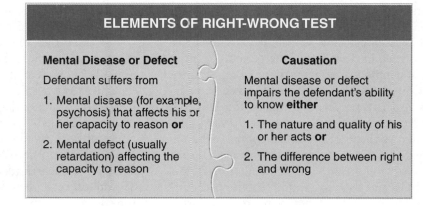

ELEMENTS OF RIGHT-WRONG TEST

Mental Disease or Defect

Defendant suffers from

1. Mental disease (for example, psychosis) that affects his or her capacity to reason **or**

2. Mental defect (usually retardation) affecting the capacity to reason

Causation

Mental disease or defect impairs the defendant's ability to know **either**

1. The nature and quality of his or her acts **or**

2. The difference between right and wrong

1. The defendant had a mental disease or defect at the time of the crime, and

2. The disease or defect caused the defendant to not know either
   a. The nature and the quality of his or her actions, or
   b. That what he or she was doing is wrong.[3]

Several terms in the test need defining. "Mental disease" means psychosis, like the paranoia from which M'Naghten himself suffered, and schizophrenia. It doesn't include personality disorders like psychopathic and sociopathic personalities that lead to criminal or antisocial conduct. Mental "defect" refers to retardation severe enough to make it impossible to know what you're doing, or to know that it is wrong. In most states, "know" means simple awareness: cognition. Some states require more than simple awareness, demanding the ability to understand or appreciate, namely to grasp the true significance of an act. Some states don't define the term, leaving it to juries to define it by applying it to the facts of specific cases. "Nature and quality of the act" means that you don't know what you're doing. In law school we learned the meaning of this by an example: "If a man believes he's squeezing lemons when in fact he's strangling his wife" he doesn't know the nature and quality of his act.[4]

The meaning of "wrong" has created problems. Some states require that defendants didn't know their conduct was *legally* wrong; others say it means *morally* wrong. Consider someone who kills another person under the insane delusion that her being convicted of murder will save the human race. She knew that killing was a crime but she believed it was morally right. If "wrong" means "legal," she's guilty; if it means "moral," she's insane. The court applied the right-wrong test in *Sharrieff v. State*.[5]

C A S E   Was He Insane When He Assaulted the Officer?

Sharrieff v. State
1999 Wl 956691 (Tex.App. 1999)

Saladene Sharrieff ("Sharrieff") was convicted of one count of aggravated assault of a peace officer and one count of assault of a peace officer. Sharrieff challenged his convictions on the basis that the jury's rejection of his insanity defense is against the

great weight and preponderance of the evidence. We affirm the trial court's judgment.

STONE, J.

FACTS

On April 9, 1997, Sharrieff was in the men's clothing department of the Dillard's Department Store in Central Park Mall in San Antonio, Texas, where he was observed walking into a dressing room with several items of clothing. Concerned because Sharrieff had been in there for a long period of time, a Dillard's employee contacted in-store security. Bexar County Sheriff Deputy Stephen Benoy, working as a part-time security officer for Dillard's, responded to the call. The employee directed Officer Benoy to Sharrieff's dressing room. As he approached the room, Officer Benoy smelled strong body odor and heard "metal being pried" and "plastic and paper being ripped," both noises that indicate security devices are being removed from clothing. At trial, Sharrieff explained that he attempted to break the security device in half because he had never seen it done. Officer Benoy knocked on the door, identified himself, and asked Sharrieff if he was okay. Sharrieff did not respond. Officer Benoy knocked twice more before Sharrieff opened the door wearing two pairs of pants, a black shirt, which the Dillard's employee identified as store merchandise, and concealing a second shirt. Believing Sharrieff was attempting to shoplift, Officer Benoy questioned him several times about the multiple layers of clothing. He did not respond. Officer Benoy described Sharrieff as confused.

Officer Benoy handcuffed Sharrieff and escorted him to a training office, a room adjacent to the manager's office, where Officer Benoy advised him he was under arrest. Inside the office, Officer Benoy uncuffed Sharrieff and ordered him to take off the store merchandise. Cooperating, Sharrieff took off the shirts, remaining in a bra that apparently belonged to him and the store's pants. He refused to remove the store's pants and became violent when Officer Benoy insisted that he do so. At trial, Sharrieff explained that he became agitated because he was not wearing underwear; he did not want to disrobe in front of the officers. Sharrieff hit Officer Benoy in the chest and face and then pushed him. With the help of Michael Lamb, a Dillard's operations manager, Officer Benoy attempted to restrain Sharrieff and handcuff him. Sharrieff broke free, grabbed a fire extinguisher, assumed a kick-box stance, and sprayed the extinguisher in the office. Sharrieff explained that he took such measures in order to protect himself from the officers. He testified that he feared for his life. Officer Benoy cleared employees out of both the training room and the manager's office; the store manager

phoned the San Antonio Police Department. Visibility in the area was significantly reduced.

Sharrieff then ran from the training room into the manager's office where he began lighting paper or clothing on fire and throwing the objects outside the office. At trial, Sharrieff explained that he lit the fires so that the fire department would respond to the crisis. He believed the firemen, as opposed to police officers, would treat him fairly. By the time San Antonio police officers arrived on the scene, Sharrieff had barricaded himself inside the office. Several officers identified themselves as law enforcement and directed Sharrieff to open the door. Officer Tucker, lead person in a rugby-like scrum formation, momentarily gained entry into the office before Sharrieff struck him in the face with a heavy metal object, breaking his glasses and gashing one of his upper eyelids.

Officers eventually entered the office and discovered that Sharrieff had climbed into the crawl space in the ceiling, where he remained for approximately forty-five minutes. At trial, Sharrieff explained that he went into the ceiling with the intention of heading toward the dressing room area where he could jump down and leave the area. While in the ceiling crawl space, San Antonio police officer Benny Johnson attempted to coax Sharrieff down from the ceiling. His efforts, however, ended disastrously when Sharrieff threw a urine-filled condom at him. Officer Johnson testified that without warning Sharrieff threw a condom at him. He attempted to block himself, but it hit him in the face, breaking on contact. Sharrieff was eventually apprehended by a San Antonio Police Department S.W.A.T. team.

For his role in the April 9, 1997 melee, Sharrieff was charged with one count of aggravated assault of a peace officer and one count of assault of a peace officer. Prior to trial, Sharrieff's defense counsel filed a motion requesting that Sharrieff be examined both for competency to stand trial and sanity at the time of the offense. On September 26, 1997, and again on January 13, 1998, Sharrieff was found incompetent to stand trial. He was committed to Vernon State Hospital during his period of incompetency. On May 12, 1998, Sharrieff was found to be competent; trial to a jury began in August 1998.

At trial, Sharrieff asserted the affirmative defense of insanity, which the jury implicitly rejected through its guilty verdict. On appeal, Sharrieff complains that the trial court abused its discretion in denying his motion for new trial in which he argued that the jury's rejection of his insanity defense was against the great weight and preponderance of the evidence.

OPINION

To establish the affirmative defense of insanity, the defendant must prove by a preponderance of the evidence that he did not know that his conduct was wrong at the time of the offense as a result of a severe mental disease or defect. Tex.Penal Code Ann. § 8.01 (Vernon 1994). Although the defense concerns a mental condition, the issue of insanity is not strictly medical. See *Graham v. State,* 566 S.W.2d 941, 948-49 (Tex.Crim.App.1978). As explained by the *Graham* court:

> Ultimately the issue of insanity . . . lies in the province of the jury, not only as to the credibility of the witnesses and weight of the evidence, but also as to the limits of the defense itself. . . . In deciding whether the abnormal mental condition of the accused will excuse criminal responsibility, the jury is not restricted to medical science theories of causation.

Thus, although expert witnesses may aid the jury in its determination of whether a mental condition should excuse holding the defendant responsible for his crime, the jury may accept or reject any or all of the opinion testimony of physicians, and can accept lay testimony over that of experts.

In determining whether the defendant has established his defense by a preponderance of the evidence, we consider all the evidence and determine whether the judgment is so against the great weight and preponderance of the evidence so as to be manifestly unjust.

In support of his affirmative defense, Sharrieff called Dr. John Sparks to testify about Sharrieff's sanity at the time of the offense. Dr. John Sparks, the director of correctional health for Bexar County, first evaluated Sharrieff at the Bexar County Adult Detention Center several days after his arrest. Dr. Sparks' evaluation from that first meeting indicated that Sharrieff was uncooperative, responding inappropriately to instruction, and generally unaware of his actions. Dr. Sparks described

Sharrieff as agitated and noted that he appeared to be ill. Sharrieff did not seem elated or depressed; he seemed self-absorbed. And he was speaking in what is clinically referred to as "clang speech." Sharrieff would say a word and then repeatedly make a sound that mimicked the word. Based on his evaluation, Dr. Sparks concluded that Sharrieff was insane at the time of the offense. This conclusion was based on Dr. Sparks' belief that Sharrieff was severely impaired by schizophrenia, and that as a result of that disease, he did not know that his conduct was wrong.

On cross-examination, Dr. Sparks explained that mentally ill people are not categorically insane. He stated that some mentally ill people are very clear on what they are doing; they understand that their actions are wrong. In the instant case, Dr. Sparks' conclusion regarding Sharrieff's sanity was based on the belief that Sharrieff lacked a clear understanding of what he had done. With respect to the shoplifting, Sharrieff told Dr. Sparks he did not know why he put on the clothes. With respect to Sharrieff's violent post-arrest reaction, Sharrieff indicated that he was acting out of fear of being harmed. Based on his conversations with Sharrieff, Dr. Sparks concluded that Sharrieff, as a result of his schizophrenic condition, did not know that his conduct was wrong. However, when presented with additional facts concerning both Sharrieff's arrest for shoplifting and the ensuing post-arrest fracas, Dr. Sparks' conclusion changed.

The prosecutor explained that Sharrieff had removed security tags from layers of store clothing he was found wearing. Acknowledging that he was unaware of those facts, Dr. Sparks agreed that such behavior would suggest that Sharrieff knew his actions were wrong; thus precluding application of the statutory affirmative defense of insanity. Sharrieff, however, as pointed out by Dr. Sparks, was not prosecuted for shoplifting. He was prosecuted for the assaults committed during his apparent attempted escape.

Turning to the circumstances surrounding that activity, the prosecutor inquired of Dr. Sparks whether an attempt to escape is consistent with someone who knows his conduct is wrong. Dr. Sparks responded affirmatively. The prosecutor also questioned Dr. Sparks about the urine-filled condom. According to Dr. Sparks that offensive gesture was not a calculated diversionary tactic.

Dr. Sparks indicated that Sharrieff urinated in a condom out of necessity and simply discarded it by throwing it through an opening in the ceiling. Such a scenario, in Dr. Sparks' opinion, suggested that Sharrieff neither understood the nature of actions nor that those actions are wrong. But when asked if his opinion would change if it was established that Sharrieff deliberately threw the condom at Officer Johnson, Dr. Sparks agreed that it would. Dr. Sparks admitted he did not know Officer Johnson's version of events, and stated that "if the facts are that [Sharrieff] was looking at the officer and he threw [the condom] in the officer's face directly . . . that would change my opinion."

Understandably frustrated with being presented new facts at trial, Dr. Sparks stated:

> There are two different sets of fact. I don't know which is the correct story. If I assume that Mr. Sharrieff told the truth about what happened, then I believe he was insane at the time. If I assume Mr. Sharrieff was mentally able to lie to me about that time, then I have a conflict, because if he was that sick, why was he not insane? And the third is, if he was mentally ill, but not so ill at that time that he did know the officer was there, did [he] know what was happening and did have some reason to put all those clothes on, then he was certainly sane.
>
> And I have to say it's somewhat confusing to hear additional facts that I haven't heard before. The facts I thought were facts and I tried to corroborate, say that at the time he did not know he was throwing [the condom] at an officer, that he got rid of it, and so he did not know he was doing something wrong by that explanation.
>
> What you've added to it puts a different light on that explanation. Now I'm not certain that he was insane. Finding him insane is a very positive thing. Everything is negative. He wasn't, he wasn't, he wasn't. I have to say there is some fact that makes me come to that conclusion. Now I'm not certain. At that time I went through this, I thought he was definitely unaware and that he definitely didn't have intent to do some wrong.

The prosecutor then turned to the circumstances regarding the events that transpired before Sharrieff climbed into the ceiling. Dr. Sparks testified that although Sharrieff's behavior suggested a great deal of confusion, he acted as if he knew he was doing something wrong. That is, "he acted as if he needed to escape from the scene. . . . When someone acts as if they know it was wrong, I have no other way of saying it's not wrong unless that person is acting as a result of a delusion that clearly says this is not real, I'm going to act because God is here, or whatever the delusion is, it's here causing me to do this. That did not happen in this case."

At the close of his questioning, the prosecutor posed a final clarifying question:

> So the only thing—What you're telling this jury, then, so that we're clear, is that if [Sharrieff] filled the condom with urine because he had to urinate and was merely tossing it away and not deliberately throwing it at an officer, that's the only conduct that you could describe that would tell this jury that he was insane at the time these offenses occurred?

Dr. Sparks answered affirmatively.

Considering all the evidence presented on the issue of Sharrieff's sanity, we are unable to conclude that the judgment, and thus the jury's implicit finding of sanity, was so against the great weight and preponderance of the evidence that it was manifestly unjust. Dr. Sparks' opinion, although not binding upon the jury, was less than definitive. The jury heard Dr. Sparks change and or qualify his initial opinion as the prosecutor presented a fuller picture of Sharrieff's behavior. The jury, like Dr. Sparks, was free to believe that, although Sharrieff was exhibiting bizarre behavior, Sharrieff understood that his actions were wrong. The jury was free to believe that Sharrieff created a great deal of confusion and mayhem in an attempt to escape from the department store and evade arrest for shoplifting. Attempts to evade police or attempts to conceal evidence, both circumstances present in the instant case, may persuade a jury that a defendant understood that his actions were wrong. The jury in the instant case was also free to disbelieve Sharrieff's benign explanation regarding the thrown condom. Thus, while the evidence suggested that Sharrieff suffered from a schizophrenic disorder, the jury was free to believe that by barricading himself in an office, striking an officer with a heavy metal object, and then climbing into a ceiling crawl space so that he could, according to his own testimony, leave the area, Sharrieff knew his actions were wrong. While this court may have reached a different decision, we do not sit as thirteenth jurors, and in the face of factually sufficient evidence, we must affirm the jury's verdict. Sharrieff's sole point of error is overruled.

The judgment of the trial court is affirmed.

QUESTIONS FOR DISCUSSION

1. State the right-wrong test as the Texas court understands it.

2. List all of the facts in the case relevant to the question of Sharrieff's sanity.

3. Apply the right-wrong test to the facts of the case. Make sure that you refer to both prongs of the test, and to the meaning of "disease" and "wrong."

4. If you were defining the right-wrong test how would you define "disease" and "wrong." Would Sharrieff be guilty under your test? Explain your answer.

The right-wrong test has generated long-drawn-out argument. One line of criticism began in the 1950s when many social reformers thought that Freudian psychology could cure many individual and social ills. A widely cited case from that era, *Durham v. United States,* reflects the influence of Freud. According to the court:

> The science of psychiatry now recognizes that a man is an integrated personality and that reason, which is only one element in that personality, is not the sole determinant of his conduct. The right-wrong test, which considers knowledge or reason alone, is therefore an inadequate guide to mental responsibility for criminal behavior.[6]

The court rejected the right-wrong test and replaced it with the **product test of insanity**, also known as the **Durham rule.** According to the new test, acts that are the products of mental disease or defect excuse criminal liability. The court stretched the concept of insanity beyond the purely intellectual knowledge in the right-wrong test to deeper areas of cognition and will. Only New Hampshire (where the test originated in 1871), the federal court of appeals for the District of Columbia (which decided *Durham*), and Maine ever adopted the product test. The federal court and Maine have since abandoned the test, leaving it in effect only in New Hampshire.[7]

Defenders of the right-wrong test say that the product test misses the point of insanity. They maintain that the right-wrong test shouldn't substitute mental illness for insanity. Rather, mental illness is only an instrument to determine which mental states ought to relieve persons of criminal responsibility. Two articulate defenders put it this way:

> It is always necessary to start any discussion of *M'Naghten* by stressing that the case does not state a test of psychosis or mental illness. Rather, it lists conditions under which those who are mentally diseased will be relieved from criminal responsibility. Thus, criticism of *M'Naghten* based on the proposition that the case is premised on an outdated view of mental disease is inappropriate. The case can only be criticized justly if it is based on an outdated view of the mental conditions that ought to preclude application of criminal sanction.[8]

Another line of criticism focuses on the purely intellectual basis of the test. According to this line of criticism, the right-wrong test, by focusing on reason, neglects two important dimensions of criminal responsibility. One is that knowing something is wrong is not enough; you have to *appreciate* that it's wrong. A five year old probably knows in her head that it's wrong to steal from her mother's purse, but she doesn't appreciate the criminality of the act. Second, looking only at reason overlooks will. Just because you know something is wrong, even if you fully appreciate its wrongfulness, doesn't mean that you can stop yourself from doing it. I used to be fat. I knew and fully appreciated the wrongfulness of overeating. I can remember so many times knowing that those french fries were really bad for me but I just couldn't stop myself from shoving them in. According to the criticism, we can neither blame nor deter people who *because of a mental disease or defect* can't conform their conduct to what the law requires. The law of civil commitment can protect society from them and treat them without resorting to criminal sanctions.

IRRESISTIBLE IMPULSE TEST

Several jurisdictions have responded to the criticism that the insanity defense should look at will as well as reason by supplementing the right-wrong test with what we call the **irresistible impulse test**. According to the test, even if defendants know what they're doing and that it is wrong, they are entitled to a verdict of not guilty by reason of insanity if they have a mental disease or defect that at the time of the crime kept them from controlling their conduct.[9]

In 1877, the court in *Parsons v. State* spelled out the application of the right-wrong test with its irresistible impulse supplement:

1. At the time of the crime was the defendant afflicted with "a disease of the mind"?

2. If so, did the defendant know right from wrong with respect to the act charged? If not, the law excuses the defendant.

3. If the defendant did have such knowledge, the law will still excuse the defendant if two conditions concur:
   a. if mental disease caused the defendant to so far lose the power to choose between right and wrong and to avoid doing the alleged act that the disease destroyed the defendant's free will, and
   b. if the mental disease was the sole cause of the act.[10]

Some critics say that the irresistible impulse supplement doesn't go far enough. First, they claim (but supporters deny) that it includes only sudden impulses although it should also include conduct "characterized by brooding and reflection." Second, they claim that the irresistible requirement implies that defendants have to lack control totally. In practice, however, juries do acquit defendants who have some control; rarely do juries demand an utter lack of control.

Other critics say that the irresistible impulse test goes too far. By allowing people who lack self-control to escape punishment, the test cripples both retribution and de-

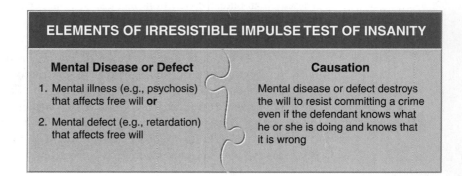

ELEMENTS OF IRRESISTIBLE IMPULSE TEST OF INSANITY

Mental Disease or Defect	Causation
1. Mental illness (e.g., psychosis) that affects free will **or** 2. Mental defect (e.g., retardation) that affects free will	Mental disease or defect destroys the will to resist committing a crime even if the defendant knows what he or she is doing and knows that it is wrong

terrence. They point to the high-profile case of John Hinckley, Jr., acquitted because the jury found him insane when he attempted to assassinate President Ronald Reagan to get Jodie Foster's attention. Shortly after Hinckley's trial, Harvard criminal law professor Charles Nesson wrote:

> To many Mr. Hinckley seems like a kid who had a rough life and who lacked the moral fiber to deal with it. This is not to deny that Mr. Hinckley is crazy but to recognize that there is a capacity for craziness in all of us. Lots of people have tough lives, many tougher than Mr. Hinckley's, and manage to cope. The Hinckley verdict let those people down. For anyone who experiences life as a struggle to act responsibly in the face of various temptations to let go, the Hinckley verdict is demoralizing, an example of someone who let himself go and who has been exonerated because of it.[11]

Since the attempted murder of former President Reagan, several jurisdictions have abolished the irresistible impulse defense on the ground that juries can't distinguish between irresistible impulses that should excuse criminal conduct and merely unresisted impulses that shouldn't. The federal statute abolishing irresistible impulse in federal cases provides as follows:[12]

> It is an affirmative defense to a prosecution under any Federal statute that, at the time of the commission of the acts constituting the offense, the defendant, as a result of a severe mental disease or defect, was unable to appreciate the nature and quality or the wrongfulness of his acts. Mental disease or defect does not otherwise constitute a defense.[13]

SUBSTANTIAL CAPACITY TEST

The right-wrong test, either supplemented by the irresistible impulse test or not, was the rule in most states until the 1960s, after which the **substantial capacity test** became the majority rule. Following John Hinckley's "not guilty by reason of insanity" verdict in his trial for attempting to assassinate President Ronald Regan, the right-wrong test has enjoyed something of a comeback.

The substantial capacity test is supposed to remove the objections to the right-wrong test and the irresistible impulse supplement to it just discussed. But the test preserves the legal nature of both those tests. It emphasizes both qualities in insanity that affect culpability: reason and will.[14]

As the name of the test indicates, defendants have to lack *substantial*, not total, mental capacity. Both the right-wrong and irresistible impulse tests are ambiguous on

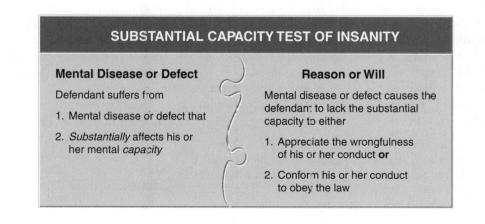

SUBSTANTIAL CAPACITY TEST OF INSANITY

Mental Disease or Defect

Defendant suffers from

1. Mental disease or defect that

2. *Substantially* affects his or her mental *capacity*

Reason or Will

Mental disease or defect causes the defendant to lack the substantial capacity to either

1. Appreciate the wrongfulness of his or her conduct **or**

2. Conform his or her conduct to obey the law

this point, leading some to maintain that both require total lack of knowledge and control. So, people who can only modestly tell right from wrong and who have only a feeble will to resist are insane. Most states follow the *Model Penal Code*'s definition of substantial capacity:

> A person is not responsible for criminal conduct if at the time of such conduct as a result of mental disease or defect he lacks substantial capacity either to appreciate the criminality [wrongfulness] of his conduct or to conform his conduct to the requirements of law.[15]

The use of "appreciate" instead of "know" makes clear that mere intellectual awareness isn't enough to create culpability. Affective or emotional components of understanding are required. The phrase "conform his conduct" removes the requirement of a "sudden" lack of control. In other words, the code provision eliminates the suggestion that losing control means losing it on the spur of the moment, as the irresistible impulse test implies. The code's definition of "mental disease or defect" excludes psychopathic personalities, habitual criminals, and antisocial personalities from the defense. The Connecticut Supreme Court reviewed the application of the substantial capacity test to the facts of *State v. Quinet*.

C A S E   **Did He Lack "Substantial Capacity" of Reason and Will?**

State v. Quinet
253 Conn. 392, 752 A.2d 490 (2000)

Corey Quinet was convicted of attempted murder and attempted sexual assault after bench trial in the Superior Court, Judicial District of Fairfield. He was sentenced to a total effective term of imprisonment of forty years, suspended after twenty years, and five years probation. He appealed. On transfer from the Appellate Court, the Supreme Court affirmed.
    PALMER, J.

FACTS

After a trial to the court, the defendant, Corey Quinet, was convicted of two counts of attempted murder and one count of attempted sexual assault in the first degree. On appeal, the defendant claims that the trial court improperly . . . rejected his affirmative defense of insanity under General Statutes § 53a-13. General Statutes § 53a-13 provides in relevant part:

> (a) In any prosecution for an offense, it shall be an affirmative defense that the defendant, at the time he committed the proscribed act or acts, lacked substantial capacity, as a result of mental disease or defect, either to appreciate the wrongfulness of

his conduct or to control his conduct within the requirements of the law. . . .

General Statutes § 53a-12 (b) provides that a defendant has the burden of establishing an affirmative defense by a preponderance of the evidence.

On Friday, April 29, 1994, the defendant, then a 19-year-old 1993 graduate of the Hopkins School (Hopkins) in New Haven (a private, coeducational school), conceived a plan to rape and murder twenty-seven of his former female classmates and, thereafter, to flee to Australia, where he intended to commit suicide. One of these former classmates, hereinafter referred to as the victim, was a seventeen year old senior at Hopkins with whom the defendant was acquainted (defendant and the victim had worked on the school newspaper together and had attended several of the same classes) and who once had rejected the defendant's request for a date. The defendant decided that she would be his first victim.

On Saturday, April 30, 1994, the defendant purchased a number of items that he intended to use to rape, torture and murder the victim, including a knife, a glue gun, duct tape, rope, and metal and bamboo skewers. On Monday, May 2, the defendant rented three films containing graphic violence to "get [himself] in the mood" to rape and kill the victim that day. These videotapes are entitled "Faces of Death," "Death Faces," and "Slaughter High."

At approximately 5 p.m. on May 2, the defendant drove to the vicinity of the victim's home and observed the residence from a distance. The defendant did not approach the home immediately because he believed that a car parked in the driveway belonged to the victim's brother and, in addition, because he was not certain that the victim was inside. At about 7:15 p.m., the defendant drove to a nearby pay telephone and called the victim to determine whether she was home. Upon learning that the victim was there, the defendant drove back to the victim's home, walked up to the front door and rang the doorbell. The victim's father answered the door, and the defendant explained that his car had broken down and asked the victim's father if he could use a telephone to call for assistance. The victim's father agreed and, when the defendant entered the house, she recognized him as a former classmate who had graduated from Hopkins the previous year.

The defendant then pretended to use the telephone to call for assistance. The victim's father offered the defendant some food and a drink, which the defendant accepted. The defendant and the victim then engaged in conversation.

The defendant had been at the victim's home for approximately one-half hour when he suddenly pulled out a gun and placed it against the victim's head. It subsequently was determined that the weapon was an unloaded pellet gun. The defendant ordered the victim to lie on the floor and, when the victim's father walked into the room, demanded that he do the same. Both the victim and her father complied with the defendant's command. As the defendant was removing some duct tape from a duffel bag that he had brought with him into the victim's home, the victim's father jumped up from the floor, wrested the gun from the defendant and subdued him. The victim's father then ordered the defendant to lie facedown on the floor and the defendant complied. The defendant remained in that position, motionless and silent, until the police arrived.

[Footnote. The duffel bag also contained some torn sheets, two packages of metal skewers, two packages of bamboo skewers, moisturizing cream, a glue gun, two glue sticks, two rolls of duct tape, lubricating lotion, rope and a knife with an eight-inch blade. The defendant told the police that he had purchased the items and had brought them with him to the victim's home to use in the rape, torture and murder of the victim. In particular, the defendant stated that he intended to use the knife, rather than a gun, to kill the victim in order to inflict more pain. The defendant further explained that, after raping the victim, he had planned to insert the skewers and the glue into the victim's vagina to cause her additional pain and suffering.]

After the police had advised the defendant of his rights, he readily admitted that his purpose in going to the victim's home was to torture, rape and kill her. He further stated that he intended to kill the victim's father and her brother, who also were home at the time, because they would have been able to identify the defendant as the victim's assailant. The defendant also confessed that he had planned to rape and murder twenty-six other female students at Hopkins. Additional facts will be set forth as necessary.

The defendant was charged with three counts of attempted murder for allegedly attempting to kill the victim, her father and her brother, two counts of kidnapping in the first degree in violation of General Statutes § 53a-92 (a)(2), for allegedly abducting the victim and her father and restraining them with the intent to sexually assault the victim, and one count of attempted sexual assault in the first degree for allegedly attempting to compel the victim to engage in sexual intercourse with him by the use or threat of use of force. The defendant, who elected to be tried by the court, raised the affirmative defense of insanity. At the conclusion of the trial, the court rejected the defendant's insanity defense and found him guilty of two counts of attempted murder and one count of attempted sexual assault in the first degree. The trial court rendered judgment sentencing the defendant to a total effective term of imprisonment of forty years, suspended after twenty years, and five years probation. This appeal followed.

OPINION

The defendant first contends that the evidence he adduced at trial established, as a matter of law, that, due to a mental disease or defect, he lacked substantial capacity to control his conduct within the requirements of the law.

[Footnote: The defendant never has claimed that he lacked the capacity to appreciate the wrongfulness of his conduct on May 2, 1994. Indeed, on appeal, the defendant concedes that he understood the wrongfulness of his actions. Thus, he makes no claim under the cognitive prong of the insanity defense; his claim is limited to the volitional prong of that test.]

We reject the defendant's claim.

The following additional facts are relevant to our resolution of this issue. At trial, the defendant did not deny committing the acts alleged by the state. He claimed, rather, that, as a result of his mental disease or defect, he was unable to conform his conduct to the requirements of the law when he engaged in the proscribed conduct. In support of his affirmative defense, the defendant presented the testimony of Madelene Baranoski, a clinical psychologist, and Paul Amble, a psychiatrist. The defendant also adduced evidence tending to establish that he had suffered from a progressively more serious mental illness that culminated in his unsuccessful effort to rape and kill the victim on May 2, 1994.

Baranoski conducted a psychological evaluation of the defendant that consisted of a number of psychological tests, a clinical interview and a review of the defendant's psychiatric history. On the basis of her inquiry into the defendant's mental condition on May 2, 1994, Baranoski opined that the defendant was suffering from paranoid schizophrenia at that time. Baranoski also stated that the behavior of a person suffering from that mental illness "would be more likely to be impulsive when the disease is not under good control either by medication or close psychiatric observation." Baranoski further opined that the defendant "was having difficulty with rational thought" and had "an impairment of judgment and . . . difficulty controlling his behavior" between April 30 and May 2, 1994. According to Baranoski, the defendant also had frequent delusions that an external entity was controlling his mind, another common trait of individuals suffering from paranoid schizophrenia. Among other examples of the defendant's delusional ideation, Baranoski testified that the defendant, during a psychiatric hospitalization in the fall of 1993, had stated that an "evil entity" was "controlling his mind by putting in . . . rape fantasies. . . ." Finally, Baranoski stated that the ability to plan and organize also was a recognized characteristic associated with paranoid schizophrenia.

Amble conducted a psychiatric examination of the defendant and, in addition, reviewed his men-

tal health history and the results of the psychological tests that Baranoski had administered to the defendant. Amble concluded that the defendant suffered from a "psychotic disorder not otherwise specified," a mental illness that, according to Amble, is characterized by bizarre delusions, a separation from reality and a deterioration in functioning. Amble testified that, although he could not make a definitive diagnosis of paranoid schizophrenia because, in his view, the defendant's disorder was continuing to evolve, his evaluation of the defendant did "seem to strongly point towards . . . chronic paranoid schizophrenia." Amble also testified that the defendant suffered from sexual sadism and, further, that he did not believe that the defendant was malingering. Finally, Amble opined that from April 29 through May 2, 1994, the defendant lacked the ability to control his behavior and that the defendant believed that he was under the influence of an outside force.

The defendant also adduced evidence regarding his treatment and hospitalization for mental problems during the six month period prior to May 2, 1994. Specifically, the defendant, while attending Vassar College (Vassar) in Poughkeepsie, New York, in 1993, after graduating from Hopkins, became obsessed with a young woman that he had met at Vassar. The defendant, distraught because the woman refused his request for a date, decided to fly to Belgium to commit suicide. The defendant purchased an airline ticket to Belgium and boarded the plane, but when the flight was canceled due to a mechanical problem, he contacted his therapist at Vassar and returned to Poughkeepsie. Several days later, however, the woman again rejected the defendant's overture, and the defendant devised a plan to rape and kill her. The defendant had invited the young woman to a campus classroom, ostensibly to show her a computer program. She arrived, accompanied by a friend, and observed that the defendant was talking to himself and appeared to be confused. The defendant told her that he had a knife in his bag with which he planned to injure her but that he then decided to use on himself. Campus and local police were called, and the defendant was transported and involuntarily committed to St. Francis Hospital (St. Francis) in Poughkeepsie on November 20, 1993. Upon his admission to the hospital, he was diagnosed with major depression and borderline personality disorder.

The defendant was discharged from St. Francis on November 24, 1993, and, on that very same day, was admitted to Silver Hill Hospital (Silver Hill) in New Canaan. The defendant remained there as an inpatient until December 20, when he was discharged to outpatient care. He was readmitted to Silver Hill as an inpatient on December 29, however, because he could not control his suicidal ideation. The defendant was discharged from Silver Hill on January 24, 1994, but, because he still was unable to control his suicidal impulses, he was admitted to Four Winds Hospital (Four Winds) in Katonah, New York, on January 28, where he remained until his discharge on February 22. The defendant continued to receive treatment at Four Winds on an outpatient basis until March 11, when he entered an outpatient program at Greenwich Hospital. The defendant remained a participant in that program until his arrest on May 2, 1994.

In rebuttal to the defendant's insanity defense, the state relied primarily on its cross-examination of the defendant's two experts, and on the conduct and statements of the defendant before, during and after the events of May 2, 1994. The state also relied on the notes and records of the various institutions at which the defendant had received treatment or counseling, and on the observations of several persons familiar with the defendant's activities and conduct immediately prior to May 2. Finally, the state emphasized the uncontroverted fact that many of the mental health professionals who had examined the defendant offered differing diagnoses of the defendant's psychiatric condition, including the defendant's own experts, Baranoski and Amble.

In particular, Baranoski acknowledged on cross-examination that she did not have enough information to render an opinion as to whether the defendant was unable to control his conduct at any time between April 29 and May 2, 1994. Baranoski also conceded that her diagnosis of the defendant differed from those of a number of other mental health professionals, including Amble, and, further, that she disagreed with some of those diagnoses. Finally, Baranoski noted that the defendant had told her that, upon executing his plan to kill twenty-seven people, he would become famous.

Amble stated on cross-examination that he had not previously testified concerning the sanity of a person accused of a crime. Amble further stated that he was not board certified in psychiatry, that, as of the time of trial, he had been engaged in the practice of forensic psychiatry only for about two years, and that he never had treated the defendant. Amble also conceded that he was the only mental health professional to have diagnosed the defendant as suffering from sexual sadism, and that the other examining psychiatrists and psychologists, including Baranoski, had offered diagnoses of the defendant that differed from his own.

In addition, Amble acknowledged that the defendant had felt the need to rent several violent films to "get [himself] in the mood" to rape and kill the victim. Amble also acknowledged that the defendant initially had not planned to kill the victim's father and brother, but later decided to do so, not out of any compulsion to harm them, but because they would have been able to identify him as the victim's assailant. Amble further acknowledged that the defendant originally had planned to kill only himself, but, thereafter, decided that, if he was going to commit suicide, he would fulfill some of his violent sexual fantasies before doing so. Moreover, because the defendant had demonstrated a measure of self-control in executing his criminal plan, Amble could not say that the defendant would have been compelled to proceed in accordance with his plan if, for example, there had been a law enforcement officer at the victim's home when the defendant arrived there on the evening of May 2, 1994. Amble also conceded that the defendant knew that what he was doing was wrong, and that he was not suffering from any hallucinations, or otherwise out of touch with reality, during the several days leading up to and including May 2. Finally, during closing arguments, the prosecutor noted that Amble agreed that a mental disease or illness can result in a lowering of a person's inhibitions without causing that person to lose control over his or her conduct.

The state also relied on other evidence to support its contention that the defendant was able to control his conduct within the requirements of the law. For example, during several interviews with the police immediately after his arrest, the defendant answered all questions calmly and responsively. In one of these interviews, the defendant, when asked why he had attempted to rape and murder the victim, explained that he "had the will to do it" and, further, that he "has a criminal mind." In this interview, the defendant also stated that, if he had been able to execute his plan to rape and murder the victim, he would have felt "fulfilled in a sense. My brain would have been fulfilled because I feel that was what I . . . intended to do. It was intended for me to do that." In addition, the defendant indicated that he had the desire to act out his violent sexual fantasies because, according to him, "nature made my brain a certain way."

Subsequent to his arrest, the defendant also told the police that he had rented the three videotapes on May 2 to "expose [himself] to violence" for the purpose of "get[ting] [himself] in the mood" to assault and kill the victim. The defendant further explained that, in light of his previous struggles with such thoughts, it was "time to cross the line." The defendant indicated that he had become impatient waiting to have his first sexual relationship with a woman, and that he had "tried to cross the line twice and . . . failed," referring to the incidents involving the victim and the young woman at Vassar.

Finally, the state maintained that Amble's opinion regarding the defendant's inability to control himself lacked support in the evidence. In particular, the state noted that the defendant had exhibited self-control by waiting from Friday until Monday to execute his plan to rape and kill the victim and also noted that the defendant, again, demonstrated self-restraint on Monday by postponing his entry into the victim's home for several hours. In addition, the records of the defendant's treatment at Greenwich Hospital during the period preceding the May 2 incident, and those of the Bridgeport correctional center for the period immediately thereafter, contain nothing to indicate that the defendant believed that he was being controlled by an outside force or forces.

Furthermore, the defendant, in responding to a psychological test administered to him while an inpatient at Four Winds in February, 1994, denied that he was possessed by evil spirits; had very peculiar and strange experiences; has something wrong with his mind; often feels as if things are not real; has never seen a vision; and wishes that he were not bothered by thoughts about sex. The state also introduced a letter that had been retrieved from the defendant's laptop computer, in which the defendant, presumably writing to a friend sometime prior to his arrest, indicates that he is doing fine and learning to cope with his problems. The letter, addressed to "Jay," reads as follows:

Oh boy, does it feel good to be out of the hospital and back home where I can take this opportunity to write you. Things are going just fine here, Jay. I got to tell you I feel like a new man. At my last stay in the hospital I really thought over a lot of things. First, it was a big mistake to call [to apologize to the young woman from Vassar]. I knew I would get in trouble for it and I did but what's done is done and we've got to move on. In group therapy I really opened up and talked about my problems. I talked about the loss of my dad and how I really miss him. It was surprising how well I handled it.

The state, moreover, adduced evidence indicating that the defendant had been able to sleep and work normally, and enjoy dinner with his friends, in the days immediately prior to May 2. For example, the defendant, who was employed by the Darien YMCA as a swimming instructor and lifeguard until his arrest, worked there on Sunday, May 1, 1994, without incident. . . .

In light of the totality of the evidence, the court reasonably could have rejected the opinion of Amble, the lone witness to testify that the defendant, due to his mental illness, was unable to control his conduct within the requirements of the law on May 2, 1994. In addition, the court reasonably could have concluded that, even though the evidence indicated that the defendant was suffering from a mental illness, he nevertheless had the capacity to refrain from acting on his desire to commit rape and murder. In particular, that conclusion is supported by the fact that the defendant felt the need to "get [himself] in the mood" in advance of attempting to commit those crimes by viewing videotapes depicting graphic violence. That conclusion is further supported by evidence indicating that the defendant decided to act out his sadistic sexual fantasies only after he had resolved to accomplish his primary objective, namely, to kill himself. The assistant state's attorney made the following remarks regarding this point in his rebuttal closing argument:

As [the defendant] thought about [committing suicide] more and planned it more thoroughly, he had the idea that, if he were going to die anyway, he would fulfill some of his sexual fantasies. The sexual fantasies no longer have to be controlled, because he's not going to be around to be apprehended. That doesn't indicate that he lacks . . . control. It indicates that he doesn't wish to put it off any longer and there's a distinction. His focus is to commit suicide and, as long as he's going to do that, there's no reason to control [himself] any longer with regard to the fantasies.

The defendant also asserts that the trial court, in rejecting his affirmative defense, placed undue emphasis on the fact that the defendant was able carefully to plan his attack on the victim over a period of several days. In particular, the defendant contends that his ability to plan cannot be viewed as inconsistent with his claim that, due to the particular nature of his mental illness, he could not control his conduct within the requirements of the law. In support of his claim, the defendant relies on the following portion of the trial court's statement explaining its verdict:

> The defendant, by the evidence, the court can so find, carefully planned his course of conduct. He made deliberate preparations to seek out [the victim] and other classmates by use of the Hopkins yearbook and handbook, whereby he obtained their addresses and used maps and atlases to determine their locations. He purchased all of the items he felt he needed to carry out his plan. That includes . . . the rope, the duct tape, skewers, lubricants and, of course, the knife, which he indicated was the intended fatal weapon. "He prepared an escape plan by making a plane reservation for Australia four days hence. He concocted a ruse . . . to gain entrance to the [the victim's] home. He surveyed that home and made the conscious decision not to immediately go up to the house, because he saw a car and believed that the victim's brother may be at home. He thereupon, called from the railroad station to verify that [the victim] was at home. He proceeded to the house. He entered by deceit and eventually attempted to carry out his planned mayhem, which was thwarted by [the] . . . actions [of the victim's father].

> Surely, one can perceive this type of conduct as unusual and even bizarre, but the court, taking into account the calculated and precise planning and movements of the defendant and his acknowledgement in the statement to the police that he was a criminal and was escaping to Australia and [the trial court quotes], "because I wanted to get

far away from here, I would be a criminal and I wanted to be as far away as possible from this country," and also that he would [have killed the victim's father and brother] because, again quot[ing the defendant] "they would have seen me," all suggest . . . to the court that the defendant appreciated the wrongfulness of his actions and was able to conform his conduct to the requirements of the law even though he suffered from some mental illness.

Of course, an accused who suffers from a mental disease or illness may be able to establish that he was unable to control his conduct according to law even though he had the capacity to plan that illegal conduct. Whether the capacity to plan a course of criminal conduct is probative of an accused's ability to control his behavior within legal requirements necessarily depends upon the specific facts and circumstances of the case, and ultimately is a determination for the trier of fact. Indeed, we previously have indicated that an accused's ability to formulate a plan to kill is relevant to a determination of whether the accused has the capability of conforming his conduct to the requirements of the law. We see no persuasive reason why the court was prohibited from drawing such an inference in this case.

The judgment is affirmed.

QUESTIONS FOR DISCUSSION

1. State the "substantial capacity" as the court defines it in the case.

2. List all of the facts relevant to deciding whether Corey Quinet was insane when he committed the crimes.

3. Relying on the facts, did Corey Quinet at the time he committed the crimes, "lack substantial capacity, as a result of mental disease or defect, either to appreciate the wrongfulness of his conduct or to control his conduct within the requirements of the law . . ."?

✳ 8-2 "Multiple Personality" as a Form of Insanity

BURDEN OF PROOF

The defense of insanity not only poses definition problems but also gives rise to difficulties in application. States vary as to who has to prove insanity, and how convincingly they have to do so. The Hinckley trial made these questions the subject of heated debate and considerable legislative reform in the 1980s. Federal law required that the government prove Hinckley's sanity beyond a reasonable doubt. So, if Hinckley's lawyers could raise a doubt in jurors' minds about his sanity, the jury had to acquit. That means that even though the jury thought Hinckley was sane, if they weren't convinced beyond a reasonable doubt that he was, they had to acquit him. And that's just what happened: They thought he was sane but had their doubts, so they acquitted him. In 1984, the federal Comprehensive Crime Control Act shifted the burden of proof from the government's having to prove sanity beyond a reasonable doubt to defendants' having to prove they were insane by clear and convincing evidence.[16]

Most states don't follow the federal standard; they call insanity an affirmative defense. As an affirmative defense, sanity and responsibility are presumed. The defense has the burden to offer *some* evidence of insanity. If they do, the burden shifts to the government to prove sanity. States differ as to how heavy the government's burden to prove sanity is. Some states require proof beyond a reasonable doubt; some clear and convincing evidence; and some, a preponderance of the evidence. There is a trend in favor of shifting the burden to defendants and making that burden heavier. This is both because Hinckley's trial generated antagonism toward the insanity defense and because of growing hostility toward rules that the public believes coddle criminals.[17]

DIMINISHED CAPACITY

Some defendants suffer from mental diseases or defects that diminish their mental capacity but not enough to make them insane. Can they claim the defense of their **diminished capacity**? In other words, can they claim that their diseases or defects diminished their capacity enough to prevent them from forming the required *mens rea*? Most states say no. Defendants are either sane or insane. For example, California, in the wake of public hostility to mental excuses, enacted the following provision to replace its diminished capacity provision:

> The defense of diminished capacity is hereby abolished. In a criminal action . . . evidence concerning an accused person's intoxication, mental illness, disease, or defect shall not be admissible to show or negate capacity to form the particular purpose, intent, motive, malice aforethought, knowledge, or other mental state required for the commission of the crime charged. . . . Notwithstanding the foregoing, evidence of diminished capacity or of a mental disorder may be considered by the court at the time of sentencing or other disposition or commitment.[18]

At the other extreme, the *Model Penal Code* provision admits evidence of impaired mental capacity to negate *mens rea* in all crimes. For example, if a mental disease or defect not serious enough to amount to insanity caused a defendant to believe a television set she took belonged to her, the disease negates the specific intent to take "another's property," the *mens rea* required by the crime of stealing.

The few jurisdictions that allow the defense restrict it to first-degree murder. A defendant in these jurisdictions can introduce evidence that a mental disease or defect destroyed the capacity to premeditate (plan in advance) a homicide but not the intent to kill. The effect of this is to excuse the defendant from first-degree murder, requiring premeditation, but to hold her responsible for second-degree murder, requiring the intent to kill. Fewer states go further, permitting diminished capacity to reduce murder to voluntary manslaughter if a mental disease or defect caused the "heat of passion" required to convict for voluntary manslaughter (Chapter 9).[19]

INTOXICATION

Johnny James went quietly to his death by lethal injection . . . inside the Texas prison system's Huntsville Unit. His crimes? Abducting two women, forcing them to have sex with each other, and then shooting them both in the head. One died, the other lived to identify him at trial. The Texas courts turned a deaf ear to James's plea that he was too drunk to know what he was doing when he abducted, raped, and shot his victims.[20]

According to Professor George Fletcher, the defense of intoxication is "buffeted between two conflicting principles":

1. *Accountability.* Those who get drunk should take the consequences of their actions. Someone who gets drunk is liable for the violent consequences.

2. *Culpability.* Criminal liability and punishment depend on blameworthiness.[21]

The common-law approach focused on the first principle:

As to artificial, voluntarily contracted madness, by drunkenness or intoxication, which, depriving men of their reason, puts them in a temporary frenzy; our law looks upon this as an aggravation of the offense, rather than as an excuse for any criminal misbehavior.[22]

The Johnny James case is only one dramatic example that the common law principle is alive and well in 2001. John Gibeaut, who wrote about the James case in an article entitled, "Sobering Thoughts," notes the contemporary emphasis on accountability in the subtitle to his article: "Legislatures and courts increasingly are just saying no to intoxication as a defense or mitigating factor." Section §13-503 of the Arizona code is a typical accountability statute:

Temporary intoxication resulting from the voluntary ingestion, consumption, inhalation or injection of alcohol, an illegal substance under chapter 34 of this title or other psychoactive substances or the abuse of prescribed medications does not constitute insanity and is not a defense for any criminal act or requisite state of mind.[23]

Between November 1996 and May 1997, at least ten states introduced bills similar to the Arizona statute. According to a member of the Prosecution Function Committee of the American Bar Association's Criminal Justice Section, "The fight goes back to the ancient struggle over just how much free will one has."[24]

What we have said so far applies only to *voluntary* intoxication. Involuntary intoxication is an excuse to criminal liability in all states. Involuntary intoxication

---

ELEMENTS OF THE EXCUSE OF INTOXICATION

Voluntary Intoxication

1. Voluntary intoxication is not a defense **but**

2. Can negate specific intent

3. Can reduce the degree of the crime

Involuntary Intoxication

1. Involuntary intoxication is an excuse **if**

2. Intoxication is induced by extreme duress

includes cases in which defendants don't know they are taking intoxicants, or know but are forced to take them. In one case, a man took what his friend told him were "breath perfumer" pills; in fact, they were cocaine tablets. While under their influence, he killed someone. The court allowed the defense of intoxication. Involuntary intoxication applies only under extreme conditions. According to one authority, "a person would need to be bound hand and foot and the liquor literally poured down his throat, or . . . would have to be threatened with immediate serious injury." In another case where the defendant claimed involuntary intoxication, an eighteen-year-old man was traveling with an older man across the desert. The older man insisted that the young man drink some whiskey with him. When he said no, the older man got abusive. Afraid that the older man would throw him out of the car in the middle of the desert without any money, he drank the whiskey, got drunk and killed the older man. The court rejected his defense of involuntary intoxication because the older man had not compelled the youth "to drink against his will and consent."[25]

The United States Supreme Court dealt with the constitutionality of a Montana statute that abolished the defense of voluntary intoxication in *Montana v. Egelhoff.*

C A S E   Was He Too Drunk to Intend to Kill?

Montana v. Egelhoff
116 S.Ct. 2013 (1996)

Steven Egelhoff was convicted of two counts of deliberate homicide, and he appealed. The Montana Supreme Court reversed. The Supreme Court reversed.

SCALIA, J., announced the judgment of the Court and delivered an opinion, joined by REHNQUIST, CJ., and KENNEDY and THOMAS, JJ.

FACTS

In July 1992, while camping out in the Yaak region of northwestern Montana to pick mushrooms, respondent made friends with Roberta Pavola and John Christenson, who were doing the same. On Sunday, July 12, the three sold the mushrooms they had collected and spent the rest of the day and evening drinking, in bars and at a private party in Troy, Montana. Some time after 9 P.M., they left the party in Christenson's 1974 Ford Galaxy station wagon. The drinking binge apparently continued, as respondent was seen buying beer at 9:20 P.M. and recalled "sitting on a hill or a bank passing a bottle of Black Velvet back and forth" with Christenson.

At about midnight that night, officers of the Lincoln County, Montana, sheriff's department, responding to reports of a possible drunk driver, discovered Christenson's station wagon stuck in a ditch along U.S. Highway 2. In the front seat were Pavola and Christenson, each dead from a single gunshot to the head. In the rear of the car lay respondent, alive and yelling obscenities. His blood-alcohol content measured .36 percent over one hour later. On the floor of the car, near the brake pedal, lay respondent's .38 caliber handgun, with four loaded rounds and two empty casings; respondent had gunshot residue on his hands.

Respondent was charged with two counts of deliberate homicide, a crime defined by Montana law as "purposely" or "knowingly" causing the death of another human being. Mont.Code Ann. § 455102 (1995). A portion of the jury charge, uncontested here, instructed that "a person acts purposely when it is his conscious object to engage in conduct of that nature or to cause such a result," and that "a person acts knowingly when he is aware of his conduct or when he is aware under the circumstances his conduct constitutes a crime; or, when he is aware there exists the high probability that his conduct will cause a specific result." Respondent's defense at trial was that an unidentified fourth person must have committed the murders; his own extreme intoxication, he claimed, had rendered him physically incapable of committing the murders, and accounted for his inability to recall the events of the night of July 12. Although respondent was allowed to make this use of the evidence that he was intoxicated, the jury was instructed, pursuant to Mont.Code Ann. § 452203 (1995), that it could not consider respondent's "intoxicated condition . . . in determining the existence of a mental state which is an element of the offense." The jury found respondent guilty on both counts, and the court sentenced him to 84 years' imprisonment.

The Supreme Court of Montana reversed. It reasoned

> (1) that respondent "had a due process right to present and have considered by the jury all relevant evidence to rebut the State's evidence on all elements of the offense charged," and
> (2) that evidence of respondent's voluntary intoxication was "clearly . . . relevant to the issue of whether [respondent] acted knowingly and purposely."

Because § 452203 prevented the jury from considering that evidence with regard to that issue, the court concluded that the State had been "relieved of part of its burden to prove beyond a reasonable doubt every fact necessary to constitute the crime charged," and that respondent had therefore been denied due process. We granted certiorari.

OPINION

The cornerstone of the Montana Supreme Court's judgment was the proposition that the Due Process Clause guarantees a defendant the right to present and have considered by the jury "all relevant evidence to rebut the State's evidence on all elements of the offense charged." Respondent does not defend this categorical rule; he acknowledges that the right to present relevant evidence "has not been viewed as absolute." That is a wise concession, since the proposition that the Due Process Clause guarantees the right to introduce all relevant evidence is simply indefensible. . . . Of course, to say that the right to introduce relevant evidence is not absolute is not to say that the Due Process Clause

places no limits upon restriction of that right. But it is to say that the defendant asserting such a limit must sustain the usual heavy burden that a due process claim entails:

> Preventing and dealing with crime is much more the business of the States than it is of the Federal Government, and . . . we should not lightly construe the Constitution so as to intrude upon the administration of justice by the individual States. Among other things, it is normally "within the power of the State to regulate procedures under which its laws are carried out," . . . and its decision in this regard is not subject to proscription under the Due Process Clause unless "it offends some principle of justice so rooted in the traditions and conscience of our people as to be ranked as fundamental." *Patterson v. New York*, 432 U.S. 197, 201–202, 97 S.Ct. 2319, 2322, 53 L.Ed.2d 281 (1977) (citations omitted).

Respondent's task, then, is to establish that a defendant's right to have a jury consider evidence of his voluntary intoxication in determining whether he possesses the requisite mental state is a "fundamental principle of justice."

Our primary guide in determining whether the principle in question is fundamental is, of course, historical practice. Here that gives respondent little support. By the laws of England, wrote Hale, the intoxicated defendant "shall have no privilege by this voluntarily contracted madness, but shall have the same judgment as if he were in his right senses." 1 M. Hale, *Pleas of the Crown*. According to Blackstone and Coke, the law's condemnation of those suffering from *dementia affectata* was harsher still: Blackstone, citing Coke, explained that the law viewed intoxication "as an aggravation of the offence, rather than an excuse for any criminal misbehaviour." 4 W. Blackstone, *Commentaries*. This stern rejection of inebriation as a defense became a fixture of early American law as well. The American editors of the 1847 edition of Hale wrote:

> Drunkenness, it was said in an early case, can never be received as a ground to excuse or palliate an offence: this is not merely the opinion of a speculative philosopher, the argument of counsel, or the obiter dictum of a single judge, but it is a sound and long established maxim of judicial policy, from which perhaps a single dissenting voice cannot be found. But if no other authority could be adduced, the uniform decisions of our own

Courts from the first establishment of the government, would constitute it now a part of the common law of the land.

In an opinion citing the foregoing passages from Blackstone and Hale, Justice STORY rejected an objection to the exclusion of evidence of intoxication as follows:

> This is the first time, that I ever remember it to have been contended, that the commission of one crime was an excuse for another. Drunkenness is a gross vice, and in the contemplation of some of our laws is a crime; and I learned in my earlier studies, that so far from its being in law an excuse for murder, it is rather an aggravation of its malignity. *United States v. Cornell*, 25 F. Cas. 650, 657–658 (No. 14,868) (CC R.I. 1820).

The historical record does not leave room for the view that the common law's rejection of intoxication as an "excuse" or "justification" for crime would nonetheless permit the defendant to show that intoxication prevented the requisite *mens rea*. . . .

Against this extensive evidence of a lengthy common-law tradition decidedly against him, the best argument available to respondent is the one made by his *amicus* and conceded by the State: Over the course of the 19th century, courts carved out an exception to the common law's traditional across-the-board condemnation of the drunken offender, allowing a jury to consider a defendant's intoxication when assessing whether he possessed the mental state needed to commit the crime charged, where the crime was one requiring a "specific intent.". . . As late as 1878, the Vermont Supreme Court upheld the giving of the following instruction at a murder trial:

> The voluntary intoxication of one who without provocation commits a homicide, although amounting to a frenzy, that is, although the intoxication amounts to a frenzy, does not excuse him from the same construction of his conduct, and the same legal inferences upon the question of premeditation and intent, as affecting the grade of his crime, which are applicable to a person entirely sober. *State v. Tatro*, 50 Vt. 483, 487 (1878).

. . . On the basis of this historical record, respondent's *amicus* argues that "the old common-law rule . . . was no longer deeply rooted at the time the Fourteenth Amendment was ratified." Brief for National Association of Criminal Defense Lawyers as *Amicus Curiae* 23. That conclusion is questionable, but we need not pursue the point, since the argument of *amicus* mistakes the nature of our inquiry. It is not the State which bears the burden of demonstrating that its rule is "deeply rooted," but rather respondent who must show that the principle of procedure violated by the rule (and allegedly required by due process) is "so rooted in the traditions and conscience of our people as to be ranked as fundamental." Thus, even assuming that when the Fourteenth Amendment was adopted the rule Montana now defends was no longer generally applied, this only cuts off what might be called an *a fortiori* [much stronger] argument in favor of the State. The burden remains upon respondent to show that the "new common law" rule—that intoxication may be considered on the question of intent—was so deeply rooted at the time of the Fourteenth Amendment (or perhaps has become so deeply rooted since) as to be a fundamental principle which that Amendment enshrined.

That showing has not been made. Instead of the uniform and continuing acceptance we would expect for a rule that enjoys "fundamental principle" status, we find that fully one-fifth of the States either never adopted the "new common-law" rule at issue here or have recently abandoned it. . . .

It is not surprising that many States have held fast to or resurrected the common-law rule prohibiting consideration of voluntary intoxication in the determination of *mens rea*, because that rule has considerable justification—which alone casts doubt upon the proposition that the opposite rule is a "fundamental principle." A large number of crimes, especially violent crimes, are committed by intoxicated offenders; modern studies put the numbers as high as half of all homicides, for example. Disallowing consideration of voluntary intoxication has the effect of increasing the punishment for all unlawful acts committed in that state, and thereby deters drunkenness or irresponsible behavior while drunk. The rule also serves as a specific deterrent, ensuring that those who prove incapable of controlling violent impulses while voluntarily intoxicated go to prison. And finally, the rule comports with and implements society's moral perception that one who has voluntarily impaired his own faculties should be responsible for the consequences. . . .

There is, in modern times, even more justification for laws such as § 452203 than there used to be. Some recent studies suggest that the connection between drunkenness and crime is as much cultural as pharmacological—that is, that drunks are violent not simply because alcohol makes them that way, but because they are behaving in accord with their learned belief that drunks are violent. This not only adds additional support to the traditional view that an intoxicated criminal is not deserving of exoneration, but it suggests that juries—who possess the same learned belief as the intoxicated offender—will be too quick to accept the claim that the defendant was biologically incapable of forming the requisite *mens rea*. Treating the matter as one of excluding misleading evidence therefore makes some sense.

In sum, not every widespread experiment with a procedural rule favorable to criminal defendants establishes a fundamental principle of justice. Although the rule allowing a jury to consider evidence of a defendant's voluntary intoxication where relevant to *mens rea* has gained considerable acceptance, it is of too recent vintage, and has not received sufficiently uniform and permanent allegiance to qualify as fundamental, especially since it displaces a lengthy common-law tradition which remains supported by valid justifications today. . . .

The doctrines of *actus reus, mens rea,* insanity, mistake, justification, and duress have historically provided the tools for a constantly shifting adjustment of the tension between the evolving aims of the criminal law and changing religious, moral, philosophical, and medical views of the nature of man. This process of adjustment has always been thought to be the province of the States. *Powell v. Texas* [*Powell v. Texas* is excerpted in Chapter 3 in the section on *actus reus*.]

The people of Montana have decided to resurrect the rule of an earlier era, disallowing consideration of voluntary intoxication when a defendant's state of mind is at issue. Nothing in the Due Process Clause prevents them from doing so, and the judgment of the Supreme Court of Montana to the contrary must be reversed.

It is so ordered.

DISSENT

O'CONNOR, joined by STEVENS, SOUTER, and BREYER, JJ.

The Montana Supreme Court unanimously held that Mont.Code Ann. § 452203 (1995) violates due process. I agree. Our cases establish that due process sets an outer limit on the restrictions that may be placed on a defendant's ability to raise an effective defense to the State's accusations. Here, to impede the defendant's ability to throw doubt on the State's case, Montana has removed from the jury's consideration a category of evidence relevant to determination of mental state where that mental state is an essential element of the offense that must be proved beyond a reasonable doubt. Because this disallowance eliminates evidence with which the defense might negate an essential element, the State's burden to prove its case is made correspondingly easier. The justification for this disallowance is the State's desire to increase the likelihood of conviction of a certain class of defendants who might otherwise be able to prove that they did not satisfy a requisite element of the offense. In my view, the statute's effect on the criminal proceeding violates due process. . . .

Due process demands that a criminal defendant be afforded a fair opportunity to defend against the State's accusations. Meaningful adversarial testing of the State's case requires that the defendant not be prevented from raising an effective defense, which must include the right to present relevant, probative evidence. To be sure, the right to present evidence is not limitless; for example, it does not permit the defendant to introduce any and all evidence he believes might work in his favor. . . . Nevertheless, "an essential component of procedural fairness is an opportunity to be heard. That opportunity would be an empty one if the State were permitted to exclude competent, reliable evidence" that is essential to the accused's defense. Section 452203 forestalls the defendant's ability to raise an effective defense by placing a blanket exclusion on the presentation of a type of evidence that directly negates an element of the crime, and by doing so, it lightens the prosecution's burden to prove that mental-state element beyond a reasonable doubt. . . .

I would afford more weight to principles enunciated in our case law than is accorded in the Court's opinion today. It seems to me that a State may not first determine the elements of the crime it wishes to punish, and then thwart the accused's defense by categorically disallowing the very evidence that would prove him innocent. . . .

The Due Process Clause protects those "principles of justice so rooted in the traditions and conscience of our people as to be ranked as fundamental." At the time the Fourteenth Amendment was ratified, the common-law rule on consideration of intoxication evidence was in flux. The Court argues that rejection of the historical rule in the 19th century simply does not establish that the "new common law" rule is a principle of procedure so "deeply rooted" as to be ranked "fundamental." But to determine whether a fundamental principle of justice has been violated here, we cannot consider only the historical disallowance of intoxication evidence, but must also consider the "fundamental principle" that a defendant has a right to a fair opportunity to put forward his defense, in adversarial testing where the State must prove the elements of the offense beyond a reasonable doubt. As concepts of *mens rea* and burden of proof developed, these principles came into conflict, as the shift in the common law in the 19th century reflects. . . .

SOUTER, J.

The plurality opinion convincingly demonstrates that when the Fourteenth Amendment's Due Process Clause was added to the Constitution in 1868, the common law as it then stood either rejected the notion that voluntary intoxication might be exculpatory, or was at best in a state of flux on that issue. That is enough to show that Montana's rule that evidence of voluntary intoxication is inadmissible on the issue of culpable mental state contravenes no principle "so rooted in the traditions and conscience of our people," as they stood in 1868, "as to be ranked as fundamental." But this is not the end of the due process enquiry. Justice HARLAN'S dissenting opinion in *Poe v. Ullman,* 367 U.S. 497, 542, 81 S.Ct. 1752, 1776, 6 L.Ed.2d 989 (1961), teaches that the "tradition" to which we are tethered "is a living thing." What the historical practice does not rule out as inconsistent with "the concept of ordered liberty," *Palko v. Connecticut,* 302 U.S. 319, 325, 58 S.Ct. 149, 152, 82 L.Ed. 288 (1937), must still pass muster as rational in today's world. . . .

BREYER, J., joined by STEVENS, J.

I join Justice O'CONNOR's dissent. As the dissent says, and as Justice SOUTER agrees, the Montana Supreme Court did not understand Montana's statute to have redefined the mental element of deliberate homicide. In my view, however, this circumstance is not simply happenstance or a technical matter that deprives us of the power to uphold that statute. To have read the statute differently—to treat it as if it had redefined the mental element—

would produce anomalous results. A statute that makes voluntary intoxication the legal equivalent of purpose or knowledge but only where external circumstances would establish purpose or knowledge in the absence of intoxication, is a statute that turns guilt or innocence not upon state of mind, but upon irrelevant external circumstances. An intoxicated driver stopped at an intersection who unknowingly accelerated into a pedestrian would likely be found guilty, for a jury unaware of intoxication would likely infer knowledge or purpose. An identically intoxicated driver racing along a highway who unknowingly sideswiped another car would likely be found innocent, for a jury unaware of intoxication would likely infer negligence. Why would a legislature want to write a statute that draws such a distinction, upon which a sentence of life imprisonment, or death, may turn? If the legislature wanted to equate voluntary intoxication, knowledge, and purpose, why would it not write a statute that plainly says so, instead of doing so in a roundabout manner that would affect, in dramatically different ways, those whose minds, deeds, and consequences seem identical? I would reserve the question of whether or not such a hypothetical statute might exceed constitutional limits.

QUESTIONS FOR DISCUSSION

1. If the degree of intoxication was as great as the facts say it was, was Egelhoff capable of forming the intent to commit murder?

2. Summarize the arguments of the plurality in favor of the power of states to abolish the defense of voluntary intoxication without violating the due process clause.

3. Summarize the arguments of the dissents that abolishing the defense of voluntary intoxication violates due process.

4. Which arguments persuade you?

5. Does your answer depend on the heinousness of the murder that Egelhoff committed?

6. Or does it depend on his capacity to form the intent to commit first-degree murder?

7. Or does it depend on whether he was capable of committing the voluntary act (*actus reus*) of first-degree murder?

8. Can you blame someone who is as intoxicated as Egelhoff was?

9. Which of the conflicting principles enunciated by Professor Fletcher at the outset of this section does the plurality adopt?

10. Which does the dissent adopt?

11. Do you agree with the majority or with the dissent?

✸ 8-3 *Montana v. Egelhoff*, Oral Argument, Transcript of Oral Argument, and Briefs

✸ 8-4 California "Insanity Due to Long-Term Intoxication"

Alcohol is the main but not the only intoxicant covered by the defense of intoxication. In most states, it includes all "substances" that disturb mental and physical capacities. In *State v. Hall*, Hall's friend gave him a pill that his friend told him was only a "little sunshine" to make him feel "groovy." In fact, the pill contained LSD (lysergic acid diethylamide). A car picked up Hall while he was hitchhiking. At that time, the drug caused Hall to hallucinate that the driver was a rabid dog. Under this sad delusion, Hall shot and killed the driver. The court said that criminal responsibility recognizes no difference between alcohol and other intoxicants.[26]

AGE

A four-year-old boy stabs a two-year-old girl in a murderous rage. Is this a criminal assault? What if the boy is eight? Twelve? Sixteen? Eighteen? At the other end of the age spectrum, what if he is eighty-five? At how early an age are people liable for criminal conduct? And when, if ever, does someone become too old for criminal responsibility? Age—both old and young—does affect criminal liability, sometimes to excuse it, sometimes to mitigate it, and sometimes even to aggravate it.

Ever since the early days of the English common law, immaturity has excused criminal liability. A rigid but sensible scheme for administering the defense was developed in the sixteenth century. The law divided people into three age groups—under 7 years; 7 to 14 years; over 14 years. Children under seven could not form criminal intent, that is, there was an **irrebuttable presumption** that they lacked the mental capacity to commit crimes. Between seven and fourteen, the presumption became a **rebuttable presumption**; that is, children were presumed to lack the capacity to form criminal intent. The prosecution could rebut the presumption by proving that defendants between seven and fourteen had in fact formed *mens rea*. The presumption of incapacity was strong at age seven but gradually weakened until it disappeared at age fourteen. At fourteen, children were conclusively presumed to have the mental capacity to commit crimes.

About half the states adopted the common-law approach but altered the specific ages within it. Some states excluded serious crimes—usually offenses carrying the death penalty or life imprisonment. States have integrated the age of criminal responsibility with the jurisdiction of the juvenile courts. Some grant the juvenile court exclusive jurisdiction up to a specific age, usually between fifteen and sixteen. Then, from sixteen to eighteen (although occasionally up to twenty-one), juvenile court judges can transfer, or certify, cases to adult criminal courts. The number of cases certified has increased with the public recognition that youths can and do commit serious felonies. In *State v. K.R.L.*, the Washington state supreme court grappled with the capacity of an eight-year-old boy to form *mens rea*.[27]

C A S E   Was He Too Young to Commit Burglary?

State v. K.R.L.
67 Wash.App. 721, 840 P.2d 210 (Wash. App. 1992)

K.R.L., an eight-year-old boy, was convicted of res-idential burglary by the Superior Court, Clallam County, and he appealed. The Court of Appeals reversed.

ALEXANDER, J.

FACTS

In July 1990, K.R.L., who was then 8 years and 2 months old, was playing with a friend behind a business building in Sequim. Catherine Alder, who lived near the business, heard the boys playing and she instructed them to leave because she believed the area was dangerous. Alder said that K.R.L.'s re-sponse was belligerent, the child indicating that he would leave "in a minute." Losing patience with the boys, Alder said "no, not in a minute, now, get out of there now." The boys then ran off. Three days later, during daylight hours, K.R.L. entered Alder's home without her permission. He pro-ceeded to pull a live goldfish from her fishbowl, chopped it into several pieces with a steak knife and "smeared it all over the counter. He then went into Alder's bathroom and clamped a "plugged in" hair curling iron onto a towel.

Upon discovering what had taken place, Alder called the Sequim police on the telephone and re-ported the incident. A Sequim police officer con-tacted K.R.L.'s mother and told her that he suspected that K.R.L. was the perpetrator of the of-fense against Alder. K.R.L.'s mother confronted the child with the accusation and he admitted to her that he had entered the house. She then took K.R.L. to the Sequim Police Department where the child was advised of his constitutional rights by a Sequim police officer. This took place in the pres-ence of K.R.L.'s mother who indicated that she did not believe "he really understood." K.R.L. told the police officer that he knew it was wrong to enter Alder's home. [The statement given by K.R.L. to the officer was not offered by the State to prove guilt. Initially, the State took the position that K.R.L. fully understood those rights and that he had made a free and voluntary waiver of rights.

Defense counsel objected to the admission of the statements and eventually the State withdrew its offer of the evidence, concluding that the evidence was cumulative in that K.R.L.'s admissions were al-ready in evidence through the testimony of his mother.]

K.R.L. was charged in Clallam County Juve-nile Court with residential burglary, a class B felony. At trial, considerable testimony was devoted to the issue of whether K.R.L. possessed sufficient capac-ity to commit that crime. The juvenile court judge heard testimony in that regard from K.R.L.'s mother, Catherine Alder, two school officials, a Se-quim policeman who had dealt with K.R.L. on two prior occasions as well as the incident leading to the charge, one of K.R.L.'s neighbors and the neighbor's son.

K.R.L.'s mother, the neighbor, the neighbor's son and the police officer testified to an incident that had occurred several months before the al-leged residential burglary. This incident was re-ferred to by the police officer as the "Easter Candy Episode." Their testimony revealed that K.R.L. had taken some Easter candy from a neighbor's house without permission. As a consequence, the Sequim police were called to investigate. K.R.L. re-sponded to a question by the investigating officer, saying to him that he "knew it was wrong and he wouldn't like it if somebody took his candy." The same officer testified to another incident involving K.R.L. This was described as the "joyriding inci-dent," and it occurred prior to the "Easter Candy Episode." It involved K.R.L. riding the bicycles of two neighbor children without having their per-mission to do so. K.R.L. told the police officer that he "knew it was wrong" to ride the bicycles.

The assistant principal of K.R.L.'s elementary school testified about K.R.L.'s development. He said that K.R.L. was of "very normal" intelligence. K.R.L.'s first grade teacher said that K.R.L. had "some difficulty" in school. He said that he would put K.R.L. in the "lower age academically." K.R.L.'s mother testified at some length about her son and, in particular, about the admissions he made to her regarding his entry into Alder's home. Speaking of that incident, she said that he admitted to her that what he did was wrong "after I beat him with a belt, black and blue." She also said that her son told her "that the Devil was making him do bad things."

The juvenile court rejected the argument of K.R.L.'s counsel that the State had not presented sufficient evidence to show that K.R.L. was capable of committing a crime. It found him guilty, saying:

> From my experience in my eight, nine years on the bench, it's my belief that the so-called juvenile criminal system is a paper tiger and it's not going to be much of a threat to Mr. [K.R.L.], so I don't think that for that reason there is a whole lot to protect him from.

OPINION

There is only one issue—did the trial court err in concluding that K.R.L. had the capacity to commit the crime of residential burglary? [Residential burglary is defined in RCW 9A.52.025 as: "A person is guilty of residential burglary if, with intent to commit a crime against a person or property therein, the person enters or remains unlawfully in a dwelling. . . ." RCW 9A.04.050 speaks to the capability of children to commit crimes and, in pertinent part, provides:

> Children under the age of eight years are incapable of committing crime. Children of eight and under twelve years of age are presumed to be incapable of committing crime, but this presumption may be removed by proof that they have sufficient capacity to understand the act or neglect, and to know that it was wrong.

This statute applies in juvenile proceedings.

Because K.R.L. was 8 years old at the time he is alleged to have committed residential burglary, he was presumed incapable of committing that offense. The burden was, therefore, on the State to overcome that presumption and that burden could only be removed by evidence that was "clear and convincing." Thus, on review we must determine if there is evidence from which a rational trier of fact could find capacity by clear and convincing evidence. There are no reported cases in Washington dealing with the capacity of 8-year-old children to commit crimes. That is not too surprising in light of the fact that up to age 8, children are deemed incapable of committing crimes. Two cases involving older children are, however, instructional. In *State v. Q.D.* . . . our Supreme Court looked at a case involving a child who was charged with commit-

ting indecent liberties. In concluding that there was clear and convincing circumstantial evidence that the child understood the act of indecent liberties and knew it to be wrong, the court stressed the fact that the child was only 3 months shy of age 12, the age at which capacity is presumed to exist. The court also placed stock in the fact that the defendant used stealth in committing the offense as well as the fact that she had admonished the victim, a 4½-year-old child whom she had been babysitting, not to tell what happened.

In another case, *State v. S.P.,* 49 Wash.App. 45, 746 P.2d 813 (1987), rev'd on other grounds, 110 Wash.2d 886, 756 P.2d 1315 (1988), Division One of this court upheld a trial judge's finding that a child, S.P., had sufficient capacity to commit the crime of indecent liberties. In so ruling, the court noted that (1) S.P. was 10 years of age at the time of the alleged acts; (2) S.P. had had sexual contact with two younger boys during the prior year; (3) in treatment for the earlier incident, S.P. acknowledged that sexual behavior was wrong; (4) S.P. was aware that if convicted on the present charge, detention could result; and (5) experts concluded that S.P. had an extensive knowledge of sexual terms and understood the wrongfulness of his conduct toward the victims.

None of the factors that the courts highlighted in the two aforementioned cases is present here. Most notably, K.R.L. is considerably younger than either of the children in the other two cases. In addition, we know almost nothing about what occurred when K.R.L. went into Alder's home. Furthermore, there was no showing that he used "stealth" in entering Alder's home. We know only that he entered her home in daylight hours and that while he was there he committed the act. Neither was there any showing that K.R.L. had been previously treated for his behavior, as was the case in *State v. S.P.*

The State emphasizes the fact that K.R.L. appeared to appreciate that what he did at Alder's home and on prior occasions was wrong. When K.R.L. was being beaten "black and blue" by his mother, he undoubtedly came to the realization that what he had done was wrong. We are certain that this conditioned the child, after the fact, to know that what he did was wrong. That is a far different thing than one appreciating the quality of his or her acts at the time the act is being committed.

In arguing that it met its burden, the State placed great reliance on the fact that K.R.L. had exhibited bad conduct several months before during the so-called "Easter Candy" and "Joyriding" incidents. Again, we do not know much about these incidents, but it seems clear that neither of them involved serious misconduct and they shed little light on whether this child understood the elements of the act of burglary or knew that it was wrong. In *State v. Q.D.*, our Supreme Court emphasized that a capacity determination must be made in reference to the specific act charged. If the State shows no more than a general understanding of the justice system, the State does not meet its burden of showing an understanding of the act and knowledge that it was wrong. Indeed, the court indicated that an understanding of the wrongfulness of one crime does not alone establish capacity in regard to another crime.

Here, we have a child of very tender years—only two months over 8 years. While the State made a valiant effort to show prior bad acts on the part of the child, an objective observer would have to conclude that these were examples of behavior not uncommon to many young children. Furthermore, there was no expert testimony in this case from a psychologist or other expert who told the court anything about the ability of K.R.L. to know and appreciate the gravity of his conduct. Although two school officials testified, one of them said K.R.L. was of an age lower than 8, "academically." In short, there is simply not enough here so that we can say that in light of the State's significant burden, there is sufficient evidence to support a finding of capacity.

Reversed.

QUESTIONS FOR DISCUSSION

1. Was the trial judge or the supreme court of Washington right in the ruling on the capacity of K.R.L. to form criminal intent?

2. Back up your answer with facts from the case.

3. Did K.R.L. know what he was doing intellectually yet not sufficiently *appreciate* what he was doing?

4. What facts support this conclusion?

5. Should it matter whether he appreciated what he did so long as he knew what he did? Explain your answer.

Youth doesn't always either excuse criminal responsibility or mitigate punishment. Sometimes it makes the crime worse. For example, 17-year-old Miguel Muñoz was convicted of possessing a switchblade under a New York City ordinance that prohibited youths under twenty-one from carrying such knives. Had Muñoz been over twenty-one, what he did would not have been a crime. The Florida Court of Appeals examined the constitutionality of a Dade County, Florida, ordinance that made carrying "jumbo markers" a crime when juveniles carried them but not when adults did so in *D.P. v. State*.[28]

| C A S E | Can He Be Punished for Carrying a "Jumbo Marker"? |

D. P. v. State
705 So.2d 593 (Fla. App. 1998)

D.P. was adjudicated a delinquent by the Circuit Court, Dade County and he appealed. The District Court of Appeal affirmed.

    COPE, J.

FACTS

Dade County passed a comprehensive anti-graffiti ordinance, which forbids the sale to minors of spray paint cans and broadtipped markers ("jumbo markers"). A broad-tipped marker is an indelible felt tip marker having a writing surface of one-half inch or greater. . . . The ordinance does not prohibit the possession of ordinary-sized felt tip markers. The ordinance provides that minors can possess spray paint or jumbo markers on public property only if accompanied by a responsible adult. On private property, the minor must have the consent of the property owner, but need not be accompanied by an adult. It is a misdemeanor for a minor to possess spray paint or a jumbo marker without the required supervision or consent.

D.P. challenges the facial constitutionality of the provisions of the anti-graffiti ordinance that restrict minors' possession of spray paint or jumbo markers. We conclude that the ordinance is constitutional and affirm the adjudication of delinquency.

> The ordinance prohibits the sale of spray paint or broad-tipped markers to minors. See id. § 21-30.01(f)(1). The ordinance makes it a misdemeanor to possess spray paint or jumbo markers with intent to make graffiti.

The ordinance then sets forth special provisions pertaining to minors. Subdivision (e)(2) of the ordinance addresses possession of spray paint and jumbo markers by minors on public property, while subdivision (e)(3) addresses possession on private property: (e) Possession of Spray Paint and Markers . . .

> (2) Possession of spray paint and markers by minors on public property prohibited. No person under the age of eighteen (18) shall have in his or her possession any aerosol container or spray paint or broad-tipped indelible marker while on any public property, highway, street, alley or way except in the company of a supervising adult.
> (3) Possession of spray paint and markers by minors on private property prohibited without consent of owner. No person under the age of eighteen (18) shall have in his or her possession any aerosol container of spray paint or broad-tipped indelible marker while on any private property unless the owner, agent, or manager, or person in possession of the property knows of the minor's possession of the aerosol container or marker and has consented to the minor's possession while on his or her property.

A petition for delinquency was filed against D.P., alleging violations of subdivisions (e)(2) and (3). D.P. entered a plea of no contest, reserving the right to appeal the trial court order holding the ordinance constitutional.

OPINION

. . . D.P. suggests that it is impermissible to treat minors differently than adults. That suggestion is clearly incorrect. There are many activities that are legal for adults but prohibited to minors: drinking, and driving under legal age, being the most obvious examples. Some supervisory requirements apply to minors that do not apply to adults, such as compulsory school attendance and the curfew ordinance. See *Metropolitan Dade County v. Pred*, 665 So.2d 252, 253-54 (Fla. 3d DCA 1995), review denied, 676 So.2d 413 (Fla.1996) (curfew ordinance). . . .

No fundamental right is implicated in the possession of spray paint and jumbo markers. See *National Paint & Coatings Association v. City of Chicago*, 45 F.3d 1124 (1995) ("One could scan the most wild-eyed radical's list of candidates for the status of fundamental rights without encountering spray paint."). Nor is youth a suspect classification. *White Egret Condominium, Inc. v. Franklin,* 379 So.2d 346, 351 (Fla.1979) ("The law is now clear that restriction of individual rights on the basis of age need not pass the strict scrutiny test, and therefore age is not a suspect class."); *Metropolitan Dade County v. Pred,* 665 So.2d 252 (Fla. 3d DCA 1995)[, review denied, 676 So.2d 413 (Fla.1996)]. ("Under both the Florida and United States Constitution, children, due to their special nature and vulnerabilities, do not enjoy the same quantum or quality of rights as adults.").

The Court's review is therefore limited to the rational basis test. The rational basis test does not turn on whether this Court agrees or disagrees with the legislation at issue, and this Court will not attempt to impose on a duly-elected legislative body his reservations about the wisdom of the subject ordinance. Instead, the rational basis test focuses narrowly on whether a legislative body could rationally believe that the legislation could achieve a legitimate government end. The end of controlling the blight of graffiti is obviously legitimate and the Juvenile does not challenge this fact.

In addition, a legislative body could rationally conclude that the subject prohibition of possession by minors of spray paint and jumbo markers without supervision on public property or permission of the private-property owner would serve to control and limit incidences of graffiti. Indeed, the prohibition at issue is less restrictive than the prohibitions on spray paint and jumbo markers upheld in *National Paint*. The Court notes that juveniles can avoid the restrictions at issue by using markers less than one-half inch in [writing surface] or markers that contain water-soluble ink.

For the above reasons, the Court finds that the challenged graffiti ordinance does not offend the due process or equal protection provisions of either the Florida or Federal Constitutions. Accordingly, the Juvenile's Motion to Dismiss is denied. We concur with the trial court's ruling that the statute is constitutional.

Affirmed.

DISSENT

GREEN, J.

. . . The majority points out that it is not constitutionally impermissible to treat minors differently from adults. While that is certainly true, it is true only in some delineated areas. Our United States Supreme Court has recognized as a general proposition, that "a child, merely on account of his [or her] minority, is not beyond the protection of the Constitution." For example, in criminal juvenile proceedings, juveniles are afforded the constitutional safeguards of proof beyond a reasonable doubt, notice of the charges, right to counsel, rights of confrontation and examination and the privilege against self-incrimination. Notwithstanding these general principles, the constitutional rights of minors are still not co-equal with those of adults. The Court cited three reasons for not equating the constitutional rights of children with those of adults, namely, "the peculiar vulnerability of children; their inability to make critical decisions in an informed, mature manner; and the importance of the parental role in child rearing."

The central rationale for finding diminished constitutional rights of minors, in limited circumstances, appears to be for the personal protection of the child or the personal protection of others from the acts of minors. For example, in *T.M. v. State,* 689 So.2d 443 (Fla. 3d DCA 1997), we found section 790.22(9)(a), Florida Statutes, which mandates the imposition of a five-day detention period on any juvenile who commits any offense involving the use or possession of a firearm, to be

constitutional notwithstanding the fact that an adult who similarly commits any such offense is not subject to the same mandatory incarceration period. The statute in *T.M.,* unlike the graffiti subsections in this case, was attempting to regulate a minor's possession and/or use of an inherently dangerous item. In *Metropolitan Dade County v. Pred,* 665 So.2d 252, 253 (Fla. 3d DCA 1995), review denied, 676 So.2d 413 (Fla.1996), we similarly upheld the power of the county to impose a curfew for minors, for the personal well-being of minors. Likewise, the laws which prohibit minors from drinking and driving under the legal age limit are constitutionally permissible because they are for the purpose of protecting minors from inherently dangerous activities.

Thus, although the constitutional rights of minors are not co-equal with those of adults under certain circumstances, I must conclude that those factors which generally tend to support a reduction of the rights of minors are simply not present in this case. The purpose of the challenged subsections of the graffiti ordinance is wholly unrelated to the personal protection of minors or others. The county's sole aim is to protect property from graffiti artists. While that is certainly a legitimate and laudable objective, I do not believe that it can be pursued by the county at the expense and deprivation of fundamental due process rights which both adults and minors share. . . .

QUESTIONS FOR DISCUSSION

1. List the majority's arguments in favor of making age an aggravating circumstance under the graffiti ordinance.
2. List the dissent's arguments against making age an aggravating circumstance under the ordinance.
3. Review *Allam v. State* in the equal protection section of Chapter 2.
4. Assume you are the judge and write an opinion deciding whether the ordinance is constitutional.

NOTE CASE

A prosecutor was faced with the question whether the other end of the age spectrum, old age, should affect the capacity to commit crimes:

You have this married couple, married for over 50 years, living in a retirement home. The guy sends his wife out for bagels and while the wife can still get around she forgets and brings back onion rolls. Not a capital offense, right? Anyway, the guy goes berserk and he axes his wife; he kills the poor woman with a Boy Scout-type axe! What do we do now? Set a high bail? Prosecute? Get a conviction and send the fellow to prison? You tell me! We did nothing. The media dropped it quickly and, I hope, that's it.[29]

Do you agree? Explain your answer based on the discussion of age.

DURESS

Professor Hyman Gross admirably states the problem in the defense of **duress** (also called **compulsion**):

> Sometimes people are forced to do what they do. When what they are forced to do is wrong it seems that the compulsion ought to count in their favor. After all, we say, such a person wasn't free to do otherwise—he couldn't help himself, not really. No claim to avoid blame appeals more urgently to our moral intuitions, yet none presents more problems of detail. There are times, after all, when we ought to stand firm and run the risk of harm to ourselves instead of taking a way out that means harm to others. In such a situation we must expect to pay the price if we cause harm when we prefer ourselves, for then the harm is our fault even though we did not mean it and deeply regret it.[30]

Professor Gross's comments suggest three grounds for the defense of duress.

1. There is no *actus reus* because there is no voluntary act. This ground doesn't apply when people intentionally, recklessly, or negligently put themselves in a position where others can coerce them.

2. There is no *mens rea*. The criminal intent is really that of the person who forces, not of the person forced to act.

3. The defense is sound public policy. The criminal law can't force people to act against their self-interest. Faced with enough pressure, people will always act to save their own lives even if that requires hurting someone else.

The main argument against the defense of duress is that denying the excuse of duress encourages people to resist the pressure to commit crimes.

The grounds for and the argument against the excuse of duress explains a long-standing disagreement over whether and when to allow the defense. The nineteenth-century English jurist and historian of the criminal law, Sir James F. Stephen, took the extreme position that duress should never excuse criminal liability because "it is at the moment when temptation is strongest that the law should speak most clearly and emphatically to the contrary." But Stephen said that duress was a mitigating

ELEMENTS OF THE DEFENSE OF DURESS

Nature of the Threat	Timing of the Threat	Crimes Excused
Duress requires threats of death or great bodily harm	The threat must be of immediate or instant harm	Duress excuses 1. Minor crimes usually 2. Murder never

circumstance that allowed judges to reduce sentences. Professor Glanville Williams went to the other extreme, claiming that duress should always excuse, no matter what the crime or the threat, because the law can't affect people's choices when they're "in thrall to some power." Professor Jerome Hall took the middle ground, arguing that duress should excuse minor crimes committed under the threat of death.[31]

The defense of duress varies from state to state on the points made by the scholars just referred to. As for the crimes that qualify, some states say only minor crimes, others say all but murder. Some require threats to kill, as for example when a robber holds a gun to someone's head and says, "If you don't take her purse, I'll pull this trigger!" Other states accept threats of serious bodily harm: "If you don't steal that jacket, I'll break your kneecaps!" In all states, threats to property—"If you don't steal that stereo I'll smash your car"—don't count. Neither do threats to reputation, like "If you don't sell me some marijuana, I'll tell your boss you're gay." In some states, threats to harm others don't count either—"If you don't mug her, I'll kill your mother."[32]

The timing of the threat is also important, but the degree of immediacy required varies from state to state. In Minnesota, for example, only threats of "instant death" qualify. In most states an imminent threat is enough. The definition of immediate threat is not always clear. For example, in *Regina v. Hudson,* while they were outside the courtroom Hudson threatened to stab a woman if she didn't go into court and lie to give him an alibi. He sat in court while she committed the perjury. The trial court ruled that his threat wasn't immediate because he couldn't stab her at the very moment she was lying in court. The appellate court disagreed:

> In the present case the threats of Hudson were likely to be no less compelling because their execution could not be effected in the court room, if they could be carried out in the streets of Salford the same night.[33]

States also vary as to whether to measure threats objectively or subjectively. Some states accept proof of the honest belief of defendants; others demand proof of their reasonable belief *and* honest belief. A few states speak of actual compulsion. In *State v. Irons,* the Kansas Supreme Court applied the defense of duress in the setting where it often occurs, escape from custody.[34]

C A S E   Did He Escape under Duress?

State v. Irons
250 Kan. 302, 827 P.2d 722 (1992)

Brandon Irons, the defendant-appellant, was convicted before the District Court, Sedgwick County of aggravated escape from custody, and he appealed. The Court of Appeals affirmed, and defendant petitioned for review. The Supreme Court reversed and remanded.

HERD, J.

FACTS

In 1982, at the age of 19, Brandon N. Irons was convicted of burglary and felony theft in Butler County. He was sentenced to 2 to 10 years' imprisonment. He was sent to the Kansas State Industrial Reformatory (KSIR) in Hutchinson for 18 months and was then paroled. Irons eventually moved to Colorado with his wife and child. There, Irons worked with one of his brothers as a high-rise window washer. In 1988, he was stopped in Colorado for driving under the influence of alcohol. He became belligerent with the police and, as a consequence, his parole was revoked and he was sent back to Hutchinson. Irons was then sent to the Wichita Community Residential Center (CRC) in May 1989. CRC was a privately owned work release facility where inmates were transferred from KSIR and Lansing within a year of their release date. Formerly the old stockyards building, CRC housed between 150 and 200 inmates, primarily those convicted of felonies. There were only three or four security guards on duty around the clock. None of the dormitory rooms were locked and the inmates could move around within the building as they needed. The inmates were required to get jobs and were allowed to sign in and out of CRC in order to go to work. The facility was closed in August 1989.

On June 6, 1989, Irons gave an interview to television station KAKE regarding CRC. Although the interview lasted 20 minutes, the television station only showed a few seconds. During this interview, Irons stated he did not believe that CRC was "that bad of a program." The next day, the other inmates told Irons he had been stupid to give the interview, and they were very angry with him. No one physically threatened Irons that night, but their anger was such that he was frightened about returning to his dorm room which he shared with 10 other inmates. Instead, Irons slept hidden between a soda machine and a wall in another part of the facility. During the night some inmates urinated on Irons' bunk.

The next morning, Irons returned to his dormitory room. Other inmates questioned where he had been the night before and began accusing him of being a "snitch." They called him a woman and said any snitch could be turned into a woman. They told Irons they were going "to punk [him] out" and "dry heave" him. This was slang for sodomize. The inmates were in Irons' room, moving him toward the back door, when one said, "Why don't we just take you out and why don't we just bend you over." Another one slapped him on the ear. At this point, one of Irons' friends said a counselor was coming, causing the other inmates to back off. Irons then went down and stood by the security office until he signed out to go to work. While he waited at the bus stop, two inmates appeared and began chasing him. He ran to a 7-Eleven, where they stopped chasing him but told him they were going to kill him when he returned.

Irons was working at the cinema at Towne West Shopping Center. Once he arrived at work, Irons called Judge JAWORSKI in Butler County, who had sentenced him. Judge JAWORSKI said he could not do anything and suggested Irons call security at CRC. Irons then called CRC and talked to Officer Sharon Willits, the shift supervisor. He told

her he was having some problems and wanted to talk to the "top person." She advised Irons to come in and talk to CRC personnel. Irons told her if he came back the other inmates would get him, particularly if they saw him go to a guard. He had previously witnessed one inmate beat up two guards. Willits let Irons talk to Mark Ryan, CRC assistant administrator.

Irons told Ryan what had happened and that the other inmates were going to kill him. Ryan said he could move Irons to another room, but Irons replied they would still get him and did not feel he could safely come back to the facility. Ryan said he could have Irons transferred to Topeka in about a week. Irons again said he could not come back to CRC. Ryan told Irons he would call him later that evening at work. Irons waited until 5:00 or 6:00 p.m. and then called Ryan. Irons was told Ryan had left for the evening and had left no messages for Irons. Irons told CRC personnel he was not coming back and asked if he could have his return time extended from 6:00 a.m. until 9:00 a.m. It was extended until 7:00 a.m.

The following morning, June 9, 1989, Irons called Ryan at 7:00 a.m. at CRC, but Ryan was not there. Irons then called at 8:00 a.m., and Ryan was still not in. Irons called again at 10:00 or 10:30 a.m., and his counselor told him he was wanted for escape. Irons told her that Ryan was going to get him moved, but she replied Ryan was in a meeting and had said simply that Irons must return. Irons tried to explain his situation, but the counselor replied that she had no authority as to security. Irons told her he was not coming back, and he went to Texas, where he remained until he was taken into custody five months later.

Also on the morning of June 9, 1989, Officer Willits called Irons' workplace and found he was not there. She then notified the Wichita police department of Irons' escape. Irons was formally charged on June 13, 1989, with one count of aggravated escape from custody, K.S.A. 21-3810.

Prior to trial the State made a motion in limine [a motion made at the beginning of a jury trial that requests the court to issue an interlocutory order which prevents an opposing party from introducing or referring to potentially irrelevant, prejudicial, or otherwise inadmissible evidence] requesting the court not to admit evidence regarding Irons' motives for escaping, specifically the threats he had received from other inmates. During the hearing on the motion in limine, Irons proffered testimony regarding the threats made to him before his escape and his attempts to talk to Ryan. Irons argued this testimony supported his defense of compulsion. The trial court granted the State's motion in limine, finding the threats were not "imminent," and thus, as a matter of law the defense of compulsion was not available to Irons. Prior to presentation of the defense's case, the defendant unsuccessfully moved the court to reconsider the motion in limine. At that time, Irons also proffered testimony of Bradley Bates, a man who worked with defendant at the movie theatre, and to whom the defendant had relayed his fears.

Irons was convicted by a jury on May 30, 1990. He filed a motion for acquittal and a motion for new trial on June 5, 1990. The motion for new trial again raised the issues of the compulsion defense and the trial court's failure to give an instruction on compulsion. Both motions were denied and Irons was sentenced to one to five years' imprisonment, to run consecutively with the previous Butler County conviction. Irons' appeal followed.

OPINION

The first issue is whether the trial court abused its discretion by granting the State's motion in limine, thereby denying Irons a chance to present the defense of compulsion. Irons had planned to present evidence at trial to support his claim of the defense of compulsion. Compulsion is statutorily defined at K.S.A. 21 3209 as follows:

> "(1) A person is not guilty of a crime other than murder or voluntary manslaughter by reason of conduct which he performs under the compulsion or threat of the imminent infliction of death or great bodily harm, if he reasonably believes that death or great bodily harm will be inflicted upon him or upon his spouse, parent, child, brother or sister if he does not perform such conduct.
> "(2) The defense provided by this section is not available to one who willfully or wantonly places himself in a situation in which it is probable that he will be subjected to compulsion or threat."

The State, however, made a motion in limine requesting that any evidence of Irons' motives for leaving CRC not be admitted. . . . The State argued Irons was not in imminent fear of death or great bodily harm and, therefore, could not claim compulsion. . . . The trial court agreed with the State's analysis that once Irons got to work at Towne West

he was no longer in imminent danger. Thus, the trial court found as a matter of law the proffered testimony did not constitute facts which would satisfy the requirements of the defense of compulsion and granted the State's motion in limine. Therefore, at trial Irons, Willits, Ryan, and Bates were not allowed to testify to any threats toward Irons made by other inmates nor to any phone calls Irons had made to CRC on June 8 and 9.

On appeal, the Court of Appeals applied the rules of law pertaining to the compulsion defense stated in *State v. Pichon*, 15 Kan.App.2d 527, 811 P.2d 517, rev. denied 249 Kan.—(June 27, 1991), which also dealt with a defendant charged with aggravated escape from custody. . . . In *Pichon*, the Court of Appeals [stated] . . . the conditions that must exist before a prison escapee can claim the defense of compulsion. . . . The conditions are:

> (1) The prisoner is faced with a threat of imminent infliction of death or great bodily harm;
> (2) there is no time for a complaint to the authorities or there exists a history of futile complaints which makes any result from such complaints illusory;
> (3) there is no time or opportunity to resort to the courts;
> (4) there is no evidence of force or violence used towards prison personnel or other "innocent" persons in the escape; and
> (5) the prisoner immediately reports to the proper authorities when he has attained a position of safety from the immediate threat.

When considering Irons' appeal, the Court of Appeals further explained:

> This court held that all of the five conditions must exist before the defense is available. Other courts have held that the existence of all five is not required before the defendant may present the defense. Those courts held that the existence or nonexistence of the factors goes only to the weight and credibility of the defendant's evidence of duress or necessity."

Relying upon *State v. Hundley*, 236 Kan. 461, 693 P.2d 475 (1985), the Court of Appeals discussed at length the difference between "immediate" and "imminent." *Hundley* was a murder case involving the battered woman syndrome in which the defendant argued the defense of self-defense. On appeal, the defendant contended the self-defense instruction used was reversible error because it stated the defendant must reasonably believe she is faced with "immediate use of unlawful force" rather than the "imminent use of unlawful force" as stated in the statute. This court stated:

> Thus, the question is whether the instruction allows the jury to consider "all the evidence" or whether the use of the word "immediate" rather than "imminent" precludes the jury's consideration of the prior abuse. "Immediate" is defined in *Webster's Third New International Dictionary* (1961): "Occurring, acting or accomplished without loss of time." "Imminent" is defined as: "Ready to take place . . . or impending." Therefore, the time limitations in the use of the word "immediate" are much stricter than those with the use of the word "imminent."

The Court of Appeals acknowledged the inmates had threatened Irons immediately before he left CRC. But . . . the threats were not for some indefinite time in the future. Therefore, the Court of Appeals concluded Irons was in imminent threat of death or great bodily harm and "the trial court erred by refusing the testimony for this reason."

The Court of Appeals went on to determine whether Irons was able to meet the other four conditions required by *Pichon*. It found Irons could meet the second requirement of making complaints to the authorities or showing there exists a history of futility when complaints are registered, the third requirement that there is no time or opportunity to resort to the courts, and the fourth requirement that there is no evidence of force or violence used in the escape. The Court of Appeals, however, found Irons could not meet the fifth requirement of immediately reporting to the proper authorities once he reached safety. Thus, the Court of Appeals affirmed the trial court on this issue because the trial court reached the right result for the wrong reason.

Judge DAVIS dissented, stating he believed "all conditions of *Pichon* have been satisfied." Judge DAVIS further stated:

> Whether it was a viable defense depends upon the jury's determination of the evidence at trial. To say under the facts of this case that the defense of compulsion is not available is to deny the defendant a fair trial by preventing him from presenting to the jury the only theory of defense he had.
>
> I believe *Pichon* to be good law but I read it more restrictively than the majority. In my opinion, it is not enough to say that, since the defen-

dant did not immediately report to the proper authorities when reaching Texas, he forfeits his defense of compulsion. This is especially true under the facts of this case where the defendant sought to report the danger he perceived. The authorities offered a solution that not only failed to alleviate the danger but virtually guaranteed that the threat he perceived would be carried out if he returned. I believe that, in this case, the last requirement of *Pichon* was met by the defendant when, safe at his place of employment and before returning to the facility, he reported to the proper authorities.

. . . We agree with Judge DAVIS. The trial court and the Court of Appeals assumed Irons did not escape until he reached Texas, even though Irons repeatedly told authorities he would not return to CRC. Viewing the evidence in the light most favorable to the defendant, Irons reported the threats to the authorities, who offered him no viable alternative, forcing him to fail to return. Moreover, motions in limine are not to be used to "choke off a valid defense in a criminal action." Irons' escape occurred when he did not return to CRC by 7:00 a.m. He made every effort to report to Ryan at that time and previously. Thus, he met the requirements of all the conditions entitling him to the defense of compulsion.

We find the trial court abused its discretion in granting the State's motion in limine. Irons proffered evidence which would satisfy each of the five requirements of *Pichon,* and his defense of compulsion should have been presented to the jury with appropriate instructions. We adopt the conditions set out in *Pichon* with one modification. Condition (5) should contain the phrase "imminent threat," rather than "immediate threat," to conform to K.S.A. 21-3209.

The judgments of the Court of Appeals and the district court are reversed, and the case is remanded for new trial.

QUESTIONS FOR DISCUSSION

1. List the elements in the Kansas statute's duress defense.
2. List all of the facts relevant to those elements.
3. Can you distinguish between "imminent" and "immediate"? How would you do it?
4. Do you believe that Irons's escape should be excused by duress? Defend your answer.

MISTAKE

Everybody knows that "ignorance of the law is no excuse." What most people don't know is that ignorance of *fact* can be an excuse. For example, if I take from a restaurant coatroom a coat that I honestly and reasonably believe is mine, I haven't stolen the coat because I don't have the requisite intent, namely the intent to deprive the owner of his property (Chapter 12). So, if I took the coat because it's where I left mine an hour ago, it's the same color and size as mine, and no other coat hanging there looks like it, I've honestly and reasonably mistaken the coat for mine.

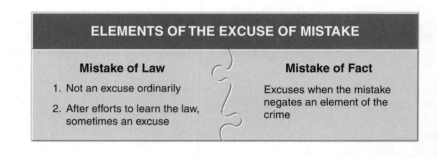

ELEMENTS OF THE EXCUSE OF MISTAKE

Mistake of Law

1. Not an excuse ordinarily

2. After efforts to learn the law, sometimes an excuse

Mistake of Fact

Excuses when the mistake negates an element of the crime

Mistake of law doesn't excuse criminal responsibility. Why? Three reasons:

1. We can't let individuals define crimes for themselves.
2. Punishing ignorance encourages people to know the law.
3. Almost anyone could escape punishment because as a practical matter, most people don't know the details of criminal statutes and court decisions interpreting them.[35]

This is how U.S. Supreme Court justice and legal philosopher Oliver Wendell Holmes summed up the reasons why ignorance of the law is not a defense:

> The true explanation of the rule is the same as that which accounts for the law's indifference to a man's particular temperament, faculties, and so forth. Public policy sacrifices the individual to the general good. It is desirable that the burden of all should be equal, but it is still more desirable to put an end to robbery and murder. It is no doubt true that there are many cases in which the criminal could not have known that he was breaking the law, but to admit the excuse at all would be to encourage ignorance where the law-maker has determined to make men know and obey, and justice to the individual is rightly outweighed by the larger interests on the other side of the scales.[36]

ENTRAPMENT

Ancient tyrants and modern dictators have relied on secret agents as a law enforcement tool. From the days of Henry VIII to the era of Hitler and Stalin, to Saddam Hussein and Slobodon Milosevic in our own time, the world's police states have relied on entrapment to catch and then crush their opponents. But inducement isn't only a tool of dictators. All societies rely on it even though it violates a basic purpose of government in free societies. The great Victorian British Prime Minister William Gladstone admonished government to make it easy to do right and difficult to do wrong. Inducement to criminality also flies in the face of the entreaty of the Lord's Prayer to "lead us not into temptation, but deliver us from evil."[37]

For a long time United States courts rejected the idea that **entrapment** (government agents getting people to commit crimes they wouldn't otherwise commit) excused criminal liability. In 1864, the New York Supreme Court explained why:

> Even if inducements to commit crime could be assumed to exist in this case, the allegation of the defendant would be but the repetition of the pleas as ancient as the world, and first interposed in Paradise: "The serpent beguiled me and I did eat." That defense was overruled by the great Lawgiver, and whatever estimate we may form, or whatever judgment pass upon the character or conduct of the tempter, this plea has never since availed to shield crime or give indemnity to the culprit, and it is safe to say that under any code of civilized, not to say Christian ethics, it never will.[38]

In 1904, another court summed up the acceptance of entrapment this way:

> We are asked to protect the defendant, not because he is innocent, but because a zealous public officer exceeded his powers and held out a bait. The courts do not look to see who held out the bait, but to see who took it.[39]

The earlier attitude was based on indifference to government encouragement to commit crimes. After all, "once the crime is committed, why should it matter what particular incentives were involved and who offered them?" Attitudes have shifted from indifference to both a "limited sympathy" toward entrapped defendants and a growing intolerance of government inducements to entrap otherwise law-abiding people.[40]

The present law of entrapment balances criminal predisposition and law enforcement practices. In other words, it aims to catch habitual criminals but not at the expense of punishing law-abiding people. The entrapment defense arose because of the difficulty in enforcing consensual crimes like drug offenses, pornography, official wrongdoing, and prostitution.

Law enforcement encouragement occurs when law enforcement officers:

1. Pretend they are victims.
2. Intend to entice suspects to commit crimes.
3. Communicate the enticement to suspects.
4. Influence the decision to commit crimes.[41]

The idea of encouragement is to make sure that officers are there to get evidence first-hand to convict consensual crimes. It's usually not enough for officers to provide an opportunity to commit crimes, or even to ask their targets to commit crimes. They have to actively encourage their targets because most people who are about to commit crimes are wary of strangers. Active encouragement includes such tactics as

- Making repeated requests to commit a crime.
- Forming personal relationships with suspects.
- Appealing to personal considerations.
- Promising benefits from committing the crime.
- Supplying contraband.
- Helping to obtain contraband.[42]

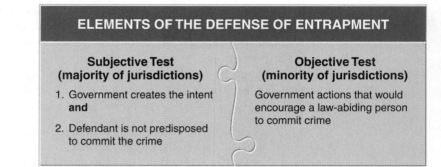

Encouragement turns into entrapment when it crosses the line from acceptable to *un*acceptable encouragement. Entrapment is a defense to crime; it is not a constitutional right. The U.S. Supreme Court has held that Congress didn't intend to let law enforcement officers lure innocent people into committing crimes. In most states entrapment is an affirmative defense, meaning that defendants have to show some evidence that they were entrapped. If they do this, the burden shifts to the prosecution to prove that defendants were not entrapped. The jury—or the judge in trials without juries—decides whether officers in fact entrapped defendants.

The majority of state and all federal courts have adopted a **subjective test of entrapment**. The subjective test focuses on the predisposition of defendants to commit crimes. According to this view, only defendants who acted under the following conditions could claim the defense of entrapment:

1. Initially, defendants had no desire to commit crimes.

2. The government induced defendants into criminality.

The crucial question in the subjective test is, Where did criminal intent originate? If it originated with the defendant, then the government didn't entrap the defendant. If it originated with the government, then the government did entrap the defendant. For example, in the leading case of *Sherman v. United States,* Kalchinian, a government informant and undercover agent, met Sherman in a drug treatment center. He struck up a friendship with Sherman and eventually asked Sherman to get him some heroin. Sherman, an addict, first refused. Following weeks of persistent begging and pleading, Sherman finally gave in and got Kalchinian some heroin. The police promptly arrested Sherman. The U.S. Supreme Court found that the intent originated with the government. According to the Court, Sherman was hardly predisposed to commit a drug offense since he was seriously committed to a drug treatment program to cure his addiction.[43]

Defendants have to present some evidence that a government agent persuaded them to commit a crime. If they do, then the government has to prove that defendants were predisposed to commit the crime. The government can do this by proving one of the following:

1. Defendants' prior convictions for similar offenses, or

2. Defendants' willingness to commit similar offenses, or

3. Defendants' display of criminal expertise in carrying out the offense, or

4. Defendants' readiness to commit the crime.

As the list indicates, proving predisposition can depend on either the character of defendants or their past and present conduct. The Minnesota Court of Appeals applied the subjective test of entrapment to the facts of *State v. Johnson.*

CASE | Was He Predisposed to Sell the Marijuana?

State v. Johnson
511 N.W.2d 753 (Minn. App. 1994)

Mark Johnson was convicted in the District Court, Douglas County, of various drug offenses, and he appealed. The Minnesota Court of Appeals reversed.

DAVIES, J.

FACTS

After Mark Hagberg was arrested and charged with driving while intoxicated, authorities agreed to drop the charges if Hagberg participated in a "reverse sting" operation by setting up a certain quota of drug deals. Pursuant to this arrangement, Hagberg called appellant Mark Steven Johnson in April 1991 shortly after Johnson returned to Minnesota from Alaska. Hagberg thought Johnson might be interested in buying marijuana because they had been involved in some marijuana transactions in the early 1970s. Hagberg asked Johnson whether he wanted to buy any marijuana. Johnson testified that he simply told Hagberg that he was not interested, that he had no desire to buy any marijuana. Hagberg agreed that Johnson did not indicate any interest in buying any drugs at that time, but testified that Johnson nonetheless went so far as to inquire about the price and quantity.

A recording established that when Hagberg called back later, Johnson again indicated that he did not want any marijuana for himself, but that he would check to see if anyone else was interested. Johnson testified that Hagberg at some time offered a two-for-one (or half-price) deal. Hagberg initially denied making any two-for-one offers, but conceded that, if Johnson had believed the street (or resale) value for a pound was $2,500, then Hagberg's price of $1,200 would have been like getting two for one. But when the defense recalled Hagberg, he testified that he had in fact told Johnson that the price was like getting two for one. Then, on re-redirect, Hagberg maintained that a reasonable price at the time for the transaction he proposed was in fact anywhere from $1,000 to $1,500 per pound.

After several more calls and a meeting with undercover agents, Johnson assented to a transaction.

Claiming to be acting only as a conduit, Johnson gave Hagberg $1,200 and instructed him to put the marijuana in the trunk of a car owned by and registered to someone else. The police placed the marijuana in the car trunk, retrieving it later.

Johnson was arrested and charged with an attempt to commit a controlled substance crime in the fifth degree in violation of Minn.Stat. §§ 152.025, subds. 2(1), 3(a), and 609.17, subds. 1, 4(2) (1990), and conspiracy to commit a controlled substance crime in the fifth degree in violation of Minn.Stat. §§ 152.025, subds. 2(1), 3(a), and 152.096, subd. 2 (1990).

Johnson agreed to have the issue of entrapment decided by the court. The trial court denied the entrapment defense, concluding that the authorities did not induce the crime and that the state knew of Johnson's "prior criminal activity and reputation for dealing in marijuana before any attempt was made to contact defendant." A jury subsequently found Johnson guilty as charged.

OPINION

Minnesota adheres to the subjective approach to entrapment. Under the two-part subjective approach, a successful entrapment defense requires, first, that the defendant show that the government induced the crime, after which the government must fail to show beyond a reasonable doubt that the defendant was predisposed to commit the crime. Accordingly, an entrapment defense exists where the government has lured the accused into committing an offense which he otherwise would not have committed and had no intention of committing.

On the other hand, no matter how involved the government is in inducing the commission of a crime, the defense of entrapment [fails] if the government can prove beyond a reasonable doubt that the defendant was predisposed to commit the crime.

The defendant bears the burden of proving government inducement by a fair preponderance of the evidence. The government's action in inducing the crime must go beyond mere solicitation. Inducement requires "something in the nature of persuasion, badgering or pressure by the state." In the present case, Johnson has shown by a fair preponderance of the evidence that the government induced the crime. Not only did the government solicit the encounter by initiating the "reverse sting," it also continued to press its offer even after Johnson initially refused to buy any marijuana.

Once the defendant has adequately shown government inducement, the burden shifts to the government to show beyond a reasonable doubt that the defendant was predisposed to commit the crime. Predisposition may be established by: (1) the defendant's active solicitation to commit the crime; (2) defendant's prior criminal convictions; (3) defendant's prior criminal activity not resulting in a conviction; (4) defendant's criminal reputation, or (5) any other adequate means. A defendant's ready response to the government's solicitation of the crime satisfies the "other adequate means" basis for predisposition.

Here, the state claims it established predisposition beyond a reasonable doubt by Johnson's prior criminal activity. We disagree. A predisposition to engage in drug trafficking at the time of solicitation—the only relevant time—cannot be established by showing involvement in drugs some 20 years earlier. Otherwise, anyone ever involved with drugs would—for entrapment purposes—be forever "predisposed" to sell drugs.

Furthermore, the United States Supreme Court recently clarified that the state must prove the defendant was predisposed "prior to first being approached by government agents." *Jacobson v. United States,* 503 U.S. 540, —, 112 S.Ct. 1535, 1540, 118 L.Ed.2d 174 (1992) When the Government's quest for convictions leads to the apprehension of an otherwise law-abiding citizen who, if left to his own devices, likely would have never run afoul of the law, the courts should intervene.

Here, Johnson refused to buy any marijuana when first solicited by Hagberg in April 1991. Johnson testified that he had no desire to buy marijuana because he had just returned to Minnesota from Alaska and no longer knew anyone to sell it to. He also testified that he planned to stay in Minnesota only briefly, and he believed it would be foolish to attempt to transport marijuana back across the Canadian border. (A witness testified that Johnson did not sell marijuana during the approximately nine-year period he lived in Alaska.)

Furthermore, Johnson told Hagberg that the marijuana sale was not important to him because the marijuana was not for himself. Johnson testified that he proceeded with the deal only to accommo-

date a friend, and that his friend supplied the money used to purchase the marijuana. This point is only relevant to the fact that Johnson was not predisposed to commit the crime prior to the government inducement. We, of course, do not suggest that participating in criminal activity to accommodate a friend creates a license to violate the law.

The prosecution failed to show that Johnson would have purchased marijuana absent Hagberg's inducements. Accordingly, the state failed to establish beyond a reasonable doubt that Johnson was predisposed to commit the crime prior to the government's solicitation as a matter of law. There was entrapment.

Reversed.

QUESTIONS FOR DISCUSSION

1. State the subjective test or entrapment as the Minnesota court defines it.

2. List all of the facts that show that the state encouraged Johnson to sell the marijuana.

3. Identify the four factors that the state can prove to show predisposition.

4. Do you agree with the court that the state didn't prove predisposition beyond a reasonable doubt? Back up your answer with specific facts from the case.

NOTE CASES

1. A man on trial in federal court for distributing cocaine claimed that he was entrapped by an old high school friend, who, unknown to the defendant, was a government informant. The informant repeatedly asked the defendant to get him some cocaine. The man finally agreed. The government offered proof that the man, now twenty-five, had been convicted of distributing a small amount of cocaine when he was nineteen, that he was able to obtain a quarter ounce of cocaine quickly and with no difficulty, and that when he transferred the cocaine to the informant he was cool, smooth, relaxed, and confident. The jury rejected the entrapment defense and convicted the defendant.

2. An undercover agent for the FBI, with the knowledge of other federal agents, developed a sexual relationship with a target. After de-

veloping the relationship, she asked the target to sell drugs to some "friends" who, unknown to the target, were also FBI agents. The Ninth Circuit Court of Appeals said that it saw "no principled way to identify a fixed point along the continuum from casual physical contact to intense physical bonding beyond which the relationship becomes 'shocking' when entertained by an informant." The court rejected the due process claim.[44]

3. Narcotics agents offered a five-year-old child $5 to tell where her mommy hid her heroin. The court rejected the due process claim.[45]

4. Defendant's friend and former brother-in-law, an informer, persuaded defendant over a period of time to go in on a drug deal. The informer claimed that he desperately needed money to care for himself and his family. The court denied the defense of entrapment.[46]

5. An undercover agent told defendant that he worked for a dentist whose son was an addict. Because of a change in the law, the dentist could no longer write prescriptions for narcotics to supply his son. The officer said his boss needed to get good heroin off the street because the son "was in pretty bad shape [and they] didn't think he would live very long." After twenty requests, defendant purchased narcotics and resold them to the undercover agent without a profit. A majority of the court upheld the conviction.[47]

6. Which of the following police activities violate due process?
   a. Agents arrange for sales of drugs to other agents.
   b. They assist in illegally importing drugs.
   c. They threaten buyers in their role as drug dealers.
   d. They assist the manufacture of illegal drugs.

Answer: None, according to various lower federal courts.

Consensual crimes, especially drug offenses, are the usual target of law enforcement inducement tactics. But a few local police departments have also used it to combat street mugging. The Nevada Supreme Court dealt with two street mugging decoy cases operating in an area of Las Vegas with a high population of "street people."

C A S E   Were They Entrapped?

Oliver v. State
101 Nev. 308, 703 P.2d 869 (1985)

Ernest Oliver was convicted of larceny from the person in the Eighth Judicial District Court and sentenced to 10 years in prison. He appealed. The Supreme Court reversed.
   GUNDERSON, J.

FACTS

On the night of Oliver's arrest, three policemen undertook to conduct a "decoy operation" near the intersection of Main and Ogden in Las Vegas. That corner is in a downtown area frequented by substantial numbers of persons commonly characterized as "street people," "vagrants," and "derelicts." It appears Oliver, a black man, is one of these.

Disguised as a vagrant in an old Marine Corps jacket, the decoy officer slumped against a palm tree, pretending to be intoxicated and asleep. His associates concealed themselves nearby. The decoy prominently displayed a ten-dollar bill, positioning it to protrude from the left breast pocket of his jacket. This was done, the decoy later testified, "to provide an opportunity for a dishonest person to prove himself."

Oliver, who had the misfortune to come walking down the street, saw the decoy and evidently felt moved to assist him. Shaking and nudging the decoy with his foot, Oliver attempted to warn the decoy that the police would arrest him if he did not move on. The decoy did not respond, and Oliver stepped away. Up to this point, Oliver had shown no pre-disposition whatever to commit any criminal act.

Then, Oliver saw the ten-dollar bill protruding from the decoy's pocket. He reached down and took it. "Thanks, home boy," he said. Thereupon, he was arrested by the decoy and the two other officers. Following the trial, a jury convicted Oliver of larceny from the person, and he has been sentenced to ten years imprisonment. This appeal followed.

OPINION

Oliver's counsel contends he was entrapped into committing the offense in question. We agree. . . . Government agents or officers may not employ extraordinary temptations or inducements. They may not manufacture crime. We have repeatedly endorsed the following concept:

> Entrapment is the seduction or improper inducement to commit a crime for the purpose of instituting a criminal prosecution, but if a person in good faith and for the purpose of detecting or discovering a crime or offense, furnishes the opportunity for the commission thereof by one who has the requisite criminal intent, it is not entrapment.

Thus, because we discern several facts which we believe combined to create an extraordinary temptation, which was inappropriate to apprehending merely those bent on criminal activity, we feel constrained to reverse Oliver's conviction. We note, first of all, that the decoy portrayed himself as completely susceptible and vulnerable. He did not respond when Oliver attempted to wake him, urging him to avoid arrest by moving to another location. Moreover, the decoy displayed his ten dollar-bill in a manner calculated to tempt any needy person in the area, whether immediately disposed to crime or not. In the case of Oliver, the police succeeded in tempting a man who apparently did not approach the decoy with larceny in mind, but rather to help him. Even after being lured into petty theft by the decoy's open display of currency and apparent helplessness, Oliver did not go on to search the decoy's pockets or to remove his wallet.

On this record, then, we think the activities of the officers, however well intentioned, accomplished an impermissible entrapment. The Florida court's comments in *State v. Holliday*, 431 So.2d 309 (Fla.Dist.Ct.App.1983) . . . are noteworthy:

> There is no evidence of any prior conduct of the defendant that would have shown predisposition. There is no evidence that he was engaging in criminal activity before he took the money from the decoy. [Citations omitted.] No ready acquiescence is shown; on the contrary, the defendant's acts . . . demonstrate only that he succumbed to temptation. The record, as such, reveals that the decoy did not detect or discover, nor could he reasonably be intended to discover, the type of crime the police were attempting to prevent by the use of the decoy, i.e., robberies and purse snatchings. Indeed, lifting some money protruding from the pocket of a seemingly unconscious, drunken bum is just not sufficiently similar to either robbery or purse snatchings. Upon these facts, the decoy simply provided the opportunity to commit a crime to anyone who succumbed to the lure of the bait.

Similarly, in the instant case, through the state's own witnesses at trial, Oliver's counsel established a *prima facie* showing that Oliver's criminal act was instigated by the state. There was no countervailing evidence whatever. Accordingly, on this record, we must conclude as a matter of law that Oliver was entrapped, and we reverse his conviction.

C A S E | **Was He "Predisposed" to Steal?**

DePasquale v. State
104 Nev. 338, 757 P.2d 367 (1988)

Vincent DePasquale was convicted of larceny from person in the Eighth Judicial District Court, Clark County and sentenced to ten years in prison. He appealed and the Nevada Supreme Court affirmed.
YOUNG, J.

FACTS

Four officers on the LVMPD's S.C.A.T. Unit (Street Crime Attack Team) were performing a decoy operation near the intersection of Fremont Street and Casino Center Blvd. in Las Vegas on April 30, 1983, at 11:45 p.m. Officer Debbie Gautwier was the decoy, and Officers Shalhoob, Young, and Harkness were assigned to "back-up."

Officer Gautwier was dressed in plain clothes and was carrying a tan shoulder bag draped over her left shoulder. Within one of the side, zippered pockets of the bag, she had placed a $5 bill and $1 bill wrapped with a simulated $100 bill. The money, including the numbers of the simulated $100 bill, were exposed so as to be visible to persons near by; however, the zipper was pulled tight against the money so as to require a concentrated effort to remove it.

Officer Young, also in plain clothes, was standing approximately six to seven feet away from Officer Gautwier (the decoy), near the entrance of the Horseshoe Club, when Randall DeBelloy approached Officer Gautwier from behind and asked if he could borrow a pen. Officer Gautwier stated that she did not have a pen, and DeBelloy retreated eight to ten feet. Within a few seconds he approached a second time, asking for a piece of paper. Again the response was "no." During these approaches Officer Young observed DeBelloy reach around Officer Gautwier toward the exposed cash.

DeBelloy again retreated eight to ten feet from Officer Gautwier. He then motioned with his hand to two men who were another eight to ten feet away, and the trio huddled together for 15 to 30 seconds. As DeBelloy talked with the two men, he looked up and over in the direction of Officer Gautwier. Vincent DePasquale was one of the two men who joined DeBelloy in this huddle.

While this trio was conversing, Officer Gautwier had been waiting for the walk signal at the intersection. When the light changed, she crossed Fremont Street and proceeded southbound on the west sidewalk of Casino Center Blvd. DePasquale and DeBelloy followed her, 15 to 20 feet behind. After crossing the street, Officer Gautwier looked back briefly and saw DeBelloy following her. DePasquale was four to seven feet behind DeBelloy and to his right.

As they walked in this formation, DePasquale yelled out, "Wait lady, can I talk to you for a minute." As Officer Gautwier turned to her right in response—seeing DePasquale whom she identified in court—DeBelloy took a few quick steps to her left side, took the money with his right hand and ran. DeBelloy was arrested, with the marked money in his possession, by Officers Harkness and Shalhoob. DePasquale was arrested by Officers Gautwier and Young. Both were charged with larceny from the person and convicted by a jury.

OPINION

DePasquale argues that he was entrapped, that the district court erred in its instruction to the jury on the law of entrapment, that the evidence fails to support the verdict, and that the sentence of ten years is disproportionate and, therefore, cruel and unusual.

In *Shrader v. State,* 101 Nev. 499, 504, 706 P.2d 834, 837 (1985), we stated that "entrapment encompasses two elements: (1) an opportunity to commit a crime is presented by the state (2) to a person not predisposed to commit the act." Thus, this subjective approach focuses upon the defendant's predisposition to commit the crime.

In *Oliver v. State,* 101 Nev. 308, 703 P.2d 869 (1985), the decoy was disguised as an intoxicated or sleeping vagrant. His money was exposed temptingly from a pocket which was readily accessible. . . . The decoy was apparently helpless, intoxicated, and feigned unconsciousness with cash hanging from his pocket. It is this degree of vulnerability, exemplified . . . by the decoy's feigned lack of consciousness, which cloaks any suggestion of the defendant's predisposition. Furthermore, the entire scenario of the decoy operations was devoid of any relation to an identified crime pattern.

In contrast, in the present case, the cash, although exposed, was zipped tightly to the edge of a zippered pocket, not hanging temptingly from the pocket of an unconscious derelict. Admittedly, the money was exposed; however, that attraction alone fails to cast a pall over the defendant's predisposition. The exposed valuables (money) were presented in a realistic situation, an alert and well-dressed woman walking on the open sidewalks in the casino area. The fact that the money was exposed simply presented a generally identified social predator with a logical target. These facts suggest that DePasquale was predisposed to commit this crime. Furthermore, the fact that DePasquale had no contact with the decoy but rather succumbed to the apparent temptation of his co-defendant to systematically stalk their target, evidences his predisposition. . . .

Lastly, DePasquale complains that his sentence was disproportionate to the crime and, therefore, cruel and unusual punishment. In *Schmidt v. State,* 94 Nev. 665, 668, 584 P.2d 695, 697 (1978), we stated . . . a sentence is unconstitutional "if it is so disproportionate to the crime for which it is inflicted that it shocks the conscience and offends fundamental notions of human dignity. . . ." While the punishment authorized in Nevada is strict, it is not cruel and unusual. . . .

Accordingly, we affirm the judgment of conviction.

QUESTIONS FOR DISCUSSION

1. State the test for entrapment according to Nevada law.
2. What facts led the court to conclude that Oliver was entrapped but DePasquale wasn't?
3. Is the entrapment defense more appropriate in street muggings than in consensual crimes like *State v. Johnson*? Explain your answer.

A minority of courts follow an **objective test of entrapment**. The objective test of entrapment focuses not on the predisposition of defendants but instead on the actions that government agents take to induce individuals to commit crimes. According to the objective test, if the government engages in conduct that would tempt an "ordinarily law-abiding" person to commit the crime, the court should dismiss the case. This test is a prophylactic rule aimed to deter "unsavory police methods."[48]

SYNDROMES

Since the 1970s, a range of "syndromes" affecting mental states have led to novel defenses in criminal law. The most bizarre of these include the policeman's, love, fear, chronic brain, and holocaust syndromes. Law professor and famous defense attorney Alan Dershowitz has written a book about these novel defenses. Its title, *The Abuse Excuse and Other Cop-Outs, Sob Stories, and Evasions of Responsibility,* makes clear Dershowitz's opinion of these defenses. Dershowitz worries that these excuses are "quickly becoming a license to kill and maim." His is probably a needless worry because defendants rarely plead these excuses, and except for a few notorious cases picked up by television and the newspapers, defendants rarely succeed when they do plead syndromes and other "abuse excuses."[49]

When San Francisco city official Dan White was tried for killing his fellow official Harvey Milk and Mayor George Moscone, the defense introduced the junk food syndrome, popularly called the "Twinkie defense." White's lawyer argued that junk food diminished White's mental faculties. One psychiatrist testified as follows concerning White's frequent depressions:

> During these spells he'd become quite withdrawn, quite lethargic. He would retreat to his room. Wouldn't come to the door. Wouldn't answer the phone. And during these periods he found that he could not cope with people. Any confrontations would cause him to kind of become argumentative. Whenever he felt things were not going right he would abandon his usual program of exercise and good nutrition and start gorging himself on junk foods. Twinkies, Coca Cola.
>
> Mr. White had always been something of an athlete, priding himself on being physically fit. But when something would go wrong he'd hit the high sugar stuff. He'd hit the chocolate and the more he consumed the worse he'd feel, and he'd respond to his ever-growing depression by consuming even more junk food. The more junk food he consumed, the worse he'd feel. The worse he'd feel, the more he'd gorge himself.

The defense argued that these depressions, which junk food aggravated, sufficiently diminished White's capacity to reduce his responsibility. The jury returned a verdict of manslaughter, and White was sentenced to a relatively short prison term. After his release from prison, he committed suicide. No one has ventured to blame his suicide on junk food. During the White case, much public comment—most of it negative—was directed at this "Twinkie defense." Despite that derision, substantial evidence exists to suggest that white sugar does indeed diminish capacity. Whether or not it does so to sufficiently reduce responsibility is a highly controversial and far-from-settled question.[50]

Women have relied on the battered spouse syndrome to justify killing spouses in self-defense, even though the defendants were not in imminent danger (see Chapter 7). Occasionally, women have also used premenstrual syndrome (PMS) to excuse their crimes. In a New York case, Shirley Santos called the police, telling them, "My little girl is sick." The medical team in the hospital emergency room diagnosed the welts on the girl's legs and blood in her urine as the results of child abuse. The police arrested Santos, who explained, "I don't remember what happened. . . . I would never hurt my baby . . . I just got my period." At a preliminary hearing, Santos asserted PMS as a complete defense to assault and endangering the welfare of a child, both felonies. She admitted beating her child but argued that she had blacked out owing to PMS, hence she could not have formed the intent to assault or endanger her child's welfare. After lengthy plea bargaining, the prosecutor dropped the felony charges and Santos pleaded guilty to the misdemeanor of harassment. Santos received no sentence, not even probation or a fine, even though her daughter spent two weeks in the hospital from the injuries. The plea bargaining prevented a legal test of the PMS defense in this case. Nevertheless, the judge's leniency suggests that PMS affected the outcome informally.[51]

Three difficulties ordinarily stand in the way of proving the PMS defense:

1. Defendants have to prove that PMS is a disease; little medical research exists to prove that it is.
2. The defendant has to suffer from PMS; rarely do medical records document the condition.
3. The PMS has to cause the mental impairment that excuses the conduct; too much skepticism still surrounds PMS to expect ready acceptance that it excuses criminal conduct.[52]

The years since the Vietnam War have revealed that combat soldiers suffered more lasting and serious casualties than physical injury. The war took a heavy emotional and mental toll on the veterans. The effects have created what some call a "mental health crisis which has had a dramatic impact on the incidence of major crime." Medical research has established a complex relationship between the stress of the combat tour in guerilla type, as opposed to conventional, warfare and later antisocial conduct. At the same time, lawyers have begun to consider the effect the Vietnam vet syndrome has on criminal responsibility.

Occasionally, defendants have also sought to excuse their criminal liability by means of what might be called a cultural norms defense. This defense is based on the claim that criminal behavior in the United States is normal behavior in an immigrant's homeland. Therefore, although what they may have done is wrong, they aren't responsible for acting according to their cultural norms. The New York Court of Appeals dealt with a cultural norm defense in *People v. Aphaylath.*

C A S E   Was Laotian Culture an Excuse?

People v. Aphaylath
68 N.Y.2d 945, 502 N.E.2d 998, 510 N.Y.S.2d
83 (1986)

May Aphaylath was convicted of second-degree murder, and he appealed. The Supreme Court, Appellate Division, affirmed. Aphaylath appealed. The Court of Appeals reversed.

Per Curiam ["by the court," meaning a brief opinion not written by an individual justice]:

FACTS

Defendant, a Laotian refugee living in this country for approximately two years, was indicted and tried for the intentional murder of his Laotian wife of one month. At trial, defendant attempted to establish the affirmative defense of extreme emotional disturbance to mitigate the homicide (Penal Law § 125.25[1h][a] on the theory that the stresses resulting from his status of a refugee caused a significant mental trauma, affecting his mind for a substantial period of time, simmering in the unknowing subconscious and then inexplicably coming to the fore. (*People v. Patterson*, 39 N.Y.2d 288, 303, 383 N.Y.S.2d 573, 347 N.E.2d 898) Although the immediate cause for the defendant's loss of control was his jealousy over his wife's apparent preference for an ex-boyfriend, the defense argued that under Laotian culture the conduct of the victim wife in displaying affection for another man and receiving phone calls from an unattached man brought shame on defendant and his family sufficient to trigger defendant's loss of control.

OPINION

The defense was able to present some evidence of the Laotian culture through the cross-examination of two prosecution witnesses and through the testimony of defendant himself, although he was hampered by his illiteracy in both his native tongue and English. Defendant's ability to adequately establish his defense was impermissibly curtailed by the trial court's exclusion of the proffered testimony of two expert witnesses concerning the stress and disorientation encountered by Laotian refugees in attempting to assimilate into the American culture. It appears from the record before us that the sole basis on which the court excluded the expert testimony was because "neither one was going to be able to testify as to anything specifically relating to this defendant." It is unclear from this ruling whether the Trial Judge determined that she had no discretion to allow the testimony because the experts had no knowledge of this particular defendant or that she declined to exercise her discretion because of the experts' lack of knowledge of the defendant or his individual background and characteristics. Under either interpretation, however, the exclusion of this expert testimony as a matter of law was erroneous because the admissibility of expert testimony that is probative of a fact in issue does not depend on whether the witness has personal knowledge of a defendant or a defendant's particular characteristics. Whether or not such testimony is sufficiently relevant to have probative value is a determination to be made by the Trial Judge in the exercise of her sound discretion.

Accordingly, because the court's ruling was not predicated on the appropriate standard and the defendant may have been deprived of an opportunity to put before the jury information relevant to his defense, a new trial must be ordered.

QUESTIONS FOR DISCUSSION

1. Should defendants be allowed the "opportunity to put before the jury information" about cultural norms? Why or why not?

2. A variation of the cultural norms defense is what Alan Dershowitz calls the "urban survival syndrome." This excuse is that some neighborhoods are so dangerous as to require living by the motto, "Kill or be killed." In one Texas case, a lawyer used the defense. Although it did not produce a "not guilty" verdict, it nevertheless caused a hung jury. Should the conditions of your neighborhood excuse your criminal liability? Act as both prosecutor and defense attorney and argue your case.[53]

SUMMARY

The defenses of excuse are based on the idea that human frailty ought to lessen the harshness of the criminal law. So, even though what defendants did was wrong, there are circumstances that excuse their responsibility for the wrong. The best-known excuse is insanity, but there is a long list of others, including diminished capacity, intoxication, age, mistake, entrapment, and syndromes. In criminal law as in ordinary life, excuses are not popular. So, although the list of excuses is long, in practice most defendants fail when they try to escape criminal liability by pleading an excuse that absolves them of responsibility for their wrongdoing.

Most of the excuses, like the justifications, have the same practical effect—they free defendants. But not always. The major exception is insanity. Defendants who are found insane can be—and often are—locked in maximum security hospitals until they are sane. Many insane people spend more time confined to these hospitals (really prisons) than they would spend serving their sentences in prison. Some excuses, like diminished capacity, can reduce the degree of an offense, usually murder, from first-degree to second-degree. Others, like age, can aggravate an offense as well as mitigate it.

 Go to the Criminal Law 7e CD-ROM for Internet exercises.

REVIEW QUESTIONS

1. Distinguish between the defenses of justification and the defenses of excuse.

2. How does the defense of insanity differ from the other defenses?

3. Explain the extent to which the insanity defense is used and is successful, then describe the consequences of successful insanity pleas.

4. Identify the tests of insanity.

5. State the major elements of each of the tests of insanity.

6. Compare and contrast the tests of insanity as they relate to reason and will.

7. Explain different ways in which the burden of proof works in insanity cases.

8. Define diminished capacity. Under what conditions is it a defense to criminal liability? Explain the extent and limits of the defense.

9. Identify and briefly explain the possible effects of intoxication on criminal liability.

10. Explain the circumstances under which intoxication is, and is not, a defense.

11. Identify the two conflicting principles underlying the defense of voluntary intoxication.

12. Briefly describe the trend in the law regarding the conflicting principles underlying the defense of intoxication.

13. When is age an excuse for criminal liability, and why?

14. Explain why age can be an aggravating circumstance.

15. According to Professor Hyman Gross, what is the problem with the defense of duress?

16. List and briefly explain the differing resolutions to the five main issues in the defense of duress.

17. Identify and describe the three rationales for the defense of duress.

18. Explain when mistake is, and is not, a defense of excuse.

19. Define entrapment, then identify and explain the three main tests for determining when entrapment is a defense to criminal liability.

20. Explain the impact of various syndromes on the defenses of excuse in criminal law.

KEY TERMS

civil commitment—the government can invoke its power to lock up dangerous people by means of the noncriminal proceeding.

diminished capacity—mental capacity less than "normal" but more than "insane."

duress or **compulsion**—when people are forced to commit crimes that they do not want to do.

Durham rule, or **product test of insanity**—an insanity test to determine whether a crime was a product of mental disease or defect.

entrapment—government actions that induce individuals to commit crimes that they otherwise would not commit.

irrebuttable presumption—a conclusive assumption that requires a finding of a presumed fact once the fact is introduced into evidence.

irresistible impulse test—impairment of the will that makes it impossible to control the impulse to do wrong.

objective test of entrapment—focuses on the actions that government agents take to induce individuals to commit crimes.

M'Naghten rule, or **right-wrong test**—a defense pleading insanity due to mental disease or defect that impairs the capacity to distinguish right from wrong.

rebuttable presumption—an assumption of fact that can be overturned upon sufficient proof.

subjective test of entrapment—focuses on the predisposition of defendants to commit crimes.

substantial capacity test—insanity due to mental disease or defect impairing the substantial capacity either to appreciate the wrongfulness of conduct or to conform behavior to the law.

SUGGESTED READINGS

1. David G. Bromley and James T. Richardson, *The Brainwashing/Deprogramming Controversy: Sociological, Psychological, Legal, and Historical Perspectives* (New York: Edwin Mellen Press, 1983). Discusses brainwashing from a multidisciplinary perspective, covering many topics relevant to the defense of brainwashing.

2. Peter Meyer, *The Yale Murder* (New York: Empire Books, 1982). A compelling narrative relating the "fatal romance" of Yale student Richard Herrin and Bonnie Garland. Meyer gives a detailed account of the trial, the insanity plea, the jury deliberations, and the verdict. Written for the general reader, this is an excellent journalistic account revealing much about the insanity plea.

3. Joseph Livermore and Paul Meehl, "The Virtues of M'Naghten," *Minnesota Law Review* 51 (1967):800. A well-argued, articulate defense of the right-wrong test. Although intended for specialists, it is well worth the novice's efforts.

4. Mike Weiss, *Double Play: The San Francisco City Hall Killings* (Reading, Mass.: Addison-Wesley, 1984). A detailed account of former San Francisco city supervisor Dan White's shooting of Mayor George Moscone and fellow supervisor Harvey Milk in San Francisco City Hall, and of the trial that followed. Weiss gives an excellent description of the diminished capacity defense, which came to be called the Twinkie defense because it was based on the argument that White's excessive use of junk foods, particularly those containing white sugar, led to his erratic behavior.

NOTES

1. Rorie Sherman, "Insanity Defense: A New Challenge," *The National Law Journal*, March 28, 1994, 1, p. 24.

2. Mich. Stat. Ann. § 28.1059(1).

3. *M'Naghten's Case*, 8 Eng.Rep. 718 (1843).

4. Herbert M. Fingarette, *The Meaning of Criminal Insanity* (Berkeley: University of California, 1972), contains a full treatment of the subject. A good introduction is Abraham S. Goldstein, "Insanity," in *Encyclopedia of Crime and Justice*, ed. Sanford Kadish (New York: Free Press, 1983), pp. 735–742; American Law Institute, *Model Penal Code and Commentaries*, vol. 1, pt. I, pp. 174–176.

5. *People v. Schmidt*, 110 N.E. 945 (1915).

6. 214 F.2d 862 (D.C.Cir.1954).

7. 18 U.S.C.A. § 17 adopted the right-wrong test; *United States v. Brawner*, 471 F.2d 969 (D.C.Cir.1972) rejected the *Durham* rule for that circuit; adopted by Maine Rev. Stat. Ann. tit. 15, § 102 (1964), superseded by Maine Rev. Stat. Ann. tit. 17–A, § 58 adopting the substantial capacity test.

8. Joseph Livermore and Paul Meehl, "The Virtues of M'Naghten," *Minnesota Law Review* 51 (1967):800.

9. LaFave and Scott, *Criminal Law,* p. 283.

10. 2 So. 854 (Ala.1877).

11. "A Needed Verdict: Guilty but Insane," *New York Times* (July 1, 1982), p. 29.

12. See Slovenko, "The Insanity Defense in the Wake of the Hinckley Trial," *Rutgers Law Journal* 14 (1983):373.

13. 18 U.S.C.A. § 17.

14. Robert F. Schopp, "Returning to *M'Naghten* to Avoid Moral Mistakes: One Step Forward, or Two Steps Backward for the Insanity Defense?" *Arizona Law Review* 30 (1988):135.

15. *Model Penal Code,* § 4.01(1).

16. Federal Criminal Code and Rules (St. Paul, Minn.: West Publishing Co., 1988), § 17(b).

17. American Law Institute, *Model Penal Code and Commentaries,* vol. 2, pt. I, p. 226.

18. California Penal Code, § 25 (b); (c).

19. *People v. Colavecchio,* 11 A.D.2d 161, 202 N.Y.S.2d 119 (1960) (mental disease negatives the specific intent to take another's property).

20. Related in John Gibeaut, "Sobering Thoughts: Legislatures and courts increasingly are just saying no to intoxication as a defense or mitigating factor," *American Bar Association Journal,* May 1997, 56.

21. Fletcher, *Rethinking Criminal Law,* p. 846.

22. Blackstone, *Commentaries,* pt. IV, pp. 25–26.

23. Arizona Criminal Code §13.503 at http://www.azleg.state.az.us/ars/13/205.htm.

24. Gibeaut, "Sobering Thoughts," pp. 56–57.

25. *People v. Penman,* 271 Ill. 82, 110 N.E. 894 (1915) Hall, *General Principles of Criminal Law,* p. 540: *Burrows v. State,* 38 Ariz. 99, 297 P. 1029 (1931).

26. 214 N.W.2d 205 (Iowa 1974).

27. American Law Institute, *Model Penal Code and Commentaries,* vol. 1, pt. I, pp. 273–279.

28. *People v. Munoz,* 22 Misc.2d 1078, 200 N.Y.S.2d 957 (1960).

29. Taken from Fred Cohen, *Criminal Law Bulletin* 21 (1985):9.

30. Hyman Gross, *A Theory of Criminal Justice* (New York: Oxford University Press, 1978), p. 276.

31. Jerome Hall, *General Principles of Criminal Law,* 2d ed. (Indianapolis, Ind.: Bobbs-Merrill, 1960), pp. 437–444; Glanville Williams, *Criminal Law: The General Part,* 2d ed. rev. (London: Stevens and Sons, 1961), pp. 765–766; American Law Institute, *Model Penal Code and Commentaries,* vol. 1, pt. I, 372–373.

32. American Law Institute, *Model Penal Code and Commentaries,* vol. 1, pt. I, pp. 380–381.

33. *Regina v. Hudson,* 2 All E.R. 244 (1971).

34. American Law Institute, *Model Penal Code and Commentaries,* vol. 1, pt. I, pp. 368–380; Gross, *A Theory of Criminal Justice,* pp. 276–292; Wayne R. LaFave and Austin W. Scott, Jr., *Criminal Law* (St. Paul, Minn.: West Publishing Co., 1972), pp. 434–439; George Fletcher, *Rethinking Criminal Law* (Boston: Little, Brown and Co., 1978), pp. 429–435.

35. Rollin M. Perkins and Ronald N. Boyce, *Criminal Law,* 3d ed. (Mineola, N.Y.: Foundation Press, 1982), p. 1030.

36. Oliver Wendell Holmes, Jr., *The Common Law* (Boston: Little, Brown, and Company, 1963), p. 41.

37. Jonathan C. Carlson, "The Act Requirement and the Foundations of the Entrapment Defense," *Virginia Law Review* 73 (1987):1011.

38. *Board of Commissioners v. Backus,* 29 How. Pr. 33, 42 (1864).

39. *People v. Mills,* 178 N.Y. 274, 70 N.E. 786, 791 (1904).

40. Paul Marcus, "The Development of Entrapment Law," *Wayne Law Review* 33 (1986):5.

41. *United States v. Jenrette,* 744 F.2d 817 (D.C.Cir.1984) (one of the Abscam cases); "Gershman, Abscam, the Judiciary, and the Ethics of Entrapment," *Yale Law Journal* 91 (1982):1565 (history of Abscam); L. Tiffany and others, Detection of Crime (Boston: Little, Brown and Co., 1967) (quote defining encouragement).

42. Wayne R. LaFave and Jerold H. Israel, *Criminal Procedure* (St. Paul: West Publishing Co., 1984), 1:412–13.

43. 356 U.S. 369, 78 S.CT. 819, 2 L.ED.2d 848 (1958).

44. *United States v. Simpson,* 813 F.2d 1462 (9th Cir. 1987).

45. Noted in Ibid.

46. *United States vs. Struyf,* 701 F.2d 875 (11th Cir. 1983).

47. *People v. Toler,* 26 Ill.2d 100, 185 N.E.2d 874 (1962).

48. American Law Institute. *Model Penal Code and Commentaries* (Philadelphia: American Law Institute, 1985), Part I, 1:411-12, 406-7.

49. Alan Dershowitz, *The Abuse Excuse and Other Cop-Outs, Sob Stories, and Evasions of Responsibility* (Boston: Little, Brown and Company, 1994), p. 3.

50. Mike Weiss, *Double Play: The San Francisco City Hall Killings* (Reading, Mass.: Addison-Wesley, 1984), pp. 349–350.

51. "Not Guilty Because of PMS?" *Newsweek* (November 8, 1982):111.

52. Robert Mark Carney and Brian D. Williams, "Premenstrual Syndrome: A Criminal Defense," *Notre Dame Law Review* 59 (1983):263–269.

53. Dershowitz, *Abuse Excuse*, p. 73.

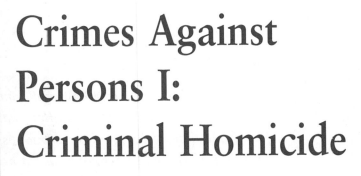

CHAPTER 9

Crimes Against Persons I: Criminal Homicide

Chapter Outline

I. Introduction

II. History of Criminal Homicide

III. Elements of Criminal Homicide

IV. Murder

V. Manslaughter

VI. Summary

CHAPTER MAIN POINTS

1. The law of criminal homicide involves the most complex grading in the criminal law.

2. The law of criminal homicide applies the general principles of *actus reus, mens rea,* and causing a particular result—the death of another person.

3. The *actus reus* of criminal homicide requires the killing of another live human being.

4. Definitions of "live human being" raise fundamental moral, legal, and policy issues in specifying both when life begins and when it ends.

5. Criminal homicide refines the general principle of *mens rea* to the highest degree in criminal law.

6. First-degree murders include premeditated, deliberate killings, especially brutal murders, and felony murders.

7. According to the modern law of homicide, premeditated killings don't require long-term planning; even a few seconds satisfies the requirement in most states.

8. Second-degree murder is a catchall category that includes all intentional criminal homicides that are neither voluntary nor first-degree murders.

9. Felony murder creates problems of determining both what felonies to include and of determining the relationship between the felony committed and the death of the person occurring during its commission.

10. Establishing *mens rea* and causation are major problems in applying murder statutes to corporations.

11. In most states, words are never adequate provocation to reduce murder to voluntary manslaughter.

12. Involuntary manslaughter is criminal homicide committed without the intent to kill or inflict serious bodily harm; it includes grossly reckless and grossly negligent homicides and, in some states, deaths that occur during the commission of illegal acts.

13. Some states have adopted special vehicular homicide statutes that require something less than gross criminal negligence and for which both the penalty and stigma are milder than for manslaughter.

Did He Murder His Wife?

Schnopps and his wife were having marital problems. Among the problems was that his wife was having an affair with a man at work. Schnopps found out about the affair. Mrs. Schnopps moved out of the house, taking their children with her. Schnopps asked his wife to come to their home and talk over their marital difficulties. Schnopps told his wife that he wanted his children at home, and that he wanted the family to remain intact. Schnopps cried during the conversation, and begged his wife to let the children live with him and to keep their family together. His wife replied, "No, I am going to court, you are going to give me all the furniture, you are going to have to get the Hell out of here, you won't have nothing." Then, pointing to her crotch, she said, "You will never touch this again, because I have got something bigger and better for it."

On hearing those words, Schnopps claims that his mind went blank, and that he went "berserk." He went to a cabinet and got out a pistol he had bought and loaded the day before, and he shot his wife and himself. Schnopps survived the shooting but his wife died.

INTRODUCTION

Crimes against persons include a number of offenses that deprive people of their lives, their liberty, and their privacy. Chapter 10 examines crimes committed by criminals who don't kill their victims. Here we examine crimes that do. Criminal homicide is unique. To be sure, crimes that don't kill people, crimes against homes and property, and crimes against public order and morals hurt their victims and society. However, these injuries are to worldly things. Causing death, on the other hand, deprives a person of life itself. According to the distinguished professor of criminal law, George P. Fletcher,

> Killing another human being is not only a worldly deprivation; in the Western conception of homicide, killing is an assault on the sacred, natural order. In the Biblical view, the person who slays another was thought to acquire control over the blood—the life force—of the victim. The only way that this life force could be returned to God, the origin of all life, was to execute the slayer himself. In this conception of crime and punishment, capital execution for homicide served to expiate the desecration of the natural order.[1]

Much of the law of homicide is devoted to answering questions like: Is this murder first- or second-degree? Is that killing murder or manslaughter? Is this manslaughter voluntary or involuntary? Students ask: "Does it really matter?" Certainly not to the victim—who's already and always dead! But it does make a big practical difference. The punishment for criminal homicide depends on the degrees of murder and types of manslaughter. These degrees and types are determined according to three elements:

1. *Mens rea* (Chapter 4)
2. *Actus reus* (Chapter 3)
3. Special circumstances

HISTORY OF CRIMINAL HOMICIDE

The law of criminal homicide took centuries to develop. In the beginning there was only one form of criminal homicide: all killings that were not justified or excused. Eventually, criminal homicide was divided into murder and manslaughter. This division depended entirely on *mens rea*. Murder was killing someone "with **malice aforethought**." "Malice" meant intentional killing without excuse or justification. "Aforethought" meant planning in advance to kill, what we now call **premeditated** killing. The typical examples were poisoning and lying in wait to kill. Manslaughter was killing in the sudden heat of passion when the victim provoked the passion.

As time went by, murder came to include not only premeditated killing but all intentional, "**deliberate**" killing, deliberate meaning not in the sudden heat of passion. Gradually added to the list of criminal homicides were some kinds of unintentional killing, like deaths during the commission of felonies, and extremely reckless and negligent killings (called "depraved-heart killing"). Last in this long history from its "malice aforethought" beginning, the judges ruled that the intent to inflict "serious bodily harm" was enough to satisfy the *mens rea* of criminal homicide.

So, in order to understand the modern law of criminal homicide we need to consider at least the following separate crimes:

1. First-degree murder
2. Second-degree murder
3. Voluntary manslaughter
4. Involuntary manslaughter

✳ 9-1 Criminal Homicide Statutes

ELEMENTS OF CRIMINAL HOMICIDE

Homicide—killing another live human being—began as a common-law crime, meaning that English and then American judges created it, not the legislatures of England or the United States. Now, as then, there were three types of common law homicide:

1. **Justifiable homicides**, such as killing in self-defense, capital punishment, and police use of deadly force (Chapter 7).
2. **Excusable homicides**, such as accidental killings and killing while insane (Chapter 8).
3. **Criminal homicides**, all homicides that are neither justified nor excused (this chapter).

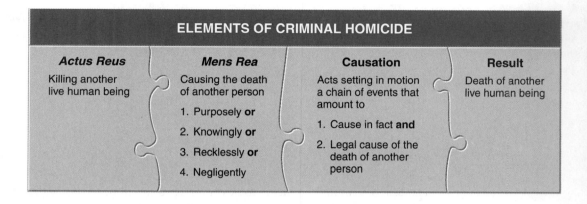

TAKING A LIFE

Criminal homicide requires taking the life of another live human being. What is "another live human being"? "Another" is easy enough to understand; it doesn't include suicide. "Live human being" is another story. The definition depends on how the law defines when life begins and ends. According to common law criminal homicide, life begins when babies are "born alive." But some states have pushed the definition of life back into the period before birth. Some statutes say that life begins at conception; others say that only "viable fetuses," such as those twenty-eight weeks past conception, are live human beings.[2]

When Does Life Begin?

Fetal death statutes (laws defining when life begins for purposes of the law of criminal homicide) have generated heated debate because they've gotten mixed up with the deep controversy over abortion. But fetal death statutes and definitions of abortion differ fundamentally. Abortion is the termination of pregnancy by a medical professional with the woman's consent. Fetal death statutes deal with killing a fetus without the woman's consent outside normal medical practice. Many who oppose making abortion a form of criminal homicide support fetal death statutes because of these differences. One more point: it would violate the Constitution to make it a crime to either perform or have a medically performed consensual abortion. In *Roe v. Wade,* the U.S. Supreme Court upheld the right of women to terminate their pregnancies under some conditions.[3]

In the end, the definition of when life begins for purposes of criminal homicide is a tough public policy question, too important to be left to lawyers and doctors. And that's as it should be. Public policy requires that legislators decide when life in its earliest—and latest—stages is valuable enough that taking it is the major felony of criminal homicide. No amount of medical knowledge or skill in the techniques of law can answer this question. One art student captured the dilemma in a poster. Under a drawing of a just-fertilized egg inside a happy, laughing fourteen-year-old girl is a caption that reads, "Which life is worth more?" Minnesota's fetal death statute didn't resolve this dilemma, as the opinion and dissents make clear in *State v. Merrill.*[4]

C A S E Did He Kill an "Unborn Child"?

State v. Merrill
450 N.W.2d 318 (Minn.1990)

Sean Patrick Merrill, the defendant, was indicted for the first- and second-degree murder of Gail Anderson and also for the first- and second-degree murder of her "unborn child." The trial court denied Merrill's motion to dismiss the charges. Merrill was ultimately convicted of second-degree intentional fetal homicide and sentenced to 29 years and 6 months in prison.

SIMONETT, J.

FACTS

On November 13, 1988, Gail Anderson died from gunshot wounds allegedly inflicted by Sean Patrick Merrill. An autopsy revealed Ms. Anderson was pregnant with a 27- or 28-day-old embryo. The coroner's office concluded that there was no abnormality which would have caused a miscarriage, and that death of the embryo resulted from the death of Ms. Anderson. At this stage of development, a 28-day-old embryo is 4- to 5-millimeters long and, through the umbilical cord, completely dependent on its mother. The Anderson embryo was not viable. Up to the eighth week of development, it appears that an "unborn child" is referred to as an embryo; thereafter it is called a fetus. The evidence indicates that medical science generally considers a fetus viable at 28 weeks following conception although some fetuses as young as 20 or 21 weeks have survived.

The record is unclear in this case whether either Ms. Anderson or defendant Merrill knew she was pregnant at the time she was assaulted. Defendant was indicted for the death of Anderson's "unborn child" under two statutes entitled, respectively, "Murder of an Unborn Child in the First Degree" and "Murder of an Unborn Child in the Second Degree."

These two statutes, enacted by the legislature in 1986, followed precisely the language of our murder statutes, except that "unborn child" is substituted for "human being" and "person." The term "unborn child" is defined as "the unborn offspring of a human being conceived, but not yet born." Minn.Stat. § 609.266(a) (1988).

[Footnote: "Minn.Stat. § 609.2661 (1988), provides in part: Whoever does any of the following is guilty of murder of an unborn child in the first degree and must be sentenced to imprisonment for life:
(1) causes the death of an unborn child with premeditation and with intent to effect the death of the unborn child or of another; . . .

Minn.Stat. § 609.2662 (1988), provides in part:

Whoever does either of the following is guilty of murder of an unborn child in the second degree and may be sentenced to imprisonment for not more than 40 years: (1) causes the death of an unborn child with intent to effect the death of that unborn child or another, but without premeditation; . . ."]

OPINION

This legislative approach to a fetal homicide statute is most unusual and raises the constitutional questions certified to us. Of the 17 states that have codified a crime of murder of an unborn, 13 create criminal liability only if the fetus is "viable" or "quick." Additionally, two noncode states have expanded their definition of common-law homicide to include viable fetuses [Massachusetts and South Carolina]. Arizona and Indiana impose criminal liability for causing the death of a fetus at any stage, as does Minnesota, but the statutory penalty provided upon conviction is far less severe. Ariz.Rev.Stat.Ann. § 13–1103(A)(5) (1989) (5-year sentence); Ind.Code Ann. § 35–42–1–6 (Burns 1985) (2-year sentence).

Before discussing the Minnesota statutes, three preliminary observations must be made. First, to challenge successfully the constitutional validity of a statute, the challenger bears the very heavy burden of demonstrating beyond a reasonable doubt that the statute is unconstitutional. Second, there are no common-law crimes in this state. Minnesota is a code state, i.e., the legislature has exclusive province to define by statute what acts constitute a crime. *State v. Soto,* 378 N.W.2d 625, 627 (Minn.1985). And, third, the role of the judiciary is limited to deciding whether a statute is constitutional, not whether it is wise or prudent legislation. We do not sit as legislators with a veto vote, but as judges deciding whether the legislation, presumably constitutional, is so.

Defendant first contends that the unborn child homicide statutes violate the Equal Protection Clause. Defendant premises his argument on *Roe v. Wade,* 410 U.S. 113, 93 S.Ct. 705, 35 L.Ed.2d 147 (1973), which, he says, holds that a nonviable fetus is not a person. He then argues that the unborn child criminal statutes have impermissibly "adopted a classification equating viable fetuses and nonviable embryos with a person.". . .

The state's interest in protecting the "potentiality of human life" includes protection of the unborn child, whether an embryo or a nonviable or viable fetus, and it protects, too, the woman's interest in her unborn child and her right to decide whether it shall be carried in utero. The interest of a criminal assailant in terminating a woman's pregnancy does not outweigh the woman's right to continue the pregnancy. In this context, the viability of the fetus is "simply immaterial" to an equal protection challenge to the feticide statute.

We conclude that sections 609.2661(1) and 609.2662(1) do not violate the Fourteenth Amendment by failing to distinguish between a viable and a nonviable fetus.

A more difficult issue, as the trial court noted, is whether the unborn child criminal statutes are so vague as to violate the Due Process Clause of the Fourteenth Amendment. Defendant claims the statutes are unconstitutionally vague because they fail to give fair warning of the prohibited conduct and because they encourage arbitrary and discriminatory enforcement. . . .

Defendant first contends that the statutes fail to give fair warning to a potential violator. Defendant argues it is unfair to impose on the murderer of a woman an additional penalty for murder of her unborn child when neither the assailant nor the pregnant woman may have been aware of the pregnancy. . . .

In this case, defendant seems to be arguing that an intent to kill the mother is not transferable to the fetus because the harm to the mother and the harm to the fetus are not the same. We think, however, the harm is substantially similar. The possibility that a female homicide victim of childbearing age may be pregnant is a possibility that an assaulter may not safely exclude. We conclude, however, that the statutes provide the requisite fair warning.

Defendant next contends that the unborn child criminal statutes are fatally vague because they do not define the phrase "causes the death of an unborn child." As a result, defendant argues, the statutes invite or permit arbitrary and discriminatory enforcement. Defendant argues that the statute leaves uncertain when "death" occurs, or, for that matter, when "life" begins. . . .

Some background is necessary to put the issue in its proper perspective. In 1985 this court, in *State v. Soto,* 378 N.W.2d 625 (Minn.1985), held that when the legislature referred to the death of a "human being" in the homicide statutes, the term "human being" was being used in its well-established common-law sense of a person born alive. Consequently, we held that the homicide statutes did not apply to the death of an 8-month-old fetus yet unborn. The legislature was free, of course, if it wished to do so, to create a crime to cover feticide. Traditionally, the crime of feticide imposed criminal liability for the death of a "viable" fetus, that is, a fetus at that stage of development which permits it to live outside the mother's womb, or a fetus that has "quickened," that is, which moves within the mother's womb.

Apparently in response to *Soto,* the legislature has enacted criminal statutes to cover feticide. In so doing, it has enacted very unusual statutes which go beyond traditional feticide, both in expanding the definition of a fetus and in the severity of the penalty imposed. The statutes in question impose the criminal penalty for murder on whoever causes the death of "the unborn offspring of a human being conceived, but not yet born." Whatever one might think of the wisdom of this legislation, and notwithstanding the difficulty of proof involved, we do not think it can be said the offense is vaguely defined. An embryo or nonviable fetus when it is within the mother's womb is "the unborn offspring of a human being."

Defendant argues, however, that to cause the death of an embryo, the embryo must first be living; if death is the termination of life, something which is not alive cannot experience death. In short, defendant argues that causing the death of a 27-day-old embryo raises the perplexing question of when "life" begins, as well as the question of when "death" occurs.

The difficulty with this argument, however, is that the statutes do not raise the issue of when life as a human person begins or ends. The state must prove only that the implanted embryo or the fetus in the mother's womb was living, that it had life, and that it has life no longer. To have life, as that term is commonly understood, means to have the property of all living things to grow, to become. It is not necessary to prove, nor does the statute require, that the living organism in the womb in its embryonic or fetal state be considered a person or a human being. People are free to differ or abstain on the profound philosophical and moral questions of whether an embryo is a human being, or on whether or at what stage the embryo or fetus is ensouled or acquires "personhood." These questions are entirely irrelevant to criminal liability under the statute. Criminal liability here requires only that the genetically human embryo be a living organism that is growing into a human being. Death occurs when the embryo is no longer living, when it ceases to have the properties of life.

Defendant wishes to argue that causing the death of a living embryo or nonviable fetus in the mother's womb should not be made a crime. This is an argument, however, that must be addressed to the legislature. Our role in the judicial branch is limited solely to whether the legislature has defined a crime within constitutional parameters. Indeed, in this case, our role is further limited to answering only the two specific questions certified to us for a ruling. We answer both questions no.

Certified questions answered.

DISSENT

KELLY, J.

. . . It cannot be gainsaid that few topics today compel as fierce public debate and evoke the passionate convictions of as many of our citizens as does the issue of when "life" in a fetus begins. In view of the stridency of that debate, it appears conceivable, perhaps even predictable, that two juries having the same evidence could arrive at the same factual conclusions, but due to divergent and strongly held beliefs arrived at a dissimilar legal result.

By way of example, in the case before us, one jury sharing a common viewpoint of when life commences could find the defendant guilty of fetal murder, whereas another whose members share the view that life was nonexistent in a 26- to 28-day-old embryo, could exonerate the appellant.

The likelihood of discriminatory enforcement is further enhanced when the discretionary charging function possessed by a grand jury is considered. The decision to charge must be concurred in by only a majority of the panel. Thus, the decision to charge or not may well pivot on the personal philosophical and moral tenets of a majority of the potential panel—a majority whose beliefs may vary from grand jury panel to grand jury panel. . . . I think the proper forum for defining life's onset and its cessation in these feticide statutes is the legislature. . . .

WAHL, J.

The trial court . . . noted that "the Minnesota crimes against unborn children statutes represent the most sweeping legislative attempt in the country to criminalize actions of third parties which harm fetuses and embryos." . . .

Defendant is charged with murder of an unborn child in the first degree carrying a sentence of life imprisonment, Minn.Stat. § 609.2661(1), and murder of an unborn child in the second degree, carrying a sentence of imprisonment for not more than 40 years, Minn.Stat. § 609.2662(1). These statutes track, respectively, the language and sentences of murder in the first degree, Minn.Stat. § 609.185(1) (1988), and murder in the second degree, Minn.Stat. § 609.19(1) (1988), with one exception. In both §§ 609.2661(1) and 609.2662(1), the actor, to be guilty of murder and to be sentenced for murder, must cause the death, not of a human being, but of an unborn child. An unborn child is the unborn offspring of a human being conceived, but not yet born. Minn.Stat. § 609.266(a) (1988). Thus an unborn child can be a fertilized egg, an embryo, a nonviable fetus or a viable fetus.

The law with regard to murder is clear. Murder is the "unlawful killing of a human being by another. . . ." *Black's Law Dictionary* 918 (5th ed. 1979). The term murder implies a felonious homicide, which is the wrongful killing of a human being. A nonviable fetus is not a human being, nor is an embryo a human being, nor is a fertilized egg a human being. None has attained the capability of independent human life. Each has the potentiality of human life. In this potential human life the state has an important and legitimate interest—an interest which becomes compelling at viability. Only at viability does the fetus have the "capability of meaningful life outside the mother's womb.". . .

The underlying rationale of *Roe v. Wade* . . . is that until viability is reached, human life in the legal sense has not come into existence. Implicit in *Wade* is the conclusion that as a matter of constitutional law the destruction of a non-viable fetus is not a taking of human life. It follows that such destruction cannot constitute murder or other form of homicide, whether committed by a mother, a father (as here), or a third person. . . .

The fundamental right involved in the case before us as far as defendant is concerned is his liberty. He is charged with two counts of murder of a woman who was 26 to 28 days pregnant at the time of her death. For the death of the 28-day embryo he is further charged with murder of an unborn child in the first degree and murder of an unborn child in the second degree for which he may be sentenced to life imprisonment and 40 years. The state does not have a compelling interest in this potential human life until the fetus becomes viable. . . .

QUESTIONS FOR DISCUSSION

1. What objections did the defendant make to the unborn child homicide statutes?

2. How does the majority answer these objections?

3. Why does the dissent disagree with the majority?

4. Isn't the statute perfectly clear—that life begins at conception? Why does it therefore give the court so much difficulty?[5]

5. Do you agree that the penalties should be the same for killing embryos? Fetuses? Born babies? Adults? Why or why not?

6. Who should resolve these questions? Legislatures? Courts? Public opinion polls? Doctors? Lawyers? Priests, ministers, and rabbis?

✳ 9-2 Minnesota's Fetal Death and Fetal Assault Statutes

When Does Life End?

Determining when life ends has become increasingly complex as organ transplants and sophisticated artificial life support mechanisms make it possible to maintain vital life signs. To kill a dying person, to accelerate a person's death, or to kill a "worthless" person are clearly homicide under current law. So, a doctor who removed a vital organ too soon committed criminal homicide. And anyone who kills another by purposely disconnecting a respirator has also committed criminal homicide.[6]

Historically, *alive* meant breathing and having a heartbeat. The concept of brain death has gained prominence over the past several years, with implications not only for medicine and morals but also for criminal law. If artificial supports alone maintain breathing and heartbeat while brain waves remain minimal or flat, brain death has occurred. The Uniform Brain Death Act provides that an individual who has suffered irreversible cessation of all brain functions, including those of the brain stem, is dead.[7]

More difficult are cases involving individuals with enough brain functions to sustain breathing and heartbeat but nothing more, such as patients in a deep coma. They may breathe and their hearts may beat, but are they alive according to the criminal law? Troubling cases arise in which patients in deep coma have been described by medical specialists as "vegetables" but regain consciousness and live for a considerable time afterward. A Minneapolis police officer was shot and written off for dead after more than a year in a deep coma, but then regained consciousness and lived several years. We hear of similar cases from time to time.

As was true for defining when life begins, defining death need not be fastened to traditional legal doctrine or medical practice. Definitions that satisfy the purposes of criminal law should rather depend on the underlying values that homicide statutes are meant to preserve. Resolving definition problems therefore requires policymakers and legislators to grapple with how to determine what worth they ultimately attribute to continuing life for the critically and hopelessly injured, the gravely mentally ill, and other victims of advanced disease and life's vicissitudes. The New York Court of Appeals dealt with the difficult question of when life ends in homicide law in *People v. Eulo* and *People v. Borillo*.

C A S E Were They "Dead"?

People v. Eulo
63 N.Y.2d 34, 482 N.Y.S.2d 436,
472 N.E.2d 286 (1984)

John Eulo was indicted for second-degree murder. Following a jury trial he was convicted of manslaughter. He appealed. The appellate court affirmed his conviction. In a second case, Robert Bonillo was indicted for second-degree murder and was convicted of first-degree manslaughter. He appealed and the appellate court affirmed his conviction.

COOKE, CJ.

People v. Eulo

FACTS

On the evening of July 19, 1981, defendant and his girlfriend attended a volunteer firemen's fair in Kings Park, Suffolk County. Not long after they arrived, the two began to argue, reportedly because defendant was jealous over one of her former suitors, whom they had seen at the fair. The argument continued through the evening; it became particularly heated as the two sat in defendant's pick-up truck, parked in front of the home of the girlfriend's parents. Around midnight, defendant shot her in the head with his unregistered handgun.

The victim was rushed by ambulance to the emergency room of St. John's Hospital. A gunshot wound to the left temple causing extreme hemorrhaging was apparent. A tube was placed in her windpipe to enable artificial respiration and intravenous medication was applied to stabilize her blood pressure.

Shortly before 2:00 A.M., the victim was examined by a neurosurgeon, who undertook various tests to evaluate damage done to the brain. Painful stimuli were applied and yielded no reaction. Various reflexes were tested and, again, there was no response. A further test determined that the victim

was incapable of spontaneously maintaining respiration. An electroencephalogram (EEG) resulted in "flat," or "isoelectric," readings indicating no activity in the part of the brain tested.

Over the next two days, the victim's breathing was maintained solely by a mechanical respirator. Her heartbeat was sustained and regulated through medication. Faced with what was believed to be an imminent cessation of these two bodily functions notwithstanding the artificial maintenance, the victim's parents consented to the use of certain of her organs for transplantation.

On the afternoon of July 23, a second neurosurgeon was called in to evaluate whether the victim's brain continued to function in any manner. A repetition of all of the previously conducted tests led to the same diagnosis: the victim's entire brain had irreversibly ceased to function. This diagnosis was reviewed and confirmed by the Deputy Medical Examiner for Suffolk County and another physician.

The victim was pronounced dead at 2:20 P.M. on July 23, although at that time she was still attached to a respirator and her heart was still beating. Her body was taken to a surgical room where her kidneys, spleen, and lymph nodes were removed. The mechanical respirator was then disconnected, and her breathing immediately stopped, followed shortly by a cessation of the heartbeat.

Defendant was indicted for second degree murder. After a jury trial, he was convicted of manslaughter. The Appellate Division unanimously affirmed the conviction, without opinion.

People v. Bonilla

FACTS

At approximately 10:30 P.M. on February 6, 1979, a New York City police officer found a man lying faceup on a Brooklyn street with a bullet wound to the head. The officer transported the victim in his patrol car to the Brookdale Hospital, where he was placed in an intensive care unit. Shortly after arriving at the hospital, the victim became comatose and was unable to breathe spontaneously. He was placed on a respirator and medication was administered to maintain his blood pressure.

The next morning, the victim was examined by a neurologist. Due to the nature of the wound, routine tests were applied to determine the level, if any, of the victim's brain functions. The doctor found no reflex reactions and no response to painful stimuli. The mechanical respirator was disconnected to test for spontaneous breathing. There was none, and the respirator was reapplied. An EEG indicated an absence of activity in the part of the brain tested. In the physician's opinion, the bullet wound had caused the victim's entire brain to cease functioning.

The following day, the tests were repeated and the same diagnosis was reached. The victim's mother had been informed of her son's condition and had consented to a transfer of his kidneys and spleen. Death was pronounced following the second battery of tests and, commencing at 9:25 P.M., the victim's kidneys and spleen were removed for transplantation. The respirator was then disconnected, and the victim's breathing and heartbeat stopped.

An investigation led to defendant's arrest. While in police custody, defendant admitted to the shooting. He was indicted for second degree murder and criminal possession of a weapon. A jury convicted him of the weapons count and of first degree manslaughter. The conviction was affirmed by a divided Appellate Division.

OPINION

. . . Death has been conceptualized by the law as, simply, the absence of life: "Death is the opposite of life; it is the termination of life." But, while erecting death as a critical milepost in a person's legal life, the law has had little occasion to consider the precise point at which a person ceases to live. Ordinarily, the precise time of death has no legal significance. . . . Within the past two decades, machines that artificially maintain cardiorespiratory functions have come into widespread use. This technical accomplishment has called into question the universal applicability of the traditional legal and medical criteria for determining when a person has died.

These criteria were cast into flux as the medical community gained a better understanding of human physiology. It is widely understood that the human brain may be anatomically divided, generally, into three parts: the cerebrum, the cerebellum, and the brain stem. The cerebrum, known also as the "higher brain," is deemed largely to control cognitive functions such as thought, memory, and consciousness. The cerebellum primarily controls motor coordination. The brain stem, or "lower brain," which itself has three parts known as the midbrain, pons, and medulla, controls reflexive or spontaneous functions such as breathing, swallowing, and "sleep-wake" cycles.

In addition to injuries that directly and immediately destroy brain tissue, certain physical traumas may indirectly result in a complete and irreversible cessation of the brain's functions. For example, a direct trauma to the head can cause great swelling of the brain tissue, which, in turn, will stem the flow of blood to the brain. A respiratory arrest will similarly cut off the supply of oxygen to the blood and, hence, the brain. Within a relatively short period after being deprived of oxygen, the brain will irreversibly stop functioning. With the suffocation of the higher brain all cognitive powers are lost and a cessation of lower brain functions will ultimately end all spontaneous bodily functions.

Notwithstanding a total irreversible loss of the entire brain's functioning, contemporary medical techniques can maintain, for a limited period, the operation of the heart and the lungs. Respirators or ventilators can substitute for the lower brain's failure to maintain breathing. This artificial respiration, when combined with a chemical regimen, can support the continued operation of the heart. This is so because, unlike respiration, the physical contracting or "beating" of the heart occurs independently of impulses from the brain: so long as blood containing oxygen circulates to the heart, it may continue to beat and medication can take over the lower brain's limited role in regulating the rate and force of the heartbeat.

It became clear in medical practice that the traditional "vital signs"—breathing and heartbeat—are not independent indicia of life, but are, instead, part of an integration of functions in which the brain is dominant. As a result, the medical community began to consider the cessation of brain activity as a measure of death.

The movement in law towards recognizing cessation of brain functions as criteria for death followed this medical trend. The immediate motive for adopting this position was to ease and make more efficient the transfer of donated organs. Organ transfers, to be successful, require a "viable, intact organ." Once all of a person's vital functions have ceased, transferable organs swiftly deteriorate and lose their transplant value. The technical ability to artificially maintain respiration and heartbeat after the entire brain has ceased to function was sought to be applied in cases of organ transplant to preserve the viability of donated organs. . . .

Professional and quasi-governmental groups (including the American Bar Association, the American Medical Association, the President's Commission for the Study of Ethical Problems in Medicine and Biomedical and Behavioral Research, and the National Conference of Commissioners on Uniform State Laws) have jointly indorsed a single standard that includes both cardiorespiratory and brain-based criteria.

The recommended standard provides:

> An individual who has sustained either (1) irreversible cessation of circulatory and respiratory functions, or (2) irreversible cessation of all functions of the entire brain, including the brain stem, is dead. A determination of death must be made in accordance with accepted medical standards.

In New York, the term "death," although used in many statutes, has not been expressly defined by the Legislature. This raises the question of how this court may construe these expressions of the term "death" in the absence of clarification by the Legislature. When the Legislature has failed to assign definition to a statutory term, the courts will generally construe that term according to "its ordinary and accepted meaning as it was understood at the time.". . .

We hold that a recognition of brain-based criteria for determining death is not unfaithful to prior judicial definitions of "death," as presumptively adopted in the many statutes using that term. Close examination of the common-law conception of death and the traditional criteria used to determine when death has occurred leads inexorably to this conclusion.

Courts have not engaged in a metaphysical analysis of when life should be deemed to have passed from a person's body, leaving him or her dead. Rather, they have conceptualized death as the absence of life, unqualified and undefined. On a practical level, this broad conception of death as "the opposite of life" was substantially narrowed through recognition of the cardiorespiratory criteria for determining when death occurs. Under these criteria, the loci of life are the heart and the lungs: where there is no breath or heartbeat, there is no life. Cessation manifests death.

Considering death to have occurred when there is an irreversible and complete cessation of the functioning of the entire brain, including the brain stem, is consistent with the common-law conception of death (see *Commonwealth v. Golston*, 373 Mass. 249, 254, 366 N.E.2d 744). Ordinarily, death will be determined according to the traditional criteria of irreversible cardiorespiratory repose. When, however, the respiratory and circulatory functions are maintained by mechanical means, their significance, as signs of life, is at best ambiguous. Under such circumstances, death may nevertheless be deemed to occur when, according to accepted medical practice, it is determined that the entire brain's function has irreversibly ceased. . . .

In each case, the order of the Appellate Division should be affirmed. . . . Order affirmed.

QUESTIONS FOR DISCUSSION

1. What facts indicate death in the cases?
2. What facts indicate the victims were still alive?
3. What determines death, according to the court's criteria?
4. How would you define death for purposes of the law of homicide?
5. Is putting another in a deep coma murder?
6. The underlying idea in brain death is that insufficient activity exists to appreciate life. Do you agree?
7. What about killing other people in somewhat similar circumstances?
8. What about persons who are born so retarded or so seriously brain damaged that they cannot ever hope to perform life's most basic tasks? Are they "live" human beings?
9. What about psychotics so deep in paranoia that they have no lucid intervals? Are such tragic persons "alive" in a meaningful sense?
10. How would you define death for homicide purposes?

CAUSING ANOTHER'S DEATH

Causing another's death is an element in criminal homicide that can create difficulties. Some killers never touch their victims but still cause their deaths. For example, if I invite my blind enemy to step over the edge of a cliff he can't see and he dies from the fall, I've caused his death. If I expose my helpless child to freezing temperatures, I've caused her death. Such bizarre cases hardly ever come up. The more common problem cases are when several causes contribute to a death. This usually happens when victims don't die immediately. One man beaten almost to death was taken to a hospital where, in a delirious state, he pulled out his life support plugs and died. Another victim was so stunned from a beating that he stumbled in front of a speeding car and was killed. Factual cause exists in these killings because the assailants set in motion chains of events that eventually resulted in death. Whether the assailants legally caused their victims' deaths depends on whether it is fair, just, and expedient to impose liability for criminal homicide (see Chapter 4). In *Commonwealth v. Golston* (treated as a note case later in this chapter), the court ruled that even if a doctor's negligence contributed to the victim's death, Golston's brutal attack with a baseball bat amounted to enough evidence for the jury to find Golston's actions the legal cause of death. According to the ancient **year-and-a-day rule**, still followed in some states, no act occurring more than one year and one day before death can be the legal cause of death. According to the year-and-a-day rule, the law conclusively presumes that death was due to "natural causes," not the defendant's acts. *State v. Minster* deals with applying the ancient rule in the context of modern medical realities.[8]

C A S E	Did He Cause Her Death?

State v. Minster
302 Md. 240, 486 A.2d 1197 (1985)

Larry Minster was indicted for first-degree murder. The Circuit Court for Prince Georges County dismissed the indictment. The state appealed. The Maryland supreme court affirmed.

COUCH, J.

FACTS

On July 8, 1982, Minster shot Cheryl Dodgson in the neck. As a result of the shooting, Ms. Dodgson became a quadriplegic. Minster was charged in Prince George's County Circuit Court with attempted first degree murder, assault with intent to murder, assault and battery and use of a handgun in a crime of violence. He was brought to trial in April of 1983. Minster was convicted of attempted first-degree murder and the use of a handgun in a crime of violence. He was sentenced to 20 years

imprisonment for attempted murder and received a 10 year concurrent sentence for the handgun violation. The Court of Special Appeals affirmed his conviction in an unreported per curiam opinion.

On October 3, 1983, Ms. Dodgson died from injuries the State contends resulted directly from Minster's actions on July 8, 1982 one year and eighty-seven days before the victim's death. One month after Ms. Dodgson's death, Minster was indicted for first degree murder. The Circuit Court for Prince George's County dismissed the indictment because the death of Ms. Dodgson occurred more than a year and a day after the shooting. Judge Johnson [the trial judge] noted that *State v. Brown*, 21 Md.App. 91, 318 A.2d 257 (1974), which held that the year and a day rule was valid in Maryland, barred the indictment. The State appealed the dismissal to the Court of Special Appeals. We granted certiorari prior to consideration by the Court of Special Appeals in order to address an issue of public importance.

OPINION

The State's issue is simply stated: should the prosecution of Minster for the murder of Cheryl Dodgson be barred by the year-and-a-day rule. It argues that the common law rule is now archaic and, in light of medical advances in life-saving techniques, there is no sound reason for retaining the rule today. Minster argues that there are legitimate justifications for the rule's continued application; moreover, because of the number of alternatives available to replace the year-and-a-day rule, a change in the rule should be left to the legislature.

In *Brown,* this identical issue came before the Court of Special Appeals. . . . The Court held that the rule was part of our common law and, although no Maryland case had previously addressed the issue, the rule was "in full force and effect in Maryland." In addition, "if change is to be made in the rule it should be by the General Assembly because expression and weighing of divergent views, consideration of potential effect, and suggestion of adequate safeguards, are better suited to the legislative forum." We are in accordance with this view.

We agree with Minster that there are a number of sound justifications for retaining this rule. As Chief Judge ORTH stated in *Brown,*

> abolition of the rule may well result in imbalance between the adequate protection of society and justice for the individual accused, and there would remain a need for some form of limitation on causation.

Justice MUSMANNO, who dissented from the judicial abrogation of the rule in *Commonwealth v. Ladd,* 402 Pa. 164, 166 A.2d 501 (1960), stated this concern more fully:

> Dorothy Pierce, the alleged victim, died of pneumonia. It is possible, of course, that her weakened condition, due to the alleged hurt received thirteen months before, made her more susceptible to the attack of pneumonia. On the other hand, there is the likely possibility that the pneumonia had no possible connection with the injury allegedly inflicted by the defendant.
>
> Suppose that the pneumonia occurred two years after the physical injury, would it still be proper to charge the defendant with murder? If a murder charge can be brought two years after a blow has been struck, will there ever be a time when the Court may declare that the bridge between the blow and death has now been irreparably broken? May the Commonwealth indict a man for murder when the death occurs ten years after the blow has fallen? Twenty years? Thirty years? One may search the majority opinion through every paragraph, sentence, clause, phrase and comma, and find no answer to this very serious question. The majority is content to open a Pandora's box of interrogation and let it remain unclosed, to the torment and possible persecution of every person who may have at one time or another injured another. I don't doubt that an "expert" of some kind can be found to testify that a slap in the face was the cause of a death fifteen years later.
>
> If there is one thing which the criminal law must be, if it is to be recognized as just, it must be specific and definitive.

We are reminded of the oft-cited explanation for the rule's existence: "If he died after that time [of a year and a day], it cannot be discerned, as the law presumes, whether he died of the stroke or poison, etc. or of a natural death; and in the case of life, the rule of law ought to be certain." 3 Coke, *Institutes of the Laws of England* at 52 (1797)

In addition, a person charged with attempted first degree murder (as was the case here) can be sentenced to life imprisonment. Moreover, a sentencing judge may always consider the seriousness of the injury to, or the subsequent death of, the victim. The only additional conceivable punishment a first degree murder conviction entails is the death penalty.

We do not believe this distinction is a sufficient reason to rescind a common law rule which has existed for over seven hundred years.

[Footnote: The rule has been traced back to the Statutes of Gloucester (1278) in the reign of King Edward I.]

Assuming, arguendo [for the sake of argument], that we abrogate this rule, with what do we replace it? In *People v. Stevenson,* 416 Mich. 383, 331 N.W.2d 143 (1982), the court addressed the identical issue we address today. Five alternatives to the rule were offered to that court:

1. The Court could retain the year and a day rule.

2. The Court could modify the rule by extending the span of time, for example, to three years and a day. California Penal Code § 194.

3. The Court could extend the rule to any length of time it chooses, perhaps two years, five years, or ten years.

4. The Court could change the rule from an irrebuttable presumption to a rebuttable one, but with a higher burden of proof. Cf., *Serafin v. Serafin,* 401 Mich. 629, 258 N.W.2d 461 (1977), requiring clear and convincing evidence.

5. Finally, the Court could simply abolish the rule entirely, leaving the issue of causation to the jury in light of the facts and arguments in each particular case.

Similarly, in *State v. Young,* 77 N.J. 245, 390 A.2d 556 (1978), the justices were split between three alternatives: four justices favoring abrogation, two justices favoring retention, and one justice favoring a compromise "three years and a day" rule. In fact, two jurisdictions, California and Washington, have enacted a three year and a day rule.

Thus we find there is a great difference of opinion surrounding the appropriate length of the period after which prosecution is barred and some doubt whether the rule should exist at all. Consequently, we believe it is the legislature which should mandate any change in the rule, if indeed any change is appropriate in Maryland. The legislature may hold hearings on this matter; they can listen to the testimony of medical experts; and they may determine the viability of this rule in modern times.

We also observe that if there is any discernible trend towards abrogation of the year and a day rule, the trend is towards abrogation by act of the legislature, not the judiciary. Of the thirteen jurisdictions which had enacted the year and a day rule by statute in 1941, only four jurisdictions retain the rule today. In addition, in two jurisdictions (New York and Oregon) the judiciary has held that the legislature abrogated the rule by failing to include it in the comprehensive revision of the state's Criminal Code. Thus, in eleven jurisdictions the rule has been abrogated by legislative action or omission. In contrast, judicial abrogation has occurred in only five jurisdictions.

> [Footnote: "The statistical breakdown of the above analysis is as follows:
> A. Jurisdictions legislatively retaining the rule— California, Idaho, Nevada and South Carolina (reckless manslaughter by vehicle).
> B. Jurisdictions legislatively abrogating the rule— Arizona, Arkansas, Colorado, Delaware, Illinois, Montana, North Dakota, Texas, and Utah.
> C. Jurisdictions judicially abrogating the rule— Massachusetts, Michigan, New Jersey, Ohio and Pennsylvania."]

We recognize the cogency of the State's argument concerning medical advances in lifesaving techniques, and we are aware that other courts have been persuaded by this argument. Yet recent decisions have affirmed the viability of the year and a day rule, and, by our count, the rule remains extant in twenty-six states.

In sum, we uphold the application of the year and a day rule in Maryland. Accordingly, we affirm the trial court's dismissal of the indictment. Judgment affirmed; costs to be paid by appellant.

QUESTIONS FOR DISCUSSION

1. What reasons does the court give for maintaining the year-and-a-day rule?

2. Do they make sense in the twenty-first century? Why or why not?

3. Why does the court believe that if Maryland wishes to change the year-and-a-day rule, the legislature should make the change?

4. Do you agree?

5. Is it important that this rule has existed for more than seven hundred years? Does its longevity argue in favor of keeping this rule or rejecting it?

MURDER

In the sixteenth century, the English judge Sir Edward Coke defined common-law murder as

> when a man of sound memory and of the age of discretion unlawfully kills any reasonable creature in being, and under the King's peace, with malice aforethought, either express or implied by the law, the death taking place within a year and a day.[9]

Express or implied malice aforethought was a broad term that included all of the following mental states:

1. Intent to kill.
2. Intent to inflict serious bodily harm.
3. Intent to commit dangerous felonies.
4. Intent to resist arrest by force.
5. Creation of a greater than reckless risk of death or serious bodily harm (sometimes called "depraved heart murder," such as shooting into a crowd of people).

FIRST-DEGREE MURDER

The common law didn't recognize degrees of murder; all criminal homicides were capital felonies. Pennsylvania was the first state to depart from the common law, enacting a statute in 1794 that divided murder into first- and second-degree murder. The Pennsylvania statute provided that

> all murder, which shall be perpetrated by means of poison, lying in wait, or by any other kind of willful, deliberate or premeditated killing, or which shall be committed in the perpetration, or attempt to perpetrate any arson, rape, robbery or burglary shall be deemed murder in the first degree; and all other kinds of murder shall be deemed murder in the second degree.[10]

The impetus for the statute was the first wave of opposition to the death penalty in the United Sates. Until the Pennsylvania statute, all criminal homicides were capital offenses. First-degree murder limited the death penalty to the worst killings. That remains the reason for today's first-degree murder statutes. Most states quickly followed Pennsylvania's example. In states that abolished the death penalty, first-degree murder became a life imprisonment felony.

"Premeditated" and "Deliberate Murder"

First-degree murder depends on a narrow definition of the intent to kill. Most statutes define the *mens rea* of murder as the premeditated and deliberate killing of another person. Premeditated means that the murderer planned the murder in advance. Deliberate means that the murderer killed in "cold blood," not in a sudden burst of rage. Of course, you can't plan a killing in advance and kill deliberately unless you have the specific intent to kill. But you can specifically intend to kill without advance planning

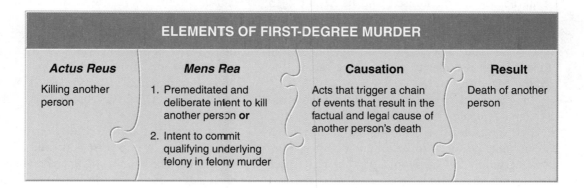

ELEMENTS OF FIRST-DEGREE MURDER

Actus Reus	Mens Rea	Causation	Result
Killing another person	1. Premeditated and deliberate intent to kill another person **or** 2. Intent to commit qualifying underlying felony in felony murder	Acts that trigger a chain of events that result in the factual and legal cause of another person's death	Death of another person

and deliberation—the definition of second-degree murder, as we'll see in the next section. Courts are not consistent in their definitions of premeditation and deliberation. Only a few courts require defendants to have taken enough time and exercised cold rational thinking to concoct a well-laid plan to kill. One court put it this way:

> A verdict of murder in the first degree . . . is proper only if the slayer killed "as a result of careful thought and weighing of considerations; as a deliberate judgment or plan; carried on coolly and steadily, according to a preconceived design."[11]

The majority of courts, however, virtually eliminate the element of advanced planning and cool deliberation by holding that premeditation includes killings that take place even instantly after forming the intent to kill. One judge said that a defendant premeditated deliberately when his intent to kill arose "at the very moment the fatal shot was fired." The Idaho Supreme Court dealt with the meaning of premeditated deliberate murder in the **capital murder** case of *State v. Snowden*.[12]

C A S E	Did He "Premeditate" the Killing?

State v. Snowden
79 Idaho 266, 313 P.2d 706 (1957)

Ray Snowden pleaded guilty to first-degree murder. The trial judge sentenced him to death. He appealed to the Idaho supreme court. The supreme court affirmed.

   MCQUADE, J.

FACTS

Ray Snowden had been playing pool and drinking in a Boise pool room early in the evening. With a companion, one Carrier, he visited a club near Boise, then went to nearby Garden City. There the two men visited a number of bars, and defendant had several drinks. Their last stop was the HiHo Club. Witnesses related that while defendant was in the HiHo Club he met and talked to Cora Lucyle Dean. The defendant himself said he hadn't been acquainted with Mrs. Dean prior to that time, but he had "seen her in a couple of the joints up town." He danced with Mrs. Dean while at the HiHo Club. Upon departing from the tavern, the two left together.

   In statements to police officers, that were admitted in evidence, defendant Snowden said after they left the club Mrs. Dean wanted him to find a cab and take her back to Boise, and he refused because he didn't feel he should pay her fare. After some words, he related: "She got mad at me so I got pretty hot and I don't know whether I back

handed her there or not. And, we got calmed down and decided to walk across to the gas station and call a cab."

   They crossed the street, and began arguing again. Defendant said: "She swung and at the same time she kneed me again. I blew my top." Defendant said he pushed the woman over beside a pickup truck which was standing near a business building. There he pulled his knife—a pocket knife with a two-inch blade—and cut her throat.

   The body, which was found the next morning, was viciously and sadistically cut and mutilated. An autopsy surgeon testified the voice box had been cut, and that this would have prevented the victim from making any intelligible outcry. There were other wounds inflicted while she was still alive—one in her neck, one in her abdomen, two in the face, and two on the back of the neck. The second neck wound severed the spinal cord and caused death. There were other wounds all over her body, and her clothing had been cut away. The nipple of the right breast was missing. There was no evidence of a sexual attack on the victim; however, some of the lacerations were around the breasts and vagina of the deceased. A blood test showed Mrs. Dean was intoxicated at the time of her death.

   Defendant took the dead woman's wallet. He hailed a passing motorist and rode back to Boise with him. There he went to a bowling alley and changed clothes. He dropped his knife into a sewer, and threw the wallet away. Then he went to his hotel and cleaned up again. He put the clothes he had worn that evening into a trash barrel.

OPINION

By statute, murder is defined as the unlawful killing of a human being with malice aforethought. Degrees of murder are defined by statute as follows:

> All murder which is perpetrated by means of poison, or lying in wait, torture, or by any other kind of willful, deliberate and premeditated killing, or which is committed in the perpetration of, or attempt to perpetrate arson, rape, robbery, burglary, kidnapping or mayhem, is murder of the first degree. All other murders are of the second degree.

The defendant admitted taking the life of the deceased. The principal argument of the defendant pertaining to . . . [premeditation] is that the defendant did not have sufficient time to develop a desire to take the life of the deceased, but rather this action was instantaneous and a normal reaction to the physical injury which she had dealt him. . . . The test to determine if the killing was willful, deliberate, and premeditated has been set out in *State v. Shuff* . . . :

> The unlawful killing must be accompanied with a deliberate and clear intent to take life, in order to constitute murder of the first degree. The intent to kill must be the result of deliberate premeditation. It must be formed upon the pre-existing reflection, and not upon a sudden heat of passion sufficient to preclude the idea of deliberation. . . .

The Supreme Court of Arizona held in the case of *Macias v. State*:

> There need be no appreciable space of time between the intention to kill and the act of killing. They may be as instantaneous as successive thoughts of the mind. It is only necessary that the act of killing be preceded by a concurrence of will, deliberation, and premeditation on the part of the slayer, and, if such is the case, the killing is murder in the first degree.

In the present case, the trial court had no other alternative than to find the defendant guilty of willful, deliberate, and premeditated killing with malice aforethought in view of the defendant's acts in deliberately opening up a pocket knife, next cutting the victim's throat, and then hacking and cutting until he had killed Cora Lucyle Dean and expended himself. The full purpose and design of defendant's conduct was to take the life of the deceased. . . . [Snowden objected to the imposition of the death penalty. Idaho provides the following punishment for murder:]

> Every person guilty of murder in the first degree shall suffer death or be punished by imprisonment in the state prison for life, and the jury may decide which punishment shall be inflicted. . . .

The trial court could have imposed life imprisonment, or, as in the instant case, sentenced the defendant to death. It is abuse of discretion we are dealing with, and in particular the alleged abuse of discretion in prescribing the punishment for murder in the first degree as committed by the defendant. To choose between the punishments of life imprisonment and death there must be some distinction between one homicide and another. This case exemplifies an abandoned and malignant heart and sadistic mind, bent upon taking human life. It is our considered conclusion, from all the facts and circumstances, the imposition of the death sentence was not an abuse of discretion by the trial court. The judgment is affirmed.

QUESTIONS FOR DISCUSSION

1. The Idaho Supreme Court upheld the trial court's finding that Snowden premeditated Dean's death. In fact, in a part of the opinion not included here, the court approved the trial judge's death sentence over life imprisonment because it was satisfied that Snowden clearly premeditated Dean's murder. Do you agree?

2. If you were defining premeditation in a criminal statute, would you say it is sufficient that the deed followed instantly upon the intention?

3. What practical meaning does premeditation have according to that definition?

4. Do you think the court used premeditation as an "excuse" to make it possible to sentence Snowden to death for the especially brutal way he murdered Dean? (When you read about second-degree murder, rethink how you defined premeditation in first-degree murder.)

5. As for the sentence, do you find any mitigating circumstances, such as Snowden's intoxication, Dean's provocation, and Snowden's quick response to Dean's provocation?

THE REST OF THE STORY   *Ray Snowden's Story*

LIFE BEFORE THE MURDER

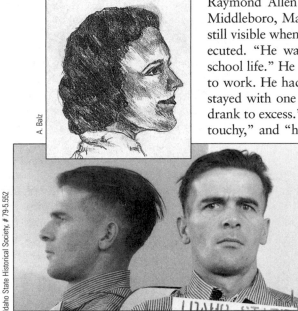

A. Balz

Idaho State Historical Society, # 79-5-552

Raymond Allen Snowden was born on October 22, 1921 in Middleboro, Massachusetts. He was beaten as a boy, the scars still visible when he was 36 years old in prison waiting to be executed. "He was in the principal's office a good deal of his school life." He quit school in his first year in high school to go to work. He had many jobs as "a general laborer but he never stayed with one job more than six months." He "smoked and drank to excess." In his own words, he "fights easily and is very touchy," and "has a tendency to tear things up." He admitted to stabbing two women before he murdered Cora Dean.

March 24, 1941.

Snowden joined the U.S. Army.

December 15, 1942.

Snowden was dishonorably discharged from the army for assaulting and breaking his staff sergeant's jaw.

Tuesday evening, September 10, 1956.

Boise police officer Frank Boor got a call from a woman six months pregnant. She said she had been accosted by a man in an alley outside a downtown bar. She said he had "held a knife to the back of her neck and threatened to cut out her unborn child unless she submitted to him." She identified the man as Raymond Snowden, 36, and said he lived at the Milner Hotel. Two detectives went to the hotel. Snowden denied the charge.

Later in the evening the hotel night clerk called police to report a disturbance in Snowden's apartment. The officers went back and found Snowden lying on the bed, holding a hand over his eye in pain, and the woman's husband standing over him. "Snowden got to his feet, crying like a child," Officer Boor reported." Snowden threatened to have the man arrested. But neither the woman's husband nor Snowden were arrested. The woman and her husband said they'd be in the next morning to file a complaint against Snowden. But they never reappeared.

September 10–September 21, 1956.

Snowden drank heavily for the next 10 days. A hotel guest encountered him in the lobby a few evenings later and inquired casually what had become of Marcy. Marcy was Snowden's girlfriend who had run off a few months before. The question triggered an emotional reaction. His eyes blazing, Snowden replied: "I know where she is, but I wouldn't spend two dollars to get her back."

FROM CORA DEAN'S MURDER TO PRISON

Saturday night, September 21, 1956.

Snowden spent the morning and afternoon shooting pool and drinking beer. In the early evening he and a friend named Red climbed into the latter's car, a "souped up" Ford. He'd heard that Marcy was back in town. They went to the Collister Club, then to the Pink Elephant in Garden City, then to the Alpine Club, then to Don & Dell's, then to another place, then to the Hi-Ho Club. "I'm looking for a girl," Snowden told Red. "And if I find her I'm going to cut her heart out."

Snowden was looking for Marcy. But he found Cora Lucyle Dean instead. Dean was a recently divorced 48-year-old alcoholic. She was currently engaged to marry a Boise man. But they had fought that evening when he had returned home and found her drunk. She took a taxi to the Garden City night club strip, vowing she "would have herself a good time."

Snowden and Dean's encounter began "as a chance meeting of two drunks." He didn't even know her name until after he murdered her. Later, he couldn't remember whether he'd bought her a drink. They talked idly for a while. Then Snowden, noticing that Red had disappeared, asked the bartender to call a cab to take him to town. The bartender didn't hear him, so Snowden left, hoping to hail one himself. Mrs. Dean followed him out of the club.

During the course of a seven-hour interrogation, Snowden told the police that "She asked if I was going to catch a cab to town. I said I was going to see if I could find one. And then we got to arguing about going to town, and she got mad. She said she wanted to go up town and drink, and we had a bit of an argument." The interrogation also exposed the awful details of the murder and the mutilation that followed it:

Q. What was the argument about, Ray?

A. Well, it was about whether I should pay the cab fare up town and buy drinks for her all night. I figured her boyfriend might be in town, and I didn't figure I should go up there and set up her whiskey all night. So she said something about I should for a lady and I told her that was all the more reason why I shouldn't.

So, she got mad at me so I got pretty hot and I don't know whether I back-handed her there or not. We got calmed down and decided to walk across to the gas station to call a cab. . . . We got across the street and started arguing some more and I said, "The hell with it," or something like that. I would take her back to the Hi-Ho. I am going back to town the best I could. We started walking back to the Hi-Ho. She swung, and at the same time she kneed me again. I blew my top.

Q. And then what happened?

A. I pushed her over by the pickup and pulled my knife out and cut her throat . . . She let out a squeal and fell over backwards. . . . She was moaning and groaning so I wanted to stop the noise so I cut her throat again.

Q. What did you do then?

A. After that I don't remember much of anything. . . . When I became aware of what I had done I began to realize what . . . what I'd done, so I went on. I don't, know how to put it in words. . . . I must have cut her up because there was blood all over the place.

Q. Do you remember how many times you cut her?

A. I don't know.

Q. Do you remember cutting her nipple from her . . . breast?

A. Yes.

Q. Can you tell us what you did with that nipple?

A. I ate it.

Q. You ate it, you say?

A. Yes.

Q. Did you have in mind when you cut it off you were going to eat it?

A. No.

Q. What caused you to eat it?

A. I don't know.

Outside of court, a Boise lawyer asked Snowden why he killed Dean. Snowden answered, "She kicked me in the nuts, and so I killed her."

Early Sunday morning, September 22, 1956.

A young boy, out looking for empty bottles to return for deposit, found Dean's mutilated body in the alley where Snowden left her.

September 24, 1956.

Snowden was arrested and charged with first-degree murder.

October 5, 1956.

Snowden pleaded not guilty.

October 18, 1956.

Snowden, against the advice of his court-appointed attorney, "sabotaged his own defense" by changing his initial "not guilty" plea to "guilty."

October 26, 1956.

Snowden was convicted and sentenced to death.

November 18, 1956.

Snowden's attorney filed a notice of appeal in the Idaho Supreme Court.

July 24, 1957.

The Idaho Supreme Court affirmed the trial court's judgment of conviction and his sentence of death.

September 18, 1957.

The Ada County trial court re-sentenced Snowden to death.

WAITING TO DIE

While he was on death row, none of the prison officials who came in contact with Snowden remembers him as troublesome or vicious. Lew Clapp who left the penitentiary in 1966 after serving 20 years as warden, recalls him as "a quiet man who said little. Unlike many serving lesser sentences, he appeared to be resigned to his lot."

Snowden spoke little to the guards who took turns on the 24-hour "death watch" outside his cell, which was across a hallway from the execution chamber on death row, on the second floor of the maximum security building.

Following a lifetime habit, he read voraciously. Within a few months he had exhausted the meager stock of the prison library. He had few visitors, but those who had occasion to call brought him books. An attorney once scooped up an armful of paperbacks at random in a Boise drugstore and took them to Snowden's cell. The prisoner's eye fell on one of the titles, and he looked up with a sardonic scowl. "You son of a bitch," he said. The title was *The First One Hundred Years*.

Time hung heavily on Snowden's hands as the weeks stretched into months while the State Supreme Court pondered his appeal.

The man who came to know him best as a prisoner was Orvil Stiles, who was then the prison chaplain and since 1967 has become the warden of the penitentiary. Snowden said little to Stiles in the first few weeks. But one day he asked the chaplain to bring him a book of crossword puzzles. Stiles brought the book on his next visit and then watched open-mouthed as Snowden snapped it open and began filling in tile blanks. "I have never seen anything like it in my life," Stiles recalled much later. "He worked those puzzles as fast as a man can write and never glanced at a dictionary. He had a phenomenal mind."

It was one of several feats of intellect which Snowden exhibited to Stiles. The chaplain brought him a Bible correspondence course. He passed it and asked for something tougher. He took a Bible memory course and learned 120 verses in less than a week. "My lord, what a memory that man had! One day I told him I was going to Nebraska for my vacation. He told me the names and locations of all the businesses in Ogallala. I guess he'd been there as a truck driver."

A brother, one of Snowden's seven siblings, came out from Massachusetts and visited him in his prison cell. The brother told Stiles that Snowden recounted the details of a fishing trip the two had taken 10 years earlier, a trip that he himself had long forgotten.

As spring gave way to summer, a bond grew up between the prisoner and the chaplain. They chatted cagily about inconsequential things. But Snowden was unusually somber and quiet on the day the news reached him that the Supreme Court had upheld his conviction and sentence.

"I asked him, 'Do you think your crime was so bad that not even God can find it in his heart to forgive you?' He looked at me and for the first time we weren't talking about crossword puzzles or things like that. All he said was, 'Yes.' I saw him every day after that." Snowden was determined to get the conviction over with.

As the final days slipped by on death row he lay quietly on his bunk, reading the Bible.

October 17, 1957.

Warden Clapp summoned Stiles to his office and asked him if the prisoner were ready. "Warden," said Stiles, "this man is as well prepared as any man I know."

Snowden ate his last meal in his cell, only 60 feet from the gallows where he would be hanged. The meal:

Boiled lobster with drawn butter
Sweet potatoes, asparagus, tossed combination salad with French dressing
Cranberry sauce, hot rolls
Tea
Strawberry shortcake

October 18, 1957, a few minutes after midnight.

12:05 A.M. Snowden entered the death chamber.
12:05:45 seconds A.M. Twelve people watched Snowden drop through the trap door in the execution chamber of the Idaho State Penitentiary.
12:25:25 seconds A.M. Neither the twelve official witnesses nor anyone else who watched the hanging has ever described the nearly twenty minutes it took to kill Snowden. Nor has anyone explained why it took that long.

Not everyone agrees that premeditated killings are the worst murders. According to the nineteenth-century English judge and criminal law reformer, James F. Stephen:

> As much cruelty, as much indifference to the life of others, a disposition at least as dangerous to society, probably even more dangerous, is shown by sudden as by premeditated murders. The following cases appear to me to set this in a clear light. A man, passing along the road, sees a boy sitting on a bridge over a deep river and, out of mere wanton barbarity, pushes him into it and so drowns him. A man makes advances to a girl who repels him. He deliberately but instantly cuts her throat. A man civilly asked to pay a just debt pretends to get the money, loads a rifle and blows out his creditor's brains. In none of these cases is there premeditation unless the word is used in a sense as unnatural as "aforethought" in "malice aforethought," but each represents even more diabolical cruelty and ferocity than that which is involved in murders premeditated in the natural sense of the word.[13]

Heinous or Atrocious Murder

Some first-degree murder statutes focus not only on intent but also on the act of killing, defining first-degree murders as intentional killing by means of "heinous or atrocious" acts. This usually means especially brutal murders or torture murders intended to cause lingering death. The Florida Supreme Court applied the state's "heinous, atrocious, or cruel" aggravating circumstance provision to determine whether Charles Donaldson should receive the death penalty in *Donaldson v. State.*

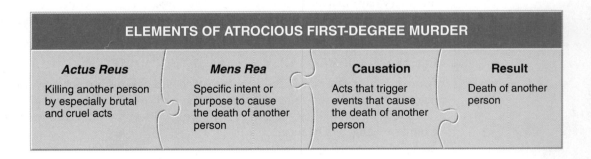

ELEMENTS OF ATROCIOUS FIRST-DEGREE MURDER			
Actus Reus	*Mens Rea*	**Causation**	**Result**
Killing another person by especially brutal and cruel acts	Specific intent or purpose to cause the death of another person	Acts that trigger events that cause the death of another person	Death of another person

CASE   "Was the Murder Heinous, Atrocious, and Cruel?"

Donaldson v. State
722 So.2d 177 (Fla. 1998)

Charles Donaldson, the defendant, was convicted in the Circuit Court, Okaloosa County of first-degree murder, kidnapping with a firearm, and aggravated child abuse with a firearm for the death of two child victims. Following jury recommendation, Donaldson was sentenced to death for the murders, life imprisonment for the kidnapping and 30 years imprisonment for aggravated child abuse. He appealed. The Florida Supreme Court affirmed the convictions, reversed the sentences, and remanded the case.

PER CURIAM (By the court)

FACTS

On July 9, 1994, Charles Donaldson (the defendant) and three others, Ruben Cisneros, Joseph Wengert, and William Purcell Straham, sat in Donaldson's home for most of the day drinking alcoholic beverages. Donaldson was a street level drug dealer involved in selling crack cocaine. From the record, in fact, it appears that virtually everyone, including the victims and the State's witnesses, were involved in illicit drug activity. At one point that evening, Donaldson called thirteen-year-old Lawanda Latisha Campbell, who was at a friend's house with fifteen-year-old Donnta Lamar Head, and told her to "go stand in front of her daddy's house and that he would be by to shoot her." Campbell and Head then left the friend's house and walked to Donaldson's home.

In the meantime, Donaldson spoke on the telephone with Campbell's father, Tommy Gainer, and argued with him. Wengert took the phone from Donaldson and continued to argue with Gainer when the phone line suddenly went dead. At the same time, Campbell and Head arrived at Donaldson's home. Afraid he was about to be robbed by Campbell and Head, Donaldson ordered everyone to exit the house from the back door. Wengert testified that Cisneros then put a gun on Head, walked him inside and seated him in a two-seat wicker chair in the living room. Donaldson then ordered Cisneros and Wengert to retrieve Campbell who had run to the corner and was hiding behind

a car. She, too, was forced into the house at gunpoint and seated in the wicker chair with Head. Although Wengert testified that everyone was armed with a firearm, Straham testified to the contrary, that he did not see any guns during the entire episode. Head and Campbell were not armed.

Apparently, Donaldson had been the victim of several prior attempted robberies, at least one of which involved Campbell and Head just a few days before the murders. Wengert testified that he, Donaldson, and Cisneros proceeded to interrogate Head and Campbell about the prior robberies, during which time Donaldson held a 9-mm handgun on his lap and Cisneros and Wengert held two firearms each—a .22 caliber and a .25 caliber automatic. According to Wengert, Campbell looked scared and asked if she was going to die. Both he and Donaldson assured her that she was not. Straham sat in the dining room drinking and watching a video, and recalled hearing Donaldson and Wengert talking to the victims about prior robberies but did not see Donaldson with a gun.

Campbell was allowed to leave the room to use the bathroom, and afterward she sat in the dining room talking to Straham. At that point Donaldson said, "I don't care about that bitch," to which Cisneros responded, "Well if you don't care about that bitch, that means that you don't care what I do." He then struck Campbell, knocking her down, and kicked her. Head and Campbell again asked if they were going to die, and everyone, including Donaldson, answered no.

According to Wengert, Donaldson's pager beeped and, when Donaldson returned the call, he told the person on the other end to sit tight as he might be needed for a favor. Cisneros and Straham were then sent by Donaldson to pick up that person and returned later with Joseph Sykosky. Wengert testified that before Sykosky arrived, Donaldson had asked him to kill the victims. However, Wengert thought Donaldson was kidding. Apparently, Sykosky owed Donaldson quite a bit of money for drugs. Wengert claims Donaldson told Sykosky that "if he did the job and done it right, that his debt would be clean." Sykosky asked Donaldson if these (indicating Head and Campbell) were the ones Donaldson wanted him to "take care of." Donaldson said yes, handed Sykosky a gun, and told him to wait until Wengert increased the volume on the stereo. Sykosky then shot and killed the two victims in rapid succession. Straham, who was in the other room and heard five gunshots, testified that he did not hear anyone order Sykosky to kill the victims and did not see the shooting. He did notice, however, a shocked or stunned look on Donaldson's face after the shootings.

Afterwards, the victims' bodies were placed in the trunk of Donaldson's car and Donaldson, Cisneros, and Wengert left to dispose of the bodies and the contents of the trunk. Upon their return, they all cleaned the house and Donaldson told Sykosky to dispose of the murder weapon. The weapon was never found. At trial, a firearms expert testified that the victims were killed with a 9 by 18 Makarov. Subsequent DNA analysis on blood found in Donaldson's house and the trunk of his car was consistent with that of the victims.

After hearing all of the evidence, the jury found Donaldson guilty of two counts of first-degree murder, two counts of kidnapping with a firearm, and two counts of aggravated child abuse with a firearm. The jury recommended death by a vote of eight to four for the murder of Head and by a vote of nine to three for the murder of Campbell. The judge followed the jury's recommendation, finding five aggravating circumstances for each victim, no statutory mitigating circumstances, and several nonstatutory mitigating circumstances.

[Footnote: Nonstatutory mitigating circumstances: (1) The triggerman, Joseph Sykosky, received a life sentence for his involvement in the murders (little, if any, weight); (2) Donaldson has a good prison record (some weight); (3) Donaldson and his family suffered numerous robbery attempts (slight weight); (4) Donaldson's family background and trauma suffered as a young boy due to the loss of his older brother (slight weight); (5) Donaldson's capacity for hard work (slight weight); and (6) Donaldson's church attendance as a boy (no weight).]

The trial court sentenced Donaldson to death for the murders and sentenced him to life imprisonment for the kidnapping charges and thirty years imprisonment for the aggravated child abuse charges.

OPINION

. . . Donaldson argues the trial court erred in finding the murder heinous, atrocious, and cruel (HAC) under section 921.141(5)(h). In *State v. Dixon*, 283 So.2d 1 (1973), this Court stated:

> It is our interpretation that heinous means extremely wicked or shockingly evil; that atrocious means outrageously wicked and vile; and, that cruel means designed to inflict a high degree of pain with utter indifference to, or even enjoyment of, the suffering of others. What is intended to be included are those capital crimes where the actual commission of the capital felony was accompanied by such additional acts as to set the crime apart from the norm of capital felonies—the conscienceless or pitiless crime which is unnecessarily torturous to the victim.

Stated another way, the heinous, atrocious or cruel aggravator "is proper only in torturous murders—those that evince extreme and outrageous depravity as exemplified either by the desire to inflict a high degree of pain or utter indifference to or enjoyment of the suffering of another."

On the other hand, we have held that "an instantaneous or near-instantaneous death by gunfire" does not satisfy the HAC aggravating factor. "Execution style killings are not generally HAC unless the state has presented other evidence to show some physical or mental torture of the victim." Indeed, we have rejected application of the HAC aggravator where the evidence indicated that the defendant had not intended to cause the victim any prolonged suffering and, in fact, had assured the victims that they would not be killed.

Here, the trial judge relied on the fact the victims were forced into the house at gunpoint, kept there against their will for several hours while Donaldson and his accomplices interrogated them. Further, the trial court speculated that the victims undoubtedly heard Donaldson order Sykosky to kill them. In contrast, the evidence reveals that the victims were assured repeatedly that they were not going to die and the murders occurred quickly. As in *Robinson*, the evidence in this case does not establish that the defendant intended or that the victims suffered an acute awareness of their impending deaths, or that Donaldson intended to cause them unnecessary pain or prolonged suffering. Mere speculation that the victims may have realized that Donaldson intended to do more than interrogate them is insufficient. Accordingly we find the evidence insufficient to establish the HAC aggravator as the murders in this case did not fall outside the norm of capital felonies.

. . . We affirm Donaldson's convictions for two counts of first-degree murder, kidnapping and aggravated child abuse. However, based upon our rejection of the heinous, atrocious and cruel aggravator . . . we reverse his sentences of death and remand this case to the trial court with instructions to hold a new penalty phase proceeding before a new jury in accord with this opinion.

It is so ordered.

DISSENT

WELLS, J.

I dissent from that portion of the majority's decision that holds that these murders were not heinous, atrocious, or cruel (HAC). The majority correctly acknowledges that execution-style murders resulting in instantaneous or near instantaneous death are not usually HAC unless there has been physical or mental torture of the victim, yet dismisses the trial court's finding that the victims were acutely aware of their impending deaths as "speculation."

In an instantaneous death situation, fear and emotional strain may be considered as contributing to the heinous nature of the murder. We have upheld the HAC aggravator where victims have been murdered by gunshot and have died instantaneously but before being killed were subjected to agony over the prospect that death was soon to occur.

In its sentencing order, the trial court made the following findings regarding the HAC aggravator:

> The murders were committed in an especially heinous, atrocious, or cruel manner. These two teenagers were kidnapped at gunpoint and held for several hours and interrogated extensively by the Defendant and his cohorts as both [Campbell] and [Head] asked on more than one occasion if they were "going to die." The testimony indicates without question that both victims were obviously in fear of dying at the hands of the Defendant for several hours before the arrival of the triggerman, Joseph Sykosky. We will never know the amount of fear and anxiety suffered by these two children when they witnessed the arrival of Joseph Sykosky, the Defendant handing him the gun, and the Defendant directing George Wengert to go turn on the stereo and then to turn it up louder. If the victims had suspicions earlier that they might die, as evidenced by their questions, "Are we going to die?", certainly they knew from the time of Mr. Sykosky's arrival that he was there for the purpose

of murdering them. While the evidence is not clear which child was shot first, it is abundantly clear that one child watched as their friend was executed with full knowledge and understanding that they would be next. Even though the deaths of these victims may have been quick rather than lingering, they were subjected to hours of terror and at least minutes of excruciating and heightened anguish and fear before their death. This aggravating circumstance has been proved beyond a reasonable doubt as to each count.

Contrary to the majority, I find that these findings are not based upon "speculation" but are supported by competent, substantial evidence. Moreover, I conclude that, based on these findings, the law supports the trial court's conclusion that the murders were especially heinous, atrocious, or cruel.

In this case, the record establishes the following. Before the day of the murders, Campbell and Head were involved in an attempted robbery of Donaldson. Although Donaldson suspected that the two were involved in the attempted robbery, Campbell and Head had no reason to know that Donaldson suspected them. On the day of the murders, Campbell and Head decided to go to Donaldson's house to try to obtain some drugs. They were kidnapped at gunpoint and interrogated about the attempted robbery.

At this time, the testimony indicates that Campbell at first did not answer any questions; she just sat there "looking scared [as if she were about] to start crying." She repeatedly asked everyone if she was going to die. The trial court properly inferred from the evidence that she may not have believed her captors when they told her she was not going to be killed. If she had believed what she was being told, she would not have repeatedly asked whether she was going to die. In fact, Wengert testified that when Donaldson told Campbell she would not die, he said it with "a serious look on his face like he went crazy or something." One possible inference is that Donaldson was teasing the victim with her own life.

At one point during her detention, Campbell was in the kitchen with Straham and Wengert when Wengert heard Donaldson say, "I don't care about that bitch." Cisneros replied, "Well, seeing that you don't care about that bitch, that means you don't care what I do." Cisneros then entered the kitchen and knocked Campbell out of her chair and kicked her.

When Sykosky arrived, he stood in front of the children, and Donaldson handed him his 9-mm handgun. Sykosky then asked, "Are these the ones you want me to do in?" At this time, Campbell and Head surely knew their fate. Donaldson responded positively by saying, "Kill them," but told Sykosky to wait while Wengert turned on the stereo. After Wengert returned from turning on the stereo, Donaldson instructed him to go back and turn it up louder. Then one child watched while the executioner killed the other, knowing that his or her execution would soon follow. . . . I find that the terror and fear that the children must have felt throughout this abominable sequence of events "beyond description by the written word" because the victims undoubtedly agonized over the prospect that death was soon to occur. . . .

I conclude that *Henyard v. State*, 689 So.2d 239, 254 (Fla.1996), cert. denied, 522 U.S. 846, 118 S.Ct. 130, 139 L.Ed.2d 80 (1997), supports the trial court's legal conclusion that the murders were especially heinous, atrocious, or cruel. In *Henyard,* the defendant and an accomplice abducted a woman and her two daughters, ages three and seven, from a Winn-Dixie Store. After raping the woman, the abductors shot her four times and left her for dead on the side of the road. The little girls were each executed with a single gunshot to the head. In affirming the trial court's finding of HAC we wrote:

> In this case, the trial court found the [HAC] aggravating factor to be present based upon the entire sequence of events, including the fear and emotional trauma the children suffered during the episode culminating in their deaths. . . .

In the instant case, it is clear that the trial court's conclusion was based upon the entire sequence of events, including the fear and emotional trauma the victims suffered during the episode that culminated in their deaths. Therefore, I would conclude that the record fully supports a finding that these murders were especially heinous, atrocious, or cruel.

QUESTIONS FOR DISCUSSION

1. How does the court define "heinous, atrocious, and cruel?"

2. List the facts in the case that are relevant to deciding whether this was a "heinous, atrocious, and cruel" murder.

3. Summarize the arguments of both the majority and dissent in favor of and against classifying this as a "heinous, cruel, and atrocious" murder.

✳ 9-3 Oral Argument and Briefs of *Donaldson v. State*

NOTE CASES

1. About 2 P.M. on Sunday, August 24, 1975, a white man about thirty-four years old came out of a store and walked toward his car. Siegfried Golston, a nineteen-year-old African American man, tiptoed up behind the victim and hit him on the head with a baseball bat. A witness testified to the sound made by Golston's blow to the victim's head: "Just like you hit a wet, you know, like a bat hit a wet baseball, that's how it sounded." Golston then went into a building, changed his clothes, and crossed the street to the store, where he worked. When asked why he had hit the man, Golston replied, "For kicks." The victim later died. Was this atrocious murder, a form of first-degree murder that qualified Golston for the death penalty? According to the court, it was.

> There was evidence of great and unusual violence in the blow, which caused a four-inch cut on the side of the skull. . . . There was also evidence that after he was struck the victim fell to the street, and that five minutes later he tried to get up, staggered to his feet and fell again to the ground. He was breathing very hard and a neighbor wiped vomit from his nose and mouth. Later, according to the testimony, the defendant said he did it, "For kicks."

> There is no requirement that the defendant know that his act was extremely atrocious or cruel, and no requirement of deliberate premeditation. A murder may be committed with extreme atrocity or cruelty even though death results from a single blow. Indifference to the victim's pain, as well as actual knowledge of it and taking pleasure in it, is cruelty; and extreme cruelty is only a higher degree of cruelty. *Commonwealth v. Golston,* 373 Mass. 249, 366 N.E.2d 744 (1977)

2. On February 15, 1982, Lloyd Duest, carrying a knife in the waistband of his pants, boasted

that he was going to a gay bar to "roll a fag." Duest was later seen at a predominantly gay bar with John Pope. Pope and Duest left the bar and drove off in Pope's gold Camaro. Several hours later, Pope's roommate returned home and found the house unlocked, the lights on, the stereo on loud, and blood on the bed. The sheriff was contacted. Upon arrival, the deputy sheriff found Pope on the bathroom floor in a pool of blood with multiple stab wounds. Duest was found and arrested on April 18, 1982. He was tried and found guilty of first-degree murder. In accordance with the jury's advisory recommendation, the trial judge imposed the death sentence. Duest argued that this was not a particularly heinous or atrocious killing. The court wrote:

We disagree with the defendant. The evidence presented at trial shows that the victim received eleven stab wounds, some of which were inflicted in the bedroom and some inflicted in the bathroom. The medical examiner's testimony revealed that the victim lived some few minutes before dying.

Duest v. State, 462 So.2d 446 (Fla.1985)

SECOND-DEGREE MURDER

First-degree murders are the most serious, but second-degree murders are more common. Most **second-degree murder** statutes include all deaths caused by intentional killings that are not premeditated, justified, or excused. For example, Washington state's second-degree murder provision which reads, "A person is guilty of murder in the second degree when . . . with intent to cause the death of another person but without premeditation, he causes the death of such person. . . ." But most second-degree murder statutes go further than this. For example, Arizona's second-degree murder statute includes the following types of second-degree murder:

A person commits second degree murder if without premeditation:

1. Such person intentionally causes the death of another person; or
2. Knowing that his conduct will cause death or serious physical injury, such person causes the death of another person; or
3. Under circumstances manifesting extreme indifference to human life, such person recklessly engages in conduct which creates a grave risk of death and thereby causes the death of another person.[14]

Broader than most, Alaska's second-degree murder statute provides:

(a) A person commits the crime of murder in the second degree if
(1) with intent to cause serious physical injury to another person or knowing that the conduct is substantially certain to cause death or serious physical injury to another person, the person causes the death of any person;

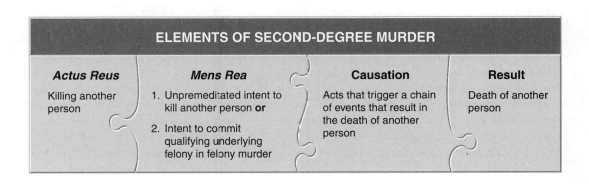

ELEMENTS OF SECOND-DEGREE MURDER			
Actus Reus	***Mens Rea***	**Causation**	**Result**
Killing another person	1. Unpremeditated intent to kill another person **or** 2. Intent to commit qualifying underlying felony in felony murder	Acts that trigger a chain of events that result in the death of another person	Death of another person

(2) the person knowingly engages in conduct that results in the death of another person under circumstances manifesting an extreme indifference to the value of human life;

(3) under circumstances not amounting to murder in the first degree . . . while acting either alone or with one or more persons, the person commits or attempts to commit arson in the first degree, kidnapping, sexual assault in the first degree, sexual assault in the second degree, sexual abuse of a minor in the first degree, sexual abuse of a minor in the second degree, burglary in the first degree, escape in the first or second degree, robbery in any degree, or misconduct involving a controlled substance . . . and, in the course of or in furtherance of that crime or in immediate flight from that crime, any person causes the death of a person other than one of the participants;

(4) acting with a criminal street gang, the person commits or attempts to commit a crime that is a felony and, in the course of or in furtherance of that crime or in immediate flight from that crime, any person causes the death of a person other than one of the participants; or

(5) the person with criminal negligence causes the death of a child under the age of 16 . . .[15]

Michigan has a catchall provision: All murders that aren't first-degree are second-degree murders. The Michigan Penal Code first-degree murder section includes premeditated deliberate murders, felony murder, and killing a "peace officer or corrections officer." The second-degree murder section provides that "All other kinds of murder shall be murder of the second degree, and shall be punished by imprisonment in the state prison for life, or any term of years, in the discretion of the court trying the same." The Michigan Court of Appeals applied Michigan's murder provisions in *People v. Thomas*.[16]

C A S E   Did He Intend to Kill?

People v. Thomas
85 Mich. App. 618, 272 N.W.2d 157 (1978)

Daniel Thomas was charged with second-degree murder. The jury convicted him of involuntary manslaughter. The trial judge sentenced Thomas to five to fifteen years in prison. Thomas appealed. The Michigan Court of Appeals affirmed.

D. E. HOLBROOK, JR., J.

FACTS

The victim, a 19-year-old male "catatonic schizophrenic," was at the time of his death a resident of Oak Haven, a religious practical training school. When it appeared he was not properly responding to ordinary treatment, defendant, the work coordinator at Oak Haven, obtained permission from the victim's parents to discipline him if such seemed necessary. Thereafter defendant, together with another supervisor at Oak Haven, took decedent to the edge of the campus, whereupon decedent's pants were taken down, following which he was spanked with a rubber hose. Such disciplinary session lasted approximately 15 to 30 minutes. During a portion thereof decedent's hands were tied behind his back for failure to cooperate.

Following the disciplinary session aforesaid, defendant testified that the young man improved for awhile but then commenced to backslide. Defendant again received permission from decedent's parents to subject him to further discipline. On September 30, 1976, defendant again took decedent to the approximate same location, removed his pants, bound his hands behind him with a rope looped over a tree limb and proceeded to beat him with a doubled-over rubber hose. This beating lasted approximately 45 minutes to an hour. While the evidence conflicted, it appears that the victim was struck between 30 to 100 times. The beating resulted in severe bruises ranging from the victim's waist to his feet. Decedent's roommate testified that decedent had open bleeding sores on his thighs. On the date of death, which was nine days after the beating, decedent's legs were immobile. At no time did defendant obtain medical attention for the victim.

Defendant admitted he had exercised poor judgment, after seeing the bruises, in continuing the discipline. He further testified that in the two days following the discipline, decedent seemed to be suffering from the flu, but by Sunday was up and walking and was in apparent good health until one week following the beating, when decedent became sick with nausea and an upset stomach. These symptoms continued for two days, when decedent died.

As a result of the autopsy, one Dr. Clark testified that the bruises were the result of a trauma and that decedent was in a state of continuous traumatization because he was trying to walk on his injured legs. Dr. Clark testified that decedent's legs were swollen to possibly twice their normal size. He further testified that the actual cause of death was acute pulmonary edema, resulting from the aspiration of stomach contents. Said aspiration caused a laryngeal spasm, causing decedent to suffocate on his own vomit. Although pulmonary edema was the direct cause of death, Dr. Clark testified that said condition usually had some underlying cause and that, while there were literally hundreds of potential underlying causes, it was his opinion that in the instant case the underlying cause was the trauma to decedent's legs.

In explaining how the trauma ultimately led to the pulmonary edema, Dr. Clark testified that the trauma to the legs produced "crush syndrome" or "blast trauma," also known as "tubular necrosis." "Crush syndrome" is a condition caused when a part of the body has been compressed for a long period of time and then released. In such cases, there is a tremendous amount of tissue damage to the body part that has been crushed. When the compression is relieved, the tissues begin to return to their normal position, but due to the compression, gaps appear between the layers of tissues, and these areas fill up with blood and other body fluids, causing swelling. In the present case, Dr. Clark estimated that about 10–15% of decedent's entire body fluids were contained in the legs, adding an additional ten pounds in weight to the normal weight of the legs and swelling them to twice their normal size. This extra blood and body fluid de-

creased the amount of blood available for circulation in the rest of the body and would cause the person to become weak, faint and pass out if he attempted to sit up or do other activities. Decedent was sitting up when he died.

It was Dr. Clark's opinion that the causal connection between the trauma and death was more than medically probable and that it was "medically likely." He further testified he could say with a reasonable degree of medical certainty that the trauma to the legs was the cause of death. . . .

OPINION

. . . Appellant claims that the prosecution failed to establish the malice element of second-degree murder. We disagree. Malice or intent to kill may be inferred from the acts of the defendant. In *People v. Morrin,* . . . Justice LEVIN, stated that the intent to kill may be implied where the actor actually intends to inflict great bodily harm or the natural tendency of his behavior is to cause death or great bodily harm. In the instant case defendant's savage and brutal beating of the decedent is amply sufficient to establish malice. He clearly intended to beat the victim and the natural tendency of defendant's behavior was to cause great bodily harm. . . .

Affirmed.

QUESTIONS FOR DISCUSSION

1. Michigan Penal Code Section 750.316 defines first-degree murder this way: "A person who commits any of the following is guilty of first degree murder and shall be punished by imprisonment for life: (a) Murder perpetrated by means of poison, lying in wait, or any other willful, deliberate, and premeditated killing." Section 750.317. defines second-degree murder as "All other kinds of murder shall be murder of the second degree, and shall be punished by imprisonment in the state prison for life, or any term of years, in the discretion of the court trying the same." Although the jury found Thomas guilty of involuntary manslaughter, the Michigan court of appeals ruled that the jury could have found Thomas guilty of second-degree murder because the facts supported the conclusion that Thomas intended to "inflict great bodily harm" on the deceased. Do the quoted

provisions mean this? Or do they require the specific intent to kill? Should the intent "to beat someone within an inch of his or her life" satisfy the *mens rea* of murder? Defend your answer.

2. How would you define Thomas's state of mind with respect to the student's death?

Knowing? Reckless? Negligent? An accident?

3. What facts support your answer?

4. Does this case mean that reckless homicide is murder? Explain.

5. Do you think it should be?

FELONY MURDER

Killing someone you didn't mean to kill while committing *some* felonies is called **felony murder.** What felonies? States vary widely, but the most common are criminal sexual conduct, kidnapping, robbery, arson, and burglary. What degree of murder? Here, too, states vary. In some states, first-degree, in others, second-degree. Alabama's felony murder provisions are representative:[17]

Alabama Criminal Code
Section 13A-6-2

(a) A person commits . . . murder if . . .

He commits or attempts to commit arson in the first degree, burglary in the first or second degree, escape in the first degree, kidnapping in the first degree, rape in the first degree, robbery in any degree, sodomy in the first degree or any other felony clearly dangerous to human life and, in the course of and in furtherance of the crime that he is committing or attempting to commit, or in immediate flight therefrom, he, or another participant if there be any, causes the death of any person.

(c) Murder is a Class A felony; provided, that the punishment for murder or any offense committed under aggravated circumstances, as provided by Article 2 of Chapter 5 of this title, is death or life imprisonment without parole, which punishment shall be determined and fixed as provided by Article 2 of Chapter 5 of this title or any amendments thereto.

Chapter 5, Article 2, Section 13A-5-40

a) The following are capital offenses:

(1) Murder by the defendant during a kidnapping in the first degree or an attempt thereof committed by the defendant.

(2) Murder by the defendant during a robbery in the first degree or an attempt thereof committed by the defendant.

(3) Murder by the defendant during a rape in the first or second degree or an attempt thereof committed by the defendant; or murder by the defendant during sodomy in the first or second degree or an attempt thereof committed by the defendant.

ELEMENTS OF FELONY MURDER

Actus Reus	Mens Rea	Circumstance	Causation	Result
Killing another person	Intent to commit a qualifying felony	Death during the commission of a qualifying felony	Act of committing a qualifying felony that triggers a chain of events that result in the death of another person	Death of another person

(4) Murder by the defendant during a burglary in the first or second degree or an attempt thereof committed by the defendant. . . .

(12) Murder by the defendant during the act of unlawfully assuming control of any aircraft by use of threats or force with intent to obtain any valuable consideration for the release of said aircraft or any passenger or crewmen thereon or to direct the route or movement of said aircraft, or otherwise exert control over said aircraft. . . .

Felony murder doesn't require the intent either to kill or to inflict serious bodily harm. In fact, most felony murderers don't intend either to kill or to injure their victims. The intent to commit the felony substitutes for the intent to kill. For example, if a robber fires a gun during the robbery and kills a convenience store clerk without the intent to kill, the intent to rob is blameworthy enough to satisfy the *mens rea* of felony murder. Felony murder laws are supposed to accomplish three policy goals:

- *Deter offenders:* The added threat of a murder conviction is supposed to prevent would-be felons from committing felonies that can lead to death.

- *Reduce violence:* The threat of a murder conviction is supposed to curtail the use of violence during the commission of felonies by inducing felons to act more carefully during robberies and other felonies fraught with the risk of injury and death.

- *Punish wrongdoers:* People who intentionally commit felonies, creating high risks of death or injury while they do so, should suffer the most serious possible consequences for their actions.

Research hasn't shown that the rule either deters dangerous felons or reduces the number of deaths during the commission of felonies. Four states—Ohio, Hawaii, Michigan, and Kentucky—have abolished felony murder. Other states have restricted felony murder to deaths that were foreseeable during the commission of the underlying felony. In *State v. Noren*, during a robbery, Monte Noren punched his victim three times in the head so hard that Noren's knuckles bled. The victim was extremely drunk, which Noren knew. The court decided that the victim's death was foreseeable. In the course of its opinion, the court explained why felony murder is limited to foreseeable deaths. According to the court,

> The statutory requirement that death be a probable consequence of a felony is intended to limit felony-murder liability to situations where the defendant's conduct creates some measure of foreseeable risk of death. Under the predecessor felony-murder statute, a defendant committed murder when death resulted from the commission of any felony. This rule was modified because it imposed severe criminal sanctions without considering the moral culpability of the defendant. . . . [Therefore,] the acts causing death must be inherently dangerous to life. We apply this test to felony-murder because it requires a high degree of foreseeability, thereby implicitly requiring greater culpability than lesser grades of homicide. Our supreme court applied this standard under the predecessor felony-murder statute when it stated that the act constituting the felony must be in itself dangerous to life.[18]

What if the victim, police officers, or a co-felon cause someone's death during a felony? Some states say deaths caused by third persons aren't felony murder. For example, when a resisting victim shot and killed one of two burglars, the court ruled that the surviving burglar couldn't be found guilty of felony murder. Similarly, when a cabdriver and a police officer shot and killed one of two men attempting to rob the driver, the surviving attempted robber was not guilty of felony murder. Some states have created an exception to the third-party exclusion to the felony murder rule when a resisting victim causes the death. In one case, a felony assault victim shot and killed one of his attackers. The court ruled that the surviving attacker could be found guilty of felony murder under the resisting victim exception.[19]

Felony murder applies only to deaths that happen during the commission of *dangerous* felonies. For example, the California Supreme Court held that a chiropractor was not guilty of felony murder when he fraudulently treated a cancer patient with chiropractic and the patient died. The court ruled that although a felony, fraud was not a "dangerous" felony. The Rhode Island Supreme Court examined the meaning of "dangerous felonies" in *State v. Stewart*.[20]

C A S E   Did She Commit an "Inherently Dangerous" Felony?

State v. Stewart
663 A.2d 912 (RI. 1995)

Twenty-year-old Tracy Stewart was convicted in the Superior Court, Providence County, of second-degree felony murder. She appealed. The Supreme Court affirmed the conviction.
WEISBERGER, CJ.

FACTS

On August 31, 1988, twenty-year-old Tracy Stewart gave birth to a son, Travis Young (Travis). Travis's father was Edward Young, Sr. (Young). Stewart and Young, who had two other children together, were not married at the time of Travis's birth. [Subsequent to her trial, Stewart married Young. Several months later she filed for divorce.] Travis lived for only fifty-two days, dying on October 21, 1988, from dehydration.

During the week prior to Travis's death, Stewart, Young, and a friend, Patricia McMasters (McMasters), continually and repeatedly ingested cocaine over a two-to three-consecutive-day period at the apartment shared by Stewart and Young. The baby, Travis, was also present at the apartment while Stewart, Young, and McMasters engaged in this cocaine marathon. Young and McMasters injected cocaine intravenously and also smoked it while Stewart ingested the cocaine only by smoking it. The smoked cocaine was in its strongest or base form, commonly referred to as "crack." When the three exhausted an existing supply of cocaine, they would pool their money and Young and McMasters would go out and buy more with the accumulated funds. The primary source of funds from which the three obtained money for this co-

caine spree was Stewart's and McMasters's Aid to Families with Dependent Children (AFDC) checks. Stewart and McMasters had each just received the second of their semimonthly AFDC checks. They both cashed their AFDC checks and gave money to Young, which he then used to purchase more cocaine. After all the AFDC funds had been spent on cocaine and the group had run out of money, McMasters and Young committed a robbery to obtain additional money to purchase more cocaine.

The cocaine binge continued uninterrupted for two to three days. McMasters testified that during this time neither McMasters nor Stewart slept at all. McMasters testified that defendant was never far from her during this entire two- to three-day period except for the occasions when McMasters left the apartment to buy more cocaine. During this entire time, McMasters saw defendant feed Travis only once. Travis was in a walker, and defendant propped a bottle of formula up on the walker, using a blanket, for the baby to feed himself. McMasters testified that she did not see defendant hold the baby to feed him nor did she see defendant change Travis's diaper or clothes during this period.

Ten months after Travis's death defendant was indicted on charges of second-degree murder, wrongfully causing or permitting a child under the age of eighteen to be a habitual sufferer for want of food and proper care (hereinafter sometimes referred to as "wrongfully permitting a child to be a habitual sufferer"), and manslaughter. The second-degree-murder charge was based on a theory of felony murder. The prosecution did not allege that defendant intentionally killed her son but rather that he had been killed during the commission of an inherently dangerous felony, specifically, wrongfully permitting a child to be a habitual sufferer. Moreover, the prosecution did not allege that defendant intentionally withheld food or care from her son. Rather the state alleged that because of defendant's chronic state of cocaine intoxication, she may have realized what her responsibilities were but simply could not remember whether she had fed her son, when in fact she had not.

At defendant's trial both the prosecution and the defense presented expert medical witnesses who testified concerning what they believed to be the cause of Travis's death. The experts for both sides agreed that the cause of death was dehydration, but they strongly disagreed regarding what caused the dehydration. The prosecution expert witnesses believed that the dehydration was caused by insufficient intake of food and water, that is, malnutrition. The defense expert witnesses, conversely, believed that the dehydration was caused by a gastrointestinal virus known as gastroenteritis which manifested itself in an overwhelming expulsion of fluid from the baby's body.

The defendant was found guilty of both second-degree murder and wrongfully permitting a child to be a habitual sufferer. A subsequent motion for new trial was denied. This appeal followed. . . .

OPINION

. . . At the pretrial hearing on the motion to dismiss, defendant argued that the law in Rhode Island is moving toward the approach used in California to determine if a felony is inherently dangerous. This approach examines the elements of a felony in the abstract. . . . In denying the motion to dismiss, the trial justice stated that "nothing . . . in my examination of Rhode Island case law, leads the Court to conclude that the Rhode Island Supreme Court is moving toward the California concept." Rather than determine if the crime of wrongfully permitting a child to be a habitual sufferer was inherently dangerous in the abstract, the trial justice ruled that the state would have the opportunity to prove at trial that the crime was inherently dangerous in the manner that it was committed. The trial justice committed no error in so ruling. . . .

The defendant moved for judgment of acquittal . . . at the close of the state's case and again at the close of all the evidence. In regard to the felony-murder charge defendant claimed that the evidence was insufficient to prove (1) that the crime of wrongfully permitting a child to be a habitual sufferer is an inherently dangerous felony and (2) that defendant intentionally committed the crime of wrongfully permitting a child to be a habitual sufferer. The motions for judgment of acquittal were denied on both grounds. The defendant claims that the denial of her motions for judgment of acquittal was reversible error.

Rhode Island's murder statute, § 11231, enumerates certain crimes that may serve as predicate felonies to a charge of first-degree murder. A felony that is not enumerated in § 11231 can, however, serve as a predicate felony to a charge of second-degree murder. Thus the fact that the crime of wrongfully permitting a child to be a habitual sufferer is not specified in § 11231 as a predicate felony to support a charge of first-degree murder does not preclude such crime from serving as a predicate to support a charge of second-degree murder.

In Rhode Island, second-degree murder has been equated with common-law murder. At common law, where the rule is unchanged by statute, "homicide is murder if the death results from the perpetration or attempted perpetration of an inherently dangerous felony." To serve as a predicate felony to a charge of second-degree murder, a felony that is not specifically enumerated in § 11231 must therefore be an inherently dangerous felony.

The defendant contends that wrongfully permitting a child to be a habitual sufferer is not an inherently dangerous felony and cannot therefore serve as the predicate felony to a charge of second-degree murder. In advancing her argument, defendant urges this court to adopt the approach used by California courts to determine if a felony is inherently dangerous. This approach requires that the court consider the elements of the felony "in the abstract" rather than look at the particular facts of the case under consideration. With such an approach, if a statute can be violated in a manner that does not endanger human life, then the felony is not inherently dangerous to human life. Moreover, the California Supreme Court has defined an act as "inherently dangerous to human life when there is 'a high probability that it will result in death.'"

In *People v. Caffero*, 207 Cal.App.3d 678, 68384, 255 Cal.Rptr. 22, 25 (1989) . . . a two-and-one-half-week-old baby died of a massive bacterial infection caused by lack of proper hygiene that was due to parental neglect. The parents were charged with second-degree felony murder and felony-child-abuse, with the felony-child-abuse charge serving as the predicate felony to the second-degree-murder charge. Examining California's felony-child-abuse statute in the abstract, instead of looking at the particular facts of the case, the court held that because the statute could be violated in ways that did not endanger human life, felony-child abuse was not inherently dangerous to human life. By way of example, the court noted that a fractured limb, which comes within the ambit of the felony-child-abuse statute, is unlikely to endanger the life of an infant, much less of a seventeen-year-old. . . . Because felony-child-abuse was not inherently dangerous to human life, it could not properly serve as a predicate felony to a charge of second-degree felony murder.

The defendant urges this court to adopt the method of analysis employed by California courts to determine if a felony is inherently dangerous to life. . . . We decline defendant's invitation to adopt the California approach in determining whether a felony is inherently dangerous to life and thus capable of serving as a predicate to a charge of second-degree felony murder. We believe that the better approach is for the trier of fact to consider the facts and circumstances of the particular case to determine if such felony was inherently dangerous in the manner and the circumstances in which it was committed, rather than have a court make the determination by viewing the elements of a felony in the abstract. We now join a number of states that have adopted this approach. . . .

The proper procedure for making such a determination is to present the facts and circumstances of the particular case to the trier of fact and for the trier of fact to determine if a felony is inherently dangerous in the manner and the circumstances in which it was committed. This is exactly what happened in the case at bar. The trial justice instructed the jury that before it could find defendant guilty of second-degree murder, it must first find that wrongfully causing or permitting a child to be a habitual sufferer for want of food or proper care was inherently dangerous to human life "in its manner of commission." This was a proper charge. By its guilty verdict on the charge of second-degree murder, the jury obviously found that wrongfully permitting a child to be a habitual sufferer for want of food or proper care was indeed a felony inher-

ently dangerous to human life in the circumstances of this particular case. . . .

. . . We are of the opinion that the evidence offered by the state was sufficient to prove beyond a reasonable doubt each of the elements of second-degree felony murder, including that the crime of wrongfully permitting a child to be a habitual sufferer was an inherently dangerous felony in its manner of commission. The defendant's motions for judgment of acquittal on the felony-murder charge on the ground that wrongfully permitting a child to be a habitual sufferer is not an inherently dangerous felony were properly denied.

The theory of felony murder is that a defendant does not have to have intended to kill one who dies during the course of certain statutorily enumerated felonies, or other inherently dangerous felonies, in order to be charged with murder. The intent to commit the underlying felony will be imputed to the homicide, and a defendant may thus be charged with murder on the basis of the intent to commit the underlying felony.

The defendant claims that the evidence presented at trial failed to establish that she intentionally committed the crime of wrongfully permitting a child to be a habitual sufferer. She claims that absent an intent to commit this felony, it cannot serve as a predicate to support a charge of second-degree felony murder because there would then be no intent to be imputed from the underlying felony to the homicide. We agree with defendant that intent to commit the underlying felony is a necessary element of felony murder. However, we believe the circumstances surrounding the events preceding Travis's death support a finding that defendant did indeed intentionally permit her son to be a habitual sufferer for want of food or proper care.

The defendant's addiction to and compulsion to have cocaine were the overriding factors that controlled virtually every aspect of her life. She referred to the extended periods that she was high on cocaine as "going on a mission." Although she was receiving public assistance and did not have much disposable income, she nevertheless spent a great deal of money on cocaine, including her AFDC money. She shoplifted and traded the stolen merchandise for cocaine. She stole food because she had used the money that she should have been using to purchase food to purchase cocaine. The compulsion to have cocaine at any cost took precedence over every facet of defendant's life including caring for her children.

Although defendant did not testify at trial, she did testify before the grand jury. A redacted tape of her grand jury testimony was admitted into evidence and played for the jury at trial. During the days preceding Travis's death, defendant had been on a two- to three-day cocaine binge, a mission, as she referred to it. Her grand jury testimony indicated that she knew that during such periods she was unable to care for her children properly. The defendant testified that whenever she would go on a mission, her mother, who lived only a few houses away, would take and care for the children. This testimony evinced a knowledge on the part of defendant that she was incapable of properly caring for her children during these periods of extended cocaine intoxication. In addition, defendant was prone to petit mal seizures, which were exacerbated by her cocaine use. During such seizures she would "black out" or "go into a coma state." She testified before the grand jury that she was aware that taking cocaine brought on more seizures and that the weekend before Travis died she had in fact blacked out and "went into a coma state."

Despite her grand jury testimony to the contrary, Travis remained with defendant at her apartment during the entire two- to three-day binge. He died two or three days later. The defendant's repeated voluntary and intentional ingestion of crack cocaine while her seven-week-old son was in her care, in addition to her testimony that she knew that she was incapable of properly caring for her children during these extended periods of cocaine intoxication, support a finding that she intentionally permitted her son to be a habitual sufferer for want of food and proper care. We make the distinction between a finding that defendant intentionally deprived her son of food and proper care, which even the state does not allege, and a finding that defendant intentionally permitted her son to be a habitual sufferer for want of food or proper care, which we find to be supported by the evidence adduced at trial. . . .

Two or three days after the cocaine binge had ended, defendant went to McMasters's apartment and informed her that Travis had died that morning. The defendant was carrying a bag containing cans of baby formula and asked McMasters if she knew where she (defendant) could exchange the unused formula for cocaine. McMasters told defendant that she did not know where the formula could be exchanged for cocaine but suggested that

she take it to a local supermarket to get a cash refund. McMasters then accompanied defendant to a supermarket in Pawtucket where they attempted to return the formula for cash. They were unsuccessful in this attempt, however, because they did not have a receipt for the formula and store policy dictated that no cash refunds be given for returns without a receipt for the merchandise. The defendant told the assistant store manager that her baby had just died, and the manager gave defendant $20 out of his own pocket because he felt sorry for her. The defendant used this $20 to purchase cocaine. The defendant and McMasters then went to McMasters's apartment and smoked cocaine. . . .

In order for the crime of wrongfully permitting a child to be a habitual sufferer to serve as a predicate felony to a charge of second-degree felony murder, the accused must have had the intent to commit the underlying felony. Although it is true that the trial justice did not specifically instruct the jury that in order to find defendant guilty of second-degree murder, it must find as one of the elements of the crime that she intentionally caused or permitted her son to be a habitual sufferer for want of food or proper care, we believe that the instructions given were substantially equivalent. The trial justice instructed the jury that it must find that defendant wrongfully, that is, without legal justification or without legal excuse, caused or permitted Travis to be a habitual sufferer. She also instructed that it must find that defendant knew or was aware beforehand that there was a likelihood that Travis's life would be endangered as a result of permitting or causing him to be a habitual sufferer for want of food or proper care. We believe that these two instructions in combination, requiring that the jury find that defendant had no legal justification or no legal excuse for causing her son to be a habitual sufferer and also requiring that the jury find that defendant knew or was aware beforehand that causing or permitting her son to be a habitual sufferer for want of food or proper care was likely to endanger his life, were the functional equivalent to an instruction requiring the jury to find that defendant intentionally caused or permitted her son to be a habitual sufferer. "This failure to distinguish between intent . . . and knowledge is probably of little consequence in many areas of the law, as often there is good reason for imposing liability whether the defendant desired or merely knew of the practical certainty of the results." LaFave and

Scott, *Substantive Criminal Law,* § 3.5(b) at 305 (1986); see also *Model Penal Code* § 2.02 cmt. 2 at 234 (1985) (the "distinction [between acting purposely and knowingly] is inconsequential for most purposes of liability; acting knowingly is ordinarily sufficient"). The trial justice committed no error in refusing to give the requested instruction.

For the foregoing reasons the defendant's appeal is denied and dismissed, and the judgment of conviction is affirmed. The papers in the case may be remanded to the Superior Court.

QUESTIONS FOR DISCUSSION

1. Explain California's approach of determining "inherently dangerous felony" in the abstract.

2. Why did the Rhode Island court reject the California approach?

3. What test did the Rhode Island court use in determining whether the felony of wrongfully permitting a child to suffer is inherently dangerous?

4. In your opinion, which is the better test? Why?

5. List all of the facts in this case relevant to determining whether Tracy Stewart was guilty of felony murder.

6. Assume you are a defense attorney in California. Relying on the relevant facts, argue that Stewart is not guilty of felony murder.

7. Assume you are a prosecutor in Rhode Island. Relying on the facts, argue that Stewart is guilty of felony murder.

NOTE CASES

1. Harry Cline, Dennis Smith, and Arthur Bragg got together to "do drugs." Cline had illegally obtained phenobarbital tablets and the three shared them. Bragg seemed unable to get high on them, so he asked for more, which Cline readily supplied. Later in the evening, after taking a total of 52 tablets, Bragg lapsed into unconsciousness. A few days later, Bragg died from a central nervous system depression caused by barbiturate intoxication. The state of California prosecuted Cline for felony murder, and he was convicted. Cline maintained that the underlying

felony—illegal use of narcotics—was not inherently dangerous to human life. On appeal, the California Supreme Court held:

A homicide that is a direct causal result of the commission of a felony inherently dangerous to human life (other than the six felonies enumerated in Pen.Code, § 189) constitutes at least second-degree murder. However, there can be no deterrent where the felony is not inherently dangerous, since the potential felon will not anticipate that any injury or death might arise solely from the fact that he will commit the felony. . . . The crucial issue that must be resolved in this appeal is, as pointed out by both parties, whether the felony of furnishing a restricted dangerous drug in violation of § 11912 of the Health and Safety Code is inherently dangerous to human life.

The trial judge found that defendant's act in furnishing a restricted dangerous drug to the deceased in violation of law was inherently dangerous to human life. His finding in this respect is amply supported by the evidence. It was the uncontroverted testimony of the pathologist that the consumption of phenobarbital in unknown strength was dangerous to human life. There was clear evidence that within a period of one-half hour this drug was consumed in considerable quantity by Bragg in defendant's presence and with his knowledge. Even defendant admitted that the deceased consumed 15 of these pills within one-half hour. It is also significant that the Legislature has defined this type of drug as "dangerous." (Health & Saf.Code, § 11901.)

People v. Cline, 75 Cal.Rptr. 459 (1969)

2. Lee Swatsenbarg had been diagnosed by the family physician as suffering from terminal leukemia. Unable to accept impending death, the twenty-four-year-old Swatsenbarg unsuccessfully sought treatment from a variety of traditional medical sources. He and his wife then began to participate in Bible study, hoping that through faith Lee might be cured. Finally, on the advice of a mutual acquaintance who had heard of defendant's ostensible successes in healing others, Lee turned to defendant for treatment.

During the first meeting between Lee and defendant, the latter described his method of curing cancer. This method included consumption of a unique "lemonade," exposure to colored lights, and a brand of vigorous massage administered by defendant. Defendant remarked that he had successfully treated "thousands" of people, including a number of physicians. He suggested the Swatsenbargs purchase a copy of his book, *Healing for the Age of Enlightenment.* If after reading the book Lee wished to begin defendant's unorthodox treatment, defendant would commence caring for Lee immediately. During the thirty days designated for the treatment, Lee would have to avoid contact with his physician.

Lee read the book, submitted to the conditions delineated by defendant, and placed himself under defendant's care. Defendant instructed Lee to drink the lemonade, salt water, and herb tea, but consume nothing more for the ensuing thirty days. At defendant's behest, the Swatsenbargs bought a lamp equipped with some colored plastic sheets, to bathe Lee in various tints of light. Defendant also agreed to massage Lee from time to time, for an additional fee per session.

Rather than improve, within two weeks Lee's condition began rapidly to deteriorate. He developed a fever and was growing progressively weaker. Defendant counseled Lee that all was proceeding according to plan and convinced the young man to postpone a bone marrow test urged by his doctor. During the next week Lee became increasingly ill. He was experiencing severe pain in several areas, including his abdomen, and vomiting frequently. Defendant administered "deep" abdom-inal massages on two successive days, each time telling Lee he would soon recuperate. Lee did not recover as defendant expected, however, and the patient began to suffer from convulsions and excruciating pain. He vomited with increasing frequency. Despite defendant's constant attempts at reassurance, the Swatsenbargs began to panic when Lee convulsed for a third time after the latest abdominal massage.

Three and a half weeks into the treatment, the couple spent the night at defendant's house, where Lee died of a massive hemorrhage of the mesentery in the abdomen. The evidence presented at trial strongly suggested the hemorrhage was the direct result of the massages performed by defendant.

Did Burroughs commit a felony murder? In deciding that he did not, the California Supreme Court noted:

the few times we have found an underlying felony inherently dangerous (so that it would support a conviction of felony murder), the offense has been tinged with malevolence totally absent from the facts of this case.

People v. Burroughs, 35 Cal.3d 824, 201 Cal.Rptr. 319, 678 P.2d 894 (1984)

CORPORATE MURDER

Can corporations commit murder? Yes, according to a few prosecutors who have prosecuted corporations for murder. Probably the most publicized corporate murder case involved three young women who were killed on an Indiana highway when their Ford Pinto exploded after being struck from behind by another vehicle. The explosion followed several other similar incidents involving Pintos that led to grisly deaths. Published evidence revealed that Ford may have known that the Pinto gas tanks were not safe but took the risk that they would not explode and injure or kill anyone. Following the three young women's deaths, the state of Indiana indicted Ford Motor Company for reckless homicide, charging that Ford had recklessly authorized, approved, designed, and manufactured the Pinto and allowed the car to remain in use with defectively designed fuel tanks. These tanks, the indictment charged, killed the three young women in Indiana. For a number of reasons not related directly to whether corporations can commit murder, the case was later dismissed.[21]

In another case that drew wide public attention during the 1980s, Autumn Hills Convalescent Centers, a corporation that operated nursing homes, went on trial for charges that it had murdered an eighty-seven-year-old woman by neglect. David Marks, a Texas assistant attorney general, said, "From the first day until her last breath, she was unattended to and allowed to lie day and night in her own urine and waste." The case attracted attention because of allegations that as many as sixty elderly people had died from substandard care at the Autumn Hills nursing home near

Galveston, Texas. The indictment charged that the company had failed to provide nutrients, fluids, and incontinent care for Mrs. Breed and neglected to turn and reposition her regularly to combat bedsores. One prosecution witness testified that Mrs. Breed's bed was wet constantly and the staff seldom cleaned her. The corporation defended against the charges, claiming that Mrs. Breed had died from colon cancer, not improper care.[22]

Most state criminal codes apply to corporate criminal homicide in the same way that they apply to other crimes committed for the corporation's benefit. Specifically, both corporations and high corporate officers acting within the scope of their authority and for the benefit of a corporation can commit murder. Practically speaking, however, prosecutors rarely charge corporations or their officers with criminal homicide, and convictions rarely follow.

The reluctance to prosecute corporations for murder, or for any homicide requiring the intent to kill or inflict serious bodily injury, is due largely to the hesitation to view corporations as persons. Although theoretically the law clearly makes that possible, in practice prosecutors and courts have drawn the line at involuntary manslaughter, a crime whose *mens rea* is negligence and occasionally recklessness. As for corporate executives, the reluctance to prosecute stems from vicarious liability and the questions it raises about culpability (see Chapter 4). It has been difficult to attribute deaths linked with corporate benefit to corporate officers who were in charge generally but didn't order or authorize a killing, didn't know about it, or even didn't want it to happen.

Only in egregious cases that receive widespread public attention, such as the Pinto and nursing home cases mentioned earlier, do prosecutors risk acquittal by trying corporations and their officers for criminal homicide. In these cases, prosecutors aren't hoping to win the case in traditional terms, meaning to secure convictions. Business law professor William J. Maakestad says: "At this point, success of this type of corporate criminal prosecution is defined by establishing the legitimacy of the case. If you can get the case to trial, you have really achieved success."

People v. O'Neil involves one of the few prosecutions of a corporation and its officers for murder.[23]

C A S E   Did They "Murder" Their Employee?

People v. O'Neil
194 Ill.App.3d 79, 550 N.E.2d 1090 (1990)

Following a joint bench trial [trial without a jury], Steven O'Neil, Charles Kirschbaum, and Daniel Rodriguez, agents of Film Recovery Systems, Inc. (Film Recovery), were convicted of the murder of Stefan Golab, a Film Recovery employee, from cyanide poisoning stemming from conditions in Film Recovery's plant in Elk Grove Village, Illinois. Corporate defendants Film Recovery and its sister corporation Metallic Marketing Systems, Inc. (Metallic Marketing), were convicted of involuntary manslaughter in the same death. O'Neil, Kirschbaum, and Rodriguez each received sentences of 25 years' imprisonment for murder. O'Neil and Kirschbaum were also each fined $10,000 with respect to the murder convictions. Corporate defendants Film Recovery and Metallic Marketing were each fined $10,000 with respect to the convictions for involuntary manslaughter. The defendants appealed, and the appellate court reversed the convictions.

LORENZ, J.

FACTS

...In 1982, Film Recovery occupied premises at 1855 and 1875 Greenleaf Avenue in Elk Grove Village. Film Recovery was there engaged in the business of extracting, for resale, silver from used x-ray and photographic film. Metallic Marketing operated out of the same premises on Greenleaf Avenue and owned 50% of the stock of Film Recovery. The recovery process was performed at Film Recovery's plant located at the 1855 address and involved "chipping" the film product and soaking the granulated pieces in large open bubbling vats containing a solution of water and sodium cyanide. The cyanide solution caused silver contained in the film to be released. A continuous flow system pumped the silver laden solution into polyurethane tanks which contained electrically charged stainless steel plates to which the separated silver adhered. The plates were removed from the tanks to another room where the accumulated silver was scraped off. The remaining solution was pumped out of the tanks and the granulated film, devoid of silver, shoveled out.

On the morning of February 10, 1983, shortly after he disconnected a pump on one of the tanks and began to stir the contents of the tank with a rake, Stefan Golab became dizzy and faint. He left the production area to go rest in the lunchroom area of the plant. Plant workers present on that day testified Golab's body had trembled and he had foamed at the mouth. Golab eventually lost consciousness and was taken outside of the plant. Paramedics summoned to the plant were unable to revive him. Golab was pronounced dead upon arrival at Alexian Brothers Hospital.

The Cook County medical examiner performed an autopsy on Golab the following day. Although the medical examiner initially indicated Golab could have died from cardiac arrest, he reserved final determination of death pending examination of results of toxicological laboratory tests on Golab's blood and other body specimens. After receiving the toxicological report, the medical examiner determined Golab died from acute cyanide poisoning through the inhalation of cyanide fumes in the plant air.

Defendants were subsequently indicted by a Cook County grand jury. The grand jury charged defendants O'Neil, Kirschbaum, Rodriguez, Pett, and Mackay with murder, stating that, as individuals and as officers and high managerial agents of Film Recovery, they had, on February 10, 1983, knowingly created a strong probability of Golab's death. Generally, the indictment stated the individ-

ual defendants failed to disclose to Golab that he was working with substances containing cyanide and failed to advise him about, train him to anticipate, and provide adequate equipment to protect him from, attendant dangers involved. The grand jury charged Film Recovery and Metallic Marketing with involuntary manslaughter stating that, through the reckless acts of their officers, directors, agents, and others, all acting within the scope of their employment, the corporate entities had, on February 10, 1983, unintentionally killed Golab. Finally, the grand jury charged both individual and corporate defendants with reckless conduct as to 20 other Film Recovery employees based on the same conduct alleged in the murder indictment, but expanding the time of that conduct to "on or about March 1982 through March 1983."

Proceedings commenced in the circuit court in January 1985 and continued through the conclusion of trial in June of that year. In the course of the 24-day trial, evidence from 59 witnesses was presented, either directly or through stipulation of the parties. That testimony is contained in over 2,300 pages of trial transcript. The parties also presented numerous exhibits including photographs, corporate documents and correspondence, as well as physical evidence.

On June 14, 1985, the trial judge pronounced his judgment of defendants' guilt. The trial judge found that "the mind and mental state of a corporation is the mind and mental state of the directors, officers and high managerial personnel because they act on behalf of the corporation for both the benefit of the corporation and for themselves." Further, "if the corporation's officers, directors and high managerial personnel act within the scope of their corporate responsibilities and employment for their benefit and for the benefit of the profits of the corporation, the corporation must be held liable for what occurred in the work place."

Defendants filed timely notices of appeal, the matters were consolidated for review, and arguments were had before this court in July 1987. . . .

OPINION

. . . We find it helpful to set out the pertinent statutory language of the offenses for which the defendants were convicted. The Criminal Code of 1961 defines murder as follows:

A person who kills an individual without lawful justification commits murder if, in performing the acts which cause the death: He knows that such acts create a strong probability of death or great bodily harm to that individual. (Ill.Rev.Stat.1981, ch. 38, par.9–1(a)(2).)

Involuntary manslaughter is defined as:

A person who unintentionally kills an individual without lawful justification commits involuntary manslaughter if his acts whether lawful or unlawful which cause the death are such as are likely to cause death or great bodily harm to some individual, and he performs them recklessly. (Ill.Rev.Stat.1981, ch. 38, par. 9–3(a).)

Reckless conduct is defined as:

A person who causes bodily harm to or endangers the bodily safety of an individual by any means, commits reckless conduct if he performs recklessly the acts which cause the harm or endanger safety, whether they otherwise are lawful or unlawful. (Ill.Rev.Stat.1981, ch. 38, par. 12–5(a)).

. . .

. . . In Illinois, a corporation is criminally responsible for offenses "authorized, requested, commanded, or performed by the board of directors or by a high managerial agent acting within the scope of his employment." (Ill.Rev.Stat.1981, ch. 38, par. 5–4(a)(2).) A high managerial agent is defined as "an officer of the corporation, or any other agent who has a position of comparable authority for the formulation of corporate policy or the supervision of subordinate employees in a managerial capacity." (Ill.Rev.Stat. 1981, ch. 38, par. 5–4(c)(2).) Thus, a corporation is criminally responsible whenever any of its high managerial agents possess the requisite mental state and is responsible for a criminal offense while acting within the scope of his employment. . . .

. . .

Evidence at trial indicated Golab died after inhaling poisonous cyanide fumes while working in a plant operated by Film Recovery and its sister corporation Metallic Marketing where such fumes resulted from a process employed to remove silver from used x-ray and photographic film. The record contains substantial evidence regarding the nature of working conditions inside the plant. Testimony established that air inside the plant was foul smelling and made breathing difficult and painful. Plant workers experienced dizziness, nausea, headaches,

and bouts of vomiting. There is evidence that plant workers were not informed they were working with cyanide. Nor were they informed of the presence of, or danger of breathing, cyanide gas. Ventilation in the plant was poor. Plant workers were given neither safety instruction nor adequate protective clothing. Finally, testimony established that defendants O'Neil, Kirschbaum, and Rodriguez were responsible for operating the plant under those conditions. For purposes of our disposition, we find further elaboration on the evidence unnecessary. Moreover, although we have determined evidence in the record is not so insufficient as to bar retrial, our determination of the sufficiency of the evidence should not be in any way interpreted as a finding as to defendants' guilt that would be binding on the court on retrial.

Reversed and remanded.

QUESTIONS FOR DISCUSSION

1. What are the relevant facts in determining whether the corporation and the individuals were guilty of murder or involuntary manslaughter?

2. Why did the court reverse and remand the case?

3. On remand, would you find the defendants guilty of murder? Explain your answer.

4. Do you agree that it is inconsistent to find that the corporation had one state of mind and the individuals another?

5. Consider the following remarks made after the convictions in the original trial.

Following the conviction in the original trial, then attorney Richard M. Daley said the verdicts meant that employers who knowingly expose their workers to dangerous conditions leading to injury or even death can be held criminally responsible for the results of their actions. Ralph Nader, consumer advocate lawyer, said:

The public is pretty upset with dangerously defective products, bribery, toxic waste, and job hazards. The polls all show it. The verdict today will encourage other prosecutors and judges to take more seriously the need to have the criminal law catch up with corporate crime.

Professor John Coffee, Columbia University Law School, said, "When you threaten the principal adequately, he will monitor the behavior of his agent." A California deputy district attorney put it more bluntly: "A person facing a jail sentence is the best deterrent against wrongdoing." Joseph E. Hadley, Jr., a corporate lawyer who specializes in health and safety issues, said the decision would not send shock waves through the corporate community: "I don't think corporate America should be viewed as in the ballpark with these folks. This was a highly unusual situation, but now people see that where the egregious situation occurs, there could be a criminal remedy."

Robert Stephenson, a lawyer defending another corporation, said, "I don't believe these statutes [murder and aggravated battery] were ever meant to be used in this way."

Utah's governor, Scott M. Matheson, refused to extradite Michael T. McKay, a former Film Recovery vice-president then living in Utah, because he was an "exemplary citizen who should not be subjected to the sensational charges in Illinois."[24]

Which of the statements best describes what you think is proper policy regarding corporate executive murder prosecutions? Defend your answer.

MANSLAUGHTER

Manslaughter, like murder, is an ancient common-law crime that was created by judges, not legislatures. At first, all manslaughters were treated alike. Later, courts and then legislatures divided manslaughter into two main categories: intentional or voluntary heat-of-passion manslaughter and unintentional or involuntary manslaughter.[25]

VOLUNTARY MANSLAUGHTER

Voluntary manslaughter is the intentional killing of another live human being under extenuating circumstances. One extenuating circumstance is imperfect self-defense, that is, the intentional killing of another in the honest—but not reasonable—belief that self-defense required the use of deadly force (see Chapter 7). Practically speaking, this means that the honest belief in the need to use deadly force can reduce first-degree murder to voluntary manslaughter. According to one court, "A person is guilty of voluntary manslaughter, if, in taking another's life, he believes that he is in danger of losing his own life or suffering great bodily harm but his belief is unreasonable."[26]

Provocation is the most common extenuating circumstance that reduces murder to voluntary manslaughter. While the criminal law aims to bridle passions and build self-control, at the same time it doesn't ignore the frailty of human nature. So, an

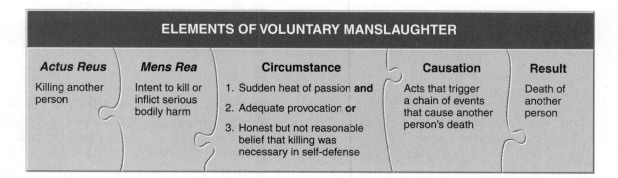

ELEMENTS OF VOLUNTARY MANSLAUGHTER

Actus Reus	*Mens Rea*	Circumstance	Causation	Result
Killing another person	Intent to kill or inflict serious bodily harm	1. Sudden heat of passion **and** 2. Adequate provocation **or** 3. Honest but not reasonable belief that killing was necessary in self-defense	Acts that trigger a chain of events that cause another person's death	Death of another person

intentional killing that the victim provoked, while still a serious felony, isn't murder. The law of voluntary manslaughter doesn't reward individuals who give in to their rages by letting them walk, but it does make what they did somewhat less serious. And it makes the killing less serious only under the severe limits of the **adequate provocation rule**. According to the rule, the killing has to meet all of the following conditions. It was committed:

1. During a sudden "heat of passion"
2. Without time for the passion to "cool off"
3. Where the provocation caused the passion and killing
4. Because of a provocation that is specifically recognized by law[27]

Not everyone who flies into a rage and suddenly kills someone has committed voluntary manslaughter instead of murder. The law of voluntary manslaughter recognizes only *adequate* provocation, namely the provocations specifically recognized by the law. These include:

1. Mutual combat (fighting)
2. Assault and battery (Chapter 10)
3. Tespass (Chapter 11)
4. Adultery

Only serious fights are adequate provocation; scuffles don't qualify. The fight has to create a sudden passion without reasonable time to cool off before the killing. And the provocation has to cause the passion and the death. Some batteries—but not all offensive touching (see Chapter 10)—are adequate provocation. Pistol whipping on the head, striking hard with fists in the face, and "staggering" body blows qualify. Mere slaps or shoves don't.

Assault without body contact is sometimes adequate provocation. In one case, a man shot at the defendant and missed him. The defendant was so enraged that he shot his attacker in the back as the assailant ran away. The court ruled that the shot in the back wasn't justified as self-defense, but it was provocative enough to reduce murder to manslaughter.[28]

Insulting gestures by themselves aren't adequate provocation. However, if they indicate an intent to attack with deadly force they are. So, using a well-known obscene gesture is not adequate provocation, but waving a gun around in a threatening manner can be. Trespasses are adequate provocation only if trespassers invade the homes of slayers and put the slayers in danger. In *State v. Watson*, the North Carolina supreme court examined the ancient rule that words are never adequate provocation.[29]

C A S E   Were the Racial Slurs Adequate Provocation?

State v. Watson
287 N.C. 147, 214 S.E.2d 85 (1975)

Rufus Watson, Jr. was convicted of second-degree murder and was sentenced to life imprisonment. He appealed, arguing that he was legally provoked. The conviction was affirmed.

COPELAND, J.

FACTS

At the time of this incident, defendant, a black, was twenty-years-old. He was serving a twenty-five year prison sentence on judgment imposed at the October, 1972, Session of Rockingham County Superior Court upon his plea of guilty to second-degree murder. The decedent Samples, was white.

Neither Samples' age nor the basis for his incarceration appears from the record. The defendant was called "Duck" by his fellow prisoners in I-Dorm. Samples, the decedent, was known as "Pee Wee." Although Samples was referred to as "Pee Wee," there appeared to be no relation between this nickname and his physical size. In fact, he was a strong man who worked out daily with weights.

The "hearsay" among the residents of I-Dorm was to the effect that Watson and Samples were "swapping-out." "Swapping-out" is a prison term that means two inmates are engaging in homosexual practices. Generally, prisoners that are "swapping-out" try to hide the practice from their fellow inmates. In particular, they try to hide it from any "home-boys" that may be in their particular unit. A "home-boy," in the prison vernacular, is a fellow inmate from one's own hometown or community. One of the State's witnesses, Johnny Lee Wilson, a resident of I-Dorm on the date of the offense, was Samples' "home-boy."

It appears that Watson and Samples had been "swapping-out" for several months. Approximately a month or so prior to the date of the killing, Watson and Samples had engaged in a "scuffle" while working in the prison kitchen. This appears to have been nothing more than a fist-fight. Samples was the winner. Although it is by no means clear from the record, it appears that this "scuffle" arose out of Samples' suspicion that Watson had been "swapping-out" with another prisoner.

At approximately 4:30 P.M. on the afternoon of the killing, Johnny Lee Wilson, Samples' "home-boy," saw Watson and Samples sitting together on a bunk in the back of I-Dorm. At this time, "they were close talking, they were close." Apparently, assuming that they were about to "swap-out," and not wanting to embarrass Samples, Wilson quickly turned around and left the dorm.

Shortly before the lights were to be dimmed (10:00 P.M.), Watson and Samples began to argue. After several minutes, Watson got up and walked across the aisle, a distance of approximately seven feet, to his bunk. Samples subsequently followed him and renewed the dispute. At this time, both parties were seated on Watson's bottom bunk. During the course of the renewed argument, Samples was verbally abusing Watson and challenging him to fight. At one point, he said: "Nigger, nigger, you're just like the rest of them." He also told Watson that he was too scared to fight him and that all

he was going to do was tremble and stay in his bunk. Finally, Samples made several derogatory and obscene references to Watson's mother. The prisoners refer to this as "shooting the dove." Generally, when a prisoner "shoots the dove," he expects the other party to fight. At this point, Watson told Johnny Lee Wilson, whose bunk was nearby on Watson's side of the room: "You better get your home-boy straightened out before I f— him up." Responding to this statement, Samples said: "Why don't you f— me up if that's what you want to do. All you're gonna do is tremble, nigger."

As Samples was making the above quoted statement, he was walking over to Wilson's bunk. Samples borrowed a cigarette from Wilson and then proceeded to his own bed. He got up in his bunk (top) and was more or less half sitting up with his back propped up against the wall. At this point, he renewed the argument with Watson, who was still in his bottom bunk on the opposite side of the room. He called Watson a "nigger" and "a black mother f—." While this was going on, Watson, without saying a word, either walked or ran across the aisle between the two rows of bunks and violently and repeatedly stabbed Samples with a kitchen-type paring knife. According to the State's witnesses, this occurred approximately two (2) to ten (10) minutes after Samples had left Watson's bed.

After summarizing the evidence, and prior to fully instructing on first-degree murder, the court stated: "Let me say here, that mere words will not form a justification or excuse for a crime of this sort." In instructing the jury on voluntary manslaughter, the court stated:

> The defendant must satisfy you that this passion was produced by acts of Samples which the law regards as adequate provocation. This may consist of anything which has a natural tendency to produce such passion in a person of average mind and disposition. However, words and gestures alone, where no assault is made or threatened, regardless of how insulting or inflammatory those words or gestures may be, does not constitute adequate provocation for the taking of a human life.

OPINION

[After reviewing several voluntary manslaughter decisions, the court wrote:] These decisions establish the following rules as to the legal effect of abusive language:

(1) Mere words, however abusive, are never sufficient legal provocation to mitigate a homicide to a lesser degree; and

(2) A defendant, prosecuted for a homicide in a difficulty that he has provoked by the use of language "calculated and intended" to bring on the encounter, cannot maintain the position of perfect self-defense unless, at a time prior to the killing, he withdrew from the encounter within the meaning of the law.

These two rules are logically consistent and demonstrate that abusive language will not serve as a legally sufficient provocation for a homicide in this State.

These well-settled rules are clearly controlling in the instant case. Hence, if defendant had provoked an assault by the deceased through the use of abusive language and had thereafter killed the deceased, then it would have been for the jury to determine if the language used by defendant, given the relationship of the parties, the circumstances surrounding the verbal assertions, etc., was "calculated and intended" to bring on the assault. If the jury had found this to be the case, then defendant would not have had the benefit of the doctrine of perfect self-defense, even though the deceased instigated the actual physical attack. But, here there was no evidence that defendant killed the deceased in self-defense. In fact, all of the evidence tends to show that the fatal attack was brought on by the continued verbal abuses directed toward defendant by the deceased. Under these circumstances, there was no basis for a jury determination of whether any of the words were "calculated and intended" to bring on the difficulty.

At this point, we note that in those few jurisdictions that permit abusive language to mitigate the degree of homicide, the majority hold that the words are only deemed sufficient to negate premeditation, thereby reducing the degree of homicide from first to second. Most of these courts reason that since the deceased had made no attempt to endanger the life of the accused, the action of the latter in meeting the insulting remarks with sufficient force (deadly or otherwise) to cause the death of the former, was beyond the bounds of sufficient retaliation to constitute sufficient provocation to reduce the homicide to manslaughter. Although we expressly decline to adopt this minority view, we note that the jury in the instant case ap-

parently applied the same reasoning and found defendant guilty of second-degree murder. Thus, even if the minority rule applied in this State, defendant would not be entitled to a new trial as a result of the instructions here given.

Defendant contends that the trial court committed prejudicial error in charging the jury as follows:

> Now, ladies and gentlemen of the jury, this case is to be tried by you under the laws of the State of North Carolina, and not upon the rules and regulations and customs and unwritten code that exists within the walls of the North Carolina Department of Correction. I can't charge you on that law because I don't know that law. I think I know this one, and this is the law that you are trying this case under.

Defendant argues that this instruction "tends to discount as a matter of law all of the factual information" that the jury was "entitled to consider, not as law, but as a part of the factual background situation within which the incident took place." We find nothing in the charge to support such an inference. During the course of the trial, several of the State's witnesses (either present or former prison inmates) testified about a "prison code," i.e., a set of unwritten rules developed by the prisoners themselves. For example, one of the State's witnesses made the following statements on cross-examination:

> In the prison system, if Watson had not fought after Samples had called him nigger, nigger, and talked about his mother, I guess, you know, everybody else probably would be jugging at him. What I mean by "jugging at him," I mean, messing with him, you know. Taking advantage of the fact that he won't stand up for himself. It is important that you stand up for yourself in the system because if you don't, somebody might get you down in the shower, you know. You might get dead-ended. It means if you don't take up for yourself, everybody picks on you.

Apparently, standing up for oneself was a vital part of this so-called "prison code." In this context, the import of the above instruction was clearly to inform the jurors that the case—like all other criminal cases tried in the North Carolina General Courts of Justice—had to be tried under the laws of this State and not upon any unwritten prisoners' code that existed within the walls of North Carolina's prisons. It is certainly not error for a trial judge to so instruct a jury. Furthermore, it appears that defendant's conduct even constituted a violation of the prisoners' code. We refer to the following redirect testimony of the same witness previously quoted above: "Standing up for yourself in the prison system would not necessarily include using a knife. He could have run over there and fought with bare fists, that would have been standing up for himself."

Defendant's contention under this assignment is without merit. Therefore, it is overruled. Affirmed.

QUESTIONS FOR DISCUSSION

1. List the specific provocations that prompted Watson to kill Samples.

2. The court states flatly that words are never adequate provocation to reduce murder to manslaughter, although they may be adequate to reduce murder from first to second degree. Do you think this is a good rule for this case?

3. Especially, is it good when the prison code called on Watson to stand up for himself or be mistreated in the future?

4. In fact, if the unwritten prison code does call for him to stand up for himself, was it the words or fears for his personal safety that provoked him?

5. If you were the judge, would you have interpreted the provocation rule differently? Why or why not?

According to the common-law **paramour rule**, a husband who caught his wife in the act of adultery had adequate provocation to kill: "There could be no greater provocation than this." Many cases have held that it is voluntary manslaughter for a husband to kill his wife, her paramour, or both in the first heat of passion following the sight of the wife's adultery. Some statutes went further than the common-law rule and called paramour killings justifiable homicide. The paramour rule did not apply to both spouses. Wives couldn't claim it; only husbands could.

In early times, the rule applied only when husbands caught their wives in the act of adultery and flew into a murderous rage. Husbands who killed when someone told them their wives had committed adultery couldn't claim the benefit of the rule. However, a few modern courts have created an exception to the words-can-never-provoke rule: Information that the killer's spouse has committed adultery. The case of *Commonwealth v. Schnopps* deals with a husband who killed his wife when she bragged about her adultery.[30]

C A S E   Did He Commit First-Degree Murder?

Commonwealth v. Schnopps
390 Mass. 722, 459 N.E.2d 98 (1983)

George Schnopps, the defendant, was convicted before the Superior Court, Berkshire County, of first-degree murder of his estranged wife and of unlawfully carrying a firearm. At a retrial, the defendant, George A. Schnopps, again was convicted of murder in the first degree and he appealed. The Supreme Judicial Court affirmed.

ABRAMS, J.

FACTS

On October 13, 1979, the defendant fatally shot his wife of fourteen years. The victim and the defendant began having marital problems approximately six months earlier when Schnopps became suspicious that his wife was seeing another man. Schnopps and his wife argued during this period over his suspicion that she had a relationship with a particular man, whom the defendant regarded as a "bum." On a few occasions the defendant threatened to harm his wife with scissors, with a knife, with a shotgun, and with a plastic pistol. A few days prior to the slaying, Schnopps threatened to make his wife suffer as "she had never suffered before." However, there is no evidence that Schnopps physically harmed the victim prior to October 13.

On October 12, 1979, while at work, the defendant asked a coworker to buy him a gun. He told the coworker he had been receiving threatening telephone calls. After work, Schnopps and the coworker went to Pownal, Vermont, where the coworker purchased a .22 caliber pistol and a box of ammunition for the defendant. The defendant purchased a starter pistol to scare the caller if there was an attempted break-in. The defendant stated he wanted to protect himself and his son, who had moved back with him.

The defendant and his coworker had some drinks at a Vermont bar. The coworker instructed the defendant in the use of the .22 caliber pistol. The defendant paid his coworker for the gun and the ammunition. While at the bar the defendant told the coworker that he was "mad enough to kill." The coworker asked the defendant "if he was going to get in any trouble with the gun." Schnopps replied that "a bullet was too good for her, he would choke her to death."

Schnopps testified that his wife had left him three weeks prior to the slaying. He claims that he first became aware of problems in his fourteen-year marriage at a point about six months before the slaying. According to the defendant, on that occasion he took his wife to a club to dance, and she spent the evening dancing with a coworker. On arriving home, the defendant and his wife argued over her conduct. She told him that she no longer loved him and that she wanted a divorce. Schnopps became very upset. He admitted that he took out his shotgun during the course of this argument, but he denied that he intended to use it.

During the next few months, Schnopps argued frequently with his wife. The defendant accused her of seeing another man, but she steadfastly denied the accusations. On more than one occasion Schnopps threatened his wife with physical harm. He testified he never intended to hurt his wife but only wanted to scare her so that she would end the relationship with her coworker.

One day in September, 1979, the defendant became aware that the suspected boyfriend used a "signal" in telephoning Schnopps' wife. Schnopps used the signal, and his wife answered the phone with "Hi, Lover." She hung up immediately when she recognized Schnopps' voice. That afternoon she did not return home. Later that evening, she informed Schnopps by telephone that she had moved to her mother's house and that she had the children with her. On that day she moved to her mother's home and took their three children with her. (The children were two daughters, age thirteen and age four, and a son, age eleven. On October 6, the son returned to his father's home.) She told Schnopps she would not return to their home. Thereafter she "froze [him] out," and would not talk to him. During this period, the defendant spoke with a lawyer about a divorce and was told that he had a good chance of getting custody of the children, due to his wife's "desertion and adultery."

On the day of the slaying, the defendant told a neighbor he was going to call his wife and have her come down to pick up some things. He said he was thinking of letting his wife have the apartment. This was the first time the defendant indicated he might leave the apartment. He asked the neighbor to keep the youngest child with her if his wife brought her so he could talk with his wife. Schnopps had asked his wife to come to their home and talk over their marital difficulties. Schnopps told his wife that he wanted his children at home, and that he wanted the family to remain intact. Schnopps cried during the conversation, and begged his wife to let the children live with him and to keep their family together. His wife replied, "No, I am going to court, you are going to give me all the furniture, you are going to have to get the Hell out of here, you won't have nothing." Then, pointing to her crotch, she said, "You will never touch this again, because I have got something bigger and better for it."

The defendant said that these words "cracked" him. He explained that everything went "around" in his head, that he saw "stars." He went "toward the guns in the dining room." He asked his wife, "Why don't you try" (to salvage the marriage). He told her, "I have nothing more to live for," but she replied, "Never, I am never coming back to you." The victim jumped up to leave and the defendant shot her. He was seated at that time. He told her she would never love anyone else. After shooting the victim, the defendant said, "I want to go with you," and he shot himself.

Shortly before 3 P.M., the defendant called a neighbor and said he had shot his wife and also had tried to kill himself. The defendant told the first person to arrive at his apartment that he shot his wife "because of what she had done to him." Neighbors notified the police of the slaying. On their arrival, the defendant asked an officer to check to see if his wife had died. The officer told him that she had, and he replied, "Good." A police officer took the defendant to a hospital for treatment of his wounds. The officer had known the defendant for twenty-nine years. The defendant said to the officer that he would not hurt a fly. The officer advised Schnopps not to say anything until he spoke with a lawyer. The defendant then said, "The devil made me do it." The officer repeated his warning at least three times. The defendant said that he "loved [his] wife and [his] children." He added, "Just between you and I, . . . I did it because she was cheating on me."

The victim died of three gunshot wounds, to the heart and lungs. Ballistic evidence indicated that the gun was fired within two to four feet of the victim. The evidence also indicated that one shot had been fired while the victim was on the floor.

The defense offered evidence from friends and coworkers who noticed a deterioration in the defendant's physical and emotional health after the victim had left the defendant. The defendant wept at work and at home; he did not eat or sleep well; he was distracted and agitated. On two occasions, he was taken home early by supervisors because of emotional upset and agitation. He was drinking. The defendant was diagnosed at a local hospital as suffering from a "severe anxiety state." He was given Valium. The defendant claimed he was receiving threatening telephone calls.

The defendant and the Commonwealth each offered expert testimony on the issue of criminal responsibility. The defendant's expert claimed the defendant was suffering from a "major affective disorder, a major depression," a "psychotic condition," at the time of the slaying. The expert was of the opinion the defendant was not criminally responsible. The Commonwealth's expert claimed that the defendant's depression was a grief reaction, a reaction generally associated with death. The expert was of the opinion the defendant was grieving, over the breakup of his marriage, but that he was criminally responsible.

The judge instructed the jurors on every possible verdict available on the evidence. The jurors were told they could return a verdict of murder in the first degree on the ground of deliberately premeditated malice aforethought; murder in the second degree; manslaughter; not guilty by reason of insanity; or not guilty.

OPINION

On appeal, the defendant "does not now quarrel with that range of possible verdicts nor with the instruction which the trial court gave to the jury . . . . [Nor] does . . . [the defendant] now dispute that there may be some view of . . . some of the evidence which might support the verdict returned in this matter." Rather, the defendant claims that his case is "not of the nature that judges and juries, in weighing evidence, ordinarily equate with murder in the first degree." The defendant therefore concludes that this is an appropriate case in which to exercise our power under G.L. c. 278, § 33E. We do not agree.

Pursuant to G.L. c. 278, § 33E, we consider whether the verdict of murder in the first degree was against the weight of the evidence, considered in a large or nontechnical sense. Our power under § 33E is to be used with restraint. Moreover, "we do not sit as a second jury to pass anew on the question of the defendant's guilt."

The defendant argues that the evidence as a whole demonstrates that his wife was the emotional aggressor, and that her conduct shattered him and destroyed him as a husband and a father. The defendant points to the fact that he was not a hoodlum or gangster, that he had no prior criminal record, and that he had a "good relationship" with his wife prior to the last six months of their marriage. The defendant concludes these factors should be sufficient to entitle him to a new trial or the entry of a verdict of a lesser degree of guilt.

The Commonwealth argues that the evidence is more than ample to sustain the verdict. The Commonwealth points out that at the time of the killing there was not a good relationship between the parties; that the defendant had threatened to harm his wife physically on several occasions; and that he had threatened to kill his wife. The defendant obtained a gun and ammunition the day before the killing. The defendant arranged to have his younger child cared for by a neighbor when his wife came to see him. The jury could have found that Schnopps lured his wife to the apartment by suggesting that he might leave and let her live in it with the children. The evidence permits a finding that the killing occurred within a few minutes of the victim's arrival at the defendant's apartment and before she had time to take off her jacket. From the facts, the jury could infer that the defendant had planned to kill his wife on October 13, and that the killing was not the spontaneous result of the quarrel but was the result of a deliberately premeditated plan to murder his wife almost as soon as she arrived.

Ballistic evidence indicated that as the victim was lying on the floor, a third bullet was fired into her. From the number of wounds, the type of weapon used, as well as the effort made to procure the weapon, the jurors could find that the defendant had "a conscious and fixed purpose to kill continuing for a length of time."

If conflicting inferences are possible, "it is for the jury to determine where the truth lies." There was ample evidence which suggested the jurors' conclusion that the defendant acted with deliberately premeditated malice aforethought. On appeal, the defendant complains that the prosecutor's summation, which stressed that premeditated murder requires "a thought and an act," could have confused the jurors by suggesting that if "at any time earlier [the defendant] merely thought about killing that person," that was sufficient to constitute deliberately "premeditated malice aforethought." We do not read the prosecutor's argument as suggesting that conclusion. The prosecutor focused on the Commonwealth's evidence of deliberately premeditated malice aforethought throughout his argument. There was no error. In any event, the argument, read as a whole, does not create a "substantial likelihood of a miscarriage of justice."

The defendant's domestic difficulties were fully explored before the jury. The jurors rejected the defendant's claim that his domestic difficulties were an adequate ground to return a verdict of a lesser degree of guilt. The degree of guilt, of course, is a jury determination. The evidence supports a conclusion that the defendant, angered by his wife's conduct, shot her with deliberately premeditated malice aforethought. The jurors were in the best position to determine whether the domestic difficulties were so egregious as to require a verdict of a lesser degree of guilt. We conclude, on review of the record as a whole, that there is no reason for us to order a new trial or direct the entry of a lesser verdict.

Judgment affirmed.

QUESTIONS FOR DISCUSSION

1. The paramour rule was adopted to cover cases where husbands found their wives in bed with other men. The provocation was the sight of the adultery itself. Thus, the passion was immediately connected to the adulterous act. If you were a juror, could you in good conscience say that Schnopps was adequately provoked?

2. If so, was it the adultery that provoked him or the provocative words his wife used to describe her adulterous relationship?

3. Do you think the prohibition against provocative words makes sense?

4. If you were writing a manslaughter law, how would you treat cases like Schnopps?

NOTE CASE

Jerry Elder and Lynn Mallas had an intimate relationship, but were never married. Mallas broke off the relationship and moved out of Elder's apartment some time in March or April of 1990. On June 2, 1990, Elder saw Mallas, her two-year-old daughter Angela, and her fiance, Tom Wicks, in an automobile. Elder, in a rented car, followed them to Wicks' apartment. Elder blocked Mallas's exit from the car, and they exchanged words. As Mallas tried to get past him, Elder shot her twice in the back, killing her in front of her two-year-old daughter. After seeing that Mallas was shot, Wicks fled on foot. Elder chased after Wicks and caught up to him when Wicks tripped and fell in a nearby field. Elder then shot Wicks in the chest. Wicks rolled onto his stomach, and Elder shot him again in the back. After Elder fled the scene, Wicks managed to return to his apartment and tell a neighbor to call the police. Wicks was seriously injured, but he survived.

Elder was convicted of first-degree murder and of attempted first-degree murder and sentenced to 60 years in prison. Elder claims that he was entitled to a second-degree murder conviction (second-degree murder has replaced manslaughter in Illinois) because of adequate provocation. Do you agree? According to the Illinois Supreme Court:

... In Illinois, only four categories of provocation have been recognized as sufficiently serious to reduce the crime of first degree murder to second degree murder. They are: (1) substantial physical injury or assault; (2) mutual quarrel or combat; (3) illegal arrest; and (4) adultery with the offender's spouse. The defendant has the burden of establishing some evidence of serious provocation, or the trial court may properly deny a second-degree murder instruction.

The facts of this case do not fall under any of the four categories of serious provocation recognized in Illinois. The first three categories clearly do not apply. Under the fourth category, there is obviously no evidence of adultery with the offender's spouse since the defendant and the victim were not married.

The defendant argues that this last category should be expanded to include the "special relationship" between the defendant and the victim. ... Although Mallas and the defendant had previously enjoyed an intimate relationship, that relationship had ended two months before the homicide occurred. Additionally, there is no evidence in this case to suggest that the defendant was acting under a "sudden and intense passion." In fact, the evidence here suggests that the defendant literally stalked the murder victim. The defendant carried a loaded gun and followed Mallas in a rented car. This conduct suggests that he was not suddenly provoked when he shot Mallas, but rather that he was completing a contemplated plan. The trial court's decision not to instruct the jury on second-degree murder was proper.

State v. Elder, 579 N.E.2d 420 (Ill.App. 1991)

Adequate provocation means *reasonable* provocation. But reasonable to whom? Reasonableness can mean how the majority of people *would* react under similar circumstances. Or, it can mean how the person *should* have reacted under the circumstances. Sometimes defendants in special circumstances argue that the standard should be whether the circumstances would have provoked a reasonable person in their special category. In *People v. Washington,* for example, Merle Francis Washington shot his gay partner following a lover's quarrel, brought on by the victim's unfaithfulness. The court instructed the jury on provocation as follows:

The jury was instructed that to reduce the homicide from murder to manslaughter upon the ground of sudden quarrel or heat of passion, the conduct must be tested by the ordinarily reasonable man test. Defendant argues without precedent that to so instruct was error because, "Homosexuals are not at present a curiosity or a rare commodity. They are a distinct third sexual class between that of male and female, are present in almost every field of endeavor, and are fast achieving a guarded recognition not formerly accorded them. The heat of their passions in dealing with one another should not be tested by standards applicable to the average man or the average woman, since they are aberrant hybrids, with an obvious diminished capacity.

Defendant submits that since the evidence disclosed that he was acting as a servient homosexual during the period of his relationship with the victim, that his heat of passion should have been tested, either by a standard applicable to a female, or a standard applicable to the average homosexual, and that it was prejudicial error to instruct the jury to determine his heat of passion defense by standards applicable to the average male."

We do not agree. In the present condition of our law it is left to the jurors to say whether or not the facts and circumstances in evidence are sufficient to lead them to believe that the defendant did, or to create a reasonable doubt in their minds as to whether or not he did, commit his offense under a heat of passion. The jury is further to be admonished and advised by the court that this heat of passion must be such a passion as would naturally be aroused in the mind of an ordinarily reasonable person under the given facts and circumstances, and that, consequently, no defendant may set up his own standard of conduct and justify or excuse himself because in fact his passions were aroused, unless further the jury believe that the facts and circumstances were sufficient to arouse the passions of the ordinarily reasonable man. Thus no man of extremely violent passion could so justify or excuse himself if the exciting cause be not adequate, nor could an excessively cowardly man justify himself unless the circumstances were such as to arouse the fears of the ordinarily courageous man. Still further, while the conduct of the defendant is to be measured by that of the ordinarily reasonable man placed in identical circumstances, the jury is properly to be told that the exciting cause must be such as would naturally tend to arouse the passion of the ordinarily reasonable man.[31]

Voluntary manslaughter requires killing in the "sudden heat of passion" with no "cooling off" period. The actual time between provocation and killing, whether seconds, hours, or even days, depends upon the facts of the individual case. Courts usually apply an objective test: Would a reasonable person under the same circumstances have had time to cool off? If defendants had reasonable time for their murderous rages to subside, the law views their killings as murders even if the provocations were adequate to reduce those killings to manslaughter had they taken place immediately following the provocations.

Using the same objective test, the time for cooling off may be considerable. In one case, a man's wife told him her father had raped her. The court ruled that the husband's passion had not reasonably cooled even after he walked all night to his father-in-law's house and killed him the next day! The court said the heinous combination of incest and rape was sufficient to keep a reasonable person in a murderous rage for at least several days.[32]

To prove voluntary manslaughter, the prosecution not only has to prove adequate provocation and sudden intentional killing, but also that the provocation *caused* the passion and the killing. Suppose that Sonny intends to kill his wife Carly because she lied to him. He goes to her bedroom, finds her in bed with his worst enemy, and shoots her to death. Is it voluntary manslaughter or murder? Murder, because Carly's lie, not her adultery, provoked Sonny to kill her.

INVOLUNTARY MANSLAUGHTER

The distinguishing characteristic of **involuntary manslaughter** is its *mens rea*: unintentional killing. There are three kinds of involuntary manslaughter:

1. Criminal recklessness manslaughter.
2. Criminal negligence manslaughter
3. Unlawful act manslaughter, also called misdemeanor manslaughter.

ELEMENTS OF INVOLUNTARY MANSLAUGHTER				
Actus Reus	*Mens Rea*	**Circumstance**	**Causation**	**Result**
Killing another person	Creating the risk of killing or seriously injuring another person 1. Recklessly **or** 2. Negligently	Death during the commission of an unlawful act	Acts that trigger a chain of events that lead to another person's death	Death of another person

Because of the seriousness of the offense of involuntary manslaughter, many states limit involuntary manslaughter to reckless manslaughter. These states usually create a separate, lesser offense of criminal negligent homicide.

 9-4 Involuntary Manslaughter

Criminal Reckless and Criminal Negligent Manslaughter

As we learned in Chapter 4, criminal recklessness means the conscious creation of a substantial and unjustifiable risk. As we also learned in Chapter 4, criminal negligence (also called **gross criminal negligence**) means creating a substantial and unjustifiable risk that the defendant *should have been* but in fact wasn't aware of. In criminal reckless and **negligent homicide** the risk is of death or serious bodily injury. Reckless and negligent homicide statutes range across a wide field, including deaths caused by using firearms, handling explosives, operating vehicles, practicing medicine, and even allowing vicious animals to run free. The Ohio Court of Appeals dealt with an unusual case of involuntary manslaughter under its vehicular homicide statute in *State v. Mays*.

C A S E   Did He Commit Aggravated Vehicular Homicide?

State v. Mays
2000 WL 1033098 (Ohio App. 1 Dist., 2000)

DOAN, J.

Nicholas A. Mays was convicted of aggravated vehicular homicide and tampering with evidence, both felonies of the third degree, in Hamilton County Court of Common Pleas. He was sentenced to consecutive terms of incarceration. He appealed. The Ohio Court of Appeals, First District, reversed the sentences in part and remanded the case to the Court of Common Pleas for resentencing.

FACTS

On August 19, 1999, nineteen-year-old Nicholas Mays was operating an automobile in which his cousin was a passenger. At approximately 1:45 a.m., they saw a pedestrian, later identified as Michael Boumer, in a grocery-store parking lot. According to Mays, Boumer appeared to be intoxicated, and the two young men decided that they would "mess with" Boumer by appearing to offer him a ride. Mays intended to nudge Boumer with the vehicle and then drive away. Investigating officers confirmed that Boumer had consumed some alcohol. However, the record also indicates that Boumer was mentally handicapped. Mays did drive the vehicle in the direction of Boumer, but instead of merely nudging him, he inadvertently ran over him, causing him fatal injuries. Upon seeing that Boumer was injured, Mays

drove to another location and called for emergency aid. He then went to a car wash, where he cleaned the vehicle to remove evidence of the fatal collision.

On the day after the incident, Mays took a planned trip to Florida, during which his mother convinced him that he should report his involvement in the crime. Mays did so, returning to Cincinnati and giving a full confession to the police. In October 1999, Mays entered guilty pleas to one count each of aggravated vehicular homicide and tampering with evidence. The trial court sentenced him to five years' incarceration for the aggravated vehicular homicide and to four years' incarceration for tampering with evidence, with the terms to run consecutively.

OPINION

[The Ohio Revised Code vehicular homicide statute (Section 2903.06) reads in part:

(A) No person, while operating or participating in the operation of a motor vehicle, motorcycle, snowmobile, locomotive, watercraft, or aircraft, shall cause the death of another or the unlawful termination of another's pregnancy in any of the following ways:

. . .

    (2) Recklessly;
    (3) Negligently;

. . .

(B)(1) Whoever violates division (A) . . . (2) of this section is guilty of aggravated vehicular homicide and shall be punished as provided in divisions (B)(1) . . . (b) of this section. . . .

> (b) Except as otherwise provided in this division, aggravated vehicular homicide committed in violation of division (A)(2) of this section is a felony of the third degree. . . . In addition to any other sanctions imposed, the court shall suspend the offender's driver's license, commercial driver's license, temporary instruction permit, probationary license, or nonresident operating privilege for a definite period of three years to life. . . .
>
> (2) Whoever violates division (A)(3) of this section is guilty of vehicular homicide. Except as otherwise provided in this division, vehicular homicide is a misdemeanor of the first degree. . . .]

Mays argues that the trial court erred in imposing the maximum term of incarceration for the aggravated vehicular homicide and in imposing consecutive sentences. Mays concedes that the sentences were within the range allowed by law for third-degree felonies and that the trial court made the requisite findings for the imposition of the sentences. . . . The sole issue posed in the assignment of error, therefore, is whether the record supports the trial court's findings.

Mays first argues that the court erred in imposing terms of incarceration greater than the minimum. To impose a prison term more than the minimum for the offender's first prison term, the court must find that the minimum sentence would demean the seriousness of the offense or not adequately protect the public from future crime. Here, the trial court found both to be applicable.

We hold that the trial court's finding with respect to the seriousness of the offenses is supported by the record. Mays conceded that his intention was to "mess with" a person whom he perceived to be impaired in some way, and in doing so, he deprived the thirty-nine-year-old victim of his life. Mays did not immediately seek help for Boumer, but instead thought first of his own interest in evading detection for the crime. His concealment of the crime was compounded when he washed the car and left the jurisdiction. Under these circumstances, the trial court reasonably concluded that the minimum term would demean the seriousness of the offenses. Because the trial court's finding with respect to the seriousness of the offenses was proper, we need not address Mays's argument concerning the adequate protection of the public.

In his second argument, Mays claims that the trial court erred in imposing the maximum sentence for aggravated vehicular homicide. Before imposing the maximum term of incarceration for an offense, the court must find that the offender has committed the worst form of the offense, poses the greatest likelihood of recidivism, or is of a certain class of repeat offenders. In the case at bar, the court found that Mays had committed the worst form of aggravated vehicular homicide. We disagree.

In past cases, this court has grappled with the somewhat vague concept of what constitutes the "worst form" of an offense. And while the concept is difficult to define in concrete terms, we hold that Mays's conduct in the case at bar did not constitute the worst form of aggravated vehicular homicide. Though the evidence certainly indicates that Mays exercised extremely poor judgment in carrying out his wish to "mess with" Boumer, there is no indication that he harbored any malice toward the victim. Instead, the record indicates that Mays's conduct started as a reckless, poorly conceived prank and ended in tragedy. And while we in no way wish to minimize the loss of a human life or to condone Mays's actions, this is not the type of conduct for which the legislature has reserved the maximum sentence.

Furthermore, although he admittedly thought of his own interests before seeking help for Boumer, Mays did take steps to ensure that emergency personnel were notified promptly. His actions therefore did not reflect an utter lack of concern for Boumer or otherwise demonstrate a perversity of character that would justify the imposition of the maximum sentence. Further, there is no indication that the victim suffered for a prolonged period of time before he died or suffered to a greater degree than any other victim of a vehicular homicide. Finally, Mays surrendered to authorities and confessed to the crimes. Under these circumstances, we cannot say that Mays committed the worst form of the offense. . . . We therefore hold that the trial court erred in imposing the maximum term for that offense.

Mays next argues that the trial court erred in imposing consecutive sentences. To impose consecutive terms of imprisonment, the court must find that consecutive sentences are necessary to protect the public from future crime and that consecutive sentences are not disproportionate to the offender's conduct and to the danger the offender poses to the public. The trial court must also find one of the following: that the offenses occurred while the offender was under community control; that the harm caused was great or unusual; or that the offender's criminal history requires consecutive sentences. Of the latter factors, the court in the instant case found that the harm caused was unusual or great.

We agree with Mays that the trial court's findings with respect to consecutive sentences are not supported by the record. Concerning the protection of the public from future crime, Mays's criminal record included no adult convictions and only one juvenile delinquency adjudication. Thus, there is little indication that Mays is likely to recidivate. Also, the trial court revoked Mays's operator's license, thereby reducing the likelihood that future vehicular offenses would occur. Further, as to the finding that consecutive terms were not disproportionate to Mays's conduct and to the danger that he posed to the public, we have already noted that Mays's conduct, while reckless and ill-conceived, was not the product of malice. Also, given the revocation of Mays's license, his confession, and his demonstrated remorse, the conduct also appears not likely to be repeated. The investigating officers and the author of the presentence-investigation report indicated that Mays was genuinely remorseful. Finally, the harm caused by the offense, while senseless and tragic, was not greater than the harm caused in every other aggravated-vehicular-homicide case. Under these circumstances, we hold that the trial court erred in imposing consecutive sentences.

Having held that the trial court erred in imposing the maximum sentence for the aggravated vehicular homicide and in otherwise imposing consecutive sentences, we hereby reverse those parts of the trial court's judgment and remand the cause for resentencing in accordance with law.

Judgment affirmed in part and reversed in part, and cause remanded.

DISSENT

HILDEBRANDT, P.J., concurring in part and dissenting in part.

I concur with the conclusion that the trial court properly imposed greater than the minimum terms of incarceration. However, because I believe that the trial court was also correct in imposing the maximum sentence on the first count and in imposing consecutive sentences, I would affirm the judgment in its entirety.

The very fact that the term "worst form of the offense" is a vague concept should cause this court to accord great deference to the trial court's finding with respect to that statutory factor. In the case at bar, Mays senselessly took the life of the victim because he wished to "mess with" him. The wantonness of that conduct alone could have justified the trial court in imposing the maximum sentence. However, Mays compounded his misconduct by leaving the scene of the collision, thereby making it clear that he valued his own interest in evading detection above the life of Boumer. The majority concedes as much, yet persists in holding that Mays did not commit the worst form of the offense. His eventual call for emergency aid and his subsequent remorse for his actions did not erase the fact that his conduct was egregious and deserving of the greatest punishment.

For many of the same reasons, I believe that the imposition of consecutive sentences was proper. The utter lack of regard for human life that Mays exhibited by using his automobile to "mess with" a person whom he believed to be impaired provided ample support for the trial court's conclusion that consecutive sentences were necessary to prevent future crimes and to protect the public. Moreover, the fact that death is caused in all aggravated-vehicular-homicide cases should not prevent a finding that the harm caused in the instant case was great or unusual. Mays's taking of a life in such a wanton manner justified the court in finding that the harm done was great or unusual, and I would not disturb that finding. In my view, nine years of incarceration is not excessive when weighed against the taking of a human life under these circumstances. I therefore respectfully dissent in part.

QUESTIONS FOR DISCUSSION

1. How does Ohio define vehicular homicide?
2. Relying on the facts of the case and referring to the Ohio provision, explain why Nicholas Mays was guilty of aggravated vehicular homicide.
3. If you were defining vehicular homicide how would you do it?
4. Do you agree with the majority opinion's reasons for reversing the sentence? Or, do the dissent and the trial court have the better arguments? Back up your answer.

✱ 9-5 Criminal Reckless and Negligent Homicides

Unlawful Act Involuntary Manslaughter

In 1260, long before the division between murder and manslaughter was created by the common-law judges, the great jurist Bracton wrote that unintended deaths during unlawful acts are criminal homicides. Some time after the judges created the offense of manslaughter, unlawful act homicides became involuntary manslaughter. In modern times, courts have restricted unlawful act manslaughter because it is considered too harsh. In fact, there is a trend to abolish unlawful act manslaughter, leaving reckless and negligent manslaughter as the only form of involuntary manslaughter. Michigan has resisted the trend to abolish, choosing instead to restrict the reach of unlawful act manslaughter to deaths following assaults. The Michigan Supreme Court majority and dissenting opinions debate the merits of abolition in *People v. Datema.*[33]

C A S E   Was Her Death Unlawful Act Manslaughter?

People v. Datema
448 Mich. 585, 533 N.W.2d 272 (1995)

Gregory Datema, the defendant, was convicted in the Circuit Court, Kent County, of involuntary manslaughter. Datema appealed. The Court of Appeals affirmed. The Supreme Court granted leave to appeal and affirmed.

BOYLE, J.

FACTS

In the early morning hours of December 22, 1988, defendant and his wife, Pamela Datema, were sitting in their living room with two friends. All four had been smoking marijuana and both defendant and his wife had been drinking throughout the evening.

As the evening wore on, the conversation turned to the topic of previous romances, and the defendant and his wife began to argue about various paramours with whom they had slept. During the argument, Mrs. Datema started to rise from her chair, claiming to have had sexual intercourse with other men in front of defendant's sons. As she rose, defendant slapped her once across the face with an open hand. Mrs. Datema slumped back into her chair, screamed that she hoped defendant would "go to Florida and stay there," then slipped from the chair onto the floor. Initially, defendant and the two others present in the room thought that Mrs. Datema had passed out from drinking too much but, after five to ten minutes, they became con-cerned and tried to wake her. When they were unable to do so, they called an ambulance. Mrs. Datema never regained consciousness and died soon after.

The medical examiner testified that Mrs. Datema had a blood-alcohol level between 0.03 and 0.05 percent. He stated that death was caused by a tear in an artery in the head that occurred as a result of defendant's blow. (Most people, when slapped, reflexively stiffen their necks and avoid serious injury. Occasionally, however, when a person is intoxicated, the reflexes do not react quickly enough, and a blow could result in a tearing. Generally, a higher blood-alcohol level is necessary, but the ingested marijuana, which was not able to be tested, was undoubtedly a contributing factor.) Although the three eyewitnesses called by the prosecution testified that defendant had slapped his wife once with an open hand and that the slap was not a hard one, the medical examiner testified that to cause death, even under the circumstances, the blow had to have been a powerful one and "would have to be with probably all the force that one could muster."

After the defense presented its case, defense counsel requested that the jury be instructed consistent with the jury instruction that defines the *mens rea* element of involuntary manslaughter exclusively in terms of gross negligence. The trial judge refused defense counsel's request, modified the instruction, and charged the jury that, to prove involuntary manslaughter, the prosecution would have to prove beyond a reasonable doubt that the defendant committed an assault and battery on Mrs. Datema with intent to injure her, that she died, and that the cause of her death was defendant's assault and battery. The court explained the modification of the charge as encompassing both the *mens rea* of the underlying misdemeanor and the requirement of specific intent. The court specifically charged the jury with regard to the defendant's lack of specific intent due to drunkenness and on self-defense.

The jury convicted defendant of involuntary manslaughter. Defendant was convicted as a second-felony offender (Defendant's prior felony conviction was for malicious destruction of property in a building.) and sentenced to 7 to 22½ years in prison. Defendant filed an appeal, contending that, if the unlawful act that results in death is not committed recklessly or with gross negligence, the crime should no longer be recognized as a form of common-law involuntary manslaughter. The Court of Appeals disagreed and affirmed the decision of the trial court in an unpublished opinion. On June 30, 1994, we granted leave to appeal.

OPINION

. . . The law of manslaughter as it exists today has been adopted from the old English common law. Common-law manslaughter has two broad categories: voluntary and involuntary. These two categories entail distinct elements and apply in different circumstances, but are often misapplied. Confusion is present because Michigan courts, ours included, have been less than precise in the use of language denoting voluntary or involuntary manslaughter.

. . . Involuntary manslaughter is a catch-all concept including all manslaughter not characterized as voluntary: Every unintentional killing of a human being is involuntary manslaughter if it is neither murder nor voluntary manslaughter nor within the scope of some recognized justification or excuse. To this . . . statement must be added the caveat [warning] that led to our grant of leave in this case. At common law, if an unlawful act was *malum in se*, inherently wrong, the only *mens rea* required was the *mens rea* of the underlying act. . . . [The caveat is a statement of the misdemeanor-manslaughter rule. The court concluded that assault is inherently wrong, and that the misdemeanor-manslaughter rule applies to this case.]

We conclude that if an assault and battery is committed with a specific intent to inflict injury and causes unintended death, the actor may be found guilty of (at least) involuntary manslaughter. We express no opinion with regard to the merits of the misdemeanor-manslaughter rule in contexts other than assault and battery. . . .

We reject the suggestion that progressive notions of jurisprudence require absolution for an unintended death under circumstances from which the fact finder may infer from a powerful blow an intent to injure that factually causes death. While we agree with the dissent that "Misdemeanors are crimes, and defendants who commit them are subject to punishment under the law," when one strikes another with "probably all the force that one can muster," the proper charge is manslaughter and not assault.

DISSENT

CAVANAGH, J.

Respectfully dissent. . . . Gross negligence should be recognized as the *mens rea* standard for all common-law forms of involuntary manslaughter. . . . In the instant case, the defendant's conviction must be reversed because the jury instructions did not provide a valid basis for an involuntary manslaughter conviction, and I would find that error prejudicial.

In *State v. Aaron* [in which the Michigan supreme court abolished the felony-murder rule], we recognized that it is inherently unjust to presume the existence of the *mens rea* for murder merely on a showing of the *mens rea* required for an underlying felony. Specifically, our holdings in *Aaron* were premised on the following principle of criminal jurisprudence: "If one had to choose the most basic principle of criminal law . . . it would be that criminal liability for causing a particular result is not justified in the absence of some culpable mental state in respect to that result. . . ."

Applying that principle to the crime of murder, we recognized that culpability for murder should require the establishment of a link between the murder (the result) and the defendant's *mens rea*. Stated otherwise, to hold a defendant accountable for murder requires a showing that the defendant had a *mens rea* with regard to the murder. The felony murder rule violated that principle because the rule, in effect, permitted the intent to commit the underlying felony, in itself, to serve as the *mens rea* for murder. This violation led us to abolish the common-law felony murder rule, and to hold that murder liability could be imposed only on an independent showing that the defendant had a *mens rea* for murder, which we decided was malice.

Like the common-law felony murder rule, the unlawful-act misdemeanor-manslaughter rule violates the principle set forth in *Aaron,* and it too should be abrogated. Pursuant to the unlawful-act misdemeanor-manslaughter rule, a defendant may be convicted of involuntary manslaughter where it has been shown that the defendant committed the unlawful act that proximately caused death. Proof of the *mens rea* for manslaughter is presumed to exist on the basis of a showing of the *mens rea* required for the underlying misdemeanor. Contrary to the principle that we endorsed in *Aaron,* liability for a homicide is imposed without an independent showing of a *mens rea* with regard to the homicide. To eliminate the perpetuation of such an injustice, this Court should abolish the unlawful-act misdemeanor-manslaughter rule. Because the Court has already recognized the suitability of a gross negligence standard for the other forms of common-law involuntary manslaughter, I would now adopt a uniform gross negligence standard to be applied to all forms of common-law involuntary manslaughter.

To recognize an exception, where the underlying misdemeanor is an assault and battery requiring proof of a specific intent to injure, would be inconsistent with the principle of *Aaron* because the requisite link between the homicide, and the *mens rea* with regard to the homicide, would not be established in all cases. While such an exception would require the establishment of a culpable mental state, it would not be the mental state required for involuntary manslaughter—which must be gross negligence.

I reject the majority's contention that the gross negligence *mens rea* standard for involuntary manslaughter is, at the most, comparable to, but no greater than, the specific intent-to-injure *mens rea* standard for assault and battery. ("Gross negligence does not require a greater level of criminal culpability than the specific intent to injure.) In my view, gross negligence would not necessarily be shown in every case simply because there is a showing of a specific intent to injure—to whatever de-

gree, and regardless of whether the injury is physical or mental in nature.

To hold a defendant accountable for involuntary manslaughter on the basis that he was "grossly negligent" requires a showing that the defendant willfully disregarded not just a high risk of injury, but a high risk of death or serious bodily injury. . . . We elaborated on this view of gross negligence in *People v. Orr,* 243 Mich. 300, 307, 220 N.W. 777 (1928), in which we listed three elements that had to be established to show gross negligence for a lawful-act involuntary-manslaughter conviction:

> (1) Knowledge of a situation requiring the exercise of ordinary care and diligence to avert injury to another.
> (2) Ability to avoid the resulting harm by ordinary care and diligence in the use of the means at hand.
> (3) The omission to use such care and diligence to avert the threatened danger when to the ordinary mind it must be apparent that the result is likely to prove disastrous to another.

. . . Imposing a uniform gross negligence standard would not preclude the possibility of an involuntary manslaughter conviction of a defendant who commits an assault and battery resulting in death. Depending on the circumstances, proof of a specific intent to injure may also manifest a willful disregard of a high risk of death or serious bodily injury. However, that would not be true in all cases, making it inappropriate to conclusively presume the existence of gross negligence. For example, a defendant may intentionally inflict bodily harm on another person by a moderate blow with his fist; the person may then fall to the sidewalk, fracture his skull, and unexpectedly die. While the defendant in that situation clearly had a specific intent to injure, the defendant may not have demonstrated a willful disregard of a high risk of death or serious bodily injury. Both the degree of risk and the defendant's awareness of that risk would have to be considered before a proper determination regarding gross negligence could be made.

The instant case is another example of a situation in which it could be shown that the defendant had a specific intent to injure, but perhaps[it] could not be shown that the defendant willfully disregarded a high risk of death or serious bodily injury. The prosecutor's medical expert testified that the cause of death in this case was "very rare," and "very unusual," and that people could receive "similar blows frequently and [not] die and perhaps [not even be] severely injured." (Specifically, Dr. Stephen Cohle testified: I can say this is a very rare cause of death. It is very unusual. . . . And I will say, early on, I can't prove beyond a reasonable doubt all of the reasons why she did die from this blow, because it is very unusual. And I'm sure people receive similar blows frequently and don't die and perhaps aren't even severely injured. . . .) This testimony strongly suggests that a high risk of death or serious bodily injury was not created when the "defendant slapped [his wife] once across the face with an open hand." Notably, the prosecutor characterizes the victim's death in this case as "entirely unexpected."

If a defendant is not shown to have been grossly negligent with respect to human life, but is shown to have had a specific intent to injure and death proximately resulted from his acts, the defendant would not be allowed to escape all punishment—contrary to the majority's suggestion otherwise. Misdemeanors are crimes, and defendants who commit them are subject to punishment under the law. In this case, the defendant committed an assault and battery. The defendant's "conduct in causing or intending to cause injury is a crime . . . and should be dealt with as such, i.e., as a crime defined in reference to the specific evil of bodily injury that it portends." In this way, the law ensures that the punishment correlates with the crime. For the law to properly impose punishment for a homicide, culpability regarding the homicide must be shown in every case.

. . . The principle embraced by this Court in *Aaron* dictates the elimination of the unlawful-act misdemeanor-manslaughter rule. After *Aaron,* culpability for homicide may not be presumed from the commission of another crime. The majority's special category is unacceptable because it equates a specific intent to injure—to whatever degree and kind—with a willful disregard of a high risk of death or serious bodily injury, and, in effect, violates the principles of *Aaron*. This case provides the Court with an excellent opportunity to abolish the unlawful-act misdemeanor-manslaughter rule once and for all. I would do so now, and thereby ensure that common-law liability for homicide will only be imposed where culpability for death has been proven.

QUESTIONS FOR DISCUSSION

1. List the facts relevant to deciding Gregory Datema's state of mind when he hit his wife.

2. How would you characterize Datema's state of mind with respect to injuring his wife? Intentional? Knowing? Reckless? Grossly negligent? Negligent? Back up your answer with facts that you listed in 1.

3. How would you characterize Datema's state of mind with respect to his wife's death? Intentional? Knowing? Reckless? Grossly negligent? Negligent? Back up your answer with facts that you listed in 1.

4. Summarize the reasons that the majority declined to abolish the misdemeanor-manslaughter rule.

5. Summarize the dissent's arguments for extending the court's abolition of the felony-murder rule to misdemeanor-manslaughter.

6. Do you agree with the majority or with the dissent? Back up your answer with the majority and/or dissent's arguments.

SUMMARY

The following outline summarizes the complicated and intricate elements in criminal homicide.

I. Criminal homicide is divided into two main categories: murder and manslaughter.

II. Murder requires taking another's life with malice aforethought.

A. The precise points at which life begins and ends for purposes of criminal homicide are difficult to determine.

B. Malice aforethought includes five distinct mental states—the specific intent to do one of the following:
   1. Kill another person,
   2. Seriously injure another person,
   3. Forcibly resist a lawful arrest,
   4. Commit specified dangerous felonies,
   5. Create a higher than criminally reckless risk of death or serious bodily injury.
C. Murder is divided into two degrees.
   1. First-degree murder:
      a. Premeditated, deliberate killings,
      b. Killings that take place while committing dangerous felonies (in some states),
      c. Particularly brutal or cruel murders (in some states).
   2. Second-degree murder:
      a. Intentional killing without premeditation,
      b. Killings resulting from the intent to do serious bodily injury,
      c. Killings resulting from the resisting of lawful arrest,
      d. Killings taking place during the commission of less serious felonies.
III. Manslaughter is either voluntary or involuntary.
A. Voluntary manslaughter is the intentional killing of another in the following circumstances:
   1. Under provocation, where such provocation
      a. is actual and adequate,
      b. occurs in the heat of passion,
      c. occurs before an adequate cooling off period.
   2. Where defendants believe they acted in self-defense but where it was unreasonable to do so.
B. Involuntary manslaughter is the killing of another person unintentionally, either
   1. with gross criminal recklessness or
   2. with gross criminal negligence
   3. while committing certain illegal acts
C. Negligent homicide is causing death by less than gross negligence; usually the deaths are related to the operation of vehicles.

✳ Go to the Criminal Law 7e CD-ROM for Internet exercises.

REVIEW QUESTIONS

1. Relate each of the elements of criminal homicide to each of the general principles of criminal liability.

2. Identify and describe the problems with defining life for purposes of the law of criminal homicide.

3. Identify all of the mental elements associated with the law of criminal homicide.

4. Explain the effect of *mens rea* on the law of criminal homicide.

5. Identify and explain the homicides included within first-degree murder.

6. According to the modern law of homicide, what are the definitions of premeditated killings and deliberate killings?

7. Identify the types and the elements of second-degree murder.

8. Why have states either modified or abolished felony murder?

9. What are the main problems with applying murder statutes to corporations?

10. Identify and describe the elements of voluntary manslaughter.

11. Identify and describe the elements of involuntary manslaughter.

12. Identify and describe the elements of vehicular homicide.

KEY TERMS

adequate provocation rule—the rule that only certain defined circumstances will reduce murder to voluntary manslaughter.

capital murder—first-degree murders for which the penalty is either death or life imprisonment.

criminal homicides—homicides that are neither justified nor excused.

"depraved-heart" murder—deaths resulting from purposely or consciously creating substantial and unjustifiable risks that someone will either die or suffer serious injury.

deliberate—meeting the requirement in murder *mens rea* that killings must be committed with a cool, reflecting mind.

excusable homicides—accidental killings and killing while insane.

felony murder—deaths occurring during the commission of felonies.

fetal death statutes—laws defining when life begins for purposes of the law of criminal homicide.

first-degree murder—premeditated, deliberate killings and other particularly heinous capital murders.

gross criminal negligence—very great negligence; actions without even slight care but not amounting to intentional or conscious wrongdoing.

homicide—the killing of one live human being by another.

involuntary manslaughter—criminal homicides caused either by recklessness or gross criminal negligence.

justifiable homicides—killing in self-defense, capital punishment, and police use of deadly force.

malice aforethought—the common-law designation for murder *mens rea* that covered a broad range of states of mind.

negligent homicide—unintentional killings in which actors should have known they were creating substantial and unjustified risks of death by conduct that grossly deviated from ordinary care.

paramour rule—the rule that a husband's witnessing his wife in the act of adultery is adequate provocation to reduce murder to manslaughter.

premeditated—the requirement in first-degree murder *mens rea* that killings must be planned in advance.

second-degree murder—a catchall offense including killings that are neither manslaughter nor first-degree murder.

voluntary manslaughter—intentional killings committed in the sudden heat of passion upon adequate provocation.

year-and-a-day rule—the rule that no act occurring more than one year and one day before death is the legal cause of death.

SUGGESTED READINGS

1. Rollin M. Perkins and Ronald N. Boyce, *Criminal Law*, 3d ed. (Mineola, N.Y.: Foundation Press, 1982), pp. 46–151. Thoroughly covers criminal homicide, using many cases and examples to illustrate the complicated elements in criminal homicide. In addition, discusses developments in the law, including the *Model Penal Code* approach to negligent homicide.

2. George Fletcher, *Rethinking Criminal Law* (Boston: Little, Brown, 1978), chaps. 4 and 5. Fletcher takes a critical look at criminal homicide, stressing the uniqueness of homicide as a crime because of its irreversibility. He goes into the philosophical underpinnings of homicide law. These chapters enhance much of what Fletcher says in this text about various homicides, including the *mens rea* and circumstances surrounding them.

3. American Law Institute, *Model Penal Code and Commentaries*, vol. 1 (Philadelphia: American Law Institute, 1980), pt. II, pp. 1–90. This volume develops the *Model Penal Code's* reconstruction of homicide law, doing away with degrees and replacing them with three classifications: murder,

manslaughter, and negligent homicide. It is a thorough, thought-provoking discussion, well worth the serious student's efforts.

NOTES

1. George Fletcher, *Rethinking Criminal Law* (Boston: Little, Brown, 1978), pp. 235–236.

2. Rollin M. Perkins and Ronald N. Boyce, *Criminal Law*, 3d ed. (Mineola, N.Y.: Foundation Press, 1982), pp. 49–53.

3. 410 U.S. 113, 93 S.Ct. 705, 35 L.Ed.2d 147 (1973); American Law Institute, *Model Penal Code and Commentaries*, vol. 1 (Philadelphia: American Law Institute, 1980), pt. II, pp. 11–13, maintains that abortion and fetal death statutes should be kept distinct.

4. I am grateful to Randall Rogers, the poster's creator, for this idea.

5. Minnesota Statutes Annotated § 609.266(a).

6. *State v. Fierro*, 124 Ariz. 182, 603 P.2d 74, 77–78 (1979); Perkins and Boyce, *Criminal Law*, pp. 48–49.

7. American Law Institute, *Model Penal Code and Commentaries*, vol. 1, pt. II, pp. 10–11, discusses this and summarizes recent legislation on the subject.

8. Perkins and Boyce, *Criminal Law*, 822–824; 373 Mass. 249, 366 N.E.2d 744 (1977).

9. American Law Institute, *Model Penal Code and Commentaries*, vol. 1, pt. II, pp. 6–7; Quoted in American Law Institute, *Model Penal Code and Commentaries*, vol. 1, pt. 11, p. 14.

10. Pa. Laws of 1794, ch. 257, §§ 1,2 (1794); Herbert Wechsler and Jerome Michael discuss this development thoroughly in "A Rationale of the Law of Homicide I," *Columbia Law Review* 37 (1937):703–717.

11. *Goodman v. State*, 573 P.2d 400 (Wyo.1977); Perkins and Boyce, *Criminal Law*, pp. 131–134; Quoted in *People v. Anderson*, 70 Cal.2d 15, 73 Cal.Rptr. 550, 447 P.2d 942 (1968).

12. *State v. Hall*, 54 Nev. 213, 13 P.2d 624 (1932) (intent formed when shot fired); *People v. Wolff*, 61 Cal.2d 795, 40 Cal.Rptr. 271, 394 P.2d 959 (1964).

13. Sir James F. Stephen, *History of the Criminal Law* (New York: Burt Franklin, 1973), p. 94.

14. RCW 9A.32.050; Arizona Statutes, 11-1304.

15. AS 11.41.110.

16. Michigan Penal Code, §§ 750.316, 750.317.

17. *State v. Weisengoff*, 85 W.Va. 271, 101 S.E. 450 (1919) (accidental death); Jerome Hall, "The Substantive Law of Crimes—1187–1936," *Harvard Law Review* 50 (1937):616, 642.

18. 125 Wis.2d 204, 371 N.W.2d 381 (1985).

19. *State v. Crane*, 247 Ga. 779, 279 S.E.2d 695 (1981) (victim shooting burglar); *Campbell v. State*, 293 Md. 438, 444 A.2d 1034 (1982) (victim cabdriver and police officer); *State v. O'Dell*, 684 S.W.2d 453 (Mo.App.1984) (victim of felonious assault).

20. *People v. Phillips*, 64 Cal.2d 574, 51 Cal.Rptr. 225, 414 P.2d 353 (1966).

21. Francis T. Cullen, William J. Maakestad, and Gray Cavender, *Corporate Crime under Attack: The Ford Pinto Case and Beyond* (Cincinnati, Ohio: Anderson Publishing Company, 1987).

22. "Texas Nursing Home on Trial in Death," *New York Times* (October 1, 1985); and (March 18, 1986), 11.

23. "Business and the Law," *New York Times* (March 5, 1985), 30; and (May 19, 1985).

24. "Three Executives Convicted of Murder for Unsafe Workplace Conditions," *New York Times* (June 14, 1985), 1, 9.

25. Sir William Blackstone, *Commentaries* (University of Chicago Press, 1979), IV:191.

26. *People v. Davis*, 33 Ill.App.3d 105, 337 N.E.2d 256 (1975); also *State v. Grant*, 418 A.2d 154 (Me.1980); but to the contrary see *State v. Tuzon*, 118 Ariz. 205, 575 P.2d 1231 (1978).

27. Perkins and Boyce, *Criminal Law*, p. 85.

28. *Beasley v. State*, 64 Miss. 518, 8 So. 234 (1886).

29. Perkins and Boyce, *Criminal Law*, pp. 95–96.

30. *Manning's Case*, 83 Eng. Rep. 112 (1793); *Palmore v. State*, 283 Ala. 501, 218 So.2d 830 (1969) (husband killed wife); *Dabney v. State*, 113 Ala. 38, 21 So. 211 (1897) (husband killed both wife and paramour).

31. *People v. Washington*, 58 Cal.App.3d 620, 130 Cal.Rptr. 96 (1976).

32. *State v. Flory*, 40 Wyo. 184, 276 P. 458 (1929).

33. Wayne R. LaFave and Austin W. Scott, Jr., *Criminal Law*, 2d ed. (St. Paul: West Publishing Company, 1986), p. 675.

Crimes Against Persons II: Criminal Sexual Conduct and Others

Chapter Outline

I. Introduction

II. Criminal Sexual Conduct

III. The Elements of Modern Rape

IV. Assault and Battery

V. False Imprisonment

VI. Kidnapping

VII. Summary

CHAPTER MAIN POINTS

1. Sex offenses cover a broad spectrum, including everything from violent assaults to nonviolent private sex between consenting adults.

2. Rape is both a violent crime and a sexual violation.

3. Criminal sexual conduct statutes have expanded traditional rape law, making sexual violations, no matter what their nature, gender-neutral crimes.

4. Violence is not always required in rape.

5. Battery is the crime of offensive physical contact.

6. Assault is either an attempted battery or a threatened battery.

7. Injury and the use of weapons aggravate simple battery and assault.

8. False imprisonment is the misdemeanor of illegal detention against the victim's will.

9. Kidnapping is the use of force or fear of force to move or keep in secret another person beyond the reach of help from the law or friends.

Did He Rape Her?

A college student left her class, went to her dormitory room where she drank a martini, and then went to a lounge to wait for her boyfriend. When her boyfriend didn't show up, she went to another dormitory to find a friend, Earl Hassel. She knocked on the door, but no one answered. She tried the doorknob and, finding it unlocked, went in and found a man sleeping on the bed. At first, she thought the man was Hassel, but he turned out to be Hassel's roommate, Robert Berkowitz. Berkowitz asked her to stay for a while and she agreed. He asked for a backrub and she turned him down. He suggested that she sit on the bed, but she said no and sat on the floor instead.

Berkowitz moved to the floor beside her, lifted up her shirt and bra and massaged her breasts. He then unfastened his pants and unsuccessfully attempted to put his penis in her mouth. They both stood up, and he locked the door. He came back, pushed her onto the bed, and removed her undergarments from one leg. He then penetrated her vagina with his penis. After withdrawing and ejaculating on her stomach, he stated, "Wow, I guess we just got carried away," to which she responded, "No, we didn't get carried away, you got carried away."

INTRODUCTION

Crimes against persons threaten three fundamental values—life, liberty, and privacy. The law of homicide, the subject of Chapter 9, examined the special nature of criminal conduct that takes life itself. The crimes against persons examined in this chapter encompass conduct that doesn't take life itself but still injures others by wounding them physically, invading their sexual integrity, invading their privacy and liberty, or putting them in fear.

Criminal sexual conduct is a lot like other crimes against persons, but both the law and society treat sex offenses as especially serious. Criminal sexual conduct stands only slightly below murder in both public recognition and law as the most serious crime against a person. One indication of this special recognition is that criminal sexual conduct is a serious crime even if the victim suffers no physical injury. The reason is that criminal sexual conduct violates intimacy in a way that physical injury doesn't. Even offensive sexual touching, such as pinching buttocks or fondling breasts, bears the mark of a special violation. Offensive sexual contacts short of rapes are universally regarded by the law and society as more serious than other offensive touching found in the law of battery. An unwanted erotic caress can offend more than an insulting spit in the face.[1]

Criminal homicide and criminal sexual conduct are clearly the most serious crimes against persons. But nonsexual assault and battery far outnumber them. Also, kidnapping and its relative, false imprisonment, invade two fundamental values in a free society—liberty and privacy.

CRIMINAL SEXUAL CONDUCT

Historically, the criminal law recognized only two crimes of sexual conduct—rape and sodomy. At common law, rape was defined as forced heterosexual penetration; sodomy meant consensual homosexual conduct. Modern court opinions have relaxed the strict definitions of rape, and statutes have expanded criminal sexual conduct so that now it embraces a wide range of nonconsensual penetrations and contacts that fall short of violence. Furthermore, public attention and criminal justice agencies have gone beyond their prior narrow focus on rape by strangers—the classic case of the lurking evil strange man who jumps from the shadows on a dark street at night and attacks a defenseless woman. Another type of rape—long unacknowledged, and therefore virtually unknown except to its victims and perpetrators—has come to public attention. Public attention in turn has brought changes in both the law of rape and the criminal justice response to it. This is rape of women by men they know. Today, it is widely accepted that there are two kinds of rape. The first kind we'll call **aggravated rape**, namely rape by strangers or by men with weapons, or where rapists physically injure their victims. The other kind we'll label **unarmed acquaintance rape**, involving "dates, lovers, neighbors, co-workers, employers, and so on."[2]

The criminal justice system deals fairly well with aggravated rapes. But it hasn't done so well with the unarmed acquaintance rapes. Why? For several reasons. Victims aren't likely to report them, or don't recognize them as rapes. If victims report them, the police are less likely to believe the victims of unarmed acquaintance rape than the victims of aggravated rape. Prosecutors are less likely to charge unarmed acquaintance rapists, and juries are less likely to convict them. Appeals court decisions are more likely to cause controversy. Finally, unarmed acquaintance rapists are most likely to escape punishment if their victims don't follow the rules of middle-class morality. According to Professor David P. Bryden,

> An acquaintance rapist is most likely to escape justice if his victim violated traditional norms of female morality and prudence: for example, by engaging in casual sex, drinking heavily, or hitchhiking. When the victim is a norm-violating woman, people often blame her rather than the rapist.

The criminal justice system's poor performance in dealing with unarmed acquaintance rapes would be a serious problem in any case, but it is made worse because the overwhelming number of rapes are unarmed acquaintance rapes. In one survey of women who didn't report rapes to the police, more than 80 percent said they were raped by men they knew. In three separate surveys of college women, one in five reported being "physically forced" to have sexual intercourse by her date. Another aspect of the social reality of rape is that a substantial number of rapes are committed against men.[3]

HISTORY OF RAPE

As early as 1800, rape was a capital offense in the common law of Anglo-Saxon England. The common law defined rape as the carnal knowledge (sexual intercourse) by a man with force and without the consent of a woman who was not his wife. This definition of rape includes four elements:

1. Intentional sexual intercourse
2. Between a man and a woman who is not his wife
3. Achieved by force or a threat of severe bodily harm
4. Without the woman's consent[4]

The common law required proof beyond a reasonable doubt of all four elements because, as Lord Hale, the highly regarded seventeenth-century lawyer and legal scholar of the criminal law, noted:

> It must be remembered, that it is an accusation to make, hard to be proved, and harder to be defended by the party accused, though innocent. . . . The heinousness of the offence many times transporting the judge and jury with so much indignation, that they are overhastily carried to the conviction of the person accused thereof, by the confident testimony of sometimes false and malicious witnesses.[5]

The common law allowed rape victims to testify against accused rapists, leaving the jury to determine the credibility of the victim witnesses. However, credibility depended on three conditions regarding the victim, all of them difficult, and often impossible, to satisfy:

1. The chastity of the victim.
2. Prompt reporting of the rape by the victim.
3. Corroboration of the rape by witnesses other than the victim.

Blackstone, the leading eighteenth-century authority on the common law in both England and the American colonies, boldly asserted that even prostitutes could be of good fame, but then made the assertion meaningless by adding the warning that if the victim

> be of evil fame, and stand unsupported by others; if she concealed the injury for any considerable time after she had opportunity to complain; if the place where the fact was alleged to be committed, was where it was possible she might have been heard, and she made no outcry; these and the like circumstances carry a strong, but not conclusive, presumption that her testimony is false or feigned.[6]

Force and Resistance Standard

From seventeenth-century England to the 1970s in the United States, the law of rape concentrated on the element of consent. Women had to prove by their resistance that they didn't consent to the unwanted sexual advances. According to an early frequently cited case, *Reynolds v. State*:

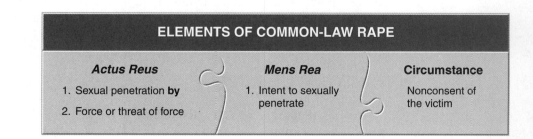

ELEMENTS OF COMMON-LAW RAPE

Actus Reus	***Mens Rea***	**Circumstance**
1. Sexual penetration **by**	1. Intent to sexually penetrate	Nonconsent of the victim
2. Force or threat of force		

> Voluntary submission by the woman, while she has power to resist, no matter how reluctantly yielded, removes from the act an essential element of the crime of rape . . . if the carnal knowledge was with the consent of the woman, no matter how tardily given, or how much force had theretofore been employed, it is not rape.[7]

Proof of nonconsent by resistance is peculiar to the law of rape. In no other crime where lack of consent is an element of the crime does the law treat passive acceptance as consent. Robbery requires taking someone's property by force or threat of force. But it is outrageous even to think that the element of force requires victims to prove that they resisted. Entering an unlocked apartment house without consent to commit a crime is burglary; it would be absurd to demand that renters prove they didn't consent to the entry. Similarly in car theft. According to Lani Anne Remick,

> A common defense to a charge of auto theft . . . is that the car's owner consented to the defendant's use of the vehicle. A mere showing that the owner never gave the defendant permission to take the car is enough to defeat this defense; no showing that the owner actually told the defendant not to take the car is necessary. In rape law, however, the "default" position is consent. Proof of the absence of affirmative indications by the victim is not enough to defeat a consent defense; instead, the prosecution must show that the alleged victim indicated to the defendant through her overt actions and/or words that she did not wish to participate in sexual activity with him. Thus, "the law presumes that one will not give away that which is his to a robber, but makes no similar presumption as to the conduct of women and rapists." In fact, quite the opposite is true: in the context of sexual activity the law presumes consent. For example, proving both that a woman did not verbally consent and that her actions consist of lying still and not moving does not raise a presumption of nonconsent but of consent. Only through evidence of some sort of overt behavior such as a verbal "no" or an attempt to push away the defendant can the prosecution meet its burden of proving nonconsent.[8]

The amount of resistance required to prove lack of consent has changed over time. From the nineteenth century until the 1950s, the **utmost resistance standard** prevailed. According to the standard, women had to use all the power at their command to physically resist. In *Brown v. State*, a sixteen-year-old virgin testified that her neighbor grabbed her, tripped her to the ground, and forced himself on her.

> I tried as hard as I could to get away. I was trying all the time to get away just as hard as I could. I was trying to get up; I pulled at the grass; I screamed as hard as I could, and he told me to shut up, and I didn't, and then he held his hand on my mouth until I was almost strangled.

The jury convicted the neighbor of rape. On appeal, the Wisconsin Supreme Court reversed because the victim hadn't resisted enough:

> Not only must there be entire absence of mental consent or assent, but there must be the most vehement exercise of every physical means or faculty within the woman's power to resist the penetration of her person, and this must be shown to persist until the offense is consummated.[9]

In another case, the Nebraska Supreme Court made the standard even tougher:

> The general rule is that a mentally competent woman must in good faith resist to the utmost with the most vehement exercise of every physical means or faculty naturally within her power to prevent carnal knowledge, and she must persist in such resistance as long as she has the power to do so until the offense is consummated.[10]

Strict as the utmost resistance standard was, the law didn't require physical resistance in all cases. Intercourse with a woman who was incapacitated by intoxication, mental deficiency, or insanity was regarded as rape regardless of whether the perpetrator used force or the victim consented. Sexual penetration obtained by fraud wasn't rape either. But the fraud had to relate to getting consent, not to the nature of the act. For example, if a doctor told a woman he needed to insert an instrument into her vagina for treatment but in fact was engaging in intercourse, the law didn't recognize her consent. On the other hand, if a woman consented to sexual intercourse because a doctor convinced her that it was good for her health, the law recognized this consent because the woman was defrauded about the benefits, not the act of sexual intercourse (see the discussion in Chapter 12 on fraud in the inducement). Finally, sexual intercourse with a minor who consented and did not resist was rape.[11]

In the 1950s courts began to relax the utmost resistance test. Its replacement, the **reasonable resistance standard,** allowed for differences in the amount of resistance required. According to the standard, the totality of circumstances in each case determines how much a victim had to resist. For example, the Virginia Supreme Court ruled that a "woman is not required to resist to the utmost of her physical strength if she reasonably believes that resistance would be useless and result in serious bodily injury."[12]

Rape Law Reform

The 1970s and 1980s were a time of major rape law reform. In the procedural law of rape, many states abolished the requirement that the prosecution has to provide corroboration for rape victims' testimony. In addition, most states passed **rape shield statutes,** which prohibit introducing evidence of victims' past sexual conduct. Many states also relaxed the requirement that prohibited prosecution unless women promptly report rapes. A few states abolished the marital exception.

States have also made changes in the substantive law of rape. Criminal sexual conduct statutes have shifted the emphasis away from consent of the victim. The Pennsylvania Superior Court, for example, ruled that the common-law emphasis on lack of consent had "worked to the unfair disadvantage of the woman who, when threatened with violence, chose quite rationally to submit to her assailant's advances rather than risk death or serious bodily injury."[13]

The *Model Penal Code* provision eliminated consent as an element in rape because of its "disproportionate emphasis upon objective manifestations by the woman." However, the drafters of the code also recognized that a complex relationship exists between force and consent. Unlike the acts in all other criminal assaults, the drafters noted, under ordinary circumstances victims may desire the physical act in rape—sexual intercourse:

> This unique feature of the offense requires drawing a line between forcible rape on the one hand and reluctant submission on the other, between true aggression and desired intimacy. The difficulty in drawing this line is compounded by the fact that there will often be no witness to the event other than the participants and that their perceptions may change over time. The trial may turn as much on an assessment of the motives of the victim as of the actor.[14]

Criminal sexual conduct statutes have replaced rape statutes and expanded the definition of sex offenses to include all sexual penetrations: vaginal, anal, and oral. In addition, they have created a lesser offense of criminal sexual contact that falls short of penetration. Under criminal sexual conduct statutes, sex offenses are gender-neutral; men can commit criminal sexual conduct against men or women, and women can commit criminal sexual conduct against women or men.[15]

Despite these advances in the law of rape, Professor David Bryden concludes:

> Most legislatures and courts still define rape narrowly. In acquaintance rape cases, in most states, nonconsensual sex is not rape unless the perpetrator employs force or a threat of force, or the victim is unconscious, badly drunk, underage, or otherwise incapacitated. Even if the victim verbally declines sex, the encounter is not rape in most states unless the man employs "force." Sex obtained by nonviolent threats ("you'll lose your job," etc.), or by deception, usually is not a crime.[16]

 10-1 Criminal Sexual Conduct Statutes

THE ELEMENTS OF MODERN RAPE

Most states define rape as intentional sexual activity with another person by force and without the other person's consent. So, rape in most jurisdictions consists of four elements:

1. The *actus reus* of sexual penetration between perpetrator and victim.
2. The *actus reus* of the use of force, or the threat of force, by the perpetrator as the means to accomplish the sexual penetration.
3. The circumstance of nonconsent of the victim.
4. The *mens rea* of intentional sexual activity.

 10-2 Bryden, "Redefining Rape"

THE *ACTUS REUS* OF RAPE

The rape *actus reus* consists of two elements:

1. sexual penetration
2. by force or the threat of force

Sexual penetration has never meant full sexual intercourse to emission, and it still doesn't. The common-law phrase "penetration however slight" still describes the modern requirement. So, a defendant who "put his fingers between folds of skin over his victim's vagina, but didn't insert his fingers" satisfied the penetration requirement.[17]

Courts have adopted two standards to determine whether penetration was accomplished by force:

1. Extrinsic force standard
2. Intrinsic force standard

The **extrinsic force standard** requires some force in addition to the physical effort needed to accomplish the penetration. The amount of force required varies according to the circumstances of particular cases. The **intrinsic force standard** requires only the amount of physical effort necessary to accomplish the penetration. The following two case excerpts apply the extrinsic and intrinsic force requirements, respectively. We look first at the Pennsylvania Supreme Court's application of the extrinsic force standard to the facts of *Commonwealth v. Berkowitz*.[18]

C A S E   Did He Have Sex by Force?

Commonwealth v. Berkowitz
537 Pa. 143, 641 A.2d 1161 (1994)

Robert Berkowitz, the defendant, was convicted in the Court of Common Pleas, Monroe County, of rape and indecent assault and he appealed. The Superior Court, Philadelphia 1990, affirmed. The Pennsylvania Supreme Court affirmed.
    CAPPY, J.

FACTS

The complainant, a female college student, left her class, went to her dormitory room where she drank a martini, and then went to a lounge to await her boyfriend. When her boyfriend failed to appear, she went to another dormitory to find a friend, Earl Hassel. She knocked on the door, but received no answer. She tried the doorknob and, finding it unlocked, entered the room and discovered a man sleeping on the bed. The complainant originally believed the man to be Hassel, but it turned out to be Hassel's roommate, Robert Berkowitz, the appellee. Berkowitz asked her to stay for a while and she agreed. He requested a backrub and she declined. He suggested that she sit on the bed, but she declined and sat on the floor.

    Berkowitz then moved to the floor beside her, lifted up her shirt and bra and massaged her breasts. He then unfastened his pants and unsuccessfully attempted to put his penis in her mouth. They both stood up, and he locked the door. He returned to push her onto the bed, and removed her undergarments from one leg. He then penetrated her vagina with his penis. After withdrawing and ejaculating on her stomach, he stated, "Wow, I guess we just got carried away," to which she responded, "No, we didn't get carried away, you got carried away."

OPINION

In reviewing the sufficiency of the evidence, this Court must view the evidence in the light most favorable to the Commonwealth as verdict winner, and accept as true all evidence and reasonable inferences that may be reasonably drawn therefrom, upon which, if believed, the jury could have relied in reaching its verdict. If, upon such review, the

Court concludes that the jury could not have determined from the evidence adduced that all of the necessary elements of the crime were established, then the evidence will be deemed insufficient to support the verdict.

    The crime of rape is defined as follows:

§ 3121. Rape
A person commits a felony of the first degree when he engages in sexual intercourse with another person not one's spouse:
(1) by forcible compulsion;
(2) by threat of forcible compulsion that would prevent resistance by a person of reasonable resolution;
(3) who is unconscious; or
(4) who is so mentally deranged or deficient that such person is incapable of consent.

    The victim of a rape need not resist. "The force necessary to support a conviction of rape . . . need only be such as to establish lack of consent and to induce the [victim] to submit without additional resistance. . . . The degree of force required to constitute rape is relative and depends on the facts and particular circumstance of the case." *Commonwealth v. Rhodes*, 510 Pa. 537, 554, 510 A.2d 1217 (1986)

    In regard to the critical issue of forcible compulsion, the complainant's testimony is devoid of any statement which clearly or adequately describes the use of force or the threat of force against her. In response to defense counsel's question, "Is it possible that [when Appellee lifted your bra and shirt] you took no physical action to discourage him," the complainant replied, "It's possible." When asked, "Is it possible that [Berkowitz] was not making any physical contact with you . . . aside from attempting to untie the knot [in the drawstrings of complainant's sweatpants]," she answered, "It's possible." She testified that "He put me down on the bed. It was kind of like—He didn't throw me on the bed. It's hard to explain. It was kind of like a push but not—I can't explain what I'm trying to say." She concluded that "it wasn't much" in reference to whether she bounced on the bed, and further detailed that their movement to the bed "wasn't slow like a romantic kind of thing, but it wasn't a fast shove either. It was kind of in the middle." She agreed that Appellee's hands were not restraining her in any manner during the actual penetration, and that the weight of his body on top of her was the only force applied. She testified that at no time did Appellee verbally threaten her. The complainant did testify that she sought to leave the room, and said "no" throughout the encounter. As to the complainant's desire to leave the room, the record clearly demonstrates that the door could be unlocked easily from the inside, that she was aware of this fact, but that she never attempted to go to the door or unlock it.

As to the complainant's testimony that she stated "no" throughout the encounter with Appellee, we point out that, while such an allegation of fact would be relevant to the issue of consent, it is not relevant to the issue of force. In *Commonwealth v. Mlinarich,* 518 Pa. 247, 542 A.2d 1335 (1988) (plurality opinion), this Court sustained the reversal of a defendant's conviction of rape where the alleged victim, a minor, repeatedly stated that she did not want to engage in sexual intercourse, but offered no physical resistance and was compelled to engage in sexual intercourse under threat of being recommitted to a juvenile detention center. The Opinion in Support of Affirmance acknowledged that physical force, a threat of force, or psychological coercion may be sufficient to support the element of "forcible compulsion," if found to be enough to "prevent resistance by a person of reasonable resolution." However, under the facts of *Mlinarich,* neither physical force, the threat of physical force, nor psychological coercion were found to have been proven, and this Court held that the conviction was properly reversed by the Superior Court. Accordingly, the ruling in *Mlinarich* implicitly dictates that where there is a lack of consent, but no showing of either physical force, a threat of physical force, or psychological coercion, the "forcible compulsion" requirement under 18 Pa.C.S. § 3121 is not met. The Opinion in Support of Reversal in *Mlinarich* did not take issue with the implicit holding of the Opinion in Support of Affirmance that something more than a lack of consent is required to prove "forcible compulsion." The Opinion in Support of Reversal acknowledged a general legislative intent to introduce an objective standard regarding the degree of physical force, threat of physical force, or psychological coercion required under 18 Pa.C.S. § 3121, in that it must be sufficient to "prevent resistance by a person of reasonable resolution," but argued that the "peculiar situation" of the victim and other subjective factors should be considered by the court in determining "resistance," "assent," and "consent," and that under the specific circumstances in *Mlinarich* sufficient facts were set forth to allow a finding of the requisite degree of psychological coercion to support the forcible compulsion element of 18 Pa.C.S. § 3121.

Moreover, we find it instructive that in defining the related but distinct crime of "indecent assault" under 18 Pa.C.S. § 3126, the Legislature did not employ the phrase "forcible compulsion" but rather chose to define indecent assault as "indecent contact with another . . . without the consent of the other person." The phrase "forcible compulsion" is explicitly set forth in the definition of rape under 18 Pa.C.S. § 3121, but the phrase "without the consent of the other person," is conspicuously absent. The choice by the Legislature to define the crime of indecent assault utilizing the phrase "without the consent of the other" and to not so define the crime of rape indicates a legislative intent that the term "forcible compulsion" under 18 Pa.C.S. § 3121, be interpreted as something more than a lack of consent. Moreover, we note that penal statutes must be strictly construed to provide fair warning to the defendant of the nature of the proscribed conduct.

Reviewed in light of the above described standard, the complainant's testimony simply fails to establish that the Appellee forcibly compelled her to engage in sexual intercourse as required under 18 Pa.C.S. § 3121. Thus, even if all of the complainant's testimony was believed, the jury, as a matter of law, could not have found Appellee guilty of rape. Accordingly, we hold that the Superior Court did not err in reversing Appellee's conviction of rape. . . .

Accordingly, the order of the Superior Court reversing the rape conviction is affirmed.

QUESTIONS FOR DISCUSSION

1. Explain how the court came to the conclusion that the Pennsylvania rape statute required extrinsic force.

2. List the facts that the court used to conclude that Robert Berkowitz did not satisfy the extrinsic force requirement.

3. Assume you are the prosecution. Argue that Robert Berkowitz did use extrinsic force to achieve sexual penetration.

The New Jersey Supreme Court applied the intrinsic force standard in *State in the Interest of M.T.S.*

| C A S E | Did He Use Force to Rape? |

State in the Interest of M.T.S.
609 A.2d 1266 (N.J. 1992)

The trial court determined that M.T.S., a juvenile, was delinquent for committing a sexual assault. The Appellate Division reversed the disposition of delinquency, concluding that nonconsensual penetration does not constitute sexual assault unless it is accompanied by some level of force more than that necessary to accomplish the penetration. The New Jersey Supreme Court granted the State's petition for certification to review the law regarding the element of force in rape. The supreme court reversed.

HANDLER, J.

FACTS

On Monday, May 21, 1990, fifteen-year-old C.G. was living with her mother, her three siblings, and several other people, including M.T.S. and his girlfriend. A total of ten people resided in the three-bedroom town home at the time of the incident. M.T.S., then age seventeen, was temporarily residing at the home with the permission of C.G.'s mother; he slept downstairs on a couch. C.G. had her own room on the second floor. At approximately 11:30 P.M. on May 21, C.G. went upstairs to sleep after having watched television with her mother, M.T.S., and his girlfriend. When C.G. went to bed, she was wearing underpants, a bra, shorts, and a shirt. At trial, C.G. and M.T.S. offered very different accounts concerning the nature of their relationship and the events that occurred after C.G. had gone upstairs. The trial court did not credit fully either teenager's testimony.

C.G. stated that earlier in the day, M.T.S. had told her three or four times that he "was going to make a surprise visit up in her bedroom." She said that she had not taken M.T.S. seriously and considered his comments a joke because he frequently teased her. She testified that M.T.S. had attempted to kiss her on numerous other occasions and at least once had attempted to put his hands inside of

her pants, but that she had rejected all of his previous advances.

C.G. testified that on May 22, at approximately 1:30 A.M., she awoke to use the bathroom. As she was getting out of bed, she said, she saw M.T.S., fully clothed, standing in her doorway. According to C.G., M.T.S. then said that "he was going to tease [her] a little bit." C.G. testified that she "didn't think anything of it"; she walked past him, used the bathroom, and then returned to bed, falling into a "heavy" sleep within fifteen minutes. The next event C.G. claimed to recall of that morning was waking up with M.T.S. on top of her, her underpants and shorts removed. She said "his penis was into [her] vagina." As soon as C.G. realized what had happened, she said, she immediately slapped M.T.S. once in the face, then "told him to get off [her], and get out." She did not scream or cry out. She testified that M.T.S. complied in less than one minute after being struck; according to C.G., "he jumped right off of [her]." She said she did not know how long M.T.S. had been inside of her before she awoke.

C.G. said that after M.T.S. left the room, she "fell asleep crying" because "[she] couldn't believe that he did what he did to [her]." She explained that she did not immediately tell her mother or anyone else in the house of the events of that morning because she was "scared and in shock." According to C.G., M.T.S. engaged in intercourse with her "without [her] wanting it or telling him to come up [to her bedroom]." By her own account, C.G. was not otherwise harmed by M.T.S.

At about 7:00 A.M., C.G. went downstairs and told her mother about her encounter with M.T.S. earlier in the morning and said that they would have to "get [him] out of the house." While M.T.S. was out on an errand, C.G.'s mother gathered his clothes and put them outside in his car; when he returned, he was told that "[he] better not even get near the house." C.G. and her mother then filed a complaint with the police.

According to M.T.S., he and C.G. had been good friends for a long time, and their relationship "kept leading on to more and more." He had been living at C.G.'s home for about five days before the incident occurred; he testified that during the three days preceding the incident they had been "kissing and necking" and had discussed having sexual intercourse. The first time M.T.S. kissed C.G., he said, she "didn't want him to, but she did after that." He said C.G. repeatedly had encouraged him to "make a surprise visit up in her room."

M.T.S. testified that at exactly 1:15 A.M. on May 22, he entered C.G.'s bedroom as she was walking to the bathroom. He said C.G. soon returned from the bathroom, and the two began "kissing and all," eventually moving to the bed. Once they were in bed, he said, they undressed each other and continued to kiss and touch for about five minutes. M.T.S. and C.G. proceeded to engage in sexual intercourse. According to M.T.S., who was on top of C.G., he "stuck it in" and "did it [thrust] three times, and then the fourth time [he] stuck it in, that's when [she] pulled [him] off of her." M.T.S. said that as C.G. pushed him off, she said "stop, get off," and he "hopped off right away."

According to M.T.S., after about one minute, he asked C.G. what was wrong; she replied with a backhand to his face. He recalled asking C.G. what was wrong a second time, and her replying, "how can you take advantage of me or something like that." M.T.S. said that he proceeded to get dressed and told C.G. to calm down, but that she then told him to get away from her and began to cry. Before leaving the room, he told C.G., "I'm leaving . . . I'm going with my real girlfriend, don't talk to me . . . I don't want nothing to do with you or anything, stay out of my life . . . don't tell anybody about this . . . it would just screw everything up." He then walked downstairs and went to sleep.

On May 23, 1990, M.T.S. was charged with conduct that if engaged in by an adult would constitute second-degree sexual assault of the victim, contrary to N.J.S.A. 2C:142c(1). . . .

Following a two-day trial on the sexual assault charge, M.T.S. was adjudicated delinquent. After reviewing the testimony, the court concluded that the victim had consented to a session of kissing and heavy petting with M.T.S. The trial court did not find that C.G. had been sleeping at the time of penetration, but nevertheless found that she had not consented to the actual sexual act. Accordingly, the court concluded that the State had proven second-degree sexual assault beyond a reasonable doubt.

On appeal, following the imposition of suspended sentences on the sexual assault and the other remaining charges, the Appellate Division determined that the absence of force beyond that involved in the act of sexual penetration precluded a finding of second-degree sexual assault. It therefore reversed the juvenile's adjudication of delinquency for that offense.

OPINION

The issues in this case are perplexing and controversial. We must explain the role of force in the contemporary crime of sexual assault and then define its essential features. We then must consider what evidence is probative to establish the commission of a sexual assault. The factual circumstances of this case expose the complexity and sensitivity of those issues and underscore the analytic difficulty of those seemingly-straightforward legal questions.

Under New Jersey law a person who commits an act of sexual penetration using physical force or coercion is guilty of second degree sexual assault. The sexual assault statute does not define the words "physical force." The question posed by this appeal is whether the element of "physical force" is met simply by an act of nonconsensual penetration involving no more force than necessary to accomplish that result.

That issue is presented in the context of what is often referred to as "acquaintance rape." The record in the case discloses that the juvenile, a seventeen-year-old boy, engaged in consensual kissing and heavy petting with a fifteen-year-old girl and thereafter engaged in actual sexual penetration of the girl to which she had not consented. There was no evidence or suggestion that the juvenile used any unusual or extra force or threats to accomplish the act of penetration.

The trial court determined that the juvenile was delinquent for committing a sexual assault. The Appellate Division reversed the disposition of delinquency, concluding that nonconsensual penetration does not constitute sexual assault unless it is accompanied by some level of force more than that necessary to accomplish the penetration.

The New Jersey Code of Criminal Justice, N.J.S.A. 2C:142c(1), defines "sexual assault" as the commission "of sexual penetration" "with another person" with the use of "physical force or coercion." An unconstrained reading of the statutory language indicates that both the act of "sexual penetration" and the use of "physical force or coercion" are separate and distinct elements of the offense. Neither the definitions section of N.J.S.A. 2C:141 to 8, nor the remainder of the Code of Criminal Justice provides assistance in interpreting the words "physical force." The initial inquiry is, therefore, whether the statutory words are unambiguous on their face and can be understood and applied in accordance with their plain meaning. The answer to that inquiry is revealed by the conflicting decisions of the lower courts and the arguments of the opposing parties. The trial court held that "physical force" had been established by the sexual penetration of the victim without her consent. The Appellate Division believed that the statute requires some amount of force more than that necessary to accomplish penetration.

The parties offer two alternative understandings of the concept of "physical force" as it is used in the statute. The State would read "physical force" to entail any amount of sexual touching brought about involuntarily. A showing of sexual penetration coupled with a lack of consent would satisfy the elements of the statute. The Public Defender urges an interpretation of "physical force" to mean force "used to overcome lack of consent." That definition equates force with violence and leads to the conclusion that sexual assault requires the application of some amount of force in addition to the act of penetration. . . .

. . . Pre-reform rape law in New Jersey, with its insistence on resistance by the victim, greatly minimized the importance of the forcible and assaultive aspect of the defendant's conduct. Rape prosecutions turned then not so much on the forcible or assaultive character of the defendant's actions as on the nature of the victim's response. "If a woman assaulted is physically and mentally able to resist, is not terrified by threats, and is not in a place and position that resistance would have been useless, it must be shown that she did, in fact, resist the assault." Under the prereform law, the resistance offered had to be "in good faith and without pretense, with an active determination to prevent the violation of her person, and must not be merely passive and perfunctory." That the law put the rape victim on trial was clear. . . .

The New Jersey Code of Criminal Justice [reformed the law of rape in 1978. Among other things, it changed the name of rape to "sexual assault," extended the range of penetrations included in the definition of sexual assault, and made sexual assault gender neutral]. The Code does not refer to force in relation to "overcoming the will" of the victim, or to the "physical overpowering" of the victim, or the "submission" of the victim. It does not require the demonstrated nonconsent of the victim. As we have noted, in reforming the rape laws, the Legislature placed primary emphasis on the assaultive nature of the crime, altering its constituent elements so that they focus exclusively on the forceful or assaultive conduct of the defendant.

The Legislature's concept of sexual assault and the role of force was significantly colored by its understanding of the law of assault and battery. As a general matter, criminal battery is defined as "the unlawful application of force to the person of another." 2 Wayne LaFave & Austin Scott, *Criminal Law*, § 7.15 at 301 (1986). The application of force is criminal when it results in either (a) a physical injury or (b) an offensive touching. Id. at 30102. Any "unauthorized touching of another [is] a battery." *Perna v. Pirozzi*, 92 N.J. 446, 462, 457 A.2d 431 (1983). Thus, by eliminating all references to the victim's state of mind and conduct, and by broadening the definition of penetration to cover not only sexual intercourse between a man and a woman but a range of acts that invade another's body or compel intimate contact, the Legislature emphasized the affinity between sexual assault and other forms of assault and battery. . . . We are thus satisfied that an interpretation of the statutory crime of sexual assault to require physical force in addition to that entailed in an act of involuntary or unwanted sexual penetration would be fundamentally inconsistent with the legislative purpose to eliminate any consideration of whether the victim resisted or expressed nonconsent.

We note that the contrary interpretation of force—that the element of force need be extrinsic to the sexual act—would not only reintroduce a resistance requirement into the sexual assault law, but also would immunize many acts of criminal sexual contact short of penetration. The characteristics that make a sexual contact unlawful are the same as those that make a sexual penetration unlawful. An actor is guilty of criminal sexual contact if he or she commits an act of sexual contact with another using "physical force" or "coercion." N.J.S.A. 2C:143(b). That the Legislature would have wanted to decriminalize unauthorized sexual intrusions on the bodily integrity of a victim by requiring a showing of force in addition to that entailed in the sexual contact itself is hardly possible.

Because the statute eschews any reference to the victim's will or resistance, the standard defining the role of force in sexual penetration must prevent the possibility that the establishment of the crime will turn on the alleged victim's state of mind or responsive behavior. We conclude, therefore, that any act of sexual penetration engaged in by the defendant without the affirmative and freely given permission of the victim to the specific act of penetration constitutes the offense of sexual assault. Therefore, physical force in excess of that inherent in the act of sexual penetration is not required for such penetration to be unlawful. The definition of "physical force" is satisfied under N.J.S.A. 2C:142c(1) if the defendant applies any amount of force against another person in the absence of what a reasonable person would believe to be affirmative and freely-given permission to the act of sexual penetration. . . .

Our understanding of the meaning and application of "physical force" under the sexual assault statute indicates that the term's inclusion was neither inadvertent nor redundant. The term "physical force," like its companion term "coercion," acts to qualify the nature and character of the "sexual penetration." Sexual penetration accomplished through the use of force is unauthorized sexual penetration. That functional understanding of "physical force" encompasses the notion of "unpermitted touching" derived from the Legislature's decision to redefine rape as a sexual assault. As already noted, under assault and battery doctrine, any amount of force that results in either physical injury or offensive touching is sufficient to establish a battery. Hence, as a description of the method of achieving "sexual penetration," the term "physical force" serves to define and explain the acts that are offensive, unauthorized, and unlawful. . . .

Today the law of sexual assault is indispensable to the system of legal rules that assures each of us the right to decide who may touch our bodies, when, and under what circumstances. The decision to engage in sexual relations with another person is one of the most private and intimate decisions a person can make. Each person has the right not only to decide whether to engage in sexual contact with another, but also to control the circumstances and character of that contact. No one, neither a spouse, nor a friend, nor an acquaintance, nor a stranger, has the right or the privilege to force sexual contact. See "Definition of Forcible Rape," *Va.L.Rev.* (arguing that "forcible rape is viewed as a heinous crime primarily because it is a violent assault on a person's bodily security, particularly degrading because that person is forced to submit to an act of the most intimate nature").

We emphasize as well that what is now referred to as "acquaintance rape" is not a new phenomenon. Nor was it a "futuristic" concept in 1978 when the sexual assault law was enacted. Current concern over the prevalence of forced sexual intercourse between persons who know one another reflects both greater awareness of the extent of such behavior and a growing appreciation of its gravity. Notwithstanding the stereotype of rape as a violent attack by a stranger, the vast majority of sexual assaults are perpetrated by someone known to the victim. One respected study indicates that more than half of all rapes are committed by male relatives, current or former husbands, boyfriends or lovers. Similarly, contrary to common myths, perpetrators generally do not use guns or knives and victims generally do not suffer external bruises or cuts. Acquaintance Rape, supra, at 10. Although this more realistic and accurate view of rape only recently has achieved widespread public circulation, it was a central concern of the proponents of reform in the 1970s.

The insight into rape as an assaultive crime is consistent with our evolving understanding of the wrong inherent in forced sexual intimacy. It is one that was appreciated by the Legislature when it reformed the rape laws, reflecting an emerging awareness that the definition of rape should correspond fully with the experiences and perspectives of rape victims. Although reformers focused primarily on the problems associated with convicting defendants accused of violent rape, the recognition that forced sexual intercourse often takes place between persons who know each other and often involves little or no violence comports with the understanding of the sexual assault law that was embraced by the Legislature. Any other interpretation of the law, particularly one that defined force in relation to the resistance or protest of the victim, would directly undermine the goals sought to be achieved by its reform. . . .

The Appellate Division was correct in recognizing that a woman's right to end intimate activity without penetration is a protectable right the violation of which can be a criminal offense. However, it misperceived the purpose of the statute in believing that the only way that right can be protected is by the woman's unequivocally expressed desire to end the activity. The effect of that requirement would be to import into the sexual assault statute the notion that an assault occurs only if the victim's will is overcome, and thus to reintroduce the requirement of nonconsent and victim resistance as a constituent material element of the crime. Under the reformed statute, a person's failure to protest or resist cannot be considered or used as justification for bodily invasion.

We acknowledge that cases such as this are inherently fact sensitive and depend on the reasoned judgment and common sense of judges and juries. The trial court concluded that the victim had not expressed consent to the act of intercourse, either through her words or actions. We conclude that the record provides reasonable support for the trial court's disposition.

Accordingly, we reverse the judgment of the Appellate Division and reinstate the disposition of juvenile delinquency for the commission of second degree sexual assault. For reversal and reinstatement—Chief Justice WILENTZ, and Justices CLIFFORD, HANDLER, POLLOCK, O'HERN, GARIBALDI and STEIN—7. Opposed—None.

QUESTIONS FOR DISCUSSION

1. List all of the facts relevant to determining whether M.T.S. satisfied the intrinsic force element of the New Jersey sexual assault statute.

2. Summarize the reasons the court gives for adopting the intrinsic force standard.

3. Taking into account the facts, decision, and reasoning of *Commonwealth v. Berkowitz,* which do you think is the better approach to the force requirement—intrinsic or extrinsic force? Defend your answer.

4. Should legislatures or courts decide whether to adopt the intrinsic or extrinsic force standard? Defend your answer.

Actual force isn't required to satisfy the force requirement. The *threat* of force is enough. The prosecution has to prove two things about the threat:

1. The victim was placed in real fear of imminent and serious bodily harm.

2. The fear was reasonable under the circumstances.

Brandishing a weapon satisfies the requirement. So do verbal threats, such as threats to kill, seriously injure, or kidnap. But the threat doesn't have to include showing weapons or express words. Courts can consider all of the following in deciding whether the victim's fear was reasonable:

- Respective ages of the perpetrator and the victim.
- Physical sizes of the perpetrator and the victim.
- Mental condition of the perpetrator and the victim.
- Physical setting of the assault.
- Position of authority, domination, or custodial control of the perpetrator over the victim.[19]

Not even the threat of force is required in cases where perpetrators obtain consent fraudulently, or when a minor, a mentally deficient, or an insane person consents. In these cases, the penetration alone is enough.

THE *MENS REA* OF RAPE

Most people think of rape as a specific intent crime, namely that the rapist intended to use force to have sex. The leading case on the point is *Regina v. Morgan.* In the widely publicized case, four companions were drinking in a bar. When they failed to "find some women," Morgan invited the other three to come home with him to have sexual intercourse with his wife. Morgan told the others not to worry if she struggled because she was "kinky"; the struggle "turned [her] on." The trial court convicted the men, and the intermediate appellate court upheld the conviction. The House of Lords, England's highest appeal court, overturned the conviction because the defendants didn't specifically intend to have sexual intercourse by force and without consent. Why? Because they believed that Morgan's wife wanted the struggle.[20]

Regina v. Morgan generated a storm of debate. Although England has adhered to the specific intent requirement, American statutes and decisions barely mention intent, except in attempted rape where intent is the essence of the crime. Where courts face the intent question, they vary in their response. The Maine Supreme Judicial Court has ruled that rape is a strict liability crime:

> Certain crimes are defined to expressly include a culpable state of mind and others are not. The more forceful or egregious sexual conduct, including rape compelled by force, is defined without reference to the actor's state of mind. The legislature, by carefully defining the sex offenses in the criminal code, and by making no reference to a culpable mental state for rape, clearly indicated that rape compelled by force or threat requires no culpable state of mind.[21]

Other courts have adopted a reckless or negligent standard with regard to the sexual penetration, saying that rapists have to either be aware that they are risking coerced sexual intercourse or should know that their victims haven't consented. Critics argue that rape is too serious a charge and the penalties are too severe to allow convictions on anything less than specific intent. Law professor Susan Estrich, a rape law scholar and herself a rape victim, disagrees:

> If inaccuracy or indifference to consent is "the best that this man can do" because he lacks the capacity to act reasonably, then it might well be unjust and ineffective to punish him for it. . . . More common is the case of the man who could have done better but did not; heard her refusal or saw her tears, but decided to ignore them. The man who has the inherent capacity to act reasonably but fails to has, through that failure, made a blameworthy choice for which he can justly be punished. The law has long punished unreasonable action which leads to the loss of human life as manslaughter—a lesser crime than murder, but a crime nonetheless. . . . The injury of sexual violation is sufficiently great, the need to provide that additional incentive pressing enough, to justify negligence liability for rape as for killing.[22]

Can defendants satisfy the *mens rea* requirement of criminal sexual conduct even if they didn't intend to sexually assault their victims? The Wisconsin supreme court answered this question in *State v. Bonds*.

CASE | Did He Intend to Rape Her?

State v. Bonds
165 Wis.2d 27, 477 N.W.2d 265 (1991)

Anthony Bonds, the defendant, was convicted of second-degree assault. Judgment was entered in the Circuit Court, Milwaukee County. Bonds appealed. The Court of Appeals reversed and further appeal was taken. The Supreme Court reversed.
STEINMETZ, J.

FACTS

The victim was confronted by Bonds in the boarding house where she resided. Bonds had previously lived in the building but because of certain problems was told to move. When the victim saw Bonds, she told him that a guard was waiting for him downstairs. She then proceeded to return to her room. Bonds began to utter profanities and followed her back to her apartment. The victim could not recall exactly what was said; however, she considered the verbiage to be threatening. When the victim turned to confront Bonds, he reached out his hand, grabbed the nipple of her left breast, squeezed and pulled it, causing pain. She responded by knocking Bonds' hand away. Bonds then attempted to bring his fist toward her face. The victim grabbed Bonds' hand and bit it.

The defendant negotiated a guilty plea and was sentenced to six years in prison. The defendant claimed at the plea hearing that when he squeezed and pulled the victim's nipple he did so intending to hurt her, not to violate her sexually. On appeal, the court of appeals held that the defendant's actions did not constitute sexual contact "by use or threat of force or violence" and therefore did not fall under second-degree sexual assault. The court of appeals reversed Bonds' conviction and remanded the case to the trial court with specific directions. The directions were as follows: "First, Bonds is to be permitted to withdraw his guilty plea. Second, the felony-bind over is to be vacated. . . ." This court concludes that the defendant's actions constitute second-degree sexual assault, and we thereby reverse the decision of the court of appeals.

OPINION

The issue in this case is whether a defendant's use of force in making sexual contact with his victim by forcibly grabbing her nipple and then squeezing and pulling it, constitutes the crime of second-degree sexual. Under § 940.225(2)(a), one is guilty of a Class C felony for second-degree sexual assault when an individual "has sexual contact or sexual intercourse with another person without consent of that person by use or threat of force or violence."

Bonds asserts that he should be charged with a misdemeanor rather than a felony. Bonds argues that he should have been charged with either the misdemeanor under sec. 940.225(3m), Stats., fourth-degree sexual assault, or under sec. 940.19(1), battery. Fourth-degree sexual assault does not require a showing of force, violence or injury. Second-degree sexual assault, however, is classified as a felony and requires a showing of force, violence or injury. The defendant argues that the statutory element "by use or threat of force or violence" in sec. 940.225(2)(a), Stats., requires that a causal relationship exists between the "use or threat of force

or violence" and the sexual contact or intercourse. He contends that the statutory requirement of sexual contact or intercourse "by use or threat of force or violence" is not satisfied where, as in the present situation, the force used is the force applied in the sexual contact. It is argued that the statutory element could be satisfied only where the force used or threatened was the means or mechanism by which the sexual contact or intercourse was accomplished. The court of appeals agreed and reasoned:

> The legislature's use of the word "by" is not ambiguous. Rather, it clearly requires that there be a cause and effect relationship between the "use or threat of force or violence" and the prohibited sexual contact or intercourse. Simply put, it is not enough that the sexual contact or sexual intercourse be forceful or violent; the "use or threat of force or violence" must be the means by which the sexual assault is accomplished.

The court of appeals refers to *State v. Baldwin*, 101 Wis.2d 441, 451, 304 N.W.2d 742 (1981), which states that the force threatened and force applied concept encompassed by the words "by use or threat of force or violence" means action that is "directed toward compelling the victim's submission." The court opined that the force applied by Bonds was not directed toward compelling her submission to the grabbing and pinching of her nipple. The court of appeals stated that: "it is not enough that the sexual contact . . . be forceful or violent; the 'use or threat of force or violence' must be the means by which the sexual assault is accomplished." We find no support for this conclusion and disagree with the court of appeals interpretation of sec. 940.225(2)(a), Stats.

In statutory construction, courts are to give effect to the intent of the legislature. This begins with the language of the statute itself. We give the language its ordinary and accepted meaning. By its very terms, § 940.225(2)(a), Stats. prohibits nonconsensual sexual contact "by use or threat of force or violence." Sexual contact under this section includes "actual or attempted battery." "Sexual contact" is defined in sec. 940.225(5)(b), Stats., as

> any intentional touching by the complainant or defendant, either directly or through clothing by the use of any body part or object, of the complainant's or defendant's intimate parts if that intentional touching is either for the purpose of sexually degrading or for the purpose of sexually

humiliating the complainant or sexually arousing or gratifying the defendant or if the touching contains the elements of actual or attempted battery under s. 940.19(1).

"Intimate parts" is defined in sec. 939.22(19), Stats., and includes any of the following: "breast, buttock, anus, groin, scrotum, penis, vagina or pubic mound of a human being."

Battery occurs when one "causes bodily harm to another by an act done with intent to cause bodily harm to that person or another without the consent of the person so harmed. . . ." See sec. 940.19(1), Stats.

The defendant admitted using force and conceded that he had intended to hurt his victim. Section 940.225(2)(a), Stats., does not state that the force used or threatened may not be the force employed in the actual nonconsensual contact. Nor does it state that the force must be directed toward compelling the victim's submission. The phrase "by use of force" includes forcible contact or the force used as the means of making contact.

We recognize that the force element of sexual assault maintains the proscription against force or compulsion not as separate and distinct forms of conduct, but as a more generalized concept of conduct, including force threatened and force applied, directed toward compelling the victim's submission. Force used at the time of contact can compel submission as effectively as force or threat occurring before contact. Regardless of when the force is applied, the victim is forced to submit. When force is used at the time of contact, the victim has no choice at the moment of simultaneous use of force and making of contact. When force is used before contact, the choice is forced. In both cases, the victim does not consent to the contact. Consent under sec. 940.225(4), Stats., reads in part as: "words or overt actions by a person who is competent to give informed consent indicating a freely given agreement to have sexual intercourse or sexual contact. . . ."

We conclude that based on the plain language of the statute, the defendant falls within second-degree sexual assault because he made sexual contact of a complainant's intimate part through the means of actual or attempted battery. The defendant's guilty plea for the crime of second-degree sexual assault is reinstated as is his conviction and sentence.

The decision of the court of appeals is reversed.

QUESTIONS FOR DISCUSSION

1. What exactly was Anthony Bonds's intent in this case?

2. Explain the court's reasoning for deciding that Anthony Bonds committed second-degree sexual assault.

3. In your opinion, do the facts in this case justify a conviction for *sexual* assault? Or should it be a case of nonsexual assault? Defend your answer.

✳ 10-3 Wisconsin Court of Appeals Decision

The Element of Nonconsent

According to the law, the prosecution has to prove beyond a reasonable doubt that the victim didn't consent to sex. Practically speaking, consent almost always arises as a defense to rape. In the typical case, defendants claim either that their victims consented or that defendants mistakenly believed that they consented. This doesn't mean that victims have to consent in writing or even specifically "announce their consent." Consent can be and often is indicated by actions not words. No state has gone so far as the guidelines for student sexual conduct adopted by Antioch College. One critic of the guidelines wrote:

> Deep among the cornfields and pig farms of central Ohio in the town of Yellow Springs, Antioch prides itself on being "A Laboratory for Democracy." The dress code is grunge and black; multiple nose rings are *de rigueur,* and green and blue hair are preferred (if you have hair). Seventy percent of the student body are womyn (for the uninitiated, that's women—without the dreaded m-e-n). And the purpose of the Sexual Offense Policy is to empower these students to become equal partners when it comes time to mate with males. The goal is 100 percent consensual sex, and

it works like this: it isn't enough to ask someone if she'd like to have sex, as an Antioch women's center advocate told a group of incoming freshmen this fall. You must obtain consent every step of the way. "If you want to take her blouse off, you have to ask. If you want to touch her breast, you have to ask. If you want to move your hand down to her genitals, you have to ask. If you want to put your finger inside her, you have to ask."

How silly this all seems; how sad. It criminalizes the delicious unexpectedness of sex—a hand suddenly moves to here, a mouth to there. What is the purpose of sex if not to lose control? (To be unconscious, no.) The advocates of sexual correctness are trying to take the danger out of sex, but sex is inherently dangerous. It leaves one exposed to everything from euphoria to crashing disappointment. That's its great unpredictability. But of course, that's sort of what we said when we were all made to use seat belts. What is implicit in the new sex guidelines is that it's the male who does the initiating and the woman who at any moment may bolt. Some young women rankle at that. "I think it encourages wimpy behavior by women and [the idea] that women need to be handled with kid gloves," says Hope Segal, 22, a fourth-year Antioch student. Beware those boys with their swords, made deaf by testosterone and, usually, blinded by drink.[23]

 10-4 "Sexual Correctness"

Statutory Rape

Statutory rape means having sex with minors. Statutory rapists don't have to use force; the victim's immaturity takes the place of force. Furthermore, nonconsent is not an element, nor is consent a defense because minors can't *legally* consent to sex. In other words, statutory rape is a strict liability crime. A few states, such as California and Alaska, however, do permit the defense of mistake. The defense applies if a man reasonably believes that his victim is over the age of consent. In other words, negligence is the required *mens rea*. A divided Maryland supreme court refused to adopt the defense of mistake in statutory rape in *Garnette v. State*.

C A S E   Did He Rape Her?

Garnett v. State
332 Md. 571, 632 A.2d 797 (1993)

Raymond Leonard Garnett, the defendant, was convicted in the Circuit Court, Montgomery County, of second-degree rape under the statute proscribing sexual intercourse between persons under 14 and another at least four years older than the victim. Garnett appealed. Maryland's supreme court, The Court of Appeals, granted certiorari prior to intermediate appellate review by the Court of Special Appeals to consider the important issue presented in the case. The Court of Appeals affirmed Garnett's conviction.

MURPHY, CJ.

FACTS

Raymond Lennard Garnett is a young retarded man. At the time of the incident in question he was 20 years old. He has an I.Q. of 52. His guidance counselor from the Montgomery County public school system, Cynthia Parker, described him as a mildly retarded person who read on the third-grade level, did arithmetic on the 5th-grade level, and interacted with others socially at school at the level of someone 11 or 12 years of age. Ms. Parker added that Raymond attended special education classes and for at least one period of time was educated at home when he was afraid to return to school due to his classmates' taunting. Because he could not understand the duties of the jobs given him, he failed to complete vocational assignments; he sometimes lost his way to work. As Raymond was unable to pass any of the State's functional tests required for graduation, he received only a certificate of attendance rather than a high-school diploma.

In November or December 1990, a friend introduced Raymond to Erica Frazier, then aged 13; the two subsequently talked occasionally by telephone. On February 28, 1991, Raymond, apparently wishing to call for a ride home, approached the girl's house at about nine o'clock in the evening. Erica opened her bedroom window, through which Raymond entered; he testified that "she just told me to get a ladder and climb up her window." The two talked, and later engaged in sexual intercourse. Raymond left at about 4:30 a.m. the following morning. On November 19, 1991, Erica gave birth to a baby, of which Raymond is the biological father.

Raymond was tried before the Circuit Court for Montgomery County (Miller, J.) on one count of second degree rape under § 463(a)(3) proscribing sexual intercourse between a person under 14 and another at least four years older than the complainant. At trial, the defense twice proffered evidence to the effect that Erica herself and her friends had previously told Raymond that she was 16 years old, and that he had acted with that belief. The trial court excluded such evidence as immaterial, explaining:

> Under 463, the only two requirements as relate to this case are that there was vaginal intercourse, and that . . . Ms. Frazier was under 14 years of age and that . . . Mr. Garnett was at least four years older than she. In the Court's opinion, consent is no defense to this charge. The victim's representation as to her age and the defendant's belief, if it existed, that she was not under age, what amounts to what otherwise might be termed a good faith defense, is in fact no defense to what amounts to statutory rape. It is in the Court's opinion a strict liability offense.

The court found Raymond guilty. It sentenced him to a term of five years in prison, suspended the sentence and imposed five years of probation, and ordered that he pay restitution to Erica and the Frazier family. Raymond noted an appeal; we granted certiorari prior to intermediate appellate review by the Court of Special Appeals to consider the important issue presented in the case.

OPINION

Maryland's "statutory rape" law prohibiting sexual intercourse with an underage person is codified in Maryland Code (1957, 1992 Repl.Vol.) Art. 27, § 463, which reads in full:

> "Second degree rape.
> (a) What constitutes.—A person is guilty of rape in the second degree if the person engages in vaginal intercourse with another person:
> (1) By force or threat of force against the will and without the consent of the other person; or
> (2) Who is mentally defective, mentally incapacitated, or physically helpless, and the person performing the act knows or should reasonably know the other person is mentally defective, mentally incapacitated, or physically helpless; or
> (3) Who is under 14 years of age and the person performing the act is at least four years older than the victim.
> (b) Penalty.—Any person violating the provisions of this section is guilty of a felony and upon conviction is subject to imprisonment for a period of not more than 20 years."

. . . Now we consider whether under the present statute, the State must prove that a defendant knew the complaining witness was younger than 14 and, in a related question, whether it was error at trial to exclude evidence that he had been told, and believed, that she was 16 years old. . . .

Section 463(a)(3) does not expressly set forth a requirement that the accused have acted with a criminal state of mind, or *mens rea*. The State insists that the statute, by design, defines a strict liability offense, and that its essential elements were met in the instant case when Raymond, age 20, engaged in vaginal intercourse with Erica, a girl under 14 and more than 4 years his junior. Raymond replies that the criminal law exists to assess and punish morally culpable behavior. He says such culpability was absent here. He asks us either to engraft onto subsection (a)(3) an implicit *mens rea* requirement, or to recognize an affirmative defense of reasonable mistake as to the complainant's age. Raymond argues that it is unjust, under the circumstances of this case which led him to think his conduct lawful, to brand him a felon and rapist.

Raymond asserts that the events of this case were inconsistent with the criminal sexual exploitation of a minor by an adult. As earlier observed, Raymond entered Erica's bedroom at the girl's invitation; she directed him to use a ladder to reach her window. They engaged voluntarily in sexual intercourse. They remained together in the room for more than seven hours before Raymond departed at dawn. With an I.Q. of 52, Raymond functioned at approximately the same level as the 13-year-old Erica; he was mentally an adolescent in an adult's body. Arguably, had Raymond's chronological age, 20, matched his socio-intellectual age, about 12, he and Erica would have fallen well within the four-year age difference obviating a violation of the statute, and Raymond would not have been charged with any crime at all.

The precise legal issue here rests on Raymond's unsuccessful efforts to introduce into evidence testimony that Erica and her friends had told him she was 16 years old, the age of consent to sexual relations, and that he believed them. Thus the trial court did not permit him to raise a defense of reasonable mistake of Erica's age, by which defense Raymond would have asserted that he acted innocently without a criminal design. At common law, a crime occurred only upon the concurrence of an individual's act and his guilty state of mind. In this regard, it is well understood that generally there are two components of every crime, the *actus reus* or guilty act and the *mens rea* or the guilty mind or mental state accompanying a forbidden act. The requirement that an accused have acted with a culpable mental state is an axiom of criminal jurisprudence. . . .

To be sure, legislative bodies since the mid-19th century have created strict liability criminal offenses requiring no *mens rea*. Almost all such statutes responded to the demands of public health and welfare arising from the complexities of society after the Industrial Revolution. Typically misdemeanors involving only fines or other light penalties, these strict liability laws regulated food, milk, liquor, medicines and drugs, securities, motor vehicles and traffic, the labeling of goods for sale, and the like. See Richard G. Singer, The Resurgence of *Mens Rea*: III—The Rise and Fall of Strict Criminal Liability, 30 *B.C.L.Rev.* 337, 340-373 (1989) (suggesting, however, that strict liability doctrine in the United States in the late 19th cen-

tury was motivated largely by moralistic fervor, such as found in the prohibitionist movement). Statutory rape, carrying the stigma of felony as well as a potential sentence of 20 years in prison, contrasts markedly with the other strict liability regulatory offenses and their light penalties.

Modern scholars generally reject the concept of strict criminal liability. . . . Conscious of the disfavor in which strict criminal liability resides, the *Model Penal Code* states generally as a minimum requirement of culpability that a person is not guilty of a criminal offense unless he acts purposely, knowingly, recklessly, or negligently, i.e., with some degree of *mens rea*. The Code allows generally for a defense of ignorance or mistake of fact negating *mens rea*. The *Model Penal Code* generally recognizes strict liability for offenses deemed "violations," defined as wrongs subject only to a fine, forfeiture, or other civil penalty upon conviction, and not giving rise to any legal disability.

With respect to the law of statutory rape, the *Model Penal Code* strikes a compromise with its general policy against strict liability crimes. The Code prohibits the defense of ignorance or a reasonable mistake of age when the victim is below the age of ten, but allows it when the critical age stipulated in the offense is higher than ten. *Model Penal Code,* supra, at §§ 213.1, 213.6(1). The drafters of the Code implicitly concede that sexual conduct with a child of such extreme youth would, at the very least, spring from a criminally negligent state of mind. The available defense of reasonable mistake of age for complainants older than ten requires that the defendant not have acted out of criminal negligence.

The commentators similarly disapprove of statutory rape as a strict liability crime. In addition to the arguments discussed above, they observe that statutory rape prosecutions often proceed even when the defendant's judgment as to the age of the complainant is warranted by her appearance, her sexual sophistication, her verbal misrepresentations, and the defendant's careful attempts to ascertain her true age. Voluntary intercourse with a sexually mature teen-ager lacks the features of psychic abnormality, exploitation, or physical danger that accompanies such conduct with children.

Two sub-parts of the rationale underlying strict criminal liability require further analysis at this point. Statutory rape laws are often justified on the "lesser legal wrong" theory or the "moral wrong" theory; by such reasoning, the defendant acting without *mens rea* nonetheless deserves punishment for having committed a lesser crime, fornication, or for having violated moral teachings that prohibit sex outside of marriage. Maryland has no law against fornication. It is not a crime in this state. Moreover, the criminalization of an act, performed without a guilty mind, deemed immoral by some members of the community rests uneasily on subjective and shifting norms. "Determining precisely what the 'community ethic' actually is is not an easy task in a heterogeneous society in which our public pronouncements about morality often are not synonymous with our private conduct.". . .

We acknowledge here that it is uncertain to what extent Raymond's intellectual and social retardation may have impaired his ability to comprehend imperatives of sexual morality in any case.

The legislatures of 17 states have enacted laws permitting a mistake of age defense in some form in cases of sexual offenses with underage persons. . . . In the landmark case of *People v. Hernandez*, 61 Cal.2d 529, 39 Cal.Rptr. 361, 393 P.2d 673 (1964), the California Supreme Court held that, absent a legislative directive to the contrary, a charge of statutory rape was defensible wherein a criminal intent was lacking; it reversed the trial court's refusal to permit the defendant to present evidence of his good faith, reasonable belief that the complaining witness had reached the age of consent. In so doing, the court first questioned the assumption that age alone confers a sophistication sufficient to create legitimate consent to sexual relations: "the sexually experienced 15-year-old may be far more acutely aware of the implications of sexual intercourse than her sheltered cousin who is beyond the age of consent." The court then rejected the traditional view that those who engage in sex with young persons do so at their peril, assuming the risk that their partners are underage:

> If [the perpetrator] participates in a mutual act of sexual intercourse, believing his partner to be beyond the age of consent, with reasonable grounds for such belief, where is his criminal intent? In such circumstances he has not consciously taken any risk. Instead he has subjectively eliminated the risk by satisfying himself on reasonable evidence that the crime cannot be committed. If it occurs that he has been misled, we cannot realistically

conclude for such reason alone the intent with which he undertook the act suddenly becomes more heinous. . . . The courts have uniformly failed to satisfactorily explain the nature of the criminal intent present in the mind of one who in good faith believes he has obtained a lawful consent before engaging in the prohibited act.

The Supreme Court of Alaska has held that a charge of statutory rape is legally unsupportable unless a defense of reasonable mistake of age is allowed. *State v. Guest,* 583 P.2d 836, 838-839 (Alaska 1978). The Supreme Court of Utah construed the applicable unlawful sexual intercourse statute to mean that a conviction could not result unless the state proved a criminal state of mind as to each element of the offense, including the victim's age. *State v. Elton,* 680 P.2d 727, 729 (Utah 1984) (Utah Criminal Code since amended to disallow mistake of age as a defense to unlawful sexual intercourse). The Supreme Court of New Mexico determined that a defendant should have been permitted at trial to present a defense that his partner in consensual sex told him she was 17, not 15, that this had been confirmed to him by others, and that he had acted under that mistaken belief. *Perez v. State,* 111 N.M. 160, 803 P.2d 249, 250-251 (1990). Two-fifths of the states, therefore, now recognize the defense in cases of statutory sexual offenses.

We think it sufficiently clear, however, that Maryland's second-degree rape statute defines a strict liability offense that does not require the State to prove *mens rea*; it makes no allowance for a mistake-of-age defense. The plain language of § 463, viewed in its entirety, and the legislative history of its creation lead to this conclusion. . . .

Section 463(a)(3) prohibiting sexual intercourse with underage persons makes no reference to the actor's knowledge, belief, or other state of mind. As we see it, this silence as to *mens rea* results from legislative design. First, subsection (a)(3) stands in stark contrast to the provision immediately before it, subsection (a)(2) prohibiting vaginal intercourse with incapacitated or helpless persons. In subsection (a)(2), the Legislature expressly provided as an element of the offense that "the person performing the act knows or should reasonably know the other person is mentally defective, mentally incapacitated, or physically helpless." Code, § 463(a)(2). In drafting this subsection, the Legislature showed itself perfectly capable of recognizing and allowing for a defense that obviates criminal intent; if the defendant objectively did not understand that the sex partner was impaired, there is no crime. That it chose not to include similar language in subsection (a)(3) indicates that the Legislature aimed to make statutory rape with underage persons a more severe prohibition based on strict criminal liability.

Second, an examination of the drafting history of § 463 during the 1976 revision of Maryland's sexual offense laws reveals that the statute was viewed as one of strict liability from its inception and throughout the amendment process. As originally proposed, Senate Bill 358 defined as a sexual offense in the first degree a sex act committed with a person less than 14 years old by an actor four or more years older. The Senate Judicial Proceedings Committee then offered a series of amendments to the bill. Among them, Amendment # 13 reduced the stipulated age of the victim from less than 14 to 12 or less. Amendment # 16 then added a provision defining a sexual offense in the second degree as a sex act with another "under 14 years of age, which age the person performing the sexual act knows or should know." These initial amendments suggest that, at the very earliest stages of the bill's life, the Legislature distinguished between some form of strict criminal liability, applicable to offenses where the victim was age 12 or under, and a lesser offense with a *mens rea* requirement when the victim was between the ages of 12 and 14.

Senate Bill 358 in its amended form was passed by the Senate on March 11, 1976. 1976 Senate Journal, at 1566. The House of Delegates' Judiciary Committee, however, then proposed changes of its own. It rejected the Senate amendments, and defined an offense of rape, without a *mens rea* requirement, for sexual acts performed with someone under the age of 14. The Senate concurred in the House amendments and S.B. 358 became law. Thus the Legislature explicitly raised, considered, and then explicitly jettisoned any notion of a *mens rea* element with respect to the complainant's age in enacting the law that formed the basis of current § 463(a)(3). In the light of such legislative action, we must inevitably conclude that the current law imposes strict liability on its violators.

This interpretation is consistent with the traditional view of statutory rape as a strict liability crime designed to protect young persons from the dangers of sexual exploitation by adults, loss of chastity, physical injury, and, in the case of girls, pregnancy. The majority of states retain statutes which impose strict liability for sexual acts with underage complainants. We observe again, as earlier, that even among those states providing for a mistake-of-age defense in some instances, the defense often is not available where the sex partner is 14 years old or less; the complaining witness in the instant case was only 13. The majority of appellate courts, including the Court of Special Appeals, have held statutory rape to be a strict liability crime.

Maryland's second-degree rape statute is by nature a creature of legislation. Any new provision introducing an element of *mens rea,* or permitting a defense of reasonable mistake of age, with respect to the offense of sexual intercourse with a person less than 14, should properly result from an act of the Legislature itself, rather than judicial fiat. Until then, defendants in extraordinary cases, like Raymond, will rely upon the tempering discretion of the trial court at sentencing.

JUDGMENT AFFIRMED, WITH COSTS.

DISSENT

BELL, J.

. . . I do not dispute that the legislative history of Maryland Code (1957, 1992 Repl.Vol.), Art. 27, section 463 may be read to support the majority's interpretation that subsection (a)(3) was intended to be a strict liability statute. Nor do I disagree that it is in the public interest to protect the sexually naive child from the adverse physical, emotional, or psychological effects of sexual relations. I do not believe, however, that the General Assembly, in every case, whatever the nature of the crime and no matter how harsh the potential penalty, can subject a defendant to strict criminal liability. To hold, as a matter of law, that section 463(a)(3) does not require the State to prove that a defendant possessed the necessary mental state to commit the crime, i.e. knowingly engaged in sexual relations with a female under 14, or that the defendant may not litigate that issue in defense, "offends a principle of justice so rooted in the traditions of conscience of our people as to be ranked as fundamental" and is, therefore, inconsistent with due process.

In . . . this case . . . , according to the defendant, he intended to have sex with a 16-, not a 13-, year-old girl. This mistake of fact was prompted, he said, by the prosecutrix herself; she and her friends told him that she was 16 years old. Because he was mistaken as to the prosecutrix's age, he submits, he is certainly less culpable than the person who knows that the minor is 13 years old, but nonetheless engages in sexual relations with her. Notwithstanding, the majority has construed section 463(a)(3) to exclude any proof of knowledge or intent. But for that construction, the proffered defense would be viable. I would hold that the State is not relieved of its burden to prove the defendant's intent or knowledge in a statutory rape case and, therefore, that the defendant may defend on the basis that he was mistaken as to the age of the prosecutrix. Generally, a culpable mental state, often referred to as *mens rea,* or intent, is, and long has been, an essential element of a criminal offense. A crime ordinarily consists of prohibited conduct and a culpable mental state; a wrongful act and a wrongful intent must concur to constitute what the law deems a crime, the purpose being to avoid criminal liability for innocent or inadvertent conduct. Historically, therefore, unless the actor also harbored an evil, or otherwise culpable, mind, he or she was not guilty of any crime.

The [U.S.] Supreme Court in *Morissette v. U.S.* [1952] recognized that ordinarily, a defendant cannot be convicted when he or she lacks the mental state which is an element of the offense charged. That concept—crime as a compound concept—gained early acceptance in the English Common law and "took deep and early root in American soil." In that case, Mr. Justice JACKSON stated the proposition thusly:

> The contention that an injury can amount to a crime only when inflicted by intention is no provincial or transient notion. It is as universal and persistent in mature systems of law as belief in freedom of the human will and a consequent ability and duty of the normal individual to choose between good and evil. A relation between some mental element and punishment for a harmful act is almost as instinctive as the child's familiar exculpatory "But I didn't mean to," and has afforded the rational basis for a tardy and unfinished substitution of deterrence and reformation in place of retaliation and vengeance as the motivation for public prosecution. Unqualified acceptance of this doctrine by English common law in the Eighteenth Century was indicated by Blackstone's sweeping statement that to constitute any crime there must first be a "vicious will."

. . . More recently, in *Anderson v. State,* 328 Md. 426, 444, 614 A.2d 963, 972 (1992), we held that the trial court improperly convicted the defendant for carrying concealed, a utility knife without considering the intent with which the utility knife was being carried. Noting that the utility knife could be used both as a tool and as a weapon, we rejected the State's argument that no intent was required. We said instead that, when the object is not a dangerous weapon per se, to convict a defendant of carrying a concealed dangerous weapon requires proof that the defendant intended to use the object as a weapon.

Although it recognized that Congress could dispense with the intent requirement if it did so specifically, the Court made clear that that power was not without limit. Thus, when a legislature wants to eliminate intent as an element of a particular crime, it should expressly so state in the statute. Legislative imposition of strict criminal liability, however, must be within constitutional limits; it cannot be permitted to violate the Due Process requirement of the Fourteenth Amendment, or a comparable state constitutional provision.

Strict liability crimes are recognized exceptions to the "guilty mind" rule in that they do not require the actor to possess a guilty mind, or the *mens rea,* to commit a crime. His or her state of mind being irrelevant, the actor is guilty of the crime at the moment that he or she does the prohibited act.

In the evolution of the statutory criminal law, two classes of strict liability crimes have emerged. One of them consists of "public welfare" offenses. Typical of this class are statutes involving, for example, the sale of food, drugs, liquor, and traffic offenses, designed to protect the health, safety, and welfare of the community at large; violation of such statutes "depend[s] on no mental element but consists only of forbidden acts or omissions." In the case of public welfare offenses, strict liability is justified on several bases, including: (1) only strict liability can deter profit-driven manufacturers from ignoring the well-being of the consuming public; (2) an inquiry into *mens rea* would exhaust the resources of the courts; (3) imposition of strict liability is not inconsistent with the moral underpinnings of the criminal law because the penalties are small and carry no stigma; and (4) the legislature is constitutionally empowered to create strict liability crimes for public welfare offenses. . . .

The second class of strict liability offenses, having a different justification than public welfare offenses, consists of narcotic, bigamy, adultery, and statutory rape crimes. State legislatures have historically used two theories to justify imposing strict liability in this class of offense: "lesser legal wrong" and "moral wrong." The lesser legal wrong theory posits that a defendant who actually intended to do some legal or moral wrong is guilty not only of the crime intended but of a greater crime of which he or she may not have the requisite mental state. . . .

A man who engages in consensual intercourse in the reasonable belief that his partner has reached [the age of consent] evidences no abnormality, no willingness to take advantage of immaturity, no propensity to corruption of minors. In short, he has demonstrated neither intent nor inclination to violate any of the interests that the law of statutory rape seeks to protect. At most, he has disregarded religious precept or social convention. In terms of mental culpability, his conduct is indistinguishable from that of any other person who engages in fornication. Whether he should be punished at all depends on a judgment about continuing fornication as a criminal offense, but at least he should not be subject to felony sanctions for statutory rape.

In utilizing the moral wrong theory, State legislatures seek to justify strict criminal liability for statutory rape when non-marital sexual intercourse is not a crime on the basis of society's characterization of it as immoral or wrong, i.e., *malum in se.* [Fornication is not a crime in Maryland.] The intent to commit such immoral acts supplies the *mens rea* for the related, but unintended crime; the outrage upon public decency or good morals, not conduct that is wrong only because it is prohibited by legislation, i.e., *malum prohibitum,* is the predicate.

There are significant problems with the moral wrong theory. First, it is questionable whether morality should be the basis for legislation or interpretation of the law. Immorality is not synonymous with illegality; intent to do an immoral act does not equate to intent to do a criminal act. Inferring criminal intent from immorality, especially when the accused is not even aware that the act is criminal, seems unjustifiable and unfair. In addition, the values and morals of society are ever evolving. Because sexual intercourse between consenting unmarried adults and minors who have reached the age of consent is not now clearly considered to be immoral, the moral wrong theory does not support strict criminal liability for statutory rape.

Second, classifying an act as immoral, in and of itself, divorced from any consideration of the actor's intention, is contrary to the general consensus of what makes an act moral or immoral. Ordinarily, an act is either moral or immoral depending on the intention of the actor. Holmes, Early Forms of Liability, in *The Common Law* 7 ("Even a dog distinguishes between being stumbled over and being kicked.").

Third, the assertion that the act alone will suffice for liability without the necessity of proving criminal intent is contrary to the traditional demand of the criminal law that only the act plus criminal intent is sufficient to constitute a crime. "Moral duties should not be identified with criminal duties," and, thus, when fornication is itself not criminal it should not become criminal merely because the defendant has made a reasonable mistake about the age of the girl with whom he has had intercourse.

Therefore, although in the case *sub judice,* the defendant engaged in sexual relations with a girl 13 years old, a minor below the age of consent, his conduct is not *malum in se,* and, so, strict liability is not justified.

Generally, a mistake of fact negates the mental state required to establish a material element of the crime. A person who engages in proscribed conduct is relieved of criminal liability if, because of ignorance or mistake of fact, he or she did not entertain the culpable mental state required for the commission of the offense.

Statutory rape is defined as sexual intercourse, by a person four or more years older, with a person under the age of 14. That statute conclusively presumes that a person under that age is incapable of legally consenting to sexual intercourse. That the female is incapable of consenting means that any act of intercourse in which she engages, even with her consent, is conclusively presumed to have been against her will. Consequently, a person engaging in intercourse with a female, whom he knows to be under 14 may not set up her consent as a defense. This does not mean, however, that one who does not know that the female is under 14 should not be able to set up his mistake of fact as a defense. This is because the closer a minor is to the age of consent, the more the appearance and behavior of that minor can be expected to be consistent with persons who have attained the age of consent. Indeed, one may plausibly mistake a minor 13 years old as being of the statutory age of consent.

The inadequacy of age as a demarcation line actually points up the flaws in the strict criminal liability analysis. First, it would seem reasonable to allow the accused to introduce evidence of the minor's maturity, sophistication, and past sexual experience, since maturity, not age, is the chief concern, age being but a factor. Second, the age standard (unless it is low enough) with its universal application draws an arbitrary line, resulting in the imposition of disproportionate penalties. Thus, for example, pursuant to section 463(a)(3) sexual intercourse with a person under 14 years of age, if the actor is at least four years older than the victim, is a second-degree rape offense punishable by a possible twenty years imprisonment. Under section 464C, defining a fourth-degree sexual offense, the same conduct if committed with a child 14 or 15 is punishable by a possible 1 year sentence. Thus, the law creates a potential disparity of up to 19 years for a difference of as little as one day in the victim's age. Third, placing the age standard too high may result in the anomaly of a female being legally able to consent to marriage, but unable to consent to intercourse.

A girl 13 years old may appear to be, and, in fact, may represent herself as being, over 16. If she should appear to be the age represented, a defendant may suppose reasonably that he received a valid consent from his partner, whom he mistakenly believes to be of legal age, only to find that her consent is legally invalid. In this situation, the majority holds, his reasonable belief as to the girl's age and consequent lack of criminal intent are no defense; the act alone suffices to establish guilt. But it is when the minor plausibly may represent that she has attained the age of consent that need for a defendant to be able to present a defense based on his or her belief that the minor was of the age to consent is the greatest. . . .

Thus, it has been observed that, "by the middle teens most girls have reached a point of maturity which realistically enables them to give meaningful, although not legal, consent." It is for this reason that "intercourse with a girl who is in her middle to late teens lacks the qualities of abnormality and physical danger that are present when she is still a child. . . . It is clear that the element of 'victimization' decreases as the girl grows older and more sophisticated.". . .

In this case . . . the defendant does not dispute that he had sexual relations with the 13-year-old prosecutrix. He seeks only to be able to defend himself against being labeled a rapist. He may only do so, however, if he is allowed to present evidence that he acted under a mistake of fact as to the prosecutrix's age, that he believed, and reasonably so, that she was above the age of consent. The proof he proposed to present to prove his defense was that the victim and her friends told him that the victim was 16 years old. He should have been allowed to show that he lacked the "guilty mind" to have sex with a 13-year-old.

A State legislature does have the power to define the elements of the criminal offenses recognized within its jurisdiction. In fact, the Supreme Court has said: "There is wide latitude in lawmakers to declare an offense and to exclude elements of knowledge and diligence from its definition." Accordingly, a State legislature may constitutionally prescribe strict liability for public welfare offenses, discussed supra, committed within its boundaries. But "far more than the simple omission of the appropriate phrase from the statutory definition is necessary to justify dispensing with an intent requirement."

To recognize that a State legislature may, in defining criminal offenses, exclude *mens rea,* is not to suggest that it may do so with absolute impunity, without any limitation whatsoever. The validity of such a statute necessarily will depend on whether it violates any provision of the federal constitution. It is ordinarily the due process clause, either of the federal constitution, or the corresponding provision of the appropriate state constitution, which will determine its validity.

The phrase "Law of the land" has been held to be equivalent to "due process" of the law, as used in the 14th Amendment to the United States Constitution. In that regard, therefore, Supreme Court cases on that subject are practically direct authority for the meaning of the Maryland provision. The essential elements of due process as it relates to a judicial proceeding are notice and opportunity to defend.

Due process, whether pursuant to that clause of the Fourteenth Amendment or the corresponding clause in a state constitution, protects an accused from being convicted of a crime except upon proof beyond a reasonable doubt of every element necessary to constitute the crime with which the accused is charged. It thus implicates the basic characteristics, if not the fundamental underpinnings, of the accusatorial system.

Under our system of justice, a person charged with a crime is presumed innocent until he or she is found guilty beyond a reasonable doubt. That means that he or she may not be found guilty until the State has produced evidence sufficient to convince the trier of fact, to the required extent, of that person's guilt. Moreover, although not required to do so, the defendant may present a defense, in which event the evidence the defendant produces must be assessed along with that of the State in determining whether the State has met its burden. The State's burden is not reduced or changed in any way simply because the defendant elects not to interpose a defense. In those cases, the defendant may still seek to convince the trier of fact that the State has not met its burden of proof by arguing that the inferences to be drawn from the evidence the State has produced simply is not sufficient to support guilt. . . .

The prosecution of statutory rape in Maryland necessarily brings into conflict the State's interests in protecting minors and defendants' due process rights because section 463(a)(3) operates "to exclude elements of knowledge and diligence from its definition," and, thus, removes reasonable ignorance of the girl's age and consequent lack of criminal intent as a defense. The failure of section 463(a)(3) to require proof of a culpable mental state conflicts both with the substantive due process ideal requiring that defendants possess some level of fault for a criminal conviction of statutory rape and the procedural due process ideal requiring that the prosecution overcome the presumption of innocence by proof of the defendant's guilt beyond a reasonable doubt. Notwithstanding the maxim that criminal statutes dispensing with the intent requirement and criminal offenses requiring no *mens rea* have a "generally disfavored status," the rationale of parts V and VI of the majority opinion is that the legislature has absolute authority to create strict liability crimes. For the reasons reviewed, I do not agree. On the contrary, I believe that due process both under the Fourteenth Amendment and under the Declaration of Rights, precludes strict criminal liability for statutory rape. Interpreting section 463(a)(3) as the majority does has the effect of largely relieving the State of its burden of proof and burden of persuasion. By making the defendant's intent, and, hence, blameworthiness, irrelevant, the Legislature has made inevitable, the petitioner's conviction. Moreover, upon conviction of the felony offense of statutory rape under section 463(a)(3), in addition to a substantial penalty of up to 20 years imprisonment, a defendant's reputation will be gravely besmirched. Where there is no issue as to sexual contact, which is more likely than not to be the case in statutory rape prosecutions, proof of the prosecutrix's age is not only proof of the defendant's guilt, it is absolutely dispositive of it and, at the same time, it is fatal to the only defense the defendant would otherwise have. So interpreted, section 463(a)(3) not only destroys absolutely the concept of fault, but it renders meaningless, in the statutory rape context, the presumption of innocence and the right to due process.

I respectfully dissent.

QUESTIONS FOR DISCUSSION

1. List all of the facts relevant to determining both the *actus reus* and the *mens rea* of rape in the case.

2. Did Raymond Garnett intend to rape Erica Frazier? Did he rape her recklessly? Negligently? Back up your answer with facts from the case.

3. According to the majority, why is Raymond's intent irrelevant? According to the dissent, why is it relevant?

4. Should statutory rape be a strict liability crime? Defend your answer.

Criminal Sexual Conduct Statutes

In the 1970s a combination of civil rights activists, feminists, and some criminal law reformers raised a strong and unified voice for abolishing existing rape laws. In their place, they recommend that legislatures create a group of new, gender-neutral offenses that would emphasize the aspects of violence and invasion of privacy more than the erotic nature of sexual assault. Some states have done this, enacting what are called criminal sexual conduct laws. One of the earliest and best known of these laws is Michigan's 1974 statute that provides:

> 1st degree: This consists of "sexual penetration," defined as sexual intercourse, cunnilingus, fellatio, anal intercourse, "or any other intrusion, however slight, of any part of a person's body or of any object into the genital or anal openings of another person's body." In addition one of the following must have occurred:
> 1. the defendant must have been armed with a weapon;
> 2. force or coercion was used and the defendant was aided by another person; or
> 3. force or coercion was used and personal injury to the victim was caused.
> 2nd degree: This consists of "sexual contact," defined as the intentional touching of the victim's or actor's personal parts or the intentional touching of the clothing covering the immediate area of the victim's intimate parts, for purposes of sexual arousal or gratification. "Intimate parts" is defined as including the primary genital area, groin, inner thigh, buttock, or breast. In addition, one of the circumstances required for 1st degree criminal sexual conduct must have existed.
> 3rd degree: This consists of sexual penetration accomplished by force or coercion.
> 4th degree: This consists of sexual contact accomplished by force or coercion.[24]

As the Michigan statute indicates, the new legislation covers all violent and otherwise offensive sexual penetration and contact without regard to the gender of victims and offenders.

Grading Rape

Most statutes divide rape into two degrees: simple or second-degree rape, and aggravated or first-degree rape. Aggravated rape involves at least one of the following:

- The victim suffers serious bodily injury.
- A stranger commits the rape.
- The rape occurs in connection with another crime.
- The rapist is armed.
- The rapist has accomplices.
- The victim is a minor and the rapist is several years older.

All other rapes are "simple" rapes for which the penalties are less severe. The criminal sexual conduct statutes have added more degrees in order to accommodate the distinction between penetration and contact. Aggravated penetration is first-degree criminal sexual conduct, aggravated contact is second degree, simple criminal penetration is third degree, and simple criminal contact is fourth degree.

ASSAULT AND BATTERY

Assault and battery, although combined in most statutes, were distinct offenses at common law. A **battery** is an unjustified offensive touching. Central to battery is body contact. An **assault** is either an attempted or a threatened battery. The essential difference between assault and battery is that assault requires no physical contact; an assault is complete before the offender touches the victim.

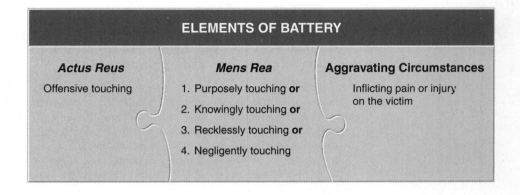

THE ELEMENTS OF BATTERY

The *actus reus* of battery consists of offensive touching. Not all offensive touching is battery. Spanking children is offensive, at least to the children who get the spanking, but it's not battery. Why? Because the law recognizes it as a justified act of disciplining children. So, only unjustified offensive touching is battery. Unjustified offensive touching covers a wide spectrum. Brutal attacks with baseball bats, kicking with heavy boots, and staggering blows with fists obviously fall within its scope. At the other extreme, some courts have included spitting in the face of someone you want to insult.[25]

Existing law doesn't clearly specify the battery *mens rea*. At common law, battery was an intentionally inflicted injury. Modern courts and statutes extend battery *mens rea* to include reckless and negligent contacts. The *Model Penal Code* defines battery to include "purposely, recklessly, or negligently causing bodily injury," or "negligently causing bodily injury . . . with a deadly weapon." Some state statutes call this expanded offense by a different name. Louisiana, for example, provides that "inflicting any injury upon the person of another by criminal negligence" is "negligent injuring." The court in *State v. Glenn* dealt with the required *mens rea* of assault and battery.[26]

| C A S E | Did He Intend to Assault and Batter? |

State v. Glenn
492 S.E.2d 393 (S.C.App. 1997)

HOWELL, J.

David L. Glenn appealed from his conviction for assault and battery with intent to kill. The South Carolina Supreme Court affirmed.

FACTS

Sara LeCroy lives approximately four miles from Interstate 85 on Old Dobbins Bridge Road in Anderson County. Glenn lives in the same area as

LeCroy. In March 1994, LeCroy removed a white porcelain toilet from her house and placed it in her yard behind the mailbox. LeCroy and her daughter-in-law placed potting soil in the toilet and planted flowers in it. On Saturday night, April 9, 1994, the toilet was still in LeCroy's yard. Sometime after midnight that night, LeCroy was awakened by a loud car or truck "taking off." The next morning, the toilet was gone.

At approximately 2:00 A.M. on Sunday, April 10, 1994, Gene Allen was traveling northbound on Interstate 85. He was driving a tractor trailer from Gainesville, Georgia, to Sagamore Beach, Massachusetts. As he approached an interstate overpass at the five-mile marker in Anderson County, Allen saw two young white males and a car on the overpass. One of the men was standing at the front of the car, while the other was standing at the rear of the car on the passenger side. As Allen was coming to the overpass, his vehicle was hit by a large white object, coming through the windshield and roof of the tractor. Although Allen was severely injured, he managed to stop his rig. Allen testified that he never actually saw the object before it hit his truck; however, the record makes clear that the object was a toilet containing some fertilizer or potting soil.

Allen's truck was towed from the scene by a local towing company. The trucking company then picked up the truck and returned it to its terminal in Norcross, Georgia.

After hearing about the incident, Larry Duckett, Glenn's cousin, contacted the victim and the police, telling them that Glenn was the only person in the community that Duckett thought might be capable of committing the crime. Duckett reached this conclusion because, sometime during the previous year, Glenn told Duckett that he had been throwing items at moving vehicles. According to Duckett, Glenn thought his pranks were funny. Glenn also told Duckett that he wondered what it would feel like to kill someone.

. . . Samuel Duckett, Larry's brother, also testified. In response to the solicitor's question about whether Glenn told Samuel that he had a desire to throw things into moving vehicles, Samuel responded:

> No, it ain't exactly like a craving, like he wanted to do something like this or something. He didn't really, you know, like was put like [sic] a big desire or anything to do something like this. It's just something spur of the moment.

OPINION

. . . Glenn argues the trial court erred in denying his motion for directed verdict. Glenn contends his motion for directed verdict should have been granted because the State failed to prove that Glenn acted with malice. Glenn also argues that the State failed to establish that Glenn acted willfully and with a specific intent to kill. . . . We disagree.

Assault and battery with intent to kill (ABIK) is the unlawful act of a violent nature to the person of another with malice aforethought, either express or implied. *State v. Foust,* S.C., 479 S.E.2d 50 (1996). Assault and battery with intent to kill contains all the elements of murder except the actual death of the person assaulted. Before a person can be convicted of ABIK, the jury must be satisfied beyond a reasonable doubt that if the party assaulted had died from the injury, the defendant would have been guilty of murder. Accordingly, ABIK requires an intent to kill accompanied with malice. With respect to the intent to kill, it is sufficient for the State to show a general intent as opposed to a specific intent to kill.

In this case, we conclude that the evidence as outlined above was sufficient to allow the jury to conclude that Glenn acted with malice and with an intent to kill. Clearly, the jury could have reasonably inferred that Glenn acted with malice, particularly in light of the evidence establishing that Glenn waited on the overpass for a motorist to pass by and then intentionally dropped a heavy item onto the moving vehicle. See, e.g., *State v. Bell,* 305 S.C. 11, 406 S.E.2d 165 (1991) (Malice is the doing of a wrongful act intentionally and without just cause or excuse.), cert. denied, 502 U.S. 1038 (1992); *State v. Johnson,* 291 S.C. 127, 128, 352 S.E.2d 480, 481 (1987) ("Malice has been defined as the wrongful intent to injure another and indicates a wicked or depraved spirit intent on doing wrong.").

The evidence was likewise sufficient to support a finding that Glenn acted with an intent to kill. In *State v. Hayes,* 272 S.C. 256, 250 S.E.2d 342 (1979), the defendant was convicted of assault and battery with intent to kill as a result of injury to a passing motorist who was struck by a brick thrown by the defendant from an overpass onto the interstate. With respect to the element of intent to kill, the Supreme Court agreed with the trial court's conclusion that the act was of such gross recklessness as to be tantamount to intent. Thus, the Court held that the intent to kill could be inferred from the surrounding circumstances. The evidence presented in this case establishes a similar act of gross recklessness and, therefore, is sufficient to support a finding that Glenn intended to kill. See also *Foust,* S.C. at, 479 S.E.2d at 52, n. 4 (Evidence of the character of the means or instrument used, the manner in which it was used, the purpose to be accomplished, and resulting wounds or injuries are admissible to show the intent with which an assault was committed.). The trial court, therefore, did not err by denying Glenn's motion for directed verdict.

Accordingly, for the foregoing reasons, the judgment below is hereby AFFIRMED.

QUESTIONS FOR DISCUSSION

1. How does the court define the *mens rea* of assault and battery with the intent to kill?

2. List all of the facts relevant to determining whether David Glenn satisfied the *mens rea* of assault and battery with the intent to kill.

3. How would you define the *mens rea* of assault and battery with intent to kill?

4. Do you think that David Glenn committed assault and battery with the intent to kill? Defend your answer.

NOTE CASE

Cheryl thought her live-in boyfriend, Harrod, was at work and invited her other boyfriend, Calvin, over. Unknown to Cheryl, Harrod had left work, gone to a back room in the house, and fallen asleep. Harrod awoke and discovered Calvin. When Calvin refused to leave, Harrod threw a hammer at him, Calvin ducked, and the hammer hit the wall just over Harrod's baby son's crib. Of course Harrod assaulted Calvin, but did he assault his baby Christopher, whom he did not intend to hurt and who had no idea his father threw a hammer at him? The Maryland Court of Special Appeals, reversing Harrod's conviction for assault against Christopher, held that attempted battery assault required the specific intent to harm Christopher, which Harrod lacked. *Harrod v. State*, 65 Md.App. 128, 499 A.2d 959 (1985)

GRADING BATTERY

Battery requires some injury. Batteries that cause minor physical injury or emotional injury are misdemeanors in most states. Batteries that cause serious bodily injury are felonies. The *Model Penal Code* departs from existing law by requiring at least some bodily injury; offensive touching by itself is not a crime. Supporters of the code admit that insulting touching causes real psychological and emotional suffering but maintain that tort law and informal sanctions more appropriately deal with those harms.

Some code provisions are directed at injuries caused by special circumstances. Injuries caused by pit bulls prompted the Minnesota legislature to enact the following provision:

> Section 609.26. A person who causes great or substantial bodily harm to another by negligently or intentionally permitting any dog to run uncontrolled off the owner's premises, or negligently failing to keep it properly confined is guilty of a petty misdemeanor. . . .
>
> Subd. 3. If proven by a preponderance of the evidence, it shall be an affirmative defense to liability under this section that the victim provoked the dog to cause the victim's bodily harm.[27]

Injuries and deaths resulting from drug abuse have led the same legislature to enact the following provision:

> 609.228 Whoever proximately causes great bodily harm by, directly or indirectly, unlawfully selling, giving away, bartering, delivering, exchanging, distributing, or administering a controlled substance . . . may be sentenced to imprisonment for not more than ten years or to payment of a fine of not more than $20,000, or both.[28]

The *Model Penal Code* grades bodily harm offenses as follows:

> § 211.1
> 2. Bodily injury is a felony when
>   a. such injury is inflicted purposely or knowingly with a deadly weapon; or

b. serious bodily injury is inflicted purposely, or knowingly or recklessly under circumstances manifesting extreme indifference to the value of human life.

c. except as provided in paragraph (2), bodily injury is a misdemeanor, unless it was caused in a fight or scuffle entered into by mutual consent, in which case it is a petty misdemeanor.

THE ELEMENTS OF ASSAULT

Assault includes two types of offense: attempted batteries and threatened batteries. **Attempted battery assault** consists of the specific intent to commit a battery and substantial steps toward carrying out the attempt without actually completing it. **Threatened battery assault**, sometimes called intentional scaring, requires only that actors intend to frighten their victims, thus expanding assault beyond attempted battery. Threatened battery doesn't require the intent to actually physically injure their victims, the intent to frighten victims into believing the actor will hurt them is enough.

Victims' awareness is critical in threatened battery assault. Specifically, victims have to reasonably fear an *immediate* battery. Words alone aren't assaults; threatening gestures have to accompany them. This requirement isn't always just. For example, what if an assailant approaches from behind a victim, saying, "Don't move, or I'll shoot!" These words obviously are grounds to reasonably fear imminent injury, but they aren't assault because they are only words.

Conditional threats aren't enough because they're not immediate. The conditional threat, "I'd punch you out if you weren't a kid," is not immediate because it depends on the victim's age. In a few jurisdictions, a present ability to carry out the threat has to exist. But in most, even a person who approaches a victim with a gun she knows is unloaded, points the gun at the victim, and pulls the trigger (intending only to frighten her victim) has committed threatened battery.[29]

Both threatened and attempted battery assaults address two somewhat distinct harms. Attempted battery assault deals with an incomplete or inchoate physical injury (see Chapter 6). Threatened battery assault is directed at a present psychological or emotional harm: putting a victim in fear. So, in attempted battery assault, a victim's awareness doesn't matter; in threatened battery assault, it's indispensable.

The *Model Penal Code* deals with threatened and attempted battery assaults as follows:

§ 211.1 Simple Assault.

A person is guilty of assault if he:

a. attempts to cause bodily injury to another; or

b. attempts by physical menace to put another in fear of imminent serious bodily harm.

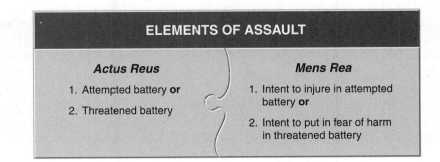

ELEMENTS OF ASSAULT	
Actus Reus	***Mens Rea***
1. Attempted battery **or**	1. Intent to injure in attempted battery **or**
2. Threatened battery	2. Intent to put in fear of harm in threatened battery

Simple assault is a misdemeanor unless committed in a fight or scuffle entered into by mutual consent, in which case the assault is a petty misdemeanor.

Historically, all assaults were misdemeanors. However, modern statutes have created several aggravated or felonious assaults. Most common are assaults with the intent to commit violent felonies (murder, rape, and robbery, for example), assaults with deadly weapons (such as guns and knives), and assaults on police officers. In *Commonwealth v. Sexton,* the court dealt with a bizarre form of "deadly weapon."

C A S E   Was the Pavement a Deadly Weapon?

Commonwealth v. Sexton
680 N.E.2d 23 (Mass. 1997)

Everett Sexton was convicted of assault and battery by means of a dangerous weapon and wilful and malicious destruction of property. On appeal, the Appeals Court reversed his conviction. The Massachusetts Supreme Judicial Court granted the Commonwealth's application for further appellate review and affirmed the conviction by the Superior Court.

FRIED, J.

FACTS

On the evening of August 28, 1992, Jeffrey Czyzewski and a female companion went to a bar in Holyoke. At the bar, Czyzewski played a game of pool with the wife of Donald Sexton. Czyzewski briefly left the pool table. On his return, he accused Sexton's wife of cheating by moving the pool balls during his absence. Ending the game, Czyzewski left the pool table and was thereafter approached three separate times by an agitated Donald Sexton, who demanded an apology. Czyzewski testified that after the second request, the defendant, Everett Sexton, the brother of Donald Sexton, approached Czyzewski and said that he would stand by his brother if anything happened. On the third occasion, Donald Sexton smashed a beer bottle on the bar, but was restrained before he could threaten Czyzewski further. Following this incident, the defendant, his brother, and his brother's wife left the bar.

Shortly thereafter, Czyzewski and his companion went out to the parking lot and got into their car. Immediately a van pulled up alongside them

and the defendant, his brother, and a third man got out. The defendant and his brother kicked in the window on the passenger side where Czyzewski was sitting. The defendant reached through the shattered window to grab Czyzewski, attempting to pull him through the window. At that moment, Czyzewski's companion was able to start the car and drove out of the parking lot. As they pulled out, the Sextons said, "Let's go get him," and returned to the van to follow Czyzewski. Because their car was about to run out of gas, Czyzewski and his companion were forced to return to the parking lot, with the van following behind. Czyzewski left the vehicle and Donald Sexton, the defendant, and their companion left their van. The defendant and his brother immediately approached Czyzewski; they began to push and shove him. The defendant restrained Czyzewski by lifting Czyzewski's jacket over his head and the brothers threw Czyzewski to the ground. On the ground, Donald Sexton banged Czyzewski's head against the pavement a number of times while the defendant repeatedly kicked him. The beating was interrupted by the bar owner and another man. The Sexton brothers left before the police arrived.

OPINION

. . . This case presents an issue of first impression, in that we have not previously addressed whether stationary objects can be considered dangerous weapons in Massachusetts. The statute, G.L. c. 265, § 15A, does not define the term "dangerous weapon," but we have stated previously that there are things which are dangerous per se and those which are dangerous as used. We have defined the former class as "instrumentalities designed and constructed to produce death or great bodily harm." In the latter class are things which become dangerous weapons because they are "used in a dangerous fashion." In such cases it is generally "a question for the fact finder whether the instrument was so used in a particular case." In evaluating different situations, the determination has invariably turned on "use," and our courts have repeatedly held that ordinarily innocuous items can be considered dangerous weapons when used in an improper and dangerous manner. See *Commonwealth v. Scott*, 408 Mass. 811, 822–823, 564 N.E.2d 370 (1990) (gag); *Commonwealth v. Barrett*, 386 Mass. 649, 655–656, 436 N.E.2d 1219 (1982) (aerosol spray can); *Commonwealth v. Appleby*, 402 N.E.2d 1051 (riding crop); *Commonwealth v. Tarrant*, 367 Mass. 411, 418, 326 N.E.2d 710 (1975) (German shepherd dog); *Commonwealth v. Farrell*, 78 N.E.2d 697 (lighted cigarettes); *Commonwealth v. Mercado*, 24 Mass.App.Ct. 391, 395, 509 N.E.2d 300 (1987) (baseball bat); *Commonwealth v. LeBlanc*, 3 Mass.App.Ct. 780, 780, 334 N.E.2d 647 (1975) (automobile door swung knocking police officer down).

Our courts have also noted, with approval, decisions in other jurisdictions which have found otherwise innocent items to fit this classification when used in a way which endangers another's safety. See *United States v. Loman*, 551 F.2d 164, 169 (7th Cir.), cert. denied, 433 U.S. 912, 97 S.Ct. 2982, 53 L.Ed.2d 1097 (1977) (walking stick); *United States v. Johnson*, 324 F.2d 264, 266 (4th Cir. 1963) (chair brought down upon victim's head); *People v. White*, 212 Cal.App.2d 464, 465, 28 Cal.Rptr. 67 (1963) (a rock); *Bennett v. State*, 237 Md. 212, 216, 205 A.2d 393 (1964) (microphone cord wrapped around victim's neck); *People v. Buford*, 69 Mich.App. 27, 30, 244 N.W.2d 351 (1976) (dictum) (automobile, broomstick, flashlight and lighter fluid may all be dangerous weapons as used).

We do not agree with the Appeals Court that, to be a dangerous weapon, the defendant must be able to wield the item at issue, nor do we think it relevant that the pavement was present as part of the environment in which the defendant chose to participate in this assault. Prior to the Appeals Court's decision in *Commonwealth v. Shea*, supra, the only explicit restriction on our use-based categorization of dangerous weapons held that human teeth and other parts of the human body were not

dangerous weapons because they are not "instrumentalities apart from the defendant's person." *Commonwealth v. Davis*, 406 N.E.2d 417. In *Shea*, a case in which the defendant pushed two women from his boat and sped off, leaving them five miles off shore, the Appeals Court found that, while "the ocean can be and often is dangerous, it cannot be regarded in its natural state as a weapon within the meaning of § 15A," because "in its natural state it cannot be possessed or controlled." *Commonwealth v. Shea*, 644 N.E.2d 244. We believe that this is too narrow a reading of the instrumentality and use language we have employed when we have defined dangerous weapons as "an instrument or instrumentality which, because of the manner in which it is used, or attempted to be used, endangers the life or inflicts great bodily harm." *Commonwealth v. Farrell*, 78 N.E.2d 697. While one might not be able to possess the ocean or exercise authority over it in a traditional sense, *Commonwealth v. Shea*, 644 N.E.2d 244, one could certainly use it to inflict great harm, such as by holding another's head underwater.

Likewise, it is obvious that one could employ concrete pavement, as the defendant and his brother did here, to cause serious bodily harm to another by banging the victim's head against the hard surface. As the Commonwealth points out, there would be no problem in convicting a defendant of assault and battery by means of a dangerous weapon if he used a broken slab of concrete to bludgeon his victim. We see no reason to hold that such a conviction cannot stand merely because the instrumentality in question is a fixed thing at the time of its dangerous use.

A number of other jurisdictions which have considered this question have also held that an object's stationary character does not prevent its use as a dangerous weapon. *United States v. Murphy*, 35 F.3d 143, 147 (4th Cir.1994), cert. denied, 513 U.S. 1135, 115 S.Ct. 954, 130 L.Ed.2d 897 (1995) (steel cell bars); *State v. Brinson*, 337 N.C. 764, 766, 448 S.E.2d 822 (1994) (cell bars and floor); *People v. O'Hagan*, 176 A.D.2d 179, 179, 574 N.Y.S.2d 198 (1991) (cell bars); *People v. Coe*, 165 A.D.2d 721, 722, 564 N.Y.S.2d 255 (1990) (plate glass window); *State v. Reed*, 101 Or.App. 277, 279–280, 790 P.2d 551 (1990) (sidewalk); *People v. Galvin*, 65 N.Y.2d 761, 762–763, 492 N.Y.S.2d 25, 481 N.E.2d 565 (1985) (same). As North

Carolina recognized, an item's dangerous propensities "often depend entirely on its use," and not its mobility, for "whether the pitcher hits the stone or the stone hits the pitcher, it will be bad for the pitcher." *State v. Reed,* 790 P.2d 551, quoting Cervantes, *Don Quixote,* Part II, ch. 43 (1615). We hold that one who intentionally uses concrete pavement as a means of inflicting serious harm can be found guilty of assault and battery by means of a dangerous weapon.

Finally, we agree with the Appeals Court that the jury was presented with sufficient evidence to find that the defendant possessed the requisite intent and knowledge to be guilty of assault and battery by means of a dangerous weapon under a joint venture theory. From the defendant's statements and actions it is apparent that he possessed the intent to engage in an assault and battery with his brother. While he may not initially have had knowledge that his brother intended to use the pavement to effectuate the attack, as the Appeals Court noted, "there is no need to prove an anticipatory compact between the parties to establish joint venture," if, "at the climactic moment the parties consciously acted together in carrying out the criminal endeavor." *Commonwealth v. Young,*

35 Mass.App.Ct. 427, 435, 621 N.E.2d 1180 (1993). The defendant continuously kicked and punched Czyzewski while his brother repeatedly slammed Czyzewski's head into the pavement. At no time during this conflict did the defendant seek to withdraw.

The conviction of assault and battery by means of a dangerous weapon is affirmed. So ordered.

QUESTIONS FOR DISCUSSION

1. Exactly what does the court mean by the distinction between things that are dangerous *per se* and things that are dangerous as used?

2. What is the problem with including stationary objects within the meaning of the term deadly weapon?

3. Do you agree with the court that the pavement is a dangerous weapon? Defend your answer.

4. How many of the many objects that the court lists from other cases cited in the opinion do you think are deadly weapons?

5. How would you define the term?

A COMPREHENSIVE MODEL ASSAULT AND BATTERY STATUTE

The *Model Penal Code* includes a comprehensive assault and battery statute, integrating, rationalizing, and grading assault and battery. It takes into account *actus reus, mens rea,* circumstance elements, and intended harm. Note the careful attention paid to these critical elements:

§ 211.2
A person is guilty of aggravated assault if he:
a. attempts to cause serious bodily injury to another, or causes such injury purposely, knowingly or recklessly under circumstances manifesting extreme indifference to the value of human life; or
b. attempts to cause or purposely or knowingly causes bodily injury to another with a deadly weapon.

Aggravated assault under paragraph (a) is a felony of the second degree; aggravated assault under paragraph (b) is a felony of the third degree.
§ 211.3
A person commits a misdemeanor if he recklessly engages in conduct which places or may place another person in danger of death or serious bodily injury. Recklessness and danger shall be presumed where a person knowingly points a firearm at or in the direction of another, whether or not the actor believed the firearm to be loaded.

FALSE IMPRISONMENT

False imprisonment is a harm to two fundamental rights:

1. Liberty: the right to come and go as we please, sometimes called the right of locomotion.
2. Privacy: the right to be left alone by the government.

Some states have enacted false imprisonment statutes to protect against invasions of these rights. For example, in California "the unlawful violation of the personal liberty of another" is a misdemeanor carrying a one-year jail term.[30]

False imprisonment is a specific intent crime. Prosecutors have to prove that defendants meant to take away their victims' liberty forcibly and unlawfully. The *Model Penal Code* provides that knowingly restraining someone is enough to prove *mens rea* in, false imprisonment. Motive doesn't matter. For example, if police officers make unlawful arrests, they can be prosecuted for false imprisonment even if they believed the arrests were lawful. Whether the unlawful arrest was due to recklessness, negligence, or just an honest mistake causes problems.

Most forcible detentions or confinements are false imprisonment under existing law. However, this doesn't include restraints authorized by law, like when police officers lawfully arrest suspects, parents restrict their children's activities, or victims detain their victimizers.

The *Model Penal Code* requires the restraint to "interfere substantially with the victim's liberty." Although physical force often accomplishes the detention, it isn't essential; threatened force is enough. So, the threat, "If you don't come with me, I'll break your arm," is enough. Even nonthreatening words can qualify, such as when a police officer who has no right to do so orders someone on the street into a squad car, asserting, "You're under arrest."

ELEMENTS OF FALSE IMPRISONMENT	
Actus Reus	***Mens Rea***
Restraining another person's liberty	Specific intent to restrain the liberty of another person

KIDNAPPING

Like false imprisonment, kidnapping invades someone's privacy and takes away their liberty. You can think of kidnapping as aggravated false imprisonment. Originally, kidnapping was the "forcible abduction or stealing away of man, woman or child from their own country." Although kidnapping was only a misdemeanor, Blackstone called it a "heinous crime" because "it robs the king of his subjects, banishes a man from his country, and may in its consequences be productive of the most cruel and disagreeable hardships."[31]

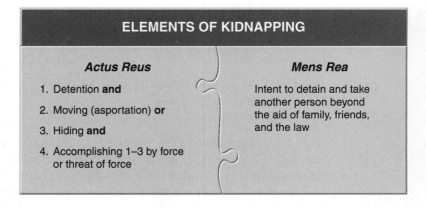

Until the twentieth century, kidnapping was a capital offense in some jurisdictions in the United States, mainly as a result of events during the first half of the century. During Prohibition (1919 to 1933), kidnapping was prevalent in the organized crime world. One gang member might abduct a rival, "take him for a ride," and kill him. Much more frequently, rivals were captured and held hostage for ransom. Before long, law-abiding citizens were being abducted, especially the spouses and children of wealthy and otherwise prominent citizens.

The most famous early case was the ransom kidnap and murder of Charles Lindbergh's son. Lindbergh was an aviator who captured Americans' hearts and imaginations when he flew solo across the Atlantic Ocean. Kidnapping was only a misdemeanor in New Jersey in 1932 when the crime occurred. The tremendous sympathy that Lindbergh's popular hero status generated and the public outrage toward what was perceived as a rampant increase in random kidnappings of America's "pillars of wealth and virtue" led legislatures to enact harsh new kidnapping statutes. These statutes are largely in force today, even though they were passed in an emotional overreaction to a few notorious cases.[32]

Another widely publicized case breathed new life into these harsh statutes. In 1974, Patricia Hearst, heiress to newspaper tycoon William Randolph Hearst, was kidnapped. The case met with public outrage, not only because of sympathy for the prominent Hearst family but also because of shock at the psychological and physical dimensions of the crime. The kidnappers were self-styled revolutionaries calling themselves the Symbionese Liberation Army. One of the SLA's first demands was that William Randolph Hearst distribute $1 million in food to the poor of California. Later on, much to her parents' and the public's horror, Patricia Hearst converted to the SLA, participating in bank robberies to raise money for the "revolution." This all happened during a time when radicalism and violence were much feared and when the Vietnam War protest and airline hijackings for terrorist political purposes were very much on the public's mind. Hence, the public saw not only Patty Hearst's capture and her family's deep trauma but also a threat to destroy American society.

The Hearst case brought kidnapping's heinous side into bold relief. It drew together in one story capture and detention, terror, violence, and political radicalism. The details were trumpeted sensationally every day in newspapers and on radio and television. Hope that existing harsh and sweeping kidnapping legislation would be reflectively reassessed vanished in this inflamed, emotional atmosphere. President Nixon expressed his hope—a hope that many others shared—that the Supreme Court would not declare capital punishment for kidnapping to be unconstitutional. Then–California Governor Reagan reflected the deep public outrage against kidnapping when he wished aloud that the kidnappers' demand for a free food program would set off a botulism epidemic among the poor.

Like false imprisonment, the offense from which it descended, kidnapping is a crime against personal liberty. At common law its main elements were

1. seizing,
2. confining, and
3. carrying away (asporting)
4. another person
5. by force, threat of force, fraud, or deception.

The critical difference between false imprisonment and kidnapping is the carrying away, or asportation, of victims. Since at least the eighteenth century, as Blackstone makes clear, carrying a victim into a foreign country where no friends or family could give aid and comfort, and the law could not protect the victim, added a particularly terrifying dimension to kidnapping. In the early days, the victim had to be carried at least as far as another county and usually across its border.

Modern interpretations leave the asportation requirement virtually meaningless. The famous case of *People v. Chessman* illustrates how broadly asportation is interpreted by courts faced with especially revolting cases. Caryl Chessman was a serial rapist who, in one instance, forced a young woman to leave her car and get into his, which was only twenty-two feet away. The court held that the mere fact of moving the victim, not the distance moved, is enough to satisfy the asportation requirement. They upheld Chessman's conviction for kidnapping, a capital crime in California. After many years of fighting the decision, Chessman eventually was executed.[33]

Modern statutes in some states have removed the asportation requirement, usually replacing it with the requirement that kidnappers intend to confine, significantly restrain, or hold their victims in secret. The Wisconsin statute, for example, defines a kidnapper as one who "seizes or confines another without his consent and with intent to cause him to be secretly confined." Whatever the changes, the heart of the crime remains to "isolate the victim from prospect of release or friendly intervention." The court dealt with the meaning of asportation in the carjacking case of *People v. Allen*.[34]

C A S E   Did He Move Her a "Substantial" Distance?

People v. Allen
64 Cal.Rptr.2d 497 (1997)

Tyrone Allen was convicted in the Superior Court, City and County of San Francisco, of, among other offenses, carjacking and kidnapping of a person under the age of 14. He appealed. The Court of Appeal affirmed the conviction for kidnapping.

RUVOLO, J.

FACTS

On August 7, 1995, May SunYoung and her family lived at 2951 Treat Street in San Francisco. That morning, Ms. SunYoung was on her way to take her 7-year-old daughter, Kirstie, to summer camp and stopped her automobile briefly in the driveway to close her garage door manually as she was backing out onto the street.

As Ms. SunYoung closed her garage door, a man approached her from behind and said, "Excuse me, can you do me a favor?" While turning around she saw the man later identified as appellant getting into her vehicle, whose engine was still running. He then locked the car doors. Kirstie was still in the vehicle with her seatbelt on and began crying. Because the driver's side window was rolled down about seven inches, Ms. SunYoung put her arms through the window and struggled with appellant in an attempt to reach the ignition key and turn off the engine.

Appellant then released the parking brake, put the vehicle in reverse, and backed out of the driveway with Kirstie inside and Ms. SunYoung running alongside the vehicle still attempting to reach the ignition key. The vehicle backed across Treat Street, which was a two-lane road with two parking lanes, until it hit the opposite curb and came to a stop. Appellant estimated the vehicle movement was 30–40 feet. While respondent now claims this estimate to be "speculation," both sides at different times suggested that the distance moved was approximately 5 car lengths, or 50 feet. Appellant exited the vehicle, threw the car keys onto the ground, shoved Ms. SunYoung against a fence, and ran down the street carrying her purse which had been left in the vehicle. Shortly thereafter, a neighbor on Treat Street several blocks away saw a man run by. In response to the neighbor's attempts to stop the man, the fleeing suspect stated, "Stay back, I got a gun." After a brief struggle, the man ran off but was later apprehended by San Francisco police officers and identified as appellant.

The jury instruction given regarding the simple kidnapping count was CALJIC No. 9.52, which sets forth the elements of kidnapping of a person under 14 years of age as follows: "Every person who unlawfully and with physical force or by any other means of instilling fear moves any other person under 14 years of age without her consent for a substantial distance, that is, a distance more than slight or trivial, is guilty of the crime of kidnapping. . . ." (Pen. Code, § 208, subd. (b); all further statutory references are to the Penal Code unless otherwise indicated.)

OPINION

The only element of the crime for which appellant asserts there was insufficient evidence and inadequate jury instructions is asportation. For "simple" kidnapping, that is, a kidnapping not elevated to a statutory form of "aggravated" kidnapping, the movement needed must be "substantial," or a distance that is more than "trivial, slight, or insignificant."

Appellant . . . argues that his conviction for simple kidnapping must be reversed because the minimum distance requirement for asportation is not met. He asserts the movement of Ms. SunYoung's vehicle 30–50 feet down her driveway and across Treat Street with Kirstie inside as a matter of law cannot be "substantial," or a distance that is more than "trivial, slight or insignificant."

Appellant is correct that under most cases decided pre-1981 which have examined only the actual distance involved, the movement here would not meet the legal test of substantiality. In *People v. Brown* (1974) 11 Cal.3d 784, 114 Cal.Rptr. 426, 523 P.2d 226 (Brown), after breaking into the victim's residence, the defendant forced the victim to accompany him through a search of her house for her husband. When the victim's husband was not found, the defendant moved the victim outside and along a passageway next to the house until a neighbor's intervention caused the defendant to abandon the victim and flee alone. The total distance the victim was moved was unascertained. The Supreme Court held the asportation of the victim was insufficient to satisfy the "substantial" requirement and was no more than trivial.

. . . Those cases which have considered the quality and character of the movement in addition to its absolute distance have weighed the purpose for the movement, whether it posed an increased risk of harm to the victim, and the "context of the environment in which the movement occurred." Purposes for movement found to be relevant have been those undertaken to facilitate the commission of a further crime, to aid in flight, or to prevent detection. We believe these factors are appropriate considerations. "Substantiality" implies something more than only measured distance. While "slight" is consistent with a quantitative analysis, the term "trivial" is a qualitative term suggestive of the conclusion that more is envisioned in determining whether a kidnapping occurs than simply how far the victim is moved. The legal requirement for asportation is satisfied by a finding of either. (CALJIC No. 9.52.)

In so holding, we conclude that while in absolute footage the distance moved here may have been empirically short, it was of a character sufficient to justify a finding of "substantiality" by the jury. The movement, in part, was plainly made to prevent Ms. SunYoung from regaining possession of her vehicle and to facilitate appellant's flight from the area with Kirstie. In addition to evasion of capture, the vehicle was moved from a position of relative safety onto a thoroughfare. The boundary crossed was significant because it placed Kirstie at greater risk of injury. We confirm these factors, coupled with the distance traveled, are sufficient to satisfy the "substantial movement" requirement for the crime of simple kidnapping. . . . [Affirmed.]

DISSENT

KLINE, J.

. . . The majority essentially concedes the movement in this case does not meet the legal test of substantiality if only actual distance is considered. In light of this, I need not belabor the manifest insufficiency of the evidence to satisfy the asportation requirement properly applicable to simple kidnapping.

It deserves emphasis, however, that movement as short a distance as that shown here—30 to 40 feet—has never been held to satisfy the asportation requirement of kidnapping. Indeed, considerably greater distances have often been held insufficient. As the majority opinion points out, movement of 90 feet, nearly three times the distance the victim in this case was moved, was held insufficient in *People v. Green* (1980) 27 Cal.3d 1, 164 Cal.Rptr. 1, 609 P.2d 468, where the Supreme Court noted that "the shortest distance this court has ever held to be 'substantial' for this purpose was a full city block."

People v. Brown (1974) 11 Cal.3d 784, 114 Cal.Rptr. 426, 523 P.2d 226 also dramatically demonstrates that the movement in the present case must be deemed trivial as a matter of law. The defendant in Brown had gone to the victim's residence in search of her husband, whose name he had discovered in the home of his estranged wife. He forced the victim to accompany him in a search of the house for her husband. When a neighbor who heard the victim scream telephoned and asked if she needed help, the defendant dragged her out of the house and along a narrow passageway between her house and the house next door. A neighbor then ordered the defendant to release the victim and told him the police were on their way. Defendant released her and fled. "All in all he had taken her approximately 40 to 75 feet from the back door of her house." A unanimous Supreme Court had little difficulty concluding that "the asportation of the victim within her house and for a brief distance outside the house must be regarded as trivial." "Under the particular facts of this case," the

court said, "the movement of the victim did not constitute a forcible taking 'into another part of the same county' and . . . the conviction of simple kidnapping must be reversed."

The movement in the present case is about half the distance which in *Brown* was held "trivial." Further, the victim in *Brown* was moved out of one area, the house, into another; and the movement of the victim was much more clearly intentional than that here, as it is not even clear appellant knew a child was in the vehicle when he moved it across the street.

I think it unreasonable to conclude that, when it enacted Penal Code section 207, the Legislature contemplated that backing up a car 30 to 40 feet across a street constitutes asportation "into another part of the same county" within the meaning of that statute. It must be remembered that the only definition of kidnapping that appears in the California Penal Code is that which appears in section 207. As the Supreme Court has noted on several occasions, the verb "kidnaps" used in section 209 (as well as in other statutes prescribing increased punishments for aggravated kidnappings, such as section 208 and 209.5) means kidnapping as defined in section 207. When the Legislature enacted section 209.5 in 1993 it not only adopted the section 207 definition of kidnapping, but explicitly incorporated into the new statute the "substantial distance" requirement imposed by the courts. (Pen.Code, § 209.5, subd. (b).) The Legislature must be deemed to have been aware of the distances considered by the courts too "slight" or "trivial" to satisfy this requirement. . . .

The fact that the Legislature punished aggravated kidnapping more severely than simple kidnapping has nothing to do with the distance the victim is moved but only to the greater harm to which the victim is exposed when a kidnapping is related to certain other serious offenses. If the Legislature felt aggravated kidnapping required movement over a greater distance than would suffice for simple kidnapping it would not have adopted the section 207 definition of kidnapping in an aggravated kidnapping statute, as it has, nor applied to aggravated kidnapping the same substantial distance requirement applicable to simple kidnapping, as it also has done. (Pen.Code, § 290.5, subd. (b).)

I agree that by moving the child in the vehicle across the street appellant committed a crime other than carjacking and the various other offenses of which he was properly convicted; that crime was not kidnapping, however, but false imprisonment (Pen.Code, § 236), which does not require any movement. . . . As the Supreme Court has repeatedly observed, "the Legislature did not intend to apply criminal sanctions [for any form of kidnapping] where the 'slightest movement' is involved."

Because the asportation in this case was trivial within the meaning of the applicable case law, I would reverse the judgment of conviction of simple kidnapping for lack of evidentiary support. I agree that in all other respects the judgment should be affirmed.

QUESTIONS FOR DISCUSSION

1. What test did the court establish in order to determine the distance required to satisfy the asportation element of the kidnapping *actus reus*?

2. What reasons does the majority give to support its definition of asportation?

3. How does the dissent's definition differ from that of the majority?

4. What reasons does the dissent give for its definition?

5. Do you agree with the majority or the dissent's definition of asportation? Defend your answer.

Kidnapping is usually divided into two degrees: simple and aggravated. The most common aggravating circumstances include kidnapping for the purpose of:

- Sexual invasions
- Obtaining a hostage
- Obtaining ransom
- Robbing the victim
- Murdering the victim
- Blackmail
- Terrorizing victims
- Obtaining political aims

The penalty for aggravated kidnapping is usually life imprisonment and, until recently, occasionally even death.

Can you kidnap your own children? This question is a problem of modern life with large numbers of separated families and the participation of both parents in child rearing. Noncustodial parents sometimes aren't willing to endure long periods without seeing their children. In fact, some can't even accept the noncustodial role. They take desperate measures to get their children, often illegally. The court dealt with such a kidnapping in *State v. McLaughlin*.

C A S E   Did He Abduct the Children?

State v. McLaughlin
125 Ariz. 505, 611 P.2d 92 (1980)

McLaughlin was convicted of child abduction. He appealed. The conviction was affirmed.

HAYS, J.

FACTS

On February 18, 1977, Dr. Stephen Zang, a physician and attorney admitted to practice in both Arizona and Nevada, obtained a default divorce from his spouse, Cheryl Zang, in Las Vegas, Nevada.

Pursuant to the terms of the dissolution, Dr. Zang was awarded custody of the two minor children of the marriage, subject to a right of visitation; however, the decree provided for subsequent review of the custody issue upon termination of the school semester. On February 20, 1977, Dr. Zang and the children moved to Arizona and shortly thereafter he had the Nevada decree entered on the Arizona dockets. Although the record at this point is unclear, the transcripts do establish the existence of a written order of the Maricopa County Superior Court granting custody of the children to Dr. Zang and suspending the visitation rights of his former spouse.

Apparently dissatisfied with the custody decrees, Ms. Zang allegedly decided to covertly remove the children from Arizona and her husband's possession. In furtherance of this scheme, she contacted appellant, the owner and operator of the local security guard service, requesting protection from interference by Dr. Zang. Although again the record is not clear, it is apparent that appellant was shown at least the Nevada decree of dissolution and possibly the order of the Arizona court.

On the morning of October 12, 1977, appellant, along with two employee security guards, met with Ms. Zang and a male companion at a Phoenix restaurant in order to finalize plans to remove the Zang children from their Tempe school. Appellant outlined the proposed course of action on a napkin which was subsequently introduced into evidence. In essence, the strategy involved the blocking of Dr. Zang's driveway with a purportedly inoperative automobile and the removal of the children from the schoolyard at the first appropriate moment. Ms. Zang wore a blond wig, sunglasses and a security guard shirt supplied her by appellant as a method of concealing her identity from school officials.

Pursuant to the scheme, appellant, a guard and Ms. Zang proceeded to the school, arriving at approximately 10:30 A.M. Appellant approached the school's principal, informed her that he was seeking a younger cousin and inquired regarding the lunch hour of the second grade. Nothing more occurred until noon recess, when Ms. Zang, accompanied by one of appellant's guards, removed one of her children from the lunch line and directed him towards a waiting auto. It was only the immediate pursuit of the child's teacher and a nearby resident which prevented the successful completion of the plan and forced the parties to await the arrival of police.

OPINION

On appeal, appellant alleges that he has violated no law. He contends that jurisdiction in the Nevada divorce proceedings was fraudulently obtained and that any decree issued pursuant thereto was void and without effect. Based upon this premise, appellant would have us hold that there could thus have been no attempt at removing the youngster from a "person having lawful charge of the child" within the meaning A.R.S. § 13–841 (1956) of our previous Criminal Code. In our opinion, however, although the record before us is void of evidence other than defendant's testimony regarding the validity or invalidity of the Nevada decree, we find this contention of little significance.

A.R.S. § 13–841 provides in part:

> A person who maliciously, forcibly or fraudulently takes or entices away a child under the age of seventeen years with intent to detain and conceal the child from its parent, guardian or other person having lawful charge of the child, shall be punished by imprisonment.

The . . . language establishes clearly the *mens rea* sufficient for conviction of child abduction. There must be an intent to detain and conceal the minor from a person in lawful control. In this regard, it must thus suffice if the accused knows that he is removing the child from the custody of one who appears to have lawful custody.

[Conviction affirmed.]

QUESTIONS FOR DISCUSSION

1. Do you think McLaughlin was guilty of child abduction?

2. Should Cheryl Zang be prosecuted, too?

3. How serious a crime do you think child abduction is under these circumstances?

4. Is it simple kidnapping, aggravated kidnapping, or a separate, less serious offense when parents kidnap their own children?

SUMMARY

Homicide and criminal sexual conduct are the most serious crimes against persons, threatening life, liberty, and privacy. Criminal sexual conduct includes the ancient common-law crimes of rape and sodomy as well as a range of other criminal sexual penetrations and contacts. Originally, rape was a crime against strangers, limited to the forcible penetration of the vagina of a woman by a man not her husband. Sodomy was directed at homosexual sexual conduct.

Today, there are two kinds of rape—aggravated rapes and unarmed acquaintance rapes. To accommodate the emphasis on nonviolent acquaintance rapes, many states have relaxed the force and nonconsent requirements and tightened the consent defense. Furthermore, to accommodate a growing intolerance to other kinds of sexual misconduct and to recognize the growing tolerance of more than one sexual orientation, criminal sexual conduct statutes have created a variety of gender-neutral offenses of sexual penetration and contact.

Although criminal homicide and criminal sexual conduct comprise the most serious crimes against persons, they are not the only crimes against persons. Measured in sheer numbers, assault and battery far outnumber homicides and criminal sexual conduct. Although often considered one crime, battery and assault are separate offenses. Batteries are offensive touching, ranging from severe beatings to insulting contacts. Assaults are attempted batteries or threatened batteries, in which no physical contact is required to complete the crime.

Another harm to persons covered by criminal law is deprivation of liberty. Short detentions without asportations are misdemeanors called false imprisonment. More serious detentions accompanied by asportation are kidnappings, ancient offenses generally associated with carrying off important persons for ransom. Aggravated kidnapping generally involves some circumstance that generates public outrage, such as kidnappings accompanied by rape, murder, and terror. Related to simple kidnapping is child abduction, a growing phenomenon as noncustodial parents are unwilling to accept separation from their children.

Restraints on liberty take three forms under existing criminal law. The misdemeanor of false imprisonment is a brief detention without asportation, the penalty for which is generally a fine or a short jail term. Simple kidnapping is a significant detention accompanied by asportation, however slight. The penalty for simple kidnapping is usually up to ten years' imprisonment. Aggravated kidnapping is reserved for cases touching off the most public outrage: kidnappings associated with murder, rape, ransom, blackmail, and terror. For aggravated kidnapping, the penalty is severe: usually life imprisonment and occasionally even death, at least until recently.

 Go to the Criminal Law 7e CD-ROM for Internet exercises.

REVIEW QUESTIONS

1. What values in a free society do crimes against persons threaten?

2. Identify, compare, and contrast the main crimes against persons.

3. Compare aggravated rape and unarmed acquaintance rape.

4. To what conditions was common-law rape limited?

5. According to Lord Hale, what was the justification for requiring proof of the conditions in question 4?

6. Upon what three conditions did the credibility of common-law rape charges depend?

7. What element of rape was most important until the 1970s?

8. Summarize the main changes in the law of rape that took place during the 1970s and 1980s.

9. Describe the *actus reus* of rape.

10. Describe the "storm of debate" over the *mens rea* of rape generated by *Regina v. Morgan*.

11. Summarize the majority opinion in *State v. Garnett* and the California rule regarding statutory rape.

12. Identify and briefly describe the main provisions of the Michigan criminal sexual conduct statute and explain how it differs from traditional rape law.

13. List the main circumstance elements that can raise simple rape to aggravated rape.

14. State the *actus reus,* the *mens rea,* and the harm in battery.

15. What is the essential difference between assault and battery?

16. Identify and describe the two kinds of assault.

17. What are the basic interests that false imprisonment and kidnapping threaten?

18. Identify the elements of false imprisonment and kidnapping.

19. Contrast false imprisonment and kidnapping.

KEY TERMS

aggravated rape—rape by strangers, or men with weapons, or where rapists physically injure their victims.

assault—an attempt to commit a battery, or intentionally putting another in fear.

attempted battery assault—the crime of assault that focuses on *actus reus*.

battery—offensive bodily contact.

extrinsic force standard—requires some force in addition to the amount needed to accomplish the penetration.

intrinsic force standard—requires only the amount of force necessary to accomplish the penetration.

rape shield statutes—statutes that prohibit introducing evidence of victims' past sexual conduct.

reasonable resistance standard—the requirement that women must use the amount of resistive force required by the totality of the circumstances surrounding sexual assault.

statutory rape—carnal knowledge with a person under the age of consent whether or not accomplished by force.

threatened battery assault—the crime of assault that focuses on the *mens rea*.

unarmed acquaintance rape—rape involving dates, lovers, neighbors, coworkers, employers, and so on.

utmost resistance standard—the requirement that rape victims must use all the physical strength they have in order to prevent penetration.

SUGGESTED READINGS

1. Rollin M. Perkins and Ronald N. Boyce, *Criminal Law,* 3d ed. (Mineola, N.Y.: Foundation Press, 1982), pp. 197–224 and 453–477. The authors discuss all matters in this chapter, including recent developments in the law.

2. American Law Institute, *Model Penal Code and Commentaries,* vol. 1 (Philadelphia: American Law Institute, 1980), pt. II, pp. 273–439. Summarizes the legal points and the debate surrounding revision of rape laws. It is worth reading for the arguments raised for and against various definitions of the sex offenses.

3. Battelle Law and Justice Study Center, *Forcible Rape: A National Survey* (Washington, D.C.: National Institute of Law Enforcement and Criminal Justice, March 1977). An excellent study of how rape is viewed by criminal justice professionals and how rape law is enforced. This work shows rape law in action as opposed to what the books say rape law should be. It develops some important points concerning prosecutors' attitudes toward rape victims.

4. Susan Estrich, *Real Rape* (Cambridge, Mass.: Harvard University Press, 1987). A stimulating history and critique of rape law in the United States with particular attention to rape by acquaintances. The author writes forcefully and convincingly, stimulating readers to think about the definition and enforcement of rape laws.

NOTES

1. For the feminist position regarding the special significance of the sexual component in rape, see Diana Russell, *The Politics of Rape: The Victim's Perspective* (New York: Stein and Day, 1975); Anra Medea and Kathleen Thompson, *Against Rape* (New York: Farrar, Straus and Giroux, 1974).

2. David P. Bryden, "Redefining Rape," *Buffalo Criminal Law Review,* 3 (2000):318.

3. Ibid.; Linda S. Williams, "The Classic Rape: When Do Victims Report?" *Social Problems* 31 (April 1984):464; Diana E. H. Russell, *Sexual Exploitation* (Beverly Hills, Calif.: Sage, 1984); Judy Foreman, "Most Rape Victims Know Assailant, Don't Report to Police, Police Report Says," *Boston Globe* (April 16, 1986), p. 27; *Parade Magazine* (September 22, 1985), p. 10; Lani Anne Remick, "Read Her Lips: An Argument for a Verbal Consent Standard in Rape," *University of Pennsylvania Law Review,* 141(1993):1103; Richie McMullen, Male Rape: Breaking the Silence on the Last Taboo (London: Gay Men Press, 1990).

4. Sir William Blackstone, *Commentaries* (University of Chicago Press, 1979), book IV, p. 210.

5. Quoted in Blackstone, *Commentaries,* p. 215.

6. Ibid., pp. 213–214.

7. *Reynolds v. State,* 27 Neb. 90, 42 N.W. 903, 904 (1889).

8. Remick, "Read Her Lips," p. 1111.

9. 127 Wis. 193, 106 N.W. 536, 538 (1906).

10. *Casico v. State,* 147 Neb. 1075, 25 N.W.2d 897, 900 (1947).

11. *State v. Ely,* 114 Wash. 185, 194 P. 988 (1921) (fraud as to nature of the act); *Moran v. People,* 25 Mich. 356 (1872) (told intercourse beneficial).

12. *Satterwhite v. Commonwealth,* 201 Va. 478, 111 S.E.2d 820 (1960).

13. *Commonwealth v. Mlinarich,* 345 Pa.Super. 269, 498 A.2d 395, 397 (1985)

14. American Law Institute, *Model Penal Code and Commentaries,* vol. 1 (Philadelphia: American Law Institute, 1980), pt. II, pp. 279–281.

15. For example, see Minnesota Statutes Annotated § 609.341, subd. 12 (St. Paul, Minn.: West Publishing Company, 1987).

16. Bryden, "Redefining Rape," 321.

17. *State v. Shamp,* 422 N.W.2d 520 (Minn.App.1988).

18. *Model Penal Code and Commentaries,* vol. 1, pt. II, 281; Joshua Mark Fried, "Forcing the Issue: An Analysis of the Various Standards of Forcible Compulsion in Rape," *Pepperdine Law Review* 23 (1996):120, 123–127.

19. Daphne Edwards, "Acquaintance Rape and the 'Force' Element: When 'No' is Not Enough," *Golden Gate Law Review,* 26 (1996):241, 260–261.

20. *Regina v. Morgan,* [1975] 2. W.L.R. 923 (H.L.).

21. *State v. Reed,* 479 A.2d 1291, 1296 (Me.1984).

22. Estrich, *Real Rape,* pp. 97–98.

23. Sarah Crichton, "Sexual Correctness: Has It Gone Too Far?" *Newsweek,* Oct. 25, 1993, 52, 54.

24. M.C.L.A. § 750(a) through (g).

25. *State v. Humphries,* 21 Wash.App. 405, 586 P.2d 130 (1978).

26. Louisiana Stat.Ann.—Rev. Stat. tit. 17—A, 14.39 (1974); American Law Institute, *Model Penal Code,* tentative draft no. 11.

27. Ibid.

28. Minn.Stat.Ann. § 609.26 (1987) (1989 Cumulative Supplement).

29. *Encyclopedia of Crime and Justice* (New York: Free Press, 1983), 1:89.

30. West's Ann. Cal. Penal Code § 236 (St. Paul, Minn.: West Publishing Company, 1988).

31. Blackstone, *Commentaries,* book IV, p. 219.

32. *State v. Hauptmann,* 115 N.J.L. 412, 180 A. 809 (1935)

33. 38 Cal.2d 166, 238 P.2d 1001 (1951).

34. *Model Penal Code and Commentaries,* vol. II, pp. 211–212.

Crimes Against Habitation: Burglary and Arson

Chapter Outline

I. Introduction

II. Burglary

III. Arson

IV. Summary

CHAPTER MAIN POINTS

1. Burglary and arson law protect both personal security and property.

2. The harm in burglary is the *invasion* of homes, other structures, and vehicles.

3. The harm in arson is the *damage* and *destruction* to homes, other structures, and personal property.

4. The structures subject to burglary and arson cover a broad spectrum.

5. Burglary is a specific intent crime.

6. Arson is a general intent crime.

Did He Burglarize the Apartment?

An apartment manager was visited by a man who said he was looking to rent a one-bedroom apartment. The manager showed the man the community room and the laundry facilities. She then took the man to a one-bedroom, upper-level apartment that had been vacant for approximately one month. She unlocked the door with her master keys and walked into the kitchen. As she turned around to face the man she saw he had a gun pointed at her. The man instructed her to do as she was told. He ordered her to walk down a hallway into the bedroom. There, he pushed her down on the floor, tied a scarf around her mouth and placed her in handcuffs. He removed her boots, slacks and pantyhose. He then tied her ankles together with the pantyhose and fondled her. The man took her keys and asked for money. When she was sure he had left the apartment, the manager escaped to another apartment and called the police.

INTRODUCTION

The ancient English proverb, "A man's home is his castle," is not just a popular belief. Two common-law felonies, burglary and arson, were created to protect people's houses. Common-law burglary protected dwellings from night-time intruders; arson protected them from "malicious and willful" burning. For many people, their homes are their most valuable if not their only material asset. But homes are more than property that is worth money. Perhaps the novelist Sinclair Lewis best expressed this non-monetary value when he wrote that "a house is not a home." He meant that a house is the material thing worth money; a home is the haven of refuge where security and privacy from the outside world are possible. Modern burglary and arson have grown far beyond their common-law origin of protecting homes. Now, all kinds of structures and even vehicles fall within their scope. But at their core remain the serious harms of invading, damaging, and destroying homes.

BURGLARY

The famous seventeenth-century English jurist Sir Edward Coke defined common-law burglary as follows:

> A felon, that in the night breaketh and entereth into the mansion house of another, with intent to kill some reasonable creature, or to commit some other felony within the same, whether his felonious intent be executed or not.[1]

According to this definition, common law burglary consists of the following elements:

1. breaking and entering
2. dwellings
3. at night
4. and inside the dwelling
5. the intent to commit a felony.

The sentiment that people's homes are their castles ran deep in English culture. The common law reflected this sentiment. Not even the king's majesty and power could thwart this protection. According to Lord Pitt's famous speech in the British House of Commons:

> The poorest man may in his cottage bid defiance to all the forces of the Crown. It may be frail—its roof may shake—the wind may blow through it—the storm may enter—but the King of England cannot enter—all his force dares not cross the threshold of the ruined tenement.

Reflecting that idea, debate over unreasonable searches and seizures in homes began long before the Fourth Amendment to the United States guaranteed protection against them. In 1575, for example, an irate burgess from Colchester (an English town from which many American settlers originated) successfully challenged the right of Queen Elizabeth's officers to enter his home to search for seditious libels against a local public figure. When the officers tried to enter the burgess's front door without a warrant, he met them armed with a sword. The burgess warned that officers who had earlier tried to come in without a warrant were heavily fined in the Queen's court for trespass. At this announcement, the officers disbanded, leaving the burgess alone for the time being.

The definition of burglary has varied greatly over the centuries. Medieval burglary was a broad offense that protected any place likely to attract people (churches, houses, even walled towns) against intrusions, no matter what their purpose. Sometime in the sixteenth century, the offense started to resemble Lord Coke's narrower definition. The more general trespass from medieval times became the nighttime invasion of a home to commit a felony. Burglary was a felony, punishable by death. Mere invasions into homes without the intent to commit further crimes inside were lumped with other trespasses. Trespass was a misdemeanor, punishable by fines.

ELEMENTS OF BURGLARY

Actus Reus	*Mens Rea*	Circumstances
1. Breaking **and** 2. Entering **or** 3. Unlawfully remaining	Specific intent to commit a crime in addition to breaking and entering or unlawfully remaining	1. Type of structure **and/or** 2. Nighttime **and/or** 3. Occupied structure **and/or** 4. Intended crime beyond the breaking and entering

From Lord Coke's time to modern times, burglary gradually returned to its medieval origins. Both legislation and judicial decisions have broadened its sixteenth-century meaning. So, modern burglary consists of the following elements:

1. Breaking and entering *and* also simply remaining in
2. Homes *and* also any structure with four walls and a roof *and* even most vehicles
3. During the night *and* during the day
4. With the intent to commit felonies *and* also most other crimes.

BURGLARY *ACTUS REUS*

The *actus reus* of burglary consists of two elements—breaking and entering. At one time, breaking meant a violent entry, but very early on it came to include much more than knocking down doors and smashing windows. By the eighteenth century, the common-law authority Sir William Blackstone wrote that breaking included "picking a lock, or opening it with a key; nay, by lifting up the latch of a door, or unloosing any other fastening which the owner has provided." Even if an outer door wasn't locked, it was breaking if a felon had to loosen the door to get in. However, walking through a wide open door wasn't breaking.

By 1900, the common-law element of breaking had become a mere technicality. Entering structures in an unusual manner, such as through a chimney, was called a **constructive breaking**. So was opening a door for an accomplice. Some retreat from constructive breaking has prevented the total collapse of the breaking requirement. The *Model Penal Code* provides that

> a person is guilty of burglary if he enters a building or occupied structure, or separately secured or occupied portion thereof, with purpose to commit a crime
> therein, unless the premises are at the time open to the public or the actor is licensed to enter. It is an affirmative defense to prosecution for burglary that the building or structure was abandoned.

A number of states have adopted the Code's recommended **unprivileged entry** definition of burglary *actus reus*: entering a structure without right, license, or permission.[2]

Entering, like breaking, has a broad meaning in burglary law. From about 1650, partial entry was enough. One court ruled that a burglar "entered" a house because his finger was inside the windowsill when he was caught. In another case, an intruder who assaulted an owner on the owner's threshold "entered" the house because his pistol crossed over the doorway. In Texas a man who never got inside a building at all, but who fired a gun into it intending to injure an occupant, "entered" by means of the bullet.[3]

Some statutes completely remove the entering element by providing that *remaining* in a structure lawfully entered is enough. So, it's burglary to go into a store during business hours and wait in a rest room until the store closes, with the intent to steal. Some states don't even require burglars to get inside; it's enough if they try. So, one man who got a door ajar but never set foot inside was convicted because the state's burglary statute didn't require entering or remaining. To some criminal law reformers, substituting remaining for breaking and entering badly distorts burglary's core idea—nighttime invasions into homes.[4]

The *Model Penal Code* and several jurisdictions take a middle ground between the old common law of actual entry and the total elimination of the entering seen in some modern statutes. They have adopted a **surreptitious remaining** element. Surreptitious remaining means that the perpetrator entered lawfully (like going into a bank during business hours) with the purpose to wait inside to commit a crime. This requirement distinguishes between invited guests and potential criminals who enter lawfully but remain in order to commit crimes. It also prevents injustices like prosecuting for burglary an invited guest who later gets into a fight with the owner and refuses to leave.

CIRCUMSTANCE ELEMENTS

"Structure"

A material circumstance in burglary is what structures qualify. Modern law goes far beyond the common-law restriction to dwellings. The structures included in burglary today stand somewhere between the sweeping medieval "any place where people are likely to congregate" and the narrow sixteenth-century "dwelling." Even in the sixteenth century, however, dwelling included more than finished standard houses; it meant any place where someone lived. In one case, a dwelling consisted of "a sheet stretched over poles and fastened to boards nailed to posts for sides, being closed at one end and having an old door at the other." Unfinished houses were also included.[5]

Most modern burglary statutes cover an almost limitless array of structures. Definitions such as "any structure" or "any building" are common. One writer who surveyed the subject concluded that any structure with "four walls and a roof" was included. Many statutes also include vehicles. These sweeping definitions have led to bizarre results. For example, in California, if you break into a car and steal a camera from the glove compartment you've committed burglary, punishable by up to fifteen years in prison. However, if you steal the entire car, including its contents, you've committed grand larceny, punishable by up to ten years.[6]

The *Model Penal Code* definition limits burglary to *occupied* structures. According to the authors, this limit covers "intrusions that are typically the most alarming and dangerous." According to *Model Penal Code* Section 221.0, "occupied structure" means "any structure, vehicle, or place adapted for overnight accommodations of persons, or for carrying on business therein, whether or not a person is actually present." A few states follow the *Model Penal Code* approach and limit burglary to occupied structures, whether or not people are present when the burglary occurs. The Ohio Court of Appeals dealt with the problem of defining "occupied structure" in the unpublished opinion of *State v. Burns*.[7]

C A S E   Did He Burglarize an "Occupied" Apartment?

State v. Burns
1997 WL 152074 (Ohio App. 6 Dist. 1997)

Robert Burns was found guilty of aggravated burglary and other felonies. He appealed and the Ohio Court of Appeals affirmed.

FACTS

On January 8, 1996, an apartment manager of a one hundred thirty-eight unit complex in Maumee, Ohio was visited by a man who said he was looking to rent a one-bedroom apartment. The manager showed the man the community room and the laundry facilities. She then took the man to a one-bedroom, upper level apartment that had been vacant for approximately one month. She unlocked the door with her master keys and walked into the kitchen. As she turned around to face the man she saw he had a gun pointed at her. The man instructed her to do as she was told. He ordered her to walk down a hallway into the bedroom. There, he pushed her down on the floor, tied a scarf around her mouth and placed her in handcuffs. He removed her boots, slacks and pantyhose. He then tied her ankles together with the pantyhose and fondled her. The man took her keys and asked for money. When she was sure he had left the apartment, the manager escaped to another apartment and called the police. The manager identified appellant as the man who had attacked her.

A jury found appellant guilty of aggravated burglary, aggravated robbery, kidnaping and gross sexual imposition. The jury further found that the state had proven the specification that appellant used a firearm in the commission of these offenses. The court sentenced appellant to twelve to twenty-five concurrent years for aggravated burglary, aggravated robbery and kidnapping. He received a consecutive three to five year term of imprisonment for the offense of gross sexual imposition and a three year term of imprisonment for the firearm specification. The firearm specification sentence was ordered to be served consecutively to all the other sentences. In total, appellant was sentenced to not less than eighteen years nor more than thirty-three years.

OPINION

On appeal, appellant asserts . . . [that] the convictions are against the manifest weight of the evidence. The standard of review for manifest weight arguments is as follows:

> An appellate court's function when reviewing the sufficiency of the evidence to support a criminal conviction is to examine the evidence admitted at trial to determine whether such evidence, if believed, would convince the average mind of the defendant's guilt beyond a reasonable doubt. The relevant inquiry is whether, after viewing the evidence in a light most favorable to the prosecution, any rational trier of fact could have found the essential elements of the crime proven beyond a reasonable doubt.

Appellant presents one argument for this court to consider. Appellant contends the state failed to prove the elements of aggravated burglary in that a vacant apartment is not an "occupied structure" pursuant to R.C. 2911.11. The elements of aggravated burglary, a violation of R.C. 2911.11 are as follows:

> (A) No person, by force, stealth, or deception, shall trespass in an occupied structure, as defined in section 2909.01 of the Revised Code, or in a separately secured or separately occupied portion thereof, with purpose to commit therein any theft offense, as defined in section 2913.01 of the Revised Code, or any felony, when any of the following apply:
> (1) The offender inflicts, or attempts or threatens to inflict physical harm on another;
> (2) The offender has a deadly weapon or dangerous ordnance, as defined in section 2923.11 of the Revised Code, on or about his person or under his control;
> (3) The occupied structure involved is the permanent or temporary habitation of any person, in which at the time any person is present or likely to be present.

R.C. 2909.01(C) defines occupied structure as:

> any house, building, outbuilding, watercraft, aircraft, railroad car, truck, trailer, tent, or other structure, vehicle, or shelter, or any portion thereof, to which any of the following applies:
> (1) It is maintained as a permanent or temporary dwelling, even though it is temporarily unoccupied and whether or not any person is actually present.

The court's jury instruction regarding "occupied structure" mirrored the above definition.

The Tenth District Court of Appeals addressed a similar issue in *State v. Green* (1984), 18 Ohio App.3d 69. The court stated:

> It is obvious that the General Assembly, in adopting the definition of 'occupied structure' found in R.C. 2909.01, intended to broaden the concept of the offense of burglary from one of an offense against the security of habitation, to one concerned with the serious risk of harm created by the actual or likely presence of a person in a structure of any nature. In that context, it is noteworthy that the General Assembly utilized the word 'maintained' in division (A), as opposed to 'occupied,' although it did use that latter word in division (B), which deals with structures other than dwellings. We believe that the distinction between 'maintained' and 'occupied' is significant, in the sense that the former alludes more to the character or type of use for which the dwelling is intended to be subjected, whereas the latter is more closely related to the actual use to which the structure is presently being subjected.
>
> Thus, a structure which is dedicated and intended for residential use, and which is not presently occupied as a person's habitation, but, which has neither been permanently abandoned

nor vacant for a prolonged period of time, can be regarded as a structure 'maintained' as a dwelling within the meaning of division (A). In this context, then, division (A) includes a dwelling whose usual occupant is absent on prolonged vacation, a dwelling whose usual occupant is receiving longterm care in a nursing home, a summer cottage, or a residential rental unit which is temporarily vacant. In all these examples, even though the dwelling is not being presently occupied as a place of habitation, that situation is temporary, and persons are likely to be present from time to time to look after the property to help 'maintain' its character as a dwelling.

Applying this analysis to the instant case, we conclude that there was sufficient evidence to support a finding that the apartment at issue was an 'occupied structure' as that term is used in R.C. 2911.11. Accordingly, appellant's sole assignment of error is found not well-taken.

On consideration whereof, the court finds that appellant was not prejudiced or prevented from having a fair trial, and the judgment of the Lucas County Court of Common Pleas is affirmed. It is ordered that appellant pay the court costs of this appeal.

QUESTIONS FOR DISCUSSION

1. List all of the facts relevant to deciding whether Robert Burns broke and entered an "occupied structure."
2. How did the Ohio Court of Appeals define "occupied structure"?
3. What policy interests does this definition promote?
4. Do you agree that Robert Burns committed burglary of an occupied structure? Explain your answer.

"Of Another"

Another circumstance element in burglary stems from the common-law requirement that burglars have to break and enter the dwelling of another. Modern law has expanded the common-law definition. For example, landlords can burglarize their tenants' apartments. And, in *Jewell v. State,* the court dealt with the problem of whether you can burglarize your own home.

| **C A S E** | Did He Burglarize His Own Home? |

Jewell v. State
672 N.E.2d 417 (Ind.App. 1996)

Barry L. Jewell, after a jury trial, was convicted of burglary with a deadly weapon resulting in serious bodily injury, a class A felony, and battery resulting in serious bodily injury, a class C felony. Jewell was sentenced to an aggregate term of 48 years imprisonment. After a re-trial Jewell appealed. The Indiana Court of Appeals affirmed.

ROBERTSON, J.

FACTS

In 1989, Bridget Fisher, who later married Jewell and changed her name to Bridget Jewell, purchased a home on contract in her maiden name from her relatives. Bridget and Jewell lived in the house together on and off before and after they married in 1990. Jewell helped fix the house up, and therefore, had some "sweat equity" in the house.

Jewell and Bridget experienced marital difficulties and dissolution proceedings were initiated. Jewell moved out of the house and Bridget changed the locks so that Jewell could not reenter. At a preliminary hearing in the dissolution proceedings, Bridget's attorney informed Jewell that Bridget wanted a divorce and wanted Jewell to stop coming by the house. Jewell moved into a friend's house, agreeing to pay him $100.00 per month in rent and to split the utility expenses.

Bridget resumed a romantic relationship with her former boyfriend, Chris Jones. Jewell told a friend that he wanted to get Jones in a dark place, hit him over the head with a 2x4 (a board), and cut his "dick" off. Jewell confronted Jones at his place of employment and threatened to kill him if he were to continue to see Bridget. Jewell was observed on numerous occasions watching Bridget's house. Jewell used a shortwave radio to intercept and listen to the phone conversations on Bridget's cordless phone.

At approximately 4:00 A.M. on the morning of June 13, 1991, Jewell gained entry to Bridget's house through the kitchen window after having removed a window screen. Bridget and Jones were inside sleeping. Jewell struck Jones over the head with a 2x4 until he was unconscious, amputated Jones' penis with a knife, and fed the severed penis to the dog. Bridget awoke and witnessed the attack, but she thought she was having a bad dream and went back to sleep. Bridget described the intruder as the same size and build as Jewell and as wearing a dark ski mask similar to one she had given Jewell. She observed the assailant hit Jones on the head with a board, and stab him in the lower part of his body.

A bloody 2x4 was found at the scene. The sheets on the bed where Bridget and Jones had been sleeping were covered in blood. Bridget discovered that one of her kitchen knives was missing. However, the police did not preserve the sheets or take blood samples and permitted Bridget to dispose of the sheets. A police officer involved explained that the possibility that any of the blood at the crime scene could have come from anyone other than Jones had not been considered.

Jones' severed penis was never found and he underwent reconstructive surgery. His physicians fashioned him a new penis made from tissue and bone taken from his leg. Jones experienced complications and the result was not entirely satisfactory.

OPINION

. . . Jewell attacks the sufficiency of evidence supporting his conviction of Burglary, which is defined as:

> A person who breaks and enters the building or structure of another person, with intent to commit a felony in it, commits burglary. Ind. Code 354321

Jewell argues he was improperly convicted of breaking into his own house.

When reviewing the sufficiency of the evidence, we neither reweigh the evidence nor judge the credibility of witnesses. Rather, we examine only the evidence most favorable to the judgment, along with all reasonable inferences to be drawn therefrom, and if there is substantial evidence of probative value to support the conviction, it will not be set aside. It is for the fact-finder to resolve conflicts in the evidence and determine which witnesses to believe.

The Burglary statute's requirement that the dwelling be that "of another person" is satisfied if the evidence demonstrates that the entry was unauthorized. *Ellyson v. State,* 603 N.E.2d 1369, 1373 (Ind. Ct.App.1992). In *Ellyson,* we held a husband was properly convicted of burglary for breaking into the house in which he and his estranged wife had lived previously with the intent of raping his wife. We noted that dissolution proceedings had been initiated and that wife alone controlled access to the home. We upheld the husband's burglary conviction even though he may have had a right to possession of the house co-equal with his wife at the time of the breaking and entering.

In the present case, Bridget had purchased the house in her own name before the marriage. When she and Jewell experienced marital difficulties, Jewell moved out and Bridget changed the locks to prevent Jewell from reentering the house. Bridget alone controlled access to the house. Jewell entered the house at 4:00 A.M. through the kitchen window after having removed the screen. The evidence supports the conclusion that the entry was unauthorized; and, therefore, we find no error. . . .

Judgment affirmed.

QUESTIONS FOR DISCUSSION

1. List all of the facts relevant to determining whether Barry Jewell burglarized his own home.

2. How does the state of Indiana define the "of another" element?

3. How did the court arrive at the conclusion that Barry Jewell burglarized his own home?

4. What is the reason for the "unauthorized entry" requirement?

5. Do you agree with it? Defend your answer.

"Nighttime"

At common law, burglaries had to take place at night. The requirement of the circumstance of nighttime was based on three considerations. First, it's easier to commit crimes at night. Second, it's harder to identify suspects you've seen at night. Third, and probably most important, nighttime intrusions frighten victims more than daytime intrusions. At least eighteen states retain the nighttime requirement. Some do so by making nighttime an element of the crime. Others treat nighttime invasions as an aggravating circumstance. However, some have eliminated the nighttime requirement entirely.

BURGLARY *MENS REA*

Burglary is a specific intent crime. The prosecution has to prove two *mens rea* elements:

1. The intent to commit the *actus reus* of breaking and entering or remaining;
2. The intent to commit a crime once inside the structure broken into, entered, or remained in.

In other words, burglars not only have to intend to invade someone else's structure, they also have to intend to commit additional crimes once they get inside.

As in the other burglary elements, the list of crimes burglars have to intend to commit has grown enormously since the sixteenth century. In Lord Coke's time, the intended crime had to be serious. Although some law books emphasized violent felonies like murder and rape, the cases routinely involve breaking and entering with the intent to steal. Modern statutes also routinely focus on invasions with the intent to steal. Some statutes limit the *mens rea* to invasions with the intent to commit "a felony or any larceny." Under such a statute, if you enter a store with the intent to steal only a #2 pencil worth 50 cents in order to take your machine-graded criminal law exam, you've committed burglary. Some jurisdictions extend the burglary *mens rea* still further, making it burglary to invade with the intent to commit "any crime," "any public offense," and sometimes "any misdemeanor."[8]

Notice that it's not necessary to complete or even attempt to commit the intended crime. So, if I break into my enemy's house with the intent to murder him, change my mind just inside the front door, and return home without hurting anyone, I've committed burglary. Since the *mens rea* of intent to kill was present when I entered, the burglary was complete at the moment I entered the house. While completing the intended crime is not an element of the crime, it might well be evidence of *mens rea*. For example, if I'm caught leaving a house with my arms loaded with valuable silver, jurors can infer that I entered the house in order to steal the silver.

GRADING BURGLARY

Because burglary is defined so broadly, many states divide it into several degrees. In Minnesota, for example, first-degree burglary includes burglary of dwellings, if someone is in the house, if the burglar possesses a weapon, or if the burglar assaults a person within the building. Burglary of a dwelling, a bank, or a pharmacy dealing in controlled substances constitutes second-degree burglary. Third-degree burglary includes burglary of any building with an intent to steal or commit any felony or gross misdemeanor. Fourth-degree burglary includes burglary of a building with an intent to commit a misdemeanor other than theft.[9]

Despite efforts to grade burglary according to seriousness, the broad scope of the offense invites injustices in most statutes. This is true in large part because burglary punishes the invasion and not the predicate crime, namely the crime the burglar entered to commit. In many cases, the penalty for burglary is a lot harsher than the penalty for the intended crime. The difference between a five-year sentence and a twenty-year sentence sometimes depends upon the largely philosophical question of whether a thief intended to steal before or after entering a building.

 11-1 Burglary Statutes

ARSON

Burglary is directed at *invasions* of homes and other structures. Arson, on the other hand, aims at *damage* or *destruction* to homes and other buildings.

HISTORY AND RATIONALE OF ARSON

> If any person shall wittingly, and willingly set on fire any dwelling house, meeting house, store house or any out house, barn, stable, stack of hay, corn or wood, or any thing of like nature, whereby any dwelling house, meeting house or store house, cometh to be burnt shall be put to death, and to forfeit so much of his lands, goods, or chattels, as shall make full satisfaction, to the victim.[10]

This 1652 Massachusetts Bay Colony statute making arson a capital offense shows clearly that the colonists considered arson a serious crime.

Arson is still a serious crime because it poses a threat to life and property. Arson kills hundreds and injures thousands of people annually. It damages and destroys more than a billion dollars in property and in lost taxes and jobs. It has also significantly increased insurance rates throughout the United States. Most states prescribe harsh penalties for arson. In North Dakota and Hawaii, the maximum penalty is ten years. In other states, such as Texas and Alabama, arson is punishable by life imprisonment.

ELEMENTS OF ARSON				
Actus Reus	**Mens Rea**	**Circumstances**	**Causation**	**Harm**
Setting fire to a structure	Intent to burn	1. Kind of structure 2. Amount of damage to structure	Setting fire causes damage to or destruction of structure	Damage and/or destruction caused by burning

BURNING: THE ARSON *ACTUS REUS*

At common law, burning had its obvious meaning, namely setting a building on fire. Just setting the fire wasn't enough; the fire had to reach the structure and burn it. Burning didn't mean burning to the ground. Once the building caught on fire, arson was complete, however slight the actual burning was. Modern statutes adopt the common-law rule, and the cases pour great effort into deciding whether the smoke from the fire only blackened or discolored buildings, whether the fire scorched them, or whether the fire burned only the outside wall or the wood under it.

The *Model Penal Code* tries to clear up many of the technical questions in common law arson by providing that burning means "starting a fire," even if the fire never touches the structure it was aimed at. The drafters justify this expansion of common-law burning on the ground that there is no meaningful difference between a fire that has already started but hasn't reached the structure and a fire that has reached the structure but hasn't done any real damage to it. Burning also includes explosions, even though the phrase "set on fire" doesn't usually mean "to explode." The Indiana Court of Appeals dealt with some of the problems in defining "burning" in *Williams v. State*.[11]

| **C A S E** | **Did She Burn the House?** |

Williams v. State
600 N.E.2d 962 (Ind. App. 1992)

Tonyia Dee Williams, the defendant, was convicted of arson, a Class B felony, following a jury trial in the St. Joseph Superior Court. She appealed. The Court of Appeals affirmed.
GARRARD, J.

FACTS

On December 31, 1990, Carol Hines hosted a New Year's Eve gathering at the home of her sister, Annette Hines. Annette was in Chicago at the time and Carol was left in charge of the house and Annette's three children. During the course of the evening the guests were playing cards and drinking. Shortly before midnight, Tonyia Dee Williams arrived at the house and asked about some money that Annette had been holding for her and requested use of the telephone. Williams went upstairs to use the telephone, but found that Annette's teenage son, Lamont, was already on the phone with his girlfriend. After arguing over use of the phone, Williams was allowed to use it.

At the stroke of midnight, the partygoers began to celebrate by shaking up beer containers and pouring beer onto one another. Lamont joined in the revelry by pouring a beer onto the head of Williams. Williams, taking heated exception to being doused with beer, pulled the phone cord out of the wall and chased Lamont down the stairs and into the basement. Lamont locked himself in one of the rooms in the basement while Williams proceeded to pound on the door with the telephone. Carol, after observing Williams and Lamont run past her and into the basement, went downstairs and asked Williams to leave. Williams, however, refused to leave. Carol and Lamont then went upstairs, leaving Williams alone in the basement. Shortly after this, Chaka Jennings, Carol's daughter, overheard Williams say through a furnace vent: "I hope all you mother fuckers burn up."

Soon after these events Carol went back to check on Williams and when she opened the basement door, a ball of smoke met her at the door. The house was then evacuated and one of the guests, William Sanders, put out the fire by throwing dirty laundry onto the flames to smother it. The only physical damage caused by the fire, besides the burned clothes, was smoke throughout the house and soot and smoke damage to one of the walls in the basement.

Williams had meanwhile left the house through a side door and was five houses down the street before Carol could catch up with her. When

Carol caught up with her the two argued again and Carol accused Williams of starting the fire. Carol Hines and the children were unable to stay in the house that night because of all the smoke.

On April 25, 1991, a jury found Tonyia Dee Williams guilty of Arson, a class B felony. Williams appeals her conviction and we affirm.

OPINION

Williams presents three issues for appeal which we restate as follows:

I. Whether soot and smoke damage constitute "damages" within the meaning of IC 35-43-1-1(a).

II. Whether the trial court erred in prohibiting defense counsel from inquiring into a previous unrelated fire at the house.

III. Whether the trial court erred in denying the defendant's motion for a mistrial.

Williams contends that the soot and smoke damage to the wall of the basement do not constitute "damages" within the meaning of IC 35-43-1-1(a). We disagree. IC 35-43-1-1(a) reads: "A person who, by means of fire or explosive, knowingly or intentionally damages: (1) a dwelling of another person without his consent. . . ." Ind.Code Ann. § 35-43-1-1(a) (West 1986). The word "damages" is not further defined by the statute.

It is Williams' contention that this offense requires proof of burning or charring as was the case at common law. Traditionally the common law rigidly required an actual burning. The fire must have been actually communicated to the object to such an extent as to have taken effect upon it. In general, any charring of the wood of a building, so that the fiber of the wood was destroyed, was enough to constitute a sufficient burning to complete the crime of arson. However, merely singeing, smoking, scorching, or discoloring by heat were not considered enough to support a conviction.

The State contends that the word "damages" in our present statute is not tied to the common law definition of the word "burning" and should therefore be construed in its plain and ordinary sense. Any damage, even smoke damage, would therefore be enough to satisfy the requirements of the statute. We agree with the State.

First, in construing statutes, words and phrases must be given their plain, ordinary, and usual meaning, unless a contrary purpose is clearly shown by the statute itself. In this case, there is no indication from the statute that any special meaning is to be given to the word "damages." *Webster's Third New International Dictionary* (1976), defines damage to mean: "loss due to injury: injury or harm to person, property, or reputation: hurt, harm." In this case, there is clearly some harm done to the basement wall by the smoke damage and soot.

Secondly, other states with similar statutes have held that smoke damage is enough to meet a requirement of "damage" in their statutes. For example, Georgia's first degree arson statute reads: "A person commits the offense of arson in the first degree when, by means of fire or explosive, he knowingly damages . . . (1) Any dwelling house of another without his consent . . ." Ga.Code Ann. § 16-7-60(a) (1992). The Court of Appeals of Georgia, interpreting this statute, stated:

> It was shown at the trial that the only damage to the building was heavy smoke damage which required special machinery to remove it from the building. The jail itself was not charred or burned. . . . The verb "damages" is an ordinary word and when it is used in a statute it must be given its ordinary signification. [cite omitted] Webster defines 'damage' as 'To hurt; impair.' Thus, causing smoke damage to the jail building falls within this definition and constitutes arson in the first degree if the other elements of the crime are present. *Smith v. State* (1976), 140 Ga.App. 200, 230 S.E.2d 350, 350.

New York is similar. New York's fourth-degree arson statute reads: "1. A person is guilty of arson in the fourth degree when he recklessly damages a building or motor vehicle by intentionally starting a fire or causing an explosion." N.Y. Penal Law § 150.05 (McKinney 1992). The appellate division, in *People v. Fleming* (1990), 164 A.D.2d 942, 560 N.Y.S.2d 50, 51, interpreted this statute:

> The fire caused smoke damage to the ceiling and walls and heat damage to a light fixture in the ceiling. . . . The defendant contends on appeal that there was no 'damage' to the building so as to support the arson conviction [under] Penal Law § 150.05(1). . . . It is not necessary that a building 'burn' in order for there to be arson in the fourth degree. The slightest damage to a building caused by fire which is intentionally set is sufficient to es-

tablish the damage element of this crime [cite omitted] and the smoke and heat damage did so here.

We find the authorities cited above persuasive and therefore find that the smoke damage and the soot on the basement wall were enough to support a conviction for arson under IC 35-43-1-1(a).

Williams contends that the trial court erred in prohibiting defense counsel from inquiring into a previous unrelated fire at the house. We disagree. During cross-examination of the State's witness, Annette Hines, the following occurred:

"Q: Now, she [Williams] wasn't in your house earlier in 1990 when you had a house fire then, was she?

A: No, she wasn't.

Q: How was that fire started?

THE STATE: Objection, Your Honor, it's irrelevant.

THE COURT: Whoa, both attorneys come up here.
(SIDE BAR CONFERENCE)"

Evidence is relevant when it throws or tends to throw light on the guilt or innocence of an accused even though its tendency to do so may be slight. It is well settled, however, that rulings on the relevancy of evidence are entrusted to the broad discretion of the trial judge. A defendant may, of course, establish his innocence by showing that some other person or persons committed the crime charged, instead of himself. But the mere possibility that some third person did the act is not enough. Evidence tending to incriminate another must be competent and confined to substantive facts which create more that a mere suspicion that such other person committed the particular offense in question.

In the case at bar, the testimony that the defendant desired to introduce would have tended to show that the children of Annette Hines had set a previous fire in the house. Specifically, the defendant's offer of proof showed that the defense had a witness that had heard a statement from Annette Hines that her children had set a fire that occurred in the house six months prior to the New Year's Eve fire. This evidence would have been, at most, hearsay evidence designed to cast a mere suspicion over Williams' involvement in the fire. The trial court did not err in excluding this testimony.

Finally, Williams contends that the trial court erred in denying the defendant's motion for a mis-

trial. We disagree. The trial court in this case admonished defense counsel in front of the jury. The full exchange reads as follows:

"Q: Now, she [Williams] wasn't in your house earlier in 1990 when you had a house fire then, was she?

A: No, she wasn't.

Q: How was that fire started?

THE STATE: Objection, Your Honor, it's irrelevant.

THE COURT: Whoa, both attorneys come up here.

(SIDE BAR CONFERENCE)

THE COURT: Exactly what do you think you're doing? Now, if the State did that, that would be a mistrial.

MR. DRENDALL: This isn't about the Defendant. This is not prejudicial to anyone.

THE COURT: You're out of order. You go sit down and don't get into that again.

(END OF SIDE BAR CONFERENCE)

THE COURT: Ladies and gentlemen of the jury, disregard that. That is totally inappropriate. It has nothing to do with this case, and it was wrong to bring it into this case.

MR. DRENDALL: We object to the Court's admonition.

THE COURT: Well, Mr. Drendall, you are a practicing attorney, and you know the rules, and if you wanted to bring that up in front of this jury, you knew perfectly well you were to do that outside the presence of this jury—

MR. DRENDALL: I have nothing else.

THE COURT: —and get a ruling, and that was wrong to do. And jury disregard it and ignore it. Anybody have a problem with that? We're not trying this lady for other crimes. We're not trying this lady for anything. We're concerned about the 31st of December and the 1st of January and that's all.

MR. DRENDALL: I don't have any more questions of this witness."

The next morning, defense counsel moved for a mistrial outside the presence of the jury. The trial court denied the motion. In general, whether to grant a mistrial is within the trial court's discretion and on review, great deference is accorded to the trial judge as he is in the best position to gauge the surrounding circumstances of an event and its impact on a jury. Granting a mistrial is an extreme remedy and is warranted only when the defendant is placed in a position of grave peril to which he should not have been subjected.

On the other hand, a trial judge should be an impartial person whose conduct and remarks do not give the jury an impression of partiality. Not all untoward remarks by a judge, however, constitute reversible error. Id. The remarks must harm the complaining party or interfere with the right to a fair trial. Id. In addition, the trial judge has a responsibility to preside over the trial and control the proceedings by taking responsible steps to insure proper order and discipline. Implicit in the judge's duty to control the proceedings is the power to give reasonable admonitions to the witnesses and counsel.

In this case, we find nothing in the brief exchange between the court and Mr. Drendall that placed Williams in grave peril or prejudiced her right to a fair trial. It was within the trial judge's

discretion to exclude the testimony in this instance and admonish the jury to disregard the question asked by the defendant. While we are sure that the trial judge could have accomplished his purposes in a more genteel fashion, we cannot say that his remarks rose to the level of reversible error.

For the foregoing reasons the judgment of the trial court is affirmed.

QUESTIONS FOR DISCUSSION

1. What definition of burning did the state argue for?
2. Why did the court adopt the state's definition?
3. Compare the court's definition with the *Model Penal Code*. Which definition is better? Defend your answer.
4. How much damage, if any, would you require if you were writing an arson statute? Explain your answer.

ARSON *MENS REA*

Most arson statutes follow the common-law *mens rea* requirement that arsonists "maliciously and willfully" burn or set fire to buildings. Some courts call the arson *mens rea* general intent. Here is one example:

> Arson is a crime of general, rather than specific, criminal intent. The requirement that defendant act "willfully and maliciously" does not signify that defendant must have actual subjective purpose that the acts he does intentionally shall produce either (1) a setting afire or burning of any structure or (2) damage to or destruction of said structure. So long as defendant has actual subjective intention to do the act he does and does it in disregard of a conscious awareness that such conduct involves highly substantial risks that will be set afire, burned or caused to be burned—notwithstanding that defendant does not "intend" such consequences in the sense that he has no actual subjective purpose that his conduct produce them— defendant acts "willfully and maliciously."[12]

According to the general intent standard, purpose refers to the *act* in arson (burning or setting fire to buildings), not to the resulting harm (burning buildings). So, a prisoner who burned a hole in his cell to escape was guilty of arson because he purposely started the fire. So was a sailor who lit a match to find his way into a dark hold in a ship in order to steal rum. The criminal intent in arson is general—an intent to start a fire, even if there is no intent to burn a specific structure.

Burning property to defraud an insurer raises a special *mens rea* concern. The *Model Penal Code* divides arson into two degrees, according to defendants' blameworthiness. Most blameworthy are defendants who intend to destroy buildings and not merely to set fire to or burn them; these are first-degree arsonists. Second-degree arsonists are defendants who set buildings on fire for other purposes. For example, if I burn a wall with an acetylene torch because I want to steal valuable fixtures attached to the wall, I'm guilty of second-degree arson for "recklessly" exposing the building to destruction even though I meant only to steal fixtures.[13]

Motive is a special problem in arson because arsonists act for a variety of motives. Some are so consumed by rage that they burn down their enemies' homes. Then there are the pyromaniacs, whose psychotic compulsion drives them to set buildings on fire for thrills. And there are the rational, but equally deadly, arsonists who burn down their own buildings or destroy their own property to collect insurance. Finally, and most deadly and difficult to catch, the professional torch commits arson for hire. Statutory provisions don't usually grade arson according to motive, but motive probably ought to affect sentencing.

❋ 11-2 Arson Statutes

PROPERTY IN ARSON

Common-law arson, like common-law burglary, was aimed at the protection of dwellings. Modern arson law, like modern burglary law, has vastly expanded the types of structures it protects. Sometimes, it goes as far as the protection of personal property. For example, Arizona's arson statute provides:

13-1703. Arson of a structure or property
A. A person commits arson of a structure or property by knowingly and unlawfully damaging a structure or property by knowingly causing a fire or explosion.
B. Arson of a structure is a class 4 felony. Arson of property is a class 4 felony if the property had a value of more than one thousand dollars. Arson of property is a class 5 felony if the property had a value of more than one hundred dollars but not more than one thousand dollars. Arson of property is a class 1 misdemeanor if the property had a value of one hundred dollars or less.[14]

GRADING ARSON

As the Arizona statute indicates, arson is usually divided into degrees. Typically, there are three degrees of arson, not the two that Arizona has enacted. Most serious (first-degree arson) is burning homes or other occupied structures (such as schools, offices, and churches) where there is a possible danger to human life. Second-degree arson includes setting fire to, or burning, unoccupied structures and vehicles (such as boats and automobiles). Third-degree arson includes setting fire to or burning personal property.

Common-law arson was originally aimed at the protection of the *security* of dwellings. So, setting fire to your own house wasn't arson. Today, arson is a crime against possession and occupancy, not just against ownership. So, where owners aren't in possession or don't occupy their own property, they can commit arson against it. For example, if I'm a landlord and I set fire to my house in order to collect insurance on it, I've committed arson because I transferred occupancy to my tenant.

SUMMARY

Burglary and arson laws are both aimed at protecting homes, other occupied structures, vehicles, and many other valuable properties. Their definitions have expanded since the sixteenth century. Both felonies protect three basic interests: personal security, homes, and property. Burglary's harm to these interests results from intrusion; arson's, from damage and destruction.

The actus reus in burglary includes illegally entering someone else's property. Whether committed at night, to homes, or to occupied structures, violence or harm to occupants aggravates the offense. The *actus reus* in arson is setting fire to or burning various structures. In some cases, it even means throwing a lighted match at a structure. The *mens rea* in burglary is the specific intent to intrude in order to commit a crime. The *mens rea* in arson is the general intent to burn or set fire to various structures.

 Go to the Criminal Law 7e CD-ROM for Internet exercises.

REVIEW QUESTIONS

1. Define and give examples of the elements of breaking and entering in the law of burglary.
2. Trace the changes in the definition of burglary since medieval times.
3. What interests does the law of burglary protect?
4. Identify the criteria used to grade burglary.
5. What is the *actus reus* of arson?
6. What structures does arson include?
7. Identify the criteria used to grade arson.

KEY TERMS

constructive breaking—entering structures in an unusual manner.
surreptitious remaining—entering a structure lawfully with the intent to commit a crime inside.
unprivileged entry—entering a structure without right, license, or permission.

SUGGESTED READINGS

1. American Law Institute, *Model Penal Code and Commentaries,* vol. 2 (Philadelphia: American Law Institute, 1980), pt. II, pp. 3–94. The most detailed, up-to-date survey of arson and burglary and all the offenses related to them. It compares various recent statutory developments, argues for reforms in the law, suggests grading the crimes, and includes model provisions for them. Meant for professionals, it is still worth the serious student's effort.

2. Rollin M. Perkins and Ronald N. Boyce, *Criminal Law,* 3d ed. (Mineola, N.Y.: Foundation Press, 1982), chap. 3. This book extensively surveys arson and burglary. It includes a good history, thoroughly analyzes the material elements in both arson and burglary, and analyzes recent changes in the law.

3. Wayne R. LaFave and Austin W. Scott, Jr., *Handbook on Criminal Law* (St. Paul, Minn.: West Publishing Co., 1972). A good analysis of burglary's material elements.

4. James Inciardi, "The Adult Firesetter: A Typology," *Criminology* 8 (August 1970): 145–155. A sociologist's effort to divide arsonists into types using considerably more detail than appears in this text. Inciardi discusses not only the professional torch, the pyromaniac, and the businesspeople who burn down buildings to collect insurance, but also adolescent thrill seekers, revenge-seeking firesetters, political arsonists, and others. This is an excellent article that puts arson into a broader context than a strictly legal one.

NOTES

1. Sir Edward Coke, *The Third Part of the Institutes of the Laws of England* (London: 1797), p. 63.

2. American Law Institute, *Model Penal Code and Commentaries* (Philadelphia: American Law Institute, 1985), § 221.1.

3. *Rex v. Bailey,* Crown Cases Reserved (1818); Matthew Hale, Pleas of the Crown, London: 1670 553; *Nalls v. State,* 219 S.W. 473 (Tex.Cr.App.1920).

4. *State v. Myrick,* 306 N.C. 110, 291 S.E.2d 577 (1982).

5. Rollin M. Perkins and Ronald N. Boyce, *Criminal Law,* 3d ed. (Mineola, N.Y.: Foundation Press, 1982), p. 201.

6. Note, "Statutory Burglary: The Magic of Four Walls and a Roof," *University of Pennsylvania Law Review* 100 (1951):411.

7. American Law Institute, *Model Penal Code and Commentaries,* vol. 2, pt. II, 72, 6.

8. Note, "Statutory Burglary," p. 420.

9. Minn.Stat.Ann 609.52 (1987).

10. William Whitmore, ed., *The Colonial Laws of Massachusetts* (Boston: 1887), p. 52.

11. *Model Penal Code and Commentaries,* vol. 2, pt. II, p. 3.

12. State v. O'Farrell, 355 A.2d 396,398 (Me.1976).

13. *Crow v. State,* 136 Tenn. 333, 189 S.W. 687 (1916); *Regina v. Harris,* 15 Cox C.C. 75 (1882).

14. http://www.azleg.state.az.us/ars/13/title13.htm

12 Crimes Against Property

Chapter Outline

I. Introduction

II. History of Theft

III. Larceny

IV. Embezzlement

V. False Pretenses—Stealing by Deceit

VI. General Theft Statutes

VII. Computer Crime

VIII. Receiving Stolen Property

IX. Forgery and Uttering

X. Robbery and Extortion

XI. Summary

C H A P T E R   M A I N   P O I N T S

1. Understanding property crimes depends more on history than on logic.

2. All property crimes originated in the ancient felony of larceny.

3. Consolidated theft statutes have rationalized the crimes of getting other people's property by basing their elements more on logic than history.

4. Theft law protects both possession and ownership of property.

5. It's a crime not only to take, convert, and get property by lies and tricks but also to receive property already wrongfully gotten by someone else.

6. Forgery and uttering statutes protect not only property but also confidence in the authenticity of documents.

7. Robbery and extortion are crimes against both property and persons.

8. The growth in the use of computers and the rapidly growing Internet have created complex and expanded ways to invade, damage, and take intellectual property.

9. Both broader application of theft law and special computer crime statutes are responses to the increasing computer use and the rapidly growing Internet.

Did He Receive Stolen Property?

A 1992 Chevrolet Astrovan automobile was stolen from a mobile home park in Spalding County. The van was subsequently utilized in a drive-by shooting on August 28, 1996. Later on the same day, Corporal Bradshaw of the Spalding County Sheriff's Department observed the van and recognized it as being similar to one that was reported stolen, as well as one that was reported as being involved in a drive-by shooting a few hours earlier. Corporal Bradshaw followed the van and could see four to five black males inside; he could not determine who was driving. While Corporal Bradshaw was following the van, the van abruptly turned into a driveway, where two or three men jumped out of the van and ran from the scene. Without the driver, the van, which was left in the "drive" mode, rolled backwards into the patrol car. Then, two young men, one of whom was the appellant, attempted to exit the van through the passenger door but were caught by Corporal Bradshaw before they could flee and were arrested at the scene.

The arresting officer was never able to determine who the driver had been or who had been in control of the stolen vehicle. The car keys were never found. When questioned by an investigator after receiving Miranda *warnings, C.W. stated that he had only been along for a ride and did not know that the van was stolen. At the hearing, appellant's co-defendant, D.L.S., testified that C.W. had only gone for a ride in the van and did not have control of the vehicle at any time.*

INTRODUCTION

Crimes against property include invasion, damage, destruction, and theft (**misappropriation**). Burglary and arson are directed at invading, damaging, and destroying property (see Chapter 11). Theft includes several offenses with a long history. In fact, understanding theft depends a lot more on history than it does on logic. The major **theft** offenses include larceny, embezzlement, false pretenses, receiving stolen property, robbery, and extortion. All of these crimes aim at the same basic harm: wrongfully taking and using someone else's property. For that reason, several states have consolidated at least some of these crimes into one general theft offense. Computers and the Internet create special problems of invasion, damage, destruction, and misappropriation.

HISTORY OF THEFT

Larceny (stealing) is the oldest crime against property. All other theft offenses descend from this ancient crime of sneaking away with someone else's property. Larceny developed at common law as a protection of the ancient Anglo-Saxons' most valuable possession—livestock. People on the western frontier in the United States placed a similar value on cattle and horses. The disgrace attached to offenders against these valuable possessions still lingers in the epithet "horse thief," to signify a dishonest or untrustworthy person. People who stole (sneaked off with) other people's property were considered evil not only because of the loss to property owners but also because they threatened community peace and harmony. Cheaters, on the other hand, were seen in a different light. They weren't condemned. On the contrary they were called clever. Besides, they didn't deserve the law's support because "a fool and his money are soon parted."[1]

Larceny, which focused on sneaking away with someone else's property, left two big gaps in the protection of property. Taking someone else's property by force instead of sneaking away with it, and keeping property that the owner had voluntarily handed over to a caretaker. Early in its history, taking property by force grew into the separate offense we still call robbery, a violent felony against both people and their property. Taking property voluntarily handed over to caretakers became an enormous problem as society grew more complex. Larceny couldn't protect the exploding range and amounts of valuable possessions (tangible property) and money, checks, and other valuable paper (intangible property) that clever people could get into their hands. Complex urban, commercial, and industrial society with its banks, businesses, services, and concentrated populations created a need to rely on others to conduct the daily business of ordinary life. Both those who owned and those who possessed property left it with caretakers for a number of purposes: safekeeping, shipping, repair, and storage. They trusted these caretakers to carry out the purpose for which the property was left with them. The criminal law grew so those who abused that trust could be punished.[2]

LARCENY

For 500 years, larceny has included five elements:

1. Wrongfully taking and
2. Carrying away
3. The property
4. Of another
5. With the intent to permanently deprive the holder of its possession.

Notice that larceny is a crime against possession as well as ownership; and it is a crime against permanent, not temporary, possession.

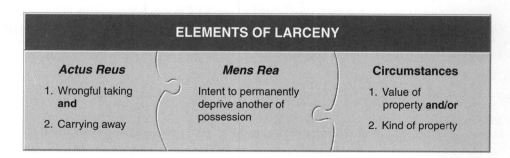

ELEMENTS OF LARCENY

Actus Reus	*Mens Rea*	Circumstances
1. Wrongful taking **and** 2. Carrying away	Intent to permanently deprive another of possession	1. Value of property **and/or** 2. Kind of property

LARCENY *ACTUS REUS*

Larceny *actus reus* consists of two elements:

1. Taking.
2. Carrying away (sometimes called **asportation**).

The element of taking requires getting control—if only briefly—of someone else's property. Taking includes direct actions like picking a pocket, lifting objects from a shop, or stealing a car. But sometimes, indirect takings are enough. For example, suppose I see someone's unlocked bicycle parked outside a shop. I offer to sell the bicycle to an unsuspecting passerby for forty dollars. She accepts my offer, pays me the money, and gets on the bicycle. In most states, I've taken the bicycle as soon as the passerby gets on the bicycle, even though I never touched it.

Carrying away means that someone else's property is moved from the place where it was taken. Carrying the property a short distance, even a few inches, is enough. All that is required is that the property actually move from the exact spot where it was taken. A pickpocket who got the money only partway out wasn't guilty because he didn't move it from its original position. Another man who tried to steal a barrel wasn't guilty because he'd only turned the barrel on its side so he could pick it up more easily. A woman who tried to walk off with a watch that she didn't know was chained to the counter in a store took but didn't "carry away" the watch.

Larceny violates possession, and it requires that actors wrongfully dispossess property. In the language of the common law, "There must be a trespass in the taking." Problems arise when a person who takes and carries away another person's property already lawfully possesses that property. Common examples are repair shop operators who have items in their possession, parking lot attendants who have their customers' car keys, and bank tellers who are authorized to handle money. In the ordinary sense of possession, all these persons possess another's property. Therefore, they could not wrongfully "take and carry away" the property because they already possess it.

The law doesn't define possession as the simple fact that the property is physically under someone's control. Instead, it looks to the kind of possession. In the law of larceny, physical custody for a particular purpose (such as when a bank teller holds the money to cash a check) differs from legal possession (such as owning a television set, leasing a car, or renting a computer). Custodians for particular purposes can wrongfully take and carry away property they have in their possession so they can commit larceny. However, lawful possessors can't commit larceny because they can't "take" what they already have.

Possession is a technical concept, involving both complex historical and property law questions. Distinguishing between mere custody and lawful possession isn't easy, but three rules shed light on the meaning of larcenous "taking":

1. Employees don't possess their employers' goods; they have mere custody of them.
2. Those who hand over their personal property for repairs haven't given up possession.
3. Money given to tellers or others for change doesn't transfer possession, only custody. The court in *People v. Olivo* dealt with the element of taking.

| C A S E | Did the Shoplifters Wrongfully Take the Property? |

People v. Olivo
52 N.Y. 2d 309, 438 N.Y.S.2d 242
420 N.E. 2d 40 (1981)

Ronald Olivo, Stefan Gasparik, and George Spatzier were convicted of petit larceny.
    COOKE, CJ.

FACTS

In *People v. Olivo,* the defendant was observed by a security guard in the hardware area of a department store. Initially conversing with another person, defendant began to look around furtively when his acquaintance departed. The security agent continued to observe and saw defendant assume a crouching position, take a set of wrenches and secret it in his clothes. After again looking around, defendant began walking toward an exit, passing a number of cash registers en route. When defendant did not stop to pay for the merchandise, the officer accosted him a few feet from the exit. In response to the guard's inquiry, he denied having the wrenches, but as he proceeded to the security office, defendant removed the wrenches and placed them under his jacket. At trial, defendant testified that he had placed the tools under his arm and was in line at a cashier when apprehended. The jury returned a verdict of guilty on the charge of petit larceny. The conviction was affirmed by Appellate Term.

In *People v. Gasparik,* defendant was in a department store trying on a leather jacket. Two store detectives observed him tear off the price tag and remove a "sensormatic" device designed to set off an alarm if the jacket were carried through a detection machine. There was at least one such machine at the exit of each floor. Defendant placed the tag and the device in the pocket of another jacket on the merchandise rack. He took his own jacket, which he had been carrying with him, and placed it on a table. Leaving his own jacket, defendant put on the leather jacket and walked through the store, still on the same floor, bypassing several cash registers. When he headed for the exit from that floor, in the direction of the main floor, he was apprehended by security personnel. At trial, defendant denied removing the price tag and the sensormatic

device from the jacket, and testified that he was looking for a cashier without a long line when he was stopped. The court, sitting without a jury, convicted defendant of petit larceny. Appellate Term affirmed.

In *People v. Spatzier,* defendant entered a bookstore on Fulton Street in Hempstead carrying an attaché case. The two co-owners of the store observed the defendant in a ceiling mirror as he browsed through the store. They watched defendant remove a book from the shelf, look up and down the aisle, and place the book in his case. He then placed the case at his feet and continued to browse. One of the owners approached defendant and accused him of stealing the book. An altercation ensued and when defendant allegedly struck the owner with the attaché case, the case opened and the book fell out. At trial, defendant denied secreting the book in his case and claimed that the owner had suddenly and unjustifiably accused him of stealing. The jury found defendant guilty of petit larceny, and the conviction was affirmed by the Appellate Term.

OPINION

These cases present a recurring question in this era of the self-service store which has never been resolved by this court: may a person be convicted of larceny for shoplifting if the person is caught with goods while still inside the store? For reasons outlined below, it is concluded that a larceny conviction may be sustained, in certain situations, even though the shoplifter was apprehended before leaving the store.

The primary issue in each case is whether the evidence, viewed in the light most favorable to the prosecution, was sufficient to establish the elements of larceny as defined by the Penal Law.

[§ 155.05 of New York Penal Law, subdivision 1, provides: "A person steals property and commits larceny when, with intent to deprive another of property or to appropriate the same to himself or to a third person, he wrongfully takes, obtains or withholds such property from an owner thereof."]

To resolve this common question, the development of the common-law crime of larceny and its evolution into modern statutory form must be briefly traced.

Larceny at common law was defined as a trespassory taking and carrying away of the property of another with intent to steal it. The early common-law courts apparently viewed larceny as defending society against breach of the peace, rather than protecting individual property rights, and therefore placed heavy emphasis upon the requirement of a trespassory taking.

As the reach of larceny expanded, the intent element of the crime became of increasing importance, while the requirement of a trespassory taking became less significant. As a result, the bar against convicting a person who had initially obtained lawful possession of property faded. In *King v. Pear*, for instance, a defendant who had lied about his address and ultimate destination when renting a horse was found guilty of larceny for later converting the horse. Because of the fraudulent misrepresentation, the court reasoned, the defendant had never obtained legal possession. Thus, "larceny by trick" was born.

Later cases went even further, often ignoring the fact that a defendant had initially obtained possession lawfully, and instead focused upon his later intent. The crime of larceny then encompassed, not only situations where the defendant initially obtained property by a trespassory taking, but many situations where an individual, possessing the requisite intent, exercised control over property inconsistent with the continued right of the owner. During this evolutionary process, the purpose served by the crime of larceny obviously shifted from protecting society's peace to general protection of property rights.

Modern penal statutes generally have incorporated these developments under a unified definition of larceny (see e.g., American Law Institute, *Model Penal Code* [Tent Draft No. 1], § 206.1 [theft is appropriation of property of another, which includes unauthorized exercise of control]). Case law, too, now tends to focus upon the actor's intent and the exercise of dominion and control over the property. Indeed, this court has recognized, in construing the New York Penal Law, that the "ancient common-law concepts of larceny" no longer strictly apply.

This evolution is particularly relevant to thefts occurring in modern self-service stores. In stores of that type, customers are impliedly invited to examine, try on, and carry about the merchandise on display. Thus in a sense, the owner has consented to the customer's possession of the goods for a limited purpose. That the owner has consented to that possession does not, however, preclude a conviction for larceny. If the customer exercises dominion and control wholly inconsistent with the continued rights of the owner, and the other elements of the crime are present, a larceny has occurred. Such conduct on the part of a customer satisfies the "taking" element of the crime. It is this element that forms the core of the controversy in these cases. The defendants argue, in essence, that the crime is not established, as a matter of law, unless there is evidence that the customer departed the shop without paying for the merchandise.

Although this court has not addressed the issue, case law from other jurisdictions seems unanimous in holding that a shoplifter need not leave the store to be guilty of larceny. This is because a shopper may treat merchandise in a manner inconsistent with the owner's continued rights—and in a manner not in accord with that of prospective purchaser—without actually walking out of the store.

Under these principles, there was ample evidence in each case to raise a factual question as to the defendants' guilt. In *People v. Olivo*, defendant not only concealed goods in his clothing, but he did so in a particularly suspicious manner. And, when defendant was stopped, he was moving towards the door, just three feet short of exiting the store.

In *People v. Gasparik*, defendant removed the price tag and sensor device from a jacket, abandoned his own garment, put the jacket on and ultimately headed for the main floor of the store. Removal of the price tag and sensor device, and careful concealment of those items, is highly unusual and suspicious conduct for a shopper. Coupled with defendant's abandonment of his own coat and his attempt to leave the floor, those factors were sufficient to make out a prima facie case of taking.

In *People v. Spatzier*, defendant concealed a book in an attaché case. Unaware that he was being observed in an overhead mirror, defendant looked furtively up and down the aisle before secreting the book. In these circumstances, given the manner in which defendant concealed the book and his suspicious behavior, the evidence was not insufficient as a matter of law.

In sum, in view of the modern definition of the crime of larceny, and its purpose of protecting individual property rights, a taking of property in the self-service store context can be established by evidence that a customer exercised control over merchandise wholly inconsistent with the store's continued rights. Quite simply, a customer who crosses the line between the limited right he or she has to deal with merchandise and the store owner's rights may be subject to prosecution for larceny. Such a rule should foster the legitimate interests and continued operation of self-service shops, a convenience which most members of the society enjoy.

Accordingly, in each case, the order of the Appellate Term should be affirmed.

QUESTIONS FOR DISCUSSION

1. The court says that larceny originally stressed possession, but modern convenience shopping requires that the emphasis shift to intent. Why does the court say this?
2. Under strict taking and carrying away requirements, do you think these defendants committed larceny?
3. Is the court right in adopting a rule that doesn't require shoplifters to leave the store before they have "taken" the property?
4. What rule would you adopt?

One final note on larceny *actus reus*. Larceny law doesn't follow the old rhyme, "Finders keepers, losers weepers." Owners who lose their property keep possession for the purposes of larceny law. So, those who take and carry away lost money or other property satisfy the *actus reus* of larceny.

THE PROPERTY AND ITS VALUE

Common-law larceny applied only to personal property. So, you couldn't steal real estate or anything attached to it, stocks and bonds, services, and labor. Modern statutes have greatly expanded the property you can steal. The Texas statute includes:

1. Real property.
2. Tangible or intangible personal property including anything severed from the land.
3. Documents, including money, that represent or embody anything of value.
4. Theft of service, including labor or professional services; telecommunication, public utility, and transportation services; lodging, restaurant services, and entertainment; and the supply of a motor vehicle or other property for use.[3]

The value of the property stolen usually determines the seriousness of the crime: the higher the value, the more serious the larceny. Grand larceny, a felony punishable by one year or more in prison, includes property exceeding a dollar amount, typically between $100 and $400. Property worth less than the designated amount for grand larceny is usually included in the misdemeanor of petty larceny, which is punishable by less than one year in jail or a fine, or both. The dividing line between grand and petty larceny differs from state to state. In South Carolina, for example, the critical amount is only $1,000; in Pennsylvania it's $2,000.[4]

Money value doesn't necessarily determine the grade of larceny. Sometimes it's the method used to take the property. Pickpocketing, for example, is always a felony, and so is taking property from someone's home. These cases involve more interests than mere property; harms to both persons and habitation are present. The item taken can also determine the seriousness of the larceny. In Texas, for example, stealing natural oil, no matter what the value, is grand larceny. California provides that grand larceny is stealing property worth more than $400. But it's also grand larceny to steal avocados, olives, citrus or deciduous fruits, vegetables, artichokes, nuts, or other farm crops worth more than $100.

LARCENY *MENS REA*

Common law larceny is a crime of purpose. Thieves had to intend to permanently deprive rightful possessors of their property. For example, suppose I see a lawn mower on my neighbor's lawn, and I believe it's the one I loaned him last month. In fact, it's his. If I take the mower and sell it, I haven't committed larceny because I didn't intend to keep his lawn mower, I intended to take mine back. Most states permit me to invoke the defense called **claim of right** that allows me to claim that I didn't intend to permanently take my neighbor's lawnmower.[5]

Intent to temporarily take someone else's property isn't common-law larceny either. But statutes have filled that gap in common-law larceny by making some temporary misappropriations separate crimes. Joyriding statutes are the typical example. It's a crime, although not as serious as larceny, to take a vehicle to drive for a short while, fully intending to return it. The joyrider lacks the larceny *mens rea*—the intent to permanently deprive the owner of possession.[6]

EMBEZZLEMENT

Historically, you couldn't take property that someone voluntarily handed over to you. For example, carriers (persons hired to deliver someone else's goods to third parties) couldn't "take" the goods while they were in the carriers' possession. Similarly, bank employees who removed money from an account couldn't "take" the money, because the owner had voluntarily deposited it. Larceny's ancient origins explain why these clearly wrongful acts weren't criminal. There were no carriers, banks, and other modern institutions at the time. The English Parliament created **embezzlement** during the period when temporary possessors (legally known as **bailees**) were becoming common. With the onset of banking, industrialization, and modern society, many more types of embezzlement were possible, and conversion became increasingly common. The crime of embezzlement brought larceny up to date by making it a crime for parking lot attendants, dry cleaners, auto repair people, bank tellers, and others to lawfully get possession of someone else's property and later converted it to their own use.

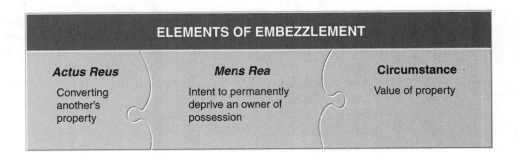

ELEMENTS OF EMBEZZLEMENT		
Actus Reus	***Mens Rea***	**Circumstance**
Converting another's property	Intent to permanently deprive an owner of possession	Value of property

Legally speaking, converting in embezzlement substitutes for taking in larceny. Notice that **conversion** can only happen after possession is lawfully acquired. Embezzlers acquire possession for a specific purpose—to repair a computer, dry-clean clothes, and so on—and then convert the property to their own use or profit. Conversion breaches the trust placed in caretakers. The breach of trust is just as bad, some say worse, than sneaking away with (taking) someone else's property.

FALSE PRETENSES—STEALING BY DECEIT

Larceny covers those who sneak away with someone else's property. Embezzlement covers those who have a temporary right to possess someone else's property. But what about owners who are tricked into parting with possession because they're deceived into giving up title or ownership? The deceivers don't have any right to possess the property, but they haven't "taken" it because the owners willingly gave it to them. And they haven't converted it because they didn't even have a temporary right to possess it. The crime of **false pretenses** (in modern law often called theft by deceit) fills the gap between larceny and embezzlement created by getting someone else's property by trick or deceit.

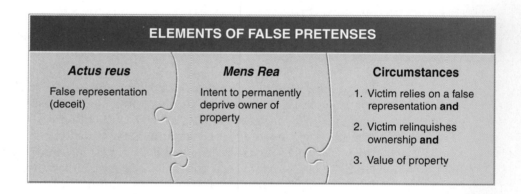

ELEMENTS OF FALSE PRETENSES

Actus reus	*Mens Rea*	Circumstances
False representation (deceit)	Intent to permanently deprive owner of property	1. Victim relies on a false representation **and** 2. Victim relinquishes ownership **and** 3. Value of property

Trick replaces taking in larceny and converting in embezzlement as the *actus reus*. Trick requires a lie, like a promise to deliver something the person making it can't or doesn't intend to keep. The law often expresses this as falsely representing a material past or existing fact. The false pretenses *mens rea* requires the purpose or specific intent to obtain title or ownership by deceit and lies; these are the false pretenses that give the crime its name. False pretenses also has two circumstance elements. First, victims have to part with possession and *ownership* because they believe and rely on the false representation. Note the difference between false pretenses and larceny by trick. In larceny by trick, the possessor has to part only with possession. In false pretenses, the owner has to part with possession *and* ownership. The Missouri Court of Appeals applied the Missouri statute on false pretenses in *State v. Watson*.

C A S E	Did He Attempt to Steal by Deceit?

State v. Watson
1997 WL 342497 (Mo.App. W.D. 1997)

Following a jury trial before the Circuit Court, Clay County, Andre Watson was convicted of attempted stealing by deceit and was sentenced to one year in the county jail. He appealed. The Court of Appeals affirmed the conviction.

ULRICH, CJ.

FACTS

In June 1995, Andre Watson was employed by A.B. May Sales and Service Company, a heating and air retailer, as an installer's helper. A.B. May purchases furnaces, air conditioners, humidifiers, and other parts used to repair and maintain equipment from Comfort Products, a distributor in Missouri and Kansas for Carrier Heating and Air. A.B. May places its orders with Comfort Products over the telephone using a purchase order system. Purchase order numbers are generated by A.B. May at the time an order is placed.

Bobbie Brakenbury, an employee of Comfort Products, received an order by telephone from a man named "Brian" on June 6, 1995. The man said he worked for A.B. May. The man placed an order for six condensing units, six furnaces, six coils, and six humidifiers. The caller ascribed A.B. May purchase order number 9400 to the order. The cost of the order was approximately $12,000.

Later, Ms. Brakenbury discovered that the coils ordered by the man did not match the size of the furnaces. She called A.B. May and asked to speak with "Brian." There was no employee at A.B. May named "Brian," however, so Ms. Brakenbury spoke with Trent Bryant who normally places the equipment orders for A.B. May. Mr. Bryant informed her that purchase order number 9400 was assigned to Lennox, another vendor, and not Comfort Products. The order was then "put on hold" until the validity of the order was determined.

Mr. Watson was working on an installation job in Prairie Village as an installer's helper on the same day. Just before lunch, the installer and Mr. Watson determined what additional parts they would need to complete the job. Mr. Watson was then sent to acquire the parts. During the lunch hour, Mr. Watson was involved in an automobile accident and did not return to work.

The next day, June 7, 1995, Mr. Watson arrived at Comfort Products requesting to pick up the six systems ordered by Brian. The warehouse manager, Thomas Dunmire, recognized Mr. Watson because he had been to Comfort Products on many occasions to get parts and equipment. Mr. Watson drove an A.B. May truck and was dressed in shorts and an A.B. May shirt with the name "Bill" printed on it.

Because the order was on hold, Mr. Dunmire informed Mr. Watson that there was a problem with the paper work and that he would have to wait a few minutes. Mr. Watson made a phone call, said he would be back in fifteen minutes, and departed. He did not return.

In the meantime, Ms. Brakenbury called Shane Coughlin, the chief financial officer at A.B. May, to confirm the order. Because the purchase order number was assigned to a different vendor and the cost of the order was approximately ten times larger than the normal $1500 order to Comfort Products, appropriate authority at Comfort Products concluded the order was not legitimate. Further inquiry at A.B. May disclosed that no one at the company was authorized to purchase six air conditioners and furnaces from Comfort Products on June 6 or 7, 1995.

Mr. Watson did not return to work at A.B. May except for part of a day on June 15, 1995. Attempts by A.B. May personnel to contact Mr. Watson by telephone failed. Ultimately, Mr. Watson was charged with attempted stealing by deceit. At trial, Mr. Watson testified in his own defense. He claimed that on June 7, 1995, he was at home recuperating from the automobile accident that occurred the previous day.

OPINION

. . . Mr. Watson was convicted of attempted stealing by deceit. "A person is guilty of attempt to commit an offense when, with the purpose of committing the offense, he does any act which is a substantial step towards the commission of the offense." 564.011.1, RSMo 1994. The crime of stealing is committed if a person

> appropriates property or services of another with the purpose to deprive him thereof, either without his consent or by means of deceit or coercion. 570.030.1, RSMo 1994.

Deceit is defined as

> purposely making a representation which is false and which the actor does not believe to be true and upon which the victim relies, as to a matter of fact, law, value, intention or other state of mind. 570.010(6), RSMo 1994.

Mr. Watson contends that the evidence was insufficient to prove that he had the intent to deceive or that he knew or should have known that he did not have authority to pick up the furnaces and air conditioners. The subjective intent of a defendant to deceive may be proven by circumstantial evidence. The evidence presented in this case showed that an invalid order for six systems consisting of furnaces, air conditioners, coils, and humidifiers was placed with Comfort Products on June 6, 1995, by a man who identified himself as "Brian" from A.B. May. A.B. May did not have an employee named Brian on June 6, 1995, and no A.B. May employee had authority on June 6 or 7, 1995, to purchase six systems. The purchase order number provided was 9400, and the value of the six systems was about $12,000.00.

The evidence also established that Mr. Watson was working in Prairie Village for A.B. May on June 6 and was asked by his supervisor to order parts to complete the job and to get them. He did not return to work that day because he was involved in an automobile accident.

The next day, Mr. Watson arrived at Comfort Products to obtain six systems that included six furnaces, six coils and six air conditioners. He wore an A.B. May shirt with the name "Bill" printed on it and was not wearing the pants that are the normal uniform A.B. May employees wear. He was informed that the order was "on hold" because of a problem with the paper work. Mr. Watson left and did not return. Mr. Watson did not return to work at A.B. May except for part of June 15.

This evidence was sufficient for a reasonable juror to have concluded that Mr. Watson made a substantial act to steal six systems by deceit. From the evidence, a reasonable inference could have been drawn that Mr. Watson knowingly made a false representation that he had A.B. May's authorization to acquire the furnaces and air conditioners from Comfort Products. The trial court, therefore, did not err in overruling Mr. Watson's motion for judgment of acquittal at the close of all the evidence.

The judgment of conviction is affirmed.

QUESTIONS FOR DISCUSSION

1. The critical issue in the case is determining whether Andre Watson intended to deceive Comfort Products in order to get the air conditioning equipment. In other words, did he use false pretenses to get the merchandise?

2. He argued that he did know he lacked the authority to purchase the merchandise. Does the evidence presented convince you that he meant to deceive Comfort Products in order to get the merchandise?

GENERAL THEFT STATUTES

In most criminal codes, larceny, embezzlement, and obtaining property by false pretenses were distinct offenses until the 1970s. Although all three involved wrongfully getting other people's property, taking in larceny, converting in embezzlement, and fraud in false pretenses were considered different enough to require separate treatment under criminal codes. But as we noted earlier, it was a lot more history than logic that drove the law of crimes against property. Supreme Court Justice Oliver Wendell Holmes put it simply: "In law a page of history is worth a volume of logic."

Most states have made some effort to turn away from history and toward logic. Most have done so by consolidating larceny, embezzlement, and false pretenses into one offense called theft. These **consolidated theft statutes** do away with the artificial need to decide whether property was "taken and carried away," "converted," or "swindled." They accept the social reality that they are all aimed at the same criminal offense—wrongfully getting someone else's property.

Some statutes are even more ambitious. The *Model Penal Code,* for example, has a single theft article that covers not only larceny, embezzlement, and false pretenses but also extortion, blackmail, and receiving stolen property. Thus, the code combines all nonviolent misappropriations in one provision. Only robbery—because it is a violent crime—is treated in a separate provision. Other consolidated theft statutes include some or all of the following thefts: taking, conversion, deception, extortion, lost property, receiving stolen property, theft of services, failure to make required deposits, and unauthorized vehicle use.[7]

The California consolidated theft statute provides

> every person who shall feloniously steal the personal property of another, or who shall fraudulently appropriate property which has been entrusted to him, or who shall knowingly and designedly, by any false or fraudulent representation or pretense, defraud any other person of money, labor or real or personal property, shall be guilty of theft.[8]

Commenting on the provision, the California Supreme Court wrote:

> Included within § 484 is not only the offense of taking personal property (larceny), but also "embezzlement," theft by trick and device, and theft by false pretenses [of both personal and real property].[9]

COMPUTER CRIME

Consolidated theft statutes only begin to respond to the rapidly developing opportunities to misappropriate property at the beginning of the twenty-first century. Electronics has created not only new value but also new methods to misappropriate it. The vast expansion of computers and the exponential growth of the Internet are already making it difficult for the laws of privacy, copyright, and the relationship between states and the federal government to keep up with the real world. The same is true of the law of theft. Every day, new opportunities to misappropriate **intellectual property**—information and services stored in and transmitted to and from electronic data banks—demonstrate how far short even the most advanced theft laws fall.

Some states have attempted to deal with computer crimes by expanding the interpretation of the elements of the common-law crimes of larceny, embezzlement, and false pretenses. In *Hancock v. Texas,* the court ruled that computer programs are property for purposes of larceny. The Washington Supreme Court applied the law of theft to stealing computer software in *State v. Smith.*

C A S E   Did He "Take" the Software?

State v. Smith
798 P.2d 1146 (Wash. 1990)

John Smith was convicted of the theft of a copyrighted computer software package by the Superior Court, Thurston County. He appealed. The Washington Court of Appeals and the Washington Supreme Court affirmed the conviction.

DOLLIVER, J.

FACTS

On December 20, 1985, defendant John P. Smith contacted MicroFocus, Incorporated and inquired into purchasing a software package called "Professional Cobal." At the time, defendant was a student at The Evergreen State College (TESC). After MicroFocus informed defendant he could not examine the software free of charge, he agreed to purchase it C.O.D. The marketing representative who took defendant's order testified that defendant represented himself as being a professor at TESC, thereby entitling him to a 20 percent discount off the $3,000 market price of the program.

On December 23, 1985, the United Parcel Service (UPS) attempted to deliver the program to defendant at TESC. The UPS driver spoke with the campus police sergeant who informed him the address on the package was actually student housing rather than an on-campus office address. The driver eventually located the correct address and delivered the program and instruction manual to defendant. Both the program and the manual were copyrighted. Defendant wrote a personal check to MicroFocus for the purchase in the amount of $2,407, even though the account upon which the check was issued had a balance of only $472.52. Defendant also maintained another bank account which had a balance of approximately $7,062 at the time. Almost immediately after receiving the program, defendant made a copy of it and the instruction manual.

Defendant testified that the following morning he realized the program did not work on his computer. At some point after this, defendant called his bank and stopped payment on the check he had written to MicroFocus. Defendant then returned the items to MicroFocus, marking the package with the notation, "Unauthorized purchase, returned."

After investigation into the attempted misdelivery of the MicroFocus package, the campus police sergeant at TESC obtained a warrant to search defendant's apartment. During the execution of the warrant, officers uncovered multiple complete sets of the MicroFocus software defendant had ordered and returned, as well as a copy of the instruction manual which accompanied the software. These items, plus copies of additional programs defendant had ordered from other manufacturers but then returned, were seized and later produced at trial.

Defendant was charged in Thurston County Superior Court under RCW 9A.56.030(1)(a) and RCW 9A.56.020(1)(a) or (1)(b) with one count of first degree theft. Before trial, defendant moved to dismiss the charge, arguing federal copyright law preempted the State's jurisdiction to prosecute him for the offense. The trial court denied the motion. Defendant did not renew his motion. Defendant also moved to suppress reference to a charge for welfare fraud pending against him in Jefferson County. The trial court granted the motion contingent upon defendant not opening the subject up.

During trial, defendant admitted he had received five other software packages in the mail, paid for them, and then later stopped payment on the checks. He also testified to having made backup copies for all of the ordered programs but one, which he stated could not be copied. Defendant testified his original intention was to keep each of the programs he ordered, but he returned them because he later realized none of them ran properly on his computer. He also testified he copied the programs because the software manuals suggested doing this in case the master program was damaged or destroyed. He testified he copied the manuals in order to protect himself from theft or other loss. Although he kept copies of the materials after returning them to the manufacturers, he testified he never intended to use them.

When defendant was questioned about receiving the goods at a discount, he testified he had told a college official that he "understood how the system worked and how to manipulate it," but what he meant was that he was getting software at a wholesale price rather than the retail price and thereby "cutting out the middle man." Defendant also testified he merely told MicroFocus that he was "with" TESC and not that he was a professor there.

The jury found defendant guilty as charged. The defendant appealed to the Court of Appeals. In an unpublished opinion, the Court of Appeals affirmed the trial court. We granted review and affirm, although in part for reasons other than those set out by the Court of Appeals.

OPINION

. . . RCW 9A.56.030(1) defines first degree theft as follows:

> A person is guilty of theft in the first degree if he commits theft of:
> (a) Property or services which exceeds one thousand five hundred dollars in value; or
> (b) Property of any value taken from the person of another.

"Theft," according to RCW 9A.56.020(1), means:

> (a) To wrongfully obtain or exert unauthorized control over the property or services of another or the value thereof, with intent to deprive him of such property or services; or
> (b) By color or aid of deception to obtain control over the property or services of another or the value thereof, with intent to deprive him of such property or services . . .

Subsection (a) is known as theft by taking while subsection (b) is known as theft by deception. Here, defendant was charged under both subsections (a) and (b). "Deprive," in addition to its common meaning, also includes making "unauthorized use or an unauthorized copy of records, information, data, trade secrets, or computer programs . . ." RCW 9A.56.010(5).

We . . . find erroneous the Court of Appeals' conclusion that theft by taking requires a trespass. . . . Trespass is not required for statutory theft by taking. "The Legislature may define crimes. Where it does so, its statutory definition may supersede common law." Both this court and the Court of Appeals have affirmed convictions for theft by taking under RCW 9A.56.020(1)(a) without requiring evidence of a trespass. See *State v. Britten,* 46 Wash.App. 571, 731 P.2d 508 (1986) (involving theft by taking which occurred in a department store); *State v. Komok,* supra (also involving theft in a department store). Vargas and any other decision inferring the contrary is disapproved. As we find theft by taking as defined by statute does not include the common-law element of trespass, the contention of the Court of Appeals and defendant that there was insufficient evidence to convict under the taking statute is not valid. There was sufficient evidence for conviction of theft either by taking (RCW 9A.56.020(1)(a)) or deception (RCW 9A.56.020(1)(b)). . . .

The Court of Appeals is affirmed.

QUESTIONS FOR DISCUSSION

1. How has the Washington statute modified the elements of common-law larceny?
2. Is it possible to define modern theft without referring to common-law larceny? Explain.

Most states have concluded that trying to shoehorn computer crime into the law of theft isn't enough. So, most states have enacted specific computer crimes statutes. The Arkansas legislature stated its purpose for enacting a specific computer crime statute:

> It is found and determined that computer-related crime poses a major problem for business and government; that losses for each incident of computer-related crime are potentially astronomical; that the opportunities for computer-related crime in business and government through the introduction of fraudulent records into a computer system, the unauthorized use of computers, alteration or destruction of computerized information or files, and the stealing of financial instruments, data, and other assets, are great; that computer-related crime has a direct effect on state commerce; and that, while various forms of computer-related crime might possibly be the subject of criminal charges based on other provisions of law, it is appropriate and desirable that a statute be enacted which deals directly with computer-related crime.[10]

Kansas has adopted the following computer crime statute as part of Article 37 of the Kansas Criminal Code, "Crimes Against Property:"

§ 21—3755. Computer crime; computer password disclosure; computer trespass.

(a) As used in this section:

(1) 'Access' means to instruct, communicate with, store data in, retrieve data from or otherwise make use of any resources of a computer, computer system or computer network.

(2) 'Computer' means an electronic device which performs work using programmed instruction and which has one or more of the capabilities of storage, logic, arithmetic or communication and includes all input, output, processing, storage, software or communication facilities which are connected or related to such a device in a system or network.

(3) 'Computer network' means the interconnection of communication lines, including microwave or other means of electronic communication, with a computer through remote terminals, or a complex consisting of two or more interconnected computers.

(4) 'Computer program' means a series of instructions or statements in a form acceptable to a computer which permits the functioning of a computer system in a manner designed to provide appropriate products from such computer system.

(5) 'Computer software' means computer programs, procedures and associated documentation concerned with the operation of a computer system.

(6) 'Computer system' means a set of related computer equipment or devices and computer software which may be connected or unconnected.

(7) 'Financial instrument' means any check, draft, money order, certificate of deposit, letter of credit, bill of exchange, credit card, debit card or marketable security.

(8) 'Property' includes, but is not limited to, financial instruments, information, electronically produced or stored data, supporting documentation and computer software in either machine or human readable form.

(9) 'Services' includes, but is not limited to, computer time, data processing and storage functions and other uses of a computer, computer system or computer network to perform useful work.

(10) 'Supporting documentation' includes, but is not limited to, all documentation used in the construction, classification, implementation, use or modification of computer software, computer programs or data.

(b)(1) Computer crime is:

(A) Intentionally and without authorization accessing and damaging, modifying, altering, destroying, copying, disclosing or taking possession of a computer, computer system, computer network or any other property;

(B) using a computer, computer system, computer network or any other property for the purpose of devising or executing a scheme or artifice with the intent to defraud or for the purpose of obtaining money, property, services or any other thing of value by means of false or fraudulent pretense or representation; or

(C) intentionally exceeding the limits of authorization and damaging, modifying, altering, destroying, copying, disclosing or taking possession of a computer, computer system, computer network or any other property.

(2) Computer crime is a severity level 8, nonperson felony.

(3) In any prosecution for computer crime, it is a defense that the property or services were appropriated openly and avowedly under a claim of title made in good faith.

(c) (1) Computer password disclosure is the unauthorized and intentional disclosure of a number, code, password or other means of access to a computer or computer network.

(2) Computer password disclosure is a class A nonperson misdemeanor.

(d) Computer trespass is intentionally, and without authorization accessing or attempting to access any computer, computer system, computer network or computer software, program, documentation, data or property contained in any computer, computer system or computer network. Computer trespass is a class A nonperson misdemeanor.

The Kansas Supreme Court applied the computer crime statute in *State v. Allen.*

C A S E   Did He Commit Computer Crime?

State v. Allen
260 Kan. 107, 917 P.2d 848 (1996)

Anthony Allen, the defendant, was charged with felony computer crime. The Johnson District Court dismissed complaint, and the state appealed. The Kansas Supreme Court affirmed.

LARSON, J.

FACTS

Allen admitted to Detective Kent Willnauer that he had used his computer, equipped with a modem, to call various Southwestern Bell computer modems. The telephone numbers for the modems were obtained by random dialing. If one of Allen's calls were completed, his computer determined if it had been answered by voice or another computer. These were curiosity calls of short duration.

The State presented no evidence which showed that Allen ever had entered any Southwestern Bell computer system. Detective Willnauer was unable to state that Allen had altered any programs, added anything to the system, used it to perform any functions, or interfered with its operation. Willnauer specifically stated he had no evidence that the Southwestern Bell computer system had been damaged.

Ronald W. Knisley, Southwestern Bell's Regional Security Director, testified Allen had called two different types of Southwestern Bell computer equipment—SLC-96 system environmental controls and SMS-800 database systems. The telephone numbers for the SLC-96 systems were thought to be known only to Southwestern Bell employees or agents on a need-to-know basis. Access to the SLC-96 systems required knowledge of a password. If one connected to the system it displayed "KEYWORD?" without any identification

or warning. No evidence existed that Allen attempted to respond to the prompt.

Testimony confirmed Allen also called and connected 28 times with the SMS-800 systems at several different modem numbers. Each call but two was under 1 minute. Upon connection with this system, a person would see a log on request and a "banner." The banner identifies the system that has answered the incoming call and displays that it is Southwestern Bell property and that access is restricted. Entry into the system itself then requires both a user ID and a password which must agree with each other. No evidence indicated Allen went beyond this banner or even attempted to enter a user ID or password.

Knisley testified that if entry into an SMS-800 system were accomplished and proper commands were given, a PBX system could be located which would allow unlimited and nonchargeable long distance telephone calls. There was no evidence this occurred, nor was it shown that Allen had damaged, modified, destroyed, or copied any data.

James E. Robinson, Function Manager responsible for computer security, testified one call to an SMS-800 system lasted 6 minutes and 35 seconds. Although the system should have retained information about this call, it did not, leading to speculation the record-keeping system had been overridden. Robinson speculated Allen had gained entry into the system but admitted he had no evidence that Allen's computer had done anything more than sit idle for a few minutes after calling a Southwestern Bell modem number.

Robinson testified that Southwestern Bell was unable to document any damage to its computer equipment or software as a result of Allen's activities. However, as a result of its investigation, Southwestern Bell decided that prudence required it to upgrade its password security system to a more secure "token card" process. It was the cost of this investigation and upgrade that the State alleges comprises the damage caused by Allen's actions. Total investigative costs were estimated at $4,140. The cost of developing deterrents was estimated to be $1,656. The cost to distribute secure ID cards to employees totaled $18,000. Thus, the total estimated damage was $23,796.

In closing arguments, the State admitted Allen did not get into the computer system, nor did he modify, alter, destroy, copy, disclose, or take possession of anything. See K.S.A. 21-3755(b)(1). Instead, the State argued Allen's conduct in acquiring the unlisted numbers and calling them constituted an "approach" to the systems, within the meaning of K.S.A. 21-3755(a)(1), which questioned the integrity of the systems and resulted in the altered or added security precautions.

In its oral ruling, the trial court noted K.S.A. 21-3755 was unclear. The court then held the mere fact Allen made telephone calls, a legal activity, which resulted in the connection of two modems, was insufficient to prove he had "gained access" to Southwestern Bell's computer systems as the K.S.A. 21-3755(b)(1) charge required. In addition, the court held Southwestern Bell's investigative expenses and voluntary security upgrade costs did not constitute damage to the computer systems or other property as defined in the statute.

OPINION

In this first impression case, we are presented with the question of whether a person's telephonic connections that prompt a computer owner to change its security systems constitute felony computer crime in violation of K.S.A. 21-3755(b).

The charges against Anthony A. Allen arose from several telephonic connections he made with Southwestern Bell Telephone Company's computers in early 1995. After preliminary hearing, the trial court dismissed the complaint, finding no probable cause existed to believe Allen had committed any crime. The State has appealed pursuant to K.S.A. 22-3602(b)(1). We affirm the trial court.

The legal standard to be applied in a preliminary hearing is clear. If it appears from the evidence presented that a crime has been committed and there is probable cause to believe the defendant committed it, K.S.A. 22-2902(3) requires that the defendant be bound over for trial. If there is not

sufficient evidence, the defendant must be discharged. From the evidence presented, the trial court must draw the inferences favorable to the prosecution, and the evidence need only establish probable cause. "Probable cause at a preliminary hearing signifies evidence sufficient to cause a person of ordinary prudence and caution to conscientiously entertain a reasonable belief of the accused's guilt."

Allen was charged under K.S.A. 21-3755, which in applicable part provides:

> (a) As used in this section, the following words and phrases shall have the meanings respectively ascribed thereto:
> (1) 'Access' means to approach, instruct, communicate with, store data in, retrieve data from, or otherwise make use of any resources of a computer, computer system or computer network.
> (2) 'Computer' means an electronic device which performs work using programmed instruction and which has one or more of the capabilities of storage, logic, arithmetic or communication and includes all input, output, processing, storage, software or communication facilities which are connected or related to such a device in a system or network.
> (3) 'Computer network' means the interconnection of communication lines, including microwave or other means of electronic communication, with a computer through remote terminals, or a complex consisting of two or more interconnected computers.
>
> . . . .
>
> (6) 'Computer system' means a set of related computer equipment or devices and computer software which may be connected or unconnected.
>
> . . . .
>
> (8) 'Property' includes, but is not limited to, financial instruments, information, electronically produced or stored data, supporting documentation and computer software in either machine or human readable form.
>
> . . . .
>
> (b) Computer crime is:
> (1) Intentionally and without authorization gaining or attempting to gain access to and damaging, modifying, altering, destroying, copying, disclosing or taking possession of a computer, computer system, computer network or any other property;
>
> . . . .
>
> (c) . . .

(2) Computer crime which causes a loss of the value of at least $500 but less than $25,000 is a severity level 9, nonperson felony.

. . . .

(e) Criminal computer access is intentionally, fraudulently and without authorization gaining or attempting to gain access to any computer, computer system, computer network or to any computer software, program, documentation, data or property contained in any computer, computer system or computer network. Criminal computer access is a class A nonperson misdemeanor."

Allen was charged with a violation of K.S.A. 21-3755(b)(1), with the second amended complaint alleging that he

did then and there intentionally and without authorization gain access and damage a computer, computer system, computer network or other computer property which caused a loss of the value of at least $500.00 but less than $25,000.00, a severity level 9 non-person felony.

Felony computer crime as it is charged in this case under K.S.A. 21-3755(b)(1) required the State to prove three distinct elements: (1) intentional and unauthorized access to a computer, computer system, computer network, or any other property (as property is defined in K.S.A. 21-3755[a] [8]); (2) damage to a computer, computer system, computer network, or any other property; and (3) a loss in value as a result of such crime of at least $500 but less than $25,000. The trial court found that the State failed to show probable cause as to each of these elements.

Did the trial court err in ruling there was insufficient evidence to show Allen gained "access" to Southwestern Bell's computers?

After finding the evidence showed Allen had done nothing more than use his computer to call unlisted telephone numbers, the trial court ruled there was insufficient evidence to show Allen had gained access to the computer systems. Although a telephone connection had been established, the evidence showed Allen had done nothing more. The trial court reasoned that unless and until Allen produced a password that permitted him to interact with the data in the computer system, he had not "gained access" as the complaint required.

The State argues the trial court's construction of the statute ignores the fact that "access" is defined in the statute, K.S.A. 21-3755(a)(1), as "to approach, instruct, communicate with, store data in, retrieve data from, or otherwise make use of any resources of a computer, computer system or computer network." By this definition, the State would lead us to believe that any kind of an "approach" is criminal behavior sufficient to satisfy a charge that Allen did in fact "gain access" to a computer system.

The problem with the State's analysis is that K.S.A. 21-3755(b)(1) does not criminalize "accessing" (and, thus, "approaching") but rather "gaining or attempting to gain access." If we were to read "access" in this context as the equivalent of "approach," the statute would criminalize the behavior of "attempting to gain approach" to a computer or computer system. This phrase is lacking in any common meaning such that an ordinary person would have great difficulty discerning what conduct was prohibited, leading to an effective argument that the statute was void for vagueness.

The United States Department of Justice has commented about the use of "approach" in a definition of "access" in this context: "The use of the word 'approach' in the definition of 'access,' if taken literally, could mean that any unauthorized physical proximity to a computer could constitute a crime." National Institute of Justice, *Computer Crime: Criminal Justice Resource Manual,* p. 84 (2d ed.1989).

We read certain conduct as outside a statute's scope rather than as proscribed by the statute if including it within the statute would render the statute unconstitutionally vague. Consequently, although K.S.A. 21-3755 defines "access," the plain and ordinary meaning should apply rather than a tortured translation of the definition that is provided. See *State Dept. of SRS v. Public Employee Relations Board,* 249 Kan. 163, 168, 815 P.2d 66 (1991) (statutory words presumed used in ordinary and common meanings).

In addition, K.S.A. 21-3755 is certainly rendered ambiguous by the inclusion of the definition of "access" as a verb when its only use in the statute is as a noun. As a criminal statute, any ambiguity is to be resolved in favor of the accused. See *State v. JC Sports Bar, Inc.,* 253 Kan. 815, 818, 861 P.2d 1334 (1993) (criminal statutes construed strictly against the State).

Webster's defines "access" as "freedom or ability to obtain or make use of." *Webster's New Collegiate Dictionary,* p. 7 (1977). This is similar to the construction used by the trial court to find that no evidence showed that Allen had gained access to Southwestern Bell's computers. Until Allen proceeded beyond the initial banner and entered appropriate passwords, he could not be said to have had the ability to make use of Southwestern Bell's computers or obtain anything. Therefore, he cannot be said to have gained access to Southwestern Bell's computer systems as gaining access is commonly understood. The trial court did not err in determining the State had failed to present evidence showing probable cause that Allen had gained access to Southwestern Bell's computer system.

Did the trial court err in ruling that no evidence showed Allen had damaged any computer, computer system, computer network, or any other property?

The State acknowledges it cannot meet the damage element of the crime it has charged by any means other than evidence showing Allen's actions resulted in expenditures of money by Southwestern Bell. It is crystal clear there is absolutely no evidence Allen modified, altered, destroyed, copied, disclosed, or took possession of anything. The State's evidence clearly shows Allen did not physically affect any piece of computer equipment or software by his telephone calls. All the State was able to show was that Southwestern Bell made an independent business judgment to upgrade its security at a cost of $23,796. The State argues this is sufficient.

The State's argument is clearly flawed. The trial court reasoned by a fitting analogy that the State is essentially saying that a person looking at a no trespassing sign on a gate causes damage to the owner of the gate if the owner decides as a result to add a new lock. The trial court has clearly and correctly pointed to the correct analysis of this issue.

The State's circular theory is that if someone incurs costs to investigate whether an activity is criminal, it becomes criminal because investigative costs were incurred. Although computer crime is not, for obvious reasons, a common-law crime, it nevertheless has a common-law predicate which helps us to understand the legislature's intent. K.S.A. 21-3755 was not designed to update criminal trespass or malicious mischief statutes to the computer age but "to address inadequacies in the present theft statute related to prosecution of computer related crimes. Specifically, present theft statutes make prosecution difficult among crimes in which the computer owner was not actually deprived of the computer or its software." Kansas Legislature Summary of Legislation 1985, p. 80.

Theft, as defined in K.S.A. 21-3701, is not concerned with mere occupation, detention, observation, or tampering, but rather requires permanent deprivation. The intent required for theft is an "intent to deprive the owner permanently of the possession, use, or benefit of the owner's property." K.S.A. 21-3701(a). One may have wrongful intent, such as intent to trespass, without having the intent required for a theft. In addition, at common law, the thing of which the victim was deprived had to be something of value. The second element of computer crime mirrors this common-law requirement of the deprivation of something of value in a larceny action. As in a larceny action, the extent of the deprivation determines the severity level of the crime. This element of computer crime, as with other theft statutes, cannot be satisfied where there is no deprivation as in this case.

The State argues that investigative costs qualify as damages under the statute because investigative costs may be recovered from the perpetrator of computer crime as restitution. In our case, the issue is whether Allen's conduct is rendered criminal because it was investigated, not whether restitution for conduct already determined to be criminal includes investigative costs. *Lindsly* has no application to the present case.

The degree of a theft crime is established by the value of the stolen property. Restitution, in contrast, can include not only the fair market value of the property lost, but other costs in connection with the theft as well. The amount of restitution can be greater than the damages used to classify the crime. It requires only a causal connection between the crime proved and the loss on which restitution is based. We will not utilize the State's "restitution" theory to determine if there is probable cause to determine that the damage elements of a crime have been shown.

Southwestern Bell's computer system was not "damaged" in the sense the statute requires. Southwestern Bell was not deprived of property in the manner required to support a criminal charge. The fact an independent business judgment that Southwestern Bell's computer systems might be accessible was made after Allen's conduct was discovered does not support the second and third elements of the crime charged. The trial court correctly determined the State failed to meet its probable cause burden on these issues as well.

Affirmed.

QUESTIONS FOR DISCUSSION

1. State the elements of the statute that relate to the facts of the case.
2. List all of the facts relevant to deciding whether Anthony Allen was guilty of computer crime.
3. Summarize the state's arguments in favor of Anthony Allen's guilt.
4. Do you agree with the supreme court's decision upholding the lower court's decision? Defend your answer.
5. Was Anthony Allen guilty of "criminal computer access"? Back up your answer by stating the elements of the crime and applying the facts of the case to the elements.
6. Why do you think the state didn't charge Anthony Allen with "criminal computer access"?

RECEIVING STOLEN PROPERTY

Not only is it a crime to take or convert someone else's property or to get it by deception, it's also a crime to receive property after it's been criminally misappropriated. Called **receiving stolen property**, this offense aims to punish those who stand to benefit from someone else's property even though he or she didn't participate in the wrongful acquisition in the first place. Most who benefit are **fences**, those who sell stolen merchandise for profit. But so do the people who buy the stolen stuff at greatly reduced prices.

Fences have the facilities to buy, store, and market property. As go-betweens, they're as indispensable as middlemen in legitimate operations are to farmers, manufacturers, and other producers. Large-city fences trade a remarkably large volume and variety in stolen property, ranging from narcotics and weapons to appliances and computers and even clothes. Receiving stolen property is aimed primarily at these large-scale operations.

The *actus reus* in receiving stolen property is receiving the property. Receiving means that receiver has to control the property, at least briefly. Receiving doesn't mean that the receiver has to personally possess the property. So, if I buy a stolen TIVO for a friend and the fence hands it over directly to my friend, I've received the drive even though I've never seen or touched it. If my friend gives the TIVO to her friend, my friend has also received the stolen TIVO. Also, fences as well as friends who hide stolen goods temporarily for thieves have received the stolen goods.

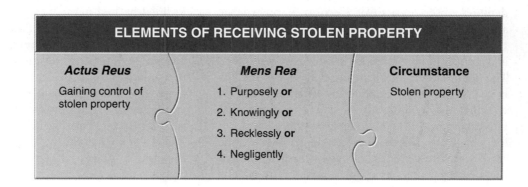

ELEMENTS OF RECEIVING STOLEN PROPERTY		
Actus Reus	**Mens Rea**	**Circumstance**
Gaining control of stolen property	1. Purposely **or** 2. Knowingly **or** 3. Recklessly **or** 4. Negligently	Stolen property

A circumstance element in receiving stolen property is that someone in fact wrongfully took, converted, or acquired the property in the first place. So, if you believe you're hiding stolen CDs but in fact they weren't stolen, you haven't received stolen property.

Receiving stolen property *mens rea* varies. Some states require actual knowledge that the goods are stolen. In others, an honest belief that the goods are stolen is enough. In all jurisdictions, knowledge may be inferred from surrounding circumstances, like receiving goods from a known thief or buying goods at a fraction of their real value (like buying a top of the line digital audio recording system for $75). Some jurisdictions require only that receivers were reckless or negligent about whether the property was stolen. Recklessness and negligence as to whether the property was stolen is often directed at likely fences, usually junk dealers and pawn shop operators.

Another aspect of the *mens rea* of receiving stolen property is that receivers have to intend to keep the property permanently. This means that police officers who knowingly accept stolen property and secretly place it in the hands of suspected fences in order to catch them haven't received stolen property because they don't intend to keep it.

C A S E   Did He Receive the Stolen Car?

Hurston v. State
414 S.E.2d 303 (Ga. App. 1991)

Illya Hurston and Demetrious Reese were convicted by a jury of theft by receiving stolen property before the Rockdale County Superior Court. Hurston appealed the denial of his motion for a new trial. The Court of Appeals affirmed.

ANDREWS, J.

FACTS

A silver 1986 Pontiac Fiero belonging to Stella Burns was stolen from a parking lot at Underground Atlanta on June 11, 1989, between 10:35 and 11:05 P.M. Two Rockdale County sheriff's deputies observed a silver Fiero at a convenience store later that night at approximately 1:20 A.M. Hurston's co-defendant, Reese, was driving the car and appellant was slumped in the passenger seat. The deputies became suspicious because of the late hour, the cautious manner in which Reese was walking after exiting the car, and the fact that Hurston appeared to be hiding, and decided to follow the Fiero. When Reese drove away from the store with the deputies following in their marked car, he crossed the centerline of the highway. The

deputies, who by this time had ascertained from computer records that the car was stolen, turned on the blue lights and siren of their automobile. Reese refused to stop, drove away from the deputies at a speed in excess of 100 miles per hour and attempted at one point to run the police vehicle into a wall. The deputies pursued the Fiero until Reese lost control and wrecked in a field. Reese ran from the scene and was pursued and apprehended by one deputy. Another officer apprehended Hurston, who had gotten out of the car immediately after the accident and appeared to be ready to run.

At trial, Hurston testified that he spent the day at his former girlfriend's home watching television with her and a friend of hers. Later in the day, the friend called her boyfriend, Reese, whom Hurston testified he had never met, to join them. Hurston testified Reese came to the house and stayed for awhile, left for several hours, and then returned and invited Hurston to ride in the Fiero with him to a relative's home. Hurston recalled that he was suspicious about the ownership of the vehicle because Reese, a teenager, seemed too young to own such a nice car, but that in response to his inquiry Reese stated that the car belonged to his cousin. Hurston testified that after they left the convenience store and Reese saw the deputies in pursuit, he began to speed, and admitted to Hurston for the first time that the car was stolen. Hurston's trial testimony differed somewhat from an earlier statement he gave regarding the evening's events.

Burns, the vehicle's owner, testified that the vehicle was driven without keys and that the steering wheel had been damaged, which was consistent with it having been stolen. She testified that various papers, including the car registration and business cards bearing the owner's name and address, had been removed from the glove compartment and were on the floor of the car; that grass, mud, food, drink and cigarettes were scattered in the car; and that a picture of her daughter was displayed on a visor. Hurston denied noticing the personal items or the damaged steering wheel.

OPINION

OCGA § 1687(a) provides:

> a person commits the offense of theft by receiving stolen property when he receives, disposes of, or retains stolen property which he knows or should know was stolen unless the property is received, disposed of, or retained with intent to restore it to the owner. 'Receiving' means acquiring possession or control. . . .

Unexplained possession of recently stolen property, alone, is not sufficient to support a conviction for receiving stolen property but guilt may be inferred from possession in conjunction with other evidence of knowledge. Guilty knowledge may be inferred from circumstances which would excite suspicion in the mind of an "ordinary prudent man." "Possession, as we know it, is the right to exercise power over a corporeal thing. . . ." Furthermore, "if there is any evidence of guilt, it is for the jury to decide whether that evidence, circumstantial though it may be, is sufficient to warrant a conviction."

Construed most favorably for the State, there was sufficient evidence for a jury to find Hurston guilty of receiving stolen property. First, there was sufficient evidence for a jury to find that Hurston knew, or should have known, that the vehicle was stolen. At trial, Hurston admitted that he doubted that the vehicle belonged to Reese. There was evidence from which the jury could reasonably have concluded that Hurston was aware during the two hours that he spent in the small vehicle that it was stolen, in that the vehicle was being driven without keys, the steering wheel was damaged and the interior was disorderly, which was inconsistent both with Reese's ownership of the vehicle and with his explanation that he borrowed it from a relative. Hurston's suspicious behavior at the convenience store and his attempt to flee also indicated that he knew the vehicle was stolen.

There was also evidence from which the jury could conclude that Hurston possessed, controlled or retained the vehicle. Although Hurston was only a passenger in the vehicle, the inquiry does not end here, for in some circumstances, a passenger may possess, control or retain a vehicle for purposes of OCGA § 1687. Here, there was sufficient evidence that Hurston exerted the requisite control over the vehicle in that Reese left Hurston alone in the car with the vehicle running when he went into the convenience store.

"Questions as to reasonableness are generally to be decided by the jury which heard the evidence and where the jury is authorized to find that the evidence, though circumstantial, was sufficient to exclude every reasonable hypothesis save that of guilt, the appellate court will not disturb that finding, unless the verdict of guilty is unsupportable as a matter of law."

. . . Judgment affirmed.

DISSENT

SOGNIER, C.J.

I respectfully dissent, for I find the evidence was insufficient to establish the essential element of "receiving" beyond a reasonable doubt. "A person commits the offense of theft by receiving stolen property when he receives, disposes of, or retains stolen property which he knows or should know was stolen. . . . 'Receiving' means acquiring possession or control . . . of the property." OCGA § 1687(a). Here, the record is devoid of evidence that appellant exercised or intended to exercise any dominion or control over the car or that he ever acquired possession of it. The "mere presence" of a defendant in the vicinity of stolen goods "furnishes only a bare suspicion" of guilt, and thus is insufficient to establish possession of stolen property. Evidence that a defendant was present as a passenger in a stolen automobile, without more, is insufficient to establish possession or control. *Abner v. State,* 196 Ga.App. 752753, 397 S.E.2d 36 (1990) (conviction for theft by receiving automobile upheld where defendant was in actual possession of car). I disagree with the majority that the circumstantial evidence that appellant, the automobile passenger, was observed to be "slumped" in the seat while Reese parked the car and entered a store was sufficient to constitute the type of "other incriminating circumstances" that would authorize a rejection of the general principle that "the driver of the [stolen] automobile [is] held prima facie in exclusive possession thereof.". . .

Moreover, the evidence also did not meet the standard required for a conviction based on circumstantial evidence—i.e., that the evidence exclude every reasonable hypothesis except the guilt of the accused. The only evidence offered by the State to connect appellant to the stolen car was that he was a passenger in the car several hours after it was stolen. In response, appellant offered his explanation of his activities. "While neither the jury nor this court is required to accept these explanations, in the absence of any other valid explanation, we cannot ignore the only explanation offered. I conclude that there is no circumstantial evidence of guilt on which to base a conviction beyond a reasonable doubt." Accordingly, I would reverse. . . .

QUESTIONS FOR DISCUSSION

1. Identify all of the facts relevant to determining whether Illya Hurston received stolen property.
2. State the elements of receiving stolen property according to the Georgia statute.
3. What reasons does the dissenting judge give for dissenting?
4. Do you agree with the dissent or the majority? Defend your answer.

NOTE CASE

A 1992 Chevrolet Astrovan automobile was stolen from a mobile home park in Spalding County. The van was subsequently utilized in a drive-by shooting on August 28, 1996. Later on the same day, Corporal Bradshaw of the Spalding County Sheriff's Department observed the van and recognized it as being similar to one that was reported stolen, as well as one that was reported as being involved in a drive-by shooting a few hours earlier. Corporal Bradshaw followed the van and could see four to five black males inside; he could not determine who was driving. While Corporal Bradshaw was following the van, the van abruptly turned into a driveway, where two or three men jumped out of the van and ran from the scene. Without the driver, the van, which was left in the "drive" mode, rolled backwards into the patrol car. Then, two young men, one of whom was the appellant, attempted to exit the van through the passenger door but were caught by Corporal Bradshaw before they could flee and were arrested at the scene.

The arresting officer was never able to determine who the driver had been or who had been in control of the stolen vehicle. The car keys were never found. When questioned by an investigator after receiving *Miranda* warnings, C.W. stated that he had only been along for a ride and did not know that the van was stolen. At the hearing, appellant's co-defendant, D.L.S., testified that C.W. had only gone for a ride in the van and did not have control of the vehicle at any time.

The juveniles were charged with theft by receiving stolen property because they had been in the stolen vehicle. They were tried in Spalding County Juvenile Court on October 23, 1996. The juvenile court judge determined that C.W. was delinquent and sentenced him to 90 days in custody. Appellant timely appealed, asserting that the adjudication of delinquency was contrary to the law and to the evidence.

Did C.W. receive the stolen van? No, according to the Georgia Court of Appeals. The court wrote:

> Mere proximity to stolen property is insufficient to establish possession or control. *Williamson v. State,* 134 Ga.App. 329, 331, 214 S.E.2d 415 (1975). In a similar vein, riding in a stolen van or automobile as a passenger does not support a conviction for theft by receiving unless the accused also, at some point, acquires possession of or controls the vehicle, i.e., has " 'the right to exercise power over a corporeal thing,' [cit.]" Therefore, one cannot be convicted of the crime of receiving stolen property absent exercise of control over the stolen goods, or if one is a passenger, intentionally aiding and abetting the commission of the crime.
> . . . No evidence was presented by the state that the appellant ever retained, disposed of, acquired possession of, or controlled the stolen van, nor was any evidence presented of any affirmative act by the appellant that rose to the level of aiding

and abetting the crime. The undisputed evidence indicates that the appellant got into the van while it was driven by an acquaintance, known as "Rat," and that Rat previously had acquired the van from a "Geek Monster," i.e., a crack addict, who apparently traded the van for cocaine. Appellant denied ever driving the van, an assertion supported by his co-defendant, D.L.S. In addition, there was no evidence that appellant ever exercised control over the van, i.e., determined where it would go, who it would transport, etc., or that the appellant otherwise actively aided and abetted the crime. All evidence indicates that appellant was simply along for the ride. While appellant admitted being in the van while another passenger shot at an acquaintance in a drive by shooting, appellant was not charged with being an accessory to that offense. Therefore, lacking evidence that the appellant ever possessed or controlled the van under OCGA § 1687(A) or affirmatively acted as a party to the crime under OCGA § 16220(B), his adjudication of delinquency for the offense of theft by receiving stolen property must be reversed.

Judgment reversed. *In the Interest of C.W., a child,* 485 S.E.2d 561, (Ga.App. 1997)

FORGERY AND UTTERING

The crime of **forgery** includes making false legal documents or altering existing ones—such as checks, deeds, stocks, bonds, and credit cards. Uttering means to pass false documents on to others. Forgery and uttering both misappropriate and destroy property. They harm not only the individuals directly involved but also society in general. Because day-to-day business in modern society relies on legal instruments for its smooth and efficient operation, impairing confidence in the authenticity of those instruments can lead to serious disruption in business, commercial, and financial transactions. It is this general harm, as much as individual losses, that forgery and uttering laws are designed to protect against.

FORGERY

The subject matter of forgery is false writing. Documents subject to forgery make up a long list, because the law defines fraudulent or false writings broadly. Many forgeries, such as forged checks, clearly and directly misappropriate property. These forgeries are obviously property offenses. Other forgeries are not so obviously harms to property. For example, a university might lose more reputation than property from forged diplomas. Injury to reputation and impairment of normal transactions make forgery more than a mere property offense.

California's approach to forgery is found in the California Penal Code, § 470.

> Every person who, with intent to defraud, signs the name of another person, or of a fictitious person, knowing that he has no authority so to do, or falsely makes,

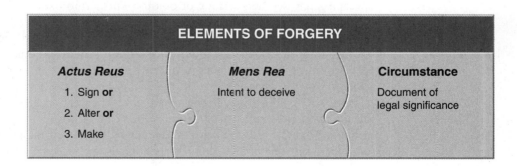

ELEMENTS OF FORGERY		
Actus Reus	**Mens Rea**	**Circumstance**
1. Sign **or**	Intent to deceive	Document of legal significance
2. Alter **or**		
3. Make		

alters, forges, or counterfeits, any charter, letters patent, deed, lease, indenture, writing obligatory, will, testament, codicil, bond, covenant, bank bill or note, post note, check, draft, bill of exchange, contract, promissory note, due bill for the payment of money or property, receipt for money or property, passage ticket, trading stamp, power of attorney, or any certificate of any share, right, or interest in the stock of any corporation or association, or any controller's warrant for the payment of money at the treasury, county order or warrant, or request for the payment of money, or the delivery of goods or chattels of any kind, or for the delivery of any instrument of writing, or acquittance, release, or receipt for money or goods, or any acquittance, release, or discharge of any debt, account, suit, action, demand, or other thing, real or personal, or any transfer or assurance of money, certificates of shares of stock, goods, chattels, or other property whatever, or any letter of attorney, or other power to receive money, or to receive or transfer certificates of shares of stock or annuities, or to let, lease, dispose of, alien, or convey any goods, chattels, lands, or tenements, or other estate, real or personal, or any acceptance or endorsement of any bill of exchange, promissory note, draft, order, or any assignment of any bond, writing obligatory, promissory note, or other contract for money or other property; or counterfeits or forges the seal or handwriting of another; or utters, publishes, passes, or attempts to pass, as true and genuine, any of the above named false, altered, forged, or counterfeited matters, as above specified and described, knowing the same to be false, altered, forged, or counterfeited, with intent to prejudice, damage, or defraud any person; or who, with intent to defraud, alters, corrupts, or falsifies any record of any will, codicil, conveyance, or other instrument, the record of which is by law evidence, or any record of any judgment of a court or the return of any officer to any process of any court, is guilty of forgery.[11]

California's is not the only approach to defining forgery. Other states don't list documents by name; instead, they use phrases such as "any writing," "any writing having legal efficacy or commonly relied on in business or commercial transactions," or "any written instrument to the prejudice of another's right." Either approach, however, indicates the legislatures' intention to cover written documents broadly.

When the *Model Penal Code* drafters wrote a sweeping forgery definition, they aimed the code's forgery provision against three harms: direct property loss, damage to reputation, and impaired business and commercial confidence. Except in grading forgery, the *Model Penal Code* abandons a significant traditional requirement: that a forged document must have legal or evidentiary significance. So, it includes doctors' prescriptions, identification cards, diaries, and letters, not just deeds, wills, contracts, stocks, and bonds. Furthermore, more than documents can be forged. You can forge coins, tokens, paintings, and antiques. According to the Code commentary, "Anything which could be falsified in respect of 'authenticity' can be the subject of forgery."[12]

Defenders of the *Model Penal Code* provision maintain that the serious harms caused by forgery and the difficulty in separating various forms of forgery justify the sweeping phrase, "any writing or object." Furthermore, even critics admit that those who forge checks or fake antiques probably respond more to deterrence and rehabilitation than other criminals do. However, there is no clear evidence that this is so, leaving some critics uneasy about sweeping forgery provisions.

Making a false document or altering an authentic one is the forgery *actus reus*. Contrary to the apparent logic of the *Model Penal Code* provision, most states limit forgery to making false writings that have apparent legal significance. "Making" means making documents or parts of documents from scratch. But it also means altering a basic part of an authentic document. So, if you make out and sign a check on either someone else's account or a nonexistent account, you've forged it because you falsified the whole check. Most existing forgery laws require that either the whole document or some material part be falsified.

Merely presenting false information on an otherwise authentic document is not forgery. So, if I change only the amount on a check made out and signed by the checking account's owner, I haven't committed forgery because the check itself is genuine. Similarly, if a properly authorized payroll clerk alters payrolls by adding hours, it's not forgery because the payroll is still good. Checks drawn on insufficient funds are not forgeries for two reasons. First, they're not false; second, unless the writer of the check doesn't intend to back up the checks with a later deposit, they lack the forgery *mens rea*.

Forgery is a specific intent crime. The forger has to intend to defraud others with a false writing. It's not necessary to intend to defraud specific individuals; a general purpose to fraudulently use the falsified document is good enough. Furthermore, forgery doesn't require the falsifier to intend to obtain *money* fraudulently. Intending to secure any advantage will do. So, a false letter of recommendation intended to gain membership in a desirable professional organization satisfies the forgery *mens rea*.

Once documents are falsified or altered with proper fraudulent intent, forgery is complete. Forgers need not actually gain from their falsifications and fraudulent intent. The reason is that the harm of forgery lies in undermining confidence in the authenticity of documents and the consequent disruption created by such undermined confidence.

UTTERING

Forgery means making false documents in order to defraud, even if the forger never defrauds anyone. **Uttering** means passing or using documents that someone else may have falsified—even if the utterer never altered anything on the documents—with the intent to defraud others. So, forgery and uttering are two distinct offenses. Forgery is directed at making and altering documents in order to defraud. Uttering is directed at passing and using forged documents in order to defraud.

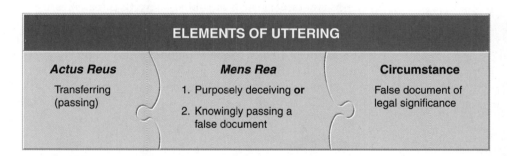

ELEMENTS OF UTTERING

Actus Reus	Mens Rea	Circumstance
Transferring (passing)	1. Purposely deceiving **or** 2. Knowingly passing a false document	False document of legal significance

ROBBERY AND EXTORTION

Robbery and extortion are more than property crimes; they are also crimes against persons, and as such they constitute aggravated property crimes. In fact, they are violent or threatened violent thefts. They are therefore more serious than ordinary thefts and usually carry much heavier penalties.

ROBBERY

Robbery consists of six elements:

1. taking and
2. carrying away
3. the property of others
4. from their person or in their presence
5. by immediate force or threatened immediate force
6. with the intent to permanently dispossess the rightful possessor.

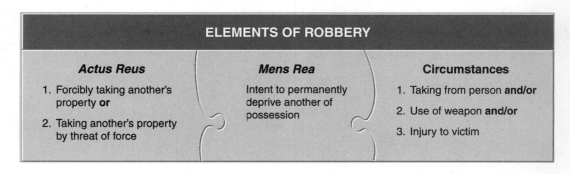

ELEMENTS OF ROBBERY

Actus Reus
1. Forcibly taking another's property **or**
2. Taking another's property by threat of force

Mens Rea
Intent to permanently deprive another of possession

Circumstances
1. Taking from person **and/or**
2. Use of weapon **and/or**
3. Injury to victim

Any force beyond the amount needed to take and carry away someone else's property is enough. Picking a pocket isn't robbery because picking pockets requires only enough force to remove the contents of the pocket. But even slightly mishandling the victim (such as shoving) turns the pickpocket into a robber. Robbery doesn't require actual force; threatened force is enough. Also, robbers don't have to threaten victims themselves; threats to family members will do. However, robbers do have to threaten their victims with death or great bodily injury. Threats to property aren't enough, although there is some authority that threats to homes are.

Most statutes say that robbers have to threaten to use force immediately, not in the future. Furthermore, victims have to give up their property because they honestly and reasonably fear robbers' threats. Critics maintain that honest fear should be enough. Whether robbery requires real, honest, or reasonable fear (or a combination) raises the question of how far criminal law ought to go in punishing potential harm (see Chapter 5). The court in *State v. Curley* dealt with the element of force.

C A S E   **Did He Take Property by Force?**

State v. Curley
1997 WL 242286 (N.M.App. 1997)

Erwin Curley was convicted in the District Court of robbery. He appealed. The Court of Appeals reversed and remanded for new trial.

PICKARD, J.

FACTS

The victim was walking out of a mall with her daughter when Defendant grabbed her purse and ran away. The victim described the incident as follows: "I had my purse on my left side ... and I felt kind of a shove of my left shoulder where I had my purse strap with my thumb through it and I kind of leaned—was pushed—toward my daughter, and this person came and just grabbed the strap of my purse and continued to run." The victim used the words "grab" or "pull" to describe the actual taking of the purse and "shove" or "push" to describe what Defendant did as he grabbed or "pulled [the purse] from her arm and hand." However, there was also evidence that the victim's thumb was not through the strap of the purse, but was rather on the bottom of the purse. The purse strap was not broken, and the victim did not testify that she struggled with Defendant for the purse in any way or that any part of her body offered any resistance or even moved when the purse was pulled from her arm and hand. Defendant presented evidence that he was drunk and did not remember the incident at all.

OPINION

Robbery is theft by the use or threatened use of force or violence. NMSA 1978, § 30162 (Repl. Pamp.1994). Because the words "or violence" refer to the unwarranted exercise of force and do not substantively state an alternative means of committing the offense, we refer simply to "force" in this opinion. The force must be the lever by which the property is taken. Although we have cases saying . . . that even a slight amount of force, such as jostling the victim or snatching away the property, is sufficient, we also have cases in which a taking of property from the person of a victim has been held not to be robbery, see *State v. Sanchez,* 78 N.M. 284, 285, 430 P.2d 781, 782 (Ct.App.1967) (wallet taken from victim's pocket while victim was aware that the defendant was taking the wallet).

A defendant is entitled to a lesser-included-offense instruction when there is some evidence to support it. There must be some view of the evidence pursuant to which the lesser offense is the highest degree of crime committed, and that view must be reasonable. Thus, in this case, to justify giving Defendant's larceny instruction, there must be some view of the evidence pursuant to which force sufficient to constitute a robbery was not the lever by which Defendant removed the victim's purse.

Defendant contends that such evidence exists in that the jury could have found that Defendant's shoving of the victim was part of his drunkenness, and then the purse was taken without force sufficient to constitute robbery. We agree. We are persuaded by an analysis of our own cases, as well as cases from other jurisdictions, that the applicable rule in this case is as follows: when property is attached to the person or clothing of a victim so as to cause resistance, any taking is a robbery, and not larceny, because the lever that causes the victim to part with the property is the force that is applied to break that resistance; however, when no more force is used than would be necessary to remove property from a person who does not resist, then the offense is larceny, and not robbery.

In our cases where we have not found sufficient force to be involved, the victim did not resist the property being taken from his person. See, e.g., *Sanchez,* 78 N.M. at 285, 430 P.2d at 782 (defendant took wallet from victim's pants, but force was not lever by which wallet was taken); see also *State v. Aldershof,* 220 Kan. 798, 556 P.2d 371, 372, 376 (1976) (purse lifted from victim's lap while she sat at a table). On the other hand, the evidence of a snatching of a purse was sufficient to establish robbery in *State v. Clokey,* 89 N.M. 453, 553 P.2d 1260 (1976), but the issue in that case was not whether there was evidence justifying a lesser-included-offense instruction.

The general rule from other jurisdictions is stated in 4 Charles E. Torcia, *Wharton's Criminal Law Section 465,* at 4749 (15th ed. 1996) that a mere snatching of property from a victim is not robbery unless the property is attached to the person or clothes of the owner so as to afford resistance. A minority position is represented by the analysis in *Commonwealth v. Jones,* 362 Mass. 83, 283 N.E.2d 840, 844 (1972). There, the court held that the values sought to be protected by the crime of robbery, as opposed to larceny, are equally present when any property is taken from a person as long as that person is aware of the application of force which relieves the person of property and the taking is therefore, at least to some degree, against the victim's will. See also *Commonwealth v. Ahart,* 37 Mass.App. Ct. 565, 641 N.E.2d 127, 131 (the snatching of a purse necessarily involves the use of force), certs. denied, 419 Mass. 1101, 644 N.E.2d 225 (1994).

The minority rule adopted by Massachusetts, however, appears inconsistent with our earlier cases. Pursuant to the Massachusetts rule, any purse snatching not accomplished by stealth would be robbery. We are not inclined to overrule cases such as *Sanchez,* in which we held that the taking of a wallet accompanied by just so much force as is necessary to accomplish the taking from a person who was not resisting was not robbery. Rather, we adhere to what we perceive to be the majority rule.

According to the majority rule, robbery is committed when attached property is snatched or grabbed by sufficient force so as to overcome the resistance of attachment. In cases such as this one, where one view of the facts appears to put the case on the border between robbery and larceny, it is necessary to further explore what is meant by the concept of "the resistance of attachment." Our exploration is informed by the interests protected by the two crimes.

In *Fuentes,* 119 N.M. at 106, 108, 888 P.2d at 988, 990, we said that robbery is a crime "primarily" directed at protecting property interests. That statement, however, was made in the context of contrasting the crime of robbery with the crime of assault, which is directed exclusively toward protecting persons. In this case, contrasting the crime of robbery with the crime of larceny, we could similarly say that robbery is directed "primarily" at protecting persons inasmuch as larceny is directed exclusively at protecting property interests. In truth, it is probably inaccurate to say that the crime of robbery is directed "primarily" at either personal or property interests. That is because it is directed at both interests. See Torcia, supra, 454 at 5 ("By definition, then, robbery may be classified not only as an offense against property but also as an offense against the person."). It is the aspect of the offense that is directed against the person which distinguishes the crime of robbery from larceny and also justifies an increased punishment. See W. LaFave & A. Scott, Jr., *Substantive Criminal Law* 8.11 at 437 (2d ed. 1986). Thus, "the resistance of attachment" should be construed in light of the idea that robbery is an offense against the person, and something about that offense should reflect the increased danger to the person that robbery involves over the offense of larceny.

LaFave and Scott state:

> The great weight of authority, however, supports the view that there is not sufficient force to constitute robbery when the thief snatches property from the owner's grasp so suddenly that the owner cannot offer any resistance to the taking. On the other hand, when the owner, aware of an impending snatching, resists it, or when, the thief's first attempt being ineffective to separate the owner from his property, a struggle for the property is necessary before the thief can get possession thereof, there is enough force to make the taking robbery. Taking the owner's property by stealthily picking his pocket is not taking by force and so is not robbery; but if the pickpocket or his confederate jostles the owner, or if the owner, catching the pickpocket in the act, struggles unsuccessfully to keep possession, the pickpocket's crime becomes robbery. To remove an article of value, attached to the owner's person or clothing, by a sudden snatching or by stealth is not robbery unless the article in question (e.g., an earring, pin or watch) is so attached to the person or his clothes as to require some force to effect its removal.

Thus, it would be robbery, not larceny, if the resistance afforded is the wearing of a necklace around one's neck that is broken by the force used to remove it and the person to whom the necklace is attached is aware that it is being ripped from her neck. On the other hand, it would be larceny, not robbery, if the resistance afforded is the wearing of a bracelet, attached by a thread, and the person to whom the bracelet is attached is not aware that it is being taken until she realizes that it is gone.

While the difference . . . might appear to be the amount of force necessary to break the necklace or string, respectively, that is not how we distinguish the cases. Subtle differences in the amount of force used, alone, is neither a clear nor reasonable basis to distinguish the crime of robbery from that of larceny. However, if we remember that the reason for the distinction in crimes is the increased danger to the person, then an increase in force that makes the victim aware that her body is resisting could lead to the dangers that the crime of robbery was designed to alleviate. A person who did not know that a bracelet was being taken from her wrist by the breaking of a string would have no occasion to confront the thief, thereby possibly leading to an altercation. A person who knows that a necklace is being ripped from her neck might well confront the thief. As stated in the Florida cases, the law is well settled that snatching a purse or picking a pocket is "not robbery if no more force or violence is used than is necessary to remove the property from a person who does not resist."

We now apply these rules to the facts of this case. Although the facts in this case are simply stated, they are rich with conflicting inferences. Either robbery or larceny may be shown, depending on the jury's view of the facts and which inferences it chooses to draw.

In the light most favorable to the State, Defendant shoved the victim to help himself relieve her of the purse, and the shove and Defendant's other force in grabbing the purse had that effect. This view of the facts establishes robbery, and if the jury believed it, the jury would be bound to find Defendant guilty of robbery.

However, there is another view of the facts. Defendant contends that the evidence that he was drunk allows the jury to infer that the shove was unintentional and that the remaining facts show the mere snatching of the purse, thereby establishing larceny. Two issues are raised by this contention that we must address:

(1) is there a reasonable view of the evidence pursuant to which the shove was not part of the robbery? and (2) even disregarding the shove, does the remaining evidence show only robbery?

We agree with Defendant that the jury could have inferred that the shove was an incidental touching due to Defendant's drunkenness. Defendant's testimony of his drunkenness and the lack of any testimony by the victim or any witness that the shove was necessarily a part of the robbery permitted the jury to draw this inference. Once the jury drew the inference that the shove was independent of the robbery, the jury could have found that Defendant formed the intent to take the victim's purse after incidentally colliding with her. Alternatively, the jury could have found that Defendant intended to snatch the purse without contacting the victim and that the contact (the shove) was not necessary to, or even a part of, the force that separated the victim from her purse. The victim's testimony (that she felt "kind of a shove" and then Defendant grabbed her purse) would allow this inference. Thus, the jury could have found that the shove did not necessarily create a robbery.

The question would then remain, however, whether the grabbing of the purse was still robbery because more force was used than would have been necessary to remove the purse if the victim had not resisted. Under the facts of this case, in which the victim did not testify that she held the strap tightly enough to resist and in which there was some evidence that she was not even holding the strap, we think that there was a legitimate, reasonable view of the evidence that, once the shove is eliminated from consideration, Defendant used only such force as was necessary to remove the purse from a person who was not resisting. Under this view of the facts, Defendant took the purse by surprise from a person who was not resisting, and not by force necessary to overcome any resistance. Therefore, the trial court should have given Defendant's tendered larceny instructions.

. . . Accordingly, Defendant's conviction is reversed and remanded for a new trial.

IT IS SO ORDERED.

QUESTIONS FOR DISCUSSION

1. List all of the facts relevant to determining whether the purse snatching was a robbery.
2. State both the majority and the minority rule regarding the element of force in purse snatching.
3. In your opinion, which is the better rule? Defend your answer. See the note case below.

NOTE CASE

About 7:30 P.M., June 10, 1994, two elderly women, Nancy Colantonio and Vera Croston, returned in Croston's 1981 Chevrolet Citation automobile to their home at 36 Webster Street, Haverhill. Croston, upon entering the driveway, located by the side of the stairs leading to the porch and front door, stopped the car to let Colantonio out. Colantonio walked up the stairs. She felt James Zingari snatch her purse from under her arm. She was stunned. Turning, she saw Zingari running down Webster Street in the direction of Summer Street. She said she couldn't believe what she was seeing.

Was Zangari guilty of purse snatching? Yes, according to the Appeals Court of Massachusetts. According to the court:

Where the snatching or sudden taking of property from a victim is sufficient to produce awareness, there is sufficient evidence of force to permit a finding of robbery. In pickpocketing, which is accomplished by sleight of hand, such evidence is lacking. The difference accounts for the perceived greater severity of the offense of unarmed robbery in contrast with larceny. The [minority rule followed in Massachusetts] . . . was firmly adopted in the face of contrary authority in some States. It seems that a division continues to the present although, as usual, one can anticipate that a classification of jurisdictions may falter somewhat when the decisions are examined in detail. Judgment affirmed.

✳ 12-1 *Commonwealth v. Zangari,* 677 N.E.2d 702 (Mass. App. 1997).

Most states have divided robbery into degrees according to the injury caused and the force or threat used. For example, New York grades robbery into three degrees. Robbers commit first-degree robbery if they carry deadly weapons, seriously injure their victims, threaten the immediate use of dangerous instruments, or display what "appears to be a pistol, revolver, shotgun, machine gun or other firearm." In other words, play weapons will do. Second-degree robbery occurs if robbers rob with accomplices, cause any injury, or display "what appears to be a pistol, revolver, rifle, shotgun, machine gun or firearm." Third-degree robbery is unarmed robbery or "forcible stealing"; that is, it occurs when the actor "uses or threatens the immediate use of force upon another person."[13]

EXTORTION

At common law, **extortion** applied only to public officials who used their influence illegally to collect fees. Most modern extortions were not known to the common law, although unusually extreme threats to get property (such as the threat to accuse another of sodomy in one case) were considered robbery. The *actus reus* of extortion (blackmail), like robbery, is a threat to get someone else's property by doing the person harm. The time of the harm distinguishes blackmail from robbery. Robbery is a threat to hurt someone right now. Extortion is a threat to hurt someone later. The line between extortion and robbery can be fine, making it difficult to separate them in real cases.

Threats to harm victims in three ways satisfy the requirements of extortion:

1. To inflict future bodily harm
2. To damage property
3. To expose victims to shame or ridicule

The *mens rea* of extortion is the specific intent to obtain property by threat. Some statutes require the circumstance element that blackmailers get the desired property. Others say it's enough to make threats with a present intention to carry them out.

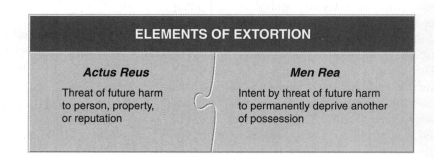

ELEMENTS OF EXTORTION	
Actus Reus	*Men Rea*
Threat of future harm to person, property, or reputation	Intent by threat of future harm to permanently deprive another of possession

According to these statutes, extortionists have to actually put their victims in fear that the extortionist will carry out the threat. The Texas Court of Criminal Appeals applied the elements of extortion to sexual harassment in *Sanchez v. State*.

C A S E	Did He Commit Sexual Extortion?

Sanchez v. State
995 S.W.2d 677 (Texas 1999)

Arthur Garcia Sanchez, Chairman of the San Antonio metropolitan transit board was convicted in the 144th Judicial District Court, Bexar County, of official oppression based on sexual harassment, and he appealed. The San Antonio Court of Appeals reversed, finding the sexual harassment provision unconstitutional. On discretionary review, the Court of Criminal Appeals reversed and remanded.

KELLER, J.

FACTS

The complainant Gonzalez was hired by the Board of Trustees of the VIA Metropolitan Transit in San Antonio as an assistant to the Board in securing federal grant money. She was placed in the Public Affairs Division of VIA, with instructions to report to appellant, the Board Chairman. Appellant, during the period of time in which the events resulting in the charge against him took place, was chairman of the Board of VIA, the public transportation system for the City of San Antonio. Complainant was employed by the Board as an assistant for governmental affairs. As such, complainant reported to appellant as her de facto supervisor.

At trial, the complainant testified appellant began making sexual advances toward her. These advances began in June of 1994. During August of 1994, according to the complainant, appellant's behavior escalated into requests for sex (complainant was married at the time, a fact known to appellant), or an affair, and threats that should she not comply she could lose her job. She declined his advances. Appellant told her he had had an affair with her predecessor and she had to do likewise. The complainant testified appellant repeated his demand that they have an affair during a business trip to Washington, D.C. in September of 1994. When she declined his advances again, complainant testi-

fied appellant gave another employee of VIA the larger office that had been promised to her by appellant.

During October of 1994, complainant testified, she spoke to a coworker, Zamora, about the situation and thereafter appellant's sexual advances stopped for awhile. She also spoke with VIA's in-house EEOC person, who, she testified, was not helpful and told her, in effect, appellant was very powerful. Complainant subsequently testified appellant's advances became more frequent and more intense in December of 1994. On several occasions he told her she would be fired if she refused to have sex with him, and he would touch her on various parts of her body. He also belittled her marital status, talked about her legs, and, on one occasion, said a bruise on her leg was a result of rough sex. Complainant testified she continually told him to leave her alone; his response was, essentially, he was the chairman, had lots of power, and could do whatever he wanted.

During January of 1995, complainant told Zamora about appellant's latest advances; Zamora told complainant she should get appellant's advances on tape but, other than that, given appellant's power, there was not much she could do about it. Other testimony established complainant never received a promised raise, secretarial support or more office space.

During February of 1995, complainant filed complaints with the EEOC. On March 10, 1995, complainant gave a written statement to a San Antonio Police detective concerning this matter, describing the events that gave rise to the charge filed against appellant.

OPINION

The "sexual harassment" portion of the official oppression statute provides: "A public servant acting under color of his office or employment commits an offense if he . . . intentionally subjects another to sexual harassment." A public servant acts under color of his office or employment "if he acts or purports to act in an official capacity or takes advantage of such actual or purported capacity." § 39.03(b). "Sexual harassment" is specifically defined as meaning:

> unwelcome sexual advances, requests for sexual favors, or other verbal or physical conduct of a sexual nature, submission to which is made a term or condition of a person's exercise or enjoyment of any right, privilege, power, or immunity, either explicitly or implicitly. § 39.03(c).

In proposing the sexual harassment provision, the sponsor and supporters related an incident in which a municipal judge purportedly offered to dismiss a woman's traffic tickets in return for sexual favors. The woman went to the judge's office to arrange a payment schedule because she did not have enough money to pay the full amount all at once. The judge offered to take the woman in his truck for a ride and "see what they could work out." After consulting law enforcement authorities, the woman went to the judge's office again, this time wearing a hidden microphone. The judge told the woman he would take care of her ticket in exchange for oral sex. The woman asked if there was anything else she could do, such as maintenance work around the courthouse, but the judge said, "No, I have something else in mind for you." The hearings indicated that the municipal judge was originally prosecuted for official oppression, but that indictment was quashed, and the judge pled guilty to a lesser offense. One of the supporters of the bill contended that a public official should be held to a higher standard of care and subject to higher sanctions than someone "on the street.". . . [The Court of Appeals, among other things, held that the statute violated the free speech clause of the First Amendment.] . . .

Where First Amendment freedoms are implicated, the law must be sufficiently definite to avoid chilling protected expression. The question in the present case is whether the sexual harassment provision reaches protected expression. . . . The offense proscribed is in many ways similar to bribery or extortion. Under the common law, extortion by public officials was essentially a form of bribery: the official took money that was not due him for the performance of official duties. Congress incorporated this common law definition into its Hobbs Act statute. Congress also provided for an offense of extortion involving private individuals in which property is taken by means of force, fear, or threats.

Bribery and extortion, while involving "speech," are not protected by the First Amendment. "Threats and bribes are not protected simply because they are written or spoken; extortion is a crime although it is verbal." "It may categorically be stated that extortionate speech has no more constitutional protection than that uttered by a robber while ordering his victim to hand over the money, which is no protection at all."

As with official extortion—what we would now call bribery—the sexual harassment provision is concerned with the use of official power to obtain a benefit to which the official was not otherwise entitled. In a bribery/official extortion case, that benefit was traditionally money or tangible property, but the receipt of someone's submission to sexual conduct seems to be as legitimate an object of government regulation. The First Amendment does not give an official the right to trade official services for sexual favors or for submission to conduct of a sexual nature.

Further, the sexual harassment statute goes beyond mere bribery due to the requirement that the conduct be "unwelcome." With that requirement, the sexual harassment provision encompasses coercive conduct—analogous to private extortion. Sexual harassment under the statute is essentially sexual extortion: an official uses his official position to coerce submission to conduct of a sexual nature. And the statute criminalizes sexual harassment that is intentional. To be liable, the official must intend the sexual nature of his conduct, he must be aware that the conduct is unwelcome, and he must intend submission to the conduct to be made a term or condition of enjoying something of value to the recipient or another person—something of value that the official is in a position to withhold or provide. In other words, the official must intend to carry out sexual extortion. The First Amendment is not implicated by such activity.

The judgment of the Court of Appeals is reversed, and the case is remanded for proceedings consistent with this opinion.

CONCURRING OPINION

MANSFIELD, J., delivered a concurring opinion.

Texas Penal Code § 6.02 states that a person does not commit an offense unless he intentionally, knowingly, recklessly, or with criminal negligence engages in conduct delineated in the definition of the offense. The only way that a definition of an offense may dispense with the requirement of a culpable mental state is if that definition plainly dispenses with any mental element. Tex. Penal Code, § 6.02(b). Section 39.03(a)(3) clearly describes the mental state necessary for an individual to commit the offense of official oppression by sexual harassment: the actor must intentionally subject another to "sexual harassment." Furthermore, "sexual harassment" is carefully and specifically defined in § 39.03(c) as "unwelcome sexual advances. . . ."

Appellant's conduct in the present case was blatantly intentional: testimony established he continually made advances toward the complainant despite her repeated pleas for him to stop. Such behavior is commonly referred to as *"quid pro quo"* sexual harassment, i.e., the harasser tells the harassee that failure to submit will result in adverse employment-related consequences for the harassee. Complainant sustained adverse job-related consequences due to her refusal to submit, namely, the loss of a raise, a bigger office and secretarial assistance. She also was threatened with the loss of her job itself. There is little doubt that such *quid pro quo* sexual harassment suffered by complainant might well give rise to redress under civil law. Section 39.03 criminalizes only *quid pro quo* sexual harassment that is "intentional." The other major category of sexual harassment is so-called "hostile work environment" sexual harassment. Examples of hostile work environment sexual harassment might include leaving sexually-suggestive materials around the workplace, making comments on fellow employees' appearance and/or dress, etc. It does not involve any threats of loss of employment or other rights or privileges. . . .

Testimony at trial established the required culpable mental state: appellant intentionally persisted in making unwelcome sexual advances despite complainant's requests that he cease doing so. Testimony at trial also established appellant told complainant that failure to comply with his demands would result in loss of her job (she did lose a promised raise and other job-related benefits), which meets the requirement of § 39.03(c) that the sexual harassment involve a threat to a valuable right or privilege of the victim (such as a job) should she not submit.

Certainly, § 39.03(c) does not criminalize protected speech, such as asking a coworker out for a date, making a comment about someone's dress or even what might amount to hostile work environment sexual harassment. In effect, all § 39.03(c) does is criminalize what is intentional sexual harassment coupled with extortion: either do what I want or else something bad will happen to you. It is difficult to see how this statute is either vague or runs afoul of the First Amendment, given how narrowly-drafted it really is.

QUESTIONS FOR DISCUSSION

1. State the elements of the crime of official oppression.

2. Do you agree that these elements amount to sexual extortion? Do they compare to the elements of extortion discussed in the text?

3. List all of the facts relevant to deciding whether Arthur Sanchez committed sexual extortion.

4. Was Arthur Sanchez guilty of sexual extortion? Back up your answer with facts from the case.

5. Explain why the court concluded that the statute didn't violate the First Amendment. Do you agree? Explain your answer.

SUMMARY

The crime of taking someone else's property began with the ancient common-law felony of larceny. Larceny meant sneaking away with or stealing other people's property. At first, larceny applied only to stealing livestock. Then, as society advanced, it was extended to all kinds of personal property. Out of larceny grew several other crimes, created to keep pace with new ways to take other people's property created by opportunities in an increasingly complex society. Embezzlement made it a crime to wrongfully convert property entrusted to caretakers. False pretenses made it a crime to get other people's property by tricks and lies. Receiving stolen property made it a crime to get other people's property even if you weren't the original thief. Forgery and uttering made it a crime to create, alter, and pass false documents. Robbery made it a felony to take other people's property by force or threats of *immediate* force. Extortion extended the felony to getting other people's property by threats of *future* harm.

Since the 1970s, consolidated theft statutes have rationalized the crimes of misappropriating other people's property. They join together what used to be larceny, embezzlement, and false pretenses into a new offense called theft. They are based on the idea that taking, converting, using tricks and lies to get other people's property all amount to the same evil.

Although larceny, embezzlement, false pretenses, and receiving stolen property protect property almost exclusively, forgery, uttering, extortion, and robbery protect other interests as well. Forgery and uttering protect society in general from the disruptive effects created by impairing confidence in the authenticity of documents. They protect not only property but also society's interest in smoothly operating business in modern, complex society. Robbery and extortion are crimes against persons as well as property, because they involve violence or threatened violence. Sometimes called aggravated larceny, their laws punish violent property misappropriations. By punishing when victims suffer fear but sustain no property loss, they demonstrate a wider application than for misappropriated property offenses.

The rise of computers and the rapid growth of the Internet have created highly complex and vastly expanded opportunities to commit property and other crimes as well. Some states tried to shoehorn these new harms into existing property crime statutes. But it hasn't worked well. So, almost all states have passed special computer crime statutes to respond not only to taking intellectual property but also to damaging it or even "accessing" it.

  Go to the Criminal Law 7e CD-ROM for Internet exercises.

REVIEW QUESTIONS

1. Briefly describe the origins and development of the crimes against property.

2. Distinguish between and explain why there were (and still are in some states) separate property crimes of larceny, embezzlement, and false pretenses.

3. Identify and explain the elements in larceny, embezzlement, and false pretenses.

4. Explain the content of and rationale for consolidated theft statutes.

5. Explain the response of criminal law to the rise of computers and the Internet.

6. Identify and explain the elements in the crime of receiving stolen property.

7. Is receiving stolen property more serious than, as serious as, or less serious than theft? Explain your answer.

8. Identify and explain the elements in forgery and uttering.

9. Identify and explain the elements of robbery. How is robbery different from the other property crimes?

10. Identify and explain the elements of extortion. How is extortion different from and similar to robbery?

KEY TERMS

asportation—the carrying away of another's property.

bailee—a temporary possessor who had control over others' property (a term operative when English Parliament created embezzlement).

claim of right—the belief that property taken rightfully belongs to the taker.

consolidated theft statutes—statutes consolidating larceny, embezzlement, and false pretenses into one offense called theft, accepting the social reality that they are all aimed at the same criminal offense—wrongfully getting someone else's property.

conversion—illegal use of another's property.

embezzlement—crime of lawfully gaining possession of someone else's property and later converting it to one's own use.

extortion—misappropriation of another's property by means of threat to inflict bodily harm in the future.

false pretenses—in modern law often called theft by deceit.

fences—those who sell stolen merchandise for profit.

forgery—making false writings or materially altering authentic writings.

intellectual property—information and services stored in and transmitted to and from electronic data banks; a rapidly developing area of property crimes.

misappropriation—gaining possession of another's property.

receiving stolen property—benefiting from someone else's property without having participated in the wrongful acquisition in the first place.

robbery—taking and carrying away another's property by force or threat of force with the intent to permanently deprive the owner of possession.

theft—consolidated crimes of larceny, embezzlement, and false pretenses.

uttering—knowing or conscious use or transfer of false documents.

SUGGESTED READINGS

1. Jerome Hall, *Theft, Law, and Society,* 2d ed. (Indianapolis, Ind.: Bobbs-Merrill, 1952). An excellent demonstration of the relationship between law and society in historical development. Hall convincingly shows that larceny and other misappropriation crimes grew out of English social history. This is an interesting and authoritative work written for the general reader as well as the specialist.

2. Rollin M. Perkins and Ronald N. Boyce, *Criminal Law,* 3d ed. (Mineola, N.Y.: Foundation Press, 1982), chap. 4. Surveys in detail all the property crimes, analyzes their development, discusses new developments, and presents arguments concerning most reforms.

3. Wayne R. LaFave and Austin W. Scott, Jr., *Handbook on Criminal Law,* 2d ed. (St. Paul, Minn.: West Publishing Co., 1986). This book has a useful chapter on property crimes.

4. American Law Institute, *Model Penal Code and Commentaries,* vol. 2 (Philadelphia: American Law Institute, 1980), pt. II. Deals with property crimes. This is the most comprehensive treatment of the history and content of property crimes. The commentary treats extensively its recommended consolidated theft provision, compares that provision with the consolidated theft statutes of various states, and discusses the influence of the *Model Penal Code* provision on those statutes.

NOTES

1. Rollin M. Perkins and Ronald N. Boyce, *Criminal Law,* 3d ed. (Mineola, N.Y.: Foundation Press, 1982), chap. 4; Wayne R. LaFave and Austin W. Scott, Jr., *Handbook on Criminal Law,* 2d ed. (St. Paul, Minn.: West Publishing Co., 1986), chap. 8.

2. Perkins and Boyce, *Criminal Law,* p. 289; Jerome Hall, *Theft, Law, and Society,* 2d ed. (Indianapolis, Ind.: Bobbs-Merrill, 1952).

3. V.T.C.A., Penal Code §§ 31.01, 31.02, 31.03. 7th ed. (St. Paul, Minn.: West Publishing Co., 1988).

4. I am grateful to David J. Cooper, Jr., Director of Research, South Carolina Legislative Council, for the reference to the South Carolina law, § 16-13-30, Code of Laws of South Carolina, 1976, as amended.

5. American Law Institute, *Model Penal Code and Commentaries,* vol. 2 (Philadelphia: American Law Institute, 1980), pt. II, p. 151.

6. Ibid., p. 175-176.

7. *Model Penal Code,* Arts. 223.0 to 223.9.

8. Quoted in *People v. Shirley,* 78 Cal.App.3d 424, 144 *Cal.Rptr.* 282, 289 (1978).

9. Ibid.

10. Quoted in Carl Benson, Andrew J. Jablon, Paul J. Kaplan, and Mara Elena Rosenthal, "Computer Crimes," *American Criminal Law Review,* 34 (1997):409, 431, n. 147.

11. West's Ann.Cal. Penal Code (1970), enacted 1872, amended by Stats. 1905, c. 515, 673, 1; Stats. 1968, c. 713, 1414, 1.

12. American Law Institute, *Model Penal Code,* tentative draft no. 11 (Philadelphia: American Law Institute, 1960).

13. New York Penal Code, §§ 160.00-160.15.

Crimes Against Public Order and Morals

Chapter Outline

I. Introduction

II. Street People

III. Street Gangs

IV. Summary

CHAPTER MAIN POINTS

1. Balancing the community interest in order and the individual interest in liberty is a fundamental requirement of our constitutional system.

2. Ancient public order and morals offenses are altered to suit the social reality of life at the start of the twenty-first century.

3. Quality of life crimes are intended to enforce minimum standards of decent behavior in public.

4. Controversy over the quality of life crimes stems from the belief that they are used to keep "undesirables" from bothering "respectable" people, and that they violate the right of free expression, the right of peaceable assembly, the right against cruel and unusual punishment, and the right not to be deprived of liberty without due process of law.

5. The "broken windows" theory posits that behavior that threatens the quality of life can lead not only to increased disorder but also to more serious crime.

6. National attention focuses on the serious crimes, while local attention centers on the quality of life crimes.

7. Both the criminal law and the civil action of injunction to abate public nuisances are used to regulate behavior in public.

8. A number of state and municipal governments have enacted laws making gang-related behavior criminal.

9. For centuries, the ancient vagrancy and loitering laws have made the status of being poor a crime.

10. Modern laws affecting poor people are aimed at specific behavior, such as sleeping in public.

11. The regulation of panhandling represents another effort to improve the quality of life in cities by means of regulating begging in public.

12. Blanket prohibitions on panhandling probably are not constitutional; prohibitions against aggressive panhandling probably are constitutional.

Are They "Quality of Life" Criminals?

Rocksprings is an urban war zone. The four-square-block neighborhood, claimed as the turf of a gang variously known as Varrio Sureno Town, Varrio Sureno Treces (VST), or Varrio Sureno Locos (VSL), is an occupied territory. Gang members, all of whom live elsewhere, congregate on lawns, on sidewalks, and in front of apartment complexes at all hours of the day and night. They display a casual contempt for notions of law, order, and decency—openly drinking, smoking dope, sniffing toluene, and even snorting cocaine laid out in neat lines on the hoods of residents' cars. The people who live in Rocksprings are subjected to loud talk, loud music, vulgarity, profanity, brutality, fistfights, and the sound of gunfire echoing in the streets. Gang members take over sidewalks, driveways, carports, and apartment parking areas, and impede traffic on the public thoroughfares to conduct their drive-up drug bazaar. Murder, attempted murder, drive-by shootings, assault and battery, vandalism, arson, and theft are commonplace.

The community has become a staging area for gang-related violence and a dumping ground for the weapons and instrumentalities of crime once the deed is done. Area residents have had their garages used as urinals; their homes commandeered as escape routes; their walls, fences, garage doors, sidewalks, and even their vehicles turned into a sullen canvas of gang graffiti. The people of this community are prisoners in their own homes. Violence and the threat of violence are constant. Residents remain indoors, especially at night. They do not allow their children to play outside. Strangers wearing the wrong color clothing are at risk. Relatives and friends refuse to visit. The laundry rooms, the trash dumpsters, the residents' vehicles, and their parking spaces are used to deal and stash drugs. Verbal harassment, physical intimidation, threats of retaliation, and retaliation are the likely fate of anyone who complains of the gang's illegal activities or tells police where drugs may be hidden.

INTRODUCTION

Both order and liberty are essential values in a constitutional democracy. But they are values in conflict. So, they create a natural tension. The United States Supreme Court has recognized the need to balance these two values by repeatedly holding that "ordered liberty" is a fundamental requirement of our constitutional system. In this chapter, **order** refers to behavior in public that complies with minimum community standards of good manners. **Liberty** refers to the right of individuals to come and go as they please without government interference. Specifically, we examine laws limiting behavior in public places like sidewalks, streets, and parks. Significant numbers of people across the spectrum of age, sex, race, ethnicity, and class believe that bad manners in public places create disorder and threaten the quality of life of ordinary people. Others believe that making bad manners a crime violates individual liberty.

Called crimes against public order and morals during most of our history, these breaches of minimum standards of decent behavior in public, are now usually referred to as **quality of life crimes**. Despite their ancient roots, crimes against public order and morals didn't cause much controversy until the Great Depression of the 1930s. The list of public order and morals offenses is long, and embraces a wide range of behavior. Among other offenses, it includes public drinking and drunkenness; begging and aggressive panhandlng; threatening behavior and harassment; blocking streets and public places; graffiti and vandalism; street prostitution; public urination and defecation; unlicensed vending; and even "squeegeeing"—washing the windshields of stopped cars and demanding money for the "service."

In the 1980s, two prominent scholars sensed a deep public yearning for what they called a lost sense of decency and order, particularly in our largest cities. Professors James Q. Wilson and George L. Kelling suggested that what were labeled "petty crimes" were not only upsetting law-abiding people but could also trigger rises in serious crime. They called this connection between disorderly conduct and serious crime the **broken windows theory**. According to Kelling, research conducted since the article was written in 1982 has demonstrated "a direct link between disorder and crime . . ." Wilson described the broken windows theory in 1996 more cautiously. In the foreword to a book written by Kelling and Catherine M. Coles, entitled *Fixing Broken Windows,* Wilson wrote:

> We used the image of broken windows to explain how neighborhoods might decay into disorder and even crime if no one attends faithfully to their maintenance. If a factory or office window is broken, passersby observing it will conclude that no one cares or no one is in charge. In time, a few will begin throwing rocks to break more windows. Soon all the windows will be broken, and now passersby will think that, not only is no one in charge of the building no one is in charge of the street on which it faces. Only the young, the criminal, or the foolhardy have any business on an unprotected avenue, and so more and more citizens will abandon the street to those they assume prowl it. Small disorders lead to larger and larger ones, and perhaps even to crime.[1]

Professor Wesley G. Skogan, the author of some of the research on which Kelling relies, has also characterized his and others' research more cautiously than Kelling:

> Our concern with common crime is limited to whether disorder is a cause of it. . . .
> Neighborhood levels of disorder are closely related to crime rates, to fear of crime, and the belief that serious crime is a neighborhood problem. *This relationship could reflect the fact that the link between crime and disorder is a causal one, or that both are dependent on some third set of factors (such as poverty or neighborhood instability).* [italics added][2]

Despite the caution Skogan maintained that the data

> support the proposition that disorder needs to be taken seriously in research on neighborhood crime, and that both directly and through crime, it plays an important role in neighborhood decline.[3]

Most of the national debate over crime, criminal law books (this one included), and criminal justice courses concentrate on the serious crimes analyzed in Chapters 9 through 12. But there is a disconnect between the national debate, criminal law books, and criminal justice courses on one side and local concern on the other. Of course mayors and the residents of local communities worry about murder, rape, burglary, and theft. But they also care a lot about order on their streets, in their parks, and in other public places. In a careful and extensive survey of a representative sample of high and low crime neighborhoods in major cities, public drinking, followed closely by loitering youths, top the list of worries among all classes, races, and ethnic groups, men and women. Survey participants also listed begging, street harassment, noisy neighbors, vandalism, street prostitution, and illegal vending.[4]

Any examination of criminal law has to recognize quality of life crimes as part of the social reality of life at the beginning of the twenty-first century. Beginning in the 1980s, state statutes and city ordinances have reinvigorated and molded the old crimes against public order and morals to fit the public demand that criminal justice preserve, protect, and even restore the quality of life in their communities. The courts have assumed the burden of balancing the social interest in public order and decency against the social interest in individual liberty and privacy. This chapter examines how states and localities have shaped traditional public order and morals laws to control the public behavior of two groups—"street people" and street gangs.[5]

STREET PEOPLE

For at least 600 years, vagrancy and loitering statutes have made crimes out of the idleness of poor people who are either standing around with no apparent purpose or roaming around without visible means of support. The Articles of Confederation specifically denied paupers rights that other citizens enjoyed—the right to travel from state to state and the right to the equal protection of the laws. In 1837, the United States Supreme Court approved the efforts by the state of New York to exclude paupers arriving by ship. The Court noted that it is

> as necessary for a state to provide precautionary measures against the moral pestilence of paupers, vagabonds, and possibly convicts as it is to guard against the physical pestilence, which may arise from unsound and infectious articles.

Every state in the union had and enforced vagrancy and loitering statutes that wrote these views into law.[6]

These laws against poor people and the attitudes behind them began to change during the Great Depression of the 1930s. In 1941, the United States Supreme Court struck down a statute that prohibited the importation of paupers into California. In response to the argument that the regulation of paupers enjoyed a long history, the Court dismissed the earlier decisions as out of date. According to the Court, "We do not think that it will now be seriously contended that because a person is without employment and without funds he constitutes a 'moral pestilence.'" In a concurring opinion, Justice Robert Jackson encouraged the Court to

> say now, in no uncertain terms, that a mere property status, without more, cannot be used by a state to test, qualify, or limit his rights as a citizen of the United States.[7]

During the 1960s and 1970s, courts began to strike down vagrancy laws because they unfairly discriminated against the poor. The following excerpt from an opinion written by Chief Justice Thompson of the Nevada Supreme Court reflects this trend.

It is simply not a crime to be unemployed, without funds, and in a public place. To punish the unfortunate for this circumstance debases society. The comment of [U.S. Associate Supreme Court] Justice Douglas is relevant: "How can we hold our heads high and still confuse with crime the need for welfare or the need for work?"[8]

Finally, in 1972, in *Papichristou v. City of Jacksonville,* the United States Supreme Court struck down the Jacksonville, Florida, vagrancy ordinance, an ordinance nearly identical to virtually every other vagrancy law in the country. Writing for an unanimous Court, Justice Douglas wrote that the ordinance was void for vagueness because it both failed to give adequate notice to individuals and it encouraged arbitrary law enforcement. The Court warned that criminal statutes aimed at the poor

teach that the scales of justice are so tipped that even-handed administration of the law is not possible. The rule of law, evenly applied to minorities as well as majorities, to the poor as well as the rich, is the great mucilage that holds society together.[9]

LOITERING

In the important 1983 decision, *Kolender v. Lawson,* the United States Supreme Court tightened the constitutional restrictions on loitering statutes. The counterpart to vagrancy, which means to roam about with no visible means of support, **loitering** means to "remain in one place with no apparent purpose." In *Kolender,* the Court struck down a California statute that combined ancient vagrancy and loitering into a new crime: wandering the streets and failing to produce credible identification when a police officer asked for it. As it did in *Papichristou,* the Court ruled that the statute was void for vagueness.[10]

According to Harry Simon, staff attorney, Legal Aid Society, Orange County, Santa Ana,

With the Supreme Court's decisions in *Papichristou* and *Kolender,* loitering and vagrancy laws ceased to be effective tools to punish and control the displaced poor. While judicial attitudes on vagrancy and loitering laws had changed, local officials perceived the invalidation of these laws as a dangerous assault on their authority to enforce social order.[11]

According to Robert C. Ellickson, Professor of Property and Urban Law at the Yale Law School:

Many judges at the time seemed blind to the fact that their constitutional rulings might adversely affect the quality of urban life and the viability of city centers. It is one thing to protect unpopular persons from wrongful confinement; it is another to imply that these persons have no duty to behave themselves in public places. In addition, federal constitutional rulings are one of the most centralized and inflexible forms of lawmaking. In a diverse and dynamic nation committed to separation of powers and federalism, there is much to be said for giving state and local legislative bodies substantial leeway to tailor street codes to city conditions, and for giving state judges ample scope to interpret the relevant provisions of state constitutions.[12]

At the same time these decisions eased control over the behavior of poor people in public, other events were creating a spiraling—and to many a frightening—underclass. Mental institutions were in the midst of major deinstitutionalization of the mentally ill; family breakdowns and breakups were steeply increasing; crack cocaine was readily available on the streets; hard economic times were upon us; and budgets for social programs were tightening. By the late 1980s, this rising underclass and its public presence and behavior led many city dwellers to conclude that "things had gone too far." The liberal columnist Ellen Goodman, in a piece entitled "Swarms of Beggars Cause 'Compassion Fatigue,'" captured this "things have gone too far" attitude when she wrote, "Today at least, this tourist, walking from one block to another, one cup to another, one city to another wants to join in a citizens' chorus: 'Enough's enough.'" Municipal codes reflected this growing intolerance of the behavior of street people. By the late 1990s, Juliette Smith, found that "at least thirty-nine American cities had initiated or continued policies that criminalize activities associated with homelessness."[13]

Enforcing the laws regulating the behavior of homeless and other "street people" generates controversy because these laws seem to target the poorest and weakest members of the community in order to provide for the comfort and convenience of better-off residents. But James Q. Wilson defends laws that target the misbehavior of street people. He notes that the special competence of courts lies in defining and applying rights. Courts typically hear the cases of "an individual beggar, sleeper, or solicitor." Such an individual rarely poses a threat to anyone, "and so the claims of communal order often seem, in the particular case, to be suspect or overdrawn."

> But the effects on a community of many such individuals taking advantage of the rights granted to an individual (or often, as the court sees it, an abstract depersonalized individual) are qualitatively different from the effects of a single person. A public space—a bus stop, a market square, a subway entrance—is more than the sum of its parts; it is a complex pattern of interactions that can become dramatically more threatening as the scale and frequency of those interactions increase. As the number of unconventional individuals increases arithmetically, the number of worrisome behaviors increases geometrically.[14]

San Francisco was one of many cities whose officials enforced the "quality of life" laws against the public misbehavior of street people. But it is also a city where a few individuals turned to the courts to fight for the individual rights of homeless people. In *Joyce v. City of San Francisco,* Federal District Judge Lowell Jensen heard a motion to grant a preliminary injunction to stop the city of San Francisco from continuing its Matrix Program, which was designed to preserve the quality of life on San Francisco streets and other public places. A **preliminary injunction** is "not a decision on the merits of the plaintiff's suit. It is merely a decision that the suit has enough merit—which need not be great merit—to justify an order that will freeze the situation, in the plaintiff's favor, for such time as it may take to determine whether the suit is, or is not, meritorious."[15]

C A S E   Did the Program Violate the Rights of Homeless People?

Joyce v. City and County of San Francisco
846 F.Supp. 843 (N.D. Cal 1994)

Bobby Joe Joyce, Timothy E. Smith, Thomas O'Halloran, and Jim Tullah, homeless persons, brought an action against the city seeking a preliminary injunction against the Matrix Program which targeted violation of certain ordinances and thus allegedly penalized homeless persons for engaging in life sustaining activities. U.S. District

Judge LOWELL JENSEN denied the plaintiffs' motion for a preliminary injunction.
JENSEN, J.

FACTS

Plaintiffs to this action seek preliminary injunctive relief on behalf of themselves and a class of homeless individuals alleged to be adversely affected by the City and County of San Francisco's (the "City's") "Matrix Program." While encompassing a wide range of services to the City's homeless, the Program simultaneously contemplates a rigorous law enforcement component aimed at those violations of state and municipal law which arguably are committed predominantly by the homeless. Plaintiffs endorse much of the Program, challenging it not in its entirety, but only insofar as it specifically penalizes certain "life sustaining activities" engaged in by the homeless.

Institution of the Matrix Program followed the issuance of a report in April of 1992 by the San Francisco Mayor's Office of Economic Planning and Development, which attributed to homelessness a $173 million drain on sales in the City. In August of 1993, the City announced commencement of the Matrix Program, and the San Francisco Police Department began stringently enforcing a number of criminal laws.

The City describes the Program as "initiated to address citizen complaints about a broad range of offenses occurring on the streets and in parks and neighborhoods. . . . [The Matrix Program is] a directed effort to end street crimes of all kinds." The program addresses offenses including public drinking and inebriation, obstruction of sidewalks, lodging, camping or sleeping in public parks, littering, public urination and defecation, aggressive panhandling, dumping of refuse, graffiti, vandalism, street prostitution, and street sales of narcotics, among others.

An illustration of the enforcement efforts characteristic of the Program can be found in a four-page intradepartmental memorandum addressed to the Police Department's Southern Station Personnel. That memorandum, dated August 10, 1993 and signed by acting Police Captain Barry Johnson, defines "Quality of Life" violations and establishes a concomitant enforcement policy. Condemning a "type of behavior [which] tends to make San Francisco a less desirable place in which to live, work or visit," the memorandum directs the vigorous enforcement of eighteen specified code sections, including prohibitions against trespassing, public inebriation, urinating or defecating in public, removal and possession of shopping carts, solicitation on or near a highway, erection of tents or structures in parks, obstruction and aggressive panhandling.

Pursuant to the memorandum,

All station personnel shall, when not otherwise engaged, pay special attention and enforce observed "Quality of Life" violations. . . . One Officer . . . shall, daily, be assigned specifically to enforce all "Quality of Life" violations. . . .

Officers are to stop and advise all individuals pushing shopping carts that said carts are the property of local stores (Grocery/Drug etc.) and that these carts are never sold: Therefore the carts will, in the near future, be confiscated for return to their rightful owner or otherwise disposed of by the police. . . . Note: This phase of the "Quality of Life" operation will be implemented when appropriate containers, for the contents of the shopping carts, are available. . . .

In a Police Department Bulletin entitled "Update on Matrix Quality of Life Program," dated September 17, 1993, Deputy Chief Thomas Petrini paraphrased General Order D6, the source of the intended nondiscriminatory policy of the Program's enforcement measures:

All persons have the right to use the public streets and places so long as they are not engaged in specific criminal activity. Factors such as race, sex, sexual preference, age, dress, unusual or disheveled or impoverished appearance do not alone justify enforcement action. Nor can generalized complaints by residents or merchants or others justify detention of any person absent such individualized suspicion.

The memorandum stated that the "rights of the homeless must be preserved," and included as an attachment a Department Bulletin on "Rights of the Homeless," which stated that:

[All members of the Department] are obligated to treat all persons equally, regardless of their economic or living conditions. The homeless enjoy the same legal and individual rights afforded to others. Members shall at all times respect these rights. . . .

The Police Department has, during the pendency of the Matrix Program, conducted continuing education for officers regarding nondiscriminatory enforcement of the Program. When, in mid-August of 1993, concerns were raised by interests outside the Department about proper enforcement of the ordinances prohibiting lodging and sleeping in public parks, the Department issued a clarification of its policies. Again, in mid-November of 1993, inquiries were made of the Police Department concerning the confiscation of grocery store shopping carts. Police Chief Anthony Ribera responded with the issuance of a Department Bulletin establishing topical guidelines.

Since implementation of the Matrix Program, the City estimates that "according to unverified statistics kept by the Department," approximately sixty percent of enforcement actions have involved public inebriation and public drinking, and that other "significant categories" include felony arrests for narcotics and other offenses, and arrests for street sales without a permit. Together, enforcement actions concerning camping in the park . . . , sleeping in the park during prohibited hours . . . , and lodging . . . have constituted only approximately 10% of the total.

Plaintiffs, pointing to the discretion inherent in policing the law enforcement measures of the Matrix Program, allege certain actions taken by police to be "calculated to punish the homeless." As a general practice, the Program is depicted by plaintiffs as "targeting hundreds of homeless persons who are guilty of nothing more than sitting on a park bench or on the ground with their possessions, or lying or sleeping on the ground covered by or on top of a blanket or cardboard carton." On one specific occasion, according to plaintiffs, police "cited and detained more than a dozen homeless people, and confiscated and destroyed their possessions, leaving them without medication, blankets or belongings to cope with the winter cold."

The City contests the depiction of Matrix as a singularly focused, punitive effort designed to move "an untidy problem out of sight and out of mind." Instead, the City characterizes the Matrix Program as

> an interdepartmental effort . . . [utilizing] social workers and health workers . . . and offering shelter, medical care, information about services and general assistance. Many of those on the street refuse those services, as is their right; but Matrix makes the choice available. . . .

The City emphasizes its history as one of the largest public providers of assistance to the homeless in the State, asserting that "individuals on general assistance in San Francisco are eligible for larger monthly grants than are available almost anywhere else in California." Homeless persons within the City are entitled to a maximum general assistance of $345 per month—an amount exceeding the grant provided by any of the surrounding counties. General assistance recipients are also eligible for up to $109 per month in food stamps. According to the City, some 15,000 City residents are on general assistance, of whom 3,000 claim to be homeless.

The City's Department of Social Services encourages participation in a Modified Payments Program offered by the Tenderloin Housing Clinic. Through this program, a recipient's general assistance check is paid to the Clinic, which in turn pays the recipient's rent and remits the balance to the recipient. The Clinic then negotiates with landlords of residential hotels to accept general assistance recipients at rents not exceeding $280 per month.

By its own estimate, the City will spend $46.4 million for services to the homeless for 1993–94. Of that amount, over $8 million is specifically earmarked to provide housing, and is spent primarily on emergency shelter beds for adults, families, battered women and youths. An additional $12 million in general assistance grants is provided to those describing themselves as homeless, and free health care is provided by the City to the homeless at a cost of approximately $3 million.

The City contends that "few of the Matrix-related offenses involve arrest." Those persons found publicly inebriated, according to the City, are taken to the City's detoxification center or district stations until sober. "Most of the other violations result in an admonishment or a citation."

Since its implementation, the Matrix Program has resulted in the issuance of over 3,000 citations to homeless persons. Plaintiffs contend these citations have resulted in a cost to the City of over $500,000. Citations issued for encampment and sleeping infractions are in the amount of $76, according to Alissa Riker, Director of the Supervised Citation Release Program ("SCRP") with the Center for Juvenile and Criminal Justice. Those cited must pay or contest the citation within twenty-one days; failure to do so results in a $180 warrant for the individual's arrest, which is issued approximately two months after citation of the infraction. Upon the accrual of $1,000 in warrants, which equates roughly to the receipt of six citations, an individual becomes ineligible for citation release and may be placed in custody. The typical practice, however, is that those arrested for Matrix-related offenses are released on their own recognizance or with "credit for time served" on the day following arrest. [Seventeen homeless persons were held in custody as a result of high bail amounts accruing from Matrix-identified infraction warrants.] In each instance, the individual was released after being sentenced to "credit for time served." Plaintiffs characterize the system as one in which "homeless people are cycled through the criminal justice system and released to continue their lives in the same manner, except now doing so as 'criminals'."

According to plaintiffs, the City has conceded the inadequacy of shelter for its homeless. Plaintiffs have cited as supporting evidence an application made to the State Department of Housing and Community Development in which the City's Director of Homeless Services described an "emergency situation" created by the closure of the Transbay Terminal, which had served as "the largest de facto shelter for homeless individuals."

Plaintiffs have proffered estimates as to the number of homeless individuals unable to find nightly housing. Plaintiffs cite a survey conducted by Independent Housing Services, a nonprofit agency which among its aims seeks the improvement of access to affordable housing for the homeless. Begun in July of 1990 and conducted most recently in August of 1993, the survey tracks the number of homeless individuals turned away each night from shelters in the San Francisco area due to a lack of available bed space. Based on the data of that survey, plaintiffs contend that from January to July of 1993, an average of 500 homeless persons was turned away nightly from homeless shelters. That number, according to plaintiffs, increased to 600 upon the closing of the Transbay Terminal. . . .

OPINION

Plaintiffs have at this time moved the Court to preliminarily enjoin the City's enforcement of certain state and municipal criminal measures which partially define the Matrix Program. Given this posture of the litigation, the Court is called upon to decide whether to grant a preliminary injunction in the exercise of its equitable powers [a court acting according to a set of principles that determine whether or not to issue a court order requiring parties to the suit to do something, in this case stop acting until the court decides the case]. Such relief constitutes an extraordinary use of the Court's powers, and is to be granted sparingly and with the ultimate aim of preserving the status quo pending trial on the merits.

As the Court is acting in equity, the decision whether to grant preliminary injunctive relief is largely left to its discretion. However, this discretion has been circumscribed by the presence or not of various factors, notably, the likelihood that the moving party will prevail on the merits and the likelihood of harm to the parties from granting or denying the injunctive relief. At the extremes, a party seeking injunctive relief must show either (1) a combination of probable success on the merits and the possibility of irreparable harm, or (2) that serious questions are raised and the balance of hardships tips sharply in the moving party's favor. . . .

The injunction sought by plaintiffs at this juncture of the litigation must be denied for each of two independent reasons. First, the proposed injunction lacks the necessary specificity to be enforceable, and would give rise to enforcement problems sufficiently inherent as to be incurable by modification of the proposal. Second, those legal theories upon which plaintiffs rely are not plainly applicable to the grievances sought to be vindicated, with the effect that the Court cannot find at this time that, upon conducting the required balance of harm and merit, plaintiffs have established a sufficient probability of success on the merits to warrant injunctive relief.

. . .

[Only the discussion of the second reason is included in this case excerpt.]

II. Under the Posited Legal Theories, Plaintiffs Have Not Demonstrated a Clear Probability of Success on the Merits

A. Whether the Eighth Amendment Prohibits Enforcement of Matrix as Punishing "Status"

Plaintiffs contend enforcement of the Matrix Program unconstitutionally punishes an asserted "status" of homelessness. The central thesis is that since plaintiffs are compelled to be on the street involuntarily, enforcement of laws which interfere with their ability to carry out life sustaining activities on the street must be prohibited. This argument, while arguably bolstered by decisions of courts in other jurisdictions, has not been adopted by any case within the Ninth Circuit. Moreover, it is the opinion of this Court that plaintiffs' position, if adopted, would represent an improper reach by this Court into matters appropriately governed by the State of California and the City of San Francisco. . . .

[The court summarized the holdings of *Robinson v. California* and *Powell v. Texas*. *Robinson v. California* held that it was cruel and unusual punishment to make the disease of drug addiction a crime. *Powell v. Texas* held that it was not cruel and unusual punishment to make the act of drinking in public a crime, even though the person who was drunk in public is an alcoholic. These cases are discussed in Chapter 3 in the section on status as a criminal act. You should review that discussion before reading further.]

Plaintiffs argue, however, on the basis of Justice WHITE'S concurring opinion, that *Powell* was decided as it was solely because the convicted defendant had not been shown to be on the streets involuntarily. In casting the fifth vote to uphold the appellant's conviction in *Powell,* Justice WHITE wrote,

> The fact remains that some chronic alcoholics must drink and hence must drink somewhere. Although many chronics have homes, many others do not. For all practical purposes the public streets may be home for these unfortunates, not because their disease compels them to be there, but because, drunk or sober, they have no place else to go and no place else to be when they are drinking. This is more a function of economic station than of disease, although the disease may lead to destitution and perpetuate that condition. For some of these alcoholics I would think a showing could be made that resisting drunkenness is impossible and that avoiding public places when intoxicated is also impossible. As applied to them this statute is in effect a law which bans a single act for which they may not be convicted under the Eighth Amendment—the act of getting drunk.

Plaintiffs contend on the basis of this concurring opinion that, had the appellant in *Powell* been homeless, five justices would have voted to reverse his conviction. "*Powell* effectively establishes that a person who is involuntarily in public may not be punished for doing an act or being in a condition that he or she is powerless to avoid."...

This Court is unable to conclude at this time that the extension of the Eighth Amendment to the "acts" at issue here is warranted by governing authorities. Plaintiffs argue that the failure of the City to provide sufficient housing compels the conclusion that homelessness on the streets of San Francisco is cognizable as a status. This argument is unavailing at least for the fundamental reason that status cannot be defined as a function of the discretionary acts of others.

As an analytical matter, more fundamentally, homelessness is not readily classified as a "status." Rather, as expressed for the plurality in *Powell* by Justice MARSHALL, there is a "substantial definitional distinction between a 'status' . . . and a 'condition,'. . ." While the concept of status might elude perfect definition, certain factors assist in its determination, such as the involuntariness of the acquisition of that quality (including the presence or not of that characteristic at birth), and the degree to which an individual has control over that characteristic.

Examples of such "status" characteristics might include age, race, gender, national origin and illness. The reasoning of the Court in including drug addiction as status involved the analogy of drug addiction to a disease or an illness which might be contracted involuntarily. While homelessness can be thrust upon an unwitting recipient, and while a person may be largely incapable of changing that condition, the distinction between the ability to eliminate one's drug addiction as compared to one's homelessness is a distinction in kind as much as in degree. To argue that homelessness is a status and not a condition, moreover, is to deny the efficacy of acts of social intervention to change the condition of those currently homeless.

The Court must approach with hesitation any argument that science or statistics compels a conclusion that a certain condition be defined as a status. The Supreme Court has determined that drug addiction equals a status, and this Court is so bound. But the Supreme Court has not made such a determination with respect to homelessness, and because that situation is not directly analogous to drug addiction, it would be an untoward excursion by this Court into matters of social policy to accord to homelessness the protection of status.
. . .

B. *Whether Matrix Violates the Equal Protection Clause*

Predicate to an equal protection clause violation is a finding of governmental action undertaken with an intent to discriminate against a particular individual or class of individuals. Such intent may be evinced by statutory language, or in instances where an impact which cannot be explained on a neutral ground unmasks an invidious discrim-ination. Under the latter approach, a neutral law found to have a disproportionately adverse effect upon a minority classification will be deemed un-constitutional only if that impact can be traced to a discriminatory purpose.

In the present case, plaintiffs have not at this time demonstrated a likelihood of success on the merits of the equal protection claim, since the City's action has not been taken with an evinced intent to discriminate against an identifiable group. As discussed above, various directives is-sued within the Police Department mandate the nondiscriminatory enforcement of Matrix. See, e.g., "Update on Matrix Quality of Life Program," Petrini Decl., Exh. A at 12 (providing that "rights of the homeless must be preserved"); Department Bulletin on "Rights of the Homeless," discussed in Petrini Decl. at 2 (stating that "[all members of the Department] are obligated to treat all persons equally, regardless of their economic or living con-ditions. The homeless enjoy the same legal and in-dividual rights afforded to others. Members shall at all times respect these rights. . . ."). Further, the Police Department has, during the pendency of the Matrix Program, conducted continuing education for officers regarding nondiscriminatory enforce-ment of the Program.

It has not been proven at this time that Matrix was implemented with the aim of discriminating against the homeless. That enforcement of Matrix will, de facto, fall predominantly on the homeless does not in itself effect an equal protection clause violation. . . .

Even were plaintiffs able at this time to prove an intent to discriminate against the homeless, the challenged sections of the Program might nonethe-less survive constitutional scrutiny. Only in cases where the challenged action is aimed at a suspect classification, such as race or gender, or premised upon the exercise of a fundamental right, will the governmental action be subjected to a heightened scrutiny.

Counsel for plaintiff proposed at the hearing that this Court should be the first to recognize as a fundamental right the "right to sleep." This is an invitation the Court, in its exercise of judicial re-straint, must decline. Despite the seeming inno-cence of a right so defined, the natural corollary to recognition of a right is an obligation to enforce it. The discovery of a right to sleep concomitantly re-quires prohibition of the government's interference with that right. This endeavor, aside from creating a jurisprudential morass, would involve this un-elected branch of government in a legislative role for which it is neither fit, nor easily divested once established. . . .

C. Whether the Matrix Program Impermissibly Burdens the Right to Travel

This argument proffered by plaintiffs is essentially a subset of equal protection analysis, in which the right to travel is deemed a fundamental right which a state government may not abridge unless neces-sary to achieve a compelling state interest. The right to travel has found its strongest expression in the context of attempts by states to discourage the immigration of indigents. The application of strict scrutiny to such laws, however, has been limited to those which are facially discriminatory [namely, hold-ing unconstitutional a statutory provision requiring welfare assistance applicants to reside in a state at least one year im-mediately preceding application for assistance; curtailing im-migration of new residents to a state; and denying medical services to new state residents]. The Matrix Program does not facially discriminate between those who are, and those who might be, the City's residents. Accordingly, the application of strict scrutiny to the Program would be unwarranted. . . .

Assuming the right to travel encompasses pro-tection to intrastate travel, it is nevertheless doubt-ful that facially neutral laws impacting intrastate travel should be subjected to such strict scrutiny. "Both the United States Supreme Court and [the California Supreme Court] have refused to apply the strict construction test to legislation . . . which does not penalize travel and resettlement [through disparate treatment] but merely makes it more dif-ficult for the outsider to establish his residence in the place of his choosing.". . .

D. Whether the Matrix Program Violates Plaintiffs' Rights to Due Process of Law

Plaintiffs contend the Matrix Program has been en-forced in violation of the due process clause . . . of the United States . . . Constitution. . . . Plaintiffs specifically argue that due process has been vio-lated by employing punitive policing measures against the homeless for sleeping in public parks; plaintiffs also argue that certain state codes are un-constitutionally vague.

1. Punishing the Homeless for Sitting or Sleeping in Parks

Plaintiffs claim that San Francisco Park Code section 3.12 has been applied by police in an unconstitutional manner. That section provides,

> No person shall construct or maintain any building, structure, tent or any other thing in any park that may be used for housing accommodations or camping, except by permission from the Recreation and Park Commission.

Plaintiffs contend the Police Department has impermissibly construed this provision to justify citing, arresting, threatening and "moving along" those "persons guilty of nothing more than sitting on park benches with their personal possessions or lying on or under blankets on the ground." Plaintiffs have submitted declarations of various homeless persons supporting the asserted application of the San Francisco Park Code section. See, e.g., Homeless Decls. at 34 (lying down atop blankets eating lunch), 121 ("sleeping on bench"), 125 ("sleeping on boxes").

It appears, if plaintiffs have accurately depicted the manner in which the section is enforced, that the section may have been applied to conduct not covered by the section and may have been enforced unconstitutionally. . . .

2. . . . Vagueness Challenges to Enforcement Measures

Plaintiffs also contend that San Francisco Park Code section 3.12, discussed supra, and California Penal Code Section 647(i) [Every person who commits any of the following acts is guilty of disorderly conduct, a misdemeanor: . . . Who lodges in any building, structure, vehicle, or place, whether public or private, without the permission of the owner or person entitled to the possession or in control thereof. Cal. Penal Code _ 647(i).] are unconstitutionally overbroad and vague." . . .

The possible success of the vagueness challenge is also in doubt, as it seems readily apparent the measure is not "impermissibly vague in all of its applications. . . ." This likely failing follows from plaintiffs' inability to prove at this stage that police have been granted an excess of discretion pursuant to the statute. Plaintiffs assert vagueness in the San Francisco Park Code prohibition against maintaining "any other thing" that "may be used for . . . camping," and in enforcing the Penal Code prohi-

bition against one "who lodges in . . . public," claiming "the vagueness of these [Park Code] terms has apparently allowed San Francisco police officers to determine that blankets or possessions in carts are sufficiently connected to 'camping' to violate the ordinance." Plaintiffs have also submitted declarations of homeless persons supporting these assertions, and a concession by Assistant District Attorney Paul Cummins to the effect that the standards for enforcement are vague. . . .

Similarly, the challenged Penal Code section cannot be concluded by the Court at this time to be unconstitutionally vague. Read in conjunction with supplemental memoranda, the challenged measures appear, as a constitutional matter, sufficiently specific. Police officers were specifically cautioned in a September 17, 1993 memorandum that "the mere lying or sleeping on or in a bedroll of and in itself does not constitute a violation." While plaintiffs argue the additional memoranda were circulated too late to save the enforcement measures from vagueness, and also that they do not eliminate the confusion, it is far from clear that plaintiffs could meet the requisite showing that the measure was impermissibly vague in all its applications. Accordingly, even if the limits of permissible enforcement of these sections have not been perfectly elucidated, preliminary injunctive relief is inappropriate at this stage of the litigation.

Conclusion

In common with many communities across the country, the City is faced with a homeless population of tragic dimension. Today, plaintiffs have brought that societal problem before the Court, seeking a legal judgment on the efforts adopted by the City in response to this problem.

The role of the Court is limited structurally by the fact that it may exercise only judicial power, and technically by the fact that plaintiffs seek extraordinary pretrial relief. The Court does not find that plaintiffs have made a showing at this time that constitutional barriers exist which preclude that effort. Accordingly, the Court's judgment at this stage of the litigation is to permit the City to continue enforcing those aspects of the Matrix Program now challenged by plaintiffs.

The Court therefore concludes that the injunction sought, both as it stands now and as plaintiffs have proposed to modify it, is not sufficiently specific to be enforceable. Further, upon conducting the required balance of harm and merit, the Court finds that plaintiffs have failed to establish a sufficient probability of success on the merits to warrant injunctive relief. Accordingly, plaintiffs' motion for a preliminary injunction is DENIED.

IT IS SO ORDERED.

QUESTIONS FOR DISCUSSION

1. Describe the main elements of the Matrix Program.

2. Why did San Francisco adopt the Matrix Program?

3. What are the plaintiffs' objections to the Matrix Program?

4. Why does the court grant injunctions rarely?

5. Do you agree with the reasons given for granting injunctions "sparingly"?

6. What requirements must the plaintiffs satisfy before they can obtain an injunction in this case?

7. Do you think the plaintiffs have satisfied the requirements? Defend your answer.

8. Assume you are the attorney for San Francisco. Argue why the court should deny the injunction.

9. Assume you are the attorney for the homeless people. Argue why the court should issue the injunction.

10. If you could, what terms would you include in an injunction in this case?

PANHANDLING

> On the concrete plaza outside [San Francisco] City Hall here, day or night, dozens of homeless men and women shuffle from bench to grate dragging blankets or pushing shopping carts stuffed with all they own. They beg, they bicker, they sleep. It is a ragged, aimless procession that never ends. It is also a sight that this ever-tolerant city is tired of seeing. Frustrated by how difficult it is to end homelessness even in robust economic times, and facing pressure to make neighborhoods and business centers safe and clean, San Francisco has become the latest in a growing number of cities deciding that it is time to get tougher.[16]

So wrote *Washington Post* reporter Renee Sanchez in 1998 about the continuing backlash against the so-called rights revolution of the 1960s and 1970s. According to Robert Tier, General Counsel of the American Alliance for Rights and Responsibilities:

> Many City Councils have been convinced to adopt new and innovative controls on anti-social behavior to maintain minimal standards of public conduct and to keep public spaces safe and attractive. . . . One of the most common examples of these efforts are ordinances aimed at aggressive begging.[17]

These "new and innovative controls" rely on ancient laws against begging. At the outset, keep in mind that the new anti-begging ordinances don't apply to organized charities. So, although it's a crime for a private beggar to panhandle for money, it's legal for the Salvation Army to ring their bells to get contributions. Why the distinction? Supporters say that the rights revolution has simply gone too far. It's reached the point, they say, where the rights of a minority of offensive individuals trump the quality of life of the whole community. Associate Supreme Court Justice Clarence Thomas, commenting on "how judicial interpretations of the First Amendment and of 'unenumerated' constitutional rights have affected the ability of urban communities to deal with crime, disorder, and incivility on their public streets," told the Federalist Society in 1996:

> Vagrancy, loitering, and panhandling laws were challenged [during the rights revolution] because the poor and minorities could be victims of discrimination under the guise of broad discretion to ensure public safety. Moreover, as a consequence of

the modern tendency to challenge society's authority to dictate social norms, the legal system began to prefer the ideal of self-expression without much attention to self-discipline or self control. What resulted was a culture that declined to curb the excesses of self-indulgence—vagrants and others who regularly roamed the streets had rights that could not be circumscribed by the community's sense of decency or decorum.[18]

"Hey, buddy, can you spare some change?" is clearly speech. And, of course the First Amendment guarantees individuals freedom of speech. However, free speech doesn't mean you can say anything you want anywhere at anytime (see Chapter 2). The United States Supreme Court has "rejected the notion that a city is powerless to protect its citizens from unwanted exposure to certain methods of expression which may legitimately be deemed a public nuisance."[19]

The Court has established a number of tests to determine whether ordinances violate the First Amendment guarantee of free speech. One is to look at the place where the speech takes place. In **traditional public forums**—streets, sidewalks, and parks—where people have since ancient times expressed their views, the freedom to solicit is virtually unrestricted. In **designated public forums**—places the government chooses to make available to the public—the government has more leeway to regulate solicitation. In **nonpublic forums**—airports, bus stations, railroad stations, subways, and shopping malls—the government has broad power to restrict and even prohibit solicitation.[20]

Second, the First Amendment free speech clause permits "time, place, and manner" regulations. According to the Supreme Court, time, place, and manner restrictions are valid if

1. They aren't based on the *content* of the speech.
2. They serve a significant government interest, like maintaining the free flow of pedestrian traffic.
3. They leave open other channels of expression.[21]

The first part of the test means that the regulation can't be an excuse for suppressing any message about social conditions that panhandlers are trying to convey. Part 2 of the test is often hotly debated. Advocates for panhandlers argue that the regulation of panhandling is really a government policy of removing "unsightly" poor people from public view. Others maintain that the "purpose is to permit people to use the streets, sidewalks, and public transportation free from the borderline robbery and pervasive fraud which characterizes so much of today's panhandling." The third part of the test requires that the regulation allow panhandlers to beg in other ways. So, a panhandling ordinance that prohibits only "aggressive panhandling" leaves panhandlers free to beg peaceably. Prohibitions against fraudulent panhandling or panhandling in subways also permit alternative means of solicitation.[22]

In addition to forum and time, place, and manner restrictions, the First Amendment gives the government considerable leeway to regulate nonverbal expression, the so-called "expressive conduct" (Chapter 2). In panhandling, this includes approaching a person or blocking the sidewalk in order to beg or receiving the money solicited.

Finally, the First Amendment grants commercial speech less protection than other types of speech. Since begging relies on talking listeners into handing over their money, panhandling is commercial speech. The United States Court of Appeals for the Seventh Circuit decided whether an Indianapolis ordinance restricting panhandling violated the First Amendment right to free speech in *Gresham v. Peterson*.

C A S E — Was the Panhandling Ordinance Vague and Did It Violate Free Speech?

Gresham v. Peterson
225 F.3d 899 (7th Cir. 2000)

Jimmy Gresham challenged an Indianapolis ordinance that limits street begging in public places and prohibits entirely activities defined as "aggressive panhandling." Gresham believes that the ordinance infringes his First Amendment right to free speech and his Fourteenth Amendment right to due process. The city considers the ordinance a reasonable response to the public safety threat posed by panhandlers. The district court found that a state court could construe the ordinance in such a way to render it sufficiently clear and specific and granted the city summary judgment on Gresham's request for a permanent injunction. The U.S. Circuit Court affirmed.

Before WOOD, EASTERBROOK, KANNE, Circuit Judges.

KANNE, J.

FACTS

In June 1999, the City of Indianapolis amended an ordinance regarding solicitation in public places. The ordinance, which became effective on July 6, 1999, reads as follows:

(a) As used in this section, panhandling means any solicitation made in person upon any street, public place or park in the city, in which a person requests an immediate donation of money or other gratuity from another person, and includes but is not limited to seeking donations:

(1) By vocal appeal or for music, singing, or other street performance; and,

(2) Where the person being solicited receives an item of little or no monetary value in exchange for a donation, under circumstances where a reasonable person would understand that the transaction is in substance a donation.

However, panhandling shall not include the act of passively standing or sitting nor performing music, singing or other street performance with a sign or other indication that a donation is being sought, without any vocal request other than in response to an inquiry by another person.

(b) It shall be unlawful to engage in an act of panhandling on any day after sunset, or before sunrise.

(c) It shall be unlawful to engage in an act of panhandling when either the panhandler or the person being solicited is located at any of the following locations; at a bus stop; in any public transportation vehicle or public transportation facility; in a vehicle which is parked or stopped on a public street or alley; in a sidewalk cafe; or within twenty (20) feet in any direction from an automatic teller machine or entrance to a bank.

(d) It shall be unlawful to engage in an act of panhandling in an aggressive manner, including any of the following actions:

(1) Touching the solicited person without the solicited person's consent.

(2) Panhandling a person while such person is standing in line and waiting to be admitted to a commercial establishment;

(3) Blocking the path of a person being solicited, or the entrance to any building or vehicle;

(4) Following behind, ahead or alongside a person who walks away from the panhandler after being solicited;

(5) Using profane or abusive language, either during the solicitation or following a refusal to make a donation, or making any statement, gesture, or other communication which would cause a reasonable person to be fearful or feel compelled; or,

(6) Panhandling in a group of two (2) or more persons.

(e) Each act of panhandling prohibited by this section shall constitute a public nuisance and a separate violation of this Code. Each violation shall be punishable as provided in section 103-3 of the Code, and the court shall enjoin any such violator from committing further violations of this section.

City-County General Ordinance No. 78 (1999), Revised Code of Indianapolis and Marion County § 407-102.

Section 103-3 provides that a person convicted of violating the ordinance will be fined not more than $2,500 for each violation. The ordinance does not provide for imprisonment of violators, except, of course, a past offender who violates the mandatory injunction provided in Paragraph (e) could be jailed for contempt.

Jimmy Gresham is a homeless person who lives in Indianapolis on Social Security disability benefits of $417 per month. He supplements this income by begging, using the money to buy food. He begs during both the daytime and nighttime in downtown Indianapolis. Because different people visit downtown at night than during the day, it is important to him that he be able to beg at night. Gresham approaches people on the street, tells them he is homeless and asks for money to buy food. Gresham has not been cited for panhandling under the new ordinance, but he fears being cited for panhandling at night or if an officer interprets his requests for money to be "aggressive" as defined by the law.

Gresham filed this class action shortly after the ordinance took effect, requesting injunctive and declaratory relief. Gresham moved for a preliminary injunction barring enforcement of the ordinance on the grounds that it was unconstitutionally vague and violated his right to free speech. The district court, after hearing oral argument . . . entered a final order denying the motion for preliminary injunction and dismissing the case.

In the order, the district court construed the list of six actions that constitute aggressive panhandling as exclusive, eliminating the danger that someone could be cited for other, unenumerated acts. The court further ruled that the proscription in Paragraph (d)(5) against actions that make a person "fearful or feel compelled" was not unconstitutionally vague because it could be interpreted to mean "fear for his safety or feel compelled to donate." The court held that because the ordinance was civil in nature and the actions prohibited under aggressive panhandling were not related to speech interests, no intent element was necessary. Finally, the court found the ordinance to be a valid content-neutral regulation. . . . ["Content neutral" means that the government regulation isn't an excuse to censor the message of the speech.]

OPINION

On appeal, Gresham raises two principal arguments. First, he contends that the provisions defining aggressive panhandling are vague because they fail to provide clear criteria to alert panhandlers and authorities of what constitutes a violation and because they fail to include an intent element. Second, he argues that the statute fails the test for content-neutral time, place and manner restrictions on protected speech. We review de novo the question of whether a state law violates the Constitution.

A. The First Amendment

Laws targeting street begging have been around for many years, but in the last twenty years, local communities have breathed new life into old laws or passed new ones. Cities, such as Indianapolis, have tried to narrowly draw the ordinances to target the most bothersome types of street solicitations and give police another tool in the effort to make public areas, particularly downtown areas, safe and inviting.

While the plaintiff here has focused the inquiry on the effects of the ordinance on the poor and homeless, the ordinance itself is not so limited. It applies with equal force to anyone who would solicit a charitable contribution, whether for a recognized charity, a religious group, a political candidate or organization, or for an individual. It would punish street people as well as Salvation Army bell ringers outside stores at Christmas, so long as the appeal involved a vocal request for an immediate donation.

The ordinance bans panhandling by beggars or charities citywide on any "street, public place or park" in three circumstances. First, it would prohibit any nighttime panhandling § 407-102(b). Second, it would prohibit at all times—day or night—panhandling in specified areas. § 407-102(c). Third, it would prohibit "aggressive panhandling" at all times. § 407-102(d)(1)-(6). The defendants emphatically point out that the ordinance allows a great deal of solicitation, including "passive" panhandling, which does not include a vocal appeal, street performances, legitimate sales transactions and requests for donations over the telephone or any other means that is not "in person" or does not involve an "immediate donation." Under the ordinance, one could lawfully hold up a sign that says "give me money" and sing "I am cold and starving," so long as one does not voice words to the effect of "give me money."

Several courts before us, as well as many commentators, have grappled with understanding panhandling laws in light of the First Amendment guarantee of free speech and the constitutional right to due process. See, e.g., *Smith v. City of Fort Lauderdale*, 177 F.3d 954 (11th Cir.1999); *Loper v. New York City Police Dep't*, 999 F.2d 699 (2d Cir.1993). To this point, the Supreme Court has not resolved directly the constitutional limitations on such laws as they apply to individual beggars, but has provided clear direction on how they apply to organized charities, not-for-profits and political groups.

To the extent the Indianapolis ordinance could be enforced against organized charities, such as the United Way, Salvation Army or others, the Supreme Court's holding in *Schaumburg* would control resolution of the case. In *Schaumburg*, the Supreme Court considered a local prohibition on solicitation by charities that did not use a certain percentage of their contributions for charitable purposes. 444 U.S. at 623-24, 100 S.Ct. 826. As a threshold consideration, the Court determined that solicitations by organized charities were entitled to First Amendment protection. The Court found that charities often engage in core First Amendment speech while soliciting donations, and that without such appeals for support, the flow of information on many social, economic, political and cultural topics would cease. As such, the solicitations by organized charities were "within the protection of the First Amendment" although "subject to reasonable regulation."

The Court placed charitable solicitations by organizations in a category of speech close to the heart of the First Amendment, and distinguished it from "purely commercial speech" which is "primarily concerned with providing information about the characteristics and costs of goods and services." Commercial speech, on the other hand, has been placed lower in the First Amendment food chain, somewhere between political speech and pornography. It deserves protection, but authorities are more free to regulate commercial speech than core-value speech.

Other courts examining issues similar to those at hand did not distinguish between solicitation for organized charities and solicitation by individual beggars. The Eleventh Circuit held that "like other charitable solicitation, begging is speech entitled to First Amendment protection." *Smith,* 177 F.3d at 956 (citing *Schaumburg,* 444 U.S. at 632, 100 S.Ct. 826). The Second Circuit likewise held that for First Amendment purposes, the distinction between begging for a charity and begging for one's self is not significant. *Loper,* 999 F.2d at 704. "We see little difference between those who solicit for organized charities and those who solicit for themselves in regard to the message conveyed." Both

Smith and *Loper* held that limitations on panhandling must be analyzed under the same *Schaumburg* framework as limitations for charities.

Indeed, the Court's analysis in *Schaumburg* suggests little reason to distinguish between beggars and charities in terms of the First Amendment protection for their speech. Solicitation, the Court reasoned, "is characteristically intertwined with informative and perhaps persuasive speech" which the First Amendment protects. Because they are intimately connected, solicitation cannot be restricted without also risking the flow of information. Importantly, the *Schaumburg* Court expressly rejected the suggestion that the message and the solicitation could be considered severable [could be separated]. The village had argued that the ordinance prohibited only the request for money and left the charity free to propagate its views, but the Court called this view of the First Amendment protection for solicitors "too limited." After extensively reviewing its own case law on the subject, the Court held that restrictions on a charity's request for money necessarily implicate restrictions on speech itself.

Similarly, the Indianapolis ordinance protects the communication of ideas by solicitors and limits only the bare request for cash. Yet the two can be closely intertwined. Beggars at times may communicate important political or social messages in their appeals for money, explaining their conditions related to veteran status, homelessness, unemployment and disability, to name a few. Like the organized charities, their messages cannot always be easily separated from their need for money. While some communities might wish all solicitors, beggars and advocates of various causes be banished from the streets, the First Amendment guarantees their right to be there, deliver their pitch and ask for support. See *Schaumburg,* 444 U.S. at 632, 100 S.Ct. 826 ("Charitable appeals for funds, on the street or door to door, involve a variety of speech interests . . . that are within the protection of the First Amendment."). Neither the parties to this appeal nor any authorities found by this Court suggest we should distinguish between restrictions on organized charities and individuals for purposes of understanding the First Amendment guarantees. Therefore, assuming for the purposes of this appeal that some panhandler speech would be protected by the First Amendment, we find that *Schaumburg* provides the appropriate standard to analyze this claim.

As an aside, we note that the Court in *Schaumburg* distinguished solicitation from commercial speech, which is "primarily concerned with providing information about the characteristics and costs of goods and services." The Eleventh Circuit, noting that the parties did not raise the argument, declined to reach the issue of whether panhandling could be considered commercial speech and therefore subject to more regulation. We too will follow that prudent approach and not decide an issue the parties declined to raise. See generally Robert C. Ellickson, Controlling Chronic Misconduct in City Spaces: Of Panhandlers, Skid Rows, and Public-Space Zoning, 105 *Yale L.J.* 1165, 1229 (1996) (discussing possibility of treating begging as commercial speech). In any event, considering the Supreme Court's definition of commercial speech as outlined in *Schaumburg,* we doubt panhandling falls into this classification.

After recognizing a First Amendment right to solicit money in public places, the *Schaumburg* Court held that a government may enact "reasonable regulations" so long as they reflect "due regard" for the constitutional interests at stake. The parties assume that the proper analysis to determine whether the Indianapolis ordinance is one such reasonable regulation is that set out for "time, place and manner" restrictions in *Perry,* 460 U.S. at 45, 103 S.Ct. 948. Because the Indianapolis ordinance does not ban all panhandling, we agree that the law could be understood as a time, place or manner regulation. Under *Perry,* governments may "enforce regulations of the time, place and manner of expression which are content neutral, are narrowly tailored to serve a significant government interest, and leave open ample alternative channels of communication.". . .

Colorable arguments could be made both for and against the idea that the Indianapolis ordinance is a content-neutral time, place or manner restriction. The Supreme Court has held that "government regulation of expressive activity is content neutral so long as it is 'justified without reference to the content of the regulated speech.'" *Ward v. Rock Against Racism,* 491 U.S. 781, 791, 109 S.Ct. 2746, 105 L.Ed.2d 661 (1989) To help apply this somewhat circular definition, the Court instructed that the principal inquiry is "whether the government has adopted a regulation of speech because of disagreement with the message it conveys.". . . Whether a solicitor violates the ordinance depends on whether he asked for cash rather than for something else. On one side of the argument, the city ordinance does not prohibit all solicitation on city streets, only solicitations for immediate cash donations. One could, for instance, ask passers-by for their signatures, time, labor or anything else, other than money. Only by determining the specific content of a solicitor's speech could authorities determine whether they violated the ordinance, which would seem to be a content-based restriction. But as *Ward* and more recently *Hill v. Colorado,* —— U.S. ——, ——,120 S.Ct. 2480, 2491, 147 L.Ed.2d 597 (2000), emphasized, the inquiry into content neutrality in the context of time, place or manner restrictions turns on the government's justification for the regulation. Because the parties here agree that the regulations are content neutral, we need not decide whether the Indianapolis ordinance can be justified without reference to the content of the regulated speech. Thus the Indianapolis ordinance should be upheld if it is narrowly tailored to achieve a significant governmental purpose and leaves open alternate channels of communication.

The city has a legitimate interest in promoting the safety and convenience of its citizens on public streets. See *Madsen v. Women's Health Center,* 512 U.S. 753, 768, 114 S.Ct. 2516, 129 L.Ed.2d 593 (1994) (holding that the state "also has a strong interest in ensuring the public safety and order, in promoting the free flow of traffic on public streets and sidewalks . . ."); *Heffron v. International Soc. for Krishna Consciousness, Inc.,* 452 U.S. 640, 650, 101 S.Ct. 2559, 69 L.Ed.2d 298 (1981) (recognizing state interest in safety and convenience of citizens using public fora); *Cox v. New Hampshire,* 312 U.S. 569, 574, 61 S.Ct. 762, 85 L.Ed. 1049 (1941) (recognizing state interest in safety and convenience on public roads); *Ayres v. City of Chicago,* 125 F.3d 1010, 1015 (7th Cir.1997) ("There are unquestionable benefits from regulating peddling, First Amendment or otherwise, [including] the control of congestion."). The plaintiff concedes this much, but argues that a total nighttime ban on verbal requests for alms is substantially broader than necessary and therefore cannot be considered narrowly tailored. However, a government regulation can be considered narrowly tailored "so long as the . . . regulation promotes a substantial government interest that would be achieved less effectively absent the regulation." This means the regulation need not be a perfect fit for the government's needs, but cannot burden substantially more speech than necessary. Furthermore, a time, place or manner restriction need not be the least restrictive means of achieving the government purpose, so long as it can be considered narrowly tailored to that purpose.

The city determined that vocal requests for money create a threatening environment or at least a nuisance for some citizens. Rather than ban all panhandling, however, the city chose to restrict it only in those circumstances where it is considered especially unwanted or bothersome—at night, around banks and sidewalk cafes, and so forth. These represent situations in which people most likely would feel a heightened sense of fear or alarm, or might wish especially to be left alone. By limiting the ordinance's restrictions to only those certain times and places where citizens naturally would feel most insecure in their surroundings, the city has effectively narrowed the application of the law to what is necessary to promote its legitimate interest.

Finally, the plaintiff contends that the statute fails to provide ample alternative channels of communication. We disagree. An adequate alternative does not have to be the speaker's first or best choice, or one that provides the same audience or impact for the speech. However, the Court has "shown special solicitude for forms of expression that are much less expensive than feasible alternatives," and so an alternative must be more than merely theoretically available. It must be realistic as well. Furthermore, an adequate alternative cannot totally foreclose a speaker's ability to reach one audience even if it allows the speaker to reach other groups. See *Bery v. City of New York,* 97 F.3d 689, 698 (2d Cir.1996) (holding that total ban on sidewalk art does not leave open alternative means of communication because alternative display in galleries or museums would not reach the same audience.)

The Indianapolis ordinance allows many feasible alternatives to reach both the daytime and nighttime downtown Indianapolis crowds. Under the ordinance, panhandlers may ply their craft vocally or in any manner they deem fit (except for those involving conduct defined as aggressive) during all the daylight hours on all of the city's public streets. Gresham contends that soliciting at night is vital to his survival, a fact we do not dispute, but the ordinance leaves open many reasonable ways for him to reach the nighttime downtown crowd. He may solicit at night, so long as he does not vocally request money. He may hold up signs requesting money or engage in street performances, such as playing music, with an implicit appeal for support. Although perhaps not relevant to street beggars, the ordinance also permits telephone and door-to-door solicitation at night. Thus to the extent that "give me money" conveys an idea the expression of which is protected by the First Amendment, solicitors may express themselves vocally all day, and in writing, by telephone or by other non-vocal means all night. Furthermore, they may solicit in public places on all 396.4 square miles of the city, except those parts occupied by sidewalk cafes, banks, ATMs and bus stops. This is a far cry from the total citywide ban on panhandling overturned by the court in *Loper,* 999 F.2d at 705 ("A statute that totally prohibits begging in all public places cannot be considered 'narrowly tailored.'"), or the total ban on panhandling in a five-mile area of public beach upheld by the court in *Smith,* 177 F.3d at 956.

B. Vagueness

Gresham next challenges certain provisions of the ordinance as unconstitutionally vague. Specifically, he contends that the definition[s] of aggressive panhandling in sections (d)(4) and (d)(5) are not sufficiently clear to direct authorities on the enforcement of the law, nor to allow panhandlers such as Gresham to avoid violating the law. Section (d)(4) prohibits "following behind, ahead or alongside a person who walks away from the panhandler after being solicited." Gresham argues hypothetically that police could cite a person for inadvertently violating this section merely by walking in the same direction as the solicited person, without intending to engage in "aggressive panhandling." Also, section (d)(5) refers to making a person "fearful or feel compelled" without defining what the terms mean in relation to panhandling. A generalized guilt at economic inequality might make one "feel compelled" even by the meekest request for money.

The void-for-vagueness doctrine forbids the enforcement of a law that contains "terms so vague that [persons] of common intelligence must necessarily guess at its meaning and differ as to its application." Legislative enactments must articulate terms "with a reasonable degree of clarity" to reduce the risk of arbitrary enforcement and allow individuals to conform their behavior to the requirements of the law. A statute that "vests virtually complete discretion in the hands of the police" fails to provide the minimal guidelines required for due process. See *Kolender v. Lawson,* 461 U.S. 352, 358, 103 S.Ct. 1855, 75 L.Ed.2d 903 (1983).

In assessing the constitutionality of an allegedly vague state law or ordinance, "a federal court must, of course, consider any limiting construction that a state court or enforcement agency has proffered." In this case, the Indiana courts have not yet had an opportunity to interpret the terms of the Indianapolis ordinance, and so we have no authoritative judicial construction of its terms. However, the rule that federal courts should defer to state court interpretations of state laws, also discourages federal courts from enjoining statutes that could be easily narrowed by a state court to avoid constitutional problems. Therefore, we will not hold a vague statute unconstitutional if a reasonable interpretation by a state court could render it constitutional in some application.

Laws must contain a "reasonable degree of clarity" so that people of "common intelligence" can understand their meaning. Furthermore, because the penalties for noncompliance are less severe, laws imposing civil rather than criminal penalties do not demand the same high level of clarity. Like the civil sanction at issue in *Hoffman Estates,* Gresham faces only a fine for noncompliance with the Indianapolis law. However, this lowered burden is mitigated by the fact that the Indianapolis ordinance potentially interferes with the right of free speech, suggesting that a "more stringent vagueness test should apply."

The challenged provisions in this case define what the City Council meant by the term "aggressive panhandling" and must be read in that context. The district court was rightly concerned that Paragraph (d) could be construed as offering an incomplete list of examples of prohibited behavior, leaving open the possibility that other unspecified actions might also be considered illegal, which would raise serious due process concerns. The district court suggested that the list might be exclusive rather than illustrative, a reasonable interpretation which, if adopted by the Indiana courts, would save it from a vagueness challenge.

Likewise, Paragraphs (d)(4) and (d)(5) are subject to reasonable interpretations that answer the vagueness challenge. A state court interpreting Paragraph (d)(4) may read it to prohibit "following" only in the context of a continued request for money such that the victim reasonably interprets the behavior as a threat. A continuing request for a donation coupled with "following" would be prohibited, but walking in the same direction as the solicited person would not be against the law if the walking were divorced from the request. Construed this way, the statute would prohibit the type of harassing behavior that governments routinely outlaw. See, e.g., Ind.Code § 35-45-2-1 (prohibiting as intimidation a threat by words or action that forces a person to engage in conduct against their will); Ind.Code § 35-45-10-1 (prohibiting as stalking a "course of conduct involving repeated or continuing harassment of another person that would cause a reasonable person to feel terrorized, frightened, intimidated, or threatened."); *Johnson v. State,* 648 N.E.2d 666, 670 (Ind.Ct.App.1995) (upholding stalking statute against vagueness challenge). Numerous cases hold that governments may proscribe threats, extortion, blackmail and the like, "despite the fact that they criminalize utterances because of their expressive content." See, e.g., *Watts v. United States,* 394 U.S. 705, 707, 89 S.Ct. 1399, 22 L.Ed.2d 664 (1969) (upholding constitutionality of law against threatening life of the President); *United States v. Velasquez,* 772 F.2d 1348, 1357 (7th Cir.1985) (holding that threats of physical violence are not protected by First Amendment); see also *R.A.V. v. City of St. Paul,* 505 U.S. 377, 420, 112 S.Ct. 2538, 120 L.Ed.2d 305 (1992) (STEVENS, J., concurring) (quoting Frederick Schauer, Categories and the First Amendment: A Play in Three Acts, 34 *Vand. L.Rev.* 265, 270 (1981)) ("Although the First Amendment broadly protects 'speech,' it does not protect the right to 'fix prices, breach contracts, make false warranties, place bets with bookies, threaten, or extort.'").

Paragraph (d)(5) could be construed to prohibit "any statement, gesture, or other communication" that makes a reasonable person feel they face danger if they refuse to donate, that they are being compelled out of physical fear. The possibility that a polite request for a donation might be heard as a threatening demand by an unusually sensitive or timid person is eliminated by the "reasonable person" standard included in the ordinance. A statement that makes a reasonable person feel compelled to donate out of physical fear amounts to a prohibition on robbery or extortion, which of course would be constitutional. While it is not a certainty that the state courts would adopt constitutional interpretations of the panhandling provisions, they are entitled to the opportunity to do so, and we will not interfere with that right. The district court did not err in refusing to enjoin the ordinance based on the vagueness concerns.

Conclusion

For the foregoing reasons, we Affirm the district court's denial of a permanent injunction and dismissal of Gresham's complaint.

QUESTIONS FOR DISCUSSION

1. Identify the main elements in Indianapolis's new panhandling ordinance.
2. Summarize the positions of the city of Indianapolis and Jimmy Gresham regarding the ordinance.
3. Should there be a distinction between organized charities and individual beggars when it comes to asking for money in this ordinance? Explain your answer.
4. According to the court, what is the difference between solicitation and commercial speech? What is the significance of distinguishing between them?
5. According to the court, why doesn't the ordinance violate the free speech clause of the First Amendment?
6. Should panhandling be considered speech? Defend your answer.
7. Assuming that panhandling is speech, is this ordinance a reasonable "time, place, and manner" regulation of free speech?
8. Summarize the arguments the court gives for ruling that the ordinance is not unconstitutionally vague. Do you agree? Defend your answer.

STREET GANGS

"Bands of loitering youth," seriously threaten their quality of life, say many city residents. Gangs can include everything from casual groups of kids who are just hanging out drinking a little bit all the way to "organized fighting squads" who terrorize neighborhoods. The casual groups do little more than "bother" residents. According to one observer: "They are neighborhood kids and they sometimes make a nuisance of themselves. Actually they stand there because they have no place to go." Gangs composed of older, rowdier members are more threatening. According to a resident in a neighborhood with one of these gangs:

> Sometimes I walk out of my house and start to try to walk down the street, and a gang will cross the street and try to scare me and my mother. A gang used to sit and drink beer and smoke pot in front of our stairs. My mom used to come out and tell them to get off; they would, and then when she would go into the house they'd come back, sit down, and look at us. Actually we're afraid to walk around in the neighborhood after it gets dark. I stay right in front of the house where my mom can see me.

A number of state and city governments have passed criminal laws to regulate gang behavior. In some places, it's a crime to participate in a gang. Some statutes and ordinances have stiffened the penalties for crimes committed by gang members. Others make it a crime to encourage minors to participate in gangs. Some have applied organized crime statutes to gangs. A few have punished parents for their children's gang activities. Cities have also passed ordinances banning gang members from certain public places, particularly city parks.

In addition to criminal penalties, cities have also turned to civil remedies in order to control gang activity. For example, the ancient civil remedy—**injunction to abate public nuisances**—is available. In these actions, city attorneys ask courts to declare gang activities and gang members public nuisances, and to issue **injunctions** (court orders) to abate (eliminate) the **public nuisance**. According to the California Supreme Court, in *People ex rel. Gallo v. Acuna,* a public nuisance may be any act

> which alternatively is injurious to health or is indecent, or offensive to the senses; the result of the act must interfere with the comfortable enjoyment of life or property; and those affected by the act may be an entire neighborhood or a considerable number of people.

The city attorney in *People ex rel. Gallo v. Acuna* asked for an injunction ordering gang members to stop doing all of the following:

(a) Standing, sitting, walking, driving, gathering or appearing anywhere in public view with any other defendant herein, or with any other known 'VST' (Varrio Sureno Town or Varrio Sureno Locos) member;

(b) Drinking alcoholic beverages in public excepting consumption on properly licensed premises or using drugs;

(c) Possessing any weapons including but not limited to knives, dirks, daggers, clubs, nunchukas, BB guns, concealed or loaded firearms, and any other illegal weapons as defined in the California Penal Code, and any object capable of inflicting serious bodily injury including but not limited to the following: metal pipes or rods, glass bottles, rocks, bricks, chains, tire irons, screwdrivers, hammers, crowbars, bumper jacks, spikes, razor blades, razors, sling shots, marbles, ball bearings;

(d) Engaging in fighting in the public streets, alleys, and/or public and private property;

(e) Using or possessing marker pens, spray paint cans, nails, razor blades, screwdrivers, or other sharp objects capable of defacing private or public property;

(f) Spray painting or otherwise applying graffiti on any public or private property, including but not limited to the street, alley, residences, block walls, vehicles and/or any other real or personal property;

(g) Trespassing on or encouraging others to trespass on any private property;

(h) Blocking free ingress and egress to the public sidewalks or street, or any driveways leading or appurtenant thereto in 'Rocksprings';

(i) Approaching vehicles, engaging in conversation, or otherwise communicating with the occupants of any vehicle or doing anything to obstruct or delay the free flow of vehicular or pedestrian traffic;

(j) Discharging any firearms;

(k) In any manner confronting, intimidating, annoying, harassing, threatening, challenging, provoking, assaulting and/or battering any residents or patrons, or visitors to 'Rocksprings', or any other persons who are known to have complained about gang activities, including any persons who have provided information in support of this Complaint and requests for Temporary Restraining Order, Preliminary Injunction and Permanent Injunction;

(l) Causing, encouraging, or participating in the use, possession and/or sale of narcotics;

(m) Owning, possessing or driving a vehicle found to have any contraband, narcotics, or illegal or deadly weapons;

(n) Using or possessing pagers or beepers in any public space;

(o) Possessing channel lock pliers, picks, wire cutters, dent pullers, sling shots, marbles, steel shot, spark plugs, rocks, screwdrivers, 'slim jims' and other devices capable of being used to break into locked vehicles;

(p) Demanding entry into another person's residence at any time of the day or night;

(q) Sheltering, concealing or permitting another person to enter into a residence not their own when said person appears to be running, hiding, or otherwise evading a law enforcement officer;

(r) Signaling to or acting as a lookout for other persons to warn of the approach of police officers and soliciting, encouraging, employing or offering payment to others to do the same;

(s) Climbing any tree, wall, or fence, or passing through any wall or fence by using tunnels or other holes in such structures;

(t) Littering in any public place or place open to public view;

(u) Urinating or defecating in any public place or place open to public view;

(v) Using words, phrases, physical gestures, or symbols commonly known as hand signs or engaging in other forms of communication which describe or refer to the gang known as 'VST' or 'VSL' as described in this Complaint or any of the accompanying pleadings or declarations;

(w) Wearing clothing which bears the name or letters of the gang known as 'VST' or 'VSL';

(x) Making, causing, or encouraging others to make loud noise of any kind, including but not limited to yelling and loud music at any time of the day or night."

The California trial court issued the injunction and the California Supreme Court upheld the injunction against challenges that it both violated freedom of association and was void for vagueness. Injunctions, like crimes that outlaw gang activities, call for balancing community and individual rights. The community interest in the quality of life requires peace, quiet, order, and a sense of security. At the same time, even members of street gangs have the right to associate, express themselves, travel freely, and be free from vague laws (see the section on the void-for-vagueness doctrine in Chapter 2).

In 1992, Chicago was facing a skyrocketing increase in crime rates that many outspoken people blamed on street gangs. However, unlike the sweeping injunction approved in California, the Chicago City Council passed a modern version of the ancient loitering ordinances discussed in the section on street people. As we saw in that section, loitering means to "remain in one place with no apparent purpose." Chicago's ordinance gave its police the power to take back street corners from gangs. Under its provisions, police officers could order groups of loiterers to disperse or face arrest if officers reasonably believed that one of the loiterers was a gang member.[23]

No one was surprised when the ordinance set off an angry debate. Mayor Richard Daley, Jr. expressed one view, "In some areas of the city, street gangs are terrorizing residents and laying claim to whole communities." Bobbie Crawford, a waitress, expressed another view, "When kids reach a certain age they hang around on street corners. I sure wouldn't like my children taken to a police station for hanging around." And Joan Suglich, mother of six, asked, "What if somebody asks his boys to walk him home so gang members don't jump him. Are police going to arrest them?" Nor was anyone surprised when the debate ended up in the United States Supreme Court. A divided Court decided the constitutionality of the ordinance in *City of Chicago v. Morales*.

C A S E   Was the Loitering Ordinance Void for Vagueness?

Chicago v. Morales
527 U.S. 41, 119 S.Ct. 1849 (1999)

After they were charged with violating the city's gang loitering ordinance, Jesus Morales moved to dismiss the actions. The Circuit Court, Cook County, granted the motion. The City appealed. The Appellate Court affirmed, and granted the city's subsequent request for a certificate of importance. After the defendants in another set of actions were charged with violating the ordinance, the Circuit Court dismissed the charges. On review, the Appellate Court affirmed. The City petitioned for a leave to appeal. In a further set of actions, the defendants were convicted in the Circuit Court of violating the ordinance and were sentenced to jail terms. The defendants appealed. The Appellate Court reversed. The City petitioned for leave to appeal. After granting the petitions and consolidating the cases, the Supreme Court of Illinois affirmed. Granting certiorari, the United States Supreme Court affirmed the judgment of the Illinois Supreme Court.

STEVENS, J. announced the judgment of the Court and delivered the opinion of the Court with respect to Parts I, II, and V, and an opinion with respect to Parts III, IV, and VI, joined by SOUTER and GINSBURG, JJ.

FACTS

In 1992, the Chicago City Council enacted the Gang Congregation Ordinance, which prohibits "criminal street gang members" from "loitering" with one another or with other persons in any public place. The question presented is whether the Supreme Court of Illinois correctly held that the ordinance violates the Due Process Clause of the Fourteenth Amendment to the Federal Constitution.

I

Before the ordinance was adopted, the city council's Committee on Police and Fire conducted hearings to explore the problems created by the city's street gangs, and more particularly, the consequences of public loitering by gang members. Witnesses included residents of the neighborhoods where gang members are most active, as well as some of the aldermen who represent those areas. Based on that evidence, the council made a series of findings that are included in the text of the ordinance and explain the reasons for its enactment.

The council found that a continuing increase in criminal street gang activity was largely responsible for the city's rising murder rate, as well as an escalation of violent and drug related crimes. It noted that in many neighborhoods throughout the city, "the burgeoning presence of street gang members in public places has intimidated many law abiding citizens." 177 Ill.2d 440, 445, 227 Ill.Dec. 130, 687 N.E.2d 53, 58 (1997). Furthermore, the council stated that gang members "establish control over identifiable areas . . . by loitering in those areas and intimidating others from entering those areas; and . . . members of criminal street gangs avoid arrest by committing no offense punishable under existing laws when they know the police are present. . . ." It further found that "loitering in public places by criminal street gang members creates a justifiable fear for the safety of persons and property in the area" and that "aggressive action is necessary to preserve the city's streets and other public places so that the public may use such places without fear." Moreover, the council concluded that the city "has an interest in discouraging all persons from loitering in public places with criminal gang members."

The ordinance creates a criminal offense punishable by a fine of up to $500, imprisonment for not more than six months, and a requirement to perform up to 120 hours of community service. Commission of the offense involves four predicates. First, the police officer must reasonably believe that at least one of the two or more persons present in a "public place" is a "criminal street gang member." Second, the persons must be "loitering," which the ordinance defines as "remain[ing] in any one place with no apparent purpose." Third, the officer must then order "all" of the persons to disperse and remove themselves "from the area." Fourth, a person must disobey the officer's order. If any person, whether a gang member or not, disobeys the officer's order, that person is guilty of violating the ordinance. The ordinance states in pertinent part:

(a) Whenever a police officer observes a person whom he reasonably believes to be a criminal street gang member loitering in any public place with one or more other persons, he shall order all such persons to disperse and remove themselves from the area. Any person who does not promptly obey such an order is in violation of this section.

(b) It shall be an affirmative defense to an alleged violation of this section that no person who was observed loitering was in fact a member of a criminal street gang.

(c) As used in this section:

(1) 'Loiter' means to remain in any one place with no apparent purpose.

(2) 'Criminal street gang' means any ongoing organization, association in fact or group of three or more persons, whether formal or informal, having as one of its substantial activities the commission of one or more of the criminal acts enumerated in paragraph

(3) and whose members individually or collectively engage in or have engaged in a pattern of criminal gang activity. . . .

(5) 'Public place' means the public way and any other location open to the public, whether publicly or privately owned.

. . .

(e) Any person who violates this Section is subject to a fine of not less than $100 and not more than $500 for each offense, or imprisonment for not more than six months, or both. In addition to or instead of the above penalties, any person who violates this section may be required to perform up to 120 hours of community service pursuant to section 1-4-120 of this Code. Chicago Municipal Code § 8-4-015 (added June 17, 1992).

Two months after the ordinance was adopted, the Chicago Police Department promulgated General Order 92-4 to provide guidelines to govern its enforcement. That order purported to establish limitations on the enforcement discretion of police officers "to ensure that the anti-gang loitering ordinance is not enforced in an arbitrary or discriminatory way." The limitations confine the authority to arrest gang members who violate the ordinance to sworn "members of the Gang Crime Section" and certain other designated officers, and establish detailed criteria for defining street gangs and membership in such gangs. In addition, the order directs district commanders to "designate areas in which the presence of gang members has a demonstrable effect on the activities of law abiding persons in the surrounding community," and provides that the ordinance "will be enforced only within the designated areas." The city, however, does not release the locations of these "designated areas" to the public.

II

During the three years of its enforcement, the police issued over 89,000 dispersal orders and arrested over 42,000 people for violating the ordinance. In the ensuing enforcement proceedings, two trial judges upheld the constitutionality of the ordinance, but eleven others ruled that it was invalid. In respondent Youkhana's case, the trial judge held that the "ordinance fails to notify individuals what conduct is prohibited, and it encourages arbitrary and capricious enforcement by police."

The city believes that the ordinance resulted in a significant decline in gang-related homicides. It notes that in 1995, the last year the ordinance was enforced, the gang-related homicide rate fell by 26%. In 1996, after the ordinance had been held invalid, the gang-related homicide rate rose 11%. However, gang-related homicides fell by 19% in 1997, over a year after the suspension of the ordinance. Given the myriad factors that influence levels of violence, it is difficult to evaluate the probative value of this statistical evidence, or to reach any firm conclusion about the ordinance's efficacy. Cf. Harcourt, Reflecting on the Subject: A Critique of the Social Influence Conception of Deterrence, the Broken Windows Theory, and Order-Maintenance Policing New York Style, 97 *Mich. L.Rev.* 291, 296 (1998) (describing the "hotly contested debate raging among . . . experts over the causes of the decline in crime in New York City and nationally").

The Illinois Appellate Court affirmed the trial court's ruling in the Youkhana case, consolidated and affirmed other pending appeals in accordance with Youkhana, and reversed the convictions of respondents Gutierrez, Morales, and others. The Appellate Court was persuaded that the ordinance impaired the freedom of assembly of non-gang members in violation of the First Amendment to the Federal Constitution and Article I of the Illinois Constitution, that it was unconstitutionally vague, that it improperly criminalized status rather than conduct, and that it jeopardized rights guaranteed under the Fourth Amendment.

The Illinois Supreme Court affirmed. It held "that the gang loitering ordinance violates due process of law in that it is impermissibly vague on its face and an arbitrary restriction on personal liberties." 177 Ill.2d, at 447, 227 Ill.Dec. 130, 687 N.E.2d, at 59. The court did not reach the contentions that the ordinance "creates a status offense, permits arrests without probable cause or is overbroad." In support of its vagueness holding, the court pointed out that the definition of "loitering" in the ordinance drew no distinction between innocent conduct and conduct calculated to cause harm.

The ordinance defines "loiter" to mean "to remain in any one place with no apparent purpose." People with entirely legitimate and lawful purposes will not always be able to make their purposes apparent to an observing police officer. For example, a person waiting to hail a taxi, resting on a corner during a job, or stepping into a doorway to evade a rain shower has a perfectly legitimate purpose in all these scenarios; however, that purpose will rarely be apparent to an observer. Moreover, the definition of "loiter" provided by the ordinance does not assist in clearly articulating the proscriptions of the ordinance.

Furthermore, it concluded that the ordinance was "not reasonably susceptible to a limiting construction which would affirm its validity." It stated,

> Although the proscriptions of the ordinance are vague, the city council's intent in its enactment is clear and unambiguous. The city has declared gang members a public menace and determined that gang members are too adept at avoiding arrest for all the other crimes they commit. Accordingly, the city council crafted an exceptionally broad ordinance which could be used to sweep these intolerable and objectionable gang members from the city streets.

We granted certiorari, and now affirm. Like the Illinois Supreme Court, we conclude that the ordinance enacted by the city of Chicago is unconstitutionally vague.

OPINION

III

The basic factual predicate for the city's ordinance is not in dispute. As the city argues in its brief,

> the very presence of a large collection of obviously brazen, insistent, and lawless gang members and hangers-on on the public ways intimidates residents, who become afraid even to leave their homes and go about their business. That, in turn, imperils community residents' sense of safety and security, detracts from property values, and can ultimately destabilize entire neighborhoods.

The findings in the ordinance explain that it was motivated by these concerns. We have no doubt that a law that directly prohibited such intimidating conduct would be constitutional, but this ordinance broadly covers a significant amount of additional activity. Uncertainty about the scope of that additional coverage provides the basis for respondents' claim that the ordinance is too vague.

In fact the city already has several laws that serve this purpose. See, e.g., Ill. Comp. Stat. ch. 720 §§ 5/12-6 (1998) (Intimidation); 570/405.2 (Streetgang criminal drug conspiracy); 147/1 et seq. (Illinois Streetgang Terrorism Omnibus Prevention Act); 5/25-1 (Mob action). Deputy Superintendent Cooper, the only representative of the police department at the Committee on Police and Fire hearing on the ordinance, testified that, of the kinds of behavior people had discussed at the hearing, "90 percent of those instances are actually criminal offenses where people, in fact, can be arrested."

We are confronted at the outset with the city's claim that it was improper for the state courts to conclude that the ordinance is invalid on its face. The city correctly points out that imprecise laws can be attacked on their face . . . [if they fail] to establish standards for the police and public that are sufficient to guard against the arbitrary deprivation of liberty interests. *Kolender v. Lawson,* 461 U.S. 352, 358, 103 S.Ct. 1855, 75 L.Ed.2d 903 (1983). . . . The freedom to loiter for innocent purposes is part of the "liberty" protected by the Due Process Clause of the Fourteenth Amendment. We have expressly identified this "right to remove from one place to another according to inclination" as "an attribute of personal liberty" protected by the Constitution. *Williams v. Fears,* 179 U.S. 270, 274, 21 S.Ct. 128, 45 L.Ed. 186 (1900); see also *Papachristou v. Jacksonville,* 405 U.S. 156, 164, 92 S.Ct. 839, 31 L.Ed.2d 110 (1972). Indeed, it is apparent that an individual's decision to remain in a public place of his choice is as much a part of his liberty as the freedom of movement inside frontiers that is "a part of our heritage" or the right to move "to whatsoever place one's own inclination may direct" identified in Blackstone's *Commentaries.*

There is no need, however, to decide whether the impact of the Chicago ordinance on constitutionally protected liberty alone would suffice to support a facial challenge under the overbreadth doctrine. For it is clear that the vagueness of this enactment makes a facial challenge appropriate. This is not an ordinance that "simply regulates business behavior and contains a scienter requirement." It is a criminal law that contains no *mens rea* requirement, and infringes on constitutionally protected rights. When vagueness permeates the text of such a law, it is subject to facial attack.

Vagueness may invalidate a criminal law for either of two independent reasons. First, it may fail to provide the kind of notice that will enable ordinary people to understand what conduct it prohibits; second, it may authorize and even encourage arbitrary and discriminatory enforcement. Accordingly, we first consider whether the ordinance provides fair notice to the citizen and then discuss its potential for arbitrary enforcement.

IV

"It is established that a law fails to meet the requirements of the Due Process Clause if it is so vague and standardless that it leaves the public uncertain as to the conduct it prohibits. . . ." The Illinois Supreme Court recognized that the term "loiter" may have a common and accepted meaning, but the definition of that term in this ordinance— "to remain in any one place with no apparent purpose"—does not. It is difficult to imagine how any citizen of the city of Chicago standing in a public place with a group of people would know if he or she had an "apparent purpose." If she were talking to another person, would she have an apparent purpose? If she were frequently checking her watch and looking expectantly down the street, would she have an apparent purpose?

Since the city cannot conceivably have meant to criminalize each instance a citizen stands in public with a gang member, the vagueness that dooms this ordinance is not the product of uncertainty about the normal meaning of "loitering," but rather about what loitering is covered by the ordinance and what is not. The Illinois Supreme Court emphasized the law's failure to distinguish between innocent conduct and conduct threatening harm. One of the trial courts that invalidated the ordinance gave the following illustration:

> Suppose a group of gang members were playing basketball in the park, while waiting for a drug delivery. Their apparent purpose is that they are in the park to play ball. The actual purpose is that they are waiting for drugs. Under this definition of loitering, a group of people innocently sitting in a park discussing their futures would be arrested, while the 'basketball players' awaiting a drug delivery would be left alone.

Its decision followed the precedent set by a number of state courts that have upheld ordinances that criminalize loitering combined with some other overt act or evidence of criminal intent. See, e.g., *Tacoma v. Luvene,* 118 Wash.2d 826, 827 P.2d 1374 (1992) (upholding ordinance criminalizing loitering with purpose to engage in drug-related activities); *People v. Superior Court,* 46 Cal.3d 381, 394-395, 250 Cal.Rptr. 515, 758 P.2d 1046, 1052 (1988) (upholding ordinance criminalizing loitering for the purpose of engaging in or soliciting lewd act). However, state courts have uniformly invalidated laws that do not join the term "loitering" with a second specific element of the crime. See, e.g., *State v. Richard,* 108 Nev. 626, 629, 836 P.2d 622, 624, n. 2 (1992) (striking down statute that made it unlawful "for any person to loiter or prowl upon the property of another without lawful business with the owner or occupant thereof").

The city's principal response to this concern about adequate notice is that loiterers are not subject to sanction until after they have failed to comply with an officer's order to disperse. "Whatever problem is created by a law that criminalizes conduct people normally believe to be innocent is solved when persons receive actual notice from a police order of what they are expected to do." We find this response unpersuasive for at least two reasons.

First, the purpose of the fair notice requirement is to enable the ordinary citizen to conform his or her conduct to the law. "No one may be required at peril of life, liberty or property to speculate as to the meaning of penal statutes." *Lanzetta v. New Jersey,* 306 U.S. 451, 453, 59 S.Ct. 618, 83 L.Ed. 888 (1939). Although it is true that a loiterer is not subject to criminal sanctions unless he or she disobeys a dispersal order, the loitering is the conduct that the ordinance is designed to prohibit. . . . Because an officer may issue an order only after prohibited conduct has already occurred, it cannot provide the kind of advance notice that will protect the putative loiterer from being ordered to disperse.

Such an order cannot retroactively give adequate warning of the boundary between the permissible and the impermissible applications of the law.

Second, the terms of the dispersal order compound the inadequacy of the notice afforded by the ordinance. It provides that the officer "shall order all such persons to disperse and remove themselves from the area." This vague phrasing raises a host of questions. After such an order issues, how long must the loiterers remain apart? How far must they move? If each loiterer walks around the block and they meet again at the same location, are they subject to arrest or merely to being ordered to disperse again? As we do here, we have found vagueness in a criminal statute exacerbated by the use of the standards of "neighborhood" and "locality."... Both terms are elastic and, dependent upon circumstances, may be equally satisfied by areas measured by rods or by miles.

Lack of clarity in the description of the loiterer's duty to obey a dispersal order might not render the ordinance unconstitutionally vague if the definition of the forbidden conduct were clear, but it does buttress our conclusion that the entire ordinance fails to give the ordinary citizen adequate notice of what is forbidden and what is permitted. The Constitution does not permit a legislature to "set a net large enough to catch all possible offenders, and leave it to the courts to step inside and say who could be rightfully detained, and who should be set at large." This ordinance is therefore vague "not in the sense that it requires a person to conform his conduct to an imprecise but comprehensible normative standard, but rather in the sense that no standard of conduct is specified at all."

V

The broad sweep of the ordinance also violates " 'the requirement that a legislature establish minimal guidelines to govern law enforcement.' " *Kolender v. Lawson,* 461 U.S., at 358, 103 S.Ct. 1855. There are no such guidelines in the ordinance. In any public place in the city of Chicago, persons who stand or sit in the company of a gang member may be ordered to disperse unless their purpose is apparent. The mandatory language in the enactment directs the police to issue an order without first making any inquiry about their possible purposes. It matters not whether the reason that a gang member and his father, for example, might loiter near Wrigley Field is to rob an unsuspecting fan or

just to get a glimpse of Sammy Sosa leaving the ballpark; in either event, if their purpose is not apparent to a nearby police officer, she may—indeed, she "shall"—order them to disperse.

Recognizing that the ordinance does reach a substantial amount of innocent conduct, we turn, then, to its language to determine if it "necessarily entrusts lawmaking to the moment-to-moment judgment of the policeman on his beat." As we discussed in the context of fair notice, the principal source of the vast discretion conferred on the police in this case is the definition of loitering as "to remain in any one place with no apparent purpose."

As the Illinois Supreme Court interprets that definition, it "provides absolute discretion to police officers to determine what activities constitute loitering." We have no authority to construe the language of a state statute more narrowly than the construction given by that State's highest court. "The power to determine the meaning of a statute carries with it the power to prescribe its extent and limitations as well as the method by which they shall be determined."

Nevertheless, the city disputes the Illinois Supreme Court's interpretation, arguing that the text of the ordinance limits the officer's discretion in three ways. First, it does not permit the officer to issue a dispersal order to anyone who is moving along or who has an apparent purpose. Second, it does not permit an arrest if individuals obey a dispersal order. Third, no order can issue unless the officer reasonably believes that one of the loiterers is a member of a criminal street gang.

Even putting to one side our duty to defer to a state court's construction of the scope of a local enactment, we find each of these limitations insufficient. That the ordinance does not apply to people who are moving—that is, to activity that would not constitute loitering under any possible definition of the term—does not even address the question of how much discretion the police enjoy in deciding which stationary persons to disperse under the ordinance. Similarly, that the ordinance does not permit an arrest until after a dispersal order has been disobeyed does not provide any guidance to the officer deciding whether such an order should issue. The "no apparent purpose" standard for making that decision is inherently subjective because its application depends on whether some purpose is "apparent" to the officer on the scene.

Presumably an officer would have discretion to treat some purposes—perhaps a purpose to engage in idle conversation or simply to enjoy a cool breeze on a warm evening—as too frivolous to be apparent if he suspected a different ulterior motive. Moreover, an officer conscious of the city council's reasons for enacting the ordinance might well ignore its text and issue a dispersal order, even though an illicit purpose is actually apparent.

It is true, as the city argues, that the requirement that the officer reasonably believe that a group of loiterers contains a gang member does place a limit on the authority to order dispersal. That limitation would no doubt be sufficient if the ordinance only applied to loitering that had an apparently harmful purpose or effect, or possibly if it only applied to loitering by persons reasonably believed to be criminal gang members. Not all of the respondents in this case, for example, are gang members. The city admits that it was unable to prove that Morales is a gang member but justifies his arrest and conviction by the fact that Morales admitted "that he knew he was with criminal street gang members." But this ordinance, for reasons that are not explained in the findings of the city council, requires no harmful purpose and applies to non-gang members as well as suspected gang members. It applies to everyone in the city who may remain in one place with one suspected gang member as long as their purpose is not apparent to an officer observing them. Friends, relatives, teachers, counselors, or even total strangers might unwittingly engage in forbidden loitering if they happen to engage in idle conversation with a gang member.

Ironically, the definition of loitering in the Chicago ordinance not only extends its scope to encompass harmless conduct, but also has the perverse consequence of excluding from its coverage much of the intimidating conduct that motivated its enactment. As the city council's findings demonstrate, the most harmful gang loitering is motivated either by an apparent purpose to publicize the gang's dominance of certain territory, thereby intimidating nonmembers, or by an equally apparent purpose to conceal ongoing commerce in illegal drugs. As the Illinois Supreme Court has not placed any limiting construction on the language in the ordinance, we must assume that the ordinance means what it says and that it has no application to loiterers whose purpose is apparent. The relative importance of its application to harmless loitering is magnified by its inapplicability to loitering that has an obviously threatening or illicit purpose.

Finally, in its opinion striking down the ordinance, the Illinois Supreme Court refused to accept the general order issued by the police department as a sufficient limitation on the "vast amount of discretion" granted to the police in its enforcement. We agree. That the police have adopted internal rules limiting their enforcement to certain designated areas in the city would not provide a defense to a loiterer who might be arrested elsewhere. Nor could a person who knowingly loitered with a well-known gang member anywhere in the city safely assume that they would not be ordered to disperse no matter how innocent and harmless their loitering might be.

VI

In our judgment, the Illinois Supreme Court correctly concluded that the ordinance does not provide sufficiently specific limits on the enforcement discretion of the police "to meet constitutional standards for definiteness and clarity." We recognize the serious and difficult problems testified to by the citizens of Chicago that led to the enactment of this ordinance. "We are mindful that the preservation of liberty depends in part on the maintenance of social order." However, in this instance the city has enacted an ordinance that affords too much discretion to the police and too little notice to citizens who wish to use the public streets.

Accordingly, the judgment of the Supreme Court of Illinois is Affirmed.

DISSENT

SCALIA, J.

The citizens of Chicago were once free to drive about the city at whatever speed they wished. At some point Chicagoans (or perhaps Illinoisans) decided this would not do, and imposed prophylactic speed limits designed to assure safe operation by the average (or perhaps even subaverage) driver with the average (or perhaps even subaverage) vehicle. This infringed upon the "freedom" of all citizens, but was not unconstitutional.

Similarly, the citizens of Chicago were once free to stand around and gawk at the scene of an accident. At some point Chicagoans discovered that this obstructed traffic and caused more accidents. They did not make the practice unlawful, but they did authorize police officers to order the crowd to disperse, and imposed penalties for refusal to obey such an order. Again, this prophylactic measure infringed upon the "freedom" of all citizens, but was not unconstitutional.

Until the ordinance that is before us today was adopted, the citizens of Chicago were free to stand about in public places with no apparent purpose—to engage, that is, in conduct that appeared to be loitering. In recent years, however, the city has been afflicted with criminal street gangs. As reflected in the record before us, these gangs congregated in public places to deal in drugs, and to terrorize the neighborhoods by demonstrating control over their "turf." Many residents of the inner city felt that they were prisoners in their own homes. Once again, Chicagoans decided that to eliminate the problem it was worth restricting some of the freedom that they once enjoyed. The means they took was similar to the second, and more mild, example given above rather than the first: Loitering was not made unlawful, but when a group of people occupied a public place without an apparent purpose and in the company of a known gang member, police officers were authorized to order them to disperse, and the failure to obey such an order was made unlawful. The minor limitation upon the free state of nature that this prophylactic arrangement imposed upon all Chicagoans seemed to them (and it seems to me) a small price to pay for liberation of their streets.

The majority today invalidates this perfectly reasonable measure by . . . elevating loitering to a constitutionally guaranteed right, and by discerning vagueness where, according to our usual standards, none exists. . . . The fact is that the present ordinance is entirely clear in its application, cannot be violated except with full knowledge and intent, and vests no more discretion in the police than innumerable other measures authorizing police orders to preserve the public peace and safety. As suggested by their tortured analyses, and by their suggested solutions that bear no relation to the identified constitutional problem, the majority's real quarrel with the Chicago Ordinance is simply that it permits (or indeed requires) too much harmless conduct by innocent citizens to be proscribed.

. . . Justice O'CONNOR's concurrence says with disapprobation, "the ordinance applies to hundreds of thousands of persons who are not gang members, standing on any sidewalk or in any park, coffee shop, bar, or other location open to the public." But in our democratic system, how much harmless conduct to proscribe is not a judgment to be made by the courts. So long as constitutionally guaranteed rights are not affected, and so long as the proscription has a rational basis, all sorts of perfectly harmless activity by millions of perfectly innocent people can be forbidden—riding a motorcycle without a safety helmet, for example, starting a campfire in a national forest, or selling a safe and effective drug not yet approved by the FDA. All of these acts are entirely innocent and harmless in themselves, but because of the risk of harm that they entail, the freedom to engage in them has been abridged. The citizens of Chicago have decided that depriving themselves of the freedom to "hang out" with a gang member is necessary to eliminate pervasive gang crime and intimidation—and that the elimination of the one is worth the deprivation of the other. This Court has no business second-guessing either the degree of necessity or the fairness of the trade.

I dissent from the judgment of the Court.

THOMAS, J. joined by REHNQUIST, CJ. and SCALIA, J.

The duly elected members of the Chicago City Council enacted the ordinance at issue as part of a larger effort to prevent gangs from establishing dominion over the public streets. By invalidating Chicago's ordinance, I fear that the Court has unnecessarily sentenced law-abiding citizens to lives of terror and misery. The ordinance is not vague. "Any fool would know that a particular category of conduct would be within its reach." *Kolender v. Lawson*, 461 U.S. 352, 370, 103 S.Ct. 1855, 75 L.Ed.2d 903 (1983) (WHITE, J., dissenting). Nor does it violate the Due Process Clause. The asserted "freedom to loiter for innocent purposes," is in no way "'deeply rooted in this Nation's history and tradition,'" I dissent.

The human costs exacted by criminal street gangs are inestimable. In many of our Nation's cities, gangs have "virtually overtaken certain neighborhoods, contributing to the economic and social decline of these areas and causing fear and lifestyle changes among law-abiding residents." Gangs fill the daily lives of many of our poorest and most vulnerable citizens with a terror that the Court does not give sufficient consideration, often relegating them to the status of prisoners in their own homes. "From the small business owner who is literally crippled because he refuses to pay 'protection' money to the neighborhood gang, to the families who are hostages within their homes, living in neighborhoods ruled by predatory drug trafficking gangs, the harmful impact of gang violence . . . is both physically and psychologically debilitating."

The city of Chicago has suffered the devastation wrought by this national tragedy. Last year, in an effort to curb plummeting attendance, the Chicago Public Schools hired dozens of adults to escort children to school. The youngsters had become too terrified of gang violence to leave their homes alone. The children's fears were not unfounded. In 1996, the Chicago Police Department estimated that there were 132 criminal street gangs in the city. Between 1987 and 1994, these gangs were involved in 63,141 criminal incidents, including 21,689 nonlethal violent crimes and 894 homicides. Many of these criminal incidents and homicides result from gang "turf battles," which take place on the public streets and place innocent residents in grave danger. "While street gangs may specialize in entrepreneurial activities like drug-dealing, their gang-related lethal violence is more likely to grow out of turf conflicts."

Before enacting its ordinance, the Chicago City Council held extensive hearings on the problems of gang loitering. Concerned citizens appeared to testify poignantly as to how gangs disrupt their daily lives. Ordinary citizens like Ms. D'Ivory Gordon explained that she struggled just to walk to work:

> When I walk out my door, these guys are out there. . . . They watch you. . . . They know where you live. They know what time you leave, what time you come home. I am afraid of them. I have even come to the point now that I carry a meat cleaver to work with me. . . . I don't want to hurt anyone, and I don't want to be hurt. We need to clean these corners up. Clean these communities up and take it back from them.

Eighty-eight-year-old Susan Mary Jackson echoed her sentiments, testifying, "We used to have a nice neighborhood. We don't have it anymore. . . . I am scared to go out in the daytime. . . . you can't pass because they are standing. I am afraid to go to the store. I don't go to the store because I am afraid. At my age if they look at me real hard, I be ready to holler." Another long-time resident testified:

> I have never had the terror that I feel everyday when I walk down the streets of Chicago. . . . I have had my windows broken out. I have had guns pulled on me. I have been threatened. I get intimidated on a daily basis, and it's come to the point where I say, well, do I go out today. Do I put my ax in my briefcase. Do I walk around dressed like a bum so I am not looking rich or got any money or anything like that.

Following these hearings, the council found that "criminal street gangs establish control over identifiable areas . . . by loitering in those areas and intimidating others from entering those areas." It further found that the mere presence of gang members "intimidates many law abiding citizens" and "creates a justifiable fear for the safety of persons and property in the area." It is the product of this democratic process—the council's attempt to address these social ills—that we are asked to pass judgment upon today.

As part of its ongoing effort to curb the deleterious effects of criminal street gangs, the citizens of Chicago sensibly decided to return to basics. The ordinance does nothing more than confirm the well-established principle that the police have the duty and the power to maintain the public peace, and, when necessary, to disperse groups of individuals who threaten it. The plurality, however, concludes that the city's commonsense effort to combat gang loitering fails constitutional scrutiny for two separate reasons—because it infringes upon gang members' constitutional right to "loiter for innocent purposes," and because it is vague on its face. A majority of the Court endorses the latter conclusion. I respectfully disagree.

We recently reconfirmed that "our Nation's history, legal traditions, and practices . . . provide the crucial 'guideposts for responsible decision-making' that direct and restrain our exposition of the Due Process Clause." Only laws that infringe "those fundamental rights and liberties which are, objectively, 'deeply rooted in this Nation's history and tradition'" offend the Due Process Clause. The plurality asserts that "the freedom to loiter for innocent purposes is part of the 'liberty' protected by the Due Process Clause of the Fourteenth Amendment." Yet it acknowledges—as it must—that "antiloitering ordinances have long existed in this country."

Loitering and vagrancy statutes have been utilized throughout American history in an attempt to prevent crime by removing 'undesirable persons' from public before they have the opportunity to engage in criminal activity. . . . The plurality asserts that this history fails to "persuade us that the right to engage in loitering that is entirely harmless . . . is not a part of the liberty protected by the due process clause." Apparently, the plurality believes it sufficient to rest on the proposition that antiloitering laws represent an anachronistic throwback to an earlier, less sophisticated, era. For example, it expresses concern that some antivagrancy laws carried the penalty of slavery. But this fact is irrelevant to our analysis of whether there is a constitutional right to loiter for innocent purposes. This case does not involve an antiloitering law carrying the penalty of slavery. The law at issue in this case criminalizes the failure to disobey a police officer's order to disperse and imposes modest penalties, such as a fine of up to $500 and a prison sentence of up to six months.

The plurality's sweeping conclusion that this ordinance infringes upon a liberty interest protected by the Fourteenth Amendment's Due Process Clause withers when exposed to the relevant history: Laws prohibiting loitering and vagrancy have been a fixture of Anglo-American law at least since the time of the Norman Conquest. The American colonists enacted laws modeled upon the English vagrancy laws, and at the time of the founding, state and local governments customarily criminalized loitering and other forms of vagrancy. Vagrancy laws were common in the decades preceding the ratification of the Fourteenth Amendment, and remained on the books long after. . . .

The Court concludes that the ordinance is also unconstitutionally vague because it fails to provide adequate standards to guide police discretion and because, in the plurality's view, it does not give residents adequate notice of how to conform their conduct to the confines of the law. I disagree on both counts.

At the outset, it is important to note that the ordinance does not criminalize loitering per se. Rather, it penalizes loiterers' failure to obey a police officer's order to move along. A majority of the Court believes that this scheme vests too much discretion in police officers. Nothing could be further from the truth. Far from according officers too much discretion, the ordinance merely enables police officers to fulfill one of their traditional functions. Police officers are not, and have never been,

simply enforcers of the criminal law. They wear other hats—importantly, they have long been vested with the responsibility for preserving the public peace. Nor is the idea that the police are also peace officers simply a quaint anachronism. In most American jurisdictions, police officers continue to be obligated, by law, to maintain the public peace. . . .

In order to perform their peace-keeping responsibilities satisfactorily, the police inevitably must exercise discretion. Indeed, by empowering them to act as peace officers, the law assumes that the police will exercise that discretion responsibly and with sound judgment. That is not to say that the law should not provide objective guidelines for the police, but simply that it cannot rigidly constrain their every action. By directing a police officer not to issue a dispersal order unless he "observes a person whom he reasonably believes to be a criminal street gang member loitering in any public place," Chicago's ordinance strikes an appropriate balance between those two extremes. . . .

In concluding that the ordinance adequately channels police discretion, I do not suggest that a police officer enforcing the Gang Congregation Ordinance will never make a mistake. Nor do I overlook the possibility that a police officer, acting in bad faith, might enforce the ordinance in an arbitrary or discriminatory way. But our decisions should not turn on the proposition that such an event will be anything but rare. Instances of arbitrary or discriminatory enforcement of the ordinance, like any other law, are best addressed when (and if) they arise, rather than prophylactically through the disfavored mechanism of a facial challenge on vagueness grounds.

The plurality's conclusion that the ordinance "fails to give the ordinary citizen adequate notice of what is forbidden and what is permitted," is similarly untenable. There is nothing "vague" about an order to disperse. While "we can never expect mathematical certainty from our language," it is safe to assume that the vast majority of people who are ordered by the police to "disperse and remove themselves from the area" will have little difficulty understanding how to comply.

Assuming that we are also obligated to consider whether the ordinance places individuals on notice of what conduct might subject them to such an order . . . I subscribe to the view of retired Justice WHITE—"If any fool would know that a particular category of conduct would be within the reach of the statute, if there is an unmistakable core that a reasonable person would know is forbidden by the law, the enactment is not unconstitutional on its face." *Kolender*, 461 U.S., at 370-371, 103 S.Ct. 1855 (dissenting opinion). This is certainly such a case. As the Illinois Supreme Court recognized, "persons of ordinary intelligence may maintain a common and accepted meaning of the word 'loiter.'"

The plurality also concludes that the definition of the term loiter—"to remain in any one place with no apparent purpose," fails to provide adequate notice. "It is difficult to imagine," the plurality posits, "how any citizen of the city of Chicago standing in a public place . . . would know if he or she had an 'apparent purpose.'" The plurality underestimates the intellectual capacity of the citizens of Chicago. Persons of ordinary intelligence are perfectly capable of evaluating how outsiders perceive their conduct, and here "it is self-evident that there is a whole range of conduct that anyone with at least a semblance of common sense would know is [loitering] and that would be covered by the statute." Members of a group standing on the corner staring blankly into space, for example, are likely well aware that passersby would conclude that they have "no apparent purpose." In any event, because this is a facial challenge, the plurality's ability to hypothesize that some individuals, in some circumstances, may be unable to ascertain how their actions appear to outsiders is irrelevant to our analysis. Here, we are asked to determine whether the ordinance is "vague in all of its applications." The answer is unquestionably no.

Today, the Court focuses extensively on the "rights" of gang members and their companions. It can safely do so—the people who will have to live with the consequences of today's opinion do not live in our neighborhoods. Rather, the people who will suffer from our lofty pronouncements are people like Ms. Susan Mary Jackson; people who have seen their neighborhoods literally destroyed by gangs and violence and drugs. They are good, decent people who must struggle to overcome their desperate situation, against all odds, in order to raise their families, earn a living, and remain good citizens. As one resident described, "There is only about maybe one or two percent of the people in the city causing these problems maybe, but it's keeping 98 percent of us in our houses and off the streets and afraid to shop." By focusing exclusively on the imagined "rights" of the two percent, the Court today has denied our most vulnerable citizens the very thing that Justice STEVENS, elevates above all else—the "freedom of movement." And that is a shame.

I respectfully dissent.

QUESTIONS FOR DISCUSSION

1. List the four elements in the Chicago gang loitering ordinance.

2. List the specific arguments the majority gave to support its conclusion that the ordinance was vague.

3. Explain specifically all of the reasons why the dissenting judges disagreed.

4. Would "any fool know" what conduct this ordinance prohibited? Defend your answer.

5. Did the majority properly balance the interest in community order with the individual liberty? Explain your answer.

6. If the majority didn't properly strike the balance, how would you do it differently? Explain your answer.

13-1 *Chicago v. Morales,* Oral Arguments and Briefs

SUMMARY

The ancient crimes against public order and decency were used for centuries to control public misbehavior. Although the list of public order and morals offenses is long, the most frequently used among them included public drunkenness, vagrancy, loitering, prostitution, nuisance, and begging. Some of these offenses, such as public drunkenness and nuisance, were aimed primarily at conduct. However, most of them were also used to control "undesirable" groups—the poor, particularly the unemployed wandering poor, prostitutes, drunks, and panhandlers. In other words, they were status offenses.

Until the twentieth century, these minor offenses aroused little attention and certainly no controversy. Beginning in the 1930s, the crimes against public order and morals were criticized as discriminatory weapons of the wealthy to keep the poor out of sight, or at least off the streets. Then, as a result of the Civil Rights movement of the 1960s and the so-called rights revolution that followed in its aftermath, the public order and morals offenses came under fire in the courts. State courts first struck down vagrancy and loitering statutes. Then the United States Supreme Court declared that the typical vagrancy and loitering statutes not only were void for vagueness but also denied equal protection of the laws to the poor and the weak. Furthermore, the high court ruled that status offenses denied members of the criminalized group life, liberty, or property without due process of law.

During the 1980s, a combination of developments turned the tide against the rights offensive. Economic hard times, court rulings that deinstitutionalized the mentally ill, lack of housing, and other factors not yet fully identified combined with the rights revolution to increase the numbers and visibility of people in public places, apparently without anywhere else to go. The behavior of these "street people" and of their highly vocal advocates created a backlash across a broad social spectrum of employed "respectable" people—men and women, minorities and whites, rich and poor. Academic support for the backlash came from the "broken windows" theory that suggested a link between these minor offenses against public order and morals and serious crimes against persons, their homes, and property.

The backlash found legislative expression in a rash of new city ordinances and some state statutes. These new laws have tailored some of the old public order offenses to meet the social reality of the United States—particularly of city life—at the beginning of the twenty-first century. And these new laws have called upon not only the traditional criminal law but also upon the civil remedy of injunctions to abate public nuisances in order to control public misbehavior. Both the criminal laws and the civil remedies are based on the idea that state and municipal governments are responsible for preserving the quality of life by enforcing a minimum level of decent conduct in public. The quality of life crimes and their enforcement challenge criminal law to preserve the fundamental requirement of our constitutional democracy—ordered liberty—by balancing individual rights and community order. In other words, individual rights cannot trump the community interest in preserving the quality of life. It remains to be seen whether the new laws and remedies can prevent the community interest in the quality of life from trumping the rights of unconventional but law-abiding individuals who "bother" "respectable" people.

   Go to the Criminal Law 7e CD-ROM for Internet exercises.

REVIEW QUESTIONS

1. Identify and explain the fundamental requirement of our constitutional system in formulating its crimes against public order.

2. Explain how the ancient public order and morals offenses have been altered to suit the social reality of life at the turn of the twenty-first century.

3. Define, describe, and list the purposes of quality of life crimes.

4. Describe and explain the controversy over the quality of life crimes.

5. Describe the "broken windows" theory and the degree of empirical support for it.

6. Identify and explain the disconnect between national attention and local concerns regarding serious crimes and quality of life offenses.

7. Define injunctions and explain their role in regulating behavior in public.

8. Explain the purposes of and the differences between the ancient vagrancy and loitering laws and modern laws affecting the poor.

9. Describe modern panhandling laws and discuss which ones are probably constitutional and which types are probably not constitutional.

KEY TERMS

"broken windows" theory—the theory that minor offenses can lead to a rise in serious crime.

designated public forums—places the government chooses to make available to the public.

injunction—a court order to do or to stop doing something.

injunction to abate public nuisances—an action in which city attorneys ask the courts to declare gang activities and gang members public nuisances and to issue injunctions to abate the public nuisance.

liberty—the right of individuals to go about in public free of undue interference.

loitering—remaining in one place with no apparent purpose.

nonpublic forums—places, such as airports, bus terminals, railway stations, and subways, where the government has broad power to restrict or even prohibit solicitation.

order—behavior in public that comports with minimum community standards of civility.

preliminary injunction—a temporary order issued by a court after notice and hearing.

public nuisance—offense against, or interference with, the exercise of rights common to the public.

quality of life crimes—breaches of minimum standards of decent behavior in public.

traditional public forums—streets, sidewalks, parks, and other places where people have since ancient times expressed their views.

NOTES

1. James Q. Wilson and George L. Kelling, "Broken Windows," *Atlantic Monthly,* March 1982; James Q. Wilson, Foreword, George L. Kelling and Catherine M. Coles, *Fixing Broken Windows* (New York: Free Press, 1996), p. xiv.

2. Wesley G. Skogan, *Disorder and Decline* (New York: Free Press, 1990), 10.

3. Ibid., p. 75.

4. Ibid., ch. 2.

5. Ibid., p. 21.

6. Harry Simon, "Towns Without Pity: A Constitutional and Historical Analysis of Official Efforts to Drive Homeless Persons from American Cities," *Tulane Law Review* 66 (1992): 631 (1992); *Mayor of New York v. Miln,* 36 U.S. (11 Pet.) 102 (1837).

7. *Edwards v. California,* 314 U.S. 162 (1941), 174, 184.

8. *Parker v. Municipal Judge,* 427 P.2d 642 (Nev. 1967).

9. 405 U.S. 156 (1972), quote from 169.

10. 461 U.S. 352 (1983).

11. Simon, "Towns without Pity," p. 645.

12. Robert C. Ellickson, "Controlling Chronic Misconduct in City Spaces: of Panhandlers, Skid Rows, and Public-Space Zoning," *Yale Law Journal,* 105 (1996):1213–1214.

13. Goodman quote, ibid., p. 1218; Juliette Smith, "Arresting the Homeless for Sleeping in Public: A Paradigm for Expanding the Robinson Doctrine," *Columbia Journal of Law and Social Problems,* 29 (1996):293.

14. Kelling and Coles, p. xiv.

15. *Ayers v. City of Chicago,* 125 F.3rd 1010 (7th Cir. 1997), 1013.

16. Renee Sanchez, "City of Tolerance Tires of Homeless: San Francisco Aims to Roust Street Dwellers," *The Washington Post,* 28 November 1998, p. A03.

17. Robert Tier, "Maintaining Safety and Civility in Public Spaces: A Constitutional Approach to Aggressive Begging," *Lousiana Law Review,* 54 (1993):287.

18. Clarence Thomas, "Federalist Society Symposium: The Rights Revolution," *Michigan Law and Policy Review,* 1(1996):269.

19. Kent S. Scheidegger, *A Guide to Regulating Panhandling* (Sacramento, Calif.: Criminal Justice Legal Foundation, 1993), p. 7.

20. Ibid., pp. 7–9.

21. *R.A.V. v. St. Paul*, 112 S.Ct. 2538 (1992).

22. Scheidegger, *A Guide*, pp. 10–11.

23. *Black's Law* Dictionary, 7th ed. (St. Paul: West Group, 1999) (loitering defined); Peter W. Poulos, "Chicago's Ban on Gang Loitering: Making Sense Out of Vagueness and Overbreadth in Loitering Laws," *California Law Review*, 83 (1995): 379–381.

Constitution of the United States

PREAMBLE

We the People of the United States, in Order to form a more perfect Union, establish Justice, insure domestic Tranquility, provide for the common defence, promote the general Welfare, and secure the Blessings of Liberty to ourselves and our Posterity, do ordain and establish this Constitution for the United States of America.

ARTICLE I

Section 1 All legislative Powers herein granted shall be vested in a Congress of the United States, which shall consist of a Senate and House of Representatives.

Section 2 The House of Representatives shall be composed of Members chosen every second Year by the People of the several States, and the Electors in each State shall have the Qualifications requisite for Electors of the most numerous Branch of the State Legislature.

No Person shall be a Representative who shall not have attained to the Age of twenty five Years, and been seven Years a Citizen of the United States, and who shall not, when elected, be an Inhabitant of that State in which he shall be chosen.

Representatives and direct Taxes shall be apportioned among the several States which may be included within this Union, according to their respective Numbers, which shall be determined by adding to the whole Number of free Persons, including those bound to Service for a Term of Years, and excluding Indians not taxed, three fifths of all other Persons. The actual Enumeration shall be made within three Years after the first Meeting of the Congress of the United States, and within every subsequent Term of ten Years, in such Manner as they shall by Law direct. The Number of Representatives shall not exceed one for every thirty Thousand, but each State shall have at Least one Representative; and until such enumeration shall be made, the State of New Hampshire shall be entitled to choose three, Massachusetts eight, Rhode Island and Providence Plantations one, Connecticut five, New York six, New Jersey four, Pennsylvania eight, Delaware one, Maryland six, Virginia ten, North Carolina five, South Carolina five, and Georgia three.

When vacancies happen in the Representation from any State, the Executive Authority thereof shall issue Writs of Election to fill such Vacancies.

The House of Representatives shall choose their Speaker and other Officers; and shall have the sole Power of Impeachment.

Section 3 The Senate of the United States shall be composed of two Senators from each State, chosen by the Legislature thereof, for six Years; and each Senator shall have one Vote.

Immediately after they shall be assembled in Consequence of the first Election, they shall be divided as equally as may be into three Classes. The Seats of the Senators of the first Class shall be vacated at the Expiration of the second Year, of the second Class at the Expiration of the fourth Year, and of the third Class at the Expiration of the sixth Year, so that one third may be chosen every second Year; and if Vacancies happen by Resignation, or otherwise, during the Recess of the Legislature of any State, the Executive thereof may make temporary Appointments until the next Meeting of the Legislature, which shall then fill such Vacancies.

No Person shall be a Senator who shall not have attained to the Age of thirty Years, and been nine Years a Citizen of the United States, and who shall not, when elected, be an Inhabitant of that State for which he shall be chosen.

The Vice President of the United States shall be President of the Senate, but shall have no Vote, unless they be equally divided.

The Senate shall choose their other Officers, and also a President pro tempore, in the Absence of the Vice President, or when he shall exercise the Office of President of the United States.

The Senate shall have the sole Power to try all Impeachments. When sitting for that Purpose, they shall be on Oath or Affirmation. When the President of the United States is tried, the Chief Justice shall preside: And no Person shall be convicted without the Concurrence of two thirds of the Members present.

Judgment in Cases of Impeachment shall not extend further than to removal from Office, and disqualification to hold and enjoy any Office of honor, Trust, or Profit under the United States: but the Party convicted shall nevertheless be liable and subject to Indictment, Trial, Judgment, and Punishment, according to Law.

Section 4 The Times, Places and Manner of holding Elections for Senators and Representatives, shall be prescribed in each State by the Legislature thereof; but the Congress may at any time by Law make or alter such Regulations, except as to the Places of choosing Senators.

The Congress shall assemble at least once in every Year, and such Meeting shall be on the first Monday in December, unless they shall by Law appoint a different Day.

Section 5 Each House shall be the Judge of the Elections, Returns, and Qualifications of its own Members, and a Majority of each shall constitute a Quorum to do Business; but a smaller Number may adjourn from day to day, and may be authorized to compel the Attendance of absent Members, in such Manner, and under such Penalties as each House may provide.

Each House may determine the Rules of its Proceedings, punish its Members for disorderly Behavior, and, with the Concurrence of two thirds, expel a Member.

Each House shall keep a Journal of its Proceedings, and from time to time publish the same, excepting such Parts as may in their Judgment require Secrecy; and the Yeas and Nays of the Members of either House on any question shall, at the Desire of one fifth of those Present, be entered on the Journal.

Neither House, during the Session of Congress, shall, without the Consent of the other, adjourn for more than three days, nor to any other Place than that in which the two Houses shall be sitting.

Section 6 The Senators and Representatives shall receive a Compensation for their Services, to be ascertained by Law, and paid out of the Treasury of the United States. They shall in all Cases, except Treason, Felony and Breach of the Peace, be privileged from Arrest during their Attendance at the Session of their respective Houses, and in going to and returning from the same; and for any Speech or Debate in either House, they shall not be questioned in any other Place.

No Senator or Representative shall, during the Time for which he was elected, be appointed to any civil Office under the Authority of the United States, which shall have been created, or the Emoluments whereof shall have been increased during such time; and no Person holding any Office under the United States, shall be a Member of either House during his Continuance in Office.

Section 7 All Bills for raising Revenue shall originate in the House of Representatives; but the Senate may propose or concur with Amendments as on other Bills.

Every Bill which shall have passed the House of Representatives and the Senate, shall, before it become a Law, be presented to the President of the United States; If he approve he shall sign it, but if not he shall return it, with his Objections to the House in which it shall have originated, who shall enter the Objections at large on their Journal, and proceed to reconsider it. If after such Reconsideration two thirds of that House shall agree to pass the Bill, it shall be sent together with the Objections, to the other House, by which it shall likewise be reconsidered, and if approved by two thirds of that House, it shall become a Law. But in all such Cases the Votes of both Houses shall be determined by Yeas and Nays, and the Names of the Persons voting for and against the Bill shall be entered on the Journal of each House respectively. If any Bill shall not be returned by the President within ten Days (Sundays excepted) after it shall have been presented to him, the Same shall be a Law, in like Manner as if he had signed it, unless the Congress by their Adjournment prevent its Return in which Case it shall not be a Law.

Every Order, Resolution, or Vote, to which the Concurrence of the Senate and House of Representatives may be necessary (except on a question of Adjournment) shall be presented to the President of the United States; and before the Same shall take Effect, shall be approved by him, or being disapproved by him, shall be repassed by two thirds of the Senate and House of Representatives, according to the Rules and Limitations prescribed in the Case of a Bill.

Section 8 The Congress shall have Power To lay and collect Taxes, Duties, Imposts and Excises, to pay the Debts and provide for the common Defence and general Welfare of the United States; but all Duties, Imposts and Excises shall be uniform throughout the United States;

To borrow Money on the credit of the United States;

To regulate Commerce with foreign Nations, and among the several States, and with the Indian Tribes;

To establish an uniform Rule of Naturalization, and uniform Laws on the subject of Bankruptcies throughout the United States;

To coin Money, regulate the Value thereof, and of foreign Coin, and fix the Standard of Weights and Measures;

To provide for the Punishment of counterfeiting the Securities and current Coin of the United States;

To establish Post Offices and post Roads;

To promote the Progress of Science and useful Arts, by securing for limited Times to Authors and Inventors the exclusive Right to their respective Writings and Discoveries;

To constitute Tribunals inferior to the supreme Court;

To define and punish Piracies and Felonies committed on the high Seas, and Offenses against the Law of Nations;

To declare War, grant Letters of Marque and Reprisal, and make Rules concerning Captures on Land and Water;

To raise and support Armies, but no Appropriation of Money to that Use shall be for a longer Term than two Years;

To provide and maintain a Navy;

To make Rules for the Government and Regulation of the land and naval Forces;

To provide for calling forth the Militia to execute the Laws of the Union, suppress Insurrections and repel Invasions;

To provide for organizing, arming, and disciplining, the Militia, and for governing such Part of Them as may be employed in the Service of the United States, reserving to the States respectively, the Appointment of the Officers, and the Authority of training the Militia according to the discipline prescribed by Congress;

To exercise exclusive Legislation in all Cases whatsoever, over such District (not exceeding ten Miles square) as may, by Cession of particular States, and the Acceptance of Congress, become the Seat of the Government of the United States, and to exercise like Authority over all Places purchased by the Consent of the Legislature of the State in which the Same shall be, for the Erection of Forts, Magazines, Arsenals, dock-Yards, and other needful Buildings;—And

To make all Laws which shall be necessary and proper for carrying into Execution the foregoing Powers, and all other Powers vested by this Constitution in the Government of the United States, or in any Department or Officer thereof.

Section 9 The Migration or Importation of such Persons as any of the States now existing shall think proper to admit, shall not be prohibited by the Congress prior to the Year one thousand eight hundred and eight, but a Tax or duty may be imposed on such Importation, not exceeding ten dollars for each Person.

The privilege of the Writ of Habeas Corpus shall not be suspended, unless when in Cases of Rebellion or Invasion the public Safety may require it.

No Bill of Attainder or ex post facto Law shall be passed.

No Capitation, or other direct, Tax shall be laid, unless in Proportion to the Census or Enumeration herein before directed to be taken.

No Tax or Duty shall be laid on Articles exported from any State.

No Preference shall be given by any Regulation of Commerce or Revenue to the Ports of one State over those of another: nor shall Vessels bound to, or from, one State be obliged to enter, clear, or pay Duties in another.

No Money shall be drawn from the Treasury, but in Consequence of Appropriations made by Law; and a regular Statement and Account of the Receipts and Expenditures of all public Money shall be published from time to time.

No Title of Nobility shall be granted by the United States: And no Person holding any Office of Profit or Trust under them, shall, without the Consent of the Congress, accept of any present, Emolument, Office, or Title, of any kind whatever, from any King, Prince, or foreign State.

Section 10 No State shall enter into any Treaty, Alliance, or Confederation; grant Letters of Marque and Reprisal; coin Money; emit Bills of Credit; make any Thing but gold and silver Coin a Tender in Payment of Debts; pass any Bill of Attainder, ex post facto Law, or Law impairing the Obligation of Contracts, or grant any Title of Nobility.

No State shall, without the Consent of the Congress, lay any Imposts or Duties on Imports or Exports, except what may be absolutely necessary for executing it's inspection Laws: and the net Produce of all Duties and Imposts, laid by any State on Imports or Exports, shall be for the Use of the Treasury of the United States; and all such Laws shall be subject to the Revision and Control of the Congress.

No State shall, without the Consent of Congress, lay any Duty of Tonnage, keep Troops, or Ships of War in time of Peace, enter into any Agreement or Compact with another State, or with a foreign Power, or engage in War, unless actually invaded, or in such imminent Danger as will not admit of delay.

ARTICLE II

Section 1 The executive Power shall be vested in a President of the United States of America. He shall hold his Office during the Term of four Years, and, together with the Vice President, chosen for the same Term, be elected, as follows:

Each State shall appoint, in such Manner as the Legislature thereof may direct, a Number of Electors, equal to the whole Number of Senators and Representatives to which the State may be entitled in the Congress; but no Senator or Representative, or Person holding an Office of Trust or Profit under the United States, shall be appointed an Elector.

The Electors shall meet in their respective States, and vote by Ballot for two Persons, of whom one at least shall not be an Inhabitant of the same State with themselves. And they shall make a List of all the Persons voted for, and of the Number of Votes for each; which List they shall sign and certify, and transmit sealed to the Seat of the Government of the United States, directed to the President of the Senate. The President of the Senate shall, in the Presence of the Senate and House of Representatives, open all the Certificates, and the Votes shall then be counted. The Person having the greatest Number of Votes shall be the President, if such Number be a Majority of the whole Number of Electors appointed; and if there be more than one who have such Majority, and have an equal Number of Votes, then the House of Representatives shall immediately choose by Ballot one of them for President; and if no Person have a Majority, then from the five highest on the List the said House shall in like Manner choose the President. But in choosing the President, the Votes shall be taken by States, the Representation from each State having one Vote; A quorum for this Purpose shall consist of a Member or Members from two thirds of the States, and a Majority of all the States shall be necessary to a Choice. In every Case, after the Choice of the President, the Person having the greater Number of Votes of the Electors shall be the Vice President. But if there should remain two or more who have equal Votes, the Senate shall choose from them by Ballot the Vice President.

The Congress may determine the Time of choosing the Electors, and the Day on which they shall give their Votes; which Day shall be the same throughout the United States.

No person except a natural born Citizen, or a Citizen of the United States, at the time of the Adoption of this Constitution, shall be eligible to the Office of President; neither shall any Person be eligible to that Office who shall not have attained to the Age of thirty five Years, and been fourteen Years a Resident within the United States.

In Case of the Removal of the President from Office, or of his Death, Resignation or Inability to discharge the Powers and Duties of the said Office, the same shall devolve on the Vice President, and the Congress may by Law provide for the Case of Removal, Death, Resignation or Inability, both of the President and Vice President, declaring what Officer shall then act as President, and such Officer shall act accordingly, until the Disability be removed, or a President shall be elected.

The President shall, at stated Times, receive for his Services, a Compensation, which shall neither be increased nor diminished during the Period for which he shall have been elected, and he shall not receive within that Period any other Emolument from the United States, or any of them.

Before he enter on the Execution of his Office, he shall take the following Oath or Affirmation: "I do solemnly swear (or affirm) that I will faithfully execute the Office of President of the United States, and will to the best of my Ability, preserve, protect and defend the Constitution of the United States."

Section 2 The President shall be Commander in Chief of the Army and Navy of the United States, and of the Militia of the several States, when called into the actual Service of the United States: he may require the Opinion, in writing, of the principal Officer in each of the executive Departments, upon any Subject relating to the Duties of their respective Offices, and he shall have Power to grant Reprieves and Pardons for Offenses against the United States, except in Cases of Impeachment.

He shall have Power, by and with the Advice and Consent of the Senate to make Treaties, provided two thirds of the Senators present concur; and he shall nominate, and by and with the Advice and Consent of the Senate, shall appoint Ambassadors, other public Ministers and Consuls, Judges of the supreme Court, and all other Officers of the United States, whose Appointments are not herein otherwise provided for, and which shall be established by Law; but the Congress may by Law vest the Appointment of such inferior Officers, as they think proper, in the President alone, in the Courts of Law, or in the Heads of Departments.

The President shall have Power to fill up all Vacancies that may happen during the Recess of the Senate, by granting Commissions which shall expire at the End of their next Session.

Section 3 He shall from time to time give to the Congress Information of the State of the Union, and recommend to their Consideration such Measures as he shall judge necessary and expedient; he may, on extraordinary Occasions, convene both Houses, or either of them, and in Case of Disagreement between them, with Respect to the Time of Adjournment, he may adjourn them to such Time as he shall think proper; he shall receive Ambassadors and other public Ministers; he shall take Care that the Laws be faithfully executed, and shall Commission all the Officers of the United States.

Section 4 The President, Vice President and all civil Officers of the United States, shall be removed from Office on Impeachment for, and Conviction of, Treason, Bribery, or other high Crimes and Misdemeanors.

ARTICLE III

Section 1 The judicial Power of the United States, shall be vested in one supreme Court, and in such inferior Courts as the Congress may from time to time ordain and establish. The Judges, both of the supreme and inferior Courts, shall hold their Offices during good Behavior, and shall, at stated Times, receive for their Services a Compensation, which shall not be diminished during their Continuance in Office.

Section 2 The judicial Power shall extend to all Cases, in Law and Equity, arising under this Constitution, the Laws of the United States, and Treaties made, or which shall be made, under their Authority;—to all Cases affecting Ambassadors, other public Ministers and Consuls;—to all Cases of admiralty and maritime Jurisdiction;—to Controversies to which the United States shall be a Party;—to Controversies between two or more States;—between a State and Citizens of another State;—between Citizens of different States;—between Citizens of the same State claiming Lands under Grants of different States, and between a State, or the Citizens thereof, and foreign States, Citizens or Subjects.

In all Cases affecting Ambassadors, other public Ministers and Consuls, and those in which a State shall be a Party, the supreme Court shall have original Jurisdiction. In all the other Cases before mentioned, the supreme Court shall have appellate Jurisdiction, both as to Law and Fact, with such Exceptions, and under such Regulations as the Congress shall make.

The Trial of all Crimes, except in Cases of Impeachment, shall be by Jury; and such Trial shall be held in the State where the said Crimes shall have been committed; but when not committed within any State, the Trial shall be at such Place or Places as the Congress may by Law have directed.

Section 3 Treason against the United States, shall consist only in levying War against them, or, in adhering to their Enemies, giving them Aid and Comfort. No Person shall be convicted of Treason unless on the Testimony of two Witnesses to the same overt Act, or on Confession in open Court.

The Congress shall have Power to declare the Punishment of Treason, but no Attainder of Treason shall work Corruption of Blood, or Forfeiture except during the Life of the Person attainted.

ARTICLE IV

Section 1 Full Faith and Credit shall be given in each State to the public Acts, Records, and judicial Proceedings of every other State. And the Congress may by general Laws prescribe the Manner in which such Acts, Records and Proceedings shall be proved, and the Effect thereof.

Section 2 The Citizens of each State shall be entitled to all Privileges and Immunities of Citizens in the several States.

A Person charged in any State with Treason, Felony, or other Crime, who shall flee from Justice, and be found in another State, shall on Demand of the executive Authority of the State from which he fled, be delivered up, to be removed to the State having Jurisdiction of the Crime.

No Person held to Service or Labour in one State, under the Laws thereof, escaping into another, shall, in Consequence of any Law or Regulation therein, be discharged from such Service or Labor, but shall be delivered up on Claim of the Party to whom such Service or Labor may be due.

Section 3 New States may be admitted by the Congress into this Union; but no new State shall be formed or erected within the Jurisdiction of any other State; nor any State be formed by the Junction of two or more States, or Parts of States, without the Consent of the Legislatures of the States concerned as well as of the Congress.

The Congress shall have Power to dispose of and make all needful Rules and Regulations respecting the Territory or other Property belonging to the United States;

and nothing in this Constitution shall be so construed as to Prejudice any Claims of the United States, or of any particular State.

Section 4 The United States shall guarantee to every State in this Union a Republican Form of Government, and shall protect each of them against Invasion; and on Application of the Legislature, or of the Executive (when the Legislature cannot be convened) against domestic Violence.

ARTICLE V

The Congress, whenever two thirds of both Houses shall deem it necessary, shall propose Amendments to this Constitution, or, on the Application of the Legislatures of two thirds of the several States, shall call a Convention for proposing Amendments, which, in either Case, shall be valid to all Intents and Purposes, as part of this Constitution, when ratified by the Legislatures of three fourths of the several States, or by Conventions in three fourths thereof, as the one or the other Mode of Ratification may be proposed by the Congress; Provided that no Amendment which may be made prior to the Year One thousand eight hundred and eight shall in any Manner affect the first and fourth Clauses in the Ninth Section of the first Article; and that no State, without its Consent, shall be deprived of its equal Suffrage in the Senate.

ARTICLE VI

All Debts contracted and Engagements entered into, before the Adoption of this Constitution shall be as valid against the United States under this Constitution, as under the Confederation.

This Constitution, and the Laws of the United States which shall be made in Pursuance thereof; and all Treaties made, or which shall be made, under the Authority of the United States, shall be the supreme Law of the Land; and the Judges in every State shall be bound thereby, any Thing in the Constitution or Laws of any State to the Contrary notwithstanding.

The Senators and Representatives before mentioned, and the Members of the several State Legislatures, and all executive and judicial Officers, both of the United States and of the several States, shall be bound by Oath or Affirmation, to support this Constitution; but no religious Test shall ever be required as a Qualification to any Office or public Trust under the United States.

ARTICLE VII

The Ratification of the Conventions of nine States shall be sufficient for the Establishment of this Constitution between the States so ratifying the Same.

AMENDMENT I [1791]

Congress shall make no law respecting an establishment of religion, or prohibiting the free exercise thereof; or abridging the freedom of speech, or of the press; or the right of the people peaceably to assemble, and to petition the Government for a redress of grievances.

AMENDMENT II [1791]

A well regulated Militia, being necessary to the security of a free State, the right of the people to keep and bear Arms, shall not be infringed.

AMENDMENT III [1791]

No Soldier shall, in time of peace be quartered in any house, without the consent of the Owner, nor in time of war, but in a manner to be prescribed by law.

AMENDMENT IV [1791]

The right of the people to be secure in their persons, houses, papers, and effects, against unreasonable searches and seizures, shall not be violated, and no Warrants shall issue, but upon probable cause, supported by Oath or affirmation, and particularly describing the place to be searched, and the persons or things to be seized.

AMENDMENT V [1791]

No person shall be held to answer for a capital, or otherwise infamous crime, unless on a presentment or indictment of a Grand Jury, except in cases arising in the land or naval forces, or in the Militia, when in actual service in time of War or public danger; nor shall any person be subject for the same offence to be twice put in jeopardy of life or limb; nor shall be compelled in any criminal case to be a witness against himself, nor be deprived of life, liberty, or property, without due process of law; nor shall private property be taken for public use, without just compensation.

AMENDMENT VI [1791]

In all criminal prosecutions, the accused shall enjoy the right to a speedy and public trial, by an impartial jury of the State and district wherein the crime shall have been committed, which district shall have been previously ascertained by law, and to be informed of the nature and cause of the accusation; to be confronted with the witnesses against him; to have compulsory process for obtaining witnesses in his favor, and to have the Assistance of Counsel for his defence.

AMENDMENT VII [1791]

In Suits at common law, where the value in controversy shall exceed twenty dollars, the right of trial by jury shall be preserved, and no fact tried by jury, shall be otherwise re-examined in any Court of the United States, than according to the rules of the common law.

AMENDMENT VIII [1791]

Excessive bail shall not be required, nor excessive fines imposed, nor cruel and unusual punishments inflicted.

AMENDMENT IX [1791]

The enumeration in the Constitution, of certain rights, shall not be construed to deny or disparage others retained by the people.

AMENDMENT X [1791]

The powers not delegated to the United States by the Constitution, nor prohibited by it to the States, are reserved to the States respectively, or to the people.

AMENDMENT XI [1798]

The Judicial power of the United States shall not be construed to extend to any suit in law or equity, commenced or prosecuted against one of the United States by Citizens of another State, or by Citizens or Subjects of any Foreign State.

AMENDMENT XII [1804]

The Electors shall meet in their respective states, and vote by ballot for President and Vice-President, one of whom, at least, shall not be an inhabitant of the same state with themselves; they shall name in their ballots the person voted for as President, and in distinct ballots the person voted for as Vice-President, and they shall make distinct lists of all persons voted for as President, and of all persons voted for as Vice-President, and of the number of votes for each, which lists they shall sign and certify, and transmit sealed to the seat of the government of the United States, directed to the President of the Senate;—The President of the Senate shall, in the presence of the Senate and House of Representatives, open all the certificates and the votes shall then be counted;—The person having the greatest number of votes for President, shall be the President, if such number be a majority of the whole number of Electors appointed; and if no person have such majority, then from the persons having the highest numbers not exceeding three on the list of those voted for as President, the House of Representatives shall choose immediately, by ballot, the President. But in choosing the President, the votes shall be taken by states, the representation from each state having one vote; a quorum for this purpose shall consist of a member or members from two thirds of the states, and a majority of all states shall be necessary to a choice. And if the House of Representatives shall not choose a President whenever the right of choice shall devolve upon them, before the fourth day of March next following, then the Vice-President shall act as President, as in the case of the death or other constitutional disability of the President.—The person having the greatest number of votes as Vice-President, shall be the Vice-President, if such number be a majority of the whole number of Electors appointed, and if no person have a majority, then from the two highest numbers on the list, the Senate shall choose the Vice-President; a quorum for the purpose shall consist of two thirds of the whole number of Senators, and a majority of the whole number shall be necessary to a choice. But no person constitutionally ineligible to the office of President shall be eligible to that of Vice-President of the United States.

AMENDMENT XIII [1865]

Section 1 Neither slavery nor involuntary servitude, except as a punishment for crime whereof the party shall have been duly convicted, shall exist within the United States, or any place subject to their jurisdiction.

Section 2 Congress shall have power to enforce this article by appropriate legislation.

AMENDMENT XIV [1868]

Section 1 All persons born or naturalized in the United States, and subject to the jurisdiction thereof, are citizens of the United States and of the State wherein they reside. No State shall make or enforce any law which shall abridge the privileges or immunities of citizens of the United States; nor shall any State deprive any person of life, liberty, or property, without due process of law; nor deny to any person within its jurisdiction the equal protection of the laws.

Section 2 Representatives shall be apportioned among the several States according to their respective numbers, counting the whole number of persons in each State, excluding Indians not taxed. But when the right to vote at any election for the choice of electors for President and Vice President of the United States, Representatives in Congress, the Executive and Judicial officers of a State, or the members of the Legislature thereof, is denied to any of the male inhabitants of such State, being twenty-one years of age, and citizens of the United States, or in any way abridged, except for participation in rebellion, or other crime, the basis of representation therein shall be reduced in the proportion which the number of such male citizens shall bear to the whole number of male citizens twenty-one years of age in such State.

Section 3 No person shall be a Senator or Representative in Congress, or elector of President and Vice-President, or hold any office, civil or military, under the United States, or under any State, who having previously taken an oath, as a member of Congress, or as an officer of the United States, or as a member of any State legislature, or as an executive or judicial officer of any State, to support the Constitution of the United States, shall have engaged in insurrection or rebellion against the same, or given aid or comfort to the enemies thereof. But Congress may by a vote of two thirds of each House, remove such disability.

Section 4 The validity of the public debt of the United States, authorized by law, including debts incurred for payment of pensions and bounties for services in suppressing insurrection or rebellion, shall not be questioned. But neither the United States nor any State shall assume or pay any debt or obligation incurred in aid of insurrection or rebellion against the United States, or any claim for the loss or emancipation of any slave; but all such debts, obligations and claims shall be held illegal and void.

Section 5 The Congress shall have power to enforce, by appropriate legislation, the provisions of this article.

AMENDMENT XV [1870]

Section 1 The right of citizens of the United States to vote shall not be denied or abridged by the United States or by any State on account of race, color, or previous condition of servitude.

Section 2 The Congress shall have power to enforce this article by appropriate legislation.

AMENDMENT XVI [1913]

The Congress shall have power to lay and collect taxes on incomes, from whatever source derived, without apportionment among the several States, and without regard to any census or enumeration.

AMENDMENT XVII [1913]

Section 1 The Senate of the United States shall be composed of two Senators from each State, elected by the people thereof, for six years; and each Senator shall have one vote. The electors in each State shall have the qualifications requisite for electors of the most numerous branch of the State legislatures.

Section 2 When vacancies happen in the representation of any State in the Senate, the executive authority of such State shall issue writs of election to fill such vacancies: Provided, That the legislature of any State may empower the executive thereof to make temporary appointments until the people fill the vacancies by election as the legislature may direct.

Section 3 This amendment shall not be so construed as to affect the election or term of any Senator chosen before it becomes valid as part of the Constitution.

AMENDMENT XVIII [1919]

Section 1 After one year from the ratification of this article the manufacture, sale, or transportation of intoxicating liquors within, the importation thereof into, or the exportation thereof from the United States and all territory subject to the jurisdiction thereof for beverage purposes is hereby prohibited.

Section 2 The Congress and the several States shall have concurrent power to enforce this article by appropriate legislation.

Section 3 This article shall be inoperative unless it shall have been ratified as an amendment to the Constitution by the legislatures of the several States, as provided in the Constitution, within seven years from the date of the submission hereof to the States by the Congress.

AMENDMENT XIX [1920]

Section 1 The right of citizens of the United States to vote shall not be denied or abridged by the United States or by any State on account of sex.

Section 2 Congress shall have power to enforce this article by appropriate legislation.

AMENDMENT XX [1933]

Section 1 The terms of the President and Vice President shall end at noon on the 20th day of January, and the terms of Senators and Representatives at noon on the 3d day of January, of the years in which such terms would have ended if this article had not been ratified; and the terms of their successors shall then begin.

Section 2 The Congress shall assemble at least once in every year, and such meeting shall begin at noon on the 3d day of January, unless they shall by law appoint a different day.

Section 3 If, at the time fixed for the beginning of the term of the President, the President elect shall have died, the Vice President elect shall become President. If the President shall not have been chosen before the time fixed for the beginning of his term, or if the President elect shall have failed to qualify, then the Vice President elect shall act as President until a President shall have qualified; and the Congress may by law provide for the case wherein neither a President elect nor a Vice President elect shall have qualified, declaring who shall then act as President, or the manner in which one who is to act shall be selected, and such person shall act accordingly until a President or Vice-President shall have qualified.

Section 4 The Congress may by law provide for the case of the death of any of the persons from whom the House of Representatives may choose a President whenever the right of choice shall have devolved upon them, and for the case of the death of any of the persons from whom the Senate may choose a Vice-President whenever the right of choice shall have devolved upon them.

Section 5 Sections 1 and 2 shall take effect on the 15th day of October following the ratification of this article.

Section 6 This article shall be inoperative unless it shall have been ratified as an amendment to the Constitution by the legislatures of three-fourths of the several States within seven years from the date of its submission.

AMENDMENT XXI [1933]

Section 1 The eighteenth article of amendment to the Constitution of the United States is hereby repealed.

Section 2 The transportation or importation into any State, Territory, or possession of the United States for delivery or use therein of intoxicating liquors, in violation of the laws thereof, is hereby prohibited.

Section 3 This article shall be inoperative unless it shall have been ratified as an amendment to the Constitution by conventions in the several States, as provided in the Constitution, within seven years from the date of the submission hereof to the States by the Congress.

AMENDMENT XXII [1951]

Section 1 No person shall be elected to the office of the President more than twice, and no person who has held the office of President, or acted as President, for more than two years of a term to which some other person was elected President shall be elected to the office of President more than once. But this Article shall not apply to any person holding the office of President when this Article was proposed by the Congress, and shall not prevent any person who may be holding the office of President, or acting as President, during the term within which this Article becomes operative from holding the office of President or acting as President during the remainder of such term.

Section 2 This article shall be inoperative unless it shall have been ratified as an amendment to the Constitution by the legislatures of three-fourths of the several States within seven years from the date of its submission to the States by the Congress.

AMENDMENT XXIII [1961]

Section 1 The District constituting the seat of Government of the United States shall appoint in such manner as the Congress may direct:

A number of electors of President and Vice President equal to the whole number of Senators and Representatives in Congress to which the District would be entitled if it were a State, but in no event more than the least populous state; they shall be in addition to those appointed by the states, but they shall be considered, for the purposes of the election of President and Vice President, to be electors appointed by a state; and they shall meet in the District and perform such duties as provided by the twelfth article of amendment.

Section 2 The Congress shall have power to enforce this article by appropriate legislation.

AMENDMENT XXIV [1964]

Section 1 The right of citizens of the United States to vote in any primary or other election for President or Vice President, for electors for President or Vice-President, or for Senator or Representative in Congress, shall not be denied or abridged by the United States, or any State by reason of failure to pay any poll tax or other tax.

Section 2 The Congress shall have power to enforce this article by appropriate legislation.

AMENDMENT XXV [1967]

Section 1 In case of the removal of the President from office or of his death or resignation, the Vice President shall become President.

Section 2 Whenever there is a vacancy in the office of the Vice President, the President shall nominate a Vice President who shall take office upon confirmation by a majority vote of both Houses of Congress.

Section 3 Whenever the President transmits to the President pro tempore of the Senate and the Speaker of the House of Representatives his written declaration that he is unable to discharge the powers and duties of his office, and until he transmits to them a written declaration to the contrary, such powers and duties shall be discharged by the Vice President as Acting President.

Section 4 Whenever the Vice President and a majority of either the principal officers of the executive departments or of such other body as Congress may by law provide, transmit to the President pro tempore of the Senate and the Speaker of the House of Representatives their written declaration that the President is unable to discharge the powers and duties of his office, the Vice President shall immediately assume the powers and duties of the office as Acting President.

Thereafter, when the President transmits to the President pro tempore of the Senate and the Speaker of the House of Representatives his written declaration that no inability exists, he shall resume the powers and duties of his office unless the Vice President and a majority of either the principal officers of the executive department or of such other body as Congress may by law provide, transmit within four days to the President pro tempore of the Senate and the Speaker of the House of Representatives their written declaration and the President is unable to discharge the powers and duties of his office. Thereupon Congress shall decide the issue, assembling within forty-eight hours for that purpose if not in session. If the Congress, within twenty-one days after receipt of the latter written declaration, or, if Congress is not in session, within twenty-one days after Congress is required to assemble, determines by two thirds vote of both Houses that the President is unable to discharge the powers and duties of his office, the Vice President shall continue to discharge the same as Acting President; otherwise, the President shall resume the powers and duties of his office.

AMENDMENT XXVI [1971]

Section 1 The right of citizens of the United States, who are eighteen years of age or older, to vote shall not be denied or abridged by the United States or by any State on account of age.

Section 2 The Congress shall have power to enforce this article by appropriate legislation.

AMENDMENT XXVII
[PROPOSED 1789; RATIFIED 1992]

No law, varying the compensation for the services of Senators and Representatives, shall take effect until an election of Representatives have intervened.

Glossary

accessory the party liable for separate, lesser offenses following a crime.

accomplices the parties liable as principals before and during a crime.

actual possession physical possession; on the possessor's person.

actus reus the criminal act or the physical element in criminal liability.

adequate provocation rule the rule that only certain defined circumstances will reduce murder to voluntary manslaughter.

affirm to uphold a trial court's decision.

affirmative defense a defense in which the defendant bears the burden of production.

aggravated rape rape by strangers, or men with weapons, or where rapists physically injure their victims.

alibi a defense that places defendants in a different place from the scene at the time of the crime.

American bystander rule there is no legal duty to rescue or call for help to aid someone who is in danger even if helping poses no risk whatsoever to the potential rescuer.

appellant a party who appeals a lower court decision.

appellate court a court that reviews decisions of trial courts.

appellee the party against whom an appeal is filed.

arbitrary action unreasonable action.

asportation the carrying away of another's property.

assault an attempt to commit a battery, or intentionally putting another in fear.

attempt taking steps toward but not completing a crime.

attempted battery assault the crime of assault that focuses on *actus reus*.

bailee a temporary possessor who had control over others' property (a term operative when English Parliament created embezzlement).

battery offensive bodily contact.

"broken windows" theory the theory that minor offenses can lead to a rise in serious crime.

burden of persuasion the responsibility to convince the fact finder of the truth of the defense.

burden of production the responsibility to introduce initial evidence to support a defense.

burden of proof the affirmative duty to prove a point in dispute; the responsibility to produce the evidence to persuade the fact finder.

"but for" or sine qua non causation the actor's conduct sets in motion a chain of events that, sooner or later, leads to a result.

capital felonies felonies punishable by death or life imprisonment without parole.

capital murder first-degree murders for which the penalty is either death or life imprisonment.

castle exception the principle stating that defenders have no need to retreat when attacked in their homes.

causation concurrence between criminal conduct and criminal result; the requirement that criminal conduct cause a particular result.

cause in fact actual cause of the harmful result.

certiorari an order to a lower court from the U.S. Supreme Court to send the record of the lower court to the Supreme Court for review.

choice-of-evils defense or the principle of necessity defense of making the right choice, namely choosing the lesser of two evils.

circumstantial evidence indirect evidence.

citation a reference to the published report of a case.

civil commitment   the government can invoke its power to lock up dangerous people by means of the noncriminal proceeding.

civil law   the law that deals with private rights and remedies.

claim of right   the belief that property taken rightfully belongs to the taker.

clear and present danger doctrine   criminal statutes can prohibit words that threaten a serious public danger that rises above public inconvenience, annoyance, and unrest

codified   put into writing.

collateral attack   a proceeding asking an appellate court to rule against the trial court's jurisdiction to decide a question or case.

common law   the body of law consisting of all the statutes and case law background of England and the colonies before the American Revolution, based on principles and rules that derive from usages and customs of antiquity.

common-law crimes   crimes originating in the English common law.

common-law jurisdictions   jurisdictions that still recognize the common-law crimes.

concurrence   the requirement that *actus reus* must join with *mens rea* to produce criminal conduct or that conduct cause a harmful result.

concurring opinion   an opinion that supports the court's result but not its reasoning.

conflict-elitist theory   assumes that society operates according to conflict among interest groups.

consolidated theft statutes   statutes consolidating larceny, embezzlement, and false pretenses into one offense called theft, accepting the social reality that they are all aimed at the same criminal offense—wrongfully getting someone else's property.

conspiracy   agreeing to commit a crime.

constructive breaking   entering structures in an unusual manner.

constructive intent   intent in which the actors do not intend any harm but should have known that their behavior created a high risk of injury.

constructive possession   legal possession or custody of an item or substance.

conversion   illegal use of another's property.

crime of criminal conduct   an act triggered by criminal intent.

crimes of cause and result   crimes in which criminal conduct (the joining of a criminal act with a criminal intent) causes a harm that the law specifically prohibits.

criminal homicides   homicides that are neither justified nor excused.

criminal omission   two forms: (1) mere failure to act or (2) failure to intervene in order to prevent a serious harm.

culpability   blameworthiness based on *mens rea*; deserving of punishment because of individual responsibility for actions.

damages   money awarded in civil lawsuits for injuries.

defendant   the person against whom a civil or criminal action is brought.

defenses   justifications and excuses to criminal liability.

deliberate   meeting the requirement in murder *mens rea* that killings must be committed with a cool, reflecting mind.

democratic-consensus theory   originating in the insights of the great French sociologist Emile Durkheim, holds that elected representatives define crime.

designated public forums   places the government chooses to make available to the public.

deterrence theory   states that rational human beings will not commit crimes if they know that the pain of punishment outweighs the pleasure gained from committing crimes.

diminished capacity   mental capacity less than "normal" but more than "insane."

dissent   the opinion of the minority of justices.

distinguish cases   to find that facts differ enough from those in a prior case to release judges from the precedent of the decision in that case.

doctrine of complicity   the principle regarding parties to crime that establishes the conditions under which more than one person incurs liability before, during, and after committing crimes.

due process clauses   clauses within the U.S. Constitution stating that government cannot deny citizens life, liberty, or property without notice, hearing, and other established procedures.

duress or compulsion   when people are forced to commit crimes that they do not want to do.

Durham rule, or product test of insanity   An insanity test to determine whether a crime was a product of mental disease or defect.

elements of crime   the parts of a crime that the prosecution must prove beyond a reasonable doubt, such as *actus reus*, *mens rea*, concurrence, causation, and harmful result.

embezzlement   crime of lawfully gaining possession of someone else's property and later converting it to one's own use.

entrapment government actions that induce individuals to commit crimes that they otherwise would not commit.

equivocality approach the theory that attempt *actus reus* requires an act that can have no other purpose than the commission of a crime.

ethical core theory assumes that crime is the embodiment of universal, permanent, inherent evil.

***ex post facto* laws** laws passed after the occurrence of the conduct constituting the crime.

excusable homicides accidental killings and killing while insane.

excuse a defense admitting wrongdoing without criminal responsibility.

expressive conduct conduct that communicates an idea or emotion without using words

extortion misappropriation of another's property by means of threat to inflict bodily harm in the future.

extraneous factor a condition beyond the attempter's control.

extrinsic force standard requires some force in addition to the amount needed to accomplish the penetration.

factual causation conduct that in fact leads to a harmful result.

factual impossibility the defense that some extraneous factor makes it impossible to complete a crime.

false pretenses in modern law often called theft by deceit.

felonies serious crimes generally punishable by one year or more in prison.

felony murder deaths occurring during the commission of felonies.

fences those who sell stolen merchandise for profit.

fetal death statutes laws defining when life begins for purposes of the law of criminal homicide.

fighting words words likely to provoke the average person to breaching the peace by retaliation

first-degree murder premeditated, deliberate killings and other particularly heinous capital murders.

forgery making false writings or materially altering authentic writings.

general deterrence or prevention preventing crime by threatening potential lawbreakers.

general intent intent to commit the *actus reus*—the act required in the definition of the crime.

general part of criminal law principles that apply to all crimes.

general principles of criminal liability The theoretical foundation for the elements of *actus reus*, *mens rea*, concurrence, causation, and harm.

Good Samaritan doctrine doctrine that imposes a legal duty to render or summon aid for imperiled strangers.

gross criminal negligence very great negligence; actions without even slight care but not amounting to intentional or conscious wrongdoing.

gross misdemeanor offense with a maximum penalty of close to one year in jail.

habeas corpus a request for a court action to review an individual's detention by the government.

harmful result a harm defined by criminal law.

hedonism human beings seek pleasure and avoid pain.

holding the legal principle or rule that a case enunciates.

homicide the killing of one live human being by another.

imperfect defense defense reducing but not eliminating criminal liability.

incapacitation punishment by imprisonment, mutilation, and even death.

inchoate offenses offenses based on crimes not yet completed.

injunction a court order to do or to stop doing something.

injunction to abate public nuisances an action in which city attorneys ask the courts to declare gang activities and gang members public nuisances and to issue injunctions to abate the public nuisance.

intellectual property information and services stored in and transmitted to and from electronic data banks; a rapidly developing area of property crimes.

intervening or supervening cause the cause that either interrupts a chain of events or substantially contributes to a result.

intrinsic force standard requires only the amount of force necessary to accomplish the penetration.

involuntary manslaughter criminal homicides caused either by recklessness or gross criminal negligence.

irrebuttable presumption a conclusive assumption that requires a finding of a presumed fact once the fact is introduced into evidence.

irresistible impulse test impairment of the will that makes it impossible to control the impulse to do wrong.

justifiable homicides killing in self-defense, capital punishment, and police use of deadly force.

justification a defense deeming acceptable under the circumstances what is otherwise criminal conduct.

knowing possession awareness of physical possession.

legal causation cause recognized by law to impose criminal liability.

legal impossibility   the defense that what the actor attempted was not a crime.

lex non scripta   based on local community customs and mores.

libel   defamation expressed in print.

liberty   the right of individuals to go about in public free of undue interference.

living standard analysis   classification based on injury to quality of life.

loitering   remaining in one place with no apparent purpose.

M'Naghten rule, or right-wrong test   a defense pleading insanity due to mental disease or defect that impairs the capacity to distinguish right from wrong.

majority opinion   the opinion of the majority of justices.

malice aforethought   the common-law designation for murder *mens rea* that covered a broad range of states of mind.

malum in se   a crime inherently bad, or evil.

malum prohibitum   a crime not inherently bad, or evil, but merely prohibited.

manifest criminality   the requirement in law that intentions have to turn into criminal deeds to be punishable.

medical model of punishment   crime as a disease.

mens rea   the mental element in crime, including purpose, knowledge, recklessness, and negligence.

mere possession   physical possession.

mere presence rule   that a person's presence at the scene of a crime doesn't by itself satisfy the *actus reus* requirement of accomplice liability.

misappropriation   gaining possession of another's property.

misdemeanor   a minor crime for which the penalty is usually less than one year in jail or a fine.

mitigating circumstances   facts that reduce but do not eliminate culpability.

Model Penal Code   the code developed by the American Law Institute to guide reform in criminal law.

Model Penal Code standard   the precept that attempt *actus reus* requires substantial steps that strongly corroborate the actor's purpose.

motive   the reason why a defendant commits a crime.

negligence   the unconscious creation of substantial and unjustifiable risks.

negligent homicide   unintentional killings in which actors should have known they were creating substantial

and unjustified risks of death by conduct that grossly deviated from ordinary care.

nonpublic forums   places, such as airports, bus terminals, railway stations, and subways, where the government has broad power to restrict or even prohibit solicitation.

objective test of entrapment   focuses on the actions that government agents take to induce individuals to commit crimes.

obscenity   material whose predominant appeal is to nudity, sex, or excretion

order   behavior in public that comports with minimum community standards of civility.

overruling a case   throwing out a precedent.

paramour rule   the rule that a husband's witnessing his wife in the act of adultery is adequate provocation to reduce murder to manslaughter.

perfect defense   a defense that leads to outright acquittal.

petty misdemeanor   offense punishable by a jail sentence of up to thirty days.

physical proximity doctrine   the principle that the number of remaining acts in attempt determines attempt *actus reus*.

Pinkerton rule   the rule that conspiracy and the underlying crime are separate offenses.

plaintiff   the person who sues another party in a civil action.

plurality opinion   an opinion that announces the result of the case but whose reasoning does not command a majority of the court.

precedent   prior court decision that guides judges in deciding future cases.

preliminary injunction   a temporary order issued by a court after notice and hearing.

premeditated   the requirement in first-degree murder *mens rea* that killings must be planned in advance.

preponderance of the evidence   this means that more than 50 percent of the evidence proves justification or excuse.

prevention   the punishing of offenders in order to prevent crimes in the future.

principle of legality   a principle stating that there can be no crime or punishment if there are no specific laws forewarning citizens that certain specific conduct will result in a particular punishment.

principle of limited methods   criminal law is the last resort of social control.

principle of proportionality a principle of law stating that the punishment must be proportionate to the crime committed.

principle of utility allows only the minimum amount of pain necessary to prevent crime.

probable desistance approach an approach that considers whether the act in attempt would naturally lead to the commission of the crime.

profanity irreverence toward sacred things.

proximate cause the main cause of the result of criminal conduct.

public nuisance offense against, or interference with, the exercise of rights common to the public.

punitive damages payments to injured parties intended to punish the wrongdoer.

quality of life crimes breaches of minimum standards of decent behavior in public.

rape shield statutes statutes that prohibit introducing evidence of victims' past sexual conduct.

rational criminal law if informal private sanctions can secure compliance, criminal law has no role to play.

rationalism desire to maximize pleasure and minimize pain.

reasonable resistance standard the requirement that women must use the amount of resistive force required by the totality of the circumstances surrounding sexual assault.

reasoning the reasons a court gives to support its holding.

rebuttable presumption an assumption of fact that can be overturned upon sufficient proof.

receiving stolen property benefiting from someone else's property without having participated in the wrongful acquisition in the first place.

reckless or "depraved heart" murder deaths resulting from purposely or consciously creating substantial and unjustifiable risks that someone will either die or suffer serious injury.

recklessness the conscious creation of substantial and unjustifiable risk.

rehabilitation prevention of crime by treatment.

remand to send a case back to a trial court for further proceedings consistent with the reviewing court's decision.

respondeat superior the doctrine that employers are responsible for their employees' actions.

retreat rule you have to retreat, but only if you reasonably believe that backing off won't unreasonably put you in danger of death or serious bodily harm.

retribution punishment based on just deserts.

reverse to set aside the decision of the trial court and substitute a different decision.

robbery taking and carrying away another's property by force or threat of force with the intent to permanently deprive the owner of possession.

rule of law the principles that require that established written rules and procedures define, prohibit, and prescribe punishments for crimes.

second-degree murder a catchall offense including killings that are neither manslaughter nor first-degree murder.

self-defense the use of force to prevent attacks against individuals, their homes, and their property.

slander defamation by spoken word.

solicitation trying to get someone to commit a crime.

special deterrence the threat of punishment aimed at individual offenders in the hope of deterring future criminal conduct.

special part of criminal law defines the elements of specific crimes.

specific intent the intent to do something beyond the *actus reus*.

stand-your-ground rule says that if you didn't start the fight, you can stand your ground and kill.

stare decisis the principle that binds courts to stand by prior decisions and to leave undisturbed settled points of law.

statutory rape carnal knowledge with a person under the age of consent whether or not accomplished by force.

strict liability liability without fault, or in the absence of *mens rea*.

strict scrutiny statutory classifications that require proof that they further a compelling state interest.

subjective test of entrapment focuses on the predisposition of defendants to commit crimes.

substantial capacity test insanity due to mental disease or defect impairing the substantial capacity either to appreciate the wrongfulness of conduct or to conform behavior to the law.

surreptitious remaining entering a structure lawfully with the intent to commit a crime inside.

theft consolidated crimes of larceny, embezzlement, and false pretenses.

threatened battery assault the crime of assault that focuses on the *mens rea*.

tort a legal wrong for which the injured party may sue the injuring party.

traditional public forums streets, sidewalks, parks, and other places where people have since ancient times expressed their views.

transferred intent actor intends to harm one victim but instead harms another.

unarmed acquaintance rape rape involving dates, lovers, neighbors, coworkers, employers, and so on.

unprivileged entry entering a structure without right, license, or permission.

utmost resistance standard the requirement that rape victims must use all the physical strength they have in order to prevent penetration.

uttering knowing or conscious use or transfer of false documents.

vicarious liability the principle regarding liability for another based on relationship.

violation a minor legal infraction subject to a small fine.

void-for-overbreadth doctrine the principle that a statute is unconstitutional if it includes in its definition of undesirable behavior conduct protected under the U.S. Constitution.

void-for-vagueness doctrine the principle that statutes violate due process if they do not clearly define crime and punishment in advance.

voluntary manslaughter intentional killings committed in the sudden heat of passion upon adequate provocation.

Wharton's rule the principle that more than two parties must conspire to commit crimes that naturally involve at least two parties.

writ of certiorari discretionary Supreme Court order to review lower court decisions.

year-and-a-day rule the rule that no act occurring more than one year and one day before death is the legal cause of death.

Table of Cases

A

Aaron, State v., 377, 378, 379
Abner v. State, 465–466
Acuna, People ex rel. Gallo v., 502–503
Agnello, People v., 205–207
Ahart, Commonwealth v., 471
Akers, State v., 168–170
Aldershof, State v., 471
Allam v. State, 47, 48–49
Allen, People v., 419–422
Allen, State v., 459–463
Amado, State v., 217
Anderson v. State (1977), 48
Anderson v. State (1992), 405
Aphaylath, People v., 317, 318
Appleby, Commonwealth v., 415
Arizona, Miranda v., 250
Armitage, People v., 139–140
Ayres v. City of Chicago, 498

B

Bailey v. United States, 148
Bakolas, People v., 45
Baldwin, State v., 398
Barnes, State v., 125, 126–127
Barnes v. Glen Theatre, Inc., et al., 55
Barnette, Commonwealth v., 122–125
Barnette, West Virginia Board of Education v., 62
Barrett, Commonwealth v., 415
Barry, State v., 164
Bauer v. Cole, 161
Beard v. United States, 250
Bell, State v., 411
Bennett v. State, 415

Berg, People v., 95
Berkowitz, Commonwealth v., 389, 390–391
Bery v. City of New York, 499
Bonds, State v., 397–399, CD-ROM
Bonilla, People v., 331–333
Borras v. State, 69
Bowers v. Hardwick, 58–64
Bradshaw, People v., 54
Brinson, State v., 415
Britten, State v., 457
Brown, Commonwealth v., 121
Brown, People v., 420, 421
Brown, Reginald, State v., 269
Brown, State v., 334, 335
Brown v. State, 387
Brown v. United States, 140
Bruno, United States v., 197
Buford, People v., 415
Burns, State v., 431–433
Burroughs, People v., 358–359
Byfield, United States v., 107, 108, 109–110

C

Cabey v. Goetz, 228–229
Caffero, People v., 355–356
California, Robinson v., 70–71, 86, 88, 89–90, 490, CD-ROM
Casey's General Stores, Inc. and Hy-Vee, Inc., State v., 160–163
Celli, State v., 264–265
Chessman, People v., 419
Chiarello, State v., 218
Chicago v. Morales, 503, 504–513
Chism, State v., 155–157
Citizens for a Better Environment, Village of Schaumburg v., 497

City and County of San Francisco, Joyce v., 486–493
City of Chicago, Ayres v., 498
City of Chicago, National Paint and Coatings Association v., 301, 302
City of Fort Lauderdale, Smith v., 496, 497, 499
City of Jacksonville, Papichristou v., 485, 506
City of New York, Bery v., 499
City of St. Paul, R.A.V. v., 53, 54, 500
Clark, State v., 110–111
Clavis, United States v., 109
Cleppe, State v., 111
Cline, People v., 358
Clokey, State v., 471
Clowes, State v., 263
Coe, People v., 415
Cogdon, King v., 83–84
Coker v. Georgia, 72, 73, 74, CD-ROM
Cole, Bauer v., 161
Cole, State v., 263, 264
Colorado, Hill v., 498
Commonwealth, Dunn v., 158
Commonwealth, Thacker v., 178
Commonwealth v. Ahart, 471
Commonwealth v. Appleby, 415
Commonwealth v. Barnette, 122–125
Commonwealth v. Barrett, 415
Commonwealth v. Berkowitz, 389, 390–391
Commonwealth v. Brown, 121
Commonwealth v. Davis, 415
Commonwealth v. Farrell, 415
Commonwealth v. Gilliam, 184–185

Commonwealth v. Golston, 333, 334, 348
Commonwealth v. Jones, 471
Commonwealth v. Ladd, 335
Commonwealth v. LeBlanc, 415
Commonwealth v. Mercado, 415
Commonwealth v. Mlinarich, 391
Commonwealth v. Peaslee, 181, 185
Commonwealth v. Rhodes, 390
Commonwealth v. Schnopps, 367–370
Commonwealth v. Scott, 415
Commonwealth v. Sexton, 414–416
Commonwealth v. Shea, 415
Commonwealth v. Tarrant, 415
Commonwealth v. Young, 416
Commonwealth v. Zangari, 473–474, CD-ROM
Connecticut, Griswold v., 57–58, 59, 61
Connecticut, Palko v., 59, 296
Cornell v. State, 95
Cornell, United States v., 294
Cox v. New Hampshire, 498
Cramer, State v., 234–237
Crawford v. State, 249
Curley, State v., 470–473

D
D.P. v. State, 300–302
Damms, State v., 186–190, 192
Datema, People v., 376–379
Davis, Commonwealth v., 415
Dawkins v. State, 111
Decina, People v., 84
DePasquale v. State, 314–316
Diana, State v., 263, 264
Dixon, State v., 346
Donaldson v. State, 344, 345–348, CD-ROM
Dover, People v., 264
Dudley and Stephens, Queen v., 260
Duest v. State, 348–349
Dulles, Trop v., 72
Dunn v. Commonwealth, 158
Durham v. United States, 281

E
East Cleveland, Moore v., 59, 61
Egelhoff, Montana v., 292–296, CD-ROM
Elder, State v., 370–371
Ellyson v. State, 434
Elton, State v., 403

Emmund v. Florida, 73
Eulo, People v., 331

F
Farmer, State v., 122
Farrell, Commonwealth v., 415
Fears, Williams v., 506
Fleming, People v., 438–439
Flipside, Hoffman Estates, Inc., Village of Hoffman Estates v., 500
Florida, Emmund v., 73
Floyd, State v., 268
Foster, State v., 154–155
Foust, State v., 411
Franklin, White Egret Condominium, Inc. v., 301
Fransua, State v., 269–270
Freer, People v., 268
Friedman, State v., 45–46
Fuentes, State v., 472
Fulcher v. State, 85
Fullmer v. Tague, 161–162
Furman v. Georgia, 74
Furr, State v., 207

G
Gallegos, State v., 237–238
Galvin, People v., 415
Garner, Tennessee v., 251, 252, 253–254
Garnett v. State, 400–408
Gasparik, People v., 448, 449
George v. State, 84
Georgia, Coker v., 72, 73, 74, CD-ROM
Georgia, Furman v., 74
Georgia, Gregg v., 72, 74
Georgia, Stanley v., 58, 59–60, 61
Gilliam, Commonwealth v., 184–185
Gitlow v. New York, 50
Glen Theatre, Inc., et al., Barnes v., 55
Glenn, State v., 410–412
Goetz, Cabey v., 228–229
Goetz, People v., 219–222
Golston, Commonwealth v., 333, 334, 348
Goodwin, Hudson v., 20
Graham v. State, 279
Graven, People v., 136
Green, People v., 421
Green, State v., 432–433
Gregg v. Georgia, 72, 74
Gresham v. Peterson, 494, 495–501

Griswold v. Connecticut, 57, 59, 61
Guest, State v., 403

H
Haines, State v., 121
Hall, State v., 297
Hanby v. State, 48
Hancock v. Texas, 455
Hardwick, Bowers v., 58–64
Harrod v. State, 412
Hatatley, United States v., 97
Hatch v. Superior Court, 111–112
Hayes, State v., 411
Heffron v. International Society for Krishna Consciousness, Inc., 498
Helton v. State, 267
Hemmer, State v., 178–179
Henyard v. State, 348
Hernandez, People v., 403
Herron, State v., 193
Hill v. Colorado, 498
Hiott, State v., 269
Holland, State v., 46
Holliday, State v., 314
Holmes, State v., 218
Hudson, Regina v., 304
Hudson v. Goodwin, 20
Hundley, State v., 306–307
Hurston v. State, 464–466
Hutchinson, People v., 136

I
In the Interest of C.W., a child, 466–467
International Society for Krishna Consciousness, Inc., Heffron v., 498
Iowa City, Nolan v., 163–166
Irons, State v., 304–307

J
Jacobson v. United States, 312
Jahnke v. State, 232, 238–240
Jantzi, State v., 128
JC Sports Bar Inc., State v., 461
Jerrett, State v., 85
Jewell v. State, 433–434
Johnson, Mark, State v., 310, 311–313
Johnson, State v., 411
Johnson, Texas v., 55–57
Johnson, United States v., (1963), 415
Johnson, United States v., (1992), 109
Johnson v. State, 500
Jones, Commonwealth v., 471

Jones, State v., 94
Joyce v. City and County of San Francisco, 486–493

K
K.R.L., State v., 297, 298–300
Katz v. United States, 61, 62
Keeler v. Superior Court, 21
Kibbe, People v., 141–142
Kimball, People v., 176–178
King v. Cogdon, 83–84
King v. Pear, 449
Knapp, People v., 153–154
Kolender v. Lawson, 39, 485, 500, 506, 508, 510, 513, CD-ROM
Komok, State v., 457
Koppersmith v. State, 130–132
Kuntz, State v., 97–99

L
Ladd, Commonwealth v., 335
Lanzetta v. New Jersey, 39, 507
Law v. State, 245–250
Lawson, Kolender v., 39, 485, 500, 506, 508, 510, 513, CD-ROM
Le Barron v. State, 191–192
LeBlanc, Commonwealth v., 415
Lenti, People v., 267
Lewis et al. v. State, 154
Lindsly, State v., 462
Loge, State v., 134–136
Loman, United States v., 415
Loper v. New York City Police Department, 496, 497, 499
Lucas, United States v., 106–109
Luvene, Tacoma v., 507

M
Macias v. State, 339
Madsen v. Women's Health Center, 498
Mays, State v., 373–375
McCart, State v., 197, 198–202
McLaughlin, State v., 422–423
Mercado, Commonwealth v., 415
Merrill, State v., 326, 327–330
Metropolitan Dade County v. Pred, 301, 302
Metzger, State v., 46–47
Michael M. v. Superior Court of Sonoma County, 47
Michaud, State v., 133
Minster, State v., 334–336
Miranda, State v., 92–96
Miranda v. Arizona, 250

Mitchell, Wisconsin v., 53–54
Mlinarich, Commonwealth v., 391
Mobley v. State, 151
Montana v. Egelhoff, 292–296, CD-ROM
Moore v. East Cleveland, 59, 61
Morales, Chicago v., 503, 504–513
Morgan, Regina v., 396–397
Morgan, State v., 97
Morissette v. United States, 165, 166, 405
Morrin, People v., 351
Morse, State v., 135
Murphy, United States v., 415
Musser, State v., 196

N
National Paint and Coatings Association v. City of Chicago, 301, 302
New Hampshire, Cox v., 498
New Jersey, Lanzetta v., 39, 507
New York, Gitlow v., 50
New York, Patterson v., 293
New York City Police Department, Loper v., 496, 497, 499
New York City Transit Authority, Young v., 55
Nitz, People v., 53, 54
Nolan v. Iowa City, 163–166
Noren, State v., 353
Norman, State v., 232

O
O'Hagan, People v., 415
O'Neil, People v., 360–362
Oliver, People v., 99
Oliver v. State, 313–314, 315
Olivo, People v., 447, 448–450
Olmstead v. United States, 61, 62
Onick, United States v., 108
Orr, People v., 378
Ownbey, State v., 262–264

P
Pace, State v., 151
Palko v. Connecticut, 59, 296
Papichristou v. City of Jacksonville, 485, 506
Parsons v. State, 282
Patterson, People v., 318
Patterson v. New York, 293
Pear, King v., 449
Peaslee, Commonwealth v., 181, 185
People, Sanchez v., 218

People ex rel. Gallo v. Acuna, 502–503
People v. Agnello, 205–207
People v. Allen, 419–422
People v. Aphaylath, 317, 318
People v. Armitage, 139–140
People v. Bakolas, 45
People v. Berg, 95
People v. Bonilla, 331–333
People v. Bradshaw, 54
People v. Brown, 420, 421
People v. Buford, 415
People v. Burroughs, 358–359
People v. Caffero, 355–356
People v. Chessman, 419
People v. Cline, 358
People v. Coe, 415
People v. Datema, 376–379
People v. Decina, 84
People v. Dover, 264
People v. Eulo, 331
People v. Fleming, 438–439
People v. Freer, 268
People v. Galvin, 415
People v. Gasparik, 448, 449
People v. Goetz, 219–222
People v. Graven, 136
People v. Green, 421
People v. Hernandez, 403
People v. Hutchinson, 136
People v. Kibbe, 141–142
People v. Kimball, 176–178
People v. Knapp, 153–154
People v. Lenti, 267
People v. Morrin, 351
People v. Nitz, 53, 54
People v. O'Hagan, 415
People v. O'Neil, 360–362
People v. Oliver, 99
People v. Olivo, 447, 448–450
People v. Orr, 378
People v. Patterson, 318
People v. Poplar, 152–154
People v. Rizzo, 181, 185
People v. Roberts, 151–152
People v. Rokicki, 51–55
People v. Shields, 178
People v. Silva, 216–219
People v. Spatzier, 448, 449
People v. Stanciel, 93
People v. Stark, 50
People v. Stevenson, 335–336
People v. Strong, 132–133
People v. Superior Court, 507
People v. Thomas, 350–351

People v. Washington, 371–372
People v. White (1963), 415
People v. White (1980), 239
Perez v. State, 403
Perna v. Pirozzi, 394
Perry Education Association v. Perry Local Educators' Association, 498
Perry Local Educators' Association, Perry Education Association v., 498
Peters, State v., 94
Petersen, State v., 141
Peterson, Gresham v., 494, 495–501
Peterson, State v., 138
Peterson, United States v., 241–244
Pichon, State v., 306, 307
Pinkerton v. United States, 148
Pirozzi, Perna v., 394
Poe v. Ullman, 296
Poplar, People v., 152–154
Powell, State v., CD-ROM
Powell v. Texas, 86–90, 164, 295, 490
Pred, Metropolitan Dade County v., 301, 302
Public Employee Relations Board, State Department of SRS v., 461

Q
Q.D., State v., 299, 300
Queen v. Dudley and Stephens, 260
Quinet, State v., 284–289

R
R.A.V. v. City of St. Paul, 53, 54, 500
Ravin v. State, 48
Reed, State v., 415, 416
Regina v. Hudson, 304
Regina v. Morgan, 396–397
Rex v. Scofield, 174
Reynolds v. State, 386–387
Rhodes, Commonwealth v., 390
Richard, State v., 507
Rizzo, People v., 181, 185
Roberts, People v., 151–152
Roberts v. United States Jaycees, 62
Robinson v. California, 70–71, 86, 88, 89–90, 490, CD-ROM
Robinson v. State, 346
Robinson v. United States, 44
Rock Against Racism, Ward v., 498
Roe v. Wade, 244, 326, 328, 330

Rokicki, People v., 51–55
Rosencrantz, CD-ROM
Rousseau, State v., 256, 258

S
S.P., State v., 299
Sanchez, State v., 471, 472
Sanchez v. People, 218
Sanchez v. State, 475–477
Schmidt v. State, 316
Schnopps, Commonwealth v., 367–370
Scofield, Rex v., 174
Scott, Commonwealth v., 415
Scroggins v. State, 121
Seeley v. State, 264
Serafin v. Serafin, 336
Sexton, Commonwealth v., 414–416
Sharrieff v. State, 277–281
Shea, Commonwealth v., 415
Shelley, State v., 266–268, 269
Sherman v. United States, 310
Shields, People v., 178
Shrader v. State, 315
Shuff, State v., 339
Silva, People v., 216–219
Simmons, State v., 267
Smith, State v., 455, 456–457
Smith v. City of Fort Lauderdale, 496, 497, 499
Smith v. State (1976), 438
Smith v. State (1980), 93
Snowden, State v., 338–339
Sodders, State v., 179
Soto, State v., 327, 328
Spatzier, People v., 448, 449
Staley, State v., 106
Stanciel, People v., 93
Stanley v. Georgia, 58, 59–60, 61
Staples v. United States, 135
Stark, People v., 50
Stark, State v., 119, 120–122
State, Abner v., 465–466
State, Allam v., 47, 48–49
State, Anderson v., (1977), 48
State, Anderson v., (1992), 405
State, Bennett v., 415
State, Borras v., 69
State, Brown v., 387
State, Cornell v., 95
State, Crawford v., 249
State, D.P. v., 300–302
State, Dawkins v., 111
State, DePasquale v., 314–316

State, Donaldson v., 344, 345–348, CD-ROM
State, Duest v., 348–349
State, Ellyson v., 434
State, Fulcher v., 85
State, Garnett v., 400–408
State, George v., 84
State, Graham v., 279
State, Hanby v., 48
State, Harrod v., 412
State, Helton v., 267
State, Henyard v., 348
State, Hurston v., 464–466
State, Jahnke v., 232, 238–240
State, Jewell v., 433–434
State, Johnson v., 500
State, Koppersmith v., 130–132
State, Law v., 245–250
State, Le Barron v., 191–192
State, Lewis et al. v., 154
State, Macias v., 339
State, Madsen v. Women's Health Center, 498
State, Mobley v., 151
State, Oliver v., 313–314, 315
State, Parsons v., 282
State, Perez v., 403
State, Ravin v., 48
State, Reynolds v., 386–387
State, Robinson v., 346
State, Sanchez v., 475–477
State, Schmidt v., 316
State, Scroggins v., 121
State, Seeley v., 264
State, Sharrieff v., 277–281
State, Shrader v., 315
State, Smith v., (1976), 438
State, Smith v., (1980), 93
State, Sterling v., 39, 40, 41, 43, 44–45
State, T. M. v., 302
State, Velazquez v., 140–141
State, Williams v., 437–440
State, Williamson v., 466
State, Young v., 182–184
State, Zule v., 121
State Department of SRS v. Public Employee Relations Board, 461
State in the Interest of M.T.S., 392–396
State v. Aaron, 377, 378, 379
State v. Akers, 168–170
State v. Aldershof, 471
State v. Allen, 459–463
State v. Amado, 217

State v. Baldwin, 398
State v. Barnes, 125, 126–127
State v. Barry, 164
State v. Bell, 411
State v. Bonds, 397–399, CD-ROM
State v. Brinson, 415
State v. Britten, 457
State v. Brown, 334, 335
State v. Brown, Reginald, 269
State v. Burns, 431–433
State v. Casey's General Stores, Inc. and Hy-Vee, Inc., 160–163
State v. Celli, 264–265
State v. Chiarello, 218
State v. Chism, 155–157
State v. Clark, 110–111
State v. Cleppe, 111
State v. Clokey, 471
State v. Clowes, 263
State v. Cole, 263, 264
State v. Cramer, 234–237
State v. Curley, 470–473
State v. Damms, 186–190, 192
State v. Diana, 263, 264
State v. Dixon, 346
State v. Elder, 370–371
State v. Elton, 403
State v. Farmer, 122
State v. Floyd, 268
State v. Foster, 154–155
State v. Foust, 411
State v. Fransua, 269–270
State v. Friedman, 45–46
State v. Fuentes, 472
State v. Furr, 207
State v. Gallegos, 237–238
State v. Glenn, 410–412
State v. Green, 432–433
State v. Guest, 403
State v. Haines, 121
State v. Hall, 297
State v. Hayes, 411
State v. Hemmer, 178–179
State v. Herron, 193
State v. Hiott, 269
State v. Holland, 46
State v. Holliday, 314
State v. Holmes, 218
State v. Hundley, 306–307
State v. Irons, 304–307
State v. Jantzi, 128
State v. JC Sports Bar Inc., 461
State v. Jerrett, 85
State v. Johnson, 411
State v. Johnson, Mark, 310, 311–313

State v. Jones, 94
State v. K.R.L., 297, 298–300
State v. Komok, 457
State v. Kuntz, 97–99
State v. Lindsly, 462
State v. Loge, 134–136
State v. Mays, 373–375
State v. McCart, 197, 198–202
State v. McLaughlin, 422–423
State v. Merrill, 326, 327–330
State v. Metzger, 46–47
State v. Michaud, 133
State v. Minster, 334–336
State v. Miranda, 92–96
State v. Morgan, 97
State v. Morse, 135
State v. Musser, 196
State v. Noren, 353
State v. Norman, 232
State v. Ownbey, 262–264
State v. Pace, 151
State v. Peters, 94
State v. Petersen, 141
State v. Peterson, 138
State v. Pichon, 306, 307
State v. Powell, CD-ROM
State v. Q.D., 299, 300
State v. Quinet, 284–289
State v. Reed, 415, 416
State v. Richard, 507
State v. Rousseau, 256, 258
State v. S.P., 299
State v. Sanchez, 471, 472
State v. Shelley, 266–268, 269
State v. Shuff, 339
State v. Simmons, 267
State v. Smith, 455, 456–457
State v. Snowden, 338–339
State v. Sodders, 179
State v. Soto, 327, 328
State v. Staley, 106
State v. Stark, 119, 120–122
State v. Stewart, Peggy, 230, 231–233, 236
State v. Stewart, Tracy, 354–358
State v. Tatro, 294
State v. Thames, 179–180
State v. Thomas, (1978), 257
State v. Thomas, (1981), 239
State v. Tomaino, 166–167
State v. Tunney, CD-ROM
State v. Turley, 236
State v. Ulvinen, 149–151
State v. Valentine, 255–259, CD-ROM

State v. Wagner, 190
State v. Walden, 93, 148
State v. Watson, Andre, 452, 453–454
State v. Watson, Rufus, 364–367
State v. Westlund, 257
State v. Williams (1996), 258
State v. Williams (1998), 263–264
State v. Williquette, 93–94
State v. Wilson, 71–74
State v. Young, 336
Sterling v. State, 39, 40, 41, 43, 44–45
Stevenson, *People v.*, 335–336
Stewart, Peggy, *State v.*, 230, 231–233, 236
Stewart, Tracy, *State v.*, 354–358
Strong, *People v.*, 132–133
Superior Court of Sonoma County, Michael M. *v.*, 47
Superior Court, Hatch *v.*, 111–112
Superior Court, Keeler *v.*, 21
Superior Court, *People v.*, 507

T
T. M. v. State, 302
Tacoma v. Luvene, 507
Tague, Fullmer *v.*, 161–162
Tarrant, Commonwealth *v.*, 415
Tatro, *State v.*, 294
Tennessee v. Garner, 251, 252, 253–254
Texas, Hancock *v.*, 455
Texas, Powell *v.*, 86–90, 164, 295, 490
Texas v. Johnson, 55–57
Thacker v. Commonwealth, 178
Thames, *State v.*, 179–180
Thomas, *People v.*, 350–351
Thomas, *State v.*, (1978), 257
Thomas, *State v.*, (1981), 239
Tomaino, *State v.*, 166–167
Trop v. Dulles, 72
Tunney, *State v.*, CD-ROM
Turley, *State v.*, 236

U
Ullman, Poe *v.*, 296
Ulvinen, *State v.*, 149–151
United States, Bailey *v.*, 148
United States, Beard *v.*, 250
United States, Brown *v.*, 140
United States, Durham *v.*, 281
United States, Jacobson *v.*, 312
United States, Katz *v.*, 61, 62

United States, Morissette v., 165, 166, 405
United States, Olmstead v., 61, 62
United States, Pinkerton v., 148
United States, Robinson v., 44
United States, Sherman v., 310
United States, Staples v., 135
United States, Watts v., 500
United States, Weems v., 70, 71
United States Jaycees, Roberts v., 62
United States v. Bruno, 197
United States v. Byfield, 107, 108, 109–110
United States v. Clavis, 109
United States v. Cornell, 294
United States v. Hatatley, 97
United States v. Johnson (1963), 415
United States v. Johnson (1992), 109
United States v. Loman, 415
United States v. Lucas, 106–109
United States v. Murphy, 415
United States v. Onick, 108
United States v. Peterson, 241–244
United States v. Velasquez, 500
United States v. Zeigler, 108

V

Valentine, State v., 255–259, CD-ROM
Velasquez, United States v., 500
Velazquez v. State, 140–141
Village of Hoffman Estates v. Flipside, Hoffman Estates, Inc., 500
Village of Schaumburg v. Citizens for a Better Environment, 497

W

Wade, Roe v., 244, 326, 328, 330
Wagner, State v., 190
Walden, State v., 93, 148
Ward v. Rock Against Racism, 498
Washington, People v., 371–372
Watson, Andre, State v., 452, 453–454
Watson, Rufus, State v., 364–367
Watts v. United States, 500
Weems v. United States, 70, 71
West Virginia Board of Education v. Barnette, 62
Westlund, State v., 257

White, People v., (1963), 415
White, People v., (1980), 239
White Egret Condominium, Inc. v. Franklin, 301
Williams, State v., (1996), 258
Williams, State v., (1998), 263–264
Williams v. Fears, 506
Williams v. State, 437–440
Williamson v. State, 466
Williquette, State v., 93–94
Wilson, State v., 71–74
Wisconsin v. Mitchell, 53–54

Y

Young, Commonwealth v., 416
Young, State v., 336
Young v. New York City Transit Authority, 55
Young v. State, 182–184

Z

Zangari, Commonwealth v., 473–474, CD-ROM
Zeigler, United States v., 108
Zule v. State, 121

Index

A

Abandonment, 176, 191–193, CD-ROM

Abortion, fetal death statutes and, 326–330, CD-ROM

Access, computer crimes and, 458, 459–461

Accessory
  after the fact, 147, 155–158
  before the fact, 147
  definition of, 147, 171
  liability, 147, 155–158

Accomplice, 147–152, 171

Accomplice liability, 147–148, CD-ROM
  actus reus, 148–152
  vs. conspiracy, 147–148
  elements of, 147
  mens rea of, 152–155
  mere presence rule, 148, 171
  words as, 148–151

Accountability, intoxication defense and, 291

Acquaintance rape, unarmed. *See* Rape

Actual possession, 105, 114

Actus reus, 6, 80–81, 82–84
  accomplice liability, 148–152
  arson and, 437–440
  assault and, 413
  attempt and, 180–185
  battery and, 410
  bodily movements and, 83
  burglary and, 80, 430–431
  causation and, 81
  concurrence and, 80–81
  condition and, 85–90
  conspiracy, 194–195

criminal conduct and, 6, 79–83
criminal omission, 91
definition of, 114
degrees of homicide and, 325
duress and, 303
extortion and, 474
failure to act, 91, CD-ROM
false pretenses and, 452
forgery, 468
free will and, 83
homicide and, 326, 344
larceny, 447, 450
legal duty and, 91–103
Model Penal Code and, 81–82
omission, 82
passive state and, 112–113
possession, 82, 105–106, 112–113
prior voluntary act, 86–90
public drunkenness as, 86–90
purpose of requirement, 82
rape and, 389
receipt of stolen property, 463
requirements of, 81–82
robbery and, 470
seriousness of the offense and, 142
solicitation, 204
status as, 85–90
thoughts and, 82
voluntariness, 81, 83–85

Adequate provocation, 364–371, 381
  adultery as, 367–371
  assault as, 364
  battery as, 364
  insulting gestures as, 364
  objective test of, 371–372
  rule, 364–367, 381
  trespasses as, 364

words as, 364–367

Adultery, paramour rule, 367–372, 381

Affirm, 43, 75

Affirmative defense, 213, 271

Age
  classifications, 47
  distinction, equal protection clause and, 47, 48–49
  excuse, 297–303
  mens rea and, 297

Agent Orange, *actus reus* and, 85

Aggravated rape, 385, 409, 425

Agreement, in conspiracy *actus reus*, 194–195, 198–202

Alcohol
  intoxication defense and, 291–297
  public drunkenness and, 86–90

Alcoholism, as status, 86–90

ALI (American Law Institute), 20, 22, 81, 129

Alibi, 212, 271

Allen, Barry, 226

Amendments, Constitutional, 524–532

American bystander rule, 91, 114

American flag burning, 55–57

American Law Institute (ALI), 20, 22, 81, 129

Andenaes, Johannes, 13

Anti-begging ordinances, 493–501

Anti-panhandling ordinances, 493–501

Appellant, 40, 75

Appellate court, 40, 75

Appellee, 40, 75

Aquinas, St. Thomas, 118

Arbitrary action, 38, 75

Arrest
  executing, use of force and,
    253–254
  unlawful, resisting, 255–259
Arson, 436–441
  actus reus, 437–440
  attempted, 181, 185
  degrees of, 440–441
  elements of, 436
  grading, 441
  history of, 436
  law, rationale for, 436
  mens rea, 440–441
  Model Penal Code, 437, 440–441
  motive and, 441
  property in, 441
  statutes, 441, CD-ROM
Asportation, 447, 479
  carjacking and, 419–422
  in kidnapping, 419–422
  in larceny, 447
Assault, 409–416, 425
  actus reus, 413
  attempted battery assault, 413, 425
  vs. battery, 409
  with deadly weapons, 414–416
  definition of, 409, 425
  elements of, 413–414
  mens rea, 410–412, 413
  Model Penal Code, 413–414, 416
  as provocation, 364
  threatened battery assault, 413,
    425
  words as, 413
Atrocious murder, 344–349
Attacks
  consent defense and, 266–270
  excessive force and, 215, 240–241
  future, 215
  imminent, 215, 229–233
  Model Penal Code and, 229
  present danger and, 229
  provoked, self-defense and,
    215–219
  reasonable belief and, 215
  retreat doctrine and, 241–244
  self-defense and, 214–223,
    229–233
Attempt, 173–194, 208
  abandonment, 191–193
  actus reus, 175, 180–185
  definition of, 208
  elements of, 175
  equivocality approach, 180, 181,
    209

factual impossibility, 185–190, 209
history of law, 174–175
legal impossibility, 185–186, 209
mens rea, 175, 176–180
Model Penal Code standard, 180,
    181–184, 209
physical proximity doctrine, 180,
    181, 209
vs. preparation, 182
probable desistance approach,
    180, 181, 209
statutes, CD-ROM
substantial steps, 180, 181–184,
    209
summary of law, 194
theories of, 175
Attempted battery assault, 413, 425
Automatism, *actus reus* and, 85
Autonomy, retribution and, 10

B
Bacon, Francis, 174
Bacon, Sir Nicholas, 24
Bailees, 451, 479
Bank robbery, attempt and, 182–184
Barbarism, retribution as, 11
Battered woman's syndrome,
    230–238, 317
Battery, 409–416, 425
  actus reus, 410
  vs. assault, 409
  definition of, 409, 425
  elements of, 410
  grading, 412–413
  injury from, 412–413
  mens rea, 410–412
  Model Penal Code, 410, 412–413,
    416
  as provocation, 364
Begging, 493–501. *See also*
    Panhandling
  First Amendment and, 496–499
  free speech and, 494–501
  time, place, and manner
    regulations, 494
Benefit, from receiving stolen
    property, 463
Bentham, Jeremy, 12, 15
Blackmail. *See* Extortion
Blackouts, *actus reus* and, 84
Blackstone, Sir William, 18, 20, 245,
    386, 417, 430
Blameworthiness. *See* Culpability
Bodily movements, *actus reus* and,
    83

Bracton, 174, 259, 376
Brain death, 330–333
Brain injury, *actus reus* and, 84
Breaking, burglary and, 429,
    430–431, 433
Broken windows theory, 483, 515
Bryden, David, 385, 389, 400,
    CD-ROM
Burden of persuasion, 213, 271
Burden of production, 213, 271
Burden of proof
  challenging constitutionality of
    laws and, 37
  definition of, 76, 212, 271
  insanity defense and, 289–290
Burglary, 5, 428–436, CD-ROM
  actus reus, 430–431
  circumstance elements, 431–435
  constructive breaking, 430, 442
  dwellings, 428–430
  elements of, 429–430
  grading, 435–436
  history of, 428–429
  mens rea, 435
  Model Penal Code, 430–431
  "nighttime" element, 428, 429,
    435
  occupied structure, 431–433
  "of another," 433–434
  statutes, CD-ROM
  structure element, 431–433
  surreptitious remaining element,
    430–431, 442
  vs. trespass, 429
  unprivileged entry, 430, 442
Burning, arson and, 437–440
"But for" (*sine qua non*) causation,
    137, 143
Butler, Samuel, 85–86

C
California "insanity due to long
    term intoxication," CD-ROM
Canty, Troy, 225–226
Capital felonies, 6, 30
Capital felonies, punishment for, 6
Capital murder, 337–339, 381
Capital punishment, 13
  as justifiable homicide, 325
Cardozo, Benjamin, 18–19
Carjacking, asportation and, 419–422
Carnal knowledge, 385
Carrying away. *See* Asportation
Cases
  briefing, 42–43

distinguish, 19, 30
distinguishing on its facts, 19
finding, 43–44
importance, 39–40
overruling, 19, 30
reading, 39–42
"Casing a joint," 181
Castle exception, 241–244, 271
Causation, 80, 114
  actus reus and, 81
  criminal liability and, 137–142
  definition of, 143
  as element in crime, 80–81, 137
Cause
  in fact, 137, 139–142, 143
  intervening, 138–142, 143
  legal, 137, 139–142, 143
  proximate cause, 137–138,
    139–140, 143
  supervening, 138–142, 143
Certiorari, 58, 76
Chance, influence on criminal law,
  25–26
Change, criminal law and, 28
Chapter exercises, CD-ROM
Chatham, Earl of, 244–245
Child abuse, 91, 92–96
Child custody battles, kidnapping
  and, 422–423
Choice-of-evils defense, 259–265
  burglary and, 264–265
  elements of, 261
  marijuana, medical use and,
    262–264
  Model Penal Code and, 262
  provisions, CD-ROM
  speeding and, 264
Circumstances, mitigating, 213–214,
  271
Circumstantial evidence, 118, 143
Citation, 41, 43, 76
Civil commitment, 276, 320
Civil law, 5, 30
  vs. criminal law, 4, 5
Claim of right, 451, 479
Clarke, Ramsey, 252
Classifying crimes, 4–8
Clear and present danger doctrine,
  51, 76
Codification movement, 20
Codified, 19, 30
Coffee, John, 362–363
Coke, Sir Edward, 37, 244, 336, 428
Coleridge, Lord, 260–261
Coles, Catherine M., 483

Collateral attack, 41, 76
Coma patient, ending life of,
  330–333
Common law, 18
  abolishment of, 19–21
  codification movement, 20
  definition of, 30
  jurisdictions, problems with,
    21–22
  Model Penal Code and, 20
  reception statues, 19
Common-law crimes, 18
  abolishment of, 19–20
  definition of, 30
  history of, 18–19
  modern criminal law and, 20–22
Common-law jurisdictions, 21–22,
  30
Common-law rape, 385–388
Community service, 9
Complicity
  doctrine of, 146, 147, 171
  following crime, 155–158
Comprehensive Crime Control Act
  of 1984, 290
Compulsion. *See* Duress.
Computer software, theft and,
  455–457
Computer software, theft of,
  455–457
Computer-related crime, 455–463
  access in, 458, 459–461
  specific statutes, 457, 458–459,
    459–463
  theft law and, 455–457
Concurrence, 80–81, 114, 137, 143
Concurring opinion, 42, 76
Condition, *actus reus* and, 85–90
Confessions, *mens rea* and, 118
Conflict elitist theory, 23–25, 30
Connecticut defense of consent
  statute, CD-ROM
Consensus, criminal law and, 23–24
Consent, defense of, 265–270
  athletic events and, 265, 266–269
  circumstances and, 265
  Connecticut statute, CD-ROM
  elements of, 265
Consent, rape and, 386–389,
  399–400
Consolidated theft statutes,
  454–455
Conspiracy, 173, 194–203, 209
  vs. accomplice liability, 147–148
  actus reus, 194–195, 198–202

criticism of, 202–203
drug trafficking and, 197,
  198–202
elements of, 194, 195
mens rea, 194, 195–196
Model Penal Code, 196, 203
objective of, 196–202
parties to, 197–202
summary of law, 202–203
Wharton's rule, 197, 209
Constitution of the United States,
  517–538. *See also specific*
  amendments
  limits to criminal law, 36–37
Constitutional democracy, 36
  criminal law in, 4, 36–37
Constitutional limits, 36–37
Constructive breaking, 430, 442
Constructive intent, 118, 143
Constructive possession, 105,
  106–109, 114
Contraceptives, privacy rights and,
  57–58
Conversion, 451, 452, 479
Conviction, 4
Corporate crime, 159–163
Corporate liability, vicarious,
  159–163
Corporate murder, 359–362
Corporate officer, vicarious liability
  and, 159–163
Cressey, Donald R., 25
Crichton, Susan, CD-ROM
Crimes, 6. *See also specific crimes*
  of cause and result, 79, 80, 114
  classification schemes, 6–8
  classifying and grading, 4–8
  common-law, 18–22
  of criminal conduct, 79–80, 114
  elements of, 79–82, 114
  grading schemes, 6–8
  against habitation, 428–441
  against persons, 324–379,
    384–423
  against property, 445–477
  against public order & morals. *See*
    Quality of life crimes
  social conditions and, 11
  social control and, 5–6
  as torts, 5
  types of, 79
Criminal codes, 16–17, 19–20,
  CD-ROM
Criminal codes, differences among
  jurisdictions, 16–17

Criminal conduct, crimes of, 79–80, 114
Criminal convictions, review of, 40
Criminal court structure, 40
Criminal homicide. *See* Homicide
Criminal law
  change and, 28
  characteristics, 4
  vs. civil law, 4, 5
  common-law crimes, 20–22
  common-law origins of, 18–19
  consensus and, 23–24
  differences among jurisdictions, 16–17
  in a constitutional democracy, 4, 36–37
  ethical core, influence of 27–28
  in federal system, 16–17
  general part, 6, 30
  grading schemes, 6–7
  history, influence of, 26–27
  ideology, influence of, 23–25
  irrationality, influence of, 25–26
  as last resort, 5–6
  nature of, 4, 134
  nonlegal influences on, 23–28
  offenses, grading, 6–7
  parts of, 6
  purposes of, 2
  rational, 5, 22–23, 31
  reasons for, 2
  sources of, 17–18
  special part, 6, 31
  study of, 5, 23
Criminal liability
  actus reus and, 81–83
  causation and, 137–142
  concurrence and, 81, 137
  general principles of, 80–81, 114
  harmful result and, 81
  mens rea and, 117
Criminal liability, defenses to, alibi, 212, 271
  excuses. *See* Excuses
  justifications. *See* Justifications
Criminal negligence manslaughter, 372–373
Criminal negligent homicide, 373, 381
Criminal omission, 91–103, 114
Criminal punishment. *See* Punishment
Criminal recklessness manslaughter, 372–373
Criminal sexual conduct statutes, 408–409, CD-ROM

Criminal sexual conduct. *See* Sexual conduct, criminal
Cruel and unusual punishment, 70–74
  disease and, 86
  status and, 86–90
Culpability, 10, 30, 119, 128, 143
  corporate murder and, 360
  definition of, 10, 30
  insanity and, 276, 283
  intoxication defense and, 291
  levels of, 119
  requirements, 119
  retribution and, 10, 11
  strict liability and, 133–134
Cultural norms defense, 317–318
Custody, escape from, 304–307

D
Daley, Richard, 362
Damages, 5, 30
  vs. fines, 5
  punitive, 5, 31
Danger, reasonable belief in, 215, 219–222
Dangerous conduct rationale, 175
Dangerous persons rationale, 175
Deadly force usage as justifiable homicide, 325
Deadly weapon, defining, 414–416
Death penalty, 9, 337
  electrocution, 70
  for rape, 15, 70–74
Death risk, creation of, 130–133
Death
  causation and, 137–142
  causing another's, 334–336
  foreseeable, 353
Defendant
  definition of, 5, 30
  ex post facto clause and, 38
  in torts, 5
Defender-provoked attacks, 216–219
Defense of home and property, 244–250
  deadly force and, 245–250
  Texas provisions, CD-ROM
Defenses
  affirmative, 213, 271
  age, 297–303
  alibi, 212, 271
  choice-of-evils, 259–265
  claim of right, 451
  consent, 265–270
  cultural norms, 317–318

definition of, 212, 271
  diminished capacity, 290, 320
  duress, 303–307
  entrapment, 308–316
  excuses. *See* Excuses
  execution of public duties, 251–254
  against felonies, 215, 219–222
  of home and property, 244–250, CD-ROM
  imperfect, 213, 271
  insanity, 275–290
  intoxication, 291–297
  justifications. *See* Justifications
  mistake, 308, 400–408
  mitigating circumstances, 213–214, 271
  necessity, 259–265
  of others, 244
  perfect, 213, 271
  self-defense, 214–251
  syndromes, 316–317
  types of, 212–213
Deliberate killing, 325, 381
Democratic-consensus theory, 23–25, 30
"Depraved heart" (reckless) murder, 325, 381
Dershowitz, Alan, 316, 318
Designated public forums, 494, 515
Detentions, forcible, 417
Determinism, 11
Deterrence, 12–13
  criticism of, 13
  general deterrence (prevention), 8, 12, 30
  historical aspects, 15–16
  special deterrence, 8, 12, 31
Deterrence theory, 12–13, 30
Diminished capacity, 290, 320
Disease, as an act, 86
Dissenting opinion, 42, 76
Distinguishing cases, 19, 30
Doctrines. *See specific doctrines*
Double jeopardy clause, 5
Drag racing and vehicular homicide, cause of, 140–141
Drowning, causation of, 139–142
Drug abuse, injuries/deaths from, 412
Drug possession, 105–113
Drunkenness, as act, 86–90
Due process clauses, 38, 76
  vicarious liability and, 159–160
  void-for-vagueness doctrine and, 38–39

Duress, 303–307, 320
  consent, defense of and, 265
  definition of, 320
  elements of, 303
  escape from custody and,
    304–307
  threats and, 304
Durham rule (product test of
  insanity), 281, 320
Durkheim, Emile, 23
Dwelling requirement, for burglary,
  429, 431

E
Earl of Chatham, 244–245
Eighteenth Amendment, 528–529
Eighth Amendment, 526
  cruel and unusual punishment
    and, 14, 15, 70
Elements of crime, 79–82, 114
Eleventh Amendment, 526
Ellickson, Robert C., 485
Embezzlement, 451–452
Emotionalism, punishment and,
  12–13
Encouragement, to commit crimes,
  308–312
End of life, 330–333
Enforcement, selective, 24–25
English Bill of Rights, 70
English common law. *See* Common
  law
Enlightenment, influence of, 12
Entering, burglary and, 429,
  430–431, 433
Enticement
  attempt and, 181
  by government to commit crimes,
    308–312
Entrapment, 308–313, 320
  affirmative defense, 310
  defense of, 308–316, 320
  drugs and, 311–312
  elements of, 310
  encouragement and, 308–309
  larceny and, 313–316
  objective test, 310–316
  subjective test, 310–316
Epileptic seizure, while driving, 84
Equal protection clause, 47–50
  age distinction and, 47, 48–49
  rational basis and, 47
  strict scrutiny and, 47
Equivocality approach, 180, 181,
  209

Erwhonians, criminal code, 85–86
Escape from custody, 304–307
Estrich, Susan, 397
Ethical core, influence on criminal
  law, 27–28
Ethical core theory, 27–28
"Evil act." *See Actus reus*
"Evil mind." *See Mens rea*
Excessive force, 240–241
Excusable homicide, 325, 381
Excuses, 212, 271
  age, 297–303
  cultural norms, 317–318
  diminished capacity, 290
  duress, 303–307
  entrapment, 308–316
  insanity, 275–290
  intoxication, 291–297
  vs. justifications, 213
  mistake, 308
  syndromes, 316–317
Execution of public duties, 251–252
Ex post facto laws, 36, 37
  definition of, 76
  goals of prohibition against, 37
  U.S. Supreme Court interpretation
    of clause, 37–38
Expressive conduct, 50, 51, 76
Extortion, 469, 474–477
  actus reus, 474
  mens rea, 474–475
  vs. robbery, 474
  sexual, 475–477
  threats and, 474
Extraneous factor, 185, 209
Extrinsic force standard, 389,
  390–391, 425

F
Factual causation, 137, 143
Factual impossibility, 185–190, 209
Failure
  to act, 91, 92–99, CD-ROM
  to intervene, 91, 99–103
False imprisonment, 417, 419
False pretenses, 452–454, 479
Federal criminal code, 16, 17–18
Federal Criminal Justice Reform Act
  of 1973, 28
Federal system, criminal law in,
  16–17
Felonies
  capital, 6
  common-law, 18
  defense against, 215, 219–222

  definition of, 6, 30
  inherently dangerous, 354–358
  vs. misdemeanors, 6–7
  noncapital, 6
Felony murder, 352–359, 381
Fences, 463, 479
Fetal death statutes, 326–330, 381,
  CD-ROM
Fifteenth Amendment, 528
Fifth Amendment, 525
  privacy and, 57
Fighting words, 51, 76
Fines, 5, 9
First Amendment, 524–525
  categories of expression not
    protected, 50–51
  commercial speech, 494
  expressive conduct, 50, 51, 76, 494
  extortion and, 476–477
  flag burning and, 55–57
  forum regulations, 494
  freedom of speech, 50–51
  hate crimes and, 51–55
  nude dancing, 55
  panhandling, 55, 493–501
  privacy and, 57
First-degree murder, 337–349, 381
  atrocious or heinous, 344–348
  elements of, 337
  mens rea, 337–339
  premeditated or deliberate,
    337–339
Flag burning, 55–57
Fletcher, George, 91, 213, 222–223,
  229, 291, 324
Force
  excessive, 240–241
  robbery and, 470–474
Forgery, 467–469, 479
  actus reus, 468
  elements of, 467
  mens rea, 467, 469
  Model Penal Code, 468–469
  vs. uttering, 467, 469
Fourteenth Amendment, 47–48,
  527–528
  panhandling, 495–501
  privacy, 57
Fourth Amendment, 525
  deadly force by police, 251
  privacy, 57
Fraud
  rape and, 388
  theft and. *See* False pretenses
Free will, retribution and, 10, 11

Freedom of speech, 50–57, 493–501
Fundamental right
  definition, 50
  free speech, 50
  nature of, 59
  privacy, 57
Future harm
  attempt and, 173, 175, 180–182
  possession and, 112–113

G

Gang-related violence. *See* Street
  gangs
Gangs, 501–513. *See also* Street
  gangs
Gender classifications, 47
General deterrence, 8, 12, 30
General intent, 118, 143
General prevention. *See* General
  deterrence
General principles of criminal
  liability, 80–81, 114
  in state codes, CD-ROM
Genovese, Catherine (Kitty), 100–103
Gestures, insulting or obscene, 364
Gladstone, William, 309
Goetz, Bernhard, 219–222, 223–229
Good Samaritan doctrine, 91, 114
Goodman, Ellen, 486
Government inducement to commit
  crime. *See* Entrapment
Grading. *See also specific crimes*
  classifications according to subject,
  7
  crimes, 4–8
  felonies, misdemeanors and
    violations, 6
  living standard analysis, 7, 30
  offenses, 142
  problems with, 7
  schemes, 6–8
  wrongs *mala in se* and *mala
    prohibita*, 7
Grand larceny, 450. *See also* Larceny
Gross criminal negligence, 373, 381
Gross misdemeanor, 7, 30
Gross, Hyman, 303
Guilty, but mentally ill verdict, 276
Gun, accidental discharge, *actus reus*
  and, 84

H

Habeas corpus, 41, 76
Habitation, crimes against. *See*
  Arson; Burglary

Hadley, Jr., Joseph E., 363
Hale, Lord, 386
Hall, Jerome, 304
Hand, Learned, 147, 257
Hardwick, Michael, 64–69
Harm
  actual vs. intended, 118
  future. *See* Future harm
  negligence and, 129–130
  recklessness and, 129
Harmful result, 81, 114
Hart, Henry M. Jr., 4
Hate crimes, 51–55
Hearst, Patricia, 418
Heat of passion, voluntary
  manslaughter and, 363,
  367–372
Hedonism, 12, 30
Heinous murder, 344–349
History, influence on criminal law,
  26–27
HIV exposure, 120–122
Holding, 42, 76
Holmes, Oliver Wendell, 13, 26, 37,
  51, 83, 117, 176, 183, 194, 308,
  454
Home, defense of, 244–250,
  CD-ROM
Homeless people. *See* Street people
Homicide. *See also* Murder;
  Manslaughter
  actus reus and, 326, 344
  attempted, 179–180
  causing another's death, 334–336
  common-law and, 325
  criminal, 325–379
  criminal reckless and negligent,
    CD-ROM
  definition of, 325, 381
  degrees of, 325
  determining the degree, 324–325
  elements of, 81, 326
  excusable, 325. *See also* Excuses
  fetal death statutes, 326–330,
    381, CD-ROM
  general principles of liability and,
    81
  history of, 325
  justifiable, 325. *See* also
    Justifications
  manslaughter, 363–379
  mens rea, 325, 326
  murder, 336–363
  negligent, 373
  statutes, CD-ROM

taking a life, 326–333
  types, 325
  vehicular, 373–375
  year and a day rule and, 334–336
Homosexual activity, privacy rights
  and, 58–64
Hospitalization as a penalty, 8,
  275–276
Hypnosis, *actus reus* and, 85

I

Ideology, influence on criminal law,
  23–25
Ignorance of fact. *See* Mistake,
  defense of
Ignorance of law. *See* Mistake,
  defense of
Imminent attacks, 229
Imperfect defense, 213, 271
Imprisonment, false, 417, 419
Incapacitation, 8, 12, 30
  criticisms of, 14
  historical aspects, 15–16
  as prevention, 13–14
Incarceration, 9
Inchoate offenses
  attempt, 173–194, 209
  conspiracy, 194–203, 209
  definition of, 173, 209
  doctrine of, 173
  solicitation, 203–207, 209
Incomplete criminal conduct, 173.
  See Inchoate offenses
Incomplete offenses. *See* Inchoate
  offenses
Inherently dangerous felonies,
  murder and, 354–358
Injunction to abate public nuisances,
  502, 515
Injury from battery, 412–413
Insanity, 275–290
  affirmative defense and, 290
  burden of proof, 289–290
  civil commitment and, 276
  diminished capacity and, 290
  Durham rule, 281–282
  institutionalization and, 275–276
  irresistible impulse test, 282–283
  as legal concept, 276
  long term intoxication
    (California), CD-ROM
  M'Naghten rule, 276
  mens rea and, 276
  vs. mental illness, 276
  multiple personality and, CD-ROM

product test of insanity, 281–282
right-wrong test, 276–281, 230
substantial capacity test, 283–289,
320
Institutionalization, and insanity
plea, 275–276
Intellectual property, 455, 479
Intent to frighten, 413
Intent, 82, 118. *See also Mens rea*
Intentional scaring, 413
Intermittent confinement, 9
Intervening causes, 138, 139–140,
143
Intoxication defense, 291–297
accountability, 291
culpability, 291
elements of, 291
excuse, 291–297
involuntary vs. voluntary,
291–292
long term (California), CD-ROM
mens rea and, 291, 292–296
voluntary, 292–297
Intrinsic force standard, 389,
392–396, 425
Involuntary intoxication, defense of,
291–292
Involuntary manslaughter, 372–379,
381
Irrationality, influence on criminal
law, 25–26
Irrebuttable presumption, 297, 320
Irresistible impulse test, 282, 320
elements of, 282
vs. right-wrong test, 282

J
Jackson, Robert, 195, 484
Jareborg, Nils, 7–8
Jefferson, Thomas, 20
Junk food syndrome, 316–317
Jurisdiction
common-law, 21–22, 30
diminished capacity defense and,
290
penalties and, 17
Justice
preventive, 112–113
retribution and, 11
Justifiable homicide, 325, 381
Justifications, 212, 213, 271
choice-of-evils, 259–265
consent, 265–270
vs. excuses, 213
execution of public duties, 251–254

necessity, 259–265
New York's provision, CD-ROM
resisting unlawful arrest, 255–259
self-defense, 214–251

K
Kelling, George L., 483
Kidnapping, 417–422
aggravated, 422
asportation, 419–422
children, one's own, 422–423
degrees of, 422
elements of, 419
vs. false imprisonment, 417, 419
history of, 418–419
simple, 422
Knowing possession, 105, 114
Knowledge, 119, 125–129
as culpability requirement, 119
determining, standards for, 128

L
LaFave, Wayne, 91, 161, 213, 472
Larceny, 445–451. *See also* Theft
actus reus, 447, 450
asportation, 447
claim of right, 451, 479
consolidated statutes, 454–455
elements of, 446
grading, 450–451
grand, 450
history of, 26–27, 449
mens rea, 451
petty, 450
possession and, 447
property and, 450
shoplifting and, 448, 450
taking, element of, 447–450
Law. *See* Civil law; Criminal law
Lawful possession, 447
Legal cause, 137, 143
Legal duty, 91–103
American bystander rule, 91
failure to perform, 91–92, 99–100
Good Samaritan doctrine, 91
Legal impossibility, 185, 209
Legality, principle of, 25, 36, 76
Lesly, Mark, 226–228
Lewis, C.S., 15
Lewis, Sinclair, 428
Lex non scripta, 18, 30
Liability
accessory, 147, 155–157
accomplice. *See* Accomplice
liability

general principles of, 80–81, 114,
CD-ROM
for omissions, 91
parents, 167–170 CD-ROM
strict, 133–137, 143, 159
vicarious, 146, 158–170, 171
Libel, 51, 76
Liberty
constitutional democracy and, 482
definition of, 482, 515
false imprisonment and, 417
vs. order, 482–483
Life
beginning of, defining, 326–330
end of, defining, 330–333
taking a life, 326
Limited methods, principle of, 22
Lindbergh, Charles, 418
Living standard analysis, 7, 30
Locomotion, right of. *See* Liberty
Loitering, 485–493
definition of, 485, 515
due process and, 507–509,
512–513
history of, 484–486
vagueness and, 503, 504–513

M
M'Naghten rule, 276–281, 320
Maakestad, William J., 360
Madison, James, 36
Magna Carta, 70
Maitland, William, 26
Majority opinion, 42, 76
Mala in se (malum in se), 7, 30
Mala prohibita (malum prohibita),
7, 30
Malice aforethought, 325, 381
Malum in se (mala in se), 7, 30
Malum prohibita (mala prohibita),
7, 30
Manifest criminality, 82, 114
Manslaughter
adequate provocation rule,
364–367, 381
creation of death risk and,
373–375
involuntary, 363, 372–376, 381
paramour rule and, 367–372, 381
self-defense and, 363
unlawful act, 376–379
voluntary, 363–372
Marijuana
age distinction, equal protection
clause, 47, 48–49

Marijuana (*continued*)
  choice-of-evils defense and,
    262–264
  in home, privacy and, 69
Marshall, Thurgood, 39
Matrix program, 486–493
  due process and, 491
  equal protection clause and,
    490–491
  status and, 489–490
  void-for-vagueness, 492
Medical model of punishment, 14
Mens rea, 80–81, 117–136
  accomplice liability, 152–155
  age and, 297
  arson and, 440–441
  assault and, 410–412, 413
  atrocious or heinous murder,
    344–349
  attempt and, 175, 176–180
  battery and, 410–412
  burglary and, 80
  complexity of, 117
  concurrence and, 137
  conspiracy and, 194, 195–196
  constructive intent, 118
  definition of, 114, 143
  degrees of homicide and, 325
  determining, 118
  diminished capacity and, 290
  duress, 303
  false pretenses and, 452–454
  felony murder and, 352–353
  first-degree murder, 337–339,
    344–349
  forgery and, 467, 469
  general intent, 118
  hate crime, 122–125
  inchoate offenses, 173
  insanity defense and, 276
  intoxication and, 291, 292–296
  irrebuttable presumption, 297
  knowledge, 119, 125–129
  larceny and, 451
  levels of, 118–119
  mental states of, 118–119
  mistakes and, 308, 400–408
  Model Penal Code, 118–119
  vs. motive, 214, 271
  negligence, 119, 129–133
  objective standard, 128–129
  purpose, 119–125, 128–129
  rape and, 396–399
  rebuttable presumption, 297
  receipt of stolen property,
    463–464

  recklessness, 119, 129–133
  second-degree murder, 349–351
  seriousness of offense and, 142
  solicitation, 204
  strict liability and, 133–137
  subjective standard, 128
  transferred intent, 118
Mental capacity, impaired or
    diminished, 290
Mental element. *See Mens rea*
Mental illness vs. insanity, 276
Mental states. *See Mens rea*
Mental status, syndromes and,
    316–318
Mercy killing, 214
Mere custody, 447
Mere possession, 105, 114
Mere presence rule, 148, 171
Minnesota fetal death and fetal
    assault statutes, 327–330,
    CD-ROM
Misappropriation, 445, 479. *See
    also* Theft
  temporary, 451
Misdemeanor manslaughter. *See*
    Manslaughter, unlawful act
Misdemeanor
  common-law, 18
  definition of, 6, 30
  vs. felony, 6–7
  gross misdemeanor, 7, 30
  petty misdemeanor, 7, 30
Mistake, defense of, 308
  of fact, 308, 400–408
  of law, 308
  rape and, 400–408
Mitigating circumstances, 213–214,
    271
*Model Penal Code and
    Commentaries*, 16, 22–23
  abolishment of common-law
    crimes, 20
  actus reus, 81–82
  arson, 437, 440–441
  assault, 413–414, 416
  attacks and, 229
  attempt, 181–182
  battery, 410, 412–413, 416
  bodily harm offenses and,
    412–413
  burglary, 430–431
  choice-of-evils defense, 261–262
  common law and, 20
  conspiracy, 196, 203
  definition of, 30
  diminished capacity and, 290

  false imprisonment, 417
  forgery, 468–469
  knowledge and, 119
  mens rea and, 118–119
  negligence and, 119
  purpose and, 119
  rape, 388
  rational criminal code, 22–23
  recklessness and, 119
  restraint and, 417
  self-defense and, 229
  solicitation, 204
  standard, for attempt, 180,
    181–184, 209
  substantial steps, 180, 181–182,
    209
  surreptitious remaining and,
    430–431
  theft, 455
  threatened battery assault and,
    413–414
  voluntary abandonment and, 191
Moral duties, failure to perform, 91
Moseley, Winston, 100–103,
    103–105
Motive, 214, 271
Motor vehicle accident, epileptic
    seizures and, 84
Multiple personality as insanity,
    CD-ROM
Municipal codes, 18
Municipal ordinances, 18, CD-ROM
Murder, 336. *See also* Homicide;
    Manslaughter
  accomplice to, 149–151
  atrocious or heinous, 344–349
  capital, 337, 381
  common-law and, 337
  conspiracy and, 194–195
  corporate, 359–362
  deliberate, 381
  "depraved heart," 325, 381
  diminished capacity and, 290
  elements of, 337, 344, 349, 352
  felony, 352–359, 381
  first-degree, 337–349, 381
  heinous or atrocious, 344–349
  malice aforethought, 325, 381
  premeditated or deliberate, 325,
    337–339, 381
  reckless, 325, 381
  second-degree, 349–351, 381
  solicitation and, 203, 204
  statutes, CD-ROM
  while asleep, 83–84
  year-and-a-day rule and, 334, 381

N

Nader, Ralph, 362
Necessity, defense of, 259–265
Negligence, 119, 129–133, 143
    as culpability requirement, 119
    vs. recklessness, 129–130, 131
Negligent homicide, 373, 381
Nesson, Charles, 283
New York's "Defense of Justification"
    provision, CD-ROM
"Nighttime" element for burglary,
    428, 429, 435
Nineteenth Amendment, 529
Ninth Amendment, 526
    privacy and, 57
Nonconsent, rape and, 387, 399–400
Nonpublic forums, 494, 515
Nude dancing, 55

O

Objective element. *See Actus reus*
Objective standard,
    mens rea, 128–129
Objective test, 372
    of entrapment, 310, 316, 320
Obscenity, 50, 76
Offenses, grading, 142
Omission, failure to act, 82, 91,
    92–103
    criminal, 91, 92–99
    noncriminal, 91, 99–103
Open bottle laws, CD-ROM
Opinion, 42
Order, 482, 515
    vs. liberty, 482–483
Ordered liberty, 482–483
Overruling a case, 19, 31

P

Packer, Herbert, 8, 14
Pain
    intentional infliction of, 8, 12
    vs. pleasure, 8
Paine, Thomas, 258–259
Palgrave, Sir Francis, 14–15
Panhandling, 493–501
    as commercial speech, 494
    First Amendment and, 496–499
    free speech and, 494–501
    time, place and manner
        regulations, 494
    vagueness and, 499–501
Paramour rule, 367–372, 381
Parents, vicarious liability for
    offenses committed by children,
    167–170, CD-ROM

Parties to conspiracy, 197–202
Parties to crime,
    doctrine of, 146, 147
    types, 147–148
Penalties
    criteria for, 8
    jurisdictional differences in, 17
Perfect defenses, 213, 271
Perkins, Rollin M., 267
Petitioners, 41
Petty larceny, 450. *See also* Larceny
Petty misdemeanor, 7, 30
Physical element. *See Actus reus*
Physical proximity doctrine, 180,
    181, 209
Pinkerton rule, 147–148, 171
Pitt, Lord, 429
Plaintiff, 5, 30
Plato, 174
Plurality opinion, 42, 76
PMS defense (premenstrual
    syndrome defense), 317
Police, public duty defense and,
    251–254
Political demonstrations, American
    flag burning, 55–57
Poor people. *See* Street people
Pornography
    possession and, 111–112
    privacy rights and, 58
Possession, 105–113
    actual, 105, 114
    actus reus, 82, 105–106, 112–113
    constructive, 105, 106–110, 114
    future harm and, 112–113
    knowing, 105, 114
    lawful, 447
    limited definition, 112–113
    mere, 105, 114
    passive state and, 112–113
    privacy rights and, 58
    unwitting, 106
    wrongful, 447
Power, influence on criminal law,
    23–25
Precedent, 18–19, 26, 31
Prejudice, influence on criminal law,
    24–25
Preliminary injunction, 486, 489,
    515
Premeditated killings, 325, 337–339,
    381
Premenstrual syndrome defense
    (PMS defense), 317
Preponderance of the evidence, 213,
    271

Present danger, 229
Prevention
    forms of, 8, 12–15
    general deterrence or prevention,
        8, 12, 30
    historical aspects, 15–16
    incapacitation, 12, 13–14, 30
    justifications for, 12
    rehabilitation, 8, 14–15, 31
    vs. retribution, 12, 13
    special deterrence, 8, 12, 31
Preventive justice, 112
Principals
    in first degree, 147
    in second degree, 147
Principles, legal, 6. *See also specific*
        principles
    actus reus, 80–82
    causation, 81, 137–142
    concurrence, 80–81, 114, 137,
        143
    harmful result, 81
    legality, 25, 37, 76
    limited methods, 220
    manifest criminality, 82, 114
    mens rea, 80–81, 117–136
    necessity, 259
    proportionality, 70–71, 76
    rule of law, 36, 37, 76
    utility, 12, 31
Privacy, right to, 57–64, 69, 417
    contraceptives and, 57–58
    false imprisonment and, 417
    pornography and, 58
    provisions, 69
    sodomy, 58–64
    state constitutions, 69, CD-ROM
Probable desistance approach, 180,
    181, 209
Probation, 9
Product test of insanity, 281–282,
    320
Profanity, 50, 76
Prohibition, kidnapping and, 418
Property
    aggravated property crimes,
        469–477
    crimes against, 445–477
    defense of, 244–250, CD-ROM
    in larceny, 450
    misappropriation of, 445
    obtaining by false pretenses,
        452–454
    stolen, receiving, 463–467, 479
Proportionality, principle of, 70–71,
    76

Provocation
  reasonable, 371–372
  voluntary manslaughter and,
    363–367, 371
Proximate cause, 137–138, 139–140,
  143
Public drunkenness, as act, 86–90
Public duty defense, 251–252
Public nuisance, 502, 515
Public order offenses. *See* Quality of
  life crimes
Punishment, 4, 8–16
  barbaric, 70, 71, 72
  characteristics of criminal
    punishment, 8
  constitutionality and, 14, 15
  cruel and unusual, 70–74
  degrees of homicide and,
    324–235
  emotionalism and, 12–13
  forms of, 8
  goals of, 73
  as grading scheme, 6
  medical model, 14
  pain and, 8
  prevention and, 8, 12–15
  proportionality of, 70–74
  purposes of, 8
  retribution and, 8, 10–11
  threatened, 12, 13
  vs. treatment, 8
  trends in, 15–16
  utility, principle of, 12
Punitive damages, 5, 31
Purpose, 119–125, 129
  conspiracy *mens rea* and, 196
  as culpability requirement, 119
  determining, standards for, 128
  HIV exposure and, 120–122

Q
Quality of life crimes, 483–513, 515
  begging, 493–501
  gangs and, 501–513
  history of, 483–486
  loitering, 485–493
  panhandling, 493–501
  vagrancy, 483–486

R
Race classifications, 47
Racketeer Influenced and Corrupt
  Organizations Act (RICO), 203
Racketeering, 203
Rape, 385–409

acquaintance rape, unarmed, 385,
  425
actus reus, 389
  aggravated, 385, 409, 425
  common-law, 385–388
  consent and, 386–389, 399–400
  criminal sexual conduct statutes,
    408–409, CD-ROM
  degrees of, 409
  elements of, 389
  extrinsic force standard, 389,
    390–391, 425
  force and, 389–396
  fraud and, 388
  grading, 409
  history of, 385–389
  intrinsic force standard, 389,
    392–396, 425
  law reform, 388–389
  mens rea, 396–399
  mistake, defense of and, 400–408
  Model Penal Code, 388
  nonconsent, element of, 397,
    399–400
  reasonable resistance standard,
    386, 425
  shield statutes, 389, 425
  simple, 409
  statutory, 11, 400–408, 425
  strict liability and, 397, 400–408
  unarmed acquaintance rape, 385,
    425
  utmost resistance standard, 387,
    425
  voluntary abandonment and,
    191–192
Rape shield statutes, 389, 425
Rational criminal law, 5, 22–23, 31
Rationalism, 12, 30
Reasonable force in executing arrest,
  253–254
Reasonable resistance standard, 386,
  425
Reasoning, 42, 76
Rebuttable presumption, 297, 320
Receiving stolen property, 463–466,
  479
Reckless ("depraved heart") murder,
  325, 381
Recklessness, 119, 129–133
  as culpability requirement, 119
  definition of, 143
  vs. negligence, 129–130, 131
  two-pronged test, 129
Reconnoitering, 181

"Redefining rape," Bryden,
  CD-ROM
Rehabilitation, 8, 12
  aims of, 14
  assumptions, 14–15
  criticisms, 15
  definition of, 31
  determinism and, 14
  historical aspects, 15–16
Remanded, 43, 76
Remick, Lani Anne, 387
Resisting arrest. *See* Arrest
Resisting unlawful arrest, 255–259
Respondeat superior, 165, 171
Responses to social harms, 5
Restitution, 9
Restraints authorized by law, 417
Resulting harm. *See* Harmful result
Retreat rule, 241–244, 271
Retribution, 8, 10–11
  assumptions underlying, 10–11
  autonomy and, 10
  benefits of, 10
  culpability and, 11
  definition of, 31
  determinism and, 11
  free will and, 10, 11
  historical aspects, 15–16
  vs. prevention, 12, 13
Reverse, 41, 43, 76
RICO (Racketeer Influenced and
  Corrupt Organizations Act),
  203
Right
  constitutional, expanding, 69
  against cruel and unusual
    punishment, 70–74
  to due process, 37
  to equal protection, 47–50
  free speech, 50–57, 493–501
  to privacy, 57–64, 69, CD-ROM
Rights revolution of the 1970s,
  493–494
Right-wrong test (M'Naghten rule),
  276–281, 320
  Durham rule and, 281–282
  elements of, 277
  insanity and, 276–282
  vs. product test of insanity,
    281–282
  vs. substantial capacity test, 276,
    283–284
Risk, creation of, 119, 129–133
Robbery, 469–474, 479
  actus reus, 470

attempted, 176–178, 182–184, 185
degrees of, 474
elements of, 470
force and, 470–474
mens rea, 470
Rule of law, 36, 37
definition of, 76
self-defense and, 214

S

Safire, William, 203
Sanchez, Renee, 493
Sayre, Francis, 117
Scene of crime, presence at, 148, 151, 171
Schwartz, Louis B., 28
Scott, Austin, 91, 213, 472
Searches, unreasonable, 429
Second Amendment, 525
Second-degree murder, 349–352, 381
Seizures, epileptic, *actus reus* and, 84, 85
Seizures, unreasonable, 429
Selective enforcement, 24–25
Self-defense, 214–251, 271, CD-ROM
attacks and, 229–233
battered woman's syndrome and, 230–238
belief in danger, 219–222
danger and, 215, 229–233
defender-provoked attacks, 216–219
elements of, 215
excessive force and, 215, 240–241
against felonies, 219–223
of homes and property, 244–251
imminent danger, 215, 229–233
imperfect, 363
initial aggressors and, 216–219
as justifiable homicide, 325
of others, 244
preemptive strikes and, 215
present danger, 229
reasonable belief and, 215, 219
retaliation and, 215
retreat doctrine and, 241–244
stand-your-ground rule, 241
Sentences, typical, 9–10
Seventeenth Amendment, 528
Seventh Amendment, 525–526
Sex psychopath legislation, 25–26

Sexual conduct, criminal, 385–389. *See also* Rape
aggravated rape, 385, 425
consent, element of, 386–389
force and resistance standard, 386–388
history of, 385–389
mens rea, 397–399
nonconsent, proving, 386–389
rape, common-law, 385–388
rape, history of, 385–386
rape law reform, 388–389
reasonable resistance standard, 388, 425
sodomy, 58–64, 385
statutes, 408–409, CD-ROM
unarmed acquaintance rape, 385, 425
utmost resistance standard, 387, 425
"Sexual Correctness," CD-ROM
Sexual penetration,
definition of, 409
force and, 389–396
rape and, 397, 389, 409
Shaw, George Bernard, 12
Shock probation, 9
Shoplifting, larceny and, 448–450
Simon, Harry, 485
Sine qua non ("but for") causation, 137, 143
Sixteenth Amendment, 528
Sixth Amendment, 525
Skilton, Robert H., 188
Skogan, Wesley, 483
Slander, 51, 76
Sleeping in public, 484–493
Sleepwalking, *actus reus* and, 83–85
Smith, Juliette, 486
Snowden, Ray, 340–344
Social class, influence on criminal law, 23–25
Social conditions, crime and, 11
Social control, 5–6
Society, retribution and, 10
Sodomy, 58–64, 385
privacy rights and, 58–64
Software, computer, theft of, 455–457
Solicitation, 173, 203–207, 209
Special deterrence, 8, 12, 31
Specific intent, 118, 143
Speech,
commercial, 494

expressive conduct as, 50, 51, 76, 494
forum regulations, 494
freedom of, 50–57, 493–501
hate crimes and, 51–55
panhandling and, 55, 493–501
time, place and manner restrictions, 494
Split sentences, 9
Stand-your-ground rule, 241, 271
Standards for determining purpose and knowledge, 128
Stare decisis, 18–19, 31
State constitutions, privacy rights and, 69, CD-ROM
State criminal code, 16–17, CD-ROM
Status, *actus reus* and, 85–90
Statutes
arson, 441, CD-ROM
attempt, CD-ROM
burglary, CD-ROM
common-law and, 20–22
computer-related crime, 457, 458–459, 459–463
fetal death, 326–330, CD-ROM
homicide, CD-ROM
murder, CD-ROM
rape shield, 389, 425
reception, 19
sexual conduct, criminal, 408–409, CD-ROM
theft, consolidated, 454–455
vagrancy, 27
Statutory rape, 11, 400–408, 425
Stealing by deceit. *See* False pretenses
Stealing. *See* Theft; Larceny
Stephen, Sir James F., 10, 260, 303–304, 344
Stephenson, Robert, 363
Stolen property, receiving, 463–466, 479
Street gangs, 501–513
Street people, 484–501
equal protection clause and, 490–491
Matrix program and, 486–493
punishing as a status, 489–490
treatment of, 484–486
Strict liability, 133–137, 143, 159
rape and, 397, 400
Strict scrutiny, 47, 76
Structure element, for burglary, 431–433

Subject classifications, for crime, 7
Subjective element. *See Mens rea*
Subjective standard, *mens rea*, 128
Subjective test of entrapment, 310, 311–316, 320
Substantial capacity test, 283–289, 320
Substantial steps standard, 180, 181–182
Supervening causes, 138, 143
Surreptitious remaining, 430–431, 442
Syndromes, 316–318

T

Taking, element of, 447–450
Tenth Amendment, 526
Texas provisions, force to protect property and, CD-ROM
Theft
  age excuse and, 297–300
  computer-related crime, 455–463
  consolidated statutes, 454–455
  definition of, 445, 479
  embezzlement and, 451–452
  extortion, 474–477
  by false pretenses, 452–454
  general statutes, 454–455
  history of, 445–446
  intellectual property, 455, 479
  larceny and, 445, 447–451
  law, 26–27
  misappropriation, temporary, 451
  Model Penal Code, 455
  receiving stolen property, 463–467, 479
  robbery, 469–474
  stealing by deceit, 452–454
Third Amendment, 525
  privacy and, 57
Thirteenth Amendment, 527
Thomas, Clarence, 493–494
Thoughts, punishing, 82
Threatened battery assault, 413, 425
Threats
  duress and, 304
  extortion and, 474
  rape and, 389
  timing, 304
Tier, Robert, 493

Tort, 5, 31
Touching, unjustified offensive, 410. *See also* Battery
Traditional public forums, 494, 515
Trafficking in drugs, conspiracy and, 197, 198–202
Transferred intent, 118, 143
Trespass, 429
Twelfth Amendment, 526–527
Twentieth Amendment, 529
Twenty-fifth Amendment, 531
Twenty-first Amendment, 530
Twenty-fourth Amendment, 530–531
Twenty-second Amendment, 531
Twenty-seventh Amendment, 532
Twenty-sixth Amendment, 531–532
Twenty-third Amendment, 530
Twinkie defense, 316–317

U

Unarmed acquaintance rape. *See* Rape
Uncompleted crimes. *See* Attempt; Conspiracy; Solicitation
Uniform Brain Death Act, 330
Uniform Determinate Sentencing Law, 16
United States Criminal Code, 16, 17–18
United States Supreme Court, structure, 40
United States, Constitution of, 517–538
Unlawful act manslaughter, 376–379
Unlawful arrest. *See* Arrest
Unprivileged entry, 430, 442
Urban survival syndrome, 318
Utility, principle of, 12, 31
Utmost resistance standard, 387, 425
Uttering, 467, 469, 479

V

Vagrancy
  history of, 484–485
  legislation, 24
  statutes, 27
Vehicular homicide, 373–375
Vengeance, retribution as, 11

Vicarious liability, 146, 158–170, 171
  corporate, 159–163
  due process and, 159–160
  individual, 163–167
  parents, 167–170, CD-ROM
Victim compensation, 9
Victims Crime Act of 1984, 10
Vietnam vet syndrome, 317
Violation, 7, 31
Void-for-overbreadth doctrine, 51, 54, 76
Void-for-vagueness doctrine, 38, 76
  due process clauses and 38–39
  two-pronged test, 38–39
  vagrancy and, 485
Voluntariness, *actus reus* and, 81, 83–85
Voluntary abandonment, 191–193, CD-ROM
Voluntary intoxication, defense of, 291–297
  abolishment of, 292–296
  accountability and, 291
  culpability and, 291
  elements of, 291
Voluntary manslaughter, 363–372
  definition of, 363, 381
  elements of, 363
  heat of passion and, 363, 367–371, 372
  vs. involuntary manslaughter, 372
  objective test, 372
  provocation and, 363–367, 371
Von Hirsch, Andrew, 7–8

W

Wealth, influence on criminal law, 23–25
Weapons
  bringing to scene of crime, 182
  deadly, 414–416
Wechsler, Herbert, 7
Wharton's rule, 197, 209
Wiehofen, Henry, 11
Williams, Glanville, 260, 304
Wilson, James Q., 14, 483, 486

Y

Year-and-a-day rule, 334, 381